THE **MGMT** SOLUTION

Print + Online

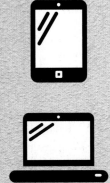

MGMT¹⁰ delivers all the key terms and core concepts for the **Principles of Management** course.

MGMT Online provides the complete narrative from the printed text with additional interactive media and the unique functionality of **StudyBits**—all available on nearly any device!

What is a StudyBit™? Created through a deep investigation of students' challenges and workflows, the StudyBit™ functionality of **MGMT Online** enables students of different generations and learning styles to study more effectively by allowing them to learn their way. Here's how they work:

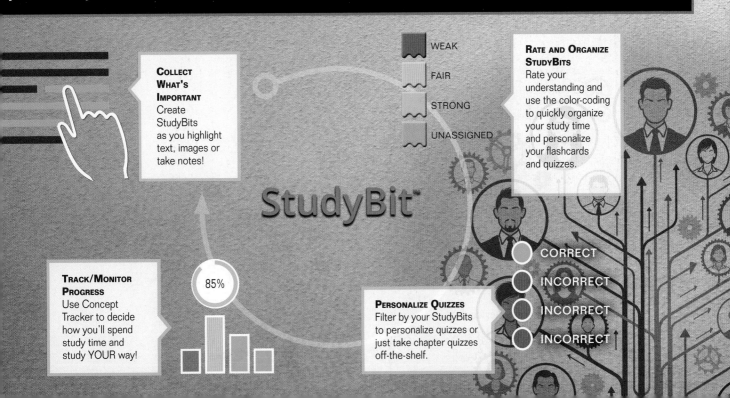

COLLECT WHAT'S IMPORTANT
Create StudyBits as you highlight text, images or take notes!

WEAK

FAIR

STRONG

UNASSIGNED

RATE AND ORGANIZE STUDYBITS
Rate your understanding and use the color-coding to quickly organize your study time and personalize your flashcards and quizzes.

StudyBit™

CORRECT

INCORRECT

INCORRECT

INCORRECT

TRACK/MONITOR PROGRESS
Use Concept Tracker to decide how you'll spend study time and study YOUR way!

85%

PERSONALIZE QUIZZES
Filter by your StudyBits to personalize quizzes or just take chapter quizzes off-the-shelf.

MGMT 10
Chuck Williams

Vice President, General Manager:
  Lauren Murphy

Product Manager: Laura Redden

Content/Media Developer: Colin Grover

Product Assistant: Lauren Dame

Marketing Manager: Charisse Darin

Marketing Coordinator: Casey Binder

Sr. Content Project Manager: Kim Kusnerak

Manufacturing Planner: Ron Montgomery

Production Service: MPS Limited

Sr. Art Director: Bethany Casey

Internal Design: Tippy McIntosh

Cover Design: Lisa Kuhn: Curio Press, LLC/
  Trish & Ted Knapke: Ke Design

Cover Image: iStockphoto.com/
  AlonzoDesign

Title Page, Back Cover, and In Book Ad Images:
  Computer/tablet illustration: iStockphoto.
  com/furtaev; Smart Phone illustration:
  iStockphoto.com/dashadima; Students:
  Rawpixel.com/Shutterstock.com

Doing the Right Thing Checkmark: Zorana
  Matijasevic/Shutterstock.com

Intellectual Property Analyst: Diane Garrity

Intellectual Property Project Manager:
  Erika Mugavin

Unless otherwise noted, all items © Cengage Learning

Library of Congress Control Number: 2016957447

Student Edition ISBN: 978-1-337-11676-3

Student Edition with Online ISBN: 978-1-337-11675-6

Cengage Learning
20 Channel Center Street
Boston, MA 02210
USA

Cengage Learning is a leading provider of customized learning solutions with employees residing in nearly 40 different countries and sales in more than 125 countries around the world. Find your local representative at **www.cengage.com.**

Cengage Learning products are represented in Canada by Nelson Education, Ltd.

To learn more about Cengage Learning Solutions, visit **www.cengage.com.**

Purchase any of our products at your local college store or at our preferred online store **www.cengagebrain.com.**

Printed in the United States of America
Print Number: 01   Print Year: 2017

iStockPhoto.com/AlonzoDesign

Contents

Part 2
Planning

Part 3
Organizing

Jirsak/Shutterstock.com

Part 4
Leading

Part 5
Controlling

Dirk Ercken/Shutterstock.com

1 Management

Jan Faukner/Shutterstock.com

LEARNING OUTCOMES

1-1 Describe what management is.

1-2 Explain the four functions of management.

1-3 Describe different kinds of managers.

1-4 Explain the major roles and subroles that managers perform in their jobs.

1-5 Explain what companies look for in managers.

1-6 Discuss the top mistakes that managers make in their jobs.

1-7 Describe the transition that employees go through when they are promoted to management.

1-8 Explain how and why companies can create competitive advantage through people.

After you finish this chapter, go to **PAGE 21** for

STUDY TOOLS

MANAGEMENT IS …

Management issues are fundamental to any organization: How do we plan to get things done, organize the company to be efficient and effective, lead and motivate employees, and put controls in place to make sure our plans are followed and our goals met? Good management is basic to starting a business, growing a business, and maintaining a business after it has achieved some measure of success.

To understand how important *good* management is, think about this. Sears, one of the oldest retailers in the United States, has lost $8.2 billion since 2011. In 2015 alone, Sears saw revenues decline 20 percent—a $6 billion drop. The company lost $1.1 billion that year and was forced to close 562 stores. Without the $9.5 billion it raised from selling Lands End clothing, Sears Hometown and Outlet Stores, and 327 profitable Sears stores, Sears would be hemorrhaging cash and filing for bankruptcy. Robert Futterman, CEO of RKF, a retail leasing and consulting company, said, "Retailers invest in their best stores and refurbish them, they don't sell them."[1]

Ah, bad managers and bad management. Is it any wonder that companies pay management consultants nearly $210 billion a year for advice on basic management issues such as how to outperform competitors to earn customers' business, lead people effectively, organize the company efficiently, and manage large-scale projects and processes?[2] This textbook will help you understand some of the basic issues that management consultants help companies resolve. (And it won't cost you billions of dollars.)

Many of today's managers got their start welding on the factory floor, clearing dishes off tables, helping customers fit a suit, or wiping up a spill in aisle 3. Similarly, lots of you will start at the bottom and work your way up. There's no better way to get to know your competition, your customers, and your business. But whether you begin your career at the entry level or as a supervisor, your job as a manager is not to do the work but to help others do theirs. **Management** is getting work done through others.

Vineet Nayar, CEO of IT services company HCL Technologies, doesn't see himself as the guy who has to do everything or have all the answers. Instead, he sees himself as "the guy who is obsessed with enabling employees to create value." Rather than coming up with solutions himself, Nayar creates opportunities for collaboration, for peer review, and for employees to give feedback on ideas and work processes. Says Nayar, "My job is to make sure everybody is enabled to do what they do well."[3]

Sears is so cash strapped that it has sacrificed future earnings for short-term needs by selling a dozen profitable stores.

Nayar's description of managerial responsibilities suggests that managers also have to be concerned with efficiency and effectiveness in the work process. **Efficiency** is getting work done with a minimum of effort, expense, or waste. At aircraft manufacturer Airbus, lasers help workers join massive fuselage pieces together 30 percent faster (and 40 percent cheaper). Similarly, rather than reaching up for hours to assemble and install overhead luggage bins, workers now assemble these parts at waist-high benches and then bolt them to the plane's ceiling. Besides being easier for workers, this process is 30 percent faster. When testing a plane's electrical circuitry, engineers previously used probes to validate electrical connections, hand recording the results of 35,000 such tests on each plane's paper blueprints. Today, wireless probes paired to computer tablets test each connection, automatically recording the results onto the plane's digital blueprints. Finally, by using a massive ink-jet printer, Airbus has cut the time it takes to paint airline logos on plane tail fins from 170 to 17 hours.

Efficiency alone, however, is not enough to ensure success. Managers must also strive for **effectiveness**, which is accomplishing tasks that help fulfill organizational objectives such as customer service and satisfaction. Time Warner Cable (TWC) recently reduced its eight-hour service-call window to just one hour by outfitting technicians with iPads that geolocate the nearest customer needing service. Company spokesman Bobby Amirshahi

---

Management getting work done through others

Efficiency getting work done with a minimum of effort, expense, or waste

Effectiveness accomplishing tasks that help fulfill organizational objectives

Ken Wolter/Shutterstock.com

said, "We know when a tech is finishing up at one home, the one-hour window somewhere near them is starting to open for another customer, so we can dynamically dispatch that technician to the next job."[5] The focus on improving customer service is paying off. Today, TWC technicians arrive within the set one-hour window 98 percent of the time. TWC's TechTracker app provides customers with the technician's arrival time, name, identification number, and photo. Thanks to improvements in TWC reliability, repair-related visits dropped by 15 percent and the number of pay-TV subscribers increased.[6] TWC Chairman Rob Marcus said, "Our customers expect and deserve the best customer experience we can deliver."[7]

1-2 MANAGEMENT FUNCTIONS

Henri Fayol, who was a managing director (CEO) of a large steel company in the early 1900s, was one of the founders of the field of management. You'll learn more about Fayol and management's other key contributors when you read about the history of management in Chapter 2. Based on his 20 years of experience as a CEO, Fayol argued that "the success of an enterprise generally depends much more on the administrative ability of its leaders than on their technical ability."[8] A century later, Fayol's arguments still hold true. During a two-year study code-named Project Oxygen, Google analyzed performance reviews and feedback surveys to identify the traits of its best managers. According to Laszlo Bock, Google's vice president for people operations, "We'd always believed that to be a manager, particularly on the engineering side, you need to be as deep or deeper a technical expert than the people who work for you. It turns out that that's absolutely the least important thing." What was most important? "Be a good coach." "Empower; Don't micromanage." "Be product and results-oriented." "Be a good communicator and listen to your team." "Be interested in [your] direct reports' success and well-being." In short, Google found what Fayol observed: administrative ability, or management, is key to an organization's success.[9]

According to Fayol, managers need to perform five managerial functions in order to be successful: planning, organizing, coordinating, commanding, and controlling.[10] Most management textbooks today have updated this list by dropping the coordinating function and referring to Fayol's commanding function as "leading." Fayol's management functions are thus known today in this updated form as planning, organizing, leading, and controlling. Studies indicate that managers who perform these management functions well are more successful, gaining promotions for themselves and profits for their companies. For example, the more time CEOs spend planning, the more profitable their companies are.[11] A 25-year study at AT&T found that employees with better planning and decision-making skills were more likely to be promoted into management jobs, to be successful as managers, and to be promoted into upper levels of management.[12]

The evidence is clear. Managers serve their companies well when they plan, organize, lead, and control. So we've organized this textbook based on these functions of management, as shown in Exhibit 1.1.

*Now let's take a closer look at each of the management functions: **1-2a planning, 1-2b organizing, 1-2c leading, and 1-2d controlling**.*

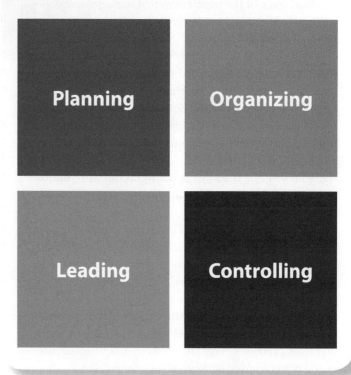

Exhibit 1.1
The Four Functions of Management

Planning	Organizing
Leading	Controlling

1-2a Planning

Planning involves determining organizational goals and a means for achieving them. As you'll learn in Chapter 5, planning is one of the best ways to improve performance. It encourages people to work harder, to work for extended periods, to engage in behaviors directly related to goal accomplishment, and to think of better ways to do their jobs. But most importantly, companies that plan have larger profits and faster growth than companies that don't plan.

For example, the question "What business are we in?" is at the heart of strategic planning. You'll learn about this in Chapter 6. If you can answer the question "What business are you in?" in two sentences or fewer, chances are you have a very clear plan for your business. But getting a clear plan is not so easy. As the manufacturer of backpacks for industry leading brands like JanSport, North Face, Timberland, and Eastpak, VF Corporation dominates the $2.7 billion backpack business. The increasing digitalization of textbooks and other documents has led VF to reassess how customers use its backpacks. According to JanSport director of research and design Eric Rothenhaus, "We realized we needed to forget everything we knew about the category.... We started to ask: What are the things we carry with us? How do we carry them? And how is that changing?"[13] VF studied college students, homeless people, and extreme mountaineers, learning that they had surprisingly similar requirements: water-resistance, flexibility, storage for electronics, and the ability to pack and unpack several times a day. So rather than making bags to carry things from point A to point B, VR's JanSport backpacks are designed for people who move *and* work in multiple locations—classrooms, coffee shops, shared office spaces, and beyond. "When you need to be on the go," Rothenhaus said, "you need a backpack."[14]

You'll learn more about planning in Chapter 5 on planning and decision making, Chapter 6 on organizational strategy, Chapter 7 on innovation and change, and Chapter 8 on global management.

1-2b Organizing

Organizing is deciding where decisions will be made, who will do what jobs and tasks, and who will work for whom in the company. In other words, organizing is about determining how things get done. In the retail industry, that usually means matching staffing levels to customer traffic, increasing staffing when busy, and then decreasing staffing when slow. Walmart recently implemented software to match the schedules of its 2.2 million associates with the flows of its 260 million weekly customers. While this dynamic, just-in-time approach sounds like a great idea, it resulted in highly fragmented schedules for thousands of store employees who could be sent home from work after just a few hours (due to unexpectedly slow customer traffic) or called back unexpectedly (when customer traffic increased). These unpredictable work schedules, which effectively put many associates perpetually on call, produced backlash from employees, advocacy groups, and unions alike. In response, Walmart reconfigured its schedules using three types of shifts: open, fixed, and flex. Managers schedule open shift employees during times that they previously indicated that they would be available for. Fixed shifts, which are offered first to long-time employees, guarantee the same weekly hours for up to a year. Finally, flex shifts let employees build their own schedules in two- to three-week blocks. Walmart is also developing an app that will allow employees to view, update, and set their schedules using a smartphone. Walmart managers have high hopes for the new shift structures, which reduced absenteeism by 11 percent and employee turnover by 14 percent during a two-year test.[15]

You'll learn more about organizing in Chapter 9 on designing adaptive organizations, Chapter 10 on managing teams, Chapter 11 on managing human resources, and Chapter 12 on managing individuals and a diverse workforce.

1-2c Leading

Our third management function, **leading**, involves inspiring and motivating workers to work hard to achieve organizational goals. Eileen Martinson, CEO of software developer Sparta Systems, believes that it is important for leaders to clearly communicate what an organization's goals are. She says, "A boss taught me a long time ago that people are going to remember only two to three things." So at her first company-wide

Planning determining organizational goals and a means for achieving them

Organizing deciding where decisions will be made, who will do what jobs and tasks, and who will work for whom

Leading inspiring and motivating workers to work hard to achieve organizational goals

MANAGEMENT TIPS FROM THE PROS

The functions of planning, organizing, leading, and controlling all seem straightforward enough, but how do managers do all of them simultaneously? Today's managers are busy; as you'll learn later in the chapter, managers spend as little as two minutes on a task before having to switch to another! Here are some techniques seasoned managers use to be more efficient and effective as they execute on the four functions of management.

▸ *Planning*: Carlos Ghosn is CEO of two automakers with headquarters halfway around the world from each other: Nissan (in Japan) and Renault (in France). He is also the chairman of a third—AvtoVaz (in Russia). To balance all his responsibilities, he plans his schedule out more than a year in advance.

▸ *Organizing*: One of the ways Adora Cheung, CEO of Homejoy, stays

PepsiCo CEO Indra Nooyi speaks at a conference in Miami, Florida.

iStockphoto.com/EdStock

organized is by crowdsourcing meeting agendas. She asks coworkers to add agenda items to an online spreadsheet, and then during the meeting, covers only the topics listed—no more.

▸ *Leading*: Indra Nooyi, CEO of PepsiCo, handwrites notes to roughly 200 of the company's top employees and even to top recruits. She also sends notes to the parents of her direct reports, thanking them for their child.

▸ *Controlling*: Birchbox CEO Katia Beauchamp insists her coworkers give her a deadline for every question they ask her, no matter how simple. That way, she can prioritize her responses and stay on track.

Source: J. McGregor, "How 10 CEOs Work Smarter, Manage Better, and Get Things Done Faster," *Washington Post*, January 2, 2015, https://www.washingtonpost.com/news/on-leadership/wp/2015/01/02/how-10-ceos-work-smarter-manage-better-and-get-things-done-faster/.

meeting, she communicated just one goal—doubling revenues over the next few years.[16] Martinson says, "The employees completely understand where we are going, and we've built a culture around that. If you have to come in and show me 45 charts and go through a lot of mumbo jumbo that neither of us understands, it's not going to work."[17]

You'll learn more about leading in Chapter 13 on motivation, Chapter 14 on leadership, and Chapter 15 on managing communication.

1-2d Controlling

The last function of management, **controlling**, is monitoring progress toward goal achievement and taking corrective action when progress isn't being made. The basic control process involves setting standards to achieve goals, comparing actual performance to those standards, and then making changes to return performance to those

Controlling monitoring progress toward goal achievement and taking corrective action when needed

standards. When traveling, Indians are much more likely to stay with friends or family than in a hotel. In fact, there are just two hotel rooms for every 10,000 people in India (compared to 40 in China and 200 in the United States). Why is this? Analyst Chetan Kapoor says, "There are lots of hotels where customers go in thinking, 'Will there be rats in my room?'"[18] Roughly 60 percent of those rooms are located in independent budget hotels, which vary dramatically in quality. Oyo Rooms is aiming to change that with its new hotel inspection service. Oyo inspects hotels across 200 dimensions, including linen quality, mattress comfort, cleanliness, shower water temperature, and staff appearance. Hotels agree to maintain those standards as a condition of staying in Oyo's 175 city database. Oyo Rooms founder Ritesh Agarwal says that inspections encourage hoteliers to make repairs and upgrade facilities. As a result, he says, "When you book a room through Oyo, you know exactly what you're going to get."[19]

You'll learn more about the control function in Chapter 16 on control, Chapter 17 on managing information, and Chapter 18 on managing service and manufacturing operations.

1-3 KINDS OF MANAGERS

Not all managerial jobs are the same. The demands and requirements placed on the CEO of Facebook are significantly different from those placed on the manager of your local Chipotle restaurant.

As shown in Exhibit 1.2, there are four kinds of managers, each with different jobs and responsibilities: 1-3a top managers, 1-3b middle managers, 1-3c first-line managers, and 1-3d team leaders.

1-3a Top Managers

Top managers hold positions such as chief executive officer (CEO), chief operating officer (COO), chief financial officer (CFO), and chief information officer (CIO) and are responsible for the overall direction of the organization. Top managers have three major responsibilities.[20] First, they are responsible for creating a context for change. When R. J. Dourney was hired as **Cosi's** CEO, the sandwich chain had struggled for 12 years under nine CEOs who never posted a profit. After just two days on the job, Dourney announced to the company's corporate employees that its Chicago headquarters would close and be relocated in Boston, where Dourney had been a successful franchiser of thirteen Cosi stores before becoming CEO. Dourney immediately closed ten unprofitable stores, updated the menu, and changed Cosi's stock-incentive program to be performance based. He then rolled out a more efficient serving system to serve customers quickly at all locations. In less than a year, those same store sales rose 20 percent while the company's stock price rose 160 percent per share.[21]

Indeed, in both Europe and the United States, 35 percent of all CEOs are eventually fired because of their inability to successfully change their companies.[22] Creating a context for change includes forming a long-range vision or mission for the company. When Satya Nadella was appointed CEO of **Microsoft**, the company was perceived as a shortsighted, lumbering behemoth. Nadella reoriented the company with a series of acquisitions and innovations, including purchasing **Mojang**, maker of the **Minecraft** video game, and a 3D-hologram feature for controlling Windows. After following Microsoft for years, one analyst noted about Nadella's new direction for the company, "Microsoft hasn't really shown any sort of vision like this in a long, long time."[23] As one CEO said, "The CEO has to think about the future more than anyone."[24]

After that vision or mission is set, the second responsibility of top managers is to develop employees' commitment to and ownership of the company's performance. That is, top managers are responsible for creating employee buy-in. Third, top managers must create a positive organizational culture through language and action. Top managers impart company values, strategies, and lessons through what they do and say to others both inside and outside the company. Indeed, no matter what they communicate, it's critical for them to send and reinforce clear, consistent messages.[25] When Phil Martens became CEO of aluminum producer Novelis, he spent his first 100 days visiting plants around the world and discovered that the company, with 11,000 employees, had highly fragmented business practices, operations, and strategies. To clearly communicate, "that we're going to move from a fragmented, regional company to a globally integrated company," Martens had shirts with the slogan, "One Novelis," distributed so that a symbolic picture of the leadership team could be taken. For the picture, said Martens, "We stood in a very defined triangle, very precise, because I wanted to create the image of order, and that we are together."[26] Likewise, it's important to actively manage internal organizational communication. As part of the One Novelis program, Martens created a global safety program, called Together We Are Safe, which monitored health and safety practices across Novelis's global sites, identified best practices, and then adopted and communicated them as a global standard. As a result, from 2009 to 2013, Novelis saw injuries, illnesses, and fatalities drop by over 40 percent.[27]

Finally, top managers are responsible for monitoring their business environments. This means that top managers must closely monitor customer needs, competitors' moves, and long-term business, economic, and social trends.

1-3b Middle Managers

Middle managers hold positions such as plant manager, regional manager, or divisional manager. They are responsible for setting objectives consistent with top management's goals and for planning and implementing subunit strategies for achieving those objectives.[28] Or as one middle manager put it, a middle manager is, "the implementer of the company's strategy" who figures out the "how" to do the "what."[29] Ryan Carson founded online learning company Treehouse Island without managers because he believed that his 100 employees

Top managers executives responsible for the overall direction of the organization

Middle managers responsible for setting objectives consistent with top management's goals and for planning and implementing subunit strategies for achieving these objectives

Exhibit 1.2
What the Four Kinds of Managers Do

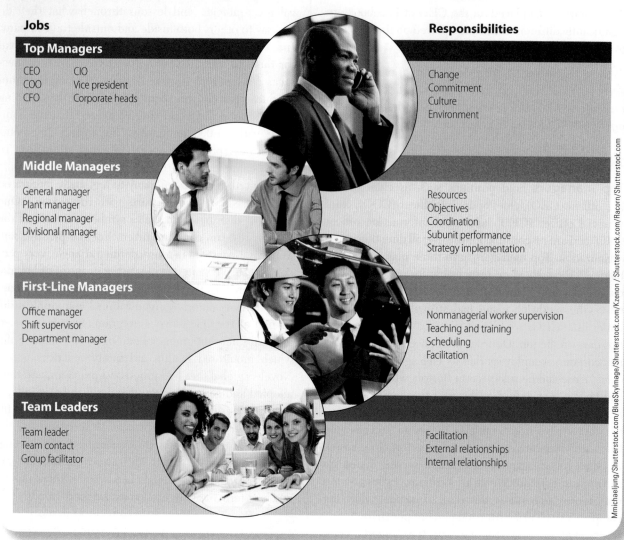

Jobs		Responsibilities
Top Managers		
CEO	CIO	Change
COO	Vice president	Commitment
CFO	Corporate heads	Culture
		Environment
Middle Managers		
General manager		Resources
Plant manager		Objectives
Regional manager		Coordination
Divisional manager		Subunit performance
		Strategy implementation
First-Line Managers		
Office manager		Nonmanagerial worker supervision
Shift supervisor		Teaching and training
Department manager		Scheduling
		Facilitation
Team Leaders		
Team leader		Facilitation
Team contact		External relationships
Group facilitator		Internal relationships

Mmichaeljung/Shutterstock.com/BlueSkyImage/Shutterstock.com/Kzenon/Shutterstock.com/Racorn/Shutterstock.com

could make decisions better and faster by themselves. However, that decision was severely tested when rapid growth resulted in 100,000 students enrolled in Treehouse Island's online courses. Employees, unsure of their responsibilities, became increasingly frustrated as endless meetings never seemed to result in meaningful action or decisions. Tasks and projects that were necessary to keep up with demand started to fall behind schedule. Carson fixed the situation by creating roles for middle managers. "That [managerless] experiment broke," said Carson. "I just had to admit it."[30]

One specific middle management responsibility is to plan and allocate resources to meet objectives. A second major responsibility is to coordinate and link groups, departments, and divisions within a company.

One middle manager described his job as, "A man who can discuss strategy with [the] CXO at breakfast and [then] eat lunch with workers."[31]

A third responsibility of middle management is to monitor and manage the performance of the subunits and individual managers who report to them. Finally, middle managers are also responsible for implementing the changes or strategies generated by top managers. Why? Because they're closer to the managers and employees who work on a daily basis with suppliers to effectively and efficiently deliver the company's product or service. In short, they're closer to the people who can best solve problems and implement solutions. How important are middle managers to company performance? A study of nearly 400 video-game companies conducted at the University of Pennsylvania's Wharton School of Business found that middle managers' effectiveness accounted for 22 percent of the differences in performance across companies. In fact, middle managers were three times as important as the video-game designers who develop game characters and storylines. Professor Ethan Mollick, who conducted the study, said that middle managers are the key to "making sure the people at the bottom and the top [of the organization] are getting what they need."[32] As for Treehouse Island, revenue is up, the number of instructional videos has increased, and response times to student questions have been cut in half. According to teacher Craig Dennis, things are "light years better" with middle managers in place.[33]

1-3c First-Line Managers

First-line managers hold positions such as office manager, shift supervisor, or department manager. The primary responsibility of first-line managers is to manage the performance of entry-level employees who are directly responsible for producing a company's goods and services. Thus, first-line managers are the only managers who don't supervise other managers. The responsibilities of first-line managers include monitoring, teaching, and short-term planning.

First-line managers encourage, monitor, and reward the performance of their workers. First-line managers are also responsible for teaching entry-level employees how to do their jobs. They also make detailed schedules and operating plans based on middle management's intermediate-range plans. In contrast to the long-term plans of top managers (three to five years out) and the intermediate plans of middle managers (six to eighteen months out), first-line managers engage in plans and actions that typically produce results within two weeks.[34] Consider the typical convenience store manager (e.g., 7-Eleven) who starts the day by driving past competitors' stores to inspect their gasoline prices and then checks the outside of his or her store for anything that might need maintenance, such as burned-out lights or signs, or restocking, such as windshield washer fluid and paper towels. Then comes an inside check, where the manager determines what needs to be done for that day. (Are there enough donuts and coffee for breakfast or enough sandwiches for lunch?) After the day is planned, the manager turns to weekend orders. After accounting for the weather (hot or cold) and the sales trends at the same time last year, the manager makes sure the store will have enough beer, soft drinks, and snack foods on hand. Finally, the manager looks seven to ten days ahead for hiring needs. Because of strict hiring procedures (basic math tests, drug tests, and background checks), it can take that long to hire new employees. Said one convenience store manager, "I have to continually interview, even if I am fully staffed."[35]

1-3d Team Leaders

The fourth kind of manager is a team leader. This relatively new kind of management job developed as companies shifted to self-managing teams, which, by definition, have no formal supervisor. In traditional management hierarchies, first-line managers are responsible for the performance of nonmanagerial employees and have the authority to hire and fire workers, make job assignments, and control resources. In this new structure, the teams themselves perform nearly all of the functions performed by first-line managers under traditional hierarchies.[36]

Team leaders are primarily responsible for facilitating team activities toward accomplishing a goal. This doesn't mean team leaders are responsible for team performance. They aren't. The team is. So how do team leaders help their teams accomplish their goals? Avinoam Nowogrodski, CEO at Clarizen, a software company, says, "Great leaders ask the right questions. They recognize . . . that a team is much better at figuring out the answers."[37] Team leaders help their team members plan and schedule work, learn to solve problems, and work effectively with each other. Management consultant Franklin Jonath says, "The idea is for the team leader to be at the service of the group." It should be clear that

Andrey_Popov/Shutterstock.com

First-line managers
responsible for training and supervising the performance of nonmanagerial employees who are directly responsible for producing the company's products or services

Team leaders managers responsible for facilitating team activities toward goal accomplishment

the team members own the outcome. The leader is there to bring intellectual, emotional, and spiritual resources to the team. Through his or her actions, the leader should be able to show the others how to think about the work that they're doing in the context of their lives. It's a tall order, but the best teams have such leaders.[38]

Relationships among team members and between different teams are crucial to good team performance and must be well managed by team leaders, who are responsible for fostering good relationships and addressing problematic ones within their teams. Getting along with others is much more important in team structures because team members can't get work done without the help of teammates. Clarizen CEO Avinoam Nowogrodski agrees, saying, "Innovation is created with people who you respect. It will never happen in a group of people who hate each other. If you want to have innovation within your company, you need to have a culture of respect."[39] And, Nowogrodski adds, that starts with the team leader. "If you respect other people, they'll respect you."[40] Tim Clem emerged as a team leader at **GitHub**, a San Francisco—based software company that provides collaborative tools and online work spaces for people who code software. GitHub, itself, also uses team structures and team leaders to decide the software projects on which its 170 employees will work. After only a few months at the company, Clem, who had not previously led a team, convinced his GitHub colleagues to work on a new product he had designed for Microsoft Windows. Without their approval, he would not have gotten the go-ahead and the resources to hire people to do the project. By contrast, a manager, and not the team, would have likely made this decision in a traditional management structure.[41]

Team leaders are also responsible for managing external relationships. Team leaders act as the bridge or liaison between their teams and other teams, departments, and divisions in a company. For example, if a member of Team A complains about the quality of Team B's work, Team A's leader is responsible for solving the problem by initiating a meeting with Team B's leader. Together, these team leaders are responsible for getting members of both teams to work together to solve the problem. If it's done right, the problem is solved without involving company management or blaming members of the other team.[42]

In summary, because of these critical differences, team leaders who don't understand how their roles are different from those of traditional managers often struggle in their jobs.

You will learn more about teams in Chapter 10.

1-4 MANAGERIAL ROLES

Although all four types of managers engage in planning, organizing, leading, and controlling, if you were to follow them around during a typical day on the job, you would probably not use these terms to describe what they actually do. Rather, what you'd see are the various roles managers play. Professor Henry Mintzberg followed five American CEOs, shadowing each for a week and analyzing their mail, their conversations, and their actions. He concluded that managers fulfill three major roles while performing their jobs—interpersonal, informational, and decisional.[43]

In other words, managers talk to people, gather and give information, and make decisions. Furthermore, as shown in Exhibit 1.3, these three major roles can be subdivided into ten subroles.

*Let's examine each major role—**1-4a interpersonal roles, 1-4b informational roles,** and **1-4c decisional roles**—and their ten subroles.*

1-4a Interpersonal Roles

More than anything else, management jobs are people-intensive. When asked about her experience as a

Exhibit 1.3
Mintzberg's Managerial Roles

Interpersonal Roles
- Figurehead
- Leader
- Liaison

Informational Roles
- Monitor
- Disseminator
- Spokesperson

Decisional Roles
- Entrepreneur
- Disturbance Handler
- Resource Allocator
- Negotiator

Source: Adapted from "The Manager's Job: Folklore and Fact," by Mintzberg, H. *Harvard Business Review*, July–August 1975.

Seven Deadlies—Things Great Bosses Avoid

A manager is responsible not only for providing direction and guidance to employees but also for making sure to create a work environment that allows them to be the best. Author and columnist Jeff Haden identifies seven things that managers often do that create an uncomfortable and unproductive work atmosphere:

1. Pressuring employees to attend social events. When your employees are with people from work, even at some party, it might just end up feeling like "work."

2. Pressuring employees to give to charity.

3. Not giving employees time to eat during mealtime hours.

4. Asking employees to do self-evaluations.

5. Asking employees to evaluate their coworkers.

6. Asking employees to do something that you don't want to do.

7. Asking employees to reveal personal information in the spirit of "team building."

Source: J. Haden "7 Things Great Bosses Never Ask Employees to Do" *Inc.com*, March 12, 2015, accessed March 28, 2015. http://www.inc.com/jeff-haden/7-things-the-best-bosses-refuse-to-ask-employees-to-do.html.

Brues/Shutterstock.com

---

first-time CEO, Kim Bowers, CEO of CST Brands, said, "We have 12,000 employees. [So,] I spend a lot of time out in the field with them."[44] Estimates vary with the level of management, but most managers spend between two-thirds and four-fifths of their time in face-to-face communication with others.[45] If you're a loner, or if you consider dealing with people a pain, then you may not be cut out for management work. In fulfilling the interpersonal role of management, managers perform three subroles: figurehead, leader, and liaison.

In the **figurehead role**, managers perform ceremonial duties such as greeting company visitors, speaking at the opening of a new facility, or representing the company at a community luncheon to support local charities. When **Fendi**, the Italian fashion house, launched a design initiative to raise money for charity, CEO Pietro Beccari hosted a gala at the company's recently opened flagship store in New York City.[46]

In the **leader role**, managers motivate and encourage workers to accomplish organizational objectives (see box "Seven Deadlies—Things Great Bosses Avoid"). One way managers can act as leaders is to establish challenging goals. William Xu, the enterprise division chief of Chinese telecom equipment maker Huawei Enterprises, gave his division a 40 percent sales growth target for 2013. Xu said, "The (2013) target was very ambitious to motivate staff."[47]

In the **liaison role**, managers deal with people outside their units. Studies consistently indicate that managers spend as much time with outsiders as they do with their own subordinates and their own bosses. For example, CEOs often sit on other companies' boards. CEO Stephen Zarrilli, of Safeguard Scientifics, which invests in high-growth health care and technology firms, says, "When you sit on another company's board, you gain perspective—not only about the company and its industry—but, more importantly, about other operating methodologies, governance, and viewpoints that can be very beneficial when you bring them back to your company."[48] Indeed, companies in low-growth, highly competitive industries whose CEOs sit on outside boards earn an average return on assets 15 percent higher than companies with CEOs who don't sit on outside boards![49]

Figurehead role the interpersonal role managers play when they perform ceremonial duties

Leader role the interpersonal role managers play when they motivate and encourage workers to accomplish organizational objectives

Liaison role the interpersonal role managers play when they deal with people outside their units

1-4b Informational Roles

Not only do managers spend most of their time in face-to-face contact with others, they spend much of it obtaining and sharing information. Mintzberg found that the managers in his study spent 40 percent of their time giving and getting information from others. In this regard, management can be viewed as gathering information by scanning the business environment and listening to others in face-to-face conversations, processing that information, and then sharing it with people both inside and outside the company. Mintzberg described three informational subroles: monitor, disseminator, and spokesperson.

In the **monitor role**, managers scan their environment for information, actively contact others for information, and, because of their personal contacts, receive a great deal of unsolicited information. Besides receiving firsthand information, managers monitor their environment by reading local newspapers and the *Wall Street Journal* to keep track of customers, competitors, and technological changes that may affect their businesses. Today's managers can subscribe to electronic monitoring and distribution services that track the news wires (Associated Press, Reuters, and so on) for stories and social media posts related to their businesses. These services deliver customized news that only includes topics the managers specify. Business Wire (http://www.businesswire.com) monitors and distributes daily news headlines from major industries (for example automotive, banking and financial, health, high tech).[50]

CyberAlert (http://www.cyberalert.com) keeps round-the-clock track of new stories in categories chosen by each subscriber. It also offers CyberAlert Social, which monitors roughly 25 million individual social media posts daily across 190 million social media sources worldwide. Brandwatch and Viral-Heat are additional tools

H.J. Heinz Company CEO Bernardo Hees acts as a spokesperson for his company. Here, Hees speaks at an exhibition at the Senator John Heinz History Center in Pittsburgh, Pennsylvania.

AP Images/Keith Srakocic

for monitoring social media.[51] Another site, Federal News Service (http://fednews.com), provides subscribers with daily electronic news clips from more than 10,000 online news sites.[52]

Because of their numerous personal contacts and their access to subordinates, managers are often hubs for the distribution of critical information. In the **disseminator role**, managers share the information they have collected with their subordinates and others in the company. At **Qualtrics**, a software company that provides sophisticated online survey research tools, CEO Ryan Smith makes sure that everyone in the company is clear on company goals and plans. Every Monday, employees are asked via email to respond to two questions: "What are you going to get done this week? And what did you get done last week that you said you were going to do?" Smith says, "Then that rolls up into one email that the entire organization gets. So if someone's got a question, they can look at that for an explanation. We share other information, too—every time we have a meeting, we release meeting notes to the organization. When we have a board meeting, we write a letter about it afterward and send it to the organization." Qualtrics also uses an internal database where each quarter employees enter their plans for meeting the company's objectives. Those plans are then made visible to everyone else at Qualtrics.[53]

In contrast to the disseminator role, in which managers distribute information to employees inside the company, managers in the **spokesperson role** share information with people outside their departments or companies. One of the most common ways that CEOs act as spokespeople for their companies is speaking at annual meetings and on conference calls with shareholders or boards of directors. CEOs also serve as spokespeople to the media when their companies are involved in major news stories. When Kraft Foods merged with H.J. Heinz Company in 2015, managers began working to reduce spending. They announced 5,000 layoffs and implemented zero-based budgeting, which requires even the smallest expenses to be justified every

Monitor role the informational role managers play when they scan their environment for information

Disseminator role the informational role managers play when they share information with others in their departments or companies

Spokesperson role the informational role managers play when they share information with people outside their departments or companies

year. With earnings dropping and revenue down nearly 10 percent, CEO Bernardo Hees told the media and investors, "We are instituting routines that represent discipline, accountability, and methodology for how we will operate. The actions under the resulting plan will take us two years to be [sic] complete, but will make us more globally competitive and accelerate our future growth."[54]

Tupungato/Shutterstock.com

1-4c Decisional Roles

Mintzberg found that obtaining and sharing information is not an end in itself. Obtaining and sharing information with people inside and outside the company is useful to managers because it helps them make good decisions. According to Mintzberg, managers engage in four decisional subroles: entrepreneur, disturbance handler, resource allocator, and negotiator.

In the **entrepreneur role**, managers adapt themselves, their subordinates, and their units to change. For years, **Whole Foods Market**, was the top—and only—organic grocery retailer. When traditional chains, such as Kroger and Walmart, began offering organic produce, meat, and packaged foods for cheaper prices, Whole Foods—sometimes called "Whole Paycheck" due to its high prices—became vulnerable and earnings plummeted. Co-CEO Walter Robb said, "All of a sudden . . . you can get the same stuff in many other places and you could get it cheaper." So the company cut prices, which, "Will tell customers what we are about: values and value," says founder and Co-CEO John Mackey. Whole Foods also launched its first national advertising campaign, started a customer loyalty program, and partnered with **Instacart** to deliver groceries to customers' homes in fifteen cities. Co-CEO Robb says that changes—and lower prices—will continue.[55]

In the **disturbance handler role**, managers respond to pressures and problems so severe that they demand immediate attention and action. In December 2014, Brian Cornell, Target's new CEO, went on a solo tour of the company's Canadian retail stores. Target Canada, the company's first international expansion, had lost $2 billion since starting in 2011. Cornell, CEO for just four months, wanted to see the struggling Canadian stores firsthand. On returning home, he reviewed Target Canada's sales numbers, and just a few weeks later, in January 2015, announced Target would spend $600 million to liquidate all 133 Canadian stores, lay off 17,000 employees, and take a $5.4 billion writedown. Cornell said, "Simply put, we were losing money every day," and could not, "find a realistic scenario that got Target Canada to profitability until at least 2021."[56]

In the **resource allocator role**, managers decide who will get what resources and how many resources they will get. Ford's F-series truck, the best selling vehicle in the U.S. for 32 consecutive years, generates $22 billion in sales a year and accounts for 12 percent of Ford's global sales and 40 percent of its global profits. In 2009, Ford committed to a multibillion-dollar investment to redesign the F-series, whose prices range from $24,000 to $50,000, to be built with a completely aluminum body, something found only in much more expensive cars, such as the the $70,000 Tesla Model S or the $75,000 Audi A8. Ford Chairman Bill Ford, says, "Some people might say, 'Aren't you taking a chance with your best-selling vehicle?' But that's what you have to do." He said, "I would have had much more anxiety if they had come in with business-as-usual." The 2015 F-series is 700 lbs. lighter, which allowed Ford engineers to replace a 6.2 liter V8 with a 3.5-liter turbocharged V6. While still capable of towing 8,000 pounds, overall gas mileage rose by 16 percent from 19 mpg to 22 mpg, making the F-series the most fuel efficient gas-powered vehicle in its class."[57]

In the **negotiator role**, managers negotiate schedules, projects, goals, outcomes, resources, and employee raises. When low-cost Dublin-based airline **Ryanair** was shopping for 200 new planes in 2014, it pressed Boeing and Airbus to add an extra eight to eleven seats per plane. Doing so cuts costs by 20 percent and earns an extra 1 million euros per plane each year. CEO Michael O'Leary traveled from Ireland to Seattle to personally negotiate the deal and acknowledged pitting Ryanair's longtime supplier Boeing against Airbus, saying, "We were very close to going to Airbus in the spring [of 2014]." O'Leary left Boeing with a deal for 200 planes, each with eight extra seats, and a hefty discount off the $104 million retail price of Boeing's 737-MAX

Entrepreneur role the decisional role managers play when they adapt themselves, their subordinates, and their units to change

Disturbance handler role the decisional role managers play when they respond to severe pressures and problems that demand immediate action

Resource allocator role the decisional role managers play when they decide who gets what resources and in what amounts

Negotiator role the decisional role managers play when they negotiate schedules, projects, goals, outcomes, resources, and employee raises

jet (still in development) that brought the total price tag down from $20.8 billion to $11 billion.[58]

1-5 WHAT COMPANIES LOOK FOR IN MANAGERS

I didn't have the slightest idea what my job was. I walked in giggling and laughing because I had been promoted and had no idea what principles or style to be guided by. After the first day, I felt like I had run into a brick wall. (Sales Representative #1)

Suddenly, I found myself saying, boy, I can't be responsible for getting all that revenue. I don't have the time. Suddenly you've got to go from [taking care of] yourself and say now I'm the manager, and what does a manager do? It takes awhile thinking about it for it to really hit you . . . a manager gets things done through other people. That's a very, very hard transition to make. (Sales Representative #2)[59]

The preceding statements were made by two star sales representatives who, on the basis of their superior performance, were promoted to the position of sales manager. As their comments indicate, at first they did not feel confident about their ability to do their jobs as managers. Like most new managers, these sales managers suddenly realized that the knowledge, skills, and abilities that led to success early in their careers (and were probably responsible for their promotion into the ranks of management) would not necessarily help them succeed as managers. As sales representatives, they were responsible only for managing their own performance. But as sales managers, they were now directly responsible for supervising all of the sales representatives in their sales territories. Furthermore, they were now directly accountable for whether those sales representatives achieved their sales goals. If performance in nonmanagerial jobs doesn't necessarily prepare you for a managerial job, then what does it take to be a manager?

When companies look for employees who would be good managers, they look for individuals who have technical skills, human skills, conceptual skills, and the motivation to manage.[60] Exhibit 1.4 shows the relative importance of these four skills to the jobs of team leaders, first-line managers, middle managers, and top managers.

Technical skills are the specialized procedures, techniques, and knowledge required to get the job done. For the sales managers described previously, technical skills involve the ability to find new sales prospects, develop accurate sales pitches based on customer needs, and close sales. For a nurse supervisor, technical skills include being able to insert an IV or operate a crash cart if a patient goes into cardiac arrest.

Technical skills are most important for team leaders and lower-level managers because they supervise the workers who produce products or serve customers. Team leaders and first-line managers need technical knowledge and skills to train new employees

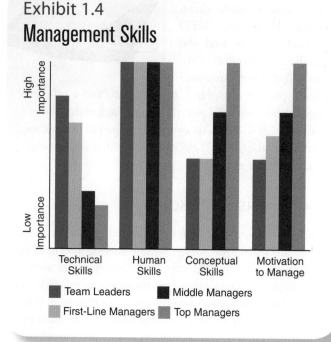

Exhibit 1.4
Management Skills

Chart with vertical axis labeled from Low Importance to High Importance, and horizontal axis categories: Technical Skills, Human Skills, Conceptual Skills, Motivation to Manage. Legend: Team Leaders, Middle Managers, First-Line Managers, Top Managers.

Viorel Sima/Shutterstock.com

Technical skills the specialized procedures, techniques, and knowledge required to get the job done

HOW TO BE AN EFFECTIVE EXECUTIVE IN THE AGE OF BRILLIANT MACHINES

In the era of big data, powerful analytics, enterprise software tools, and apps that do just about anything, there's no denying that technology has made many jobs obsolete. Could the same be true for managers? Could technology make management obsolete?

As data science and artificial intelligence begin to permeate business organizations, it will become increasingly critical for managers to have strong human skills. In this era of brilliant machines, managers make the biggest difference by doing the following:

▶ Asking questions—It takes judgment to know who to ask, what questions to ask, and when to ask them.

▶ Attacking exceptions—An algorithm might identify exceptions, but good managers will chase them down to resolve them.

▶ Tolerating ambiguity—The bigger and broader a problem, the better suited it is to a manager who can tolerate ambiguity and has a high level of discernment.

▶ Employing soft skills—Humans have the advantage when it comes to interpersonal skills such as empathy, inspiration, and coaching.

In the era of brilliant machines, the managers who master human skills will be the ones who have the edge.

Source: Irving Wladawksy-Berger, "As Big Data and AI Take Hold, What Will It Take to Be an Effective Executive," *Wall Street Journal*, January 23, 2015. http://blogs .wsj.com/cio/2015/01/23/as-big-data-and-ai-take-hold-what-will-it-take-to-be -an-effective-executive/tab/print/.

and help employees solve problems. Technical knowledge and skills are also needed to troubleshoot problems that employees can't handle. Technical skills become less important as managers rise through the managerial ranks, but they are still important.

Human skills can be summarized as the ability to work well with others. Managers with human skills work effectively within groups, encourage others to express their thoughts and feelings, are sensitive to others' needs and viewpoints, and are good listeners and communicators. Human skills are equally important at all levels of management, from team leaders to CEOs. However, because lower-level managers spend much of their time solving technical problems, upper-level managers may actually spend more time dealing directly with people. On average, first-line managers spend 57 percent of their time with people, but that percentage increases to 63 percent for middle managers and 78 percent for top managers.[61]

Conceptual skills are the ability to see the organization as a whole, to understand how the different parts of the company affect each other, and to recognize how the company fits into or is affected by its external environment such as the local community, social and economic forces, customers, and the competition. Good managers have to be able to recognize, understand, and reconcile multiple complex problems and perspectives. In other words, managers have to be smart! In fact, intelligence makes so much difference for managerial performance that managers with above-average intelligence typically outperform managers of average intelligence by approximately 48 percent.[62] Clearly, companies need to be careful to promote smart workers into management. Conceptual skills increase in importance as managers rise through the management hierarchy.

Good management involves much more than intelligence, however. For example, making the department genius a manager can be disastrous if that genius lacks technical skills, human skills, or one other factor known as the motivation to manage. **Motivation to manage** is an assessment of how motivated employees are to interact with superiors, participate in competitive situations, behave assertively toward others, tell others what to do, reward good behavior and punish poor behavior, perform actions that are highly visible to others, and handle and organize administrative tasks. Managers typically have a stronger motivation to manage than their subordinates, and managers at higher levels usually have a stronger motivation to manage than managers at lower levels. Furthermore, managers with a stronger motivation to manage are promoted faster, are rated as better managers by their employees, and earn more money than managers with a weak motivation to manage.[63]

Human skills the ability to work well with others

Conceptual skills the ability to see the organization as a whole, understand how the different parts affect each other, and recognize how the company fits into or is affected by its environment

Motivation to manage an assessment of how enthusiastic employees are about managing the work of others

1-6 MISTAKES MANAGERS MAKE

Another way to understand what it takes to be a manager is to look at the mistakes managers make. In other words, we can learn just as much from what managers shouldn't do as from what they should do. Exhibit 1.5 lists the top ten mistakes managers make.

Several studies of U.S. and British managers have compared "arrivers," or managers who made it all the way to the top of their companies, with "derailers," or managers who were successful early in their careers but were knocked off the fast track by the time they reached the middle to upper levels of management.[64] The researchers found that there were only a few differences between arrivers and derailers. For the most part, both groups were talented, and both groups had

Exhibit 1.5
Top Ten Mistakes Managers Make

1. Insensitive to others: abrasive, intimidating, bullying style
2. Cold, aloof, arrogant
3. Betrays trust
4. Overly ambitious: thinking of next job, playing politics
5. Specific performance problems with the business
6. Overmanaging: unable to delegate or build a team
7. Unable to staff effectively
8. Unable to think strategically
9. Unable to adapt to boss with different style
10. Overdependent on advocate or mentor

Source: M. W. McCall, Jr., and M. M. Lombardo, "What Makes a Top Executive?" *Psychology Today*, February 1983, 26–31.

Chrisdorney/Shutterstock.com

Werner Heiber/Shutterstock.com

The top mistake made by derailers is having an abrasive, intimidating, and bullying management style.

weaknesses. But what distinguished derailers from arrivers was that derailers possessed two or more fatal flaws with respect to the way they managed people. Although arrivers were by no means perfect, they usually had no more than one fatal flaw or had found ways to minimize the effects of their flaws on the people with whom they worked.

The top mistake made by derailers was that they were insensitive to others by virtue of their abrasive, intimidating, and bullying management style. The authors of one study described a manager who walked into his subordinate's office and interrupted a meeting by saying, "I need to see you." When the subordinate tried to explain that he was not available because he was in the middle of a meeting, the manager barked, "I don't give a damn. I said I wanted to see you now."[65] Not surprisingly, only 25 percent of derailers were rated by others as being good with people, compared to 75 percent of arrivers.

The second mistake was that derailers were often cold, aloof, or arrogant. Although this sounds like insensitivity to others, it has more to do with derailed managers being so smart, so expert in their areas of knowledge, that they treated others with contempt because they weren't experts, too.[66] For example, AT&T called in an industrial psychologist to counsel its vice president of human resources because she had been blamed for "ruffling too many feathers" at the company.[67] Interviews with the vice president's coworkers and subordinates revealed that they thought she was brilliant, was "smarter and faster than other people," "generates a lot of ideas," and "loves to deal with complex issues." Unfortunately, these smarts were accompanied by a cold, aloof, and arrogant management style. The people she worked with complained that she does "too much too fast," treats coworkers with "disdain," "impairs teamwork," "doesn't always show her warm side," and has "burned too many bridges."[68]

The third mistake made by derailers involved betraying a trust. Betraying a trust doesn't mean being dishonest. Instead, it means making others look bad by not doing what you said you would do when you said you would do it. That mistake, in itself, is not fatal because managers and their workers aren't machines. Tasks go undone in every company every single business day. There's always too much to do and not enough time, people, money, or resources to do it. The fatal betrayal of trust is failing to inform others when things will not be done right or on time. This failure to admit mistakes, failure to quickly inform others of the mistakes, failure to take responsibility for the mistakes, and failure to fix the mistakes without blaming others clearly distinguished the behavior of derailers from arrivers.

The fourth mistake was being overly political and ambitious. Managers who always have their eye on their next job rarely establish more than superficial relationships with peers and coworkers. In their haste to gain credit for successes that would be noticed by upper management, they make the fatal mistake of treating people as though they don't matter. An employee with an overly ambitious boss described him this way: "He treats employees coldly, even cruelly. He assigns blame without regard to responsibility, and takes all the credit for himself. I once had such a boss, and he gave me a new definition of shared risk: If something I did was successful, he took the credit. If it wasn't, I got the blame."[69]

The fatal mistakes of being unable to delegate, build a team, and staff effectively indicate that many derailed managers were unable to make the most basic transition to managerial work: to quit being hands-on doers and get work done through others. In fact, according to an article in *Harvard Business Review*, up to 50 percent of new managers fail because they cannot make the transition from producing to managing.[70] Two things go wrong when managers make these mistakes. First, when managers meddle in

decisions that their subordinates should be making—when they can't stop being doers—they alienate the people who work for them. Rich Dowd, founder of Dowd Associates, an executive search firm, admits to constantly monitoring and interrupting employees because they weren't doing the job "in the way I saw fit, even when their work was outstanding." According to Richard Kilburg of Johns Hopkins University, when managers interfere with workers' decisions, "You . . . have a tendency to lose your most creative people. They're able to say, 'Screw this. I'm not staying here.'"[71] Indeed, one employee told Dowd that if he was going to do her job for her, she would quit. Second, because they are trying to do their subordinates' jobs in addition to their own, managers who fail to delegate will not have enough time to do much of anything well. An office assistant to a Washington politician came in to work every day to find a long to-do list waiting on her desk, detailing everything she was expected to get done that day, along with how to do it, who to call, and when to give her boss updates on her progress. She said, "Sometimes, this list was three or four pages long. It must have taken him at least an hour to create."[72]

1-7 THE TRANSITION TO MANAGEMENT: THE FIRST YEAR

In her book *Becoming a Manager: Mastery of a New Identity*, Harvard Business School professor Linda Hill followed the development of nineteen people in their first year as managers. Her study found that becoming a manager produced a profound psychological transition that changed the way these managers viewed themselves and others. As shown in Exhibit 1.6, the evolution of the managers' thoughts, expectations, and realities over the course of their first year in management reveals the magnitude of the changes they experienced.

Initially, the managers in Hill's study believed that their job was to exercise formal authority and to manage tasks—basically being the boss, telling others what to do, making decisions, and getting things done. One of the managers Hill interviewed said, "Being the manager means running my own office, using my ideas and thoughts." Another said, "[The office is]

Exhibit 1.6
Stages in the Transition to Management

MANAGERS' INITIAL EXPECTATIONS			AFTER SIX MONTHS AS A MANAGER			AFTER A YEAR AS A MANAGER					
JAN	FEB	MAR	APR	MAY	JUN	JUL	AUG	SEP	OCT	NOV	DEC

MANAGERS' INITIAL EXPECTATIONS	AFTER SIX MONTHS AS A MANAGER	AFTER A YEAR AS A MANAGER
◉ Be the boss	◉ Initial expectations were wrong	◉ No longer a doer
◉ Formal authority	◉ Fast pace	◉ Communication, listening, and positive reinforcement
◉ Manage tasks	◉ Heavy workload	◉ Learning to adapt to and control stress
◉ Job is not managing people	◉ Job is to be problem solver and troubleshooter for subordinates	◉ Job is people development

Source: L.A. Hill, *Becoming a Manager: Mastery of a New Identity* (Boston: Harvard Business School Press, 1992).

my baby. It's my job to make sure it works."[73] In fact, most of the new managers were attracted to management positions because they wanted to be in charge. Surprisingly, the new managers did not believe that their job was to manage people. The only aspects of people management mentioned by the new managers were hiring and firing.

After six months, most of the new managers had concluded that their initial expectations about managerial work were wrong. Management wasn't just about being the boss, making decisions, and telling others what to do. The first surprise was the fast pace and heavy workload involved. Said one of Hill's managers, "This job is much harder than you think. It is 40 to 50 percent more work than being a producer! Who would have ever guessed?" The pace of managerial work was startling, too. Another manager said, "You have eight or nine people looking for your time . . . coming into and out of your office all day long." A somewhat frustrated manager declared that management was "a job that never ended . . . a job you couldn't get your hands around."[74]

Informal descriptions like these are consistent with studies indicating that the average first-line manager spends no more than two minutes on a task before being interrupted by a request from a subordinate, a phone call, or an email. The pace is somewhat less hurried for top managers, who spend an average of approximately nine minutes on a task before having to switch to another. In practice, this means that supervisors may perform thirty tasks per hour, while top managers perform seven tasks per hour, with each task typically different from the one that preceded it. A manager described this frenetic level of activity by saying, "The only time you are in control is when you shut your door, and then I feel I am not doing the job I'm supposed to be doing, which is being with the people."[75]

The other major surprise after six months on the job was that the managers' expectations about what they should do as managers were very different from their subordinates' expectations. Initially, the managers defined their jobs as helping their subordinates perform

IQoncept/Shutterstock.com

their jobs well. For the managers, who still defined themselves as doers rather than managers, assisting their subordinates meant going out on sales calls or handling customer complaints. One manager said, "I like going out with the rep, who may need me to lend him my credibility as manager. I like the challenge, the joy in closing. I go out with the reps and we make the call and talk about the customer; it's fun."[76] But when the managers "assisted" in this way, their subordinates were resentful and viewed their help as interference. The subordinates wanted their managers to help them by solving problems that they couldn't solve themselves. After the managers realized this distinction, they embraced their role as problem solver and troubleshooter. Thus, they could help without interfering with their subordinates' jobs.

After a year on the job, most of the managers thought of themselves as managers and no longer as doers. In making the transition, they finally realized that people management was the most important part of their job. One of Hill's interviewees summarized the lesson that had taken him a year to learn by saying, "As many demands as managers have on their time, I think their primary responsibility is people development. Not production, but people development."[77] Another indication of how much their views had changed was that most of the managers now regretted the rather heavy-handed approach they had used in their early attempts to manage their subordinates. "I wasn't good at managing . . . , so I was bossy like a first-grade teacher." "Now I see that I started out as a drill sergeant. I was inflexible, just a lot of how-tos." By the end of the year, most of the managers had abandoned their authoritarian approach for one based on communication, listening, and positive reinforcement.

Finally, after beginning their year as managers in frustration, the managers came to feel comfortable with their subordinates, with the demands of their jobs, and with their emerging managerial styles. While being managers had made them acutely aware of their limitations and their need to develop as people, it also provided them with an unexpected reward of coaching and developing the people who worked for them. One manager said, "It gives me the best feeling to see somebody do something well after I have helped them. I get excited." Another stated, "I realize now that when I accepted the position of branch manager that it is truly an exciting vocation. It is truly awesome, even at this level; it can be terribly challenging and terribly exciting."[78]

1-8 COMPETITIVE ADVANTAGE THROUGH PEOPLE

If you walk down the aisle of the business section in your local bookstore, you'll find hundreds of books that explain precisely what companies need to do to be successful. Unfortunately, the best-selling business books tend to be faddish, changing dramatically every few years. One thing that hasn't changed, though, is the importance of good people and good management: companies can't succeed for long without them.

In his books *Competitive Advantage through People: Unleashing the Power of the Work Force* and *The Human Equation: Building Profits by Putting People First*, Stanford University business professor Jeffrey Pfeffer contends that what separates top-performing companies from their competitors is the way they treat their workforces—in other words, their management style.[79]

Pfeffer found that managers in top-performing companies used ideas such as employment security, selective hiring, self-managed teams and decentralization, high pay contingent on company performance, extensive training, reduced status distinctions (between managers and employees), and extensive sharing of financial information to achieve financial performance that, on average, was 40 percent higher than that of other companies. These ideas, which are explained in detail in Exhibit 1.7, help organizations develop workforces that are smarter, better trained, more motivated, and more committed than their competitors' workforces. And—as indicated by the phenomenal growth and return on investment earned by these companies—smarter, better trained, more motivated, and more committed workforces provide superior products and service to customers. Such customers keep buying and, by telling others about their positive experiences, bring in new customers.

According to Pfeffer, companies that invest in their people will create long-lasting competitive advantages that are difficult for other companies to duplicate. Other studies also clearly demonstrate that sound management practices can produce substantial advantages in four critical areas of organizational performance: sales revenues, profits, stock market returns, and customer satisfaction.

In terms of sales revenues and profits, a study of nearly 1,000 U.S. firms found that companies that use *just some* of the ideas shown in Exhibit 1.7 had $27,044 more sales per employee and $3,814 more profit per employee than companies that didn't. For a 100-person company, these differences amount to $2.7 million more in sales and nearly $400,000 more in annual profit! For a 1,000-person company, the difference grows to $27 million more in sales and $4 million more in annual profit![80]

Another study that considers the effect of investing in people on company sales found that poorly performing companies were able to improve their average return on

Exhibit 1.7
Competitive Advantage Through People: Management Practices

1. Employment Security—Employment security is the ultimate form of commitment companies can make to their workers. Employees can innovate and increase company productivity without fearing the loss of their jobs.

2. Selective Hiring—If employees are the basis for a company's competitive advantage, and those employees have employment security, then the company needs to aggressively recruit and selectively screen applicants in order to hire the most talented employees available.

3. Self-Managed Teams and Decentralization—Self-managed teams are responsible for their own hiring, purchasing, job assignments, and production. Self-managed teams can often produce enormous increases in productivity through increased employee commitment and creativity. Decentralization allows employees who are closest to (and most knowledgeable about) problems, production, and customers to make timely decisions. Decentralization increases employee satisfaction and commitment.

4. High Wages Contingent on Organizational Performance—High wages are needed to attract and retain talented workers and to indicate that the organization values its workers. Employees, like company founders, shareholders, and managers, need to share in the financial rewards when the company is successful. Why? Because employees who have a financial stake in their companies are more likely to take a long-run view of the business and think like business owners.

5. Training and Skill Development—Like a high-tech company that spends millions of dollars to upgrade computers or research and development labs, a company whose competitive advantage is based on its people must invest in the training and skill development of its people.

6. Reduction of Status Differences—A company should treat everyone, no matter what the job, as equal. There are no reserved parking spaces. Everyone eats in the same cafeteria and has similar benefits. The result is improved communication as employees focus on problems and solutions rather than on how they are less valued than managers.

7. Sharing Information—If employees are to make decisions that are good for the long-term health and success of the company, they need to be given information about costs, finances, productivity, development times, and strategies that was previously known only by company managers.

Source: J. Pfeffer, *The Human Equation: Building Profits by Putting People First* (Boston: Harvard Business School Press, 1996).

The CFO: Not Just a Bean Counter

Having served as CFO at ADT Corp., Nalco Holdings Co., UAL Corp., and Xerox Corp., Kathryn Mikells knows a thing or two about the challenges of being a new CFO. Mikells describes several keys that can help new CFOs be successful. One of the most important steps is taking the time to talk to senior management and get a sense of where the company is and what challenges it faces. She also believes that the CFO should involve herself in strategic planning. "Strategy tends to tie directly into resource allocation and capital allocation," she says. "It's really important that [they] all link together." She also stresses the importance of getting a good feel for your team. A new CFO wants to quickly figure out what direction the team is going and what kind of skills the members have.

Source: K. Mikells, "Xerox CFO; An Atmosphere for Transformation," Interview by N. Knox, *The Wall Street* Journal, April 4, 2014, accessed April 9, 2014. http://blogs.wsj.com/cfo/2014/04/04/xerox-cfo-an-atmosphere-for-transformation/?mod=WSJ_business_cfo.

investment from 5.1 percent to 19.7 percent and increase sales by $94,000 per employee. They did this by adopting management techniques as simple as setting performance expectations (establishing goals, results, and schedules), coaching (informal, ongoing discussions between managers and subordinates about what is being done well and what could be done better), reviewing employee performance (annual, formal discussion about results), and rewarding employee performance (adjusting salaries and bonuses based on employee performance and results).[81] Two decades of research across 92 companies indicates that the average increase in company performance from using these management practices is typically around 20 percent.[82] So, in addition to significantly improving the profitability of healthy companies, sound management practices can turn around failing companies.

To determine how investing in people affects stock market performance, researchers matched companies on *Fortune* magazine's list of "100 Best Companies to Work for in America" with companies that were similar in industry, size, and—this is key—operating performance. Both sets of companies were equally good performers; the key difference was how well they treated their employees. For both sets of companies, the researchers found that employee attitudes such as job satisfaction changed little from year to year. The people who worked for the "100 Best" companies were consistently much more satisfied with their jobs and employers year after year than were employees in the matched companies. More importantly, those stable differences in employee attitudes were strongly related to differences in stock market performance. Over a three-year period,

an investment in the "100 Best" would have resulted in an 82 percent cumulative stock return compared with just 37 percent for the matched companies.[83] This difference is remarkable given that both sets of companies were equally good performers at the beginning of the period.

Finally, research also indicates that managers have an important effect on customer satisfaction. Many people find this surprising. They don't understand how managers, who are largely responsible for what goes on inside the company, can affect what goes on outside the company. They wonder how managers, who often interact with customers under negative conditions (when customers are angry or dissatisfied), can actually improve customer satisfaction. It turns out that managers influence customer satisfaction through employee satisfaction. When employees are satisfied with their jobs, their bosses, and the companies they work for, they provide much better service to customers.[84] In turn, customers are more satisfied, too. In fact, customers of companies on *Fortune*'s list of "100 Best," where employees are much more satisfied with their jobs and their companies, have much higher customer satisfaction scores than do customers of comparable companies that are not on *Fortune*'s list. Over an eight-year period, that difference in customer satisfaction also resulted in a 14 percent annual stock market return for the "100 Best" companies compared to a 6 percent return for the overall stock market.[85]

You will learn more about the service-profit chain in Chapter 18 on managing service and manufacturing operations.

STUDY TOOLS 1

LOCATED IN TEXTBOOK
☐ Rip out and review chapter review card

LOCATED AT WWW.CENGAGEBRAIN.COM
☐ Review key term flashcards and create your own from StudyBits
☐ Track your knowledge and understanding of key concepts, using the concept tracker

☐ Complete practice and graded quizzes to prepare for tests
☐ Complete interactive content within the exposition
☐ View chapter highlight box content at the beginning of each chapter

2 The History of Management

ea Golovney/Shutterstock.com

LEARNING OUTCOMES

2-1 Explain the origins of management.

2-2 Explain the history of scientific management.

2-3 Discuss the history of bureaucratic and administrative management.

2-4 Explain the history of human relations management.

2-5 Discuss the history of operations, information, systems, and contingency management.

After you finish

this chapter, go

to **PAGE 43** for

STUDY TOOLS

2-1 THE ORIGINS OF MANAGEMENT

Each day, managers are asked to solve challenging problems with a limited amount of time, people, or resources. Yet it's still their responsibility to get things done on schedule and within budget. Tell today's managers to "reward workers for improved production or performance," "set specific goals to increase motivation," or "innovate to create and sustain a competitive advantage," and they'll respond, "Duh! Who doesn't know that?" A mere 125 years ago, however, business ideas and practices were so different that today's widely accepted management ideas would have been as self-evident as space travel, smart phones, and flying drones. In fact, management jobs and careers didn't exist 125 years ago, so management was not yet a field of study. Now, of course, managers and management are such an important part of the business world that it's hard to imagine organizations without them. So if there were no managers 125 years ago, but you can't walk down the hall today without bumping into one, where did management come from?

Although we can find the seeds of many of today's management ideas throughout history, not until the past few centuries did systematic changes in the nature of work and organizations create a compelling need for managers.

2-1a Management Ideas and Practices throughout History

Examples of management thought and practice can be found throughout history.[1] For example, the earliest recorded instance of information management dates to ancient Sumer (modern Iraq), *circa* 8000–3000 BCE. Sumerian businesses used small clay tokens to calculate quantities of grain and livestock—and later, value-added goods such as perfume or pottery—that they owned and traded in temples and at city gates. Different shapes and sizes represented different types and quantities of goods. The tokens were also used to store data. They were kept in small clay envelopes, and the token shapes were impressed on the outside of the envelope to indicate what was inside. Eventually, someone figured out that it was easier to just write these symbols with a stylus on a tablet instead of using the tokens. In the end, the new technology of *writing* led to more efficient management of the business of Sumerian temples.[2]

A task as enormous as building the great pyramids in Egypt was bound to present practical problems that would lead to the development of management ideas. Egyptians recognized the need for planning, organizing, and controlling; for submitting written requests; and for consulting staff for advice before making decisions. The enormity of the task they faced is evident in the pyramid of King Khufu, which contains 2.3 million blocks of stone. Each block had to be quarried, cut to precise size and shape, cured (hardened in the sun), transported by boat for two to three days, moved to the construction site, numbered to identify where it would be placed, and then shaped and smoothed so that it would fit perfectly into place. It took 20,000 workers 23 years to complete this pyramid; more than 8,000 were needed just to quarry and transport the stones. A typical quarry expedition might include 100 army officers, 50 government and religious officials, and 200 members of the king's court to lead; 130 stonemasons to cut the stones; and 5,000 soldiers, 800 barbarians, and 2,000 bond servants to load and unload the stones from the ships.[3]

Exhibit 2.1 shows how other management ideas and practices throughout history relate to the management functions we discuss in this textbook.

2-1b Why We Need Managers Today

Working from 8:00 a.m. to 5:00 p.m., coffee breaks, lunch hours, crushing rush hour traffic, and punching a time clock are things we associate with today's working world. Work hasn't always been this way, however. In fact, the design of jobs and organizations has changed dramatically over the past 500 years. For most of humankind's history, for example, people didn't commute to work.[4] Work usually occurred in homes or on farms. In 1720, almost 80 percent of the 5.5 million people in England lived and worked in the country. And as recently as 1870, two-thirds of Americans earned their living from agriculture. Even most of those who didn't earn their living from agriculture didn't commute to work. Blacksmiths, furniture makers, leather goods makers, and other skilled tradespeople or craftspeople who formed trade guilds (the historical predecessors of labor unions) in England as early as 1093 typically worked out of shops in or next to their homes.[5] Likewise, cottage workers worked with each other out of small homes that were often built in a semicircle. A family in each cottage would complete a different production step, and work passed from one cottage to the next until production was complete. With small, self-organized work groups, no commute, no bosses, and no common building, there wasn't a strong need for management.

Exhibit 2.1
Management Ideas and Practices throughout History

Time	Individual or Group	Planning	Organizing	Leading	Controlling	Contributions to Management Thought and Practice
5000 BCE	Sumerians				√	Written record keeping
4000 BCE to 2000 BCE	Egyptians	√	√		√	Planning, organizing, and controlling to build the pyramids; submitting requests in writing; making decisions after consulting staff for advice
1800 BCE	Hammurabi				√	Controls and using witnesses in legal cases
600 BCE	Nebuchadnezzar		√	√		Wage incentives and production control
500 BCE	Sun Tzu	√		√		Strategy and identifying and attacking opponents' weaknesses
400 BCE	Xenophon	√	√	√	√	Management as separate art
400 BCE	Cyrus		√	√	√	Human relations and motion study
175	Cato		√			Job descriptions
284	Diocletian		√			Delegation of authority
900	al-Farabi			√		Leadership traits
1100	Ghazali			√		Managerial traits
1418	Barbarigo		√			Different organizational forms/structures
1436	Venetians				√	Numbering, standardization, and interchangeability of parts
1500	Sir Thomas More			√		Critique of poor management and leadership
1525	Machiavelli	√	√			Cohesiveness, power, and leadership in organizations

Source: C. S. George, Jr., *The History of Management Thought* (Englewood Cliffs, NJ: Prentice Hall, 1972).

During the Industrial Revolution (1750–1900), however, jobs and organizations changed dramatically.[6] First, unskilled laborers running machines began to replace high-paid, skilled artisans. This change was made possible by the availability of power (steam engines and, later, electricity) as well as numerous related inventions, including Darby's coke-smelting process and Cort's puddling and rolling process (both for making iron), as well as Hargreaves's spinning jenny and Arkwright's water frame (both for spinning cotton). Whereas artisans made entire goods by themselves by hand, this new production system was based on a division of labor: each worker, interacting with machines, performed separate, highly specialized tasks that were but a small part of all the steps required to make manufactured goods. Mass production was born as rope- and chain-driven assembly lines moved work to stationary workers who concentrated on performing one small task over and over again. While workers focused on their singular tasks, managers were needed to coordinate the different parts of the production system and optimize its overall performance. Productivity skyrocketed at companies that understood this. At **Ford Motor Company**, where the assembly line was developed, the time required to assemble a car dropped from 12.5 work hours to just 93 minutes after switching to mass production.[7]

Second, instead of being performed in fields, homes, or small shops, jobs occurred in large, formal organizations where hundreds, if not thousands, of people worked under one roof.[8] In 1849, for example, **Chicago Harvester** (the predecessor of International Harvester) ran the largest factory in the United States with just 123 workers. Yet by 1913, Henry Ford employed 12,000 employees in his Highland Park, Michigan, factory alone. Because the number of people working in manufacturing quintupled from 1860 to 1890, and individual factories employed so many workers under one roof, companies now had a strong need for disciplinary rules to impose order and structure. For the first time, they needed managers who knew how to organize large groups, work with employees, and make good decisions.

SCIENTIFIC MANAGEMENT

Before 1880, business educators taught only basic book-keeping and secretarial skills, and no one published books or articles about management.[9] Today you can turn to dozens of academic journals (such as the Academy of Management's *Journal* or *Review*, *Administrative Science Quarterly*, the *Strategic Management Journal*, and the *Journal of Applied Psychology*), hundreds of business school and practitioner journals (such as *Harvard Business Review*, *MIT Sloan Management Review*, and the *Academy of Management Perspectives*), and thousands of books and articles if you have a question about management. In the next four sections, you will learn about some important contributors to the field of management and how their ideas shaped our current understanding of management theory and practice.

Bosses, who were hired by the company owner or founder, used to make decisions by the seat of their pants—haphazardly, without any systematic study, thought, or collection of information. If the bosses decided that workers should work twice as fast, little or no thought was given to worker motivation. If workers resisted, the bosses often resorted to physical beatings to get workers to work faster, harder, or longer. With no incentives for bosses and workers to cooperate with one another, both groups played the system by trying to take advantage of each other. Moreover, each worker did the same job in his or her own way with different methods and different tools. In short, there were no procedures to standardize operations, no standards by which to judge whether performance was good or bad, and no follow-up to determine whether productivity or quality actually improved when changes were made.[10]

This all changed, however, with the advent of **scientific management**, which involved thorough study and testing of different work methods to identify the best, most efficient ways to complete a job.

Let's find out more about scientific management by learning about 2-2a Frederick W. Taylor, the father of scientific management; 2-2b Frank and Lillian Gilbreth and motion studies; and 2-2c Henry Gantt and his Gantt charts.

2-2a Father of Scientific Management: Frederick W. Taylor

Frederick W. Taylor (1856–1915), the father of scientific management, began his career as a worker at **Midvale**

Frederick W. Taylor was affected by his three-year struggle to get the men who worked for him to do, as he called it, "a fair day's work."

ullstein bild/Getty Images

Steel Company. He was promoted to patternmaker, supervisor, and then chief engineer. At Midvale, Taylor was deeply affected by his three-year struggle to get the men who worked for him to do, as he called it, "a fair day's work." Taylor, who had worked alongside the men as a coworker before becoming their boss, said, "We who were the workmen of that shop had the quantity output carefully agreed upon for everything that was turned out in the shop. We limited the output to about, I should think, one third of what we could very well have done." Taylor explained that, as soon as he became the boss, "the men who were working under me . . . knew that I was onto the whole game of **soldiering**, or deliberately restricting output."[11] When Taylor told his workers, "I have accepted a job under the management of this company and I am on the other side of the fence . . .

> **Scientific management** thoroughly studying and testing different work methods to identify the best, most efficient way to complete a job
>
> **Soldiering** when workers deliberately slow their pace or restrict their work output

Exhibit 2.2
Taylor's Four Principles of Scientific Management

First:	Develop a science for each element of a man's work, which replaces the old rule-of-thumb method.
Second:	Scientifically select and then train, teach, and develop the workman, whereas in the past, he chose his own work and trained himself as best he could.
Third:	Heartily cooperate with the men so as to ensure all of the work being done is in accordance with the principles of the science that has been developed.
Fourth:	There is an almost equal division of the work and the responsibility between the management and the workmen. The management take over all the work for which they are better fitted than the workmen, while in the past, almost all of the work and the greater part of the responsibility were thrown upon the men.

Source: F. W. Taylor, *The Principles of Scientific Management* (New York: Harper, 1911).

I am going to try to get a bigger output," the workers responded, "We warn you, Fred, if you try to bust any of these rates [a **rate buster** was someone who worked faster than the group] we will have you over the fence in six weeks."[12]

Over the next three years, Taylor tried everything he could think of to improve output. By doing the job himself, he showed workers that it was possible to produce more output. He hired new workers and trained them himself, hoping they would produce more. But "very heavy social pressure" from the other workers kept them from doing so. Pushed by Taylor, the workers began breaking their machines so that they couldn't produce. Taylor responded by fining them every time they broke a machine and for any violation of the rules, no matter how small, such as being late to work. Tensions became so severe that some of the workers threatened to shoot Taylor. Looking back at the situation, Taylor reflected, "It is a horrid life for any man to live, not to be able to look any workman in the face all day long without seeing hostility there and feeling that every man around one is his virtual enemy." He said, "I made up my mind either to get out of the business entirely and go into some other line of work or to find some remedy for this unbearable condition."[13]

The remedy that Taylor eventually developed was scientific management. Taylor, who once described scientific management as "seventy-five percent science and twenty-five percent common sense," emphasized that the goal of scientific management was to use systematic study to find the "one best way" of doing each task. To do that, managers had to

Rate buster a group member whose work pace is significantly faster than the normal pace in his or her group

follow the four principles shown in Exhibit 2.2. The first principle was to "develop a science" for each element of work. Study it. Analyze it. Determine the "one best way" to do the work. For example, one of Taylor's controversial proposals at the time was to give rest breaks to factory workers doing physical labor. We take morning, lunch, and afternoon breaks for granted, but in Taylor's day, factory workers were expected to work without stopping.[14] When Taylor said that breaks would increase worker productivity, no one believed him. Nonetheless, through systematic experiments, he showed that workers receiving frequent rest breaks were able to greatly increase their daily output.

Second, managers had to scientifically select, train, teach, and develop workers to help them reach their full potential. Before Taylor, supervisors often hired on the basis of favoritism and nepotism. Who you knew was often more important than what you could do. By contrast, Taylor instructed supervisors to hire "first-class" workers on the basis of their aptitude to do a job well. In one of the first applications of this principle, physical reaction times were used to select bicycle ball-bearing inspectors, who had to be able to examine ball bearings as fast as they were produced on a production line. For similar reasons, Taylor also recommended that companies train and develop their workers—a rare practice at the time.

The third principle instructed managers to cooperate with employees to ensure that the scientific principles were actually implemented. Labor unrest was widespread at the time; the number of labor strikes against companies doubled between 1893 and 1904. As Taylor knew from personal experience, workers and management more often than not viewed each other as enemies. Taylor's advice ran contrary to the common

Taylor's Rest Break Now Includes Napping

While rest breaks traditionally involve sitting or taking a brief walk, some employers now see a rest break as an opportunity for a quick snooze. Lampooned in movies, television, and even the business press, napping at work is nonetheless a proven way to increase focus, memory, and alertness on the job. A recent study from the University of Michigan found that a one-hour nap during the workday produced all those benefits—and more. As numerous as the benefits of napping are said to be, the challenges of napping at work are even more so. Not only is it difficult to break pace during the workday long enough to actually fall asleep, but finding a *place* to sleep can be challenging as well. Only 6 percent of companies have dedicated spaces for napping, and many employees work in loud, crowded spaces with stiff, uncomfortable chairs. Sleep experts do have some advice for people working at companies that embrace workday naps. First, when deciding what time to close your eyes, figure out the midpoint of your previous night's rest and add 12 hours. (For example, if you slept from 11 p.m. to 7 a.m., then your ideal nap time the next day is 3 p.m.) Once you know when to nap, sleep either for 20 or 90 minutes—ideal times for a re-energizing nap. Anything in between or beyond those two durations will leave the napper feeling groggy and ineffective, counteracting the point of the nap in the first place.

Source: R. Greenfield, "Napping at Work Can Be So Exhausting," *Bloomberg Businessweek*, August 20, 2015, http://www.bloomberg.com/news/articles/2015-08-20/napping-at-work-can-be-so-exhausting, accessed March 26, 2016.

wisdom of the day. He said, "The majority of these men believe that the fundamental interests of employees and employers are necessarily antagonistic. Scientific management, on the contrary, has for its very foundation the firm conviction that the true interests of the two are one and the same; that prosperity for the employer cannot exist through a long term of years unless it is accompanied by prosperity for the employee and vice versa; and that it is possible to give the workman what he most wants—high wages—and the employer what he wants—a low labor cost for his manufactures."[15] (See the MGMT Trends box for more on this point.)

The fourth principle of scientific management was to divide the work and the responsibility equally between management and workers. Prior to Taylor, workers alone were held responsible for productivity and performance. But, said Taylor, "Almost every act of the workman should be preceded by one or more preparatory acts of the management, which enable him to do his work better and quicker than he otherwise could. And each man should daily be taught by and receive the most friendly help from those who are over him, instead of being, at the one extreme, driven or coerced by his bosses, and at the other left, to his own unaided devices."[16]

Above all, Taylor believed these principles could be used to determine a "fair day's work," that is, what an average worker could produce at a reasonable pace, day in and day out. After that was determined, it was management's responsibility to pay workers fairly for that fair day's work. In essence, Taylor was trying to align management and employees so that what was good for employees was also good for management. In this way, he believed, workers and managers could avoid the conflicts he had experienced at Midvale Steel.

Although Taylor remains a controversial figure among some academics who believe that his ideas were bad for workers, his key ideas have stood the test of time.[17] These include using systematic analysis to identify the best methods; scientifically selecting, training, and developing workers; promoting cooperation between management and labor; developing standardized approaches and tools; setting specific tasks or goals and then rewarding workers with financial incentives; and giving workers shorter work hours and frequent breaks. In fact, his ideas are so well accepted and widely used that we take most of them for granted. As eminent management scholar Edwin Locke said, "The point is not, as is often claimed, that he was 'right in the context of his time,' but is now outdated, but that *most of his insights are still valid today*."[18]

2-2b Motion Studies: Frank and Lillian Gilbreth

The husband and wife team of Frank and Lillian Gilbreth are best known for their use of motion studies to simplify work, but they also made significant contributions to the employment of disabled workers and to the field of industrial psychology. Like Taylor, their early experiences significantly shaped their interests and contributions to management.

Frank and Lillian Gilbreth are best known for their use of motion studies to simplify work.

Though admitted to MIT, Frank Gilbreth (1868–1924) began his career as an apprentice bricklayer. While learning the trade, he noticed the bricklayers using three different sets of motions—one to teach others how to lay bricks, a second to work at a slow pace, and a third to work at a fast pace.[19] Wondering which was best, he studied the various approaches and began eliminating unnecessary motions. For example, by designing a stand that could be raised to waist height, he eliminated the need to bend over to pick up each brick. Turning to grab a brick was faster and easier than bending down. By having lower-paid workers place all the bricks with their most attractive side up, bricklayers didn't waste time turning a brick over to find it. By mixing a more consistent mortar, bricklayers no longer had to tap each brick numerous times to put it in the right position. Together, Gilbreth's improvements raised productivity from 120 to 350 bricks per hour and from 1,000 bricks to 2,700 bricks per day.

As a result of his experience with bricklaying, Gilbreth and his wife, Lillian, developed a long-term interest in using motion study to simplify work, improve productivity, and reduce the level of effort required to safely perform a job. Indeed, Frank Gilbreth said, "The greatest waste in the world comes from needless, ill-directed, and ineffective motions."[20] **Motion study** broke each task or job into separate motions and then eliminated those that were unnecessary or repetitive. Because many motions were completed very quickly, the Gilbreths used motion-picture films, then a relatively new technology, to analyze jobs. Most film cameras at that time were hand cranked and thus variable in their film speed, so Frank invented the microchronometer, a large clock that could record time to 1/2,000th of a second. By placing the microchonometer next to the worker in the camera's field of vision and attaching a flashing strobe light to the worker's hands to better identify the direction and sequence of key movements, the Gilbreths could use film to detect and precisely time even the slightest, fastest movements. Motion study typically yielded production increases of 25–300 percent.[21]

Taylor also strove to simplify work, but he did so by managing time rather than motion as the Gilbreths did.[22] Taylor developed time study to put an end to soldiering and to determine what could be considered a fair day's work. **Time study** worked by timing how long it took a "first-class man" to complete each part of his job. A standard time was established after allowing for rest periods, and a worker's pay would increase or decrease depending on whether the worker exceeded or fell below that standard.

Lillian Gilbreth (1878–1972) was an important contributor to management in her own right. She was the first woman to receive a PhD in industrial psychology as well as the first woman to become a member of the Society of Industrial Engineers and the American Society of Mechanical Engineers. When Frank died in 1924, she continued the work of their management consulting company (which they had shared for over a dozen years). Lillian, who was concerned with the human side of work, was one of the first contributors to industrial psychology, originating ways to improve office communication, incentive programs, job satisfaction, and management training. Her work also convinced the government to enact laws regarding workplace safety, ergonomics, and child labor.

2-2c Charts: Henry Gantt

Henry Gantt (1861–1919) was first a protégé and then an associate of Frederick W. Taylor. Gantt is best known for the Gantt chart, but he also made significant contributions to management with respect to pay-for-

Motion study breaking each task or job into its separate motions and then eliminating those that are unnecessary or repetitive

Time study timing how long it takes good workers to complete each part of their jobs

Exhibit 2.3
Gantt Chart for Starting Construction on a New Headquarters

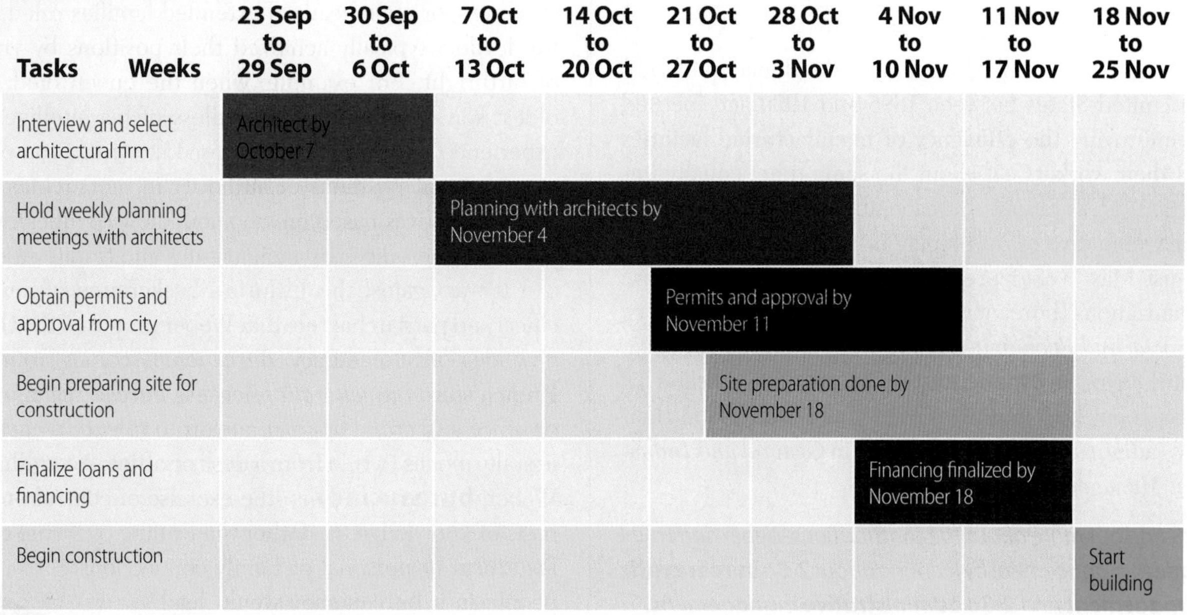

Tasks	Weeks	23 Sep to 29 Sep	30 Sep to 6 Oct	7 Oct to 13 Oct	14 Oct to 20 Oct	21 Oct to 27 Oct	28 Oct to 3 Nov	4 Nov to 10 Nov	11 Nov to 17 Nov	18 Nov to 25 Nov
Interview and select architectural firm		Architect by October 7								
Hold weekly planning meetings with architects				Planning with architects by November 4						
Obtain permits and approval from city							Permits and approval by November 11			
Begin preparing site for construction								Site preparation done by November 18		
Finalize loans and financing									Financing finalized by November 18	
Begin construction										Start building

performance plans and the training and development of workers. As shown in Exhibit 2.3, a **Gantt chart** visually indicates what tasks must be completed at which times in order to complete a project. It accomplishes this by showing time in various units on the x-axis and tasks on the y-axis. For example, Exhibit 2.3 shows that the following tasks must be completed by the following dates: in order to start construction on a new company headquarters by the week of November 18, the architectural firm must be selected by October 7, architectural planning done by November 4, permits obtained from the city by November 11, site preparation finished by November 18, and loans and financing finalized by November 18.

Though simple and straightforward, Gantt charts were revolutionary in the era of seat-of-the-pants management because of the detailed planning information they provided. As Gantt wrote, "By using the graphical forms, its [the Gantt chart's] value is very much increased, for the general appearance of the sheet is sufficient to tell how closely the schedule is being lived up to; in other words, whether the plant is being run efficiently or not."[23] Gantt said, "Such sheets show at a glance where the delays occur, and indicate what must have our attention in order to keep up the proper output." The use of Gantt charts is so widespread today that nearly all project management software and computer spreadsheets have the capability to create charts that track and visually display the progress being made on a project.

Finally, Gantt, along with Taylor, was one of the first to strongly recommend that companies train and develop their workers.[24] In his work with companies, he found that workers achieved their best performance levels if they were trained first. At the time, however, supervisors were reluctant to teach workers what they knew for fear that they could lose their jobs to more knowledgeable workers. Gantt overcame the supervisors' resistance by rewarding them with bonuses for properly training all of their workers. Said Gantt, "This is the first recorded attempt to make it in the financial interest of the foreman to teach the individual worker, and the importance of it cannot be overestimated, for it changes the foreman from a driver of men to their friend and helper."[25] Gantt's approach to training was straightforward: "(1) A scientific investigation in detail of each piece of work, and the determination of the best method and the shortest time in which the work can be done. (2) A teacher capable of teaching the best method and the shortest time. (3) Reward for both teacher and pupil when the latter is successful."[26]

> **Gantt chart** a graphical chart that shows which tasks must be completed at which times in order to complete a project or task

2-3 BUREAUCRATIC AND ADMINISTRATIVE MANAGEMENT

The field of scientific management developed quickly in the United States between 1895 and 1920 and focused on improving the efficiency of manufacturing facilities and their workers. At about the same time, equally important ideas about bureaucratic and administrative management were developing in Europe. German sociologist Max Weber presented a new way to run entire organizations (bureaucratic management) in *The Theory of Social and Economic Organization*, published in 1922. Henri Fayol, an experienced French CEO, published his ideas about how and what managers should do in their jobs (administrative management) in *General and Industrial Management* in 1916.

Let's find out more about the contributions Weber and Fayol made to management by learning about 2-3a bureaucratic management and 2-3b administrative management.

2-3a Bureaucratic Management: Max Weber

Today, when we hear the term *bureaucracy*, we think of inefficiency and red tape, incompetence and ineffectiveness, and rigid administrators blindly enforcing nonsensical rules. When German sociologist Max Weber (1864–1920)

Bureaucracy the exercise of control on the basis of knowledge, expertise, or experience

first proposed the idea of bureaucratic organizations, however, these problems were associated with monarchies and patriarchies rather than bureaucracies. In monarchies, where kings, queens, sultans, and emperors ruled, and patriarchies, where a council of elders, wise men, or male heads of extended families ruled, the top leaders typically achieved their positions by virtue of birthright. For example, when the queen died, her oldest son became king, regardless of his intelligence, experience, education, or desire. Likewise, promotion to prominent positions of authority in monarchies and patriarchies was based on who you knew (politics), who you were (heredity), or ancient rules and traditions.

It was against this historical background of monarchical and patriarchal rule that Weber proposed the then-new idea of bureaucracy. *Bureaucracy* comes from the French word *bureaucratie*. Because *bureau* means desk or office and *cratie* or *cracy* means to rule, *bureaucracy* literally means to rule from a desk or office. According to Weber, **bureaucracy** is "the exercise of control on the basis of knowledge."[27] Rather than ruling by virtue of favoritism or personal or family connections, people in a bureaucracy would lead by virtue of their rational-legal

Exhibit 2.4
Elements of Bureaucratic Organizations

Qualification-based hiring:	Employees are hired on the basis of their technical training or educational background.
Merit-based promotion:	Promotion is based on experience or achievement. Managers, not organizational owners, decide who is promoted.
Chain of command:	Each job occurs within a hierarchy, the chain of command, in which each position reports and is accountable to a higher position. A grievance procedure and a right to appeal protect people in lower positions.
Division of labor:	Tasks, responsibilities, and authority are clearly divided and defined.
Impartial application of rules and procedures:	Rules and procedures apply to all members of the organization and will be applied in an impartial manner, regardless of one's position or status.
Recorded in writing:	All administrative decisions, acts, rules, and procedures will be recorded in writing.
Managers separate from owners:	The owners of an organization should not manage or supervise the organization.

Source: M. Weber, *The Theory of Social and Economic Organization*, trans. A. Henderson and T. Parsons (New York: The Free Press, 1947), 329–334.

Maxx-Studio/Shutterstock.com/Wavebreakmedia/Shutterstock.com/Ryan McVay/Photodisc/Getty Images/Michaeljung/Shutterstock.com/XRoigs/Shutterstock.com/Pressmaster/Shutterstock.com/Andy Dean Photography/Shutterstock.com

authority—in other words, their knowledge, expertise, or experience. Furthermore, the aim of bureaucracy is not to protect authority but to achieve an organization's goals in the most efficient way possible.

Exhibit 2.4 shows the seven elements that, according to Weber, characterize bureaucracies. First, instead of hiring people because of their family or political connections or personal loyalty, they should be hired because their technical training or education qualifies them to do the job well. Second, along the same lines, promotion within the company should no longer be based on who you know (politics) or who you are (heredity) but on your experience or achievements. And to further limit the influence of personal connections in the promotion process, *managers* rather than organizational owners should decide who gets promoted. Third, each position or job is part of a chain of command that clarifies who reports to whom throughout the organization. Those higher in the chain of command have the right, if they so choose, to give commands, take action, and make decisions concerning activities occurring anywhere below them in the chain. Unlike in many monarchies or patriarchies, however, those lower in the chain of command are protected by a grievance procedure that gives them the right to appeal the decisions of those in higher positions. Fourth, to increase efficiency and effectiveness, tasks and responsibilities should be separated and assigned to those best qualified to complete them. Authority is vested in these task-defined positions rather than in people, and the authority of each position is clearly defined in order to reduce confusion and conflict. If you move to a different job in a bureaucracy, your authority increases or decreases commensurate with the responsibilities of that job. Fifth, because of his strong distaste for favoritism, Weber believed that an organization's rules and procedures should apply to all the members regardless of their position or status. Sixth, to ensure consistency and fairness over time and across different leaders and supervisors, all rules, procedures, and decisions should be recorded in writing. Finally, to reduce favoritism, "professional" managers rather than company owners should manage or supervise the organization.

When viewed in historical context, Weber's ideas about bureaucracy represent a tremendous improvement in how organizations should be run. Fairness supplanted favoritism, the goal of efficiency replaced the goal of personal gain, and logical rules and procedures took the place of traditions or arbitrary decision making.

Today, however, after more than a century of experience, we recognize that bureaucracy has limitations as well. Weber called bureaucracy the "iron cage" and said, "Once fully established, bureaucracy is among those social structures which are the hardest to destroy."[28] In bureaucracies, managers are supposed to influence employee behavior by fairly rewarding or punishing employees for compliance or noncompliance with organizational policies, rules, and procedures. In reality, however, most employees would argue that bureaucratic managers emphasize punishment for noncompliance much more than rewards for compliance. Ironically, bureaucratic management was created to prevent just this type of managerial behavior.

2-3b Administrative Management: Henri Fayol

Though his work was not translated and widely recognized in the United States until 1949, Frenchman Henri Fayol (1841–1925) was as important a contributor to the field of management as Taylor. Like Taylor and the Gilbreths, Fayol's work experience significantly shaped his thoughts and ideas about management. But, whereas Taylor's ideas changed companies from the shop floor up, Fayol's ideas were shaped by his experience as a managing director (CEO) and generally changed companies from the board of directors down.[29] Fayol is best known for developing five functions of managers and 14 principles of management, as well as for his belief that management can and should be taught to others.

The most formative events in Fayol's business career came during his 20+ years as the managing director of Compagnie de Commentry-Fourchambault et Décazeville, commonly known as **Comambault**, a vertically integrated steel company that owned several coal and iron ore mines and employed 10,000–13,000 workers. Fayol was initially hired by the board of directors to shut down the "hopeless" steel company. The company was facing increased competition from English and German steel companies, which had lower costs, and from new steel mills in northern and eastern France, which were closer to major markets and thus could avoid the high shipping costs incurred by Fayol's company, located in central France.[30] In the five years before Fayol became CEO, production had dropped more than 60 percent, from 38,000 to 15,000 annual metric tons. Comambault had exhausted a key supply of coal needed for steel production, had already shut down one steel mill, and was losing money at another.[31] The company had quit paying dividends to shareholders and had no cash to invest in new technology, such as blast furnaces, that could lower its costs and increase productivity.

So the board hired Fayol as CEO to quickly dissolve and liquidate the business. But, after "four months of reflection and study," he presented the board with a plan, backed by detailed facts and figures, to save the company.[32] With little to lose, the board agreed. Fayol then began the process of turning the company around by obtaining supplies of key resources such as coal and iron ore; using research to develop new steel alloy products; carefully selecting key subordinates in research, purchasing, manufacturing, and sales and then delegating responsibility to them; and cutting costs by moving the company to a better location closer to key markets.[33] Looking back ten years later, Fayol attributed his and the company's success to changes in management practices. He wrote, "When I assumed the responsibility for the restoration of Décazeville, I did not rely on my technical superiority.... I relied on my ability as an organizer [and my] skill in handling men."[34]

Based on his experience as a CEO, Fayol argued that "the success of an enterprise generally depends much more on the administrative ability of its leaders than on their technical ability."[35] And, as you learned in Chapter 1, Fayol argued that managers need to perform five managerial functions if they are to be successful: planning, organizing, coordinating, commanding, and controlling.[36] Because most management textbooks have dropped the coordinating function and now refer to Fayol's commanding function as "leading," these functions are widely known as planning (determining organizational goals and a means for achieving them), organizing (deciding where decisions will be made, who will do what jobs and tasks, and who will work for whom), leading (inspiring and motivating workers to work hard to achieve organizational goals), and controlling (monitoring progress toward goal achievement and taking corrective action when needed). In addition, according to Fayol, effective management is based on the 14 principles in Exhibit 2.5.

Exhibit 2.5
Fayol's 14 Principles of Management

1. **Division of work**

   Increase production by dividing work so that each worker completes smaller tasks or job elements.

2. **Authority and responsibility**

   A manager's authority, which is the "right to give orders," should be commensurate with the manager's responsibility. However, organizations should enact controls to prevent managers from abusing their authority.

3. **Discipline**

   Clearly defined rules and procedures are needed at all organizational levels to ensure order and proper behavior.

4. **Unity of command**

   To avoid confusion and conflict, each employee should report to and receive orders from just one boss.

5. **Unity of direction**

   One person and one plan should be used in deciding the activities to be carried out to accomplish each organizational objective.

6. **Subordination of individual interests to the general interests**

   Employees must put the organization's interests and goals before their own.

7. **Remuneration**

   Compensation should be fair and satisfactory to both the employees and the organization; that is, don't overpay or underpay employees.

8. **Centralization**

   Avoid too much centralization or decentralization. Strike a balance depending on the circumstances and employees involved.

9. **Scalar chain**

   From the top to the bottom of an organization, each position is part of a vertical chain of authority in which each worker reports to just one boss. For the sake of simplicity, communication outside normal work groups or departments should follow the vertical chain of authority.

10. **Order**

    To avoid confusion and conflict, order can be obtained by having a place for everyone and having everyone in his or her place; in other words, there should be no overlapping responsibilities.

11. **Equity**

    Kind, fair, and just treatment for all will develop devotion and loyalty. This does not exclude discipline, if warranted, and consideration of the broader general interests of the organization.

12. **Stability of tenure of personnel**

    Low turnover, meaning a stable work force with high tenure, benefits an organization by improving performance, lowering costs, and giving employees, especially managers, time to learn their jobs.

13. **Initiative**

    Because it is a "great source of strength for business," managers should encourage the development of initiative, or the ability to develop and implement a plan, in others.

14. ***Esprit de corps***

    Develop a strong sense of morale and unity among workers that encourages coordination of efforts.

Sources: H. Fayol, *General and Industrial Management* (London: Pittman & Sons, 1949); M. Fells, "Fayol Stands the Test of Time," *Journal of Management History* 6 (2000): 345–360; C. Rodrigues, "Fayol's 14 Principles of Management Then and Now: A Framework for Managing Today's Organizations Effectively," *Management Decision* 39 (2001): 880–889.

DOING THE RIGHT THING

C.C. Spaulding: "Mr. Cooperation," African-American CEO, and Early Contributor to Management

Thanks to new archival research by Professors Leon Prieto and Simone Phipps, Charles Clinton (C.C.) Spaulding is now recognized as a significant early contributor to the field of management. Spaulding, a successful African American business executive, was born ten years (1874) after the end of the American Civil War and died 12 years (1952) before passage of the 1964 Civil Rights Act outlawing discrimination.

Like Henry Fayol and Chester Barnard, Spaulding's experience as president of the North Carolina Mutual Life Insurance Company—then the largest African American insurance company in the United States—shaped his views about management. However, Spaulding wrote his eight fundamental necessities of business administration in a 1927 article titled "The Administration of Big Business" before Barnard's (1938) and Fayol's (1949) ideas were first published in the United States. His ideas on conflict and cooperation are consistent with those of Mary Parket Follett, which were also published during the 1920s. Spaulding's eight fundamental necessities of management are, in the author's own words:

▶ Necessity 1: Cooperation and Teamwork. "Not only should executives confer daily with each other, disclosing all the facts and circumstances attendant upon their operations, but they ought to keep constant check upon the activities and liabilities of their associates . . . "

▶ Necessity 2: Authority and Responsibility. "There must always be some responsible executive who must pass upon every issue that is fundamental; he must be the final authority from whom there is no appeal except to the entire group in conference."

▶ Necessity 3: Division of Labor. "Departmental divisions function separately under the direction of experts who may or may not be executive officers."

▶ Necessity 4: Adequate Manpower. "First and foremost success in business depends upon adequate manpower. Our schools are turning out only partially trained young people with no business experience whatsoever, and while many of them are good technicians they are for the most part helpless in their new jobs because there is little correlation between the classroom and the business office."

▶ Necessity 5: Adequate Capital. "Initial capital must not only be sufficient to commence operations, but must be sustaining over a given period . . . Even large scale corporations frequently dissipate their surplus earnings in hurried dividends instead of re-investing the surplus for the extension of the business."

▶ Necessity 6: Feasibility Analysis. "Frequently it happens that as soon as one person or group appears successful in a given line [of business] another person or group organizes a new enterprise in the same line without ascertaining the advisability of such a move, as reflected in the needs and resources of the community."

▶ Necessity 7: Advertising Budget. "[. . .] when it comes to advertising, a large number of our organizations are depriving themselves of the most effective means of propagation . . . Very few of these have an annual appropriation for advertisement."

▶ Necessity 8: Conflict Resolution. "Personal contact and business contact, if not properly directed and if not based on mutual goodwill and intelligence derived from a common sense education, will develop personal conflict and business conflict instead of personal cooperation and business cooperation."

Sources: L.C. Prieto & S.T.A. Phipps, "Re-discovering Charles Clinton Spaulding's 'The Administration of Big Business,' Insight Into Early 20th Century African-American Management Thought," *Journal of Management History* 22 (1) (2016): 73–90; A. Rutledge, "They call him 'Co-operation,'" *The Saturday Evening Post*, March 27, 1943, p. 15; C.C. Spaulding, "The Administration of Big Business," *The Pittsburgh Courier*, August, 13, 1927, 4; C.C. Spaulding, "The Administration of Big Business," *The Pittsburgh Courier*, August, 20, 1927, 8; H. Fayol, *General and Industrial Management* (London: Pittman & Sons, 1949); P. Graham, ed., *Mary Parker Follett—Prophet of Management: A Celebration of Writings from the 1920s* (Boston: Harvard Business School Press, 1995); C. I. Barnard, *The Functions of the Executive* (Cambridge, MA: Harvard University Press, 1938).

2-4 HUMAN RELATIONS MANAGEMENT

As we have seen, scientific management focuses on improving efficiency; bureaucratic management focuses on using knowledge, fairness, and logical rules and procedures; and administrative management focuses on how and what managers should do in their jobs. The human relations approach to management focuses on *people*, particularly the psychological and social aspects of work. This approach to management sees people not as just extensions of machines but as valuable organizational resources in their own right. Human relations management holds that people's needs are important and that their efforts, motivation, and performance are affected by the work they do and their relationships with their bosses, coworkers, and work groups. In other words, efficiency alone is not enough. Organizational success also depends on treating workers well.

*Let's find out more about human relations management by learning about **2-4a Mary Parker Follett's theories of constructive conflict and coordination, 2-4b Elton Mayo's Hawthorne Studies,** and **2-4c Chester Barnard's theories of cooperation and acceptance of authority.***

2-4a Constructive Conflict and Coordination: Mary Parker Follett

Mary Parker Follett (1868–1933) was a social worker with a degree in political science who, in her 50s, after 25 years of working with schools and nonprofit organizations, began lecturing and writing about management and working extensively as a consultant for business and government leaders in the United States and Europe. Although her contributions were overlooked for decades, perhaps because she was a woman or perhaps because they were so different, many of today's "new" management ideas can clearly be traced to her work.

Follett believed that the best way to deal with conflict was not **domination**, where one side wins and the other loses, or **compromise**, where each side gives up some of what it wants, but integration. Said Follett, "There is a way beginning now to be recognized at least, and even occasionally followed: when two desires are *integrated*, that means that a solution has been found in which both desires have found a place that neither side has had to sacrifice anything."[37] So, rather than one side dominating the other or both sides compromising, the point of **integrative conflict resolution** is to have both parties indicate their preferences and then work together to find an alternative that meets the needs of both. According to Follett, "Integration involves invention, and the clever thing is to recognize this, and not to let one's thinking stay within the boundaries of two alternatives which are mutually exclusive." Indeed, Follett's ideas about the positive use of conflict and an integrative approach to conflict resolution predate accepted thinking in the negotiation and conflict resolution literature by six decades (see the best-selling book *Getting to Yes: Negotiating Agreement without Giving In* by Roger Fisher, William Ury, and Bruce Patton).

Exhibit 2.6 summarizes Follett's contributions to management in her own words. She casts power as "with" rather than "over" others. Giving orders involves

Domination occurs when one party satisfies its desires and objectives at the expense of the other party's desires and objectives.

discussing instructions and dealing with resentment. Authority flows from job knowledge and experience rather than position. Leadership involves setting the tone for the team rather than being aggressive and dominating, which may be harmful. Coordination and control should be based on facts and information. In the end, Follett's contributions added significantly to our understanding of the human, social, and psychological sides of management. Peter Parker, the former chairman of the London School of Economics, said about Follett: "People often puzzle about who is the father of management. I don't know who the father was, but I have no doubt about who was the mother."[38]

2-4b Hawthorne Studies: Elton Mayo

Australian-born Elton Mayo (1880–1948) is best known for his role in the famous Hawthorne Studies at the **Western Electric Company**. The Hawthorne Studies were conducted in several stages between 1924 and 1932 at a Western Electric plant in Chicago. Although Mayo didn't join the studies until 1928, he played a significant role thereafter, writing about the results in his book, *The Human Problems of an Industrial Civilization*.[39] The first stage of the Hawthorne Studies investigated the

Domination an approach to dealing with conflict in which one party satisfies its desires and objectives at the expense of the other party's desires and objectives

Compromise an approach to dealing with conflict in which both parties give up some of what they want in order to reach agreement on a plan to reduce or settle the conflict

Integrative conflict resolution an approach to dealing with conflict in which both parties indicate their preferences and then work together to find an alternative that meets the needs of both

Exhibit 2.6

Mary Parker Follett says . . .

On constructive conflict...

"As conflict—difference—is here in this world, as we cannot avoid it, we should, I think, use it to work for us. Instead of condemning it, we should set it to work for us."

On power...

"It seems to me that whereas power usually means power-over, the power of some person or group over some other person or group, it is possible to develop the conception of power-with, a jointly developed power, a co-active, not a coercive power."

On the giving of orders...

"An advantage of not exacting blind obedience, of discussing your instructions with your subordinates, is that if there is any resentment, any come-back, you get it out into the open, and when it is in the open, you can deal with it."

On authority...

"Authority should go with knowledge and experience, that is where obedience is due, no matter whether it is up the line or down."

On leadership...

"Of the greatest importance is the ability to grasp a total situation. . . . Out of a welter of facts, experience, desires, aims, the leader must find the unifying thread. He must see a whole, not a mere kaleidoscope of pieces. . . . The higher up you go, the more ability you have to have of this kind."

On coordination...

"The most important thing to remember about unity is—that there is no such thing. There is only unifying. You cannot get unity and expect it to last a day—or five minutes. Every man in a business should be taking part in a certain process and that process is unifying."

On control...

"Central control is coming more and more to mean the co-relation of many controls rather than a superimposed control."

Source: M. Parker Follett, *Mary Parker Follett—Prophet of Management: A Celebration of Writings from the 1920s*, ed. P. Graham (Boston: Harvard Business School Press, 1995).

iStockphoto.com/Kokoroyuki

effects of lighting levels and incentives on employee productivity in the Relay Test Assembly Room, where workers took approximately a minute to put "together a coil, armature, contact springs, and insulators in a fixture and secure the parts by means of four machine screws."[40]

Two groups of six experienced female workers, five to do the work and one to supply needed parts, were separated from the main part of the factory by a ten-foot partition and placed at a standard work bench with the necessary parts and tools. Over the next five years, the experimenters introduced various levels and combinations of lighting, financial incentives, and rest pauses (work breaks) to study the effect on productivity. Curiously, however, production levels increased whether the experimenters increased or decreased the lighting, paid workers based on individual production or group production, or increased or decreased the number and length of rest pauses. In fact, Mayo and his fellow researchers were surprised that production steadily increased from 2,400 relays per day at the beginning of the study to 3,000 relays per day five years later. The question was: Why?

Mayo and his colleagues eventually concluded that two things accounted for the results. First, substantially more attention was paid to these workers than to workers in the rest of the plant. Mayo wrote, "Before every change of program [in the study], the group is consulted. Their comments are listened to and discussed; sometimes their objections are allowed to negate a suggestion. The group unquestionably develops a sense of participation in the critical determinations and becomes something of a social unit."[41]

For years, the "Hawthorne Effect" has been *incorrectly* defined as increasing productivity by paying more attention to workers.[42] But it is not simply about attention from management. The Hawthorne Effect cannot be understood without giving equal importance to the social units, which became intensely cohesive groups. Mayo said, "What actually happened was that six individuals became a team and the team gave itself wholeheartedly and spontaneously to cooperation in the experiment. The consequence was that they felt themselves to be participating freely and without afterthought, and they were happy in the knowledge that they were working without coercion from above or limits from below."[43]

For the first time, human factors related to work were found to be more important than the physical conditions or design of the work. Together, the increased attention from management and the development of a cohesive work group led to significantly higher levels of job satisfaction and productivity. In short, the Hawthorne Studies found that workers' feelings and attitudes affected their work.

The next stage of the Hawthorne Studies was conducted in the Bank Wiring Room, where "the group consisted of nine wiremen, three solderers, and two inspectors. Each of these groups performed a specific task and collaborated with the other two in completion of each unit of equipment. The task consisted of setting up the banks of terminals side-by-side on frames, wiring the corresponding terminals from bank to bank, soldering the connections, and inspecting with a test set for short circuits or breaks in the wire. One solderman serviced the work of the three wiremen."[44] While productivity increased in the Relay Test Assembly Room no matter what the researchers did, productivity dropped in the Bank Wiring Room. Again, the question was: Why?

DOING THE RIGHT THING

Cooperation ≠ Collaboration

The modern work environment focuses so much on teams and groups that it can be easy to mistake pleasant, agreeable, and friendly behavior for collaboration. These traits describe cooperation, which on its own often fails to produce the desired results. True collaboration goes beyond social niceties; it requires aligning resources and goals with others and doing so in real time. To move beyond simple cooperation to true collaboration, follow these four steps:

1. Identify your goal.

2. Create the framework you need to achieve your goal by clearly stating what you need, in what form, and by when.

3. Decide if the framework is possible to implement.

4. Convene all (not just some) of the required collaborators for a work session to review, revise, and commit to the collaboration.

Getting real results requires moving beyond merely cooperating to the real work of collaborating.

Source: R. Ashkenas, "There's a Difference between Cooperation and Collaboration," *Harvard Business Review*, April 20, 2015, https://hbr.org/2015/04/theres-a-difference-between-cooperation-and-collaboration, accessed April 8, 2016.

The point of integrative conflict resolution is to have both parties indicate their preferences and then work together to find an alternative that meets the needs of both.

Mayo and his colleagues found that the differences in performance were due to group dynamics. The workers in the Bank Wiring Room had been an existing work group for some time and had already developed strong negative norms that governed their behavior. For instance, despite a group financial incentive for production, the group members decided that they would wire only 6,000–6,600 connections a day (depending on the kind of equipment they were wiring), well below the production goal of 7,300 connections that management had set for them. Individual workers who worked at a faster pace were socially ostracized from the group or "binged" (hit on the arm) until they slowed their work pace. Thus, the group's behavior was reminiscent of the soldiering that Taylor had observed. Mayo concluded, "Work [was] done in accord with the group's conception of a day's work; this was exceeded by only one individual who was cordially disliked."[45]

In the end, the Hawthorne Studies demonstrated that the workplace was more complex than previously thought, that workers were not just extensions of machines, and that financial incentives weren't necessarily the most important motivator for workers. By highlighting the crucial role, positive or negative, that groups, group norms, and group behavior play at work, Mayo strengthened Follett's point about coordination—make just one change in an organization and others, some expected and some unexpected, will occur. Thanks to Mayo and his colleagues and their work on the Hawthorne Studies, managers better understood the effect that group social interactions, employee satisfaction, and attitudes had on individual and group performance.

Organization a system of consciously coordinated activities or forces created by two or more people

2-4c Cooperation and Acceptance of Authority: Chester Barnard

Like Fayol, Chester Barnard (1886–1961) had experiences as a top executive that shaped his views of management. Barnard began his career in 1909 as an engineer and translator for AT&T, becoming a general manager at Pennsylvania Bell Telephone in 1922 and then president of New Jersey Bell Telephone in 1927.[46] Barnard's ideas, published in his classic book, *The Functions of the Executive*, influenced companies from the board of directors down. He is best known for his ideas about cooperation and the acceptance of authority.

Barnard proposed a comprehensive theory of cooperation in formal organizations. In fact, he defines an **organization** as a "system of consciously coordinated activities or forces of two or more persons."[47] In other words, organization occurs whenever two people work together for some purpose, whether it be classmates working together to complete a class project, Habitat for Humanity volunteers donating their time to build a house, or managers working with subordinates to reduce costs, improve quality, or increase sales. Barnard placed so much emphasis on cooperation because cooperation is *not* the normal state of affairs: "Failure to cooperate, failure of cooperation, failure of organization, disorganization, disintegration, destruction of organization—and reorganization—are characteristic facts of human history."[48]

According to Barnard, the extent to which people willingly cooperate in an organization depends on how workers perceive executive authority and whether they're willing to accept it. Many managerial requests or directives fall within a *zone of indifference* in which acceptance of managerial authority is automatic. For example, if your supervisor asks you for a copy of the monthly inventory report, and compiling and writing that report is part of your job, you think nothing of the request and automatically send it. In general, people will be indifferent to managerial directives or orders if they (1) are understood, (2) are consistent with the purpose of the organization, (3) are compatible with the people's personal interests, and (4) can actually be carried out by those people. Acceptance of managerial authority (that is, cooperation) is not automatic, however. Ask people to do things contrary to the organization's purpose or to their own benefit and they'll put up a fight. While many people assume that managers have the authority to do whatever they want, Barnard, referring to the "fiction of superior authority," believed that workers ultimately grant managers their authority.

2-5 OPERATIONS, INFORMATION, SYSTEMS, AND CONTINGENCY MANAGEMENT

In this last section, we review four other significant historical approaches to management that have influenced how today's managers produce goods and services on a daily basis, gather and manage the information they need to understand their businesses and make good decisions, understand how the different parts of the company work together as a whole, and recognize when and where particular management practices are likely to work.

To better understand these ideas, let's learn about 2-5a operations management, 2-5b information management, 2-5c systems management, and 2-5d contingency management.

2-5a Operations Management

In Chapter 18, you will learn about *operations management*, which involves managing the daily production of goods and services. In general, operations management uses a quantitative or mathematical approach to find ways to increase productivity, improve quality, and manage or reduce costly inventories. The most commonly used operations management tools and methods are quality control, forecasting techniques, capacity planning, productivity measurement and improvement, linear programming, scheduling systems, inventory systems, work measurement techniques (similar to the Gilbreths' motion studies), project management (similar to Gantt's charts), and cost-benefit analysis.[49]

Since the sixteenth century, skilled craftspeople made the lock, stock, and barrel of a gun by hand. After each part was made, a skilled gun finisher assembled the parts into a complete gun. But the gun finisher did not simply screw the different parts of a gun together, as is done today. Instead, each handmade part required extensive finishing and adjusting so that it would fit

together with the other handmade gun parts. Hand-fitting was necessary because, even when made by the same skilled craftspeople, no two parts were alike. In fact, gun finishers played a role similar to that of fine watchmakers who meticulously assembled expensive watches—without them, the product simply wouldn't work. Today, we would say that these parts were low quality because they varied so much from one part to another.

All this changed in 1791 when the U.S. government, worried about a possible war with France, ordered 40,000 muskets from private gun contractors. All but one contractor built handmade muskets assembled by skilled gun finishers who made sure that all the parts fit together. Thus, each musket was unique. If a part broke, a replacement part had to be handcrafted. But one contractor, Eli Whitney of New Haven, Connecticut (who is better known for his invention of the cotton gin), determined that if gun parts were made accurately enough, guns could be made with standardized, interchangeable parts. So he designed machine tools that allowed unskilled workers to make each gun part the same as the next. Said Whitney, "The tools which I contemplate to make are similar to an engraving on copper plate from which may be taken a great number of impressions perceptibly alike."[50] Years passed before Whitney delivered his 10,000 muskets to the U.S. government. But he demonstrated the superiority of interchangeable parts to President-elect Thomas Jefferson in 1801 by quickly and easily assembling complete muskets from randomly picked piles of musket parts. Today, because of Whitney's ideas, most products, from cars to toasters to space shuttles, are manufactured using standardized, interchangeable parts.

But even with this advance, manufacturers still could not produce a part unless they had seen or examined it firsthand. Thanks to Gaspard Monge, a Frenchman of modest beginnings, this soon changed. Monge's greatest achievement was his book *Descriptive Geometry*.[51] In it, he explained techniques for drawing three-dimensional objects on paper. For the first time, precise drawings permitted manufacturers to make standardized, interchangeable parts without first examining a prototype. Today, thanks to Monge, manufacturers rely on CAD (computer-aided design) and CAM (computer-aided

Truefelpix/Shutterstock.com

manufacturing) to take three-dimensional designs straight from the computer to the factory floor.

Once standardized, interchangeable parts became the norm, and after parts could be made from design drawings alone, manufacturers ran into a costly problem that they had never faced before: too much inventory. *Inventory* is the amount and number of raw materials, parts, and finished products that a company has in its possession. In fact, large factories were accumulating parts inventories sufficient for two to three months, much more than they needed on a daily basis to run their manufacturing operations. A solution to this problem was found in 1905 when the Oldsmobile Motor Works in Detroit burned down.[52] Management rented a new production facility to get production up and running as quickly as possible after the fire. But because the new facility was much smaller, there was no room to store large stockpiles of inventory (which the company couldn't afford anyway as it was short on funds). Therefore, the company made do with what it called "hand-to-mouth inventories," in which each production station had only enough parts on hand to do a short production run. Because all of its parts suppliers were close by, Oldsmobile could place orders in the morning and receive them in the afternoon (even without telephones), just as with today's computerized just-in-time inventory systems. So, contrary to common belief, just-in-time inventory systems were not invented by Japanese manufacturers. Instead, they were invented out of necessity more than a century ago because of a fire.

2-5b Information Management

For most of recorded history, information has been costly, difficult to obtain, and slow to spread. Because of the immense labor and time it took to hand copy information, books, manuscripts, and written documents of any kind were rare and extremely expensive. Word of Joan of Arc's death in 1431 took 18 months to travel from France across Europe to Constantinople (now Istanbul, Turkey).

Consequently, throughout history, organizations have pushed for and quickly adopted new information technologies that reduce the cost or increase the speed with which they can acquire, store, retrieve, or communicate information. The first technologies to truly revolutionize the business use of information were paper and the printing press. In the fourteenth century, water-powered machines were created to pulverize rags into pulp to make paper. Paper prices, which were already lower than those of animal-skin parchments, dropped dramatically. Less than a half-century later, Johannes Gutenberg invented the printing press, which greatly reduced the cost and time needed to copy

WHEN 1 + 1 = 3

One of the most common reasons for justifying mergers is synergy, namely that 1 + 1 = 3, meaning the merged companies will be more efficient, productive, and profitable together than apart. A study by Bain & Company shows that 70 percent of merger deals don't generate anticipated synergies. Why? Executives, eager to justify the mergers, strongly overestimated what could be achieved and hadn't done the rigorous analysis that would have helped them learn whether the merger would have truly produced synergies. One exception, AB InBev, the global beverage conglomerate, routinely calculates accurate—and high—synergy levels and then meets those forecasts.

Every time it acquires a company, AB InBev establishes an integration plan, an oversight program, and a change management program. It then sets standards and benchmarks and adopts the best practices of whichever company has the better operation. And when companies approach mergers like that, 1 + 1 = 3.

Source: L. Miles, "How Merging Companies Can Beat the Synergy Odds," *Forbes*, January 9, 2015, accessed April 24, 2015. www.forbes.com/sites/baininsights/2015/01/09/how-merging-companies-can-beat-the-synergy-odds/.

Lunasee Studios/Shutterstock.com

written information. In fifteenth-century Florence, Italy, a scribe would charge one florin (an Italian unit of money) to hand copy one document page. By contrast, a printer would set up and print 1,025 copies of the same document for just three florins. Within 50 years of its invention, Gutenberg's printing press cut the cost of information by 99.8 percent!

What Gutenberg's printing press did for publishing, the manual typewriter did for daily communication. Before 1850, most business correspondence was written by hand and copied using the letterpress. With the ink still wet, the letter would be placed into a tissue-paper book. A hand press would then be used to squeeze the book and copy the still-wet ink onto the tissue paper. By the 1870s, manual typewriters made it cheaper, easier, and faster to produce and copy business correspondence. Of course, in the 1980s, slightly more than a century later, typewriters were replaced by personal computers and word processing software with the same results.

Finally, businesses have always looked for information technologies that would speed access to timely information. The Medici family, which opened banks throughout Europe in the early 1400s, used post messengers to keep in contact with their more than 40 branch managers. The post messengers, who predated the U.S. Postal Service Pony Express by 400 years, could travel 90 miles per day, twice what average riders could cover, because the Medicis were willing to pay for the expense of providing them with fresh horses. This need for timely information also led companies to quickly adopt the telegraph in the 1860s, the telephone in the 1880s, and, of course, Internet technologies in the past three decades.

2-5c Systems Management

Today's companies are much more complex than they used to be. They are larger and employ more people. They most likely manufacture, service, *and* finance what they sell, not only in their home markets but in foreign markets throughout the world, too. They also operate in complex, fast-changing, competitive, global environments that can quickly turn competitive advantages into competitive disadvantages. How, then, can managers make sense of this complexity, both within and outside their organizations?

One way to deal with organizational and environmental complexity is to take a systems view of organizations. The systems approach is derived from theoretical models in biology and social psychology developed in the 1950s and 1960s.[53] A **system** is a set of interrelated elements or parts that function as a whole. Rather than

Companies generate a lot of important information, so it's critical that that information be managed properly.

viewing one part of an organization as separate from the other parts, a systems approach encourages managers to complicate their thinking by looking for connections between the different parts of the organization. Indeed, one of the more important ideas in the systems approach to management is that organizational systems are composed of parts or **subsystems**, which are simply smaller systems within larger systems. Subsystems and their connections matter in systems theory because of the possibility for managers to create synergy. **Synergy** occurs when two or more subsystems working together can produce more than they can working apart. In other words, synergy occurs when $1 + 1 = 3$.

Systems can be open or closed. **Closed systems** can function without interacting with their environments. But nearly all organizations should be viewed as **open systems** that interact with their environments and depend on them for survival. Therefore, rather than viewing what goes on within the organization as separate from what goes on outside it, the systems approach encourages managers to look for connections between

System a set of interrelated elements or parts that function as a whole

Subsystems smaller systems that operate within the context of a larger system

Synergy when two or more subsystems working together can produce more than they can working apart

Closed systems systems that can sustain themselves without interacting with their environments

Open systems systems that can sustain themselves only by interacting with their environments, on which they depend for their survival

the different parts of the organization and the different parts of its environment. Exhibit 2.7 illustrates how the elements of systems management work together.

A systems view of organizations offers several advantages. First, it forces managers to view their organizations as part of and subject to the competitive, economic, social, technological, and legal/regulatory forces in their environments.[54] Second, it forces managers to be aware of how the environment affects specific parts of the organization. Third, because of the

AVOIDING THE PITFALLS OF MERGERS

Managers interested in growth and scale often hope to reach their goals through mergers and acquisitions. Although mergers are a traditional path toward growth, several common problems arise when trying to achieve synergy through a merger.

▸ **Assuming you know what you're doing.** Managers often assume that their past experiences with mergers will automatically translate to any future merger they pursue ("I've done this before, so I can do it again—no problem."). Unfortunately, past experience is not always a predictor of future success because the strategies needed to create synergy in one merger are not necessarily universally applicable. Solve this problem by mixing up your team. A team whose members have diverse merger experiences will have a more panoramic view of the current opportunity and will be more likely to identify pitfalls early.

▸ **Breaking the bank.** Merger activity increases when companies have cash to spend. Managers who feel like their money is burning a hole in their pockets tend to overpay. Resist that urge by focusing on the metrics and logic of the merger. Ask yourself how the acquisition will create value for your company; whether your company is, in fact, the right buyer; and if the merger makes sense for your company strategically.

▸ **Understanding the real costs and benefits.** Not all synergies are equal. Synergies derived from cost savings are typically the most successful, while those related to cross-selling or vertical integration are more difficult to achieve. To avoid this pitfall, pay close attention to the costs associated with the merger (such as management time, severance for laid-off workers, and additional investments). According to experts, producing annual savings of any amount can, over time, cost twice as much to achieve. (That is, if you expect to gain $100 million in synergistic cost savings, also expect to spend $200 million over time to achieve them.)

Source: S. Finkelstein, "How to Avoid Four Common Problems in Mergers," *Wall Street Journal*, February 22, 2016, R7.

Exhibit 2.7
Systems View of Organizations

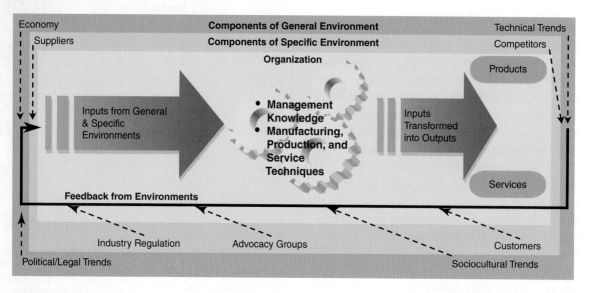

complexity and difficulty of trying to achieve synergies among different parts of the organization, the systems view encourages managers to focus on better communication and cooperation within the organization. Finally, it makes managers acutely aware that good internal management of the organization may not be enough to ensure survival. Survival also depends on making sure that the organization continues to satisfy critical environmental stakeholders such as shareholders, employees, customers, suppliers, governments, and local communities.

2-5d Contingency Management

Earlier, you learned that the goal of scientific management was to use systematic study to find the one best way of doing each task and then use that one best way everywhere. The problem, as you may have gathered from reading about the various approaches to management, is that no one in management seems to agree on what that one best way is. Furthermore, more than 100 years of management research has shown that there are clear boundaries or limitations to most management theories and practices. No management ideas or practices are universal. Although any theory or practice may work much of the time, none works all the time. How, then, is a manager to decide what theory to use? Well, it depends on the situation. The **contingency approach** to management clearly states that there are no universal management theories and that the most effective management theory or idea depends on the kinds of problems or situations that managers or organizations are facing at a particular time and place.[55] In short, the best way depends on the situation.

One of the practical implications of the contingency approach to management is that management is much harder than it looks. In fact, because of the clarity and obviousness of management theories (OK, most of them), students and workers often wrongly assume that a company's problems would be quickly and easily solved if management would take just a few simple steps. If this were true, few companies would have problems.

A second implication of the contingency approach is that managers need to look for key contingencies that differentiate today's situation or problems from yesterday's situation or problems. Moreover, it means that managers need to spend more time analyzing problems, situations, and employees before taking action to fix them. Finally, it means that as you read this text and learn about management ideas and practices, you need to pay particular attention to qualifying phrases such as "usually," "in these situations," "for this to work," and "under these circumstances." Doing so will help you identify the key contingencies that will help you become a better manager.

Wavebreakmedia/Shutterstock.com

STUDY TOOLS 2

LOCATED IN TEXTBOOK

☐ Rip out and review chapter review card

LOCATED AT WWW.CENGAGEBRAIN.COM

☐ Review key term flashcards and create your own from StudyBits

☐ Track your knowledge and understanding of key concepts, using the concept tracker

☐ Complete practice and graded quizzes to prepare for tests

☐ Complete interactive content within the exposition

☐ View chapter highlight box content at the beginning of each chapter

Contingency approach holds that there are no universal management theories and that the most effective management theory or idea depends on the kinds of problems or situations that managers are facing at a particular time and place

3 Organizational Environments and Cultures

Raywoo.com/Shutterstock.com

LEARNING OUTCOMES

3-1 Discuss how changing environments affect organizations.

3-2 Describe the four components of the general environment.

3-3 Explain the five components of the specific environment.

3-4 Describe the process that companies use to make sense of their changing environments.

3-5 Explain how organizational cultures are created and how they can help companies be successful.

After you finish this chapter, go to **PAGE 66** for

STUDY TOOLS

3-1 CHANGING ENVIRONMENTS

This chapter examines the internal and external forces that affect business. We begin by explaining how the changes in external organizational environments affect the decisions and performance of a company. Next, we examine the two types of external organizational environment: the general environment that affects all organizations and the specific environment unique to each company. Then, we learn how managers make sense of their changing general and specific environments. The chapter finishes with a discussion of internal organizational environments by focusing on organizational culture. But first, let's see how the changes in external organizational environments affect the decisions and performance of a company.

External environments are the forces and events outside a company that have the potential to influence or affect it. In most cities, taxi prices (what's charged on the meter) and taxi licenses (for drivers and cars) are highly regulated. The taxi industry, however, is threatened by Uber, a seven-year-old Internet company. After signing up as an Uber customer (name, password, credit card information), customers use the Uber app on their smartphones to order rides. Tap Uber. Enter a destination. Tap a button indicating your location. Then, the Uber app indicates the cost and how long till the car arrives. Afterwards, it sends email receipts and automatically pays the driver. No cash changes hands. Customers love Uber because it's often faster than hailing a cab on the street. Taxi drivers and companies hate it because it represents competition, which is why 30,000 taxi drivers across London, Berlin, Madrid, and Paris parked their taxis in protest. Steve McNamara, a spokesperson for London's Licensed Taxi Driver Association, said, "We have nothing against competition. But Uber is being allowed to 'operate outside the law.'"[1] So far, London's taxi regulation agency has ruled that Uber apps and cars do not have taxi meters, therefore, they can't be regulated as taxi cabs. While London's famous black cab taxi drivers disagree, the goal of these protests is to influence regulatory agencies to prevent Uber from operating, or to force Uber to buy expensive, limited-in-number taxi licenses.

Let's examine the three basic characteristics of changing external environments: 3-1a environmental change; 3-1b environmental complexity; 3-1c resource scarcity; and 3-1d the uncertainty that environmental change, complexity, and resource scarcity can create for organizational managers.

Taxi drivers in Paris, France stage a protest against ride-sharing service Uber on January 26, 2016.

Guillaume Louyot Onickz Artworks/Shutterstock.com

3-1a Environmental Change

Environmental change is the rate at which a company's general and specific environments change. In **stable environments**, the rate of environmental change is slow. The funeral business changes little from year to year. Families arrange for services for their loved ones with a funeral home, which then obtains a casket from one of three U.S. manufacturers, cares for the remains, hosts a visitation or memorial service, and organizes the burial or cremation, perhaps connecting the family with the cemetery or columbarium for purchase of a final resting place—all for an average price of $6,460. Although there have been some changes—such as cremation increasing from 4 percent in 1960 to 43 percent today, advances in embalming that are healthier (for the embalmer and the environment), and a small percentage of imported caskets (less than 10%) that have increased profits—the basic business of preparing bodies for burial, internment, or cremation hasn't changed significantly in over a century.[2]

Whereas the funeral industry has a stable environment, BlackBerry competes in an extremely dynamic external environment. In **dynamic environments**, the rate of environmental change is fast. BlackBerry competitors, such as Apple, Samsung, HTC,

External environments all events outside a company that have the potential to influence or affect it

Environmental change the rate at which a company's general and specific environments change

Stable environment an environment in which the rate of change is slow

Dynamic environment an environment in which the rate of change is fast

and Motorola, frequently updated models with innovative features and new technology. Over an 8-year span, Apple released thirteen different iPhone models—the 3G and 3GS, the 4 and 4S, the 5 and 5S, the 6 and 6 Plus, the 6S and 6S Plus, the SE, and the 7 and 7 Plus—each having better features and functionality. For instance, the new iPhone 7 Plus is water resistant, two times faster, and 25 percent brighter than the iPhone 6S Plus, has two camera lenses (wide-angle and telephoto), has stereo speakers, and will last for 13 hours of use on one charge.[3]

Although you might think that a company's external environment would be either stable or dynamic, research suggests that companies often experience both. According to **punctuated equilibrium theory**, companies go through long periods of stability (equilibrium) during which incremental changes occur; followed by short, complex periods of dynamic, fundamental change (revolutionary periods); and finishing with a return to stability (new equilibrium).[4]

The U.S. airline industry is a classic example of punctuated equilibrium, as three times in the past thirty years it has experienced revolutionary periods followed by a temporary return to stability. The first, from mid-1979 to mid-1982, occurred immediately after airline deregulation in 1978. Prior to deregulation, the federal government controlled where airlines could fly, how much they could charge, when they could fly, and the number of flights they could have on a particular route. After deregulation, these choices were left to the airlines. The large financial losses during this period clearly indicate that the airlines had trouble adjusting to the intense competition from new airlines that occurred after deregulation. By mid-1982, however, profits returned to the industry and held steady until mid-1989.

Then, after experiencing record growth and profits, U.S. airlines lost billions of dollars between 1989 and 1993 as the industry went through dramatic changes. Key expenses, including jet fuel and employee salaries, which had held steady for years, suddenly increased. Furthermore,

The iPhone 7 Plus, released September 16, 2016, can be submerged in a meter (just under 3.3 feet) of water for 30 minutes without taking damage.

Alexey Boldin/Shutterstock.com

revenues, which had grown steadily year after year, suddenly dropped because of dramatic changes in the airlines' customer base. Business travelers, who had typically paid full-price fares, made up more than half of all passengers during the 1980s. However, by the late 1980s, the largest customer base had changed to leisure travelers, who wanted the cheapest flights they could get.[5] With expenses suddenly up, and revenues suddenly down, the airlines responded to these changes in their business environment by laying off 5–10 percent of their workers, canceling orders for new planes, and eliminating unprofitable routes. Starting in 1993 and lasting until 1998, these changes helped the airline industry achieve profits far in excess of their historical levels. The industry began to stabilize, if not flourish, just as punctuated equilibrium theory predicts.[6]

The third revolutionary period for the U.S. airline industry began with the terrorist attacks of September 11, 2001, in which planes were used as missiles to bring down the World Trade Center towers and damage the Pentagon. The immediate effect was a 20 percent drop in scheduled flights, a 40 percent drop in passengers, and losses so large that the U.S. government approved a $15 billion bailout to keep the airlines in business. Heightened airport security also affected airports, the airlines themselves, and airline customers. Five years after the 9/11 attacks, United Airlines, U.S. Airways, Delta, and American Airlines had reduced staffing by 169,000 full-time jobs to cut costs after losing a combined $42 billion.[7] Due to their financially weaker position, the airlines restructured operations to take advantage of the combined effect of increased passenger travel, a sharply reduced cost structure, and a 23 percent reduction in the fleet to return their businesses to profitability.[8] But, just as the airlines were heading toward a more stable period of equilibrium in 2006 and 2007, the price of oil jumped dramatically, doubling, if not tripling, the price of jet fuel, which prompted the airlines to charge for luggage (to increase revenues and discourage heavy baggage) and cut flights using older, fuel-inefficient jets.

In 2013, however, stability and profitability largely returned. Compared to 2007, the airlines cut total seat capacity 14 percent; filled 83 percent of seats, up from

Punctuated equilibrium theory the theory that companies go through long periods of stability (equilibrium), followed by short periods of dynamic, fundamental change (revolutionary periods), and then a new equilibrium

The dairy industry is an excellent example of a simple external environment.

80 percent; and with stronger demand and fewer flights, saw round-trip fares rise by 4 percent, even after adjusting for inflation. In 2008, U.S. airlines collectively lost $23.7 billion, but by the end of 2015, they had logged their sixth consecutive year of profits.[9] Multiple airline mergers—Delta and Northwest, United and Continental, Southwest and AirTran, and U.S. Airways and American Airlines—reduced competition and routes even further. As a result, the number of domestic flights dropped 6.8 percent from 2012 to 2015, while the number of available seats increased by 2.2 percent. Why are airlines instituting these changes? So they can fly fewer flights in larger, fuller planes. Smaller U.S. airports, many in the Midwest and South, have seen dramatic cuts in flights. These hubs traditionally flew smaller planes with low passenger loads—that is—too many empty seats. Dan Landson, spokesperson for Southwest, recently justified the reduced flight traffic to these locations, saying, "We have a responsibility to maximize the productivity and profitability of our fleet."[10]

3-1b Environmental Complexity

Environmental complexity refers to the number and the intensity of external factors in the environment that affect organizations. **Simple environments** have few environmental factors, whereas **complex environments** have many environmental factors. The dairy industry is an excellent example of a relatively simple external environment. Even accounting for decades-old advances in processing, automatic milking machines, and breeding techniques, where the latter

has increased annual yield from 5,000 pounds of milk per cow in 1942 to 22,400 pounds today, milk is produced the same way today as it was 100 years ago.[11] So while food manufacturers introduce dozens of new dairy-based products each year, U.S. milk production has grown a modest 1.7 percent per year over the past decade. In short, producing milk is a highly competitive industry with a few key environmental factors.[12]

At the other end of the spectrum, few industries find themselves in more complex environments today than the personal computer (PC) business. Since the early 1980s, PC sales have grown spectacularly. But with consumers now spending technology dollars on tablets, e-readers, and smartphones (some as big as tablets and e-readers!), sales of Windows-based PCs dropped 1.7 percent from 2013 to 2014 and by 10.3 percent from 2014 to 2015. PC manufacturers saw similar trends, with HP, Dell, Acer Group, and Asus all posting double-digit declines. Microsoft's Windows 8 operating system, which brought touch-screen capabilities and design to PCs, Microsoft tablets, and smartphones, was supposed to revive PC sales, but consumers found it confusing and difficult. Reviews of Windows 10 are broadly positive and seem to indicate that Windows 10 will provide a positive, stable user experience on all device formats—PCs, Windows smartphones and tablets, and the Xbox console. Those improvements, however, have not yet turned around declining PC sales."[13]

3-1c Resource Scarcity

The third characteristic of external environments is resource scarcity. **Resource scarcity** is the abundance or shortage of critical organizational resources in an organization's external environment. Italy-based **Ferrero Group** makes **Nutella**, the popular food spread made

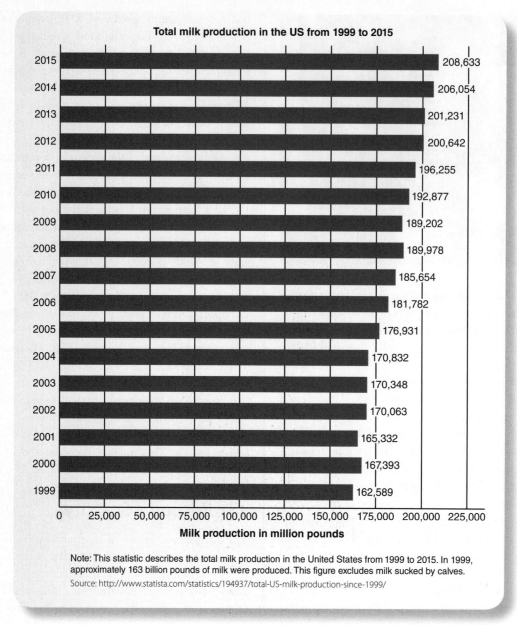

Total milk production in the US from 1999 to 2015

Year	Milk production in million pounds
2015	208,633
2014	206,054
2013	201,231
2012	200,642
2011	196,255
2010	192,877
2009	189,202
2008	189,978
2007	185,654
2006	181,782
2005	176,931
2004	170,832
2003	170,348
2002	170,063
2001	165,332
2000	167,393
1999	162,589

Milk production in million pounds

Note: This statistic describes the total milk production in the United States from 1999 to 2015. In 1999, approximately 163 billion pounds of milk were produced. This figure excludes milk sucked by calves.

Source: http://www.statista.com/statistics/194937/total-US-milk-production-since-1999/

with hazelnuts, skim milk, and cocoa. A 13-ounce jar of Nutella contains 50 hazelnuts, so Ferrero buys 100,000 tons of hazelnuts each year, roughly 25 percent of the world supply, to produce 82 million pounds of Nutella. But, with sales growing 6 percent a year and competitors, such as Hershey, Jif, and Kroger, now making their own chocolate-hazelnut spreads, demand for the limited global supply of hazelnuts, grown primarily on a narrow strip of Turkish coastland, is skyrocketing. Hazelnut prices jumped by 60 percent in 2014, thanks to growing demand and a combination of frost and hail damage. With supplies of its key ingredient at risk, Ferrero bought Turkish-based Oltan Group, the world's largest hazelnut procurer and supplier, with five production facilities in Europe.[14]

3-1d Uncertainty

As Exhibit 3.1 shows, environmental change, environmental complexity, and resource scarcity affect environmental **uncertainty**, which is how well managers can understand or predict the external changes and trends affecting their businesses. Starting at the left side of the exhibit, environmental uncertainty is lowest when environmental change and environmental complexity

Uncertainty extent to which managers can understand or predict which environmental changes and trends will affect their businesses

Exhibit 3.1
Environmental Change, Environmental Complexity, and Resource Scarcity

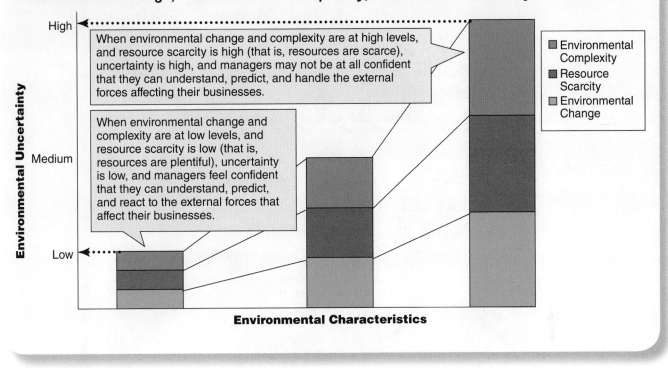

When environmental change and complexity are at high levels, and resource scarcity is high (that is, resources are scarce), uncertainty is high, and managers may not be at all confident that they can understand, predict, and handle the external forces affecting their businesses.

When environmental change and complexity are at low levels, and resource scarcity is low (that is, resources are plentiful), uncertainty is low, and managers feel confident that they can understand, predict, and react to the external forces that affect their businesses.

Environmental Complexity

Resource Scarcity

Environmental Change

Environmental Uncertainty: High / Medium / Low

Environmental Characteristics

---

are at low levels, and resource scarcity is low (that is, resources are plentiful). In these environments, managers feel confident that they can understand, predict, and react to the external forces that affect their businesses. By contrast, the right side of the exhibit shows that environmental uncertainty is highest when environmental change and complexity are extensive, and resource scarcity is a problem. In these environments, managers may not be confident that they can understand, predict, and handle the external forces affecting their businesses.

3-2 GENERAL ENVIRONMENT

As Exhibit 3.2 shows, two kinds of external environments influence organizations: the general environment and the specific environment. The **general environment** consists of the economy and the technological, sociocultural, and political/legal trends that indirectly affect *all* organizations. Changes in any sector of the general environment eventually affect most organizations. For example, when the Federal Reserve lowers its prime lending rate, most businesses benefit because banks and credit card companies often lower the interest rates they charge for loans. Consumers, who can then borrow money more cheaply, might borrow more to buy homes, cars, refrigerators, and large-screen LCD TVs.

Each organization also has a **specific environment** that is unique to that firm's industry and directly affects the way it conducts day-to-day business.

The specific environment, which will be discussed in detail in Section 3-3 of this chapter, includes customers, competitors, suppliers, industry regulation, and advocacy groups.

But first let's take a closer look at the four components of the general environment: **3-2a the economy** *and* **3-2b the technological,** **3-2c sociocultural,** *and* **3-2d political/legal trends that indirectly affect all organizations.**

> **General environment** the economic, technological, sociocultural, and political/legal trends that indirectly affect all organizations
>
> **Specific environment** the customers, competitors, suppliers, industry regulations, and advocacy groups that are unique to an industry and directly affect how a company does business

Exhibit 3.2
General and Specific Environments

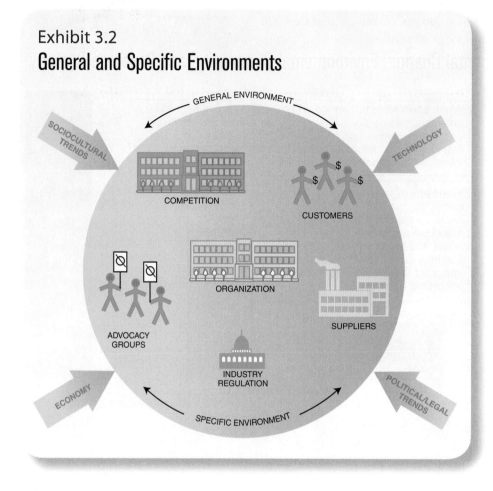

3-2a Economy

The current state of a country's economy affects virtually every organization doing business there. In general, in a growing economy, more people are working, and wages are growing, and therefore consumers have relatively more money to spend. More products are bought and sold in a growing economy than in a static or shrinking economy. Although an individual firm's sales will not necessarily increase, a growing economy does provide an environment favorable to business growth. In contrast, in a shrinking economy, consumers have less money to spend, and relatively fewer products are bought and sold. Thus, a shrinking economy makes growth for individual businesses more difficult.

For three decades, the Chinese economy averaged 10 percent annual growth. This consistent growth spurred cargo companies to buy new ships to transport goods to and from China.[15] In 2008, however, China's growth rate began declining. China's growth slowed so much that by 2015, several global shipping companies started storing, selling, or scrapping much of their fleets.[16] From 2015 to 2016, **International Shipcare** doubled its number of ships in dry dock from 51 to 102.[17] **Scorpio Bulkers**, which spent $1.5 billion in 2013 and 2014 to acquire new cargo ships, has had to sell them all at a loss of $400 million.[18] Demolition rates also rose 15 percent as shipping companies sold older vessels for scrap.[19] Regarding the shift in China's economy, Maritime advisor Basil Karatzas says, "It's a bloodbath, which calls into question the survival of many dry-bulk shipping companies."[20]

Because the economy influences basic business decisions, such as whether to hire more employees, expand production, or take out loans to purchase equipment, managers scan their economic environments for signs of significant change. Unfortunately, the economic statistics that managers rely on when making these decisions are notoriously poor predictors of *future* economic activity. The Organization for Economic Cooperation and Development (OECD), an influential, but independent, nonprofit organization that works with governments to improve economic and social well-being, regularly publishes country economic forecasts. Over the past seven years, however, the OECD found that its forecasts were consistently overly optimistic and wrong.[21] So a manager who hired ten more employees because OECD forecasts data suggested future growth, could very well have had to lay off those workers when the forecasted economic growth did not occur.

Because economic statistics can be poor predictors, some managers try to predict future economic activity by keeping track of business confidence. **Business confidence indices** show how confident actual managers are about future business growth. For example, the Conference Board's CEO Confidence Index is a quarterly survey of 100 CEOs in large companies across a variety of different industries that examines attitudes regarding future growth in the economy or particular industries.[22] Another useful index is the *Wall Street Journal (WSJ)/Vistage Small Business CEO Survey*, which surveys small business CEOS about their sentiments regarding their general economy and how optimistic they are about future revenues, profitability, and business spending.[23] Managers often prefer business confidence indices to economic statistics because they know that other managers make business decisions that are in line with their expectations concerning the economy's future. So if the Conference Board or WSJ/Vistage Small Business CEO Survey business confidence indices are dropping, a manager might decide against hiring new employees, increasing production, or taking out additional loans to expand the business.

3-2b Technological Component

Technology is the knowledge, tools, and techniques used to transform inputs (raw materials, information, and so on) into outputs (products and services). For example, the inputs of authors, editors, and artists (knowledge) and the use of equipment such as computers and printing presses (technology) transformed paper, ink, and glue (raw materials) into this book (the finished product). In the case of a service company such as an airline, the technology consists of equipment, including airplanes, repair tools, and computers, as well as the knowledge of mechanics, ticketers, and flight crews. The output is the service of transporting people from one place to another.

Changes in technology can help companies provide better products or produce their products more efficiently. Although technological changes can benefit a business, they can also threaten it. Companies must embrace new technology and find effective ways to use it to improve their products and services or decrease costs. If they don't, they will lose out to companies that do.

3-2c Sociocultural Component

The sociocultural component of the general environment refers to the demographic characteristics, general

Carnival Cruise line has increased the number of cruises sailing out of China; the industries fastest growing market.

behavior, attitudes, and beliefs of people in a particular society. Sociocultural changes and trends influence organizations in two important ways.

First, changes in demographic characteristics, such as the number of people with particular skills or the growth of or decline in the number of people with particular population characteristics (marital status, age, gender, ethnicity), affect how managers staff their businesses. With the cruise industry growing just 3–4 percent per year, Carnival Cruise Lines has increased the number of cruises sailing out of China, the industry's fastest growing market, from one in 2011 to four today. While 700,000 Chinese took cruises last year, compared to 10 million Americans, Carnival expects 20–30 percent annual growth in China, which will result in 5 million Chinese taking cruises by 2020.[24]

Second, sociocultural changes in behavior, attitudes, and beliefs also affect the demand for a business's products and services. For example, urban dwellers in their twenties and early thirties who follow the latest styles, trends, and fashions—often referred to as *hipsters*—spend more of their income on food than their parents did at the same age. But rather than buying from the commercial food and beverage companies that their parents made into household names, these young adults gravitate toward organic foods, exotic ingredients, and craft beers, spirits, and mixers. Consequently, markets that used to be considered niche are booming. Sales of organic food have doubled in little over a decade; U.S. craft beers account for

Business confidence indices indices that show managers' level of confidence about future business growth

Technology the knowledge, tools, and techniques used to transform inputs into outputs

19 percent of the total U.S. beer market; and sales of male grooming products, such as beard balm, are up nearly 10 percent.[25] Despite the economic impact that hipsters have in these markets, large consumer product companies find it difficult to get and keep their purchasing loyalty. Economist Douglas McWilliams says that hipsters have "identifiable spending patterns and homogeneous tastes. But they don't want others to copy them, so they keep up by changing their tastes, by moving on to the next things. You have to watch that if you're a consumer products company."[26]

3-2d Political/Legal Component

The political/legal component of the general environment includes the legislation, regulations, and court decisions that govern and regulate business behavior. New laws and regulations continue to impose additional responsibilities on companies. Unfortunately, many managers are unaware of these new responsibilities. For example, under the 1991 Civil Rights Act (http://www.eeoc.gov/policy /cra91.html), if an employee is sexually harassed by anyone at work (a supervisor, a coworker, or even a customer), the company—not just the harasser—is potentially liable for damages, attorneys' fees, and back pay.[27] Under the Family and Medical Leave Act (http://www.dol.gov/dol /topic/benefits-leave/fmla.htm), which applies to employers with fifty or more employees, employees who have been on the job one year are guaranteed twelve weeks of unpaid leave per year to tend to their own illnesses or to their elderly parents, a newborn baby, or a newly adopted child. Employees are guaranteed the same job, pay, and benefits when they return to work.[28] The most recent major regulation to affect U.S. businesses is the Patient Protection and Affordable Care Act (http://www.hhs.gov /healthcare/rights/), which requires businesses with more than 100 full-time employees to offer affordable health care insurance to full-time employees and their families. To demonstrate that they are in compliance, companies must file tax forms showing their individual employees' health care costs on a monthly basis. Penalties for not filing proper tax forms can be up to $3,000 per employee.[29]

Many managers are also unaware of the potential legal risks associated with traditional managerial decisions about recruiting, hiring, and firing employees. Increasingly, businesses and managers are being sued for negligent hiring and supervision, defamation, invasion of privacy, emotional distress, fraud, and misrepresentation during employee recruitment.[30] More than 14,000 suits for wrongful termination (unfairly firing employees) are filed each year.[31] In fact, wrongful termination lawsuits increased by 77 percent during the 1990s.[32] Likewise, Equal Employment Opportunity Commission filings alleging wrongful discharge average around 22,000 cases per year[33] One in four employers will at some point be sued for wrongful termination. It can cost $300,000 to settle such a case after it goes to court, but employers lose 50 percent to 70 percent of court cases,[34] and the former employee is awarded, on average, $1 million or more.[35] On the other hand, employers who settle before going to court typically pay just $10,000–$100,000 per case.[36]

Not everyone agrees that companies' legal risks are too severe. Indeed, many believe that the government should do more to regulate and restrict business behavior and that it should be easier for average citizens to sue dishonest or negligent corporations. From a managerial perspective, the best medicine against legal risk is prevention. As a manager, it is your responsibility to educate yourself about the laws, regulations, and potential lawsuits that could affect your business. Failure to do so may put you and your company at risk of sizable penalties, fines, or legal charges.

3-3 SPECIFIC ENVIRONMENT

As you just learned, changes in any sector of the general environment (economic, technological, sociocultural, and political/legal) eventually affect most organizations. Each organization also has a specific environment that is unique to that firm's industry and directly affects the way it conducts day-to-day business. For instance, if your customers decide to use another product, your main competitor cuts prices 10 percent, your best supplier can't deliver raw materials, federal regulators mandate reductions in pollutants in your industry, or environmental groups accuse your company of selling unsafe products, the impact from the specific environment on your business is immediate.

*Let's examine how the **3-3a customer**, **3-3b competitor**, **3-3c supplier**, **3-3d industry regulation**, and **3-3e advocacy group** components of the specific environment affect businesses.*

3-3a Customer Component

Customers purchase products and services. Companies cannot exist without customer support. Monitoring customers' changing wants and needs is critical to business success. There are two basic strategies for monitoring customers: reactive and proactive.

Reactive customer monitoring involves identifying and addressing customer trends and problems after they occur.

Cable and satellite providers face new competition from streaming television options like Sony's PlayStation Vue. Launched nationwide in March, 2016, Vue offers live streaming television, cloud-based DVR, and no contracts for less than $30 a month.

One reactive strategy is to listen closely to customer complaints and respond to customer concerns. **Listen360** is a company that helps businesses monitor customer satisfaction and complaints by contacting their customers and asking two questions, "How likely are you to recommend this business?" followed by an open-ended question to explain why. Customer responses fall into three categories: "promoters," who would recommend the business to others; "passives," who are neither negative nor positive; and "detractors," unhappy customers who would not recommend the business. When customers are unhappy, the business receives a report detailing what products and services the customer purchased, what it would cost the company if it lost that customer's business, and a "voice of the customer" report that scans the answers to the open-ended question for key words about specific likes, dislikes, and concerns. According to Heather Anderson, director of marketing for The Little Gym, a children's fitness franchise, "Many owners have also chosen to get an immediate notification via text message if they receive a detractor comment, so they can respond within minutes of receiving the feedback."[37]

Companies that respond quickly to customer letters of complaint (that is, reactive customer monitoring) are viewed much more favorably than companies that are slow to respond or never respond.[38] In particular, studies have shown that customers are much more likely to purchase products or services again from a company when that company sends a follow-up letter to thank the customer for writing; offers a sincere, specific response to the complaint (not a form letter, but an explanation of how the problem will be handled); and offers a small gift, coupons, or a refund to make up for the problem.[39]

Proactive monitoring of customers means identifying and addressing customer needs, trends, and issues *before* they occur. **Spotify** is the world's most popular subscription music service, with 20 million paying subscribers and 55 million ad-supported users. In 2015, Spotify unveiled Spotify Fan Insights, a data analytics tool, to help musical artists better understand their listeners and convert their fans' enthusiasm into deeper engagement. Fan Insights lists listeners' geographic locations, demographic information (such as gender and age), how they are listening (for example, to a Spotify-curated playlist or to their own collections), when they are listening (down to the time of day), and even which playlists contain the artists' music. In addition, artists can now sell concert tickets and merchandise directly through Spotify. For Spotify Chief Revenue Officer Jeff Levick, supporting artists with metrics and selling tools helps them understand their own audiences. "For artists, this can even give them the ability to better manage their tours. They can have the knowledge about where they should be playing certain songs, for example, rather than just doing the same set list everywhere."[40] This kind of information is particularly helpful for finding and catering to superfans. According to Spotify's vice president of product, Charlie Hellman, these fans "have a disproportionate impact on revenue: they're the people who'll buy tickets, VIP packages, merchandise, and will be the social evangelists for the band."[41]

3-3b Competitor Component

Competitors are companies in the same industry that sell similar products or services to customers. Ford, Toyota, Honda, Nissan, Hyundai, and Kia all compete for automobile customers. NBC, ABC, CBS, and Fox (along with hundreds of cable channels) compete for TV viewers' attention. McDonald's, Burger King, Wendy's, Hardee's, Chick-fil-A, and a host of others compete for fast-food customers' dollars. Often the difference between business success and failure comes down to whether your company is doing a better job of satisfying customer wants and needs than the competition. Consequently, companies need to keep close track of what their competitors are doing. To do this, managers perform a **competitive analysis**, which involves deciding who your competitors are, anticipating competitors' moves, and determining competitors' strengths and weaknesses.

Surprisingly, managers often do a poor job of

Competitors companies in the same industry that sell similar products or services to customers

Competitive analysis a process for monitoring the competition that involves identifying competition, anticipating their moves, and determining their strengths and weaknesses

identifying potential competitors because they tend to focus on only two or three well-known competitors with similar goals and resources.[42]

Another mistake managers may make when analyzing the competition is to underestimate potential competitors' capabilities. When this happens, managers don't take the steps they should to continue to improve their products or services. The result can be significant decreases in both market share and profits. For decades, TV viewers had two options—watch the four or five channels that could be picked up with an antenna or purchase a package from a local cable supplier, which almost always operated as a local monopoly. Then, a third choice came along—buy a package from a satellite provider, such as DirecTV or DISH Network. In the past five years, however, the television marketplace has changed dramatically, and cable TV companies now find themselves surrounded by competitors. Netflix started the process by offering an inexpensive DVD-by-mail service, which began eroding cable TV dominance. Over the past five years, however, online content providers and streaming services and devices such as Netflix, Hulu, YouTube, iTunes, Roku, Apple TV, and Amazon Instant Video allow consumers to watch their favorite TV shows and movies at a fraction of the cost of a monthly cable subscription. Cable companies have been slow to respond. From 2010 to 2014, the forty most widely distributed cable channels lost 3.2 million subscribers, as consumers trimmed their cable TV bills by cutting out popular channels such as TNT, USA, ESPN, and Disney. It's also estimated that somewhere between a quarter million and a half million cable/satellite TV customers "cut the cord" in 2014, completely dropping their subscriptions. According to Bryan Rader, CEO of Bandwidth Consulting LLC, a firm that tracks pay-TV trends, "We're at a tipping point of consumers thinking Internet first and TV second."[43]

3-3c Supplier Component

Suppliers are companies that provide material, human, financial, and informational resources to other companies. U.S. Steel buys iron ore from suppliers to make steel products. When IBM sells a mainframe computer, it also provides support staff, engineers, and other technical consultants to the company that bought the computer. If you're shopping for desks, chairs, and office supplies, chances are that Staples will be glad to help your business open a revolving charge account to pay for your purchases. When a clothing manufacturer has spent $100,000 to purchase new high-pressure water drills to cut shirt and pant patterns to precise sizes, the water drill manufacturer, as part of the purchase, will usually train the workers to use the machinery.

A key factor influencing the impact and quality of the relationship between companies and their suppliers is how dependent they are on each other.[44] **Supplier dependence** is the degree to which a company relies on that supplier because of the importance of the supplier's product to the company and the difficulty of finding other sources for that product. Even though Apple and Samsung are fierce competitors when it comes to smartphones and tablets, and they have sued and countersued each other over alleged patent infringements, Apple has been highly dependent on Samsung for the computer chips, flash drives, and high resolution touchscreens in iPhones and iPads for more than a decade. Stanford University professor Michael Marks said that Apple's choices for alternative suppliers, "aren't good, which is why they keep buying from Samsung."[45] Indeed, Apple awarded Taiwan Semiconductor the contract chips to go in its iPhone 6. Within six months of the release of the

Suppliers companies that provide material, human, financial, and informational resources to other companies

Supplier dependence the degree to which a company relies on a supplier because of the importance of the supplier's product to the company and the difficulty of finding other sources of that product

Federal Regulatory Agencies and Commissions

Consumer Product Safety Commission
Reduces risk of injuries and deaths associated with consumer products, sets product safety standards, enforces product recalls, and provides consumer education **http://www.cpsc.gov**

Department of Labor
Collects employment statistics and administers labor laws concerning safe working conditions, minimum hourly wages and overtime pay, employment discrimination, and unemployment insurance **http://www.dol.gov**

Environmental Protection Agency
Reduces and controls pollution through research, monitoring, standard setting, and enforcement activities **http://www.epa.gov**

Equal Employment Opportunity Commission
Promotes fair hiring and promotion practices **http://www.eeoc.gov**

Federal Communications Commission
Regulates interstate and international communications by radio, television, wire, satellite, and cable **http://www.fcc.gov**

Federal Reserve System
As the nation's central bank, controls interest rates and money supply and monitors the U.S. banking system

to produce a growing economy with stable prices **http://www.federalreserve.gov**

Federal Trade Commission
Restricts unfair methods of business competition and misleading advertising and enforces consumer protection laws **http://www.ftc.gov**

Food and Drug Administration
Protects the nation's health by making sure food, drugs, and cosmetics are safe **http://www.fda.gov**

National Labor Relations Board
Monitors union elections and stops companies from engaging in unfair labor practices **http://www.nlrb.gov**

Occupational Safety and Health Administration
Saves lives, prevents injuries, and protects the health of workers **http://www.osha.gov**

Securities and Exchange Commission
Protects investors in the bond and stock markets, guarantees access to information on publicly traded securities, and regulates firms that sell securities or give investment advice **http://www.sec.gov**

Staples is a prime example of a supplier.

newest iPhone, however, Apple announced that, for future iPhone models, it would go back to buying chips from Samsung.[46]

Buyer dependence is the degree to which a supplier relies on a buyer because of the importance of that buyer to the supplier's sales and the difficulty

of finding other buyers of its products. While Samsung is one of Apple's key suppliers (that is, supplier dependence), Apple, in turn, is Samsung's key buyer of computer components. Apple's purchase of $10 billion of chips, flash memory drives, and touchscreens in 2013 represented 17 percent of Samsung's $59.13 billion components business. Regaining the Apple chip order for future versions of the iPhone helped Samsung turn a $914 million loss in 2013 into a $914 million profit.[47]

A high degree of buyer or seller dependence can lead to **opportunistic behavior,** in which one party benefits at the expense of the other. Apple was concerned with the possibility of opportunistic behavior when it stopped buying touchscreens from Samsung in 2010. Technology analyst Hiroshi

Buyer dependence
the degree to which a supplier relies on a buyer because of the importance of that buyer to the supplier and the difficulty of finding other buyers for its products

Opportunistic behavior
a transaction in which one party in the relationship benefits at the expense of the other

Hayase explained, "If you buy screens from your competitor, you will be sharing some key information on your next product."[48] Consequently, Apple shifted its touchscreen orders to Sharp and Toshiba. This is also why Apple began working with Toshiba in 2009, to build flash memory for iPads and iPhones, and with TSMC (Taiwan Semiconductor Manufacturing Company) in 2010, to build computer chips.[49] As of June 2014, Apple only purchases 10 percent of its flash memory from Samsung. TSMC started chip production for Apple in 2014, which will allow Apple to significantly reduce its reliance on Samsung over the next few years.[50]

In contrast to opportunistic behavior, **relationship behavior** focuses on establishing a mutually beneficial, long-term relationship between buyers and suppliers.[51] DreamWorks Studios, which makes films and TV shows, has had a long-term strategic relationship with Hewlett-Packard (H-P), which makes computers and software. DreamWorks, the buyer, advises H-P, the supplier, on the advanced servers and data management it needs to produce animated films, or even traditional films, which today contain significant portions of computer-generated images.[52] The average DreamWorks film is created using 300 graphics workstations, 60 million rendering hours (a rendering hour is an hour of computer time used to process an image), the simultaneous use of 17,000 computer core chips, and more than 200 terabytes of storage.[53] In fact, the DreamWorks animation data center in Redwood City, California, is run completely on H-P systems.

Relationship behavior
the establishment of mutually beneficial, long-term exchanges between buyers and suppliers

Industry regulation
regulations and rules that govern the business practices and procedures of specific industries, businesses, and professions

Advocacy groups concerned citizens who band together to try to influence the business practices of specific industries, businesses, and professions

Public communications an advocacy group tactic that relies on voluntary participation by the news media and the advertising industry to get the advocacy group's message out

3-3d Industry Regulation Component

Whereas the political/legal component of the general environment affects all businesses, the **industry regulation** component consists of regulations and rules that govern the practices and procedures of specific industries, businesses, and professions. To combat rising rates of obesity, the U.S. Food and Drug Administration (FDA) established menu-labeling regulations requiring restaurants to clearly and conspicuously display calorie information next to the name and price of the menu item.[54]

Regulatory agencies affect businesses by creating and enforcing rules and regulations to protect consumers, workers, or society as a whole. The menu-labeling regulations angered the pizza industry, which serves 41 million Americans a day. Given the number of possible combinations of pizza toppings, crust types, and sauces, the pizza industry argues that posting accurate calorie information is practically impossible. (For a store offering twenty toppings, one type of crust, and one type of sauce, there are more than 24×10^{17} possible pizza combinations.) Ron Berger, CEO of Figaro's Pizza chain in Oregon, says, "Having to post that information on a menu board is a very costly exercise in humoring government bureaucrats." To make matters worse, the proposed regulations require pizzerias to post the calories for a whole pizza, not for individual slices.[55]

The nearly 100 federal agencies and regulatory commissions can affect almost any kind of business. For example, children's toys that contain high-powered magnets, such as Buckyballs, were once marketed as desktop toys for adults. But from 2009 to 2013, nearly 3,000 children visited emergency rooms after swallowing high-powered magnets, which can cause serious injury or death by pinching the intestinal track. So, in 2014, the Consumer Products Safety Commission (CPSC) ruled that high-powered magnets in toys needed to be too large to ingest or too weak to cause internal harm. Within six months, all of the magnet makers, except one, Zen Magnets, which is appealing the ruling in court, had ceased production.[56]

3-3e Advocacy Groups

Advocacy groups are groups of concerned citizens who band together to try to influence the business practices of specific industries, businesses, and professions. The members of a group generally share the same point of view on a particular issue. For example, environmental advocacy groups might try to get manufacturers to reduce smokestack pollution emissions. Unlike the industry regulation component of the specific environment, advocacy groups cannot force organizations to change their practices. Nevertheless, they can use a number of techniques to try to influence companies, including public communications, media advocacy, web pages, blogs, and product boycotts.

The **public communications** approach relies on *voluntary* participation by the news media and the advertising industry to send out an advocacy group's message. Media advocacy is much more aggressive

IT'S A BIRD! IT'S A PLANE! IT'S A DRONE!

You have likely heard news stories about drones being used in both personal and commercial applications. But are drones a recreational hobby or mass-market commercial industry? According to the U.S. Federal Aviation Administration (FAA), the answer is the latter. After receiving nearly 250 reports of drones flying dangerously close to commercial aircrafts, the FCC moved swiftly to outline rules regarding use of the unmanned aircrafts. For example, the FCC now requires that all drones be registered with the organization.

Drone pilots who pay the $5 registration fee receive a unique identification number, which must appear on every drone that person owns. By classifying drones as aircrafts, regulators are sending the message that drones are more than toys. Indeed, the new regulations empower the FAA to penalize those who don't register their drones with fines of up to $250,000 and a three-year prison sentence.

Sources: J. Nicas, "New Rules for Drone Owners," *Wall Street Journal*, December 15, 2015, B3; "The FAA Reminds You to Register Your Drone," Federal Aviation Administration, February 16, 2016, faa.gov.

Glenn Price/Shutterstock.com

---

than the public communications approach. A **media advocacy** approach typically involves framing the group's concerns as public issues (affecting everyone); exposing questionable, exploitative, or unethical practices; and creating controversy that is likely to receive extensive news coverage.

A **product boycott** is a tactic in which an advocacy group actively tries to persuade consumers not to purchase a company's product or service. Often times, advocacy groups will combine media advocacy with boycotts. This not only draws attention to concerns a group has with a company's practices or products, it also decreases the company's revenues and profits. This was the case with the LEGO Group, a family-owned Danish company that makes LEGO block and toys.

While 90 percent of LEGO players are boys, the company has launched four girl-focused toy lines since 1979—mostly for building jewelry, beach houses, and stables in pink and purple. Feminist groups criticized each line for being less challenging than the traditional LEGO bricks aimed at boys and for perpetuating gender stereotypes through "pinkification." Before making another attempt at appealing to girls, LEGO spent five years conducting observation research to better understand how they assembled and played with LEGO products. LEGO also researched how girls and their parents make purchase decisions. (As it turns out, when given the choice, they still opted for pinks and purples over gender-neutral packaging.)

The research led to the development and launch of LEGO Friends, which design director Rosario Costa described as, "a real construction toy—not dumbing it down."[57] But as with prior product lines aimed at girls, LEGO Friends was harshly criticized and boycotted. Advocacy group Spark Movement published an open letter to LEGO, beginning, "We represent the girls, the parents, the children, the fans, the hobbyists, the collectors, the friends, the big sisters and brothers, the grandparents, and your future. And we are very disappointed."[58] LEGO ultimately modified some of the LEGO Friends marketing materials, but the product remained unchanged—pink and purple bricks for building pop star houses, cupcake cafés, and a supermarket. Overall, LEGO Friends has been a tremendous success. The boycott had no effect on sales, and independent research firm NPD Group credits LEGO Friends with increasing the market for girls' building toys from $300 million to $900 million in just three years.[59] According to LEGO Senior Design Manager Benedikte Schinkel Stamp, "We just had to wait for the controversy to die out."[60]

Media advocacy an advocacy group tactic that involves framing issues as public issues; exposing questionable, exploitative, or unethical practices; and forcing media coverage by buying media time or creating controversy that is likely to receive extensive news coverage

Product boycott an advocacy group tactic that involves protesting a company's actions by persuading consumers not to purchase its product or service

Despite being harshly criticized and boycotted, LEGO friends has been a tremendous success.

3-4 MAKING SENSE OF CHANGING ENVIRONMENTS

In Chapter 1, you learned that managers are responsible for making sense of their business environments. As our discussions of the general and specific environments have indicated, however, making sense of business environments is not an easy task.

Because external environments can be dynamic, confusing, and complex, managers use a three-step process to make sense of the changes in their external environments: 3-4a environmental scanning, 3-4b interpreting environmental factors, and 3-4c acting on threats and opportunities.

3-4a Environmental Scanning

Environmental scanning involves searching the environment for important events or issues that might affect an organization. Managers scan the environment to stay up to date on important factors in their industry and to reduce uncertainty. They want to know if demand will increase, prices for key components will rise, and whether competitors sales are rising or falling. This is why Google paid $500 million to buy Skybox, a company that captures high-resolution satellite images. By 2016, Skybox will have six dedicated satellites that take complete images of the earth twice daily. By 2018, it will have twenty-four dedicated satellites that do so three times a day and can provide real-time video of trucks moving down highways. The timeliness and resolution of its images will be so good that when traveling, you'll be able to use Google Maps street view to see if you left the front porch light on at your house. That also means Walmart's sales can be accurately predicted by counting the number of cars in its parking lots. Want to know when the next iPhone will be released? You'll be able to monitor the number of trucks coming and going from Foxconn factories in Taiwan, where they're manufactured. Co-founder Dan Berkenstock says, "We think we are going to fundamentally change humanity's understanding of the economic landscape on a daily basis."[61]

Organizational strategies also affect environmental scanning. In other words, managers pay close attention to trends and events that are directly related to their company's ability to compete in the marketplace.[62] With nearly 70 percent of China's water sources polluted from industry and agriculture, consumers are understandably concerned about drinking tap water. Furthermore, water purified at Chinese treatment plants is often recontaminated by hazardous materials when transported to homes. According to Hope Lee, an analyst with Euromonitor, "You don't dare drink the tap water in China." China's water problem, however, represents a business opportunity for Nestlé's bottled water business, especially with sales flat in North America and Europe. Chinese sales of bottled water, by contrast, are expected to grow significantly from $9 billion in 2012 to $16 billion in 2017. Therefore, Nestlé is rapidly expanding in China, selling water in five-gallon jugs, often through company-owned stores that provide free delivery to consumers' homes. Nestlé's Chinese sales have jumped 27 percent from the previous year.[63]

Finally, environmental scanning is important because it contributes to organizational performance. Environmental scanning helps managers detect environmental changes and problems before they become organizational crises.[64] Furthermore, companies whose CEOs do more environmental scanning have higher profits.[65] CEOs in better-performing firms scan their firms' environments more frequently and scan more key factors in their environments in more depth and detail than do CEOs in poorer-performing firms.[66]

3-4b Interpreting Environmental Factors

After scanning, managers determine what environmental events and issues mean to the organization. Typically, managers view environmental events and issues as

Environmental scanning searching the environment for important events or issues that might affect an organization

SSL Headquarters

Skybox Headquarters

AP Images/PRNewsFoto/SSL

either threats or opportunities. When managers interpret environmental events as threats, they take steps to protect the company from further harm. For more than a century, dry cereal was found on nearly every breakfast table in the United States. At its peak, Kellogg's and its cast of cartoon cereal mascots held a dominating 45 percent share of the market. Today, however, Kellogg's sales are dropping. Instead of having cereal for breakfast, many Americans now prefer a variety of alternatives, such as a piece of fruit, a breakfast sandwich, a granola bar, or a protein shake, all of which they can eat in their car or at their desk. Kellogg's CEO John Bryant acknowledges the threat to the company, saying, "The good news is that more people are eating breakfast; the bad news is that there are more alternatives."[67] Kellogg's CEO John Bryant implemented Project K, a cost-cutting program, from which a percentage of the savings would be invested in product innovation. Kellogg's also hired additional sales people to create more attractive in-store product displays. And, the company changed how it markets some of its cereals. For example, sales of Fruit Loops rose 3 percent after they were marketed to adults as a late-night snack.[68]

With the world's population projected to grow from 7.3 billion in 2016 to 9.7 billion by 5050, farmers and food producers will need to produce an additional 455 million metric tons of meat to keep up with demand. Chicken is expected to account for the majority of that increase because of its mild taste, universal religious acceptance, and efficiency. Bringing a full-grown chicken to market requires just 30 percent of the water and feed needed to bring a cow to market.[69] Hoping to take advantage of the growing population and increased preference for chicken, Cargill has invested several billion dollars in new and expanded facilities. These high-tech operations feature automated, high-speed processing lines for breast deboning and production-line software that ensures that chicken portions are consistent in size and weight.[70] In Thailand, the company's network of more than 100 animal-friendly poultry farms has increased production 300 percent in just ten years. Cargill is now able to ship 2.6 million birds from its Thailand operations to customers in Asia and Europe every week. This amounts to an additional 100 metric tons of chicken per year, or roughly 22 percent of the amount needed to feed an additional 2.4 billion people by 2050. Cargill expects to increase its capacity in Thailand another 30 percent in the near future, and also plans to develop a similarly sized network in sub-Saharan Africa to meet growing demand for meat across Africa's swelling urban centers.[71]

Valentina_S/Shutterstock.com

Exhibit 3.3
Cognitive Maps

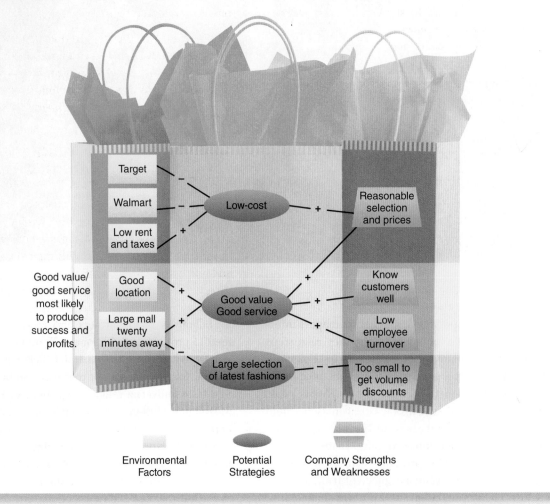

Environmental Factors   Potential Strategies   Company Strengths and Weaknesses

3-4c Acting on Threats and Opportunities

After scanning for information on environmental events and issues and interpreting them as threats or opportunities, managers have to decide how to respond to these environmental factors. Deciding what to do under conditions of uncertainty is always difficult. Managers can never be completely confident that they have all the information they need or that they correctly understand the information they have.

Because it is impossible to comprehend all the factors and changes, managers often rely on simplified models of external environments

Cognitive maps graphic depictions of how managers believe environmental factors relate to possible organizational actions

called cognitive maps. **Cognitive maps** summarize the perceived relationships between environmental factors and possible organizational actions. For example, the cognitive map shown in Exhibit 3.3 represents a small clothing-store owner's interpretation of her business environment. The map shows three kinds of variables. The first variables, shown as rectangles, are environmental factors, such as a Walmart or a large mall twenty minutes away. The second variables, shown in ovals, are potential actions that the store owner might take, such as a low-cost strategy; a good-value, good-service strategy; or a "large selection of the latest fashions" strategy. The third variables, shown as trapezoids, are company strengths, such as low employee turnover, and weaknesses, such as small size.

The plus and minus signs on the map indicate whether the manager believes there is a positive or negative relationship between variables. For example, the manager believes that a low-cost strategy won't work because Walmart and Target are nearby. Offering a large selection of the latest fashions would not work either—not with the small size of the store and that large nearby mall. However, the manager believes that a good-value, good-service strategy would lead to success and profits due to the store's low employee turnover, good knowledge of customers, reasonable selection of clothes at reasonable prices, and good location.

3-5 ORGANIZATIONAL CULTURES: CREATION, SUCCESS, AND CHANGE

We have been looking at trends and events outside of companies that have the potential to affect them. By contrast, the **internal environment** consists of the trends and events *within* an organization that affect the management, employees, and **organizational culture**. Internal environments are important because they affect what people think, feel, and do at work. The key component in internal environments is organizational culture, or the set of key values, beliefs, and attitudes shared by members of the organization.

Under Armour, the sporting apparel and accessories maker, got its start two decades ago when founder and CEO Kevin Plank, a former college football player and special teams captain, sewed shorts and shirts himself in his grandmother's Baltimore, Maryland, basement. Today, Under Armour is a fast-growing—sales increased 28 percent in 2015—$2.3 billion company that competes with Nike, Reebok, and Adidas. One of the keys to its meteoric rise may be its "faster-stronger-better" internal culture. Plank says, "We as a company don't sleep much. We work harder. We have a commitment that I think would be exhausting to someone else." To sustain that hard-driving, competitive culture, Under Armour builds camaraderie and a team orientation among employees. New employees are given big welcome breakfasts. Staff members are treated to outdoor movie nights, tuition reimbursement, and discounted tickets to sporting events, and there is a club for working mothers that offers support and advice. Says Plank, "I manage the company much like a team. Coming out of school and starting the business, sales and marketing were offense, and manufacturing was

defense, and finance and operations were like special teams. What I've come to find out is that when the company is the best, it's not that one team is playing and another team is winning on the side, it's that everyone is on the field together."[72]

*Let's take a closer look at **3-5a how organizational cultures are created and maintained, 3-5b the characteristics of successful organizational cultures,** and **3-5c how companies can accomplish the difficult task of changing organizational cultures.***

3-5a Creation and Maintenance of Organizational Cultures

A primary source of organizational culture is the company founder. Founders like Walt Disney (Disney) and Steve Jobs (Apple) created organizations in their own images and imprinted them with their beliefs, attitudes, and values. According to Professor Zeynep Ton, "The founder is in a better position than anyone else to say this is what our business is about, this is what we won't give up. They have to stick to their values 100 percent of the time, not 95 percent of the time." Founder Kip Tindell infused the **Container Store** with his personal philosophy, "Pay employees well and treat them with respect; consider suppliers and customers as family; have fun."[73] Tindell has turned that philosophy into seven Foundational Principles (see http://standfor.containerstore.com/our-foundation-principles/) that drive the Container Store's culture and actions. Not only are full-time employees given a week of training on the principles, the principles have been printed on company shopping bags, t-shirts, and packing tape. One strong sign that the principles have shaped the company culture is the low rate of employee turnover. Whereas the median turnover rate for part-time retail workers is 75 percent, at the Container Store, it is only 10 percent.[74] How are values, attitudes, and beliefs sustained in organizational cultures? Answer: stories and heroes.

People tell **organizational stories** to make sense of organizational events and changes and to emphasize culturally consistent assumptions, decisions, and actions.[75] Andreessen

Internal environment the events and trends inside an organization that affect management, employees, and organizational culture

Organizational culture the values, beliefs, and attitudes shared by organizational members

Organizational stories stories told by organizational members to make sense of organizational events and changes and to emphasize culturally consistent assumptions, decisions, and actions

Horowitz (AH) is a venture capital (VC) firm that invests millions in high-potential technology startups. AH's co-founders, Mark Andreessen and Ben Horowitz have significant experience—and success—starting high-tech companies that have sold for nearly $2 billion. Horowitz said, "When we started Andreessen Horowitz, we knew that one of the most frustrating things for entrepreneurs is that VCs do not respect their time. As entrepreneurs, every time we'd visit a VC [trying to secure funding for our companies], we'd wait in the lobby for 30–45 minutes. So at the core of the firm, we wanted a cultural tenet to be respect for the entrepreneur and the entrepreneurial process. But how do you get that into people's minds? The mechanism I came up with was to tell VCs that if you are late for a meeting with an entrepreneur, then the fine is $10 a minute. That is a very big fine. It is shocking to people who have to pay it. And that's the point. Because every time somebody pays a fine, *we get to tell the story* of why the person is paying so much money."[76]

A second way in which organizational culture is sustained is by recognizing and celebrating heroes. By definition, **organizational heroes** are organizational people admired for their qualities and achievements within the organization. Francisco D'Souza, CEO of Cognizant, an information technology firm with 170,000 employees, explains that, "Culture gets passed along not by writing it down, but through the rituals you have in the organization, the legends you refer to, and the heroes of the organization. So we institutionalized a set of things to create rituals, heroes, and legends."[77] Cognizant does that by having each regional division name an associate of the year who heroically exemplifies the company's culture. Likewise, to broaden cultural recognition beyond individuals to key teams and groups, Cognizant has each division celebrate a project of the year. D'Souza explains, "We rent stadiums around the world and bring all the employees and their families for a celebration, with entertainment and awards."[78]

3-5b Successful Organizational Cultures

Preliminary research shows that organizational culture is related to organizational success. As shown in Exhibit 3.4, cultures based on adaptability, involvement, a clear mission, and consistency can help companies achieve higher sales growth, return on assets, profits, quality, and employee satisfaction.[79]

Organizational heroes people celebrated for their qualities and achievements within an organization

Exhibit 3.4
Keys to an Organizational Culture That Fosters Success

Adaptability

Employee Involvement

Clear Mission

Consistency

de2marco/Shutterstock.com

Adaptability is the ability to notice and respond to changes in the organization's environment. Cultures need to reinforce important values and behaviors, but a culture becomes dysfunctional if it prevents change. Unfortunately, that was the case at **Mattel**, the toy company, where Barbie sales are down 18 percent this year after dropping 13 percent the year before. Sales of Fisher-Price toys have declined three straight years. With revenues shrinking, Mattel has cut $550 million in expenses just to maintain profits. New CEO Bryan Stockton is trying to turn things around by changing the PowerPoint-presentation, meeting-driven, slow-to-make decisions culture. For example, it took eight meetings and thirty design iterations to approve the school crest for the Monster High toy line. As such, Mattel drifted from its creative roots focused on fun and play toward a conservative culture focused on the bottom line. To jump-start culture change, CEO Stockton has generated new rules for meetings: No more than ten participants (except for training meetings), every meeting must have a specific purpose, and "There should be no more than a TOTAL of three meetings to make any decision."[80] Change is slow, but it took just one meeting to approve the new package designs for the 2016 Hot Wheels toys.

Company mission is the business's purpose or reason for existing. In organizational cultures with a clear

Hardcore Tech Culture

Crunchtime at a software development firm can be so intense that employees spend several days at the office without even going home. As journalist Joel Stein puts it, "Sleeping in the office is as Silicon Valley as startups in garages." Spending the night at work can be seen as a badge of commitment and dedication; not so much to a company, but to the occupation of computer coding itself. It's said that even after he was a billion-aire, Yahoo! co-founder David Filo would doze in a sleeping bag under his desk. Elon Musk of PayPal (and now Tesla and SpaceX) would do the same on a beanbag alongside Filo's sleeping bag. Aaron Levie, founder of Box.com, even moved his bed to his new office when his company (and his staff) outgrew his home. But workers who actually *live* on site are in another category altogether.

Google programmer Matthew Weaver lived in an RV in the company's parking lot for fifty-four weeks, eating at the Google-plex and showering in the company gym. His record stood until programmer Ben Discoe joined Google and lived out of a GMC van in the company parking lot for fifty-six weeks. Following Weaver's strategy, Discoe ate at the Googleplex, charged his

electronics at the office, and "badged" into the building in the middle of the night if he needed the restroom. According to Discoe, "Only a fool would pay rent in the Bay Area."

Source: J. Stein, "The Man Who Lived at Google: Thirteen Months of Working, Eating, Sleeping, and Bathing at the Googleplex. The Saga of Ben Discoe," *Bloomberg BusinessWeek,* July 27–August 2, 2015, 57–59.

company mission, the organization's strategic purpose and direction are apparent to everyone in the company. When managers are uncertain about their business environments, the mission helps guide the discussions, decisions, and behavior of the people in the company. BPV Capital Management is a Knoxville, Tennessee, mutual fund with thirty-eight employees. Alluding to the common dream of owning a retirement home with wonderful weather and a great view, founder Mike West explains that "BPV" stands for "back porch vista"; BPV exists "to help American families retire well." More specifically, its mission is, "To ensure that investors who work hard and save have the opportunity to retire comfortably, regardless of net worth." Says West, "Our values and the promise that we make to every advisor and investor are driven by that core ideology."[81]

Finally, in **consistent organizational cultures**, the company actively defines and teaches organizational values, beliefs, and attitudes. With 520 Olympic medals (220 gold), the U.S. Olympic team has dominated swimming for 25 years (Australia is a distant second with 171 medals). In 2015, **USA Swimming**, which governs the sport, commissioned a study to find out why. Said Executive Director Chuck Wielgus, "We wanted to know, what is **USA Swimming** doing so right?"[82] The answer

wasn't superior athletes or facilities, but a consistent three-part culture:

1. Build the base (develop a team environment and create a talent pipeline).

2. Promote the sport (mentor young swimmers and support mature swimmers so they can devote time to training).

3. Achieve competitive success (pair swimmers with experts and cultivate the value of serving swimming as a sport).

According to Wielgus, "Consistency is underrated. If you have consistency across your culture, you will always at least be in the top 80 percent. Then, from time to time, you might have a huge star pop up, but even if you don't, you still have your 80 percent."[83] Gold medalist Ryan Lochte agrees, "We have a system… when it comes down to it, Team USA is just the best. And I think it's because we have something in our system that we don't break."[84]

> **Company mission** a company's purpose or reason for existing
>
> **Consistent organizational culture** a company culture in which the company actively defines and teaches organizational values, beliefs, and attitudes

Exhibit 3.5
Three Levels of Organizational Culture

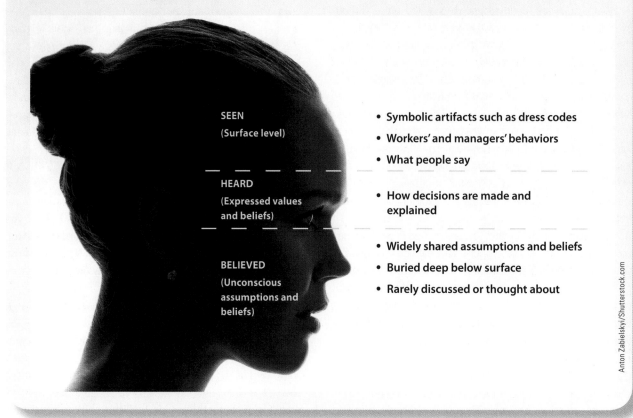

SEEN (Surface level)
- Symbolic artifacts such as dress codes
- Workers' and managers' behaviors
- What people say

HEARD (Expressed values and beliefs)
- How decisions are made and explained

BELIEVED (Unconscious assumptions and beliefs)
- Widely shared assumptions and beliefs
- Buried deep below surface
- Rarely discussed or thought about

Anton Zabielskyi/Shutterstock.com

Having a consistent or strong organizational culture doesn't guarantee good company performance. When core beliefs are widely shared and strongly held, it is very difficult to bring about needed change. Consequently, companies with strong cultures tend to perform poorly when they need to adapt to dramatic changes in their external environments. Their consistency sometimes prevents them from adapting to those changes.[85]

3-5c Changing Organizational Cultures

As shown in Exhibit 3.5, organizational cultures exist on three levels.[86] On the first, or surface, level are the reflections of an organization's culture that can be seen and observed, such as symbolic artifacts (for example, dress codes and office layouts) and workers' and managers' behaviors. Next, just below the surface, are the values and beliefs expressed by people in the company. You can't see these values and beliefs, but they become clear if you carefully listen to what people say and observe how decisions are made or explained. Finally, unconsciously held assumptions and beliefs about the company are buried deep below the surface. These are the unwritten views and rules that are so strongly held and so widely shared that they are rarely discussed or even thought about unless someone attempts to change them or unknowingly violates them. Changing such assumptions and beliefs can be very difficult. Instead, managers should focus on the parts of the organizational culture they can control. These include observable surface-level items, such as workers' behaviors, symbolic artifacts, and expressed values and beliefs, which can be influenced through employee selection. Let's see how these can be used to change organizational cultures.

One way of changing a corporate culture is to use behavioral addition or behavioral substitution to establish new patterns of behavior among managers and employees. **Behavioral addition** is the process of having managers and employees perform a new behavior, while

Behavioral addition the process of having managers and employees perform new behaviors that are central to and symbolic of the new organizational culture that a company wants to create

CONSTRUCTION AS CULTURE

Visible artifacts are, at their core, about defining corporate identity—especially, it seems, for tech companies, which are often championed as fun, relaxed, productive campuses. Apple, Facebook, and Google have taken the quest for the coolest, most collaborative headquarters to a new level. Each company has enlisted the services of an architectural icon who is reflective of its corporate culture to design its corporate offices. Apple has hired Sir Norman Foster (stoic); Google has hired Bjarke Ingels and Thomas Heatherwick (fun); and Facebook has hired Frank Gehry (expressionist). Through architecture, each company hopes to create a structure that communicates its mission, work, and personality.

Source: K. Campell-Dollaghan, "The Forgotten Offices That Shaped Apple, Google, and Facebook," Gizmodo.com, April 1, 2015. http://gizmodo.com/the-forgotten-offices-that-inspired-apple-facebook-an-1694978864.

behavioral substitution is having managers and employees perform a new behavior in place of another behavior. The key in both instances is to choose behaviors that are central to and symbolic of the old culture you're changing and the new culture that you want to create.[87] When Bob Flexon became CEO of **Dynegy**, which provides wholesale energy to utilities, energy cooperatives, and municipalities, the company was losing hundreds of millions of dollars. So, he not only cut costs, he began changing the company culture by emphasizing new behaviors. The first move was to ditch his expansive corner office—with a $15,000 marble desk and Oriental rugs—for a 64-foot cubicle identical to those used by everyone else at Dynegy's new headquarters, which is now on a single floor in a cheaper building (resulting in annual savings of $5 million). In terms of culture, Flexon and his leadership team created a new set of expectations regarding management and employee behavior. To start, employees received their first performance appraisals in two years (behavioral addition), including judgments regarding how well they were embracing the new cultural norms of safety, accountability, and agility. Next, managers and employees were expected to "Be Here Now," which means no distractions when engaging with others. For example, chief administrative officer Carolyn Burke has told employees who are tapping on their smartphones in meetings, "Hey, be here now." Likewise, CEO Flexon has a "Be Here Now" plaque underneath his computer monitor to remind him to not read emails during phone calls (behavioral substitution).[88]

Another way in which managers can begin to change corporate culture is to change the **visible artifacts** of their old culture, such as the office design and layout, company dress code, and recipients (or nonrecipients) of company benefits and perks such as stock options, personal parking spaces, or the private company dining room. Recall from Chapter 1 that Ryanair is a Dublin-based airline that offers incredibly low rates. Ryanair led the way in charging passengers for every part of the flight experience, including $50 to print a boarding pass at the airport and a "no refunds" policy for canceled flights. Ryanair's brazen policies originate from its brash CEO, Michael O'Leary. Regarding passengers who forget to print boarding passes at home, O'Leary says, "We think they should pay 60 euros for being so stupid." Regarding canceled flights, he says, "You're not getting a refund, so **** off. We don't want to hear your sob stories. What part of 'no refund' don't you understand?"[89] Unfortunately, O'Leary's unabashed statements have rubbed off on the company's staffers, whose similarly negative attitudes discourage customers from choosing the airline. To address the problem, Ryanair recently introduced the "Always Getting Better" campaign (also called the "Being Nicer" campaign) to change the company's focus from being cheap to providing a superior customer experience. The company reduced or eliminated some (but not all) of its fees; simplified online booking to require only five mouse clicks instead of seventeen; and introduced fully allocated seating to minimize congestion at the boarding gate. Previously, its "first come, first served" boarding strategy encouraged travelers to rush the gates to get better seats.[90] Crews were issued new, brightly colored uniforms, and the company moved its headquarters from a tired, dull facility to a cheerful building with colorful art on the walls. The changes dramatically improved company performance. In just one year, the number of Ryanair passengers increased 10 percent, and the load factor (the measurement of how full a jet is) reached 95 percent. O'Leary said, "If I'd known being nicer to customers was going to work so well, I'd have done it ages ago."[91]

Cultures can also be changed by hiring and selecting people with values and beliefs consistent with the company's desired culture. *Selection* is the process of gathering information about job applicants to decide who should be offered a job. As discussed in Chapter 11 on human resources,

Behavioral substitution the process of having managers and employees perform new behaviors central to the new organizational culture in place of behaviors that were central to the old organizational culture

Visible artifacts visible signs of an organization's culture, such as the office design and layout, company dress code, and company benefits and perks, such as stock options, personal parking spaces, or the private company dining room

most selection instruments measure whether job applicants have the knowledge, skills, and abilities needed to succeed in their jobs. But companies are increasingly testing job applicants to determine how they fit with the company's desired culture by using selection tests, instruments, and exercises to measure these values and beliefs in job applicants. (See Chapter 11 for a complete review of applicant and managerial selection.) During the hiring process, Amazon uses a group of employees called "Bar Raisers," who interview job candidates from other areas of the company, asking difficult and unexpected questions. Bar Raisers, who spend two to three hours on each job candidate, conducting phone and face-to-face interviews and participating in evaluation meetings, have the power to veto any applicant they've assessed. Founder Jeff Bezos started the Bar Raiser program to create a consistent corporate culture by "raising the bar" when it came to hiring talent. Rather than hiring people for particular jobs, Bezos asks Bar Raisers to focus on hiring people who can succeed in Amazon's culture. John Vlastelica, an HR consultant who worked at Amazon in its early days, says, "You want someone who can adapt to new roles in the company, not just someone who can fill the role that's vacant." Susan Harker, Amazon's vice president of global talent acquisition, says, "We want to be as objective and scientific in our hiring as possible. The point is to optimize our chances of having long-term employees." And, unlike many companies, that means hiring talented people who fit Amazon's culture. Human resource consultant Valerie Frederickson says, "There is no company that sticks to its process like Amazon does. They don't just hire the best of what they see; they're willing to keep looking and looking for the right talent."[92]

Corporate cultures are very difficult to change. Consequently, there is no guarantee that any one approach—changing visible cultural artifacts, using behavioral substitution, or hiring people with values consistent with a company's desired culture—will change a company's organizational culture. The best results are obtained by combining these methods. Together, these are some of the best tools managers have for changing culture because they send the clear message to managers and employees that "the accepted way of doing things" has changed.

Changing corporate culture can go a long way in boosting employee morale.

Blend Images/Shutterstock.com

STUDY TOOLS 3

LOCATED IN TEXTBOOK
☐ Rip-out and review chapter review card

LOCATED AT WWW.CENGAGEBRAIN.COM
☐ Review key term flashcards and create your own from StudyBits

☐ Track your knowledge and understanding of key concepts, using the concept tracker

☐ Complete practice and graded quizzes to prepare for tests

☐ Complete interactive content within the exposition

☐ View chapter highlight box content at the beginning of each chapter

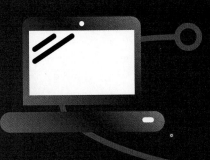

4 Ethics and Social Responsibility

LEARNING OUTCOMES

4-1 Identify common kinds of workplace deviance.

4-2 Describe the U.S. Sentencing Commission Guidelines for Organizations, and explain how they both encourage ethical behavior and punish unethical behavior by businesses.

4-3 Describe what influences ethical decision making.

4-4 Explain what practical steps managers can take to improve ethical decision making.

4-5 Explain to whom organizations are socially responsible.

4-6 Explain for what organizations are socially responsible.

4-7 Explain how organizations can respond to societal demands for social responsibility.

4-8 Explain whether social responsibility hurts or helps an organization's economic performance.

After you finish this chapter, go to **PAGE 90** for

STUDY TOOLS

WORKPLACE DEVIANCE

Today, it's not enough for companies to make a profit. We also expect managers to make a profit by doing the right things. Unfortunately, no matter what managers decide to do, someone or some group will be unhappy with the outcome. Managers don't have the luxury of choosing theoretically optimal, win-win solutions that are obviously desirable to everyone involved. In practice, solutions to ethical and social responsibility problems aren't optimal. Often, managers must be satisfied with a solution that just makes do or does the least harm. Rights and wrongs are rarely crystal clear to managers charged with doing the right thing. The business world is much messier than that.

Ethics is the set of moral principles or values that defines right and wrong for a person or group. Unfortunately, numerous studies have consistently produced distressing results about the state of ethics in today's business world. One global ethics study found that, even though business is substantially more trusted than government and that 65 percent of employees trust the company where they work, only 31 percent of people believe that companies are ethical.[1] Another study found that just 25 percent trust business leaders to honestly correct mistakes and that less than 20 percent believed that business leaders would be truthful and make ethical decisions.[2] According to the Ethics Recourse Center's National Business Ethics Survey, 41 percent of employees observed unethical behavior at work. Twenty-four percent of unethical behavior was committed by senior managers, while 60 percent was committed by managers (of all kinds). Moreover, 9 percent of employees report being pressured to compromise ethical standards at work. The good news, however, is that 63 percent of employees observing unethical behavior reported it.[3]

Other studies contain additional good news about workplace ethics. When people believe their work environment is ethical, they are six times more likely to stay with that company than if they believe they work in an unethical environment.[4] In fact, a survey by Deloitte reported that employees who were considering leaving their jobs cited "loss of trust" as the greatest factor.[5] One study asked 444 white-collar workers which qualities they considered to be important in company leaders. The results? Honesty (30%) and communication (22%) ranked by far the highest. Interestingly, these two qualities also ranked highest as areas in which business leaders needed to improve—16 percent of respondents

iStockphoto.com/Avava

said that leaders need to improve their honesty, and 11 percent cited communication.[6] According to Eduardo Castro-Wright, vice chairman of Walmart Stores Inc., "There's nothing that destroys credibility more than not being able to look someone in the eye and have them know that they can trust you."[7] In short, much needs to be done to make workplaces more ethical, but—and this is very important—most managers and employees want this to happen.

Ethical behavior follows accepted principles of right and wrong. Depending on which study you look at, one-third to three-quarters of all employees admit that

Ethics the set of moral principles or values that defines right and wrong for a person or group

Ethical behavior behavior that conforms to a society's accepted principles of right and wrong

CHAPTER 4: Ethics and Social Responsibility   69

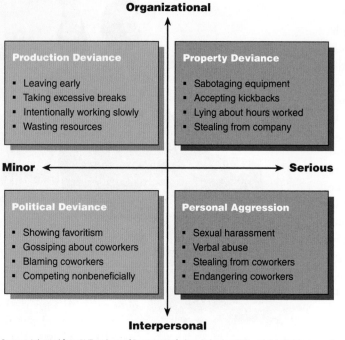

Exhibit 4.1
Types of Workplace Deviance

Organizational

Production Deviance
- Leaving early
- Taking excessive breaks
- Intentionally working slowly
- Wasting resources

Property Deviance
- Sabotaging equipment
- Accepting kickbacks
- Lying about hours worked
- Stealing from company

Minor ←———————→ **Serious**

Political Deviance
- Showing favoritism
- Gossiping about coworkers
- Blaming coworkers
- Competing nonbeneficially

Personal Aggression
- Sexual harassment
- Verbal abuse
- Stealing from coworkers
- Endangering coworkers

Interpersonal

Source: Adapted from "A Typology of Deviant Workplace Behaviors" (Figure), S. L. Robinson and R. J. Bennett. *Academy of Management Journal* 38 (1995).

both tangible and intangible assets. One kind of workplace deviance, called **production deviance**, hurts the quality and quantity of work produced. Examples include leaving early, taking excessively long work breaks, intentionally working slower, or wasting resources. Every spring, employees fill out their tournament brackets for March Madness in hopes of winning office betting pools (which are technically illegal) for most accurately predicting which teams advance during the NCAA basketball tournament. Employees commonly spend time talking about which teams made or didn't make the tournament, setting up brackets, and managing office pools. In addition, the first two days of tournament play occur on a Thursday and Friday during working hours. Outplacement firm Challenger, Gray, and Christmas estimates that 60 million American office workers participate in March Madness office pools. In 2015, as the University of Kentucky was chasing its first undefeated season in more than thirty years, John Challenger said, "If Kentucky plays their first game during the workday, it wouldn't be shocking if every single working person in the state called in sick for the day or took an extra-long lunch break." Although he was joking, with 56 percent of 60 million U.S. workers spending at least one work hour on the tournament, that lost time costs employers $1.9 billion. And that doesn't even consider how much more time employees will spend not working as they watch the games at work online, or get updates via Twitter or special sports apps on their smartphones.[10]

Property deviance is unethical behavior aimed at company property or products. Examples include sabotaging, stealing, or damaging equipment or products, and overcharging for services and then pocketing the difference. For example, in Nigeria, thieves steal 150,000 barrels a day of oil from oil company pipelines. Jacob Mandi, a diver who has grown rich stealing oil from pipelines, says, "We know which [pipeline] is gas, products, crude. We can sense whether it is hot or cold. We need nobody's help to know what's inside." Eni S.p.A., an Italian oil company, closed its production facilities in Nigeria because it was losing 60 percent of its production to thieves like Mandi.[11]

Organizational employees, however, do a significant amount of property deviance themselves.

they have stolen from their employers, committed computer fraud, embezzled funds, vandalized company property, sabotaged company projects, faked injuries to receive workers' compensation benefits or insurance, or been "sick" from work when they weren't really sick. Experts estimate that unethical behaviors like these, which researchers call *workplace deviance*, may cost companies as much as $3.7 trillion a year, or roughly 5 percent of their revenues.[8]

Workplace deviance is unethical behavior that violates organizational norms about right and wrong. As Exhibit 4.1 shows, workplace deviance can be categorized by how deviant the behavior is, from minor to serious, and by the target of the deviant behavior, either the organization or particular people in the workplace.[9]

Company-related deviance can affect

Workplace deviance
unethical behavior that violates organizational norms about right and wrong

Production deviance
unethical behavior that hurts the quality and quantity of work produced

Property deviance
unethical behavior aimed at the organization's property or products

Employee shrinkage, when employees steal company merchandise, accounts for 43 percent of theft from U.S. retailers and costs $18 billion a year. In fact, employee theft costs U.S. retailers more than shoplifters do![12] A survey of twenty-five large retailers across 23,250 stores found that one out of thirty-eight employees is caught stealing each year and that a dishonest employee steals six times as much as the typical shoplifter.[13] Likewise, 58 percent of office workers acknowledge taking company property for personal use, according to a survey conducted for lawyers.com. "Sweethearting" occurs when employees discount or don't ring up merchandise their family or friends bring to the cash register. A recent study found that sweethearting costs the retail service industry (that is, restaurants, hotels, hair salons, car washes, and so on) $80 billion annually. Of the employees surveyed, 67 percent indicated that, in the month prior to the survey, they had participated in some form of sweethearting, primarily in hopes of receiving similar deals and discounts from the customers to whom they had extended a sweetheart deal.[14] In "dumpster diving," employees unload trucks, stash merchandise in a dumpster, and then retrieve it after work.[15]

Whereas production and property deviance harm companies, political deviance and personal aggression are unethical behaviors that hurt particular people within companies. Political deviance is using one's influence to harm others in the company. Examples include making decisions based on favoritism rather than performance, spreading rumors about coworkers, or blaming others for mistakes they didn't make. Personal aggression is hostile or aggressive behavior toward others. Examples include sexual harassment, verbal abuse, stealing from coworkers, or personally threatening coworkers. Another kind of personal aggression is workplace violence. Fortunately, like nearly all kinds of crime, workplace violence has dropped significantly since 1993, when 16 of every 1,000 employees experienced nonfatal workplace violence. Today, the rate has dropped to just 5.4 incidents per 10,000 full-time workers. Furthermore, the rate of workplace violence is one-third the level of nonworkplace violence. So, overall, you are less likely to encounter violence at work. Still, 403 people were killed at work in 2014, the most recent year for which data are available. That means 9 percent of workplace deaths are homicides.[16] For more information on workplace violence, see the Bureau of Labor Statistics website, http://www.bls.gov/iif/osh_wpvs.htm.

4-2 U.S. SENTENCING COMMISSION GUIDELINES FOR ORGANIZATIONS

A male supervisor is sexually harassing female coworkers. A sales representative offers a $10,000 kickback to persuade an indecisive customer to do business with his company. A company president secretly meets with the CEO of her biggest competitor, and they agree not to compete in markets where the other has already established customers. Each of these behaviors is clearly unethical (and, in these cases, also illegal). Historically, if management was unaware of such activities, the company could not be held responsible for them. Since 1991, however, when the U.S. Sentencing Commission Guidelines for Organizations were established, companies can be prosecuted and punished *even if management didn't know about the unethical behavior*. Penalties can be substantial, with maximum fines approaching a whopping $300 million.[17] Later changes to the Guidelines resulted in much stricter ethics training requirements and emphasized the importance of creating a legal and ethical company culture.[18]

*Let's examine **4-2a to whom the guidelines apply and what they cover** and **4-2b how, according to the guidelines, an organization can be punished for the unethical behavior of its managers and employees**.*

4-2a Who, What, and Why?

Nearly all businesses are covered by the U.S. Sentencing Commission's guidelines. This includes nonprofits, partnerships, labor unions, unincorporated organizations and associations, incorporated organizations, and even pension funds, trusts, and joint stock companies. If your organization can be characterized as a business (remember, nonprofits count, too), then it is subject to the guidelines.[19] For example, World Vision, a nonprofit Christian humanitarian

Employee shrinkage employee theft of company merchandise

Political deviance using one's influence to harm others in the company

Personal aggression hostile or aggressive behavior toward others

aid organization, has a compliance program based on the U.S. sentencing guidelines. The program includes regular audits, a code of conduct, ethics standards, and anti-bribery and corruption policies (because much of its humanitarian work is carried out in third-world countries).[20]

The guidelines cover offenses defined by federal laws such as invasion of privacy, price fixing, fraud, customs violations, antitrust violations, civil rights violations, theft, money laundering, conflicts of interest, embezzlement, dealing in stolen goods, copyright infringements, extortion, and more. But it's not enough merely to stay within the law. The purpose of the guidelines is not just to punish companies *after* they or their employees break the law but also to encourage companies to take proactive steps that will discourage or prevent white-collar crime *before* it happens. The guidelines also give companies an incentive to cooperate with and disclose illegal activities to federal authorities.[21]

4-2b Determining the Punishment

The guidelines impose smaller fines on companies that take proactive steps to encourage ethical behavior or voluntarily disclose illegal activities to federal authorities. Essentially, the law uses a carrot-and-stick approach. The stick is the threat of heavy fines that can total millions of dollars. The carrot is a greatly reduced fine, but only if the company has started an effective compliance program (discussed next) to encourage ethical behavior *before* the illegal activity occurs.[22] The method used to determine a company's punishment illustrates the importance of establishing a compliance program, as illustrated in Exhibit 4.2.

The first step is to compute the *base fine* by determining what *level of offense* (that is, its seriousness) has occurred. The level of the offense varies depending on the kind of crime, the loss incurred by the victims, and how much planning went into the crime. For example, simple fraud is a level 6 offense (there are thirty-eight levels in all). But if the victims of that fraud lost more than $5 million, that level 6 offense becomes a level 22 offense. Moreover, anything beyond minimal planning to commit the fraud results in an increase of two levels to a level 24 offense. How much difference would this make to a company? As Exhibit 4.2 shows, crimes at or below level 6 incur a base fine of $8,500, whereas the base fine for level 24 is $3.5 million, a difference of $3,491,500! The base fine for level 38, the top-level offense, is a hefty $150 million.

After assessing a *base fine*, the judge computes a culpability score, which is a way of assigning blame to the company. The culpability score can range from 0.05 to 4.0. The greater the corporate responsibility in conducting, encouraging, or sanctioning illegal or unethical activity, the higher the culpability score. A company that already has a compliance program and voluntarily reports the offense to authorities will incur a culpability score of 0.05. By contrast, a company whose management secretly plans, approves, and participates in illegal or unethical activity will receive the maximum score of 4.0.

The culpability score is critical because the total fine is computed by multiplying the base fine by the culpability score. Going back to our level 24 fraud offense, the left point of the upper arrow in Exhibit 4.2 shows that a company with a compliance program that turns itself in will be fined only $175,000 ($3,500,000 × 0.05). In contrast, a company that secretly planned, approved, and participated in illegal activity will be fined $14 million ($3,500,000 × 4.0), as shown by the right point of the upper arrow. The difference is even greater for level 38 offenses. As shown by the left point of the bottom arrow, a company with a compliance program and a 0.05 culpability score is fined only $7.5 million, whereas a company with the maximum 4.0 culpability score is fined a whopping $600 million, as indicated by the right point of the bottom arrow. These differences clearly show the importance of having a compliance program in place. Over the past decade, 1,494 companies have been charged under the U.S. Sentencing Guidelines. Seventy-six percent of those charged were fined, with the average fine exceeding $2 million. Company fines are on average twenty times larger now than before the implementation of the guidelines in 1991.[23]

Fortunately for companies that want to avoid paying these stiff fines, the U.S. Sentencing Guidelines clearly spell out the seven necessary components of an effective compliance program.[24] Exhibit 4.3 lists those components. Caremark International, a managed-care service provider in Delaware, pleaded guilty to criminal charges related to its physician contracts and improper patient referrals. When shareholders sued the company for negligence and poor management, the Delaware court dismissed the case, ruling that the company's ethics compliance program, built on the components described in Exhibit 4.3, was a good-faith attempt to monitor employees and that the company did not knowingly allow illegal and unethical behavior to occur. The court went on to rule that a compliance program based on the U.S. Sentencing Guidelines was enough to shield the company from liability.[25]

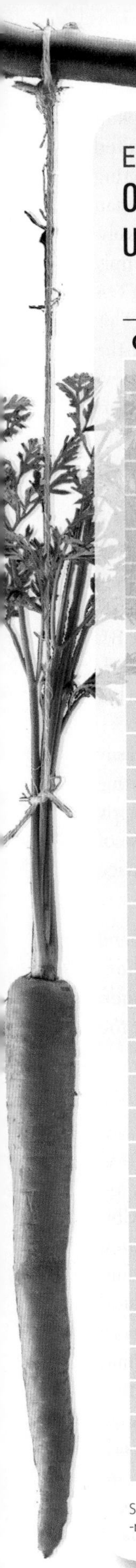

Exhibit 4.2

Offense Levels, Base Fines, Culpability Scores, and Possible Total Fines under the U.S. Sentencing Commission Guidelines for Organizations

Offense Level	Base Fine	Total Fine with a Culpability Score of					
		0.05	0.5	1.0	2.0	3.0	4.0
6 or less	$ 8,500	$ 425	$ 4,250	$ 8,500	$ 17,000	$ 25,500	$ 34,000
7	15,000	750	7,500	15,000	30,000	45,000	60,000
8	15,000	750	7,500	15,000	30,000	45,000	60,000
9	25,000	1,250	12,500	25,000	50,000	75,000	100,000
10	35,000	1,750	17,500	35,000	70,000	105,000	140,000
11	50,000	2,500	25,000	50,000	100,000	150,000	200,000
12	70,000	3,500	35,000	70,000	140,000	210,000	280,000
13	100,000	5,000	50,000	100,000	200,000	300,000	400,000
14	150,000	7,500	75,000	150,000	300,000	450,000	600,000
15	200,000	10,000	100,000	200,000	400,000	600,000	800,000
16	300,000	15,000	150,000	300,000	600,000	900,000	1,200,000
17	450,000	22,500	225,000	450,000	900,000	1,350,000	1,800,000
18	600,000	30,000	300,000	600,000	1,200,000	1,800,000	2,400,000
19	850,000	42,500	425,000	850,000	1,700,000	2,550,000	3,400,000
20	1,000,000	50,000	500,000	1,000,000	2,000,000	3,000,000	4,000,000
21	1,500,000	75,000	750,000	1,500,000	3,000,000	4,500,000	6,000,000
22	2,000,000	100,000	1,000,000	2,000,000	4,000,000	6,000,000	8,000,000
23	3,000,000	150,000	1,500,000	3,000,000	6,000,000	9,000,000	12,000,000
24	3,500,000	175,000	1,750,000	3,500,000	7,000,000	10,500,000	14,000,000
25	5,000,000	250,000	2,500,000	5,000,000	10,000,000	15,000,000	20,000,000
26	6,500,000	325,000	3,250,000	6,500,000	13,000,000	19,500,000	26,000,000
27	8,500,000	425,000	4,250,000	8,500,000	17,000,000	25,500,000	34,000,000
28	10,000,000	500,000	5,000,000	10,000,000	20,000,000	30,000,000	40,000,000
29	15,000,000	750,000	7,500,000	15,000,000	30,000,000	45,000,000	60,000,000
30	20,000,000	1,000,000	10,000,000	20,000,000	40,000,000	60,000,000	80,000,000
31	25,000,000	1,250,000	12,500,000	25,000,000	50,000,000	75,000,000	100,000,000
32	30,000,000	1,500,000	15,000,000	30,000,000	60,000,000	90,000,000	120,000,000
33	40,000,000	2,000,000	20,000,000	40,000,000	80,000,000	120,000,000	160,000,000
34	50,000,000	2,500,000	25,000,000	50,000,000	100,000,000	15,000,0000	200,000,000
35	65,000,000	3,250,000	32,500,000	65,000,000	130,000,000	195,000,000	260,000,000
36	80,000,000	4,000,000	40,000,000	80,000,000	160,000,000	240,000,000	320,000,000
37	100,000,000	5,000,000	50,000,000	100,000,000	200,000,000	300,000,000	400,000,000
38 or more	150,000,000	7,500,000	75,000,000	150,000,000	300,000,000	450,000,000	600,000,000

Source: U.S. Sentencing Commission, *Guidelines Manual*, §3E1.1 (November 2015), accessed August 4, 2016. http://www.ussc.gov/sites/default/files/pdf/guidelines-manual/2015/GLMFull.pdf.

iStockphoto.com/Terry Hankin

Exhibit 4.3
Compliance Program Steps from the U.S. Sentencing Commission Guidelines for Organizations

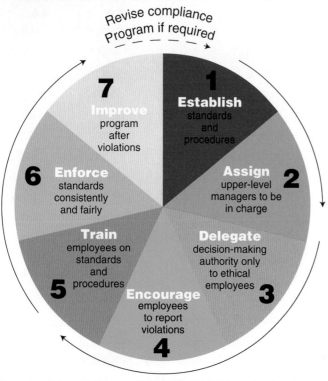

Revise compliance Program if required

7 **Improve** program after violations

1 **Establish** standards and procedures

2 **Assign** upper-level managers to be in charge

6 **Enforce** standards consistently and fairly

3 **Delegate** decision-making authority only to ethical employees

Train employees on standards and procedures 5

Encourage employees to report violations 4

Source: D. R. Dalton, M. B. Metzger, and J. W. Hill, "The 'New' U.S. Sentencing Commission Guidelines: A Wake-up Call for Corporate America," *Academy of Management Executive* 8 (1994): 7–16.

4-3 INFLUENCES ON ETHICAL DECISION MAKING

Imagine that you are CEO of Chimerix, a pharmaceutical company that is currently developing an experimental antiviral drug called brincidofovir. This drug could be an effective treatment for a range of virulent viruses, including Ebola, smallpox, and the adenovirus, which is thought to cause the common cold. Yesterday, you were contacted by the family of Josh Hardy, a seven-year-old boy

Ethical intensity the degree of concern people have about an ethical issue

who underwent a marrow stem cell transplant to treat kidney cancer. While being treated for cancer, Josh contracted a lifethreatening respiratory virus that the family thinks can be treated with brincidofovir. Unfortunately, the company must reserve its limited supply for the clinical trials needed to secure FDA approval and bring the drug to market. This is the third time the family has asked for the drug, but you and Chimerix have declined every time. A social media campaign in support of Josh erupted last week, and at last count, nearly 32,500 tweets using the hashtag #Save-Josh have been posted worldwide. Nonprofit group Kids v Cancer publicized the campaign, and its director made a public statement that it is "profoundly unethical" for you to not give Josh the drug. The company is being lambasted on social media, and according to the FBI, you personally have received several credible death threats.[26] As Chimerix's CEO, what would be the ethical thing for you to do?

Although some ethical issues are easily solved, many do not have clearly right or wrong answers. But even though the answers are rarely clear, managers do need to have a clear sense of *how* to arrive at an answer in order to manage this ethical ambiguity well.

*The ethical answers that managers choose depend on **4-3a the ethical intensity of the decision**, **4-3b the moral development of the manager**, and **4-3c the ethical principles used to solve the problem.***

4-3a Ethical Intensity of the Decision

Managers don't treat all ethical decisions the same. Chimerix's CEO, who has to decide if the company's drug treatment will go to Josh or to another ill (perhaps dying) person who has been waiting for the company's clinical trial to begin, is going to treat that decision much more seriously than the decision of how to deal with an assistant who has been taking paper home for personal use. These decisions differ in their **ethical intensity**, or the degree of concern people have about an ethical issue. When addressing an issue of high ethical intensity, managers are more aware of the impact their decision will have on others. They are more likely to view the decision as an ethical or moral decision than as an economic decision. They are also more likely to worry about doing the right thing.

Six factors must be taken into account when determining the ethical intensity of an action, as shown in Exhibit 4.4. **Magnitude of consequences** is the total harm or benefit derived from an ethical decision. The more people who are harmed or the greater the harm to those people, the larger the consequences. **Social consensus** is agreement on whether behavior is bad or good. **Probability of effect** is the chance that something will happen that results in harm to others. If we combine these factors, we can see the effect they can have on ethical intensity. For example, if there is *clear agreement* (social consensus) that a managerial decision or action is *certain* (probability of effect) to have *large negative consequences* (magnitude of consequences) in some way, then people will be highly concerned about that managerial decision or action, and ethical intensity will be high.

Temporal immediacy is the time between an act and the consequences the act produces. Temporal immediacy is stronger if a manager has to lay off workers next week as opposed to three months from now. **Proximity of effect** is the social, psychological, cultural, or physical distance of a decision maker from those affected by his or her decisions. Thus, proximity of effect is greater when a manager lays off employees he knows than when he lays off employees he doesn't know. Finally, whereas the magnitude of consequences is the total effect across all people, **concentration of effect** is how much an act affects the average person.

HOW CONVENIENCE COMPROMISES ETHICS

E-signatures are tremendously convenient. There's no need to print, sign, scan, or return anything. Just type your name in a digital field or check a box, and you're done! Because they are so fast and easy, e-signatures increase ease of use, meaning that fewer signatures are missing from key documents. However, e-signatures can also make people feel less committed to the (sometimes legally binding) documents they are signing. A recent study in the *Journal of Experimental Psychology* found that people are more likely to sign their name to a dishonest statement if they use an e-signature than if they sign traditionally with a pen. So if you want the honest truth, ask your clients to sign with a pen (or a stylus).

Source: P. Anand, "The Lies E-Sigs Tell: Research suggests people are more honest if signing by hand," *Wall Street Journal*, October 14, 2015, R5.

For instance, eliminating health care coverage for 100 employees has a greater concentration of effect than reducing the health care benefits for 1,000 employees by 10 percent.

Which of these six factors has the most impact on ethical intensity? Studies indicate that managers are much more likely to view decisions as ethical issues when the magnitude of consequences (total harm) is high and there is a social consensus (agreement) that a behavior or action is bad.[27]

4-3b Moral Development

It's Friday. Another long week of classes and studying is over, and all you want to do is sit down and relax. "A movie sounds good," you think to yourself, but you don't want to spend $12 to trek down to the megaplex. And, while it would cost less than a $1.50 to rent a DVD, you're too tired to make the short trip down to the corner drugstore's Redbox machine. Your roommate says

Exhibit 4.4
Six Factors That Contribute to Ethical Intensity

- Magnitude of consequences
- Social consensus
- Probability of effect
- Temporal immediacy
- Proximity of effect
- Concentration of effect

Source: Republished with permission of Academy of Management; P.O. Box 3020, Briar Cliff Manor, NY, 10510-8020. T.M. Jones, "Ethical Decision Making by Individuals in Organizations: An Issue Contingent Model," *Academy of Management Review* 16 (1991) 366–395; Reproduced by permission of the publisher via Copyright Clearance Center, Inc.

Magnitude of consequences the total harm or benefit derived from an ethical decision

Social consensus agreement on whether behavior is bad or good

Probability of effect the chance that something will happen that results in harm to others

Temporal immediacy the time between an act and the consequences the act produces

Proximity of effect the social, psychological, cultural, or physical distance between a decision maker and those affected by his or her decisions

Concentration of effect the total harm or benefit that an act produces on the average person

Exhibit 4.5
Kohlberg's Stages of Moral Development

Stage 1	Stage 2	Stage 3	Stage 4	Stage 5	Stage 6
Punishment and Obedience	Instrumental Exchange	Good Boy, Nice Girl	Law and Order	Social Contract	Universal Principle
Preconventional		**Conventional**		**Postconventional**	
Self-Interest		**Societal Expectations**		**Internalized Principles**	

he's got the perfect solution and gives you the URL of a website that streams all the latest blockbuster movies and TV shows for free. The writers, actors, and producers won't earn a dime if you watch the pirated copy of the movie. Furthermore, it's illegal to download or watch streamed copies of pirated shows. But how will the movie studios ever find out? Are the cops going to come through your door because you watched a pirated copy of *The Revenant*? Will you watch the movie? What are you going to do?

In part, according to psychologist Lawrence Kohlberg, your decision will be based on your level of moral development. Kohlberg identified three phases of moral development, with two stages in each phase (see Exhibit 4.5).[28] At the **preconventional level of moral development**, people decide based on selfish reasons. For example, if you are in Stage 1, the punishment and obedience stage, your primary concern will be to avoid trouble for yourself. So you won't watch the pirated movie because you are afraid of being caught and punished. Yet, in Stage 2, the instrumental exchange stage, you worry less about punishment and more about doing things that directly advance your wants and needs. So you will watch the pirated movie.

People at the **conventional level of moral development** make decisions that conform to societal expectations. In other words, they look outside themselves to others for guidance on ethical issues. In Stage 3, the "good boy, nice girl" stage, you normally do what the other "good boys" and "nice girls" are

doing. If everyone else is watching the pirated movie, you will, too. But if they aren't, you won't either. In the law and order stage, Stage 4, you again look for external guidance and do whatever the law permits, so you won't watch the movie.

People at the **postconventional level of moral development** use internalized ethical principles to solve ethical dilemmas. In Stage 5, the social contract stage, you will refuse to watch the pirated movie because, as a whole, society is better off when the rights of others—in this case, the rights of actors, producers, directors, and writers—are not violated. In Stage 6, the universal principle stage, you might or might not watch the pirated movie, depending on your principles of right and wrong. Moreover, you will stick to your principles even if your decision conflicts with the law (Stage 4) or what others believe is best for society (Stage 5). For example, those with socialist or communist beliefs would probably choose to watch the pirated movie because they believe goods and services should be owned by society rather than by individuals and corporations.

Kohlberg believed that people would progress sequentially from earlier stages to later stages as they became more educated and mature. But only 20 percent of adults ever reach the postconventional stage of moral development, where internal principles guide their decisions. Most adults are in the conventional stage of moral development, in which they look outside themselves to others for guidance on ethical issues. This means that most people in the workplace look to and need leadership when it comes to ethical decision making.[29]

4-3c Principles of Ethical Decision Making

Beyond an issue's ethical intensity and a manager's level of moral maturity, the particular ethical principles that managers use will also affect how they solve ethical

Preconventional level of moral development the first level of moral development, in which people make decisions based on selfish reasons

Conventional level of moral development the second level of moral development, in which people make decisions that conform to societal expectation

Postconventional level of moral development the third level of moral development, in which people make decisions based on internalized principles

dilemmas. Unfortunately, there is no one ideal principle to use in making ethical business decisions.

According to professor LaRue Hosmer, a number of different ethical principles can be used to make business decisions: long-term self-interest, religious injunctions, government requirements, individual rights, personal virtue, distributive justice, and utilitarian benefits.[30] All of these ethical principles encourage managers and employees to take others' interests into account when making ethical decisions. At the same time, however, these principles can lead to very different ethical actions, as we can see by using these principles to decide what Chimerix might do regarding its decision to give brincidofovir to seven-year-old Josh Hardy.

According to the **principle of long-term self-interest**, you should never take any action that is not in your or your organization's long-term self-interest. Although this sounds as if the principle promotes selfishness, it doesn't. What we do to maximize our long-term interests (save more, spend less, exercise every day, watch what we eat) is often very different from what we do to maximize short-term interests (max out our credit cards, be couch potatoes, eat whatever we want). The cost to bring a drug to market has more than doubled in the last decade. According to 2014 research conducted by the Tufts Center for the Study of Drug Development, the average cost of launching a new drug is $2.56 billion.[31] For a small, 55-employee company like Chimerix, every development dollar counts. At the time of the Hardys' request, Chimerix had no FDA-approved drugs, no source of revenue beyond investor funding, and a $173 million deficit. For any pharmaceutical company, distributing experimental drugs for free represents a significant donation. For Chimerix, it would be especially costly because the company's survival depends on its ability to bring effective drug therapies to market.[32] So, based on long-term self-interest, Chimerix should refuse individual requests for its experimental drugs.

According to the **principle of religious injunctions**, you should never take an action that is unkind or that harms

a sense of community, such as the positive feelings that come from working together to accomplish a commonly accepted goal. Using this principle, Chimerix would have given Josh the treatment—even if it would have damaged the company financially.

According to the **principle of government requirements**, the law represents the minimal moral standards of society, so you should never take any action that violates the law. To obtain approval for an experimental drug from the Food and Drug Administration (FDA), companies must follow strict protocols and must meet specific regulatory requirements. When the Hardy family first approached Chimerix, the drug was already in its last stages of clinical trials and had not yet been approved for use. Based on the principle of government requirements, Chimerix should have denied the Hardys' request because Josh was not enrolled in the trials and could not legally receive the drug.

The **principle of individual rights** holds that you should never take an action that infringes on others' agreed-upon rights. At the time the brincidofovir request was made for Josh Hardy, Chimerix was preparing to begin its Phase III trials in hopes of receiving final FDA approval in 2016.[33] While many on social media argued it was wrong for Chimerix not to give Josh the drug, the significant cost of doing so would infringe on the individual rights of investors (who expect their funds to be used prudently to produce a reasonable financial return), and patients who were already enrolled in Phase III trials (who might not receive treatment because of limited supply). Because of these violations, Chimerix should not give Josh Hardy the treatment.

The **principle of personal virtue** holds that you should never do anything that is not honest, open, and truthful and that you would not be glad to see reported in the newspapers or on TV. Using the principle of personal

POSTCONVENTIONAL LEVEL OF MORAL DEVELOPMENT

CONVENTIONAL LEVEL OF MORAL DEVELOPMENT

PRECONVENTIONAL LEVEL OF MORAL DEVELOPMENT

iStockphoto.com/Mikhail Tolstoy

Principle of long-term self-interest an ethical principle that holds that you should never take any action that is not in your or your organization's long-term self-interest

Principle of religious injunctions an ethical principle that holds that you should never take any action that is not kind and that does not build a sense of community

Principle of government requirements an ethical principle that holds that you should never take any action that violates the law, for the law represents the minimal moral standard

Principle of individual rights an ethical principle that holds that you should never take any action that infringes on others' agreed-upon rights

Principle of personal virtue an ethical principle that holds that you should never do anything that is not honest, open, and truthful and that you would not be glad to see reported in the newspapers or on TV

What's the Most Ethical Profession?

For fourteen years in a row, nurses topped Gallup's Honesty and Ethics Survey of professions. In the 2015 survey, 85 percent of respondents ranked nurses as having high ethical standards and as being highly honest. At the bottom of the rankings were members of Congress. Only 8 percent of respondents considered members of Congress to have very high or high ethical standards, while 64 percent of respondents said Congress's ethical standards were low or very low.

Source: L. Saad, "Americans' Faith in Honesty, Ethics of Police Rebounds," Gallup.com reporting results from 2015 Gallup Honesty and Ethics Survey December 21, 2015, accessed February 19, 2016, http://www.gallup.com/poll/187874/americans-faith-honesty-ethics-police-rebounds.aspx.

AP Images/Peter Cihelka

Josh Hardy plays Go Fish with his brothers Jude and Joe on January 2, 2014.

virtue, Chimerix would have quietly allocated treatment doses of brincidofovir for Josh Hardy. Had it done so, it might have avoided the social media firestorm and the subsequent publication of an article in *Bloomberg Business-Week*, which brought the story to even more people.

Under the **principle of distributive justice**, you should never take any action that harms the least fortunate among us in some way. This principle is designed to protect the poor, the uneducated, and the unemployed. Josh Hardy could certainly be considered vulnerable. Having fought kidney cancer since he was a baby, the seven-year-old contracted a life-threatening virus after receiving a marrow stem cell transplant targeting the cancer. Chimerix had a drug on hand that had been shown effective in the treatment of such viruses. Would the company want to be seen as one that had a cure and intentionally withheld it? The principle of distributive justice says it would not.

Finally, the **principle of utilitarian benefits** states that you should never take an action that does not result in greater good for society. In short, you should do whatever creates the greatest good for the greatest number. Chimerix has previously given 430 patients brincidofovir for compassionate use. That program, however, was funded by the government. When funding ended, Chimerix reallocated all of its remaining doses of the drug to the formal trials required for FDA approval. Allocating any doses to Josh might have jeopardized the FDA approval process by reducing the number of doses available for use in the formal trials. Fewer individuals would be able to participate in the trials, potentially requiring additional trial rounds, delaying approval, and preventing distribution of the life-saving drug to even more people suffering from life-threatening viral infections. Thus according to the principle of utilitarian benefit, Chimerix would be obligated to put the larger group's interests first and deny the Hardy family's request. Chimerix CEO Kenneth Moch echoed this principle, saying, "If it were my child, would I do what the Hardy's did? Absolutely, yes. As the CEO, I have to think about not just the individual but the many."[34]

So, what did Moch decide to do? He factored in many of the concerns raised by these ethical principles and worked with the FDA to create a separate clinical trial for brincidofovir with Josh Hardy as its first patient. Within a week of receiving the drug, Josh's condition improved, and he was ultimately discharged from the hospital. Three weeks into the trial, however, Moch was replaced as CEO of Chimerix. He said he would have "loved to continue to be the CEO, but the board thought otherwise."[35]

Principle of distributive justice an ethical principle that holds that you should never take any action that harms the least fortunate among us: the poor, the uneducated, the unemployed

Principle of utilitarian benefits an ethical principle that holds that you should never take any action that does not result in greater good for society

nyul/Fotolia

4-4 PRACTICAL STEPS TO ETHICAL DECISION MAKING

Companies are putting more emphasis on ethical decision making. Eighty-one percent now provide ethics training. Sixty-seven percent include ethical conduct as a standard part of performance evaluations. And, seventy-four percent communicate internally about disciplinary actions that are taken when unethical behavior occurs.[36]

Managers can encourage more ethical decision making in their organizations by 4-4a carefully selecting and hiring ethical employees, 4-4b establishing a specific code of ethics, 4-4c training employees to make ethical decisions, and 4-4d creating an ethical climate.

4-4a Selecting and Hiring Ethical Employees

As an employer, how can you increase your chances of hiring honest employees, the kind who would return a wallet filled with money to its rightful owner? **Overt integrity tests** estimate job applicants' honesty by asking them directly what they think or feel about theft or about punishment of unethical behaviors.[37] For example, an employer might ask an applicant, "Would you ever consider buying something from somebody if you knew the person had stolen the item?" or "Don't most people steal from their companies?" Surprisingly, unethical people will usually answer "yes" to such questions because they believe that the world is basically dishonest and that dishonest behavior is normal.[38]

Personality-based integrity tests indirectly estimate job applicants' honesty by measuring psychological traits such as dependability and conscientiousness. For example, prison inmates serving time for white-collar crimes (counterfeiting, embezzlement, and fraud) scored much lower than a comparison group of middle-level managers on scales measuring reliability, dependability, honesty, conscientiousness, and abiding by rules.[39] These results show that companies can selectively hire and promote people who will be more ethical.

4-4b Codes of Ethics

Today, almost all large corporations have an ethics code in place. In fact, to be listed on the New York Stock Exchange, a company must "adopt and disclose a code of business conduct and ethics for directors, officers, and employees."[40] Even if a company has a code of ethics, two things must still happen if those codes are to encourage ethical decision making and behavior.[41] First, a company must communicate its code to others both inside and outside the company.

Second, in addition to having an ethics code with general guidelines such as "do unto others as you would have others do unto you," management must also develop practical ethical standards and procedures specific to the company's line of business. Hershey's, the leading producer of chocolate and confectionary goods in North America, also does business in ninety countries. Visitors to the Hershey Company's website can download the company's "Code of Ethical Business Conduct" in eight languages. The code sets specific ethical standards on topics ranging from treatment of coworkers to protecting the environment to maintenance of financial records. For example, the code states specifically, "If management, our auditors or government investigators request information or documentation from us, we must cooperate. This means we may not conceal, alter or destroy such information. Falsifying business records, destroying documents or lying to auditors, investigators or government officials is a serious offense." Likewise, Hershey's code states that information about competitors can only be obtained in legal and ethical ways and that it is wrong to attempt to pry confidential information from others. "If a coworker, customer or business partner has competitive information that they are required to keep confidential, we must not encourage them to disclose it."[42] Specific codes of ethics such as this make it much easier for employees to decide what to do when they want to do the right thing.

4-4c Ethics Training

In addition to establishing ethical standards for the company, managers must sponsor and be involved in ethics and compliance training in order to create an ethical company culture.[43] The first objective of ethics training is to develop employees' awareness of ethics.[44] This means helping employees recognize which issues are ethical issues and then avoiding

Overt integrity test a written test that estimates job applicants' honesty by directly asking them what they think or feel about theft or about punishment of unethical behaviors

Personality-based integrity test a written test that indirectly estimates job applicants' honesty by measuring psychological traits, such as dependability and conscientiousness

rationalizing unethical behavior by thinking, "This isn't really illegal or immoral" or "No one will ever find out." Several companies have created board games, produced videos, or invited special speakers to improve awareness of ethical issues.[45] Howard Winkler, project manager for ethics and compliance at Southern Co., an Atlanta-based energy provider, uses a wide range of tools to educate and engage its employees on ethics. Like many companies, Southern's mandatory ethics training requires employees to go online, read the code of ethics, and certify they have done so. Says Winkler, "When its put online, it usually has all the charm and engagement of a software licensing agreement."[46] So Winkler replaced it with a ten-minute video where actors explained the company's policies. He varies delivery methods to keep employees interested, using videos, contests, and internal social media to communicate important ethics issues. Winkler even had a convicted felon come in to talk about how small ethical compromises eventually lead to bigger unethical behavior, such as fraud, the charges that sent him to jail for five years. "It created an enormous impression," Winkler says, because, "This person didn't start out his career looking to commit fraud. The main message was that once you make the first ethical compromise, you are embarking on a path that can lead all the way to a prison cell."[47] Winkler also regularly creates opportunities for senior executives to speak with employees about ethics issues. This multifaceted approach appears to be working, as internal surveys indicate that 93 percent of employees recognize that their continued career at Southern "depends on my ethical behavior."

The second objective for ethics training programs is to achieve credibility with employees. Not surprisingly, employees can be highly suspicious of management's reasons for offering ethics training. Some companies have hurt the credibility of their ethics programs by having outside instructors and consultants conduct the classes.[48] Employees often complain that outside instructors and consultants are teaching theory that has nothing to do with their jobs and the practical dilemmas they actually face on a daily basis. CA Technologies

made its ethics training practical and relevant by creating a series of comical training videos with a fictional manager, Griffin Peabody, who is shown facing a series of ethics issues, such as conflicts of interest, competitive intelligence, workplace harassment, client expenses, and conduct outside of the workplace (search "Griffin Peabody" at YouTube.com). Chief ethics officer Joel Katz says, "It's easy for it [that is, ethics training] to become a check-the-box exercise. We use Griffin's escapades to teach compliance lessons in a funny way." For instance, since CA Technologies acquires lots of companies—a common practice in technology industries—it's critical, and required by law, that its employees keep potential acquisitions confidential to prevent insider trading. Chief compliance officer Gary Brown says, "They think they can tell a friend, 'Guess what I was working on today.' They have to realize it is a much bigger problem." To reinforce this point, Griffin Peabody is visited by Securities and Exchange Commission investigators after publicly disclosing information about a company that is being acquired.[49]

Ethics training becomes even more credible when top managers teach the initial ethics classes to their subordinates who in turn teach their subordinates.[50] At Intuitive Research and Technology Corp., an engineering services company in Huntsville, Alabama, Howard "Hal" Brewer, the company's co-founder and president, is the company's ethics champion. Every new employee attends a session called "Let's Talk Ethics with Hal," led by Brewer and the director of human resources, Juanita Phillips. Brewer explains how employees' decisions impact the company, situations they will likely encounter with outside organizations they do business with, and then how to respond. What effect does having the co-founder and president talk to every employee about ethics? Philips says about Hal, "He makes it clear that he is the ethics officer. His strength is that he means every word of it, and he shows it in how he lives every day in terms of running the company."[51] Michael Hoffman, executive director for the Center for Business Ethics at

The overarching goals of ethics training are to develop employees' awareness of ethics, achieve credibility with employees, and teach employees a practical model of ethical decision making.

Bentley University, says that having managers teach ethics courses greatly reinforces the seriousness with which employees treat ethics in the workplace.[52]

The third objective of ethics training is to teach employees a practical model of ethical decision making. A basic model should help them think about the consequences their choices will have on others and consider how they will choose between different solutions. Exhibit 4.6 presents a basic model of ethical decision making.

4-4d Ethical Climate

Organizational culture is key to fostering ethical decision making. The 2015 National Business Ethics Survey reported that only 33 percent of employees who work

CALLING ALL TIPSTERS!

The Securities and Exchange Commission (SEC) and the Commodities Futures Trading Commission (CFTC) are looking for whistle-blowers. To encourage reports of fraud and wrongdoing, these two agencies launched programs to pay bounties for information that leads to sanctions or fines. The similarities between the two programs end there, however. While the SEC's program is working smoothly, the CFTC has paid more in administrative costs to keep its whistle-blowing program operational than it has paid bounties to actual whistle-blowers. By 2016, the SEC had paid out more than $55 million in bounties to the CFTC's $530,000. The SEC leads on the overall tip count as well—14,116 to 655 as of September 2015. Still, head of the CFTC whistle-blower office Christopher Ehrman is undeterred: "The program will continue onward. We'll get what we get and hope for the best."

Borja Andreu/Shutterstock.com

Source: J. Eaglesham, "CFTC Can't Give Whistleblower Money Away," *Wall Street Journal*, February 8, 2016, accessed February 22, 2016, www.wsj.com/articles /cftc-cant-give-whistleblower-money-away-1454876128.

Exhibit 4.6
A Basic Model of Ethical Decision Making

1. **Identify the problem.** What makes it an ethical problem? Think in terms of rights, obligations, fairness, relationships, and integrity. How would you define the problem if you stood on the other side of the fence?

2. **Identify the constituents.** Who has been hurt? Who could be hurt? Who could be helped? Are they willing players, or are they victims? Can you negotiate with them?

3. **Diagnose the situation.** How did it happen in the first place? What could have prevented it? Is it going to get worse or better? Can the damage now be undone?

4. **Analyze your options.** Imagine the range of possibilities. Limit yourself to the two or three most manageable. What are the likely outcomes of each? What are the likely costs? Look to the company mission statement or code of ethics for guidance.

5. **Make your choice.** What is your intention in making this decision? How does it compare with the probable results? Can you discuss the problem with the affected parties before you act? Could you disclose without qualm your decision to your boss, the CEO, the board of directors, your family, or society as a whole?

6. **Act.** Do what you have to do. Don't be afraid to admit errors. Be as bold in confronting a problem as you were in causing it.

Source: L. A. Berger, "Train All Employees to Solve Ethical Dilemmas," *Best's Review—Life-Health Insurance Edition* 95 (1995): 70–80.

at companies with a strong ethical culture (where core beliefs are widely shared and strongly held) have observed others engaging in unethical behavior, whereas 62 percent of those who work in organizations with weak ethical cultures (where core beliefs are not widely shared or strongly held) have observed others engaging in unethical behavior.[53] Employees of companies with strong ethical cultures are also more likely to report misconduct that they observe (87% versus 32% in weak ethical cultures).[54]

The first step in establishing an ethical climate is for managers, especially top managers, to act ethically themselves. It's no surprise that in study after study, when researchers ask, "What is the most important influence on your ethical behavior at work?" the answer comes back, "My manager."

A second step in establishing an ethical climate is for top management to be active in and committed to the company ethics program.[55] Top managers who consistently talk about the importance of ethics and back up that talk by participating in their companies' ethics programs send the clear message that ethics matter. When management engages and communicates about ethical issues, employees are less likely to break rules and more likely to report ethical violations.[56] Business writer Dayton Fandray says, "You can have ethics offices and officers and training programs and reporting systems, but if the CEO doesn't seem to care, it's all just a sham. It's not surprising to find that the companies that really do care about ethics make a point of including senior management in all of their ethics and compliance programs."[57]

A third step is to put in place a reporting system that encourages managers and employees to report potential ethics violations. **Whistle-blowing**, that is, reporting others' ethics violations, is a difficult step for most people to take.[58] Managers who have been interviewed about whistle-blowing have said, "In every organization, someone's been screwed for standing up. If anything, I figured that by taking a strong stand I might get myself in trouble. People might look at me as a goody two-shoes. Someone might try to force me out."[59] Indeed, in large companies without an effective compliance program, 62 percent of workers have observed unethical behavior, 32 percent of those have reported the misconduct, and 59 percent of those who reported the unethical behavior experienced some kind of retaliation.[60]

An AirTran Airways pilot, for example, was removed from "flight status," meaning he was ineligible to fly, after filing ten safety reports in two days, all concerning an unbalanced tire on one of AirTran's passenger jets. Three weeks later, following a seventeen-minute hearing, he was fired for allegedly not satisfactorily answering questions at the hearing. However, the Occupational Safety and Health Administration (OSHA) ruled that the firing was retaliatory, that AirTran violated whistle-blower protection laws, and that AirTran should reinstate the pilot and pay him more than $1 million in back pay and compensatory damages. OSHA Assistant Secretary of Labor Dr. David Michaels said, "Airline workers must be free to raise safety and security concerns, and companies that diminish those rights through intimidation or retaliation must be held accountable. Airline safety is of vital importance, not only to the workers, but to the millions of Americans who use our airways."[61]

A 2014 ruling by the U.S. Supreme Court greatly expands protections for whistle-blowers. The Court declared that the strong whistle-blowers protections built into the 2002 Sarbanes-Oxley Act, which apply to employees of publicly traded companies, should also apply to the employees of contractors and subcontractors that work with those public companies. This ruling extends whistle-blowers protection laws beyond the 5,000 publicly traded companies covered by Sarbanes-Oxley to an additional 6 million private companies.[62]

To encourage employees to report ethics violations, that is, to act as whistle-blowers, many companies have installed confidential ethics hotlines. The information obtained from the hotline at Paychex, a multibillion dollar payroll services firm in Rochester, New York, is reported directly to the company's board of directors and audit committee, which can then trigger an investigation independent of company management.[63]

The factor that does the most to discourage whistle-blowers from reporting problems is lack of company action on their complaints.[64] Thus, the final step in developing an ethical climate is for management to fairly and consistently punish those who violate the company's code of ethics. The key, says Paychex CEO Martin Mucci, is "to deal with it quickly, severely, and publicize it."[65] Says Mucci, "Our employees know that if they are caught cheating in any way, even if only to make a few dollars or improve their scores, they will most likely be terminated. Then we review that with the entire management team. We have done that with managers of locations, top sales representatives–we don't treat anyone differently."[66] Amazingly, though, not all companies fire ethics violators. In fact, 8 percent of surveyed companies admit that they would promote top performers even if they violated ethical standards.[67]

Whistle-blowing reporting others' ethics violations to management or legal authorities

4-5 TO WHOM ARE ORGANIZATIONS SOCIALLY RESPONSIBLE?

Social responsibility is a business's obligation to pursue policies, make decisions, and take actions that benefit society.[68] Unfortunately, because there are strong disagreements over to whom and for what in society organizations are responsible, it can be difficult for managers to know what is or will be perceived as socially responsible corporate behavior. In a recent McKinsey & Company study of 1,144 top global executives, 79 percent predicted that at least some responsibility for dealing with future social and political issues would fall on corporations, but only 3 percent said they themselves do a good job of dealing with these issues.[69] So what should managers and corporations do to be socially responsible?

There are two perspectives regarding to whom organizations are socially responsible: the shareholder model and the stakeholder model. According to the late Nobel Prize–winning economist Milton Friedman, the only social responsibility that organizations have is to satisfy their owners, that is, company shareholders. This view—called the **shareholder model**—holds that the only social responsibility that businesses have is to maximize profits. By maximizing profit, the firm maximizes shareholder wealth and satisfaction. More specifically, as profits rise, the company stock owned by shareholders generally increases in value.

Friedman argued that it is socially irresponsible for companies to divert time, money, and attention from maximizing profits to social causes and charitable organizations. The first problem, he believed, is that organizations cannot act effectively as moral agents for all company shareholders. Although shareholders are likely to agree on investment issues concerning a company, it's highly unlikely that they have common views on what social causes a company should or should not support.

The second major problem, Friedman said, is that the time, money, and attention diverted to social causes undermine market efficiency.[70] In competitive markets, companies compete for raw materials, talented workers, customers, and investment funds. A company that spends money on social causes will have less money to purchase quality materials or to hire talented workers

who can produce a valuable product at a good price. If customers find the company's product less desirable, its sales and profits will fall. If profits fall, the company's stock price will decline, and the company will have difficulty attracting investment funds that could be used to fund long-term growth. In the end, Friedman argues, diverting the firm's money, time, and resources to social causes hurts customers, suppliers, employees, and shareholders. Russell Roberts, an economist and research fellow at Stanford University's Hoover Institution, agrees, saying, "Doesn't it make more sense to have companies do what they do best, make good products at fair prices, and then let consumers use the savings for the charity of their choice?"[71]

By contrast, under the **stakeholder model**, management's most important responsibility is the firm's long-term survival (not just maximizing profits), which is achieved by satisfying the interests of multiple corporate stakeholders (not just shareholders).[72] **Stakeholders** are persons or groups with a legitimate interest in a company.[73] Because stakeholders are interested in and affected by the organization's actions, they have a stake in what those actions are. In 2013, an environmental group, As You Sow, along with company shareholders, asked Exxon Mobile via a formal shareholder proposal at Exxon's annual shareholder meeting to provide detailed information about the impact of fracking, a technique in which water is injected at high pressure into oil shale deposits to force lose oil and natural gas. Exxon declined to answer, stating, "the minimal environmental impacts of hydraulic fracturing have been well-documented." But, in the face of increased concerns about fracking, the company agreed in April 2014 to provide a report on fracking's impact on air quality, water, and chemical usage at Exxon sites. A company spokesperson said the agreement was, "a productive evolution of our relationship with some of these shareholder groups." After formally withdrawing its shareholder proposal, As You Sow president Danielle Fugere, commented, "It does feel like Exxon is changing the way it's doing business. [But if the report doesn't provide much

Social responsibility
a business's obligation to pursue policies, make decisions, and take actions that benefit society

Shareholder model a view of social responsibility that holds that an organization's overriding goal should be profit maximization for the benefit of shareholders

Stakeholder model
a theory of corporate responsibility that holds that management's most important responsibility, long-term survival, is achieved by satisfying the interests of multiple corporate stakeholders

Stakeholders persons or groups with a stake, or legitimate interest, in a company's actions

information], "we did reserve the right to bring a [shareholder] resolution next year."[74]

Stakeholder groups may try to influence the firm to advance their interests. Exhibit 4.7 shows the various stakeholder groups that the organization must satisfy to assure its long-term survival. Being responsible to multiple stakeholders raises two basic questions. First, how does a company identify organizational stakeholders? Second, how does a company balance the needs of different stakeholders? Distinguishing between primary and secondary stakeholders can help to answer these questions.[75]

Some stakeholders are more important to the firm's survival than others. **Primary stakeholders** are groups on which the organization depends for its long-term survival; they include shareholders, employees, customers, suppliers, governments, and local communities. When managers are struggling to balance the needs of different stakeholders, the stakeholder model suggests that the needs of primary stakeholders take precedence over the needs of secondary stakeholders. But among primary stakeholders, are some more important than others? According to the life cycle theory of organizations, the answer is yes. In practice, the answer is also yes, as CEOs typically give somewhat higher priority to shareholders, employees, and customers than to suppliers, governments, and local communities, no matter what stage of the life cycle a company is in.[76] Addressing the concerns of primary stakeholders is important because if a stakeholder group becomes dissatisfied and terminates its relationship with the company, the company could be seriously harmed or go out of business.

Secondary stakeholders, such as the media and special interest groups, can influence or be influenced by the company. Unlike the primary stakeholders, however, they do not engage in regular transactions with the company and are not critical to its long-term survival. Meeting the needs of primary stakeholders is therefore usually more important than meeting the needs of secondary stakeholders. Nevertheless, secondary stakeholders are still important because they can affect public perceptions and opinions about socially responsible behavior.

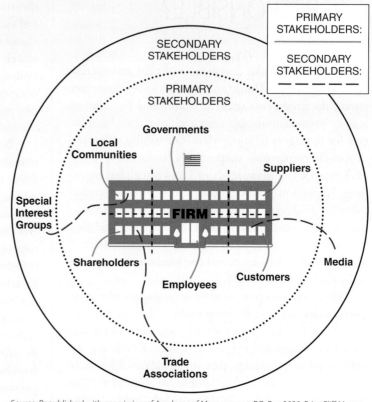

Exhibit 4.7
Stakeholder Model of Corporate Social Responsibility

Source: Republished with permission of Academy of Management, P.O. Box 3020, Briar Cliff Manor, NY, 10510-8020. "The Stakeholder Theory of the Corporation: Concepts, Evidence and Implications" (Figure), T. Donaldson and L. E. Preston, *Academy of Management Review* 20 (1995). Reproduced by permission of the publisher via Copyright Clearance Center, Inc.

Antibacterial gels, soaps, cleansers, and sanitizers make up a large segment of the $30 billion U.S. cleaning products industry. But according to nonprofit special-interest group the Natural Resources Defense Council, the key ingredient has a number of serious side effects. Triclosan, which weakens bacterial strains, is believed to alter thyroid production, aggravate asthma, decrease muscle function, and, thanks to its pervasive use, actually increase resistance to antibiotics.[77] Kaiser Permanente has banned triclosan and thirteen other antimicrobials from its hospitals because, as Environmental-Stewardship Officer Kathy Gerwig says, "We want to use our purchasing power to send a message that it's not OK to use ingredients that might be harmful to our health." Soap manufacturers have begun to take notice of the debate. Henkel (the maker

Primary stakeholder any group on which an organization relies for its long-term survival

Secondary stakeholder any group that can influence or be influenced by a company and can affect public perceptions about the company's socially responsible behavior

of Dial), Procter & Gamble, Johnson & Johnson, and Colgate Palmolive have all begun eliminating triclosan from some or all of their cleansing products in response to consumer concerns.[78]

So, to whom are organizations socially responsible? Many commentators, especially economists and financial analysts, continue to argue that organizations are responsible only to shareholders. Increasingly, however, top managers have come to believe that they and their companies must be socially responsible to their stakeholders. Today, surveys show that as many as 80 percent of top-level managers believe that it is unethical to focus just on shareholders. Twenty-nine states have changed their laws to allow company boards of directors to consider the needs of employees, creditors, suppliers, customers, and local communities, as well as those of shareholders.[79] Although there is not complete agreement, a majority of opinion makers would argue that companies must be socially responsible to their stakeholders.

4-6 FOR WHAT ARE ORGANIZATIONS SOCIALLY RESPONSIBLE?

If organizations are to be socially responsible to stakeholders, what are they to be socially responsible *for*? Companies can best benefit their stakeholders by fulfilling their economic, legal, ethical, and discretionary responsibilities.[80] Economic and legal responsibilities are at the bottom of the pyramid because they play a larger part in a company's social responsibility than do ethical and discretionary responsibilities. However, the relative importance of these various responsibilities depends on society's expectations of corporate social responsibility at a particular point in time.[81] A century ago, society expected businesses to meet their economic and legal responsibilities and little else. Today, when society judges whether businesses are socially responsible, ethical and discretionary responsibilities are considerably more important than they used to be (see box "Grooveshark Faces the Music").

Historically, **economic responsibility**, or making a profit by producing a product or service valued by society, has been a business's most basic social responsibility. Organizations that don't meet their financial and economic expectations come under tremendous pressure. For example, company boards are quick these days to fire CEOs. Typically, all it takes is two or three bad quarters in a row. **Spirit Airlines** is known for it's extremely low cost "Bare Fare" pricing. Spirit customers get cheap prices, but they don't get snacks (not even water), are charged for carry-on luggage (which is free on other airlines), and sit in crowded, non-reclining seats (more people equals lower prices). Spirit grew steadily, went public, and by September 2015, had revenues of $1.6 billion, up 11 percent over 2014. More impressively, profits rose 43 percent to nearly $243 million during that same period. Competing airlines noticed. Helped by low oil prices, they aggressively slashed fares. In turn, Spirit cut fares 17 percent to stay competitive. Its revenues, profits and stock price all declined. Three months later, CEO Ben Baldanza was abruptly replaced.[82] William Rollnick, who became acting chairman of Mattel after the company fired its previous CEO, says, "There's zero forgiveness. You screw up and you're dead."[83] According to the Conference Board, 16–29 percent of CEOs of large companies are fired each year.[84]

Legal responsibility is a company's social responsibility to obey society's laws and regulations as it tries to meet its economic responsibilities. After purchasing a controlling interest in **Yoplait**, the world's second-largest maker of fresh dairy products, **General Mills**, the U.S. food giant and maker of Cheerios, uncovered a secret. Yoplait had been part of a secret dairy cartel, the members of which met regularly at cafés around Paris, France, to fix prices, exchange information about commercial strategies, and divide sales territories. The illegal cartel represented over 90 percent of the French dairy market, and a Yoplait executive had documented the group's proceedings for years in a ruled notebook. General Mills handed over evidence to the authorities, and a company spokesperson said, "General Mills has strict corporate policies for our operations, including antitrust compliance."[85]

Ethical responsibility is a company's social responsibility to not violate accepted principles of right and wrong when conducting

Minerva Studio/Shutterstock.com

Economic responsibility a company's social responsibility to make a profit by producing a valued product or service

Legal responsibility a company's social responsibility to obey society's laws and regulations

Ethical responsibility a company's social responsibility not to violate accepted principles of right and wrong when conducting its business

Grooveshark Faces the Music

When Grooveshark co-founders Sam Tarantino and Josh Greenberg launched their free streaming music service, they did it backward. First, they uploaded thousands of songs to their platform—and urged employees to do the same—and then they tried to obtain licenses to stream the songs legally. Over seven years, the streaming site grew to have a collection of roughly 20 million songs and 30 million subscribers, yet the company never secured permissions to stream songs by artists from several major record labels. Vivendi, Sony, and Warner Music sued Grooveshark, which was ultimately found guilty of copyright infringement. Tarantino said he had been in a catch-22—record labels wouldn't license the music unless he could give them financial guarantees, and his investors wouldn't give him money

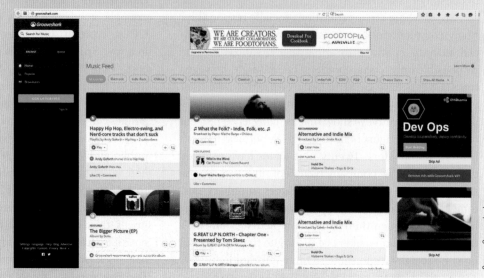

Source: Grooveshark

unless he had rights to stream the music. Tarantino said his investors told him, "You have all these lawsuits—we're not going to give you a big check."

Sources: H. Karp, "Grooveshark Tries to Play by the Rules with Online Radio App," *Wall Street Journal*, December 8, 2014, accessed March 28, 2015, http://www.wsj.com/articles/grooveshark-tries-to-play-by-the-rules-with-online-radio-app-1418014861.

its business. When pepper costs spiked, spice company McCormick & Co. reduced the amount of pepper in its aluminum tins from four ounces to three ounces. McCormick relabeled the product contents on the front label, so consumers were technically informed of the change. Still, consumers could easily have assumed that they were buying four ounces of pepper since the overall design and size of the package didn't change. The food industry calls this strategy—putting less product into the same-sized package—*weight-out*. Marketing professor and former Federal Trade Commission official Thomas J. Maronick says that legally, "the critical thing is that [McCormick & Co.] told the truth."

By contrast, consumer-fraud attorney Janine Pollack says, "When it tips the balance over to where you're kind of cheating a bit, that's when the law needs to step in."[86] Indeed, several companies have been caught going too far with weight-out, including Procter & Gamble's Old Spice and Olay brands, L'Oréal, CVS, Johnson & Johnson, Unilever's Axe brand, and ConAgra's Slim Jim brand.[87] While McCormick informed retailers and changed the bar code used for scanning, would it not have been more ethical to add a distinctive sticker informing customers as well?

Discretionary responsibilities pertain to the social roles that businesses play in society beyond their economic, legal, and ethical responsibilities. Hurricane Sandy, the largest Atlantic hurricane ever recorded, caused approximately $75 billion in damage—with New York State and New Jersey taking the brunt of the 1,100 mile-wide storm. As recovery efforts began, many companies stepped in with donations, contributions, and other forms of valuable assistance. J.P. Morgan, for example, pledged $2 million to the Red Cross, $1 million to local agencies, and $5 billion in special loans to small and mid-sized businesses. The bank also allowed storm-affected customers to skip mortgage payments for ninety days and suspended all of its foreclosure activity in storm-damaged areas. Entertainment companies Time Warner, News Corporation, Walt Disney, and Viacom each pledged to donate $1 million to $2 million.

Discretionary responsibilities the social roles that a company fulfills beyond its economic, legal, and ethical responsibilities

J.P. Morgan allowed businesses and home owners to skip mortgage payments for 90 days and suspended all of its foreclosure activities in storm-damaged areas.

Meanwhile, Adidas, the sporting goods company, donated $600,000 worth of jackets, while Terramar Sports, which makes outdoor clothing and gear, donated $500,000 worth of long underwear and thermal clothing to people displaced from their homes by the storm.[88]

Carrying out discretionary responsibilities such as these is voluntary. Companies are not considered unethical if they don't perform them. Today, however, corporate stakeholders expect companies to do much more than in the past to meet their discretionary responsibilities.

4-7 RESPONSES TO DEMANDS FOR SOCIAL RESPONSIBILITY

Social responsiveness refers to a company's strategy to respond to stakeholders' economic, legal, ethical, or discretionary expectations concerning social responsibility. A social responsibility problem exists whenever company actions do not meet stakeholder expectations. One model of social responsiveness identifies four strategies for responding to social responsibility problems: reactive, defensive, accommodative, and proactive. These strategies differ in the extent to which the company is willing to act to meet or exceed society's expectations.

A company using a **reactive strategy** will do less than society expects. For nearly two decades, the National Transportation Safety Board (NTSB) has been pressuring the helicopter industry to adopt tougher fuel-tank standards that would reduce the likelihood of fires erupting after a crash. The NTSB estimates that with these upgrades, hundreds of fatalities and serious burns caused by post-impact fires could have been prevented. The industry balked at the expense of the upgrades ($100,000 per helicopter, or $500 million industry-wide). Until, that is, a series of high-profile accidents and fatal crashes made it impossible to ignore the issue any longer. Matthew Zuccaro, president of industry trade association Helicopter Association International, acknowledges that attitudes have finally changed. "There is a major cultural shift in the international helicopter community. You got our attention, and we're going to participate," he said recently.[89] Prompted by two fatal crashes in a three-year period, **Air Methods**, the largest operator of air ambulances in the United States, has begun the process by retrofitting the fuel systems on 130 of its 400 helicopters.

By contrast, a company using a **defensive strategy** would admit responsibility for a problem but would do the least required to meet societal expectations. Foxconn is a Taiwanese electronics manufacturing company that operates Chinese factories that produce 40 percent of the world's consumer electronic products. Over the past four years, at the Foxconn factories that make iPhones and iPads, eighteen employees attempted suicide, most by leaping to their deaths. After the eleventh suicide, the company placed suicide nets that reach twenty feet out around the perimeter of each building. An extensive *New York Times* investigation found that employees often worked seven days a week, were exposed to dangerous chemicals, and lived in crowded, company-supplied dorm rooms, some with as many as twenty people per three-bedroom apartment. However, Apple, which had been conducting audits of its suppliers' manufacturing facilities for many years, was slow to respond. A consultant with Business for Social Responsibility, a company Apple hired for advice on labor issues, said, "We've spent years telling Apple there are serious problems and

Social responsiveness a company's strategy to respond to stakeholders' economic, legal, ethical, or discretionary expectations concerning social responsibility

Reactive strategy a social responsiveness strategy in which a company does less than society expects

Defensive strategy a social responsiveness strategy in which a company admits responsibility for a problem but does the least required to meet societal expectations

RESPONDING TO COMPETING SOCIAL RESPONSIBILITIES

The Colorado Correctional Industries (CCI) considers it part of its core mission to provide inmates with job and life skills as a way to facilitate their return to society and reduce recidivism. In furtherance of that mission, CCI recently collaborated with several companies to give inmates the opportunity to train for a variety of jobs. One such company, Haystack Mountain Goat Dairy, sells goat cheese to the national grocery chain Whole Foods. According to Whole Foods spokesperson Michael Silverman, "We felt that supporting supplier partners who found a way to be part of paid, rehabilitative work being done by inmates would help people get back on their feet." Michael Allen of End Mass Incarceration Houston disagrees, however. Allen believes that Whole Foods' support of products made with inmate labor is exploitative rather than socially responsible, saying, "People are incarcerated and then forced to work for pennies on the dollar—compare that to what the products are sold for." Although Whole Foods asked Haystack Mountain Goat Dairy to find an alternate source for the goat

iStockphoto.com/ivanastar

milk that goes into its cheeses, CCI and Haystack Mountain stand by the program. Haystack considers the arrangement a model prison-labor program because inmates not only earn up to $2,500 a year, they also receive teamwork and job training, giving them a new set of skills for when they are released.

Source: A. Aubrey, "Whole Foods Says It Will Stop Selling Foods Made with Prison Labor," *National Public Radio*, October 1, 2015, www.npr.org/sections/thesalt /2015/09/30/444797169/whole-foods-says-it-will-stop-selling-foods-made-by -prisoners (Accessed February 23, 2016).

recommending changes. They don't want to pre-empt problems, they just want to avoid embarrassments." A former Apple executive said, "If you see the same pattern of problems, year after year, that means the company's ignoring the issue rather than solving it. Noncompliance is tolerated, as long as the suppliers promise to try harder next time. If we meant business, core violations would disappear." After the *New York Times* story, Apple began working with the Fair Labor Association, a nonprofit organization that promotes and monitors safe working conditions. Four years after the problems began, following the Fair Labor Association's report, Apple and Foxconn agreed to increase pay, limit workers to a maximum of forty-nine hours a week, build more dormitories, and hire thousands of additional workers.[90]

A company using an **accommodative strategy** will accept responsibility for a problem and take a progressive approach by doing all that could be expected to solve the problem. Chipotle once ridiculed rivals for using artificial ingredients and boasted that it served "food with integrity." In 2015, however, the fast-casual restaurant chain was hit with a foodborne illnesses outbreak that crippled the brand's sparkling image. Between July and December 2015, hundreds of customers across nine states contracted *E. coli* and noroviruses after eating Chipotle food. In response, Chipotle not only closed the stores where outbreaks occurred but also neighboring stores. Managers and employees across the country scoured their stores to sterilize them, and thousands of ingredient samples were submitted to the Centers for Disease Control (CDC) for

Accommodative strategy a social responsiveness strategy in which a company accepts responsibility for a problem and does all that society expects to solve that problem

On February 8, 2016, Chipotle closed all of its 1,900 restaurants for four hours to have a company-wide meeting on food safety.

Helen Sessions/Alamy Stock photo

testing. Ultimately, the CDC could not point to a particular cause or source. Chipotle director of public relations Chris Arnold said, however, "If there's a silver lining in this, it is that by not knowing for sure what the cause is, it's prompted us to look at every ingredient we use with an eye to improving our practices."[91] Chipotle's beef supplier now tests meat for pathogens before shipping, and Chipotle has adopted new labeling protocols, such as unique item numbers for all its ingredients, to allow full traceability from the field to food suppliers to restaurants. To ensure that these changes stick, half of all bonuses given to Chipotle managers are now tied to food safety.[92]

Finally, a company using a **proactive strategy** will anticipate responsibility for a problem before it occurs, do more than expected to address the problem, and lead the industry in its approach. McDonald's CEO Steve Easterman announced that at its 14,350 U.S. stores, it will stop selling menu items made from chickens treated with antibiotics. Scientists and doctors have long warned that treating livestock with antibiotics to prevent infections before they occur is accelerating the development of antibiotic-resistant bacteria. Indeed, 2 million Americans a year develop bacterial infections resistant to antibiotics, and, according to the Centers for Disease Control and Prevention, 23,000 of them will die. McDonald's is making these changes even though it will significantly increase its costs (antibiotic-free chickens are two to three times more expensive to raise). McDonald's size is expected to broadly influence the chicken-growing industry to stop raising chicken with antibiotics. Gail Hansen of the Pew Charitable Trust, an organization critical of the use of antibiotics in meat, said McDonald's new policy, "Will have a ripple effect probably throughout the entire food industry."[93]

4-8 SOCIAL RESPONSIBILITY AND ECONOMIC PERFORMANCE

One question that managers often ask is, "Does it pay to be socially responsible?" In previous editions of this textbook, the answer was no, as early research indicated that there was not an inherent relationship between social responsibility and economic performance.[94] Recent research, however, leads to different conclusions. There is no trade-off between being socially responsible and economic performance.[95] And there is a small, positive relationship between being socially responsible and economic performance that strengthens with corporate reputation.[96] Let's explore what each of these results means.

First, as noted earlier, there is no trade-off between being socially responsible and economic performance.[97] Being socially responsible usually won't make a business less profitable. What this suggests is that the costs of being socially responsible—and those costs can be high, especially early on—can be offset by a better product or corporate reputation, which results in stronger sales or higher profit margins. When businesses enhance their reputations by being socially responsible, they hope to maximize *willingness to pay,* that is, customers paying more for products and services that are socially responsible. In an effort to align its business practices with its core mission, **CVS Caremark** changed its name to **CVS Health** and stopped selling cigarettes at CVS pharmacies. Researchers analyzing eighteen months of data from CVS pharmacies had found that 6 percent of people filling prescriptions for respiratory diseases, such as asthma and chronic obstructive pulmonary disorder (COPD), had bought a pack of cigarettes. Removing cigarettes from CVS stores cost the company $2 billion in annual revenues, resulting in a 4.5 percent drop in front-of-the-store sales (candy, magazines, toiletries). However, sales from pharmacy services rose 16 percent to $22.5 billion during that time. CVS attributed that increase, which offset the loss of cigarette revenue, to acquiring larger corporate and insurance clients to whom CVS now

Proactive strategy a social responsiveness strategy in which a company anticipates a problem before it occurs and does more than society expects to take responsibility for and address the problem

provides pharmacy benefits to their employees and patients. One year after making this change, CVS was still the only pharmacy chain to not sell cigarettes.[98]

Second, it usually *does* pay to be socially responsible, and that relationship becomes stronger particularly when a company or its products have a strong reputation for social responsibility.[99] Finally, even if there is generally a small positive relationship between social responsibility and economic performance that becomes stronger when a company or its products have a positive reputation for social responsibility, and even if there is no trade-off between being socially responsible and economic performance, there is no guarantee that socially responsible companies will be profitable. Simply put, socially responsible companies experience the same ups and downs in economic performance that traditional businesses do. General Motors' Chevy Volt features a plug-in hybrid engine, producing outstanding fuel efficiency of 60 miles per gallon and the ability to drive 800 miles between fill-ups. The Volt is a tremendous technological and environmental product, but it's been a disaster for GM's bottom line. GM's investment in the Volt, so far, is estimated at $1.2 billion. But, because of the technology involved, the Volt is difficult and expensive to assemble, so much so that Reuters estimates that GM loses $50,000 per Volt! Sales have been incredibly disappointing. Priced at $39,995, GM has sold only 58,000 Volts in four years, far short of its goal of 60,000 per year. Sales picked up slightly only after GM offered a 25 percent discount on top of the Volt's already steep price discounts, which are three to four times higher than the rest of the auto industry. At the end of 2014, GM dropped the price of the Volt by another $5,000, hoping to increase sales. But by March 2015, it had a 210-day inventory of unsold Volts (60 days is optimal). GM then announced it would stop production of the Volt for seven months to clear the inventory backlog. GM's attempt at building a highly fuel-efficient, environmentally friendly car may have been good for the planet, but it has been a drag on GM's profits and finances.[100]

Being socially responsible may be the right thing to do, and it is usually associated with increased profits, but it doesn't guarantee business success.

STUDY TOOLS 4

LOCATED IN TEXTBOOK

☐ Rip-out and review chapter review card

LOCATED AT WWW.CENGAGEBRAIN.COM

☐ Review key term flashcards and create your own from StudyBits

☐ Track your knowledge and understanding of key concepts, using the concept tracker

☐ Complete practice and graded quizzes to prepare for tests

☐ Complete interactive content within the exposition

☐ View chapter highlight box content at the beginning of each chapter

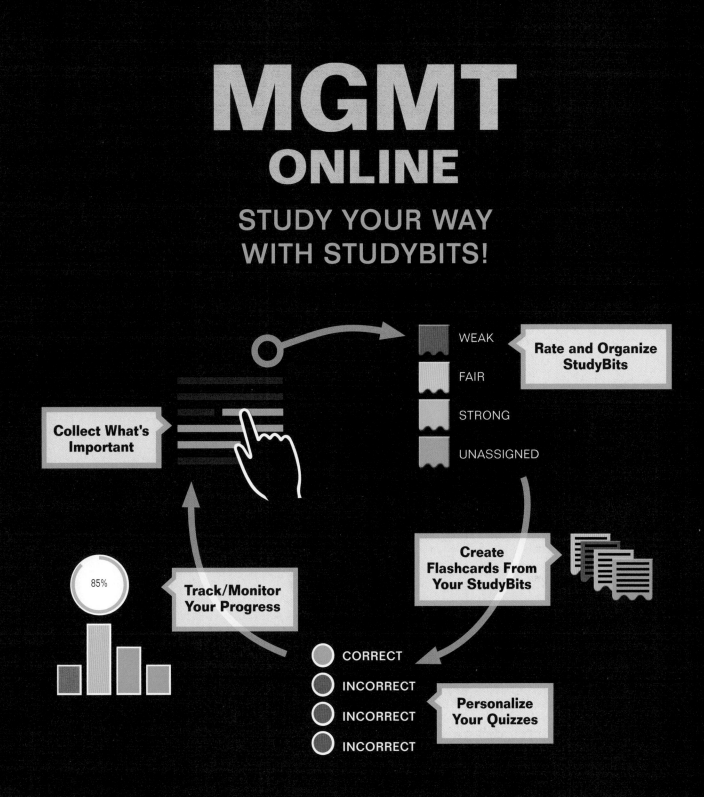

PART 2

5 Planning and Decision Making

Brian A Jackson/Shutterstock.com

LEARNING OUTCOMES

5-1 Discuss the benefits and pitfalls of planning.

5-2 Describe how to make a plan that works.

5-3 Discuss how companies can use plans at all management levels, from top to bottom.

5-4 Explain the steps and limits to rational decision making.

5-5 Explain how group decisions and group decision-making techniques can improve decision making.

After you finish

this chapter, go

to **PAGE 111** for

STUDY TOOLS

5-1 BENEFITS AND PITFALLS OF PLANNING

Even inexperienced managers know that planning and decision making are central parts of their jobs. Figure out what the problem is. Generate potential solutions or plans. Pick the best one. Make it work. Experienced managers, however, know how hard it really is to make good plans and decisions. One seasoned manager says: "I think the biggest surprises are the problems. Maybe I had never seen it before. Maybe I was protected by my management when I was in sales. Maybe I had delusions of grandeur, I don't know. I just know how disillusioning and frustrating it is to be hit with problems and conflicts all day and not be able to solve them very cleanly."[1]

Planning is choosing a goal and developing a method or strategy to achieve that goal. Thanks to strong business and defense industry growth, northern Virginia's population will rise 26 percent by 2040. The **Virginia Railway Express** (VRE), the region's commuter train service, is already feeling the effects. VRE's ridership has grown by 30 percent in the past decade, and its trains are at 90 percent capacity. To meet growing demand, VRE's goals are to add reverse peak and express trains by 2030 and double ridership by 2040. To reach those goals, it will lengthen existing trains by 20 percent, add additional stations and longer rail lines to serve more commuters, and widen a bridge to double the number of trains traveling in both directions. The total budget for the expansion is several billion dollars, and planners have created a comprehensive document, VRE System Plan 2040, to ensure that VRE meets its goals. VRE's CEO, Doug Allen, said, "More people would take VRE if the stations were more convenient, more accessible, and had more parking."[2]

Are you one of those naturally organized people who always makes a daily to-do list, writes everything down so you won't forget, and never misses a deadline because you keep track of everything with your handy time-management notebook, iPhone, or PC? Or are you one of those flexible, creative, go-with-the-flow people who dislikes planning and organizing because it restricts your freedom, energy, and performance? Some people are natural planners. They love it and can see only its benefits. Others dislike planning and can see only its disadvantages. It turns out that *both* views have real value.

Planning has advantages and disadvantages. Let's learn about 5-1a the benefits and 5-1b the pitfalls of planning.

5-1a Benefits of Planning

Planning offers several important benefits: intensified effort, persistence, direction, and creation of task strategies.[3] First, managers and employees put forth greater effort when following a plan. Take two workers. Instruct one to "do your best" to increase production, and instruct the other to achieve a 2 percent increase in production each month. Research shows that the one with the specific plan will work harder.[4]

Second, planning leads to persistence, that is, working hard for long periods. In fact, planning encourages persistence even when there may be little chance of short-term success.[5] McDonald's founder Ray Kroc, a keen believer in the power of persistence, had this quotation from President Calvin Coolidge hung in all of his executives' offices: "Nothing in the world can take the place of persistence. Talent will not; nothing is more common than unsuccessful men with talent. Genius will not; unrewarded genius is almost a proverb. Education will not; the world is full of educated derelicts. Persistence and determination alone are omnipotent."[6]

The third benefit of planning is direction. Irving Wladawsky-Berger of the Institute for Data Driven Design explains that planning through goal setting is especially important when organizations experience major transitions. "A major way of rallying the organization to embrace the needed transformation is to have a compelling target to shoot for, a kind of promised land everyone can aim for instead of wandering in the desert without a clear path forward," Wladawsky-Berger says.[7]

The fourth benefit of planning is that it encourages the development of task strategies. In other words, planning not only encourages people to work hard for extended periods and to engage in behaviors directly related to goal accomplishment, it also encourages them to think of better ways to do their jobs. Finally, perhaps the most compelling benefit of planning is that it has been proven to work for both companies and individuals. On average, companies with plans have larger profits and grow much faster than companies without plans.[8] The same holds true for individual managers and employees: There is no better way to improve the performance of the people who work in a company than to have them set goals and develop strategies for achieving those goals.

5-1b Pitfalls of Planning

Despite the significant benefits associated with planning, it is not a cure-all. Plans won't fix all

Planning choosing a goal and developing a strategy to achieve that goal

A&F made its mark with booming music, heady scents, and shuttered windows, but the stores became less popular with shoppers when logos went out of style.

organizational problems. In fact, many management authors and consultants believe that planning can harm companies in several ways.[9]

The first pitfall of planning is that it can impede change and prevent or slow needed adaptation. Sometimes companies become so committed to achieving the goals set forth in their plans or on following the strategies and tactics spelled out in them that they fail to see that their plans aren't working or that their goals need to change. When Mike Jeffries became Abercrombie & Fitch's (A&F) CEO in 1992, he recast the brand as sexy, fit, and exclusive. **Abercrombie** grew into a $4.5 billion company with 1,000 stores in 19 countries. Its preppy jeans, polos, and logo t-shirts became iconic among U.S. teens. Provocative advertising on billboards, posters, and shopping bags included images of shirtless men and scantily clad women. With booming music, heady scents, and windows darkened by shutters, A&F stores were more like a rave than shopping. By 2013, however, logos were no longer popular, and stores offering unique styles at low prices, such as H&M, thrived. When asked which brands they no longer wore, teen girls ranked A&F and Hollister (an A&F brand) second and third, respectively. Even when profits dropped by half, and A&F closed 220 mall stores (with plans to close 120 more), Jeffries refused to change the brand. Finally, in mid-2014, he allowed stores to remove the shutters and cut the scents they used by 25 percent. But with declining brand equity and flagging financials, it was too late. Jeffries was pushed out by the board.[10]

The second pitfall is that planning can create a false sense of certainty. Planners sometimes feel that they know exactly what the future holds for their competitors, their suppliers, and their companies. However, all plans are based on assumptions. "National home prices never go down. Eurozone countries don't default. Saudi Arabia won't let the price of oil crash. China's demand for raw materials is infinite." For plans to work, the assumptions on which they are based must hold true. If the assumptions turn out to be false, then the plans based on them are likely to fail. Indeed, according to the *Wall Street Journal's* Greg Ip, the four assumptions just listed were "some of the most cherished assumptions of investors and policy makers in the past decade, assumptions that have underpinned trillions of dollars of investment and debt."[11] And they were all completely wrong.

The third potential pitfall of planning is the detachment of planners. In theory, strategic planners and top-level managers are supposed to focus on the big picture and not concern themselves with the details of implementation (that is carrying out the plan). According to management professor Henry Mintzberg, detachment leads planners to plan for things they don't understand.[12] Plans are meant to be guidelines for action, not abstract theories. Consequently, planners need to be familiar with the daily details of their businesses if they are to produce plans that can work.

British-based **Tesco**, the third-largest retailer in the world, spent five years researching and planning before it spent $1.6 billion to enter the U.S. grocery business by building 199 Fresh & Easy stores. Former CEO Terry Leahy said, "Our team went over to live in the U.S. We stayed in people's homes. We went through their fridges. We did all our research, and we're good at research." Unfortunately, because they had never competed in the U.S. grocery business, Tesco's research and planning failed to account for Americans' different tastes. For example, at 10,000 square feet, or 20 percent of the size of a typical American supermarket, Fresh & Easy stores were too small and had too limited a selection, and, at first, didn't have bakeries, which Americans like. Tesco relied heavily on its Fresh & Easy brand of premade meals, popular in England but unknown in the United States, where shoppers prefer brand-name products. According to Natalie Berg, director of Planet Retail, "The main thing is that they underestimated how Americans shop."[13]

5-2 HOW TO MAKE A PLAN THAT WORKS

Planning is a double-edged sword. If done right, planning brings about tremendous increases in individual and organizational performance. If planning is done

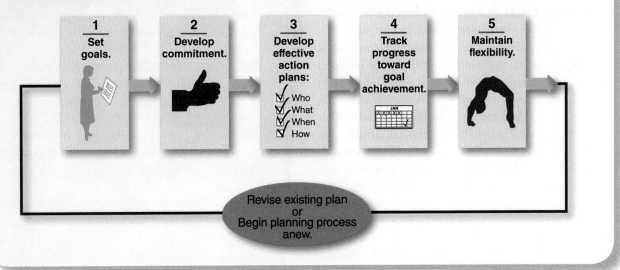

Exhibit 5.1
How to Make a Plan That Works

1 Set goals.

2 Develop commitment.

3 Develop effective action plans:
- ☑ Who
- ☑ What
- ☑ When
- ☑ How

4 Track progress toward goal achievement.

5 Maintain flexibility.

Revise existing plan
or
Begin planning process anew.

wrong, however, it can have just the opposite effect and harm individual and organizational performance.

In this section, you will learn how to make a plan that works. As depicted in Exhibit 5.1, planning consists of 5-2a setting goals, 5-2b developing commitment to the goals, 5-2c developing effective action plans, 5-2d tracking progress toward goal achievement, and 5-2e maintaining flexibility in planning.

5-2a Setting Goals

The first step in planning is to set goals. To direct behavior and increase effort, goals need to be specific and challenging.[14] For example, deciding to "increase sales this year" won't direct and energize workers as much as deciding to "increase North American sales by 4 percent in the next six months." Specific, challenging goals provide a target for which to aim and a standard against which to measure success.

One way of writing effective goals for yourself, your job, or your company is to use the S.M.A.R.T. guidelines. **S.M.A.R.T. goals** are **S**pecific, **M**easurable, **A**ttainable, **R**ealistic, and **T**imely.[15] With annual sales of $83 billion, Cincinnati-based **Procter & Gamble** is a global leader in consumer products in 180 countries. It's size, however, makes managing growth difficult. To combat this difficulty, in 2013, CEO A.G. Lafley established a goal of cutting P&G's massive brand portfolio of roughly 165 brands to 65 core brands, organized into 10 key categories, by 2016.[16] Let's see how P&G's objectives measure up to the S.M.A.R.T. guidelines for goals.

First, is the goal *Specific*? Yes, as opposed to saying that it wants to be smaller, P&G identified exactly how many brands it wants in its portfolio by 2016—its 65 best-selling brands. Is the goal *Measurable*? Yes, P&G's best-performing brands generate 95 percent of its profits, which are growing faster than the rest of P&G, while its poorer performing brands haves sales and profits that are shrinking 3 percent and 16 percent per year, respectively.[17] Whether the goal is *Attainable* or not depends on many factors. First, P&G needs to find potential buyers for the 100 brands it is selling. After it identifies potential buyers, they must agree on a purchase price (a complex task with billion-dollar businesses). Then, it must clear the financial and legal hurdles involved in transferring ownership of each brand. But, major merger and acquisitions transactions aren't new, certainly for P&G, and it's unlikely these issues will be problematic. Finally, while the goals are ambitious, they are *Timely*. When P&G announced the goal in 2013, it gave itself three years to divest 50 of the 100 brands it has identified for sale. So far P&G has made good progress. By the end of the first quarter of 2016, it had successfully sold forty three beauty brands, including Clairol and Cover Girl, to Coty for $12.5 billion.[18]

5-2b Developing Commitment to Goals

Just because a company sets a goal doesn't mean that people will try to accomplish it. If workers

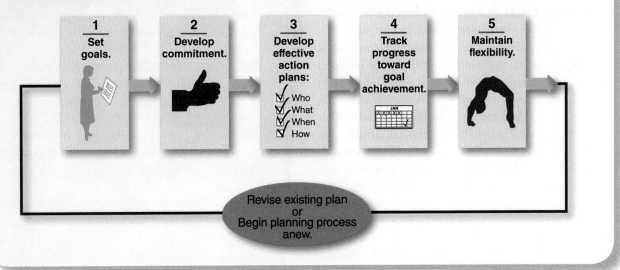
S.M.A.R.T. goals goals that are specific, measurable, attainable, realistic, and timely

don't care about a goal, that goal won't encourage them to work harder or smarter. Thus, the second step in planning is to develop commitment to goals.[19]

Goal commitment is the determination to achieve a goal. Commitment to achieve a goal is not automatic. Managers and workers must choose to commit themselves to a goal. Edwin Locke, professor emeritus of management at the University of Maryland and the foremost expert on how, why, and when goals work, tells a story about an overweight friend who lost seventy-five pounds. Locke says, "I asked him how he did it, knowing how hard it was for most people to lose so much weight." His friend responded, "Actually, it was quite simple. I simply decided that I *really wanted* to do it."[20] Put another way, goal commitment is really wanting to achieve a goal.

So how can managers bring about goal commitment? The most popular approach is to set goals participatively. Rather than assigning goals to workers ("Johnson, you've got till Tuesday of next week to redesign the flux capacitor so it gives us 10% more output"), managers and employees choose goals together. The goals are more likely to be realistic and attainable if employees participate in setting them. Another technique for gaining commitment to a goal is to make the goal public. For example, college students who publicly communicated their semester grade goals ("This semester, I'm shooting for a 3.5") to important people in their lives (usually a parent or sibling) were much more committed to achieving their grades than those who did not. Still another way to increase goal commitment is to obtain top management's support. Top management can show support for a plan or program by providing funds, speaking publicly about the plan, or participating in the plan itself.

5-2c Developing Effective Action Plans

The third step in planning is to develop effective action plans. An **action plan** lists the specific steps (how), people (who), resources (what), and time period (when) for accomplishing a goal. It takes a blackberry bush three years to produce fruit, so to add a salad with blackberries to its 2016 summer menu, Wendy's started planning well in advance, especially since sourcing blackberries was a significant challenge. Wendy's usually interviews two to five potential suppliers before selecting one, but for blackberries, its procurement team spent fourteen months reviewing over thirty growers before finding two that could supply its needs. Since most U.S. blackberries end up in supermarkets, with little left for restaurants, Wendy's worked with those two growers to plant the extra blackberry bushes to grow the nearly 2 million extra berries, or 10 percent of the total U.S. blackberry crop, needed to serve a summer's worth of salads at its nearly 6,700 North American restaurants. Wendy's COO Bob Wright admits the plan was challenging to put into action, saying, "Just to have a salad on a menu is a very difficult thing to achieve."[21]

5-2d Tracking Progress

The fourth step in planning is to track progress toward goal achievement. There are two accepted methods of tracking progress. The first is to set proximal goals and distal goals. **Proximal goals** are short-term goals or subgoals, whereas **distal goals** are long-term or primary goals.[22]

When General Motors launched a plan to produce a driverless car by 2025 (the distal goal), managers identified three proximal goals to get there:

1. In 2010, driver is in charge.
2. In 2015, driver is mostly in charge.
3. In 2020, car is mostly in charge.[23]

THE PLANNING FALLACY

One of the most common mistakes made in the planning process is underestimating the amount of time a task will take. This concept is so prevalent, in fact, that it has a name: the planning fallacy. Roger Buehler, a psychology professor at Ontario's Wilfrid Laurier University, says that the average person underestimates the time necessary to complete a task by 40 percent. Although management plans are often more complex than those involved in a single employee's job, similar tactics may be useful to reduce the effects of planning fallacy in both. A study published in the *Journal of Experimental Social Psychology* found that breaking a task down into very detailed steps can help chronically poor planners more accurately estimate the amount of time required to complete a task. Another strategy, devised from a study published in *Organizational Behavior and Human Decision Processes*, involves forming a mental image of a task from an outside perspective to improve predictions of time allotment.

Source: S. Reddy, "Why Are You Always Late? It Could Be the Planning Fallacy," *Wall Street Journal*, February 3, 2015, D1, D4.

Goal commitment the determination to achieve a goal

Action plan a plan that lists the specific steps, people, resources, and time period needed to attain a goal

Proximal goals short-term goals or subgoals

Distal goals long-term or primary goals

The second method of tracking progress is to gather and provide performance feedback. Regular, frequent performance feedback allows workers and managers to track their progress toward goal achievement and make adjustments in effort, direction, and strategies.[24] Exhibit 5.2 shows the impact of feedback on safety behavior at a large bakery company with a worker safety record that was two-and-a-half times worse than the industry average. During the baseline period, workers in the wrapping department, who measure and mix ingredients, roll the bread dough, and put it into baking pans, performed their jobs safely about 70 percent of the time (see 1 in Exhibit 5.2). The baseline safety record for workers in the makeup department, who bag and seal baked bread and assemble, pack, and tape cardboard cartons for shipping, was somewhat better at 78 percent (see 2). The company then gave workers thirty minutes of safety training, set a goal of 90 percent safe behavior, and then provided daily feedback (such as a chart similar to Exhibit 5.2). Performance improved dramatically. During the intervention period, safely performed

Exhibit 5.2
Effects of Goal Setting, Training, and Feedback on Safe Behavior in a Bread Factory

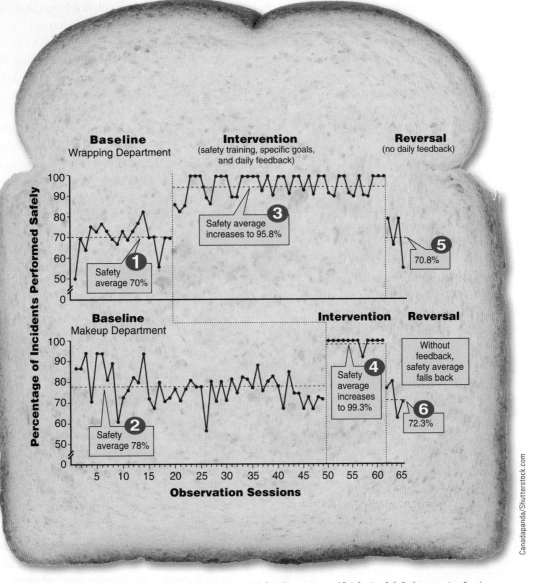

Source: J. Komaki, K. D. Barwick, and L. R. Scott. "A Behavioral Approach to Occupational Safety: Pinpointing and Reinforcing Safe Performance in a Food Manufacturing Plant," *Journal of Applied Psychology* 63 (1978).

behaviors rose to an average of 95.8 percent for wrapping workers (see 3) and 99.3 percent for workers in the makeup department (see 4), and never fell below 83 percent. Thus, the combination of training, a challenging goal, and feedback led to a dramatic increase in performance. The importance of feedback alone can be seen in the reversal stage, when the company quit posting daily feedback on safe behavior. Without daily feedback, the percentage of safely performed behaviors returned to baseline levels—70.8 percent for the wrapping department (see 5) and 72.3 percent for the makeup department (see 6). For planning to be effective, workers need both a specific, challenging goal and regular feedback to track their progress. In fact, additional research indicates that the effectiveness of goal setting can be doubled by the addition of feedback.[25]

5-2e Maintaining Flexibility

Because action plans are sometimes poorly conceived and goals sometimes turn out not to be achievable, the last step in developing an effective plan is to maintain flexibility. One method of maintaining flexibility while planning is to adopt an options-based approach.[26] The goal of **options-based planning** is to keep options open by making small, simultaneous investments in many alternative plans. Then, when one or a few of these plans emerge as likely winners, you invest even more in these plans while discontinuing or reducing investment in the others. That's exactly the strategy **Airbnb** used to go from being a company generating a meager $200 per week in revenue to being a multibillion-dollar global enterprise. Airbnb programmers have permission to make small bets on new features and measure the response. After being assigned the task—on his first day—of reevaluating the company's property rating system, a new Airbnb designer wanted to test using a heart instead of a star icon. His rationale was that Airbnb's service was aspirational and people established an emotional connection to the places they stay. The company changed the feature to a heart to test it and discovered that the heart icon increased customer engagement 30 percent over the star icon.[27]

In part, options-based planning is the opposite of traditional planning. Whereas the purpose of an action plan is to commit people and resources to a particular course of action, the purpose of options-based planning is to leave those commitments open by maintaining **slack resources**—that is, a cushion of resources, such as extra time, people, money, or production capacity, that can be used to address and adapt to unanticipated changes, problems, or opportunities.[28] Holding options open gives you choices. And choices, combined with slack resources, give you flexibility. Because it can take a year and a half to receive new equipment, U.S. power companies are funding Grid Assurance, LLC, which will buy and hold extra electrical transformers and circuit breakers to be used for emergencies when damaged power generating and transmission equipment needs replacing. Grid Assurance will also locate key equipment in secure, undisclosed locations. In case of terrorist attack, "The last thing we want is for someone to do a physical attack and wipe out our spares," says Scott Moore, vice president of transmission engineering for American Electric Power.[29] Grid Assurance will need a minimum of 100 transformers, which can cost from $2 million to $10 million each. Grid Assurance provides the equivalent of catastrophic insurance, giving power companies the extra resources needed to survive unanticipated disruptions and breakdowns.

5-3 PLANNING FROM TOP TO BOTTOM

Planning works best when the goals and action plans at the bottom and middle of the organization support the goals and action plans at the top of the organization. In other words, planning works best when everybody pulls in the same direction. Exhibit 5.3 illustrates this planning continuity, beginning at the top with a clear definition of the company purpose and ending at the bottom with the execution of operational plans.

*Let's see how **5-3a top managers create the organization's purpose statement and strategic objective, 5-3b middle managers develop tactical plans and use management by objectives to motivate employee efforts toward the overall purpose and strategic objective,** and*

Options-based planning maintaining planning flexibility by making small, simultaneous investments in many alternative plans

Slack resources a cushion of extra resources that can be used with options-based planning to adapt to unanticipated changes, problems, or opportunities

Valentyn Volkov/Shutterstock.com

Exhibit 5.3
Planning from Top to Bottom

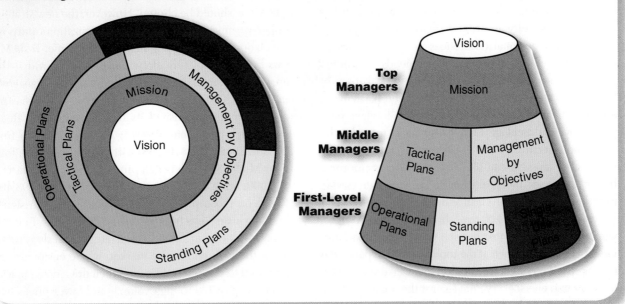

5-3c first-level managers use operational, single-use, and standing plans to implement the tactical plans.

5-3a Starting at the Top

Top management is responsible for developing long-term **strategic plans** that make clear how the company will serve customers and position itself against competitors in the next two to five years. Recall that P&G recently set a goal of cutting 100 of its brands. That goal was part of a strategic plan developed under CEO A.G. Lafley. During his first term as Twice-retired A.G. Lafley focused on acquisitions and growth. His strategic focus turned P&G into the world's largest consumer-products company. When he returned to serve as CEO for a second time, Laffley began purposefully shrinking the giant company. The reason? The company had grown too large to compete. Lafley sold Camay and Zest brands to archrival Unilever and exited the battery business by selling Duracell and the pet-food business by sell-

ing Iams. He also looked to sell Wella and Clairol, two brands that he acquired during his first term as P&G's CEO. "Decade after decade, we have to find the strategy and the business model that wins with consumers," Lafley said, and trimming P&G's portfolio "strategically resets P&G's where-to-play choices for at least the next five years."[30]

Strategic planning begins with the creation of an organizational purpose. A **purpose statement**, which is often referred to as an organizational mission or vision, is a statement of a company's purpose or reason for existing.[31] Purpose statements should be brief—no more than two sentences. They should also be enduring, inspirational, clear, and consistent with widely shared company beliefs and values. An excellent example of a well-crafted purpose statement is that of cosmetics company Avon: "To be the company that best understands and satisfies the product, service and self-fulfillment needs of women—globally."[32]

Strategic plans overall company plans that clarify how the company will serve customers and position itself against competitors over the next two to five years

Purpose statement a statement of a company's purpose or reason for existing

It guides everyone in the organization and provides a focal point for the delivery of beauty products and services to the customers, women around the world. The purpose is the same whether Avon is selling lipstick to women in India, shampoo packets to women in the Amazon, or jewelry to women in the United States. Despite these regional differences in specific strategy, the overall goal—understanding the needs of women globally—does not change. Other examples of organizational purpose statements that have been particularly effective include Walt Disney Company's "to make people happy" and Schlage Lock Company's "to make the world more secure."[33]

A clear mission can also help employees prioritize better and work more efficiently. Early in her career, president and COO of Change.org Jennifer Dulski and her team worked past 9:00 p.m. almost every day. A supervisor took notice and told her she was working too hard. His advice: "Write down at the top of a piece of paper the mission you're trying to accomplish. Now take your entire to-do list and check every item against the mission."[34]

The **strategic objective**, which flows from the purpose, is a more specific goal that unifies company-wide efforts, stretches and challenges the organization, and possesses a finish line and a time frame.[35] Collins and Porras define an organization's mission: "A mission is a clear and compelling goal that serves to unify an organization's efforts. An effective mission must stretch and challenge the organization, yet be achievable." However, many others define *mission* as an organization's purpose. In this edition, to be more specific and avoid confusion, we use Collins and Porras's term *purpose statement*, meaning a clear statement of an organization's purpose or reason for existence. Furthermore, we will continue to use Collins and Porras's definition of a mission (that is "a clear and compelling goal . . .") but instead call it "the strategic objective."

After two bankruptcies, Sbarro, a chain of Italian restaurants located in shopping mall food courts, will return to its New York–style pizza roots. CEO David Karam says, "The essence of this brand is pizza. It's what consumers buy from Sbarro and how they view Sbarro."[36] Sbarro's strategic objective is to establish neighborhood pizza restaurants that also deliver pizza. Karam explained, "There are 900 malls in the U.S. with food courts, and we're in a third of them. But instead of them representing 90 percent of our sites, I'd like them to represent less than half."[37]

Once the strategic objective has been accomplished, a new one should be chosen. However, the new strategic objective must grow out of the organization's purpose, which does not change significantly over time. Tesla Motors builds completely electric cars—not hybrids—that are faster than most gas-powered cars and can cover more than 300 miles on a full charge. But Teslas are extraordinarily expensive. Its first car, the Tesla Roadster, a high-performance sports car in production from 2008 to 2012, cost $109,000 without add-ons. The four-door Model S, which began production in 2012, starts at $70,000, but a completely loaded version costs $93,400. Based on those prices, it seems that Tesla's mission is building luxury, electric sports cars. But, it's not. Founder Elon Musk explains that, "the strategy at Tesla is to enter at the high end of the market, where customers are prepared to pay a premium, and then drive down market as fast as possible to high volume and lower prices with each successive model."[38] In other words, Musk says, "When someone buys the Tesla Roadster sports car, they are actually helping pay for development of the low-cost family car."[39] Tesla's Model X, a smaller sedan with gull-wing rear doors, debuted in 2016 and sells for $80,000–$115,500 (depending on option packages). While Tesla is on track to produce 75,000 cars in 2016, its ambitious goal is to produce 500,000 a year by 2020.[40]

5-3b Bending in the Middle

Middle management is responsible for developing and carrying out tactical plans to accomplish the organization's strategic objective. **Tactical plans** specify how a company will use resources, budgets, and people to

A Tesla Model S sits outside the company's new showroom in Paris, France.

Hadrian/Shutterstock.com

Strategic objective a more specific goal that unifies company-wide efforts, stretches and challenges the organization, and possesses a finish line and a time frame

Tactical plans plans created and implemented by middle managers that direct behavior, efforts, and attention over the next six months to two years

accomplish specific goals related to its strategic objective for the next five years. Whereas strategic plans and objectives are used to focus company efforts over the next two to five years, tactical plans and objectives are used to direct behavior, efforts, and attention over the next six months to two years. Hostess sells nearly $1.3 billion a year in Twinkies, Cupcakes, HoHos, Ding Dongs, and other snack cakes in more than 100,000 convenience stores across the United States. Still, says CEO Bill Toler, Hostess is 20,000 stores shy of reaching its strategic objective: "To be sold everywhere a candy bar is sold, whether it's an airport kiosk, or a vending machine."[41] To achieve that objective, Hostess's tactical plans include expanding in the United States, broadening distribution in Europe and the Caribbean, and launching new distribution in Mexico and Canada. Hostess has extended its brand name by placing bread and sandwich buns in drug, dollar, and convenience stores, and is also considering entering the $400 million brownie category (and perhaps the cookie category as well). These expansions have limits, however. Toler wants to keep Hostess close to its roots as a maker of treats. According to him, "We have a mindful eye into healthier trends . . . but our primary focus is on being an indulgent snack."[42]

Management by objectives is a management technique often used to develop and carry out tactical plans. **Management by objectives** is a four-step process in which managers and their employees (1) discuss possible goals; (2) collectively select goals that are challenging, attainable, and consistent with the company's overall goals; (3) jointly develop tactical plans that lead to the accomplishment of tactical goals and objectives; and (4) meet regularly to review progress toward accomplishment of those goals. In Chapter 1, we learned that on Mondays, **Qualtrics**, which sells online survey research tools, sends out a company-wide email describing each employee's goals for the coming week and whether they met their prior week's goals. Those weekly goals, however, are derived from quarterly goals containing detailed, measurable objectives and key results, such as revenue and customer satisfaction. Similar to the weekly email, Qualtrics's internal database, which is open to all who work there, shows each employee's quarterly goals and results, individual weekly goals, performance reviews and bonuses, successes and failures from which others can learn, and full career histories.[43] CEO Adam Bryant

says, "When everyone's rowing together toward the same objective, it's extremely powerful. We're trying to execute at a very high level, and we need to make sure everyone knows where we're going."[44]

5-3c Finishing at the Bottom

Lower-level managers are responsible for developing and carrying out **operational plans**, which are the day-to-day plans for producing or delivering the organization's products and services. Operational plans direct the behavior, efforts, and priorities of operative employees for periods ranging from thirty days to six months. There are three kinds of operational plans: single-use plans, standing plans, and budgets.

Single-use plans deal with unique, one-time-only events. In 1905, **General Electric Co.** set up a banking division to finance the sale of its equipment to utility companies. By the 1930s, it financed appliances sales to consumers. By 2015, GE Capital had $500 billion in assets and was the seventh-largest U.S. bank. To sharpen its strategic focus and return to its industrial roots, GE aims to obtain 90 percent of earnings from industrial businesses in 2016, up from 58 percent in 2014. Accordingly, GE created a single-use plan, called "Project Hubble," to dismantle and sell off GE Capital. Over a two-year period, GE will sell its $74 billion lending unit, including roughly $165 million in loans to companies such as Wendy's, and liquidate $26.5 billion in commercial real estate. GE will use the proceeds from this one-time only event to invest further in its remaining industrial businesses, while also rewarding shareholders with $90 billion in dividends and stock buybacks.[45]

Unlike single-use plans that are created, carried out once, and then never used again, **standing plans** save managers time because after the plans are

Management by objectives a four-step process in which managers and employees discuss and select goals, develop tactical plans, and meet regularly to review progress toward goal accomplishment

Operational plans day-to-day plans, developed and implemented by lower-level managers, for producing or delivering the organization's products and services over a thirty-day to six-month period

Single-use plans plans that cover unique, one-time-only events

Standing plans plans used repeatedly to handle frequently recurring events

> Money sends a clear message about your priorities. Budgets act as a language for communicating your goals to others.

created, they can be used repeatedly to handle frequently recurring events. If you encounter a problem that you've seen before, someone in your company has probably written a standing plan that explains how to address it. When a snowstorm hit Atlanta in 2014, **Delta Airlines** transformed a Boeing 767 into sleeping quarters for stranded employees. Instead of going to the airport hotel—or to uncomfortable cots in the terminal—employees slept on the plane's business class lie-flat seats and were rested and ready when the runways were clear in the morning. The contingency plan was so successful that Delta added it to its standard storm-response planning in 2015. Using a standing plan rather than reinventing the wheel allows Delta to save time. Delta's senior vice president of operations, Dave Holtz, says, "We don't want to limit our ability to get customers going because employees can't get there."[46] There are three kinds of standing plans: policies, procedures, and rules and regulations.

Policies standing plans that indicate the general course of action that should be taken in response to a particular event or situation

Procedures standing plans that indicate the specific steps that should be taken in response to a particular event

Rules and regulations standing plans that describe how a particular action should be performed or what must happen or not happen in response to a particular event

Policies indicate the general course of action that company managers should take in response to a particular event or situation. A well-written policy will also specify why the policy exists and what outcome the policy is intended to produce. Absenteeism means missing work, while "presenteeism" is coming to work when you're sick.[47] Ann Stevens at ClearRock, a leadership and career consulting company, says, "People get really, really ticked off at co-workers who spread germs in the workplace." But people come to work sick because of policies that reward people for good attendance or because of policies with a limited number of sick days. Use them up and you're stuck if you're sick again. Both reasons are why more companies are using paid-time-off policies that don't distinguish among sick days, personal days, or vacation days. This give employees maximum flexibility and discourages them from coming to work sick. Carol Sladek, at Aon Hewitt, a human resource consulting firm, says, "If you have the flu, stay home. Just stay home . . . ."[48]

Procedures are more specific than policies because they indicate the series of steps that should be taken in response to a particular event. All commercial airplanes require regular cleaning. With no regulatory standards, airlines set their own procedures. At **Singapore Airlines**, which flies longer international flights, a twelve-person team takes roughly forty minutes to clean a Boeing 777-300 jet during a normal stopover. At **United Airlines**, most domestic flights require a quick turn (thirty minutes or less), so the cleaning procedures focus on the following tasks:

▸ Removing visible trash and cleaning out the seat-back pockets

▸ Cleaning and restocking the bathrooms and galleys

▸ Pulling up the armrests

▸ Wiping crumbs off seats

▸ Cleaning large spills

In addition to between flights, United conducts more thorough overnight cleanings (vacuuming and cleaning restrooms and galleys) and "deep cleanings," in which the plane is "scrubbed from nose to tail," every thirty-five to fifty-five days.[49]

Rules and regulations are even more specific than procedures because they specify what must happen or not happen. They describe precisely how a particular action should be performed. For instance, many companies have rules and regulations forbidding managers from writing job reference letters for employees who have worked at their firms because a negative reference may prompt a former employee to sue for defamation of character.[50]

After single-use plans and standing plans, budgets are the third kind of operational plan. **Budgeting** is quantitative planning because it forces managers to decide how to allocate available money to best accomplish company goals. According to Jan King, author of *Business Plans to Game Plans*, "Money sends a clear message about your priorities. Budgets act as a language for communicating your goals to others."

5-4 STEPS AND LIMITS TO RATIONAL DECISION MAKING

Decision making is the process of choosing a solution from available alternatives.[51] **Rational decision making** is a systematic process in which managers define problems, evaluate alternatives, and choose optimal solutions that provide maximum benefits to their organizations. Thus, for example, your boss comes to you requesting that you define and evaluate the various options for the company's social media strategy; after all, you tweet and use Facebook, Google+, Instagram, Groupon, Reddit, and so on and he doesn't even know how to reboot his computer. Furthermore, your solution has to be optimal. Because budgets and expertise are limited, the company gets one, maybe two, tries to make its social media strategy work. If you choose incorrectly, the company's investment will just go to waste, without increasing sales and market share. What would you recommend?

*Let's learn more about each of these: **5-4a define the problem, 5-4b identify decision criteria, 5-4c weigh the criteria, 5-4d generate alternative courses of action, 5-4e evaluate each alternative,** and **5-4f compute the optimal decision.** Then we'll consider **5-4g limits to rational decision making.***

5-4a Define the Problem

The first step in decision making is identifying and defining the problem. A **problem** exists when there is a gap between a desired state (what is wanted) and an existing state (the situation you are actually facing). You're the VP of HR for Guitar Center, a music instrument retailer with 240 U.S. locations. Each store has a combination of full-time and part-time employees, who all want schedules that fit their personal lives and give them the most

hours. Furthermore, daily customer flow is steady on the weekends. But during the workweek, it's inconsistent—light in the morning (stores open at 10:00 a.m. to 11:00 a.m), heavier around lunch, then lighter till about 3:00 p.m. Customer flow becomes heavier again between 3:00 p.m and 6:00 p.m. (after school and people getting off work), and then heaviest in the evening from 6:00 p.m. until stores close at 8:00 p.m. or 9:00 p.m. Your problem, and it's not easy, is how to match employees' schedules and wishes to lighter and heavier parts of the day throughout the week so that there are enough employees to help customers, but not so many so that stores are overstaffed.[52]

The presence of a gap between an existing state and a desired state is no guarantee that managers will make decisions to solve problems. Three things must occur for this to happen.[53] First, managers have to be aware of the gap. They have to know there is a problem before they can begin solving it. For example, after noticing that people were spending more money on their pets, a new dog food company created an expensive, high-quality dog food. To emphasize its quality, the dog food was sold in cans and bags with gold labels, red letters, and detailed information about its benefits and nutrients. Yet the product did not sell very well, and the company went out of business in less than a year. Its founders didn't understand why. When they asked a manager at a competing dog food company what their biggest mistake had been, the answer was, "Simple. You didn't have a picture of a dog on the package."[54] This problem would have been easy to solve if management had only been aware of it.

Being aware of a problem isn't enough to begin the decision-making process. Managers have to be motivated to reduce the gap between a desired and an existing state. **S**ales of carbonated soda have declined as public health concerns over obesity and diabetes have grown. In response, **Pepsi Cola** and **Coca-Cola** diversified by adding water, juice, and energy drinks to their product lines. But after missing its growth target (3–4%) for two straight years, Coke CEO Muhtar Kent settled on a simple strategy

MekCar/Shutterstock.com

Budgeting quantitative planning through which managers decide how to allocate available money to best accomplish company goals

Decision making the process of choosing a solution from available alternatives

Rational decision making a systematic process of defining problems, evaluating alternatives, and choosing optimal solutions

Problem a gap between a desired state and an existing state

to close Coke's sales gap—sell more soda. The company launched Freestyle self-serve soda machines that allow consumers to custom mix more than 100 drink flavors (there are now 27,000 Freestyle machines in U.S. restaurants) and is working with **Keurig Green Mountain Inc.** to develop an in-home counter-top soda machine. Coke also announced a $3 billion cost-cutting program, including some 1,500 layoffs. Soda accounts for 70 percent of Coke's revenue, and Classic Coke and Diet Coke are the top-selling sodas in the United States. With Coke's stalled stock prices making it a potential takeover target, management is highly motivated to address flagging soft drink sales. CEO Kent says, "If we don't do what we need to do quickly, effectively, execute 100 percent, then somebody else will come and do it for us."[55]

Finally, it's not enough to be aware of a problem and be motivated to solve it. Managers must also have the knowledge, skills, abilities, and resources to fix the problem. So how did Guitar Center solve its scheduling problem? The company replaced the Excel spreadsheets that it had been using to manually manage schedules with powerful Dayforce scheduling software from Ceridian Corporation. Guitar Centers' Chris Salles says, "We load [customer traffic and transactions] in fifteen-minute intervals into Dayforce, and it generates labor-demand curves that let each store know how many people they should staff for every fifteen minutes." Plus, employees can go online to indicate their weekly availability, to see their schedules, and to swap and cover shifts with co-workers.[56]

5-4b Identify Decision Criteria

Decision criteria are the standards used to guide judgments and decisions. Typically, the more criteria a potential solution meets, the better that solution will be. Again, imagine your boss asks you to determine the best options for the company's social media strategy. What general factors would be important when selecting one social media tool over another? Are you trying to increase your search rankings? Provide customer support? Are you trying to reach a particular target market? Is it young single women ages 18–25 or, perhaps, married women ages 25–35? Are you reaching out directly to consumers or to businesses (that is business-to-business)? Will your strategy focus on visual content,

Decision criteria the standards used to guide judgments and decisions

Absolute comparisons a process in which each decision criterion is compared to a standard or ranked on its own merits

demonstrations, or detailed, complex knowledge? Answering questions like these will help you identify the criteria that will guide the social media strategy you recommend.

5-4c Weigh the Criteria

After identifying decision criteria, the next step is deciding which criteria are more or less important. Although there are numerous mathematical models for weighing decision criteria, all require the decision maker to provide an initial ranking of the criteria. Some use **absolute comparisons**, in which each criterion is compared with a standard or is ranked on its own merits. For example, *Consumer Reports* uses nine criteria when it rates and recommends new cars: predicted reliability, current owners' satisfaction, predicted depreciation (the price you could expect if you sold the car), ability to avoid an accident, fuel economy, crash protection, acceleration, ride, and front seat comfort.[57]

Different individuals will rank these criteria differently, depending on what they value or require in a car. Exhibit 5.4 shows the absolute weights that someone buying a car might use. Because these weights are absolute, each criterion is judged on its own importance using a five-point scale, with 5 representing "critically important" and 1 representing "completely unimportant."

Exhibit 5.4
Absolute Weighting of Decision Criteria for a Car Purchase

5 critically important
4 important
3 somewhat important
2 not very important
1 completely unimportant

Criterion	1	2	3	4	5
1. Predicted reliability					(5)
2. Owner satisfaction		(2)			
3. Predicted depreciation	(1)				
4. Avoiding accidents				(4)	
5. Fuel economy					(5)
6. Crash protection				(4)	
7. Acceleration	(1)				
8. Ride			(3)		
9. Front seat comfort					(5)

Exhibit 5.5
Relative Comparison of Home Characteristics

Home Characteristics	L	SSQ	IP	SR	QS	NBH
Daily commute (L)		+1	−1	−1	−1	0
School system quality (SSQ)	−1		−1	−1	−1	−1
In-ground pool (IP)	+1	+1		0	0	+1
Sun room (SR)	+1	+1	0		0	0
Quiet street (QS)	+1	+1	0	0		0
Newly built house (NBH)	0	+1	−1	0	0	
Total weight	+2	+5	−3	−2	−2	0

In this instance, predicted reliability, fuel economy, and front seat comfort were rated most important, and acceleration and predicted depreciation were rated least important.

Another method uses **relative comparisons**, in which each criterion is compared directly with every other criterion.[58] Exhibit 5.5 shows six criteria that someone might use when buying a house. Moving down the first column of Exhibit 5.5, we see that the time of the daily commute has been rated less important (−1) than school system quality; more important (+1) than having an in-ground pool, a sun room, or a quiet street; and just as important as the house being brand new (0). Total weights, which are obtained by summing the scores in each column, indicate that the school system quality and daily commute are the most important factors to this home buyer, while an in-ground pool, sun room, and a quiet street are the least important. So with relative comparison, criteria are directly compared with each other.

5-4d Generate Alternative Courses of Action

After identifying and weighting the criteria that will guide the decision-making process, the next step is to identify possible courses of action that could solve the problem. In general, at this step, the idea is to generate as many alternatives as possible. Let's assume that you're trying to select a city in Europe to be the location of a major office. After meeting with your staff, you generate a list of possible alternatives: Amsterdam, the Netherlands; Barcelona or Madrid, Spain; Berlin, Dusseldorf, Frankfurt, or Munich, Germany; Brussels, Belgium; London, England; and Paris, France.

5-4e Evaluate Each Alternative

The next step is to systematically evaluate each alternative against each criterion. Because of the amount of information that must be collected, this step can take much longer and be much more expensive than other steps in the decision-making process. When selecting a European city for your office, you could contact economic development offices in each city, systematically interview businesspeople or executives who operate there, retrieve and use published government data on each location, or rely on published studies such as Cushman & Wakefield's *European Cities Monitor*, which conducts an annual survey of more than five hundred senior European executives who rate thirty-four European cities on twelve business-related criteria.[59]

No matter how you gather the information, once you have it, the key is to use that information systematically to evaluate each alternative against each criterion. Exhibit 5.6 shows how each of the ten cities on your staff's list fared with respect to each of the twelve criteria (higher scores are better), from qualified staff to freedom from pollution. Although London has the most qualified staff, the best access to markets and telecommunications, and is the easiest city to travel to and from, it is also one of the most polluted and expensive cities on the list. Paris offers excellent access to markets and clients, but if your staff is multilingual, Brussels may be a better choice.

Relative comparisons a process in which each decision criterion is compared directly with every other criterion

iStockphoto.com/Jason Walton

Exhibit 5.6
Criteria Ratings Used to Determine the Best Location for a New Office

Criteria Weights:	Access to Markets 0.60	Qualified Staff 0.53	Telecom-munications 0.52	Easy to Travel to/from City 0.42	Cost & Value of Office Space 0.33	Cost of Staff 0.32	Available Office Space 0.25	Languages Spoken 0.21	Business Climate 0.20	Travel within City 0.20	Quality of Life 0.16	Freedom from Pollution 0.16	Weighted Average	Ranking
Amsterdam	0.42	0.40	0.39	0.68	0.30	0.19	0.30	0.96	0.47	0.34	0.44	0.63	1.72	5
Barcelona	0.23	0.32	0.16	0.29	0.52	0.59	0.52	0.23	0.31	0.47	1.08	0.42	1.45	8
Berlin	0.44	0.39	0.41	0.35	0.78	0.40	0.79	0.50	0.34	0.78	0.38	0.29	1.85	4
Brussels	0.46	0.43	0.37	0.48	0.44	0.17	0.42	0.98	0.37	0.29	0.41	0.27	1.65	7
Dusseldorf	0.30	0.30	0.23	0.21	0.37	0.14	0.28	0.18	0.17	0.22	0.20	0.26	0.97	10
Frankfurt	0.68	0.57	0.70	1.17	0.38	0.11	0.44	0.57	0.38	0.35	0.17	0.18	2.16	3
London	1.50	1.36	1.27	1.79	0.27	0.10	0.42	1.48	0.55	1.26	0.46	0.15	4.03	1
Madrid	0.45	0.46	0.27	0.41	0.52	0.61	0.67	0.22	0.29	0.53	0.67	0.13	1.70	6
Munich	0.34	0.47	0.48	0.37	0.18	0.03	0.18	0.30	0.22	0.47	0.62	0.57	1.36	9
Paris	1.09	0.84	0.89	1.36	0.22	0.10	0.37	0.58	0.30	1.07	0.52	0.12	2.83	2

Source: "European Cities Monitor 2011," *Cushion & Wakefield*, 2011, accessed 27 May 2013. http://www.berlin-partner.de/fileadmin/user_upload/01_chefredaktion/02_pdf/studien-rankings/2011/Cushman%20&%20Wakefield%20-%20European%20Cities%20Monitor%20%282011%20english%29.pdf

5-4f Compute the Optimal Decision

The final step in the decision-making process is to compute the optimal decision by determining the optimal value of each alternative. This is done by multiplying the rating for each criterion (Step 5-4e) by the weight for that criterion (Step 5-4c), and then summing those scores for each alternative course of action that you generated (Step 5-4d). For example, the 500 executives participating in Cushman & Wakefield's survey of the best European cities for business rated the twelve decision criteria in terms of importance, as shown in the first row of Exhibit 5.6. Access to markets, qualified staff, telecommunications, and easy travel to and from the city were the four most important factors, while quality of life and freedom from pollution were the least important factors. To calculate the optimal value for Paris, the weight for each category is multiplied by its score in each category (.53 × .84 in the qualified staff category, for example). Then all of these scores are added together to produce the optimal value, as follows:

$$(.60 \times 1.09) + (.53 \times .84) + (.52 \times .89) +$$
$$(.42 \times 1.36) + (.33 \times .22) + (.32 \times .10) +$$
$$(.25 \times .37) + (.21 \times .58) + (.20 \times .30) +$$
$$(.20 \times 1.07) + (.16 \times .52) + (.16 \times .12) = 2.83$$

Because London has a weighted average of 4.03 compared to 2.83 for Paris and 2.16 for Frankfurt (the cities with the next-best ratings), London clearly ranks as the best location for your company's new European office because of its large number of qualified staff; easy access to markets; outstanding ease of travel to, from, and within the city; excellent telecommunications; and top-notch business climate.

5-4g Limits to Rational Decision Making

In general, managers who diligently complete all six steps of the rational decision-making model will make better decisions than those who don't. So, when they can, managers should try to follow the steps in the rational decision-making model, especially for big decisions with long-range consequences.

To make completely rational decisions, managers would have to operate in a perfect world with no real-world constraints. Of course, it never actually works like that in the real world. Managers face time and money constraints. They often don't have time to make extensive lists of decision criteria. And they often don't have the resources to test all possible solutions against all possible criteria.

In theory, fully rational decision makers **maximize** decisions by choosing the optimal solution. In practice, however, limited resources along with attention, memory, and expertise problems make it nearly impossible for managers to maximize decisions. Consequently, most managers don't maximize—they satisfice. Whereas maximizing is choosing the best alternative, **satisficing** is choosing a "good-enough" alternative.

In the opening to this section, your boss comes to you asking for a recommendation on the best options for the company's social media strategy. With so many options and the fast pace of change, deciding isn't easy. In other words, there's no optimal solution that will satisfy all criteria. For instance, if you're trying to increase your search rankings, you should use Google+ and YouTube, both of which are owned and linked to Google and its search results. If you're interested in providing customer support, then pay close attention to what your customers are saying on Facebook and Twitter, and reach out to them when they're having problems or are dissatisfied. If your target market is teenagers, use Instagram. If it is young single women ages 18–25, use Twitter and Facebook. If it's married women ages 25–35, use Pinterest. If reaching out directly to consumers, use Pinterest and Facebook, but if reaching out to businesses, use LinkedIn and Twitter. Finally, if your strategy focuses on visual content, use Pinterest; if your intent is to demonstrate what your product or service does, use YouTube; and if you've got detailed, complex knowledge, use Twitter and blogs.[60] Your decision will be complete when you find a "good-enough alternative" that does the best job of meeting your decision criteria.

5-5 USING GROUPS TO IMPROVE DECISION MAKING

A survey of 2,044 human resources and organizational leaders found that 84 percent of companies used teams for special projects, while 74 percent used teams to address departmental issues and innovation.[61] In other words, groups were used to solve problems and make decisions. Companies rely so heavily on groups to make decisions because when done properly, group decision making can lead to much better decisions than those typically made by individuals. In fact, numerous studies show that groups consistently outperform individuals on complex tasks.

*Let's explore the **5-5a advantages and pitfalls of group decision making** and see how the following group decision-making methods—**5-5b structured conflict, 5-5c the nominal group technique, 5-5d the Delphi technique,** and **5-5e electronic brainstorming**—can be used to improve decision making.*

5-5a Advantages and Pitfalls of Group Decision Making

Groups can do a much better job than individuals in two important steps of the decision-making process: defining the problem and generating alternative solutions. Still, group decision making is subject to some pitfalls that can quickly erase these gains. One possible pitfall is groupthink. **Groupthink** occurs in highly cohesive groups when group members feel intense pressure to agree with each other so that the group can approve a proposed solution.[62] Because groupthink leads to consideration of a limited number of solutions and restricts discussion of any considered solutions, it usually results in poor decisions. Groupthink is most likely to occur under the following conditions:

▸ The group is insulated from others with different perspectives.

▸ The group leader begins by expressing a strong preference for a particular decision.

▸ The group has no established procedure for systematically defining problems and exploring alternatives.

▸ Group members have similar backgrounds and experiences.[63]

A second potential problem with group decision making is that it takes considerable time. Reconciling schedules so that group members can meet takes time. Furthermore, it's a rare group that consistently holds productive,

Maximize choosing the best alternative

Satisficing choosing a "good-enough" alternative

Groupthink a barrier to good decision making caused by pressure within the group for members to agree with each other task-oriented meetings to effectively work through the decision-making process. Some of the most common complaints about meetings (and thus group decision making) are that the meeting's purpose is unclear, participants are unprepared, critical people are absent or late, conversation doesn't stay focused on the problem, and no one follows up on the decisions that were made.

A third possible pitfall to group decision making is that sometimes one or two people, perhaps the boss or a strong-willed, vocal group member, can dominate group discussions and limit the group's consideration of different problem definitions and alternative solutions. And, unlike individual decisions where people feel personally responsible for making a good choice, another potential problem is that group members may not feel accountable for the decisions made and actions taken by the group. Ironically, a fourth pitfall to group decision making is equality bias, which causes individuals to treat all group members as equally competent. More highly competent people tend to underestimate their abilities, while less competent people overestimate theirs. A recent study showed that even though the more competent person in a pair of study participants was correct over 70 percent of the time, the more competent person would agree to the less competent partner's decision roughly 40 percent of the time. Likewise, the less competent person in the pair would agree with the more competent partner's choice only 50 percent of the time—even though the other person was correct over 70 percent of the time. Study author Dr. Bahudar Bahrami noted, "Even when we showed them exactly how competent they each were, they still gave each other more or less equal say. Incredibly, this still continued when people were rewarded with real money for making correct decisions." Bahrami suggests two key reasons for equality bias. First, individuals do not want to exclude the other group members by asserting their competence. Second, individuals may be reluctant to take responsibility for group decisions.[64]

Although these pitfalls can lead to poor decision making, this doesn't mean that managers should avoid using groups to make decisions. When done properly, group decision making can lead to much better decisions. The pitfalls of group decision making are not inevitable. Managers can overcome most of them by using the various techniques described next.

5-5b Structured Conflict

Most people view conflict negatively. Yet the right kind of conflict can lead to much better group decision making. **C-type conflict**, or "cognitive conflict," focuses on problem- and issue-related differences of opinion.[65] In c-type conflict, group members disagree because their different experiences and expertise lead them to view the problem and its potential solutions differently. C-type conflict is also characterized by a willingness to examine, compare, and reconcile those differences to produce the best possible solution. Douglas Merrill, CEO of big-data firm ZestFinance, says, "Without conflict of some sort, you can't get to better answers. The challenge is to build a culture that enables conflict without the kind of painful conflict that some companies thrive on."[66] Ray Dalio, founder and CEO of Bridgewater Associates, the world's largest hedge fund, says anyone in the company can say that what the firm is doing doesn't make sense to them. At most investment firms, he says, "people keep that [kind of criticism] to themselves." But at Bridgewater, "you have a right and an obligation to say 'I think this is terrible' and explore whether or not that's true." Ultimately, he believes that, "if you can't have independent thinking, you can't know what your weaknesses are, and sort those things out, you're not going to be successful."[67]

By contrast, **a-type conflict**, meaning "affective conflict," refers to the emotional reactions that can occur when disagreements become personal rather than professional. A-type conflict often results in hostility, anger, resentment, distrust, cynicism, and apathy. Unlike c-type conflict, a-type conflict undermines team effectiveness by preventing teams from engaging in the activities characteristic of c-type conflict that are critical to team effectiveness. Examples of a-type conflict statements are "your idea," "our idea," "my department," "you don't know what you are talking about," or "you don't

Wavebreakmedia/Shutterstock.com

A-type conflict: When disagreements become personal rather than professional understand our situation." Rather than focusing on issues and ideas, these statements focus on individuals.[68]

The **devil's advocacy** approach can be used to create c-type conflict by assigning an individual or a subgroup the role of critic. The following five steps establish a devil's advocacy program:

1. Generate a potential solution.
2. Assign a devil's advocate to criticize and question the solution.
3. Present the critique of the potential solution to key decision makers.
4. Gather additional relevant information.
5. Decide whether to use, change, or not use the originally proposed solution.[69]

When properly used, the devil's advocacy approach introduces c-type conflict into the decision-making process. Contrary to the common belief that conflict is bad, studies show that these methods lead not only to less a-type conflict but also to improved decision quality and greater acceptance of decisions after they have been made.[70]

Another method of creating c-type conflict is **dialectical inquiry**, which creates c-type conflict by forcing decision makers to state the assumptions of a proposed solution (a thesis) and then generate a solution that is the opposite (antithesis) of the proposed solution. The five steps of the dialectical inquiry process are:

1. Generate a potential solution.
2. Identify the assumptions underlying the potential solution.
3. Generate a conflicting counterproposal based on the opposite assumptions.
4. Have advocates of each position present their arguments and engage in a debate in front of key decision makers.
5. Decide whether to use, change, or not use the originally proposed solution.

5-5c Nominal Group Technique

Nominal means "in name only." Accordingly, the **nominal group technique** (NGT) received its name because it begins with a quiet time in which group members independently write down as many problem definitions and alternative solutions as possible. In other words, the NGT begins by having group members act as individuals. After the quiet time, the group leader asks each member to share one idea at a time with the group. As they are read aloud, ideas are posted on flip charts or wallboards for all to see.

This step continues until all ideas have been shared. In the next step, the group discusses the advantages and disadvantages of the ideas. The NGT closes with a second quiet time in which group members independently rank the ideas presented. Group members then read their rankings aloud, and the idea with the highest average rank is selected.[71]

IBM manager Phil Gilbert used the NGT when his team developed a new email tool called IBM Verse. Instead of instructing them to come up with the next big thing in email, Gilbert had them spend ten minutes quietly writing down what they disliked about email on sticky notes—one idea per note, and no talking. As people finished writing, they stuck their notes on a big whiteboard until there weren't any more to post. The team leader then organized the sticky notes into logical groupings for review. Then the team left (Gilbert says sometimes briefly or for days). When they returned to the whiteboard, they brought additional ideas. Regarding the NGT process, Gilbert says, "It makes for better teams, and it leads to better outcomes. When you give voice to more people, the best ideas win, not the loudest ones."[72]

The nominal group technique improves group decision making by decreasing a-type conflict. But it also restricts c-type conflict. Consequently, the nominal group technique typically produces poorer decisions than the devil's advocacy and dialectical inquiry approaches. Nonetheless, more than eighty studies have found that nominal groups produce better ideas than those produced by traditional groups.[73]

5-5d Delphi Technique

In the **Delphi technique**, the members of a panel of experts respond to questions and to each other until reaching agreement on an issue. The first step is to assemble a panel of experts. Unlike other approaches to group decision making, however, it isn't necessary to bring the panel members together in one place. Because the Delphi technique does not require the experts

Devil's advocacy a decision-making method in which an individual or a subgroup is assigned the role of critic

Dialectical inquiry a decision-making method in which decision makers state the assumptions of a proposed solution (a thesis) and generate a solution that is the opposite (antithesis) of that solution

Nominal group technique a decision-making method that begins and ends by having group members quietly write down and evaluate ideas to be shared with the group

Delphi technique a decision-making method in which members of a panel of experts respond to questions and to each other until reaching agreement on an issue

to leave their offices or disrupt their schedules, they are more likely to participate.

The second step is to create a questionnaire consisting of a series of open-ended questions for the group. In the third step, the group members' written responses are analyzed, summarized, and fed back to the group for reactions until the members reach agreement. Asking group members why they agree or disagree is important because it helps uncover their unstated assumptions and beliefs. Again, this process of summarizing panel feedback and obtaining reactions to that feedback continues until the panel members reach agreement.

5-5e Electronic Brainstorming

Brainstorming, in which group members build on others' ideas, is a technique for generating a large number of alternative solutions. Brainstorming has four rules:

1. The more ideas, the better.
2. All ideas are acceptable, no matter how wild or crazy they might seem.
3. Other group members' ideas should be used to come up with even more ideas.
4. Criticism or evaluation of ideas is not allowed.

Although brainstorming is great fun and can help managers generate a large number of alternative solutions, it does have a number of disadvantages. Fortunately, **electronic brainstorming**, in which group members use computers to communicate and generate alternative solutions, overcomes the disadvantages associated with face-to-face brainstorming.[74]

Brainstorming a decision-making method in which group members build on each others' ideas to generate as many alternative solutions as possible

Electronic brainstorming a decision-making method in which group members use computers to build on each others' ideas and generate as many alternative solutions as possible

Production blocking a disadvantage of face-to-face brainstorming in which a group member must wait to share an idea because another member is presenting an idea

Evaluation apprehension fear of what others will think of your ideas

The first disadvantage that electronic brainstorming overcomes is **production blocking**, which occurs when you have an idea but have to wait to share it because someone else is already presenting an idea to the group. During this short delay, you may forget your idea or decide that it really wasn't worth sharing. Production blocking doesn't happen with electronic brainstorming. All group members are seated at computers, so everyone can type in ideas whenever they occur. There's no waiting for your turn to be heard by the group.

The second disadvantage that electronic brainstorming overcomes is **evaluation apprehension**, that is, being afraid of what others will think of your ideas. For example, Robert Murphy, an online marketing representative, had prepared for a meeting with his boss and six coworkers by conducting research and bringing detailed notes to the meeting. Then, when the discussion began, his evaluation apprehension regarding what his boss and colleagues would say about his ideas overwhelmed his preparation. Says Murphy, "I just sat there like a lump, fixated on the fact that I was quiet."[75]

With electronic brainstorming, all ideas are anonymous. When you type in an idea and press the Enter key to share it with the group, group members see only the idea. Furthermore, many brainstorming software programs also protect anonymity by displaying ideas in random order. So if you laugh maniacally when you type "Cut top management's pay by 50 percent!" and then press the Enter key, it won't show up immediately on everyone's screen. This makes it doubly difficult to determine who is responsible for which comments.

In the typical layout for electronic brainstorming, all participants sit in front of computers around a U-shaped table. This configuration allows them to see their computer screens, the other participants, a large main screen, and a meeting leader or facilitator. Step 1 in electronic brainstorming is to anonymously generate as many ideas as possible. Groups commonly generate 100 ideas in a half-hour period. Step 2 is to edit the generated ideas, categorize them, and eliminate redundancies. Step 3 is to rank the categorized ideas in terms of quality. Step 4, the last step, has three parts: generate a series of action steps, decide the best order for accomplishing these steps, and identify who is responsible for each step. All four steps are accomplished with computers and electronic brainstorming software.[76]

Studies show that electronic brainstorming is much more productive than face-to-face brainstorming. Four-person electronic brainstorming groups produce 25–50 percent more ideas than four-person regular brainstorming groups, and twelve-person electronic brainstorming groups produce 200 percent more ideas than

Creativa Images/Shutterstock.com

Maximize Your Life Decisions Using a Spreadsheet

Maximizers, according to the *Wall Street Journal*'s Elizabeth Bernstein, "like to take their time and weigh a wide range of options—sometimes every possible one—before choosing." Satisficers, on the other hand, "would rather be fast than thorough; they prefer to quickly choose the option that fills the minimum criteria." Most of us are satisficers. But should we really make major life decisions based on what meets "minimum criteria?" Probably not. When it comes to the decisions that matter, it is in your best interest to weigh the costs and benefits of all available choices. This may sound like a daunting task, but a simple spreadsheet can help you evaluate your alternatives quickly and easily. Suppose you're looking for a new apartment. First, list the criteria you're looking for (location, cost, spaciousness) in the left-hand column and list your various alternatives at the top. As you gather information, rate each alternative against the criteria on a scale of 1–5 (1 being worst and 5 being best). Psychologist Fjola Helgadottir has used this spreadsheet method to "run 4 marathons, climb Mt Kilimanjaro, travel the world, and complete 4 university degrees." What could a spreadsheet help you decide to do with your life?

Sources: F. Helgadottir, "How Excel Can Help You Achieve Goals," The *AI-Therapy Blog*, August 27, 2012, accessed May 7, 2016, https://www.ai-therapy.com/blog/how-excel-can-help-you-achieve-goals/; R. Sanghani, "How Excel Spreadsheets Can Help You Make Major Life Decisions," *The Telegraph*, January 4, 2016, accessed May 7, 2016, http://www.telegraph.co.uk/women/life/how-excel-spreadsheets-can-help-you-make-major-life-decisions/; E. Bernstein, "How You Make Decisions Says a Lot About How Happy You Are," *Wall Street Journal*, October 6, 2014, accessed May 7, 2016, http://www.wsj.com/articles/how-you-make-decisions-says-a-lot-about-how-happy-you-are-1412614997.

dennizn/Shutterstock.com

---

regular groups of the same size! In fact, because production blocking (having to wait your turn) is not a problem in electronic brainstorming, the number and quality of ideas generally increase with group size.[77]

Even though it works much better than traditional brainstorming, electronic brainstorming has disadvantages, too. An obvious problem is the expense of computers, networks, software, and other equipment. As these costs continue to drop, however, electronic brainstorming will become cheaper.

Another problem is that the anonymity of ideas may bother people who are used to having their ideas accepted by virtue of their position (that is the boss). On the other hand, one CEO said, "Because the process is anonymous, the sky's the limit in terms of what you can say, and, as a result, it is more thought-provoking. As a CEO, you'll probably discover things you might not want to hear but need to be aware of."[78]

A third disadvantage is that outgoing individuals who are more comfortable expressing themselves verbally may find it difficult to express themselves in writing. Finally, the most obvious problem is that participants have to be able to type. Those who can't type, or who type slowly, may be easily frustrated and find themselves at a disadvantage compared to experienced typists.

STUDY TOOLS 5

LOCATED IN TEXTBOOK
☐ Rip-out and review chapter review card

LOCATED AT WWW.CENGAGEBRAIN.COM
☐ Review key term flashcards and create your own from StudyBits
☐ Track your knowledge and understanding of key concepts, using the concept tracker
☐ Complete practice and graded quizzes to prepare for tests
☐ Complete interactive content within the exposition
☐ View chapter highlight box content at the beginning of each chapter

6 Organizational Strategy

alphaspirit/Shutterstock.com

LEARNING OUTCOMES

6-1 Specify the components of sustainable competitive advantage, and explain why it is important.

6-2 Describe the steps involved in the strategy-making process.

6-3 Explain the different kinds of corporate-level strategies.

6-4 Describe the different kinds of industry-level strategies.

6-5 Explain the components and kinds of firm-level strategies.

After you finish this chapter, go to **PAGE 135** for **STUDY TOOLS**

SUSTAINABLE COMPETITIVE ADVANTAGE

Just six years ago, there was no market for tablet computers. A number of computer makers sold touchscreen laptops, but other than some programs that allowed users to handwrite notes, there was little to distinguish these machines from traditional laptops. All of that changed when Apple released the iPad, a tablet computer that is controlled by a multitouch display and can run hundreds of thousands of applications allowing users to read books, watch movies, listen to music, check the weather, or play games. With its innovative product, Apple in effect created a new market for portable, touch-based tablet computers. The iPad is not without its competitors, however. There is, for example, the Amazon Kindle Fire, Barnes & Noble's Nook HD, and Samsung's Android-based Galaxy Tab. The latest competitor is the Microsoft Surface, which comes with a touchscreen, a combination cover/detachable keyboard, and the Windows 10 operating system. Critics complain about the higher price ($1,628 for a 256GB Surface Pro 4 with a 12.3-inch screen, keyboard, and Surface Pen versus $1,450 for a 256GB iPad Pro with a 12.9-inch screen, keyboard, and the Apple Pencil), and the Surfaces's 40 percent shorter battery life. Despite its competitors, Apple still dominates tablet sales, selling 49.6 million iPads in 2015 compared to just 6 million Surfaces, 33.4 million Galaxies, and 3.3 million Kindles.[1] Likewise, a report on Web usage, meaning the percentage of tablet Web traffic (that is, surfing the Web with your tablet rather than your PC or smartphone), found that Apple generated 70.8 percent of all tablet Web traffic in North America compared to 8 percent for Amazon, 11.5 percent for Samsung, and 2 percent for Microsoft.[2]

How can a company like Apple, which dominates a particular industry, maintain its competitive advantage as strong, well-financed competitors enter the market? What steps can Apple and other companies take to better manage their strategy-making process?

Resources are the assets, capabilities, processes, employee time, information, and knowledge that an organization controls. Firms use their resources to improve organizational effectiveness and efficiency. Resources are critical to organizational strategy because they can help companies create and sustain an advantage over competitors.[3]

Organizations can achieve a **competitive advantage** by using their resources to provide greater value for customers than competitors can. For example, the iPad's competitive advantage came partly from its sleek, attractive design and partly from the reputation of Apple's iPod and iPhone as innovative, easy-to-use products.

The goal of most organizational strategies is to create and then sustain a competitive advantage. A competitive advantage becomes a **sustainable competitive advantage** when other companies cannot duplicate the value a firm is providing to customers. Sustainable competitive advantage is *not* the same as a long-lasting competitive advantage, though companies obviously want a competitive advantage to last a long time. Instead, a competitive advantage is *sustained* if competitors have tried unsuccessfully to duplicate the advantage and have, for the moment, stopped trying to duplicate it. It's the corporate equivalent of your competitors saying, "We give up. You win. We can't do what you do, and we're not even going to try to do it anymore." Four conditions must be met if a firm's resources are to be used to achieve a sustainable competitive advantage. The resources must be valuable, rare, imperfectly imitable, *and* nonsubstitutable.

Valuable resources allow companies to improve their efficiency and effectiveness. Unfortunately, changes in customer demand and preferences, competitors' actions, and technology can make once-valuable resources much less valuable. Before the iPad was introduced, netbooks appeared to be the next big thing in mobile computing. These laptops were small and light, making them ultra portable; were very affordable, averaging anywhere from $200 to $500; and let users run basic programs such as Web browsing and word processing on the go. At first, sales were brisk—in 2009, 7.5 million netbooks were sold in the United States and more than 34 million worldwide. But all that changed. The iPad had a touchscreen, an intuitive operating system, and a large selection of app software, while netbooks were often criticized for having small, hard-to-use keyboards, a slow operating system, and a lack of software options. While it took only twenty-eight days for Apple to sell its first 1 million iPads, netbook sales fell by

Resources the assets, capabilities, processes, employee time, information, and knowledge that an organization uses to improve its effectiveness and efficiency and create and sustain competitive advantage

Competitive advantage providing greater value for customers than competitors can

Sustainable competitive advantage a competitive advantage that other companies have tried unsuccessfully to duplicate and have, for the moment, stopped trying to duplicate

Valuable resource a resource that allows companies to improve efficiency and effectiveness

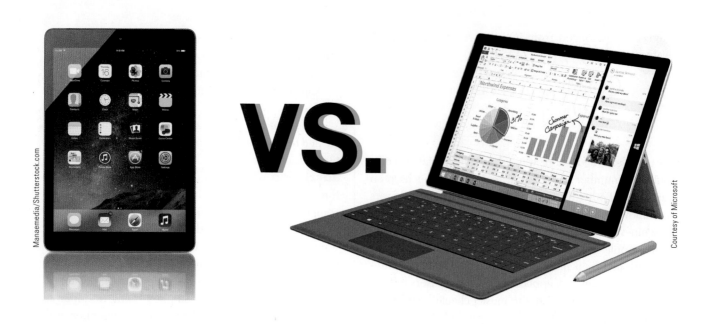

Manaemedia/Shutterstock.com

Courtesy of Microsoft

40 percent in one year.⁴ Only one year after netbook sales peaked, tablet sales passed them, and netbook sales have been steadily declining ever since.⁵

For sustained competitive advantage, valuable resources must also be rare resources. Think about it: How can a company sustain a competitive advantage if all of its competitors have similar resources and capabilities? Consequently, **rare resources**, resources that are not controlled or possessed by many competing firms, are necessary to sustain a competitive advantage. One of Apple's truly rare resources has been its ability to reconfigure existing technology into a package that is easy to use, elegantly designed, and therefore highly desired by customers. Apple used its wealth of experience from developing the iPod, iPod touch, and iPhone to create an operating system for the iPad that was easy to use and, more importantly, basically identical to what was found on its other products. In other words, it leveraged the iOS operating system into a single platform that would give users the same experience across multiple devices. An iPhone user who just purchased an iPad will have little difficulty learning how to use it. But, they might have trouble learning the macOS operating system on Apple Mac personal computers, which is substantially different. By contrast, with Windows 10, the Microsoft Surface 4 automatically and seamlessly switches apps from personal computer mode (when a keyboard is attached) to tablet mode (when used as a tablet with the keyboard detached). In other words, Apple is no longer the only software/hardware provider to create an operating system that is easily used across multiple devices.⁶

As this example shows, valuable and rare resources can create temporary competitive advantage. For sustained competitive advantage, however, other firms must be unable to imitate or find substitutes for those valuable, rare resources. **Imperfectly imitable resources** are those resources that are impossible or extremely costly or difficult to duplicate. Both Google and Amazon operate online app stores that are in some way similar to Apple's App Store. Users can log on to the sites, browse for programs, and purchase and download them to their devices. There is a big difference, however, in security. Apple's App Store is a closed platform, meaning that if a software developer wants to sell an app on Apple's site, the company first puts it through a review process to check for content and security issues. Android, however, is an open platform, which means that while Google has improved in security prescreening, it is far easier for Android developers with bad intentions to create and sell applications that can harm devices or steal personal information. According to a study conducted in 2015 by Symantec, a technology security company, 17 percent of 6.3 million available Android apps are malware.⁷ And Verizon's 2015 Data Breach Investigations report shows that, although there are extremely few malware-infested mobile devices on its network (only 100 per week), 96 percent of those are Android devices. The report states, "Android wins. Not just wins, but Android wins so hard that most of the suspi-

Rare resource a resource that is not controlled or possessed by many competing firms

Imperfectly imitable resource a resource that is impossible or extremely costly or difficult for other firms to duplicate

cious activity logged from iOS devices was just failed Android exploits."[8]

Valuable, rare, imperfectly imitable resources can produce sustainable competitive advantage only if they are also **nonsubstitutable resources**, meaning that no other resources can replace them and produce similar value or competitive advantage. From 2007 to 2012, Google Maps was the iPhone's dominant navigation app. In 2012, 91 percent of iPhone owners used Google Maps because it gave them accurate information, voice-guided direction, and the ability to map routes by car, public transportation, and walking.[9] So for five years, nothing else on the iPhone came close to providing the simple, accurate, easy-to-use navigation found in Google Maps. With 7,000 people working on Google Maps as "street view drivers, people flying planes, people drawing maps, people correcting listings, and people building new products," Google Maps was a nonsubstitutable navigation resource on the iPhone.[10] Apple set out to change that in 2012 when the company released the first version of Apple Maps for iOS. However, it was so bad and inaccurate that CEO Tim Cook apologized, saying, "We are extremely sorry for the frustration," and that iPhone users could, while Maps was being improved, "try alternatives by downloading map apps from the App Store or use Google or Nokia maps."[11] By June 2015, after acquiring a number of mapping software companies, fixing incorrect map data, and largely matching the functionality found in Google Maps, Apple reported that iPhone owners used the Apple Maps app 5 billion times per week, 3.5 times more than the "next leading maps app," Google Maps.[12] Does this mean that Apple Maps has a sustainable competitive advantage over Google Maps? No—not even close. But it does mean that Apple Maps is a worthy substitute for Google Maps, and that Google Maps lost its previously sustainable competitive advantage among iPhone users.

In summary, Apple reaped the rewards of a first-mover advantage when it introduced the iPad. The company's history of developing customer-friendly software, the innovative capabilities of the iPad, and the uniformity of experience provide customers with a service that has been valuable, rare, relatively nonsubstitutable, and, in the past, imperfectly imitable. As demonstrated by the rise of Windows 10 and the stumble of Apple Maps, however, past success is no guarantee of future success. Apple needs to continue developing and improving its products or risk being unseated by a more nimble competitor whose products are more relevant and have higher perceived value for consumers.

Exhibit 6.1
Three Steps of the Strategy-Making Process

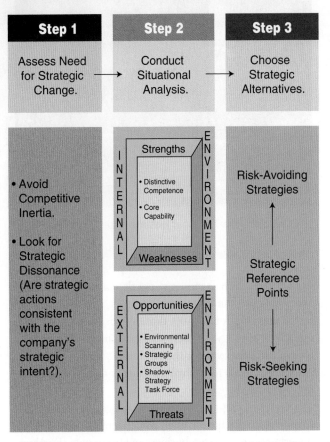

6-2 STRATEGY-MAKING PROCESS

To create a sustainable competitive advantage, a company must have a strategy.[13] Exhibit 6.1 displays the three steps of the strategy-making process:

6-2a assess the need for strategic change, 6-2b conduct a situational analysis, *and then **6-2c choose strategic alternatives.** Let's examine each of these steps in more detail.*

6-2a Assessing the Need for Strategic Change

The external business environment is much more turbulent than it

> **Nonsubstitutable resource** a resource that produces value or competitive advantage and has no equivalent substitutes or replacements

Throughout its 140-year history, Avon has used a direct-selling model.

used to be. With customers' needs constantly growing and changing, and with competitors working harder, faster, and smarter to meet those needs, the first step in creating a strategy is determining the need for strategic change. In other words, the company should determine whether it needs to change its strategy to sustain a competitive advantage.[14]

Determining the need for strategic change might seem easy to do, but it's really not. There's a great deal of uncertainty in strategic business environments. Furthermore, top-level managers are often slow to recognize the need for strategic change, especially at successful companies that have created and sustained competitive advantages. Because they are acutely aware of the strategies that made their companies successful, they continue to rely on those strategies, even as the competition changes. In other words, success often leads to **competitive inertia**—a reluctance to change strategies or competitive practices that have been successful in the past. Throughout its 140-year history, **Avon** used a direct-selling model in which customers bought beauty products, perfume, and more from their local Avon sales representatives. But since 2011, sales are down 50 percent to $8.9 billion. The company's team of 6 million sales representatives has shrunk nineteen quarters in a row.[15] And, in 2014, Avon lost nearly $400 million when sales dropped by 21 percent, even though the

direct sales industry grew globally by 3.2 percent during the same period.[16] In fact, direct selling competitors, such as Mary Kay, and store/Internet competitors, such as Ultra Salon and Sephora, are experiencing strong growth. Despite Avon's steady decline, CEO Sherilyn McCoy is committed to the company's strategy, saying, "We continue to stay the course on our plans to return Avon to sustainable, profitable growth."[17] Why has Avon stuck with a strategy that is clearly not working? Competitive inertia— because it was successful for more than 140 years. CEO Sherilyn McCoy says, "I'm not one to shy away from challenges, and Avon certainly hasn't disappointed me on that front."[18] So is Avon beginning to recognize that it fundamentally needs to change its strategy? Perhaps. In April 2015, it was exploring options to sell its North American division. Critics would contend, however, that selling a problematic part of the company doesn't represent a wholesale change in strategy.

Besides being aware of the dangers of competitive inertia, what can managers do to improve the speed and accuracy with which they determine the need for strategic change? One method is to actively look for signs of strategic dissonance. **Strategic dissonance** is a discrepancy between a company's intended strategy and the strategic actions managers take when actually implementing that strategy.[19] With Japan's shrinking population, little economic growth, stiff competition from Japan's high-speed railways, and airline deregulation leading to new low-cost airlines, **All Nippon Airways (ANA)**, Japan's largest airline, needed to cut costs and move quickly to respond to competitors. However, that intended strategy was at odds (that is, strategic dissonance) with its long-standing high-price, high-quality service strategy. So, it started two low-cost airlines, Peach Aviation and AirAsia Japan. While that provided low-cost flights to customers, an unintended benefit for ANA was seeing how Peach and AirAsia made faster decisions to respond to competition and lower costs. For example, AirAsia's top management decided to expand service to Nagoya, Japan, three months faster than planned but got the work done in one-third of the planned time! At ANA, that decision would have taken six months and involved fifty people from across the company in multiple discussions. Yoshinori Odagiri, a long-time ANA executive who became AirAsia's CEO, said, "I was taken aback by the decision-making speed." So, to overcome strategic dissonance and make sure that its new low-cost, speed-to-market strategy is infused through the entire company, ANA has now brought Peach and AirAsia directly into its organizational structure.[20]

Note, however, that strategic dissonance is not the same thing as when a strategy does not produce

Competitive inertia a reluctance to change strategies or competitive practices that have been successful in the past

Strategic dissonance a discrepancy between a company's intended strategy and the strategic actions managers take when implementing that strategy

the results that it's supposed to. When Xhibit, the maker of the SkyMall catalogs found on airplanes (and then at SkyMall.com), filed for bankruptcy, the issue wasn't strategic dissonance. It was that Sky-Mall's strategy of using catalogs to sell quirky, expensive products such as a $200 pet ramp staircase, a $170 portable icemaker, or a $60 "Tablift Hands-Free Tablet Holder" to bored travelers no longer worked. Why read the Sky-Mall catalog when you've got books, movies, and music on your smartphone or tablet? Or, when your plane has Wi-Fi, and you can surf the Internet?[21]

Aldi's business model focuses on selling a limited number of groceries and household items in a small setting.

6-2b Situational Analysis

A situational analysis can also help managers determine the need for strategic change. A **situational analysis**, also called a **SWOT analysis**, for *strengths*, *weaknesses*, *opportunities*, and *threats*, is an assessment of the strengths and weaknesses in an organization's internal environment and the opportunities and threats in its external environment.[22] Ideally, as shown in Step 2 of Exhibit 6.1, a SWOT analysis helps a company determine how to increase internal strengths and minimize internal weaknesses while maximizing external opportunities and minimizing external threats.

An analysis of an organization's internal environment, that is, a company's strengths and weaknesses, often begins with an assessment of its distinctive competencies and core capabilities. A **distinctive competence** is something that a company can make, do, or perform better than its competitors. For example, *Consumer Reports* magazine consistently ranks Toyota and Subaru cars as tops in quality, reliability, and owner satisfaction.[23] Similarly, *PC Magazine* ranked Intuit's TurboTax the best tax preparation software for its user experience, thorough coverage of tax topic, and robust help resources.[24]

Whereas distinctive competencies are tangible—for example, a product or service is faster, cheaper, or better—the core capabilities that produce distinctive competencies are not. **Core capabilities** are the less visible, internal decision-making routines, problem-solving processes, and organizational cultures that

determine how efficiently inputs can be turned into outputs. Distinctive competencies cannot be sustained for long without superior core capabilities.

For years, large retail stores such as Walmart and Target have been trying to open stores in New York City only to be met with protests. Aldi, however, recently opened two stores in the city, not only with no protests but even with some politicians in attendance. The reason that Aldi faces little opposition as it opens stores in dense, urban settings is that it is able to make money in small, high-rent inner city locations. It operates with a business model that focuses on selling a limited number of groceries and household items in a small setting; its typical stores are just 16 percent the size of a typical Walmart store and carry just 1,500 or so items, compared to 100,000 items in a superstore. Furthermore, most of its items are private brands, that is, goods that Aldi buys and packages itself. All of this means that Aldi can offer prices that are 20 percent less than Walmart's, making it an attractive place for city dwellers to shop.[25]

After examining internal strengths and weaknesses, the second part of a situational analysis is to look outside the company and assess the opportunities and threats in the external environment. In Chapter 3, you learned

Situational (SWOT) analysis an assessment of the strengths and weaknesses in an organization's internal environment and the opportunities and threats in its external environment

Distinctive competence what a company can make, do, or perform better than its competitors

Core capabilities the internal decision-making routines, problem-solving processes, and organizational cultures that determine how efficiently inputs can be turned into outputs

SHADOW-STRATEGY TASK FORCE

When looking for threats and opportunities, many managers focus on competitors in the external environment. Others, however, prefer to examine the internal environment through a **shadow-strategy task force**. This strategy involves a company actively seeking out its own weaknesses and then thinking like its competitors, trying to determine how they can be exploited for competitive advantage. To make sure that the task force challenges conventional thinking, its members should be independent-minded, come from a variety of company functions and levels, and have the access and authority to question the company's current strategic actions and intent.

Source: W. B. Werther, Jr., and J. L. Kerr, "The Shifting Sands of Competitive Advantage," *Business Horizons* (May–June 1995): 11–17.

that *environmental scanning* involves searching the environment for important events or issues that might affect the organization, such as pricing trends or new products and technology. In a situational analysis, however, managers use environmental scanning to identify specific opportunities and threats that can either improve or harm the company's ability to sustain its competitive advantage. Identification of strategic groups and formation of shadow-strategy task forces are two ways to do this (see box "Shadow-Strategy Task Force").

Strategic groups are not groups that actually work together. They are companies—usually competitors—that managers closely follow. More specifically, a **strategic group** is a group of other companies within an industry against which top managers compare, evaluate, and benchmark their company's strategic threats and opportunities.[26] (*Benchmarking* involves identifying outstanding practices, processes, and standards at other companies and adapting them to your own company.) Typically, managers include companies as part of their strategic group if they compete directly with those companies for customers or if those companies use

strategies similar to theirs. The U.S. home improvement industry has annual sales in excess of $319 billion. This market is divided into professional and consumer markets, both of which were forecast to grow roughly 5 percent in 2016.[27] It's likely that the managers at Home Depot, the largest U.S. home improvement and hardware retailer, assess strategic threats and opportunities by comparing their company to a strategic group consisting of the other major home improvement supply companies. Exhibit 6.2 shows the number of stores, the size of the typical new store, and the overall geographic distribution (states, countries) of Home Depot stores compared with Lowe's, Ace Hardware, and 84 Lumber.

In fact, when scanning the environment for strategic threats and opportunities, managers tend to categorize the different companies in their industries as core, secondary, and transient firms.[28] **Core firms** are the central companies in a strategic group. Home Depot operates 2,274 stores covering all fifty states, Puerto Rico, the U.S. Virgin Islands, Guam, Mexico, and Canada. The company has more than 350,000 employees and annual revenues of $83.2 billion. By comparison, Lowe's has more than 1,855 stores and 270,000 employees in the United States, Canada, and Mexico; stocks about 36,000 products in each store; and has annual revenues of $59.1 billion.[29] Clearly, Lowe's is the closest competitor to Home Depot and is the core firm in Home Depot's strategic group. Even though Ace Hardware has more stores (4,700) than Home Depot and appears to be a bigger multinational player (seventy different countries), Ace's different franchise structure and small, individualized stores (10,000–14,000 square feet, with each store laid out differently with a different mix of products) keep it from being a core firm in Home Depot's strategic group.[30] Likewise, Home Depot's management probably doesn't include Aubuchon Hardware in its core strategic group, because Aubuchon has only 125 stores in New England and upstate New York.[31]

When most managers scan their environments for strategic threats and opportunities, they concentrate on the strategic actions of core firms, not unrelated firms such as Aubuchon. Where does a firm like Ace Hardware fit in? As a retailer-owned cooperative, Ace Hardware is a network of independently owned stores. Ace's 20/20 vision employs a customer-focused strategy to grow the brand and improve store performance.[32]

Secondary firms are firms that use strategies related to but somewhat different from those of core firms. 84 Lumber has roughly 250 stores in thirty states, but even though its stores are open to the public, the company focuses on supplying professional contractors, to whom it sells 85 percent of its products. Without the wide variety of products on the shelves or assistance

Shadow-strategy task force a committee within a company that analyzes the company's own weaknesses to determine how competitors could exploit them for competitive advantage

Strategic group a group of companies within an industry against which top managers compare, evaluate, and benchmark strategic threats and opportunities

Core firms the central companies in a strategic group

Secondary firms the firms in a strategic group that follow strategies related to but somewhat different from those of the core firms

Exhibit 6.2
Core and Secondary Firms in the Home Improvement Industry

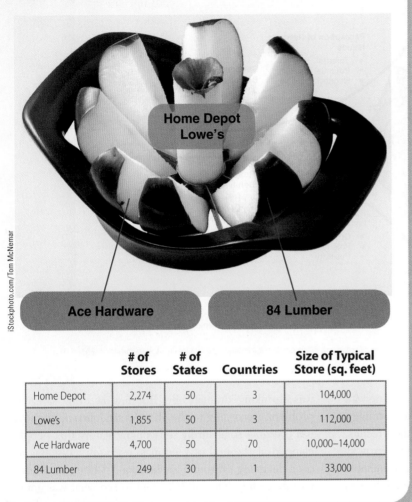

iStockphoto.com/Tom McNemar

	# of Stores	# of States	Countries	Size of Typical Store (sq. feet)
Home Depot	2,274	50	3	104,000
Lowe's	1,855	50	3	112,000
Ace Hardware	4,700	50	70	10,000–14,000
84 Lumber	249	30	1	33,000

help the company create or maintain a sustainable competitive advantage. According to *strategic reference point theory*, managers choose between two basic alternative strategies. They can choose a conservative, *risk-avoiding strategy* that aims to protect an existing competitive advantage. Or they can choose an aggressive, *risk-seeking strategy* that aims to extend or create a sustainable competitive advantage.

The choice to seek risk or avoid risk typically depends on whether top management views the company as falling above or below strategic reference points. **Strategic reference points** are the targets that managers use to measure whether their firm has developed the core competencies that it needs to achieve a sustainable competitive advantage. If a hotel chain decides to compete by providing superior quality and service, then top management will track the success of this strategy through customer surveys or published hotel ratings such as those provided by the prestigious *Mobil Travel Guide*. If a hotel chain decides to compete on price, it will regularly conduct market surveys to check the prices of other hotels. The competitors' prices are the hotel managers' strategic reference points against which to compare their own pricing strategy. If competitors can consistently underprice them, then the managers need to determine whether their staff and resources have the core competencies to compete on price.

As shown in Exhibit 6.3, when a company is performing above or better than its strategic reference points, top management will typically be satisfied with the company's strategy. Ironically, this satisfaction tends to make top management conservative and risk-averse. Because the company already has a sustainable competitive advantage, the worst thing that could happen would be to lose it, so new issues or changes in the company's external environment are viewed as threats. By contrast, when a company is performing below or worse than its strategic reference points, top management will typically be dissatisfied with

available to the average consumer, people without expertise in building or remodeling probably don't find 84 Lumber stores very accessible. Home Depot would most likely classify 84 Lumber as a secondary firm in its strategic group analysis.[33] Managers need to be aware of the potential threats and opportunities posed by secondary firms, but they usually spend more time assessing the threats and opportunities associated with core firms.

6-2c Choosing Strategic Alternatives

After determining the need for strategic change and conducting a situational analysis, the last step in the strategy-making process is to choose strategic alternatives that will

> **Strategic reference points** the strategic targets managers use to measure whether a firm has developed the core competencies it needs to achieve a sustainable competitive advantage

Exhibit 6.3
Strategic Reference Points

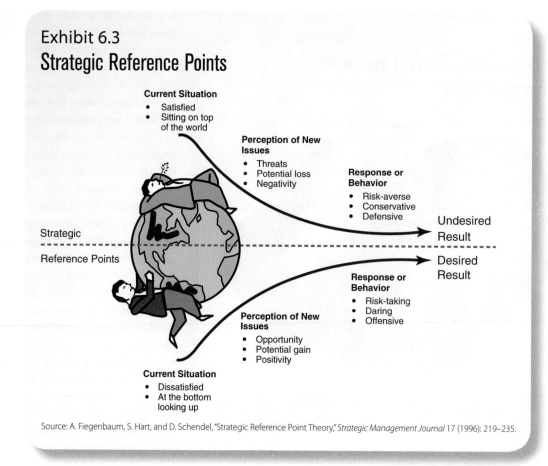

Current Situation
- Satisfied
- Sitting on top of the world

Perception of New Issues
- Threats
- Potential loss
- Negativity

Response or Behavior
- Risk-averse
- Conservative
- Defensive

Undesired Result

Strategic
- - - - - - - - - - - - - -
Reference Points

Desired Result

Response or Behavior
- Risk-taking
- Daring
- Offensive

Perception of New Issues
- Opportunity
- Potential gain
- Positivity

Current Situation
- Dissatisfied
- At the bottom looking up

Source: A. Fiegenbaum, S. Hart, and D. Schendel, "Strategic Reference Point Theory," *Strategic Management Journal* 17 (1996): 219–235.

the company's strategy. In this instance, managers are much more likely to choose a daring, risk-taking strategy. If the current strategy is producing substandard results, the company has nothing to lose by switching to risky new strategies in the hope that it can create a sustainable competitive advantage. Managers of companies in this situation view new issues or changes in the external environment as opportunities for potential gain.

Strategic reference point theory is not deterministic, however. Managers are not predestined to choose risk-averse or risk-seeking strategies for their companies. In fact, one of the most important elements of the theory is that managers *can* influence the strategies chosen by their company by *actively changing and adjusting* the strategic reference points they use to judge strategic performance. If a company has become complacent after consistently surpassing its strategic reference points, then top management can change from a risk-averse to a risk-taking orientation by raising or changing the standards of performance (that is, the strategic reference points). This is just what happened at eBay.

When John Donahoe first joined eBay, Amazon was growing, Google helped shoppers to find what they wanted on other websites, and eBay's auction business

was shrinking dramatically. But few at eBay saw the problem. According to the *Wall Street Journal*, employees "became so absurdly self-congratulatory that people clapped at the end of meetings, even after discussions over declining customer satisfaction."[34] Founder Pierre Omidyar said, "They didn't seem to see what was going on outside the company in terms of competition. They had lost their ability to innovate, to create new things."[35] In other words, success had made eBay complacent and risk averse.

When Donahoe later became eBay's CEO, he raised standards, thus changing the strategic reference points eBay had been using to assess its strategic performance. His first week on the job, he told everyone that eBay needed a major turnaround. Said Donahoe, "Our sellers hated that word. Our employees hated it. Investors hated it. But it was the first step ... we had to confront reality."[36] To encourage a daring, offensive-minded strategy, he funded a mobile app team that produced the eBay RedLaser (barcode price scanning that finds products locally and online) and eBay Motors apps, which have been downloaded 120 million times; he told his team to find a way to deliver purchased products in one day (called eBay Now); and he sent a design team offsite to create a fresh graphics-based look to its aging text-based website. His ultimate challenges, however, were to double eBay's active users to 225 million, increase revenue from $14 billion to $23.5 billion, and increase customer payments from $145 billion to $300 billion, all within the next three years. Says Donahoe, "The turnaround is behind us, and we are now playing offense."[37]

So even when (perhaps *especially* when) companies have achieved a sustainable competitive advantage, top managers must adjust or change strategic reference points to challenge themselves and their employees to develop new core competencies for the future. In the long run, effective organizations will frequently revise their strategic reference points to better focus managers' attention on the new challenges and opportunities that occur in their ever-changing business environments.

6-3 CORPORATE-LEVEL STRATEGIES

To formulate effective strategies, companies must be able to answer these three basic questions:

▶ What business are we in?

▶ How should we compete in this industry?

▶ Who are our competitors, and how should we respond to them?

These simple but powerful questions are at the heart of corporate-, industry-, and firm-level strategies.

Corporate-level strategy is the overall organizational strategy that addresses the question, "What business or businesses are we in or should we be in?" IBM CEO Virginia (Ginni) Rometty knows exactly what business her company is in: "When people say, 'What's IBM?' I say, 'it's an enterprise innovation company.'"[38] Similarly, Dr. Pepper is in the "flavored beverage business."[39]

There are two major approaches to corporate-level strategy that companies use to decide which businesses they should be in: 6-3a portfolio strategy and 6-3b grand strategies.

6-3a Portfolio Strategy

One of the standard strategies for stock market investors is **diversification**, or owning stocks in a variety of companies in different industries. The purpose of this strategy is to reduce risk in the overall stock portfolio (the entire collection of stocks). The basic idea is simple: if you invest in ten companies in ten different industries,

you won't lose your entire investment if one company performs poorly. Furthermore, because they're in different industries, one company's losses are likely to be offset by another company's gains. Portfolio strategy is based on these same ideas. We'll start by taking a look at the theory and ideas behind portfolio strategy and then proceed with a critical review which suggests that some of the key ideas behind portfolio strategy are *not* supported.

Portfolio strategy is a corporate-level strategy that minimizes risk by diversifying investment among various businesses or product lines.[40] Just as a diversification strategy guides an investor who invests in a variety of stocks, portfolio strategy guides the strategic decisions of corporations that compete in a variety of businesses. For example, portfolio strategy could be used to guide the strategy of a company such as 3M, which makes 55,000 products for five different business groups: Consumer (Post-its, Scotch tape); Electronics and Energy (electronic devices, telecoms equipment, renewable energy solutions); Health Care (medical, surgical, and dental products, health information systems); Industrial (tapes, abrasives, adhesives, specialty materials, filtration systems); and Safety and Graphics (safety and security products, track and trace solutions, graphic solutions).[41]

Just as investors consider the mix of stocks in their stock portfolio when deciding which stocks to buy or sell, managers following portfolio strategy try to acquire companies that fit well with the rest of their corporate portfolio and to sell those that don't. **Procter & Gamble** used to have a diverse portfolio of food, beverage, household, beauty, health care, pharmaceutical, pet food, and battery brands. However, when it decided to focus on its core business of household, beauty, and health care products, it began selling off brands that did not relate to its core business, a process that included the sale of Duracell to Warren Buffett's **Berkshire Hathaway** for $4.7 billion and Iams and Eukanuba pet foods to **Mars** for $2.9 billion.[42]

First, according to portfolio strategy, the more businesses in which a corporation competes, the smaller its overall chances of failing. Think of a corporation as a stool and its businesses as the legs of the stool. The more legs or businesses added to the

Corporate-level strategy the overall organizational strategy that addresses the question "What business or businesses are we in or should we be in?"

Diversification a strategy for reducing risk by buying a variety of items (stocks or, in the case of a corporation, types of businesses) so that the failure of one stock or one business does not doom the entire portfolio

Portfolio strategy a corporate-level strategy that minimizes risk by diversifying investment among various businesses or product lines

stool, the less likely it is to tip over. Using this analogy, portfolio strategy reduces 3M's risk of failing because the corporation's survival depends on essentially five different business sectors. Managers employing portfolio strategy can either develop new businesses internally or look for **acquisitions**, that is, other companies to buy. Either way, the goal is to add legs to the stool.

Second, beyond adding new businesses to the corporate portfolio, portfolio strategy predicts that companies can reduce risk even more through **unrelated diversification**—creating or acquiring companies in completely unrelated businesses (more on the accuracy of this prediction later). According to portfolio strategy, when businesses are unrelated, losses in one business or industry should have minimal effect on the performance of other companies in the corporate portfolio. For example, Newell Brands has fifty-one brands organized into ten divisions. Some of the best-known brands in those divisions are Sharpie, PaperMate, and Uni-Ball (writing); Coleman camping products, Volkl Skis, and Rawlings sporting gear (outdoor solutions); Oster kitchen appliances, Crock-Pot slow cookers, and Mr. Coffee (consumer solutions); Rubbermaid (commercial products); Graco car seats and high chairs, and Baby Jogger strollers (baby and parenting); and Yankee Candle, First Alert security systems, and Ball canning jars (branded consumables).[43]

Because most internally grown businesses tend to be related to existing products or services, portfolio strategy suggests that acquiring new businesses is the preferred method of unrelated diversification.

Third, investing the profits and cash flows from mature, slow-growth businesses into newer, faster-growing businesses can reduce long-term risk. The best-known portfolio strategy for guiding investment in a corporation's businesses is the Boston Consulting Group (BCG) matrix.[44] The **BCG matrix** is a portfolio strategy that managers use to categorize their corporation's businesses by growth rate and relative market share, which helps them decide how to invest corporate funds. The matrix, shown in Exhibit 6.4, separates businesses into four categories based on how fast the market is growing (high growth or low growth) and the size of the business's share of that market (small or large). **Stars** are companies that have a large share of a fast-growing market. To take advantage of a star's fast-growing market and its strength in that market (large share), the corporation must invest substantially in it. The investment is usually worthwhile, however, because many stars produce sizable future profits. **Question marks** are companies

Acquisition the purchase of a company by another company

Unrelated diversification creating or acquiring companies in completely unrelated businesses

BCG matrix a portfolio strategy developed by the Boston Consulting Group that categorizes a corporation's businesses by growth rate and relative market share and helps managers decide how to invest corporate funds

Star a company with a large share of a fast-growing market

Question mark a company with a small share of a fast-growing market

Exhibit 6.4
Boston Consulting Group Matrix

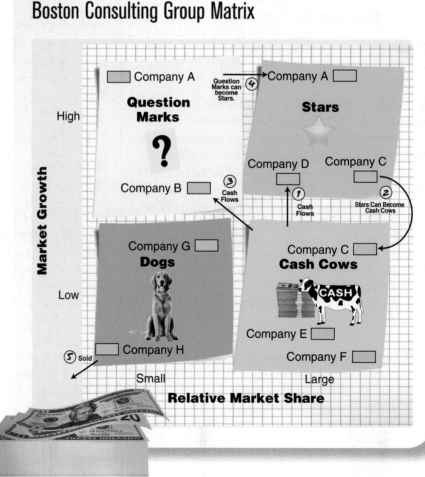

that have a small share of a fast-growing market. If the corporation invests in these companies, they may eventually become stars, but their relative weakness in the market (small share) makes investing in question marks riskier than investing in stars. **Cash cows** are companies that have a large share of a slow-growing market. Companies in this situation are often highly profitable, hence the name "cash cow." Finally, **dogs** are companies that have a small share of a slow-growing market. As the name suggests, having a small share of a slow-growth market is often not profitable.

Because the idea is to redirect investment from slow-growing to fast-growing companies, the BCG matrix starts by recommending that while the substantial cash flows from cash cows last, they should be reinvested in stars (see 1 in Exhibit 6.4) to help them grow even faster and obtain even more market share. Using this strategy, current profits help produce future profits. Over time, as their market growth slows, some stars may turn into cash cows (see 2). Cash flows should also be directed to some question marks (see 3). Though riskier than stars, question marks have great potential because of their fast-growing market. Managers must decide which question marks are most likely to turn into stars and therefore warrant further investment and which ones are too risky and should be sold. Over time, managers hope some question marks will become stars as their small markets become large ones (see 4). Finally, because dogs lose money, the corporation should "find them new owners" or "take them to the pound." In other words, dogs should either be sold to other companies or closed down and liquidated for their assets (see 5).

Although the BCG matrix and other forms of portfolio strategy are relatively popular among managers, portfolio strategy has some drawbacks. The most significant drawback is that contrary to the predictions of portfolio strategy, the evidence suggests that acquiring unrelated businesses is *not* useful. As shown in Exhibit 6.5, there is a U-shaped relationship between diversification and risk. The left side of the curve shows that single businesses with no diversification are extremely risky (if the single business fails, the entire business fails). So, in part, the portfolio strategy of diversifying is correct—competing in a variety of different businesses can lower risk. However, portfolio strategy is partly wrong, too—the right side of the curve shows that conglomerates composed of completely unrelated businesses are even riskier than single, undiversified businesses.

A second set of problems with portfolio strategy has to do with the dysfunctional consequences that can

Exhibit 6.5
U-Shaped Relationship between Diversification and Risk

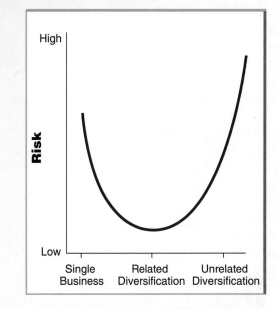

Source: M. Lubatkin & P.J. Lane, "Psst! . . . The Merger Mavens Still Have It Wrong," *Academy of Management* Executive 10 (1996) 21–39.

occur when companies are categorized as stars, cash cows, question marks, or dogs. Contrary to expectations, the BCG matrix often yields incorrect judgments about a company's potential. In other words, managers using the BCG matrix aren't very good at accurately determining which companies should be categorized as stars, cash cows, questions marks, or dogs. The most common mistake is simply miscategorizing highly profitable companies as dogs.[45] In part, this is because the BCG matrix relies on past performance (previous market share and previous market growth), which is a notoriously poor predictor of future company performance. More worrisome, however, is research that indicates the BCG matrix actually makes managers worse at judging the future profitability of a business. A study conducted in six countries over five years gave managers and business students clear information about the current and future profits (that is, slow or fast growth) of three companies and asked them to select the one that would be most successful in the future. Although not labeled this way, one company

Cash cow a company with a large share of a slow-growing market

Dog a company with a small share of a slow-growing market

Adidas—Three Stripes Are Out

When looking at the performance of the U.S. division of **Adidas AG**, it is fair to ask if the company has a bad strategy, bad execution, or both. In 2010, Adidas executives launched a strategic plan to generate sales growth of more than 45 percent by 2015. After four years, however, the company had negative sales growth and a 10 percent market share, well below Nike and Under Armour. Despite landing a contract to supply the NBA with jerseys, Adidas failed to sign key NBA players to endorse the brand, allowing Nike, adept at signing top talent, to capture more than 90 percent of the basketball-shoe retail market. Adidas faces additional challenges connecting with fickle U.S. consumers whose primary sports interest is not professional soccer. In response, Adidas is working to shorten its product development cycle from eighteen to six months. President Mark King is optimistic of Adidas's strategy and execution, saying, "We have so many assets that nobody knows about, and if we could tell those stories in a much better, U.S.-centric way, this brand . . . could definitely change its cool factor."

Source: E. E. Jervell and S. Germano, "How Adidas Aims to Get Its Cool Back," *Wall Street Journal*, March 22, 2015. http://www.wsj.com/articles/how-adidas-aims-to-get-its-cool-back-1427072066.

Nike has gained a major advantage over Adidas in the shoe and apparel industry by signing stars like Kevin Durant to large endorsement deals.

was clearly a star, another was a dog, and the last was a cash cow. Just exposing people to the ideas in the BCG matrix led them to incorrectly categorize less profitable businesses as the most successful businesses 64 percent of the time, while actually *using* the BCG matrix led to making the same mistake 87 percent of the time.[46]

Furthermore, using the BCG matrix can also weaken the strongest performer in the corporate portfolio: the cash cow. As funds are redirected from cash cows to stars, corporate managers essentially take away the resources needed to take advantage of the cash cow's new business opportunities. As a result, the cash cow becomes less aggressive in seeking new business or in defending its present business.

The Office productivity suite (Word, PowerPoint, Excel) has long been one of Microsoft's two cash cows (the other is its Windows operating system).[47] But with free alternatives, such as Google Docs, Apache's Open Office, and Apple's Pages, Numbers, and Keynote apps (free on every Mac computer, iPhone and

iPad), and strongly declining sales of PCs worldwide, Office, while still highly profitable, is facing major challenges that threaten its long-time dominance and ability to throw off cash.[48] These threats come at a time when Microsoft needs to divert cash from Office into its cloud-based file storage and Azure (cloud services, big data, servers, virtual machines, and website hosting) platforms to turn those questions marks into future stars, as well as its Surface tablets, a business which it hopes to transform from a dog to a question mark (and eventually a star). The risk, however, is that diverting cash from Office may make it less able to defend its current business or to grow by seeking new business.[49]

Finally, labeling a top performer as a cash cow can harm employee morale. Cash-cow employees realize that they have inferior status and that instead of working for themselves, they are now working to fund the growth of stars and question marks.

So, what kind of portfolio strategy does the best job of helping managers decide which companies to buy or sell? The U-shaped curve in Exhibit 6.5 indicates that, contrary to the predictions of portfolio strategy, the best approach is probably **related diversification**, in which the different business units share similar products, manufacturing, marketing, technology, or cultures. The key to related diversification is to acquire or create new companies with core capabilities that complement the core capabilities of businesses already in the corporate portfolio. Hormel Foods is an example of related diversification in the food business. The company both manufactures and markets a variety of foods, from deli meats to salsa to the infamous SPAM.

We began this section with the example of 3M and its 55,000 products sold in five different business groups. While seemingly different, most of 3M's product divisions are based in some fashion on its distinctive competencies in adhesives and tape (for example wet or dry sandpaper, Post-it notes, Scotchgard fabric protector, transdermal skin patches, and reflective material used in traffic signs). Furthermore, all of 3M's divisions share its strong corporate culture that promotes and encourages risk taking and innovation. In sum, in contrast to a single, undiversified business or unrelated diversification, related diversification reduces risk because the different businesses can work as a team, relying on each other for needed experience, expertise, and support.

6-3b Grand Strategies

A **grand strategy** is a broad strategic plan used to help an organization achieve its strategic goals.[50] Grand strategies guide the strategic alternatives that managers of individual businesses or subunits may use in deciding what businesses they should be in. There are three kinds of grand strategies: growth, stability, and retrenchment/recovery.

The purpose of a **growth strategy** is to increase profits, revenues, market share, or the number of places (stores, offices, locations) in which the company does business. Companies can grow in several ways. They can grow externally by merging with or acquiring other companies in the same or different businesses. AT&T is growing slowly at 3 percent per year. DirecTV, a satellite TV service, is growing at less than 1 percent a year. In hopes of accelerating growth for both companies, AT&T agreed to buy DirecTV for $48.5 billion. CBS News business analyst Jill Schlesinger says, "AT&T wants content. DirecTV has content."[51] AT&T is also interested in selling phone services to DirecTV's 18 million customers in Latin America. But the primary benefit that could accelerate growth for both companies is the ability to combine and discount their services for consumers. For example, instead of paying more to buy separate Internet, TV (subscription and pay TV packages), and wireless phone services, DirecTV's 20 million customers and AT&T's 107 million customers would then be able to buy those services together in a discounted bundle.[52]

Another way to grow is internally, directly expanding the company's existing business or creating and growing new businesses. In 2015, Amazon expanded its online e-tail business with several new selling platforms. Handmade at Amazon, a handicraft marketplace similar to Etsy.com, launched with 5,000 artisans from sixty countries selling 80,000 handmade items. Amazon charges vendors a 12 percent commission, but provides them with the same shipping services it offers its Marketplace sellers. Amazon Home Services, a referral service similar to Angie's List, connects consumers with professionals who perform home repairs, upkeep, and upgrades. More than 700 different services can be booked through the service, and rather than charge its customers, Amazon collects a commission on the value of the services from the professionals who provide them. Finally, in its first move away from e-commerce, Amazon recently opened the first of 400 planned brick-and-mortar stores selling books, Kindle e-readers, and Fire tablets.[53]

The purpose of a **stability strategy** is to continue doing what the company has been doing, just doing it better. Companies following a stability strategy try to improve the way in which they sell the same products or services to the same customers. Since its inception in 1909 as a window-washing company in San Francisco, **ABM Industries** has focused on providing facility services to businesses. Today, ABM's 100,000 employees in the U.S. and twenty other countries offer facility services management for electrical and lighting solutions, energy management, building maintenance and repair,

Related diversification creating or acquiring companies that share similar products, manufacturing, marketing, technology, or cultures

Grand strategy a broad corporate-level strategic plan used to achieve strategic goals and guide the strategic alternatives that managers of individual businesses or subunits may use

Growth strategy a strategy that focuses on increasing profits, revenues, market share, or the number of places in which the company does business

Stability strategy a strategy that focuses on improving the way in which the company sells the same products or services to the same customers

janitorial services, landscape and ground maintenance, security, and parking services. In short, for more than 100 years, ABM has reduced costs by keeping businesses' facilities safe, clean, comfortable, and energy efficient.[54] Companies often choose a stability strategy when their external environment doesn't change much or after they have struggled with periods of explosive growth.

The purpose of a **retrenchment strategy** is to turn around very poor company performance by shrinking the size or scope of the business or, if a company is in multiple businesses, by closing or shutting down different lines of the business. The first step of a typical retrenchment strategy might include making significant cost reductions: laying off employees; closing poorly performing stores, offices, or manufacturing plants; or closing or selling entire lines of products or services.[55] Barclays Plc, a London-based bank for more than 300 years, got its start in 1690 when founders John Freame and Thomas Gould served as goldsmith bankers that, much like today's banks, stored gold and money, made loans, transferred deposits from account to account, and handled foreign exchange currencies.[56] By 2008, Barclays aspired to become a global bank serving customers, businesses, and investors worldwide. In 2014, however, following numerous financial scandals and poor financial performance, Barclays began an aggressive retrenchment strategy. Chairman Michael Rake said, "It's just no longer doable for us to be a global, universal bank."[57] Following a strategy that Rake termed "bold simplification," Barclays will cut 19,000 employees by 2016, exit commodities trading, sell half of its investment bank, and sell its retail banking operations in France, Spain, and Italy. Rake explained that, "In the future, Barclays will be leaner, stronger, much better balanced and well positioned to deliver lower volatility, higher returns and growth. My goal is unchanged: to create a Barclays that does business in the right way, with the right values, and delivers the returns that our shareholders deserve. However, the way in which we will achieve this is different."[58]

After cutting costs and reducing a business's size or scope, the second step in a retrenchment strategy is recovery. **Recovery** consists of the strategic actions that a company takes to return to a growth strategy. This two-step process of cutting and recovery is analogous to pruning roses. Prior to each growing season, roses should be cut back to two-thirds their normal size. Pruning doesn't damage the roses; it makes them stronger and more likely to produce beautiful, fragrant flowers. The retrenchment-and-recovery process is similar.

Like pruning, the cuts are made as part of a recovery strategy intended to allow companies to eventually return to a successful growth strategy. When company performance drops significantly, a strategy of retrenchment and recovery may help the company return to a successful growth strategy.

After three years of slumping sales due to an overly complex menu and increased competition from fast-casual restaurants, McDonald's returned to basics with a recovery strategy called "Plan to Win." In addition to simplifying its menu, McDonald's took several bold steps under this initiative:

▶ Renovate existing locations rather than build new ones.

▶ Increase font sizes on orders so that cooks can read them correctly.

▶ Make the most of the core menu (by, for example, toasting hamburger buns longer and searing hamburgers so they're juicier).

▶ Institute all-day breakfast (which used to end at 10:30 a.m.).

▶ Reduce employee turnover by increasing crew pay.

CEO Steve Easterbrook said about the new strategy, "Our goal is net simplification. We want to focus on fewer, bigger decisions that generate bigger reward."[59] After nine months, same-store sales rose 6.2 percent and profits soared by 35 percent.[60]

6-4 INDUSTRY-LEVEL STRATEGIES

Industry-level strategy addresses the question, "How should we compete in this industry?"

Let's find out more about industry-level strategies by discussing 6-4a the five industry forces that determine overall levels of competition in an industry as well as 6-4b the positioning strategies and 6-4c adaptive

---

Retrenchment strategy a strategy that focuses on turning around very poor company performance by shrinking the size or scope of the business

Recovery the strategic actions taken after retrenchment to return to a growth strategy

Industry-level strategy a corporate strategy that addresses the question, "How should we compete in this industry?"

Exhibit 6.6
Porter's Five Industry Forces

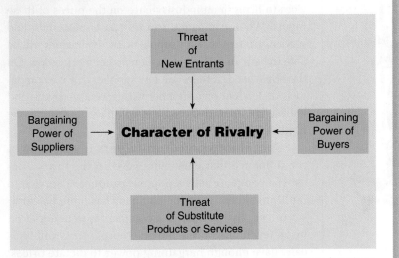

Source: Based on the Simon & Schuster, Inc. Porter, M. E. *Competitive Strategy: Techniques for Analyzing Industries and Competitors.* New York: Free Press, 1980.

strategies that companies can use to achieve sustained competitive advantage and above-average profits.

6-4a Five Industry Forces

According to Harvard professor Michael Porter, five industry forces determine an industry's overall attractiveness and potential for long-term profitability: the character of the rivalry, the threat of new entrants, the threat of substitute products or services, the bargaining power of suppliers, and the bargaining power of buyers. The stronger these forces, the less attractive the industry becomes to corporate investors because it is more difficult for companies to be profitable. Porter's industry forces are illustrated in Exhibit 6.6. Let's examine how these forces are bringing changes to several kinds of industries.

Character of the rivalry is a measure of the intensity of competitive behavior among companies in an industry. Is the competition among firms aggressive and cutthroat, or do competitors focus more on serving customers than on attacking each other? Both industry attractiveness and profitability decrease when rivalry is cutthroat. For example, selling cars is a highly competitive business. Pick up a local newspaper on Friday, Saturday, or Sunday morning, and you'll find dozens of pages of car advertising ("Anniversary Sale-A-Bration,"

"Ford March Savings!" and "$99 Down, You Choose!"). In fact, competition in new-car sales is so intense that if it weren't for used-car sales, repair work, and replacement parts, many auto dealers would actually lose money.

The **threat of new entrants** is a measure of the degree to which barriers to entry make it easy or difficult for new companies to get started in an industry. If new companies can enter the industry easily, then competition will increase, and prices and profits will fall. Altos Research provides real-time statistics and analysis of real estate markets for investors and news services such as Bloomberg Financial. Because its business relies on access to terabytes of market data, it leases computing power and data storage from Amazon Web Services (AWS), the market leader in cloud services. Without any negotiation, AWS cut its costs in half, enough to pay for two new programmers. On the other hand, if there are sufficient barriers to entry, such as large capital requirements to buy expensive equipment or plant facilities or the need for specialized knowledge, then competition will be weaker, and prices and profits will generally be higher. The automobile industry has traditionally had a high barrier to entry. So when Tesla entered the market in 2003 to manufacture a completely electric sports car, it was the first new car company in a generation. With billions of dollars in startup funding, the company hired thousands of engineers, built new manufacturing facilities, and created a complex supply chain to source, manufacture, and assemble 10,000 component parts. While its stock is valued at $30 billion, Tesla has never made a profit. In fact, the company has burned through $100 million a month in expenses since going public in 2010. With six new competitors poised to enter the automotive industry (including Apple, Google, and an upstart founded by a team of former Tesla executives), the barrier to entry is falling and competition is rising. Becoming profitable may take longer than Tesla planned as barriers to entry fall and competition rises.[61]

Character of the rivalry
a measure of the intensity of competitive behavior between companies in an industry

Threat of new entrants
a measure of the degree to which barriers to entry make it easy or difficult for new companies to get started in an industry

iStockphoto.com/bluehill75

The **threat of substitute products or services** is a measure of the ease with which customers can find substitutes for an industry's products or services. If customers can easily find substitute products or services, the competition will be greater, and profits will be lower. If there are few or no substitutes, competition will be weaker, and profits will be higher. Overnight delivery companies like UPS and DHL deliver millions of items every day. What would happen to these businesses if, instead of buying products and having them delivered, people could use 3-D printers to manufacture what they needed right at work or home? This new technology led UPS chief information officer Dave Barnes to wonder, "Should we be threatened by it or should we endorse it?"[62] To answer that question, UPS created a 3-D printing test center at its Louisville, Kentucky hub. There, UPS explored the feasibility of local production and delivery of 3-D printed items. The center's 100 industrial 3-D printers create everything from iPhone cases to replacement parts for UPS's fleet of Airbus A300 jets. DHL's initial studies show that just 2–4 percent of shipped products can reliably be 3-D printed. UPS, however, is purchasing 900 more 3-D printers for other locations. According to Barnes, "We saw the capability of a logistics company

to be challenged on one side but on the other [to] be an enabler."[63]

Bargaining power of suppliers is a measure of the influence that suppliers of parts, materials, and services to firms in an industry have on the prices of these inputs. When companies can buy parts, materials, and services from numerous suppliers, the companies will be able to bargain with the suppliers to keep prices low. On the other hand, if there are few suppliers, or if a company is dependent on a supplier with specialized skills and knowledge, then the suppliers will have the bargaining power to dictate price levels.

Bargaining power of buyers is a measure of the influence that customers have on the firm's prices. If a company sells a popular product or service to multiple buyers, then the company has more power to set prices. By contrast, if a company is dependent on just a few high-volume buyers, those buyers will typically have enough bargaining power to dictate prices. Walmart's 11,000 stores and 245 million weekly customers give it incredible bargaining power over suppliers. Walmart is far and away the largest and most important buyer (or customer) for many of its suppliers, so it is in suppliers' best interests to stay on Walmart's good side. In the past, Walmart has used its bargaining power to enforce strict guidelines regarding everything from pricing to short delivery windows to data management. In 2015, Walmart unveiled new supplier payment terms that put a greater emphasis on fast-selling items. For example, Walmart now charges suppliers for the warehouse space it uses to store their products. It also charges a premium fee for shelf space in newer Walmart locations. Amidst these changes, Walmart announced that it would discount a supplier's bill by 1 percent if the supplier paid early (before each bill came due). Some analysts suspect that there were significant discussions between Walmart and suppliers before the new program was announced, but retail analyst Budd Bugatch suspects that Walmart and its suppliers have an incredibly uneven partnership: "No supplier will happily accept less payment and/or longer payment terms . . . Walmart is clearly the senior partner."[64]

6-4b Positioning Strategies

After analyzing industry forces, the next step in industry-level strategy is to protect your company from the negative effects of industry-wide competition and to create a sustainable competitive advantage. According to Michael Porter, there are three positioning strategies: cost leadership, differentiation, and focus.

Surfer Troy Williams rides a wave off the coast of Ventura, California on a $99 Wavestorm surfboard.

Cost leadership means producing a product or service of acceptable quality at consistently lower production costs than competitors so that the firm can offer the product or service at the lowest price in the industry. Cost leadership protects companies from industry forces by deterring new entrants, who will have to match low costs and prices. Cost leadership also forces down the prices of substitute products and services, attracts bargain-seeking buyers, and increases bargaining power with suppliers, who have to keep their prices low if they want to do business with the cost leader. With entry-level surfboards costing $300 and top-of-the-line, handmade longboards going for $1,000 or more, surfing is expensive. Those high prices inspired Matt Zilinskas to create Wavestorm, an 8-foot, mass-produced soft-foam surfboard that sells for $99 at Costco. Now the industry's best-selling surfboard, Wavestorm's sales are so strong that other retailers have stopped selling more expensive soft-foam boards altogether. "Why even bother when you can go to Costco [and get one for] $100?" asked Cody Quarress, manager at the Huntington Surf & Sport.[65] Zilinkas has received complaints from competitors, but he sees his product as beneficial to the industry: "How many of the hundreds of thousands of people who bought our board have moved on to higher-end product? Ask any surfer in the water about Wavestorm. They probably own one."[66]

Differentiation means making your product or service sufficiently different from competitors' offerings that customers are willing to pay a premium price for the extra value or performance that it provides. Differentiation protects companies from industry forces by reducing the threat of substitute products. It also protects companies by making it easier to retain customers and more difficult for new entrants trying to attract new customers. Would you pay $113 for a mop? Or $26.99 for a polishing cloth? Norway-based Norwex makes premium-priced cleaning products that clean your house with water and no chemicals or cleaning agents. For instance, a Norwex Microfiber cloth contains microfibers that are 1/200th the thickness of a human hair.[67] The microfibers capture and can hold seven times their weight, which means that they capture dirt, grease, and moisture. Does it work? Microbiologist Kristen Gibson says, "A damp microfiber cloth is a really good tool for removing microorganisms, including viruses and bacteria."[68] Her research, funded by the U.S. Department of Agriculture, found that microfibers removed viruses, unlike typical cloth towels that simply spread viruses from one surface to another. Norwex advises using the cloths dry to dust and wet (with water) to clean. And while its products are expensive, with the average family spending $600–800 a year on cleaning supplies and chemicals, Norwex claims that consumers save time and money because its products are reusable.[69]

With a **focus strategy**, a company uses either cost leadership or differentiation to produce a specialized product or service for a limited, specially targeted group of customers in a particular geographic region or market segment. Focus strategies typically work in market niches that competitors have overlooked or have difficulty serving. Once a week, Mike Hallatt drives from Vancouver, B.C., to the nearest **Trader Joe's** in Bellingham, Washington, where he buys $6,000 of Trader Joe's merchandise. Hallatt marks up his purchases by an average of $2 and sells them at **Pirate Joe's**, his Vancouver grocery store that is an unapologetic knockoff of Trader Joe's. Hallett says Pirate Joe's is, "an unaffiliated unauthorized re-seller of Trader Joe's products (we were sued, they lost, now they are appealing)."[70] Because Trader Joe's has no plans to enter Canada, Hallatt is able to focus on Canadians—in Vancouver and afar (www.piratejoes.ca will soon be ready for Internet shopping)—who

Cost leadership the positioning strategy of producing a product or service of acceptable quality at consistently lower production costs than competitors can, so that the firm can offer the product or service at the lowest price in the industry

Differentiation the positioning strategy of providing a product or service that is sufficiently different from competitors' offerings that customers are willing to pay a premium price for it

Focus strategy the positioning strategy of using cost leadership or differentiation to produce a specialized product or service for a limited, specially targeted group of customers in a particular geographic region or market segment

Pirate Joe's slogan is "Unauthorized, Unaffiliated, Unafriad." This refers to the pressure by North American grocer, Trader Joe's, to change their name.

Pirate Joe's

want to buy Trader Joe's grocery products without crossing the Canadian border. Hallatt says, "We'll ship anywhere in Canada, but if we start getting orders from Japan, why not?"[71]

6-4c Adaptive Strategies

Adaptive strategies are another set of industry-level strategies. Whereas the aim of positioning strategies is to minimize the effects of industry competition and build a sustainable competitive advantage, the purpose of adaptive strategies is to choose an industry-level strategy that is best suited to changes in the organization's external environment. There are four kinds of adaptive strategies: defenders, prospectors, analyzers, and reactors.[72]

Defenders seek moderate, steady growth by offering a limited range of products and services to a well-defined set of customers. In other words, defenders aggressively "defend" their current strategic position by doing the best job they can to hold on to customers in a particular market segment.

Not surprisingly, ultra-premium carmakers, such as **Ferrari** and **Aston-Martin**, are not as interested in growth as they are in retaining the luxury brand image. That's because higher sales volume leads to ubiquity, which makes it harder to charge premium pricing. The retail price of a new Ferrari California is roughly $200,000, but a new LaFerrari model has an MSRP of $1.4 million. To retain is exclusivity, Ferrari has a self-imposed production cap of 7,000 vehicles a year. At Aston Martin, the level is much lower, at 4,000 cars per year. "This is not a car company that is ever going to be selling a lot of cars," said Andy Palmer, CEO of Aston Martin. "Part of its mystique is its exclusivity."[73]

Prospectors seek fast growth by searching for new market opportunities, encouraging risk taking, and being the first to bring innovative new products to market. Prospectors are analogous to gold miners who "prospect" for gold nuggets (that is, new products) in hope that the nuggets will lead them to a rich deposit of gold (that is, fast growth). 3M has long been known for its innovative products, particularly in the area of adhesives. Since 1904, it has invented sandpaper;

Defenders companies using an adaptive strategy aimed at defending strategic positions by seeking moderate, steady growth and by offering a limited range of high-quality products and services to a well-defined set of customers

Prospectors companies using an adaptive strategy that seeks fast growth by searching for new market opportunities, encouraging risk taking, and being the first to bring innovative new products to market

THE POSTAL SERVICE GETS BACK IN THE GAME

Having reported losses for the past twenty-one of twenty-three quarters, the **United States Postal Service** (USPS) is looking to attract new business, particularly in the online retail market. So, when FedEx and UPS announced prices increases for ground shipments ahead of the holiday season, the USPS responded by cutting its prices in half for customers who ship more than 50,000 packages a year. It's only one strategy the agency is using to increase its market share. USPS has begun offering Sunday delivery and is testing grocery delivery for Amazon in the San Francisco area. And the agency plans to invest $10 billion on new trucks and sorting equipment to help it become more competitive.

Source: L. Stevens, "U.S. Mail Cuts Prices, Chafing UPS and FedEx," *Wall Street Journal*, September 5, 2014, B1; G. Bensinger and L. Stevens, "Amazon Tries U.S. Mail for Groceries," *Wall Street Journal*, September 5, 2014, B2.

masking, cellophane, electrical, and Scotch tapes; the first commercially available audiotapes and videotapes; and its most famous invention, Post-it notes. Lately, 3M has invented a film that increases the brightness of LCD displays on laptop computers; developed a digital system for construction companies to detect underground telecommunication, gas, water, sewer, or electrical lines without digging; and created a pheromone spray that, by preventing harmful insects from mating, will protect apple, walnut, tomato, cranberry, and grape crops. For more on 3M's innovative products, see the 3M innovation archive (http://solutions.3m.com /innovation/en_US/).

Analyzers are the blend of the defender and prospector strategies. They seek moderate, steady growth and limited opportunities for fast growth. Analyzers are rarely first to market with new products or services. Instead, they try to simultaneously minimize risk and maximize profits by following or imitating the proven successes of prospectors.

When Pope Francis visited New York City in 2015, 20,000 people rented places to stay via Airbnb. Airbnb allows homeowners to market and rent rooms, entire homes, condos, and castles—yes, even castles—to travelers who might otherwise have stayed at hotels.[74] Since its founding in 2008, 60 million people have stayed at Airbnb-rented locations in 34,000 cities across 191 countries.[75] Airbnb didn't invent the business of short-term room sharing, however. In 1995, VRBO (Vacation Rentals by Owner), now part of HomeAway, began renting homes to vacation travelers. Although similar (roughly 6% of properties are listed on both sites), HomeAway rents entire homes or condos (40% owned by property management companies) in popular vacation spots, whereas Airbnb also rents independent single rooms in cities across the country. While Airbnb is one of the best-known companies in this market that uses an analyzer strategy, it is not the only one. Kidandcoe.com rents family friendly units, while Villas.com (part of Booking.com) rents more than 420,000 vacation homes, apartments, and, of course, villas.[76]

Finally, unlike defenders, prospectors, or analyzers, **reactors** do not follow a consistent strategy. Rather than anticipating and preparing for external opportunities and threats, reactors tend to react to changes in their external environment after they occur. Not surprisingly, reactors tend to be poorer performers than defenders, prospectors, or analyzers. A reactor approach is inherently unstable, and firms that fall into this mode of operation must change their approach or face almost certain failure.

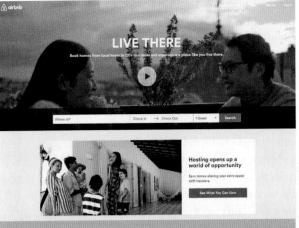

Courtesy of Airbnb

Since Airbnb's founding in 2008, 60 million people have booked rentals in 34,000 cities across 191 countries.

6-5 FIRM-LEVEL STRATEGIES

Apple unveils its Apple Watch with advanced fitness tracking and FitBit counters with the Blaze, which has a color touchscreen and syncs automatically with your phone. Starbucks Coffee opens a store, and nearby locally run coffeehouses respond by improving service, increasing portions, and holding the line on prices. In the German luxury car industry, **BMW**, **Audi**, and **Mercedes** have an intense three-way rivalry that goes well beyond sales volume to include investments in technology, quality rankings, and profitability. According to one Audi executive, to get approval for a new project, "I just have to say BMW is already doing it, and it goes through." The rivalry is just as heated over at BMW. When it comes to Audi, one BMW executive said, "We like to stick it to them."[77] Attack and respond, respond and attack. **Firm-level strategy** addresses the question, "How should we compete against a particular firm?"

Let's find out more about the firm-level strategies (direct competition between companies) by

Analyzers companies using an adaptive strategy that seeks to minimize risk and maximize profits by following or imitating the proven successes of prospectors

Reactors companies that do not follow a consistent adaptive strategy but instead react to changes in the external environment after they occur

Firm-level strategy a corporate strategy that addresses the question, "How should we compete against a particular firm?"

*reading about **6-5a the basics of direct competition** and **6-5b the strategic moves involved in direct competition between companies.***

6-5a Direct Competition

Although Porter's five industry forces indicate the overall level of competition in an industry, most companies do not compete directly with all the firms in their industry. For example, McDonald's and Red Lobster are both in the restaurant business, but no one would characterize them as competitors. McDonald's offers low-cost, convenient fast food in a seat-yourself restaurant, while Red Lobster offers mid-priced seafood dinners complete with servers and a bar.

Instead of competing with an entire industry, most firms compete directly with just a few companies within it. **Direct competition** is the rivalry between two companies offering similar products and services that acknowledge each other as rivals and take offensive and defensive positions as they act and react to each other's strategic actions.[78] Two factors determine the extent to which firms will be in direct competition with each other: market commonality and resource similarity. **Market commonality** is the degree to which two companies have overlapping products, services, or customers in multiple markets. The more markets in which there is product, service, or customer overlap, the more intense the direct competition between the two companies. **Resource similarity** is the extent to which a competitor has similar amounts and kinds of resources, that is, similar assets, capabilities, processes, information, and knowledge used to create and sustain an advantage over competitors. From a competitive standpoint, resource similarity means that your direct competitors can probably match the strategic actions that your company takes.

Direct competition the rivalry between two companies that offer similar products and services, acknowledge each other as rivals, and act and react to each other's strategic actions

Market commonality the degree to which two companies have overlapping products, services, or customers in multiple markets

Resource similarity the extent to which a competitor has similar amounts and kinds of resources

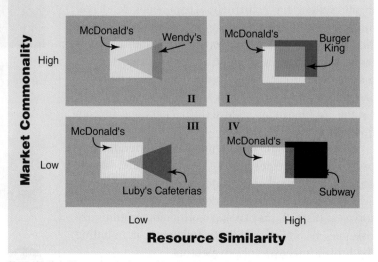

Exhibit 6.7
A Framework of Direct Competition

Source: M. Chen, "Competitor Analysis and InterFirm Rivalry: Toward a Theoretical Integration," *Academy of Management Review* 21 (1996): 100–134.

Exhibit 6.7 shows how market commonality and resource similarity interact to determine when and where companies are in direct competition.[79] The overlapping area in each quadrant (between the triangle and the rectangle, or between the differently colored rectangles) depicts market commonality. The larger the overlap, the greater the market commonality. Shapes depict resource similarity, with rectangles representing one set of competitive resources and triangles representing another. Quadrant I shows two companies in direct competition because they have similar resources at their disposal and a high degree of market commonality. These companies try to sell similar products and services to similar customers. McDonald's and Burger King would clearly fit here as direct competitors. While we normally think about them competing to sell hamburgers, with wholesale beef prices near record highs, they're also direct competitors when it comes to selling chicken. For example, after McDonald's began selling fifty chicken nuggets for $9.99 (or 20 cents each), Burger King responded by selling ten-packs of chicken nuggets for $1.49.[80]

In Quadrant II, the overlapping parts of the triangle and rectangle show two companies going after similar customers with some similar products or services but doing so with different competitive resources. McDonald's and Wendy's restaurants would fit here.

Wendy's is after the same lunchtime and dinner crowds that McDonald's is. Nevertheless, with its more expensive hamburgers, fries, shakes, and salads, Wendy's is less of a direct competitor to McDonald's than Burger King is. For example, Wendy's has recently rebranded itself more like a casual dining restaurant, redesigning its locations with lounge seating, fireplaces, Wi-Fi, and digital menu boards.[81] Wendy's goal is to convert 85 percent of its company-owned locations and 35 percent of its franchised stores by 2017.[82] Even though Wendy's competes less directly with McDonald's, there are signs that McDonald's may be shifting its strategy to compete more directly with Wendy's by upgrading its menu to include a premium burger priced around $5 and a grilled chicken sandwich with Applewood smoked bacon, caramelized onions, and an artisan roll.[83]

In Quadrant III, the very small overlap shows two companies with different competitive resources and little market commonality. McDonald's and Luby's cafeterias fit here. Although both are in the fast-food business, there's almost no overlap in terms of products and customers. Luby's sells baked chicken, turkey, roasts, meat loaf, and vegetables, none of which are available at McDonald's. Furthermore, Luby's customers aren't likely to eat at McDonald's. In fact, Luby's is not really competing with other fast-food restaurants, but with eating at home. Company surveys show that close to half of its customers would have eaten at home, not at another restaurant, if they hadn't come to Luby's.[84]

Finally, in Quadrant IV, the small overlap between the two rectangles shows that McDonald's and Subway compete with similar resources but with little market commonality. In terms of resources, sales at McDonald's are much larger, but Subway has grown substantially in the past decade and now has 43,916 stores in 98 countries, compared to McDonald's with 36,525 stores in nearly 100 countries.[85]

Though Subway and McDonald's compete, they aren't direct competitors in terms of market commonality in the way that McDonald's and Burger King are because Subway, unlike McDonald's, sells itself as a provider of healthy fast food. Thus, the overlap is much smaller in Quadrant IV than in Quadrant I. With detailed nutritional information available in its stores, and its close relationships with the American Heart Association, the American College of Cardiologists, and Heart Research UK, Subway has long focused on healthy eating and well being.[86]

6-5b Strategic Moves of Direct Competition

While corporate-level strategies help managers decide what business to be in, and industry-level strategies help them determine how to compete within an industry, firm-level strategies help managers determine when, where, and what strategic actions should be taken against a direct competitor. Firms in direct competition can make two basic strategic moves: attack and response. These moves occur all the time in virtually every industry, but they are most noticeable in industries where multiple large competitors are pursuing customers in the same market space.

T-Mobile has launched a strategic initiative aimed at removing key restrictions found in its competitors' wireless services.

Northfoto/Shutterstock.com

Dollar Shave Club is an online service that sells razor blades and accessories via subscription plans.

An **attack** is a competitive move designed to reduce a rival's market share or profits. Gillette dominates the $3.3 billion U.S. shaving business, earning an enormous 32 percent profit on each blade. Dollar Shave Club, an online service selling razor blades via subscription plans, attacked Gillette with substantially lower prices. While Gillette cartridges cost $3.50 to $6.00 each, Dollar Shave Club's entry-level plan, the Humble Twin, charges only $0.20 per cartridge and $2.00 per month for shipping. Dollar Shave Club quickly amassed nearly 53 percent of the online market for razors and blades.[87]

A **response** is a countermove, prompted by a rival's attack, that is designed to defend or improve a company's market share or profit. There are two kinds of responses.[88] The first is to match or mirror your competitor's move. This is what Gillette did when it launched the online Gillette Shave Club, which offers three subscription plans, free shipping on all orders, loyalty rewards, and sweepstakes for entertainment and major-league sports tickets.[89]

The second kind of response, however, is to respond along a different dimension from your competitor's move or attack. Wireless carriers, such at AT&T, Verizon, and Sprint, have typically responded to competitors' attacks by cutting prices, expanding coverage, or speeding up their networks. T-Mobile, the smallest of the major wireless carriers, faired poorly on those dimensions and lost 2 million customers as a result four years ago.[90] In the past three years, however, T-Mobile has grown from 33 million to 63 million customers, increasing its share of the U.S. wireless market from 10–17 percent. The company achieved this remarkable growth by responding with an "uncarrier" strategy that removes key restrictions found in its competitors' wireless services.[91] Overage charges? Not at T-Mobile, which offers unlimited minutes, texts, and data (go beyond your data "cap," and T-Mobile slows down your data rather than charge you). Exorbitant roaming charges for international plans? T-Mobile charges a meager 20 cents per minute for international calls, while providing unlimited international data and texts at no extra charge in 120 countries. Moreover, with 35 percent of U.S. international calls and 55 percent of U.S. international travel to Mexico and Canada, T-Mobile has consolidated all three countries into one North American market in which access to data plans, 4G LTE fast connections, and calling are included—at no extra cost—for T-Mobile customers. Finally, streaming music and video on your phone? Thirty minutes a day uses 900 megabytes a month against the typical 1 or 2 gigabyte data plan. At T-Mobile, though, streaming music does NOT count against data usage for more than 100 music and video services, including Amazon Video, HBO NOW, Hulu, Netflix, YouTube, Apple Music, Google Music, Pandora, Rhapsody, and Spotify.[92]

Market commonality and resource similarity determine the likelihood of an attack or response, that is, whether a company is likely to attack a direct competitor or to strike back with a strong response when attacked. When market commonality is large, and companies have overlapping products, services, or customers in multiple markets, there is less motivation to attack and more motivation to respond to an attack. The reason for this is straightforward: when firms are direct competitors in a large number of markets, they have a great deal at stake.

Airlines Air France-KLM and Lufthansa once dominated highly lucrative routes between Europe's and Asia's largest cities. That is, until Middle Eastern carriers such as Emirates Airlines and Etihad Airways attacked their market shares and profits by offering high-end amenities such as private suites, onboard showers, and a bar in first class. The European carriers quickly took note, with Air France-KLM CEO Alexandre de Juniac saying, "The Gulf carriers have significantly captured market share."[93] Market commonality is extensive in the airline industry. With so much at stake, Germany-based Lufthansa responded by spending $3.4 billion for 650 new first-class seats, 7,000 business-class seats that lie flat (for sleeping),

Attack a competitive move designed to reduce a rival's market share or profits

Response a competitive countermove, prompted by a rival's attack, to defend or improve a company's market share or profit

and upgrades to premium economy seating and in-flight entertainment. Air France-KLM responded similarly, spending $1.1 billion to install private, first-class suites on forty-four planes and replace economy-class seating.[94]

Whereas market commonality affects the likelihood of an attack or a response to an attack, resource similarity largely affects response capability, that is, how quickly and forcefully a company can respond to an attack. When resource similarity is strong, the responding firm will generally be able to match the strategic moves of the attacking firm. Consequently, a firm is less likely to attack firms with similar levels of resources because it is unlikely to gain any sustained advantage when the responding firms strike back. On the other hand, if one firm is substantially stronger than another (that is, there is low resource similarity), then a competitive attack is more likely to produce sustained competitive advantage.

In general, the more moves (that is, attacks) a company initiates against direct competitors, and the greater a company's tendency to respond when attacked, the better its performance. More specifically, attackers and early responders (companies that are quick to launch a retaliatory attack) tend to gain market share and profits at the expense of late responders. This is not to suggest that a full-attack strategy always works best. In fact, attacks can provoke harsh retaliatory responses.

When Amazon unveiled its first showrooming app, brick-and-mortar retailers were outraged. When users scanned a barcode, the app would direct them to the same product on Amazon.com and provide a coupon for a discount and free shipping. The Firefly app on Amazon's Fire phone, as well as the Amazon App for iPhone and Android phones, can now recognize more than 70 million products just by taking a picture. A mobile industry analyst calls this "showrooming on steroids." According to IDC, a market research firm, one out of five shoppers uses a mobile device to make purchases from online retailers while store shopping at brick-and-mortar retailers.[95]

Best Buy is the world's largest electronics retailer. Today, 60 percent of its consumers "showroom shop," looking at products in Best Buy stores and then checking their smartphones to find prices at online stores like Amazon. Best Buy responded aggressively to Amazon's showrooming app by matching online prices year round in its stores, offering deep Black Friday discounts the day after Thanksgiving (typically the heaviest shopping day of the year), and instituting a low-price guarantee. Best Buy's retaliatory responses, however, have come at a steep cost, with profits dropping over 90 percent and the announcement of more than fifty store closings in 2012 alone.[96] Best Buy's sales are down more than 20 percent overall, and the company has closed more than 2,500 stores in the United States and abroad. CFO Sharon McCollam expects the trend to continue saying, "We have well over 100 [lease] expirations coming [in 2016], and we will continue to do what we have been doing, which is methodically rationalize the real estate portfolio."[97] Consequently, when deciding when, where, and what strategic actions to take against a direct competitor, managers should always consider the possibility of retaliation.

STUDY TOOLS 6

LOCATED IN TEXTBOOK
☐ Rip-out and review chapter review card

LOCATED AT WWW.CENGAGEBRAIN.COM
☐ Review key term flashcards and create your own from StudyBits
☐ Track your knowledge and understanding of key concepts, using the concept tracker

☐ Complete practice and graded quizzes to prepare for tests
☐ Complete interactive content within the exposition
☐ View chapter highlight box content at the beginning of each chapter

7 Innovation and Change

Syda Productions/Shutterstock.com

LEARNING OUTCOMES

7-1 Explain why innovation matters to companies.

7-2 Discuss the different methods that managers can use to effectively manage innovation in their organizations.

7-3 Discuss why not changing can lead to organizational decline.

7-4 Discuss the different methods that managers can use to better manage change as it occurs.

After you finish this chapter, go to **PAGE 155** for **STUDY TOOLS**

7-1 WHY INNOVATION MATTERS

As you approach your office parking garage, the LED lights inside brighten. Prompted by an app on your smartphone, the garage camera matches your license plate to your personnel record, raises the gate, and locates a parking space. Inside the office, the same app finds a desk based on your schedule and preferences (standing desk, sitting desk, work booth, concentration room, or meeting room). Before setting off to your desk, you drop your coat and personal belongings in an empty locker (indicated by a green light), using your ID badge to unlock it. As you arrive at your desk, the temperature and lighting automatically adjust to the personal preferences you set in the app. A central dashboard collects data on everything from energy usage to when the espresso machines—which, naturally, remember how you like your coffee—need to be refilled. The northfacing exterior wall is glass, while the south-facing exterior wall is composed of an alternating pattern of windows and solar panels that generate more electricity than the building uses. And when everyone leaves for the day, small security robots begin their patrol while other robots clean the rooms that were most heavily used that day. Sound futuristic? It's not. This unbelievable account is routine at **the Edge**, a smart building in Amsterdam where a complex network of cables and 28,000 sensors connects the building, its mechanical structures (heating, ventilation, plumbing, and electricity), technological systems, and occupants via a smartphone app.[1] **Organizational innovation** is the successful implementation of creative ideas, like the construction of the Edge office building in Amsterdam (http://ovgrealestate.com /project-development/the-edge).

We can only guess what changes technological innovations will bring in the next twenty years. Will we carry computers in our pockets? Today's smartphones are a step in that direction. Will solar power and wind power get cheap and efficient enough so that your home can have a standalone power source off the main electrical grid? Will fully automated, self-driving cars chauffeur you (working in the back seat on a computing tablet via high-speed Internet) to work in the next decade? Who knows? The only thing we do know about the next twenty years is that innovation will continue to change our lives.

*Let's begin our discussion of innovation by learning about **7-1a technology cycles** and **7-2b innovation streams**.*

Exhibit 7.1
S-Curves and Technological Innovation

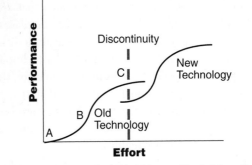

Source: R. N. Foster, *Innovation: The Attacker's Advantage* (New York: Summitt, 1986).

7-1a Technology Cycles

In Chapter 3, you learned that technology consists of the knowledge, tools, and techniques used to transform inputs (raw materials and information) into outputs (products and services). A **technology cycle** begins with the birth of a new technology and ends when that technology reaches its limits and dies as it is replaced by a newer, substantially better technology.[2] For example, technology cycles occurred when air conditioners supplanted fans, when Henry Ford's Model T replaced horse-drawn carriages, when planes replaced trains as a means of cross-country travel, when vaccines that prevented diseases replaced medicines designed to treat them, and when battery-powered wristwatches replaced mechanically powered, stem-wound wristwatches.

From Gutenberg's invention of the printing press in 1448 to the rapid advance of the Internet, studies of hundreds of technological innovations have shown that nearly all technology cycles follow the typical **S-curve pattern of innovation** shown in Exhibit 7.1.[3] Early in a technology cycle, there is still much to learn, so progress is slow, as depicted by point A on the S-curve. The flat slope indicates that increased effort

Organizational innovation the successful implementation of creative ideas in organizations

Technology cycle a cycle that begins with the birth of a new technology and ends when that technology reaches its limits and is replaced by a newer, substantially better technology

S-curve pattern of innovation a pattern of technological innovation characterized by slow initial progress, then rapid progress, and then slow progress again as a technology matures and reaches its limits

(in terms of money or research and development) brings only small improvements in technological performance.

Fortunately, as the new technology matures, researchers figure out how to get better performance from it. This is represented by point B of the S-curve in Exhibit 7.1. The steeper slope indicates that small amounts of effort will result in significant increases in performance. At point C, the flat slope again indicates that further efforts to develop this particular technology will result in only small increases in performance. More importantly, however, point C indicates that the performance limits of that particular technology are being reached. In other words, additional significant improvements in performance are highly unlikely.

Intel's technology cycles have followed this pattern. Intel spends billions to develop new computer chips and to build new facilities to produce them. Intel has found that the technology cycle for its integrated circuits is about three years. In each three-year cycle, Intel spends billions to introduce a new chip, improves the chip by making it a little bit faster each year, and then replaces that chip at the end of the cycle with a brand-new, different chip that is substantially faster than the old chip. At first, though (point A), the billions Intel spends typically produce only small improvements in performance. But after six months to a year with a new chip design, Intel's engineering and production people typically figure out how to make the new chips much faster than they were initially (point B). Yet, despite impressive gains in performance, Intel is unable to make a particular computer chip run any faster because the chip reaches its design limits.

After a technology has reached its limits at the top of the S-curve, significant improvements in performance usually come from radical new designs or new performance-enhancing materials. In Exhibit 7.1, that new technology is represented by the second S-curve. The changeover or discontinuity between the old and new technologies is represented by the dotted line. At first, the old and new technologies will likely coexist. Eventually, however, the new technology will replace the old technology. When that happens, the old technology cycle will be complete, and a new one will have started. The changeover between newer and older computer chip designs typically takes about one year. Over time, improving existing technology (tweaking the performance of the current technology cycle), combined with replacing old technology with new technology cycles (that is, new, faster computer chip designs replacing older ones), has increased the speed of

Intel's computer processors by a factor of 300. Today's super-powerful Xeon processors, which provide instantaneous processing and results, have 7.2 billion transistors compared to 3.1 million transistors for 1990s 32-bit processors, 275,000 transistors for the earliest 1980s 32-bit processors, or just 4,500 transistors for the 8-bit processors, which began personal computing in the 1970s.[4]

Though the evolution of Intel's chips has been used to illustrate S-curves and technology cycles, it's important to note that technology cycles and technological innovation don't necessarily involve faster computer chips or cleaner-burning automobile engines. Remember, *technology* is simply the knowledge, tools, and techniques used to transform inputs into outputs. So a technology cycle occurs whenever there are major advances or changes in the *knowledge*, *tools*, and *techniques* of a field or discipline, whatever it may be.

For example, one of the most important technology cycles in the history of civilization occurred in 1859, when 1,300 miles of central sewer line were constructed throughout London to carry human waste to the sea more than eleven miles away. This extensive sewer system replaced the widespread practice of dumping raw sewage directly into streets, where people walked through it and where it drained into public wells that supplied drinking water. Though the relationship between raw sewage and cholera wasn't known at the time, preventing waste runoff from contaminating water supplies stopped the spread of that disease, which had killed millions of people for centuries in cities throughout the world.[5] Safe water supplies immediately translated into better health and longer life expectancies. In fact, the water you drink today is safe thanks to this technological breakthrough. So, when you think about technology cycles, don't automatically think "high tech." Instead, broaden your perspective by considering advances or changes in *any* kind of knowledge, tools, and techniques.

7-1b Innovation Streams

In Chapter 6, you learned that organizations can create *competitive advantage* for themselves if they have a *distinctive competence* that allows them to make, do, or perform something better than their competitors. A competitive advantage becomes sustainable if other companies cannot duplicate the benefits obtained from that distinctive competence. Technological innovation, however, can enable competitors to duplicate the benefits obtained from a company's distinctive advantage. It can also quickly turn

Peter Gudella/Shutterstock.com

a company's competitive advantage into a competitive disadvantage.

Twenty-five years ago, digital cameras replaced film-based technology. But with digital camera sales down 40 percent in four years (and still dropping), digital camera makers are losing their competitive advantage to smartphones with HD photo and video capabilities far better than basic digital cameras. Shigenobu Nagamori, CEO of Nidec, which makes electric motors used in consumer electronics, says that thanks to smartphones, we should, "assume that the inexpensive cameras are dead, just like PCs."[6] Tsugio Tsuchiya, a general manager at Tamron which makes lenses for more advanced DSLRS (digital single-lens reflex cameras), worries that, "Smartphones pose a threat not just to compact cameras but entry-level DSLRS," which start at $400 and use interchangeable lenses, such as telescoping zooms.[7] But even that advantage may soon be lost. HTC's Symon Whitehorn says, "I think we're looking at about eighteen months to two years until that [zoom] lens barrier begins breaking down, and it becomes much harder to justify buying a dedicated camera outside of specialist or nostalgia reasons."[8]

Companies that want to sustain a competitive advantage must understand and protect themselves from the strategic threats of innovation. Over the long run, the best way for a company to do that is to create a stream of its own innovative ideas and products year after year. Consequently, we define **innovation streams** as patterns of innovation over time that can create sustainable competitive advantage.[9] Exhibit 7.2 shows a typical innovation consisting of a series of technology cycles. Recall that a technology cycle begins with a new technology and ends when that technology is replaced by a newer, substantially better technology. The innovation stream in Exhibit 7.2 shows three such technology cycles.

An innovation stream begins with a **technological discontinuity**, in which a scientific advance or a unique combination of existing technologies creates a significant breakthrough in performance or function. Imagine the inefficiency of just one train running on the train track between two cities. It goes to the first, returns to the second, and so on. That, however, is exactly how elevators work, up to the top, down to the bottom, just one car per elevator shaft. **ThyssenKrupp**, maker of the Multi elevator, hopes

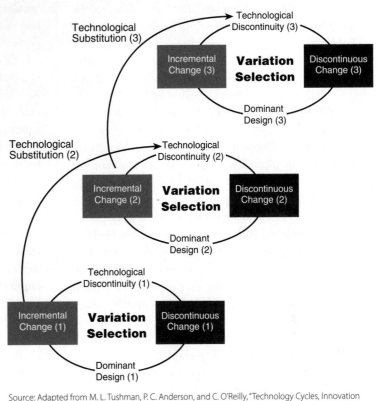

Exhibit 7.2
Innovation Streams: Technology Cycles over Time

Source: Adapted from M. L. Tushman, P. C. Anderson, and C. O'Reilly, "Technology Cycles, Innovation Streams and Ambidextrous Organizations: Organization Renewal Through Innovation Streams and Strategic Change," *On Managing Strategic Innovation and Change*, eds. M. L. Tushman and P. C. Anderson (New Oxford Press, 1997) 3–23.

to solve that problem by replacing the steel safety cable and pulleys used to move elevators with magnetic levitation (similar to that used on high-speed trains) that allows elevators cars to "float" to their destinations. This not only reduces the space needed for elevators by half, but without cables, multiple cars can use the same shaft, just like a subway line, and they can even move horizontally, from one side of a building to another, all of which will allow the design of wider, uniquely shaped buildings.[10]

Technological discontinuities are followed by a **discontinuous change**, which is characterized by technological substitution and design competition. **Technological substitution** occurs when customers purchase new technologies to replace older technologies. For example, just twenty years ago, nearly all phone calls were made via hardwired landline telephones. But, according to the U.S. National Health Interview Survey, 52.1 percent of U.S. homes don't have landline phones.[11] That's up from 17 percent in 2008.[12] Furthermore, only 3.5 percent of U.S. homes have landlines only.[13] Finally, with AT&T and Verizon replacing their old cable-based phone systems with wireless IP-based networks, landline phones won't even be an option within several years.[14] Indeed, Verizon's 10.5 million residential landline customers are already only a small fraction of its 112.1 million individual cellphone connections. Ironically, the growing number of free Wi-Fi hotspots may also pose a threat to wireless carriers by making it easy to use a smartphone without a mobile network. Charissa Struble canceled her contract with Verizon and switched to Wi-Fi only, saying, "I just got tired of paying an exorbitant bill."[15] With almost 3,100 hotspots per 100,000 people in the United States, the risk of customer defection is growing. Rick Osterloh, president of Motorola Mobility, said, "The percentage of time that a phone is in Wi-Fi coverage is very high. This is the beginning of a trend."[16]

Discontinuous change is also characterized by **design competition,** in which the old technology and several different new technologies compete to establish a new technological standard or dominant design. Because of large investments in old technology and because the new and old technologies are often incompatible with each other, companies and consumers are reluctant to switch to a different technology during a design competition. For example, the telegraph was so widely used as a means of communication in the late 1800s that at first almost no one understood why telephones would be a better way to communicate. It's hard to envision today, with everyone constantly checking cell phones for email, texts, tweets, and voice mail, but as Edwin Schlossberg explains in his book *Interactive Excellence*, "People could not imagine why they would want or need to talk immediately to someone who was across town or, even more absurdly, in another town. Although people could write letters to one another, and some could send telegraph messages, the idea of sending one's voice to another place and then instantly hearing another voice in return was simply not a model that existed in people's experience. They also did not think it was worth the money to accelerate sending or hearing a message."[17] In addition, during design competition, the older technology usually improves significantly in response to the competitive threat from the new technologies; this response also slows the changeover from older to newer technologies.

Discontinuous change is followed by the emergence of a **dominant design**, which becomes the new accepted market standard for technology.[18] Dominant designs emerge in several ways. One is critical mass, meaning that a particular technology can become the dominant design simply because most people use it, for example, Blu-ray beating out HD-DVD. Critical mass will likely determine the dominant design for wireless device charging, where instead of plugging in your device to recharge, you simply place it on top of a recharging station containing magnetic charging coils. Over the last few years, three different wireless technologies were trying to become the dominant standard: the Power Matters Alliance (PMA) backing Duracell's Powermat, a Duracell and Procter & Gamble joint venture supported by Google, AT&T, Starbucks, and McDonald's; the Alliance for Wireless Power (A4WP) and its Rezence charging mats, backed by Samsung, Broadcom, Deutsche Telekom, and Texas Instruments; and the Wireless Power Consortium (WPC) and its Qi charging mats, supported by LG Electronics, Energizer, and Nokia. However, PMA and A4WP joined forces to create a new, combined standard for wireless charging devices.[19] Again, why does this matter? It matters because the market for wireless charging, estimated at $785 million, is projected to increase to $8.5 billion by 2018. In other words, becoming the dominant standard is worth billions to the winner.[20]

The best technology doesn't always become the dominant design because a number of other factors

David Becker/Getty Images News/Getty Images

Qualcomm CEO, Steve Mollenkopf, agrees that there is a lot of work left to do when it comes to defining standards for 5G smart phones.

Technological substitution
the purchase of new technologies to replace older ones

Design competition
competition between old and new technologies to establish a new technological standard or dominant design

Dominant design a new technological design or process that becomes the accepted market standard

THE CHALLENGES OF CLIMBING THE STACK

Why do some companies with seemingly endless resources and brainpower fail when they try to innovate? Venture capitalist Anshu Sharma says that it's because of the stack fallacy—the tendency of successful companies to overvalue what they know in one area and misjudge what they need to know to innovate in another.

Imagine technology as a layer cake of capabilities. These capabilities stack on top of each other until they ultimately reach the end user. The Minecraft app on your laptop is the top of a technology stack undergirded by layers—from the operating system, to the server, to the microprocessor, to the electricity powering the device. Just because a company is successful in one layer, say, microprocessors, doesn't mean it can jump up to a higher level, such as the operating system, and have the same success. When Google tried to move from search up to social networking, the result was the failed Google+. IBM saw its revenues shrink four years in a row as it tried to move up from hardware to services. Going down the stack, however, tends to yield positive results. Google moved down the stack by creating its own data farms and servers, which solidified the company's dominance in search. Why is climbing the technology stack so much harder than descending it? Companies don't fully understand what customers on

the level above theirs actually want. However, because companies often buy products and services at the level *below* their own, they understand what customers want out of that lower layer of technology. According to Anshu Sharma, the fundamental question of who will win in a given market is, "Who understands the user better?"

Sources: C. Mims, "Why Big Companies Keep Getting Disrupted," *Wall Street Journal*, January 25, 2016, accessed March 22, 2016, http://www.wsj.com/articles/why-bigcompanies-keep-getting-disrupted-1453698061; E. Kim, "Dropbox Is Falling Prey to a Common Fallacy," *Business Insider*, March 17, 2016, accessed May 11, 2016, http://www.businessinsider.com/this-vc-says-dropboxs-recent-moves-show-why-big-companies-often-fail-to-innovate-2016-3.

come into play. For instance, a design can become dominant if it solves a practical problem. The QWERTY keyboard (named for the top left line of letters) became the dominant design for typewriters because it slowed typists who, by typing too fast, caused mechanical typewriter keys to jam. Though computers can easily be switched to the Dvorak keyboard layout, which doubles typing speed and cuts typing errors in half, QWERTY lives on as the standard keyboard. In this instance, the QWERTY keyboard solved a problem that, with computers, is no longer relevant. Yet it remains the dominant design not because it is the best technology, but because most people learned to type that way and continue to use it.

Dominant designs can also emerge through independent standards bodies. The International Telecommunication Union (ITU) (www.itu.ch) is an independent organization that establishes standards for the communications industry. The ITU was founded in Paris in 1865 because European countries all had different telegraph systems that could not communicate with each other. Messages crossing borders had to be transcribed from one country's system before they could be coded and delivered on another. After three months of negotiations,

twenty countries signed the International Telegraph Convention, which standardized equipment and instructions, enabling telegraph messages to flow seamlessly from country to country. Today, as in 1865, various standards are proposed, discussed, negotiated, and changed until agreement is reached on a final set of standards that communication industries (Internet, telephony, satellites, radio) will follow worldwide.

For example, the telecommunications industry has yet to agree on standards for 5G, or fifth-generation, service on mobile devices. Telecom operators are hoping for a 5G standard data-transmission speed of 10 gigabits per second, fast enough to download high-def movies within seconds. Another desired 5G standard is for two 5G devices to communicate with each other with a latency (or wait time) of just 1 millisecond, down from 50 milliseconds with 4G. Shorter 5G latencies would allow doctors in remote hospitals to conduct life-saving robotics-based surgeries on patients in other locations. The standards and technology are far from final, however. According to Qualcomm CEO Steve Mollenkopf, "There's still a lot to do."[21]

No matter how it happens, the emergence of a dominant design is a key event in an innovation stream. First,

Shopping for Innovations

Not all innovations are developed internally. Sometimes companies in vastly different industries connect to generate true innovations, such as when Intel CEO Brian Krzanich attends fashion week. He says, "When I show up at fashion week, what I'm trying to do is connect with these innovators to partner with them and show them what's possible. I want to know what problems they want solved so that I can go back and work on those problems." Krzanich's networking has produced results. A glove laden with Intel sensors leads the wearer through every step of changing a tire, and a robotic Spider Dress, designed by Anouk Wipprect and using Intel technology, monitors the wearer's stress levels and extends a set of protective legs if it senses someone is getting too close.

Source: R. Feitelberg, "Intel CEO Plugs into FAST A/W 2015," *WWD*, February 14, 2015, p. 2.

the emergence of a dominant design indicates that there are winners and losers. Technological innovation is both competence enhancing and competence destroying. Companies that bet on the now-dominant design usually prosper. By contrast, when companies bet on the wrong design or the old technology, they may experience **technological lockout**, which occurs when a new dominant design (that is, a significantly better technology) prevents a company from competitively selling its products or makes it difficult to do so.[22] **Adobe's** Flash software, which supports animation and video on web pages, was once installed on nearly every computer. Flash was ubiquitous in website design, and was even the foundation of YouTube and Netflix, two video streaming platforms that transformed the way we see the Web. In 2010, however, resource intensity and security issues prompted Apple to declare that it wouldn't support Flash on iPhones and iPads. According to Jeremy Allaire, CEO of video software developer Brightcove, "Immediately, the entire ecosystem of people involved in video pivoted." By 2015, Google, Mozilla, YouTube, Facebook, and countless others had removed Flash from their websites, opting for alternatives like HTML5. Today, Flash is now used on just 6 percent of Internet homepages.[23] Technological lockout is a serious threat, as more companies are likely to go out of business in a time of discontinuous change and changing standards than in an economic recession or slowdown.

Second, the emergence of a dominant design signals a shift from design experimentation and competition to **incremental change,** a phase in which companies innovate by lowering the cost and improving the functioning and performance of the dominant design. For example, manufacturing efficiencies enable Intel to cut the cost of its chips by one-half to two-thirds during a technology cycle, while doubling or tripling their speed. This focus on improving the dominant design continues until the next technological discontinuity occurs.

7-2 MANAGING INNOVATION

One consequence of technology cycles and innovation streams is that managers must be equally good at managing innovation in two very different circumstances. First, during discontinuous change, companies must find a way to anticipate and survive the technological changes that can suddenly transform industry leaders into losers and industry unknowns into powerhouses. Companies that

Technological lockout the inability of a company to competitively sell its products because it relies on old technology or a nondominant design

Incremental change the phase of a technology cycle in which companies innovate by lowering costs and improving the functioning and performance of the dominant technological design

can't manage innovation following technological discontinuities risk quick organizational decline and dissolution. Second, after a new dominant design emerges following discontinuous change, companies must manage the very different process of incremental improvement and innovation. Companies that can't manage incremental innovation slowly deteriorate as they fall further behind industry leaders.

Unfortunately, what works well when managing innovation during discontinuous change doesn't work well when managing innovation during periods of incremental change (and vice versa).

Consequently, to successfully manage innovation streams, companies need to be good at three things: **7-2a managing sources of innovation, 7-2b managing innovation during discontinuous change,** *and* **7-2c managing innovation during incremental change.**

7-2a Managing Sources of Innovation

Innovation comes from great ideas. So a starting point for managing innovation is to manage the sources of innovation, that is, where new ideas come from. One place where new ideas originate is with brilliant inventors. But only a few companies have the likes of a Thomas Edison or Alexander Graham Bell. Given that great thinkers and inventors are in short supply, what might companies do to ensure a steady flow of good ideas?

Well, when we say that innovation begins with great ideas, we're really saying that innovation begins with creativity. As we defined it at the beginning of this chapter, creativity is the production of novel and useful ideas.[24] Although companies can't command employees to be creative ("You *will* be more creative!"), they can jump-start innovation by building **creative work environments** in which workers perceive that creative thoughts and ideas are welcomed and valued. As Exhibit 7.3 shows, creative work environments have six components that encourage creativity: challenging work, organizational encouragement, supervisory encouragement, work group encouragement, freedom, and a lack of organizational impediments.[25]

Work is *challenging* when it requires effort, demands attention and focus, and is perceived as important to others in the organization. According to researcher Mihaly Csikszentmihalyi (pronounced ME-high-ee

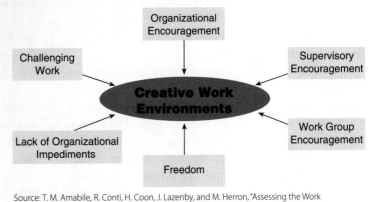

Exhibit 7.3
Components of Creative Work Environments

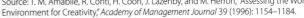

Source: T. M. Amabile, R. Conti, H. Coon, J. Lazenby, and M. Herron, "Assessing the Work Environment for Creativity," *Academy of Management Journal* 39 (1996): 1154–1184.

CHICK-sent-me-high-ee), challenging work promotes creativity because it creates a rewarding psychological experience known as "flow." **Flow** is a psychological state of effortlessness, in which you become completely absorbed in what you're doing and time seems to fly. When flow occurs, who you are and what you're doing become one. Csikszentmihalyi first encountered flow when studying artists: "What struck me by looking at artists at work was their tremendous focus on the work, this enormous involvement, this forgetting of time and body. It wasn't justified by expectation of rewards, like, 'Aha, I'm going to sell this painting.'"[26] Csikszentmihalyi has found that chess players, rock climbers, dancers, surgeons, and athletes regularly experience flow, too. Today, achieving flow is increasingly challenging. A recent study by Professor Gloria Mark at the University of California, Irvine, found that workers focus on their computer screen an average of one minute fifteen seconds before shifting their attention, down from two minutes eighteen seconds in 2008. Office furniture maker **Steelcase** has designed a workstation that, according to designer Mark McKenna, encourages flow by reducing workers' latent anxiety and distractions from physical surroundings. But Gloria Mark is skeptical, arguing that workers suffer more from digital distractions. In 2015, she found that on a daily basis, workers visited Facebook an average of twenty-one times and checked email seventy-four times.[27]

Removing distractions assists in creating an

Creative work environments workplace cultures in which workers perceive that new ideas are welcomed, valued, and encouraged

Flow a psychological state of effortlessness, in which you become completely absorbed in what you're doing, and time seems to pass quickly

environment conducive to flow. Another key part of creating flow experiences, and thus creative work environments, is to achieve a balance between skills and task challenge. Workers become bored when they can do more than is required of them. Or, they become anxious when their skills aren't sufficient to accomplish a task. When skills and task challenges are balanced, however, flow and creativity can occur.

A creative work environment requires three kinds of encouragement: organizational, supervisory, and work group. *Organizational encouragement* of creativity occurs when management encourages risk taking and new ideas, supports and fairly evaluates new ideas, rewards and recognizes creativity, and encourages the sharing of new ideas throughout different parts of the company. When David Richter became the VP of information technology at **Kimberly-Clark**, the division had just had a round of layoffs in which nearly everyone was fired. A year later, 200 IT engineers were hired back. He said, "We had very low morale and very low employee engagement. . . . People were in a self-preservation mode." Creativity, innovation, and risk taking were at a standstill because people were afraid they would lose their jobs again. He said, "There was a palpable fear that if you tried something and failed, it would damage your career forever." So Richter encouraged creativity by rewarding creative ideas with "start-up" funding. Anyone with an idea could pitch it to him in thirty minutes or less. They didn't need a PowerPoint presentation. The only requirement before the pitch was a one-page form asking for an explanation regarding the benefit, the resources it would take, and the scope of the idea. Richter said, "It's as simple as that. Make me a pitch. And, if it's good. Let's proceed." If the pilot trial of the idea succeeded, then Richter provided significant resources to implement it throughout the division. Finally, to celebrate and encourage risk taking, he shared all employees' ideas, whether they worked or not, on the division's intranet. Says Richter, "Failure is simply the opportunity to begin again, this time more intelligently. It's about what we learn from the failure. Not the failure itself. We celebrate that learning."[28]

Supervisory encouragement of creativity occurs when supervisors provide clear goals, encourage open interaction with subordinates, and actively support development teams' work and ideas. When it comes to clear goals, MIT's Andrew McAfee says be specific. He says goals such as, "We need to figure out why so many people are leaving our site before completing a transaction," or, "How can we increase sales to women in their 30s?" are much better at generating innovations than broad goals such as, "What should our next great idea be?"[29] When **General Electric** launched the Ecomagination initiative to emphasize

energy efficiency and ecologically friendly products, the company knew that clear goals were important. According to Lorraine Bolsinger, the GE executive running the program, "At a company full of engineers, a business initiative can't just be a feel-good plan. Setting hard targets made it an honest GE initiative."[30] Bolsinger's hard targets for this initiative included doubling the $700 million budget for researching clean technology, doubling the $10 million annual revenue from Ecomagination products (such as wind turbines, efficient jet engines, MRI systems, and hybrid locomotives), cutting water usage by 20 percent, and cutting greenhouse-gas emissions by 1 percent—all within five to seven years. Within five years, investment in clean technology research reached $5 billion, annual revenues from Ecomagination products hit an amazing $85 billion, water usage dropped 42 percent, and greenhouse gases dropped 31 percent.[31]

Work group encouragement occurs when group members have diverse experience, education, and backgrounds, and the group fosters mutual openness to ideas; positive, constructive challenge to ideas; and shared commitment to ideas. *Freedom* means having autonomy over one's day-to-day work and a sense of ownership and control over one's ideas. Numerous studies have indicated that creative ideas thrive under conditions of freedom.

To foster creativity, companies may also have to *remove impediments* to creativity from their work environments. Internal conflict and power struggles, rigid management structures, and a conservative bias toward the status quo can all discourage creativity. They create the perception that others in the organization will decide which ideas are acceptable and deserve support. Geography was a key impediment to creativity for **Levi Strauss**. While Levi is headquartered in San Francisco,

Levi Strauss brought its research and development team back to its headquarters in San Francisco, California to save money and improve company-wide collaboration.

FORGET MOONSHOTS—APPLE MAKES A BIG BANG WITH FEWER BUCKS

Tech companies are placing big bets on what they hope will be breakthrough innovations. IBM is focusing on artificial intelligence software Watson; Microsoft on augmented reality glasses HoloLens; Facebook on virtual-reality headsets and drones that will beam the Internet directly to devices; and Alphabet on animal-look-alike robots. While exciting, these outsized innovations come at a cost. Google spends roughly 15 percent of its $66 billion annual revenue on innovation, while Facebook spends 21 percent of its $12.5 billion revenue on innovation. While much of Silicon Valley is spending heavily on so-called *moonshots*, Apple takes a decidedly different, and thrifty, approach, spending only 3.5 percent of its $233 billion annual revenue on innovation in 2015. And even *that* amount is nearly double what the company spent in 2013. Apple co-founder Steve Jobs once said that "innovation has nothing to do with how many R&D dollars

you have." And it seems that the company still embraces that less-is-more philosophy.

Source: A. Satariano, "Apple Gets More Bank for Its R&D Buck," *Bloomberg Business-Week*, November 30–December 6, 2015, 38–39.

its research and development facility used to be located 7,000 miles away in Corlu, Turkey (a facility that, incidentally, reported to a regional office in Brussels, Belgium). California-based designers regularly shipped samples back and forth and traveled to Turkey twice a year, staying for just two weeks each trip. Levi's CEO Chip Bergh said about the arrangement, "We probably spent enough on airfare to buy a 747 just to be managing product back and forth over the ocean."[32] In 2013, Levi's senior director for technical innovation Bart Sights moved his team from Corlu to San Francisco. The move allowed Sights's team to work closely with designers to develop a new stretch-denim jean with a more comfortable, flattering fit. The Levi's 700 line, featuring the new fabric, launched in 2015 to help Levi compete against Lululemon yoga pants, whose surging popularity had led to an 8 percent decline in sales of women's jeans.

7-2b Experiential Approach: Managing Innovation during Discontinuous Change

A study of seventy-two product-development projects (that is, innovation) in thirty-six computer companies across the United States, Europe, and Asia sheds light on how to manage innovation. Companies that succeeded

in periods of discontinuous change (characterized by technological substitution and design competition, as described earlier) typically followed an experiential approach to innovation.[33] The **experiential approach to innovation** assumes that innovation is occurring within a highly uncertain environment and that the key to fast product innovation is to use intuition, flexible options, and hands-on experience to reduce uncertainty and accelerate learning and understanding. The experiential approach to innovation has five aspects: design iterations, testing, milestones, multifunctional teams, and powerful leaders.[34]

An *iteration* is a repetition. So a **design iteration** is a cycle of repetition in which a company tests a prototype of a new product or service, improves on the design, and then builds and tests the improved product or service prototype. A **product prototype** is a full-scale working model that is being tested for design, function, and

> **Experiential approach to innovation** an approach to innovation that assumes a highly uncertain environment and uses intuition, flexible options, and hands-on experience to reduce uncertainty and accelerate learning and understanding

> **Design iteration** a cycle of repetition in which a company tests a prototype of a new product or service, improves on that design, and then builds and tests the improved prototype

> **Product prototype** a full-scale, working model that is being tested for design, function, and reliability

reliability. For example, Facebook-owned Oculus VR designs virtual-reality headsets to be used in simulations and digital games. Oculus shipped 60,000 units of its first product prototype and used the resulting product feedback to develop its second prototype, the DK2, which it presold to game developers who will not only test the DK2 but also how well the digital games they're designing perform using the DK2. The DK2 prototype was followed by a much improved Crescent Bay prototype, which led to the Oculus Rift, which was released commercially in April 2016.[35]

Testing is a systematic comparison of different product designs or design iterations. Companies that want to create a new dominant design following a technological discontinuity quickly build, test, improve, and retest a series of different product prototypes. While many companies are developing driverless cars, prototype testing has occurred in controlled environments (Google's driverless car always has a driver at the wheel when on public roads—just in case) that often lack the authenticity—and chaos—of daily driving. That changed in 2015 with the opening of **M City**, a twenty-three-acre mini-metropolis in Ann Arbor, Michigan, with forty building facades, a bridge, a tunnel, a traffic circle, gravel roads, angled intersections, obstructed views, and even robotic jaywalkers pushing baby carriages. M City allows researchers to test what happens if, say, a red light fails, something they could never do on real city streets. Hideki Hada, an electronics systems manager at **Toyota**, said, "We would never do any dangerous or risky tests on the open road, so this will be a good place to test some of the next technology."[36]

By trying a number of very different designs or making successive improvements and changes in the same design, frequent design iterations reduce uncertainty and improve understanding. Simply put, the more prototypes you build, the more likely you are to learn what works and what doesn't. Also, when designers and engineers build a number of prototypes, they are less likely to fall in love with a particular prototype. Instead, they'll be more concerned with improving the product or technology as much as they can. Testing speeds up and improves the innovation process, too. When two very different design prototypes are tested against each other, or the new design iteration is tested against the previous iteration, product design strengths and weaknesses quickly become apparent. Likewise, testing uncovers errors early in the design process when they are easiest to correct.

Finally, testing accelerates learning and understanding by forcing engineers and product designers to examine hard data about product performance. When there's hard evidence that prototypes are testing well, the confidence of the design team grows. Also, personal conflict between design team members is less likely when testing focuses on hard measurements and facts rather than on personal hunches and preferences.

Milestones are formal project review points used to assess progress and performance. For example, a company that has put itself on a twelve-month schedule to complete a project might schedule milestones at the three-month, six-month, and nine-month points on the schedule. By making people regularly assess what they're doing, how well they're performing, and whether they need to take corrective action, milestones provide structure to the general chaos that follows technological discontinuities. Regularly meeting milestones gives people a sense of accomplishment and can shorten the innovation process by creating a sense of urgency that keeps people on task. **Google** spends $9.8 billion annually on research and development. But, its growth and size have slowed the pace of innovation. Eric Schmidt, executive chairman of Google's parent company, Alphabet, says, "All of us believe we could execute faster." To create a sense of urgency, Google's Advanced Technology and Projects (ATAP) now puts a strict two-year limit on research projects. After two years, unsuccessful projects are killed, while successful projects are moved inside Google, spun off, or licensed to other companies. The two-year time frame forces project teams to make fast, focused decisions. Schmidt says, "We like this model because it puts pressure on people to perform and do relevant things or stop."[37]

Multifunctional teams are work teams composed of people from different departments. Multifunctional teams accelerate learning and understanding by mixing and integrating technical, marketing, and manufacturing activities. By involving all key departments in development from the start, multifunctional teams speed innovation through early identification of new ideas or problems that would typically not have been generated or addressed until much later. **Apple** CEO Tim Cook assigned Steve Zadesky, a former Ford engineer who headed the teams that developed the iPhone and the iPad, to lead a secretive car project, code-named "Titan," to apparently compete with Tesla's electric cars. Zadesky is building a multifunctional team by drafting employees from different parts of Apple, while also recruiting outsiders with experience developing concept cars at Ford and Mercedes Benz and expertise in electric-car battery technology.[38]

Testing the systematic comparison of different product designs or design iterations

Milestones formal project review points used to assess progress and performance

Multifunctional teams work teams composed of people from different departments

Powerful leaders provide the vision, discipline, and motivation to keep the innovation process focused, on time, and on target. Powerful leaders are able to get resources when they are needed, are typically more experienced, have high status in the company, and are held directly responsible for the products' success or failure. On average, powerful leaders can get innovation-related projects done nine months faster than leaders with little power or influence.

7-2c Compression Approach: Managing Innovation during Incremental Change

Whereas the experiential approach is used to manage innovation in highly uncertain environments during periods of discontinuous change, the compression approach is used to manage innovation in more certain environments during periods of incremental change. Whereas the goals of the experiential approach are significant improvements in performance and the establishment of a *new* dominant design, the goals of the compression approach are lower costs and incremental improvements in the performance and function of the *existing* dominant design.

The general strategies in each approach are different, too. With the experiential approach, the general strategy is to build something new, different, and substantially better. Because there's so much uncertainty—no one knows which technology will become the market leader—companies adopt a winner-take-all approach by trying to create the market-leading, dominant design. With the compression approach, the general strategy is to compress the time and steps needed to bring about small, consistent improvements in performance and functionality. Because a dominant technology design already exists, the general strategy is to continue improving the existing technology as rapidly as possible. For example, after using an experiential approach and investing $50 billion to develop its groundbreaking 787 Dreamliner passenger jet, Boeing is now switching to a compression approach to innovation. Chief Operating Officer Dennis Muilenburg said, "In the past, we may have said our best engineers are working on the new thing. Now we want our best engineers working on innovative reuse."[39] Likewise, Ray Conner, CEO of Boeing's commercial airplane unit said, "It's not to say you don't innovate [but] how do you innovate to make it more producible? How do you innovate to make it more reliable?"[40]

In short, a **compression approach to innovation** assumes that innovation is a predictable process, that incremental innovation can be planned using a series of steps, and that compressing the time it takes to complete those steps can speed up innovation. The compression approach to innovation has five aspects: planning, supplier involvement, shortening the time of individual steps, overlapping steps, and multifunctional teams.[41]

In Chapter 5, *planning* was defined as choosing a goal and a method or strategy to achieve that goal. When *planning for incremental innovation*, the goal is to squeeze or compress development time as much as possible, and the general strategy is to create a series of planned steps to accomplish that goal. Planning for incremental innovation helps avoid unnecessary steps and enables developers to sequence steps in the right order to avoid wasted time and delays between steps. Planning also reduces misunderstandings and improves coordination.

Most planning for incremental innovation is based on the idea of generational change. **Generational change** occurs when incremental improvements are made to a dominant technological design such that the improved version of the technology is fully backward compatible with the older version.[42] Most computers, for instance, have USB (universal serial bus) input slots to connect and power USB thumb drives, monitors, or external hard drives used for backup storage. USB 3.1 (Gen 2), the latest USB standard, can transfer more than 10 Gbps (gigabytes per second), compared to USB 3.0 devices, which operate at 5 Gbps, or USB 2.0 devices, which operate at roughly 1/2 Gbps.[43] What happens if you buy a new computer with USB 3.1 slots, but still own a USB 3.0 external hard drive and a USB 2.0 thumb drive? Both will work, but at slower speeds, because they are backward compatible with USB 3.1.

iStockphoto.com/Edin

Because the compression approach assumes that innovation can follow a series of preplanned steps, one of the ways to shorten development time is *supplier involvement*. Delegating some of the preplanned steps in the innovation process to outside suppliers reduces the amount of work that internal

Compression approach to innovation an approach to innovation that assumes that incremental innovation can be planned using a series of steps and that compressing those steps can speed innovation

Generational change change based on incremental improvements to a dominant technological design such that the improved technology is fully backward compatible with the older technology

development teams must do. Plus, suppliers provide an alternative source of ideas and expertise that can lead to better designs. Even though **Apple** develops most of its innovations in house, it does rely on suppliers for innovation as well. The prospect of landing a large contract and supplying a crucial component to a company like Apple drives suppliers to build out their own research and development capabilities. Professor Ram Mudambi believes that Apple's size and component budget ($29.5 billion in 2016) motivate suppliers to pitch their biggest breakthroughs to the company: "Suppliers are racing with each other to get Apple's business, and part of the racing they are doing is spending more on R&D."[44]

Another way to shorten development time is simply to *shorten the time of individual steps* in the innovation process. Indian cellphone manufacturer **Micromax Informatics** does this by customizing off-the-shelf hardware rather than developing it from scratch. This allows the company to keep up with consumer trends by unveiling a new model every few weeks. In fact, while Apple typically releases two new phones a year and China's Xiaomi releases four, Micromax releases more than thirty new models every year. Because it uses existing hardware imported from China, Micromax only needs three to four months to take a phone from concept to store shelves. Indeed, only four months after deciding it wanted to launch a handset that could function seamlessly across India's twenty official languages, Micromax released the Unite. Priced at just $110, this 2015 model allows users to communicate using twenty-one different scripts, including Gujarati, Marathi, and Tamil, as well as English and Hindi. The Unite is just one of dozens of Micromax cellphones released in 2015. Others include models built on Windows, models with six-inch screens for doodling, models that boast long battery life, no-frills models, and more. According to Micromax CEO Vineet Taneja, "We turn around faster than any other company."[45]

In a sequential design process, each step must be completed before the next step begins. But sometimes multiple development steps can be performed at the same time. *Overlapping steps* shorten the development process by reducing delays or waiting time between steps.

> **Organizational decline** a large decrease in organizational performance that occurs when companies don't anticipate, recognize, neutralize, or adapt to the internal or external pressures that threaten their survival

iStockphoto/Ermingut

ORGANIZATIONAL DECLINE: THE RISK OF NOT CHANGING

Founded in 1921 in Boston as a store for ham radio enthusiasts, **RadioShack** grew to more than 7,000 stores by stocking a wide range of components used to build or repair various electronic devices. In fact, before starting **Apple**, co-founders Steve Jobs and Steve Wozniak bought parts at RadioShack to make a "blue box" device that illegally switched on free long distance calling (which mattered when long distance calls were forty cents a minute).[46] RadioShack's growth was first propelled by hobbyists (nerds like Jobs and Wozniak), then by battery sales, computers, and cell phones. The TRS-80, introduced in 1977, was one of the first broadly popular PCs. Following computers, which it stopped making in 1993, its next growth cycle came from cell phones. The phone companies at first relied on RadioShack to sign up and service customers, but this changed as they eventually established their own retail stores. RadioShack moved away from its focus on serving technology power users and hobbyists by opening unsuccessful big-box electronics and appliance stores, such as Computer City and Incredible Universe, on which it lost hundreds of millions of dollars in the 1990s. Outmaneuvered by BestBuy in brick-and-mortar retailing, and never really competitive on the Web, RadioShack filed for bankruptcy in spring 2015 after losing $936 million since 2011, the last year it was profitable.[47]

Businesses operate in a constantly changing environment. Recognizing and adapting to internal and external changes can mean the difference between continued success and going out of business. Companies that fail to change run the risk of organizational decline.[48] **Organizational decline** occurs when companies don't anticipate, recognize, neutralize, or adapt to the internal or external pressures that threaten their survival. CEO of **Netflix** Reed Hastings, whose company successfully bridged from its DVD-by-mail business to Internet streaming, said, "Most companies that are great at something—AOL dial-up or Borders bookstores—do not become great at new things people want (streaming for us) because they are afraid to hurt their initial business. Eventually, these companies realize their error of not focusing enough on the new thing, and then the company fights desperately and hopelessly to recover. Companies rarely die from moving too fast, and they frequently die from moving too slowly."[49] In other words, decline occurs when organizations don't recognize the need for change. There are five stages of organizational decline: blinded, inaction, faulty action, crisis, and dissolution.

In the *blinded stage*, decline begins because key managers fail to recognize the internal or external changes that will harm their organizations. This blindness may be due to a simple lack of awareness about changes or an inability to understand their significance. It may also come from the overconfidence that can develop when a company has been successful.

In the *inaction stage*, as organizational performance problems become more visible, management may recognize the need to change but still take no action. The managers may be waiting to see if the problems will correct themselves. Or, they may find it difficult to change the practices and policies that previously led to success. Possibly, too, they wrongly assume that they can easily correct the problems, so they don't feel the situation is urgent.

In the *faulty action stage*, faced with rising costs and decreasing profits and market share, management will announce belt-tightening plans designed to cut costs, increase efficiency, and restore profits. In other words, rather than recognizing the need for fundamental changes, managers assume that if they just run a tighter ship, company performance will return to previous levels.

In the *crisis stage*, bankruptcy or dissolution (breaking up the company and selling its parts) is likely to occur

"RadioShacks filed for bankruptcy in 2015 and was acquired by its largest lender, hedge fund, Standard General."

Ken Wolter/Shutterstock.com

unless the company completely reorganizes the way it does business. At this point, however, companies typically lack the resources to fully change how they run their businesses. Cutbacks and layoffs will have reduced the level of talent among employees. Furthermore, talented managers who were savvy enough to see the crisis coming will have found jobs with other companies, often with competitors. At this stage, hoping to generate enough cash to fund a much-needed redesign of its remaining stores, RadioShack took out $835 million in loans and closed 1,100 stores, However, during the 2014 holiday season, its corporate finances amounted to the equivalent of just $15,000 cash per store.[50]

In the *dissolution stage*, after failing to make the changes needed to sustain the organization, the company is dissolved through bankruptcy proceedings or by selling assets to pay suppliers, banks, and creditors. At this point, a new CEO may be brought in to oversee the closing of stores, offices, and manufacturing facilities; the final layoff of managers and employees; and the sale of assets. It is important to note that decline is reversible at each of the first four stages and that not all companies in decline reach final dissolution. RadioShack declared bankruptcy in February 2015, and was acquired by its largest lender, hedge fund Standard General. Seventeen hundred stores will continue operating, but 1,400 will feature Sprint/RadioShack signage and branding. Sprint and its employees will use roughly one-third of each store to sell and display Sprint mobile phones and related products.[51]

7-4 MANAGING CHANGE

According to social psychologist Kurt Lewin, change is a function of the forces that promote change and the opposing forces that slow or resist change.[52] **Change forces** lead to differences in the form, quality, or condition of an organization over time. In contrast to change forces, **resistance forces** support the status quo, that is, the existing conditions in an organization. Change is difficult under any circumstances. Production schedules on movie sets have changed dramatically as a result of directors having switched from film to digital recordings. When shooting with film, a new film reel has to be loaded every

Change forces forces that produce differences in the form, quality, or condition of an organization over time

Resistance forces forces that support the existing conditions in organizations

ten minutes, creating frequent breaks when stars would return to their trailers to read, rehearse, or rest. Because there are no film reels with digital recording, shooting can occur continuously, significantly reducing film production time and costs. A number of famous actors, however, don't like the change. Actor Robert Downey, Jr. complained, "I can't work like this. I never get to go to my trailer … I'm on my feet fourteen hours a day. I'm shooting all the time."[53]

Resistance to change is caused by self-interest, misunderstanding and distrust, and a general intolerance for change.[54] People resist change out of *self-interest* because they fear that change will cost or deprive them of something they value. Resistance might stem from a fear that the changes will result in a loss of pay, power, responsibility, or even perhaps one's job.

People also resist change because of *misunderstanding and distrust*; they don't understand the change or the reasons for it, or they distrust the people—typically management—behind the change. Resistance isn't always visible at first. In fact, some of the strongest resisters may initially support the changes in public, nodding and smiling their agreement, but then ignore the changes in private and do their jobs as they always have. Management consultant Michael Hammer calls this deadly form of resistance the "Kiss of Yes."[55]

The Kiss of Yes occurs when some of the strongest resisters support changes in public, but then ignore them in private.

Resistance may also come from a generally low tolerance for change. Some people are simply less capable of handling change than others. People with a *low tolerance for change* feel threatened by the uncertainty associated with change and worry that they won't be able to learn the new skills and behaviors needed to successfully negotiate change in their companies.

Resistance to change opposition to change resulting from self-interest, misunderstanding and distrust, and a general intolerance for change

Unfreezing getting the people affected by change to believe that change is needed

Change intervention the process used to get workers and managers to change their behaviors and work practices

Refreezing supporting and reinforcing new changes so that they stick

Because resistance to change is inevitable, successful change efforts require careful management.

*In this section, you will learn about **7-4a managing resistance to change, 7-4b what not to do when leading organizational change,** and **7-4c different change tools and techniques.***

7-4a Managing Resistance to Change

According to psychologist Kurt Lewin, managing organizational change is a basic process of unfreezing, change intervention, and refreezing. **Unfreezing** is getting the people affected by change to believe that change is needed. During the **change intervention** itself, workers and managers change their behavior and work practices. **Refreezing** is supporting and reinforcing the new changes so that they stick.

Resistance to change is an example of frozen behavior. Given the choice between changing and not changing, most people would rather not change. Because resistance to change is natural and inevitable, managers need to unfreeze resistance to change to create successful change programs. The following methods can be used to manage resistance to change: education and communication, participation, negotiation, top-management support, and coercion.[56]

When resistance to change is based on insufficient, incorrect, or misleading information, managers should *educate* employees about the need for change and *communicate* change-related information to them. Managers must also supply the information, funding, or other support employees need to make changes. For example, resistance to change can be particularly strong when one company buys another company. This is because one company in the merger usually has a higher status due to its size or its higher profitability or the fact that it is the acquiring company. These status differences are important to managers and employees, particularly if they're in the lower-status company, who worry about retaining their jobs or influence after the merger. That fear or concern can greatly increase resistance to change.[57] When PMA Companies, an insurance risk management firm, was acquired by Old Republic International, an insurance company, PMA's CEO Vince Donnelly communicated frequently with PMA's employees about the merger. Four months before the acquisition became official, he traveled to each of the company's twenty offices and gave employees a detailed description of how their day-to-day operations would change and why the acquisition was good for everyone involved. He also held quarterly updates with employees via videoconference. Said Donnelly, "It's not just one and done. Communication needs to be continual. You need to continue to reinforce the messages that you want people to internalize. So you need to understand that communication is a continuous process and not something that you do just once." He went on to say, "What you are asking people to do is trust you, [trust] that you have the best interest of everybody in mind, and [trust that] when there is news to tell, you're going to hear it directly from the CEO—good, bad, or indifferent."[58]

Another way to reduce resistance to change is to have those affected by the change *participate in planning and implementing the change process.* Employees who participate have a better understanding of the change and the need for it. Furthermore, employee concerns about change can be addressed as they occur if employees participate in the planning and implementation process. When United Airlines and Continental Airlines merged to form one of the world's largest airlines, there were thousands of decisions to be made to integrate the two companies, such as combining websites, ticketing systems, pay and promotion policies, and so on. They even had to decide which coffee to serve, as Continental served coffee from Fresh Brew, and United served Starbucks. While seemingly a small decision, United and Continental serve a combined 62 million cups of coffee each year. Sandra Pineau-Boddison, the vice president of food services, picked a fourteen-member team consisting of people from flight operations, finance, food service, and marketing to make the decision, even asking them to blindly taste twelve different coffees to identify which tasted best. Then, she took the committee's selection and asked the company's board of directors, as well as 1,100 flight attendants who also tried the new brew, for input.[59]

Employees are also less likely to resist change if they are allowed *to discuss and agree on who will do what* after change occurs. Craig Durosko, founder of **Sun Design Home Remodeling Specialists** in Burke, Virginia, says, "Unfortunately, the way most employees find out when a company isn't doing well is when their paychecks bounce or when they show up and the front doors are locked. When changes go down and they don't know about it, they can't do anything about it." So, when Sun Design's business shrank dramatically during the recession, Durosko explained the problem, sharing detailed financial information, and then asked his employees what could be done to minimize losses. He says, "No less than twenty employees gave line-by-line specific *things they could do* to make a difference."[60]

Resistance to change also decreases when change efforts receive *significant managerial support.* Managers must do more than talk about the importance of change, though. They must provide the training, resources, and autonomy needed to make change happen. Finally, resistance to change can be managed through **coercion,** or the use of formal power and authority to force others to change. Because of the intense negative reactions it can create (for example, fear, stress, resentment, sabotage of company products), coercion should be used only when a crisis exists or when all other attempts to reduce resistance to change have failed.

7-4b What Not to Do When Leading Change

So far, you've learned about the basic change process (unfreezing, change intervention, refreezing) and managing resistance to change. Harvard Business School professor John Kotter argues that knowing what *not* to do is just as important as knowing what to do when it comes to achieving successful organizational change.[61]

Managers commonly make certain errors when they lead change. The first two errors occur during the unfreezing phase, when managers try to get the people affected by change to believe that change is really needed. The first and potentially most serious error is *not establishing a great enough sense of urgency.* In fact, Kotter estimates that more than half of all change efforts fail because the people affected are not convinced that change is necessary. People will feel a greater sense of urgency if a leader in the company makes a public, candid assessment of the company's problems and weaknesses.

In 1973, Nordstrom launched Nordstrom Rack, a lower-cost outlet version of its nameplate store. Neiman Marcus Last Call, Filene's Basement, and Saks Off Fifth quickly followed.[62] While Macy's currently accounts for 40 percent of U.S. department store sales, it made a critical mistake by debating what to do about off-price stores for six years before finally opening its own version, Macy's Backstage, in 2015. While the company deliberated, off-price behemoth

Coercion the use of formal power and authority to force others to change

TJX—parent company of T.J.Maxx, Marshalls, and Homegoods—shot past it on three key financial metrics. TJX has been more profitable than Macy's since 2008 and has had higher sales revenue since 2014. Since 2005, Macy's market capitalization has shrunk by $5 billion, while TJX's has risen by $35 billion, making it three times larger than Macy's. According to researcher Craig Johnson, "Macy's has been so successful for so long with its core format that it blinded them to the ways that consumer shopping behaviors were changing . . . The fix isn't going to happen overnight."[63]

The second mistake that occurs in the unfreezing process is *not creating a powerful enough coalition*. Change often starts with one or two people. But change has to be supported by a critical and growing group of people to build enough momentum to change an entire department, division, or company. Besides top management, Kotter recommends that key employees, managers, board members, customers, and even union leaders be members of a *core change coalition* that guides and supports organizational change. For GE's Ecomagination initiative, that core change coalition included a group of engineers who were responsible for finding ways to achieve the company's overall goals of reducing emissions and water usage while increasing energy efficiency. Initiative leader Lorraine Bolsinger said, "We started doing what we called 'treasure hunts' [to] see if there were ways to use our own products at our own facilities to improve efficiency."[64] Many of these treasure hunts paid off. For example, one team at a jet engine testing facility figured out how to save 3 million gallons of jet fuel per year by moving engine tests indoors, reducing the run times needed for accurate testing, and better calculating the placement of weights used to balance the hundreds of fans on jet engines, resulting in a smoother, easier-turning, more efficient jet engine.[65]

The next four errors that managers make occur during the change phase, when a change intervention is used to try to get workers and managers to change their behavior and work practices. *Lacking a vision* for change is a significant error at this point. As you learned in Chapter 5, a *vision* (defined as a *purpose statement* in Chapter 5) is a statement of a company's purpose or reason for existing. A vision for change makes clear where a company or department is headed and why the change is occurring. Change efforts that lack vision tend to be confused, chaotic, and contradictory. By contrast, change efforts guided by visions are clear, are easy to understand, and can be effectively explained in five minutes or less.

Undercommunicating the vision by a factor of ten is another mistake in the change phase. According to Kotter, companies mistakenly hold just one meeting to announce the vision. Or, if the new vision receives heavy emphasis in

Macy's executives debated off-price stores for six years before finally opening Macy's Backstage in 2015.

executive speeches or company newsletters, senior management then undercuts the vision by behaving in ways contrary to it. Successful communication of the vision requires that top managers link everything the company does to the new vision and that they "walk the talk" by behaving in ways consistent with the vision. Furthermore, even companies that begin change with a clear vision sometimes make the mistake of *not removing obstacles to the new vision*. They leave formidable barriers to change in place by failing to redesign jobs, pay plans, and technology to support the new way of doing things. One of the biggest obstacles that Nokia CEO Stephen Elop removed soon after joining the company was Symbian, the core operating software on more than 400 million Nokia phones. Killing Symbian saved Nokia $1.4 billion a year in software maintenance and research and development costs. The software was out of date and buggy, and Nokia's computer software engineers had not delivered a new smartphone on schedule or on budget since 2009. Plus, app developers hated programming for Symbian. Tuomas Artman, who used to work at Nokia, said, "Developing for Symbian could make you want to slice your wrists."[66]

Killing Symbian not only saved billions in costs, it also allowed Nokia to strike an exclusive deal with Microsoft to use Windows Phone 7 software on its phones. Microsoft agreed to allow Nokia to innovate by creating new features for Windows Phone and injected hundreds of millions of dollars of marketing funds to support Nokia's efforts to sell new Windows-based smartphones. Unfortunately, even with these changes, Nokia's Lumia Windows phones make up just 1.1 percent of the market—a figure that Microsoft CEO Satya Nadella calls, "unsustainable."[67]

Another error in the change phase is *not systematically planning for and creating short-term wins*. Most people don't have the discipline and patience to wait two years to see if the new change effort works. Change is threatening and uncomfortable, so people need to see an immediate payoff if they are to continue to support it. Kotter recommends that managers create short-term wins by actively picking people and projects that are likely to work extremely well early in the change process.

The last two errors that managers make occur during the refreezing phase, when attempts are made to support and reinforce changes so that they stick. *Declaring victory too soon* is a tempting mistake in the refreezing phase. Managers typically declare victory right after the first large-scale success in the change process. Declaring success too early has the same effect as draining the gasoline out of a car: it stops change efforts dead in their tracks. With success declared, supporters of the change process stop pushing to make change happen. After all, why push when success has been achieved? Rather than declaring victory, managers should use the momentum from short-term wins to push for even bigger or faster changes. This maintains urgency and prevents change supporters from slacking off before the changes are frozen into the company's culture.

The last mistake that managers make is *not anchoring changes in the corporation's culture*. An *organization's culture* is the set of key values, beliefs, and attitudes shared by organizational members that determines the accepted way of doing things in a company. As you learned in Chapter 3, changing cultures is extremely difficult and slow. According to Kotter, two things help anchor changes in a corporation's culture. The first is directly showing people that the changes have actually improved performance. The second is to make sure that the people who get promoted fit the new culture. If they don't, it's a clear sign that the changes were only temporary.

7-4c Change Tools and Techniques

Imagine that your boss came to you and said, "All right, genius, you wanted it. You're in charge of turning around the division." Where would you begin? How would you encourage change-resistant managers to change? What would you do to include others in the change process? How would you get the change process off to a quick start? Finally, what approach would you use to promote long-term effectiveness and performance? Results-driven change, the General Electric workout, and organizational development are different change tools and techniques that can be used to address these issues.

One of the reasons that organizational change efforts fail is that they are activity oriented rather than results oriented. In other words, they focus primarily on changing company procedures, management philosophy, or employee behavior. Typically, there is much buildup and

Shell's new CEO, Ben van Beurden, split the company into 150 performance units, each to be evaluated on its profitability.

preparation as consultants are brought in, presentations are made, books are read, and employees and managers are trained. There's a tremendous emphasis on doing things the new way. But, with all the focus on "doing," almost no attention is paid to *results*, to seeing if all this activity has actually made a difference.

By contrast, **results-driven change** supplants the emphasis on activity with a laser-like focus on quickly measuring and improving results.[68] When Ben van Beurden became CEO of Royal Dutch Shell, one of the world's largest oil companies, he put everyone in the company on notice by proclaiming that oil refining profits were "simply too low," and that Shell needed, "better operational discipline." Furthermore, he changed managers' focus from "professional excellence," which served Shell well after a serious financial scandal, to specific results-driven goals. So Beurden split Shell into 150 performance units, each to be evaluated on its profitability, with profitable units continuing, and unprofitable units closing or being sold. Likewise, managers now had to compete for additional funds for their units by submitting formal requests to a central committee, which in turn had its spending recommendations reviewed by a "challenge committee."[69]

Another advantage of results-driven change is that managers introduce changes in procedures, philosophy, or behavior only if they are likely to improve measured performance. In other words, managers and workers actually test to see if changes make a difference. A third advantage of results-driven change is that quick, visible improvements motivate employees to continue to make additional changes to improve measured performance. Exhibit 7.4 describes the basic steps of results-driven change.

Results-driven change change created quickly by focusing on the measurement and improvement of results

The **General Electric workout** is a special kind of results-driven change. The "workout" involves a three-day meeting that brings together managers and employees from different levels and parts of an organization to quickly generate and act on solutions to specific business problems.[70] On the first morning, the boss discusses the agenda and targets specific business problems that the group will solve. Then, the boss leaves, and an outside facilitator breaks the group (typically thirty to forty people) into five or six teams and helps them spend the next day and a half discussing and debating solutions.

On day three, in what GE calls a *town meeting*, the teams present specific solutions to their boss, who has been gone since day one. As each team's spokesperson makes specific suggestions, the boss has only three options: agree on the spot, say no, or ask for more information so that a decision can be made by a specific, agreed-on date. GE boss Armand Lauzon sweated his way through a town meeting. To encourage him to say yes, his workers set up the meeting room to put pressure on Lauzon. He says, "I was wringing wet within half an hour. They had 108 proposals, I had about a minute to say yes or no to each one, and I couldn't make eye contact with my boss without turning around, which would show everyone in the room that I was chicken."[72] In the end, Lauzon agreed to all but eight suggestions. Furthermore, after those decisions were made, no one at GE was allowed to overrule them.

Organizational development is a philosophy and collection of planned change interventions designed to improve an organization's long-term health and performance. Organizational development takes a long-range approach to change; assumes that top-management support is necessary for change to succeed; creates change by educating workers and managers to change ideas, beliefs, and behaviors so that problems can be solved in new ways; and emphasizes employee participation in diagnosing, solving, and evaluating problems.[74] As shown in Exhibit 7.5, organizational development interventions begin with the recognition of a problem. Then, the company designates a **change agent** to be formally in charge of guiding the change effort. This person can be someone from within the company or a professional consultant. The change agent clarifies

General Electric workout a three-day meeting in which managers and employees from different levels and parts of an organization quickly generate and act on solutions to specific business problems

Organizational development a philosophy and collection of planned change interventions designed to improve an organization's long-term health and performance

Change agent the person formally in charge of guiding a change effort

Exhibit 7.4
How to Create a Results-Driven Change Program

1. Set measurable, short-term goals to improve performance.
2. Make sure your action steps are likely to improve measured performance.
3. Stress the importance of immediate improvements.
4. Solicit help from consultants and staffers to achieve quick improvements in performance.
5. Test action steps to see if they actually yield improvements. If they don't, discard them and establish new ones.
6. Use resources you have or that can be easily acquired. It doesn't take much.

Source: R. H. Schaffer and H. A. Thomson, "Successful Change Programs Begin with Results," *Harvard Business Review on Change* (Boston: Harvard Business School Press, 1998), 189–213.

Exhibit 7.5
General Steps for Organizational Development Interventions

1. Entry	A problem is discovered, and the need for change becomes apparent. A search begins for someone to deal with the problem and facilitate change.
2. Startup	A change agent enters the picture and works to clarify the problem and gain commitment to a change effort.
3. Assessment & feedback	The change agent gathers information about the problem and provides feedback about it to decision makers and those affected by it.
4. Action planning	The change agent works with decision makers to develop an action plan.
5. Intervention	The action plan, or organizational development intervention, is carried out.
6. Evaluation	The change agent helps decision makers assess the effectiveness of the intervention.
7. Adoption	Organizational members accept ownership and responsibility for the change, which is then carried out through the entire organization.
8. Separation	The change agent leaves the organization after first ensuring that the change intervention will continue to work.

Source: W. J. Rothwell, R. Sullivan, and G. M. McLean, *Practicing Organizational Development: A Guide for Consultants* (San Diego: Pfeiffer & Co., 1995).

Exhibit 7.6
Different Kinds of Organizational Development Interventions

Large-System Interventions	
Sociotechnical systems	An intervention designed to improve how well employees use and adjust to the work technology used in an organization.
Survey feedback	An intervention that uses surveys to collect information from the members of the system, reports the results of that survey to the members, and then uses those results to develop action plans for improvement.
Small-Group Interventions	
Team building	An intervention designed to increase the cohesion and cooperation of work group members.
Unit goal setting	An intervention designed to help a work group establish short- and long-term goals.
Person-Focused Interventions	
Counseling/coaching	An intervention designed so that a formal helper or coach listens to managers or employees and advises them on how to deal with work or interpersonal problems.
Training	An intervention designed to provide individuals with the knowledge, skills, or attitudes they need to become more effective at their jobs.

Source: W. J. Rothwell, R. Sullivan, and G. M. McLean, *Practicing Organizational Development: A Guide for Consultants* (San Diego: Pfeiffer & Co., 1995).

the problem, gathers information, works with decision makers to create and implement an action plan, helps to evaluate the plan's effectiveness, implements the plan throughout the company, and then leaves (if from outside the company) after making sure the change intervention will continue to work.

Organizational development interventions are aimed at changing large systems, small groups, or people.[73] More specifically, the purpose of *large-system interventions* is to change the character and perfor-

mance of an organization, business unit, or department. *Small-group intervention* focuses on assessing how a group functions and helping it work more effectively to accomplish its goals. *Person-focused intervention* is intended to increase interpersonal effectiveness by helping people to become aware of their attitudes and behaviors and to acquire new skills and knowledge. Exhibit 7.6 describes the most frequently used organizational development interventions for large systems, small groups, and people.

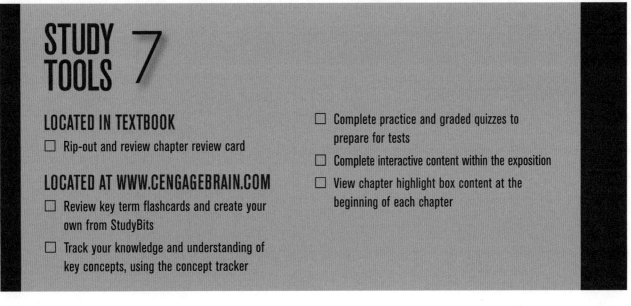

STUDY TOOLS 7

LOCATED IN TEXTBOOK
- ☐ Rip-out and review chapter review card

LOCATED AT WWW.CENGAGEBRAIN.COM
- ☐ Review key term flashcards and create your own from StudyBits
- ☐ Track your knowledge and understanding of key concepts, using the concept tracker

- ☐ Complete practice and graded quizzes to prepare for tests
- ☐ Complete interactive content within the exposition
- ☐ View chapter highlight box content at the beginning of each chapter

8 Global Management

Infocus/Dreamstime.com

LEARNING OUTCOMES

8-1 Discuss the impact of global business and the trade rules and agreements that govern it.

8-2 Explain why companies choose to standardize or adapt their business procedures.

8-3 Explain the different ways that companies can organize to do business globally.

8-4 Explain how to find a favorable business climate.

8-5 Discuss the importance of identifying and adapting to cultural differences.

8-6 Explain how to successfully prepare workers for international assignments.

After you finish this chapter, go to **PAGE 179** for **STUDY TOOLS**

8-1 GLOBAL BUSINESS, TRADE RULES, AND TRADE AGREEMENTS

Business is buying and selling of the goods or services. Buying this textbook was a business transaction. So was selling your first car and getting paid for babysitting or for mowing lawns. **Global business** is the buying and selling of goods and services by people from different countries. The Timex watch that I wore while I was writing this chapter was purchased at a Walmart in Texas. But because it was made in the Philippines, I participated in global business when I paid Walmart. Walmart, for its part, had already paid Timex, which had paid the company that employs the Filipino managers and workers who made my watch. Of course, there is more to global business than buying imported products at Walmart.

Global business presents its own set of challenges for managers. How can you be sure that the way you run your business in one country is the right way to run that business in another? This chapter discusses how organizations answer that question. We will start by examining global business in two ways: first exploring its impact on U.S. businesses and then reviewing the basic rules and agreements that govern global trade. Next, we will examine how and when companies go global by examining the trade-off between consistency and adaptation and discussing how to organize a global company. Finally, we will look at how companies decide where to expand globally, including finding the best business climate, adapting to cultural differences, and better preparing employees for international assignments.

If you want a simple demonstration of the impact of global business, look at the tag on your shirt, the inside of your shoes, and the inside of your digital camera (take out your battery). Chances are all of these items were made in different places around the world. As I write this, my shirt, shoes, and digital camera were made in Thailand, China, and Korea. Where were yours made?

*Let's learn more about **8-1a the impact of global business, 8-1b how tariff and nontariff trade barriers have historically restricted global business, 8-1c how today global and regional trade agreements are reducing those trade barriers worldwide**, and **8-1d how consumers are responding to those changes in trade rules and agreements.***

8-1a The Impact of Global Business

Multinational corporations are corporations that own businesses in two or more countries. In 1970, more than half of the world's 7,000 multinational corporations were headquartered in just two countries: the United States and the United Kingdom. There are now roughly 103,000 multinational corporations, more than fourteen times as many as in 1970, and 9,692, or 9.4 percent, are based in the United States.[1] Today, 73,144 multinationals, or 71 percent, are based in other developed countries (for example, Germany, Italy, Canada, and Japan), while 30,209, or 29.3 percent, are based in developing countries (for example, Colombia and South Africa). So, today, multinational companies can be found by the thousands all over the world!

Another way to appreciate the impact of global business is by considering direct foreign investment. **Direct foreign investment** occurs when a company builds a new business or buys an existing business in a foreign country. French information technology company **Cap Gemini** made a direct foreign investment in the U.S. when it purchased its U.S. rival IGATE for $4 billion.[2]

Of course, companies from many other countries also own businesses in the United States. As Exhibit 8.1 shows, companies from the United Kingdom, Japan, the Netherlands, Canada, Luxembourg, Switzerland, Germany, and France have the largest direct foreign investment in the United States. Overall, foreign companies invest more than $2.9 trillion a year to do business in the United States.

But direct foreign investment in the United States is only half the picture. U.S. companies also have made large direct foreign investments in countries throughout the world. **FedEx** is paying $4.8 billion to buy TNT Express, a Dutch package-delivery company. FedEx will gain TNT's door-to-door delivery routes in forty countries, doubling its European market share to over 20 percent, which will now rival the 25 percent share of its key competitor, UPS. FedEx executive Michael Glenn said, "The combination of FedEx's existing network and TNT's broad ground-based network will . . . result [in] . . . enhanced coverage, a broader portfolio, obviously, [and] better pickup and delivery cost."[3]

Global business the buying and selling of goods and services by people from different countries

Multinational corporation a corporation that owns businesses in two or more countries

Direct foreign investment a method of investment in which a company builds a new business or buys an existing business in a foreign country

Exhibit 8.1
Direct Foreign Investment in the United States

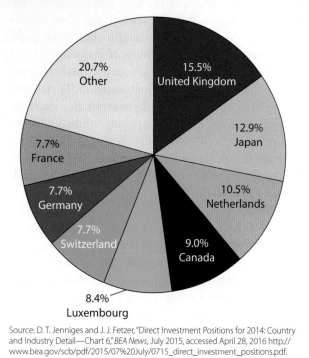

20.7% Other
15.5% United Kingdom
12.9% Japan
10.5% Netherlands
9.0% Canada
8.4% Luxembourg
7.7% Switzerland
7.7% Germany
7.7% France

Source: D. T. Jenniges and J. J. Fetzer, "Direct Investment Positions for 2014: Country and Industry Detail—Chart 6," *BEA News*, July 2015, accessed April 28, 2016 http://www.bea.gov/scb/pdf/2015/07%20July/0715_direct_investment_positions.pdf.

Exhibit 8.2
U.S. Direct Foreign Investment Abroad

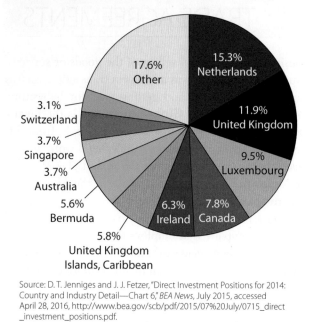

17.6% Other
15.3% Netherlands
11.9% United Kingdom
9.5% Luxembourg
7.8% Canada
6.3% Ireland
5.8% United Kingdom Islands, Caribbean
5.6% Bermuda
3.7% Australia
3.7% Singapore
3.1% Switzerland

Source: D. T. Jenniges and J. J. Fetzer, "Direct Investment Positions for 2014: Country and Industry Detail—Chart 6," *BEA News*, July 2015, accessed April 28, 2016, http://www.bea.gov/scb/pdf/2015/07%20July/0715_direct_investment_positions.pdf.

As Exhibit 8.2 shows, U.S. companies have made their largest direct foreign investments in the Netherlands, the United Kingdom, Luxembourg, Canada, and Ireland. Overall, U.S. companies invest more than $4.9 trillion a year to do business in other countries.

So, whether foreign companies invest in the United States or U.S. companies invest abroad, direct foreign investment is an increasingly important and common method of conducting global business.

Trade barriers government-imposed regulations that increase the cost and restrict the number of imported goods

Protectionism a government's use of trade barriers to shield domestic companies and their workers from foreign competition

Tariff a direct tax on imported goods

8-1b Trade Barriers

Although today's consumers usually don't care where the products they buy come from (more on this in Section 8-1d), national governments have traditionally preferred that consumers buy domestically made products in hopes that such purchases would increase the number of domestic businesses and workers. In fact, governments have done much more than hope that you will buy from domestic companies. Historically, governments have actively used **trade barriers** to make it much more expensive or difficult (or sometimes impossible) for consumers to buy or consume imported goods. For example, the Mexican government adds a 25 percent tariff to clothes, textiles, and footwear imported to Mexico. Stephen Lamar of the American Apparel & Footwear Association explained that the tariffs, ". . . will make it more expensive for our members to export to Mexico from the U.S. and everywhere. It's disappointing."[4] By establishing these restrictions and taxes, the Mexican government is engaging in **protectionism**, which is the use of trade barriers to protect local companies and their workers from foreign competition.

Governments have used two general kinds of trade barriers: tariff and nontariff barriers. A **tariff** is a direct tax on imported goods. Tariffs increase the cost of imported goods relative to that of domestic goods. The Indian import tax on raw and refined sugar is 25–40 percent, for example.[5] Countries also place tariffs on exports to discourage manufacturers from sending domestically produced goods overseas. For example, under former president Cristina Fernandez de Kirchner, Argentina placed heavy export tariffs on its agricultural products, including a 35 percent tax on soy exports, 23 percent tax on wheat, and 20 percent tax on corn. This resulted in a stockpile of crops valued at $11.4 billion.[6] When Mauricio Mauri became president in 2015, he eliminated all export tariffs on crops, saying, "We must stop being the world's barn to become the world's supermarket."[7]

Nontariff barriers are nontax methods of increasing the cost or reducing the volume of imported goods. There are five types of nontariff barriers: quotas, voluntary export restraints, government import standards, government subsidies, and customs valuation/classification. Because there are so many different kinds of nontariff barriers, they can be an even more potent method of shielding domestic industries from foreign competition.

Quotas are specific limits on the number or volume of imported products. For example, the Chinese government only allows thirty-four imported movies each year. China also limits the amount of foreign content available on video-streaming websites to no more than 30 percent. To get around the quota, films must be at least partially shot in China, co-financed by a Chinese firm, and have some Chinese cultural elements.[8]

Like quotas, **voluntary export restraints** limit the amount of a product that can be imported annually. The difference is that the exporting country rather than the importing country imposes restraints. Usually, however, the "voluntary" offer to limit exports occurs because the importing country has implicitly threatened to impose quotas. For example, to protect Brazilian auto manufacturers from less expensive Mexican-made cars, the Brazilian government convinced Mexico to "voluntarily" restrict auto exports to Brazil to no more than $1.55 billion a year for three years.[9] According to the World Trade Organization (see the discussion in Section 8-1c), however, voluntary export restraints are illegal and should not be used to restrict imports.[10]

In theory, **government import standards** are established to protect the health and safety of citizens. In reality, such standards are often used to restrict or ban imported goods. A 2014 U.S. law established elaborate safety standards for pangasius, a Vietnamese fish similar to the U.S. catfish. Vietnamese pangasius fish farmers must open their facilities to USDA inspectors, submit detailed sanitation plans, build inspection systems comparable to those in the United States, and submit their

Apparel

Festive Articles

catfish for inspection before they leave Vietnam *and* again at U.S. ports of entry.[11] Lisa Wedding of the National Fisheries Institute says the new law, "is not about food safety and never has been."[12] She says, "For years there has been an ongoing attempt to block imports and thus stifle competition. The food-safety part of the equation is a charade."[13] Imports of pangasius increased from 7 million pounds in 2014 to 215 million pounds in 2015.

Many nations also use **subsidies**, such as long-term, low-interest loans, cash grants, and tax deferments, to develop and protect companies in special industries. As part of the 1934 Sugar Act and the 2008 Farm Bill, American sugar processors, who employ 142,000 people, receive government guaranteed loans and a government subsidized price of 21 cents per pound, roughly twice the price of sugar outside the United States. Furthermore, when U.S. sugar producers aren't able to sell all of their sugar, the U.S. Department of Agriculture buys it and then sells it at a loss to ethanol producers.[14] The Competitive Enterprise Institute estimates the annual cost of subsidies at $3.5 billion a year.[15] Phillip Hayes of the U.S. Sugar Alliance says, "Other countries subsidize their sugar industries." Indeed, Brazilian sugar processors, which provide half of the world's sugar, receive $2.5 billion a year in subsidies from their government.[16]

The last type of nontariff barrier is **customs classification**. As products are imported into a country, they are examined by customs agents, who must decide which of nearly 9,000 categories they should be classified into (see the Official Harmonized Tariff Schedule of the United States at www.usitc.gov/tata/hts/index.htm for more information). The category assigned by customs

kurhan/Shutterstock.com

Nontariff barriers nontax methods of increasing the cost or reducing the volume of imported goods

Quota a limit on the number or volume of imported products

Voluntary export restraints voluntarily imposed limits on the number or volume of products exported to a particular country

Government import standard a standard ostensibly established to protect the health and safety of citizens but, in reality, is often used to restrict imports

Subsidies government loans, grants, and tax deferments given to domestic companies to protect them from foreign competition

Customs classification a classification assigned to imported products by government officials that affects the size of the tariff and the imposition of import quotas

agents can greatly affect the size of the tariff and whether the item is subject to import quotas. For example, the U.S. Customs Service classifies the various parts of a Santa Claus costume differently. The beard, wig, and hat are classified as "festive articles," which are defined as "flimsy, nondurable, and not normal articles of wearing apparel." Festive articles are exempt from import duties. The jacket, pants, gloves, and toy sacks, however, are considered apparel. They carry tariffs from 10 to 32 percent.[17]

administers trade agreements, provides a forum for trade negotiations, handles trade disputes, monitors national trade policies, and offers technical assistance and training for developing countries for its 161 member countries.

Through tremendous decreases in tariff and nontariff barriers, the Uruguay round of GATT made it much easier and cheaper for consumers in all countries to buy foreign products. First, tariffs were cut 40 percent on average worldwide by 2005. Second, tariffs were eliminated in ten specific industries: beer, alcohol, construction equipment, farm machinery, furniture, medical equipment, paper, pharmaceuticals, steel, and toys. Third, stricter limits were put on government subsidies. For example, the Uruguay round of GATT put limits on how much national governments can subsidize private research in electronic and high-tech industries (see the discussion of subsidies in Section 8-1b). Fourth, the Uruguay round of GATT established protections for intellectual property, such as trademarks, patents, and copyrights.

Protection of intellectual property has become an increasingly important issue in global trade because of widespread product piracy. For example, the International Federation of the Phonographic Industry estimates that 20 percent of "fixed-line Internet users worldwide regularly access services offering copyright infringing music."[19] Likewise, according to BSA | The Software Alliance, 43 percent of all software used in the world is pirated, costing companies $62.7 billion in lost sales.[20]

Product piracy is also costly to the movie industry, as movie studios and theaters, as well as video/DVD distributors, lose $18 billion each year to pirates. In fact, digital sales of movies rose 6–10 percent for two movie studios after Megaupload, an illegal site for downloading movies, was closed.[21]

Finally, trade disputes between countries now are fully settled by arbitration panels from the WTO. In the past, countries could use their veto power to cancel a panel's decision. For instance, the French government routinely vetoed rulings that its large cash grants to French farmers constituted unfair subsidies. Now, however, countries that are members of the WTO no longer have veto power. Thus, WTO rulings are complete and final. Exhibit 8.3 provides a brief overview of the WTO and its functions.

8-1c Trade Agreements

Thanks to the trade barriers described previously, buying imported goods has often been much more expensive and difficult than buying domestic goods. During the 1990s, however, the regulations governing global trade were transformed. The most significant change was that 124 countries agreed to adopt the **General Agreement on Tariffs and Trade (GATT)**. GATT, which existed from 1947 to 1995, was an agreement to regulate trade among (eventually) more than 120 countries, the purpose of which was "substantial reduction of tariffs and other trade barriers and the elimination of preferences."[18] GATT members engaged in eight rounds of trade negotiations, with the Uruguay Round signed in 1994 and going into effect in 1995. Although GATT itself was replaced by the **World Trade Organization (WTO)** in 1995, the changes that it made continue to encourage international trade. Today, the WTO and its member countries are negotiating what's known as the Doha Round, which seeks to advance trade opportunities for developing countries in areas ranging from agriculture to services to intellectual property rights. The WTO, headquartered in Geneva, Switzerland,

General Agreement on Tariffs and Trade (GATT) a worldwide trade agreement that reduced and eliminated tariffs, limited government subsidies, and established protections for intellectual property

World Trade Organization (WTO) the successor to GATT; the only international organization dealing with the global rules of trade between nations; its main function is to ensure that trade flows as smoothly, predictably, and freely as possible

Fabio Alcini/Shutterstock.com

Exhibit 8.3
World Trade Organization

☑ **FACT FILE**

WORLD TRADE
ORGANIZATION

Location: Geneva, Switzerland
Established: January 1, 1995
Created by: Uruguay Round
negotiations (1986–1994)
Membership: 162 countries
(on November 30, 2015)
Budget: 197 million Swiss
francs for 2013
Secretariat staff: 634
Head: Roberto Azevêdo
(Director-General)

Functions:
- Administering WTO trade agreements
- Forum for trade negotiations
- Handling trade disputes
- Monitoring national trade policies
- Technical assistance and training for developing countries
- Cooperation with other international organizations

Source: "Fact File: What Is the WTO?" *World Trade Organization*, https://www.wto.org/english/thewto_e/whatis_e/whatis_e.htm.

The second major development that has reduced trade barriers has been the creation of **regional trading zones**, or zones in which tariff and nontariff barriers are reduced or eliminated for countries within the trading zone. The largest and most important trading zones are:

▶ Africa: African Free Trade Zone Agreement (AFTZ) and Tripartite Free Trade Area (TFTA)

▶ Asia: Association of Southeast Asian Nations (ASEAN), Asia-Pacific Economic Cooperation (APEC), and Trans-Pacific Partnership (TPP)

▶ Central America: Dominican Republic-Central America Free Trade Agreement (CAFTA-DR)

▶ Europe: The Maastricht Treaty

▶ North America: North American Free Trade Agreement (NAFTA)

▶ South America: Union of South American Nations (USAN)

The map in Exhibit 8.4 shows the extent to which free-trade agreements govern global trade.

In 1992, Belgium, Denmark, France, Germany, Greece, Ireland, Italy, Luxembourg, the Netherlands, Portugal, Spain, and the United Kingdom adopted the **Maastricht Treaty of Europe**. The purpose of this treaty was to transform their twelve different economies and twelve currencies into one common economic market, called the European Union (EU), with one common currency. On January 1, 2002, a single common currency, the euro, went into circulation in twelve of the EU's members (Austria, Belgium, Finland, France, Germany, Greece, Ireland, Italy, Luxembourg, the Netherlands, Portugal, and Spain). Austria, Finland, and Sweden joined the EU in 1995, followed by Cyprus, the Czech Republic, Estonia, Hungary, Latvia, Lithuania, Malta, Poland, Slovakia, and Slovenia in 2004; Bulgaria and Romania in 2007; and Croatia in 2013, bringing the total membership to twenty-eight countries.[22] In June 2016, the UK voted to leave the EU. A final departure date, most likely sometime between 2018 and 2020, has yet to be determined. Macedonia, Iceland, Montenegro, Serbia, and Turkey have applied and are being considered for membership.

Prior to the treaty, trucks carrying products were stopped and inspected by customs agents at each border. Furthermore, because the required paperwork, tariffs, and government product specifications could be radically different in each country, companies often had to file twelve different sets of paperwork, pay twelve different tariffs, produce twelve different versions of their basic product to meet various government specifications, and exchange money in twelve different currencies. Likewise, open business travel, which we take for granted in the United States, was complicated by inspections at each border crossing. If you lived in Germany but worked in Luxembourg, your car was stopped and your passport was inspected twice every day as you traveled to and from work. Also, every business transaction required a currency exchange, for example, from German deutsche marks to Italian lira, or from French francs to Dutch guilders. Imagine all of this happening to millions of trucks, cars, and workers each day, and you can begin to appreciate the difficulty and cost of conducting business across Europe before the Maastricht Treaty. For more information about the Maastricht Treaty, the EU, and the euro, see http://europa.eu/index_en.htm.

Regional trading zones areas in which tariff and nontariff barriers on trade between countries are reduced or eliminated

Maastricht Treaty of Europe a regional trade agreement among most European countries

Exhibit 8.4
Global Map of Regional Trade Agreements

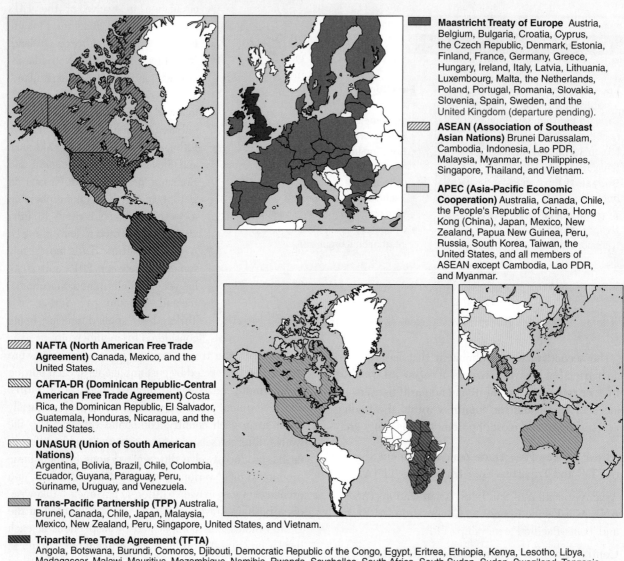

Maastricht Treaty of Europe Austria, Belgium, Bulgaria, Croatia, Cyprus, the Czech Republic, Denmark, Estonia, Finland, France, Germany, Greece, Hungary, Ireland, Italy, Latvia, Lithuania, Luxembourg, Malta, the Netherlands, Poland, Portugal, Romania, Slovakia, Slovenia, Spain, Sweden, and the United Kingdom (departure pending).

ASEAN (Association of Southeast Asian Nations) Brunei Darussalam, Cambodia, Indonesia, Lao PDR, Malaysia, Myanmar, the Philippines, Singapore, Thailand, and Vietnam.

APEC (Asia-Pacific Economic Cooperation) Australia, Canada, Chile, the People's Republic of China, Hong Kong (China), Japan, Mexico, New Zealand, Papua New Guinea, Peru, Russia, South Korea, Taiwan, the United States, and all members of ASEAN except Cambodia, Lao PDR, and Myanmar.

NAFTA (North American Free Trade Agreement) Canada, Mexico, and the United States.

CAFTA-DR (Dominican Republic-Central American Free Trade Agreement) Costa Rica, the Dominican Republic, El Salvador, Guatemala, Honduras, Nicaragua, and the United States.

UNASUR (Union of South American Nations) Argentina, Bolivia, Brazil, Chile, Colombia, Ecuador, Guyana, Paraguay, Peru, Suriname, Uruguay, and Venezuela.

Trans-Pacific Partnership (TPP) Australia, Brunei, Canada, Chile, Japan, Malaysia, Mexico, New Zealand, Peru, Singapore, United States, and Vietnam.

Tripartite Free Trade Agreement (TFTA) Angola, Botswana, Burundi, Comoros, Djibouti, Democratic Republic of the Congo, Egypt, Eritrea, Ethiopia, Kenya, Lesotho, Libya, Madagascar, Malawi, Mauritius, Mozambique, Namibia, Rwanda, Seychelles, South Africa, South Sudan, Sudan, Swaziland, Tanzania, Uganda, Zambia, and Zimbabwe.

North American Free Trade Agreement (NAFTA) a regional trade agreement among the United States, Canada, and Mexico

Dominican Republic-Central America Free Trade Agreement (CAFTA-DR) a regional trade agreement among Costa Rica, the Dominican Republic, El Salvador, Guatemala, Honduras, Nicaragua, and the United States

NAFTA, the **North American Free Trade Agreement** among the United States, Canada, and Mexico, went into effect on January 1, 1994. More than any other regional trade agreement, NAFTA has liberalized trade between countries so that businesses can plan for one market (North America) rather than for three separate markets. One of NAFTA's most important achievements was to eliminate most product tariffs *and* prevent the three countries from increasing existing tariffs or introducing new ones. Overall, Mexican and Canadian exports to the United States are up 637 percent and 212 percent, respectively, since NAFTA went into effect. U.S. exports to Mexico and Canada are up 478 percent and 212 percent, growing twice as fast as U.S. exports to any other part of the world. In fact, Mexico and Canada now account for 34 percent of all U.S. exports.[23]

CAFTA-DR, the **Dominican Republic-Central America Free Trade Agreement** among the United

States, the Dominican Republic, and the Central American countries of Costa Rica, El Salvador, Guatemala, Honduras, and Nicaragua, went into effect in August 2005. With a combined population of 51.1 million, the CAFTA-DR countries together are the thirteenth-largest U.S. export market in the world and the third-largest U.S. export market in Latin America, after Mexico and Brazil. U.S. companies export nearly $30 billion in goods each year to the CAFTA-DR countries.[24]

On May 23, 2008, twelve South American countries signed the **Union of South American Nations (UNASUR)** Constitutive Treaty, which united the countries of the Mercosur trade group (Argentina, Brazil, Paraguay, Uruguay, and Venezuela) and the countries of the Andean Community (Bolivia, Colombia, Ecuador, and Peru) with Guyana, Suriname, and Chile. UNASUR aims to create a unified South America by permitting free movement between nations, creating a common infrastructure that includes an interoceanic highway, and establishing the region as a single market by eliminating all tariffs by 2019. UNASUR is one of the largest trading zones in the world, encompassing 412 million people in South America with a combined gross domestic product (GDP) of nearly $973 billion.[25]

ASEAN, the **Association of Southeast Asian Nations**, and **APEC**, the **Asia-Pacific Economic Cooperation**, are the two largest and most important regional trading groups in Asia. ASEAN is a trade agreement among Brunei Darussalam, Cambodia, Indonesia, Lao PDR, Malaysia, Myanmar, the Philippines, Singapore, Thailand, and Vietnam, which form a market of more than 625 million people with a combined GDP of $2.4 trillion. U.S. trade with ASEAN countries exceeds $234 billion a year.[26]

In fact, the United States is ASEAN's third-largest trading partner (China is its largest), and ASEAN's member nations constitute the fourth-largest trading partner of the United States. An ASEAN free-trade area was established in 2015 for the six original countries (Brunei Darussalam, Indonesia, Malaysia, the Philippines, Singapore, and Thailand), and in 2018 for the newer member countries (Cambodia, Lao PDR, Myanmar, and Vietnam). All ten nations have committed to develop a "deeply integrated and highly cohesive ASEAN economy" by 2025.[27]

APEC is a broad agreement that includes Australia, Canada, Chile, the People's Republic of China, Hong Kong, Japan, Mexico, New Zealand, Papua New Guinea, Peru, Russia, South Korea, Taiwan, the United States, and all the members of ASEAN except Cambodia, Lao PDR, and Myanmar. APEC's twenty-one member countries have a total population of 3 billion people and combined GDP of more than $43.8 trillion.[28]

APEC countries began reducing trade barriers in 2000, though all the reductions will not be completely phased in until 2020.[29]

On February 4, 2016, twelve nations signed the **Trans-Pacific Partnership (TPP)**: Australia, Brunei, Canada, Chile, Japan, Malaysia, Mexico, New Zealand, Peru, Singapore, United States, and Vietnam. This region is home to 40 percent of the world's population and produces roughly 60 percent of global GDP.[30] As of April 2016, it is not clear when the TPP will go into effect, as the twelve signatory countries are yet to officially ratify their participation. New Zealand Prime Minister John Key says the TPP "is still just a piece of paper, or rather over 16,000 pieces of paper, until it actually comes into force." At least six countries accounting for 85 percent of the total GDP of the region must ratify the TPP within two years for it to go into effect. In other words, the United States and Japan must approve the TPP, or the agreement will fail.[31]

The **Tripartite Free Trade Agreement (TFTA)** is an African trade agreement proposed in 2015. Currently signed by twenty-seven member states and awaiting ratification, the TFTA's ultimate goal is to create a free trade area across all fifty-four African Union states by 2017.

8-1d Consumers, Trade Barriers, and Trade Agreements

The average worker earns nearly $48,420 in Finland, $61,570 in Sweden, $103,630 in Norway, and $55,230 in the United States.[32] Yet after adjusting these incomes for how much they can buy, the Finnish income is worth just $40,630, the Swedish $46,970, and the Norwegian $67,100.[33] This is the same as saying $1 of income can buy only $0.84 worth of goods in Finland, $0.76 in Sweden, and $0.65 in Norway.

Union of South American Nations (UNASUR) a regional trade agreement among Argentina, Brazil, Paraguay, Uruguay, Venezuela, Bolivia, Colombia, Ecuador, Peru, Guyana, Suriname, and Chile

Association of Southeast Asian Nations (ASEAN) a regional trade agreement among Brunei Darussalam, Cambodia, Indonesia, Laos, Malaysia, Myanmar, the Philippines, Singapore, Thailand, and Vietnam

Asia-Pacific Economic Cooperation (APEC) a regional trade agreement among Australia, Canada, Chile, the People's Republic of China, Hong Kong, Japan, Mexico, New Zealand, Papua New Guinea, Peru, Russia, South Korea, Taiwan, the United States, and all the members of ASEAN except Cambodia, Lao PDR, and Myanmar

Trans-Pacific Partnership (TPP) a proposed regional trade agreement among Australia, Brunei, Canada, Chile, Japan, Malaysia, Mexico, New Zealand, Peru, Singapore, United States, and Vietnam

Tripartite Free Trade Agreement (TFTA) a regional trade agreement among twenty-seven African countries

New trade agreements are often met with public scrutiny and protests. Here, Australian demonstrators gather on February 4, 2016, to march against the Trans-Pacific Partnership.

amount to $8.4 billion in additional costs to Japanese consumers and taxpayers.[35]

So why do trade barriers and free-trade agreements matter to consumers? They're important because free-trade agreements increase choices, competition, and purchasing power and thus decrease what people pay for food, clothing, necessities, and luxuries. Accordingly, today's consumers rarely care where their products and services come from. From seafood to diamonds, people don't care where products are from—they just want to know which brand or kind is cheaper. And why do trade barriers and free-trade agreements matter to managers? The reason, as you're about to read, is that while free-trade agreements create new business opportunities, they also intensify competition, and addressing that competition is a manager's job.

In other words, Americans can buy much more with their incomes than those in many other countries.

One reason that Americans get more for their money is that the U.S. marketplace is the third most competitive in the world (behind Switzerland and Singapore). The U.S. economy has historically been one of the easiest for foreign companies to enter.[34] Although some U.S. industries, such as textiles, have been heavily protected from foreign competition by trade barriers, for the most part, American consumers (and businesses) have had plentiful choices among American-made and foreign-made products. More important, the high level of competition between foreign and domestic companies that creates these choices helps keep prices low in the United States. Furthermore, it is precisely the lack of choice and the low level of competition that keep prices higher in countries that have not been as open to foreign companies and products. For example, Japanese trade barriers on agricultural products are high. In fact, over 45 percent of the value of Japan's agricultural industry comes from trade barriers or subsidies. The tariffs on rice alone

8-2 CONSISTENCY OR ADAPTATION?

After a company has decided that it *will* go global, it must decide *how* to go global. For example, if you decide to sell in Singapore, should you try to find a local business partner who speaks the language, knows the laws, and understands the customs and norms of Singapore's culture? Or should you simply export your products from your home country? What do you do if you are also entering Eastern Europe, perhaps starting in Hungary? Should you use the same approach in Hungary that you use in Singapore?

In this section, we return to a key issue: How can you be sure that the way you run your business in one country is the right way to run that business in another?

In other words, how can you strike the right balance between global consistency and local adaptation?

Global consistency means that a multinational company with offices, manufacturing plants, and distribution facilities in different countries uses the same rules, guidelines, policies, and procedures to run all of those offices, plants, and facilities. Managers at company headquarters value global consistency because it simplifies decisions.

Global consistency when a multinational company has offices, manufacturing plants, and distribution facilities in different countries and runs them all using the same rules, guidelines, policies, and procedures

GLOBAL TASTES INCLUDE SOGGY CORN FLAKES

Cereal sales have been declining for years in the United States, but they have been exploding in many developing nations. While this overall growth is good news for cereal manufacturer Kellogg's, it has also brought a new set of challenges. Yogurt is more widely available than milk in Colombia, so Kellogg's sells cereal attached to packets of yogurt. Kellogg's found that consumers in South Africa were boiling their Corn Flakes to give the cereal a more porridge-like consistency, so it developed Corn Flakes Instant Porridge for that market. Kara Timperley, Kellogg's marketing director for sub-Saharan Africa, said that once they realized consumer differences, reconceiving Corn Flakes as porridge was a "no-brainer." Today, nearly a third of Kellogg's $14.6 billion annual revenue comes from sales of cereal and related products in emerging markets.

Source: J. Revill and A. Gasparro, "Cereal Makers Tweak Recipes for Emerging Markets," *Wall Street Journal*, September 26, 2015, B6.

For example, rather than stock its new São Paulo, Brazil, store with apparel according to South American seasonality, **Ralph Lauren** followed the North American seasons, putting winter apparel on the shelves during the Brazilian summer.[36] By contrast, a company following a policy of **local adaptation** modifies its standard operating procedures to adapt to differences in foreign customers, governments, and regulatory agencies. For example, Netflix changed its production schedule in Europe to accommodate French and German preferences for voice dubbing, rather than subtitles. It also reworked its payment system to accept bank transfers instead of credit cards, which are unpopular in Germany. A Netflix spokesperson said, "Every market around the globe has its nuances. Our challenge is becoming a great global company where we really understand the nuances of each market and do a great job for consumers around the world."[37] Local adaptation is typically preferred by local managers who are charged with making the international business successful in their countries.

If companies lean too much toward global consistency, they run the risk of using management procedures poorly suited to particular countries' markets, cultures, and employees (that is, a lack of local adaptation). Home Depot became the biggest hardware and home improvement retailer in the United States thanks to its big-box model featuring huge stores, thousands of suburban locations, a vast range of products, and strong customer service. But, after eight years, Home Depot closed its seven Chinese stores. Unlike Americans, who are do-it-yourselfers when it comes to home improvement because it saves money, the widespread availability of low-cost labor makes China more of a "do-it-for-me culture," says a Home Depot spokesperson. Furthermore, unlike the United States, where completing DIY projects is admired, there's a stigma associated with

> **Local adaptation** modifying rules, guidelines, policies, and procedures to adapt to differences in foreign customers, governments, and regulatory agencies

performing manual labor in China. A Chinese middle-class customer said, "Poor people are the only group in China who would bother taking on a DIY project because they cannot afford to hire others."[38] And, unlike in the United States, where a much higher percentage of people own their homes, most Chinese, especially those with the discretionary income to afford home projects, rent small apartments in cities, which further diminished Home Depot's opportunities in China.[39]

If, however, companies focus too much on local adaptation, they run the risk of losing the cost effectiveness and productivity that result from using standardized rules and procedures throughout the world. Because its French stores are nearly identical to its U.S. stores, Starbucks has never been profitable in France. As a result, says Parisian Marion Bayod, "I never go into Starbucks; it's impersonal, the coffee is mediocre, and it's expensive. For us, it's like another planet." Likewise, Parisian Laurent Pauzié says Starbucks stores, "are only here to comfort tourists when they're lost." Canadian Kate Menzies, who lives in Paris, concedes that while Starbucks may not be popular for its coffee, it "is one of the few places with public toilets and free WiFi in the city."[40] Starbucks, however, is now embracing local adaptation. Rather than offering strong coffee in paper cups as in the United States, its French stores will offer a lighter-tasting "blonde" espresso in glass coffee cups (because the French prefer to sit and drink) in larger redesigned stores with sumptuous wooden bars, bright chandeliers, and velvet couches, similar to traditional Parisian cafés. While Starbucks hopes these changes will attract French customers, spending tens of millions more to adapt its stores to French tastes may also sacrifice the cost effectiveness and productivity that make it profitable in the United States.[41]

8-3 FORMS FOR GLOBAL BUSINESS

Besides determining whether to adapt organizational policies and procedures, a company must also determine how to organize itself for successful entry into foreign markets.

*Historically, companies have generally followed the phase model of globalization, in which a company makes the transition from a domestic company to a global company in the following sequential phases: **8-3a exporting, 8-3b cooperative contracts, 8-3c strategic alliances,** and **8-3d wholly***

Exporting selling domestically produced products to customers in foreign countries

***owned affiliates.** At each step, the company grows much larger, uses those resources to enter more global markets, is less dependent on home-country sales, and is more committed in its orientation to global business. Some companies, however, do not follow the phase model of globalization. Some skip phases on their way to becoming more global and less domestic. Others don't follow the phase model at all. These are known as **8-3e global new ventures.** This section reviews these forms of global business.[42]*

8-3a Exporting

When companies produce products in their home countries and sell those products to customers in foreign countries, they are **exporting**. Exporting as a form of global business offers many advantages. It makes the company less dependent on sales in its home market and provides a greater degree of control over research, design, and production decisions. **Cayuga Milk Ingredients** built a $100 million factory in New York to serve domestic customers. However, 79 percent of the plant's milk production is exported to Mexico and Saudi Arabia. CEO Kevin Ellis says, "We can't go back from the international market. There aren't enough people to consume [dairy products] in this country."[43] Today, 16 percent of U.S. milk production is exported. Over the past decade, the U.S. share of global dairy exports has risen from 7 to 20 percent.[44] Though advantageous in a number of ways, exporting also has its disadvantages. The primary disadvantage is that many exported goods are subject to tariff and nontariff barriers that can substantially increase their final cost to consumers. The second disadvantage is that transportation costs can significantly increase the price of an exported product. Chinese regulations require live imported animals to be slaughtered within fifty-five miles of their point of entry. To meet China's growing demand for fresh beef, Australian ranchers have begun flying cattle on 747 jumbo jets to ports of entry thousands of miles inland. By switching from ships to jets, exporters have been able to expand the market for fresh beef in inland China.[45] The final disadvantage of exporting is that exporters depend on foreign importers for product distribution. If, for example, the foreign importer makes a mistake on the paperwork that accompanies a shipment of imported goods, those goods can be returned to the foreign manufacturer at the manufacturer's expense.

8-3b Cooperative Contracts

When an organization wants to expand its business globally without making a large financial commitment to do so,

Franchisees pay McDonald's an initial franchise fee of $45,000 to get the rights to operate a restaurant.

it may sign a **cooperative contract** with a foreign business owner who pays the company a fee for the right to conduct that business in his or her country. There are two kinds of cooperative contracts: licensing and franchising.

Under a **licensing** agreement, a domestic company, the *licensor*, receives royalty payments for allowing another company, the *licensee*, to produce its product, sell its service, or use its brand name in a particular foreign market. It costs more than $4 million to produce a single episode of a television series like *Blacklist*, *CSI*, or *Gotham*. Payments from U.S. television networks generally only cover 50–65 percent of that, so foreign licensing agreements are critical to covering the remaining production costs. For example, in order to air these shows in the United Kingdom, Britain's Channel 5 (the licensee) pays Warner Bros. (the licensor) a $780,000-per-episode fee.[46] Forty percent of the revenue generated by popular television shows comes from foreign broadcast licenses.[47]

One of the most important advantages of licensing is that it allows companies to earn additional profits without investing more money. As foreign sales increase, the royalties paid to the licensor by the foreign licensee increase. Moreover, the licensee, not the licensor, invests in production equipment and facilities to produce the product. Licensing also helps companies avoid tariff and nontariff barriers. Because the licensee manufactures the product within the foreign country, tariff and nontariff barriers don't apply.

The biggest disadvantage associated with licensing is that the licensor gives up control over the quality of the product or service sold by the foreign licensee. Unless the licensing agreement contains specific restrictions, the licensee controls the entire business from production to marketing to final sales. Many licensors include inspection clauses in their license contracts, but closely monitoring product or service quality from thousands of miles away can be difficult.

An overeager licensor can dilute the value of a brand or damage the brand's reputation through overexposure. Luxury fashion brands like Louis Vuitton, Celine, Gucci, Yves Saint Laurent, and Burberry recently ended long-term licensing agreements, citing a lack of control over the products sold under their brand names. **Burberry** ended a forty-five-year agreement with its Japanese licensee, Sanyo Shokai, because the company opened hundreds of stores and flooded Japan with too many moderately-priced items. After canceling the contract, Burberry reduced the number of Japanese stores from more than 400 to two dozen and replaced Sanyo Shokai's mid-tier products with ones costing up to ten times more. According to CEO for Burberry in Asia, Pascal Perrier, "The license has been suffering from overexposure. We will never do that again."[48] An additional disadvantage is that licensees can eventually become competitors, especially when a licensing agreement includes access to important technology or proprietary business knowledge.

A **franchise** is a collection of networked firms in which the manufacturer or marketer of a product or service, the *franchisor*, licenses the entire business to another person or organization, the *franchisee*. For the price of an initial franchise fee plus royalties, franchisors provide franchisees with training, assistance with marketing and advertising, and an exclusive right to conduct business in a particular location. Most franchise fees run between $5,000 and $35,000. Franchisees pay McDonald's, one of the largest franchisors in the world, an initial franchise

Cooperative contract an agreement in which a foreign business owner pays a company a fee for the right to conduct that business in his or her country

Licensing an agreement in which a domestic company, the licensor, receives royalty payments for allowing another company, the licensee, to produce the licensor's product, sell its service, or use its brand name in a specified foreign market

Franchise a collection of networked firms in which the manufacturer or marketer of a product or service, the franchisor, licenses the entire business to another person or organization, the franchisee

fee of $45,000. Another $989,352 to $2,217,045 is needed beyond that to pay for food inventory, kitchen equipment, construction, landscaping, and other expenses (the cost varies by location). While franchisees typically borrow part of this cost from a bank, McDonald's requires applicants to have over $500,000 in nonborrowed assets and requires a 25–40 percent down payment in cash for the initial investment.[49] Typical royalties run from 4 percent of gross sales (plus rent at 8.5%) to 15 percent based on location and revenue.[50] So franchisors are well rewarded for the help they provide to franchisees. More than 400 U.S. companies franchise their businesses to foreign franchise partners.

Despite franchising's many advantages, franchisors face a loss of control when they sell businesses to franchisees who are thousands of miles away. Franchising specialist Cheryl Scott says, "One franchisor I know was wondering why the royalties coming from India were so small when he knew the shop was always packed. It was because the franchisee wasn't putting all of the sales through the cash register."[51]

Although there are exceptions, franchising success may be somewhat culture-bound. Because most global franchisors begin by franchising their businesses in similar countries or regions (Canada is by far the first choice for U.S. companies taking their first step into global franchising), and because 65 percent of franchisors make absolutely no change in their business for overseas franchisees, that success may not generalize to cultures with different lifestyles, values, preferences, and technological infrastructures. Customizing menus to local tastes is one of the primary ways that fast-food companies can succeed in international markets. Dunkin' Donuts struggled at first in India with its traditional coffee and donuts menu because Indians don't eat sweets for breakfast, which is eaten at home and not on the way to work. Dunkin' adjusted by changing store schedules to afternoon and evening hours and creating a new menu featuring nonbeef burgers, sandwiches, and wraps using potatoes, pepper chicken, and spicy vegetables as ingredients. It also customized its donut menu to local tastes, adding donuts with curry, pistachios, and rice pudding. Two new menu items are the Brute Tough Guy Veg burger and the It's a Mistake donut, a white-chocolate donut topped with guava and chili.[52]

Strategic alliance an agreement in which companies combine key resources, costs, risks, technology, and people

Joint venture a strategic alliance in which two existing companies collaborate to form a third, independent company

8-3c Strategic Alliances

Companies forming **strategic alliances** combine key resources, costs, risks, technology, and people. Hewlett-Packard, the world's largest electronics manufacturer, with a 28 percent share of the computer server market, and Foxconn, the Taiwanese firm that assembles some of the world's most popular electronic devices, such as the iPhone and iPad, have formed a strategic alliance to co-develop large servers that can handle cloud computing and process "big data" for multinational firms.[53] The most common strategic alliance is a **joint venture**, which occurs when two existing companies collaborate to form a third company. The two founding companies remain intact and unchanged, except that together they now own the newly created joint venture.

One of the advantages of global joint ventures is that, like licensing and franchising, they help companies avoid tariff and nontariff barriers to entry. Another advantage is that companies participating in a joint venture bear only part of the costs and the risks of that business. Many companies find this attractive because of the expense of entering foreign markets or developing new products.

Global joint ventures can be especially advantageous to smaller local partners who link up with larger, more experienced foreign firms that can bring advanced management, resources, and business skills to the joint venture.

Global joint ventures are not without problems, though. Because companies share costs and risks with their joint venture partners, they must also share profits. Managing global joint ventures can also be difficult because they represent a merging of four cultures: the country and the organizational culture of the first

In 2014, Kroger purchased Tesco's interest in Dunhumby and launched it's own market research division.

partner, and the country and the organizational culture of the second partner. Often, to be fair to all involved, each partner in the global joint venture will have equal ownership and power. But this can result in power struggles and a lack of leadership. Because of these problems, companies forming global joint ventures should carefully develop detailed contracts that specify the obligations of each party. U.S.-based **Kroger** supermarkets and UK consumer research firm **dunnhumby** (owned by UK supermarket chain **Tesco**) were fifty-fifty partners in dunnhumby USA for twelve years. The joint venture helped Kroger build customized marketing programs that resulted in a huge advantage over its competitors and forty-five straight quarters of growth. When Tesco needed cash after losing $9.52 billion in 2014, Kroger bought Tesco's interest in dunnhumby USA, ending the global joint venture. Kroger then launched 84.51°, which is its own consumer research division.[54]

8-3d Wholly Owned Affiliates (Build or Buy)

Approximately one-third of multinational companies enter foreign markets through wholly owned affiliates. In 2015, Chinese firms spent a record $15.7 billion to acquire companies or build new facilities as a way of entering the U.S. market. One of these firms, Golden Dragon Precise Copper Tube Group, entered the U.S. market by building a $120 million pipe factory in Wilcox, Alabama. The company's U.S. subsidiary, GD Copper, is completely owned by the Chinese parent company.[55] Unlike licensing arrangements, franchises, or joint ventures, **wholly owned affiliates**, such as American Standard Brands and GROHE, are 100 percent owned by their parent company, in this case, Lixil.

The primary advantage of wholly owned businesses is that the parent company receives all of the profits and has complete control over the foreign facilities. The biggest disadvantage is the expense of building new operations or buying existing businesses. Although the payoff can be enormous if wholly owned affiliates succeed, the losses can be immense if they fail because the parent company assumes all of the risk. After Hong-Kong apparel maker **TAL Group** opened a pants factory in Dongguan, China, employee wages and benefits skyrocketed 31 percent the first year, 28 percent the second year, and then rose 10–12 percent annually thereafter. After nine years, TAL Group closed the pants factory and laid off 2,400 employees. After the shutdown, CEO Roger Lee said that there was no way the Chinese factory could ever be as profitable as factories in Southeast Asia because of the higher labor costs. "We've done the calculation quite a few times," said Lee.[56]

8-3e Global New Ventures

Companies used to evolve slowly from small operations selling in their home markets to large businesses selling to foreign markets. Furthermore, as companies went global, they usually followed the phase model of globalization. Recently, however, three trends have combined to allow companies to skip the phase model when going global. First, quick, reliable air travel can transport people to nearly any point in the world within one day. Second, low-cost communication technologies such as email, teleconferencing and phone conferencing via the Internet, and cloud computing make it easier to communicate with global customers, suppliers, managers, and employees. Third, there is now a critical mass of businesspeople with extensive personal experience in all aspects of global business.[57] This combination of developments has made it possible to start companies that are global from inception. With sales, employees, and financing in different countries, **global new ventures** are companies that are founded with an active global strategy.[58]

Although there are several different kinds of global new ventures, all share two common factors. First, the company founders successfully develop and communicate the company's global vision from inception. Second, rather than going global one country at a time, new global ventures bring a product or service to market in several foreign markets at the same time. **MakerBot** 3-D printers "print" items made of rigid plastic based on specifications from computer-aided design software such as AutoDesk. NASA's Jet Propulsion Laboratory uses MakerBot's Replicator 2 (hat tip to *Star Trek*) to print prototype parts cheaply and quickly. Cofounder Bre Pettis believes that MakerBot can fundamentally disrupt global manufacturing and replace "two centuries of mass production" by giving anyone with an idea the tools to design his or her own products without a factory. Though just five years old, MakerBot, which has been global since inception, has distributors in fourteen countries, including Australia, Brazil, China, Germany, Japan, and the United Kingdom.[59]

Wholly owned affiliates foreign offices, facilities, and manufacturing plants that are 100 percent owned by the parent company

Global new ventures new companies that are founded with an active global strategy and have sales, employees, and financing in different countries

Exhibit 8.5
How Consumption of Coca-Cola Varies with Purchasing Power Around the World

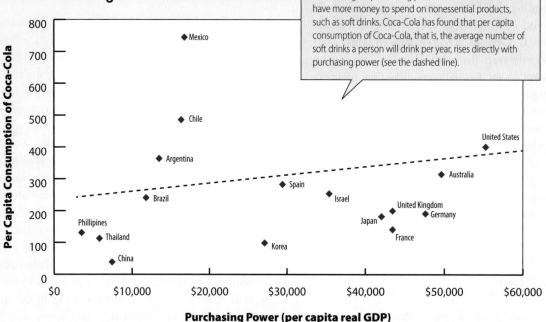

Typically, the higher the purchasing power in a country, the better that country will be for doing business. Why? Because higher purchasing power means that consumers have more money to spend on nonessential products, such as soft drinks. Coca-Cola has found that per capita consumption of Coca-Cola, that is, the average number of soft drinks a person will drink per year, rises directly with purchasing power (see the dashed line).

Sources: "Coca-Cola 2012 Annual Review," *Coca-Cola Company*, accessed June 10, 2013, http://www.coca-colacompany.com/annual-review/2012/year_in_review .html; "GNI Per Capita Ranking, Atlas Method and PPP Based," *The World Bank*, February 17, 2016, accessed April 9, 2016, http://data.worldbank.org/data-catalog /GNI-per-capita-Atlas-and-PPP-table.

8-4 FINDING THE BEST BUSINESS CLIMATE

When deciding where to go global, companies try to find countries or regions with promising business climates.

An attractive global business climate 8-4a positions the company for easy access to growing markets, 8-4b is an effective but cost-efficient place to build an office or manufacturing facility, and 8-4c minimizes the political risk to the company.

8-4a Growing Markets

The most important factor in an attractive business climate is access to a growing market. For example, no product is known and purchased by as many people throughout the world as Coca-Cola. Yet even Coke, which is available in more than 200 countries, still has tremendous potential

Purchasing power the relative cost of a standard set of goods and services in different countries

for further global growth. Coca-Cola gets 80 percent of its sales outside of North America, and emerging markets, where it has seen its fastest growth, now account for half of Coke's sales worldwide.[60]

Two factors help companies determine the growth potential of foreign markets: purchasing power and foreign competitors. **Purchasing power** is measured by comparing the relative cost of a standard set of goods and services in different countries. For example, a twenty-ounce Coke costs $5.39 in Lausanne, Switzerland. Because that same twenty-ounce Coke costs only $1.39 in the United States, the average American has more purchasing power than the average Swiss.[61] Purchasing power is growing in countries such as India and China, which have low average levels of income. This is because basic living expenses such as food, shelter, and transportation are very inexpensive in those countries, so consumers still have money to spend after paying for necessities, especially as salaries increase thanks to demand from international trade (see box "Paying for a 'Mac Attack'").

Consequently, countries with high and growing levels of purchasing power are good choices for companies looking for attractive global markets. As Exhibit 8.5

shows, Coke has found that the per capita consumption of Coca-Cola, or the number of Cokes a person drinks per year, rises directly with purchasing power. For example, in China, Brazil, and Australia, where the average person earns, respectively, $13,170, $15,590, and $42,760 annually, the number of Coca-Cola soft drinks consumed per year increases, respectively, from 39 to 241 to 315. The more purchasing power people have, the more likely they are to purchase soft drinks. And the Coca-Cola Company expects strong growth to continue in these markets, stating in its annual report, "To measure our growth potential, we look to our per capita consumption—the average number of eight-ounce servings of our beverages consumed each year in a given market. It is predicted that by the year 2020, the world will have nearly 1 billion more people whose disposable incomes will afford them choices and opportunities unthinkable a generation ago. We must discover innovative ways to connect with our traditional consumer base and this emerging global middle class—by creating new products and packaging formats for all lifestyles and occasions."[62]

The second part of assessing the growth potential of global markets involves analyzing the degree of global competition, which is determined by the number and quality of companies that already compete in a foreign market. Coffee consumption in China is growing 7 percent a year, compared to just 0.9 percent in North America. With this in mind, Starbucks decided to double its Chinese stores to 3,400 by 2019. Likewise, the UK's Costa Coffee plans to grow from 344 Chinese stores to 900 by 2020. Californian Jim Lee, who moved to Shanghai four years ago to start the Ocean Grounds coffee shop, believes that this incredible growth means that there should be plenty of business for new and old coffee houses alike. "This market is exploding," says Lee.[63]

8-4b Choosing an Office/ Manufacturing Location

Companies do not have to establish an office or manufacturing location in each country they enter. They can license, franchise, or export to foreign markets, or they can serve a larger region from one country. But there are many reasons why a company might choose to establish a location in a foreign country. Some foreign offices are established through global mergers and acquisitions, and some are established because of a commitment to grow in a new market. Chinese-owned **Volvo Cars** is building a $500 million factory in the United States to take advantage of the low cost of labor; avoid exchange rate fluctuations, which affect cars imported into the United States from other countries; and to

Volvo is building a $500 million factory in the United States, to take advantage of the low cost of labor.

Ed Aldridge/Shutterstock.com

fulfill its commitment to grow its U.S. sales.[64] CEO Håkan Samuelsson said, "Volvo Cars cannot claim to be a true global carmaker without an industrial presence in the U.S. The U.S. is an absolutely crucial part of our global transformation."[65]

Other companies choose locations by seeking a tax haven (although this is more difficult for U.S. companies due to legal concerns) or as part of creating a global brand. Ireland is a popular location to establish a company headquarters because of its corporate tax rate of 12.5 percent, which is much lower than the United Kingdom (25%), Germany (30.2%), or the United States (35%), which has the second highest corporate tax rate in the world.[66]

The criteria for choosing an office/manufacturing location are different from the criteria for entering a foreign market. Rather than focusing on costs alone, companies should consider both qualitative and quantitative factors. Two key qualitative factors are workforce quality and company strategy. Workforce quality is important because it is often difficult to find workers with the specific skills, abilities, and experience that a company needs to run its business. Workforce quality is one reason that many companies doing business in Europe locate their customer call centers in the Netherlands. Workers in the Netherlands are the most linguistically gifted in Europe, with 77 percent trilingual (speaking Dutch, English, and a third language) and 90 percent bilingual (Dutch and English). Comparable numbers across Europe are 25 percent and 54 percent.[67] Furthermore, compared to sixty countries worldwide, the Netherlands ranks fourth in terms of the supply of skilled labor, tenth for workers with financial skills, and second for competent managers (the United States ranks fifteenth, seventh, and fifth).[68]

Paying for a "Mac Attack"

Every year, *The Economist* magazine produces the Big Mac Index to illustrate differences in purchasing power across countries. By comparing the price of a single item, in this case, a Big Mac from McDonald's, the index shows how much (or how little) consumers in each country get for their money. According to the latest index, a Big Mac costs an average of $4.93 in the United States. The average cost jumps to $5.21 in Norway, $5.23 in Sweden, and $6.44 in Switzerland, meaning that residents of these countries get far less for their money than U.S. residents do. Conversely, the average cost of a Big Mac is $2.37 in Poland, $1.90 in India, $1.53 in Russia, and just $0.66 in Venezuela—the only country in which consumers pay less than a dollar for the sandwich.

Source: "The Big Mac Index," *Economist*, January 7, 2016, accessed May 18, 2016, http://www.economist.com/content/big-mac-index/.

A company's strategy is also important when choosing a location. For example, a company pursuing a low-cost strategy may need plentiful raw materials, low-cost transportation, and low-cost labor. A company pursuing a differentiation strategy (typically a higher-priced, better product or service) may need access to high-quality materials and a highly skilled and educated workforce.

Quantitative factors such as the kind of facility being built, tariff and nontariff barriers, exchange rates, and transportation and labor costs should also be considered when choosing an office/manufacturing location. In the apparel industry, low costs and short distances from field to factory are critical success factors for every manufacturer. That's why VF Corporation, owner of brands such as Wrangler, North Face, and Timberland, is sourcing products from Ethiopia. In addition to having the ability to go from fiber to factory in one country, Ethiopia also boasts a low average salary for garment workers ($21 per month versus up to $297 per month in China), low energy costs, and a free-trade agreement with the United States. The Ethiopian government built a $250 million industrial park exclusively for foreign investors in the apparel industry and is building a railroad through neighboring Djibouti to give its landlocked country access to a sea port. According to M. Raghuraman, CEO of

Brandix, Sri Lanka's largest clothing exporter, is interested in Ethiopia as a manufacturing location because "Ethiopia seems to be the best location from a government, labor, and power point of view."[69] Companies rely on studies such as FM Global's annually published "Resilience Index" to compare business climates throughout the world.[70] Exhibit 8.6 offers a quick overview of the best cities for business based on a variety of criteria. This information is a good starting point if your company is trying to decide where to put an international office or manufacturing plant.

8-4c Minimizing Political Risk

When managers think about political risk in global business, they envision burning factories and riots in the streets. Although political events such as these receive dramatic and extended coverage in the media, the political risks that most companies face usually are not covered as breaking stories on Fox News or CNN. Nonetheless, the negative consequences of ordinary political risk can be just as devastating to companies that fail to identify and minimize that risk.[71]

When conducting global business, companies should attempt to identify two types of political risk: political uncertainty and policy uncertainty.[72] **Political uncertainty** is associated with the risk of major changes in political regimes that can result from war, revolution, death of political leaders, social unrest, or other influential events. **Policy uncertainty** refers to the risk associated with changes in laws and government policies that directly affect the way foreign companies conduct business.

Political uncertainty the risk of major changes in political regimes that can result from war, revolution, death of political leaders, social unrest, or other influential events

Policy uncertainty the risk associated with changes in laws and government policies that directly affect the way foreign companies conduct business

Exhibit 8.6
World's Best Countries for Business

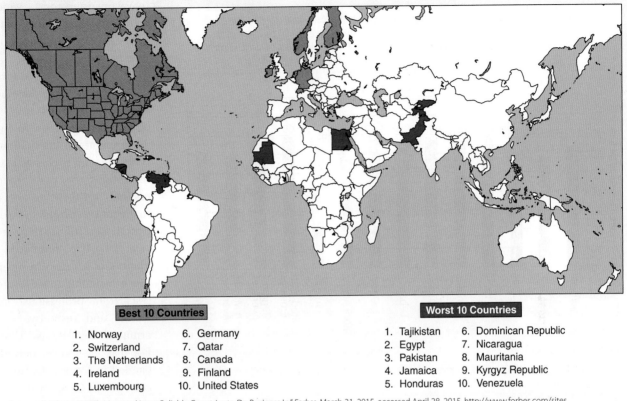

Best 10 Countries		Worst 10 Countries	
1. Norway	6. Germany	1. Tajikistan	6. Dominican Republic
2. Switzerland	7. Qatar	2. Egypt	7. Nicaragua
3. The Netherlands	8. Canada	3. Pakistan	8. Mauritania
4. Ireland	9. Finland	4. Jamaica	9. Kyrgyz Republic
5. Luxembourg	10. United States	5. Honduras	10. Venezuela

Sources: S. Adams, "2015's Most and Least Reliable Countries to Do Business In," *Forbes*, March 31, 2015, accessed April 28, 2015, http://www.forbes.com/sites /susanadams/2015/03/31/2015s-most-and-least-reliable-countries-to-do-business-in/; "Table 1: The Top 10 in 2015," Resilience Index 2015, *FM Global*, http://www .fmglobal.com/assets/pdf/Resilience_Methodology.pdf, p. 5; "Table 2: The Bottom 10 in 2015," Resilience Index 2015, *FM Global*, http://www.fmglobal.com/assets/pdf /Resilience_Methodology.pdf, p. 5.

Policy uncertainty is the most common—and perhaps most frustrating—form of political risk in global business, especially when changes in laws and government policies directly undercut sizable investments made by foreign companies. India is the third-largest retail market in the world behind the United States and China. The Indian government has long protected Indian retail stores by preventing foreign retailers from entering India unless they had a joint venture partner. So when India changed that policy, global retailers such as Walmart (United States), Carrefour (France), and Tesco (United Kingdom) began making plans to enter India on their own. The Indian government, however, reversed that decision following large protests from small-business owners and politicians who feared that huge retail stores would put locally owned mom-and-pop shops out of business. Kamlesh Gupta and her husband own such a shop, the Radha Krisna Store in Central Delhi. She said that if large retailers are allowed into India, "Everything

will be over. If they sell goods cheaper than us, who will come here? Already, we have lost 20 percent of our business since Big Bazaar and Reliance [two other Indian retailers] started operating in the last two years." As a result, the only option for foreign retailers such as Walmart, and it's not an attractive one, is to form joint ventures to establish "cash-and-carry" stores that sell to businesses but not consumers.[73]

Several strategies can be used to minimize or adapt to the political risk inherent in global business. An *avoidance strategy* is used when the political risks associated with a foreign country or region are viewed as too great. If firms are already invested in high-risk areas, they may divest or sell their businesses. If they have not yet invested, they will likely postpone their investment until the risk shrinks. Russia is an attractive market for automakers because it has a growing middle class but ranks fifty-seventh worldwide in terms of the number of cars per 1,000 people (just 300).

Exhibit 8.7
Overview of Political Risk in the Middle East

Higher scores indicate less long-term political risk, which is calculated by estimating government instability, socioeconomic conditions, internal or external conflicts, military involvement in politics, religious and ethnic tensions, foreign debt as a percent of gross domestic product, exchange rate instability, and whether there is high inflation.

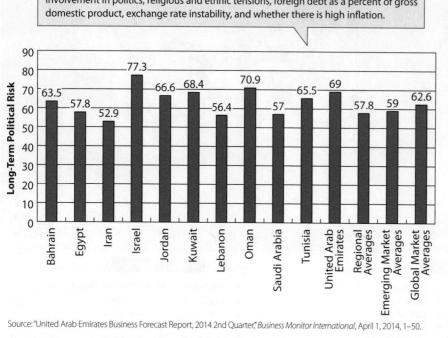

Source: "United Arab Emirates Business Forecast Report, 2014 2nd Quarter," *Business Monitor International*, April 1, 2014, 1–50.

so be sure to make risk decisions with the latest available information from resources such as the PRS Group (www.prsgroup.com), which supplies information about political risk to 80 percent of *Fortune* 500 companies.

Control is an active strategy to prevent or reduce political risks. Firms using a control strategy lobby foreign governments or international trade agencies to change laws, regulations, or trade barriers that hurt their business in that country. **Uber's** low-cost European ride-sharing service, UberPop, has faced a number of setbacks in recent years, including massive protests from professional taxi drivers and restrictive government regulations. Uber-Pop has even been outright banned in France, Germany, and Spain.[77] To deal with these setbacks, Uber hired veteran lobbyist Mark MacGann. MacGann appealed to European Union officials in Belgium, saying, "This is supposed to be a single market [but] what we're finding is that we're getting treated in completely different ways in different countries, and even within individual countries."[78] Thus far, Uber has made little progress controlling the political risks in these countries.

With the potential of a growing market, General Motors opened a manufacturing facility in St. Petersburg in 2008 to produce 98,000 cars a year. Four years later, GM was hoping to double production capacity. But by 2015, the Russian car market was shrinking and amid increasingly business-unfriendly regulations, GM closed the plant, taking a $600 million writeoff.[74] GM's president, Daniel Ammann, said, "This decision avoids significant investment into a market that has very challenging long-term prospects."[75]

Exhibit 8.7 shows the long-term political stability of various countries in the Middle East (higher scores indicate less political risk). The following factors, which were used to compile these ratings, indicate greater political risk: government instability, poor socioeconomic conditions, internal or external conflict, military involvement in politics, religious and ethnic tensions, high foreign debt as a percentage of GDP, exchange rate instability, and high inflation.[76] An avoidance strategy would likely be used for the riskiest countries shown in Exhibit 8.7, such as Iran and Saudi Arabia, but might not be needed for the less risky countries, such as Israel or Oman. Risk conditions and factors change,

Another method for dealing with political risk is *cooperation*, which involves using joint ventures and collaborative contracts, such as franchising and licensing. Although cooperation does not eliminate the political risk of doing business in a country, it can limit the risk associated with foreign ownership of a business. For example, a German company forming a joint venture with a Chinese company to do business in China may structure the joint venture contract so that the Chinese company owns 51 percent or more of the joint venture. Doing so qualifies the joint venture as a Chinese company and exempts it from Chinese laws that apply to foreign-owned businesses. However, cooperation cannot always protect against *policy risk* if a foreign government changes its laws and policies to directly affect the way foreign companies conduct business.

8-5 BECOMING AWARE OF CULTURAL DIFFERENCES

National culture is the set of shared values and beliefs that affects the perceptions, decisions, and behavior of the people from a particular country. The first step in dealing with culture is to recognize that there are meaningful differences. In recent years, Indian companies have targeted a group of mid-sized, independent, often family-owned, German companies (called Mittlestand) for acquisition. When Rail.One GmbH was acquired by PCM Group, an Indian conglomerate, the new owners didn't change the Bavarian management because, says PCM Chairman Kamal Mittal, "We didn't want to disturb the business."[79] Professor Geert Hofstede spent twenty years studying cultural differences in fifty-three different countries. His research shows that there are six consistent cultural dimensions across countries: power distance, individualism, masculinity, uncertainty avoidance, short-term versus long-term orientation, and indulgence versus restraint.[80]

Power distance is the extent to which people in a country accept that power is distributed unequally in society and organizations. In countries where power distance is weak, such as Denmark and Sweden, employees don't like their organization or their boss to have power over them or tell them what to do. They want to have a say in decisions that affect them. As Exhibit 8.8 shows, Russia, China and Nigeria, with scores of 93, 80, and 80, respectively, are much stronger in power distance than Germany (35), the Netherlands (38), and the United States (40).

Individualism is the degree to which societies believe that individuals should be self-sufficient. In individualistic societies, employees put loyalty to themselves first and loyalty to their company and work group second. In Exhibit 8.8, the United States (91), the Netherlands (80), France (71), and Germany (67) are the strongest in individualism, while Indonesia (14), China (20), and Hong Kong (25) are the weakest.

Masculinity and *femininity* capture the difference between highly assertive and highly nurturing cultures. Masculine cultures emphasize assertiveness, competition, material success, and achievement, whereas feminine cultures emphasize the importance of relationships, modesty, caring for the weak, and quality of life. In Exhibit 8.8, Japan (95), Germany (66), and China (66) have the most masculine orientations, while the Netherlands (14) has the most feminine orientation.

Manu Parpia, the CEO of Geometric, Ltd., the Indian company that acquired German engineering company 3Cap, noted that, compared to India, "German culture is more precise, very process oriented [and] quite blunt. The emphasis on process in India is much lower, because if you focused on process, nothing would get done."[81]

The cultural difference of *uncertainty avoidance* is the degree to which people in a country are uncomfortable with unstructured, ambiguous, unpredictable situations. In countries with strong uncertainty avoidance, such as Greece and Portugal, people tend to be aggressive and emotional and seek security rather than uncertainty. In Exhibit 8.8, Russia (95), Japan (92), and France (86) are strongest in uncertainty avoidance, while Hong Kong (29) and China (30) are the weakest. Rail.One CEO Jochen Riepl has noticed this dimension playing itself out during meetings with PCM officials. "In India, a 'no' is a kind of invitation to start a discussion. In Germany, a 'no' is a 'no,'" he says.[82]

The cultural dimension of *short-term/long-term orientation* addresses whether cultures are oriented to the present and seek immediate gratification or to the future and defer gratification. Not surprisingly, countries with short-term orientations are consumer-driven, whereas countries with long-term orientations are savings-driven. In Exhibit 8.8, Japan (88) and China (87) have very strong long-term orientations, while Nigeria (13) and the United States (26), have very strong short-term orientations. The cultural dimension of *indulgence versus restraint* addresses the degree to which a society allows relatively free gratification of basic drives related to enjoying life and having fun versus strict social norms that regulate and suppress gratification of needs and wants. Nigeria (81), the United States (68), and the Netherlands (68) are strongest in indulgence, while Hong Kong (17), Russia (20), and China (24) practice the most restraint. Part of what makes Mittelstand companies comfortable with new Indian owners is that Indian bidders usually offer long-term commitments. Attorney Christopher Wright says of Indian investors, "They tend to have a long-term vision and [that] gives German companies some assurance."[83]

To generate a graphical comparison of two different countries' cultures, go to http://geert-hofstede.com/countries.html. Select a "Country" from the dropdown list, and then select a "Comparison Country." A graph comparing the countries on each of Hofstede's six cultural differences will be generated automatically.

Cultural differences affect perceptions, understanding, and behavior. Recognizing cultural

> **National culture** the set of shared values and beliefs that affects the perceptions, decisions, and behavior of the people from a particular country

Exhibit 8.8
Hofstede's Six Cultural Dimensions

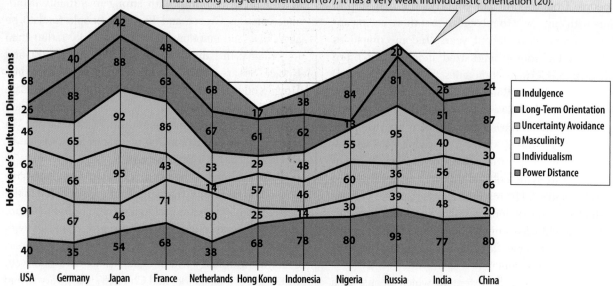

To determine the cultural characteristics of a country, compare the number and vertical distance (higher means more) of that country on a particular cultural dimension (color coded and labeled on the right side of the exihibit) with those of other countries. For example, with a score of 87, China has the second-highest long-term orientation; it is exceeded only by Japan, which has a score of 88. By contrast, with a score of 13, Nigeria has the weakest long-term orientation. Likewise, while China has a strong long-term orientation (87), it has a very weak individualistic orientation (20).

■ Indulgence
■ Long-Term Orientation
□ Uncertainty Avoidance
□ Masculinity
□ Individualism
■ Power Distance

Source: G. H. Hofstede, "Cultural Constraints in Management Theories," *Academy of Management Executive* 7, no. 1 (1993): 81–94; G. Hofstede and G. J. Hofstede, "6 Dimensions for Web Site 2015 12 08 0-100," accessed April 28, 2016, http://www.geerthofstede.eu/dimension-data-matrix.

differences is critical to succeeding in global business. Nevertheless, as Hofstede pointed out, descriptions of cultural differences are based on averages—the average level of uncertainty avoidance in Portugal, the average level of power distance in Argentina, and so forth. Accordingly, says Hofstede, "If you are going to spend time with a Japanese colleague, you shouldn't assume that overall cultural statements about Japanese society automatically apply to this person."[84] Similarly, cultural beliefs may differ significantly from one part of a country to another.[85]

After becoming aware of cultural differences, the second step is deciding how to adapt your company to those differences. Unfortunately, studies investigating the effects of cultural differences on management practices point more to difficulties than to easy solutions.

Another difficulty is that cultural values are changing, albeit slowly, in many parts of the world. The fall of communism in Eastern Europe and the former Soviet Union and the broad economic reforms in China have produced sweeping changes on two continents in the past four decades. Thanks to increased global trade resulting from free-trade agreements, major economic

transformations are also under way in India, China, Central America, and South America. Consequently, when trying to adapt management practices to cultural differences, companies must ensure that they are not basing their adaptations on outdated and incorrect assumptions about a country's culture.

8-6 PREPARING FOR AN INTERNATIONAL ASSIGNMENT

During the 2014 Winter Olympics in Sochi, Russia, American reporters discovered that Russians on the streets, at their hotels, or in restaurants, would not return their smiles. When one reporter asked why this was, a Russian told him, "In Russia, only two types of people smile: idiots and rich people." In Russia, you only smile if you have a particularly good reason. And if you smile just to be friendly, like Americans, Russians will think you're insincere, or maybe a bit crazy. Also, Russians typically don't smile while working because, well, they're at work. But, at home, with friends and family, Russian smiles and laughter are as big and hearty as anyplace in the world.[86]

If you become an **expatriate**, someone who lives and works outside his or her native country, chances are you'll run into cultural surprises just like the American reporters covering the Sochi Olympics. The difficulty of adjusting to language, cultural, and social differences is the primary reason for expatriate failure in overseas assignments. For example, although there have recently been disagreements among researchers about these numbers, it is probably safe to say that 5–20 percent of American expatriates sent abroad by their companies will return to the United States before they have successfully completed their assignments.[87] Of those who do complete their international assignments, about one-third are judged by their companies to be no better than marginally effective.[88] Because even well-planned international assignments can cost as much as three to five times an employee's annual salary, failure in those assignments can be extraordinarily expensive.[89] Furthermore, while it is difficult to find reliable indicators, studies typically show that 8–25 percent of expatriate managers leave their companies following an international assignment.[90]

*The chances for a successful international assignment can be increased through **8-6a language and cross-cultural training** and **8-6b consideration of spouse, family, and dual-career issues**.*

8-6a Language and Cross-Cultural Training

Predeparture language and cross-cultural training can reduce the uncertainty that expatriates feel, the misunderstandings that take place between expatriates and natives, and the inappropriate behaviors that expatriates unknowingly commit when they travel to a foreign country. In fact, simple things such as using a phone, locating a public toilet, asking for directions, finding out how much things cost, exchanging greetings, or understanding what people want can become tremendously complex when expatriates don't know a foreign language or a country's customs and cultures. For example, Bing, the name of Microsoft's search engine, means "illness" or "pancake" in Mandarin Chinese, so Microsoft had to change the name to "Biying" from the Chinese expression "you qui bi ying," which means, more appropriately, "seek and you shall find." Likewise, in Indonesia, an oil rig supervisor yelled to a worker to take a boat to shore. While the boss thought he was sharing instructions, the Indonesian and his workers thought he was being criticized in public, which is not done in their culture. Outraged at this behavior, they chased the supervisor with axes.[91]

Expatriates who receive predeparture language and cross-cultural training make faster adjustments to foreign cultures and perform better on their international assignments.[92] Unfortunately, only a third of the managers who go on international assignments are offered any kind of predeparture training, and only half of those actually participate in the training![93] Suzanne Bernard, director of international mobility at Bombardier Aerospace in Canada, says, "We always offer cross-cultural training, but it's very seldom used by executives leaving in a rush at the last minute."[94] This is somewhat surprising given the failure rates for expatriates and the high cost of those failures. Furthermore, with the exception of some language courses, predeparture training is not particularly expensive or difficult to provide. Three methods can be used to prepare workers for international assignments: documentary training, cultural simulations, and field experiences.

Documentary training focuses on identifying specific critical differences between cultures. For example, when sixty workers at Axcelis Technologies in Beverly, Massachusetts, were preparing to do business in India, they learned that while Americans make eye contact and shake hands firmly when greeting others, Indians, as a sign of respect, do just the opposite, avoiding eye contact and shaking hands limply.[95]

After learning specific critical differences through documentary training, trainees can participate in *cultural simulations*, in which they practice adapting to cultural differences. EMC, a global provider of information storage solutions, uses cultural simulations to train its people. In its early days, EMC was largely based in the United States, but with research labs, offices, and customers on every continent, cross-cultural interactions are a daily part of business. EMC's cultural simulations use photos and audio and video clips to present real-world situations. EMC employees must decide what to do and then learn what happened as a result of their choices. Whether it's interacting with customers or dealing with EMC employees from other countries, at every step they have the opportunity to learn good and bad methods of responding to cultural differences. EMC requires its worldwide workforce of 40,500 people to regularly use the cultural simulations. Louise Korver-Swanson, EMC's global head of executive development, said, "This is about ensuring

Expatriate someone who lives and works outside his or her native country

After learning specific critical differences through documentary training, trainees can participate in cultural simulations, in which they practice adapting to cultural differences.

that we're truly a global company. We need everyone in the organization to be tuned in."[96]

Finally, *field simulation* training, a technique made popular by the U.S. Peace Corps, places trainees in an ethnic neighborhood for three to four hours to talk to residents about cultural differences. For example, a U.S. electronics manufacturer prepared workers for assignments in South Korea by having trainees explore a nearby South Korean neighborhood and talk to shopkeepers and people on the street about South Korean politics, family orientation, and day-to-day living.

8-6b Spouse, Family, and Dual-Career Issues

Not all international assignments are difficult for expatriates and their families, but the evidence clearly shows that how well an expatriate's spouse and family adjust to the foreign culture is the most important factor in determining the success or failure of an international assignment.[97] In fact, a *Harvard Business Review* study found that 32 percent of those offered international assignments turned them down because they did not want their families to have to relocate, while 28 percent turned them down "to protect their marriages."[98] Unfortunately, despite its importance, there has been little systematic research on what does and does not help expatriates' families successfully adapt. A number of companies, however, have found that adaptability screening and intercultural training for families can lead to more successful overseas adjustment.

Adaptability screening is used to assess how well managers and their families are likely to adjust to foreign cultures. For example, Prudential Relocation Management's international division has developed an "Overseas Assignment Inventory" (OAI) to assess a spouse and family's open-mindedness, respect for others' beliefs, sense of humor, and marital communication. The OAI was initially used to help the U.S. Peace Corps, the U.S. Navy, and the Canadian International Development Agency select people who could adapt well in foreign cultures. Success there led to its use in helping

EXPAT ASSIGNMENT AS CAREER BUILDER

Among U.S. companies, expatriate assignments are becoming more common and even de rigueur for managers who want to advance their careers. Accepting foreign assignments gives managers the opportunity to test their mettle and gain deeper understandings about global markets. Before becoming CFO of Starwood Hotels, Thomas Mangas oversaw finances for Procter & Gamble in ten countries while working in Turkey and Central Asia. He says, "The experience of being in another country is essential. I don't believe you can get there by being there a week or two and flying back out."

Source: K. Johnson, "Career Builder: A Stint Abroad," *Wall Street Journal*, February 10, 2015, B7.

companies assess whether managers and their spouses were good candidates for international assignments.[99] Likewise, Pennsylvania-based AMP, a worldwide producer of electrical connectors, conducts extensive psychological screening of expatriates and their spouses when making international assignments. But adaptability screening does not just involve a company assessing an employee; it can also involve an employee screening international assignments for desirability. Because more employees are becoming aware of the costs of international assignments (spouses having to give up or change jobs, children having to change schools, everyone having to learn a new language), some companies are willing to pay for a preassignment trip so the employee and his or her spouse can investigate the country *before* accepting the international assignment.[100]

Only 40 percent of expatriates' families receive language and cross-cultural training, yet such training is just as important for the families of expatriates as for the expatriates themselves.[101] In fact, it may be more important because, unlike expatriates, whose professional jobs often shield them from the full force of a country's culture, spouses and children are fully immersed in foreign neighborhoods and schools. Households must be run, shopping must be done, and bills must be paid. When Judy Holland's husband was transferred to Shanghai, his company sent the family to a two-day cultural immersion class in the United Kingdom, where the family learned about business etiquette, the cultural importance of the number 8, the Chinese zodiac, and how to eat with chopsticks. The class even prepared the Hollands for differences they might not have anticipated, such as, in China, it's uncommon to find men's shoes in sizes larger than a U.S. 9.5 (Holland's husband wore a U.S. 11.5). Holland was grateful for the instruction, saying, "Nothing can fully prepare you for China, but it certainly took the shock out of arriving." Soon after arriving, however, her sense of confidence eroded. "I remember standing in a house with no furniture, not knowing anyone, and wishing they had buddied me up with someone from my husband's company."[102] In addition to helping families prepare for the cultural differences they will encounter, language and cross-cultural training can help reduce uncertainty about how to act and decrease misunderstandings between expatriates and their families and locals. For example, in the West, people enjoy a fairly large circle of personal space and are only comfortable with family and intimate friends being within inches of their bodies. But in China, where personal space is measured in inches and not feet, the constant jostling by strangers can be perceived as an encroachment and unhinge many Westerners. New Zealander Marita Light, who spent five years in China, found that recalibrating her xpectations and being intentionally open helped. "Letting go of my judgments and consciously being more open enabled more creativity in how I dealt with awkward situations. It was a much more rewarding way to live in China."[103]

STUDY TOOLS 8

LOCATED IN TEXTBOOK
☐ Rip-out and review chapter review card

LOCATED AT WWW.CENGAGEBRAIN.COM
☐ Review key term flashcards and create your own from StudyBits
☐ Track your knowledge and understanding of key concepts, using the concept tracker
☐ Complete practice and graded quizzes to prepare for tests
☐ Complete interactive content within the exposition
☐ View chapter highlight box content at the beginning of each chapter

PART 3

9 Designing Adaptive Organizations

Jirsak/Shutterstock.com

LEARNING OUTCOMES

9-1 Describe the departmentalization approach to organizational structure.

9-2 Explain organizational authority.

9-3 Discuss the different methods for job design.

9-4 Explain the methods that companies are using to redesign internal organizational processes (that is, intraorganizational processes).

9-5 Describe the methods that companies are using to redesign external organizational processes (that is, interorganizational processes).

After you finish this chapter, go to **PAGE 201** for

STUDY TOOLS

9-1 DEPARTMENTALI-ZATION

Organizational structure is the vertical and horizontal configuration of departments, authority, and jobs within a company. Organizational structure is concerned with questions such as, "Who reports to whom?" and "Who does what?" and "Where is the work done?" **Thomson Reuters**, which provides critical information for businesses and professionals, is organized into four separate business units: Financial & Risk ($6.1 billion in annual revenues), which provides information to traders, investors, and marketplaces; Legal ($3.4 billion), which provides information to global businesses, law firms, governments, and universities; Tax & Accounting ($1.4 billion), which provides information to tax professionals, companies, and governments; and Intellectual Property & Science ($1 billion), which provides information to life sciences companies, scientific and scholarly researchers, and those in need of intellectual property solutions. The company's former CEO Thomas Glocer said that these changes will "streamline our organization and enable us to work better across business units to achieve growth and capture operating efficiencies from scale. The professional markets in which we operate are marked by increasing collaboration among specialists,

and Thomson Reuters must operate with the speed and agility needed to serve these demanding professionals."[1]

You can see Thomson Reuters's organizational structure in Exhibit 9.1. In the first half of the chapter, you will learn about the traditional vertical and horizontal approaches to organizational structure, including departmentalization, organizational authority, and job design.

An **organizational process** is the collection of activities that transform inputs into outputs that customers value.[2] Organizational process asks, "How do things get done?" For example, Microsoft uses basic internal and external processes, shown in Exhibit 9.2, to write computer software. The process starts when Microsoft gets feedback from customers through Internet discussion forums, tweets, emails, and phone calls. This information helps Microsoft understand customers' needs and problems and identify important software issues and needed changes and functions. Microsoft then rewrites the software, testing it internally at the company and then externally through its beta testing process, in which customers who volunteer or are selected by Microsoft give the company extensive feedback. The feedback is then used to make improvements to the software. For example, Microsoft made three versions of Windows 10 available for a public beta test over a year before releasing it for sale. Over 2 million consumers and businesses downloaded and installed the beta, and then posted the bugs or errors they found on Microsoft's forums. Microsoft hoped the beta test for Windows 10 went as well as the beta test for Windows 7, during which users found and reported 2,000 bugs, all of which Microsoft corrected before releasing the software.[3] The beta testing process may take as long as a year and involve thousands of knowledgeable people. After final corrections are made to the software, the

Exhibit 9.1
Organizational Chart at Thomson Reuters

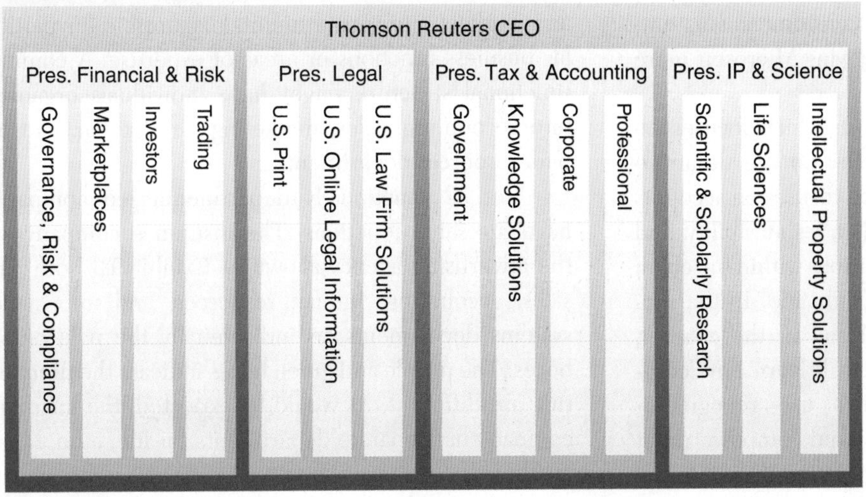

Thomson Reuters CEO			
Pres. Financial & Risk	Pres. Legal	Pres. Tax & Accounting	Pres. IP & Science
Governance, Risk & Compliance / Marketplaces / Investors / Trading	U.S. Print / U.S. Online Legal Information / U.S. Law Firm Solutions	Government / Knowledge Solutions / Corporate / Professional	Scientific & Scholarly Research / Life Sciences / Intellectual Property Solutions

The organizational chart displays the horizontal and vertical dimensions at Thomson Reuters.

Source: "Thomson Reuters Fact Book 2015," accessed April 14, 2016, http://ir.thomsonreuters.com/phoenix.zhtml?c=76540&p=irol-factbook.

Organizational structure the vertical and horizontal configuration of departments, authority, and jobs within a company

Organizational process the collection of activities that transforms inputs into outputs that customers value

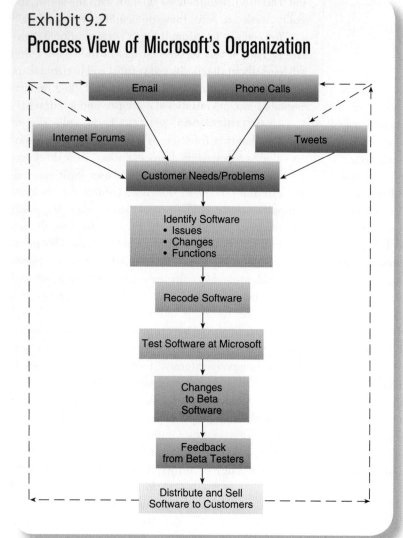

Exhibit 9.2
Process View of Microsoft's Organization

Email

Phone Calls

Internet Forums

Tweets

Customer Needs/Problems

Identify Software
- Issues
- Changes
- Functions

Recode Software

Test Software at Microsoft

Changes
to Beta
Software

Feedback
from Beta Testers

Distribute and Sell
Software to Customers

are redesigning their external processes, that is, how they are changing to improve their interactions with those outside the company. In that discussion, you will explore the basics of modular and virtual organizations.

Traditionally, organizational structures have been based on some form of departmentalization. **Departmentalization** is a method of subdividing work and workers into separate organizational units that take responsibility for completing particular tasks.[4] EBay has separate departments or divisions for payment systems, warehousing and logistics, and marketplaces and selling.[5]

Traditionally, organizational structures have been created by departmentalizing work ac-cording to five methods: 9-1a functional, 9-1b product, 9-1c customer, 9-1d geographic, and 9-1e matrix.

9-1a Functional Departmentalization

One of the most common organizational structures is functional departmentalization. Companies tend to use this structure when they are small or just starting out, but nearly a quarter of large companies (50,000 or more employees) also use functional departmentalization.[6] **Functional departmentalization** organizes work and workers into separate units responsible for particular business functions or areas of expertise. A common functional structure might have individuals organized into accounting, sales, marketing, production, and human resources departments.

Not all functionally departmentalized companies have the same functions. The insurance company and the advertising agency shown in Exhibit 9.3 both have sales, accounting, human resources, and information systems departments, as indicated by the pale orange boxes. The purple and green boxes indicate the functions that are different. As would be expected, the insurance company has separate departments for life, auto, home, and health insurance. The advertising agency has departments for artwork, creative work, print advertising, and Internet advertising. So the functional departments in a company that uses functional structure depend, in part, on the business or industry a company is in.

company distributes and sells it to customers. Customers then start the process again by giving Microsoft more feedback.

This process view of Microsoft, which focuses on how things get done, is very different from the hierarchical view of Thomson Reuters, which focuses on accountability, responsibility, and positions within the chain of command. In the second half of the chapter, you will learn how companies use reengineering and empowerment to redesign their internal organizational processes. The chapter ends with a discussion about the ways in which companies

Departmentalization
subdividing work and workers into separate organizational units responsible for completing particular tasks

Functional departmentalization organizing work and workers into separate units responsible for particular business functions or areas of expertise

Exhibit 9.3
Functional Departmentalization

Functional departmentalization has some advantages. First, it allows work to be done by highly qualified specialists. While the accountants in the accounting department take responsibility for producing accurate revenue and expense figures, the engineers in research and development can focus their efforts on designing a product that is reliable and simple to manufacture. Second, it lowers costs by reducing duplication. When the engineers in research and development come up with a fantastic new product, they don't have to worry about creating an aggressive advertising campaign to sell it. That task belongs to the advertising experts and sales representatives in marketing. Third, with everyone in the same department having similar work experience or training, communication and coordination are less problematic for departmental managers.

At the same time, functional departmentalization has a number of disadvantages. To start, cross-department coordination can be difficult. Managers and employees are often more interested in doing what's right for their function than in doing what's right for the entire organization. A good example is the traditional conflict between marketing and manufacturing. Marketing typically pushes for spending more money to make more products with more capabilities to meet customer needs. By contrast, manufacturing pushes for fewer products with simpler designs so that manufacturing facilities can ship finished products on time and keep costs within expense budgets. As companies grow, functional departmentalization may also lead to slower decision making and produce managers and workers with narrow experience and expertise.

9-1b Product Departmentalization

Product departmentalization organizes work and workers into separate units responsible for producing particular products or services. Exhibit 9.4 shows the product departmentalization structure used by United Technologies Corporation (UTC), which is organized along four different areas each with its own product line: Climate, Controls & Security (Carrier heating, ventilating, and air-conditioning; Fire safety, security products and services; and food/transport refrigeration), Pratt & Whitney jet engines (Pratt & Whitney Commercial Engines, Pratt & Whitney Military Engines, Pratt & Whitney Canada, and Pratt & Whitney AeroPower), UTC Aerospace Systems (wing and cockpit controls, landing systems and sensors, aerostructures, electric power systems and plane interiors), and Otis (elevators, escalators, and moving walkways).[7]

One of the advantages of product departmentalization is that, like functional departmentalization, it allows managers and workers to specialize in one area of expertise. Unlike the narrow expertise and experiences in functional departmentalization, however, managers and workers develop a broader set of experiences and expertise related to an entire product line. Likewise, product departmentalization makes it easier for top managers to assess work-unit performance. Because of the clear separation of their four different product divisions, UTC's top managers can easily compare the performance of UTC Aerospace Systems division and the Pratt & Whitney aircraft engines division. In 2015, Pratt & Whitney generated the same sales volume as UTC Aerospace ($14.1 billion). However UTC Aerospace had a profit of $1.9 billion (a 13.4% margin) compared to Pratt & Whitney's profit of $861 million (6.1% margin).[8]

Product departmentalization organizing work and workers into separate units responsible for producing particular products or services

Exhibit 9.4
Product Departmentalization: UTC

UTC Climate, Controls & Security			Pratt & Whitney				UTC Aerospace Systems	Otis
Carrier HVAC	Fire Safety and Security	Food & Transport Refrigeration	Pratt & Whitney Commercial Engines	Pratt & Whitney Military Engines	Pratt & Whitney Canada	Pratt & Whitney Aero-Power	Wing and cockpit controls, landing systems and sensors, aerostructures, electric power systems and plane interiors.	Elevators, escalators, and moving walkways
— Customer Service — Engineering — Human Resources — Information Technology — Legal — Maintenance & Field Operations — Manufacturing — Marketing & Sales — Sourcing & Logistics			— Administrative Services — Communication & Public Relations — Customer Service & Support — E-Business — Engineering — Enterprise Resource Planning — Environmental Health & Safety — Facilities & Services — Human Resources — Legal — Manufacturing — Procurement — Quality					

Source: "At a Glance," *UTC*, accessed April 29, 2016, http://www.utc.com/Our-Businesses/Pages/At-A-Glance.aspx.

Finally, decision making should be faster because managers and workers are responsible for the entire product line rather than for separate functional departments; in other words, there are fewer conflicts compared to functional departmentalization.

The primary disadvantage of product departmentalization is duplication. You can see in Exhibit 9.4 that both the UTC Climate, Controls & Security division and the Pratt & Whitney division have customer service, engineering, human resources, legal, manufacturing, and procurement (similar to sourcing and logistics) departments. Duplication like this often results in higher costs. If UTC were instead organized by function, one lawyer could handle matters related to both air conditioners and aircraft engines rather than working on only one or the other.

A second disadvantage is the challenge of coordinating across the different product departments. UTC would probably have difficulty standardizing its policies and procedures in product departments as different as the Carrier (heating, ventilating, and air-conditioning) and UTC Aerospace (cockpit controls and landing systems) divisions.

9-1c Customer Departmentalization

Customer departmentalization organizes work and workers into separate units responsible for particular kinds of customers. For example, as Exhibit 9.5 shows, Swisscom AG, Switzerland's leading telecommunications provider, is organized into departments by type of customer: residential customers (fixed line and voice, mobile and voice, broadband Internet, and digital TV), small- and medium-sized businesses (fixed line and voice, mobile line and voice, Internet and data services, and maintenance and operation of IT infrastructure), enterprise customers (fixed line, voice and data; mobile line and tablets, voice and

Customer departmentalization organizing work and workers into separate units responsible for particular kinds of customers

Exhibit 9.5
Customer Departmentalization: Swisscom AG

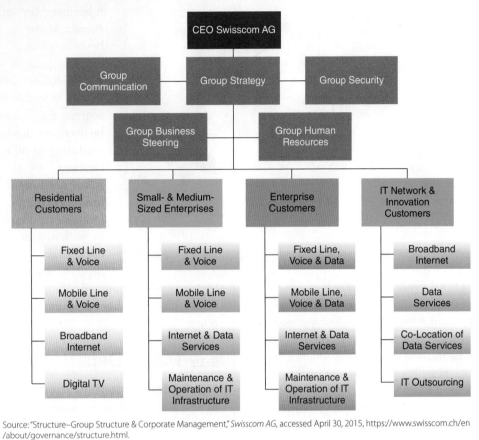

Source: "Structure–Group Structure & Corporate Management," *Swisscom AG*, accessed April 30, 2015, https://www.swisscom.ch/en /about/governance/structure.html.

data; Internet and data services; and maintenance and operation of IT infrastructure), and IT network and innovation (broadband Internet, data services, co-location of data services, and storage to wholesale customers).[9]

The primary advantage of customer departmentalization is that it focuses the organization on customer needs rather than on products or business functions. Furthermore, creating separate departments to serve specific kinds of customers allows companies to specialize and adapt their products and services to customer needs and problems. The primary disadvantage of customer departmentalization is that, like product departmentalization, it leads to duplication of resources. This is why Swisscom AG also has five "group" functions— communication, strategy, security, business steering, and human resources—that support each of its four customer departments, and avoids the disadvantage of duplication common to customer departmentalization structures. It

can be difficult to achieve coordination across different customer departments, as is also the case with product departmentalization. Finally, the emphasis on meeting customers' needs may lead workers to make decisions that please customers but hurt the business.

9-1d Geographic Departmentalization

Geographic departmentalization organizes work and workers into separate units responsible for doing business in particular geographic areas. Exhibit 9.6 shows the geographic departmentalization used by **AB InBev**, the largest beer brewer in the world. AB InBev has 156 beverage plants in twenty-five countries, 155,000 employees, and annual revenue

> **Geographic departmentalization** organizing work and workers into separate units responsible for doing business in particular geographic areas

Exhibit 9.6
Geographic Departmentalization: AB InBev Company

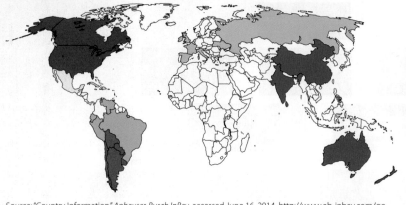

Source: "Country Information," *Anheuser-Busch InBev*, accessed June 16, 2014, http://www.ab-inbev.com/go /about_abinbev/country_information.

of $43.6 billion.[10] As shown in Exhibit 9.6, AB InBev has six regional groups: North America, Mexico, Latin America North, Latin America South, Europe, and Asia Pacific. Each of these regions would be a sizable company by itself. The smallest region, Latin America South, for instance, sold 36 million hectoliters of beverages for an annual revenue of $3.46 billion.

The primary advantage of geographic departmentalization is that it helps companies respond to the demands of different markets. This can be especially important when the company sells in different countries. For example, while AB InBev has three brands sold worldwide (Budweiser, Stella Artois, and Corona), and three sold in multiple countries (Beck's, Hoegaarden, and Leffe), most of its brands are local. You'll find the Antarctica and Brahma brands in Brazil, the Belle-Vue and Jupiler brands in Belgium, and the Sibirskaya Korona and Klinskoye brands in Russia.[11]

Another advantage is that geographic departmentalization can reduce costs by locating unique organizational resources closer to customers. For instance, it is cheaper in the long run for AB InBev to build bottling plants in each region than to, for example, transport beer to Mexico, where it has seven beverage plants, after it has been brewed and bottled in Brazil, where it has twenty-five beverage plants.[12]

The primary disadvantage of geographic departmentalization is that it can lead to duplication of resources. For example, while it may be necessary to adapt products and marketing to different geographic locations, it's doubtful that AB InBev needs significantly different inventory tracking systems from location to location. Also, even more than with the other forms of departmentalization, it can be difficult to coordinate departments that are literally thousands of miles from each other and whose managers have very limited contact with each other.

9-1e Matrix Departmentalization

Matrix departmentalization is a hybrid structure in which two or more forms of departmentalization are used together. The most common matrix combines the product and functional forms of departmentalization, but other forms may also be used. Exhibit 9.7 shows the matrix structure used by Procter & Gamble, which has 110,000 employees working in seventy different countries.[13] Across the top of Exhibit 9.7, you can see that the company uses a product structure where it groups its twenty-one billion-dollar brands into four business units: Baby, Feminine & Family Care; Health & Grooming; Fabric & Home Care; and Beauty, Hair & Personal Care. Each of these units is responsible for developing, manufacturing, and marketing its brands to consumers. As such, each unit operates its own research and development department and product supply initiative. The left side of the figure shows that the company also uses a functional structure based on five functions—finance, human resources (HR), communications, legal, and information technology (IT)—and a set of shared global

Matrix departmentalization a hybrid organizational structure in which two or more forms of departmentalization, most often product and functional, are used together

iStockphoto.com/Micropic

Exhibit 9.7
Matrix Departmentalization: Procter & Gamble

	Business Units									
	Baby, Feminine, & Family Care			Health & Grooming		Fabric & Home Care			Beauty, Hair, & Personal Care	
	Baby Care	Family Care	Feminine Care	Oral Care	Personal Health Care	Shave Care	Fabric Care	Home Care	Hair Care	Skin & Personal Care
Finance	Pampers	Bounty	Tampax	Crest	Vicks	Gillette	Tide	Swiffer	Pantene	Old Spice
Human resources										
Communications										
Legal										
Information technology										
Global business services										

Selling & Market Operations (SMOs)

Source: "Corporate Structure," *Procter & Gamble*, accessed April 14, 2016, http://us.pg.com/who_we_are/structure_governance/corporate_structure.

business services including payroll, purchases, data analytics, benefits, and facilities management. The right side of the figure shows that the selling and market operation functions (SMOs) are external to the brand units but are not part of the other functional groups. SMOs make sure that a product is sold, distributed, shelved, and priced well within a particular region of the world. P&G's SMO regions include Asia Pacific; Europe; Greater China; Latin America; North America; and India, the Middle East, and Africa (IMEA).[14]

The boxes in Exhibit 9.7 represent the matrix structure created by the combination of the product and functional structures. For example, P&G's Gillette Group (Gillette is a global brand for men's grooming products within the Shave Care segment of the Health & Grooming unit) would work with SMOs to sell, market, and distribute Gillette products worldwide; use global business services to work with suppliers and keep costs down; and then rely on corporate functions for assistance in hiring employees, billing customers, and paying suppliers. Similar matrix combinations are shown for Pampers, Bounty, Tampax, Crest, Vicks, Tide, Swiffer, Pantene, and Old Spice within each of the segments of P&G's four global business units. As shown in Exhibit 9.8, P&G envisions

its complex matrix as a set of concentric circles: the business functions at the core, then the brands, then the selling and market operations on the circle closest to the customer.

Several things distinguish matrix departmentalization from the other traditional forms of departmentalization.[15] First, most employees report to two bosses, one from each core part of the matrix. For example, in Exhibit 9.7 a manager on the Pampers team responsible for marketing would report to a boss in the baby care segment of the Baby, Feminine, & Family Care global business unit as well as to a manager in the market development function. Second, by virtue of their hybrid design, matrix structures lead to much more cross-functional interaction than other forms of departmentalization. In fact, while matrix workers are typically members of only one functional department (based on their work experience and expertise), they are also commonly members of several ongoing project, product, or customer groups. Third, because of the high level of cross-functional interaction, matrix departmentalization requires significant coordination between managers in the different parts of the matrix. In particular, managers have the complex job of tracking and managing the

Exhibit 9.8
Procter & Gamble's Concentric Matrix

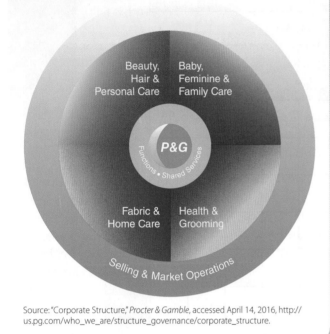

Beauty, Hair & Personal Care

Baby, Feminine & Family Care

P&G
Functions • Shared Services

Fabric & Home Care

Health & Grooming

Selling & Market Operations

Source: "Corporate Structure," *Procter & Gamble*, accessed April 14, 2016, http://us.pg.com/who_we_are/structure_governance/corporate_structure.

Matrix structures are notorious for confusion and conflict between project bosses in different parts of the matrix.

multiple demands (project, product, customer, or functional) on employees' time.

The primary advantage of matrix departmentalization is that it allows companies to manage in an efficient manner large, complex tasks such as researching, developing, and marketing pharmaceuticals or carrying out complex global businesses. Efficiency comes from avoiding duplication. For example, rather than having an entire marketing function for each project, the company simply assigns and reassigns workers from the marketing department (or market development at P&G) as they are needed at various stages of product completion. More specifically, an employee may simultaneously be part of five different ongoing projects but may be actively completing work on only a few projects at a time. Another advantage is the pool of resources available to carry out large, complex tasks. Because of the ability to quickly pull in expert help from all the functional areas of the company, matrix project managers have a much more diverse set of expertise and experience at their disposal than managers in the other forms of departmentalization.

The primary disadvantage of matrix departmentalization is the high level of coordination required to manage the complexity involved in running large, ongoing projects at various levels of completion. Matrix structures are notorious for confusion and conflict between project bosses in different parts of the matrix. Disagreements or misunderstandings about schedules, budgets, available resources, and the availability of employees with particular functional expertise are common in matrix structures. Because of these problems, many matrix structures evolve from a **simple matrix**, in which managers in different parts of the matrix negotiate conflicts and resources directly, to a **complex matrix**, in which specialized matrix managers and departments are added to the organizational structure. In a complex matrix, managers from different parts of the matrix might report to the same matrix manager, who helps them sort out conflicts and problems.

9-2 ORGANIZATIONAL AUTHORITY

The second part of traditional organizational structures is authority. **Authority** is the right to give commands, take action, and make decisions to achieve organizational objectives.[16]

Simple matrix a form of matrix departmentalization in which managers in different parts of the matrix negotiate conflicts and resources

Complex matrix a form of matrix departmentalization in which managers in different parts of the matrix report to matrix managers, who help them sort out conflicts and problems

Authority the right to give commands, take action, and make decisions to achieve organizational objectives

*Traditionally, organizational authority has been characterized by the following dimensions: **9-2a chain of command, 9-2b line versus staff authority, 9-2c delegation of authority,** and **9-2d degree of centralization.***

9-2a Chain of Command

Consider again the United Technologies organizational structure. A manager in any of the corporation's divisions ultimately reports to the head of that division. That division head, in turn, reports to the corporation's CEO Gregory Hayes. This line, which vertically connects every job in the company to higher levels of management, represents the chain of command. The **chain of command** is the vertical line of authority that clarifies who reports to whom throughout the organization. People higher in the chain of command have the right, *if they so choose*, to give commands, take action, and make decisions concerning activities occurring anywhere below them in the chain. In the following discussion about delegation and decentralization, you will learn that managers don't always choose to exercise their authority directly.[17]

One of the key assumptions underlying the chain of command is **unity of command**, which means that workers should report to just one boss.[18] In practical terms, this means that only one person can be in charge at a time. Matrix organizations, in which employees have two bosses, automatically violate this principle. This is one of the primary reasons that matrix organizations are difficult to manage. Unity of command serves an important purpose: to prevent the confusion that might arise when an employee receives conflicting commands from two different bosses. Companies don't necessarily have to have a matrix organization to violate unity of command—they can do so by appointing two CEOs. **Chipotle, Fox** studios and television, **Whole Foods, WME** talent agency, **Oracle**, and online eyewear company **Warby Parker** all have co-CEOs. In some instances, such as at Chipotle and Whole Foods, the dual role results from a founder CEO retaining the title and maintaining an inspirational role while a second CEO with more management experience handles operations. At Oracle, each CEO heads up a group of related functions. **Amazon** actually has three CEOs: Jeff Wilke is the CEO of Worldwide Consumer; Andy Jassy is the CEO of Amazon Web Services (AWS); and Jeff Bezos is an uber-CEO with authority over them both.[19] While co-CEO arrangements sometimes work well, they are rare and often short-lived because, according to research from Professor Lindred Greer, having co-CEOs "causes conflict," leads to "negative performance by [executive] teams, and may likely result in the development of 'hostile mindsets' as the co-CEOs struggle to work together.[20]

9-2b Line versus Staff Authority

A second dimension of authority is the distinction between line and staff authority. **Line authority** is the right to command immediate subordinates in the chain of command. For example, Thomson Reuters CEO James C. Smith has line authority over the president of the company's Financial & Risk Information division. Smith can issue orders to that division president and expect them to be carried out. In turn, the president of the Financial & Risk Information division can issue orders to his subordinates, who run the trading, investors, marketplaces, and governance, risk, and compliance divisions, and expect them to be carried out. By contrast, **staff authority** is the right to advise but not command others who are not subordinates in the chain of command. For example, a manager in human resources at Thomson Reuters might advise the manager in charge of the Thomson Reuters Tax & Accounting group on a hiring decision but cannot order him or her to hire a certain applicant.

Warby Parker co-founders and co-CEOs Neil Blumenthal (left) and Dave Gilboa attend a Warby Parker store opening in Los Angeles, California.

Michael Buckner/Getty Images

Chain of command the vertical line of authority that clarifies who reports to whom throughout the organization

Unity of command a management principle that workers should report to just one boss

Line authority the right to command immediate subordinates in the chain of command

Staff authority the right to advise, but not command, others who are not subordinates in the chain of command

The terms *line* and *staff* are also used to describe different functions within the organization. A **line function** is an activity that contributes directly to creating or selling the company's products. So, for example, activities that take place within the manufacturing and marketing departments would be considered line functions. A **staff function**, such as accounting, human resources, or legal services, does not contribute directly to creating or selling the company's products but instead supports line activities. For example, marketing managers might consult with the legal staff to ensure the wording of an advertisement is within the law.

9-2c Delegation of Authority

Managers can exercise their authority directly by completing tasks themselves, or they can choose to pass on some of their authority to subordinates. **Delegation of authority** is the assignment of direct authority and responsibility to a subordinate to complete tasks for which the manager is normally responsible.

When a manager delegates work, three transfers occur, as illustrated in Exhibit 9.9. First, the manager transfers full responsibility for the assignment to the subordinate. At Apple, when you've been delegated to a certain task, you become the DRI, or the "directly responsible individual." As a former Apple employee explains, "Any effective meeting at Apple will have an action list. Next to each action item will be the DRI," who of course, is responsible for completing that delegated responsibility. Furthermore, when you're trying to figure out who to contact to get something done in Apple's corporate structure, people simply ask, "Who's the DRI on that?"[21]

Many managers, however, find giving up full responsibility somewhat difficult. When Lori Lord was COO of **Spectrum Health Care**, she stayed up all night writing and reviewing 400-page requests for proposals (RFPs), upon which the company's sales and growth depended. Lord maintained tight control over the RFPs because she considered them critical to the company's success and believed that she was the only person who could do it right. "These were so important for our organization and I wouldn't let anyone else put the document[s]

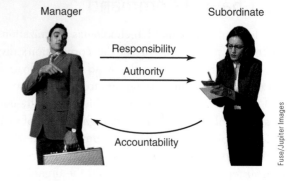

Exhibit 9.9
Delegation: Responsibility, Authority, and Accountability

Manager   Subordinate

Responsibility →
Authority →
← Accountability

Fuse/Jupiter Images

Source: C. D. Pringle, D. F. Jennings, and J. G. Longenecker, *Managing Organizations: Functions and Behaviors* (Columbus, Ohio: Merrill Publishing, 1984).

together."[22] One reason it is difficult for some managers to delegate is that they often fear that the task won't be done as well as if they did it themselves. However, one CEO says, "If you can delegate a task to somebody who can do it 75 percent to 80 percent as well as you can today, you delegate it immediately." Why? Many tasks don't need to be done perfectly; they just need to be *done*. And delegating tasks that someone else can do frees managers to assume other important responsibilities. After Lori Lord learned to delegate the RFP review along with other day-to-day activities, she could attend key meetings, focus on the future of the organization, and concentrate on growth, all activities critical to her new role as the company's CEO. She says that she lost five years of her life from not delegating and that now, "I'm glad I don't have to be here at 3 a.m. anymore."[23] Delegating authority can generate a related problem: micromanaging. Sometimes managers delegate only to interfere later with how the employee is performing the task. But delegating full responsibility means that the employee—not the manager—is now completely responsible for task completion. Good managers need to trust their subordinates to do the job.

The second transfer that occurs with delegation is that the manager gives the subordinate full authority over the budget, resources, and personnel needed to do the job. To do the job effectively, subordinates must have the same tools and information at their disposal that managers had when they were responsible for the same task. In other words, for delegation to work, delegated authority must be commensurate with delegated responsibility.

Line function an activity that contributes directly to creating or selling the company's products

Staff function an activity that does not contribute directly to creating or selling the company's products but instead supports line activities

Delegation of authority the assignment of direct authority and responsibility to a subordinate to complete tasks for which the manager is normally responsible

The third transfer that occurs with delegation is the transfer of accountability. The subordinate now has the authority and responsibility to do the job and, in return, is accountable for getting the job done. In other words, managers delegate their managerial authority and responsibility to subordinates in exchange for results.

9-2d Degree of Centralization

Centralization of authority is the location of most authority at the upper levels of the organization. In a centralized organization, managers make most decisions, even the relatively small ones. Store managers at Whole Foods' 430 locations have long been responsible for deciding what to sell in their own stores. To compete more efficiently against Kroger and Costco, however, **Whole Foods** has decided to centralize purchasing responsibilities for meat, produce, and many nonperishable items at the company's Austin, Texas, headquarters. Co-CEO John Mackey says of the change, "We want to evolve the structure in such a way that we take out redundancy and waste."[24]

Decentralization is the location of a significant amount of authority in the lower levels of the organization. An organization is decentralized if it has a high degree of delegation at all levels. In a decentralized organization, workers closest to problems are authorized to make the decisions necessary to solve the problems on their own.

McDonald's is moving away from centralized decision making regarding menu items in its U.S. stores. Whereas it used to offer the same menu items in Louisiana, such as sweet tea (a standard item at southern restaurants), as it did in Minnesota, it will now leave menu and marketing decisions up to managers in twenty-two different regions. McDonald's U.S. President Mike Andres said, "We must

As Toyota became the largest automaker in the world, car quality declined as it increased its use of unstandardized parts across different cars and continents.

evolve our culture and organizational structure to put decision making closer to our customers."[25]

Decentralization has a number of advantages. It develops employee capabilities throughout the company and leads to faster decision making and more satisfied customers and employees. Furthermore, a study of 1,000 large companies found that companies with a high degree of decentralization outperformed those with a low degree of decentralization in terms of return on assets (6.9% versus 4.7%), return on investment (14.6% versus 9.0%), return on equity (22.8% versus 16.6%), and return on sales (10.3% versus 6.3%). Surprisingly, the same study found that few large companies actually are decentralized. Specifically, only 31 percent of employees in these 1,000 companies were responsible for recommending improvements to management. Overall, just 10 percent of employees received the training and information needed to support a truly decentralized approach to management.[26]

With results like these, the key question is no longer *whether* companies should decentralize, but *where* they should decentralize. One rule of thumb is to stay centralized where standardization is important and to decentralize where standardization is unimportant. **Standardization** is solving problems by consistently applying the same rules, procedures, and processes. Toyota became the largest auto manufacturer in the world by producing highly reliable cars at competitive costs. But as the company grew, it significantly increased the number of kinds of parts used in its cars, for example, using 100 different radiators in the cars it made around the world. Using that many varieties for the same part not only increased costs, it decreased quality, which then reduced Toyota sales. Toyota's leadership addressed this issue by using standardization to significantly reduce the variety of kinds of basic parts. For example, it used just 21 different kinds of radiators in its cars rather than 100, as before. This led to greater volume for each part and lower costs. Standardization has proven so successful that Toyota aims to reduce the variety of parts it uses across all its car models by 75 percent by grouping 100 different model platforms and 800 different engine types into larger, but many fewer, model families.[27]

Centralization of authority the location of most authority at the upper levels of the organization

Decentralization the location of a significant amount of authority in the lower levels of the organization

Standardization solving problems by consistently applying the same rules, procedures, and processes

9-3 JOB DESIGN

Could you stand to do the same simple tasks an average of 50 times per hour, 400 times per day, 2,000 times per week, 8,000 times per month? Few can. Fast-food workers rarely stay on the job more than six months. In fact, McDonald's and other fast-food restaurants have well over 70 percent employee turnover each year.[28] As a drive through employee at McDonald's you would repeatedly perform the following steps:

1. "Welcome to McDonald's. May I have your order please?"

2. Listen to the order. Repeat it for accuracy. State the total cost. "Please drive to the second window."

3. Take the money. Make change.

4. Give customers cups, straws, and napkins.

5. Give customers food.

6. "Thank you for coming to McDonald's."

In this section, you will learn about **job design**—the number, kind, and variety of tasks that individual workers perform in doing their jobs.

You will learn 9-3a why companies continue to use specialized jobs such as the McDonald's drive-through job and 9-3b how job rotation, job enlargement, job enrichment, and 9-3c the job characteristics model are being used to overcome the problems associated with job specialization.

9-3a Job Specialization

Job specialization occurs when a job is composed of a small part of a larger task or process. Specialized jobs are characterized by simple, easy-to-learn steps; low variety; and high repetition, such as the McDonald's drive-through window job just described. One of the clear disadvantages of specialized jobs is that, being so easy to learn, they quickly become boring. This, in turn, can lead to low job satisfaction and high absenteeism and employee turnover, all of which are very costly to organizations.

> **Job design** the number, kind, and variety of tasks that individual workers perform in doing their jobs
>
> **Job specialization** a job composed of a small part of a larger task or process
>
> **Job rotation** periodically moving workers from one specialized job to another to give them more variety and the opportunity to use different skills
>
> **Job enlargement** increasing the number of different tasks that a worker performs within one particular job

Why, then, do companies continue to create and use specialized jobs? The primary reason is that specialized jobs are very economical. As we learned from Frederick W. Taylor and Frank and Lillian Gilbreth in Chapter 2, after a job has been specialized, it takes little time to learn and master. Consequently, when experienced workers quit or are absent, the company can replace them with new employees and lose little productivity. For example, next time you're at McDonald's, notice the pictures of the food on the cash registers. These pictures make it easy for McDonald's trainees to quickly learn to take orders. Likewise, to simplify and speed operations at the drive-through, the drink dispensers are set to automatically fill drink cups. Put a medium cup below the dispenser. Punch the medium drink button. The soft-drink machine then fills the cup to within a half-inch of the top, while the worker goes to get your fries. At McDonald's, every task has been simplified in this way. Because the work is designed to be simple, wages can remain low because it isn't necessary to pay high salaries to attract highly experienced, educated, or trained workers.

9-3b Job Rotation, Enlargement, and Enrichment

Because of the efficiency of specialized jobs, companies are often reluctant to eliminate them. Consequently, job redesign efforts have focused on modifying jobs to keep the benefits of specialized jobs while reducing their obvious costs and disadvantages. Three methods—job rotation, job enlargement, and job enrichment—have been used to try to improve specialized jobs.[29]

Job rotation attempts to overcome the disadvantages of job specialization by periodically moving workers from one specialized job to another to give them more variety and the opportunity to use different skills. For example, an office receptionist who does nothing but answer phones could be systematically rotated to a different job, such as typing, filing, or data entry, every day or two. Likewise, the "mirror attacher" in an automobile plant might attach mirrors in the first half of the work shift and then install bumpers during the second half. Because employees simply switch from one specialized job to another, job rotation allows companies to retain the economic benefits of specialized work. At the same time, the greater variety of tasks makes the work less boring and more satisfying for workers.

Another way to counter the disadvantages of specialization is to enlarge the job. **Job enlargement** increases the number of different tasks that a worker performs within one particular job. Instead of being assigned just one task, workers with enlarged jobs are given several

Exhibit 9.10
Job Characteristics Model

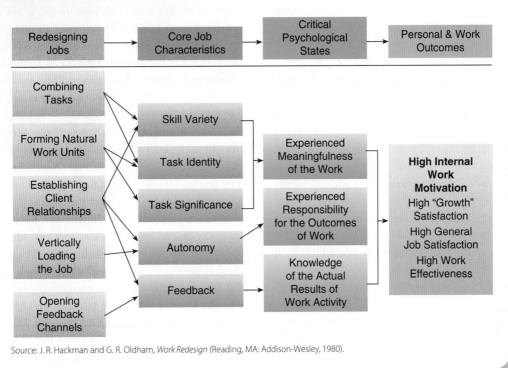

Source: J. R. Hackman and G. R. Oldham, *Work Redesign* (Reading, MA: Addison-Wesley, 1980).

tasks to perform. For example, an enlarged "mirror attacher" job might include attaching the mirror, checking to see that the mirror's power adjustment controls work, and then cleaning the mirror's surface. Though job enlargement increases variety, many workers report feeling more stress when their jobs are enlarged. Consequently, many workers view enlarged jobs as simply more work, especially if they are not given additional time to complete the additional tasks.

Job enrichment attempts to overcome the deficiencies in specialized work by increasing the number of tasks *and* by giving workers the authority and control to make meaningful decisions about their work.[30]

9-3c Job Characteristics Model

In contrast to job rotation, job enlargement, and job enrichment, which focus on providing variety in job tasks, the **job characteristics model (JCM)** is an approach to job redesign that seeks to formulate jobs in ways that motivate workers and lead to positive work outcomes.[31]

As shown in Exhibit 9.10, the primary goal of the model is to create jobs that result in positive personal and work outcomes, such as internal work motivation, satisfaction with one's job, and work effectiveness. Of these,

the central concern of the JCM is internal motivation. **Internal motivation** is motivation that comes from the job itself rather than from outside rewards such as a raise or praise from the boss. If workers feel that performing the job well is itself rewarding, then the job has internal motivation. Statements such as "I get a nice sense of accomplishment" or "I feel good about myself and what I'm producing" are examples of internal motivation.

In Exhibit 9.10, you can see that the JCM specifies three critical psychological states that must occur for work to be internally motivating. First, workers must *experience the work as meaningful*; that is, they must view their job as being important. Second, they must *experience responsibility for work outcomes*—they must feel personally responsible for the work being done well. Third, workers must have *knowledge of results*; that is, they must know how well they are performing their jobs. All three critical psychological states must occur for work to be internally motivating.

For example, grocery store cashiers usually have knowledge of results. When you're slow, your checkout line grows long. If you make a mistake, customers point it out: "No, I think that's on sale for $2.99, not $3.99." Likewise, cashiers experience responsibility for work outcomes. At the end of the day, the register is totaled, and the money is counted. Ideally, the money matches the total sales in the register. If the money in the till is less than what's recorded in the register, most stores make the cashier pay the difference. Consequently, most cashiers are very careful to avoid being caught short at the end of the day. Nonetheless, despite knowing the results and experiencing responsibility for work outcomes, most grocery store cashiers (at least where I shop) aren't internally motivated because they don't experience the work as meaningful. With scanners, it takes little skill to learn or do the job. Anyone can do it. In addition, cashiers have few decisions to make, and the job is highly repetitive.

What kinds of jobs produce the three critical psychological states? Moving another step to the left in Exhibit 9.10, you can see that these psychological states arise from jobs that are strong on five core job characteristics: skill variety, task identity, task significance, autonomy, and feedback. **Skill variety** is the number of different activities performed in a job. **Task identity** is the degree to which a job, from beginning to end, requires completion of a whole and identifiable piece of work. **Task significance** is the degree to which a job is perceived to have a substantial impact on others inside or outside the organization. **Autonomy** is the degree to which a job gives workers the discretion, freedom, and independence to decide how and when to accomplish the work. Finally, **feedback** is the amount of

information the job provides to workers about their work performance.

To illustrate how the core job characteristics work together, let's use them to assess more thoroughly why the McDonald's drive-through window job is not particularly satisfying or motivating. To start, skill variety is low. Except for the size of an order or special requests ("no onions"), the process is the same for each customer. At best, task identity is moderate. Although you take the order, handle the money, and deliver the food, others are responsible for a larger part of the process—preparing the food. Task identity will be even lower if the McDonald's has two drive-through windows because each drive-through window worker will have an even more specialized task. The first is limited to taking the order and making change, while the second just delivers the food.

Task significance, the impact you have on others, is probably low. Autonomy is also very low: McDonald's has strict rules about dress, cleanliness, and procedures. But the job does provide immediate feedback such as positive and negative customer comments, car horns honking, the amount of time it takes to process orders, and the number of cars in the drive-through. With the exception of feedback, the low levels of the core job characteristics show why the drive-through window job is not internally motivating for many workers.

What can managers do when jobs aren't internally motivating? The far left column of Exhibit 9.10 lists five job redesign techniques that managers can use to strengthen a job's core characteristics. *Combining tasks* increases skill variety and task identity by joining separate, specialized tasks into larger work modules. For example, some trucking firms are now requiring truck drivers to load their rigs as well as drive them. The hope is that involving drivers in loading will ensure that trucks are properly loaded, thus reducing damage claims.

Work can be formed into *natural work units* by arranging tasks according to logical or meaningful groups. Although many trucking companies randomly assign drivers to trucks, some have begun assigning drivers to particular geographic locations (for example, the Northeast or Southwest) or to truckloads that require special driving skill (for example, oversized loads or hazardous chemicals). Forming natural work units increases task identity and task significance. *Establishing client relationships* increases skill variety, autonomy, and feedback by giving

Skill variety the number of different activities performed in a job

Task identity the degree to which a job, from beginning to end, requires the completion of a whole and identifiable piece of work

Task significance the degree to which a job is perceived to have a substantial impact on others inside or outside the organization

Autonomy the degree to which a job gives workers the discretion, freedom, and independence to decide how and when to accomplish the job

Feedback the amount of information the job provides to workers about their work performance

Karen Katrjyan/Shutterstock.com

employees direct contact with clients and customers. In some companies, truck drivers are expected to establish business relationships with their regular customers. When something goes wrong with a shipment, customers are told to call drivers directly.

Vertical loading means pushing some managerial authority down to workers. For truck drivers, this means that they have the same authority as managers to resolve customer problems. In some companies, if a late shipment causes problems for a customer, the driver has the authority to fully refund the cost of that shipment without first obtaining management's approval.

The last job redesign technique offered by the model, *opening feedback channels*, means finding additional ways to give employees direct, frequent feedback about their job performance. For example, with advances in electronics, many truck drivers get instantaneous data as to whether they're on schedule and driving their rigs in a fuel-efficient manner. Likewise, the increased contact with customers also means that many drivers now receive monthly data on customer satisfaction.

9-4 INTRAORGANIZATIONAL PROCESSES

More than forty years ago, Tom Burns and G. M. Stalker described how two kinds of organizational designs, mechanistic and organic, are appropriate for different kinds of organizational environments.[32] **Mechanistic organizations** are characterized by specialized jobs and responsibilities; precisely defined, unchanging roles; and a rigid chain of command based on centralized authority and vertical communication. This type of organization works best in stable, unchanging business environments. By contrast, **organic organizations** are characterized by broadly defined jobs and responsibilities; loosely defined, frequently changing roles; and decentralized authority and horizontal communication based on task knowledge. This type of organization works best in dynamic, changing business environments.

The organizational design techniques described in the first half of this chapter—departmentalization, authority, and job design—are better suited for mechanistic organizations and the stable business environments that were more prevalent before 1980. By contrast, the organizational design techniques discussed in the second part of the chapter, are more appropriate for organic organizations and the increasingly dynamic environments in which today's businesses compete. The key

difference between these approaches is that mechanistic organizational designs focus on organizational structure, whereas organic organizational designs are concerned with **intraorganizational process**, which is the collection of activities that take place within an organization to transform inputs into outputs that customers value.

*Let's take a look at how companies are using **9-4a reengineering** and **9-4b empowerment** to redesign intraorganizational processes like these.*

9-4a Reengineering

In their best-selling book *Reengineering the Corporation*, Michael Hammer and James Champy define **reengineering** as "the *fundamental* rethinking and *radical* redesign of business *processes* to achieve *dramatic* improvements in critical, contemporary measures of performance, such as cost, quality, service and speed."[33] Hammer and Champy further explained the four key words shown in italics in this definition. The first key word is *fundamental*. When reengineering organizational designs, managers must ask themselves, "Why do we do what we do?" and "Why do we do it the way we do?" The usual answer is "Because that's the way we've always done it." The second key word is *radical*. Reengineering is about significant change, about starting over by throwing out the old ways of getting work done. The third key word is *processes*. Hammer and Champy noted that "most business people are not process oriented; they are focused on tasks, on jobs, on people, on structures, but not on processes." The fourth key word is *dramatic*. Reengineering is about achieving quantum improvements in company performance.

An example from IBM Credit's operation illustrates how work can be reengineered.[34] IBM Credit lends businesses money to buy IBM computers. Previously, the loan process began when an IBM salesperson called

Mechanistic organization an organization characterized by specialized jobs and responsibilities; precisely defined, unchanging roles; and a rigid chain of command based on centralized authority and vertical communication

Organic organization an organization characterized by broadly defined jobs and responsibilities; loosely defined, frequently changing roles; and decentralized authority and horizontal communication based on task knowledge

Intraorganizational process the collection of activities that take place within an organization to transform inputs into outputs that customers value

Reengineering fundamental rethinking and radical redesign of business processes to achieve dramatic improvements in critical measures of performance, such as cost, quality, service, and speed

OPEN FLOORPLAN'S FATAL FLAW: WORKERS WANT PRIVACY

From Silicon Valley to Wall Street, 70 percent of U.S. workplaces have some version of an open floorplan. Open offices save money and space, but they also tend to have a palpable buzz and have long been touted for increasing collaboration, productivity, and transparency while flattening organizational hierarchies. While open floorplans have many benefits, a growing body of research is revealing some significant flaws in them as well. Workers in open offices experience higher levels of job stress and workplace distraction; are more likely to be absent due to illness; and are less productive than are employees who work in private spaces. Perhaps because of these reasons, many workers are interested in returning to more traditional working conditions. In a recent study of 10,000 workers around the world, 95 percent said that they wanted more privacy at work, 85 percent loathed their company's open office plans, and 31 percent said that they had to leave the office to get work done.

Sources: S. Lui, "The Open Plan Office Trap: Why It Pays to Work Alone," *Lifehacker*, January 27, 2016, accessed April 29, 2016, http://www.lifehacker.com.au/2016/01/the-open-plan-office-trap-why-it-pays-to-work-alone/; J. McGregor, "Office Designers Find Open-Plan Spaces Are Actually Lousy for Workers," *Washington Post*, April 22, 2015, accessed April 29, 2016, https://www.washingtonpost.com/news/on-leadership/wp/2015/04/22/office-designers-find-open-plan-spaces-are-actually-lousy-for-workers/; "Privacy Crisis Engulfs the Office," *Steelcase Research*, September 14, 2014, accessed April 29, 2016, http://www.prnewswire.co.uk/news-releases/privacy-crisis-engulfs-the-office-275273621.html.

the home office to obtain credit approval for a customer's purchase. The first department involved in the process took the credit information over the phone from the salesperson and recorded it on the credit form. The credit form was sent to the credit checking department, then to the pricing department (where the interest rate was determined), and on through a total of five departments. In all, it took the five departments six days to approve or deny the customer's loan. Of course, this delay cost IBM business. Some customers got their loans elsewhere. Others, frustrated by the wait, simply canceled their orders.

Finally, two IBM managers decided to walk a loan straight through each of the departments involved in the process. At each step, they asked the workers to stop what they were doing and immediately process their loan application. They were shocked by what they found. From start to finish, the entire process took just ninety minutes! The six-day turnaround time was almost entirely due to delays in handing off the work

from one department to another. The solution: IBM redesigned the process so that one person, not five people in five separate departments, now handles the entire loan approval process without any handoffs. The results were indeed dramatic. Reengineering the credit process reduced approval time from six days to four hours and allowed IBM Credit to increase the number of loans it handled by a factor of 100!

Reengineering changes an organization's orientation from vertical to horizontal. Instead of taking orders from upper management, lower- and middle-level managers and workers take orders from a customer who is at the beginning and end of each process. Instead of running independent functional departments, managers and workers in different departments take ownership of cross-functional processes. Instead of simplifying work so that it becomes increasingly specialized, reengineering complicates work by giving workers increased autonomy and responsibility for complete processes.

In essence, reengineering changes work by changing **task interdependence**, the extent to which collective action is required to complete an entire piece of work. As shown in Exhibit 9.11, there are three kinds of task interdependence.[35] In **pooled interdependence**,

Task interdependence the extent to which collective action is required to complete an entire piece of work

Pooled interdependence work completed by having each job or department independently contribute to the whole

BUSINESS PROCESS REENGINEERING

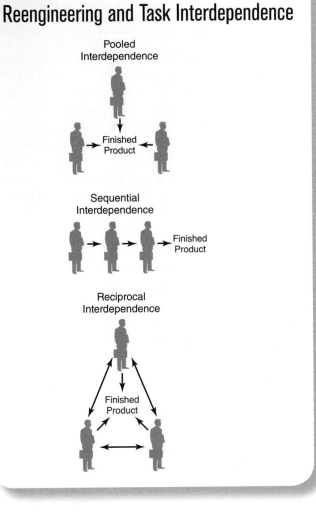

Exhibit 9.11
Reengineering and Task Interdependence

Pooled
Interdependence

Finished
Product

Sequential
Interdependence

Finished
Product

Reciprocal
Interdependence

Finished
Product

it allows a few workers to do the work formerly done by many, reengineering is simply a corporate code word for cost cutting and worker layoffs.[36] For this reason, detractors claim that reengineering hurts morale and performance. Even though ordering times were reduced from three weeks to three days, Levi Strauss ended an $850 million reengineering project because of the fear and turmoil it created in the company's workforce. One low point occurred when Levi management, encouraged by its reengineering consultants, told 4,000 workers that they would have to "reapply for their jobs" as the company shifted from its traditional vertical structure to a process-based form of organizing. Thomas Kasten, Levi Strauss's vice president for reengineering and customer service at that time, says, "We felt the pressure building up [over reengineering efforts], and we were worried about the business."[37] Today, even reengineering gurus Hammer and Champy admit that roughly 70 percent of all reengineering projects fail because of the effects on people in the workplace. Says Hammer, "I wasn't smart enough about that [the people issues]. I was reflecting my engineering background and was insufficiently appreciative of the human dimension. I've [now] learned that's critical."[38]

9-4b Empowerment

Another way of redesigning intraorganizational processes is through empowerment. **Empowering workers** means permanently passing decision-making authority and responsibility from managers to workers. For workers to be fully empowered, companies must give them the information and resources they need to make and carry out good decisions and then reward them for taking individual initiative.[39] In other words, employees won't feel very empowered if they constantly have someone looking over their shoulders. French-based Carrefour, the second largest retailer in the world, has seen its profits and market share consistently shrink over the past decade. New CEO Georges Plassat feels that Carrefour had

each job or department contributes to the whole independently. In **sequential interdependence**, work must be performed in succession because one group's or job's outputs become the inputs for the next group or job. Finally, in **reciprocal interdependence**, different jobs or groups work together in a back-and-forth manner to complete the process. By reducing the handoffs between different jobs or groups, reengineering decreases sequential interdependence. Likewise, reengineering decreases pooled interdependence by redesigning work so that formerly independent jobs or departments now work together to complete processes. Finally, reengineering increases reciprocal interdependence by making groups or individuals responsible for larger, more complete processes in which several steps may be accomplished at the same time.

As an organizational design tool, reengineering promises big rewards, but it has also come under severe criticism. The most serious complaint is that because

Sequential interdependence work completed in succession, with one group's or job's outputs becoming the inputs for the next group or job

Reciprocal interdependence work completed by different jobs or groups working together in a back-and-forth manner

Empowering workers permanently passing decision-making authority and responsibility from managers to workers by giving them the information and resources they need to make and carry out good decisions

"excess centralization preventing it from delivering results." The clearest sign of that was Carrefour headquarters determining which products to sell at what prices in each store worldwide. Today, however, Plassat says, "There is a change in culture" to empower local store managers to make these decisions. For example, the store manager, not headquarters, decides how much floor space to use to sell TVs, how many kinds of TVs to sell (a full range or only the best sellers), and how the TVs are priced. Says Plassat, "We have specialists in the store[s] who know what is selling," and top management now listens to them.[40]

When workers are given the proper information and resources and are allowed to make good decisions, they experience strong feelings of empowerment. **Empowerment** is a feeling of intrinsic motivation in which workers perceive their work to have meaning and perceive themselves to be competent, having an impact, and capable of self-determination.[41] Work has meaning when it is consistent with personal standards and beliefs. Workers feel competent when they believe they can perform an activity with skill. The belief that they are having an impact comes from a feeling that they can affect work outcomes. A feeling of self-determination arises from workers' belief that they have the autonomy to choose how best to do their work.

Empowerment can lead to changes in organizational processes because meaning, competence, impact, and self-determination produce empowered employees who take active rather than passive roles in their work. At Ritz-Carlton hotels, all employees are empowered to spend up to $2,000 to solve customer service issues. That's not $2,000 per year or $2,000 per day, it's $2,000 per incident. And, employees can spend that $2,000 without asking for managerial approval. Carmine Gallo, president of Gallo Communications Group, and his wife were eating at a particularly busy Ritz-Carlton restaurant, which meant the service was slow. Gallo says, "During one especially busy time at the hotel's restaurant, the waiter apologized for the wait, gave us complimentary appetizers, and paid for our desserts. When I asked him why he did so he said, 'I'm empowered to keep my guests happy.'"[42]

Empowerment feeling of intrinsic motivation in which workers perceive their work to have impact and meaning and perceive themselves to be competent and capable of self-determination

Interorganizational process a collection of activities that take place among companies to transform inputs into outputs that customers value

Modular organization an organization that outsources noncore business activities to outside companies, suppliers, specialists, or consultants

INTERORGANIZA-TIONAL PROCESSES

An **interorganizational process** is a collection of activities that occur *among companies* to transform inputs into outputs that customers value. In other words, many companies work together to create a product or service that keeps customers happy. Nutella, the chocolate and hazelnut spread, is headquartered in Italy, has five factories in Europe, two in South America, and one each in Russia, North America, and Australia. Those factories work with suppliers in Turkey (hazelnuts), Malaysia (palm oil), Nigeria (cocoa), Brazil (sugar), and France (vanillin). The 401,500 tons of Nutella produced each year are then sold to grocers by sales offices and sales brokers in 160 different countries.[43]

*In this section, you'll explore interorganizational processes by learning about **9-5a modular organizations** and **9-5b virtual organizations**.*

9-5a Modular Organizations

Stephen Roach, former chief economist for investment bank Morgan Stanley, says that companies increasingly want to take "functions that aren't central to their core competency" and outsource them.[44] Except for the core business activities that they can perform better, faster, and cheaper than others, **modular organizations** outsource all remaining business activities to outside companies, suppliers, specialists, or consultants. The term *modular* is used because the business activities

Amazon contracts with Integrity Staffing Solutions to fill 100,000 short-term labor positions during the hectic holiday shopping season.

purchased from outside companies can be added and dropped as needed, much like adding pieces to a three-dimensional puzzle. Exhibit 9.12 depicts a modular organization in which the company has chosen to keep training, human resources, sales, product design, manufacturing, customer service, research and development, and information technology as core business activities but has outsourced the noncore activities of product distribution, web page design, advertising, payroll, accounting, and packaging.

The primary advantage of modular organizations is that they can cost significantly less to run than traditional organizations because they pay for outsourced labor, expertise, or manufacturing capabilities only when needed. Due to a surge in online holiday shopping, **Amazon's** fourth quarter revenue is consistently 50 percent higher than that of any other quarter throughout the year. To handle the increase in shipping this creates, Amazon adds 100,000 temporary employees to the 90,000 employees already working at its seventy U.S. warehouses and shipping hubs. Amazon does not hire these seasonal workers itself, however. Instead, it contracts with Integrity

Staffing Solutions to provide short-term labor. Integrity handles background checks, tax filings, payroll, unemployment, and other legal issues, saving Amazon roughly $100 million a year on payroll taxes alone. According to former Integrity manager Robert Capo Jr., "If Amazon [was] going to do this themselves, they would have to build an entire different infrastructure."[45] To obtain cost advantages, however, modular organizations need reliable partners—vendors and suppliers with whom they can work closely and can trust.

Modular organizations have disadvantages, too. The primary disadvantage is the loss of control that occurs when key business activities are outsourced to other companies. Also, companies may reduce their competitive advantage in two ways if they mistakenly outsource a core business activity. First, as a result of competitive and technological change, the noncore business activities a company has outsourced may suddenly become the basis for competitive advantage. Second, related to that point, suppliers to whom work is outsourced can sometimes become competitors.

9-5b Virtual Organizations

In contrast to modular organizations, in which the interorganizational process revolves around a central company, a **virtual organization** is part of a network in which many companies share skills, costs, capabilities, markets, and customers with each other. Exhibit 9.13 shows a virtual organization in which, for today, the parts of a virtual company consist of product design, purchasing, manufacturing, advertising, and information technology. Unlike modular organizations, in which the outside organizations are tightly linked to one central company, virtual organizations work with some companies in the network alliance, but not with all. So, whereas a puzzle with various pieces is a fitting metaphor for a modular organization, a potluck dinner is an appropriate metaphor for a virtual organization. All participants bring their finest food dish but eat only what they want.

Another difference is that the working relationships between modular organizations and outside companies tend

Virtual organization an organization that is part of a network in which many companies share skills, costs, capabilities, markets, and customers to collectively solve customer problems or provide specific products or services

Exhibit 9.12
Modular Organization

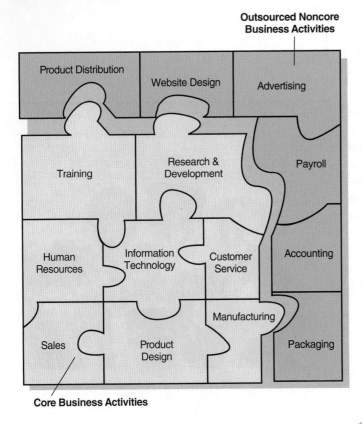

Outsourced Noncore Business Activities

Product Distribution · Website Design · Advertising · Training · Research & Development · Payroll · Human Resources · Information Technology · Customer Service · Accounting · Sales · Product Design · Manufacturing · Packaging

Core Business Activities

Exhibit 9.13
Virtual Organizations

Today, I'll have...

Purchasing

Product Design

Information Technology

Manufacturing

Advertising

Mike Powell//Photodisc/Getty Images

Democratize the Workplace to Empower Workers?

At some companies, small and large decisions are made not by managers, but by a worker vote. At software company **InContext**, for example, workers recently voted on whether to have standing desks, cubicles, or open tables. After organizing visits to two locations, marketing technology firm **MediaMath** let workers decide the location of its new headquarters. Employees at 1Sale.com voted on whether the company should continue to pay for employee lunches, or whether it should use that money to lower the cost of health insurance. According to 1Sale's Shmuli Bortunk, "They asked us, do you prefer to have your belly full or your wallet full?" While voting can take more time, it can also empower employees and improve morale. With democratized decisions, says InContext Product manager Mackenzie Siren, "People feel like they have a real voice."

Rawpixel.com/Shutterstock.com

Source: R. Silverman, "Workplace Democracy Catches On," *Wall Street Journal*, March 27, 2016, accessed April 29, 2016, http://www.wsj.com/articles/workplace-democracy-catches-on-1459117910.

to be more stable and longer lasting than the shorter, often temporary, relationships found among the virtual companies in a network alliance. The composition of a virtual organization is always changing. The combination of network partners that a virtual corporation has at any one time depends on the expertise needed to solve a particular problem or provide a specific product or service. For instance, today the business might need to focus on advertising and product design, as shown in Exhibit 9.13, but tomorrow, the business could want something completely different. In this sense, the term "virtual organization" means the organization that exists "at the moment."

Virtual organizations have a number of advantages. They let companies share costs, and because members can quickly combine their efforts to meet customers' needs, they are fast and flexible. Finally, because each member of the network alliance is the best at what it does, virtual organizations should in theory provide better products and services in all respects.

As with modular organizations, a disadvantage of virtual organizations is that after work has been outsourced, it can be difficult to control the quality of work done by network partners. The greatest disadvantage, however, is that tremendous managerial skills are required to make a network of independent organizations work well together, especially because their relationships tend to be short and based on a single task or project. Virtual organizations are using two methods to solve this problem. The first is to use a *broker*. In traditional, hierarchical organizations, managers plan, organize, and control. But with the horizontal, interorganizational processes that characterize virtual organizations, the job of a broker is to create and assemble the knowledge, skills, and resources from different companies for outside parties, such as customers.[46] The second way to make networks of virtual organizations more manageable is to use a *virtual organization agreement* that, somewhat like a contract, specifies the schedules, responsibilities, costs, payouts, and liabilities for participating organizations.[47]

STUDY TOOLS 9

LOCATED IN TEXTBOOK
- ☐ Rip-out and review chapter review card

LOCATED AT WWW.CENGAGEBRAIN.COM
- ☐ Review key term flashcards and create your own from StudyBits
- ☐ Track your knowledge and understanding of key concepts, using the concept tracker

- ☐ Complete practice and graded quizzes to prepare for tests
- ☐ Complete interactive content within the exposition
- ☐ View chapter highlight box content at the beginning of each chapter

10 Managing Teams

Rido/Shutterstock.com

LEARNING OUTCOMES

10-1 Explain the good and bad of using teams.

10-2 Recognize and understand the different kinds of teams.

10-3 Understand the general characteristics of work teams.

10-4 Explain how to enhance work team effectiveness.

After you finish this chapter, go to **PAGE 220** for **STUDY TOOLS**

10-1 THE GOOD AND BAD OF USING TEAMS

Ninety-one percent of organizations are significantly improving their effectiveness by using work teams.[1] Procter & Gamble and Cummins Engine began using teams in 1962 and 1973, respectively. Boeing, Caterpillar, Champion International, Ford Motor Company, 3M, and General Electric established work teams in the mid- to late-1980s. Today, most companies use teams to tackle a variety of issues.[2] "Teams are ubiquitous. Whether we are talking about software development, Olympic hockey, disease outbreak response, or urban warfare, teams represent the critical unit that 'gets things done' in today's world."[3]

Work teams consist of a small number of people with complementary skills who hold themselves mutually accountable for pursuing a common purpose, achieving performance goals, and improving interdependent work processes.[4] By this definition, computer programmers working on separate projects in the same department of a company would not be considered a team. To be a team, the programmers would have to be interdependent and share responsibility and accountability for the quality and amount of computer code they produced.[5] Teams are becoming more important in many industries because they help organizations respond to specific problems and challenges. Though work teams are not the answer for every situation or organization, if the right teams are used properly and in the right settings, teams can dramatically improve company performance over more traditional management approaches while also instilling a sense of vitality in the workplace that is otherwise difficult to achieve.

Let's begin our discussion of teams by learning about **10-1a the advantages of teams, 10-1b the disadvantages of teams, and 10-1c when to use and not use teams.**

10-1a The Advantages of Teams

Companies are making greater use of teams because teams have been shown to improve customer satisfaction, product and service quality, speed and efficiency in product development, employee job satisfaction, and decision making.[6] For example, one survey indicated that 80 percent of companies with more than 100 employees use teams, and 90 percent of all U.S. employees work part of their day in a team.[7] In fact, according to recent research, workers spend half again as much time in collaborative activities as they did just twenty years ago![8]

Teams help businesses increase *customer satisfaction* in several ways. One way is to create work teams that are trained to meet the needs of specific customers. 3D printing, also called additive manufacturing because one thin layer is added at a time, is now part of the production process in aviation, energy, pharmaceuticals, cars, and more. A survey of 900 manufacturers found that 14 percent use 3D printing today, and 48 percent plan to use it within a decade. Because legal issues related to additive manufacturing are different from those related to traditional manufacturing, the law practice of **Hunton & Williams** developed a cross-functional team of attorneys to assist clients who are adopting this new technology. Rather than seek out legal advice from several independent lawyers and then try to piece all the information together themselves, clients with significant investments in 3D printing can access a range of experts on product liability, taxes, intellectual property, insurance, litigation—and more—with just one phone call.[9]

Teams also help firms improve *product and service quality* in several ways.[10] In contrast to traditional organizational structures, in which management is responsible for organizational outcomes and performance, teams take direct responsibility for the quality of the products and service they produce and sell. Once considered a solo career, over-the-road (OTR) truck drivers are increasingly pairing up to keep trucks moving more than twenty hours a day. Team driver Gary Helms says that he and his partner only stop for fuel, food, and a shower—otherwise, "We want the truck to move."[11] With state regulations limiting truck drivers to no more than eleven hours a day of driving, a single driver can cover roughly 500 miles per day. Driver teams, however, can cover 1,000 miles a day, which makes them incredibly valuable to online retailers and the organic-grocery industry, both of which promise customers fast delivery and fresh products. Driver teams are so valuable, in fact, that companies are willing to pay them $6 per mile—three times the normal price. According to transportation analyst Donald Broughton, companies running driver teams can provide freight speeds at a fraction of the price.[12]

Another reason for using teams is that teamwork often leads to increased *job satisfaction*.[13] Teamwork can be more satisfying than traditional work because it gives workers a chance to improve their skills. This is often accomplished through **cross-training**,

> **Work team** a small number of people with complementary skills who hold themselves mutually accountable for pursuing a common purpose, achieving performance goals, and improving interdependent work processes
>
> **Cross-training** training team members to do all or most of the jobs performed by the other team members

AVOIDING TEAM-BUILDING FIASCOS

Regardless of where they fall on the spectrum of too boring or too extreme, corporate team-building activities are a notorious source of dread and eye rolling. According to David Jacobsen, founder of **TrivWorks** team-building company, "The worst possible outcome is having the exact opposite of what you intended happen," Jacobson says. "You've crushed morale and left your employees alienated or disconnected." Team building can be positive and meaningful, however, if overeager managers can stick to a few guidelines:

1. Clearly identify the purpose and goals of the activity and let your staff know up front.

2. Let the purpose and goals dictate the type of activity.

3. Avoid activities that simulate violence, cause harm, or humiliate the participants.

4. Draw clear connections between the activity and how the team performs in the workplace.

5. Incorporate a challenge.

The key is to make the activity relevant. "If the exercise is good, your team will take what they did or learned back to the workplace," says Jacobson. "They're going to collaborate and communicate better."

Source: J. A. Graves, "Corporate Team-Building Activities: The Good, the Bad, and the Really Ugly," *U.S. News*, September 24, 2014, accessed May 2, 2015, http://money.usnews.com/money/careers/articles/2014/09/25/corporate-team-building-activities-the-good-the-bad-and-the-really-ugly/.

in which team members are taught how to do all or most of the jobs performed by the other team members. The advantage for the organization is that cross-training allows a team to function normally when one member is absent, quits, or is transferred. The advantage for workers is that cross-training broadens their skills and increases their capabilities while also making their work more varied and interesting.

Teamwork is also satisfying because work teams often receive proprietary business information that typically is available only to managers. The **Great Little Box Company (GLBC)**, which makes corrugated boxes, custom product displays, and flexible and protective packaging for manufacturers, has an "open books" philosophy, where team members are given full access to the company's financial information. Founder Robert Meggy says, "It makes people feel more a part of the company. It instills a sense of trust. Regardless of whether the news is good or bad, people want to know and, ultimately, will try harder to make the company more profitable." After all, he says, "We want employees to run the company like their own business." Team member and customer-service representative Sandra Fung says, "If we have been profitable that month, it makes me feel good to learn that I have contributed to that." Finally, to drive home the importance of teams and teamwork, everyone receives equal monthly profit sharing checks. Says Meggy, "When it comes to teamwork, everyone is equal here. The truck drivers, the controller, office staff, plant supervisor—everybody gets the same amount."[14]

Team members also gain job satisfaction from unique leadership responsibilities that are not typically available in traditional organizations. Finally, teams share many of the advantages of group decision making discussed in Chapter 5. For instance, because team members possess different knowledge, skills, abilities, and experiences, a team is able to view problems from multiple perspectives. This diversity of viewpoints increases the odds that team decisions will solve the underlying causes of problems and not just address the symptoms. The increased knowledge and information available to teams also make it easier for them to generate more alternative solutions, a critical part of improving the quality of decisions. Because team members are involved in decision-making processes, they are also likely to be more committed to making those decisions work. In short, teams can do a much better job than individuals in two important steps of the decision-making process: defining the problem and generating alternative solutions.

10-1b The Disadvantages of Teams

Although teams can significantly improve customer satisfaction, product and service quality, speed and efficiency in product development, employee job satisfaction, and decision making, using teams does not guarantee these positive outcomes. In fact, if you've ever participated in team projects in your classes, you're probably already aware of some of the problems inherent in work teams. Despite all of their promise, teams and teamwork are also prone to these significant disadvantages: initially high turnover, social loafing, and the problems associated with group decision making.

The first disadvantage of work teams is *initially high turnover*. Teams aren't for everyone, and some workers balk at the responsibility, effort, and learning required in team settings. When Zappos, the online shoe company changed from a traditional to a team-based structure where there are no bosses and no titles and employees manage themselves (what it calls Holacracy), it offered everyone in the company three months of severance pay to leave if they decided that it wasn't right for them. Turns out that of its 1,500 employees, 14 percent decided to leave. After ten months, that figure had risen to 18 percent overall and 38 percent among members of a special technology team charged with migrating Zappos's website to Amazon servers. Zappos's John Bunch, who is managing the transition to Holacracy, said, "Whatever the number of people who took the offer was the right number as they made the decision that was right for them and right for Zappos."[15]

Social loafing is another disadvantage of work teams. **Social loafing** occurs when workers withhold their efforts and fail to perform their share of the work.[16] A nineteenth-century French engineer named Maximilian Ringlemann first documented social loafing when he found that one person pulling on a rope alone exerted an average of 139 pounds of force on the rope. In groups of three, the average force dropped to 117 pounds per person. In groups of eight, the average dropped to just 68 pounds per person. Ringlemann concluded that the larger the team, the smaller the individual effort. In fact, social loafing is more likely to occur in larger groups where identifying and monitoring the efforts of individual team members can be difficult.[17] In other words, social loafers count on being able to blend into the background, where their lack of effort isn't easily spotted.

From team-based class projects, most students already know about social loafers or "slackers," who contribute poor, little, or no work whatsoever. Not surprisingly, a study of 250 student teams found that the most talented students are typically the least satisfied with teamwork because of having to carry slackers and do a disproportionate share of their team's work.[18] A similar study of virtual teams (where team members work remotely) found that social loafing is higher among team members who are stretched by high levels of non-work obligations (such as family, volunteering, and community work).[19] Perceptions of fairness are negatively related to the extent of social loafing within teams.[20]

Finally, teams share many of the *disadvantages of group decision making* discussed in Chapter 5, such as groupthink. In *groupthink*, members of highly cohesive groups feel intense pressure not to disagree with each other so that the group can approve a proposed solution. Because groupthink restricts discussion and leads to consideration of a limited number of alternative solutions, it usually results in poor decisions. Also, team decision making takes considerable time, and team meetings can often be unproductive and inefficient. Another possible pitfall is *minority domination*, where just one or two people dominate team discussions, restricting consideration of different problem definitions and alternative solutions. Minority domination is especially likely to occur when the team leader talks so much during team discussions, effectively discouraging other team members from speaking up. When that happens, team performance drops significantly.[21] Finally, team members may not feel accountable for the decisions and actions taken by the team.

10-1c When to Use Teams

As the two previous subsections made clear, teams have significant advantages *and* disadvantages. Therefore, the question is not whether to use teams, but *when* and *where* to use teams for maximum benefit and minimum cost. As Doug Johnson, associate director at the Center for Collaborative Organizations at the University of North Texas, puts it, "Teams are a means to an end, not an end in themselves. You have to ask yourself questions first. Does the work require interdependence? Will the team philosophy fit company strategy? Will management make a long-term commitment to this process?"[22] Exhibit 10.1 provides some additional guidelines on when to use or not use teams.[23]

First, teams should be used when there is a clear, engaging reason or purpose for using them. Too many companies use teams because they're popular or because the companies assume that teams can fix all problems. Teams are much more likely to succeed if they know why they exist and what they are supposed to accomplish, and they are more likely to fail if they don't.

Second, teams should be used when the job can't be done unless people work together. This typically means that teams are needed when tasks are complex, require multiple perspectives, or require repeated interaction with others to complete. Because of the enormous complexity of today's cars, you would think that auto companies routinely use interconnected design teams. After

Social loafing behavior in which team members withhold their efforts and fail to perform their share of the work

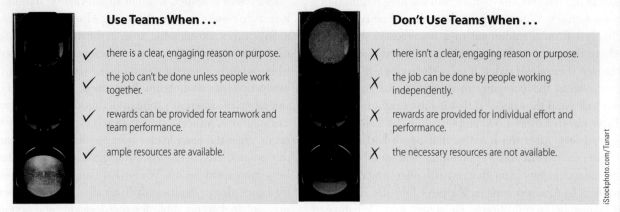

Exhibit 10.1
When to Use and When Not to Use Teams

Use Teams When . . .

✓ there is a clear, engaging reason or purpose.

✓ the job can't be done unless people work together.

✓ rewards can be provided for teamwork and team performance.

✓ ample resources are available.

Don't Use Teams When . . .

✗ there isn't a clear, engaging reason or purpose.

✗ the job can be done by people working independently.

✗ rewards are provided for individual effort and performance.

✗ the necessary resources are not available.

Source: R. Wageman, "Critical Success Factors for Creating Superb Self-Managing Teams," *Organizational Dynamics* 26, no. 1 (1997): 49–61.

all, the typical car has 30,000 parts, eighty different computer modules, indicators sensing how close other cars are when parking or going 70 mph, and the ability to automatically adjust braking, cornering, gas mileage, and acceleration. But auto companies don't routinely use interconnected design teams, as most designers are responsible for separate sections or parts of the car. Achim Badstübner, head of **Audi Group** exterior design, says, "We tend to make the mistake that we have an exterior department, an interior department and a technology department, and they all know what they're doing but the connection is not so good." Audi, however, takes a team approach. Badstübner says, "I think it's very important to basically lock them in one room, literally speaking. Then there is an interaction: you talk to the guy who does seats and he tells you something about his expertise and you might take something from him that helps you to develop a new wheel, for example." Badstübner says by connecting the teams, "you get a different result because through this method you get the best of every brain. I think you can't survive if you just depend on one brain to do a complex thing like [design] a car."[24]

Third, teams should be used when rewards can be provided for teamwork and team performance. Rewards that depend on team performance rather than individual performance are the key to rewarding team behaviors and efforts. You'll read more about team rewards later in the chapter, but for now it's enough to know that if the type of reward (individual versus team) is not matched to the type of performance (individual versus team), teams won't work.

10-2 KINDS OF TEAMS

*Let's continue our discussion of teams by learning about the different kinds of teams that companies such as Google and Maytag use to make themselves more competitive. We look first at **10-2a how teams differ in terms of autonomy, which is the key dimension that makes one team different from another**, and then at **10-2b some special kinds of teams.***

10-2a Autonomy, the Key Dimension

Teams can be classified in a number of ways, such as permanent or temporary, or functional or cross-functional. However, studies indicate that the amount of autonomy possessed by a team is the key difference among teams.[25] *Autonomy* is the degree to which workers have the discretion, freedom, and independence to decide how and when to accomplish their jobs. Exhibit 10.2 shows how five kinds of teams differ in terms of autonomy. Moving left to right across the autonomy continuum at the top of the exhibit, traditional work groups and employee involvement groups have the least autonomy, semi- autonomous work groups have more autonomy, and, finally, self-managing teams and self-designing teams have the most autonomy. Moving from bottom to top along the left side of the exhibit, note that the number of responsibilities given to each

Exhibit 10.2
Team Autonomy Continuum

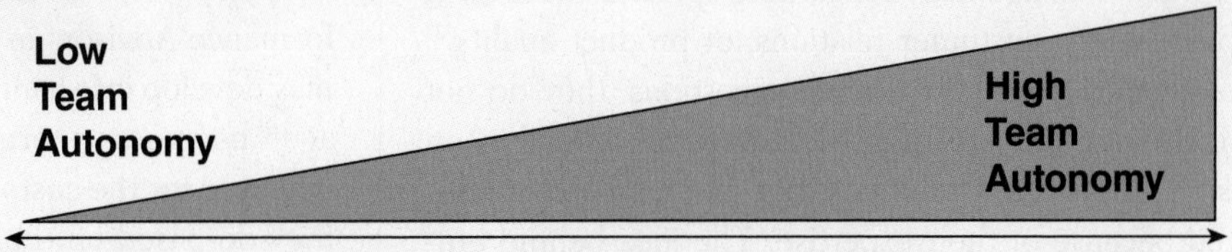

Low Team Autonomy ◄──────────────────────────► High Team Autonomy

Responsibilities	Traditional Work Groups	Employee Involvement Groups	Semi-Autonomous Work Groups	Self-Managing Teams	Self-Designing Teams
Control Design of					
Team					✓
Tasks					✓
Membership					✓
Production/Service Tasks					
Make Decisions				✓	✓
Solve Problems				✓	✓
Major Production/Service Tasks					
Make Decisions			✓	✓	✓
Solve Problems			✓	✓	✓
Information			✓	✓	✓
Give Advice/Make Suggestions		✓	✓	✓	✓
Execute Task	✓	✓	✓	✓	✓

Sources: R. D. Banker, J. M. Field, R. G. Schroeder, and K. K. Sinha, "Impact of Work Teams on Manufacturing Performance: A Longitudinal Field Study," *Academy of Management Journal* 39 (1996): 867–890; J. R. Hackman, "The Psychology of Self-Management in Organizations," in *Psychology and Work: Productivity, Change, and Employment*, ed. M. S. Pallak and R. Perlof (Washington, DC: American Psychological Association), 85–136.

kind of team increases directly with its autonomy. Let's review each of these kinds of teams and their autonomy and responsibilities in more detail.

The smallest amount of autonomy is found in **traditional work groups**, where two or more people work together to achieve a shared goal. In these groups, workers are responsible for doing the work or executing the task, but they do not have direct responsibility or control over their work. Workers report to managers, who are responsible for their performance and have the authority to hire and fire them, make job assignments, and control resources. For instance, suppose that an experienced worker blatantly refuses to do his share of the work, saying, "I've done my time. Let the younger employees do the work." In a team with high autonomy, the responsibility of getting this employee to put forth his fair share of effort would belong to his teammates. But, in a traditional work group, that responsibility belongs to the boss or supervisor. The supervisor in this situation calmly confronted the employee and told him, "We need your talent, [and] your knowledge of these machines. But if you won't work, you'll have to go elsewhere." Within days, the employee's behavior improved.[26]

> **Traditional work group** a group composed of two or more people who work together to achieve a shared goal

Employee involvement teams, which have somewhat more autonomy, meet on company time on a weekly or monthly basis to provide advice or make suggestions to management concerning specific issues such as plant safety, customer relations, or product quality.[27] Though they offer advice and suggestions, they do not have the authority to make decisions. Membership on these teams is often voluntary, but members may be selected because of their expertise. The idea behind employee involvement teams is that the people closest to the problem or situation are best able to recommend solutions. For more than three years, production of Boeing's 787 Dreamliner was delayed by multiple problems—parts shortages, improper installation, failed test flights, and more. Because of production delays, Boeing must build ten planes per month, up from the typical two and a half planes. To meet this aggressive goal, it established nearly 200 employee involvement teams to analyze the way 787s are assembled and make changes to maximize efficiency. For example, one employee involvement team found that ducts already installed in the plane were being damaged because workers were kicking and stepping on them while doing other work. The damaged ducts then had to be removed and replaced. The team recommended that temporary covers be placed over the ducts, thus eliminating delays and increased costs.[28]

Semi-autonomous work groups not only provide advice and suggestions to management but also have the authority to make decisions and solve problems related to the major tasks required to produce a product or service. Semi-autonomous groups regularly receive information about budgets, work quality and performance, and competitors' products. Furthermore, members of semi-autonomous work groups are typically cross-trained in a number of different skills and tasks. In short, semi-autonomous work groups give employees the authority to make decisions that are typically made by supervisors and managers.

That authority is not complete, however. Managers still play a role, though one that is much reduced compared with traditional work groups, in supporting the work of semi-autonomous work groups. The role a manager plays on a team usually evolves over time. "It may start with helping to transition problem-solving responsibilities to the team, filling miscellaneous requests for the team, and doing ad hoc tasks," says Steven Hitchcock, president of Axis Performance Advisors in Portland, Oregon. Later, the team may develop into a mini-enterprise, and the former manager becomes externally focused—sort of an account manager for the customer. Managers have to adjust what they do based on the sophistication of the team.[29] A lot of what managers of semi-autonomous work groups do is ask good questions, provide resources, and facilitate performance of group goals.

Self-managing teams are different from semi-autonomous work groups in that team members manage and control *all* of the major tasks *directly related* to production of a product or service without first getting approval from management. This includes managing and controlling the acquisition of materials, making a product or providing a service, and ensuring timely delivery. At Connecticut Spring & Stamping, a precision manufacturing firm, self-managing teams determine the master schedule that controls the order in which parts will flow from machines to workers, the location and proximity of machines and work stations, when and who gets overtime work (and how much), and how teams will be rewarded. For example, the teams designed a three-stage program in which constant improvement in on-time delivery is required to receive rewards. All of these decisions are made without management's input or approval.[30]

The use of self-managing teams has significantly increased productivity at a number of other companies, increasing quality by 12 percent at AT&T, reducing errors by 13 percent at FedEx, and helping 3M increase production by 300 percent at one of its manufacturing plants.[31] Seventy-two percent of *Fortune* 1,000 companies have at least one self-managing team, up from 28 percent in 1987.[32]

Self-designing teams have all the characteristics of self-managing teams, but they can also control and change the design of the teams themselves, the tasks they do and how and when they do them, and the membership of the teams. Valve, a Bellevue, Washington maker of video games, has no managers. In fact, the company defines "manager" in its employee handbook as, "The kind of people we don't have any of. So, if you see one, tell somebody, because it's probably the ghost of whoever was in this building before us."[33] "We do have a founder/president, but even he isn't your manager. This company is yours to steer—toward opportunities and away from risks. You have the power to green-light projects. You have the power to ship projects."[34] But what makes

Employee involvement team team that provides advice or makes suggestions to management concerning specific issues

Semi-autonomous work group a group that has the authority to make decisions and solve problems related to the major tasks of producing a product or service

Self-managing team a team that manages and controls all of the major tasks of producing a product or service

Self-designing team a team that has the characteristics of self-managing teams but also controls team design, work tasks, and team membership

Virtual Teams—There's an App for That! Lots, Actually

A host of productivity apps are available to make working remotely easier for people in teams. Keep the following apps in mind next time you have a group project—they might help you all work better together.

▶ **World Clock** and **Figure It Out** display multiple time zones to help teammates around the globe schedule meetings and avoid calling in the middle of the night.

▶ **Sqwiggle** takes quick snapshots of each team member via webcam every few seconds, making it easy to tell who is available if you have to call an impromptu meeting across multiple time zones. (The app can be paused during off-hours.)

▶ With annotation app **Skitch** you can add arrows, text, and more to screenshots and pictures to get your point across quickly and clearly.

▶ **15Five** lets managers send short sets of company-, project-, or user-specific questions to virtual teams to see what's on everybody's minds.

▶ With **Meldium**, remote teams can log into apps and tech platforms with a single sign-on. Team members have access to the apps but never see the actual password so the organizer can retain password control and security.

Source: O. Williams, "21 Tools That Will Help Your Remote Team Work Better Together," *The Next Web*, accessed April 20, 2016, http://thenextweb.com/apps/2014/12/06/tools-remote-teams.

Valve's team self-designing (and not just self-managing), is that they control and change the teams themselves by deciding who gets hired, fired, promoted, and what they get paid (which is determined by peer rankings regarding contributions to team projects).[35]

10-2b Special Kinds of Teams

Companies are also increasingly using several other kinds of teams that can't easily be categorized in terms of autonomy: cross-functional teams, virtual teams, and project teams. Depending on how these teams are designed, they can be either low- or high-autonomy teams.

Cross-functional teams are intentionally composed of employees from different functional areas of the organization.[36] Because their members have different functional backgrounds, education, and experience, cross-functional teams usually attack problems from multiple perspectives and generate more ideas and alternative solutions, all of which are especially important when trying to innovate or solve problems creatively.[37] Cross-functional teams can be used almost anywhere in an organization and are often used in conjunction with matrix and product organizational structures (see Chapter 9). They can also be used either with part-time or temporary team assignments or with full-time, long-term teams.

Virtual teams are groups of geographically and/or organizationally dispersed coworkers who use a combination of telecommunications and information technologies to accomplish an organizational task.[38] Virtual teams are increasingly common, and are used by 28 percent of

U.S.-based corporations and 66 percent of multinational firms.[39] Members of virtual teams rarely meet face-to-face; instead, they use email, videoconferencing, and group communication software. Virtual teams can be employee involvement teams, self-managing teams, or nearly any kind of team discussed in this chapter. Virtual teams are often (but not necessarily) temporary teams that are set up to accomplish a specific task.

Virtual teams are highly flexible because employees can work with each other regardless of physical location or time zones, but they're also much more complex than face-to-face teams when it comes to purpose, communication, and trust. Virtual teams often suffer from a lack of understanding regarding the team's purpose and team member roles. Dave Davis of RedFly Marketing has managed virtual teams for more than a decade and says, "You'd be surprised how many people will wait until halfway through a project to admit they don't understand something."[40] Because of distance and different time zones, 38 percent of virtual team members cite communication as their biggest challenge. Digital communication (email, IM, virtual conferencing) accounts for 63 percent of communication on virtual teams, yet 23 percent of team members find that long email discussion threads threaten (rather than help) effective

Cross-functional team
a team composed of employees from different functional areas of the organization

Virtual team a team composed of geographically and/or organizationally dispersed coworkers who use telecommunication and information technologies to accomplish an organizational task

Exhibit 10.3
Tips for Managing Virtual Teams

1. Establish clear expectations for communication, availability during offices hours, and frequency of check-ins.
2. Establish clear goals and milestones to help remote workers stay on track and accountable to the team.
3. Help team members set clear boundaries between work and family spaces.
4. Assign employees who have many outside obligations to teams whose members mostly have few nonwork obligations.
5. Ensure that team members have access to technology tools such as teleconferencing, file-sharing services, online meeting services, and collaboration portals.
6. Facilitate face-to-face communication with video conferencing or by requiring members of remote teams to work on-site several days each month.
7. Ensure the task is meaningful to the team and the company.
8. When building a virtual team, solicit volunteers as much as possible.

Sources: S. J. Perry, et al., "When Does Virtuality Really Work? Examining the Role of Work-Family and Virtuality in Social Loafing," *Journal of Management* 42 (2016), 449–479; C. Brooks, "4 Ways to Manage Remote Employees," *Business News Daily*, April 23, 2014, accessed April 30, 2016, http://www.businessnewsdaily.com/8895-remote-team-work.html.

project communication.[41] So, it's important for members to know when to use different communication media. Mary Ellen Slater, a manager at **Reputation Capital**, says, "At Rep Cap, we IM each other throughout the day, but there are times when a phone call or face-to-face meeting is better. A new project or something that deviates from our usual process may merit a phone call."[42] Finally, trust is critical for virtual teams to be successful. Andrea Rozman, owner of Your Gal Friday, a company that provides virtual personal assistants, says, "You have to take that leap of faith. You have to believe that once you hand them the work, they will do it, and get it done on time."[43] See Exhibit 10.3 for more information on managing virtual teams.

Project teams are created to complete specific, one-time projects or tasks within a limited time.[44] Project teams are often used to develop new products, significantly improve existing products, roll out new information systems, or build new factories or offices. The project team is typically led by a project manager who has the overall responsibility for planning, staffing, and managing the team, which usually includes employees from different functional areas. Effective project teams demand both individual and collective responsibility.[45] One advantage of project teams is that drawing employees from different functional areas can reduce or eliminate communication barriers. In turn, as long as team members feel free to express their ideas, thoughts, and concerns, free-flowing communication encourages cooperation among separate departments and typically speeds up the design process.[46] Another advantage of project teams is their flexibility. When projects are finished, project team members either move on to the next project or return to their functional units. For example, publication of this book required designers, editors, page compositors, and web designers, among others. When the task was finished, these people applied their skills to other textbook projects. Because of this flexibility, project teams are often used with the matrix organizational designs discussed in Chapter 9.

10-3 WORK TEAM CHARACTERISTICS

"Why did I ever let you talk me into teams? They're nothing but trouble."[47] Lots of managers have this reaction after making the move to teams. Many don't realize that this reaction is normal, both for them and for workers. In fact, such a reaction is characteristic of the *storming* stage of team development (discussed in Section 10-3e). Managers who are familiar with these stages and with the other important characteristics of teams will be better prepared to manage the predictable changes that occur when companies make the switch to team-based structures.

Understanding the characteristics of work teams is essential for making teams an effective part of an organization. Therefore, in this section you'll learn about 10-3a team norms, 10-3b team cohesiveness, 10-3c team size, 10-3d team conflict, and 10-3e the stages of team development.

10-3a Team Norms

Over time, teams develop **norms**, which are informally agreed-on standards that regulate team behavior.[48] Norms are valuable because they let team members know what is expected of them. While leading Orbis International, a nonprofit organization in which a DC-10 jet, converted to a "Flying Eye Hospital," transports volunteer doctors

---

Project team a team created to complete specific, one-time projects or tasks within a limited time

Norms informally agreed-on standards that regulate team behavior

HOW TO SOCIALIZE WITH COWORKERS WHEN YOU DON'T WANT TO

Being social at or after work doesn't have to mean obligatory happy hours or once-a-week group lunches. If the pressure of work group socializing stresses you out, try these tips to make it more manageable:

▶ Attend on a regular, but not necessarily frequent, basis (for example, every third or fourth event).

▶ Strike up a conversation with two people, and even prepare some conversation-starter questions ahead of time to use in the event of an awkward silence.

▶ Stay long enough to be respectful to the organizers and show that you are part of the team, but don't be afraid to be the first one to leave.

▶ Seek out colleagues with similar interests, and invite them to join you at an event sometime.

Source: S. Gawronski, "3 Easy, Introvert-Approved Ways to Socialize More with Your Co-Workers: Not Everyone Wants to Partake in Group Lunch," *Inc.*, December 30, 2015, accessed April 30, 2016, http://www.inc.com/the-muse/3-easy-introvert-approved-ways-to-socialize-more-with-your-coworkers.html.

and nurses to treat eye disease throughout the world, Jilly Stephens noticed a problem with punctuality. She said, "When I first got to the field, you would have the nurses, engineers, whoever, waiting, and you would maybe have one [person] who just couldn't drag himself out of bed and everybody's waiting." So she simply decided that there would be a new norm for the team: they leave on time. "If they aren't there [on time], the bus leaves. You get to the airport yourself. If we were in Tunisia, that meant finding a bike and cycling across the desert to get to the airport." Says Stephens, "We saw behaviors change fairly rapidly."[49]

Studies indicate that norms are one of the most powerful influences on work behavior because they regulate the everyday actions that allow teams to function effectively. Team norms are often associated with positive outcomes such as stronger organizational commitment, more trust in management, and stronger job and organizational satisfaction.[50] Effective work teams develop norms about the quality and timeliness of job performance, absenteeism, safety, and honest expression of ideas and opinions.

At **Google**, a special task force called Project Aristotle spent four years reviewing published research on teams, as well as analyzing internal data on 180 Google work teams.[51] Unable to find identifiable patterns related to the sizes, skills, or tenures of teams or their team members, Project Aristotle eventually found that Google's most successful teams had positive norms with high levels of psychological safety, a concept that Harvard Business School professor Amy Edmondson defines as "a sense of confidence that the team will not embarrass, reject or punish someone for speaking up . . . the team is safe for interpersonal risk taking."[52] Building on that study, a team of researchers led by Carnegie Mellon professor Anita Wooley found that the best-performing

teams engaged in conversational turn-taking. Woolley explained, "As long as everyone got a chance to talk, the team did well. But if only one person or a small group spoke all the time, the collective intelligence [of the team] declined."[53] Woolley's findings are consistent with the previously discussed research showing that overly dominant team leaders minimized discussion and hurt team performance. See Section 10-1b.

Norms can also influence team behavior in negative ways. For example, most people would agree that damaging organizational property; saying or doing something to hurt someone at work; intentionally doing one's work badly, incorrectly, or slowly; griping about coworkers; deliberately bending or breaking rules; and doing something to harm the company or boss are negative behaviors. A study of workers from thirty-four teams in twenty different organizations found that teams with negative norms strongly influenced their team members to engage in these negative behaviors. In fact, the longer individuals were members of a team with negative norms and the more frequently they interacted with their teammates, the more likely they were to perform negative behaviors. Because team norms typically develop early in the life of a team, these results indicate how important it is for teams to establish positive norms from the outset.[54]

10-3b Team Cohesiveness

Cohesiveness is another important characteristic of work teams. **Cohesiveness** is the extent to which team members are attracted to a team and motivated to remain in it.[55] What can be done to promote team cohesiveness? First, make

> **Cohesiveness** the extent to which team members are attracted to a team and motivated to remain in it

sure that all team members are present at team meetings and activities. Team cohesiveness suffers when members are allowed to withdraw from the team and miss team meetings and events.[56] Second, create additional opportunities for teammates to work together by rearranging work schedules and creating common workspaces. Bank of America discovered the value of cohesive teams when it did a study tracking employee behavior. When Bank of America experimented by having call center employees wear sensors monitoring their movements throughout the office, it found that the most productive employees were in cohesive teams that communicated frequently. So, to encourage more interaction, it scheduled team members to all have breaks at the same time, rather than solo breaks. As a result, worker productivity rose 10 percent.[57] When task interdependence is high, and team members have lots of chances to work together, team cohesiveness tends to increase.[58] Third, engaging in nonwork activities as a team can help build cohesion. The NBA's Golden State Warriors do something that most NBA teams don't—they eat together when on the road. Ten-year veteran center Andrew Bogut says, "We go out together and eat together way more than any other team I've been on." Why? They like each other. Center Festus Ezili says, "And you see it on the court." Indeed, the Warriors won their first NBA championship in 2015. In 2016, they set the record for most games won in a season before losing the NBA Finals to the Cleveland Cavaliers in an exciting seventh game decided in the last minute. Forward David Lee says, "Chemistry is not something you can fake. You either have it or you don't."[59] Finally, companies build team cohesiveness by making employees feel that they are part of an organization.

10-3c Team Size

The relationship between team size and performance appears to be curvilinear. Very small or very large teams may not perform as well as moderately sized teams. CEO of Amazon Jeff Bezos tends to prefer small teams, saying, "If I see more than two pizzas for lunch, the team is too big."[60] For most teams, the right size is somewhere between six and nine members.[61] A team of this size is small enough for the team members to get to know each other and for each member to have an opportunity to contribute in a meaningful way to the success of the team. At the same time, the team is large enough to take advantage of team members' diverse skills, knowledge, and perspectives. It is also easier to instill a sense of responsibility and mutual accountability in teams of this size.[62] Team size has a significant impact on the value of a company as well. Among companies with a market capitalization of $10 billion or more, those with smaller boards of directors outperform their peers by 8.5 percent, and those with larger boards underperform their peers by nearly 11 percent. With only seven directors, **Netflix's** board was able to spend nine months discussing a potential price increase. Director Jay Hoag says, "We get in-depth. That's easier with a small group." Netflix outperforms its sector peers by 32 percent.[63] The General Motors board of directors, however, has fourteen members. Its chairman, Tim Solso says, "Often you have people saying the same thing. It's just not as efficient as a smaller board."[64] Like GM, pharmaceutical company **Eli Lilly** also has fourteen members, and someone close to the company said its board "is too big to encourage the kinds of discussions you want. . . a number of people feel constrained asking a second or third question."[65]

When teams get too large, team members find it difficult to get to know one another, and the team may splinter into smaller subgroups. When this occurs, subgroups sometimes argue and disagree, weakening overall team cohesion. As teams grow, there is also a greater chance of *minority domination*, where just a few team members dominate team discussions. Even if minority domination doesn't occur, larger groups may not have time for all team members to share their input. And when team members feel that their contributions are unimportant or not needed, the result is less involvement, effort, and accountability to the team.[66] Large teams also face logistical problems such as finding an appropriate time or place to meet. Finally, the incidence of social loafing, discussed earlier in the chapter, is much higher in large teams.

Just as team performance can suffer when a team is too large, it can also be negatively affected when a team

Golden State Warriors power forward Draymond Green drives to the hoop during Game 2 of the 2016 NBA Finals in Oakland, California.

is too small. Teams with just a few people may lack the diversity of skills and knowledge found in larger teams. Also, teams that are too small are unlikely to gain the advantages of team decision making (multiple perspectives, generating more ideas and alternative solutions, and stronger commitment) found in larger teams.

What signs indicate that a team's size needs to be changed? If decisions are taking too long, if the team has difficulty making decisions or taking action, if a few members dominate the team, or if the commitment or efforts of team members are weak, chances are the team is too big. In contrast, if a team is having difficulty coming up with ideas or generating solutions, or if the team does not have the expertise to address a specific problem, chances are the team is too small.

10-3d Team Conflict

Conflict and disagreement are inevitable in most teams. But this shouldn't surprise anyone. From time to time, people who work together are going to disagree about what and how things get done. What causes conflict in teams? Although almost anything can lead to conflict—casual remarks that unintentionally offend a team member or fighting over scarce resources—the primary cause of team conflict is disagreement over team goals and priorities.[67] Other common causes of team conflict include disagreements over task-related issues, interpersonal incompatibilities, and simple fatigue.

Though most people view conflict negatively, the key to dealing with team conflict is not avoiding it, but rather making sure that the team experiences the right kind of conflict. In Chapter 5, you learned about *c-type conflict*, or *cognitive conflict*, which focuses on problem-related differences of opinion, and *a-type conflict*, or *affective conflict*, which refers to the emotional reactions that can occur when disagreements become personal rather than professional.[68] Cognitive conflict is strongly associated with improvements in team performance, whereas affective conflict is strongly associated with decreases in team performance.[69] Why does this happen? With cognitive conflict, team members disagree because their different experiences and expertise lead them to different views of the problem and solutions. Indeed, managers who participated on teams that emphasized cognitive conflict described their teammates as "smart," "team players," and "best in the business." They described their teams as "open," "fun," and "productive." One manager summed up the positive attitude that team members had about cognitive conflict by saying, "We scream a lot, then laugh, and then resolve the issue."[70] Thus, cognitive

conflict is also characterized by a willingness to examine, compare, and reconcile differences to produce the best possible solution.

By contrast, affective conflict often results in hostility, anger, resentment, distrust, cynicism, and apathy. Managers who participated on teams that experienced affective conflict described their teammates as "manipulative," "secretive," "burned out," and "political."[71] Dana Browlee, who runs a corporate training company in Atlanta, gives the example of the naysayer, who, "whatever you bring up, it will never work," and the silent plotter, who she says, "may be the quiet person sitting in the back, but as soon as the [team] meeting is over, they're over by the Coke machine, planning your demise."[72] Not surprisingly, affective conflict can make people uncomfortable and cause them to withdraw and decrease their commitment to a team.[73] Affective conflict also lowers the satisfaction of team members, may lead to personal hostility between coworkers, and can decrease team cohesiveness.[74] So, unlike cognitive conflict, affective conflict undermines team performance by preventing teams from engaging in the kinds of activities that are critical to team effectiveness.

So, what can managers do to manage team conflict? First, they need to realize that emphasizing cognitive conflict alone won't be enough. Studies show that cognitive and affective conflicts often occur together in a given team activity! Sincere attempts to reach agreement on a difficult issue can quickly deteriorate from cognitive to affective conflict if the discussion turns personal, and tempers and emotions flare. While cognitive conflict is clearly the better approach to take, efforts to engage in cognitive conflict should be managed well and checked before they deteriorate causing the team to become unproductive.

Can teams disagree and still get along? Fortunately, they can. In an attempt to study this issue, researchers examined team conflict in twelve high-tech companies. In four of the companies, work teams used cognitive conflict to address work problems but did so in a way that minimized the occurrence of affective conflict.[75]

There are several ways teams can have a good fight.[76] First, work with more, rather than less, information. A senior retail executive said, "Disagreement is great as long as it's fact-based."[77] If data are plentiful, objective, and up-to-date, teams will focus on issues, not personalities. Second, develop multiple alternatives to enrich debate. Focusing on multiple solutions diffuses conflict by getting the team to keep searching for a better solution. Positions and opinions are naturally more flexible with five alternatives than with just two. Third, establish common goals. Remember, most team conflict arises from disagreements over team goals and priorities. Therefore, common goals encourage collaboration and minimize conflict over a team's purpose. The late Steve Jobs, former CEO of Apple, explained it this way: "It's okay to spend a lot of time arguing about which route to take to San Francisco when everyone wants to end up there, but a lot of time gets wasted in such arguments if one person wants to go to San Francisco and another secretly wants to go to San Diego."[78] Fourth, inject humor into the workplace. Humor relieves tension, builds cohesion, and just makes being in teams fun. Fifth, maintain a balance of power by involving as many people as possible in the decision process. And, sixth, resolve issues without forcing a consensus. Consensus means that everyone must agree before decisions are finalized. Effectively, requiring consensus gives everyone on the team veto power. Nothing gets done until everyone agrees, which, of course, is nearly impossible. As a result, insisting on consensus usually promotes affective rather than cognitive conflict. If team members can't agree after constructively discussing their options, it's better to have the

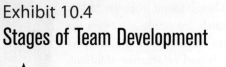

Exhibit 10.4
Stages of Team Development

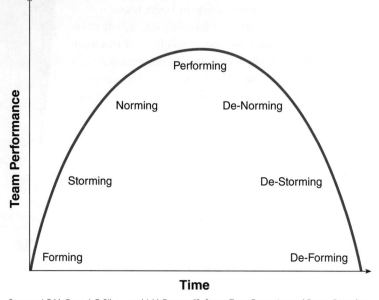

Sources: J. F. McGrew, J. G. Bilotta, and J. M. Deeney, "Software Team Formation and Decay: Extending the Standard Model for Small Groups," *Small Group Research* 30, no. 2 (1999): 209–234; B. W. Tuckman, "Development Sequence in Small Groups," *Psychological Bulletin* 63, no. 6 (1965): 384–399.

team leader make the final choice. Most team members can accept the team leader's choice if they've been thoroughly involved in the decision process.

10-3e Stages of Team Development

As teams develop and grow, they pass through four stages of development. As shown in Exhibit 10.4, those stages are forming, storming, norming, and performing.[79] Although not every team passes through each of these stages, teams that do tend to be better performers.[80] This holds true even for teams composed of seasoned executives. After a period of time, however, if a team is not managed well, its performance may start to deteriorate as the team begins a process of decline and progresses through the stages of de-norming, de-storming, and de-forming.[81]

Forming is the initial stage of team development. This is the getting-acquainted stage in which team members first meet each other, form initial impressions, and try to get a sense of what it will be like to be part of the team. Some of the first team norms will be established during this stage as team members begin to find out what behaviors will and won't be accepted by the team. During this stage, team leaders should allow time for team

Forming the first stage of team development, in which team members meet each other, form initial impressions, and begin to establish team norms

members to get to know each other, set early ground rules, and begin to set up a preliminary team structure.

Conflicts and disagreements often characterize the second stage of team development, **storming**. As team members begin working together, different personalities and work styles may clash. Team members become more assertive at this stage and more willing to state opinions. This is also the stage when team members jockey for position and try to establish a favorable role for themselves on the team. In addition, team members are likely to disagree about what the group should do and how it should do it. Team performance is still relatively low, given that team cohesion is weak and team members are still reluctant to support each other. Because teams that get stuck in the storming stage are almost always ineffective, it is important for team leaders to focus the team on team goals and on improving team performance. Team members need to be particularly patient and tolerant with each other in this stage.

During **norming**, the third stage of team development, team members begin to settle into their roles as team members. Positive team norms will have developed by this stage, and teammates should know what to expect from each other. Petty differences should have been resolved, friendships will have developed, and group cohesion will be relatively strong. At this point, team members will have accepted team goals, be operating as a unit, and, as indicated by the increase in performance, be working together effectively. This stage can be very short and is often characterized by someone on the team saying, "I think things are finally coming together." Note, however, that teams may also cycle back and forth between storming and norming several times before finally settling into norming.

In the last stage of team development, **performing**, performance improves because the team has finally matured into an effective, fully functioning team. At this point, members should be fully committed to the team and think of themselves as members of a team and not just employees. Team members often become intensely loyal to one another at this stage and feel mutual accountability for team successes and failures. Trivial disagreements, which can take time and energy away from the work of the team, should be rare. At this stage, teams get a lot of work done, and it is fun to be a team member.

The team should not become complacent, however. Without effective management, its performance may begin to decline as the team passes through the stages of **de-norming**, **de-storming**, and **de-forming**.[82] John Puckett, manufacturing vice president for circuit-board manufacturer XEL Communications, says, "The books all say you start in this state of chaos and march through these various stages, and you end up in this state of ultimate self-direction, where everything is going just great. They never tell you it can go back in the other direction, sometimes just as quickly."[83]

ENHANCING WORK TEAM EFFECTIVENESS

Making teams work is a challenging and difficult process. Nonetheless, companies can increase the likelihood that teams will succeed by carefully managing 10-4a the setting of team goals and priorities and 10-4b how work team members are selected, 10-4c trained, and 10-4d compensated.[84]

10-4a Setting Team Goals and Priorities

In Chapter 5, you learned that having specific, measurable, attainable, realistic, and timely (S.M.A.R.T.) goals is one of the most effective means for improving individual job performance. Fortunately, team goals also improve team performance. In fact, team goals lead to much higher team performance 93 percent of the time.[85]

Why is setting *specific* team goals so critical to team success? One reason is that increasing a team's performance is inherently more complex than just increasing one individual's job performance. For instance, consider that any team is likely to involve at least four different kinds of goals: each member's goal for the team, each member's goal for himself or herself on the team, the team's goal for each member, and the team's goal for itself.[86] In other

Storming the second stage of development, characterized by conflict and disagreement, in which team members disagree over what the team should do and how it should do it

Norming the third stage of team development, in which team members begin to settle into their roles, group cohesion grows, and positive team norms develop

Performing the fourth and final stage of team development, in which performance improves because the team has matured into an effective, fully functioning team

De-norming a reversal of the norming stage, in which team performance begins to decline as the size, scope, goal, or members of the team change

De-storming a reversal of the storming phase, in which the team's comfort level decreases, team cohesion weakens, and angry emotions and conflict may flare

De-forming a reversal of the forming stage, in which team members position themselves to control pieces of the team, avoid each other, and isolate themselves from team leaders

To effectively motivate teams:

1. Teams must have a high degree of autonomy.

2. Teams must be empowered with control of resources.

3. Teams need structural accommodation.

4. Teams need bureaucratic immunity.

iStockphoto.com/RoscoPhoto

words, without a specific goal for the team itself (the last of the four goals listed), team members may head off in all directions at once pursuing these other goals. Consequently, setting a specific goal *for the team* clarifies team priorities by providing a clear focus and purpose.

Challenging team goals affect how hard team members work. In particular, they greatly reduce the incidence of social loafing. When faced with difficult goals, team members necessarily expect everyone to contribute. Consequently, they are much more likely to notice and complain if a teammate isn't doing his or her share. In fact, when teammates know each other well, when team goals are specific, when team communication is good, and when teams are rewarded for team performance (discussed later in this section), there is only a one in sixteen chance that teammates will be social loafers.[87]

What can companies and teams do to ensure that team goals

Structural accommodation
the ability to change organizational structures, policies, and practices in order to meet stretch goals

Bureaucratic immunity
the ability to make changes without first getting approval from managers or other parts of an organization

lead to superior team performance? One increasingly popular approach is to give teams stretch goals. *Stretch goals* are extremely ambitious goals that workers don't know how to reach.[88] The world's largest auto company, GM, went bankrupt in 2009. Now, just seven years later, GM wants to be "the world's most valuable automotive company." How big a stretch is this goal? Pretty big. GM's value (that is, market capitalization) when this was written was $49.7 billion, sixth among the world's top nine auto companies and well behind market leader Toyota, which has a market cap of $161.2 billion. So, GM will have to more than triple its stock price relative to Toyota to achieve this goal. GM spokesman Jim Cain explains, "It's a way to get people focused around a couple of issues. We don't have competitive [profit] margins. If we can get competitive [profit] margins, it'll drive the stock price." And how will GM do that? It's not yet clear.[89]

Four things must occur for stretch goals to effectively motivate teams.[90] First, teams must have a high degree of autonomy or control over how they achieve their goals. Second, teams must be empowered with control of resources, such as budgets, workspaces, computers, or whatever else they need to do their jobs. Third, teams need structural accommodation. **Structural accommodation** means giving teams the ability to change organizational structures, policies, and practices if doing so helps them meet their stretch goals. Finally, teams need bureaucratic immunity. **Bureaucratic immunity** means that teams no longer have to go through the frustratingly slow process of multilevel reviews and sign-offs to get management approval before making changes. Once granted bureaucratic immunity, teams are immune from the influence of various organizational groups and are accountable only to top management. Research teams at Google X, Google's research lab, work on "moonshots," meaning hard to accomplish projects such as self-driving cars and Google Glass, eyeglasses that display email and can record videos and photos. Google X's teams work in two buildings half a mile from Google's main campus to separate and free them from Google's main business. With bureaucratic immunity, teams can act quickly, and even experiment, with little fear of failure. Richard DeVaul, who heads the Rapid Evaluation and Design Kitchen teams at Google X, says, "Google X is very consciously looking at things that Google in its right mind wouldn't do. They build the rocket pad far away from the widget factory, so if the rocket blows up, it's hopefully not disrupting the core business."[91]

10-4b Selecting People for Teamwork

University of Southern California management professor Edward Lawler says, "People are very naive about how easy it is to create a team. Teams are the Ferraris of work design. They're high performance but high maintenance and expensive."[92] It's almost impossible to have an effective work team without carefully selecting people who are suited for teamwork or for working on a particular team. A focus on teamwork (individualism-collectivism), team level, and team diversity can help companies choose the right team members.[93]

Are you more comfortable working alone or with others? If you strongly prefer to work alone, you may not be well suited for teamwork. Studies show that job satisfaction is higher in teams when team members prefer working with others.[94] An indirect way to measure someone's *preference for teamwork* is to assess the person's degree of individualism or collectivism. **Individualism-collectivism** is the degree to which a person believes that people should be self-sufficient and that loyalty to one's self is more important than loyalty to one's team or company.[95] *Individualists*, who put their own welfare and interests first, generally prefer independent tasks in which they work alone. In contrast, *collectivists*, who put group or team interests ahead of self-interests, generally prefer interdependent tasks in which they work with others. Collectivists would also rather cooperate than compete and are fearful of disappointing team members or of being ostracized from teams. Given these differences, it makes sense to select team members who are collectivists rather than individualists. In fact, many companies use individualism-collectivism as an initial screening device for team members. If team diversity is desired, however, individualists may also be appropriate, as discussed next. To determine your preference for teamwork, take the Team Player Inventory shown in Exhibit 10.5.

Team level is the average level of ability, experience, personality, or any other factor on a team. For example, a high level of team experience means that a team has particularly experienced team members. This does not mean that every member of the team has considerable experience, but that enough team members do to significantly raise the average level of experience on the team. Team level is used to guide selection of teammates when teams need a particular set of skills or capabilities to do their jobs well. For example, **SAP**,

Having too many people that want to be stars on your team may result in coordination issues as the team develops and faces performance challenges.

a German software company, has struggled to deliver cloud-based solutions and hopes to replicate a team approach to innovation pioneered by Xerox Parc in the 1970s. So it hired Alan Kay, a renowned technologist who was a computer scientist at Xerox Parc, to build a similar high-level team. So far, Kay has recruited twenty polymathic technologists, funded their research projects, and then given them the independence to work alone to pursue their research interests.[96] (A polymath is someone who is a genius in more than one field.) Kay understands the risks of having too many "stars." Based on his research on NBA teams, management professor Adam Galinsky says, "If you have too many people [on teams], and they all want to be stars, coordination [on the team] goes down. But if you have a bunch of star programmers all working on their own projects, and they don't need to integrate their programs with each other, then more stars is probably better."[97]

Whereas team level represents the average level or capability on a team, **team diversity** represents the variances or differences in ability, experience, personality, or any other factor on a team.[98] From a practical perspective, why is team diversity important? Andy Zynga, CEO

Individualism-collectivism the degree to which a person believes that people should be self-sufficient and that loyalty to one's self is more important than loyalty to team or company

Team level the average level of ability, experience, personality, or any other factor on a team

Team diversity the variances or differences in ability, experience, personality, or any other factor on a team

Exhibit 10.5
The Team Player Inventory

		Strongly Disagree				Strongly Agree
1.	I enjoy working on team/group projects.	1	2	3	4	5
2.	Team/group project work easily allows others to not pull their weight.	1	2	3	4	5
3.	Work that is done as a team/group is better than work done individually.	1	2	3	4	5
4.	I do my best work alone rather than in a team/group.	1	2	3	4	5
5.	Team/group work is overrated in terms of the actual results produced.	1	2	3	4	5
6.	Working in a team/group gets me to think more creatively.	1	2	3	4	5
7.	Teams/groups are used too often when individual work would be more effective.	1	2	3	4	5
8.	My own work is enhanced when I am in a team/group situation.	1	2	3	4	5
9.	My experiences working in team/group situations have been primarily negative.	1	2	3	4	5
10.	More solutions/ideas are generated when working in a team/group situation than when working alone.	1	2	3	4	5

Reverse score items 2, 4, 5, 7, and 9. Then add the scores for items 1 to 10. Higher scores indicate a preference for teamwork, whereas lower total scores indicate a preference for individual work.

Source: T. J. B. Kline, "The Team Player Inventory: Reliability and Validity of a Measure of Predisposition Toward Organizational Team-Working Environments," *Journal for Specialists in Group Work* 24, no. 1 (1999): 102–112.

of NineSigma International, an innovation consulting firm, says, "Technologists, engineers, and designers not only have their own expertise, they have their own way of applying their expertise. Ironically, the more success they've had with their approach to a solution, the harder it is to imagine a different one."[99] Team diversity ensures that strong teams not only have talented members (that is, a high team level), but those talented members also have different abilities, experiences, and personalities from which to view and solve problems.

Industrial Light & Magic's Experience Lab (xLAB) has assembled a team of artists, engineers, sound designers, and storytellers to create a virtual reality experience based on *Star Wars: The Force Awakens*. Building the future of immersive cinema requires both dreamers and rocket builders, says Vicki Dobbs Beck, the executive in charge of xLAB. "The dreamers are constantly thinking about what's possible, and the rocket builders figure out how to get us there."[100]

After the right team has been put together in terms of individualism-collectivism, team level, and team diversity, it's important to keep the team together as long as practically possible. Interesting research by the National Transportation Safety Board shows that 73 percent of serious mistakes made by jet cockpit crews are made the very first day that a crew flies together as a team and that 44 percent of serious mistakes occur on their very first flight together that day (pilot teams fly two to three flights per day). Moreover, research has shown that fatigued pilot crews who have worked together before make significantly fewer errors than rested crews who have never worked together.[101] Their experience working together helps them overcome their fatigue and outperform new teams that have not worked together before. So, after you've created effective teams, keep them together as long as possible.

10-4c Team Training

After selecting the right people for teamwork, you need to train them. To be successful, teams need significant training, particularly in interpersonal skills, decision-making and problem-solving skills, conflict resolution skills, and technical training. Organizations that create work teams *often underestimate the amount of training* required to make teams effective. This mistake occurs frequently in successful organizations where managers assume that if employees can work effectively on their

Team-Training Matchmaker

Today's team training events in corporate America go far beyond the stereotypical trust fall. From cooking to caving to paintball to mural painting, team training has become so elaborate that some companies do not have the internal resources needed to organize such exotic events. Instead, these companies outsource to **Wekudo** (pronounced "we could do"), a corporate event matchmaking service that helps companies find the best team-building experiences for their needs and culture. Wekudo draws from a wide range of third-party providers and trains them on how to reframe their activities to align with corporate goals. For example, an improv teacher might create activities for sale pitches, while a laser tag center might focus on team communication. For tea and nutritional supplement company Aloha, Wekudo proposed an outing to an Acroyoga studio. This innovative practice combines yoga and acrobatics and requires heavy doses of both cooperation and communication.

Source: J. Miller, "Mandatory Fun: Companies Are Outsourcing Employee Morale Building," *Bloomberg BusinessWeek*, February 15–21, 2016, 62.

own, they can work effectively in teams. In reality, companies that successfully use teams provide thousands of hours of training to make sure that teams work. Stacy Myers, a consultant who helps companies implement teams, says, "When we help companies move to teams, we also require that employees take basic quality and business knowledge classes as well. Teams must know how their work affects the company, and how their success will be measured."[102]

Most commonly, members of work teams receive training in interpersonal skills. **Interpersonal skills** such as listening, communicating, questioning, and providing feedback enable people to have effective working relationships with others. Consultant Peter Grazier, founder of Teambuilding Inc., says, "Teams have told us that if they had to do it over again, they would have more of the people skills up front. They don't struggle with the technical stuff. They tend to struggle with the people skills."[103] Because of teams' autonomy and responsibility, many companies also give team members training in *decision-making and problem-solving skills* to help them do a better job of cutting costs and improving quality and customer service. Many organizations also teach teams *conflict resolution skills*. Teambuilding Inc.'s Grazier explains that "the diversity of values and personalities makes a team powerful, but it can be the greatest source of conflict. If you're a detail person, and I'm not, and we

get on a team, you might say that we need more analysis on a problem before making a decision, [while I] may want to make a decision [right away]. But, if I've been trained in problem-solving and conflict resolution, then I look at your detail [focus] as something that is needed in a team because it's a shortcoming of mine."[104] Taine Moufarrige, executive director of Servcorp, a global company hosting serviced and virtual offices for about 12,000 clients, agrees. Says Moufarrige, "It's not just about disagreements, it's about working through problems, managing differences of opinion, and that's vital for moving forward."[105]

Firms must also provide team members with the *technical training* they need to do their jobs, particularly if they are being cross-trained to perform all of the different jobs on the team. Before teams were created at Milwaukee Mutual Insurance, separate employees performed the tasks of rating, underwriting, and processing insurance policies. After extensive cross-training, however, each team member can now do all three jobs.[106] Cross-training is less appropriate for teams of highly skilled workers. For instance, it is unlikely that a group of engineers, computer programmers, and systems analysts would be cross-trained for each other's jobs.

> **Interpersonal skills** skills, such as listening, communicating, questioning, and providing feedback, that enable people to have effective working relationships with others

Team leaders need training, too, as they often feel unprepared for their new duties. New team leaders face myriad problems ranging from confusion about their new roles as team leaders (compared with their old jobs as managers or employees) to not knowing where to go for help when their teams have problems. The solution is extensive training. Overall, does team training work? One recent study found that across a wide variety of settings, tasks, team types, and 2,650 teams in different organizations, team training was positively related to team performance outcomes.[107]

10-4d Team Compensation and Recognition

Compensating teams correctly is very difficult. For instance, one survey found that only 37 percent of companies were satisfied with their team compensation plans and even fewer, just 10 percent, reported being "very positive."[108] One of the problems, according to Susan Mohrman of the Center for Effective Organizations at the University of Southern California, is that "there is a very strong set of beliefs in most organizations that people should be paid for how well they do. So when people first get put into team-based organizations, they really balk at being paid for how well the team does. It sounds illogical to them. It sounds like their individuality and their sense of self-worth are being threatened."[109] Consequently, companies need to carefully choose a team compensation plan and then fully explain how teams will be rewarded. One basic requirement for team compensation to work is that the level of rewards (individual versus team) must match the level of performance (individual versus team).

Employees can be compensated for team participation and accomplishments in three ways: skill-based pay, gainsharing, and nonfinancial rewards. **Skill-based pay** programs pay employees for learning additional skills or knowledge.[110] These programs encourage employees to acquire the additional skills they will need to perform multiple jobs within a team and to share knowledge with others within their work groups.[111] For example, at the Patience & Nicholson (P&N) drill bit factory in Kaiapoi, New Zealand, workers produce 50,000 drill bits a day for export to Australia, Taiwan, Thailand, and other locations primarily in Asia. P&N uses a skill-based pay system. As employees learn how to run the various machines required to produce drill bits, their pay increases. According to operations manager Rick Smith, workers who are dedicated to learning can increase their pay by $6 an hour over the course of three or four years.[112]

In **gainsharing** programs, companies share the financial value of performance gains, such as productivity increases, cost savings, or quality improvements, with their workers.[113] *Nonfinancial rewards* are another way to reward teams for their performance. These rewards, which can range from vacations to T-shirts, plaques, and coffee mugs, are especially effective when coupled with management recognition, such as awards, certificates, and praise.[114] Nonfinancial awards tend to be most effective when teams or team-based interventions, such as total quality management (see Chapter 18), are first introduced.[115]

Which team compensation plan should your company use? In general, skill-based pay is most effective for self-managing and self-directing teams performing complex tasks. In these situations, the more each team member knows and can do, the better the whole team performs. By contrast, gainsharing works best in relatively stable environments where employees can focus on improving productivity, cost savings, or quality.

Skill-based pay compensation system that pays employees for learning additional skills or knowledge

Gainsharing a compensation system in which companies share the financial value of performance gains, such as increased productivity, cost savings, or quality, with their workers

STUDY TOOLS 10

LOCATED IN TEXTBOOK
☐ Rip-out and review chapter review card

LOCATED AT WWW.CENGAGEBRAIN.COM
☐ Review key term flashcards and create your own from StudyBits

☐ Track your knowledge and understanding of key concepts, using the concept tracker

☐ Complete practice and graded quizzes to prepare for tests

☐ Complete interactive content within the exposition

☐ View chapter highlight box content at the beginning of each chapter

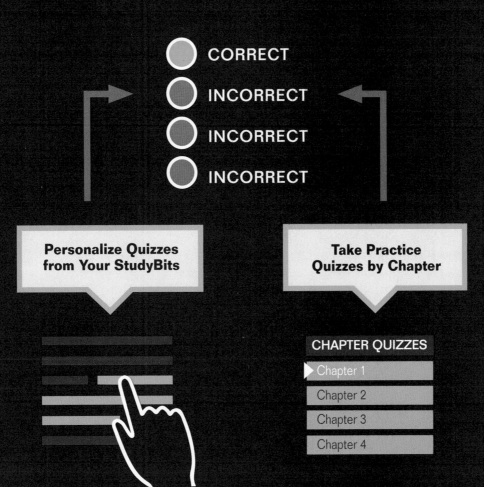

11 Managing Human Resource Systems

Kittisak Jirasittichai/Shutterstock.com

LEARNING OUTCOMES

11-1 Explain how different employment laws affect human resource practice.

11-2 Explain how companies use recruiting to find qualified job applicants.

11-3 Describe the selection techniques and procedures that companies use when deciding which applicants should receive job offers.

11-4 Describe how to determine training needs, and select the appropriate training methods.

11-5 Discuss how to use performance appraisal to give meaningful performance feedback.

11-6 Describe basic compensation strategies, and discuss the four kinds of employee separations.

After you finish

this chapter, go

to **PAGE 252** for

STUDY TOOLS

EMPLOYMENT LEGISLATION

Human resource management (HRM), or the process of finding, developing, and keeping the right people to form a qualified workforce, is one of the most difficult and important of all management tasks. This chapter is organized around the three parts of the human resource management process shown in Exhibit 11.1: attracting, developing, and keeping a qualified workforce.

This chapter will walk you through the steps of the HRM process. We explore how companies use recruiting and selection techniques to attract and hire qualified employees to fulfill human resource needs. The next part of the chapter discusses how training and performance appraisal can develop the knowledge, skills, and abilities of the workforce. The chapter concludes with a review of compensation and employee separation, that is, how companies can keep their best workers through effective compensation practices and how they can manage the separation process when employees leave the organization.

Before we explore how human resource systems work, you need to understand better the complex legal environment in which they exist. So we'll begin the chapter by reviewing the federal laws that govern human resource management decisions.

DSI Security Services, which hires and provides security guards for organizations, spends hundreds of hours each year interviewing applicants with criminal histories who are prevented by laws in twenty-three states from working as security guards. "It defies common sense," says COO and general counsel Eddie Sorrels.[1] So why does DSI interview applicants with criminal histories that it cannot hire? Because the U.S. Equal Employment Opportunity Commission (EEOC) advises that while it is appropriate to conduct background checks later in the hiring process, applicants should not be asked about criminal records on application forms. With African American men six times more likely to be incarcerated than Whites and three times more likely than Hispanics, the EEOC, as well as thirteen states, are concerned that asking about criminal records early in the hiring process could lead to racial discrimination.[2] The NAACP's ReNika Moore says, "People who are trying to work, trying to be productive citizens, are being blocked from jobs."[3] As discussed later in the chapter, however, companies use background checks to provide safe environments for employees and customers and to avoid negligent hiring lawsuits in which they may be liable for an employee's harmful actions. So, what are employers to do? Scott Fallavollita, who owns United Tool & Machine

Exhibit 11.1
The Human Resource Management Process

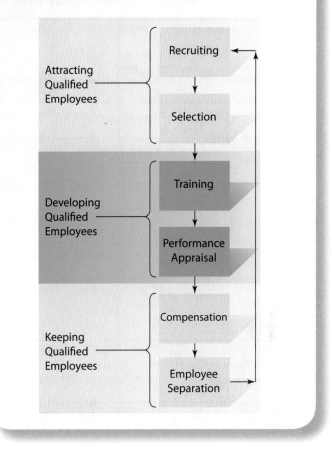

in Wilmington, Massachusetts, said, "I think most people can see both sides and really want to do the right thing."[4]

As the DSI Security Services example illustrates, the human resource planning process occurs in a very complicated legal environment.

*Let's explore employment legislation by reviewing **11-1a the major federal employment laws that affect human resource practice, 11-1b how the concept of adverse impact is related to employment discrimination**, and **11-1c the laws regarding sexual harassment in the workplace.***

11-1a Federal Employment Laws

Exhibit 11.2 lists the major federal employment laws and their websites, where you can find more detailed information. The Fair Labor Standards Act (FLSA),

> **Human resource management (HRM)** the process of finding, developing, and keeping the right people to form a qualified workforce

Exhibit 11.2
Summary of Major Federal Employment Laws

Fair Labor Standards Act (FLSA) of 1938	http://www.dol.gov/whd/flsa/index.htm	Establishes the federal minimum wage and rules related to overtime pay (eligibility and rates), recordkeeping, and child labor.
Equal Pay Act of 1963	www.eeoc.gov/laws/statutes/epa.cfm	Prohibits unequal pay for males and females doing substantially similar work.
Title VII of the Civil Rights Act of 1964	www.eeoc.gov/laws/statutes/titlevii.cfm	Prohibits employment discrimination on the basis of race, color, religion, gender, or national origin.
Age Discrimination in Employment Act of 1967	www.eeoc.gov/laws/statutes/adea.cfm	Prohibits discrimination in employment decisions against persons age 40 and older.
Pregnancy Discrimination Act of 1978	www.eeoc.gov/laws/statutes/pregnancy.cfm	Prohibits discrimination in employment against pregnant women.
Americans with Disabilities Act of 1990	www.eeoc.gov/laws/statutes/ada.cfm	Prohibits discrimination on the basis of physical or mental disabilities.
Civil Rights Act of 1991	www.eeoc.gov/laws/statutes/cra-1991.cfm	Strengthened the provisions of the Civil Rights Act of 1964 by providing for jury trials and punitive damages.
Family and Medical Leave Act of 1993	www.dol.gov/whd/fmla/index.htm	Permits workers to take up to twelve weeks of unpaid leave for pregnancy and/or birth of a new child, adoption, or foster care of a new child; illness of an immediate family member; or personal medical leave.
Uniformed Services Employment and Reemployment Rights Act of 1994	www.dol.gov/compliance/laws/comp-userra.htm	Prohibits discrimination against those serving in the armed forces reserve, the National Guard, and other uniformed services; guarantees that civilian employers will hold and then restore civilian jobs.
Genetic Information Nondiscrimination Act of 2008	www.eeoc.gov/laws/types/genetic.cfm	Prohibits discrimination on the basis of genetic information.

administered by the Department of Labor (DOL), establishes minimum wage, overtime pay, record keeping, and youth employment standards for the private sector, as well as for federal, state, and local governments. (As such, the FLSA pertains to compensation issues discussed in Section 11-6a.) Except for the Family and Medical Leave Act and the Uniformed Services Employment and Reemployment Rights Act, which are both administered by the DOL, All of these laws are administered by the EEOC (www.eeoc.gov). The general effect of this body of law, which is still evolving through court decisions, is that employers may not discriminate in employment decisions on the basis of sex, age, religion, color, national origin, race, disability, or genetic history.[5] The intent is to make these factors irrelevant in employment decisions. Stated another way, employment decisions should be based on factors that are "job related," "reasonably necessary," or a "business necessity" for successful job performance. The only time that sex, age, religion, and the like can be used to make employment decisions is when they are considered a bona fide occupational qualification. Title VII of the 1964 Civil Rights Act says that it is legal to hire and employ someone on the basis of sex, religion, or national origin when there is a **bona fide occupational qualification (BFOQ)** that is "reasonably necessary to the normal operation of that particular business." A Baptist church hiring a new minister can reasonably specify that being a Baptist rather than a Catholic or Presbyterian is a BFOQ for the position. However, it's unlikely that the church could specify race or national origin as a BFOQ. In general, the courts and the EEOC take a hard look when a business claims that sex, age, religion, color, national origin, race, or disability is a BFOQ. For example, citing the risk for sexual abuse and misconduct, the **San Francisco Sheriff's Department**

Bona fide occupational qualification (BFOQ) an exception in employment law that permits sex, age, religion, and the like to be used when making employment decisions, but only if they are "reasonably necessary to the normal operation of that particular business." BFOQs are strictly monitored by the Equal Employment Opportunity Commission

prohibited male prison guards from supervising female inmates. Dozens of deputies filed a lawsuit arguing that sex was not a BFOQ for a prison guard, and the courts agreed, ruling that background checks and psychological testing could weed out applicants likely to engage in misconduct.[6]

It is important to understand, however, that these laws apply to the entire HRM process and not just to selection decisions (for example, hiring or promotion). These laws also cover all training and development activities, performance appraisals, terminations, and compensation decisions. Employers who use sex, age, race, or religion to make employment-related decisions when those factors are unrelated to an applicant's or employee's ability to perform a job may face charges of discrimination from employee lawsuits or the EEOC.

In addition to the laws presented in Exhibit 11.2, there are two other important sets of federal laws: labor laws and the laws and regulations governing safety standards. Labor laws regulate the interaction between management and labor unions that represent groups of employees. These laws guarantee employees the right to form and join unions of their own choosing. For more information about labor laws, see the National Labor Relations Board at www.nlrb.gov.

The Occupational Safety and Health Act (OSHA) requires that employers provide employees with a workplace that is "free from recognized hazards that are causing or are likely to cause death or serious physical harm." This law is administered by the Occupational Safety and Health Administration (which, like the act, is referred to as OSHA). OSHA sets safety and health standards for employers and conducts inspections to determine whether those standards are being met. Employers who do not meet OSHA standards may be fined.[7] Even though working with wild animals has inherent risks, OSHA found that **Sea World** did not have adequate procedures in place to protect employees and supervisors properly from killer whales while riding on or swimming with the animals. Building fast-rising pool floors and emergency air systems to protect its trainers did not prevent the death of a trainer at a park in Orlando, so OSHA fined the company $25,770.[8]

For more information about OSHA, see www.osha.gov.

11-1b Adverse Impact and Employment Discrimination

The EEOC has investigatory, enforcement, and informational responsibilities. Therefore, it investigates charges of discrimination, enforces the employment discrimination laws in federal court, and publishes guidelines that organizations can use to ensure they are in compliance with the law. One of the most important guidelines, jointly issued by the EEOC, the U.S. Department of Labor, the U.S. Department of Justice, and the federal Office of Personnel Management, is the *Uniform Guidelines on Employee Selection Procedures*, which can be read in their entirety at www.uniformguidelines.com/uniformguidelines.html. These guidelines define two important criteria, disparate treatment and adverse impact, which are used in determining whether companies have engaged in discriminatory hiring and promotion practices.

Disparate treatment, which is *intentional* discrimination, occurs when people, despite being qualified, are *intentionally* not given the same hiring, promotion, or membership opportunities as other employees because of their race, color, age, sex, ethnic group, national origin, or religious beliefs.[9] Bobby Nickel, a former facilities manager at Staples, the office supply retailer, was awarded $26 million by a jury that found Staples guilty of harassing him by calling him an "old coot" and an "old goat" and firing him because he was an older employee with a higher salary.[10]

Legally, a key element of discrimination lawsuits is establishing motive, meaning that the employer intended to discriminate. If no motive can be

Disparate treatment intentional discrimination that occurs when people are purposely not given the same hiring, promotion, or membership opportunities because of their race, color, sex, age, ethnic group, national origin, or religious beliefs

established, then a claim of disparate treatment may actually be a case of adverse impact. **Adverse impact**, which is *unintentional* discrimination, occurs when members of a particular race, sex, age, or ethnic group are *unintentionally* harmed or disadvantaged because they are hired, promoted, or trained (or any other employment decision) at substantially lower rates than others.

At **Texas Roadhouse** restaurants, front-of-house employees (servers, bartenders, and hosts) are required to line dance during shifts, wear jeans, and work nights and weekends. The company hires younger workers for these positions—even though it produces a statistically adverse impact on older workers—because it considers such activities to be BFOQs.[11] The EEOC disagreed, filing a class action lawsuit against the restaurant chain for discrimination. The EEOC noted that only 1.9 percent of Texas Roadhouse's front-of-house employees were over the age of 40, a figure "well below the protected age group's representation in the general population of defendants' locations, well below the protected age group's representation in Bureau of Labor statistics data for such positions within the industry, and well below the protected age group's representation in the pool of applicants for positions with defendants."[12] How do courts determine what constitutes "well below?"

The courts and federal agencies use the **four-fifths (or 80%) rule** to determine if adverse impact has occurred. Adverse impact is de-termined by calculating the impact ratio, which divides the decision rate for a protected group of people by the decision rate for a nonprotected group (usually white males). If the impact ratio is less than 80 percent, then adverse impact may have occurred. For example, if twenty out of one hundred black applicants are hired (20/100 = 20%), but sixty white applicants are hired (60/100 = 60%), then adverse impact has occurred because the impact ratio is less than 80 percent (.20/.60 = 33%).

Violation of the four-fifths rule is not an automatic indication of discrimination, however. If an employer can demonstrate that a selection procedure or test is valid, meaning that the test accurately predicts job performance or that the test is job related because it assesses applicants on specific tasks actually used in the job, then the organization may continue to use the test. If validity cannot be established, however, then a violation of the four-fifths rule may likely result in a lawsuit brought by employees, job applicants, or the EEOC itself.

11-1c Sexual Harassment

According to the EEOC, **sexual harassment** is a form of discrimination in which unwelcome sexual advances, requests for sexual favors, or other verbal or physical conduct of a sexual nature occurs. From a legal perspective, there are two kinds of sexual harassment, quid pro quo and hostile work environment.[13]

Quid pro quo sexual harassment occurs when employment outcomes, such as hiring, promotion, or simply keeping one's job, depend on whether an individual submits to being sexually harassed. For example, in a quid pro quo sexual harassment lawsuit against First Student, a company that provides school bus transportation, four females alleged that a supervisor made explicit comments about their bodies and what he wanted to do to them. He was also alleged to have touched a female worker's breasts, exposed himself, and then rubbed himself against her. When his sexual advances were refused, he punished the women by cutting their work hours, while promising longer hours to the other women if they would do what he asked. This made it a quid pro quo case by linking sexual acts to economic outcomes.[14]

A **hostile work environment** occurs when unwelcome and demeaning sexually related behavior creates an intimidating, hostile, and offensive

Adverse impact
unintentional discrimination that occurs when members of a particular race, sex, or ethnic group are unintentionally harmed or disadvantaged because they are hired, promoted, or trained (or any other employment decision) at substantially lower rates than others

Four-fifths (or 80%) rule
a rule of thumb used by the courts and the EEOC to determine whether there is evidence of adverse impact; a violation of this rule occurs when the impact ratio (calculated by dividing the decision ratio for a protected group by the decision ratio for a nonprotected group) is less than 80 percent, or four-fifths

Sexual harassment a form of discrimination in which unwelcome sexual advances, requests for sexual favors, or other verbal or physical conduct of a sexual nature occurs while performing one's job

Quid pro quo sexual harassment a form of sexual harassment in which employment outcomes, such as hiring, promotion, or simply keeping one's job, depend on whether an individual submits to sexual harassment

Hostile work environment a form of sexual harassment in which unwelcome and demeaning sexually related behavior creates an intimidating and offensive work environment

Rommel Canlas/Shutterstock.com

work environment. In contrast to quid pro quo cases, a hostile work environment may not result in economic injury. However, it can lead to psychological injury when the work environment becomes stressful. A federal court jury found Mercy General Hospital in Sacramento, California, guilty of creating a sexually hostile work environment for Ani Chopourian, a cardiac surgery physician assistant. Chopourian was awarded $125 million in punitive damages, $3.5 million for lost wages and benefits, and $39 million for mental anguish. Chopourian was frequently subjected to touching and sex talk in the operating room. She says, "One harasser told me one day, 'You'll give in to me.' I'd look at him [and say], 'I'll never give in to you.' I'd look at my supervisor and say, 'Do something.' They'd just laugh."[15] She was fired after filing eighteen complaints in two years. Mercy General is appealing the decision.

Finally, what should companies do to make sure that sexual harassment laws are followed and not violated?[16] First, respond immediately when sexual harassment is reported. A quick response encourages victims of sexual harassment to report problems to management rather than to lawyers or the EEOC. Furthermore, a quick and fair investigation may serve as a deterrent to future harassment. A lawyer for the EEOC says, "Worse than having no sexual harassment policy is a policy that is not followed. It's merely window dressing. You wind up with destroyed morale when people who come forward are ignored, ridiculed, retaliated against, or nothing happens to the harasser."[17]

Then take the time to write a clear, understandable sexual harassment policy that is strongly worded, gives specific examples of what constitutes sexual harassment, spells outs sanctions and punishments, and is widely publicized within the company. This lets potential harassers and victims know what will not be tolerated and how the firm will deal with harassment should it occur.

Next, establish clear reporting procedures that indicate how, where, and to whom incidents of sexual harassment can be reported. The best procedures ensure that a complaint will receive a quick response, that impartial parties will handle the complaint, and that the privacy of the accused and accuser will be protected. At DuPont, Avon, and Texas Industries, employees can call a confidential hotline 24 hours a day, 365 days a year.[18]

Finally, managers should also be aware that most states and many cities or local governments have their own employment-related laws and enforcement agencies. So compliance with federal law is often not enough. In fact, organizations can be in full compliance with federal law and at the same time be in violation of state or local sexual harassment laws.

 RECUITING

RECRUITING

Frustrated by the high numbers of local candidates declining job offers, executives at **Salesforce.com**'s San Francisco headquarters developed an algorithm to collect the LinkedIn profiles of everyone in Northern California with the technical skills their jobs needed. Finding fewer candidates than anticipated, and realizing that it had already been in contact with 23 percent of them, Salesforce.com decided to look at other cities with larger talent pools. After reviewing the results, Salesforce.com recruiting head Ana Recio said, "Suddenly we were in real-estate discussions".[19]

Recruiting is the process of developing a pool of qualified job applicants.

*Let's examine **11-2a what job analysis is and how it is used in recruiting, 11-2b how companies use internal recruiting**, and **11-2c external recruiting to find qualified job applicants**.*

11-2a Defining the Job

Job analysis is a "purposeful, systematic process for collecting information on the important work-related aspects of a job."[20] A job analysis typically collects four kinds of information:

▶ Work activities, such as what workers do and how, when, and why they do it

▶ The tools and equipment used to do the job

▶ The context in which the job is performed, such as the actual working conditions or schedule

▶ The personnel requirements for performing the job, meaning the knowledge, skills, and abilities needed to do a job well[21]

Job analysis information can be collected by having job incumbents and/or supervisors complete questionnaires about their jobs, by direct observation, by interviews, or by filming employees as they perform their jobs.

Job descriptions and job specifications are two of the most important results of a job analysis. A **job description** is a written description of the basic tasks, duties, and responsibilities required of

Recruiting the process of developing a pool of qualified job applicants

Job analysis a purposeful, systematic process for collecting information on the important work-related aspects of a job

Job description a written description of the basic tasks, duties, and responsibilities required of an employee holding a particular job

Exhibit 11.3
Job Description for a Firefighter for the City of Portland, Oregon

Yes, as a firefighter you will fight fire and provide emergency medical services to your community. But it doesn't end there: your firefighting career offers you the opportunity to expand your skills to include hazardous materials response, specialty response teams (dive, rope rescue, confined space, etc.), paramedic care, public education and information, fire investigation, and fire code enforcement.

Teamwork

Professional firefighters work as a team at emergency scenes. The workday also includes training, fire station and equipment maintenance, fire prevention activities, and public education. As a firefighter, you must be in excellent physical condition to meet the demands of the job; this means you must work quickly, handling heavy equipment for long periods of time while wearing special protective gear in hot and hazardous environments. If you can meet the challenge of strenuous work and like the idea of helping people, consider applying for the position of firefighter.

Work Schedule

Portland Fire & Rescue firefighters work a 24-on/48-off shift. This means that Firefighters report to work at 8:00 a.m. the day of their shift and continue working until 8:00 a.m. the following morning. Our firefighters then have the following two days (48 hours) off. Firefighters are required to work shifts on holidays and weekends. Portland Fire & Rescue also has 40-hour-a-week firefighters who work in training, inspections/investigations, public education, logistics, and emergency management. These positions are usually filled after a firefighter has met the minimum requirements for these positions.

Source: Portland Fire and Rescue, accessed July 8, 2016. http://www.portlandoregon.gov/fire/25923.

iStockphoto.com/Kendall Griffin

an employee holding a particular job. **Job specifications**, which are often included as a separate section of a job description, are a summary of the qualifications needed to successfully perform the job. Exhibit 11.3 shows a job description for a firefighter for the city of Portland, Oregon.

Because a job analysis specifies what a job entails as well as the knowledge, skills, and abilities that are needed to do the job well, companies must complete a job analysis *before* beginning to recruit job applicants. Job analyses, job descriptions, and job specifications are the foundation on which all critical human resource activities are built. They are used during recruiting and selection to match applicant qualifications with the requirements of the job. Reddit, a news consolidation website where readers vote on which stories and discussions are the most important, wanted to hire a new programmer, but it didn't want to sort through thousands of applications from people who had no coding skills but thought it would be cool to work for the popular website. So it used the job description as a

Job specifications a written summary of the qualifications needed to successfully perform a particular job

test to make sure the company would only receive applications from highly skilled programmers. Applications for the job were to be sent to S@reddit.com, with "S" representing a real email address that applicants had to figure out by solving a series of problems and equations. If you couldn't figure it out, you couldn't send in your job application. This puzzle helped Reddit match applicant qualifications to the requirements of the job.[22]

Job descriptions are also used throughout the staffing process to ensure that selection devices and the decisions based on these devices are job related. For example, the questions asked in an interview should be based on the most important work activities identified by a job analysis. Likewise, during performance appraisals, employees should be evaluated in areas that a job analysis has identified as the most important in a job.

Job analyses, job descriptions, and job specifications also help companies meet the legal requirement that their human resource decisions be job related. To be judged *job related*, recruitment, selection, training, performance appraisals, and employee separations must be valid and be directly related to the important aspects of the job, as identified by a careful job analysis. In fact, in *Griggs v. Duke Power Co.* and *Albemarle Paper Co. v. Moody*, the U.S. Supreme Court stated that companies should use job analyses to help establish the job relatedness of their human resource procedures.[23] The EEOC's *Uniform Guidelines on Employee Selection Procedures* also recommend that companies base their human resource procedures on job analysis.

11-2b Internal Recruiting

Internal recruiting is the process of developing a pool of qualified job applicants from people who already work in the company. Internal recruiting, sometimes called "promotion from within," improves employee commitment, morale, and motivation. Recruiting current employees also reduces recruitment start-up time and costs, and because employees are already familiar with the company's culture and procedures, they are more likely to succeed in new jobs. Crédit Suisse was posting less than half of its open jobs internally until it discovered that those taking a new job within the company were more likely to stay long term. So, it now posts 80 percent of its openings internally—even cold-calling employees to let them know when jobs have opened. Doing so has resulted in promotions for 300 of its people. William Wolf, the bank's global head of talent acquisition and development, says, "We believe we've saved a number of them from taking jobs at other banks."[24] Job posting and career paths are two methods of internal recruiting.

Job posting is a procedure for advertising job openings within the company to existing employees. A job description and requirements are typically posted on a bulletin board, in a company newsletter, or in an internal computerized job bank that is accessible only to employees. Job posting helps organizations discover hidden talent, allows employees to take responsibility for career planning, and makes it easier for companies to retain talented workers who are dissatisfied in their current jobs and would otherwise leave the company.[25] In fact, a LinkedIn survey of workers who changed jobs found that 42 percent would have stayed with their former employers if a relevant position had been available.[26] LinkedIn vice president Parker Barrile says it's often the case that, "People quit their job, not the company."[27] Booz Allen Hamilton, an international consulting firm, uses an internal recruiting platform called Inside First, which lists job openings and current employee profiles indicating skills, experience, languages spoken, and willingness to relocate. Thirty percent of its positions are now filled with internal hires thanks to Inside First, compared to 10 percent before.[28]

A study of seventy large global companies found that organizations that formalize internal recruiting and

job posting have a lower average rate of turnover (11%) compared to companies that don't (15%).[29] Likewise, a University of Pennsylvania study found external hires generally are more costly, less reliable hires. Specifically, external hires get paid 18–20 percent more than internal hires, are 61 percent more likely to be fired, and are 21 percent more likely to quit their jobs.[30]

A *career path* is a planned sequence of jobs through which employees may advance within an organization. According to Brian Hoyt of RetailMeNot, an online coupon company in Austin, Texas, "Workers were saying, 'It isn't enough for me to work at a fun Internet company,' . . . they wanted to know where their career was going."[31] So the company revamped its internal recruiting system, adding to each job posting a detailed list of responsibilities, required competencies, and skills needed to get each job. Garrett Bircher, an associate product manager, said that when he when was hired, the company lacked a coherent approach. "Now, I feel more secure," he says. "I know four jobs ahead of me now where I want to go and what it takes to get there."[32]

Career paths help employees focus on long-term goals and development while also helping companies increase employee retention. As you can see in Garrett Bircher's case, career paths can also help employees gain a broad range of experience, which is especially useful at higher levels of management.

11-2c External Recruiting

External recruiting is the process of developing a pool of qualified job applicants from outside the company. Headquartered in Canton, Ohio, **Diebold** is the largest manufacturer of ATMs and voting machines in the United States. Diebold needs to expand its software and service offerings to grow, but experts in those areas don't want to move to Canton. To solve this problem, CEO Andy Mattes waived the requirement that executives relocate, saying, "We were fishing in a small pond . . . [so] we expanded the talent pool substantially. As long as they live near an airport, where they work isn't nearly as important as what they can contribute." Now, Diebold's chief strategist lives in San Jose California, the chief marketing officer in Boston, and the head of software in Dallas. Overall, nearly 40 of Diebold's top 100 executives live outside of Canton.[33]

External recruitment methods include advertising (newspapers, magazines, direct mail,

> **Internal recruiting** the process of developing a pool of qualified job applicants from people who already work in the company
>
> **External recruiting** the process of developing a pool of qualified job applicants from outside the company

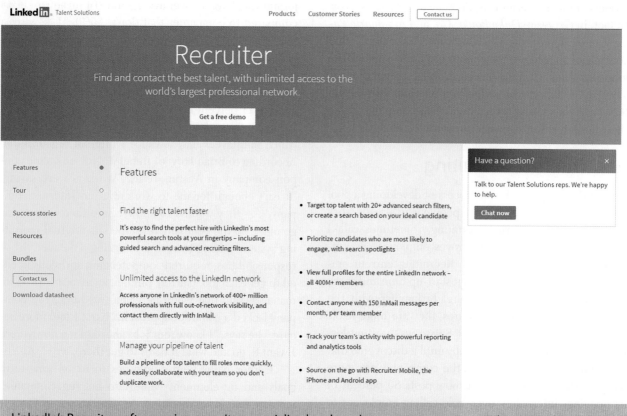

LinkedIn's Recruiter software gives recruiters specialized tools and resources to connect with potential candidates through the social media platform.

radio, or television), employee referrals (asking current employees to recommend possible job applicants), walk-ins (people who apply on their own), outside organizations (universities, technical/trade schools, professional societies), employment services (state or private employment agencies, temporary help agencies, and professional search firms), special events (career conferences or job fairs), Internet job sites (CareerBuilder.com, Indeed.com, and Monster.com), and social media (LinkedIn and Facebook), as well as career portals on company websites. Which external recruiting method should you use? Historically, studies show that employee referrals, walk-ins, advertisements, and state employment agencies tend to be used most frequently for office/clerical and production/service employees. By contrast, advertisements and college/university recruiting are used most frequently for professional/technical employees. When recruiting managers, organizations tend to rely most heavily on advertisements, employee referrals, and search firms.[34]

Recently, social media sites and industry-specific job boards have been gaining momentum at the expense of generalist job boards and newspapers. **Facebook**'s job

search platform is used effectively to recruit lower-skilled workers, and sites such as **LinkedIn** and **Ladders.com** tend to attract more highly skilled or senior-level job seekers.[35] Even though 67 percent of people seeking jobs through social media use Facebook, LinkedIn continues to be where recruiters look for promising candidates. A recent survey found that a whopping 92 percent of recruiters use social media for outreach—87 percent of whom use LinkedIn.[36]

One of the biggest trends in recruiting is identifying passive candidates, people who are not actively seeking a job but who might be receptive to a change. Why pursue passive candidates? About half of all workers would be willing to change jobs if recruited by another company.[38] Apps such as **Switch**, **Poacht**, and **Poachable** allow passive candidates to indicate they are open to jobs without letting their bosses know. Then, like online dating sites, they use algorithms and questionnaires to match people with potential jobs, to which they indicate their level of interest. Yahoo!, Walmart, Amazon, eBay—and, yes, even Facebook—have used these apps to post openings. Poachable CEO Tom Leung says, "Going on some job board feels so 1990. Now we can

LinkedIn Corporation

say we know a lot about you, [but] we don't contact you unless we have a match."[39]

Some companies are even hosting virtual job fairs, where job applicants click on recruiting booths to learn about the company, see the kinds of available jobs, and speak with company representatives via video chat or instant message. Because they don't need to send HR representatives on long trips and can interact with potential hires from all over the world, Boeing, Progressive, Citibank, and Amazon have found virtual job fairs to be an efficient, cost-effective way to find qualified candidates. Still an important part of external recruiting, job fairs are being repositioned as branding events. With nearly half of its U.S. workforce expected to retire by 2025, the insurance and risk management industry is aggressively recruiting younger workers. **Allstate** bolsters its campus recruiting and job fairs with trivia nights, free food, and hackathons to attract computer science majors. And instead of wearing business suits, its campus recruiters wear t-shirts emblazoned with "Jobhunting is Mayhem," a reference to the star character in its popular ad campaign.[40]

11-3 SELECTION

After the recruitment process has produced a pool of qualified applicants, the selection process is used to determine which applicants have the best chance of performing well on the job. From the initial review of applicants to phone screening (seven days) to group interviews (six days) to personality and skills testing, it takes an average of twenty-three to twenty-nine days to screen potential applicants and hire a new employee.[41] Software company **AppDynamics**, however, accomplishes the full selection process in less than a week. A few days after applying, strong candidates have two phone interviews, during which recruiters set expectations about compensation. Applicants then visit the office for seven hours of in-person interviews with roughly six employees. This day ends with a fifteen-minute interview with a hiring manager who may (or may not) extend an offer. Candidates who receive offers have two days to accept or decline. Luan Lam, AppDynamics' vice president of global talent, says, "Time kills deals," and notes that before implementing this speed-hiring method, AppDynamics needed thirty days to fill every open engineering position.[42]

As this example illustrates, **selection** is the process of gathering information about job applicants to

decide who should be offered a job. To make sure that selection decisions are accurate and legally defensible, the EEOC's *Uniform Guidelines on Employee Selection Procedures* recommend that all selection procedures be validated. **Validation** is the process of determining how well a selection test or procedure predicts future job performance. The better or more accurate the prediction of future job performance, the more valid a test is said to be.

*Let's examine common selection procedures such as **11-3a application forms and résumés, 11-3b references and background checks, 11-3c selection tests**, and **11-3d interviews**.*

11-3a Application Forms and Résumés

The first selection devices that most job applicants encounter when they seek a job are application forms and résumés. Both contain similar information about an applicant, such as name, address, job and educational history, and so forth. Though an organization's application form often asks for information already provided by the applicant's résumé, most organizations prefer to collect this information in their own format for entry into a **human resource information system (HRIS)**.

Employment laws apply to application forms just as they do to all selection devices. Application forms may ask applicants only for valid, job-related information. Nonetheless, application forms commonly ask applicants for non-job-related information such as marital status, maiden name, age, or date of high school graduation. One study found that 73 percent of organizations had application forms that violated at least one federal or state law.[43] Likewise, interviewers may not ask about medical histories or genetics, religious beliefs, or citizenship. Exhibit 11.4 provides a more detailed explanation and list of the kinds of information that companies may *not* request in application forms, during job interviews, or in any other part of the selection process.

Courts will assume that you use all of the

Selection the process of gathering information about job applicants to decide who should be offered a job

Validation the process of determining how well a selection test or procedure predicts future job performance; the better or more accurate the prediction of future job performance, the more valid a test is said to be

Human resource information system (HRIS) a computerized system for gathering, analyzing, storing, and disseminating information related to the HRM process

Exhibit 11.4
Don't Ask! Topics to Avoid in an Interview

1. **Children.** Don't ask applicants if they have children, plan to have them, or have or need child care. Questions about children can unintentionally single out women.

2. **Age.** Because of the Age Discrimination in Employment Act, employers cannot ask job applicants their age during the hiring process. Because most people graduate high school at the age of eighteen, even asking for high school graduation dates could violate the law.

3. **Disabilities.** Don't ask if applicants have physical or mental disabilities. According to the Americans with Disabilities Act, disabilities (and reasonable accommodations for them) cannot be discussed until a job offer has been made.

4. **Physical characteristics.** Don't ask for information about height, weight, or other physical characteristics. Questions about weight could be construed as leading to discrimination toward overweight people, and studies show that they are less likely to be hired in general.

5. **Name.** Yes, you can ask an applicant's name, but you cannot ask a female applicant for her maiden name because it indicates marital status. Asking for a maiden name could also lead to charges that the organization was trying to establish a candidate's ethnic background.

6. **Citizenship.** Asking applicants about citizenship could lead to claims of discrimination on the basis of national origin. However, according to the Immigration Reform and Control Act, companies may ask applicants if they have a legal right to work in the United States.

7. **Lawsuits.** Applicants may not be asked if they have ever filed a lawsuit against an employer. Federal and state laws prevent this to protect whistle-blowers from retaliation by future employers.

8. **Arrest records.** Applicants cannot be asked about their arrest records. Arrests don't have legal standing. However, applicants can be asked whether they have been convicted of a crime.

9. **Smoking.** Applicants cannot be asked if they smoke. Smokers might be able to claim that they weren't hired because of fears of higher absenteeism and medical costs. However, they can be asked if they are aware of company policies that restrict smoking at work.

10. **AIDS/HIV.** Applicants can't be asked about AIDS, HIV, or any other medical condition, including genetics. Questions of this nature would violate the Americans with Disabilities Act, as well as federal and state civil rights laws.

11. **Religion.** Applicants can't be asked about religious beliefs. Questions of this nature would violate federal and state civil rights laws.

12. **Genetic information.** Employers should avoid asking about genetic test results or family medical history. This would violate the Genetic Information Nondiscrimination Act, or GINA, which was designed to help encourage people to get more genetic screening done without the fear of employers or insurers using that information to deny employment or coverage.

Sources: J. S. Pouliot, "Topics to Avoid with Applicants," *Nation's Business* 80, no. 7 (1992): 57; M. Trottman, "Employers Beware When Asking about Workers' Health," *Wall Street Journal*, July 22, 2013, accessed July 9, 2014, http://blogs.wsj.com/atwork/2013/07/22/employers-beware-when-asking-about-workers-health/; L. Weber, "Hiring Process Just Got Dicier," *Wall Street Journal*, July 3, 2014, accessed July 9, 2014, http://www.wsj.com/articles/hiring-process-just-got-dicier-1404255998.

information you request of applicants even if you actually don't. Be sure to ask only those questions that relate directly to the candidate's ability and motivation to perform the job. Furthermore, using social media such as Facebook and LinkedIn at the initial stage of the hiring process can give employers access to information they're not allowed to obtain directly from applicants. Attorney James McDonald says, "I advise employers that it's not a good idea to use social media as a screening tool. You need to control the information you receive so you're only getting information that is legal for you to take into accounting."[44]

Résumés also pose problems for companies, but in a different way. A CareerBuilder survey of hiring managers found that 58 percent had found a lie on a résumé, with the most common being embellished skills, employment dates, job titles, academic degrees, and the companies one for which one has supposedly worked. Applicants in financial services (73%), leisure and hospitality (71%), and IT and health care (both 63%) were the most likely to have lies caught on resumes.[45] Therefore, managers should verify the information collected via résumés and application forms by comparing it with additional information collected during interviews and other stages of the selection process, such as references and background checks, which are discussed next.

11-3b References and Background Checks

In the United States, drivers for **Uber**'s ride-sharing service undergo an independent screening by Checkr, a company that runs each applicant's name through seven years of federal and county background checks, sex offender registries, and motor vehicle records.

Despite those checks, Uber still hired an applicant, who had spent fourteen years in federal prison on drug charges, to be a driver on its network in the Houston area. While giving a ride to a drunken female passenger, the driver allegedly took her to his home and raped her. Lara Cottingham, an administrator for the city of Houston says, "Not all background checks are created equal. It's easy to lie about your name . . . Social Security number . . . where you've lived."[46] Houston requires all drivers to undergo an FBI background check, including fingerprinting. Nearly all companies ask an applicant to provide **employment references**, such as the names of previous employers or coworkers, whom they can contact to learn more about the candidate. **Background checks** are used to verify the truthfulness and accuracy of information that applicants provide about themselves and to uncover negative, job-related background information not provided by applicants. Background checks are conducted by contacting "educational institutions, prior employers, court records, police and governmental agencies, and other informational sources, either by telephone, mail, remote computer access, or through in-person investigations."[47]

Unfortunately, previous employers are increasingly reluctant to provide references or background check information for fear of being sued by previous employees for defamation.[48] If former employers provide potential employers with unsubstantiated information that damages applicants' chances of being hired, applicants can (and do) sue for defamation. As a result, 54 percent of employers will not provide information about previous employees.[49] Many provide only dates of employment, positions held, and date of separation.

When previous employers decline to provide meaningful references or background information, they put other employers at risk of *negligent hiring* lawsuits, in which an employer is held liable for the actions of an employee who would not have been hired if the employer had conducted a thorough reference search and background check.[50] Heyl Logistics hired Washington Transportation, a trucking firm, to deliver bottled water, but its driver took drugs, fell asleep, hit a truck, and killed another driver. The killed driver's family sued Heyl Logistics for negligent hiring, alleging it should have known that Washington Transportation operated without a license, did not test its drivers for drug use, and carried no insurance. Heyl was found guilty, Washington Transportation's driver was sent to prison for negligent homicide and driving under the

influence, and the family was awarded $5.2 million in punitive damages.[51]

With previous employers generally unwilling to give full, candid references and with negligent hiring lawsuits awaiting companies that don't get such references and background information, what can companies do? They can conduct criminal record checks, especially if the job for which the person is applying involves money, drugs, control over valuable goods, or access to the elderly, people with disabilities, or people's homes.[52] According to the Society for Human Resource Management, 69 percent of organizations conduct criminal record checks, and 47 percent conduct credit checks.[53] Now that companies provide criminal record checks for $10 an applicant, pulling data from 3,100 court systems nationwide, there's no excuse to not check. Louis DeFalco, corporate director of safety, security, and investigations at ABC Fine Wine & Spirits, which has 175 stores in Florida, makes the case for criminal record checks: "If I have a guy with four arrests and bad credit versus someone who has never been in trouble in his life, who am I going to hire? It's not rocket science."[54] While companies are legally entitled to use criminal background checks at some point in the hiring process, they should, as was discussed at the beginning of the chapter, follow state laws and EEOC guidelines that restrict asking applicants about criminal records on initial application forms.[55]

Another option is to use public networking sites such as LinkedIn to identify and contact the colleagues, customers, and suppliers who are linked or connected to job applicants. LinkedIn's former CEO Dan Nye says that the company called twenty-three of his LinkedIn connections without his knowledge before offering him a face-to-face interview. With the growing use and popularity of social networking websites, Nye says such practices are "fair game." One downside to this approach is that it could unintentionally alert an applicant's current employer that the person is seeking another job. As a result, says Chuck Wardell, managing director at Korn/ Ferry International, an executive recruitment firm, "You have to be

Employment references sources such as previous employers or coworkers who can provide job-related information about job candidates

Background checks procedures used to verify the truthfulness and accuracy of information that applicants provide about themselves and to uncover negative, job-related background information not provided by applicants

careful referencing people who have jobs because you might blow them out of their jobs."[56]

After doing a background check, dig deeper for more information. Ask references to provide additional references. Next, ask applicants to sign a waiver that permits you to check references, run a background check, or contact anyone else with knowledge of their work performance or history. Likewise, ask applicants if there is anything they would like the company to know or if they expect you to hear anything unusual when contacting references.[57] This in itself is often enough to get applicants to share information they typically withhold. When you've finished checking, keep the findings confidential to minimize the chances of a defamation charge. Always document all reference and background checks, noting who was called and what information was obtained. Document everything, not just information you received. To reduce the likelihood that negligent hiring lawsuits will succeed, it's particularly important to document even which companies and people refused to share reference checks and background information.

Finally, consider hiring private investigators to conduct background checks, which can often uncover information missed by traditional background checks. For example, while traditional background checks should be able to verify applicants' academic credentials, a private investigator hired by the *Wall Street Journal* found that 7 out of 358 senior executives at publicly traded firms had falsified claims regarding the college degrees they had earned.[58] Likewise, private investigators can potentially identify when applicants hire companies that provide fake references from fake bosses (to avoid negative references from previous employers). Indeed, one such business claims, "We can replace a supervisor with a fictitious one, alter your work history, provide you with a positive employment reputation, and give you the glowing reference you need."[59]

11-3c Selection Tests

Selection tests give organizational decision makers a chance to know who will likely do well in a job and who won't. Pre-hiring assessments are growing in popularity, with 57 percent of large U.S. employers using some sort of pre-hiring test to ensure a better fit. "The incentives to screen before hiring have increased over time, while costs

have declined," says economist Steve Davis. "Both those things are encouraging employers to move away what was essentially a trial employment situation to just screening out people in advance."[60] The basic idea behind selection testing is to have applicants take a test that measures something directly or indirectly related to doing well on the job. The selection tests discussed here are specific ability tests, cognitive ability tests, biographical data, personality tests, work sample tests, and assessment centers.

Specific ability tests measure the extent to which an applicant possesses the particular kind of ability needed to do a job well. Specific ability tests are also called **aptitude tests** because they measure aptitude for doing a particular task well. For example, if you took the SAT to get into college, then you've taken the aptly named Scholastic Aptitude Test, which is one of the best predictors of how well students will do in college (that is, scholastic performances).[61] Specific ability tests also exist for mechanical, clerical, sales, and physical work. For example, clerical workers have to be good at accurately reading and scanning numbers as they type or enter data. Exhibit 11.5 shows items similar to

Exhibit 11.5
Clerical Test Items Similar to Those Found on the Minnesota Clerical Test

	Numbers/Letters		Same	
1.	3468251	3467251	Yes	No
			O	O
2.	4681371	4681371	Yes	No
			O	O
3.	7218510	7218520	Yes	No
			O	O
4.	ZXYAZAB	ZXYAZAB	Yes	No
			O	O
5.	ALZYXMN	ALZYXNM	Yes	No
			O	O
6.	PRQZYMN	PRQZYMN	Yes	No
			O	O

Source: N. W. Schmitt and R. J. Klimoski, *Research Methods in Human Resource Management* (Mason, OH: South-Western, 1991).

Specific ability tests (aptitude tests) tests that measure the extent to which an applicant possesses the particular kind of ability needed to do a job well

the Minnesota Clerical Test, in which applicants have only a short time to determine if the two columns of numbers and letters are identical. Applicants who are good at this are likely to do well as clerical or data entry workers.

Cognitive ability tests measure the extent to which applicants have abilities in perceptual speed, verbal comprehension, numerical aptitude, general reasoning, and spatial aptitude. In other words, these tests indicate how quickly and how well people understand words, numbers, logic, and spatial dimensions. Whereas specific ability tests predict job performance in only particular types of jobs, cognitive ability tests accurately predict job performance in almost all kinds of jobs.[62] Why is this so? The reason is that people with strong cognitive or mental abilities are usually good at learning new things, processing complex information, solving problems, and making decisions, and these abilities are important in almost all jobs.[63] In fact, cognitive ability tests are almost always the best predictors of job performance. Consequently, if you were allowed to use just one selection test, a cognitive ability test would be the one to use.[64] (In practice, though, companies use a battery of different tests because doing so leads to much more accurate selection decisions.)

Biographical data, or **biodata**, are extensive surveys that ask applicants questions about their personal backgrounds and life experiences. The basic idea behind biodata is that past behavior (personal background and life experience) is the best predictor of future behavior. For example, during World War II, the U.S. Air Force had to test tens of thousands of men without flying experience to determine who was likely to be a good pilot. Because flight training took several months and was very expensive, quickly selecting the right people for training was important. After examining extensive biodata, the Air Force found that one of the best predictors of success in flight school was whether students had ever built model airplanes that actually flew. This one biodata item was almost as good a predictor as the entire set of selection tests that the air force was using at the time.[65]

Most biodata questionnaires have more than 100 items that gather information about habits and attitudes, health, interpersonal relations, money, what it was like growing up in your family (parents, siblings, childhood years, teen years), personal habits, current home (spouse, children), hobbies, education and training, values, preferences, and work.[66] In general, biodata are very good predictors of future job performance, especially in entry-level jobs.

You may have noticed that some of the information requested in biodata surveys is related to those topics

Personality tests measure the extent to which applicants possess different kinds of job-related personality dimensions.

employers should avoid in applications, interviews, or other parts of the selection process. This information can be requested in biodata questionnaires provided that the company can demonstrate that the information is job related (that is, valid) and does not result in adverse impact against protected groups of job applicants. Biodata surveys should be validated and tested for adverse impact before they are used to make selection decisions.[67]

An individual's *personality* is made up of a relatively stable set of behaviors, attitudes, and emotions displayed over time. In short, it is personality that makes people different from each other. A **personality test** measures the extent to which an applicant possesses different kinds of job-related personality dimensions. In Chapter 12, you will learn that there are five major personality dimensions related to work behavior: extraversion, emotional stability, agreeableness, conscientiousness, and openness to experience.[68] Of these, only conscientiousness— the degree to which someone is organized, hardworking, responsible, persevering, thorough, and achievement oriented—predicts job performance across a wide variety of jobs.[69] Conscientiousness tests

Cognitive ability tests tests that measure the extent to which applicants have abilities in perceptual speed, verbal comprehension, numerical aptitude, general reasoning, and spatial aptitude

Biographical data (biodata) extensive surveys that ask applicants questions about their personal backgrounds and life experiences

Personality test an assessment that measures the extent to which an applicant possesses different kinds of job-related personality dimensions

work especially well in combination with cognitive ability tests, allowing companies to select applicants who are hardworking, organized, responsible, and smart!

Work sample tests, also called *performance tests*, require applicants to perform tasks that are actually done on the job. So, unlike specific ability tests, cognitive ability tests, biographical data surveys, and personality tests, which are indirect predictors of job performance, work sample tests directly measure job applicants' capability to do the job. For example, a candidate applying to be a pharmacist might be asked to consult medical databases and accurately fill prescriptions. An applicant for a sales position might have to role-play a sales pitch. **Hire Results**, which designs work sample tests, has doubled the number of work sample tests it conducts for employers over the past five years. At **Coupons.com**, only candidates who successfully complete a series of business challenges are offered an interview. Business consultant Brian Stern, who has designed application tryouts for companies such as Starbucks, Walmart, and Sherwin-Williams, says tryouts (that is, work sample tests) are gaining in popularity because, "A job tryout says 'show me your stuff.'"[70] Work sample tests are generally very good at predicting future job performance; however, they can be expensive to administer and can be used for only one kind of job. For example, an auto dealership could not use a work sample test for mechanics as a selection test for sales representatives.

Assessment centers use a series of job-specific simulations that are graded by multiple trained observers to determine applicants' ability to perform managerial work. Unlike the previously described selection tests that are commonly used for specific jobs or entry-level jobs, assessment centers are most often used to select applicants who have high potential to be good managers. Assessment centers often last two to five days and require participants to complete a number of tests and exercises that simulate managerial work.

Some of the more common assessment center exercises are in-basket exercises, role-plays, small-group presentations, and leaderless group discussions. An *in-basket exercise* is a paper-and-pencil test in which an applicant is given a manager's in-basket containing memos, phone messages, organizational policies, and other communications normally received by and available to managers. Applicants have a limited time to read through the in-basket, prioritize the items, and decide how to deal with each item. Experienced managers then score the applicants' decisions and recommendations. Exhibit 11.6 shows an item that could be used in an assessment center for evaluating applicants for a job as a store manager.

In a *leaderless group discussion*, another common assessment center exercise, a group of six applicants is given approximately two hours to solve a problem, but no one is put in charge (hence the name *leaderless* group discussion). Trained observers watch and score each participant on the extent to which he or she facilitates discussion, listens, leads, persuades, and works well with others.

Are tests perfect predictors of job performance? No, they aren't. Some people who do well on selection tests will do poorly in their jobs. Likewise, some people who do poorly on selection tests (and therefore weren't hired) would have been very good performers. Nonetheless, valid tests will minimize selection errors (hiring people who should not have been hired and not hiring people who should have been hired) while maximizing correct

---

Work sample tests tests that require applicants to perform tasks that are actually done on the job

Assessment centers a series of managerial simulations, graded by trained observers, that are used to determine applicants' capability for managerial work

---

Exhibit 11.6
In-Basket Item for an Assessment Center for Store Managers

```
February 28
Sam & Dave's Discount Warehouse
Orange, California

Dear Store Manager,

Last week, my children and I were shopping in your store.
After doing our grocery shopping, we stopped in the
electronics department and asked the clerk, whose name
is Donald Block, to help us find a copy of the latest
version of the Madden NFL video game. Mr. Block was rude,
unhelpful, and told us to find it for ourselves as he
was busy.

I've been a loyal customer for over six years and expect
you to immediately do something about Mr. Block's
behavior. If you don't, I'll start doing my shopping
somewhere else.

Sincerely,
Margaret Quinlan
```

Source: Adapted from N. W. Schmitt and R. J. Klimoski, *Research Methods in Human Resource Management* (Mason, OH: South-Western 1991).

selection decisions (hiring people who should have been hired and not hiring people who should not have been hired). Charles Handler, president of Rocket-Hire, a consulting firm on selection tests, says, "Predicting what humans will do is really . . . hard. Tests are a predictor and better than a coin toss, but you have to be realistic about them."[71] In short, tests increase the chances that you'll hire the right person for the job, that is, someone who turns out to be a good performer. So, although tests aren't perfect, almost nothing predicts future job performance as well as the selection tests discussed here.

11-3d Interviews

In **interviews**, company representatives ask job applicants job-related questions to determine whether they are qualified for the job. Interviews are probably the most frequently used and relied on selection device. There are several basic kinds of interviews: unstructured, structured, and semistructured.

In **unstructured interviews**, interviewers are free to ask applicants anything they want, and studies show that they do. Because interviewers often disagree about which questions should be asked during interviews, different interviewers tend to ask applicants very different questions.[72] Furthermore, individual interviewers even seem to have a tough time asking the same questions from one interview to the next. This high level of variety can make things difficult. As a result, while unstructured interviews do predict job performance with some success, they are about half as accurate as structured interviews at predicting which job applicants should be hired.[73]

By contrast, with **structured interviews**, standardized interview questions are prepared ahead of time so that all applicants are asked the same job-related questions.[74] Structuring interviews also ensures that interviewers ask only for important, job-related information. Not only are the accuracy, usefulness, and validity of the interview improved, but the chances that interviewers will ask questions about topics that violate employment laws (see Exhibit 11.4) are reduced.

The primary advantage of structured interviews is that comparing applicants is much easier because they are all asked the same questions. **Google** uses structured interviews by having different interviewers ask the candidate the same question. Because Google hires by committee, each member of the hiring committee will ask an identical set of questions, allowing committee members to compare how an individual candidate answered the questions each time. Laszlo Bock, head of human resources at Google, says that the practice enables easy comparisons between interviews and iden-

tification of interviewer bias.[75] Four kinds of questions are typically asked in structured interviews. Situational questions ask applicants how they would respond in a hypothetical situation ("What would you do if . . .?"). These questions are more appropriate for hiring new graduates, who are unlikely to have encountered real-work situations because of their limited work experience. Behavioral questions ask applicants what they did in previous jobs that were similar to the job for which they are applying ("In your previous jobs, tell me about . . ."). These questions are more appropriate for hiring experienced individuals. Background questions ask applicants about their work experience, education, and other qualifications ("Tell me about the training you received at . . ."). Job-knowledge questions ask applicants to demonstrate their job knowledge (for example, nurses might be asked, "Give me an example of a time when one of your patients had a severe reaction to a medication. How did you handle it?").[76]

Semistructured interviews lie between structured and unstructured interviews. A major part of the semistructured interview (perhaps as much as 80%) is based on structured questions, but some time is set aside for unstructured interviewing to allow the interviewer to probe into ambiguous or missing information uncovered during the structured portion of the interview.

How well do interviews predict future job performance? Contrary to what you've probably heard, recent evidence indicates that even unstructured interviews do a fairly good job.[77] When conducted properly, however, structured interviews can lead to much more accurate hiring decisions than unstructured interviews. In some cases, the validity of structured interviews can rival that of cognitive ability tests.

But even more important, because interviews are especially good at assessing applicants' interpersonal skills, they work particularly well with cognitive ability tests. Combining the two—using structured interviews together with cognitive ability tests to identify smart people who work well with others—leads to even better selection decisions than using either alone.[78] Exhibit 11.7 provides a set of guidelines for conducting effective structured employment interviews.

Interview a selection tool in which company representatives ask job applicants job-related questions to determine whether they are qualified for the job

Unstructured interviews interviews in which interviewers are free to ask the applicants anything they want

Structured interviews interviews in which all applicants are asked the same set of standardized questions, usually including situational, behavioral, background, and job-knowledge questions

Exhibit 11.7
Guidelines for Conducting Effective Structured Interviews

Interview Stage	What to Do
Planning the Interview	• Identify and define the knowledge, skills, abilities, and other (KSAO) characteristics needed for successful job performance. • For each essential KSAO, develop key behavioral questions that will elicit examples of past accomplishments, activities, and performance. • For each KSAO, develop a list of things to look for in the applicant's responses to key questions.
Conducting the Interview	• Create a relaxed, nonstressful interview atmosphere. • Review the applicant's application form, résumé, and other information. • Allocate enough time to complete the interview without interruption. • Put the applicant at ease; don't jump right into heavy questioning. • Tell the applicant what to expect. Explain the interview process. • Obtain job-related information from the applicant by asking those questions prepared for each KSAO. • Describe the job and the organization to the applicant. Applicants need adequate information to make a selection decision about the organization.
After the Interview	• Immediately after the interview, review your notes and make sure they are complete. • Evaluate the applicant on each essential KSAO. • Determine each applicant's probability of success, and make a hiring decision.

Source: B. M. Farrell, "The Art and Science of Employment Interviews," *Personnel Journal* 65 (1986): 91–94.

11-4 TRAINING

According to the American Society for Training and Development, a typical investment in training increases productivity by an average of 17 percent, reduces employee turnover, and makes companies more profitable.[79] Giving employees the knowledge and skills they need to improve their performance is just the first step in developing employees, however. The second step—and not enough companies do this—is giving employees formal feedback about job performance (which we will discuss in section 11-5).

Training means providing opportunities for employees to develop the job-specific skills, experience, and knowledge they need to do their jobs or improve their performance. American companies spend an estimated $164 billion a year on training.[80]

To make sure those training dollars are well spent, companies need to **11-4a determine specific training needs, 11-4b select appropriate training methods,** *and* **11-4c evaluate training.**

11-4a Determining Training Needs

Needs assessment is the process of identifying and prioritizing the learning needs of employees. Needs assessments can be conducted by identifying performance deficiencies, listening to customer complaints, surveying employees and managers, or formally testing employees' skills and knowledge.

Training developing the skills, experience, and knowledge employees need to perform their jobs or improve their performance

Needs assessment the process of identifying and prioritizing the learning needs of employees

Mind the Gap! Companies Take Training to the Schools

Roughly 2 million U.S. jobs go unfilled because of short-falls in working training, education, or skills, and by 2020, roughly one third of U.S. jobs will require more than a high-school diploma but less than a bachelor's degree. To fill that gap, companies across the country are investing in technical training at the high school and community college levels, but few initiatives compare to the vocational programs developed by German robotics company Festo, which has been building and delivering industrial training programs and growing at a rate of 8 percent per year since the 1970s. The training division, called Festo Didactic, arrived in the United States in 2015, and its managers are passionate about its ability to help fill the U.S. skills gap. Festo Didactic's strategy is to target companies, governments, colleges, and even high schools and younger, all in a quest to elevate the skill levels of U.S. workers. CEO Nader Imani says, "We feel almost like missionaries at times, but there's a hard-headed business case as well."

iStockphoto.com/Mosichev

Source: C. Gummer, "German Robots School U.S. Workers," *Wall Street Journal*, September 10, 2014, accessed May 7, 2015, http://www.wsj.com/articles/german-style-training-for-american-factory-workers-1410296094; A. Campoy, "Training Programs Target Skills Gap," *Wall Street Journal*, April 24, 2015, A3.

Note that training should never be conducted without first performing a needs assessment. Sometimes, training isn't needed at all or isn't needed for all employees. Unfortunately, however, many organizations simply require all employees to attend training whether they need to or not. As a result, employees who are not interested or don't need the training may react negatively during or after training. Likewise, employees who should be sent for training but aren't may also react negatively. Consequently, a needs assessment is an important tool for deciding who should or should not attend training. In fact, employment law restricts employers from discriminating on the basis of age, sex, race, color, religion, national origin, or disability when selecting training participants. Just like hiring decisions, the selection of training participants should be based on job-related information.

11-4b Training Methods

Assume that you're a training director for a hospital system and that you're in charge of making sure all employees in the biocontaminant unit can safely treat patients with Ebola.[81] Exhibit 11.8 lists a number of training methods you could use: films and videos, lectures, planned readings, case studies, coaching and mentoring, group discussions, on-the-job training, role-playing, simulations and games, vestibule training, and computer-based learning. Which method would be best?

To choose the best method, you should consider a number of factors, such as the number of people to be trained, the cost of training, and the objectives of the training. For instance, if the training objective is to impart information or knowledge to trainees, then you should use films and videos, lectures, and planned readings. In our example, trainees might read a manual or attend a lecture about how to put on and remove personal protective gear.

If developing analytical and problem-solving skills is the objective, then use case studies, coaching and mentoring, and group discussions. In our example, trainees might view a video documenting how a team handled exposure to the disease, talk with first responders who have worked in West Africa, and discuss what they would do in a similar situation.

If practicing, learning, or changing job behaviors is the objective, then use on-the-job training, role-playing, simulations and games, and vestibule training. Employees at the biocontainment unit of the University of Texas Southwestern Medical Center (UTSMC) role-play putting on and taking off their protective gear. Because of the number of steps involved, this is done in teams to ensure compliance so as to prevent the spread of the deadly disease. UTSMC sprays the fake Ebola patients used during the training with spicy, peppery Tabasco sauce. Dr. Bruce Myer says that if doctors and nurses get Tabasco on their skin, "it gives immediate feedback," to let them know a potentially deadly mistake has just been made.[82]

If training is supposed to meet more than one of these objectives, then your best choice may be to

Exhibit 11.8
Training Objectives and Methods

Training Objective	Training Methods
Impart Information and Knowledge	▸ *Films and videos.* Films and videos present information, illustrate problems and solutions, and effectively hold trainees' attention.
	▸ *Lectures.* Trainees listen to instructors' oral presentations.
	▸ *Planned readings.* Trainees read about concepts or ideas before attending training.
Develop Analytical and Problem-Solving Skills	▸ *Case studies.* Cases are analyzed and discussed in small groups. The cases present a specific problem or decision, and trainees develop methods for solving the problem or making the decision.
	▸ *Coaching and mentoring.* Coaching and mentoring of trainees by managers involves informal advice, suggestions, and guidance. This method is helpful for reinforcing other kinds of training and for trainees who benefit from support and personal encouragement.
	▸ *Group discussions.* Small groups of trainees actively discuss specific topics. The instructor may perform the role of discussion leader.
Practice, Learn, or Change Job Behaviors	▸ *On-the-job training.* New employees are assigned to experienced employees. The trainee learns by watching the experienced employee perform the job and eventually by working alongside the experienced employee. Gradually, the trainee is left on his or her own to perform the job.
	▸ *Role-playing.* Trainees assume job-related roles and practice new behaviors by acting out what they would do in job-related situations.
	▸ *Simulations and games.* Experiential exercises place trainees in realistic job-related situations and give them the opportunity to experience a job-related condition in a relatively low-cost setting. The trainee benefits from hands-on experience before actually performing the job, where mistakes may be more costly.
	▸ *Vestibule training.* Procedures and equipment similar to those used in the actual job are set up in a special area called a "vestibule." The trainee is then taught how to perform the job at his or her own pace without disrupting the actual flow of work, making costly mistakes, or exposing the trainee and others to dangerous conditions.
Impart Information and Knowledge; Develop Analytical and Problem-Solving Skills; and Practice, Learn, or Change Job Behaviors	▸ *Computer-based learning.* Interactive videos, software, CD-ROMs, PCs, teleconferencing, and the Internet may be combined to present multimedia-based training.

Source: A. Fowler, "How to Decide on Training Methods," *People Management* 25, no. 1 (1995): 36.

combine one of the previous methods with computer-based training. Walmart's Pathways training program uses computer games and videos to teach frontline employees how to read stock labels, the eight-steps used for collecting carts from the parking lot, plus basic information about the retail industry. Pathways supports six months of supervised on-the-job training during which managers help employees prepare to pass "gateway" assessments that can lead to a raise, a promotion to a specialty department, or acceptance into a management training program. Likewise, supervisors are being trained to support their employees and must attend a five-week managerial skills workshop. Jamie Dworackzyk, an apparel manager at the Joplin, Missouri, store for eighteen years, appreciates Walmart's new emphasis on training, saying, "In the past we didn't take the time to teach. We just expected them to know. Now I can actually manage my people."[83]

These days, many companies are adopting Internet training, or "computer-based learning." E-learning can offer several advantages. Because employees don't need to leave their jobs, travel costs are greatly reduced. Also,

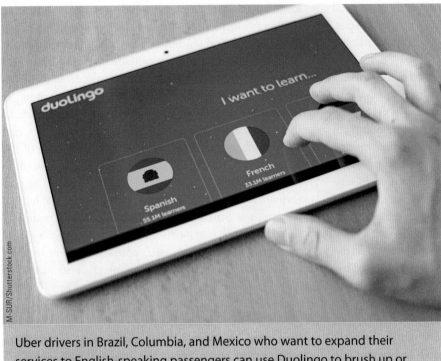

Uber drivers in Brazil, Columbia, and Mexico who want to expand their services to English-speaking passengers can use Duolingo to brush up or learn from scratch.

because employees can take training modules when it is convenient (that is, they don't have to fall behind at their jobs to attend week-long training courses), workplace productivity should increase, and employee stress should decrease. And, if a company's technology infrastructure can support it, e-learning can be much faster than traditional training methods. This is especially true of micro-learning apps. With micro-learning, training is accomplished via short, focused lessons that can generally be completed in fewer than five minutes and are often followed by a quiz to check learning. For example, **Uber** drivers in Brazil, Columbia, and Mexico can practice their English skills using **Duolingo**, a foreign language app that delivers micro-instruction through audio, video, text, and pictures. After demonstrating proficiency by advancing to a certain level in the app, a driver's vehicle is listed as an option for English-speaking passengers looking for a driver who speaks their language.[84]

There are, however, several disadvantages to e-learning. First, despite its increasing popularity, it's not always the appropriate training method. E-learning can be a good way to impart information, but it isn't always as effective for changing job behaviors or developing problem-solving and analytical skills. Second, e-learning requires a significant investment in computers and high-speed Internet and network connections for all employees. Finally, though e-learning can be faster, many employees find it so boring and unengaging that they may choose to do their jobs rather than complete e-learning courses when sitting alone at their desks. E-learning may become more interesting, however, as more companies incorporate game-like features such as avatars and competition into their e-learning courses.

11-4c Evaluating Training

After selecting a training method and conducting the training, the last step is to evaluate the training. Training can be evaluated in four ways: on *reactions* (how satisfied trainees were with the program), on *learning* (how much employees improved their knowledge or skills), on *behavior* (how much employees actually changed their on-the-job behavior because of training), or on *results* (how much training improved job performance, such as increased sales or quality, or decreased costs).[85] In general, training provides meaningful benefits for most companies if it is done well. For example, a study by the American Society for Training and Development shows that a training budget as small as $680 per employee can increase a company's total return on investment by 6 percent.[86] Chuck Runyon, CEO of Anytime Fitness, which has 2,500 locations, says, "The only thing worse than training people and having them leave is not training people and having them stay."[87]

11-5 PERFORMANCE APPRAISAL

Performance appraisal is the process of assessing how well employees are doing their jobs. Most employees and managers intensely dislike the performance appraisal process. Samuel Culbert, professor of management at UCLA, says there is nothing constructive about

Performance appraisal
the process of assessing how well employees are doing their jobs

performance appraisals and calls them a "dysfunctional pretense." Culbert says, "It's a negative to corporate performance, an obstacle to straight-talk relationships, and a prime cause of low morale at work."[88]

Many people share this view. In fact, 65 percent of employees are dissatisfied with the performance appraisal process in their companies. Likewise, according to the Society for Human Resource Management, 95 percent of human resource managers are dissatisfied with the performance appraisal systems used by their companies. Twelve percent of companies, including market leaders **Adobe** and **General Electric**, have abolished their performance appraisal systems altogether.[89] GE head of human resources Susan Peters explains the reason for the change this way: "It existed in more or less the same form since I started at the company in 1979, but we think over many years it had become more a ritual than moving the company upwards and forwards."[90] On the other hand, Paul Rubenstein, a partner at global human resources consulting firm Aon Hewitt, says, "If you get rid of the performance ratings, how are you going to get rid of a fair and equitable and measurable system to blame the distribution of pay on? Because why did performance ratings come into existence? So there's some mechanism to force pay decisions. People wonder, which came first the rating or the pay decision."[91]

Indeed, performance appraisals are used for four broad purposes: making administrative decisions (for example, pay increase, promotion, retention), providing feedback for employee development (for example, performance, developing career plans), evaluating human resource programs (for example, validating selection systems), and for documentation purposes (for example, documenting performance ratings and decisions based on those ratings).[92]

*Let's explore how companies can avoid some of these problems with performance appraisals by **11-5a accurately measuring job performance** and **11-5b effectively sharing performance feedback with employees**.*

11-5a Accurately Measuring Job Performance

Workers often have strong doubts about the accuracy of their performance appraisals— and they may be right. For example, it's widely known that assessors are prone to errors when rating worker performance. Three of the most common rating errors are central tendency, halo, and leniency. *Central tendency error* occurs when assessors rate all workers as average or in the middle of the scale. *Halo error* occurs when assessors rate all workers as performing at the same level (good, bad, or average) in all parts of their jobs. *Leniency error* occurs when assessors rate all workers as performing particularly well. One of the reasons managers make these errors is that they often don't spend enough time gathering or reviewing performance data. Mark Farrugia, vice president of human resources at **Sun Communities**, a maker of manufactured housing, is concerned that managers are giving high scores on performance appraisals to make their lives easier (and employees happier) or to maximize bonuses for employees they are worried are thinking of leaving. He says, "I'm more and more convinced that [performance appraisal] ratings are doing more harm than good," he says.[93] What can be done to minimize rating errors and improve the accuracy with which job performance is measured? In general, two approaches have been used: improving performance appraisal measures themselves and training performance raters to be more accurate.

One of the ways companies try to improve performance appraisal measures is to use as many objective performance measures as possible. **Objective performance measures** are measures of performance that are easily and directly counted or quantified. Common objective performance measures include output, scrap, waste, sales, customer complaints, and rejection rates.

But when objective performance measures aren't available (and frequently they aren't), subjective performance measures have to be used instead. **Subjective performance measures** require that someone judge or assess a worker's performance. The most common kind of subjective performance measure is the graphic rating scale (GRS) shown in Exhibit 11.9. Graphic rating scales are most widely used because they are easy to construct, but they are very susceptible to rating errors.

A popular alternative to graphic rating scales is the **behavior observation scale (BOS)**. BOSs requires raters to rate the frequency with which workers perform specific behaviors representative of the job dimensions that are critical to successful job performance. Exhibit 11.9 shows a BOS for two important job dimensions for a retail salesperson: customer service and money handling. Notice that each dimension lists several specific behaviors characteristic of a worker who excels

Objective performance measures measures of job performance that are easily and directly counted or quantified

Subjective performance measures measures of job performance that require someone to judge or assess a worker's performance

Behavior observation scales (BOSs) rating scales that indicate the frequency with which workers perform specific behaviors that are representative of the job dimensions critical to successful job performance

Exhibit 11.9
Subjective Performance Appraisal Scales

Graphic Rating Scale

	Very poor	Poor	Average	Good	Very good
Example 1: Quality of work performed is	1	2	3	4	5

	Very poor (20% errors)	Poor (15% errors)	Average (10% errors)	Good (5% errors)	Very good (less than 5% errors)
Example 2: Quality of work performed is	1	2	3	4	5

Behavioral Observation Scale

Dimension: Customer Service

	Almost Never				Almost Always
1. Greets customers with a smile and a "hello."	1	2	3	4	5
2. Calls other stores to help customers find merchandise that is not in stock.	1	2	3	4	5
3. Promptly handles customer concerns and complaints.	1	2	3	4	5

Dimension: Money Handling

	Almost Never				Almost Always
1. Accurately makes change from customer transactions.	1	2	3	4	5
2. Accounts balance at the end of the day, no shortages or surpluses.	1	2	3	4	5
3. Accurately records transactions in computer system.	1	2	3	4	5

in that dimension of job performance. (Normally, the scale would list seven to twelve items per dimension, not three, as in the exhibit.) Notice also that the behaviors are good behaviors, meaning they indicate good performance, and the rater is asked to judge how frequently an employee engaged in those good behaviors. The logic behind the BOS is that better performers engage in good behaviors more often.

Not only do BOSs work well for rating critical dimensions of performance, but studies also show that managers strongly prefer BOSs for giving performance feedback; accurately differentiating between poor, average, and good workers; identifying training needs; and accurately measuring performance. And in response to the statement, "If I were defending a company, this rating format would be an asset to my case," attorneys strongly preferred BOSs over other kinds of subjective performance appraisal scales.[94]

The second approach to improving the measurement of workers' job performance is **rater training**. The most effective is frame-of-reference training, in which a group of trainees learn how to do performance appraisals by watching a video of an employee at work. Next, they evaluate the performance of the person in the video. A trainer (an expert in the subject matter) then shares his or her evaluations, and trainees' evaluations are compared with the expert's. The expert then explains the rationales behind his or her evaluations. This process is repeated until the

> **Rater training** training performance appraisal raters in how to avoid rating errors and increase rating accuracy

differences in evaluations given by trainees and evaluations by the expert are minimized. The underlying logic behind the frame-of-reference training is that by adopting the frame of reference used by an expert, trainees will be able to accurately observe, judge, and use relevant appraisal scales to evaluate the performance of others.[95]

11-5b Sharing Performance Feedback

After gathering accurate performance data, the next step is to share performance feedback with employees. Unfortunately, even when performance appraisal ratings are accurate, the appraisal process often breaks down at the feedback stage. Employees become defensive and dislike hearing any negative assessments of their work, no matter how small. Managers become defensive, too, and dislike giving appraisal feedback as much as employees dislike receiving it. In response, many companies are asking managers to ease up on harsh feedback and instead accentuate the positive by focusing on employee strengths. In the past, Michelle Russell of **Boston Consulting Group** says, "We would bring them in and beat them down a bit."[96] Some employees would suffer a crisis of confidence and performance and then quit. At **Intel**, telling employees they "need improvement" deflates morale, says HR manager Devra Johnson, "We call them the walking wounded."[97]

What can be done to overcome the inherent difficulties in performance appraisal feedback? First, be mindful of being overly critical and making employees so defensive that they quit listening. The top half of Exhibit 11.10 offers some suggestion for being less negative and more positive in feedback sessions. Also, because performance appraisal ratings have traditionally been the judgments of just one person, the boss, another

360-degree feedback a performance appraisal process in which feedback is obtained from the boss, subordinates, peers and coworkers, and the employees themselves

possibility is to use **360-degree feedback**. In this approach, feedback comes from four sources: the boss, subordinates, peers and coworkers, and the employees themselves. The data, which are obtained anonymously (except for the boss's), are compiled into a feedback report comparing the employee's self-ratings with those of the boss, subordinates, and peers and coworkers. Usually, a consultant or human resource specialist discusses the results with the employee. The advantage of 360-degree programs is that negative feedback ("You don't listen") is often more credible when it comes from several people.

Herbert Meyer, who has been studying performance appraisal feedback for more than thirty years, recommends a list of topics to discuss in performance appraisal feedback sessions (see the bottom half of Exhibit 11.10).[98] Furthermore, managers can do three different things to make performance reviews more comfortable and productive. First, they should separate developmental feedback, which is designed to improve future performance, from administrative feedback, which is used as a reward for past performance, such as for raises. When managers give developmental feedback, they're acting as coaches, but when they give administrative feedback, they're acting as judges. These roles, coaches and judges, are clearly incompatible. As coaches, managers encourage, pointing out opportunities for growth and improvement, and employees are typically open and receptive to feedback. But as judges, managers are evaluative, and employees are typically defensive and closed to feedback.

Second, Meyer suggests that performance appraisal feedback sessions be based on self-appraisals, in which employees carefully assess their own strengths, weaknesses, successes, and failures in writing. Because employees play an active role in the review of their performance, managers can be coaches rather than judges. Also, because the focus is on future goals and development, both employees and managers are likely to be more satisfied with the process and more committed to future plans and changes. And, because the focus is on development and not administrative assessment,

PlusONE/Shutterstock.com

studies show that self-appraisals lead to more candid self-assessments than traditional supervisory reviews.[99]

Job search website **Monster.com** has put self-appraisals at the center of its performance feedback system by asking managers to conduct quarterly check-ins with their direct reports. Prior to the meetings, employees must complete a short template that includes one to three professional goals for the upcoming period, what kind of results they hope to achieve in that time frame, and how they plan to achieve them. Monster.com chief human resources officer Kim Mullaney says that "by communicating professional aspirations with their superiors, staffers will be more engaged. Knowing that you're in direct control of your goals is extremely important—as is knowing that your boss is a stakeholder in the plan."[100]

Finally, what people do with the performance feedback they receive really matters. A study of 1,361 senior managers found that managers who reviewed their 360-degree feedback with an executive coach (hired by the company) were more likely to set specific goals for improvement, ask their bosses for ways to improve, and subsequently improve their performance.[101]

A five-year study of 252 managers found that their performance improved dramatically if they met with their subordinates to discuss their

Exhibit 11.10
How and What to Discuss in a Performance Appraisal Feedback Session

How to Discuss Performance Feedback

Don't say...	Instead say...
"What are we stuck on?"	"What are we doing really well?"
"Nice work."	"You show great promise with…."
"You need to get better at…."	"This is another way that's been successful."
"We can't do this."	"We haven't done this yet."

- ✔ Overall progress—an analysis of accomplishments and shortcomings
- ✔ Problems encountered in meeting job requirements
- ✔ Opportunities to improve performance
- ✔ Long-range plans and opportunities— for the job and for the individual's career
- ✔ General discussion of possible plans and goals for the coming year

Source: H. H. Meyer, "A Solution to the Performance Appraisal Feedback Enigma," *Academy of Management Executive* 5, no. 1 (1991): 68–76; R. Feintzeig, "Everything Is Awesome! Why You Can't Tell Employees They're Doing a Bad Job." *Wall Street Journal*, February 10, 2015, accessed May 7, 2015, http://www.wsj.com/articles/everything-is-awesome-why-you-cant-tell-employees-theyre-doing-a-bad-job-1423613936.

Minerva Studio/Shutterstock.com

360-degree feedback ("You don't listen") and how they were going to address it ("I'll restate what others have said before stating my opinion"). Performance was dramatically lower for managers who never discussed their 360-degree feedback with subordinates and for managers who did not routinely do so. Why is discussing 360-degree feedback with subordinates so effective? These discussions help managers understand their weaknesses better, force them to develop a plan to improve, and demonstrate to the subordinates the managers' public commitment to improving.[102] In short, it helps to have people discuss their performance feedback with others, but it particularly helps to have them discuss their feedback with the people who provided it.

EXEMPT OR NON-EXEMPT? *THAT* IS THE QUESTION

Technology has created a never-ending workday. Many U.S. workers check their work email and voice mail accounts after hours, and with the ubiquity of smartphones, many employers tacitly suggest that their employees be available around the clock. What used to be considered overtime has become just part of the job. Until recently, only 12 percent of salaried workers—those making less than $23,660 per year—were legally eligible for overtime pay on after-hours activities. In 2016, the Department of Labor increased the cap to $47,000 per year, making many more salaried workers eligible for over-time compensation. U.S. companies lobbying to put hard limits on the forty-hour work week to prevent additional labor costs might want to follow the lead of Volkswagen AG, which prevents its email servers from delivering messages to nonexempt employees between the hours of 6:15 p.m. and 7:00 a.m.

Sources: L. Weber, "Overtime Pay for Answering Late Night Emails?" *Wall Street Journal*, May 21, 2015, B1; K. Hoover, "Dept. of Labor Makes 'Token Reduction' in New Overtime Pay Threshold (and Other News from Washington Today)," *Washington Post*, April 29, 2016, accessed May 31, 2016, http://www.bizjournals.com/boston/news/news-wire/2016/04/29/dol-makes-token-reduction-in-new-overtime-pay.html.

11-6 COMPENSATION AND EMPLOYEE SEPARATION

While China has more than a billion people, 80 percent of its manufacturers are having difficulty finding and keeping workers. Employers are responding by hiking wages, which have increased 74 percent in four years. **Pacific Resources International**, which has ten Chinese factories, pays its workers 20 percent more than minimum wage, provides insurance and free meals, and only asks employees to work forty to forty-five hours a week, which is low in China. Still, it loses employees to the insurance industry, where salaries are 40 percent larger.[103] Factories, which have already raised pay, are now addressing nonfinancial issues in hopes of becoming more attractive places to work. **Flextronics International** sponsors company picnics, talent shows (karaoke), speed-dating for unmarried workers, sports facilities for soccer and basketball, and hair salons. Chief procurement officer Tom Linton says, "If you are able to get employees connected socially, they're more likely to stay."[104]

Compensation includes both the financial and the nonfinancial rewards that organizations give employees in exchange for their work. **Employee separation** is a broad term covering the loss of an employee for any reason. *Involuntary separation* occurs when employers terminate or lay off employees. *Voluntary separation* occurs when employees quit or retire. Because employee separations affect recruiting, selection, training, and compensation, organizations should forecast the number of employees they expect to lose through terminations, layoffs, turnover, or retirements when doing human resource planning.

Let's learn more about compensation by examining the **11-6a compensation decisions that managers must make** *as well as* **11-6b termination, 11-6c downsizing, 11-6d retirement,** *and* **11-6e turnover**.

11-6a Compensation Decisions

There are three basic kinds of compensation decisions: pay level, pay variability, and pay structure.[105] *Pay-level decisions* concern whether to pay workers at a level that is below, above, or at current market wages. Companies use job evaluation to set their pay structures. **Job evaluation** determines the worth of each job by determining the market value of the knowledge, skills, and requirements needed to perform it. After conducting a job evaluation, most companies try to pay the going rate, meaning the current market wage. There are always companies, however, whose financial situation causes them to pay considerably less than current market wages.

Some companies choose to pay above-average wages to attract and keep employees. *Above-market wages* can attract a larger, more qualified pool of job applicants, increase the rate of job acceptance, decrease the time it takes to fill positions, and increase the time that employees stay.[106] While the average U.S. grocery store

Compensation the financial and nonfinancial rewards that organizations give employees in exchange for their work

Employee separation the voluntary or involuntary loss of an employee

Job evaluation a process that determines the worth of each job in a company by evaluating the market value of the knowledge, skills, and requirements needed to perform it

Prominent companies like United Airlines, Avis, and Polaroid, offer their employees a chance to "own" part of the company through ESOPs.

cashier makes $20,000 per year, entry-level cashiers at **QuikTrip**, a chain of convenience stores and gas stations, make $40,000 per year. Despite paying employees twice as much as its competitors, QuikTrip is profitable and growing. Compared to other convenience stores, its sales per square foot are 50 percent higher, and its sales per labor hour are 66 percent larger. Furthermore, Quik-Trip trains new workers for two weeks before putting them in stores, teaching them everything from the right way to clean bathrooms to ordering merchandise and tracking inventory. Finally, because the company pays well and invests in its workers, most of its managers work their way up from entry-level cashier jobs. QuikTrip's Mike Thornbrugh says, "They can see that if you work hard, if you're smart, the opportunity to grow within the company is very, very good."[107]

Pay-variability decisions concern the extent to which employees' pay varies with individual and organizational performance. Linking pay to performance is intended to increase employee motivation, effort, and job performance. Piecework, sales commissions, profit sharing, employee stock ownership plans, and stock options are common pay-variability options. For instance, under **piecework** pay plans, employees are paid a set rate for each item produced up to some standard (for example, thirty-five cents per item produced for output up to 100 units per day). After productivity exceeds the standard, employees are paid a set amount for each unit of output over the standard (for example, forty-five cents for each unit above 100 units). Under a sales **commission** plan, salespeople are paid a percentage of the purchase price of items they sell. The more they sell, the more they earn. At inventory

software company **Fishbowl**, every employee's pay is determined in part by how much he or she contributes to company sales. Employees receive a base salary discounted from the market rate, as well as a monthly commission based on how much they were able to directly influence sales. Since a company needs more than just salespeople, the significance of the commission is relative to the function within the company. Programmers receive 80 percent of their pay as base salary and 20 percent as commission, whereas salespeople receive 10 percent of their pay as base salary and 90 percent as commission. Even administrative employees earn commission. In lean months, no commissions are paid, but in good months, employees can double their base salaries through commission payouts. Overall, commissions increase Fishbowl employees' compensation by 19 percent per year.[108]

Because pay plans such as piecework and commissions are based on individual performance, they can reduce the incentive that people have to work together. Therefore, companies also use group rewards (discussed in Chapter 10) and organizational incentives, such as profit sharing, employee stock ownership plans, and stock options, to encourage teamwork and cooperation.

With **profit sharing**, employees receive a portion of the organization's profits over and above their regular compensation. Delta Airlines posted a profit of $5.9 billion in 2015. Thanks to the company's generous profit sharing plan, $1.5 billion of that was distributed to employees—the largest payout in the history of U.S. corporate profit sharing.[109]

Employee stock ownership plans (ESOPs) compensate employees by awarding them shares of the company stock in addition to their regular compensation. Central States Manufacturing, a steel-cutting firm in Lowell, Arkansas, is 100 percent owned by its 517 employees. Six and a half percent of each employee's annual pay goes into a tax-deferred ESOP account. Aaron King, a 60-year-old truck driver with the company for twenty-three years, has accumulated $1.25 million in his ESOP account. Because of the ESOP, he says, "We hold one another accountable.

Piecework a compensation system in which employees are paid a set rate for each item they produce

Commission a compensation system in which employees earn a percentage of each sale they make

Profit sharing a compensation system in which a company pays a percentage of its profits to employees in addition to their regular compensation

Employee stock ownership plan (ESOP) a compensation system that awards employees shares of company stock in addition to their regular compensation

Somebody leaving a bundle of metal where it could be run over—a $3,000 bundle—we go and get that guy and talk to him. [Because] It's going to come out of all of our paychecks."[110] Not all ESOPs are 100 percent employee owned, however. Employees at yogurt company **Chobani** receive stock grants from founder and majority owner Hamdi Ulukaya enabling them to own up to 10 percent of the $3 billion company.[111]

Stock options give employees the right to purchase shares of stock at a set price. Options work like this. Let's say you are awarded the right (or option) to buy 100 shares of stock from the company for $5 a share. If the company's stock price rises to $15 a share, you can exercise your options, sell the stock for $15 a share, come out with $1,000. When you exercise your options, you pay the company $500 (100 shares at $5 a share), but because the stock is selling for $15 in the stock market, you can sell your 100 shares for $1,500 and make $1,000. Of course, as the company's profits and share values increase, stock options become even more valuable to employees. Stock options have no value, however, if the company's stock falls below the option "grant price," the price at which the options have been issued to you. The options you have on 100 shares of stock with a grant price of $5 aren't going to do you a lot of good if the company's stock is worth $2.50. Proponents of stock options argue that this gives employees and managers a strong incentive to work hard to make the company successful. If they do, the company's profits and stock price increase, and their stock options increase in value. If they don't, profits stagnate or turn into losses, and their stock options decrease in value or become worthless. To learn more about ESOPs and stock options, see the National Center for Employee Ownership (www.nceo.org).

The incentive has to be more than just a piece of paper, however. It has to motivate employees with the real opportunity to grow the value of the company and their wealth. **Adworkshop**, a digital marketing agency that does website design and development, search marketing, media buying, and creative work, became an employee-owned company in 2007. Account supervisor Kelly Frady says the ESOP has energized employee commitment. She says, "Everyone knows that you do well, and your stock will rise. It's a driving factor in making the company succeed in the long term."[112] In the United States, 6,795 employee-owned businesses, worth $1.23 trillion, are owned by 13.9 million employees.[113]

Stock options a compensation system that gives employees the right to purchase shares of stock at a set price, even if the value of the stock increases above that price

Pay-structure decisions are concerned with internal pay distributions, meaning the extent to which people in the company receive very different levels of pay.[114] With *hierarchical pay structures*, there are big differences from one pay level to another. The highest pay levels are for people near the top of the pay distribution. The basic idea behind hierarchical pay structures is that large differences in pay between jobs or organizational levels should motivate people to work harder to obtain those higher-paying jobs. Many publicly owned companies have hierarchical pay structures, paying huge salaries to their top managers and CEOs. For example, CEOs of *Fortune* 500 companies, the 500 largest U.S. firms, now make an average of $16.3 million per year, which is 303 times the average employee salary of $53,200.[115]

By contrast, *compressed pay structures* typically have fewer pay levels and smaller differences in pay between levels. Pay is less dispersed and more similar across jobs in the company. The basic idea behind compressed pay structures is that similar pay levels should lead to higher levels of cooperation, feelings of fairness and a common purpose, and better group and team performance.

So should companies choose hierarchical or compressed pay structures? The evidence isn't straightforward, but studies seem to indicate that there are significant problems with the hierarchical approach. The most damaging finding is that there appears to be little link between organizational performance and the pay of top managers.[116] Furthermore, studies of professional athletes indicate that hierarchical pay structures (for example, paying superstars forty to fifty times as much as the lowest-paid athlete on the team) hurt the performance of teams and individual players.[117] Likewise, managers are twice as likely to quit their jobs when their companies have very strong hierarchical pay structures (that is, when they're paid dramatically less than the people above them).[118] For now, it seems that hierarchical pay structures work best for independent work, where it's easy to determine the contributions of individual performers, and little coordination with others is needed to get the job done. In other words, hierarchical pay structures work best when clear links can be drawn between individual performance and individual rewards. By contrast, compressed pay structures, in which everyone receives similar pay, seem to work best for interdependent work, which requires employees to work together. Some companies are pursuing a middle ground: combining hierarchical and compressed pay structures by giving ordinary workers the chance to earn more through ESOPs, stock options, and profit sharing.

11-6b Terminating Employees

The words "You're fired!" may have never been directed at you, but lots of people hear them, as more than 400,000 people a year get fired from their jobs. Getting fired is a terrible thing, but many managers make it even worse by bungling the firing process, needlessly provoking the person who was fired and unintentionally inviting lawsuits. Manager Craig Silverman had to fire the head of a company whom his organization had just acquired. He was specifically instructed to invite her to a meeting, which would require her to travel halfway across the country, and then fire her immediately on arrival. He said, "I literally had to tell the car service to wait. I don't think it ever entered [her] mind that [she] would be terminated."[119] When Zynga terminated almost all of the employees from OMGPOP, a startup company it had acquired a year before, one of the employees tweeted, "I learned via Facebook I was laid off today and @omgpop office is closed. Thanks @zynga for again reminding me how not to operate a business."[120] A computer systems engineer was fired on "Take Your Daughter to Work Day," with his eight-year-old daughter sitting next to him in the human resource manager's office. He and his daughter were both escorted from the building.[121] How would you feel if you had been fired in one of these ways? Though firing is never pleasant (and managers hate firings nearly as much as employees do), managers can do several things to minimize the problems inherent in firing employees.

To start, in most situations, firing should not be the first option. Instead, employees should be given a chance to change their behavior. When problems arise, employees should have ample warning and must be specifically informed as to the nature and seriousness of the trouble they're in. After being notified, they should be given sufficient time to change their behavior. Ron Cohen is CEO and founder of **Acorda Therapeutics**, a company that develops therapies to restore neurological function for people with multiple sclerosis and spinal cord injuries. Cohen first fired an em-

ployee when he was 31 years old. He says it was painful, and, "I wound up hugging the employee, and she was crying on my shoulder." Since then, however, when he fires someone, they've had plenty of opportunities to address performance issues. Says Cohen, "I've learned over the years that if the employee doesn't expect it and know it's coming, you're not doing your job as a manager."[122]

If problems continue, the employees should again be counseled about their job performance, what could be done to improve it, and the possible consequences if things don't change (such as a written reprimand, suspension without pay, or firing). Sometimes this is enough to solve the problem. If the problem isn't corrected after several rounds of warnings and discussions, however, the employee may be terminated.[123]

Second, employees should be fired only for a good reason. Employers used to hire and fire employees under the legal principle of employment at will, which allowed them to fire employees for a good reason, a bad reason, or no reason at all. (Employees could also quit for a good reason, a bad reason, or no reason whenever they desired.) As employees began contesting their firings in court, however, the principle of wrongful discharge emerged. **Wrongful discharge** is a legal doctrine that requires employers to have a job-related reason to terminate employees. In other words, like other major human resource decisions, termination decisions should be made on the basis of job-related factors such as violating company rules or consistently poor performance. And with former employees winning 68 percent of wrongful discharge cases and the average wrongful termination award at \$532,000 and climbing, managers should record the job-related reasons for the termination, document specific instances of rule violations or contin-

> **Wrongful discharge** a legal doctrine that requires employers to have a job-related reason to terminate employees

Dos and Don'ts of Conducting Layoffs in the Digital Age

▶ **DO** conduct layoffs in person. If that's not possible, conduct the layoff live over the phone or via Skype. Email should only be used as a last resort if the employee is perpetually absent and unresponsive.

▶ **DON'T** announce a mass layoff via chat, IM, or other collaborative networking platform.

▶ **DO** shut down access to internal communication systems at the same time employees are being summoned to the meeting or call during which they will learn of the layoff.

▶ **DON'T** let employees figure out that they've been laid off by seeing that their access to email, Slack, IM, or other digital platforms has been disabled.

▶ **DO** keep communication brief and to the point to minimize time for speculation and suspense.

▶ **DON'T** conduct a layoff without a representative from Human Resources present.

▶ **DO** gather the remaining team and let them know who is no longer with the company. Remember to alert remote employees and freelancers.

▶ **DON'T** discuss specifics about why an employee was let go with remaining employees.

▶ Most of all, **DO** be kind, **DO** treat people decently, and **DO** act with integrity.

iStockphoto.com/WillSelarep

Source: L. Dishman, "The New Etiquette of Firing in the Digital Age," *Fast Company*, November 19, 2015, accessed May 1, 2016, http://www.fastcompany.com/3053763/the-future-of-work/the-new-etiquette-of-firing-in-the-digital-age.

ued poor performance, and keep notes and documents from the counseling sessions held with employees.[124]

11-6c Downsizing

Downsizing is the planned elimination of jobs in a company (see box "How to Conduct Layoffs"). Whether it's because of cost cutting, declining market share, overaggressive hiring, or outsourcing, companies typically eliminate 1.11 million to 1.26 million jobs a year.[125] Two-thirds of companies that downsize will downsize a second time within a year. After struggling to successfully integrate its purchase of cellphone maker Nokia, **Microsoft** announced in January 2015 that it had completed a layoff of roughly 12,500 employees in Nokia's manufacturing division.[126] Six months later, Microsoft CEO Satya Nadella announced that the company would lay off an additional 7,800 employees in the phone division and focus on running "a more effective and focused phone portfolio

Downsizing the planned elimination of jobs in a company

while retaining capability for long-term reinvention in mobility."[127]

Does downsizing work? In theory, downsizing is supposed to lead to higher productivity and profits, better stock performance, and increased organizational flexibility. However, numerous studies demonstrate that it doesn't. For instance, a fifteen-year study of downsizing found that downsizing 10 percent of a company's workforce produced only a 1.5 percent decrease in costs; that downsizing firms increased their stock price by only 4.7 percent over three years, compared with 34.3 percent for firms that didn't; and that profitability and productivity were generally not improved by downsizing. Downsizing can also result in the loss of skilled workers who would be expensive to replace when the company grows again. These results make it clear that the best strategy is to conduct effective human resource planning and avoid downsizing altogether. Downsizing should always be a last resort.[128]

If companies do find themselves in financial or strategic situations where downsizing is required for survival, however, they should train managers how to break the news to downsized employees, have senior managers explain in detail why downsizing is necessary, and time the announcement so that employees hear it from the company and not from other sources, such as TV or online reports.[129] Finally, companies should do everything they can to help downsized employees find other jobs. One of the best ways to do this is to use **outplacement services** that provide employment counseling for employees faced with downsizing. Outplacement services often include advice and training in preparing résumés, getting ready for job interviews, and even identifying job opportunities in other companies. Sixty-nine percent of companies provide outplacement services for laid-off employees, 61 percent provide extended health coverage, and most offer up to 26 weeks of severance payments.[130] Offering this kind of assistance can soften the blow from being laid off, preserve goodwill, and lower the risk of future lawsuits.[131]

Companies also need to pay attention to the survivors, the employees remaining after layoffs have occurred. According to author Sylvia Ann Hewlett, the impact of layoffs on remaining employees' morale is severe: 64 percent of employees who survived a layoff felt demotivated, 73 percent felt demoralized, and 74 percent said they simply shut down. "In other words," she says, "just when a company needs its top performers to charge the hill, they retreat to the bunkers."[132] The key to working with layoff survivors, according to Barry Nickerson, president of Dallas-based Marlow Industries, which downsized from 800 to 200 employees, is "Communicate. Communicate. Communicate." Nickerson says, "Every time we had a change we had a meeting to explain exactly what we were doing. We were very open with our employees about where we were financially. We would explain exactly the current status and where we were."[133]

11-6d Retirement

Early retirement incentive programs (ERIPs) offer financial benefits to employees to encourage them to retire early. Companies use ERIPs to reduce the number of employees in the organization, to lower costs by eliminating positions after employees retire, to lower costs by replacing high-paid retirees with lower-paid, less-experienced employees, or to create openings and job opportunities for people inside the company. For example, the state of Wyoming offered its employees a lump-sum bonus, additional insurance benefits, and increased monthly retirement payments to encourage early retirement. Its ERIP must have been fairly attractive, because

56 percent of the state employees eligible for early retirement accepted. Thirty percent of the 437 positions vacated by the early retirees remained empty, saving the state $23.2 million over the first forty-six months of the program and a projected $65 million over eight years. After accounting for the costs of the increased early retirement benefits, the predicted savings came to more than $148,000 per retiree.[134]

Although ERIPs can save companies money, they can pose a big problem for managers if they fail to accurately predict which employees will retire—the good performers or the poor performers—and how many will retire early. Consultant Ron Nicol says, "The thing that doesn't work is just asking for volunteers. You get the wrong volunteers. Some of your best people will feel they can get a job anywhere. Or you have people who are close to retirement and are a real asset to the company."[135] When Progress Energy, in Raleigh, North Carolina, identified 450 jobs it wanted to eliminate with an ERIP, it carefully shared the list of jobs with employees, indicated that layoffs would follow if not enough people took early retirement, and then held eighty meetings with employees to answer questions. Despite this care, an extra 1,000 employees, for a total of 1,450, took the ERIP offer and applied for early retirement![136]

Because of the problems associated with ERIPs, many companies are now offering **phased retirement**, in which employees transition to retirement by working reduced hours over a period of time before completely retiring. The advantage for employees is that they have more free time but continue to earn salaries and benefits without changing companies or careers. The advantage for companies is that it allows them to reduce salaries and hiring and training costs and retain experienced, valuable workers.[137]

11-6e Employee Turnover

In 2016, 74 percent of workers with a job were either actively seeking or open to a new job.[138] **Employee turnover** is the loss of employees who voluntarily choose to leave the company. In general, most companies try to keep the rate of employee turnover low to reduce recruiting,

Outplacement services employment-counseling services offered to employees who are losing their jobs because of downsizing

Early retirement incentive programs (ERIPs) programs that offer financial benefits to employees to encourage them to retire early

Phased retirement employees transition to retirement by working reduced hours over a period of time before completely retiring

Employee turnover loss of employees who voluntarily choose to leave the company

hiring, training, and replacement costs. Not all kinds of employee turnover are bad for organizations, however. In fact, some turnover can actually be good. **Functional turnover** is the loss of poor-performing employees who choose to leave the organization.[139] Functional turnover gives the organization a chance to replace poor performers with better workers. In fact, one study found that simply replacing poor-performing workers with average workers would increase the revenues produced by retail salespeople in an upscale department store by $112,000 per person per year.[140] By contrast, **dysfunctional turnover**, the loss of high performers who choose to leave, is a costly loss to the organization. To minimize dysfunctional turnover, **VoloMetrix, Inc.** uses algorithms to identify so-called flight risks—employees who are gearing up to quit. Software examines anonymized data from employee emails and calendars to identify patterns of communication that indicate the employee is spending less time interacting with colleagues and attending only required meetings. The analysis helps the company predict a departure up to a year in advance, which is important, as the median cost of turnover for most jobs is 21 percent of the employee's annual salary.[141]

Employee turnover should be carefully analyzed to determine whether good or poor performers are choosing to leave the organization. If the company is losing too many high performers, managers should determine the reasons and find ways to reduce the loss of valuable employees. The company may have to raise salary levels, offer enhanced benefits, or improve working conditions to retain skilled workers. One of the best ways to influence functional and dysfunctional turnover is to link pay directly to performance. A study of four salesforces found that when pay was strongly linked to performance via sales commissions and bonuses, poor performers were much more likely to leave (that is, functional turnover). By contrast, poor performers were much more likely to stay when paid large, guaranteed monthly salaries and small sales commissions and bonuses.[142]

Functional turnover loss of poor-performing employees who voluntarily choose to leave a company

Dysfunctional turnover loss of high-performing employees who voluntarily choose to leave a company

STUDY TOOLS 11

LOCATED IN TEXTBOOK
☐ Rip-out and review chapter review card

LOCATED AT WWW.CENGAGEBRAIN.COM
☐ Review key term flashcards and create your own from StudyBits

☐ Track your knowledge and understanding of key concepts, using the concept tracker

☐ Complete practice and graded quizzes to prepare for tests

☐ Complete interactive content within the exposition

☐ View chapter highlight box content at the beginning of each chapter

12 Managing Individuals and a Diverse Workforce

Lewis Tse Pui Lung/Shutterstock.com

LEARNING OUTCOMES

12-1 Describe diversity and explain why it matters.

12-2 Understand the special challenges that the dimensions of surface-level diversity pose for managers.

12-3 Explain how the dimensions of deep-level diversity affect individual behavior and interactions in the workplace.

12-4 Explain the basic principles and practices that can be used to manage diversity.

After you finish this chapter, go to **PAGE 273** for

STUDY TOOLS

Exhibit 12.1
Percent of the Projected Population by Race and Hispanic Origin for the United States: 2015–2060

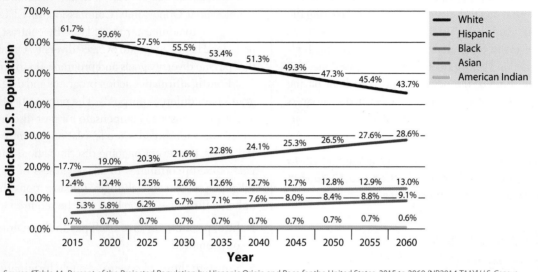

Source: "Table 11. Percent of the Projected Population by Hispanic Origin and Race for the United States: 2015 to 2060 (NP2014-T11)," *U.S. Census Bureau*, accessed May 8, 2016, https://www.census.gov/population/projections/data/national/2014/summarytables.html.

12-1 DIVERSITY: DIFFERENCES THAT MATTER

Workplace diversity as we know it is changing. Exhibit 12.1 shows predictions from the U.S. Census Bureau of how the U.S. population will change over the next forty years. The percentage of white, non-Hispanic Americans in the general population is expected to decline from 61.7 percent in 2015 to 43.7 percent by 2060. By contrast, the percentage of black Americans will increase (from 12.4 to 13%), as will the percentage of Asian Americans (from 5.3 to 9.1%). Meanwhile, the proportion of Native Americans will slightly decline (from 0.7 to 0.6%). The fastest-growing group by far, though, will be Hispanics, who are expected to increase from 17.7 percent of the total population in 2015 to 28.56 percent by 2060. Other significant changes have already occurred. For example, today women hold 46.8 percent of the jobs in the United States, up from 38.2 percent in 1970.[1] Furthermore, white males, who composed 63.9 percent of the workforce in 1950, hold just 42.8 percent of today's jobs.[2]

These rather dramatic changes have taken place in a relatively short time. And, as these trends clearly show, the workforce of the near future will be increasingly Hispanic, Asian American, and female. It will also be older, as the average baby boomer approaches the age of 70 around 2020. Because many boomers are likely to postpone retirement and work well into their 70s to offset predicted reductions in Social Security and Medicare benefits, the workforce may become even older than expected. For instance, between 1994 and 2024, 16- to 24-year olds (16.5–11.3%), 25- to 34-year olds (26.2–22.5%), and 35- to 44-year-olds (26.9–21.3%) will have become a smaller part of the U.S. labor force. By contrast, those 45- to 54-year-olds (18.6–19.4%), 55- to 64-year-olds (6.5–16.6%), 65- to 74-year-olds (2.4–6.5%), and 75 years and older (0.5–1.7%) will all have become larger parts of the U.S. labor force.[3]

Diversity means variety. Therefore, **diversity** exists in organizations when there is a variety of demographic, cultural, and personal differences among the people who work there and the customers who do business there. With 36,000 locations in ninety-two countries, few businesses have the diversity of locations and customers that McDonald's has.[4] Thanks to its global footprint, McDonald's has 160 global menu items, ranging from a

> **Diversity** a variety of demographic, cultural, and personal differences among an organization's employees and customers

Rice Burger (chicken or beef between two rice cakes) in Taiwan, to a Paneer Salsa Wrap (flatbread stuffed with fried paneer cheese, lettuce, red cabbage, celery, mayo, cheddar cheese, and salsa) in India, to McMollettes (English muffins covered with refried beans, cheese, and pico de gallo) in Mexico.[5] Former McDonald's former CEO Don Thompson said that diversity is not about "chasing the number, but chasing the insight, the experience, the background. Diversity fuels innovation, and innovation fuels success. You don't get products like what we've done, you don't create some of the newer products without having the insight." Thompson recognized, however, that progress still needed to be made, saying, "We still have a long way to go, especially as we become a more global company."[6]

You'll begin your exploration of diversity by learning 12-1a that diversity is not affirmative action and 12-1b that diversity makes good business sense.

12-1a Diversity Is Not Affirmative Action

A common misconception is that workplace diversity and affirmative action are the same, yet these concepts differ in several critical ways, including their purpose, how they are practiced, and the reactions they produce. To start, **affirmative action** refers to purposeful steps taken by an organization to create employment opportunities for minorities and women.[7] By contrast, diversity has a broader focus that includes demographic, cultural, and personal differences.

A second difference is that affirmative action is a policy for actively creating diversity, but diversity can exist even if organizations don't take purposeful steps to create it. A local restaurant located near a university in a major city is likely to have a more diverse group of employees than one located in a small town. So, organizations can achieve diversity without affirmative action. Conversely, affirmative action does not guarantee diversity. An organization can create employment opportunities for women and minorities yet not have a diverse workforce.

A third important difference is that affirmative action is required by law for private employers with fifty or more employees, whereas diversity is not. Affirmative action originated with Executive Order 11246 (www.dol.gov /ofccp/regs/compliance/fs11246.htm) but is also related to the 1964 Civil Rights Act, which bans discrimination in voting, public places, federal government programs, federally supported public education, and employment. Title VII of the Civil Rights Act (www.eeoc .gov/laws/statutes/titlevii.cfm) requires that workers have equal employment opportunities when being hired or promoted. More specifically, Title VII prohibits companies from discriminating on the basis of race, color, religion, sex, or national origin. Title VII also created the Equal Employment Opportunity Commission, or EEOC (www .eeoc.gov), to administer these laws. By contrast, there is no federal law or agency to oversee diversity. Organizations that pursue diversity goals and programs do so voluntarily.

Fourth, affirmative action programs and diversity programs have different purposes. The purpose of affirmative action programs is to compensate for past discrimination, which was widespread when legislation was introduced in the 1960s; to prevent ongoing discrimination; and to provide equal opportunities to all, regardless of race, color, religion, sex, or national origin. Organizations that fail to uphold affirmative action laws may be required to

▸ hire, promote, or give back pay to those not hired or promoted;

▸ reinstate those who were wrongly terminated;

▸ pay attorneys' fees and court costs for those who bring charges against them; or

▸ take other actions that make individuals whole by returning them to the condition or place they would have been had it not been for discrimination.[8]

Affirmative action purposeful steps taken by an organization to create employment opportunities for minorities and women

Consequently, affirmative action is basically a punitive approach.[9] By contrast, the general purpose of diversity programs is to create a positive work environment where no one is advantaged or disadvantaged, where "we" is everyone, where everyone can do his or her best work, where differences are respected and not ignored, and where everyone feels comfortable.[10] So, unlike affirmative action, which punishes companies for not achieving specific sex and race ratios in their workforces, diversity programs seek to benefit both organizations and their employees by encouraging organizations to value all kinds of differences.

Despite the overall success of affirmative action in making workplaces much fairer than they used to be, many people argue that some affirmative action programs unconstitutionally offer preferential treatment to females and minorities at the expense of other employees, a view accepted by some courts.[11] The American Civil Rights institute successfully campaigned via state ballot initiatives to ban race- and sex-based affirmative action in college admissions, government hiring, and government contracting programs in California (1996), Washington (1998), and Michigan (2006). Led by Ward Connerly, the institute backed similar efforts in Arizona, Colorado, Missouri, Nebraska, and Oklahoma in 2008. In an April 2014 decision, the U.S. Supreme Court ruled 6-2 that state ballot initiatives banning race- and sex-based action are constitutional.[12] Opponents of affirmative action, like Connerly, believe that affirmative action policies establish only surface-level diversity and, ironically, promote preferential treatment.[13]

Research shows that people who have gotten a job or promotion as a result of affirmative action are commonly viewed as unqualified, even when clear evidence of their qualifications exists.[14] This effect is so robust that those benefitting from affirmative action experience doubts about their competence.[15] So, while affirmative action programs have created opportunities for minorities and women, they unintentionally produce persistent doubts and self-doubts regarding the qualifications of those who are believed to have obtained their jobs as a result of affirmative action.

12-1b Diversity Makes Good Business Sense

Those who support the idea of diversity in organizations often ignore its business aspects altogether, claiming instead that diversity is simply the right thing to do. Yet diversity actually makes good business sense in several ways: cost savings, attracting and retaining talent, and driving business growth.[16]

Diversity helps companies with *cost savings* by reducing turnover, decreasing absenteeism, and avoiding expensive lawsuits.[17] Because of lost productivity and the cost of recruiting and selecting new workers, companies lose substantial amounts of money when employees quit their jobs. In fact, turnover costs typically amount to more than 90 percent of employees' salaries. By this estimate, if an executive who makes $200,000 leaves, the organization will have to spend approximately $180,000 to find a replacement; even the lowest-paid hourly workers can cost the company as much as $10,000 when they quit. Because turnover rates for African Americans average 40 percent higher than for whites, and since women quit their jobs at twice the rate men do, companies that manage diverse workforces well can cut costs by reducing the turnover rates of these employees.[18] And, with women absent from work 60 percent more often than men, primarily because of family responsibilities, diversity programs that address the needs of female workers can also reduce the substantial costs of absenteeism.

Diversity programs also save companies money by helping them avoid discrimination lawsuits, which have increased by a factor of twenty since 1970 and quadrupled just since 1995. In one survey conducted by the Society for Human Resource Management, 78 percent of respondents reported that diversity efforts helped them avoid lawsuits and litigation costs.[19] In fact, because companies lose two-thirds of all discrimination cases that go to trial, the best strategy from a business perspective is

Bikeriderlondon/Shutterstock.com

not to be sued for discrimination at all. When companies lose, the average individual settlement amounts to more than $600,000.[20] And settlement costs can be substantially higher in class-action lawsuits, in which individuals join together to sue a company as a group.

Diversity also makes business sense by helping companies *attract and retain talented workers*.[21] Female employees at **Google** were once twice as likely as male employees to quit the company. Company data revealed that many of the women who left were young mothers. Google head of human resources Laszlo Bock responded by substantially increasing parental leave at the company. Biological mothers now get eighteen weeks of fully paid leave for the birth of a child, and mothers who experience complications during childbirth receive twenty-two weeks. Primary caregivers, adoptive caregivers, and surrogate caregivers are also eligible for twelve weeks of fully paid time off. Now, a new mother is no more likely to leave Google than the average employee.[22] Diversity-friendly companies tend to attract better *and* more diverse job applicants. Very simply, diversity begets more diversity. Companies that make *Fortune* magazine's list of the fifty best companies for minorities or are recognized by *Working Women* and *Diversity Inc.* magazine have already attracted a diverse and talented pool of job applicants. But, after being recognized for their efforts, they subsequently experience big increases in both the quality and the diversity of people who apply for jobs. Research shows that companies with acclaimed diversity programs not only attract more talented workers but also have higher performance in the stock market.[23]

The third way that diversity makes business sense is by *driving business growth*. In the United States today, there are 42 million African Americans, 55.5 million Hispanic Americans, and 17.2 million Asian Americans with, respectively, $1 trillion, $1.2 trillion, and $713 billion in purchasing power. Given the size of those markets, it shouldn't be surprising that a survey conducted by the Society for Human Resource Management found that tapping into "diverse customers and markets" was the number-one reason managers gave for implementing diversity programs.[24] Demand for air travel in Asia is exploding as 100 million new passengers fly every year. To meet surging demand, the region's airlines will need to add 226,000 pilots over the next twenty years—far more than the current pool of job candidates. Despite needing more pilots, many Asian airlines won't hire women out of concern about male and female pilots sharing bunk space on long flights (which are common in the region). However, some carriers like **Vietnam Airlines** have begun actively recruiting women by creating flexible, family-friendly schedules. Mireille Goyer, founder of the

Carnival CEO Arnold Donald gives a toast at the Los Angeles World Cruise Center on January 24, 2016.

Institute for Women of Aviation Worldwide, believes that refusing to recruit women is shortsighted: "Arbitrarily reducing the potential pool . . . has strangled growth and led to today's situation."[25] **Boeing** executive Sherry Carbary, whose team assists Asian airlines in training pilots, agrees: "There is such an enormous demand that the gender bias will have to be pushed aside."[26]

Diversity also helps companies grow through higher-quality problem solving. Though diverse groups initially have more difficulty working together than homogeneous groups, diverse groups eventually establish a rapport and do a better job of identifying problems and generating alternative solutions, the two most important steps in problem solving.[27] When Arnold Donald became CEO of **Carnival Corporation**, his first mission was to fix operational issues and diversify the customer base. To accomplish this, he hired a wide variety of new executives at seven of the company's ten cruise lines. Now, Carnival's leadership team is a broader mix of ethnicities, genders, and sexual orientations. Emboldened by Donald's focus on diversity, president of **Princess Cruises** Jan Swartz worked with her team to redesign bedding for its typical customer—a fifty three-year-old woman going through menopause and suffering from night sweats and hot flashes. While luxurious, the new bedding doesn't trap heat and is layered so that it can easily be taken on and off. Attention to different customers' needs is exactly what Donald was aiming for: "I guarantee if you get a diverse group of people aligned around a common objective with a process to work together, they will out-engineer, out-solution a homogeneous team 90 percent of the time."[28] Carnival's stock price has risen 53 percent under Donald and its profits are up 15 percent to $1.2 billion.

12-2 SURFACE-LEVEL DIVERSITY

A survey that asked managers "What is meant by diversity to decision makers in your organization?" found that they most frequently mentioned race, culture, sex, national origin, age, religion, and regional origin.[29] When managers describe workers this way, they are focusing on surface-level diversity. **Surface-level diversity** consists of differences that are immediately observable, typically unchangeable, and easy to measure.[30] In other words, independent observers can usually agree on dimensions of surface-level diversity, such as another person's age, sex, race/ethnicity, or physical capabilities.

Most people start by using surface-level diversity to categorize or stereotype other people. But those initial categorizations typically give way to deeper impressions formed from knowledge of others' behaviors and psychological characteristics such as personality and attitudes.[31] When you think of others this way, you are focusing on deep-level diversity. **Deep-level diversity** consists of differences that are communicated through verbal and nonverbal behaviors and are learned only through extended interaction with others.[32] Examples of deep-level diversity include personality differences, attitudes, beliefs, and values. In other words, as people in diverse workplaces get to know each other, the initial focus on surface-level differences such as age, race/ethnicity, sex, and physical capabilities is replaced by deeper, more complex knowledge of coworkers.

If managed properly, the shift from surface- to deep-level diversity can accomplish two things.[33] First, 95 percent of studies on this issue show that getting to know and understand each other reduces prejudice and conflict.[34] Second, it can lead to stronger social integration. **Social integration** is the degree to which group members are psychologically attracted to working with each other to accomplish a common objective, or, as one manager put it, "working together to get the job done."

Because age, sex, race/ethnicity, and disabilities are usually immediately observable, many managers and workers use these dimensions of surface-level diversity to form initial impressions and categorizations of coworkers, bosses, customers, or job applicants. Whether intentional or not, sometimes those initial categorizations and impressions lead to decisions or behaviors that discriminate. Consequently, these dimensions of surface-level diversity pose special challenges for managers who are trying to create positive work environments where everyone feels comfortable, and no one is advantaged or disadvantaged.

Let's learn more about those challenges and the ways that **12-2a age, 12-2b sex, 12-2c race/ethnicity,** *and* **12-2d mental or physical disabilities can affect decisions and behaviors in organizations.**

12-2a Age

Age discrimination is treating people differently (for example, in hiring and firing, promotion, and compensation decisions) because of their age. The victims of age discrimination are almost always older workers, and the discrimination is based on the assumption that "you can't teach an old dog new tricks." It's commonly believed that older workers are less motivated, less productive, more prone to illness and accidents, not interested in learning new things, cost more, and make greater—more expensive—use of health care benefits.[35] Facebook founder and CEO Mark Zuckerberg once said, "I want to stress the importance of being young and technical . . . Young people are just smarter."[36] Consistent with that stereotype (and the fact that the average age of employees at Google, Facebook, LinkedIn, and Apple are 20, 28, 29, and 31 respectively), Apple, Yahoo!, and Dropbox are among the companies that have specified preferences for "new grads" in job openings. Because that clearly violates the Age Discrimination in Employment Act, companies such as Zipcar, Panasonic, and, yes, Facebook, now list being a "digital native" as a job requirement.[37]

Surface-level diversity differences such as age, sex, race/ethnicity, and physical disabilities that are observable, typically unchangeable, and easy to measure

Deep-level diversity differences such as personality and attitudes that are communicated through verbal and nonverbal behaviors and are learned only through extended interaction with others

Social integration the degree to which group members are psychologically attracted to working with each other to accomplish a common objective

Age discrimination treating people differently (for example in hiring and firing, promotion, and compensation decisions) because of their age

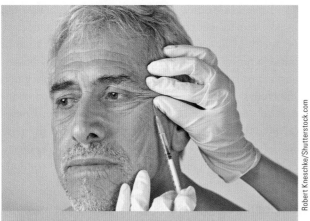

Ageism in the tech sector has caused plastic surgery to surge in Silicon Valley.

Ingrid Fredeen of **NAVEX Global**, a supplier of ethics and compliance programs, says the term makes her cringe because it implies that "only young applicants need apply."[38] The increase in age discrimination claims filed with the EEOC, 20,144 in 2015, up from 15,785 in 1997, suggests that discriminatory attitudes like this still exist. [39]

So, what's reality and what's myth? Do older employees actually cost more? In some ways, they do. The older people are and the longer they stay with a company, the more the company pays for salaries, pension plans, and vacation time. But older workers cost companies less, too, because they show better judgment, care more about the quality of their work, and are less likely to quit, show up late, or be absent, the cost of which can be substantial.[40] A meta-analysis combining the results of 118 individual studies also found that older workers are more likely to help others at work and are much less likely to use drugs or alcohol at work, engage in workplace aggression, or be involved in accidents. The authors of this study concluded, "The stereotype of older workers as difficult colleagues, then, seems largely unfounded."[41]

As for the widespread belief that job performance declines with age, the scientific evidence clearly refutes this stereotype. Performance does not decline with age, regardless of the type of job.[42]

What can companies do to reduce age discrimination?[43] To start, managers need to recognize that age discrimination is much more pervasive than they probably think. Whereas "old" used to mean mid-50s, in today's workplace "old" is closer to 40. When 773 CEOs were asked, "At what age does a worker's productivity peak?" the average age they gave was 43. Thus, age discrimination may be affecting more workers because perceptions about age have changed. In addition, with the aging of the baby boomers, age discrimination is more likely to occur simply because there are millions more older workers than there used to be. In 1992, one in twelve women worked beyond the age of 65. In 2016, one in seven do. By 2024, one in five women age 65 and older will work.[44] And, because studies show that interviewers rate younger job candidates as more qualified (even when they aren't), companies need to train managers and recruiters to make hiring and promotion decisions on the basis of qualifications, not age.

Companies also need to monitor the extent to which older workers receive training. The U.S. Bureau of Labor Statistics found that the number of training courses and number of hours spent in training drop dramatically

ONE IS THE LONELIEST NUMBER

Even as the number of women in the managerial ranks of U.S. companies is growing, in many companies, it seems there is an upper limit. Researchers have found that, if there is a woman on an executive team, then the chances of another woman joining the team drops by 51 percent. Among the 1,500 Standard & Poor's companies, 8.7 percent have a top female manager, but when one of the top five executive positions in the company is held by a woman, she is usually the only one on the team. Researcher Cristian Dezso speculates that top male managers may just want to fill a quota and "check a box. They are one and done."

Source: R. Feintzeig, "One Often Appears to Be the Limit for Women at the Top," *Wall Street Journal*, April 8, 2015, B6.

Exhibit 12.2
Women's Earnings as a Percentage of Men's, 1979–2014

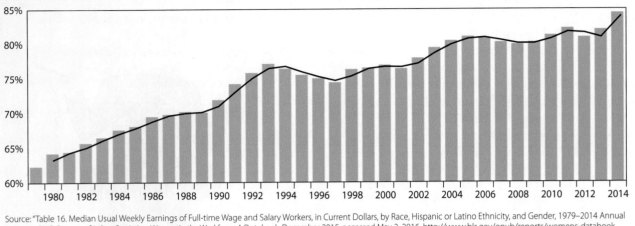

Source: "Table 16. Median Usual Weekly Earnings of Full-time Wage and Salary Workers, in Current Dollars, by Race, Hispanic or Latino Ethnicity, and Gender, 1979–2014 Annual Averages," U.S. Bureau of Labor Statistics, *Women in the Workforce: A Databook*, December 2015, accessed May 2, 2016, http://www.bls.gov/opub/reports/womens-databook /archive/women-in-the-labor-force-a-databook-2015.pdf.

after employees reach the age of 44.[45] Finally, companies need to ensure that younger and older workers interact with each other. One study found that younger workers generally hold positive views of older workers and that the more time they spent working with older coworkers, the more positive their attitudes became.[46]

12-2b Sex

Sex discrimination occurs when people are treated differently because of their sex. Sex discrimination and racial/ethnic discrimination (discussed in the next section) are often associated with the so-called **glass ceiling**, the invisible barrier that prevents women and minorities from advancing to the top jobs in organizations.

To what extent do women face sex discrimination in the workplace? Almost every year, the EEOC receives between 23,000 and 30,000 charges of sex-based discrimination.[47] In some ways, there is much less sex discrimination than there used to be. For example, whereas women held only 17 percent of managerial jobs in 1972, today they hold 52 percent of managerial and professional jobs, and they hold 47 percent of all jobs in the workplace.[48] Likewise, women own 40 percent of all U.S. businesses. Whereas women owned 2.8 million businesses in 1982 and 5.4 million businesses in 1997, today they own 9.4 million businesses, generating $1.5 trillion in sales and employing more than 7.9 million people![49] Finally, though women still earn less than men on average, the differential is narrowing, as Exhibit 12.2 shows. Women earned 83 percent of what men did in 2014, up from 63 percent in 1979.[50]

Although progress is being made, sex discrimination continues to operate via the glass ceiling at higher levels in organizations, as shown in Exhibit 12.3. For instance, while the trends are going upward, women were the top earners in just 8.1 percent of companies in 2014.[51] Likewise, only 14.6 percent of corporate officers (that is, top management) were women, and the numbers were even lower for women of color. Indra K. Nooyi, PepsiCo's CEO, and Ursula Burns, Xerox's CEO, are the only women of color heading *Fortune* 500 companies.[52] In fact, only 21 of the 500 largest companies in the United States have women CEOs.[53] Similarly, only 19.2 percent of the members of U.S. corporate boards of directors are women.[54]

Finally, a meta-analysis of 97 studies covering 378,850 employees in multiple industries over three decades found that, "Across occupations ranging from bank tellers to accountants, industries ranging from IT to healthcare, and jobs ranging from mundane to challenging, our results show that sex differences in organizational rewards were almost 14 times larger than sex differences in performance evaluations. Moreover, performance differences did not explain reward differences between men and women."[55]

Is sex discrimination the sole reason for the slow rate at which women have been rewarded and promoted to middle and upper levels of management and corporate boards? Some studies

Sex discrimination treating people differently because of their sex

Glass ceiling the invisible barrier that prevents women and minorities from advancing to the top jobs in organizations

Scrub Résumés to Remove Bias

In an effort to reduce hiring biases and improve workplace diversity, some companies have begun using a technique called blind hiring. With blind hiring, information such as a person's name and alma mater are redacted from his or her résumé and work sample before reviewing them. This way, the hiring manager can evaluate candidates based solely on their past experiences and actual work performance. The goal is to reduce unconscious biases that may result in giving preferential treatment to a candidate of a particular sex or ethnicity, or with work experience at a prominent company or a degree from an elite school, things that are not always accurate predictors of a good fit.

Source: R. Feintzeig, "Tossing Out the Résumé in Favor of 'Blind Hiring,'" *Wall Street Journal*, January 6, 2016, B1.

Exhibit 12.3
Women at *Fortune* 500 and 1000 Companies

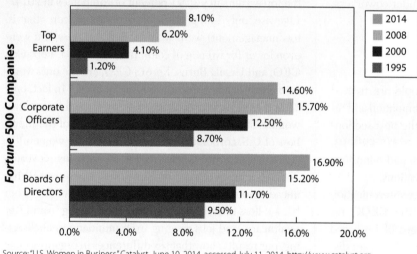

Source: "U.S. Women in Business," Catalyst, June 10, 2014, accessed July 11, 2014, http://www.catalyst.org/knowledge/us-women-business-0.

to 73 percent of women with two or more children.[58] As those numbers suggest, women are historically much more likely than men to prioritize family over work at some time in their careers. Even Indra Nooyi, PepsiCo's CEO, says, "My observation . . . is that the biological clock and the career clock are in total conflict with each other. Total, complete conflict. When you have to have kids you have to build your career. Just as you're rising to middle management your kids need you because they're teenagers, they need you for the teenage years . . . And as you grow even more, your parents need you because they're aging. So . . . we cannot have it all."[59]

indicate that it's not.[56] In some instances, the slow progress appears to be due to career and job choices. Whereas men's career and job choices are often driven by the search for higher pay and advancement, women are more likely to choose jobs or careers that also give them a greater sense of accomplishment, more control over their work schedules, and easier movement in and out of the workplace.[57] For instance, 82 percent of women without children are interested in being promoted to the next level compared

Beyond these reasons, however, it's likely that sex discrimination does play a role in women's slow progress into the higher levels of management. And even if you don't think so, many of the women you work with probably do. In fact, studies indicate that 90 percent of women believe the glass ceiling hurts their careers, and 80 percent said they left their last job because of the glass ceiling and that starting a business allows them to avoid the career limitations of the glass ceiling.[60] Discrimination is believed to be the most significant factor behind the lack of women at top levels of management.[61]

So, what can companies do to make sure that women have the same opportunities for development and advancement as men? One strategy is mentoring, or pairing promising female executives with senior executives from whom they can seek advice and support.[62] **Salesforce**, a leading customer relationship management software company, has a mentoring program for women. So, cofounder Parker Harris, who encourages Salesforce managers to speak up about their ambitions, was surprised when he discovered that Leyla Seka, who ran their mobile apps unit, was preparing to leave. Seka wanted to lead a larger division but thought her bosses didn't think she was capable, so she didn't share her aspirations. In fact, her bosses found her so capable, they hired her to run Desk.com, a company recently acquired by Salesforce, and coached her as she developed her leadership skills. "I've never had more fun at work, and I've never felt more challenged," she says. "I almost missed this opportunity by shutting the doors on myself."[63] In fact, 91 percent of female executives had a mentor at some point and felt their mentor was critical to their advancement.

Another strategy is to make sure that male-dominated social activities don't unintentionally exclude women. Nearly half (47%) of women in the workforce believe that "exclusion from informal networks" makes it more difficult to advance their careers (by contrast, just 18% of male CEOs thought this was a problem). For instance, at company conferences, **Rockwell Automation** has replaced cocktail receptions (that is, hanging out at the bar), which are a traditional social function at conferences, with alternative activities, such as chili cook-offs.[64] Another is to designate a go-to person other than their supervisors that women can talk to if they believe that they are being held back or discriminated against because of their sex. That person, of course, must have the knowledge and authority to conduct a fair, confidential internal investigation.[65]

12-2c Race/Ethnicity

Racial and ethnic discrimination occurs when people are treated differently because of their race or ethnicity. To what extent is racial and ethnic discrimination a factor in the workplace? Every year, the EEOC receives between 26,000 and 36,000 charges of racial discrimination, which is more than any other type of charge of discrimination.[66] However, it is true that since the passage of the 1964 Civil Rights Act and Title VII, there is much less racial and ethnic discrimination than there used to be. For example, twenty-five *Fortune* 500 firms had an African American (5), Hispanic (9), or Asian (9) CEO in 2016, whereas none did

in 1988.[67] Nonetheless, strong racial and ethnic disparities still exist. For instance, whereas 11.7 percent of employed Americans are black, only 9.2 percent of managers and 3.6 percent of CEOs are black. Similarly, 16.4 percent of employed Americans are Hispanic, but only 9.1 percent are managers and 5.5 percent are CEOs. By contrast, Asians, who constitute 5.8 percent of employed workers, are better represented, holding 7.7 percent of management jobs and 4.7 percent of CEO jobs.[68]

What accounts for the disparities between the percentages of minority groups in the general population and their smaller representation in management positions? Some studies have found that the disparities are due to preexisting differences in training, education, and skills. When African Americans, Hispanics, Asian Americans, and whites have similar skills, training, and education, they are much more likely to have similar jobs and salaries.[69]

Other studies, however, provide increasingly strong direct evidence of racial or ethnic discrimination in the workplace. For example, one study directly tested hiring discrimination by sending pairs of black and white males and pairs of Hispanic and non-Hispanic males to apply for the same jobs. Each pair had résumés with identical qualifications, and all were trained to present themselves in similar ways to minimize differences during interviews. The researchers found that the white males got three times as many job offers as the black males, and that the non-Hispanic males got three times as many offers as the Hispanic males.[70] Another study, which used similar methods to test hiring procedures at 149 different companies, found that whites received 10 percent more interviews than blacks. Half of the whites interviewed then received job offers, but only 11 percent of the blacks. And when job offers were made, blacks were much more likely to be offered lower-level positions, while whites were more likely to be offered jobs at higher levels than the jobs they had applied for.[71]

Critics of these studies point out that it's nearly impossible to train different applicants to give identical responses in job interviews and that differences in interviewing skills may have somehow accounted for the results. However, researchers at the University of Chicago mailed thousands of résumés to employers that were identical except for the candidate's name, which was either stereotypically black, such as "Jamal," or stereotypically white, such as "Brendan." Applicants with the "white" name were called back for interviews 50 percent more often those with "black" names.[72] Comparable studies in the United Kingdom with Indian and

> **Racial and ethnic discrimination** treating people differently because of their race or ethnicity

Pakistani applicants and in Australia with Greek and Vietnamese applicants produced similar results.[73] In short, the evidence indicates that there is strong and persistent racial and ethnic discrimination in the hiring processes of many organizations.

What can companies do to make sure that people of all racial and ethnic backgrounds have the same opportunities?[74] Start by looking at the numbers. Compare the hiring rates of whites with the hiring rates for racial and ethnic applicants. Do the same thing for promotions within the company. See if nonwhite workers quit the company at higher rates than white workers. Also, survey employees to compare white and nonwhite employees' satisfaction with jobs, bosses, and the company as well as their perceptions concerning equal treatment. Next, if the numbers indicate racial or ethnic disparities, consider employing a private firm to test your hiring system by having applicants of different races with identical qualifications apply for jobs in your company, or by data mining your application criteria.[75] Data analysis software showed **Xerox** that customer-service employees with the shortest daily commutes stayed with the company the longest. Nevertheless, managers stopped screening job applicants for commute times because they thought that doing so would put applicants from minority neighborhoods, which were generally farther from Xerox offices, at a disadvantage.[76]

Another step companies can take is to eliminate unclear selection and promotion criteria. Vague criteria allow decision makers to focus on nonjob-related characteristics that may unintentionally lead to employment discrimination. Instead, selection and promotion criteria should spell out the specific knowledge, skills, abilities, education, and experience needed to perform a job well. Finally, as explained in Chapter 11, "Managing Human Resource Systems," it is also important to train managers and others who make hiring and promotion decisions.

12-2d Mental or Physical Disabilities

According to the Americans with Disabilities Act (www.ada.gov), a **disability** is a mental or physical impairment that substantially limits one or more major life activities.[77] Approximately 39 million Americans—12.6 percent of the population—are disabled.[78] **Disability discrimination** occurs when people are treated differently because of their disabilities. To what extent is disability discrimination a factor in the workplace? Similar to studies examining racial discrimination, researchers

Disability a mental or physical impairment that substantially limits one or more major life activities

Disability discrimination treating people differently because of their disabilities

sent out 6,000 fictitious résumés and cover letters for jobs (in accounting). One résumé was for a highly qualified candidate with six years of experience, and another was for an inexperienced candidate a year out of college. One of three different cover letters accompanied each résumé: one for an applicant with no disabilities, one for an applicant with an injured spinal cord, and one for an applicant with Asperger's Syndrome, which makes interpersonal relationships and communication difficult. Overall, applicants with disabilities were 26 percent less likely to be contacted by an employer for further steps in the hiring process. Interestingly, experienced applicants were 34 percent less likely to be contacted by employers.[79] Indeed, while 76.3 percent of the U.S. population was employed in 2012, only 33.5 percent of disabled people had jobs. Individuals with sensory disabilities, such as blindness (37.7%) or deafness (50.2%), had the highest employment rates; those with self-care disabilities (16.2%), who can't dress or bathe themselves, or with independent living disabilities (15.7%), who can't do basic errands such as shopping or go to the doctor without assistance, were the least likely to work.[80]

What accounts for the disparities between those with and without disabilities? Contrary to popular opinion, it has nothing to do with how well people with disabilities can do their jobs. Studies show that as long as companies make reasonable accommodations for disabilities (for example, changing procedures or equipment), people with disabilities perform their jobs just as well as people without disabilities. Furthermore, they have better safety records and are not any more likely to be absent or quit their jobs.[81] At a recent disability summit sponsored by the state of Michigan, speakers from Walgreens, Meijer, and Trijicon said that, compared to employees without

A recent summit in Michigan gave speakers from companies like Walgreens, Meijer and Trijicon a chance to discuss the benefits of hiring employees with disabilities.

Tupungato/Shutterstock.com

disabilities, disabled employees were more dependable, took less time off, and had better safety records.[82]

What can companies do to make sure that people with disabilities have the same opportunities as everyone else? Beyond educational efforts to address incorrect stereotypes and expectations, a good place to start is to commit to reasonable workplace accommodations such as changing work schedules, reassigning jobs, acquiring or modifying equipment, or providing assistance when needed. Accommodations for disabilities needn't be expensive. According to the Job Accommodation Network, 58 percent of accommodations don't cost anything at all, while those with costs are typically just $500.[83]

At Laser Soft Info Systems, an India-based software developer, 15 percent of the staff has some disability, with causes ranging from hearing, speech, and sight impairment to cerebral palsy, polio, or accidents, and work throughout the company. "We don't have any rule that teams must take a minimum or maximum number of people with disabilities in their roles. They are recruited like any other associate," says Suresh Kamath, Laser Soft's founder and president. Laser Soft's accommodations include wheelchair ramps, wider office aisles, elevators with audio controls for the blind, and facilitators to provide physical assistance when an employee asks for it. The company also allows employees to work from home should it become difficult to make it into the office.[84]

Some of the accommodations just described involve *assistive technology* that gives workers with disabilities the tools they need to overcome their disabilities. Providing workers with assistive technology is also an effective strategy to recruit, retain, and enhance the productivity of people with disabilities. According to the National Council on Disability, 92 percent of workers with disabilities who use assistive technology report that it helps them work faster and better, 81 percent indicate that it helps them work longer hours, and 67 percent say that it is critical to getting a job.[85] To learn about assistive technologies that can help workers with disabilities, see AbleData (www.abledata.com), which lists 40,000 products, or the National Rehabilitation Information Center (www.naric.com), which provides information for specific disabilities.

Finally, companies should actively recruit qualified workers with disabilities. Numerous organizations, such as Mainstream, Kidder Resources, the American Council of the Blind (www.acb.org), the National Federation of the Blind (http://nfb.org), the National Association of the Deaf (www.nad.org), the Epilepsy Foundation (www.epilepsy.com), and the National Amputation Foundation (www.nationalamputation.org), actively work with employers to find jobs for qualified people with disabilities. Companies can also place advertisements in publications, such as *Ca-reers and the disABLED*, or on online job boards, such as Recruit AbilityJobs.com or RecruitDisability.org, that specifically target workers with disabilities.

12-3 DEEP-LEVEL DIVERSITY

As you learned in Section 12-2, people often use the dimensions of surface-level diversity to form initial impressions about others. Over time, however, as people have a chance to get to know each other, initial impressions based on age, sex, race/ethnicity, and mental or physical disabilities give way to deeper impressions based on behavior and psychological characteristics. When we think of others this way, we are focusing on deep-level diversity. *Deep-level diversity* represents differences that can be learned only through extended interaction with others. Examples of deep-level diversity include differences in personality, attitudes, beliefs, and values. In short, recognizing deep-level diversity requires getting to know and understand one another better. And that matters, because it can result in less prejudice, discrimination, and conflict in the workplace. These changes can then lead to better *social integration*, the degree to which organizational or group members are psychologically attracted to working with each other to accomplish a common objective.

Stop for a second and think about your boss (or the boss you had in your last job). What words would you use to describe him or her? Is your boss introverted or extraverted? Emotionally stable or unstable? Agreeable or disagreeable? Organized or disorganized? Open or closed to new experiences? When you describe your boss or others in this way, what you're really doing is describing dispositions and personality.

A **disposition** is the tendency to respond to situations and events in a predetermined manner. **Personality** is the relatively stable set of behaviors, attitudes, and emotions displayed over time that makes people different from each other.[86] For example, which of your aunts or uncles is a little offbeat, a little out of the ordinary? What were they like when you were small? What are they like now? Chances are that she or he is pretty much the same wacky person. In other words, the person's core personality hasn't changed. For example, as a child, Kip Tindell, CEO of the Container Store,

Disposition the tendency to respond to situations and events in a predetermined manner

Personality the relatively stable set of behaviors, attitudes, and emotions displayed over time that makes people different from each other

would reorganize the pantry or closets when his parents were out of the house. "If your house is unbelievably messy, I probably won't come back to visit. I'll meet you at a restaurant. I'm just not comfortable around mess. You don't have to be obsessive-compulsive about it. Well, OK, maybe just a tiny bit."[87] Research conducted in different cultures, different settings, and different languages has shown that five basic dimensions of personality account for most of the differences in peoples' behaviors, attitudes, and emotions (or why your boss is the way he or she is!). The *Big Five Personality Dimensions* are extraversion, emotional stability, agreeableness, conscientiousness, and openness to experience.[88]

EXTROVERT

INTROVERT

Extraversion is the degree to which someone is active, assertive, gregarious, sociable, talkative, and energized by others. In contrast to extraverts, introverts tend to be focused, thoughtful, quiet, reserved, and energized by ideas. For the best results in the workplace, introverts and extraverts should be correctly matched to their jobs. Research shows that being talkative and assertive is not correlated with greater insight, and that those who speak first and more often (usually extraverts) are not more capable than less talkative people.[89] Professor Stephen Garras is often frustrated by the premium placed on extraversion, saying, "I worry that there are people who are put in positions of authority because they're good talkers, but they don't have good ideas. It's so easy to confuse schmoozing ability with talent . . . we put too much of a premium on presenting and not enough on substance and critical thinking."[90]

Emotional stability is the degree to which someone is not angry, depressed, anxious, emotional, insecure, or excitable. People who are emotionally stable respond well to stress. In other words, they can maintain a calm, problem-solving attitude in even the toughest situations (for example, conflict, hostility, dangerous conditions, or extreme time pressures). By contrast, emotionally unstable people find it difficult to handle the most basic demands of their jobs under only moderately stressful situations and become distraught, tearful, self-doubting, and anxious. Emotional stability is particularly important for high-stress jobs such as police work, firefighting, emergency medical treatment, piloting planes, or commanding Tragically, investigators found emotional stability was a factor in the deliberate crash of a Germanwings flight that killed 150 people. The co-pilot, who had struggled with depression before, used Google, just days before to search for ways to commit suicide.[91] When the pilot left the cabin for a bathroom break, the co-pilot locked the cabin door and set the plane's auto pilot to descend to a lower altitude where it slammed into a mountain. While most Asian airlines conduct regular psychological assessments of their pilots, U.S. and European airlines only screen for emotional stability issues during initial pilot recruitment and training, or if staff members report unusual behavior.[92]

Agreeableness is the degree to which someone is cooperative, polite, flexible, forgiving, good-natured, tolerant, and trusting. Basically, agreeable people are easy to work with and be around, whereas disagreeable people are distrusting and difficult to work with and be around. A number of companies have made general attitude or agreeableness the most important factor in their hiring decisions.

Conscientiousness is the degree to which someone is organized, hardworking, responsible, persevering, thorough, and achievement oriented. One management consultant wrote about his experiences with a conscientious employee: "He arrived at our first meeting with a typed copy of his daily schedule, a sheet bearing his home and office phone numbers, addresses, and his email address. At his request, we established a timetable for meetings for the next four months. He showed up on time every time, day planner in hand, and carefully listed tasks and due dates. He questioned me exhaustively if he didn't understand an assignment and returned on schedule with the completed work or with a clear explanation as to why it wasn't done."[93] Conscientious employees are also more likely to engage in positive behaviors, such as helping new employees, coworkers, and supervisors, and are less likely to engage in negative behaviors, such as verbally or physically abusing coworkers or stealing.[94]

Extraversion the degree to which someone is active, assertive, gregarious, sociable, talkative, and energized by others

Emotional stability the degree to which someone is not angry, depressed, anxious, emotional, insecure, and excitable

Agreeableness the degree to which someone is cooperative, polite, flexible, forgiving, good-natured, tolerant, and trusting

Conscientiousness the degree to which someone is organized, hardworking, responsible, persevering, thorough, and achievement oriented

Openness to experience is the degree to which someone is curious, broadminded, and open to new ideas, things, and experiences; is spontaneous; and has a high tolerance for ambiguity. Most companies need people who are strong in terms of openness to experience to fill certain positions, but for other positions, this dimension is less important. People in marketing, advertising, research, or other creative jobs need to be curious, open to new ideas, and spontaneous. By contrast, openness to experience is not particularly important to accountants, who need to apply stringent rules and formulas consistently to make sense out of complex financial information.

Which of the Big Five Personality Dimensions has the largest impact on behavior in organizations? The cumulative results of multiple studies indicate that conscientiousness is related to job performance across five different occupational groups (professionals, police, managers, salespeople, and skilled or semiskilled workers).[95] In short, people "who are dependable, persistent, goal directed, and organized tend to be higher performers on virtually any job; viewed negatively, those who are careless, irresponsible, low achievement striving, and impulsive tend to be lower performers on virtually any job."[96] The results also indicate that extraversion is related to performance in jobs, such as sales and management, that involve significant interaction with others. In people-intensive jobs like these, it helps to be sociable, assertive, and talkative and to have energy and be able to energize others. Finally, people who are extraverted and open to experience seem to do much better in training. Being curious and open to new experiences as well as sociable, assertive, talkative, and full of energy helps people perform better in learning situations.[97]

12-4 MANAGING DIVERSITY

How much should companies change their standard business practices to accommodate the diversity of their workers? What do you do when a talented top executive has a drinking problem that seems to affect his behavior only at company business parties (for entertaining clients), where he has made inappropriate advances toward female employees? What do you do when, despite aggressive company policies against racial discrimination, employees continue to tell racist jokes and

Openness to experience the degree to which someone is curious, broad-minded, and open to new ideas, things, and experiences; is spontaneous; and has a high tolerance for ambiguity

publicly post cartoons displaying racist humor? And, because many people confuse diversity with affirmative action, what do you do to make sure that your company's diversity practices and policies are viewed as benefiting all workers and not just some workers?

No doubt about it, questions like these make managing diversity one of the toughest challenges that managers face. Nonetheless, there are steps companies can take to begin to address these issues.

As discussed earlier, diversity programs try to create a positive work environment where no one is advantaged or disadvantaged, where "we" is everyone, where everyone can do his or her best work, where differences are respected and not ignored, and where everyone feels comfortable.

*Let's begin to address those goals by learning about **12-4a different diversity paradigms, 12-4b diversity principles,** and **12-4c diversity training and practices.***

12-4a Diversity Paradigms

There are several different methods or paradigms for managing diversity: the discrimination and fairness paradigm, the access and legitimacy paradigm, and the learning and effectiveness paradigm.[98]

The *discrimination and fairness paradigm*, which is the most common method of approaching diversity, focuses on equal opportunity, fair treatment, recruitment of minorities, and strict compliance with the equal employment opportunity laws. Under this approach, success is usually measured by how well companies achieve recruitment, promotion, and retention goals for women, people of different racial/ethnic backgrounds, or other underrepresented groups. According to a recent workplace diversity practices survey conducted by the Society for Human Resource Management, 66–91 percent of companies use specialized strategies to recruit, retain, and promote talented women and minorities. The percentages increase with company size, and companies of more than 500 employees are the most likely to use these strategies. Of companies with more than 500 employees, 77 percent systematically collect measurements on diversity-related practices.[99] One manager says, "If you don't measure something, it doesn't count. You measure your market share. You measure your profitability. The same should be true for diversity. There has to be some way of measuring whether you did, in fact, cast your net widely and whether the company is better off today in terms of the experience of people of color than it was a few years ago. I measure my market share and my profitability. Why not this?"[100] The primary benefit of the discrimination and fairness paradigm is that it generally brings about fairer treatment of employees and increases demographic diversity. The primary limitation is that the focus of diversity remains on the surface-level diversity dimensions of sex, race, and ethnicity.[101]

The *access and legitimacy paradigm* focuses on the acceptance and celebration of differences to ensure that the diversity within the company matches the diversity found among primary stakeholders, such as customers, suppliers, and local communities. This is similar to the *business growth* advantage of diversity discussed earlier in the chapter. The basic idea behind this approach is to create a demographically diverse workforce that attracts a broader customer base. For example, the diversity strategy at Oshkosh, a maker of specialty trucks and truck bodies, states, "We operate and sell our products and services in over 100 countries on six continents, each with its own culture, customs, and business practices. We seek employees who are passionate about serving customers and who reflect

"We are all on the same team...

our diverse customer base so that we can truly understand our customers to better serve and delight them."[102]

The primary benefit of this approach is that it establishes a clear business reason for diversity. Like the discrimination and fairness paradigm, however, it focuses only on the surface-level diversity dimensions of sex, race, and ethnicity. Furthermore, employees who are assigned responsibility for customers and stakeholders on the basis of their sex, race, or ethnicity may eventually feel frustrated and exploited.

Whereas the discrimination and fairness paradigm focuses on assimilation (having a demographically representative workforce), and the access and legitimacy paradigm focuses on differentiation (having demographic differences inside the company match those of key customers and stakeholders), the *learning and effectiveness paradigm* focuses on integrating deep-level diversity differences, such as personality, attitudes, beliefs, and values, into the actual work of the organization. One sign that a company hasn't yet created a learning and effectiveness paradigm is that people withhold their opinions for fear of being seen as different. For example, while Helena Morrissey is the CEO of Newton Investment Management, a London firm that invests $71 billion for its clients, she admits to sometimes keeping her business opinions to herself for fear of being seen as "the annoying" woman at the table. She says, "At a recent meeting, I wasn't comfortable with a controversial point and I spoke up, but I also had a different view on the next item on the agenda but instead of speaking up I held back." Says Morrissey, "I have been conscious of feeling that where I did have different views from the rest of the [all-male] group, I may be being perceived as the 'difficult woman' rather than being listened to for what I was saying." She felt this way despite there being "no evidence that the men were actually feeling that."[103]

The learning and effectiveness paradigm is consistent with achieving organizational plurality. **Organizational plurality** is a work environment where (1) all members are empowered to contribute in a way that maximizes the benefits to the organization, customers, and themselves, and (2) the individuality of each member is respected by not segmenting or polarizing people on the basis of their membership in a particular group.[104]

The learning and effectiveness diversity paradigm offers four benefits.[105] First, it values common ground. Former Harvard Business School professor David Thomas explains, "Like the fairness paradigm, it promotes equal opportunity for all individuals. And like the access paradigm, it acknowledges cultural differences among people and recognizes the value in those differences. Yet this new model for managing diversity lets the organization internalize differences among employees so that it learns and grows because of them. Indeed, with the model fully in place, members of the organization can say, 'We are all on the same team, with our differences—not despite them.'"[106]

Second, this paradigm makes a distinction between individual and group differences. When diversity focuses only on differences between groups, such as females versus males, large differences within groups are ignored.[107] For example, think of the women you know at work. Now, think for a second about what they have in common. After that, think about how they're different. If your situation is typical, the list of differences should be just as long as the list of commonalties, if not longer. In

> **Organizational plurality**
> a work environment where (1) all members are empowered to contribute in a way that maximizes the benefits to the organization, customers, and themselves, and (2) the individuality of each member is respected by not segmenting or polarizing people on the basis of their membership in a particular group

with our differences—not despite them."

iStockphoto.com/Rawpixel Ltd

short, managers can achieve a greater understanding of diversity and their employees by treating them as individuals and by realizing that not all African Americans, Hispanics, women, or white males want the same things at work.[108]

Third, because the focus is on individual differences, the learning and effectiveness paradigm is less likely to encounter the conflict, backlash, and divisiveness sometimes associated with diversity programs that focus only on group differences. Taylor Cox, one of the leading management writers on diversity, says, "We are concerned here with these more destructive forms of conflict which may be present with diverse workforces due to language barriers, cultural clash, or resentment by majority-group members of what they may perceive as preferential and unwarranted treatment of minority-group members."[109] And Ray Haines, a consultant who has helped companies deal with the aftermath of diversity programs that became divisive, says, "There's a large amount of backlash related to diversity training. It stirs up a lot of hostility, anguish, and resentment but doesn't give people tools to deal with [the backlash]. You have people come in and talk about their specific ax to grind."[110] Not all diversity programs are divisive or lead to conflict. But by focusing on individual rather than group differences, the learning and effectiveness paradigm helps to minimize these potential problems.

Finally, unlike the other diversity paradigms that simply focus on surface-level diversity, the learning and effectiveness paradigm focuses on bringing different talents and perspectives (that is deep-level diversity) *together* to make the best organizational decisions and to produce innovative, competitive products and services.

12-4b Diversity Principles

Diversity paradigms are general approaches or strategies for managing diversity. Whatever diversity paradigm a manager chooses, diversity principles will help managers do a better job of *managing company diversity programs*.[111]

Begin by *carefully and faithfully following and enforcing federal and state laws regarding equal opportunity employment*. Diversity programs can't and won't succeed if the company is being sued for discriminatory actions and behavior. Faithfully following the law will also reduce the time and expense associated with EEOC investigations or lawsuits. Start by learning more at the EEOC website (www.eeoc.gov). Following the law also means strictly and fairly enforcing company policies.

Treat group differences as important but not special. Surface-level diversity dimensions such as age, sex, and race/ethnicity should be respected but should not be treated as more important than other kinds of differences (that is deep-level diversity). Remember, the

DIVERSITY APPS

Information technology has helped us in countless ways, but we're just beginning to discover how it can help us create a workforce that is talented, capable, and diverse. Check out these three new apps developed to increase diversity in the workplace:

▸ **Textio** is a diversity spell checker that scans job listings for biased language that might discourage a diverse applicant pool. And just like a regular spell checker, Textio suggests different wordings to help increase the number and diversity of applicants.

▸ **GapJumpers** helps companies review job applications without knowing candidates' sex or race. GapJumpers also provides companies with a number of online performance auditions so they can see how candidates perform tasks that pertain to the job in question.

▸ **Unitive** is a complete recruiting/hiring platform that tracks job applicants and assesses their fit within the company and job throughout the entire hiring process. Unitive provides visual data for easier analysis and reminds managers to implement best practices at each step to reduce bias and increase the size and quality of the applicant pool.

Source: R. Silverman and L. Gellman, "Apps Take on Workplace Bias," *Wall Street Journal*, September 30, 2015, accessed May 9, 2016, http://www.wsj.com /articles/apps-take-on-workplace-bias-1443601027.

shift in focus from surface- to deep-level diversity helps people know and understand each other better, reduces prejudice and conflict, and leads to stronger social integration with people wanting to work together and get the job done. Also, *find the common ground*. Although respecting differences is important, it's just as important, especially with diverse workforces, to actively find ways for employees to see and share commonalties.

Tailor opportunities to individuals, not groups. Special programs for training, development, mentoring, or promotion should be based on individual strengths and weaknesses, not on group status. Instead of making mentoring available for just one group of workers, create mentoring opportunities for everyone who wants to be mentored. DuPont Corporation's mentoring program, for example, is voluntary and open to all employees. Through candid and confidential conversations, DuPont's mentors help younger workers and managers with problem solving and career and leadership development.[112]

After her playing days in the WNBA, Becky Hammon has gone on to become the first female assistant coach in the NBA; due to her capabilities as a coach and not because she is a woman.

Maintain high standards. Companies have a legal and moral obligation to make sure that their hiring and promotion procedures and standards are fair to all. At the same time, in today's competitive markets, companies should not lower standards to promote diversity. This not only hurts the organizations but also feeds the stereotype that applicants who are hired or promoted in the name of affirmative action or diversity are less qualified. After a knee injury ended the career of WNBA player and Olympic medalist Becky Hammon, she became a coaching intern for the NBA's San Antonio Spurs. While rehabbing her knee, Hammon attended coaches' meetings, gave instructions during practices, and, when asked, willingly shared her opinions with head coach Gregg Popovich, who has led the Spurs to five NBA championships. Popovich told her, "As cool as it would be to hire you [as a full-time assistant coach], you'd have to be qualified, and I'd have to make sure you're qualified." She agreed. When Popovich hired her after the completion of her internship, Hammon

AP Images/John Locher

said, "Honestly, I don't think he gives two cents that I'm a woman. And, I don't want to be hired because I'm a woman . . . I'm getting hired because I'm capable."[113]

Solicit negative as well as positive feedback. Diversity is one of the most difficult management issues. No company or manager gets it right from the start. Consequently, companies should aggressively seek positive and negative feedback about their diversity programs. One way to do that is to use a series of measurements to see if progress is being made.

Set high but realistic goals. Just because diversity is difficult doesn't mean that organizations shouldn't try to accomplish as much as possible. The general purpose of diversity programs is to try to create a positive work environment where no one is advantaged or disadvantaged, where "we" is everyone, where everyone can do his or her best work, where differences are respected and not ignored, and where everyone feels comfortable. Even if progress is slow, companies should not shrink from these goals.

12-4c Diversity Training and Practices

Organizations use diversity training and several common diversity practices to manage diversity. There are two basic types of diversity training programs, skills-based and awareness. **Skills-based diversity training** teaches employees the practical skills they need for managing a diverse workforce, skills such as flexibility and adaptability, negotiation, problem solving, and conflict resolution.[114] By contrast, **awareness training** is designed to raise employees' awareness of diversity issues and to challenge underlying assumptions or stereotypes we may have about others. **Dell Inc.** enrolled several male executives in a six-month program run by Catalyst, a nonprofit group that tracks and advocates for women's advancement. The program teaches managers to recognize the hurdles facing women in the workplace. As a result of the training, Doug Hillary, a Dell vice president, checked in with a female staff member with two young children and asked her if he was adequately accommodating her family needs. She told him that, actually, he was regularly scheduling staff conference calls at an hour when she was dropping her children off at school. He changed the meeting times, saying that, previously, "He didn't pay as much attention."[115]

Skills-based diversity training training that teaches employees the practical skills they need for managing a diverse workforce, such as flexibility and adaptability, negotiation, problem solving, and conflict resolution

Awareness training training that is designed to raise employees' awareness of diversity issues and to challenge the underlying assumptions or stereotypes they may have about others

Some companies use the Implicit Association Test (IAT) for awareness training.[116] The IAT measures the extent to which people associate positive or negative thoughts (that is underlying assumptions or stereotypes) with blacks or whites, men or women, homosexuals or heterosexuals, young or old, or other groups. For the race IAT (versions also exist for weight, age, sexuality, and other ethnic groups), test takers are shown black or white faces that they must instantly pair with various words. IAT proponents argue that shorter responses generally indicate stronger associations and that the patterns of associations indicate the extent to which people are biased. For example, an early study showed that 88 percent of whites have a more positive mental association toward whites than toward blacks, but surprisingly, 48 percent of blacks showed the same bias. Do the biases measured by the IAT mean we're likely to discriminate against others? Thankfully, no, according to the consistent results of a number of recent studies.[117] But they do indicate the importance of becoming aware of our potential biases and then monitoring our workplace behavior and decision making. So, taking the IAT is a good way to increase awareness of diversity issues. To take the IAT and to learn more about the decade of research behind it, go to https://implicit.harvard.edu/implicit/demo.

Companies also use diversity audits, diversity pairing, and minority experiences for top executives to better manage diversity. **Diversity audits** are formal assessments that measure employee and management attitudes, investigate the extent to which people are advantaged or disadvantaged with respect to hiring and promotions, and review companies' diversity-related policies and procedures. According to Harvard Professor Iris Bohnet, "Using data to learn about the possible disparate treatment of employees shouldn't be controversial. No company runs its finances based just on intuition, and the same should hold for personnel decisions."[118]

Data mining software can analyze input and output variables to determine the extent to which gender gaps exist. Input variables include training, mentoring, company policies, and corporate practices; output variables include pay, recruitment, and promotions. By analyzing the actual relationships among these variables, companies like L'Oréal and Deloitte are learning how to focus on specific issues rather than simply blindly throwing resources at the problem.[119]

Earlier in the chapter, you learned that *mentoring*, pairing a junior employee with a senior employee, is a common strategy for creating learning and promotional opportunities for women. Diversity pairing is a special kind of mentoring. In **diversity pairing**, people of different cultural backgrounds, sexes, or races/ethnicities are paired for mentoring. The hope is that stereotypical beliefs and attitudes will change as people get to know each other as individuals.[120] Consultant Tom McGee, who has set up mentoring programs for numerous companies, supports diversity pairing, saying, "The assumption that people participating in diversity mentoring programs are looking for someone of the same race or gender has been proved wrong in many cases."[121]

For more than twenty years, Xerox has been fostering a culture where women and minorities are prepared and considered for top positions. CEO Ursula Burns, the first African American woman to lead a major U.S. company, worked as special assistant to Xerox's president of marketing and customer operations, Wayland Hicks. Reginald Brown, Jr., CEO of Brown Technology Group, who worked with Burns at Xerox, said, "These [appointments as special assistants] were jobs in the company that division presidents put their best people in. Most of them were white males, so to have an African American female in such a position of power, you knew early on she had great potential." Burns was then given a similar role with former Xerox CEO Paul A. Allaire. When Anne Mulcahy became CEO in 2001, Burns was gradually given control of day-to-day operations while Mulcahy repaired Xerox's financial position and customer service. Professor David Thomas, says that because of steps (such as diversity pairing) to promote diversity at Xerox, "you have a culture where having women and people of color as candidates for powerful jobs has been going on for two decades."[122]

Because top managers are still overwhelmingly white and male, a number of companies believe that it is worthwhile to *have top executives experience what it is like to be in the minority*. This can be done by having top managers go to places or events where nearly everyone else is of a different sex or racial/ethnic background. For example, managers at Raytheon are required to spend an entire day in the office in a wheelchair so that they have a better understanding of the challenges faced by their disabled colleagues. Managers and executives at Sodexho Alliance are asked to spend time working with organizations that represent minorities. One male manager became the sponsor of a women employees group at Sodexho and accompanied a female colleague to a meeting of the Women's Food Service Forum. The manager called the experience, in which he was at a conference with 1,500 women, "profound" and said that it taught him what it

Diversity audits formal assessments that measure employee and management attitudes, investigate the extent to which people are advantaged or disadvantaged with respect to hiring and promotions, and review companies' diversity-related policies and procedures

Diversity pairing a mentoring program in which people of different cultural backgrounds, sexes, or races/ethnicities are paired together to get to know each other and change stereotypical beliefs and attitudes

Xerox CEO Ursula Burns attends the Cathedral High School 110th Anniversary Gala in New York City on April 12, 2016.

Randy Brooke/Getty Images

endorses this experiential approach, saying, "To really engage people, you have to create a series of epiphanies and take leaders through those epiphanies."[123]

Finally, while there's a wealth of data on what is being done to address diversity issues, there's not much clear, consistent, scientifically rigorous evidence on effectiveness.[124] So what do we know—at this time—about what works? A review of 985 studies examining ways to reduce prejudice or bias toward others (similar to awareness training) concluded, "Psychologists are a long way from demonstrating the most effective ways to reduce prejudice," and that the evidence, so far, "does not reveal whether, when, and why interventions reduce prejudice in the world."[125]

A recent survey of 829 companies suggests that the most popular programs, diversity training, diversity performance evaluations (assessing how well managers are addressing diversity issues), and network programs (company sponsored affinity groups for women and minorities) "have no positive effects in the average workplace," and that the two least frequently used programs, diversity mentoring and appointing diversity managers responsible for diversity programs, "were among the most effective."[126]

Besides mentoring and appointing diversity managers, focusing on deep-level diversity appears to have strong positive effects. According to professors Jonathan Haidt and Lee Jussim, "In a review of more than 500 studies, published in the *Journal of Personality and Social Psychology*, Thomas Pettigrew and Linda Tropp concluded that when people of different races and ethnicities mix together and get to know each other, the effect is generally to reduce prejudice on all sides. This is a good justification for increasing diversity."[127]

feels like to be different. He also described how his experiences working with women made him more sensitive to women's feelings and even led him to change the social activities that he plans with coworkers from golf to dinner cruises. Rohini Anand, Sodexho's chief diversity officer,

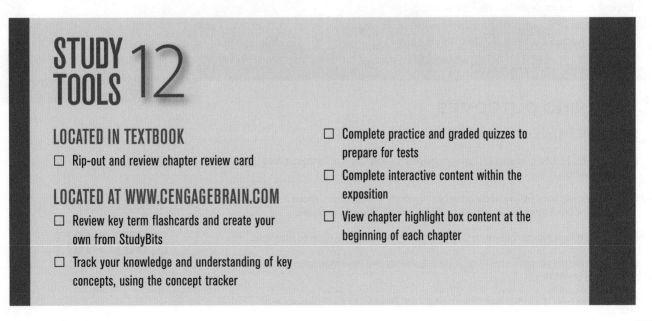

STUDY TOOLS 12

LOCATED IN TEXTBOOK

☐ Rip-out and review chapter review card

LOCATED AT WWW.CENGAGEBRAIN.COM

☐ Review key term flashcards and create your own from StudyBits

☐ Track your knowledge and understanding of key concepts, using the concept tracker

☐ Complete practice and graded quizzes to prepare for tests

☐ Complete interactive content within the exposition

☐ View chapter highlight box content at the beginning of each chapter

PART 4

13 Motivation

LEARNING OUTCOMES

13-1 Explain the basics of motivation.

13-2 Use equity theory to explain how employees' perceptions of fairness affect motivation.

13-3 Use expectancy theory to describe how workers' expectations about rewards, effort, and the link between rewards and performance influence motivation.

13-4 Explain how reinforcement theory works and how it can be used to motivate.

13-5 Describe the components of goal-setting theory and how managers can use them to motivate workers.

13-6 Discuss how the entire motivation model can be used to motivate workers.

After you finish this chapter, go to **PAGE 295** for **STUDY TOOLS**

13-1 BASICS OF MOTIVATION

What makes people happiest and most productive at work? Is it money, benefits, opportunities for growth, interesting work, or something else altogether? And if people desire different things, how can a company keep everyone motivated? It takes insight and hard work to motivate workers to join the company, perform well, and then stay with the company. In fact, a 2013 worldwide study by Gallup found that only 13 percent of employees are "engaged" or motivated at work, whereas 63 percent are "not engaged," meaning they are unmotivated and not interested in organizational goals or outcomes. Even worse, 24 percent of employees are "actively disengaged" and are "unhappy, unproductive, and liable to spread negativity."[1]

So what is motivation? **Motivation** is the set of forces that initiates, directs, and makes people persist in their efforts to accomplish a goal.[2] *Initiation of effort* is concerned with the choices that people make about how much effort to put forth in their jobs. ("Do I really knock myself out or just do a decent job?") *Direction of effort* is concerned with the choices that people make in deciding where to put forth effort in their jobs. ("I should be spending time with my high-dollar accounts instead of learning this new computer system!") *Persistence of effort* is concerned with the choices that people make about how long they will put forth effort in their jobs before reducing or eliminating those efforts. ("I'm only halfway through the project, and I'm exhausted. Do I plow through to the end, or just call it quits?") Initiation, direction, and persistence are at the heart of motivation.

Bruce Arians coaches the National Football League's Arizona Cardinals, while Pete Carroll coaches the NFL's Seattle Seahawks. Arians, a screamer and a hugger, took the Cardinals to the NFC championship, one game short of the Super Bowl. Cardinals' defensive back Tyrann Mathieu said, "I'll mess up on the practice field and he'll scream and curse at me. Then he'll find me before meetings start—he'll give me a hug, tell me it's all good and ask how my family is."[3] Pete Carroll, by contrast, coaches the Seattle Seahawks. Under Carroll, who never yells, the Seahawks have won one Super Bowl and just barely lost another. When All-Pro tight-end Jimmy Graham dropped a pass in practice, Carroll told him to focus more on what he was doing and not to worry about it. Regarding how Carroll motivates Seahawks players, Graham says, "It's literally all positive reinforcement."[4]

Under which coach, the Cardinals' Arians or the Seahawks' Carroll, would you be more motivated? Or, in Gallup's terms, are you engaged at work? Are your

co-workers? If you and your co-workers are "disengaged" or "actively disengaged," why? Are there parts of the job that interest and energize you? If so, what are they and why? Answering questions like these is at the heart of figuring out how best to motivate people at work.

Let's learn more about motivation by building a basic model of motivation out of **13-1a effort and performance, 13-1b need satisfaction,** *and* **13-1c extrinsic and intrinsic rewards** *and then discussing* **13-1d how to motivate people with this basic model of motivation.**

13-1a Effort and Performance

When most people think of work motivation, they think that working hard (effort) should lead to a good job (performance). Exhibit 13.1 shows a basic model of work motivation and performance, displaying this process. The first thing to notice about Exhibit 13.1 is that this is a basic model of work motivation *and* performance. In practice, it's almost impossible to talk about one without mentioning the other. Not surprisingly, managers often assume motivation to be the only determinant of performance, saying things such as "Your performance was really terrible last quarter. What's the matter? Aren't you as motivated as you used to be?" In fact, motivation is just one of three primary determinants of job performance. In industrial psychology, job performance is frequently represented by this equation:

$$\text{Job Performance} = \text{Motivation} \times \text{Ability} \times \text{Situational Constraints}$$

In this formula, *job performance* is how well someone performs the requirements of the job.

> **Motivation** the set of forces that initiates, directs, and makes people persist in their efforts to accomplish a goal

Exhibit 13.1
A Basic Model of Work Motivation and Performance

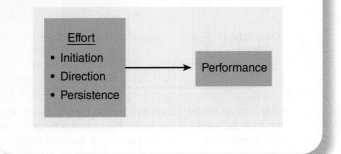

Exhibit 13.2
A Basic Model of Work Motivation and Performance

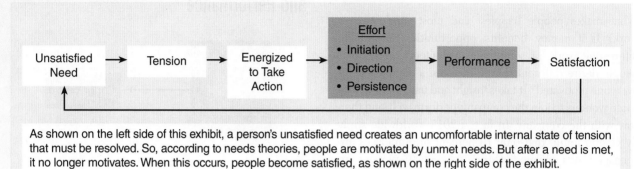

As shown on the left side of this exhibit, a person's unsatisfied need creates an uncomfortable internal state of tension that must be resolved. So, according to needs theories, people are motivated by unmet needs. But after a need is met, it no longer motivates. When this occurs, people become satisfied, as shown on the right side of the exhibit.

Motivation, as defined previously, is effort, the degree to which someone works hard to do the job well. *Ability* is the degree to which workers possess the knowledge, skills, and talent needed to do a job well. And *situational constraints* are factors beyond the control of individual employees, such as tools, policies, and resources that have an effect on job performance.

Because job performance is a multiplicative function of motivation times ability times situational constraints, job performance will suffer if any one of these components is weak. This doesn't mean that motivation doesn't matter. It just means that all the motivation in the world won't translate into high performance when an employee has little ability and high situational constraints. So, even though we will spend this chapter developing a model of work motivation, it is important to remember that ability and situational constraints affect job performance as well.

13-1b Need Satisfaction

In Exhibit 13.1 we started with a very basic model of motivation in which effort leads to job performance. But managers want to know, "What leads to effort?" Determining employee needs is the first step to answering that question.

Needs are the physical or psychological requirements that must be met to ensure survival and well-being.[5] As shown on the left side of Exhibit 13.2, a person's unmet need creates an uncomfortable, internal state of tension that must be resolved. For example, if you normally skip breakfast but

Needs the physical or psychological requirements that must be met to ensure survival and well-being

then have to work through lunch, chances are you'll be so hungry by late afternoon that the only thing you'll be motivated to do is find something to eat. So, according to needs theories, people are motivated by unmet needs. But a need no longer motivates once it is met. For example, when the author of the Mr. Everyday Dollar financial strategies website learned that he had become a millionaire at 35, he described it as a, "huge letdown," saying, "You might think when your account rolls over to seven digits that fireworks light up the sky, confetti falls, and champagne starts flowing. I can tell you that doesn't happen, in fact, it's pretty anticlimactic; I was like, 'Oh, cool,' and then went back to work." In other words, once obtained, his need for financial independence, no longer motivated him as much.[6] When this occurs, people become satisfied, as shown on the right side of Exhibit 13.2.

Note: Throughout the chapter, as we build on this basic model, the parts of the model that we've already discussed will appear shaded in color. For example, because we've already discussed the effort → performance part of the model, those components are shown with a colored background. When we add new parts to the model, they will have a white background. We're adding need satisfaction to the model at this step, so the need-satisfaction components of unsatisfied need, tension, energized to take action, and satisfaction are shown with a white background. This shading convention should make it easier to understand the work motivation model as we add to it in each section of the chapter.

Because people are motivated by unmet needs, managers must learn what those unmet needs are and address

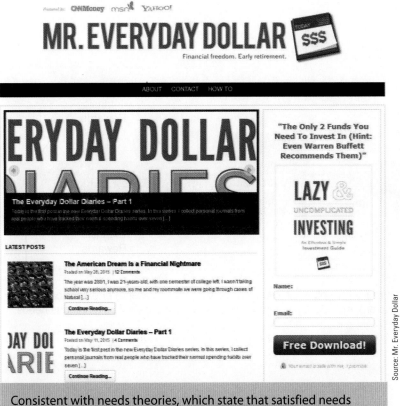

Consistent with needs theories, which state that satisfied needs no longer motivate, the owner of the website "Mr. Everyday Dollar" found out that becoming a millionaire was "anticlimactic."

them. This is not always a straightforward task, however, because different needs theories suggest different needs categories. Consider three well-known needs theories. Maslow's Hierarchy of Needs suggests that people are motivated by *physiological* (food and water), *safety* (physical and economic), *belongingness* (friendship, love, social interaction), *esteem* (achievement and recognition), and *self-actualization* (realizing your full potential) needs.[7] Alderfer's ERG Theory collapses Maslow's five needs into three: *existence* (safety and physiological needs), *relatedness* (belongingness), and *growth* (esteem and self-actualization).[8] McClelland's Learned Needs Theory suggests that people are motivated by the need for *affiliation* (to be liked and accepted), the need for *achievement* (to accomplish challenging goals), or the need for *power* (to influence others).[9]

Things become even more complicated when we consider the different predictions made by these theories. According to Maslow, needs are arranged in a hierarchy from low (physiological) to high (self-actualization). Within this hierarchy, people are motivated by their lowest unsatisfied need. As each need is met, they work their way up the hierarchy from physiological to self-actualization needs. By contrast, Alderfer says that people can be motivated by more than one need at a time. Furthermore, he suggests that

people are just as likely to move down the needs hierarchy as up, particularly when they are unable to achieve satisfaction at the next higher need level. McClelland argues that the degree to which particular needs motivate varies tremendously from person to person, with some people being motivated primarily by achievement and others by power or affiliation. Moreover, McClelland says that needs are learned, not innate. For instance, studies show that children whose parents own a small business or hold a managerial position are much more likely to have a high need for achievement.[10]

So, with three different sets of needs and three very different ideas about how needs motivate, how do we provide a practical answer to managers who just want to know what leads to effort? Fortunately, the research evidence simplifies things a bit. To start, studies indicate that there are two basic kinds of needs categories.[11] *Lower-order needs* are concerned with safety and with physiological and existence requirements, whereas *higher-order needs* are concerned with relationships (belongingness, relatedness, and affiliation), challenges and accomplishments (esteem, self-actualization, growth, and achievement), and influence (power). Studies generally show that higher-order needs will not motivate people as long as lower-order needs remain unsatisfied.[12]

For example, imagine that you graduated from college six months ago and are still looking for your first job. With money running short (you're probably living on your credit cards), and the possibility of having to move back in with your parents looming (if this doesn't motivate you, what will?), your basic needs for food, shelter, and security drive your thoughts, behavior, and choices at this point. But after you land that job, find a great place (of your own!) to live, and put some money in the bank, these basic needs should decrease in importance as you begin to think about making new friends and taking on challenging work assignments. In fact, after lower-order needs are satisfied, it's difficult for managers to predict which higher-order needs will motivate behavior.[13] Some people will be motivated by affiliation, while others will be motivated by growth or esteem. Also, the relative importance of the various needs may change over time but not necessarily in any predictable pattern. So, what leads to effort? In part, needs do. After we discuss rewards in

Exhibit 13.3
Adding Rewards to the Model

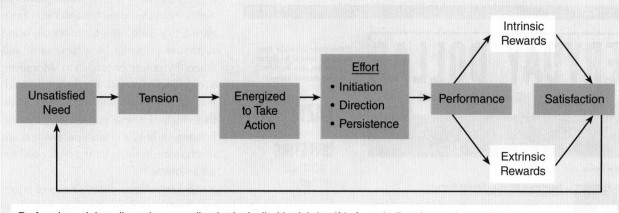

Performing a job well can be rewarding intrinsically (the job itself is fun, challenging, or interesting) or extrinsically (as you receive better pay, promotions, and so on). Intrinsic and extrinsic rewards lead to satisfaction of various needs.

Subsection 13-1c, in Subsection 13-1d, we discuss how managers can use what we know from need-satisfaction theories to motivate workers.

13-1c Extrinsic and Intrinsic Rewards

No discussion of motivation would be complete without considering rewards. Let's add two kinds of rewards, extrinsic and intrinsic, to the model in Exhibit 13.3.[14]

Extrinsic rewards are tangible and visible to others and are given to employees contingent on the performance of specific tasks or behaviors.[15] External agents (managers, for example) determine and control the distribution, frequency, and amount of extrinsic rewards, such as pay, company stock, benefits, and promotions. For example, 91 percent of large- and medium-sized U.S. companies surveyed by Hewitt Associates, a consulting company based in Lincolnshire, Illinois, offer incentives or bonuses to reward employees.[16]

Lincoln Electric, a manufacturer of arc welding tools and technology, has paid annual profit sharing bonuses to its factory workers for eighty-two straight years. In 2015, Lincoln paid out 32 percent of its pretax profits, $80 million, to employees who received bonuses of $26,291 each, worth 36 percent of total wages. In the eighty-two years in which Lincoln has paid profit-sharing bonuses, the percentage has never dropped below 25 percent of total wages and has been as high as 120 percent. Over the past decade, bonuses have averaged 40 percent of total salary.[17]

Why do companies need to offer extrinsic rewards? To get people to do things they wouldn't otherwise do. Companies use extrinsic rewards to motivate people to perform four basic behaviors: join the organization, regularly attend their jobs, perform their jobs well, and stay with the organization.[18] Think about it. Would you show up at work every day to do the best possible job that you could just out of the goodness of your heart? Very few people would.

Intrinsic rewards are the natural rewards associated with performing a task or activity for its own sake. For example, aside from the external rewards management offers for doing something well, employees often find the activities or tasks they perform interesting and enjoyable. Examples of intrinsic rewards include a sense of accomplishment or achievement, a feeling of responsibility, the chance to learn something new or interact with others, or simply the fun that comes from performing an interesting, challenging, and engaging task.

Each year, 1,300 students enter the **U.S. Military Academy at West Point**. About 1,000 will graduate, and roughly 40 percent of graduates stay beyond the Army's five years of required service. To better understand why some

Extrinsic reward a reward that is tangible, visible to others, and given to employees contingent on the performance of specific tasks or behaviors

Intrinsic reward a natural reward associated with performing a task or activity for its own sake

Cadets motivated by intrinsic rewards, such as wanting to be an Army officer, were 20 percent more likely to make it through West Point's rigorous program than those motivated by extrinsic factors.

cadets graduate and serve longer than others, a team of researchers analyzed fourteen years of data on 10,000 cadets. Regardless of race, sex, religion, scholastic achievement, or economic background, cadets who were motivated by intrinsic rewards, such as wanting to be an Army officer, were 20 percent more likely to make it through West Point's rigorous program than those motivated by extrinsic factors, such as attending West Point because their parents wanted them to. Compared to those with weak internal motivation, internally motivated cadets were also more likely to be considered for early promotion (35% vs. 16%).[19]

Which types of rewards are most important to workers in general? A number of surveys suggest that both extrinsic and intrinsic rewards are important and that employee preferences for either intrinsic or extrinsic rewards are relatively stable.[20] A 2016 Society for Human Resource Management national survey found that three extrinsic factors—pay, benefits, and job security/organizational financial stability—and four intrinsic factors—respectful treatment of employees, trust in senior management, relationships with immediate supervisors, and the chance to use one's skills and abilities in your work—were among the top factors rated as "very important" by employees.[21]

13-1d Motivating with the Basics

So, given the basic model of work motivation in Exhibit 13.3, what practical steps can managers take to motivate employees to increase their effort?

The first step is to *start by asking people what their needs are*. Jonathan Robinson, the CEO of **Freetextbooks .com**, an online college textbook seller (sorry, the textbooks aren't really free), says the key to motivating employees is finding out what they like and then giving them the rewards they want. To do that, Robinson gives each new hire a brief survey asking them about their favorite candy, restaurant, hobby, or music. Says Robinson, "You just have to know your team. We're pretty small so I have to stay in tune with the preferences and pulse of our employees. The perks are in the details." As a result, he recently gave one employee a free round of golf, another $100 to be used at a great restaurant, and another IMAX theater tickets. Because he asked, all got what they wanted.[22] So, if you want to meet employees' needs, just ask.

Next, *satisfy lower-order needs first*. Because higher-order needs will not motivate people as long as lower-order needs remain unsatisfied, companies should satisfy lower-order needs first. In practice, this means providing the equipment, training, and knowledge to create a safe workplace free of physical risks; paying employees well enough to provide financial security; and offering a benefits package that will protect employees and their families through good medical coverage and health and disability insurance. Indeed, the Society for Human Resource Management study mentioned previously found that three of the most important factors in 2016— compensation/pay (63%), job security (58%), and benefits (60%)—were all lower-order needs.[23] Consistent with the idea of satisfying lower-order needs first, a survey of 12,000 employees found that inadequate compensation is the number-one reason employees leave organizations. This is why The Container Store CEO Kip Tindell pays his employees an average salary of $48,000 per year, twice the average retail salary. As a result, says Tindell, "My employees advance on Maslow's hierarchy [from lower- to higher-order needs]." He says, "I didn't think about this when we started out. But it's the most powerful thing you can do."[24]

Third, managers should *expect people's needs to change*. As some needs are satisfied or situations change, what motivated people before may not motivate them now. Likewise, what motivates people to accept a job may not necessarily motivate them after they have the job. For instance, David Stum, president of the Loyalty Institute, says, "The [attractive] power of pay and benefits is only [strong] during the recruitment stage. After employees take the job, pay and benefits become entitlements to them. They think: 'Now that I work here, you owe me that.' "[25] Managers should also expect needs to change as people mature. For older employees, benefits are as important as pay, which is always ranked as more important by younger employees. Older employees also rank job security as more important than personal and family time, which is more important to younger employees.[26]

Finally, *as needs change and lower-order needs are satisfied, create opportunities for employees to satisfy higher-order needs.* Recall that intrinsic rewards such as accomplishment, achievement, learning something new, and interacting with others are the natural rewards associated with performing a task or activity for its own sake. And, with the exception of influence (power), intrinsic rewards correspond very closely to higher-order needs that are concerned with relationships (belongingness, relatedness, and affiliation) and challenges and accomplishments (esteem, self-actualization, growth, and achievement). Therefore, one way for managers to meet employees' higher-order needs is to create opportunities for employees to experience intrinsic rewards by providing challenging work, encouraging employees to take greater responsibility for their work, and giving employees the freedom to pursue tasks and projects they find naturally interesting.

 ## 13-2 EQUITY THEORY

We've seen that people are motivated to achieve intrinsic and extrinsic rewards. However, if employees don't believe that rewards are awarded fairly or don't believe that they can achieve the performance goals the company has set for them, they won't be very motivated.

Fairness, or what people perceive to be fair, is also a critical issue in organizations. **Equity theory** says that people will be motivated at work when they *perceive* that they are being treated fairly. In particular, equity theory stresses the importance of perceptions. So, regardless of the actual level of rewards people receive, they must also perceive that, relative to others, they are being treated fairly. For example, you learned in Chapter 11 that the CEOs of the largest U.S. firms now make $16.3 million per year, which is 303 times their average employee salary of $53,200.[27] The ten highest paid CEOs averaged earnings of

Equity theory a theory that states that people will be motivated when they perceive that they are being treated fairly

Inputs in equity theory, the contributions employees make to the organization

Outcomes in equity theory, the rewards employees receive for their contributions to the organization

Referents in equity theory, others with whom people compare themselves to determine if they have been treated fairly

$61.6 million per year, led by John H. Hammergren, the CEO of Discovery Communications, who made $156.1 million.[28] By contrast, in 2015, CEOs of companies with less than $1 billion a year in revenues averaged $220,700 in earnings, or 4.15 times what the average worker makes.[29]

Many people believe that CEO pay is obscenely high and unfair. Others believe that CEO pay is fair because the supply and demand for executive talent largely determine what CEOs are paid. They argue that if it were easier to find good CEOs, then CEOs would be paid much less. Equity theory doesn't focus on objective equity (that is, that CEOs make 303 times or 4.15 times more than average workers). Instead, equity theory says that equity, like beauty, is in the eye of the beholder.

Let's learn more about equity theory by examining **13-2a the components of equity theory, 13-2b how people react to perceived inequity,** *and* **13-2c how to motivate people using equity theory.**

13-2a Components of Equity Theory

The basic components of equity theory are inputs, outcomes, and referents. **Inputs** are the contributions employees make to the organization. They include education and training, intelligence, experience, effort, number of hours worked, and ability. **Outcomes** are what employees receive in exchange for their contributions to the organization. They include pay, fringe benefits, status symbols, and job titles and assignments. And, because perceptions of equity depend on comparisons, **referents** are other people with whom people compare themselves to determine if they have been treated fairly. The referent can be a single person (comparing yourself with a coworker), a generalized other (comparing yourself with "students in general," for example), or even yourself over time ("I was better off last year than I am this year"). Usually, people choose to compare themselves with referents who hold the same or similar jobs or who are otherwise similar in gender, race, age, tenure, or other characteristics.[30] Kevin Hallock, dean of Cornell University's School of Industrial and Labor Relations, says, "People are much more willing to talk about pay than they were even ten years ago."[31] When Brian Bader took a tech support job at Apple, he was explicitly told not to discuss his compensation with co-workers. That, he said, "Just made me more curious."[32] Bader

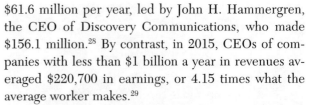

Greg Brave/Shutterstock.com

quickly learned that his co-workers were making $10 to $12 per hour (he made $12 per hour). However, publicly shared team data, such as how many problems and phone calls were successfully handled per hour showed that Bader's job performance was twice as good as the poorest-performing member of his team. Since Bader earned just 20 percent more than that employee, he said, "It irked me. If I'm doing double the work, why am I not seeing double the pay?"[33]

According to equity theory, employees compare their outcomes (the rewards they receive from the organization) with their inputs (their contributions to the organization). This comparison of outcomes with inputs is called the **outcome/input (O/I) ratio**. After an internal comparison in which they compare their outcomes with their inputs, employees then make an external comparison in which they compare their O/I ratio with the O/I ratio of a referent.[34]

When people perceive that their O/I ratio is equal to the referent's O/I ratio, they conclude that they are being treated fairly. But when people perceive that their O/I ratio is different from their referent's O/I ratio, they conclude that they have been treated inequitably or unfairly.

Inequity can take two forms, underreward and overreward. **Underreward** occurs when a referent's O/I ratio is better than your O/I ratio. In other words, you are getting fewer outcomes relative to your inputs than the referent you compare yourself with is getting. When people perceive that they have been underrewarded, they tend to experience anger or frustration. When it comes to being underrewarded, copywriter Lucy Bayly says, "You think you're satisfied [with your pay] and then all of a sudden, you find out someone is paid a little more, and it ruins your day."[35] That's what happened to Olivia Wainhouse, an account executive at New York social media analytics firm **SumAll**. When Wainhouse learned that a new hire was earning $10,000 more than she was, she felt betrayed: "My competitive drive kicked in. I thought, 'What's going on here?'"[36] To see how SumAll dealt with unsanctioned salary disclosures—and the hurt feelings that followed—see box "Transparent Pay—Not a Big Deal."

By contrast, **overreward** occurs when a referent's O/I ratio is worse than your O/I ratio. In this case, you are getting more outcomes relative to your inputs than your referent is. In theory, when people perceive that they have been overrewarded, they experience guilt. But, not surprisingly, people have a very high tolerance for overreward. It takes a tremendous amount of overpayment before people decide that their pay or benefits are more than they deserve.

13-2b How People React to Perceived Inequity

So what happens when people perceive that they have been treated inequitably at work? Exhibit 13.4 shows that perceived inequity affects satisfaction. In the case of underreward, this usually translates into frustration or anger; with overreward, the reaction is guilt. These reactions lead to tension and a strong need to take action to restore equity in some way. At first, a slight inequity may not be strong enough to motivate an employee to take immediate action. If the inequity continues, or there are multiple inequities, however, tension may build over time until a point of intolerance is reached and the person is energized to take action.

Revenues at **Plum Creek Timber** had been flat for two years and net income was dropping when CEO Rick Holley informed the company's board of directors that he was returning 44,445 restricted stock options valued at $1.85 million that the board's compensation committee had awarded him ten months earlier. Holley said, "I didn't feel comfortable taking them . . . This has been a year where total shareholder returns are down 10 percent or more. It just wasn't the right thing to do."[37]

When people perceive that they have been treated unfairly, they may try to restore equity by reducing inputs, increasing outcomes, rationalizing inputs or outcomes, changing the referent, or simply leaving. We will discuss these possible responses in terms of the inequity associated with underreward, which is much more common than the inequity associated with overreward.

People who perceive that they have been underrewarded may try to restore equity by *decreasing or withholding their inputs (that is, effort)*. After filing for bankruptcy and seeking sizable pay and benefits cuts, American Airlines pilots engaged in a sick-out that cancelled hundreds of flights. Furthermore, pilots who showed for work allegedly delayed flights by filing maintenance requests that required mechanics to inspect planes before departure. While the pilots' union denied the slowdown, its president said, "The pilots of American Airlines are angry. While AMR management continues paying lip service to needing a consensual agreement

Outcome/input (O/I) ratio in equity theory, an employee's perception of how the rewards received from an organization compare with the employee's contributions to that organization

Underreward a form of inequity in which you are getting fewer outcomes relative to inputs than your referent is getting

Overreward a form of inequity in which you are getting more outcomes relative to inputs than your referent

Exhibit 13.4
Adding Equity Theory to the Model

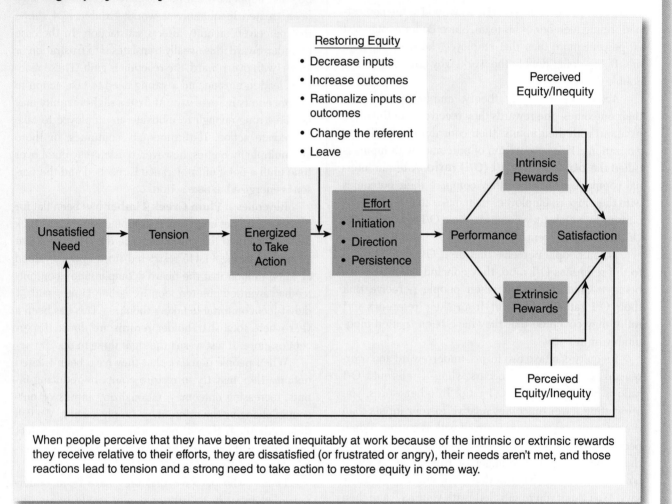

When people perceive that they have been treated inequitably at work because of the intrinsic or extrinsic rewards they receive relative to their efforts, they are dissatisfied (or frustrated or angry), their needs aren't met, and those reactions lead to tension and a strong need to take action to restore equity in some way.

with us, their punitive approach of extracting far more value than they need is hardly conducive to reaching a consensual agreement."[38]

Increasing outcomes is another way people try to restore equity. This might include asking for a raise or pointing out the inequity to the boss and hoping that he or she takes care of it. Sometimes, however, employees may go to external organizations such as labor unions, federal agencies, or the courts for help in increasing outcomes to restore equity. For instance, the U.S. Department of Labor estimates that 10 percent of workers are not getting the extra overtime pay they deserve when they work more than forty hours a week. These are known as Fair Labor Standards Act (FLSA) violations.[39] After a U.S. Department of Labor ruling, Halliburton, a global oil field services company, agreed to pay

$18.2 million in back wages to 1,106 oil and gas employees who were at first denied overtime pay after incorrectly being classified as exempt employees (who are ineligible for overtime).[40] Somewhere between 25,000 and 30,000 FLSA cases are brought each year, and employees win two-thirds of them.[41] From 2001 to 2011, the number of FLSA filings in federal court rose by nearly 500 percent.[42]

Another method of restoring equity is to *rationalize or distort inputs or outcomes*. Instead of decreasing inputs or increasing outcomes, employees restore equity by making mental or emotional adjustments in their O/I ratios or the O/I ratios of their referents. For example, suppose that a company downsizes 10 percent of its workforce. It's likely that the people who still have jobs will be angry or frustrated with company management because of the layoffs. If alternative jobs are difficult to find, however, these survivors may rationalize or distort their O/I ratios and conclude, "Well, things could be worse. At least I still have my job." Rationalizing or distorting outcomes may be used when other ways to restore equity aren't available.

Changing the referent is another way of restoring equity. In this case, people compare themselves with someone other than the referent they had been using for previous O/I ratio comparisons. Because people usually choose to compare themselves with others who hold the same or similar jobs or who are otherwise similar (that is, friends, family members, neighbors who work at other companies), they may change referents to restore equity when their personal situations change, such as a decrease in job status or pay.[43]

13-2c Motivating with Equity Theory

What practical steps can managers take to use equity theory to motivate employees? They can *start by looking for and correcting major inequities*. Among other things, equity theory makes us aware that an employee's sense of fairness is based on subjective perceptions. What one employee considers grossly unfair may not affect another employee's perceptions of equity at all. Although these different perceptions make it difficult for managers to create conditions that satisfy all employees, it's critical that they do their best to take care of major inequities that can energize employees to take disruptive, costly, or harmful actions such as decreasing inputs or leaving. So, whenever possible, managers should look for and correct major inequities.

For example, with Chinese wages rising between 10 and 15 percent per year on average and 30 percent a year where demand is high, the average factory worker in China, who makes between \$317 and \$350 a month, is generally underpaid.[44] So for two consecutive years, Lenovo CEO Yang Yuanqing has given his annual bonus to Lenovo's 10,000 employees. Approximately 90 percent of his 2013 \$3.25 million bonus will go to factory employees in China, each of whom will receive about \$325 dollars, roughly a month's salary. Lenovo spokeswoman Angela Lee said, "As you can imagine, an extra \$300 [or more] in a manufacturing environment in China does make an impact, especially to employees supporting families."[45] Lenovo's communication to employees stated, "This payment is personally funded by Yuanqing. He believes that he has the responsibility as an owner of the company, and the opportunity as our leader, to ensure all of our employees understand the impact they have on building Lenovo."[46]

Second, managers can *reduce employees' inputs*. Increasing outcomes is often the first and only strategy that companies use to restore equity, yet reducing employee inputs is just as viable a strategy. In fact, with dual-career couples working fifty-hour weeks, more and more employees are looking for ways to reduce stress and restore a balance between work and family. Consequently, it may make sense to ask employees to do less, not more; to have them identify and eliminate the 20 percent of their jobs that doesn't increase productivity or add value for customers; and to eliminate company-imposed requirements that really aren't critical to the performance of managers, employees, or the company (for example, unnecessary meetings and reports). Another way to reduce employee inputs is by committing to 40-hour work weeks. Mortgage lender United Shore Financial Services calls this the "firm 40." The deal, says chief people officer Laura Lawson, is that "You give us 40. Everything else is yours."[47] That means no online shopping at work, and no checking Facebook or Twitter. CEO Mat Isbia tells employees that they need to work as hard at 5:55 p.m. on Friday as they do on Tuesday at 10:55 a.m. But then, at 6 p.m. sharp, the office empties. Ahmed Haider, who works in client relations at USFS, says that "the parking lot is pretty much empty" by 6:05 p.m.[48] At first, Haider doubted whether the commitment to "firm 40" was real. But now, he always leaves at 6 p.m. and rarely sends emails or phones colleagues after work hours. "There's nobody to call. Everyone's at home," he says.[49]

Finally, managers should *make sure decision-making processes are fair*. Equity theory focuses on **distributive justice**, the perceived degree to

People who perceive that they have been underrewarded at the office may withhold their efforts until they feel they are fairly compensated.

Rommel Canlas/Shutterstock.com

Distributive justice the perceived degree to which outcomes and rewards are fairly distributed or allocated

which outcomes and rewards are fairly distributed or allocated. However, **procedural justice**, the perceived fairness of the procedures used to make reward allocation decisions, is just as important.[50] Procedural justice matters because even when employees are unhappy with their outcomes (that is, low pay), they're much less likely to be unhappy with company management if they believe that the procedures used to allocate outcomes were fair. For example, employees who are laid off tend to be hostile toward their employer when they perceive that the procedures leading to the layoffs were unfair. When Air France announced a plan to reduce costs by $2 billion over two years—partly by cutting 2,900 jobs—angry employees interrupted a work council meeting attended by key members of management and leaders representing the workers. Five irate employees stormed into the meeting, knocking a security guard unconscious as they attempted to assault two top managers by ripping the shirts off and jackets off their backs. Ultimately, the executives were forced to climb a fence to avoid further harm.[51] By contrast, employees who perceive layoff procedures to be fair tend to continue to support and trust their employers.[52] Also, if employees perceive that their outcomes are unfair (that is, distributive injustice) but that the decisions and procedures leading to those outcomes were fair (that is, procedural justice), they are much more likely to seek constructive ways of restoring equity, such as discussing these matters with their manager.

By contrast, if employees perceive both distributive and procedural injustice, they may resort to more destructive tactics, such as withholding effort, absenteeism, tardiness, or even sabotage and theft.[53]

13-3 EXPECTANCY THEORY

One of the hardest things about motivating people is that not everyone is attracted to the same rewards. **Expectancy theory** says that people will be motivated to the extent to which they believe that their efforts will lead to good performance, that good performance will be rewarded, and that they will be offered attractive rewards.[54]

Let's learn more about expectancy theory by examining **13-3a the components of expectancy theory** *and* **13-3b how to use expectancy theory as a motivational tool.**

13-3a Components of Expectancy Theory

Expectancy theory holds that people make conscious choices about their motivation. The three factors that affect those choices are valence, expectancy, and instrumentality.

Valence is simply the attractiveness or desirability of various rewards or outcomes. Expectancy theory recognizes that the same reward or outcome—say, a promotion—will be highly attractive to some people, will be highly disliked by others, and will not make much difference one way or the other to still others. Accordingly, when people are deciding how much effort to put forth, expectancy theory says that they will consider the valence of all possible rewards and outcomes that they

Procedural justice the perceived fairness of the process used to make reward allocation decisions

Expectancy theory the theory that people will be motivated to the extent to which they believe that their efforts will lead to good performance, that good performance will be rewarded, and that they will be offered attractive rewards

Valence the attractiveness or desirability of a reward or outcome

Fair—or Foolish?

Dan Price's announcement that he was going to cut his salary from $1 million to $70,000 per year so that he could increase the salary of his employees to $70,000 per year was met with a combination of cheers and jeers. Price is the CEO of Gravity Payments, a credit-card processing company, where his employees' average annual salary had been $48,000. And although his decision enjoyed a positive response from labor activists, others were skeptical that Price's method of creating equity would be successful. Management professor Patrick Rogers says, "Mr. Price probably thinks happy workers are productive workers. However, there's just no evidence that this is true. So he'll improve happiness, only in the short term, and will not improve productivity. Which doesn't bode well for his long-term viability as a firm."

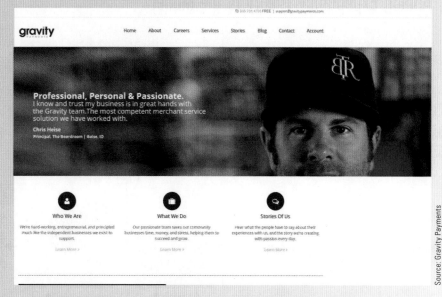

Source: Gravity Payments

Sources: P. Cohen, "Praise and Skepticism as One Executive Sets Minimum Wage to $70,000 a Year," *New York Times*, April 19, 2015, B1; A. Kaufman, "CEO Slashes $1 Million Salary to Give Lowest-Paid Workers a Raise," *Huffington Post*, April 14, 2015, accessed May 8, 2015, http://www.huffingtonpost.com/2015/04/14/gravity-payments-raise_n_7061676.html.

can receive from their jobs. The greater the sum of those valences, each of which can be positive, negative, or neutral, the more effort people will choose to put forth on the job. Consultant Carol Schultz spent nine years working for a company where the boss rewarded top-performing employees with five-day trips to expensive resorts, with the company paying for the flight, the hotel, and one dinner, leaving employees to pay for the rest of their food and all of their drinks and resort activities. Said Schultz, "It always irked me that they'd fly us to some expensive resort and expect us to pay for everything outside of our flight and hotel room. To me, this was no 'reward.'" In other words, when Schultz added up all of the valences, the positive valence of rewarding her with an expensive resort trip could not overcome the negative valence of getting stuck with large food, drink, and resort expenses.[55]

Expectancy is the perceived relationship between effort and performance. When expectancies are strong, employees believe that their hard work and efforts will result in good performance, so they work harder. By contrast, when expectancies are weak, employees figure that no matter what they do or how hard they work, they won't be able to perform their jobs successfully, so they don't work as hard.

Instrumentality is the perceived relationship between performance and rewards. When instrumentality is strong, employees believe that improved performance will lead to better and more rewards, so they choose to work harder. When instrumentality is weak, employees don't believe that better performance will result in more or better rewards, so they choose not to work as hard.

Expectancy theory holds that for people to be highly motivated, all three variables—valence, expectancy, and instrumentality—must be high. Thus, expectancy theory can be represented by the following simple equation:

$$\textbf{Motivation} =$$
$$\textbf{Valence} \times \textbf{Expectancy} \times \textbf{Instrumentality}$$

If any one of these variables (valence, expectancy, or instrumentality) declines, overall motivation will decline, too.

Exhibit 13.5 incorporates the expectancy theory variables into our motivation model. Valence and instrumentality combine to affect employees' willingness to put forth

Expectancy the perceived relationship between effort and performance

Instrumentality the perceived relationship between performance and rewards

Exhibit 13.5
Adding Expectancy Theory to the Model

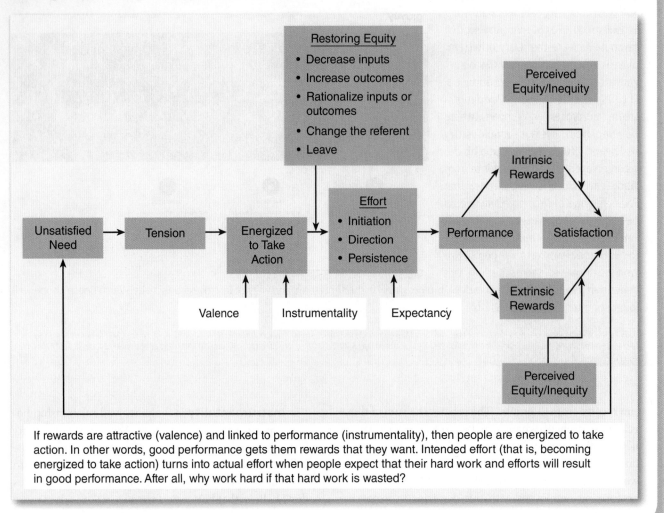

If rewards are attractive (valence) and linked to performance (instrumentality), then people are energized to take action. In other words, good performance gets them rewards that they want. Intended effort (that is, becoming energized to take action) turns into actual effort when people expect that their hard work and efforts will result in good performance. After all, why work hard if that hard work is wasted?

effort (that is, the degree to which they are energized to take action), while expectancy transforms intended effort ("I'm really going to work hard in this job") into actual effort. If you're offered rewards that you desire and you believe that you will in fact receive these rewards for good performance, you're highly likely to be energized to take action. However, you're not likely to actually exert effort unless you also believe that you can do the job (that is, that your efforts will lead to successful performance).

13-3b Motivating with Expectancy Theory

What practical steps can managers take to use expectancy theory to motivate employees? First, they can *systematically gather information to find out what employees*

want from their jobs. In addition to individual managers directly asking employees what they want from their jobs (see Subsection 13-1d, "Motivating with the Basics"), companies need to survey their employees regularly to determine their wants, needs, and dissatisfactions. Because people consider the valence of all the possible rewards and outcomes that they can receive from their jobs, regular identification of wants, needs, and dissatisfactions gives companies the chance to turn negatively valent rewards and outcomes into positively valent rewards and outcomes, thus raising overall motivation and effort. Mark Peterman, vice president of client solutions at Maritz Incentives, says that individual employees are motivated in vastly different ways: "For some, being honored in front of one's peers is a great award, but for others, the thought of being put on display in front of peers embarrasses them." And companies have a long way to go to ensure that their employees feel valued, Peterman says. A Maritz survey found that only 27 percent of employees who want to be recognized by non-monetary incentives are recognized that way.[56] Such findings suggest that employers should routinely survey employees to identify not only the range of rewards that are valued by most employees but also to understand the preferences of specific employees.

Second, managers can *take specific steps to link rewards to individual performance in a way that is clear and understandable to employees*. Unfortunately, most employees are extremely dissatisfied with the link between pay and performance in their organizations, and their companies are, too. Mercer's 2013 Pay for Performance Survey found that while 55 percent of firms say they link rewards to performance, only 42 percent measure to make sure that happens, and 48 percent say that programs linking performance to rewards need improvement.[57]

One way to establish a clear connection between pay and performance (see Chapter 11 for a discussion of compensation strategies) is for managers to publicize the way in which pay decisions are made. This is especially important given that only 52 percent of employees know how their pay increases are determined.[58] Inspired by fantasy sports leagues, **Clayton Homes** director of inside sales, David Schwall, had his sales managers become team "owners" who drafted sales representatives onto their sales teams, which competed against each other in a rotating schedule, with the best four teams moving on to the "championships." Sales reps (players) scored points by making more calls to sales leads, by increasing the percentage of leads who made appointments at Clayton Homes retail stores, and upping the percentage of leads whose phone calls were successfully transferred to a local store. Scores were tallied in real time, and the best scores were posted on TVs for everyone to see (poor scores were only visible within teams), with an individual's theme music played when sales milestones were reached. The connection between efforts and results was clear, prompting one sales rep to say, "When I saw one of my colleagues leaving, I thought—'Yes, now I can catch up and climb above him in the ranks.'" Calls rose by 18 percent, appointments jumped by 200 percent, as did visits to stores. And, after the "season" was over, employees were eager for the next season to begin, saying they missed the immediate feedback, recognition, and energy.[59]

Finally, managers should *empower employees to make decisions if management really wants them to believe that their hard work and effort will lead to good performance*. If valent rewards are linked to good performance, people should be energized to take action. However, this works only if they also believe that their efforts will lead to good performance. One of the ways that managers destroy the expectancy that hard work and effort will lead to good performance is by restricting what employees can do or by ignoring employees' ideas. In Chapter 9, you learned that *empowerment* is a feeling of intrinsic motivation in which workers perceive their work to have meaning and perceive themselves to be competent, to have an impact, and to be capable of self-determination.[60] So, if managers want workers to have strong expectancies, they should empower them to make decisions. Doing so will motivate employees to take active rather than passive roles in their work.

13-4 REINFORCEMENT THEORY

When used properly, rewards motivate and energize employees. But when used incorrectly, they can demotivate, baffle, and even anger them. Goals are supposed to motivate employees. But leaders who focus blindly on meeting goals at all costs often find that they destroy motivation.

Reinforcement theory says that behavior is a function of its consequences, that behaviors followed by positive consequences (that is, reinforced) will occur more frequently, and that behaviors either followed by negative consequences or not followed by positive consequences will occur less frequently.[61] Every holiday season, thousands of Christmas trees are cut down and stolen from private and public property. The city of Lincoln, Nebraska, is fighting back by spraying evergreen trees with fox urine. This urine produces no smell in cold weather, but emits a strong, skunk-like smell once the tree is brought into a warm home. Thanks to the noxious smell, along with prominently posted signs warning that the trees have been sprayed, thieves are no long cutting down Lincoln's evergreen trees.[62] More specifically, **reinforcement** is the process of changing behavior by changing the consequences that follow behavior.[63]

Reinforcement theory the theory that behavior is a function of its consequences, that behaviors followed by positive consequences will occur more frequently, and that behaviors followed by negative consequences, or not followed by positive consequences, will occur less frequently

Reinforcement the process of changing behavior by changing the consequences that follow behavior

One-third of U.S. employees work on vacation because they fear "getting behind," or because "no one else at my company can do my job."

Riccardo Piccinini/Shutterstock.com

Reinforcement has two parts: reinforcement contingencies and schedules of reinforcement. **Reinforcement contingencies** are the cause-and-effect relationships between the performance of specific behaviors and specific consequences. For example, if you get docked an hour's pay for being late to work, then a reinforcement contingency exists between a behavior (being late to work) and a consequence (losing an hour's pay). A **schedule of reinforcement** is the set of rules regarding reinforcement contingencies such as which behaviors will be reinforced, which consequences will follow those behaviors, and the schedule by which those consequences will be delivered.[64]

Exhibit 13.6 incorporates reinforcement contingencies and reinforcement schedules into our motivation model. First, notice that extrinsic rewards and the

Reinforcement contingencies cause-and-effect relationships between the performance of specific behaviors and specific consequences

Schedule of reinforcement rules that specify which behaviors will be reinforced, which consequences will follow those behaviors, and the schedule by which those consequences will be delivered

Positive reinforcement reinforcement that strengthens behavior by following behaviors with desirable consequences

Negative reinforcement reinforcement that strengthens behavior by withholding an unpleasant consequence when employees perform a specific behavior

schedules of reinforcement used to deliver them are the primary methods for creating reinforcement contingencies in organizations. In turn, those reinforcement contingencies directly affect valences (the attractiveness of rewards), instrumentality (the perceived link between rewards and performance), and effort (how hard employees will work).

*Let's learn more about reinforcement theory by examining **13-4a the components of reinforcement theory, 13-4b the different schedules for delivering reinforcement,** and **13-4c how to motivate with reinforcement theory.***

13-4a Components of Reinforcement Theory

As just described, *reinforcement contingencies* are the cause-and-effect relationships between the performance of specific behaviors and specific consequences. There are four kinds of reinforcement contingencies: positive reinforcement, negative reinforcement, punishment, and extinction.

Positive reinforcement strengthens behavior (that is, increases its frequency) by following behaviors with desirable consequences. Only 25 percent of U.S. employees use all of their paid time off each year. And even when on vacation, one-third work because they fear "getting behind," or because "no one else at my company can do my job." The Latin root of vacation is *vacare*, which means to "be unoccupied." That's impossible if you're working and responding to email while ostensibly on vacation. In order to prevent employees from working on vacation, Denver software company **Full Contact** pays a $7,500 time-off bonus—but only if employees resist making contact electronically, by phone, or by working in any other way during vacation.[65]

Negative reinforcement strengthens behavior by withholding an unpleasant consequence when employees perform a specific behavior. Negative reinforcement is also called *avoidance learning* because workers perform a behavior to *avoid* a negative consequence. With the cost of health care averaging $12,136 annually per employee, companies are linking positive health actions and outcomes to the avoidance of negative consequences. At Honeywell, an automation and aerospace company, employees participating in voluntary health screenings to check their cholesterol, body mass index, and more will avoid a $4,000 increase in the cost of their medical insurance. Even though the company was threatened with discrimination lawsuits, it stood by the program, saying, "Honeywell wants its employees to be

Exhibit 13.6
Adding Reinforcement Theory to the Model

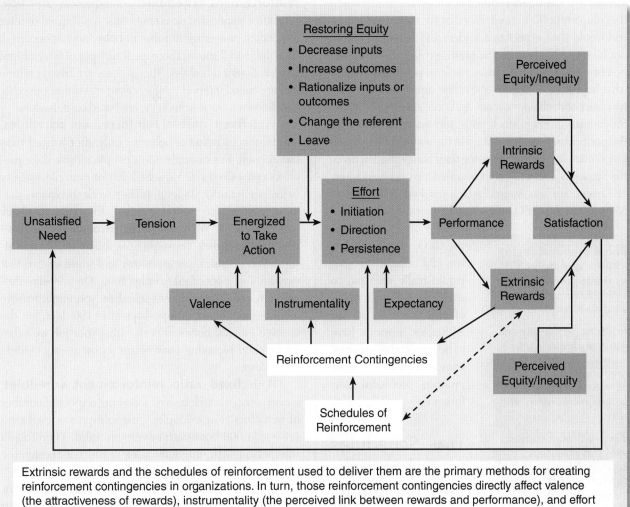

Extrinsic rewards and the schedules of reinforcement used to deliver them are the primary methods for creating reinforcement contingencies in organizations. In turn, those reinforcement contingencies directly affect valence (the attractiveness of rewards), instrumentality (the perceived link between rewards and performance), and effort (how hard employees will work).

well-informed about their health status. We don't believe that those employees who do work to lead healthier lifestyles should subsidize health care premiums for those who don't."[66] The company claims that 60 percent of those screened have found and addressed at least one health risk so far.

By contrast, **punishment** weakens behavior (that is, decreases its frequency) by following behaviors with undesirable consequences. For example, the standard disciplinary or punishment process in most companies is an oral warning ("Don't ever do that again"), followed by a written warning ("This letter is to discuss the serious problem you're having with . . ."), followed by three

days off without pay ("While you're at home not being paid, we want you to think hard about . . ."), followed by being fired ("That was your last chance"). Though punishment can weaken behavior, managers have to be careful to avoid the backlash that sometimes occurs when employees are punished at work.

Extinction is a reinforcement strategy in which a positive consequence is no longer

Punishment reinforcement that weakens behavior by following behaviors with undesirable consequences

Extinction reinforcement in which a positive consequence is no longer allowed to follow a previously reinforced behavior, thus weakening the behavior

allowed to follow a previously reinforced behavior. By removing the positive consequence, extinction weakens the behavior, making it less likely to occur. Based on the idea of positive reinforcement, most companies give company leaders and managers substantial financial rewards when the company performs well. Based on the idea of extinction, you would then expect that leaders and managers would not be rewarded (that is, the positive consequence would be removed) when companies perform poorly. This is *not* what happened at Staples, the office supply retailer. With two years of declining revenue and store sales and a below-the-industry average stock price, top managers didn't hit the performance goals required in the company's compensation plan. But instead of seeing their compensation drop, the Staples board of directors awarded top managers a new "Reinvention Cash Award," which resulted in a bonus of $300,000 to the CEO, whose total pay was $10.8 million, and a bonus of $49,000 to the CFO, whose total pay was $2.2 million.[67] If companies really want pay to reinforce the right kinds of behaviors then, unlike at Staples, rewards have to be removed when company management doesn't produce successful performance.

13-4b Schedules for Delivering Reinforcement

As mentioned earlier, a *schedule of reinforcement* is the set of rules regarding reinforcement contingencies, such as which behaviors will be reinforced, which consequences will follow those behaviors, and the schedule by which those consequences will be delivered. There are two categories of reinforcement schedules: continuous and intermittent.

With **continuous reinforcement schedules**, a consequence follows every instance of a behavior. For example, employees working on a piece-rate pay system earn money (consequence) for every part they manufacture (behavior). The more they produce, the more they earn. By contrast, with **intermittent reinforcement schedules**, consequences are delivered after a specified or average time has elapsed or after a specified or average number of behaviors has occurred. As Exhibit 13.7 shows, there are four types of intermittent reinforcement schedules. Two of these are based on time and are called *interval reinforcement schedules*; the other two, known as *ratio schedules*, are based on behaviors.

With **fixed interval reinforcement schedules**, consequences follow a behavior only after a fixed time has elapsed. For example, most people receive their paychecks on a fixed interval schedule (for example, once or twice per month). As long as they work (behavior) during a specified pay period (interval), they get a paycheck (consequence). With **variable interval reinforcement schedules**, consequences follow a behavior after different times, some shorter and some longer, that vary around a specified average time. On a 90-day variable interval reinforcement schedule, you might receive a bonus after 80 days or perhaps after 100 days, but the average interval between performing your job well (behavior) and receiving your bonus (consequence) would be 90 days.

With **fixed ratio reinforcement schedules**, consequences are delivered following a specific number of behaviors. For example, a car salesperson might receive a $1,000 bonus after every ten sales. Therefore, a salesperson with only nine sales would not receive the bonus until finally selling that tenth car.

With **variable ratio reinforcement schedules**, consequences are delivered following a different number of behaviors, sometimes more and sometimes less, that vary around a specified average number of behaviors. With a ten-car variable ratio reinforcement schedule, a salesperson might receive the bonus after seven car sales, or after twelve, eleven, or nine sales, but the average number of cars sold before receiving the bonus would be ten cars.

Which reinforcement schedules work best? In the past, the standard advice was to use continuous reinforcement when employees were learning new behaviors because reinforcement after each success leads to faster learning. Likewise, the standard advice was to use intermittent reinforcement schedules to maintain behavior after it is learned because intermittent rewards are supposed to make behavior much less subject to extinction.[68] Research shows, however, that except for interval-based systems, which usually produce weak results, the effectiveness of continuous reinforcement, fixed ratio, and variable ratio schedules differs very little.[69] In

Continuous reinforcement schedule a schedule that requires a consequence to be administered following every instance of a behavior

Intermittent reinforcement schedule a schedule in which consequences are delivered after a specified or average time has elapsed or after a specified or average number of behaviors has occurred

Fixed interval reinforcement schedule an intermittent schedule in which consequences follow a behavior only after a fixed time has elapsed

Variable interval reinforcement schedule an intermittent schedule in which the time between a behavior and the following consequences varies around a specified average

Fixed ratio reinforcement schedule an intermittent schedule in which consequences are delivered following a specific number of behaviors

Variable ratio reinforcement schedule an intermittent schedule in which consequences are delivered following a different number of behaviors, sometimes more and sometimes less, that vary around a specified average number of behaviors

organizational settings, all three consistently produce large increases over noncontingent reward schedules. So managers should choose whichever of these three is easiest to use in their companies.

13-4c Motivating with Reinforcement Theory

What practical steps can managers take to use reinforcement theory to motivate employees? University of Nebraska business professor Fred Luthans, who has been studying the effects of reinforcement theory in organizations for more than a quarter of a century, says that there are five steps to motivating workers with reinforcement theory: *identify*, *measure*, *analyze*, *intervene*, and *evaluate* critical performance-related behaviors.[70]

Identify means singling out critical, observable, performance-related behaviors. These are the behaviors that are most important to successful job performance. In addition, they must also be easily observed so that they can be accurately measured. *Measure* means determining the baseline frequencies of these behaviors. In other words, find out how often workers perform them. *Analyze* means studying the causes

Exhibit 13.7
Intermittent Reinforcement Schedules

	Fixed	**Variable**
INTERVAL (TIME)	Consequences follow behavior after a fixed time has elapsed.	Consequences follow behavior after different times, some shorter and some longer, that vary around a specific average time.
RATIO (BEHAVIOR)	Consequences follow a specific number of behaviors.	Consequences follow a different number of behaviors, sometimes more and sometimes less, that vary around a specified average number of behaviors.

CAN PUNISHMENT GET DOG OWNERS TO PICK UP AFTER FIDO?

Dog owners are doing a terrible job of cleaning up after their pets. Cities have tried dispensing free dog poop baggies and posting signs asking dog owners to "Keep [insert city name here] Clean for All." Since asking nicely didn't work, many cities are becoming more vigilant about punishing dog owners who don't pick up after their dogs. The city of Colmenar Viejo, Spain, began issuing fines after hiring private detectives to video record dogs and their offending owners. Brunete, Spain, used volunteers to identify lazy dog owners who surreptitiously collected dogs' names ("My, what a cute dog! What's her name?"). After dog names were matched to city registration records, offenders were mailed their dogs' droppings. Said Mayor Borja Gutierrez, "It's your dog, it's your dog poop. We are just returning it to you." Incidents of unscooped dog poop are now down by 70 percent.

Source: K. Brulliard, "Cities Go to Extreme Lengths to Tackle a Dog Poop Epidemic," *Washington Post*, April 27, 2016, accessed May 5, 2016, https://www.washingtonpost .com/news/animalia/wp/2016/04/27/madrid-is-the-latest-city-to-fight-a-dog -poop-epidemic-that-just-wont-go-away/.

Susan Schmitz/Shutterstock.com

and consequences of these behaviors. Analyzing the causes helps managers create the conditions that produce these critical behaviors, and analyzing the consequences helps them determine if these behaviors produce the results that they want. *Intervene* means changing the organization by using positive and negative reinforcement to increase the frequency of these critical behaviors. *Evaluate* means assessing the extent to which the intervention actually changed workers' behavior. This is done by comparing behavior after the intervention to the original baseline of behavior before the intervention.

In addition to these five steps, managers should remember three other key things when motivating with reinforcement theory. First, *Don't reinforce the wrong behaviors.* Although reinforcement theory sounds simple, it's actually very difficult to put into practice. One of the most common mistakes is accidentally reinforcing the wrong behaviors. Sometimes organizations reinforce behaviors that they don't want! To encourage green driving in Norway, the national government exempted electric cars from fees for toll roads, tunnels, ferries, and parking. With one of the highest costs of living (30% higher than the United States), not having to pay those fees has resulted in a surge of electric car usage in Norway. For example, Arne Nordbo avoids a $20 one-way fee every time he drives through the 3.5 mile undersea tunnel leading in and out of Finnoy, an island-locked Norwegian town. Finnoy borrowed $70 million to dig the tunnel, expecting drivers like Nordbo to pay off the loan via their $40-a-day tunnel fees. But with electric cars now making up 25 percent of all tunnel traffic, "We won't be able to pay down the tunnel," says Gro Skartveit, head of the company that operates the tunnel.[71] The Norwegian government now loses half a billion dollars a year in forgone tax revenue, and tunnel/ferry fees. Likewise, road operator revenues are down $40 million. Be careful what you reward!

Managers should also *correctly administer punishment at the appropriate time.* Many managers believe that punishment can change workers' behavior and help them improve their job performance. Furthermore, managers believe that fairly punishing workers also lets other workers know what is or isn't acceptable.[72] A danger of using punishment is that it can produce a backlash against managers and companies. But, if administered properly, punishment can weaken the frequency of undesirable behaviors without creating a backlash.[73] To be effective, the punishment must be strong enough to stop the undesired behavior and must be administered objectively (same rules applied to everyone), impersonally (without emotion or anger), consistently and contingently (each time improper behavior occurs), and quickly (as soon as possible following the undesirable behavior). In addition, managers should clearly explain what the appropriate behavior is and why the employee is being punished. Employees typically respond well when punishment is administered this way.[74]

Finally, managers should *choose the simplest and most effective schedule of reinforcement.* When choosing a schedule of reinforcement, managers need to balance effectiveness against simplicity. In fact, the more complex the schedule of reinforcement, the more likely it is to be misunderstood and resisted by managers and employees. For example, a forestry and logging company experimented with a unique variable ratio schedule. When tree-planters finished planting a bag of seedlings (about 1,000 seedlings per bag), they got to flip a coin. If they called the coin flip correctly (heads or tails), they were paid $4, double the regular rate of $2 per bag. If they called the coin flip incorrectly, they got nothing. The company began having problems when several workers and a manager, who was a part-time minister, claimed that the coin flip was a form of gambling. Then another worker found that the company was taking out too much money for taxes from workers' paychecks. Because the workers didn't really understand the reinforcement schedule, they blamed the payment plan associated with it and accused the company of trying to cheat them out of their money. After all of these problems, the researchers who implemented the variable ratio schedule concluded that "the results of this study may not be so much an indication of the relative effectiveness of different schedules of reinforcement as they are an indication of the types of problems that one encounters when applying these concepts in an industrial setting."[75] In short, choose the simplest, most effective schedule of reinforcement. Because continuous reinforcement, fixed ratio, and variable ratio schedules are about equally effective, continuous reinforcement schedules may be the best choice in many instances by virtue of their simplicity.

13-5 GOAL-SETTING THEORY

The basic model of motivation with which we began this chapter showed that individuals feel tension after becoming aware of an unfulfilled need. When they experience tension, they search for and select courses of action that they believe will eliminate this tension. In other words, they direct their behavior toward something. This something is a goal. A **goal** is a target, objective, or result that someone tries to accomplish. **Goal-setting theory** says that people will be motivated to the extent to which they accept specific, challenging goals and receive feedback that indicates their progress toward goal achievement.

*Let's learn more about goal setting by examining **13-5a the components of goal-setting theory** and **13-5b how to motivate with goal-setting theory**.*

13-5a Components of Goal-Setting Theory

The basic components of goal-setting theory are goal specificity, goal difficulty, goal acceptance, and performance feedback.[76] **Goal specificity** is the extent to which goals are detailed, exact, and unambiguous. Specific goals, such as "I'm going to have a 3.0 average this semester," are more motivating than general goals, such as "I'm going to get better grades this semester."

Goal difficulty is the extent to which a goal is hard or challenging to accomplish. Difficult goals, such as "I'm going to have a 3.5 average and make the dean's list this semester," are more motivating than easy goals, such as "I'm going to have a 2.0 average this semester."

Goal acceptance, which is similar to the idea of goal commitment discussed in Chapter 5, is the extent to which people consciously understand and agree to goals. Accepted goals, such as "I really want to get a 3.5 average this semester to show my parents how much I've improved," are more motivating than unaccepted goals, such as "My parents really want me to get a 3.5 average this semester, but there's so much more I'd rather do on campus than study!"

Performance feedback is information about the quality or quantity of past performance and indicates whether progress is being made toward the accomplishment of a goal. General Electric managers now use a smartphone app to give employees immediate performance feedback. The app prompts managers to provide detailed feedback using categories such as *Insights* (for current challenges), *Consider* (for changes to make), and *Continue* (for actions to keep doing). Leonardo Baldassarre and Brien Finken, of GE's Oil & Gas Turbomachinery Solutions explain, "For example, an engineer was asked to 'consider' being more open to supplier recommendations and to visit the supplier for a day. He did, and in GE's Real-Time Performance Development the following weeks the change was apparent. He championed a new approach that doubled our overall savings rate on budgeted project costs. Similarly, a procurement specialist was told to 'continue' encouraging volume pricing and other such practices among vendors to increase savings."[77]

How does goal setting work? To start, challenging goals focus employees' attention (that is, direction of effort) on the critical aspects of their jobs and away from unimportant areas. Goals also energize behavior. When faced with unaccomplished goals, employees typically develop plans and strategies to reach those goals. Goals also create tension between the goal, which is the desired future state of affairs, and where the employee or company is now, meaning the current state of affairs. This tension can be satisfied only by achieving or abandoning the goal. Finally, goals

Performance feedback—information about the quality or quantity of past performance—is key to attaining goals.

Goal a target, objective, or result that someone tries to accomplish

Goal-setting theory the theory that people will be motivated to the extent to which they accept specific, challenging goals and receive feedback that indicates their progress toward goal achievement

Goal specificity the extent to which goals are detailed, exact, and unambiguous

Goal difficulty the extent to which a goal is hard or challenging to accomplish

Goal acceptance the extent to which people consciously understand and agree to goals

Performance feedback information about the quality or quantity of past performance that indicates whether progress is being made toward the accomplishment of a goal

Exhibit 13.8
Adding Goal-Setting Theory to the Model

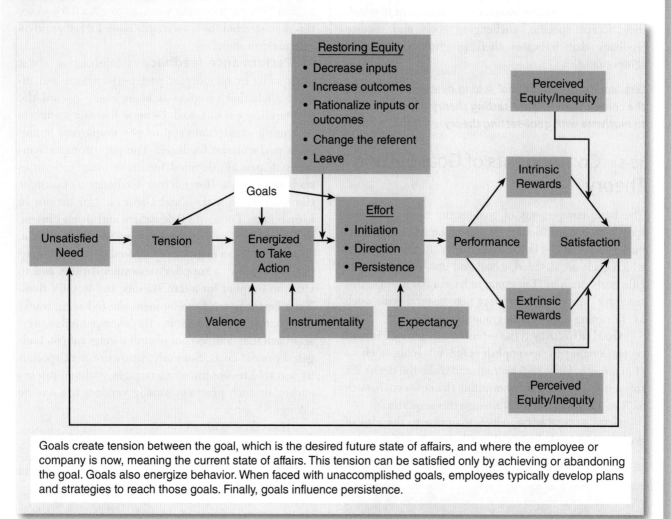

Goals create tension between the goal, which is the desired future state of affairs, and where the employee or company is now, meaning the current state of affairs. This tension can be satisfied only by achieving or abandoning the goal. Goals also energize behavior. When faced with unaccomplished goals, employees typically develop plans and strategies to reach those goals. Finally, goals influence persistence.

influence persistence. Because goals only go away when they are accomplished, employees are more likely to persist in their efforts in the presence of goals, especially with performance feedback. Exhibit 13.8 incorporates goals into the motivation model by showing how goals directly affect tension, effort, and the extent to which employees are energized to take action.

13-5b Motivating with Goal-Setting Theory

What practical steps can managers take to use goal-setting theory to motivate employees? Managers

can do three things, beginning with *assign specific, challenging goals*. One of the simplest, most effective ways to motivate workers is to give them specific, challenging goals. At **The Container Store**, every morning begins with a huddle during which sales managers announce the sales goals for the day. Because 12 percent of sales go toward their higher-than-industry-average salaries, everyone understands that sales volume is critical. Minute-by-minute status reports are posted for all stores in a particular region so that staff can see not only if they are keeping up, but how they are performing compared to other stores. And staff members who are struggling are coached by managers so that they can better contribute to meeting the goal.[78]

Second, managers should *make sure workers truly accept organizational goals*. Specific, challenging goals won't motivate workers unless they really accept, understand, and agree to the organization's goals. For this to occur, people must see the goals as fair and reasonable. Employees must also trust management and believe that managers are using goals to clarify what is expected from them rather than to exploit or threaten them ("If you don't achieve these goals . . ."). Participative goal setting, in which managers and employees generate goals together, can help increase trust and understanding and thus acceptance of goals. Furthermore, providing workers with training can help increase goal acceptance, particularly when workers don't believe they are capable of reaching the organization's goals.[79]

Finally, managers should *provide frequent, specific, performance-related feedback*. After employees have accepted specific, challenging goals, they should receive frequent performance-related feedback so that they can track their progress toward goal completion. Feedback leads to stronger motivation and effort in three ways.[80] Receiving specific feedback about the quality of their performance can encourage employees who don't have specific, challenging goals to set goals to improve their performance. After people meet goals, performance feedback often encourages them to set higher, more difficult goals. And feedback lets people know whether they need to increase their efforts or change strategies in order to accomplish their goals.

13-6 MOTIVATING WITH THE INTEGRATED MODEL

We began this chapter by defining motivation as the set of forces that initiates, directs, and makes people persist in their efforts to accomplish a goal. We also asked the basic question that managers ask when they try to figure out how to motivate their workers: What leads to effort? The answer to that question is likely to be somewhat different for each employee. So, if you're having difficulty figuring out why people aren't motivated where you work, check your Review Card for a useful, theory-based starting point.

STUDY TOOLS 13

LOCATED IN TEXTBOOK
- ☐ Rip-out and review chapter review card

LOCATED AT WWW.CENGAGEBRAIN.COM
- ☐ Review key term flashcards and create your own from StudyBits
- ☐ Track your knowledge and understanding of key concepts, using the concept tracker

- ☐ Complete practice and graded quizzes to prepare for tests
- ☐ Complete interactive content within the exposition
- ☐ View chapter highlight box content at the beginning of each chapter

14 Leadership

Yuganov Konstantin/Shutterstock.com

LEARNING OUTCOMES

14-1 Explain what leadership is.

14-2 Describe who leaders are and what effective leaders do.

14-3 Explain Fiedler's contingency theory.

14-4 Describe how path-goal theory works.

14-5 Explain the normative decision theory.

14-6 Explain how visionary leadership (that is, charismatic or transformational) helps leaders achieve strategic leadership.

After you finish this chapter, go to **PAGE 318** for **STUDY TOOLS**

LEADERS VERSUS MANAGERS

If you've ever been in charge, or even just thought about it, chances are you've considered questions such as these: Do I have what it takes to lead? What are the most important things leaders do? How can I transform a poorly performing department, division, or company? Do I need to adjust my leadership depending on the situation and the employee? Why doesn't my leadership inspire people? If you feel overwhelmed at the prospect of being a leader, you're not alone—millions of leaders in organizations across the world struggle with these fundamental leadership issues on a daily basis.

The most common view of leaders is that they are "in charge." But leadership is about more than just making decisions and giving orders. Bill Flemming, president of **Skanska USA Building**, a division of one of the world's largest construction companies, notes, "When people [I lead] ask me a question [about solving a problem], I don't always answer it with, 'Yes, this is what I want you to do,' or, 'This is what I'd do.'" He goes on, "I've seen organizations where the boss makes all the decisions. That's not leadership; that's a boss. I don't want to be the boss, I want to be the leader. So I want to get you to help me figure out what we've got to do here. Because if you're deeply immersed in the problem or the issue, you probably know a lot more about it than I'm going to know. So what do you think is going to work?"[1]

Whether you construct buildings, create and innovate to bring new products to markets, or simply help a company gain competitive advantage and thereby increase profits, **leadership** is the process of influencing others to achieve group or organizational goals. The knowledge and skills you'll learn in this chapter won't make the task of leadership less daunting, but they will help you navigate your journey as a leader.

According to late business professor Warren Bennis, the primary difference between leaders and managers is that leaders are concerned with doing the right thing, while managers are concerned with doing things right.[2] In other words, leaders begin with the question "What should we be doing?" while managers start with "How can we do what we're already doing better?" Before becoming the CEO of open source software company Red Hat, Jim Whitehurst was chief operating officer of Delta Airlines. When Whitehurst made the switch, he knew that his new job would be different. "Red Hat is a high-growth company with incredible opportunities.

My job is a lot more about developing strategies, inspiring people, inspiring creativity," he said. As CEO, Whitehurst found, "The input you receive will often conflict. Some investors may want you to focus more on short-term results than long-term growth. Different customers may want very different things. Even individual board members can have very different opinions . . . That's one of the most challenging things about the job; since you have multiple bosses with multiple agendas, you constantly wonder, 'Am I doing the right things?'"[3]

Leaders focus on vision, mission, goals, and objectives, while managers focus on productivity and efficiency. Managers see themselves as preservers of the status quo, while leaders see themselves as promoters of change and challengers of the status quo in that they encourage creativity and risk taking. Virginia Rometty, IBM's CEO, plans to keep her $100 billion company growing and innovating by doing one thing—pressing managers and employees to take risks and embrace change. Rometty recently visited a team of IBM software developers, and when the team leader assured her they would meet their year-end roll-out target, Rometty whipped around and replied, "No, no, no! Too slow. What can I do you help you move faster?" For this year's planning retreat, she told her top executives, "Your assignment: one paragraph on what is IBM 10 years from now—no constraints, no sacred cows." When IBM leaders asked for more time and money to roll out IBM's SmartCloud services, she told them, "The market is moving too fast. I can't give you more time." Finally, on a Saturday morning at Starbucks near his home, IBM VP Jeff Smith saw Rometty out of the corner of his eye and pulled his baseball cap down to avoid being seen. Rometty saw him nonetheless, walked straight over to him, lifted his cap, and asked, "What are we doing to change the company?"[4]

Another difference is that managers have a relatively short-term perspective, while leaders take a long-term view. Managers are concerned with control and limiting the choices of others, while leaders are more concerned with expanding people's choices and options.[5] Managers also solve problems so that others can do their work, while leaders inspire and motivate others to find their own solutions. Finally, managers are also more concerned with *means*, how to get things done, while leaders are more concerned with *ends*, what gets done.

Although leaders are different from managers, organizations need them both. Managers are

> **Leadership** the process of influencing others to achieve group or organizational goals

critical to getting out the day-to-day work, and leaders are critical to inspiring employees and setting the organization's long-term direction. The key issue for any organization is the extent to which it is properly led and properly managed. As Bennis said in summing up the difference between leaders and managers, "American organizations (and probably those in much of the rest of the industrialized world) are underled and overmanaged. They do not pay enough attention to doing the right thing, while they pay too much attention to doing things right."[6]

14-2 WHO LEADERS ARE AND WHAT LEADERS DO

Chuck Robbins, CEO of **Cisco**, has a strong background in sales and is known as a relationship builder who is responsive and has a warm personal style.[7] By contrast, Tony Rothman, CEO of **Sony Pictures**, is known for being a hard-nosed businessman, focused more on tasks than people, who is not afraid to cut costs or ruffle the feathers of the studio's talent to bring a movie in on or under budget.[8]

Which one is likely to be successful as a CEO? According to a survey of 1,542 senior managers, it's the extrovert. Of those 1,542 senior managers, 47 percent felt that extroverts make better CEOs, while 65 percent said that being an introvert hurts a CEO's chances of success.[9] So clearly, senior managers believe that extroverted CEOs are better leaders. But are they? Not necessarily. In fact, a relatively high percentage of CEOs, 40 percent, are introverts. Yahoo! CEO Marissa Mayer admits she is an introvert who suffers from shyness, so much so that she even wants to leave parties at her home. She says, "I will literally look at my watch and say, 'You can't leave until time X. And if you're still having a terrible time at time X, you can leave." She's learned, though, that if she stays till "time X," she relaxes and begins to enjoy herself.[10]

So, what makes a good leader? Does leadership success depend on who leaders are, such as introverts or extroverts, or on what leaders do and how they behave?

Trait theory a leadership theory that holds that effective leaders possess a similar set of traits or characteristics

Traits relatively stable characteristics, such as abilities, psychological motives, or consistent patterns of behavior

Let's learn more about who leaders are by investigating **14-2a leadership traits** *and* **14-2b leadership behaviors**.

14-2a Leadership Traits

Trait theory is one way to describe who leaders are. **Trait theory** says that effective leaders possess a similar set of traits or characteristics. **Traits** are relatively stable characteristics such as abilities, psychological motives, or consistent patterns of behavior. For example, trait theory holds that leaders are taller and more confident and have greater physical stamina (that is, higher energy levels) than nonleaders. In fact, studies show we perceive those in authority as being taller than they actually are, and that taller people see themselves as more qualified to lead.[11] Indeed, while just 14.5 percent of men are six feet tall, 58 percent of *Fortune* 500 CEOs are six feet or taller. Author Malcolm Gladwell says, "We have a sense, in our minds, of what a leader is supposed to look like, and that stereotype is so powerful that when someone fits it, we simply become blind to other considerations."[12] Likewise, in terms of physical stamina, companies whose CEOs have run and finished a marathon have a stock valuation that is 5 percent larger than those whose CEO had not.[13] Another study found a small relationship between Fortune 500 CEO face width (thought to indicate a leader's dominance, ambition, and power) and company profitability.[14] Trait theory is also known as the "great person" theory because early versions of the theory stated that leaders are born, not made. In other words, you either have the right stuff to be a leader, or you don't. And if you don't, there is no way to get it.

For some time, it was thought that trait theory was wrong and that there are no consistent trait differences

Sony CEO, Tony Rothman, is known for being a hard-nosed businessman, focused more on tasks than people.

between leaders and nonleaders, or between effective and ineffective leaders. However, more recent evidence shows that "successful leaders are not like other people," that successful leaders are indeed different from the rest of us.[15] More specifically, leaders are different from nonleaders in the following traits: drive, the desire to lead, honesty/integrity, self-confidence, emotional stability, cognitive ability, and knowledge of the business.[16]

Drive refers to high levels of effort and is characterized by achievement, motivation, initiative, energy, and tenacity. In terms of achievement and ambition, leaders always try to make improvements or achieve success in what they're doing. Because of their initiative, they have strong desires to promote change or solve problems. Leaders typically have more energy—they have to, given the long hours they put in and followers' expectations that they be positive and upbeat. Thus, leaders must have physical, mental, and emotional vitality. Leaders are also more tenacious than nonleaders and are better at overcoming obstacles and problems that would deter most of us. In an interview of Jack Ma, founder and board chair of China-based e-commerce giant **Alibaba**, veteran journalist Charlie Rose mentioned that Ma had faced a lot of rejection. Ma replied, "There's an examination for young people [in China] to go to university. I failed it three times. I failed a lot. So, I applied to thirty different jobs and got rejected. I went for a job with the police; they said, 'You're no good.' I even went to KFC when it came to my city. Twenty-four people went for the job. Twenty-three were accepted. I was the only guy. . . ."[17]

Successful leaders also have a stronger *desire to lead*. They want to be in charge and think about ways to influence or convince others about what should or shouldn't be done. *Honesty/integrity* is also important to leaders. *Honesty*, being truthful with others, is a cornerstone of leadership. Without it, leaders won't be trusted. When leaders are honest, subordinates are willing to overlook other flaws. Mike Lazzo, the executive vice president and creative director of **Comedy Central's Adult Swim**, is known for giving honest feedback directly—even when it's negative. Robert Smigel, creator of *The Jack and Triumph Show*, says, "He can be humorously blunt, which is refreshing compared to other network people who think you can't take criticism without hearing five compliments first."[18] *Integrity* is the extent to which leaders do what they say they will do. Leaders may be honest and have good intentions, but if they don't consistently deliver on what they promise, they won't be trusted.

Self-confidence, or believing in one's abilities, also distinguishes leaders from nonleaders. Self-confident leaders are more decisive and assertive and are more likely to gain others' confidence. Moreover, self-confident leaders will admit mistakes because they view them as learning opportunities rather than as refutations of their leadership capabilities. Krispy Kreme looked for candidates who demonstrated these specific qualities during a recent CEO hunt. According to chair (and former CEO) James Morgan, humility and servant leadership are strong aspects of Krispy Kreme's culture. Morgan says that Tony Thomson, who was selected to succeed him, "exhibited those two characteristics strongly." Not everyone who joins the company understands how integral this philosophy is, however. One senior manager would not collaborate with his team on new product or operation ideas, but would take credit for them and would steal the limelight when they were presented to the executive leadership team. This executive was later fired, said Morgan, because, "He didn't understand the humility part."[19]

Leaders also have *emotional stability*. Even when things go wrong, they remain even-tempered and consistent in their outlook and in the way they treat others. After experiencing disappointing results in its mobile unit, Samsung appointed DJ Koh, who is known for his even-tempered demeanor, to lead the division. Having joined Samsung out of college, Koh quickly rose through the company ranks because he was well-liked and kept a low-profile. In contrast to his hard-charging predecessor,

DOES COKE'S CEO LACK SPARKLE?

For a company whose current motto "Open Happiness" is only one in a history of upbeat, feel-good slogans, Coke's CEO Muhtar Kent can be decidedly gruff. Critics complain that he surrounds himself with "yes people" and may not realize when he's shutting down discussion. Coke veteran Sandy Douglas says, "It's a full-contact sport to argue strategy with Mr. Kent." Despite an abrupt, and perhaps autocratic, leadership style, Kent is devoted to Coke and its operations. He even carries a paint chip with the exact color of Coke red in his pocket so that, wherever he is in the world, he can compare it to delivery trucks, bottles, cans, and vending machines. And he understands the challenges facing the soft drink industry. "If we don't do what we need to do quickly, effectively, execute 100 percent," he says, "then somebody else will come and do it for us."

Source: M. Esterl, "Coke's Chief's Solution for Lost Fizz: More Soda," *Wall Street Journal*, March 18, 2015, A1, A12.

employees describe Koh as a "predictable, realistic, and reasonable executive who is hardworking and direct." One of his close colleagues adds, "He's not a screamer."[20] Leaders who can't control their emotions, who anger quickly or attack and blame others for mistakes, are unlikely to be trusted.

Leaders are also smart—they typically have strong *cognitive abilities*. This doesn't mean that leaders are necessarily geniuses—far from it. But it does mean that leaders have the capacity to analyze large amounts of seemingly unrelated, complex information and see patterns, opportunities, or threats where others might not see them. Finally, leaders also know their stuff, which means they have superior technical knowledge about the businesses they run. Leaders who have a good *knowledge of the business* understand the key technological decisions and concerns facing their companies. More often than not, studies indicate that effective leaders have long, extensive experience in their industries. Tom Staggs was with **Walt Disney Co.** nearly forty years, starting as a strategic planner. As CFO, he was involved in digital strategy and acquiring Pixar and Marvel. He ran Disney's parks and resorts division, rolling out the My Magic Plus wireless wristband technology to help park guests make purchases and better plan their trips, and oversaw the $5.5 billion construction of Disney Shanghai. He was eventually named Disney's chief operating officer—the number two position in the company.[21]

14-2b Leadership Behaviors

Thus far, you've read about who leaders *are*. But traits alone are not enough to make a successful leader. They are, however, a precondition for success. After all, it's hard to imagine a truly successful leader who lacks most of these qualities. Leaders who have these traits (or many of them) must then take actions that encourage people to achieve group or organizational goals.[22] Accordingly, we now examine what leaders *do*, meaning the behaviors they perform or the actions they take to influence others to achieve group or organizational goals.

Researchers at the University of Michigan, the Ohio State University, and the University of Texas examined the specific behaviors that leaders use to improve subordinate satisfaction and performance. Hundreds of studies were conducted, and

hundreds of leader behaviors were examined. At all three universities, two basic leader behaviors emerged as central to successful leadership: initiating structure (called *job-centered leadership* at the University of Michigan and *concern for production* at the University of Texas) and considerate leader behavior (called *employee-centered leadership* at the University of Michigan and *concern for people* at the University of Texas).[23] These two leader behaviors form the basis for many of the leadership theories discussed in this chapter.

Initiating structure is the degree to which a leader structures the roles of followers by setting goals, giving directions, setting deadlines, and assigning tasks. A leader's ability to initiate structure primarily affects subordinates' job performance. When Amazon founder and CEO Jeff Bezos bought the *Washington Post*, he instituted a data-driven focus on goals at the newspaper—similar to how Amazon is run. When a subscriber complained that the paper's mobile app took too long to download articles, he emailed the Post's chief information officer, Shailesh Prakash, saying simply, "fix it." Prakash said about the issue, "We looked at the problem and I told Jeff I thought we could improve the load time to maybe two seconds. He wrote back and said, 'It needs to be milliseconds.'"[24] Bezos had a data analytics display charting real-time web traffic patterns installed in the center of the Post's newsroom. Similar dashboards will soon be on reporter's computers. Just how important are data-driven results to Bezos? The Post's web traffic figures—which have tripled since Bezos bought the

Samsung President of Mobile Communications DJ Koh unveils the Galaxy S7 and Galaxy S7 Edge smartphones at the Mobile World Congress on February 21, 2016.

Initiating structure the degree to which a leader structures the roles of followers by setting goals, giving directions, setting deadlines, and assigning tasks

paper—are now factored into managers' and employee's performance reviews.

Consideration is the extent to which a leader is friendly, approachable, and supportive and shows concern for employees. Consideration primarily affects subordinates' job satisfaction. Specific leader consideration behaviors include listening to employees' problems and concerns, consulting with employees before making decisions, and treating employees as equals. Cheryl Bachelder, CEO of Popeye's, spends a lot of time listening to franchisees who own and run Popeye's restaurants. Before her arrival, Popeye's had suffered several years of management turnover, strained relationships with franchisees, and weak sales. To turn the chain around, Bachelder outlined a very specific plan and then consulted franchisees every step of the way. She listened when they asked to delay plans to remodel restaurants until they got their sales up and could afford the construction. Determining a national beverage supplier (that is, Coke or Pepsi) is a contentious issue in fast food, but Popeye's needed to consolidate for cost savings. So, she convened a team, with equal numbers of franchisees who sold Coke and Pepsi, and then had them listen to supplier presentations and pick the winner.[25] Asked about her leadership style, Bachelder responded, "We give dignity to human beings, and we attempt to be humble. People perform better under those conditions."[26]

Although researchers at all three universities generally agreed that initiating structure and consideration were basic leader behaviors, their interpretation differed on how these two behaviors are related to one another and which are necessary for effective leadership. The University of Michigan studies indicated that initiating structure and consideration were mutually exclusive behaviors on opposite ends of the same continuum. In other words, leaders who wanted to be more considerate would have to do less initiating of structure (and vice versa). The University of Michigan studies also indicated that only considerate leader behaviors (that is, employee-centered behaviors) were associated with successful leadership. By contrast, researchers at the Ohio State University and the University of Texas found that initiating structure and consideration were independent behaviors, meaning that leaders can be considerate and initiate structure at the same time. Additional evidence confirms this finding.[27] The same researchers also concluded that the most effective leaders were strong on both initiating structure and considerate leader behaviors.

This "high-high" approach can be seen in the upper-right corner of the Blake/Mouton leadership grid, shown in Exhibit 14.1. Blake and Mouton used two leadership

Amazon founder and Washington Post owner Jeff Bezos speaks at the grand opening of the Washington Post's new headquarters on January 28, 2016.

Chip Somodevilla/Getty Images

behaviors, concern for people (that is, consideration) and concern for production (that is, initiating structure), to categorize five different leadership styles. Both behaviors are rated on a nine-point scale, with 1 representing "low" and 9 representing "high." Blake and Mouton suggest that a "high-high," or 9,9, leadership style is the best. They call this style *team management* because leaders who use it display a high concern for people (9) and a high concern for production (9).

By contrast, leaders use a 9,1 *authority-compliance* leadership style when they have a high concern for production and a low concern for people. A 1,9 *country club* style occurs when leaders care about having a friendly, enjoyable work environment but don't really pay much attention to production or performance. The worst leadership style, according to the grid, is the 1,1 *impoverished* leader, who shows little concern for people or production and does the bare minimum needed to keep his or her job. Finally, the 5,5 *middle-of-the-road* style occurs when leaders show a moderate amount of concern for both people and production.

Is the team management style, with a high concern for production and a high concern for people, the best leadership style? Logically, it would seem so. Why wouldn't you want to show high concern for both people and production? Nonetheless, nearly fifty years of research indicates that there isn't one best leadership style. The best leadership style depends on the situation. In other words, no one leadership behavior by itself and no one combination of leadership behaviors work well across all situations and employees.

Consideration the extent to which a leader is friendly, approachable, and supportive and shows concern for employees

Exhibit 14.1
Blake/Mouton Leadership Grid

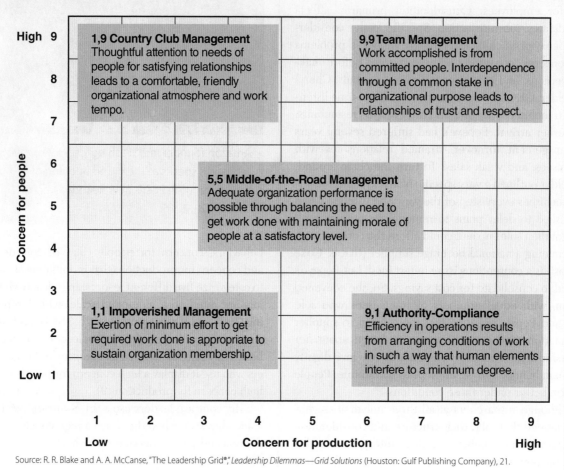

1,9 Country Club Management
Thoughtful attention to needs of people for satisfying relationships leads to a comfortable, friendly organizational atmosphere and work tempo.

9,9 Team Management
Work accomplished is from committed people. Interdependence through a common stake in organizational purpose leads to relationships of trust and respect.

5,5 Middle-of-the-Road Management
Adequate organization performance is possible through balancing the need to get work done with maintaining morale of people at a satisfactory level.

1,1 Impoverished Management
Exertion of minimum effort to get required work done is appropriate to sustain organization membership.

9,1 Authority-Compliance
Efficiency in operations results from arranging conditions of work in such a way that human elements interfere to a minimum degree.

Concern for people — High 9, 8, 7, 6, 5, 4, 3, 2, Low 1

Concern for production — Low 1 2 3 4 5 6 7 8 9 High

Source: R. R. Blake and A. A. McCanse, "The Leadership Grid®," *Leadership Dilemmas—Grid Solutions* (Houston: Gulf Publishing Company), 21.

14-3 PUTTING LEADERS IN THE RIGHT SITUATION: FIEDLER'S CONTINGENCY THEORY

After leader traits and behaviors, the situational approach to leadership is the third major method used in the study of leadership. We'll review three major situational approaches to leadership—Fiedler's contingency theory, path-goal theory, and Vroom, Yetton, and Jago's normative decision model. All assume that the effectiveness of any **leadership style**,

Leadership style the way a leader generally behaves toward followers

the way a leader generally behaves toward followers, depends on the situation.[28] A study of 130 restaurants in a pizza franchise examined the interaction between how extroverted store managers were and how involved employees were in trying "to bring about improved procedures [in the store.]" Profits were 16 percent *above* average in stores with extroverted managers and less involved employees. In those instances, the strengths of the more outgoing boss fit well with the less involved employees. By contrast, profits were 14 percent *below* average in stores with extroverted leaders and highly involved employees. Why? Because the extroverted leaders were less comfortable with employees who wanted a say in making improvements. Again, leadership success depends on the situation.[29]

According to situational leadership theories, there is no one best leadership style. But one of these situational theories differs from the other three in one significant way. Fiedler's contingency theory assumes that leadership styles are consistent and difficult to change. Therefore, leaders must be placed in or matched to a situation that fits their leadership style. By contrast, the other three situational theories all assume that leaders are capable of adapting and adjusting their leadership styles to fit the demands of different situations.

Fiedler's **contingency theory** states that in order to maximize work group performance, leaders must be matched to the right leadership situation.[30] More specifically, the first basic assumption of Fiedler's theory is that leaders are effective when the work groups they lead perform well. So, instead of judging leaders' effectiveness by what they do (that is, initiating structure and consideration) or who they are (that is, trait theory), Fiedler assesses leaders by the conduct and performance of the people they supervise. Second, Fiedler assumes that leaders are generally unable to change their leadership styles and that they will be more effective when their styles are matched to the proper situation. This explains why company founders are not always the best suited to lead their companies. Evernote, a software company known for its digital note taking applications, was growing at such a rate that it eventually surpassed founder Phil Libin's ability to lead it. Although the company is valued at roughly $1 billion, Evernote began to stumble as it transitioned from a free app to a paid subscription service for professionals. After cutting about 13 percent of its staff and closing some global operations, Libin brought in a former Google executive to be Evernote's new CEO. At the same time, Evernote's board named Jeff Shotts, a former finance executive from eBay, as its new CFO. Shotts explained the need for different leadership this way: "The company is transitioning from startup mode to a more mature organization."[31]

Third, Fiedler assumes that the favorableness of a situation for a leader depends on the degree to which the situation permits the leader to influence the behavior of group members. Fiedler's third assumption is consistent with our definition of leadership as the process of influencing others to achieve group or organizational goals. In other words, in addition to traits, behaviors, and a favorable situation to match, leaders have to be allowed to lead.

Let's learn more about Fiedler's contingency theory by examining **14-3a the least preferred coworker and leadership styles,** **14-3b situational favorableness,** and **14-3c how to match leadership styles to situations.**

14-3a Leadership Style: Least Preferred Coworker

When Fiedler refers to *leadership style,* he means the way that leaders generally behave toward their followers. Do the leaders yell and scream and blame others when things go wrong? Or do they correct mistakes by listening and then quietly but directly make their point? Do they take credit for others' work when things go right? Or do they make sure that those who did the work receive the credit they rightfully deserve? Do they let others make their own decisions and hold them accountable for the results? Or do they micromanage, insisting that all decisions be approved first by them? Fiedler also assumes that leadership styles are tied to leaders' underlying needs and personalities. Because personalities and needs are relatively stable, he assumes that leaders are generally incapable of changing their leadership styles. In other words, the way that leaders treat people now is probably the way they've always treated others. So, according to Fiedler, if your boss's first instinct is to yell and scream and blame others, chances are he or she has always done that.

Fiedler uses a questionnaire called the Least Preferred Coworker (LPC) scale to measure leadership style. When completing the LPC scale, people are instructed to consider all of the people with whom they have ever worked and then to choose the one person with whom they have worked *least* well. Fiedler explains, "This does not have to be the person you liked least well, but should be the one person with whom you have the most trouble getting the job done."[32]

Would you describe your LPC as pleasant, friendly, supportive, interesting, cheerful, and sincere? Or would you describe the person as unpleasant, unfriendly, hostile, boring, gloomy, and insincere? People who describe their LPC in a positive way (scoring 64 and above) have *relationship-oriented* leadership styles. After

Contingency theory a leadership theory states that to maximize work group performance, leaders must be matched to the situation that best fits their leadership style

all, if they can still be positive about their least preferred coworker, they must be people-oriented. By contrast, people who describe their LPC in a negative way (scoring 57 or below) have *task-oriented* leadership styles. Given a choice, they'll focus first on getting the job done and second on making sure everyone gets along. Finally, those with moderate scores (from 58 to 63) have a more *flexible* leadership style and can be somewhat relationship-oriented or somewhat task-oriented.

14-3b Situational Favorableness

Fiedler assumes that leaders will be more effective when their leadership styles are matched to the proper situation. More specifically, Fiedler defines **situational favorableness** as the degree to which a particular situation either permits or denies a leader the chance to influence the behavior of group members.[33] In highly favorable situations, leaders find that their actions influence followers. But in highly unfavorable situations, leaders have little or no success influencing the people they are trying to lead.

Three situational factors determine the favorability of a situation:

leader-member relations, task structure, and position power. The most important situational factor is **leader-member relations**, which refers to how well followers respect, trust, and like their leaders. When leader-member relations are good, followers trust the leader, and there is a friendly work atmosphere. **Task structure** is the degree to which the requirements of a subordinate's tasks are clearly specified. With highly structured tasks, employees have clear job responsibilities, goals, and procedures. **Position power** is the degree to which leaders are able to hire, fire, reward, and punish workers. The more influence leaders have over hiring, firing, rewards, and punishments, the greater their power.

Exhibit 14.2 shows how leader-member relations, task structure, and position power can be combined into eight situations that differ in their favorability to leaders. In general, Situation I, on the left side of Exhibit 14.2, is the most favorable leader situation. Followers like and trust their leaders and know what to do because their tasks are highly structured. Also, the leaders have the formal power to influence workers through hiring, firing, rewarding, and punishing them. Therefore, it's relatively easy for a leader to influence followers in Situation I. By contrast, Situation VIII, on the right side of Exhibit 14.2, is the least favorable situation for leaders. Followers don't like or trust their leaders. Plus, followers are not sure what they're supposed to be doing, given that their tasks or jobs are highly unstructured. Finally, leaders find it difficult to influence followers because they don't have the ability to hire, fire, reward, or punish the people who work for them. In short, it's very difficult to influence followers given the conditions found in Situation VIII.

Situational favorableness the degree to which a particular situation either permits or denies a leader the chance to influence the behavior of group members

Leader-member relations the degree to which followers respect, trust, and like their leaders

Task structure the degree to which the requirements of a subordinate's tasks are clearly specified

Position power the degree to which leaders are able to hire, fire, reward, and punish workers

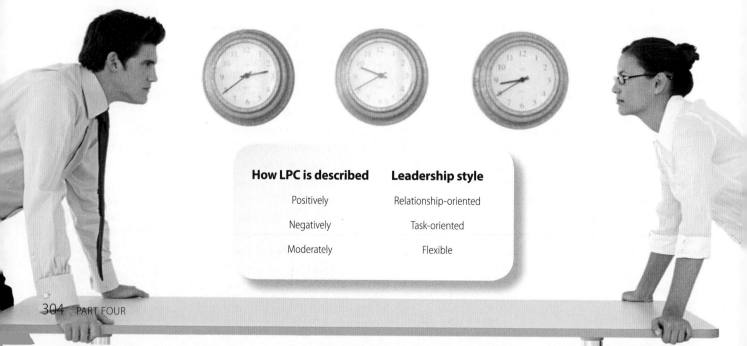

How LPC is described	Leadership style
Positively	Relationship-oriented
Negatively	Task-oriented
Moderately	Flexible

Image Source/Getty Images

14-3c Matching Leadership Styles to Situations

After studying thousands of leaders and followers in hundreds of different situations, Fiedler found that the performance of relationship- and task-oriented leaders followed the pattern displayed in Exhibit 14.3.

Relationship-oriented leaders with high LPC scores were better leaders (that is, their groups performed more effectively) under moderately favorable situations. In moderately favorable situations, the leader may be liked somewhat, tasks may be somewhat structured, and the leader may have some position power. In this situation, a relationship-oriented leader improves leader-member relations, which is the most important of the three situational factors. In turn, morale and performance improve.

By contrast, as Exhibit 14.3 shows, task-oriented leaders with low LPC scores are better leaders in highly favorable and unfavorable situations. Task-oriented leaders do well in favorable situations where leaders are liked, tasks are structured, and the leader has the power to hire, fire, reward, and punish. In these favorable situations, task-oriented leaders effectively step on the gas of a well-tuned car. Their focus on performance sets the goal for the group, which then charges forward to meet it. But task-oriented leaders also do well in unfavorable situations where leaders are disliked, tasks are unstructured, and the leader doesn't have the power to hire, fire, reward, and punish. In these unfavorable situations, the task-oriented leader sets goals, which focus attention on performance and clarify what needs to be done, thus overcoming low task structure. This is enough to jump-start performance even if workers don't like or trust the leader.

Finally, though not shown in Exhibit 14.3, people with moderate LPC scores, who can be somewhat relationship-oriented or somewhat task-oriented, tend to do fairly well in all situations because they can adapt their behavior. Typically, though, they don't perform quite as well as relationship-oriented or task-oriented leaders whose leadership styles are well matched to the situation.

Exhibit 14.2
Situational Favorableness

Leader-Member Relations	Good	Good	Good	Good	Poor	Poor	Poor	Poor
Task Structure	High	High	Low	Low	High	High	Low	Low
Position Power	Strong	Weak	Strong	Weak	Strong	Weak	Strong	Weak
Situation	I	II	III	IV	V	VI	VII	VIII
		Favorable		**Moderately Favorable**			**Unfavorable**	

Exhibit 14.3
Matching Leadership Styles to Situations

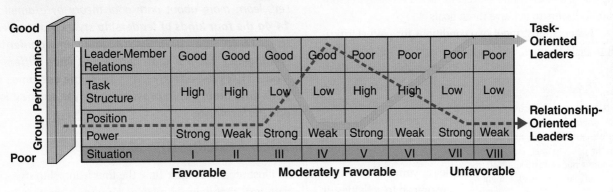

Recall, however, that Fiedler assumes leaders to be incapable of changing their leadership styles. Accordingly, the key to applying Fiedler's contingency theory in the workplace is to accurately measure and match leaders to situations or to teach leaders how to change situational favorableness by changing leader-member relations, task structure, or position power. Although matching or placing leaders in appropriate situations works particularly well, practicing managers have had little luck reengineering situations to fit their leadership styles. The primary problem, as you've no doubt realized, is the complexity of the theory.

In a study designed to teach leaders how to reengineer their situations to fit their leadership styles, Fiedler found that most of the leaders simply did not understand what they were supposed to do to change their situations. Furthermore, if they didn't like their LPC profile (perhaps they felt they were more relationship-oriented than their scores indicated), they arbitrarily changed it to better suit their view of themselves. Of course, the theory won't work as well if leaders are attempting to change situational factors to fit their perceived leadership style rather than their real leadership style.[34]

14-4 ADAPTING LEADER BEHAVIOR: PATH-GOAL THEORY

Just as its name suggests, **path-goal theory** states that leaders can increase subordinate satisfaction and performance by clarifying and clearing the paths to goals and by increasing the number and kinds of rewards available for goal attainment. Said another way, leaders need to clarify how followers can achieve organizational goals, take care of problems that prevent followers from achieving goals, and then find more and varied rewards to motivate followers to achieve those goals.[35]

Leaders must meet two conditions for path clarification, path clearing, and rewards to increase followers' motivation and effort. First, leader behavior must be a source of immediate or future satisfaction for followers. The things you do as a leader must either please your followers today or lead to activities or rewards that will satisfy them in the future. One of the key cultural principles followed by Charlie Kim, CEO of New York-based Next Jump, which runs web-based reward programs for 90,000 companies, is "Better Me + Better You = Better Us," Kim says, "The culture we're building is predicated on the concept of long-term, sustained happiness."[36] This is why Next Jump's leadership frequently asks its people what *would* make them happier. Because of the long hours they put in, employees were spending half a day per weekend in a NYC laundromat doing their laundry. So they asked if washers and dryers could be installed at work to be used (and which they would pay for) when working late hours. Recognizing the problem (not laundry, but the secondary effect of long hours resulting in lost weekend time), Next Jump now pays for laundry service. Employees bring in laundry on Fridays and it returns done on Mondays in a bag with Next Jump's logo and this phrase: "My company gets my laundry. I get my weekends back."[37] Next Jump's culture is so positive, rewarding, and satisfying that 18,000 people applied for thirty-five openings last year. Furthermore, while the quit rate in the tech industry is 22 percent per year, Next Jump has an incredibly low 1 percent quit rate.

Second, while providing the coaching, guidance, support, and rewards necessary for effective work performance, leader behaviors must complement and not duplicate the characteristics of followers' work environments. Thus, leader behaviors must offer something unique and valuable to followers beyond what they're already experiencing as they do their jobs or what they can already do for themselves.

In contrast to Fiedler's contingency theory, path-goal theory assumes that leaders *can* change and adapt their leadership styles. Exhibit 14.4 illustrates this process, showing that leaders change and adapt their leadership styles contingent on their subordinates or the environment in which those subordinates work.

*Let's learn more about path-goal theory by examining **14-4a the four kinds of leadership styles that leaders use, 14-4b the subordinate and environmental contingency factors that determine when different leader styles are effective,** and **14-4c the outcomes of path-goal theory in improving employee satisfaction and performance.***

14-4a Leadership Styles

As illustrated in Exhibit 14.4, the four leadership styles in path-goal theory are directive, supportive, participative,

Path-goal theory a leadership theory states that leaders can increase subordinate satisfaction and performance by clarifying and clearing the paths to goals and by increasing the number and kinds of rewards available for goal attainment

and achievement oriented.[38] **Directive leadership** involves letting employees know precisely what is expected of them, giving them specific guidelines for performing tasks, scheduling work, setting standards of performance, and making sure that people follow standard rules and regulations. These activities are especially important during economic downturns and periods during which a company is struggling. Recent research suggests that in more challenging economic environments (such as recessions), a more directive and authoritarian approach to leadership may produce stronger financial results for the company. More directive leaders reinforce discipline, effective coordination, and operational efficiency, so they are more likely to increase revenues during short-term crises and economic downturns.[39] Directive leadership is very similar to initiating structure.

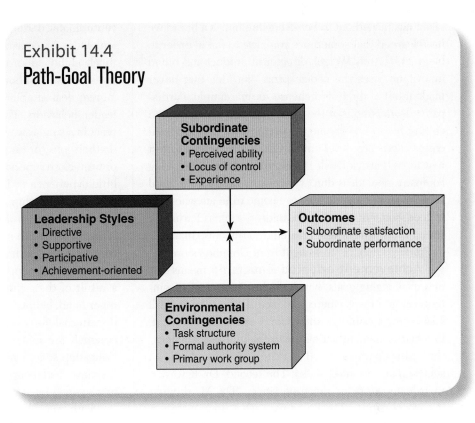

Exhibit 14.4
Path-Goal Theory

Subordinate Contingencies
• Perceived ability
• Locus of control
• Experience

Leadership Styles
• Directive
• Supportive
• Participative
• Achievement-oriented

Outcomes
• Subordinate satisfaction
• Subordinate performance

Environmental Contingencies
• Task structure
• Formal authority system
• Primary work group

Supportive leadership involves being approachable and friendly to employees, showing concern for them and their welfare, treating them as equals, and creating a friendly climate. Supportive leadership is very similar to considerate leader behavior. Supportive leadership often results in employee satisfaction with the job and with leaders. This leadership style may also result in improved performance when it increases employee confidence, lowers employee job stress, or improves relations and trust between employees and leaders.[40]

Participative leadership involves consulting employees for their suggestions and input before making decisions. Participation in decision making should help followers understand which goals are most important and clarify the paths to accomplishing them. Furthermore, when people participate in decisions, they become more committed to making them work. In Domino's Pizza's "Failure Is an Option" advertising campaign, Scott Hinshaw, Domino's EVP of operations, says, "In order to get better, in order to move ahead, you're going to make mistakes."[41] Domino's President Russell Weiner explains, "Not every risk we have

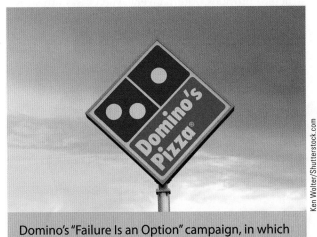

Domino's "Failure Is an Option" campaign, in which ideas can come from anywhere in the company and failures are encouraged, is an example of participatory leadership.

Ken Wolter/Shutterstock.com

Directive leadership a leadership style in which the leader lets employees know precisely what is expected of them, gives them specific guidelines for performing tasks, schedules work, sets standards of performance, and makes sure that people follow standard rules and regulations

Supportive leadership a leadership style in which the leader is friendly and approachable to employees, shows concern for employees and their welfare, treats them as equals, and creates a friendly climate

Participative leadership a leadership style in which the leader consults employees for their suggestions and input before making decisions

taken has turned out to be successful, but as a brand we have learned that sometimes you have to fail in order to be great."[42] Andy Wetzel, director of product and brand innovation, uses the cookie pizza—an idea that never made it out of the test kitchens—as an example. Participative leadership is at the heart of Domino's innovation culture because everyone in the company, down to franchisees and entry-level employees, is encouraged to test new ideas. Patrick Doyle, Domino's CEO, says, "At a big company, new ideas don't typically come from the local store level. But a great idea can come from anywhere."[43] Indeed, some of Domino's best ideas, such as Parmesan Bread Bites, which were created by a franchise manager in Findlay, Ohio, come straight from Domino's stores.[44]

Achievement-oriented leadership means setting challenging goals, having high expectations of employees, and displaying confidence that employees will assume responsibility and put forth extraordinary effort. Psychiatrist Samantha Boardman did her medical internship with two physicians. The first, Dr. M, was clearly an achievement-oriented leader. The second, Dr. F, wasn't. Boardman wrote of the experience, "Dr. M, thought the world of me. 'Dr. Boardman, what do you think?' he asked whenever there was a question about a diagnosis. 'Good work, Dr. Boardman,' he said whenever I reported lab results or presented a new patient. I thrived under his leadership and did my utmost to live up to his high expectations. It motivated me to work harder and to do my best."[45] Dr. F, she says, "thought very little of me. His low expectations became a reality. I made dumb mistakes. My mind went blank whenever he asked me questions. My confidence evaporated along with my motivation. I became a completely different person in his presence."[46]

14-4b Subordinate and Environmental Contingencies

As shown in Exhibit 14.4, path-goal theory specifies that leader behaviors should be adapted to subordinate characteristics. The theory identifies three kinds of subordinate contingencies: perceived ability, experience, and locus of control. *Perceived ability* is simply how much ability subordinates believe they have for doing their jobs well. Subordinates who perceive that they have a great deal of ability will be dissatisfied with directive leader behaviors. Experienced employees are likely to react in a similar way. Because they already know how to do their jobs (or perceive that they do), they don't need or want close supervision. By contrast, subordinates with little experience or little perceived ability will welcome directive leadership.

Locus of control is a personality measure that indicates the extent to which people believe that they have control over what happens to them in life. *Internals* believe that what happens to them, good or bad, is largely a result of their choices and actions. *Externals*, on the other hand, believe that what happens to them is caused by external forces beyond their control. Accordingly, externals are much more comfortable with a directive leadership style, whereas internals greatly prefer a participative leadership style because they like to have a say in what goes on at work.

Path-goal theory specifies that leader behaviors should complement rather than duplicate the characteristics of followers' work environments. There are three kinds of environmental contingencies: task structure, the formal authority system, and the primary work group. As in Fiedler's contingency theory, *task structure* is the degree to which the requirements of a subordinate's tasks are clearly specified. When task structure is low, and tasks are unclear, directive leadership should be used because it complements the work environment. When task structure is high and tasks are clear, however, directive leadership is not needed because it duplicates what task structure provides. Alternatively, when tasks are stressful, frustrating, or dissatisfying, leaders should respond with supportive leadership.

Achievement-oriented leadership a leadership style in which the leader sets challenging goals, has high expectations of employees, and displays confidence that employees will assume responsibility and put forth extraordinary effort

Exhibit 14.5

Path-Goal Theory: When to Use Directive, Supportive, Participative, or Achievement-Oriented Leadership

Directive Leadership	Supportive Leadership	Participative Leadership	Achievement-Oriented Leadership
Unstructured tasks	Structured, simple, repetitive tasks Stressful, frustrating tasks	Complex tasks	Unchallenging tasks
Workers with external locus of control	Workers lack confidence	Workers with internal locus of control	
Unclear formal authority system	Clear formal authority system	Workers not satisfied with rewards	
Inexperienced workers		Experienced workers	
Workers with low perceived ability		Workers with high perceived ability	

The *formal authority system* is an organization's set of procedures, rules, and policies. When the formal authority system is unclear, directive leadership complements the situation by reducing uncertainty and increasing clarity. But when the formal authority system is clear, directive leadership is redundant and should not be used.

Primary work group refers to the amount of work-oriented participation or emotional support that is provided by an employee's immediate work group. Participative leadership should be used when tasks are complex, and there is little existing work-oriented participation in the primary work group. When tasks are stressful, frustrating, or repetitive, supportive leadership is called for.

Finally, because keeping track of all of these subordinate and environmental contingencies can get a bit confusing, Exhibit 14.5 provides a summary of when directive, supportive, participative, and achievement-oriented leadership styles should be used.

14-4c Outcomes

Does following path-goal theory improve subordinate satisfaction and performance? Preliminary evidence suggests that it does.[47] In particular, people who work for supportive leaders are much more satisfied with their jobs and their bosses. Likewise, people who work for directive leaders are more satisfied with their jobs and bosses (but not quite as much as when their bosses are supportive) and perform their jobs better, too.

Does adapting one's leadership style to subordinate and environmental characteristics improve subordinate satisfaction and performance? At this point, because it is difficult to completely test this complex theory, it's too early to tell.[48] However, because the data clearly show that it makes sense for leaders to be both supportive *and* directive, it also makes sense that leaders could improve subordinate satisfaction and performance by adding participative and achievement-oriented leadership styles to their capabilities as leaders.

14-5 ADAPTING LEADER BEHAVIOR: NORMATIVE DECISION THEORY

Many people believe that making tough decisions is at the heart of leadership. Yet experienced leaders will tell you that deciding *how* to make decisions is just as important. The **normative decision theory** (also known as the *Vroom-Yetton-Jago model*) helps leaders decide how much employee participation (from none to letting employees make the entire decision) should be used when making decisions.[49]

Normative decision theory a theory that suggests how leaders can determine an appropriate amount of employee participation when making decisions

*Let's learn more about normative decision theory by investigating **14-5a decision styles** and **14-5b decision quality and acceptance**.*

14-5a Decision Styles

Unlike nearly all of the other leadership theories discussed in this chapter, which have specified *leadership* styles, that is, the way a leader generally behaves toward followers, the normative decision theory specifies five different *decision* styles, or ways of making decisions. (See Chapter 5 for a more complete review of decision making in organizations.) As shown in Exhibit 14.6, those styles vary from *autocratic decisions* (AI or AII) on the left, in which leaders make the decisions by themselves, to *consultative decisions* (CI or CII), in which leaders share problems with subordinates but still make the decisions themselves, to *group decisions* (GII) on the right, in which leaders share the problems with subordinates and then have the group make the decisions.

GE Aircraft Engines in Durham, North Carolina, uses a similar approach when making decisions. According to *Fast Company* magazine, "At GE/Durham, every decision is either an 'A' decision, a 'B' decision, or a 'C' decision. An 'A' decision is one that the plant manager makes herself, without consulting anyone."[50] One plant manager said, "I don't make very many of those, and when I do make one, everyone at the plant knows it. I make maybe ten or twelve a year."[51] "B" decisions are also made by the plant manager but with input from the people affected. "C" decisions, the most common type, are made by consensus, by the people directly involved, with plenty of discussion. With "C" decisions, the view of the plant manager doesn't necessarily carry more weight than the views of those affected.[52]

14-5b Decision Quality and Acceptance

Management consultant John Canfield says, "Leaders are responsible for improving the performance of organizations. Two significant components of [a leader's] decisions are the quality of the decision and the level of buy-in associated with it. Effective leaders want them both."[53] According to the normative decision theory, using the right degree of employee participation improves the quality of decisions and the extent to which employees accept and are committed to decisions (that is, buy-in). Exhibit 14.7 lists the decision rules that normative decision theory uses to increase the quality of a decision and the degree to which employees accept and commit to it.

The quality, leader information, subordinate information, goal congruence, and problem structure rules are used to increase decision quality. For example, the leader information rule states that if a leader doesn't have enough information to make a decision on his or her own, then the leader should not use an autocratic decision style. The commitment probability, subordinate conflict, and commitment requirement rules shown in Exhibit 14.7 are used to

Determining Your Priorities

Leaders are often asked to participate in a flood of strategic initiatives, both internal and external. According to Sandy Ogg, the former chief human resources officer at Unilever, executives often have more than 100 invitations to participate in corporate initiatives at any one time, so he devised a three-step decision tree to help busy executives identify where to invest their time and effort. First, make a list of every initiative asking for your participation. Second, rank each initiative according to the stature of its sponsor, the quality of the team, the time frame, and the budget. Finally, put less effort into low-ranking initiatives to free up time for higher-ranking initiatives.

Source: H. Ibarra, "The Way to Become a 'Strategic' Executive," *Wall Street Journal*, February 23, 2015, R7.

Exhibit 14.6
Normative Theory, Decision Styles, and Levels of Employee Participation

Leader solves the problem or makes the decision				Leader is willing to accept any decision supported by the entire group
AI	**AII**	**CI**	**CII**	**GII**
Using information available at the time, the leader solves the problem or makes the decision.	The leader obtains necessary information from employees and then selects a solution to the problem. When asked to share information, employees may or may not be told what the problem is.	The leader shares the problem and gets ideas and suggestions from relevant employees on an individual basis. Individuals are not brought together as a group. Then the leader makes the decision, which may or may not reflect their input.	The leader shares the problem with employees as a group, obtains their ideas and suggestions, and then makes the decision, which may or may not reflect their input.	The leader shares the problem with employees as a group. Together, the leader and employees generate and evaluate alternatives and try to reach an agreement on a solution. The leader acts as a facilitator and does not try to influence the group. The leader is willing to accept and implement any solution that has the support of the entire group.

Source: Table 2.1, "Decision Methods for Group and Individual Problems," in *Leadership and Decision-Making* (Pittsburgh: University of Pittsburgh Press, 1973), by V. H. Vroom and P. W. Yetton.

Exhibit 14.7
Normative Theory Decision Rules

Decision Rules to Increase Decision Quality
Quality Rule. If the quality of the decision is important, then don't use an autocratic decision style.
Leader Information Rule. If the quality of the decision is important, and if the leader doesn't have enough information to make the decision on his or her own, then don't use an autocratic decision style.
Subordinate Information Rule. If the quality of the decision is important, and if the subordinates don't have enough information to make the decision themselves, then don't use a group decision style.
Goal Congruence Rule. If the quality of the decision is important, and subordinates' goals are different from the organization's goals, then don't use a group decision style.
Problem Structure Rule. If the quality of the decision is important, the leader doesn't have enough information to make the decision on his or her own, and the problem is unstructured, then don't use an autocratic decision style.

Decision Rules to Increase Decision Acceptance
Commitment Probability Rule. If having subordinates accept and commit to the decision is important, then don't use an autocratic decision style.
Subordinate Conflict Rule. If having subordinates accept the decision is important and critical to successful implementation, and subordinates are likely to disagree or end up in conflict over the decision, then don't use an autocratic or consultative decision style.
Commitment Requirement Rule. If having subordinates accept the decision is absolutely required for successful implementation, and subordinates share the organization's goals, then don't use an autocratic or consultative style.

Sources: Adapted from V. H. Vroom, "Leadership," in *Handbook of Industrial and Organizational Psychology*, ed. M. D. Dunnette (Chicago: Rand McNally, 1976); V. H. Vroom and A. G. Jago, *The New Leadership: Managing Participation in Organizations* (Englewood Cliffs, NJ: Prentice Hall, 1988).

increase employee acceptance and commitment to decisions. For example, the commitment requirement rule says that if decision acceptance and commitment are important, and the subordinates share the organization's goals, then you shouldn't use an autocratic or consultative style. In other words, if followers want to do what's best for the company, and you need their acceptance and commitment to make a decision work, then use a group decision style and let them make the decision. As you can see, these decision rules help leaders improve decision quality and follower acceptance and commitment by eliminating decision styles that don't fit the particular decision or situation they're facing. Normative decision theory, like path-goal theory, is situational in nature. The abstract decision rules in Exhibit 14.7 are framed as yes/no questions, which makes the process of applying these rules more concrete. These questions are shown in the decision tree displayed in Exhibit 14.8. You start at the left side of the tree and answer the first question, "How important is the technical quality of this decision?" by choosing "high" or "low." Then you continue by answering each question as you proceed along the decision tree until you get to a recommended decision style.

Let's use the model to make the decision of whether to change from private offices to open offices and cubicles. The problem sounds simple, but it is actually more complex than you might think. Follow the yellow line in Exhibit 14.8 as we work through the decision in the following discussion.

How well does the normative decision theory work? A prominent leadership scholar has described it as the best supported of all leadership theories.[54] In general, the more managers violate the decision rules in Exhibit 14.7, the less effective their decisions are, especially with respect to subordinate acceptance and commitment.[55]

PROBLEM: CHANGE TO OPEN OFFICES AND CUBICLES?

1. *Quality requirement: How important is the technical quality of this decision?* High. This question has to do with whether there are quality differences in the alternatives and whether those quality differences matter. In other words: Is there a lot at stake in this decision? People have incredibly strong reactions to giving up private offices for cubicles. While companies use open offices to increase communication, workers will see this as a loss of privacy and status. Yes, there is a lot at stake.

2. *Commitment requirement: How important is subordinate commitment to the decision? High. Changes in offices, from private to open settings,* require subordinate commitment or they fail. In fact, it's not uncommon for companies to abandon open offices after trying them.

3. *Leader's information: Do you have sufficient information to make a high-quality decision?* Yes. Let's assume that you've done your homework. Much has been written about open offices and cubicles, from how to make the change to the effects it has in companies (which are mixed, sometimes positive and sometimes negative.).

4. *Commitment probability: If you were to make the decision by yourself, is it reasonably certain that your subordinate(s) would be committed to the decision?* No. Studies of companies that change from private offices to open offices find that employees' initial reactions are almost uniformly negative. Employees are likely to be angry if you change something as personal as their offices without consulting them.

5. *Goal congruence: Do subordinates share the organizational goals to be attained in solving this problem?* Probably not. The goals that usually accompany a change to open offices are a more informal culture, better communication, and less money spent on renting or buying office space (because open offices and cubicles take less square footage than private offices), none of which will matter much to employees who are losing their private offices.

6. *CII is the answer:* With a CII, or consultative decision process, the leader shares the problem with employees as a group, obtains their ideas and suggestions, and then makes the decision, which may or may not reflect their input. So, given the answers to these questions (remember, different managers won't necessarily answer these questions the same way), the normative decision theory recommends that leaders consult with their subordinates before deciding whether to change from private offices to open offices and cubicles.

Exhibit 14.8

Normative Decision Theory Tree for Determining the Level of Participation in Decision Making

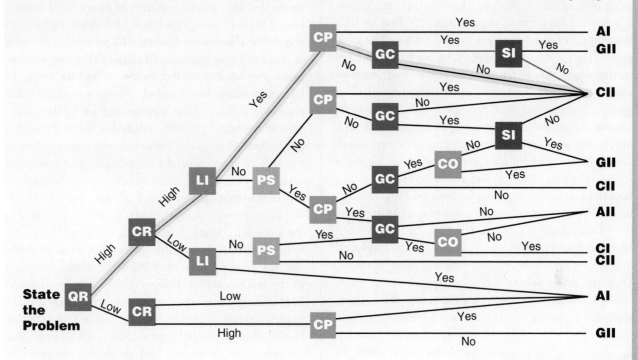

Leadership Style

Problem Attributes

QR	Quality requirement:	How important is the technical quality of this decision?
CR	Commitment requirement:	How important is subordinate commitment to the decision?
LI	Leader's information:	Do you have sufficient information to make a high-quality decision?
PS	Problem structure:	Is the problem well structured?
CP	Commitment probability:	If you were to make the decision by yourself, are you reasonably certain that your subordinate(s) would be committed to the decision?
GC	Goal congruence:	Do subordinates share the organizational goals to be attained in solving this problem?
CO	Subordinate conflict:	Is conflict among subordinates over preferred solutions likely?
SI	Subordinate information:	Do subordinates have sufficient information to make a high-quality decision?

Source: "Figure 9.3, Decision-Process Flow Chart for Both Individual and Group Problems," in *Leadership and Decision-Making* (Pittsburgh: University of Pittsburgh Press, 1973), by V. H. Vroom and P. W. Yetton.

14-6 VISIONARY LEADERSHIP

Strategic leadership is the ability to anticipate, envision, maintain flexibility, think strategically, and work with others to initiate changes that will create a positive future for an organization.[56] When he first became CEO at Ryder System, Robert Sanchez gave an ineffective one-hour speech trying to lay out his strategic priorities in truck rental and leasing, logistics and supply chain, and truck fleet management. The speech, he says, was overly complex with too many financial terms and numbers, so, "People weren't paying attention. Several front-line employees gave blank stares when I asked if they understood what we were trying to accomplish." When strategic change didn't take hold as fast as he liked, he reshaped his message into a fifteen-minute focused presentation at the company's management summit. There, he had much more success creating urgency to change when he displayed a slide with 100 trucks representing their markets. Only two were yellow, which is Ryder's color. That, he says, finally, "clicked with a lot of people."[57] Thus, strategic leadership captures how leaders inspire their companies to change and their followers to give extraordinary effort to accomplish organizational goals.

In Chapter 5, we defined a purpose statement, which is often referred to as an organizational mission or vision, as a statement of a company's purpose or reason for existing. Similarly, **visionary leadership** creates a positive image of the future that motivates organizational members and provides direction for future planning and goal setting.[58]

*Two kinds of visionary leadership are **14-6a charismatic leadership** and **14-6b transformational leadership.***

Strategic leadership the ability to anticipate, envision, maintain flexibility, think strategically, and work with others to initiate changes that will create a positive future for an organization

Visionary leadership leadership that creates a positive image of the future that motivates organizational members and provides direction for future planning and goal setting

Charismatic leadership the behavioral tendencies and personal characteristics of leaders that create an exceptionally strong relationship between them and their followers

Ethical charismatics charismatic leaders who provide developmental opportunities for followers, are open to positive and negative feedback, recognize others' contributions, share information, and have moral standards that emphasize the larger interests of the group, organization, or society

14-6a Charismatic Leadership

Charisma is a Greek word meaning "divine gift." The ancient Greeks saw people with charisma as inspired by the gods and capable of incredible accomplishments. German sociologist Max Weber viewed charisma as a special bond between leaders and followers.[59] Weber wrote that the special qualities of charismatic leaders enable them to strongly influence followers. Weber also noted that charismatic leaders tend to emerge in times of crisis and that the radical solutions they propose enhance the admiration that followers feel for them. In fact, charismatic leaders tend to have incredible influence over followers who may be inspired by their leaders and become fanatically devoted to them. From this perspective, charismatic leaders are often seen as larger-than-life or more special than other employees of the company.

Charismatic leaders have strong, confident, dynamic personalities that attract followers and enable the leaders to create strong bonds with their followers. Followers trust charismatic leaders, are loyal to them, and are inspired to work toward the accomplishment of the leader's vision. Followers who become devoted to charismatic leaders may go to extraordinary lengths to please them. Therefore, we can define **charismatic leadership** as the behavioral tendencies and personal characteristics of leaders that create an exceptionally strong relationship between them and their followers. Charismatic leaders also

▸ articulate a clear vision for the future that is based on strongly held values or morals;

▸ model those values by acting in a way consistent with the vision;

▸ communicate high performance expectations to followers; and

▸ display confidence in followers' abilities to achieve the vision.[60]

Does charismatic leadership work? Studies indicate that it often does. In general, the followers of charismatic leaders are more committed and satisfied, are better performers, are more likely to trust their leaders, and simply work harder.[61] Nonetheless, charismatic leadership also has risks that are at least as large as its benefits. The problems are likely to occur with ego-driven charismatic leaders who take advantage of fanatical followers.

In general, there are two kinds of charismatic leaders, ethical charismatics and unethical charismatics.[62] **Ethical charismatics** provide developmental opportunities for followers, are open to positive and negative

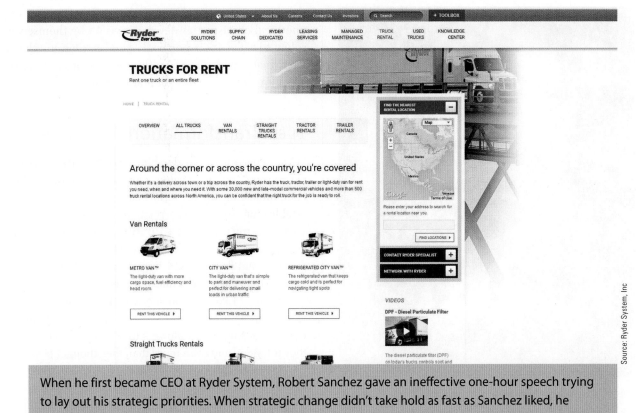

When he first became CEO at Ryder System, Robert Sanchez gave an ineffective one-hour speech trying to lay out his strategic priorities. When strategic change didn't take hold as fast as Sanchez liked, he reshaped his message into a focused fifteen-minute presentation.

feedback, recognize others' contributions, share information, and have moral standards that emphasize the larger interests of the group, organization, or society. Twenty years ago, J. J. Irani, then CEO of Tata Steel, had to close down a money-losing steel plant in Jamshedpur, India. Given that Tata not only guaranteed all employees' jobs but also jobs for their children (after you had worked at Tata twenty-five years), this was the first time that any Tata employees would lose their jobs. Rather than doing only what was best for Tata, Irani decided that laid-off employees, age 40 or under, would receive full salaries for the remainder of their working lives. Laid-off employees over 40 would get salaries plus a 20–50 percent bonus, depending on how close they were to retirement. Moreover, workers' families would receive the payments even if the workers died prior to retiring. Tata benefited, too, because it no longer had to pay payroll taxes, and part of the deal was that workers' payments would not increase over time. Over time, its labor costs shrunk, but its reputation as a caring employer among Indian managers and workers persisted.[63] As you would expect, ethical charismatics like Irani produce stronger commitment, higher satisfaction, more effort, better performance, and greater trust.

By contrast, **unethical charismatics** control and manipulate followers, do what is best for themselves instead of their organizations, want to hear only positive feedback, share information that is only beneficial to themselves, and have moral standards that put their interests before everyone else's. Steven Cohen, the billionaire owner of SAC Capital Advisors, was renowned for being acerbic and impatient with his staff of financial analysts and managers. One of his standard responses when portfolio managers couldn't answer a question about a stock was, "Do you even know how to do your f***ing job?" Once, during the first week of January, he yelled at an employee for not having come up with any good trading ideas so far that year. Cohen routinely pitted traders against each other by displaying their profits and losses in real time. He also pushed them to compete to have their picks included in his personal portfolio. Under his leadership, SAC Capital pleaded guilty to insider trading, paying $1.8 billion in fines.[64]

> **Unethical charismatics** charismatic leaders who control and manipulate followers, do what is best for themselves instead of their organizations, want to hear only positive feedback, share only information that is beneficial to themselves, and have moral standards that put their interests before everyone else's

Steven Cohen, founder and chief executive officer of SAC Capital Advisors, speaks during a Robin Hood Veterans Summit in New York City.

the development of the company vision. By contrast, unethical charismatics develop a vision by themselves solely to meet their personal agendas. One unethical charismatic said, "The key thing is that it is my idea; and I am going to win with it at all costs."[66]

14-6b Transformational Leadership

While charismatic leadership involves articulating a clear vision, modeling values consistent with that vision, communicating high performance expectations, and establishing very strong relationships with followers, **transformational leadership** goes further by generating awareness and acceptance of a group's purpose and mission and by getting employees to see beyond their own needs and self-interest for the good of the group.[67] Like charismatic leaders, transformational leaders are visionary, but they transform their organizations by getting their followers to accomplish more than they intended and even more than they thought possible.

Transformational leaders are able to make their followers feel that they are a vital part of the organization and help them see how their jobs fit with the organization's vision. By linking individual and organizational interests, transformational leaders encourage followers to make sacrifices for the organization because they know that they will prosper when the organization prospers. Transformational leadership has four components: charismatic leadership or idealized influence, inspirational motivation, intellectual stimulation, and individualized consideration.[68]

Charismatic leadership or idealized influence means that transformational leaders act as role models for their followers. Because transformational leaders put others' needs ahead of their own and share risks with their followers, they are admired, respected, and trusted, and followers want to emulate them. When Whole Foods' profit dropped 10 percent and the company needed to trim costs, co-CEO John Mackey voluntarily cut his pay by 67 percent. Likewise, Jay Leno, who hosted the Tonight Show for twenty-two years, voluntarily took a $15 million cut in pay when NBC announced that it needed to cut $20 million in costs for the show. While twenty employees were let go, Leno's voluntary pay cut absorbed 75 percent of the needed cost reduction so that many other long-time staffers on the show could keep their jobs.[69] Thus, in contrast to purely charismatic leaders (especially unethical charismatics), transformational leaders can be counted on to do the right thing and maintain high standards for ethical and personal conduct.

Because followers can become just as committed to unethical charismatics as to ethical charismatics, unethical characteristics pose a tremendous risk for companies. Professor Diane Chandler explains, "By being greatly influenced by charismatic leaders, followers are apt to agree with, feel affection for, and obey them. With charismatic leaders fostering a sense of strong identification with followers, they may likewise curry followers' inordinate allegiance to them in the face of unethical or moral leadership indiscretion."[65]

Exhibit 14.9 shows the stark differences between ethical and unethical charismatics on several leader behaviors: exercising power, creating the vision, communicating with followers, accepting feedback, stimulating followers intellectually, developing followers, and living by moral standards. For example, ethical charismatics account for the concerns and wishes of their followers when creating a vision by having followers participate in

Transformational leadership
leadership that generates awareness and acceptance of a group's purpose and mission and gets employees to see beyond their own needs and self-interests for the good of the group

Exhibit 14.9
Ethical and Unethical Charismatics

Charismatic Leader Behaviors	Ethical Charismatics . . .	Unethical Charismatics . . .
Exercising power	. . . use power to serve others.	. . . use power to dominate or manipulate others for personal gain.
Creating the vision	. . . allow followers to help develop the vision.	. . . are the sole source of vision, which they use to serve their personal agendas.
Communicating with followers	. . . engage in two-way communication and seek out viewpoints on critical issues.	. . . engage in one-way communication and are not open to suggestions from others.
Accepting feedback	. . . are open to feedback and willing to learn from criticism.	. . . have inflated egos, thrive on attention and admiration of sycophants, and avoid candid feedback.
Stimulating followers intellectually	. . . want followers to think and question status quo as well as leader's views.	. . . don't want followers to think but instead want uncritical acceptance of leader's ideas.
Developing followers	. . . focus on developing people with whom they interact, express confidence in them, and share recognition with others.	. . . are insensitive and unresponsive to followers' needs and aspirations.
Living by moral standards	. . . follow self-guided principles that may go against popular opinion and have three virtues: courage, a sense of fairness or justice, and integrity.	. . . follow standards only if they satisfy immediate self-interests, manipulate impressions so that others think they are doing the right thing, and use communication skills to manipulate others to support their personal agendas.

Source: J. M. Howell and B. J. Avolio, "The Ethics of Charismatic Leadership: Submission or Liberation?" *Academy of Management Executive 6*, no. 2 (1992): 43–54.

Inspirational motivation means that transformational leaders motivate and inspire followers by providing meaning and challenge to their work. By clearly communicating expectations and demonstrating commitment to goals, transformational leaders help followers envision future states, such as the organizational vision or mission. In turn, this leads to greater enthusiasm and optimism about the future.

Intellectual stimulation means that transformational leaders encourage followers to be creative and innovative, to question assumptions, and to look at problems and situations in new ways even if their ideas are different from those of leaders. Intolerant of mediocrity and the status quo, Sir James **Dyson**, is a unique combination of inventor, engineer, businessman, and artist. From its launch of the dual cyclone vacuum, his company has grown from a few people all using one phone to 6,000 employees in the United Kingdom, Singapore, and Malaysia booking nearly $2 billion in annual revenue from vacuums, lighting, robotics, and even agriculture. Dyson's top-secret laboratory is staffed by more than 1,000 engineers, and even though Sir James is no longer involved in the daily operation of the

Verbaska/Shutterstock.com

company, he still holds monthly "James Reviews" of new initiatives. Engineer Annmarie Nicolson says, "It can be nerve-wracking because he's so inquisitive. He'll always ask you a question you don't have an answer to. We'll sit for hours brainstorming, and we'll filter it down to what we think works best and build a prototype. James will say, 'Have you thought about this?' and we'll say, 'Well no, we haven't.'"[70]

Individualized consideration means that transformational leaders pay special attention to followers' individual needs by creating learning opportunities, accepting and tolerating individual differences, encouraging two-way communication, and being good listeners.

Finally, a distinction needs to be drawn between transformational leadership and transactional leadership. While transformational leaders use visionary and inspirational appeals to influence followers, **transactional leadership** is based on an exchange process in which followers are rewarded for good performance and punished for poor performance. When leaders administer rewards fairly and offer followers the rewards that they want, followers will often reciprocate with effort. A problem, however, is that transactional leaders often rely too heavily on discipline or threats to bring performance up to standards. This may work in the short run, but it's much less effective in the long run. Also, as discussed in Chapters 11 and 13, many leaders and organizations have difficulty successfully linking pay practices to individual performance.

Transactional leadership leadership based on an exchange process in which followers are rewarded for good performance and punished for poor performance

As a result, studies consistently show that transformational leadership is much more effective on average than transactional leadership. In the United States, Canada, Japan, and India at all organizational levels, from first-level supervisors to upper-level executives, followers view transformational leaders as much better leaders and are much more satisfied when working for them. Furthermore, companies with transformational leaders have significantly better financial performance.[71]

STUDY TOOLS 14

LOCATED IN TEXTBOOK

☐ Rip-out and review chapter review card

LOCATED AT WWW.CENGAGEBRAIN.COM

☐ Review key term flashcards and create your own from StudyBits

☐ Track your knowledge and understanding of key concepts, using the concept tracker

☐ Complete practice and graded quizzes to prepare for tests

☐ Complete interactive content within the exposition

☐ View chapter highlight box content at the beginning of each chapter

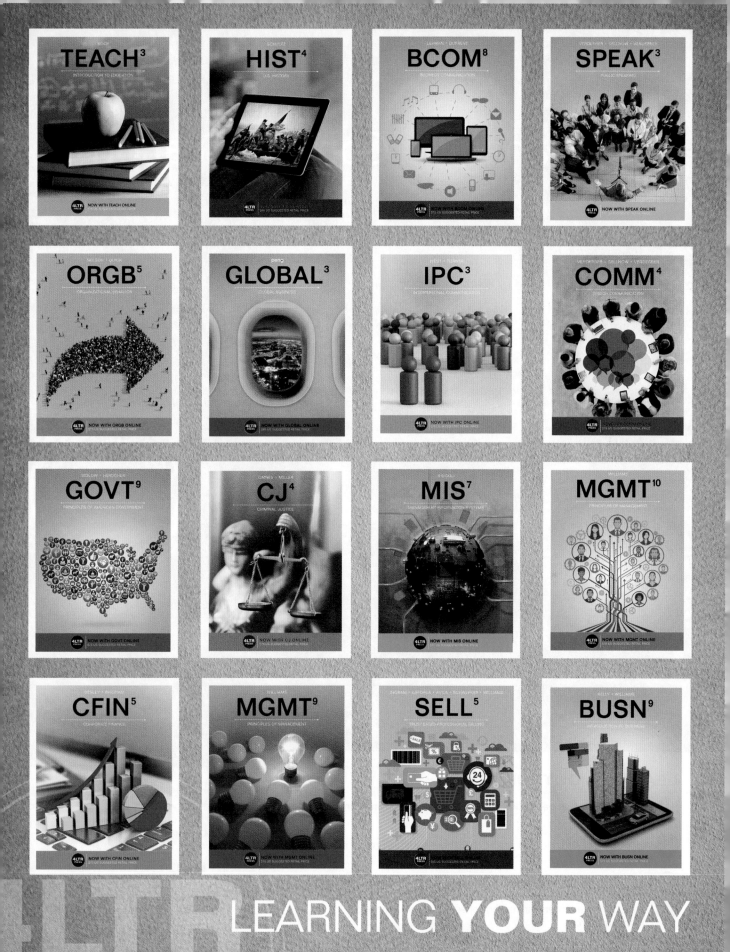

15 Managing Communication

TaraPatta/Shutterstock.com

LEARNING OUTCOMES

15-1 Explain the role that perception plays in communication and communication problems.

15-2 Describe the communication process and the various kinds of communication in organizations.

15-3 Explain how managers can manage effective one-on-one communication.

15-4 Describe how managers can manage effective organization-wide communication.

After you finish this chapter, go to **PAGE 341** for

STUDY TOOLS

15-1 PERCEPTION AND COMMUNICATION PROBLEMS

It's estimated that managers spend over 80 percent of their day communicating with others.[1] Indeed, much of the basic management process—planning, organizing, leading, and controlling—cannot be performed without effective communication. If this weren't reason enough to study communication, consider that effective oral communication—achieved by listening, following instructions, conversing, and giving feedback—is the most important skill for college graduates who are entering the workforce.[2] **Communication** is the process of transmitting information from one person or place to another. While some bosses sugarcoat bad news, smart managers understand that effective, straightforward communication between managers and employees is essential for success.

One study found that when *employees* were asked whether their supervisor gave recognition for good work, only 13 percent said their supervisor gave a pat on the back, and a mere 14 percent said their supervisor gave sincere and thorough praise. But when the *supervisors* of these employees were asked if they gave recognition for good work, 82 percent said they gave pats on the back, while 80 percent said that they gave sincere and thorough praise.[3] Given that these managers and employees worked closely together, how could they have had such different perceptions of something as simple as praise?

Let's learn more about perception and communication problems by examining **15-1a the basic perception process, 15-1b perception problems, 15-1c how we perceive others,** *and* **15-1d how we perceive ourselves.** *We'll also consider how all of these factors make it difficult for managers to communicate effectively.*

15-1a Basic Perception Process

As shown in Exhibit 15.1, **perception** is the process by which individuals attend to, organize, interpret, and retain information from their environments. And because communication is the process of transmitting information from one person or place to another, perception is obviously a key part of communication. Yet perception can also be a key obstacle to communication.

As people perform their jobs, they are exposed to a wide variety of informational stimuli such as emails, direct conversations with the boss or coworkers, rumors heard over lunch, stories about the company in the press, or a

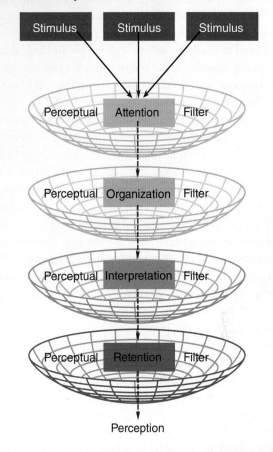

Exhibit 15.1
Basic Perception Process

video broadcast of a speech from the CEO to all employees. Just being exposed to an informational stimulus, however, is no guarantee that an individual will pay attention or attend to that stimulus. People experience stimuli through their own **perceptual filters**—the personality-, psychology-, or experience-based differences that influence them to ignore or pay attention to particular stimuli. Because of filtering, people exposed to the same information will often disagree about what they saw or heard. As shown in Exhibit 15.1, perceptual filters affect each part of the *perception process*: attention, organization, interpretation, and retention.

Attention is the process of noticing, or becoming aware of, particular

> **Communication** the process of transmitting information from one person or place to another
>
> **Perception** the process by which individuals attend to, organize, interpret, and retain information from their environments
>
> **Perceptual filters** the personality-, psychology-, or experience-based differences that influence people to ignore or pay attention to particular stimuli

stimuli. Because of perceptual filters, we attend to some stimuli and not others. For instance, a study at the University of Illinois asked viewers to watch people in black shirts and white shirts toss a basketball back and forth and to count the number of times someone in a black shirt tossed the basketball. Because their perceptual filters had narrowed to track the activities of people in black shirts, half of the viewers did not notice when the experimenters had someone in a gorilla suit walk through the midst of the people tossing the basketball back and forth.[4] *Organization* is the process of incorporating new information (from the stimuli that you notice) into your existing knowledge. Because of perceptual filters, we are more likely to incorporate new knowledge that is consistent with what we already know or believe. *Interpretation* is the process of attaching meaning to new knowledge. Because of perceptual filters, our preferences and beliefs strongly influence the meaning we attach to new information (for example, "This decision must mean that top management supports our project"). Finally, *retention* is the process of remembering interpreted information. Retention affects what we recall and commit to memory after we have perceived something. Of course, perceptual filters affect retention as much as they do organization and interpretation.

For instance, imagine that you miss the first ten minutes of a TV show and turn on your TV to see two people talking to each other in a living room. As they talk, they walk around the room, picking up and putting down various items. Some items, such as a ring, watch, and credit card, appear to be valuable, while others appear to be drug-related, such as a water pipe for smoking marijuana. In fact, this situation was depicted on videotape in a well-known study that manipulated people's perceptual filters.[5] Before watching the video, one-third of the study participants were told that the people were there to rob the apartment. Another third were told that police were on their way to conduct a drug raid and that the people in the apartment were getting rid of incriminating evidence. The remaining third of the participants were told that the people were simply waiting for a friend.

After watching the video, participants were asked to list all of the objects from the video that they could remember. Not surprisingly, the different perceptual filters (theft, drug raid, and waiting for a friend) affected what the participants attended to, how they organized the information, how they interpreted it, and ultimately which objects they remembered. Participants who thought a theft was in progress were more likely to remember the valuable objects in the video. Those who thought a drug raid was imminent were more likely to remember the drug-related objects. There was no discernible pattern to the items remembered by those who thought that the people in the video were simply waiting for a friend.

In short, because of perception and perceptual filters, people are likely to pay attention to different things, organize and interpret what they pay attention to differently, and, finally, remember things differently. Consequently, even when people are exposed to the same communications (for example, organizational memos, discussions with managers or customers), they can end up with very different perceptions and understandings. This is why communication can be so difficult and frustrating for managers. Let's review some of the communication problems created by perception and perceptual filters.

15-1b Perception Problems

Perception creates communication problems for organizations because people exposed to the same communication and information can end up with completely different ideas and understandings. Two of the most common perception problems in organizations are selective perception and closure.

At work, we are constantly bombarded with sensory stimuli: phones ringing, people talking in the background, computers dinging as new email arrives, people calling our names, and so forth. As limited processors of information, we cannot possibly notice, receive, and interpret all of this information. As a result, we attend to and accept some stimuli but screen out and reject others. This isn't a random process.

Selective perception is the tendency to notice and accept objects and information consistent with our values, beliefs, and expectations, while ignoring or screening out inconsistent information. For example, in a research study, pedestrians are stopped on a sidewalk by a man who asks for directions. Ten seconds into giving directions, two people carrying a door walk between the man who asked for directions, on the left, and the pedestrian, on the right. When the door goes by, the man who asked for directions quickly switches places with one of the young men carrying the door. The pedestrian, however, doesn't see this switch because the door blocks the view. Like the invisible gorilla example above, 50 percent of the time people don't even notice that they're talking to a different man and go right back to giving directions. Selective perception, is one of the biggest contributors to misunderstandings and miscommunication, because it strongly influences what people see, hear, read, and understand at work.[6]

Selective perception the tendency to notice and accept objects and information consistent with our values, beliefs, and expectations, while ignoring or screening inconsistent information

THE POWER OF PERCEPTION

Perception is a powerful influence on human behavior. A group of researchers testing the relationship between the size of a wine glass and the amount of wine consumed discovered that people who are served wine in a large glass drink more wine overall in one sitting than do people served the same amount of wine in a smaller wine glass. Why does this happen? Even though they are being served the same amount, the people drinking from the larger glass perceive that there is less wine in the glass. To compensate, they order more glasses throughout the evening.

Oksana Klimenkova/Shutterstock.com

Source: D. Rowland, "Large Wine Glasses Encourage More Drinking, Study Finds," *Wall Street Journal*, December 13, 2015, accessed May 7, 2016, http://www.wsj.com/articles/larger-wine-glasses-encourage-more-drinking-study-finds-1450696305.

After we have initial information about a person, event, or process, **closure** is the tendency to fill in the gaps where information is missing, that is, to assume that what we don't know is consistent with what we already do know. If employees are told that budgets must be cut by 10 percent, they may automatically assume that 10 percent of employees will lose their jobs, too, even if that isn't the case. Not surprisingly, when closure occurs, people sometimes fill in the gaps with inaccurate information, which can create problems for organizations.

15-1c Perceptions of Others

Attribution theory says that we all have a basic need to understand and explain the causes of other people's behavior.[7] In other words, we need to know why people do what they do. According to attribution theory, we use two general reasons or attributions to explain people's behavior: an *internal attribution*, in which behavior is thought to be voluntary or under the control of the individual, and an *external attribution*, in which behavior is thought to be involuntary and outside of the control of the individual.

If you've ever seen someone changing a flat tire on the side of the road and thought to yourself, "What rotten luck—somebody's having a bad day," you perceived the person through an external attribution known as the defensive bias. The **defensive bias** is the tendency for people to perceive themselves as personally and situationally similar to someone who is having difficulty or trouble.[8] When we identify with the person in a situation, we tend to use external attributions (that is, features related to the situation) to explain the person's behavior. For instance, because flat tires are common, it's easy to perceive ourselves in that same situation and put the blame on external causes such as running over a nail.

Now, let's assume a different situation, this time in the workplace:

> *A utility company worker puts a ladder on a utility pole and then climbs up to do his work. As he's doing his work, he falls from the ladder and seriously injures himself.*[9]

Answer this question: Who or what caused the accident? If you thought, "It's not the worker's fault. Anybody could fall from a tall ladder," then you interpreted the incident with a defensive bias in which you saw yourself as personally and situationally similar to someone who is having difficulty or trouble. In other words, you made an external attribution by attributing the accident to an external cause or some feature of the situation.

Most accident investigations, however, initially blame the worker (that is, an internal attribution) and not the situation (that is, an external attribution). Typically, 60–80 percent of workplace accidents each year are blamed on "operator error," that is, on the employees themselves. In reality, more complete investigations usually show that workers are responsible for only 30–40 percent of all workplace accidents.[10] Why are accident investigators so quick to blame workers? The reason is that they are committing the **fundamental attribution error**, which is the tendency to ignore external causes of behavior and to attribute other people's actions to internal causes.[11] In other words, when

Closure the tendency to fill in gaps of missing information by assuming that what we don't know is consistent with what we already know

Attribution theory the theory that we all have a basic need to understand and explain the causes of other people's behavior

Defensive bias the tendency for people to perceive themselves as personally and situationally similar to someone who is having difficulty or trouble

Fundamental attribution error the tendency to ignore external causes of behavior and to attribute other people's actions to internal causes

Exhibit 15.2
Defensive Bias and Fundamental Attribution Error

The Coworker

How can they expect us to make sales if they don't have hot-selling inventory in stock? We can't sell what's not there.

The Employee

That's the third sale I've lost this week because company management doesn't keep enough inventory in stock. I can't sell it if we don't have it.

The Boss

That new employee isn't very good. I may have to get rid of him if his sales don't improve.

Defensive Bias—
the tendency for people to perceive themselves as personally and situationally similar to someone who is having difficulty or trouble

Defensive Bias—
the tendency for people to perceive themselves as personally and situationally similar to someone who is having difficulty or trouble

Fundamental Attribution Error—
the tendency to ignore external causes of behavior and to attribute other people's actions to internal causes

investigators examine the possible causes of an accident, they're much more likely to assume that the accident is a function of the person and not the situation.

Which attribution—the defensive bias or the fundamental attribution error—are workers likely to make when something goes wrong? In general, as shown in Exhibit 15.2, employees and coworkers are more likely to perceive events and explain behavior from a defensive bias. Because they do the work themselves and see themselves as similar to others who make mistakes, have accidents, or are otherwise held responsible for things that go wrong at work, employees and coworkers are likely to attribute problems to external causes such as failed machinery, poor support, or inadequate training. By contrast, because they are typically observers (who don't do the work themselves) and see themselves as situationally and personally different from workers, managers tend to commit the fundamental attribution error and blame mistakes, accidents, and other things that go wrong on workers (that is, an internal attribution).

Consequently, workers and managers in most workplaces can be expected to take opposite views when things go wrong. Therefore, the defensive bias, which is typically used by workers, and the fundamental attribution error, which is typically made by managers, together present a significant challenge to effective communication and understanding in organizations.

15-1d Self-Perception

The **self-serving bias** is the tendency to overestimate our value by attributing successes to ourselves (internal causes) and attributing failures to others or the environment (external causes).[12] The self-serving bias can make it especially difficult for managers to talk to employees about performance problems. In general, people have a need to maintain a positive self-image. This need is so strong that when people seek feedback at work, they typically want verification of their worth (rather than information about performance deficiencies) or assurance that mistakes or problems weren't their fault.[13] People can become defensive and emotional when managerial communication threatens their positive self-image. They quit listening, and communication becomes ineffective. In the second half of the chapter, which focuses on improving communication, we'll explain ways in which managers can minimize this self-serving bias and improve effective one-on-one communication with employees.

Self-serving bias the tendency to overestimate our value by attributing successes to ourselves (internal causes) and attributing failures to others or the environment (external causes)

15-2 KINDS OF COMMUNICATION

There are many kinds of communication—formal, informal, coaching/counseling, and nonverbal—but they all follow the same fundamental process.

Let's learn more about the different kinds of communication by examining 15-2a the communication process, 15-2b formal communication channels, 15-2c informal communication channels, 15-2d coaching and counseling, or one-on-one communication, and 15-2e nonverbal communication.

15-2a The Communication Process

At the beginning of this chapter, we defined *communication* as the process of transmitting information from one person or place to another. Exhibit 15.3 displays a model of the communication process and its major components: the sender (message to be conveyed, encoding the message, transmitting the message); the receiver (receiving message, decoding the message, and the message that was understood); and noise, which interferes with the communication process.

The communication process begins when a *sender* thinks of a message he or she wants to convey to another person. For example, you had a flu shot and a pneumonia shot, and yet you've had an unexplainable fever for nine days, so you visit the doctor. The doctor asks a series of questions regarding your appetite, fatigue, tenderness in your abdomen, and whether your fever comes and goes during the day. The doctor, the sender, runs some tests and then has you, the receiver, come back the next day to provide a diagnosis and recommend a treatment.

The next step is to encode the message. **Encoding** means putting a message into a written, verbal, or symbolic form that can be recognized and understood by the receiver. In our example, this means the doctor has to take the technical language of medicine and lab test results and communicate it in a way that patients can understand. This is not easy to do. And the difficulty of doing this well is compounded by the average doctor's visit lasting less than fifteen minutes. And, while your visit might be fifteen minutes, you're not getting a full fifteen minutes to talk to the doctor. Not surprisingly, 60 percent of patients feel as if their doctor is rushing through their exam. Despite this, 58 percent of surveyed patients say their doctors do a good job of explaining things to them. But, as we'll see in a few steps, that doesn't mean communication has been effective.[14]

The sender then *transmits the message* via *communication channels*. The traditional communication channel for doctors and patients is face-to-face discussion in the doctor's office. Ironically, though, the introduction of electronic health records may be interfering with that. Dr. Rita Redberg, at the University of California San Francisco Medical Center, says, "The recent introduction of electronic health records in the office, for example, requires many doctors to spend much of a patient exam looking at a computer screen instead of the patient in order to record information." Studies show that one-third of the time, doctors forget to give patients critical information. Another critical study found that across thirty different medical conditions,

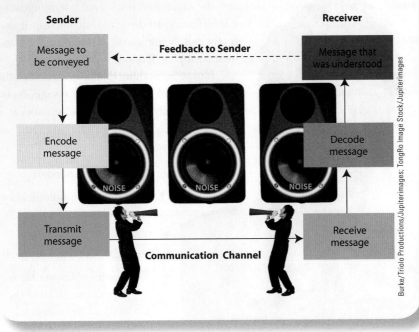

Exhibit 15.3
The Interpersonal Communication Process

Sender

Receiver

Message to be conveyed

Feedback to Sender

Message that was understood

Encode message

Decode message

NOISE   NOISE   NOISE

Transmit message

Receive message

Communication Channel

Burke/Triolo Productions/Jupiterimages; TongRo Image Stock/Jupiterimages

Encoding putting a message into a written, verbal, or symbolic form that can be recognized and understood by the receiver

patients only received all the information they needed from their doctors about 55 percent of the time.[15] Why? In an average fifteen-minute doctor's visit, the doctor will spend just 1.3 minutes telling the patient about his or her condition, prognosis, and treatment. Furthermore, as we will see, that 1.3 minutes is filled with information that is too complex and technical for the typical patient to understand.[16]

With some communication channels such as the telephone and face-to-face communication, the sender receives immediate feedback, whereas with others such as email (or text messages and file attachments), fax, beepers, voice mail, memos, and letters, the sender must wait for the receiver to respond. Unfortunately, because of technical difficulties (for example, fax down, dead battery in the cell phone, inability to read email attachments) or people-based transmission problems (for example, forgetting to pass on the message), messages aren't always transmitted.

If the message is transmitted and received, however, the next step is for the receiver to decode it. **Decoding** is the process by which the receiver translates the verbal or symbolic form of the message into an understood message. Surveys indicate that many patients clearly do not understand what their doctors are telling them. Up to 85 percent of hospitalized patients don't even know the name of the doctor in charge of their treatment. As many as 58 percent don't know why they were admitted to the hospital. Likewise, in a typical fifteen-minute doctor's appointment, half of patients will leave without understanding what their doctor has told to them to do to get better.[17] Unfortunately, even when patients seem to understand what their doctors are telling them in that fifteen-minute visit, it turns out that they immediately forget 80 percent of that medical information, and then half of what they remember is wrong![18]

The last step of the communication process occurs when the receiver gives the sender feedback. **Feedback to sender** is a return message to the sender that indicates the receiver's understanding of the message (of what the receiver was supposed to know, to do, or not to do). Feedback makes senders aware of possible miscommunications and enables them to continue communicating until the receiver understands the intended message. Because of the difficulties of communicating complex medical information in too little time, many doctors now employ the "teach-back" method at the end of a patient visit, where they ask patients to explain in their own words what they've heard the doctor say regarding their problem (diagnosis), whether they'll get better (prognosis), and what the patient is supposed to do after they leave the doctor's office (that is, treatment plan and managing medications).[19] Even so, much progress needs to be made, as about half of patients are not even asked if they have questions.[20]

Unfortunately, feedback doesn't always occur in the communication process. Complacency and overconfidence about the ease and simplicity of communication can lead senders and receivers to simply assume that they share a common understanding of the message and, consequently, to not use feedback to improve the effectiveness of their communication. This is a serious mistake, especially as messages and feedback are always transmitted with and against a background of noise. Part of the background noise in medicine is how well medical information is communicated between medical professionals. After all, medicine is a "team sport" involving various doctors, physician assistants, nurses, and other care professionals for each patient. Medical mistakes kill 500 people per day, and 80 percent of those deaths are caused by miscommunication that occurs when patients are transferred from one set of caregivers to another, for instance, the night-shift nurses not communicating key information to the day-shift nurses, or one doctor not being aware of the diagnosis and treatment plan of another doctor on a case.[21]

Noise is anything that interferes with the transmission of the intended message. Noise can occur in any of the following situations:

▸ The sender isn't sure what message to communicate.

▸ The message is not clearly encoded.

▸ The wrong communication channel is chosen.

▸ The message is not received or decoded properly.

▸ The receiver doesn't have the experience or time to understand the message.

Decoding the process by which the receiver translates the written, verbal, or symbolic form of a message into an understood message

Feedback to sender in the communication process, a return message to the sender that indicates the receiver's understanding of the message

Noise anything that interferes with the transmission of the intended message

Ollyy/Shutterstock.com

An App for Sender's Remorse

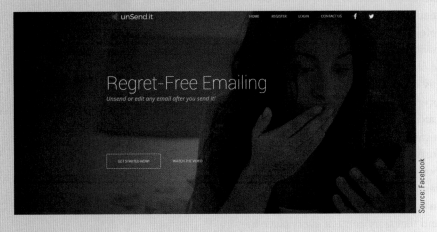

Source: Facebook

Most everyone has experienced sender's remorse—that sinking feeling you get when you send an email to the wrong person, or divulge one opinion too many about a coworker in an interoffice memo. Gmail and Outlook have features for recalling emails, but they rarely work as desired. UnSend.it is an app that aims to solve sender's remorse by converting messages to JPEG images and embedding the JPEG into the email body. Until the recipient opens the message, the sender can edit or replace the JPEG. The app does have a few practical limitations. Most Outlook and Gmail inboxes block images by default, and users of any service might find a business email containing an image with no text a little suspect. Additionally, without a CC function, UnSend.it is only suitable for direct communications to one or more recipients. But for those with overzealous sending habits, it might just provide the extra time for an email do-over.

Source: K. Wiggers, "Sent an Email to the Wrong Person? UnSend.it Lets You Remove It from Their Inbox," *Digital Trends*, April 7, 2015, accessed April 23, 2015,. http://www.digitaltrends.com/computing/unsend-it-email-app/.

Emotional outbursts are an often unrecognized type of noise. Whether yelling, crying, sulking, or table pounding, strong emotions interfere with the transmission of intended messages. The outburst itself, however, is a signal that what's being discussed touches strongly held beliefs or values. The first step in addressing noise related to strong emotions is spotting early indicators, such as body language not matching words. Acknowledge the difficulty of the issue, and then ask them to share their views. Next, listen to the response, and ask follow-up questions. Finally, work toward resolution by helping them articulate their core issues.[22] We'll cover listening and asking questions in greater detail in the "Coaching and Counseling: One-on-One Communication" section later in this chapter.

Jargon, which is vocabulary particular to a profession or group, is another form of noise that interferes with communication in the workplace. Jargon is a common cause of misunderstandings between doctors and patients. Brian Jack, chief of family medicine at Boston Medical Center, says, "We throw papers and throw words at patients. It is crazy to think they would understand."[23] The result, says Dr. David Langer, chief of neurosurgery at Lenox Hill Hospital in New York City, is that patients, "would go home and call back and say they didn't understand, and then ask me the same questions . . .

Doctors often do a terrible job at educating their patients."[24] To combat this problem, Dr. Langer and his colleagues have begun using digital videos to explain CT scans and MRIs, as well as to provide detailed post-visit medical instructions. While preparing for an upcoming surgery, Emily Monato watched the video of her brain MRI several times to better "grasp these big chunks of information."[25] She had her children, father, and friends watch it, too.

15-2b Formal Communication Channels

An organization's **formal communication channel**, is the system of official channels that carry organizationally approved messages and information. Organizational objectives, rules, policies, procedures, instructions, commands, and requests for information are all transmitted via the formal communication system or channel. There are three formal communication channels: downward communication, upward communication, and horizontal communication.[26]

> **Jargon** vocabulary particular to a profession or group that interferes with communication in the workplace
>
> **Formal communication channel** the system of official channels that carry organizationally approved messages and information

Downward communication flows from higher to lower levels in an organization. Downward communication is used to issue orders down the organizational hierarchy, to give organizational members job-related information, to give managers and workers performance reviews from upper managers, and to clarify organizational objectives and goals.[27] Michael Beer, professor emeritus at Harvard Business School, says, "You can never overcommunicate. When you think you've communicated well, go out three or four more times and communicate again." Beer's consulting firm, TruePoint, studied forty CEOs whose companies have been above-average performers for more than a decade. He found that those remarkable leaders spend an enormous amount of time in communicating downward. They have a simple story, and that story gets out every place they go."[28]

Upward communication flows from lower levels to higher levels in an organization. Upward communication is used to give higher-level managers feedback about operations, issues, and problems; to help higher-level managers assess organizational performance and effectiveness; to encourage lower-level managers and employees to participate in organizational decision making; and to give those at lower levels the chance to share their concerns with higher-level authorities. At restaurants, tables with big groups bring big tips, so competition among servers can get fierce—and unfriendly—to wait on them. The "system" of assigning tables where Michelle Burke worked as a waitress involved servers racing to the table, and whoever got there first got the table. Burke says this made her, "angry at work, and after work," and that she, "finally decided to take a stand." So she discussed the problem with her manager. First, she explained the situation and that most of the staff were upset. Then she proposed rotating the big tables among servers, which she said would be fairer, but also give customers better service. Her boss agreed and adopted her suggestion.[29]

Horizontal communication flows among managers and workers who are at the same organizational level, such as when a day shift nurse comes in at 7:30 a.m. for a half-hour discussion with the midnight nurse supervisor who leaves at 8:00 a.m. Horizontal communication helps facilitate coordination and cooperation between different parts of a company and allows coworkers to share relevant information. It also helps people at the same level resolve conflicts and solve problems without involving high levels of management. Two executives at **Business Value Group** regularly undermined each other wherever their responsibilities overlapped. Rather than complain to their boss, one of the managers, Patrick Hehir, went directly to his colleague, Paul Humphries, and said, "I'm playing games with you and you're playing games with me, yet you and I both talk with others on our team about collaborating more."[30] Humphries described his relief at finally addressing the problem as, "liberating." They discussed their concerns, agreeing to handle all future issues face-to-face.[31]

In general, what can managers do to improve formal communication? First, decrease reliance on downward communication. Second, increase chances for upward communication by increasing personal contact with lower-level managers and workers. Third, encourage much better use of horizontal communication.

15-2c Informal Communication Channels

An organization's **informal communication channel**, sometimes called the **grapevine**, is the transmission of messages from employee to employee

---

SHUT IT DOWN—HOW TO HANDLE GOSSIP (ABOUT YOU)

There can be a fine line between news and gossip, and, at some point, you might find yourself a target of the rumor mill. How should you handle it? Groundless gossip can often be extinguished with simple denial. Sometimes, however, a direct denial only attracts more attention. In those cases, consider asking the person spreading the rumors to be an advocate for you to help shut down the gossip. And as a proactive measure, maintain strong alliances with colleagues above, below, and at your own level of the organization. That way, you'll know who to enlist on your behalf to diffuse gossip about you.

Source: S. Shellenbarger, "What to Do When You Are the Subject of Office Gossip," *Wall Street Journal*, October 7, 2014, accessed May 12, 2015, http://www.wsj.com/articles/what-to-do-when-you-are-the-subject-of-office-gossip-1412701581.

There is a fine line between news and gossip. At some point, you might find yourself a target of the rumor mill.

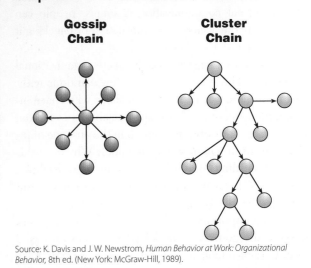

Exhibit 15.4
Grapevine Communication Networks

Gossip Chain

Cluster Chain

Source: K. Davis and J. W. Newstrom, *Human Behavior at Work: Organizational Behavior*, 8th ed. (New York: McGraw-Hill, 1989).

outside of formal communication channels. The grapevine arises out of curiosity, that is, the need to know what is going on in an organization and how it might affect you or others. To satisfy this curiosity, employees need a consistent supply of relevant, accurate, in-depth information about what is going on in the company and why. At **Net Optics**, a manufacturer of computer networking equipment, CEO Bob Shaw understands the importance of the grapevine to better communication. He says, "If there's something out there that the organization's not clear on, my role and responsibility is to make sure I fill it in with the right information." So Net Optics has a rumor jar in which employees can insert anonymous notes about the rumors they've heard. Then, at the monthly company meeting, Shaw pulls out the notes, reads them to the employees, and addresses each one. Shaw says, "I never know what's going to be in there, so it's as much a surprise for me as it is for the audience." After two employees lost their jobs (for performance reasons), notes asked if the rumor that the company was going to have layoffs was true. Shaw explained that not only was Net Optics not downsizing, it was quite successful and growing.[32]

> "THE MAIN FOCUS OF RUMOR IS TO FIGURE OUT THE TRUTH. IT'S THE GROUP TRYING TO MAKE SENSE OF SOMETHING THAT'S IMPORTANT TO THEM."

Grapevines arise out of informal communication networks such as the gossip or cluster chains shown in Exhibit 15.4. In a *gossip chain*, one highly connected individual shares information with many other managers and workers. By contrast, in a *cluster chain*, numerous people simply tell a few of their friends. The result in both cases is that information flows freely and quickly through the organization. Some believe that grapevines are a waste of employees' time, that they promote gossip and rumors that fuel political speculation, and that they are sources of highly unreliable, inaccurate information. Yet studies clearly show that grapevines are highly accurate sources of information for a number of reasons.[33] First, because grapevines typically carry "juicy" information that is interesting and timely, information spreads rapidly. During Allstate's annual Leaders Forum, a gathering of 2,000 agents and employees, CEO Thomas Wilson announced plans for reducing the company's sales force and changing sales commission rates. Later that evening, a group of employees were at the hotel bar, complaining about the changes and about Wilson, when the president of Allstate's home and auto insurance division, was allegedly overheard using two expletives in reference to Wilson. By the next day, nearly all conference attendees had heard the critical remarks. The president of that division was abruptly let go just a few weeks later.[34]

Second, because information is typically spread by face-to-face conversation, receivers can send feedback to make sure they understand the message that is being communicated. This reduces misunderstandings and increases accuracy. Third, because most of the information in a company moves along the grapevine rather than through formal communication channels, people can usually verify the accuracy of information by checking it out with others.

What can managers do to manage organizational grapevines? The very worst thing they can do is withhold information or try to punish those who share information with others. The grapevine abhors a vacuum, so rumors and anxiety will flourish in the absence of information from company management. Why does this occur? According to workplace psychologist Nicholas DiFonzo, "The main focus of rumor is to figure out the truth. It's the group trying to make sense of something that's important to them."[35] A better strategy is to embrace the grapevine and keep employees informed about possible changes and strategies. Failure to do so will just make things worse. And, in addition to using the grapevine to communicate with others, managers should not overlook the grapevine as a tremendous source of valuable information and feedback. In fact, research shows that, contrary to popular belief, grapevines are fast, accurate, and focused on information more than gossip.[36]

15-2d Coaching and Counseling: One-on-One Communication

When the Wyatt Company surveyed 531 U.S. companies undergoing major changes and restructuring, it asked the CEOs, "If you could go back and change one thing, what would it be?" The answer: "The way we communicated with our employees." The CEOs said that instead of flashy videos, printed materials, or formal meetings, they would make greater use of one-on-one communication, especially with employees' immediate supervisors instead of with higher-level executives whom employees didn't know.[37]

Coaching and counseling are two kinds of one-on-one communication. **Coaching** is communicating with someone for the direct purpose of improving the person's on-the-job performance or behavior.[38] Managers tend to make several mistakes when coaching employees. First, they wait for a problem to arise before coaching. Jim

> **Coaching** communicating with someone for the direct purpose of improving the person's on-the-job performance or behavior
>
> **Counseling** communicating with someone about non-job-related issues that may be affecting or interfering with the person's performance

Concelman, manager for leadership development at Development Dimensions International, says, "Of course, a boss has to coach an employee if a mistake has been made, but they shouldn't be waiting for the error. While it is a lot easier to see a mistake and correct it, people learn more through success than through failure, so bosses should ensure that employees are experiencing as many successes as possible. Successful employees lead to a more successful organization."[39] Second, when mistakes *are* made, managers wait much too long before talking to the employee about the problem. The late management professor Ray Hilgert said, "A manager must respond as soon as possible after an incident of poor performance. Don't bury your head. . . . When employees are told nothing, they assume everything is okay."[40] Jack Welch, who was CEO at GE for two decades, says, "I've spoken to more than 500,000 people around the world, and I always ask audiences, 'How many of you know where you stand in your organization?'" He says, "Typically no more than 10 percent raise their hands. That's criminal! As a manager, you owe candor to your people. They must not be guessing about what the organization thinks of them. My experience is that most employees appreciate this reality check, and today's 'Millenials' practically demand it."[41] In short, says Welch, "You have no right to be a leader if someone who works for you doesn't know where they stand."[42] So coach your employees about their job performance.

In contrast to coaching, **counseling** is communicating with someone about nonjob-related issues such as stress, child care, health issues, retirement planning, or legal issues that may be affecting or interfering with the person's performance. But counseling does not mean that managers should try to be clinicians, even though an estimated 20 percent of employees are dealing with personal problems at any one time. Dana Kiel, regional director in Account Management at Magellan Health, says, "We call it the quicksand. If you're a good supervisor, you do care about your employees, but it's not your job to be a therapist."[43] Instead, managers should discuss specific performance problems, listen if the employee chooses to share personal issues, and then recommend that the employee call the company's *Employee Assistance Program (EAP)*. EAPs are typically free when provided as part of a company's benefit package. In emergencies or times of crisis, EAPs can offer immediate counseling and support; they can also provide referrals to organizations and professionals that can help employees and their family members address personal issues. On the first day of her new job, Wendy Wolfson was called to pick up her first grader from school. Worried she might have to quit unless she could find childcare, Wolfson called her employer's EAP for help with this problem. Despite their proven effectiveness and a wide variety of assistance services (including mental health, substance abuse, financial counseling, and elder care services), only 4–6 percent of employees use EAPs.[44] According to Wolfson, "The problem is, you're pressed for time and you don't know where to go. It was a resource and another set of options."[45]

15-2e Nonverbal Communication

Nonverbal communication is any communication that doesn't involve words. Nonverbal communication almost always accompanies verbal communication and may either support and reinforce the verbal message or contradict it. The importance of nonverbal communication is well established. Researchers have estimated that as much as 93 percent of any message is transmitted nonverbally, with 55 percent coming from body language and facial expressions, and 38 percent coming from the tone and pitch of the voice.[46] Because many nonverbal cues are unintentional, receivers often consider nonverbal communication to be a more accurate representation of what senders are thinking and feeling than the words they use. If you have ever asked someone out on a date and been told "yes," but realized that the real answer was "no," then you understand the importance of paying attention to nonverbal communication.

Kinesics and paralanguage are two kinds of nonverbal communication.[47] **Kinesics** (from the Greek word *kinesis*, meaning "movement") are movements of the body and face.[48] These movements include arm and hand gestures, facial expressions, eye contact, folding arms, crossing legs, and leaning toward or away from another person. For example, people tend to avoid eye contact when they are embarrassed or unsure of the message they are sending. Crossed arms or legs usually indicate defensiveness or that the person is not receptive to the message or the sender. Also, people tend to smile frequently when they are seeking someone's approval.

It turns out that kinesics play an incredibly important role in communication. Studies of married couples' kinesic

Consultant, Suzanne Bales, says that some of her CEO clients check their phones so much during meetings, "it's the equivalent of not showing up for half of the meeting."

Monkey Business Images/Shutterstock.com

interactions can predict whether they will stay married with 93 percent accuracy.[49] The key is the ratio of positive to negative kinesic interactions between husbands and wives as they communicate. Negative kinesic expressions such as eye rolling suggest contempt, whereas positive kinesic expressions such as maintaining eye contact and nodding suggest listening and caring. When the ratio of positive to negative interactions drops below 5 to 1, the chances for divorce quickly increase. Kinesics operate similarly in the workplace, providing clues about people's true feelings, over and above what they say (or don't say). Unfortunately, not making or maintaining eye contact is an increasingly frequent occurrence in today's workplace. Consultant Suzanne Bates, author of *Speak Like a CEO*, says that some of her CEO clients check their phones so much during appointments that, "it's the equivalent of not showing up for half of the meeting." And that, she says, breeds resentment in others who think, "I'm just as busy as the CEO. I just have different things to juggle."[50] In fact, a survey of business professionals found that strong majorities think it is inappropriate to answer phone calls (86%) or write texts or emails (84%) in meetings or at business lunches (66%). The kinesics related to checking smartphones in these situations

Nonverbal communication any communication that doesn't involve words

Kinesics movements of the body and face

What If Your Emotions Were an Open Book?

Over the course of his career, eighty-year-old psychologist Dr. Paul Ekman built a catalog of more than 5,000 facial muscle movements that communicate one of six base emotions: anger, disgust, fear, happiness, sadness, or surprise. What started out for Ekman as an anthropological study has recently been transformed by big data, as a host of software start-ups are building programs to uncover people's hidden emotions. One software company, Emotient, has video recorded encounters with hundreds of thousands of people and extracted 90,000 data points from each frame. Rival company Affectiva has measured billions of emotional reactions from 2.4 million face videos taken in eighty countries. Enthusiastic organizations such as Procter & Gamble, Coca-Cola, and others have used the software to gauge consumers' emotional reactions to products and advertisements; law-enforcement agencies have used the software in criminal interrogations; and retailers have

LanKS/Shutterstock.com

used it to determine how people are feeling as they exit their stores. But despite their foundation on big data, emotional software programs run the risk of misinterpreting emotions or incorrectly labeling people as liars. Critics are wary, however, because people are not always aware they are being recorded. Privacy advocate Ginger McCall says, "I can see few things more invasive than trying to record someone's emotions in a database."

Source: E. Dwoskin and E. M. Rusli, "The Technology That Unmasks Your Hidden Emotions," *Wall Street Journal*, January 28, 2015, accessed May 12, 2015, http://www.wsj.com /articles/startups-see-your-face-unmask-your-emotions-1422472398.

communicate a lack of respect, attention, listening, and self-control.[51] TalentSmart's Travis Bradberry says, "Take a page out of the Old West and put a basket by the conference room door with an image of a smartphone and the message, 'Leave your guns at the door.'"[52]

Paralanguage includes the pitch, rate, tone, volume, and speaking pattern (use of silences, pauses, or hesitations) of one's voice. When people are unsure of what to say, for example, they tend to decrease their communication effectiveness by speaking softly. When people are nervous, they tend to speak faster and louder. How much does paralanguage matter? A study in which 1,000 people listened to 120 different speeches found that the tone of the speaker's voice accounted for 23 percent of the difference in listener's evaluations of the speech, compared to speech content, which accounted for only 11 percent.[53] So paralanguage was twice as important as what was actually said.

In short, because nonverbal communication is so informative, especially when it contradicts verbal communication, managers need to learn how to monitor and control their nonverbal behaviors.

Paralanguage the pitch, rate, tone, volume, and speaking pattern (that is, use of silences, pauses, or hesitations) of one's voice

Communication medium the method used to deliver an oral or written message

15-3 MANAGING ONE-ON-ONE COMMUNICATION

When it comes to improving communication, managers face two primary tasks, managing one-on-one communication and managing organization-wide communication.

On average, first-line managers spend 57 percent of their time with people, middle managers spend 63 percent of their time directly with people, and top managers spend as much as 78 percent of their time dealing with people.[54] These numbers make it clear that managers spend a great deal of time in one-on-one communication with others.

*Let's learn more about managing one-on-one communication by reading how to **15-3a choose the right communication medium, 15-3b be a good listener,** and **15-3c give effective feedback.***

15-3a Choosing the Right Communication Medium

Sometimes messages are poorly communicated simply because they are delivered using the wrong **communication medium**, which is the method used to deliver a message. For example, the wrong communication medium is being used when an employee returns from lunch, picks up the note left on her office chair, and learns she has been fired. The wrong communication medium is also being used when an employee pops into your office every ten minutes with a simple request. (An email would be better.)

There are two general kinds of communication media: oral and written communication. *Oral communication* includes face-to-face interactions and group meetings through telephone calls, videoconferencing, or any other means of sending and receiving spoken messages. Studies show that managers generally prefer oral communication over written because it provides the opportunity to ask questions about parts of the message that they don't understand. Oral communication is also a rich communication medium because it allows managers to receive and assess the nonverbal communication that accompanies spoken messages (that is, body language, facial expressions, and the voice characteristics associated with paralanguage). Furthermore, you don't need a PC and an Internet connection to conduct oral communication. Simply schedule an appointment, track someone down in the hall, or catch someone on the phone. **A&E Network** executive Mel Berning travels two weeks a month, and when he is at headquarters, he forgoes what he calls "antiseptic" formal meetings and instead prefers impromptu informal meetings in which he breezes into the offices of direct reports in the morning. "You have a conversation that is less hurried and less guarded," he says. "Face-to-face encounters are so much more revealing than a text or an email."[55] Amit Singh, president of Google for Work, agrees. He says that because "so much gets lost in translation in emails," companies should make greater use of face-to-face discussions, where there is "a clash of ideas, but a respectful clash."[56]

Former *Wall Street Journal* columnist Jason Fry worries that voice mail and email have made managers less willing to engage in meaningful, face-to-face oral communication than ever before. In fact, 67 percent of managers admit to using email as a substitute for face-to-face conversations. While there are advantages to email (for example, it creates a record of what's been said), it's often better to talk to people instead of just emailing them. Fry writes, "If you're close enough that the person you're emailing uses the plonk of your return key as a cue to look for the little Outlook envelope, [it's] best [to] think carefully about whether you should be typing instead of talking."[57] But the oral medium should not be used for *all* communication. In general, when the message is simple, such as a quick request or a presentation of straightforward information, a memo or email is often the better communication medium.

Written communication includes letters, email, and memos. Although most managers still like and use oral communication, email in particular is changing how they communicate with workers, customers, and each other. Email is the dominant form of communication in organizations primarily because of its convenience and speed. The average adult spends more than an hour each day reading and sending emails. In fact, nearly 200 billion emails are sent around the world every year.[58]

Part of the reason for email's dominance is that, as written communication, it is well suited for delivering straightforward messages and information. Furthermore, with email accessible at the office, at home, and on the road (by laptop computer, cell phone, or web-based email), managers can use email to stay in touch from anywhere at almost any time. And, because email and other written communications don't have to be sent and received simultaneously, messages can be sent and stored for reading at any time. Consequently, managers can send and receive many more messages using email than by using oral communication, which requires people to get together in person or by phone or videoconference.

Email has its own drawbacks, however. One is that it lacks the formality of paper memos and letters. It is easy to fire off a rushed email that is not well written or fully thought through. The opportunity to lash out with an angry email reply is incredibly tempting. To avoid that temptation and the damage it does to your work relationships, Pamela Rutledge of the Media Psychology Research Center recommends asking yourself, "Do I want an outcome where someone throws a cup of coffee at me? Or do I want an outcome where we work toward a solution?"[59] Another drawback to email is that it lacks nonverbal cues, making emails very easy to misinterpret. A final drawback to email is the sheer volume that employees receive each day. At global IT-services company **Atos**, workers were spending fifteen to twenty hours every week corresponding by email—and that just includes emails to and from other Atos employees. According to human resources manager Philippe Mareine, email "was becoming a burden to our employees rather than an enabler." To curb the time spent on emails, management began urging employees to use the company's internal social network, BlueKiwi. Since this move, employees' average email load has dropped to just six messages per day, and the time sales consultants take to resolve queries collaboratively has dropped from two hours (over email) to forty-five minutes (using BlueKiwi). Over the past five years, email volume has fallen 70 percent at Atos, while operating margins have increased 60 percent.[60]

Although written communication is well suited for delivering straightforward messages and information, it is not well suited to complex, ambiguous, or emotionally laden messages, which are better delivered through oral communication. At software company **Autodesk**, 62 percent of managers have at least one remote employee. Because of this, all employees are trained to makes sure that the medium fits the message. For sharing information and ideas, employees use email. For brainstorming or problem solving, they use video calls or video conferencing. For making difficult decisions or resolving conflicts, they meet face to face.[61]

15-3b Listening

Are you a good listener? You probably think so. In fact, most people, including managers, are terrible listeners. A recent study from Stanford Graduate School of Business showed that listening was among the least mentioned strengths in CEO performance evaluations.[62] You qualify as a poor listener if you frequently interrupt others, jump to conclusions about what people will say before they've said it, hurry the speaker to finish his or her point, are a passive listener (not actively working at your listening), or simply don't pay attention to what people are saying.[63] On this last point—attentiveness—college students were periodically asked to record their thoughts during a psychology course. On average, 20 percent of the students were paying attention (only 12% were actively working at being good listeners), 20 percent were thinking about sex, 20 percent were thinking about things they had done before, and the remaining 40 percent were thinking about other things unrelated to the class (for example, worries, religion, lunch, daydreaming).[64]

How important is it to be a good listener? In general, about 45 percent of the total time you spend communicating with others is spent listening. Furthermore, listening is important for managerial and business success, even for those at the top of an organization. T-Mobile CEO John Legere says that when he took the top job at the telecommunications company, he needed *Wireless for Dummies.* His response to his lack of familiarity with the industry was simple—listen. He listened to customer service calls, visited stores to listen to customers and employees, and even interacted with users over social media. Legere says, "My business philosophy is to listen to your employees, listen to your customers. Shut up and do what they tell you. And each of our uncarrier moves and the way I run my company is completely aligned with that."[65]

Listening is a more important skill for managers than ever because Generation X and Millennial employees tend to expect a high level of interaction with their supervisors. They want feedback on their performance, but they also want to offer feedback and know that it is heard. In fact, managers with better listening skills are rated more highly by their employees and are much more likely to be promoted.[66]

So, what can you do to improve your listening ability? First, understand the difference between hearing and listening. According to *Webster's New World Dictionary*, **hearing** is the "act or process of perceiving sounds," whereas **listening** is "making a conscious effort to hear." In other words, we react to sounds, such as bottles breaking or music being played too loud, because hearing is an involuntary physiological process. By contrast, listening is a voluntary behavior. So, if you want to be a good listener, you have to choose to be a good listener. Typically, that means choosing to be an active, empathetic listener.[67]

Active listening means assuming half the responsibility for successful communication by actively giving the speaker nonjudgmental feedback that shows you've accurately heard what he or she said. Active listeners make it clear from their behavior that they are listening carefully to what the speaker has to say. Active listeners put the speaker at ease, maintain eye contact, and show the speaker that they are attentively listening by nodding and making short statements.

Several specific strategies can help you be a better active listener. First, engage in immediacy behaviors, such as putting your phone away, turning off the TV, leaning forward and making eye contact, and using short words such as "yes," "uh-huh," and "okay," to encourage the speaker to continue and to demonstrate that you're listening.[68] In group settings, that means not following the "rule of three," which is that in a group of five or six people, it's acceptable to look at your phone as long as three people have their heads up and appear to be paying attention.[69] The "rule of three" is not active listening. Second, clarify responses by asking the speaker to explain confusing or ambiguous statements. Third, when there are natural breaks in the speaker's delivery, use this time to paraphrase or summarize what has been said. *Paraphrasing* is restating what has been said in your own words. *Summarizing* is reviewing the speaker's main points or emotions. Paraphrasing and summarizing give the speaker the chance to correct the message if the

Hearing the act or process of perceiving sounds

Listening making a conscious effort to hear

Active listening assuming half the responsibility for successful communication by actively giving the speaker nonjudgmental feedback that shows you've accurately heard what he or she said

Exhibit 15.5
Immediacy Behaviors, and Paraphrasing and Summarizing Responses for Active Listeners

Immediacy Behaviors	Clarifying Responses	Paraphrasing Responses	Summarizing Responses
Put your phone away.	Could you explain that again?	What you're really saying is....	Let me summarize....
Turn off the TV.	I don't understand what you mean.	If I understand you correctly....	Okay, your main concerns are....
Sit close and lean forward.	I'm not sure how....	In other words....	To recap, what you've said....
Make eye contact.	I'm confused. Would you run through that again?	So your perspective is that....	Thus far, you've discussed....
Use "yes," "uh-huh," "okay," and other short words to encourage the speaker to continue.		Tell me if I'm wrong, but what you seem to be saying is....	

Source: E. Atwater, *I Hear You*, rev. ed. (New York: Walker, 1992); E. Bernstein, "How 'Active Listening ' Makes Both Participants in a Conversation Feel Better," *Wall Street Journal*, January 12, 2015, accessed May 13, 2015, http://www.wsj.com/articles/how-active-listening-makes-both-sides-of-a-conversation-feel-better-1421082684.

active listener has attached the wrong meaning to it. Paraphrasing and summarizing also show the speaker that the active listener is interested in the speaker's message.

Exhibit 15.5 reviews immediacy behaviors and lists specific statements that listeners can use to clarify responses, paraphrase, or summarize what has been said. Active listeners also avoid evaluating the message or being critical until the message is complete. They recognize that their only responsibility during the transmission of a message is to receive it accurately and derive the intended meaning from it. Evaluation and criticism can take place after the message is accurately received. Finally, active listeners recognize that a large portion of any message is transmitted nonverbally and thus pay very careful attention to nonverbal cues (that is, immediacy behaviors) transmitted by the speaker.

Empathetic listening means understanding the speaker's perspective and personal frame of reference and giving feedback that conveys that understanding to the speaker. Empathetic listening goes beyond active listening because it depends on our ability to set aside our own attitudes or relationships to be able to see and understand things through someone else's eyes. Empathetic listening is just as important as active listening, especially for managers, because it helps build rapport and trust with others. Unfortunately, a recent analysis of 14,000 college students across seventy-two studies found a 40 percent decrease in empathy over the last thirty years.[70] Since most of that decline occurred between 2000 and today, it's clear that companies need to focus on developing their managers' ability to empathize.

Thankfully, one interesting study suggests that empathy and listening skills can quickly improve. Two groups of children were asked to accurately identify peoples' emotions in pictures and videotapes. The first group attended a five-day device-free camp (no phones, tablets, or computers), while the second group did not. After the camp, the two groups were tested again. There was little difference in the second group's scores, but the first group improved nearly 40 percent. Why? Students at camp weren't watching TV or playing video games five hours a day. Yalda Uhls, lead author of the study and senior researcher with the UCLA's Children's Digital Media Center, Los Angeles, commented, "You can't learn nonverbal emotional cues from a screen in the way you can learn it from face-to-face communication."[71] MIT Professor Sherry Turkle, author of *Reclaiming Conversation: The Power of Talk in a Digital Age*, explained the results this way: "They talked to one another. In conversation, things go best if you pay close attention and learn how to put yourself in someone else's shoes."[72]

The key to being a more empathetic listener is to show your desire to understand and to reflect people's feelings. You can *show your desire to understand* by listening, that is, asking people to talk about what's most important to them and then by giving them sufficient time to talk before responding or interrupting.

Reflecting feelings is also an important part of empathetic listening

Empathetic listening
understanding the speaker's perspective and personal frame of reference and giving feedback that conveys that understanding to the speaker

because it demonstrates that you understand the speaker's emotions. Unlike active listening, in which you restate or summarize the informational content of what has been said, the focus is on the affective part of the message. As an empathetic listener, you can use the following statements to *reflect the speaker's emotions*:

▸ So, right now it sounds like you're feeling . . . .

▸ You seem as if you're . . . .

▸ Do you feel a bit . . . ?

▸ I could be wrong, but I'm sensing that you're feeling . . . .

In the end, says management consultant Terry Pearce, empathetic listening can be boiled down to these three steps. First, wait ten seconds before you respond. It will seem an eternity, but waiting prevents you from interrupting others and rushing your response. Second, to be sure you understand what the speaker wants, ask questions to clarify the speaker's intent. Third, only then should you respond first with feelings and then facts (notice that facts *follow* feelings).[73]

A word of caution, however: Not everyone appreciates having what they said repeated back to them. Manager Candy Friesen says that whenever she did that, "I seemed to engender animosity or hostility. . . . the person to whom you're speaking may not appreciate having his thoughts paraphrased one little bit."[74] So, when applying these listening techniques, pay attention to the body language and tone of voice of the person you're communicating with to make sure they appreciate your attempts to be a better listener.

15-3c Giving Feedback

In Chapter 11, you learned that performance appraisal feedback (that is, judging) should be separated from developmental feedback (that is, coaching).[75] We can now focus on the steps needed to communicate feedback one-on-one to employees.

To start, managers need to recognize that feedback can be constructive or destructive. **Destructive feedback** is disapproving without any intention of being helpful and almost always causes a negative or defensive reaction in the recipient. By contrast, **constructive feedback** is intended to be helpful, corrective, and/or encouraging. It is aimed at correcting performance deficiencies and motivating employees. Business author Tim

For feedback to be constructive rather than destructive, it must be immediate and focused on specific behaviors and problems.

Harford says the problem with constructive feedback is that it's given like a sandwich—something nice to start with, some constructive feedback in the middle, and then something positive at the end. Harford says, "We say [to the people we're managing], 'That was a great piece of work, there was just a small problem.'" "What we tend to hear," he says, is, "That was a great piece of work."[76]

For feedback to be constructive rather than destructive, it must be immediate, focused on specific behaviors, and problem-oriented. *Immediate feedback* is much more effective than delayed feedback because manager and worker can recall the mistake or incident more accurately and discuss it in detail before it's too late to have a meaningful conversation. Employees at **PwC** use an app called Snapshot to request short, immediate assessments from their managers on everything from overall business acumen to specific technical capabilities. The feedback is visible to the employee, career coach, direct supervisor, HR manager, and the partner in charge of the team, and analytics tools assess the quality of the feedback and how quickly the manager responded. PwC vice chairman Tim Ryan says that the goal is to develop employees in real time: "We analogize it to athletes. They get feedback every time they come off the court."[77]

Specific feedback focuses on particular acts or incidents that are clearly under the control of the employee. For instance, instead of telling an employee that he or she is "always late for work," it's much more constructive to say, "In the last three weeks, you have been thirty minutes late on four occasions and more than an hour late on two others." Furthermore, specific feedback isn't very helpful unless employees have control over the problems that the

Destructive feedback
feedback that disapproves without any intention of being helpful and almost always causes a negative or defensive reaction in the recipient

Constructive feedback
feedback intended to be helpful, corrective, and/or encouraging

feedback addresses. Giving negative feedback about behaviors beyond someone's control is likely to be seen as unfair. Similarly, giving positive feedback about behaviors beyond someone's control may be viewed as insincere.

Last, *problem-oriented feedback* focuses on the problems or incidents associated with the poor performance rather than on the worker or the worker's personality. Giving feedback does not give managers the right to personally attack workers. Although managers may be frustrated by a worker's poor performance, the point of problem-oriented feedback is to draw attention to the problem in a nonjudgmental way so that the employee has enough information to correct it. For example, if an employee has body odor, a surprisingly common workplace problem, don't leave deodorant, soap, or shampoo on the person's desk (for all to see) or say, "You stink." *HR Magazine* advises handling the problem this way: "Because this is a sensitive issue and the employee will likely be uncomfortable and embarrassed in discussing it, keep the meeting private and confidential. Be compassionate but direct. Treat it as you would handle any other job-related performance issue. Explain the problem and the need to correct it. Be specific about expectations. . . . If the employer has a dress and grooming policy, refer to the policy and provide the employee with a copy."[78]

15-4 MANAGING ORGANIZATION-WIDE COMMUNICATION

Although managing one-on-one communication is important, managers must also know how to communicate effectively with a larger number of people throughout an organization.

Learn more about organization-wide communication by reading the following sections about 15-4a improving transmission by getting the message out and 15-4b improving reception by finding ways to hear what others feel and think.

15-4a Improving Transmission: Getting the Message Out

Several methods of electronic communication—email, collaborative discussion sites, televised/videotaped speeches and conferences, and broadcast voice mail—now make it easier for managers to communicate with people throughout the organization and get the message out.

Although we normally think of email, the transmission of messages via computers, as a means of one-on-one communication, it also plays an important role in organization-wide communication. With the click of a button, managers can send an email to everyone in the company via distribution lists. When Microsoft announced it would be laying off 18,000 employees, 14 percent of its workforce, CEO Satya Nadella announced the news in a speech to Microsoft employees, accompanied by a long, detailed email, in which he said, "Nothing is off the table in how we think about shifting our culture to deliver on this core strategy [to become a mobile-first, cloud-first company]. Organizations will change. Mergers and acquisitions will occur. Job responsibilities will evolve. New partnerships will be formed. Tired traditions will be questioned. Our priorities will be adjusted. New skills will be built. New ideas will be heard. New hires will be made. Processes will be simplified. And if you want to thrive at Microsoft and make a world impact, you and your team must add numerous more changes to this list that you will be enthusiastic about driving."[79] He finished by saying, "Culture change means we will do things differently. Often people think that means everyone other than them. In reality, it means all of us taking a new approach and working together to make Microsoft better."[80]

Collaborative websites are another means of electronically promoting organization-wide communication. **Online discussion forums** use web- or software-based discussion tools to allow employees across the company to easily ask questions and share knowledge with each other. The point is to share expertise and not duplicate solutions already discovered by others in the company. Furthermore, because collaborative discussion sites remain online, they provide a historical database for people who are dealing with particular problems for the first time.

Collaborative discussion sites are typically organized by topic, project, or person and can take the shape of blogs that allow readers to post comments, wikis to allow collaborative discussions, document sharing and editing, or traditional discussion forums (see Chapter 17, Managing Information, for further explanation). **Slack** is a robust group communication platform (on computers, smartphones, and tablets) that includes automatic archiving, a powerful search engine, and more informal and accessible online collaboration. Slack's "open channels" increase communication

Online discussion forums the in-house equivalent of Internet newsgroups. By using web- or software-based discussion tools that are available across the company, employees can easily ask questions and share knowledge with each other

Exhibit 15.6
Establishing Collaborative Discussion Sites

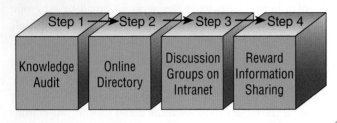

Step 1 → Step 2 → Step 3 → Step 4

| Knowledge Audit | Online Directory | Discussion Groups on Intranet | Reward Information Sharing |

transparency by making messages, files, comments, images, and video visible to everyone else in the team (or company). And with everything searchable, anyone can quickly catch up to find out where projects or discussions stand. Technology guru Walt Mossberg says, "It's sort of like a combination of Facebook, Twitter, iMessage, and Dropbox, but just for you and your co-workers."[81]. Companies have adopted Slack primarily because it increases communication effectiveness so much that email usage within teams or companies often drops by 70 or 80 percent. *New York Times* reporter Farhad Manjoo is based in California and has found that Slack helps him stay connected to "the mother ship in New York. Using Slack, I can peer into discussions that would never have been accessible to me. I can see how the producers and editors who are handling my column are discussing how to present it, and how the team overseeing the home page is thinking about my work."[82]

Exhibit 15.6 lists the steps companies need to take to establish successful collaborative discussion sites. First, pinpoint your company's top intellectual assets through a knowledge audit and spread that knowledge throughout the organization. Second, create an online directory detailing the expertise of individual workers and make it available to all employees. Third, set up collaborative discussion sites on the intranet so that managers and workers can collaborate on problem solving. Finally, reward information sharing by making the online sharing of knowledge a key part of performance ratings.

Televised/videotaped speeches and meetings are a third electronic method of organization-wide communication. **Televised/ videotaped speeches and meetings** are simply speeches and meetings originally made to a small audience that are either simultaneously broadcast to other

Televised/videotaped speeches and meetings speeches and meetings originally made to a smaller audience that are either simultaneously broadcast to other locations in the company or videotaped for subsequent distribution and viewing

locations in the company or videotaped for subsequent distribution and viewing by a broader audience.

Voice messaging, or voice mail, is a telephone answering system that records audio messages. In one survey, 89 percent of respondents said that voice messaging is critical to business communication, 78 percent said that it improves productivity, and 58 percent said they would rather leave a message on a voice messaging system than with a receptionist.[83] Nonetheless, most people are unfamiliar with the ability to *broadcast voice mail* by sending a recorded message to everyone in the company.

Broadcast voice mail gives top managers a quick, convenient way to address their workforces via oral communication—but only if people actually listen to the message, and that turns out to be a challenge with today's workers, who are much more likely to use their smartphones for social media rather than phone calls. Consequently, company leaders are increasingly using real-time messaging tools like Yammer, a Facebook-like social media platform for companies, or Skype for Business, to broadcast text or video-based messages to their workforces. When Poojan Kumar, CEO of data storage manufacturer PernixData, wanted to change how employees received internal communications, he blocked company-wide emails and insisted that messages intended for all employees be posted to Yammer instead. To encourage use, Kumar began posting snapshots of the company's equipment in action that he took during his travels. Human resources also put up a company directory with employees' photos. Getting employees to embrace a new communication platform, Kumar says, "will only happen if there's enough interesting content."[84]

15-4b Improving Reception: Hearing What Others Feel and Think

When people think of "organization-wide" communication, they think of the CEO and top managers getting their message out to people in the company. But organization-wide communication also means finding ways to hear what people throughout the organization are thinking and feeling. This is important because most employees and managers are reluctant to share their thoughts and feelings with top managers. Surveys indicate that only 29 percent of first-level managers feel that their companies encourage employees to express their opinions openly. Another study of

Slack is a robust group communication platform that increases communication transparency by making messages, files, comments, images, and video visible to everyone else in the team (or company).

twenty-two companies found that 70 percent of the people surveyed were afraid to speak up about problems they knew existed at work.

Withholding information about organizational problems or issues is called **organizational silence**. Organizational silence occurs when employees believe that telling management about problems won't make a difference or that they'll be punished or hurt in some way for sharing such information.[85] A survey of executives found that 85 percent had at some point kept quiet when they saw a serious problem at work.[86] At Jetstar Airways, an Australia-based airline, pilots were afraid to speak up about fatigue from flying too many hours. Captain Richard Woodward, then vice president of the Australian and International Pilots Association, said that his organization had received dozens of complaints from Jetstar pilots, but that the pilots were afraid to complain to Jetstar management because "there was a culture of fear and intimidation at that airline."[87] One pilot scheduler told his pilots, "Toughen up, princesses! You aren't fatigued, you are tired and can't be bothered to go into work." A report from Australia's Civil Aviation Safety Authority concluded, "There remains reluctance from a number of flight crew to report fatigue risk and/or to say no to an extension of duty based on the perceived punitive nature of taking such actions."[88]

Company hotlines, survey feedback, frequent informal meetings, surprise visits, and blogs are additional ways of overcoming organizational silence. **Company hotlines** are phone numbers that anyone in the company can call anonymously to leave information for upper management. Company hotlines are incredibly useful, as 41 percent of the calls placed to them result in an investigation and some form of corrective action within the organization. Anonymity is critical, too, because as those investigations proceeded, 59 percent of the callers did not want their identities revealed.[89]

Survey feedback is information that is collected by survey from organization members and then compiled, disseminated, and used to develop action plans for improvement. Many organizations make use of survey feedback by surveying their managers and employees several times a year. **Sunovian Pharmaceuticals**, a small drug maker in Massachusetts, which had a divided office, with employees on the second floor and executives two floors up, discovered through its annual survey that employees felt walled off from their leaders. So, chief commercial officer Rick Russell, who managed 1,100 people, put a desk in a glass-walled office in the middle of the second floor, which employees quickly dubbed "the fish bowl," where he worked every Friday without an assistant. Soon, the company's chief medical officer joined him, and the following year, survey feedback showed that employee trust in senior leadership improved. Russell says, "You have to rally the troops. You can't do it from a memo."[90]

Frequent *informal meetings* between top managers and lower-level employees are one of the best ways for top managers to hear what others think and feel. Many people assume that top managers are at the center of everything that goes on in organizations, but top managers commonly feel isolated from most of their lower-level managers and employees.[91]

Organizational silence
when employees withhold information about organizational problems or issues

Company hotlines phone numbers that anyone in the company can call anonymously to leave information for upper management

Survey feedback
information that is collected by surveys from organizational members and then compiled, disseminated, and used to develop action plans for improvement

TAKE A MEMO: THE RISE IN ANONYMOUS VENTING

A new app called Memo allows employees to vent about their employers by posting anonymous "memos" (vents). Users of the app can post new memos, comment on existing memos, and even upload photos and documents to support their memos. Employees at companies such as Delta Airline, Ernst & Young, and Hasbro are using Memo to vent about compensation, managerial inefficiency, and working from home. After a user is verified, Memo removes all identifiable data about the person's activity, making that person's posts completely anonymous. Memos (posts) are organized onto public message boards that can be seen by all users and private boards organized by company. Not all companies are thrilled at the availability of Memo. Visa, Boeing, and Hewlett-Packard have all circulated internal corporate memos (the traditional kind) discouraging employees from using the app and reminding them of the risk of proprietary information being released to the public.

Ben Schonewille/Shutterstock.com

Source: L. Gellman, "App Lets Workers Vent Anonymously," *Wall Street Journal*, January 20, 2015, accessed May 12, 2015, http://www.wsj.com/articles/memo-app-lets-workers-vent-anonymously-1421805377.

Consequently, more and more top managers are scheduling frequent informal meetings with people throughout their companies.

Mazor Robotics, an Israeli-based medical technology company, has facilities in the United States, Asia, and Europe. With employees scattered worldwide, maintaining good communication is critical. CEO Ori Hadomi says, "I think that the most constructive and the most productive way to communicate is informal communication." So once a week he has a joint one-hour phone call with people in all of the offices. With no set agenda, employees take turns explaining what is going on in their division, what was accomplished in the past few days, and what kind of issues are coming up in the near future. Says Hadomi, "So in one hour, everyone is synchronized. And when I talk with many of the employees I hear that it's a very important meeting for them because it gives them the opportunity to hear about the business."[92]

Have you ever been around when a supervisor learns that upper management is going to be paying a visit? First,

Blog a personal website that provides personal opinions or recommendations, news summaries, and reader comments

there's shock. Next, there's anxiety. And then there's panic, as everyone is told to drop what he or she is doing to polish, shine, and spruce up the workplace so that it looks perfect for the visit. Of course, when visits are conducted under these conditions, top managers don't get a realistic look at what's going on in the company. Consequently, one of the ways to get an accurate picture is to pay *surprise visits* to various parts of the organization. These visits should not just be surprise inspections but should also be used as opportunities to encourage meaningful upward communication from those who normally don't get a chance to communicate with upper management.

Blogs are another way to hear what people are thinking and saying, both inside and outside the organization. A **blog** is a personal website that provides personal opinions or recommendations, news summaries, and reader comments. When the 2.0 version of popular time-tracking app **Hours** was released with new functionality, it was featured on the Apple App Store. Within days, the app had tens of thousands of new customers. However, Hours' tech support team soon received hundreds of complaints about the app's new team functions. Company founder Jeremy Olson used the corporate blog to candidly admit the problems and how the company was trying to solve them. He also announced that Hours 2.0 would be free until a fixed version was released, and that all who had purchased a yearly subscription would get a free second year. In response, customers rallied around the company, including Aaron Whitney, who commented on Olson's post, "I've been one of the people struggling with issues since launch day . . . and, admittedly, after three weeks, was frustrated almost to the point of bailing out. This post changed my perspective. Anyone who wants to know how a company should properly handle a less than stellar customer experience should read your post. It's perfect."[93]

Monitoring social media, such as blogs, Twitter, and Facebook, written by people outside the company can be a good way to find out what others are saying or thinking about your organization or its products or actions. McDonald's put together a social media plan called "Our Food. Your Questions." to monitor and engage with both customers and critics. Laney Garcia, McDonald's manager of brand reputation and public relations, said, "What we did was audit the conversations that were happening from a social perspective. We looked at conversations that were happening on Twitter, Facebook, and we really scrubbed the data to find out when consumers have questions about our brand."[94] Common questions included, "Is your meat 100 percent beef?" "Are your eggs real?" "Does your meat include pink slime?" McDonald's prepared answers to questions already posted on social media and assembled a team of rapid responders to address new questions. The result, says Garcia, was a sizable increase in traffic, both to the company's website and to the videos where questions were answered. And, she says, "For the first time, we've seen customers really responding in the sense that they're *defending* us."[95]

Finally, in addition to being a way to deliver organizational communication, so-called *town hall meetings* can be an effective way for companies to hear feedback from employees. In 2014, Dubai-based **Emirates Airline** carried 44.5 million passengers, and by 2020, it expects that number to rise to 70 million. To meet growing demand, Emirates Airline will hire 5,000 additional cabin staff, but in the meantime, the 20,000 current cabin crew employees are working more hours on shorter layovers. Crew members who had worked their way to first-class assignments, a prestigious posting, are having to return to economy class to cover staff shortages. Many staff members have had annual leave allocations deferred. To better understand crew member complaints, the airline held three town hall meetings—the first of which lasted four hours—during which staff aired grievances to senior management. Terry Daly, Emirates' senior vice president of service delivery, announced the meetings in an email, writing that he was "aware that there are a number of subjects that are causing concern at the moment" and that the meetings would be "an opportunity to talk about these directly with me."[96]

STUDY TOOLS 15

LOCATED IN TEXTBOOK

☐ Rip-out and review chapter review card

LOCATED AT WWW.CENGAGEBRAIN.COM

☐ Review key term flashcards and create your own from StudyBits

☐ Track your knowledge and understanding of key concepts, using the concept tracker

☐ Complete practice and graded quizzes to prepare for tests

☐ Complete interactive content within the exposition

☐ View chapter highlight box content at the beginning of each chapter

PART 5

16 Control

Dirk Ercken/Shutterstock.com

LEARNING OUTCOMES

16-1 Describe the basic control process.

16-2 Discuss the various methods that managers can use to maintain control.

16-3 Describe the behaviors, processes, and outcomes that today's managers are choosing to control in their organizations.

After you finish this chapter, go to **PAGE 360** for **STUDY TOOLS**

16-1 THE CONTROL PROCESS

For all companies, past success is no guarantee of future success. Even successful companies fall short or face challenges and thus have to make changes. **Control** is a regulatory process of establishing standards to achieve organizational goals, comparing actual performance to the standards, and taking corrective action when necessary to restore performance to those standards. Control is achieved when behavior and work procedures conform to standards and when company goals are accomplished.[1] Control is not just an after-the-fact process, however. Preventive measures are also a form of control.

In a factory setting, fluorescent lighting costs $9 to $10 per square meter every year. So for a typical 600,000 square foot factory, annual lighting costs can run half a million dollars each year. This is why Quality Bicycle Products installed energy-efficient light emitting diode (LED) lighting in its new 122,000 square foot distribution facility in Lancaster, Pennsylvania. While the LED lights are two to three times more expensive to install than fluorescent lighting, they're 90 percent more efficient and can last up to twenty-five years, reducing the costs of changing burned out bulbs. Quality Bicycle also outfitted its LED lights with motion and daylight sensors so that adjust the light output based on how much natural light is entering the facility and only activate when someone is present. San Marks of Greenearth Energy says, "It's effectively having a laptop computer under each light."[2] According to Dave Smith, who runs the distribution facility for Quality Bicycle, the savings are so great that, "The payoff for our investment was a year and a half."[3]

The basic control process 16-1a begins with the establishment of clear standards of performance; 16-1b involves a comparison of performance to those standards; 16-1c takes corrective action, if needed, to repair performance deficiencies; 16-1d is a dynamic, cybernetic process; and 16-1e consists of three basic methods: feedback control, concurrent control, and feedforward control. However, as much as managers would like, 16-1f control isn't always worthwhile or possible.

16-1a Standards

The control process begins when managers set goals such as satisfying 90 percent of customers or increasing sales by 5 percent. Companies then specify the performance standards that must be met to accomplish those goals. **Standards** are a basis of comparison for measuring the extent to which organizational performance is satisfactory or unsatisfactory. For example, many pizzerias use thirty to forty minutes as the standard for delivery time. Because anything longer is viewed as unsatisfactory, they'll typically reduce the price if they can't deliver a hot pizza to you within that time period.

So how do managers set standards? How do they decide which levels of performance are satisfactory and which are unsatisfactory? The first criterion for a good standard is that it must enable goal achievement. If you're meeting the standard but still not achieving company goals, then the standard may have to be changed. One way that thieves steal money from bank accounts is by gluing down the 'enter,' 'cancel,' or 'clear' keys on ATM keypads. If a customer doesn't realize that these functions can also be accessed via the machine's touchscreen, he or she is forced to abandon the transaction with his or her PIN and card still active in the machine.[4] Because PINs are not a good standard for account security, banks have begun using the near field communication (NFC) function on smartphones to verify customers' identities. More and more, customers can open the secure bank app on their phones, choose an amount, then touch their smartphones to the NFC scanner to initiate the deposit or withdrawal. With no buttons and no threat of card skimmers, the entire process is faster and more secure.[5]

> **Control** a regulatory process of establishing standards to achieve organizational goals, comparing actual performance against the standards, and taking corrective action when necessary
>
> **Standards** a basis of comparison for measuring the extent to which various kinds of organizational performance are satisfactory or unsatisfactory

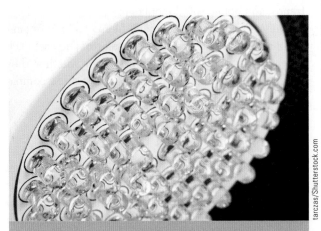

LED lights are two to three times more expensive than fluorescent lights, but they're 90 percent more efficient and can last up to 25 years.

tarczas/Shutterstock.com

KERING SETS THE STANDARD FOR SUSTAINABILITY IN FASHION

Of the dozens of brands owned by fashion conglomerate Kering, several are implementing large-scale sustainability initiatives. Stella McCartney, a longtime animal-rights activist, has developed a technique for producing real leather in a laboratory using DNA from cows. Gucci, which still uses actual hides for its leather, has developed a tanning process that uses far less pollutants, and it is sharing that technology and methodology with anyone who wants it. Across all its companies, Kering is testing a technique developed by a British firm that allows color, chemicals, and fibers to be separated so that the fiber can be recycled. The conglomerate also has a fifty-person team dedicated to sustainability that works with an associate committee of fifteen experts from the energy and transportation sectors. For CEO François-Henri Pinault, sustainability extends beyond cost-savings and brand building. Of the tanning technology, he says, "If you find a solution like this and you use it as a competitive advantage, you miss completely the point."

Source: R. Feitelberg, "Pinault Delves into Sustainability," *WWD*, April 6, 2015, 2.

Companies also determine standards by listening to customers' comments, complaints, and suggestions or by observing competitors. Sarah Beatty started Green Depot, which sells environmentally responsible construction materials, because "greenwashing"—representing products as green when they're not—was widespread among competitors. Beatty hired engineers to help Green Depot develop CLEAR standards, for **C**onservation (recycled, reclaimed, reused, or rapidly renewable resources), **L**ocal (low-carbon footprint), **E**nergy (energy-conserving or renewable resources), **A**ir quality (nontoxic, nonallergenic, or no gases or particulates), and **R**esponsibility (green jobs, worker protection, and truthful marketing). When the standards were developed, Beatty and her team sent out ten-page questionnaires to manufacturers, asking for detailed explanations regarding product production and materials. Each product is measured on each of the five standards. If a standard has been met, Green Depot displays an icon for that standard on the product's page on GreenDepot.com. As Green Depot's website explains, "Our Green Depot Icon System is designed to show at a glance why we call a particular item green."[6]

Standards can also be determined by benchmarking other companies. **Benchmarking** is the process of determining how well other companies (not just competitors) perform business functions or tasks. In other words, benchmarking is the process of determining other companies' standards. When setting standards by benchmarking, the first step is to determine what to benchmark. Organizations can benchmark anything from cycle time (how fast) to quality (how well) to price (how much). For example, based on national benchmarking studies of thousands of fire departments, many firefighters are expected to respond to an alarm within fifteen seconds 95 percent of the time. Additionally, 90 percent of the time, it should take no more than sixty seconds to leave the firehouse, and then no more than four minutes to arrive at the scene.[7]

After setting standards, the next step is to identify the companies *against which* to benchmark those standards. The last step is to collect data to determine other companies' performance standards. Intuit, maker of financial software and websites such as QuickBooks, Intuit Payroll, and TurboTax, gets nearly 40 percent of its revenues by selling its products and services to tens of thousands of small- to medium-sized businesses in different industries. Fred Shilmover, CEO of InsightSquared, which sells data-analytic tools to those businesses, says, "Intuit figured out how to leverage its internal data team for their customers, when those companies couldn't gather enough data on their own to understand the bigger [industry and business] trends."[8] And because Intuit also sells add-on products and services to help manage payroll, inventory, financing, customers, point of sale trends, and online/social media marketing, he says those businesses "can now benchmark their costs [and organizational performance in all of those areas] against each other." This benchmarking shows them whether they perform at, above, or below thousands of other companies on a number of critical dimensions.

16-1b Comparison to Standards

The next step in the control process is to compare actual performance to performance standards. Although this sounds straightforward, the quality of the comparison depends largely on the measurement and information systems a company uses to keep track of performance. The better the system, the easier it is for companies to track their progress and identify problems that need to be fixed.

Benchmarking the process of identifying outstanding practices, processes, and standards in other companies and adapting them to your company

On average, 5 percent of hospital patients catch an infection at the hospital. It costs an average of $15,000 per incident to treat such infections, and 100,000 patients will die each year from them. Why? Because in most hospitals, health care workers wash their hands only 50 percent of the time before examining or touching a patient. Because of the risks, the Center for Disease Control created a video, "Hand Hygiene Saves Lives," to be shown to patients admitted to hospitals. In the video, a patient's wife asks her husband's doctor, on entering the hospital room, to wash his hands before beginning the medical exam.[9]

So, how can a hospital measure the rate at which its employees wash their hands so it can compare the actual rate of handwashing to its goal for handwashing? At the University Health Network in Toronto, researchers electronically monitored the hand-hygiene system. Pushing the lever on a soap dispenser sent a signal time-stamping the handwashing event and logging it into a central database. Even though the hospital was able to measure the rate of handwashing digitally, it found that with the presence of an auditor—a person in a white lab coat (who did not know the purpose of the study)—the rate of handwashing nearly tripled to 3.75 washes per hour versus 1.07 washes per hour when no auditor was present.[10]

16-1c Corrective Action

The next step in the control process is to identify performance deviations, analyze those deviations, and then develop and implement programs to correct them. This is similar to the planning process discussed in Chapter 5. Regular, frequent performance feedback allows workers and managers to track their performance and make adjustments in effort, direction, and strategies.

After discovering that its ICU staff were washing their hands only 6.5 percent of the time, North Shore University Hospital decided that frequent feedback was the best way to change its health care workers' handwashing behavior. So, it provided feedback in two ways. First, an LED display by the nurses' station shows that shift's handwashing percentage and an evaluation, such as "Great Shift!" Second, the nursing shift manager receives an email with the shift's handwashing rates three hours into the shift and then again at the shift's conclusion. Since this system was installed, handwashing rates at North Shore's ICU have risen from 6.5–81 percent.[11]

16-1d Dynamic, Cybernetic Process

As shown in Exhibit 16.1, control is a continuous, dynamic, cybernetic process. Control begins by setting standards, measuring performance, and then comparing

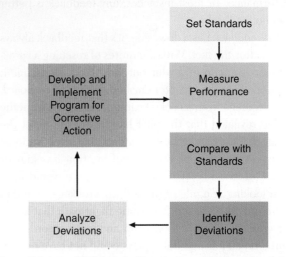

Exhibit 16.1
Cybernetic Control Process

Source: H. Koontz and R. W. Bradspies, "Managing through Feedforward Control: A Future Directed View," *Business Horizons*, June 1972, pp. 25–36.

performance to the standards. If the performance deviates from the standards, then managers and employees analyze the deviations and develop and implement corrective programs that (they hope) achieve the desired performance by meeting the standards. Managers must repeat the entire process again and again in an endless feedback loop (a continuous process). Thus, control is not a one-time achievement or result. It continues over time (that is, it is dynamic) and requires daily, weekly, and monthly attention from managers to maintain performance levels at the standard (that is, it is cybernetic). **Cybernetic** derives from the Greek word *kubernetes*, meaning "steersman," that is, one who steers or keeps on course.[12] The control process shown in Exhibit 16.1 is cybernetic because constant attention to the feedback loop is necessary to keep the company's activity on course.

16-1e Feedback, Concurrent, and Feedforward Control

The three basic control methods are feedback control, concurrent control, and feedforward control. **Feedback control** is a mechanism for gathering information about

Cybernetic the process of steering or keeping on course

Feedback control a mechanism for gathering information about performance deficiencies after they occur

performance deficiencies *after* they occur. This information is then used to correct or prevent performance deficiencies. Study after study has clearly shown that feedback improves both individual and organizational performance. In most instances, any feedback is better than no feedback.

If feedback has a downside, it's that feedback always comes after the fact. Within minutes of rescuing a snowmobiler stranded in a whiteout, an Alaska Department of Public Safety helicopter crashed, killing all on board. Video footage from a cockpit camera recovered from the rubble revealed that the pilot had incorrectly reset the device that indicates that the craft is flying level. National Transportation Safety Board chief aviation investigator John DeLisi said, "Without that video, we would have been looking at a pile of burned-up wreckage, trying to figure out what caused the erratic flight path that led to this crash."[13] The black-box data and voice recorder required on all jets and helicopters could not have provided that information. Because of this video footage, the Alaska Department of Public Safety now requires pilots to receive instrument training every ninety days. This better prepares pilots to navigate in whiteout conditions, which are common in the state. By contrast, the pilot of the crashed helicopter hadn't received instrument training in more than ten years.[14]

Concurrent control addresses the problems inherent in feedback control by gathering information about performance deficiencies *as* they occur. Thus, it is an improvement over feedback because it attempts to eliminate or shorten the delay between performance and feedback about the performance. The year after the failed launch of the Windows 8 operating system, Microsoft began developing Windows 10 by asking corporate partners to comment on the software as it was being developed. An aggressive beta-testing program involved roughly 5 million individuals, 30 percent of whom were information technology workers at large companies. An advisory board of managers from large firms (typically Microsoft's biggest customers) was formed to make recommendations and discuss the company's plans. By asking for feedback concurrently, as development occurred, Microsoft was able to fix bugs earlier and add features recommended by key customers and

Though Windows 10 has been met with critical and public acclaim, some feel that Microsoft has exhibited *too much* control in pressuring customers to upgrade to the new operating system. Users with older versions faced persistent pop-ups and reminders, and some were even upgraded without their consent. In May 2016, Teri Goldstein was awarded $10,000 after suing Microsoft for an unwanted and unauthorized update to Windows 10.

software developers. Asking so many people for feedback also created a high level of interest in the new operating system. Seventy-three percent of information technology managers indicated that their company planned to adopt Windows 10 within two years of its launch.[15]

Feedforward control is a mechanism for gathering information about performance deficiencies *before* they occur. In contrast to feedback and concurrent control, which provide feedback on the basis of outcomes and results, feedforward control provides information about performance deficiencies by monitoring inputs rather than outputs. Thus, feedforward control seeks to prevent or minimize performance deficiencies before they happen. Power companies have traditionally relied on consumers to call in power outages. Then, when repair crews arrive, fault detectors displaying a flag or a light can tell them which line is out, but the crews still have to visually inspect miles of power lines, often in weather with poor visibility, to find the precise cause of the outage. Tollgrade, however, is making sensors the size of a loaf of bread, which sit on and are powered by the electricity flowing through the wires, that can notify power companies about problems before they happen (that is, feedforward). With GPS (location) and wireless

Concurrent control
a mechanism for gathering information about performance deficiencies as they occur, thereby eliminating or shortening the delay between performance and feedback

Feedforward control
a mechanism for monitoring performance inputs rather than outputs to prevent or minimize performance deficiencies before they occur

(communication) capabilities, the sensors monitor the fluctuations in the flow of electricity—from outages to drops to normal transmissions to surge overloads—and instantaneously send text alerts to power company engineers when there are problems.[16] Pennsylvania's Orange & Rockland Utilities were alerted to an electrical line problem over a Fourth of July weekend, and the advanced notice of the outage offered ample time for repair crews to fix the issue before a single customer could complain. Haukur Asgeirsson, technology manager at DTE Energy says, "You can actually go out there and do some preemptive work before a permanent outage occurs. It looks actually very promising."[17]

16-1f Control Isn't Always Worthwhile or Possible

Control is achieved when behavior and work procedures conform to standards, and goals are accomplished. By contrast, **control loss** occurs when behavior and work procedures do not conform to standards.[18] For the first time in its 108-year history, Blue Bell Creameries experienced an outbreak of listeria, a bacterium that thrives in refrigerated conditions, which can cause fever, muscle aches, nausea, abdominal pain, and sometimes death. As a result, Blue Bell announced a voluntary, complete recall of 8 million gallons of ice cream and frozen yogurt products across twenty-three states.[19]

Maintaining control is important because control loss prevents organizations from achieving their goals. When control loss occurs, managers need to find out what, if anything, they could have done to prevent it. Usually, that means identifying deviations from standard performance, analyzing the causes of those deviations, and taking corrective action. Even so, implementing controls isn't always worthwhile or possible. Let's look at regulation costs and cybernetic feasibility to see why this is so.

To determine whether control is worthwhile, managers need to carefully assess **regulation costs**, that is, whether the costs and unintended consequences of control exceed its benefits. If a control process costs more than it benefits, it may not be worthwhile. Because glass can be recycled over and over again, and because it was profitable to recycle, waste companies paid cities for the glass they collected. In fact, to increase the amount of glass collected for recycling, the waste industry encouraged cities to allow households to mix glass, plastic, and cans together in one recycling bin. The unintended consequence of that decision, according to Curt Bucey of Strategic Materials, the largest U.S. glass recycler, is that half of the "glass" loads

headed to recycling aren't glass. Bucey says, "Now what comes with the glass are rocks, shredded paper, chicken bones people left in their takeout containers, and hypodermic needles."[20] Because very expensive equipment is needed to separate glass from other materials, Strategic Materials now charges cities from $10 to $40 per ton, depending on how "dirty" their glass recycling loads are. And for cities used to being paid for recycling glass, having to pay waste companies to take their glass comes as a high regulation cost. James Young, director of solid waste programs around Charleston, South Carolina, says, "When you're losing money and time processing glass for not much revenue, it is just a losing battle, and not sustainable."[21]

Another factor to consider is **cybernetic feasibility**, the extent to which it is possible to implement each of the three steps in the control process. If one or more steps cannot be implemented, then maintaining effective control may be difficult or impossible.

 # CONTROL METHODS

When taking college entrance exams such as the SAT, applicants present a photo ID and are warned that sharing information is prohibited, as is "the use of phones and certain other electronic devices."[22] But that hasn't stopped time zone cheating, where students in eastern time zones share test information with those taking the same exam in western time zones later that day; physical theft of tests from supposedly secure lock boxes; or online discussion following each test administration (the College Board reuses questions several times for cost and reliability reasons).[23] Chinese authorities have begun using security drones during China's National Higher Education Entrance Exam. The drones fly over testing centers, scanning for electronic signals used to transmit copies of the exam and/or provide real-time help to test takers. The Chinese education ministry arrests cheaters and bans them from taking the test for three years.[24]

Managers can use five different methods to achieve control in their organizations: 16-2a bureaucratic, 16-2b objective, 16-2c normative, 16-2d concertive, and 16-2e self-control.

Control loss the situation in which behavior and work procedures do not conform to standards

Regulation costs the costs associated with implementing or maintaining control

Cybernetic feasibility the extent to which it is possible to implement each step in the control process

16-2a Bureaucratic Control

When most people think of managerial control, what they have in mind is bureaucratic control. **Bureaucratic control** is top-down control, in which managers try to influence employee behavior by rewarding or punishing employees for compliance or noncompliance with organizational policies, rules, and procedures. Most employees, however, would argue that bureaucratic managers emphasize punishment for noncompliance much more than rewards for compliance.

As you learned in Chapter 2, bureaucratic management and control were created to prevent just this type of managerial behavior. By encouraging managers to apply well-thought-out rules, policies, and procedures in an impartial, consistent manner to everyone in the organization, bureaucratic control is supposed to make companies more efficient, effective, and fair. Ironically, it frequently has just the opposite effect. Managers who use bureaucratic control often emphasize following the rules above all else.

Another characteristic of bureaucratically controlled companies is that, due to their rule- and policy-driven decision making, they are highly resistant to change and slow to respond to customers and competitors. Recall from Chapter 2 that even Max Weber, the German philosopher who is largely credited with popularizing bureaucratic ideals in the late nineteenth century, referred to bureaucracy as the "iron cage." He said, "Once fully established, bureaucracy is among those social structures which are the hardest to destroy."[25] Of course, the national government, with hundreds of bureaus, agencies, and departments, is typically the largest bureaucracy in most countries. Under new U.S. Department of Transportation rules for long-haul truckers, drivers can now drive only seventy hours per week, down from eighty-two. And, they must take a thirty-four hour break over two nights between work weeks. Intended to increase safety by preventing tired truck drivers from getting behind the wheel, the changes are instead increasing driver turnover (ironically putting less experienced drivers on the road), putting more trucks on the road during rush hour, and forcing drivers to try to sleep when they're not tired and to drive when they are. Manny Hernandez, who has driven trucks for three decades, says the new rules prevent him from getting home to see his family. Wherever he is when the seventy hour limit kicks in, he has to stop for thirty-four hours over two nights. Says Hernandez, "It can be a nightmare of having to sit for forty-eight hours, tired, when all you want to do is get home . . . . Who made up these rules?" he asks. "Did they have any experience in driving truck[s], and traffic and dealing with customers and [the time lost from] your [truck] breakdowns? Sometimes I think they're trying to choke out the trucking industry."[26]

16-2b Objective Control

In many companies, bureaucratic control has evolved into **objective control**, which is the use of observable measures of employee behavior or output to assess performance and influence behavior. Whereas bureaucratic control focuses on whether policies and rules are followed, objective control focuses on observing and measuring worker behavior or output. Cyberloafing, wasting time online while at work, costs U.S. companies $85 billion a year due to decreased worker productivity, reduced available bandwidth, and damage from viruses and malware. Rather than blocking websites, an agricultural company uses software to divide the Internet into sites that employees can always, sometimes, or never visit. Sites that eat up too much bandwidth (such as YouTube) and those that may cause legal problems for the company (such as pornography) are forbidden. Otherwise, an on-screen warning alerts employees that a site may not be work related. Employees can browse nonwork-related sites for ten minutes at a time—up to ninety minutes per day. If they exceed this amount, they must explain to their managers why they need more time on such sites. Lead developer Jeremy Glassman says that the software "provided [employees] with a reminder of the acceptable uses for Internet resources while at work and what is expected of them."[27]

There are two kinds of objective control: behavior control and output control. **Behavior control** is regulating behaviors and actions that workers perform on the job. The basic assumption of behavior control is that if you do the right things (that is, the right behaviors) every day, then those things should lead to goal achievement. Behavior control is still management-based, however, which means that managers are responsible for monitoring and then rewarding or punishing workers for exhibiting desired or undesired behaviors.

Instead of measuring what managers and workers do, **output control** measures the results of their

Bureaucratic control the use of hierarchical authority to influence employee behavior by rewarding or punishing employees for compliance or noncompliance with organizational policies, rules, and procedures

Objective control the use of observable measures of worker behavior or outputs to assess performance and influence behavior

Behavior control the regulation of the behaviors and actions that workers perform on the job

Output control the regulation of workers' results or outputs through rewards and incentives

JPMorgan Chase realizes that culture has as much to do with control as algorithms, so it has added and designated more than 300 executives as "cultural ambassadors."

left and right turns, and whether you exceed 80 mph. Drivers who participate are eligible for discounts up to 50 percent, with their driving scores determining the size of the discount. Ed Scharlau of Austin, Texas, says, "How I drive should affect my insurance premium." Moreover, he says the program's daily feedback has him and his wife talking, "about our own driving and what we see around us: 'Oops, did we just lose points?' "[28]

16-2c Normative Control

Rather than monitoring rules, behavior, or output, another way to control what goes on in organizations is to use normative control to shape the beliefs and values of the people who work there. With **normative controls**, a company's widely shared values and beliefs guide workers' behavior and decisions.

JPMorgan Chase realizes that culture has as much to do with control as algorithms, so it has designated more than 300 executives as "cultural ambassadors" who focus on standards. The company published a memo that encouraged employees to flag any compliance concerns and emphasized that poor compliance and scandals damage the bank's reputation and affect everyone, both professionally and financially. The goal of the program is to reshape the beliefs and values of the bank's employees so that compliance and ethical financial stewardship are part of the company culture.[29]

Normative controls are created in two ways. First, companies that use normative controls are very careful about who they hire. While many companies screen potential applicants on the basis of their abilities, normatively controlled companies are just as likely to screen potential applicants based on their attitudes and values. Four Seasons hotels, a luxury five-star brand, are renowned for their exceptional guest service. Founder Isadore Sharp says, "Competence we can teach. Attitude is ingrained."[30] Former executive vice-president of HR, Nick Mutton agrees, saying, "Job skills can be taught later. The quality of our people—their attitude, professionalism, personal growth—is actually what we are as a business. Our focus on attitude is paramount because engaged employees who care about our customers create our product, and that clearly contributes directly to our bottom line."[31]

Second, with normative controls, managers and employees learn what they should and should not do by observing experienced employees and by listening to the stories they tell about the company. We learned the importance of storytelling

efforts. Whereas behavior control regulates, guides, and measures how workers behave on the job, output control gives managers and workers the freedom to behave as they see fit as long as they accomplish prespecified, measurable results. Output control is often coupled with rewards and incentives.

Three things must occur for output control to lead to improved business results. First, output control measures must be reliable, fair, and accurate. Second, employees and managers must believe that they can produce the desired results. If they don't, then the output controls won't affect their behavior. Third, the rewards or incentives tied to output control measures must truly be dependent on achieving established standards of performance. The "Drive Safe & Save" program at State Farm Insurance is based on output control. Using a device that plugs into your car's diagnostic port, State Farm tracks when you drive, and your braking, acceleration,

> **Normative control** the regulation of workers' behavior and decisions through widely shared organizational values and beliefs

Resistance Is Futile! (Or Is It?)

The easiest way to resist temptation may be to avoid it altogether. A study by researchers at Florida State gave participants the option of taking an online test in one of two formats. The standard format was static, but the stylized format included art on both sides of the screen that would change periodically. Of participants with high self-control, 67 percent selected the standard black-and-white test. By contrast, only 43 percent of the participants with low self-control chose the standard test; the majority chose the stylized test, even though they had been warned ahead of time of the potential distraction. The secret of highly disciplined people is proactive avoidance, or simply avoiding situations in which their self-control might fail.

Source: A. Lukits, "The Secret to Resisting Temptation," *Wall Street Journal*, November 24, 2014, accessed May 13, 2015, http://www.wsj.com/articles/the-secret-to-resisting-temptation-1416852990.

and organizational culture in Chapter 3. For normative controls to work, however, managers must not only select the right people, they must reward employees who honor those attitudes and values, and deal with those who don't. Elite SEM is a New York City–based search engine marketing firm that helps *Fortune* 500 companies increase their profile when potential customers do web searches. Elite SEM values hiring people with advanced technical skills and cooperative attitudes. More specifically, the company prides itself on being a "jerk-free workplace." So, there are consequences for employees and managers who, as CEO Ben Kirshner says, "don't embrace our core values." When a new employee refused to work late his first week on the job, he was let go. Kirshner says, "He was a bad seed!" And, because of the long hours people put in to meet client needs, Elite SEM has a free meal policy. So when another new employee ordered himself groceries and $30 breakfasts, Kirshner says, "Everyone jumped on him."[32]

16-2d Concertive Control

Whereas normative controls are based on beliefs that are strongly held and widely shared throughout a company, **concertive controls** are based on beliefs that are shaped and negotiated by work groups.[33] Whereas normative controls are driven by strong organizational cultures, concertive controls usually arise when companies give work groups complete autonomy and responsibility for task completion (see Chapter 10, "Managing Teams," for a complete discussion of the role of autonomy in teams and groups). The most autonomous groups operate without managers and are completely responsible for controlling work group processes, outputs, and behavior. Such groups do their own hiring, firing, worker discipline, scheduling, materials ordering, budget making and meeting, and decision making.

Concertive control the regulation of workers' behavior and decisions through work group values and beliefs

Concertive control is not established overnight. Highly autonomous work groups evolve through two phases as they develop concertive control. In phase one, group members learn to work with each other, supervise each other's work, and develop the values and beliefs that will guide and control their behavior. And because they develop these values and beliefs themselves, work group members feel strongly about following them.

In the steel industry, Nucor was long considered an upstart compared with the "biggies," U.S. Steel and Bethlehem Steel. Today, however, not only has Nucor managed to outlast many other mills, the company has bought out thirteen other mills in the past five years. Nucor has a unique culture that gives real power to employees on the line and fosters teamwork throughout the organization. This type of teamwork can be a difficult thing for a newly acquired group of employees to get used to. For example, at Nucor's first big acquisition in Auburn, New York, David Hutchins is a frontline supervisor or "lead man" in the rolling mill, where steel from the furnace is spread thin enough to be cut into sheets. When the plant was under the previous ownership, if the guys doing the cutting got backed up, the guys doing the rolling—including Hutchins—would just take a break. He says, "We'd sit back, have a cup of coffee, and complain: 'Those guys stink.'" It took six months to convince the employees at the Auburn plant that the Nucor teamwork way was better than the old way. Now, Hutchins says: "At Nucor, we're not 'you guys' and 'us guys.' It's all of us guys. Wherever the bottleneck is, we go there, and everyone works on it."[34]

The second phase in the development of concertive control is the emergence and formalization of objective rules to guide and control behavior. The beliefs and values developed in phase one usually develop into more objective rules as new members join teams. The clearer those rules, the easier it becomes for new members to figure out how and how not to behave.

Ironically, concertive control may lead to even more stress for workers to conform to expectations than bureaucratic control. Under bureaucratic control, most workers only have to worry about pleasing the boss. But with concertive control, their behavior has to satisfy the rest of their team members. For example, one team member says, "I don't have to sit there and look for the boss to be around; and if the boss is not around, I can sit there and talk to my neighbor or do what I want. Now the whole team is around me and the whole team is observing what I'm doing."[35] Plus, with concertive control, team members have a second, much more stressful role to perform: that of making sure that their team members adhere to team values and rules.

16-2e Self-Control

Self-control, also known as **self-management**, is a control system in which managers and workers control their own behavior.[36] Self-control does not result in anarchy, in which everyone gets to do whatever he or she wants. In self-control, or self-management, leaders and managers provide workers with clear boundaries within which they may guide and control their own goals and behaviors.[37] Leaders and managers also contribute to self-control by teaching others the skills they need to maximize and monitor their own work effectiveness. In turn, individuals who manage and lead themselves establish self-control by setting their own goals, monitoring their own progress, rewarding or punishing themselves for achieving or for not achieving their self-set goals, and constructing positive thought patterns that remind them of the importance of their goals and their ability to accomplish them.[38]

For example, let's assume you need to do a better job of praising and recognizing the good work that your staff does for you. You can use goal setting, self-

Alexmillos/Shutterstock.com

observation, and self-reward to manage this behavior on your own. For self-observation, write "praise/recognition" on a three-by-five-inch card. Put the card in your pocket. Put a check on the card each time you praise or recognize someone. (Wait until the person has left before you do this.) Keep track for a week. This serves as your baseline, or starting point. Simply keeping track will probably increase how often you do this. After a week, assess your baseline, or starting point, and then set a specific goal. For instance, if your baseline was twice a day, you might set a specific goal to praise or recognize others' work five times a day. Continue monitoring your performance with your cards. After you've achieved your goal every day for a week, give yourself a reward (perhaps a movie or lunch with a friend at a new restaurant) for achieving your goal.[39]

As you can see, the components of self-management, self-set goals, self-observation, and self-reward have their roots in the motivation theories you read about in Chapter 13. The key difference, though, is that the goals, feedback, and rewards originate from employees themselves and not from their managers or organizations.

 16-3 ## WHAT TO CONTROL?

In the first section of this chapter, we discussed the basics of the control process and the fact that control isn't always worthwhile or possible. In the second section, we looked at the various ways in which control can be achieved. In this third and final section, we address an equally important issue: What should managers control? Costs? Quality? Customer satisfaction? The way managers answer this question has critical implications for most businesses.

If you control for just one thing, such as costs, then other dimensions such as marketing, customer service, and quality are likely to suffer. But if you try to control for too many things, then managers and employees become confused about what's really important. In the end, successful companies find a balance that comes from doing three or four things right, such as managing costs, providing value, and keeping customers and employees satisfied.

Walmart's three key areas right now are making stores friendlier, keeping them well stocked, and reducing theft. To keep stores friendlier, the company moved its blue-vested greeters further

> **Self-control (self-management)** a control system in which managers and workers control their own behavior by setting their own goals, monitoring their own progress, and rewarding themselves for goal achievement

back from entrances so they could walk customers to the products they were looking for, direct customers to open registers, or lend a hand restocking shelves. Focusing on customers and restocking, however, resulted in an increase in theft. Barb Gertz, an overnight stocker at one Colorado store, said that once the greeters were no longer posted at the doors, "people started walking out with cartloads of stuff." One person even rode a bike out of the store.[40] Walmart lost $375 million due to theft in 2015, so the retailer reposted greeters to the front doors and gave them specialized hand held scanners. Now, greeters can keep an eye on the doors, but also check in items being returned, track merchandise, and randomly verify the receipts of people leaving the store.[41]

After reading this section, you should be able to explain **16-3a the balanced scorecard approach to control** *and how companies can achieve balanced control of company performance by choosing to control* **16-3b budgets, cash flows, and economic value added; 16-3c customer defections; 16-3d quality; and 16-3e waste and pollution.**

16-3a The Balanced Scorecard

Most companies measure performance using standard financial and accounting measures such as return on capital, return on assets, return on investments, cash flow, net income, and net margins. The **balanced scorecard** encourages managers to look beyond such traditional financial measures to four different perspectives on company performance. How do customers see us (the customer perspective)? At what must we excel (the internal perspective)? Can we continue to improve and create value (the innovation and learning perspective)? How do we look to shareholders (the financial perspective)?[42]

The balanced scorecard has several advantages over traditional control processes that rely solely on financial measures. First, it forces managers at each level of the company to set specific goals and measure performance in each of the four areas. For example, Exhibit 16.2 shows that

Southwest Airlines uses nine different measures in its balanced scorecard to determine whether it is meeting the standards it has set for itself in the control process. Of those, only three—market value, seat revenue, and plane lease costs (at various compounded annual growth rates, or CAGR)—are standard financial measures of performance. In addition, Southwest measures its Federal Aviation Administration (FAA) on-time arrival rating and the cost of its airfares compared with those of competitors (customer perspective); how much time each plane spends on the ground after landing and the percentage of planes that depart on time (internal business perspective); and the percentage of its ground crew workers, such as mechanics and luggage handlers, who own company stock and have received job training (learning perspective).

The second major advantage of the balanced scorecard approach to control is that it minimizes the chances of **suboptimization**, which occurs when performance improves in one area at the expense of decreased performance in others. Jon Meliones, medical director of pediatric cardio ICU at Duke Children's Hospital, says, "We explained the [balanced scorecard] theory to clinicians and administrators like this: if you sacrifice too much in one quadrant to satisfy another, your organization as a whole is thrown out of balance. We could, for example, cut costs to improve the financial quadrant by firing half the staff, but that would hurt quality of service, and the customer quadrant would fall out of balance. Or we could increase productivity in the internal business quadrant by assigning more patients to a nurse, but doing so would raise the likelihood of errors—an unacceptable trade-off."[43]

Let's examine some of the ways in which companies are controlling the four basic parts of the balanced scorecard: the financial perspective (budgets, cash flows, and economic value added), the customer perspective (customer defections), the internal perspective (total quality management), and the innovation and learning perspective (sustainability).

16-3b The Financial Perspective: Controlling Budgets, Cash Flows, and Economic Value Added

The traditional approach to controlling financial performance focuses on accounting tools such as cash flow analysis, balance sheets, income statements, financial ratios, and budgets. **Cash flow analysis** predicts how changes in a business will affect its ability to take in more cash than it pays out. **Balance sheets** provide a snapshot of a company's financial position at a particular time (but not the future). **Income statements**, also called

---

Balanced scorecard
measurement of organizational performance in four equally important areas: finances, customers, internal operations, and innovation and learning

Suboptimization
performance improvement in one part of an organization but only at the expense of decreased performance in another part

Cash flow analysis a type of analysis that predicts how changes in a business will affect its ability to take in more cash than it pays out

Balance sheets accounting statements that provide a snapshot of a company's financial position at a particular time

Income statements
accounting statements, also called "profit and loss statements," that show what has happened to an organization's income, expenses, and net profit over a period of time

Exhibit 16.2
Southwest Airlines–Balanced Scorecard

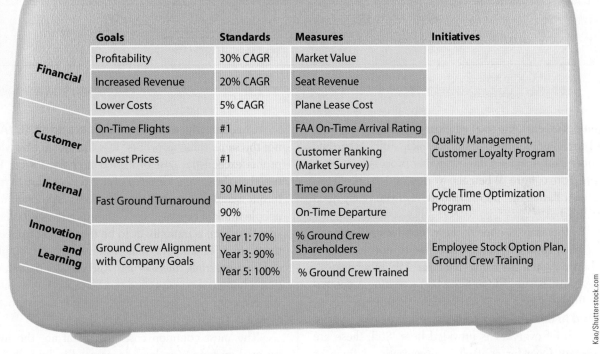

	Goals	Standards	Measures	Initiatives
Financial	Profitability	30% CAGR	Market Value	
	Increased Revenue	20% CAGR	Seat Revenue	
	Lower Costs	5% CAGR	Plane Lease Cost	
Customer	On-Time Flights	#1	FAA On-Time Arrival Rating	Quality Management, Customer Loyalty Program
	Lowest Prices	#1	Customer Ranking (Market Survey)	
Internal	Fast Ground Turnaround	30 Minutes	Time on Ground	Cycle Time Optimization Program
		90%	On-Time Departure	
Innovation and Learning	Ground Crew Alignment with Company Goals	Year 1: 70% Year 3: 90% Year 5: 100%	% Ground Crew Shareholders % Ground Crew Trained	Employee Stock Option Plan, Ground Crew Training

Kao/Shutterstock.com

Source: G. Anthes, "ROI Guide: Balanced Scorecard," *Computer World*, February 17, 2003, accessed September 5, 2008, http://www.computerworld.com/article/2579980/it-management/roi-guide--balanced-scorecard.html.

profit and loss statements, show what has happened to an organization's income, expenses, and net profit (income less expenses) over a period of time. **Financial ratios** are typically used to track a business's liquidity (cash), efficiency, and profitability over time compared with other businesses in its industry. For example, Aetna, a health insurance provider, uses a metric called the medical loss ratio. This financial ratio expresses the percentage of premiums used to pay patient medical costs—the lower the ratio, the higher the company's profits. So when the ratio dropped from 82.3–81.1 percent, it represented a 1.2 percent increase in profitability.[44] Finally, **budgets** are used to project costs and revenues, prioritize and control spending, and ensure that expenses don't exceed available funds and revenues. In a typical budgeting process, a manager uses the previous year's budget and adjusts it to reflect the current situation, but **zero-based budgeting** requires managers to outline a budget from scratch each year. In doing so, they must justify every expenditure—down to the number of color photocopies and garbage bags used—every year. Heinz, Kraft, and Anheuser-Busch all use zero-based budgeting, as does chicken-processor Pilgrim's Pride, which zealously monitors the amount of paper used to

Financial ratios calculations typically used to track a business's liquidity (cash), efficiency, and profitability over time compared to other businesses in its industry

Budgets quantitative plans through which managers decide how to allocate available money to best accomplish company goals

Zero-based budgeting a budgeting technique that requires managers to justify every expenditure every year

Exhibit 16.3
Calculating Economic Value Added (EVA)

1. Calculate net operating profit after taxes (NOPAT).	$ 3,500,000
2. Identify how much capital the company has invested (that is, spent).	$16,800,000
3. Determine the cost (that is, rate) paid for capital (usually between 5 and 8%).	10%
4. Multiply capital used (Step 2) times cost of capital (Step 3).	(10% + $16,800,000) = $1,680,000
5. Subtract the total dollar cost of capital from net profit after taxes.	$3,500,000　　NOPAT − $1,680,000　　Total cost of capital $1,820,000　　EVA

print documents, the soap employees use in washrooms, and the Gatorade workers drink each shift. According to one plant manager, the budgeting process has transformed the culture. When one worker said to him, "Hey, I need a flashlight," he responded, "Do you really need a flashlight?"[45]

By themselves, none of these tools—cash flow analyses, balance sheets, income statements, financial ratios, or budgets—tell the whole financial story of a business. They must be used together when assessing a company's financial performance. Because these tools are reviewed in detail in your accounting and finance classes, only a brief overview is provided here. Still, these are necessary tools for controlling organizational finances and expenses, and they should be part of your business toolbox. Unfortunately, most managers don't have a good understanding of these accounting tools even though they should.[46]

Though no one would dispute the importance of cash flow analyses, balance sheets, income statements, financial ratios, or budgets for determining the financial health of a business, accounting research also indicates that the complexity and sheer amount of information contained in these accounting tools can shut down the brain and glaze over the eyes of even the most experienced manager.[47] Sometimes there's simply too much information to make sense of. The balanced scorecard simplifies things by focusing on one simple question when it comes to finances: How do we look to shareholders? One way to answer that question is through something called economic value added.

Conceptually, **economic value added (EVA)** is not the same thing as profits. It is the amount by which profits exceed the cost of capital in a given year. It is based on the simple idea that capital is necessary to run a business and that capital comes at a cost. Although most people think of capital as cash, after it is invested (that is, spent), capital is more likely to be found in a business in the form of computers, manufacturing plants, employees, raw materials, and so forth. And just like the interest that a homeowner pays on a mortgage or that a college student pays on a student loan, there is a cost to that capital.

The most common costs of capital are the interest paid on long-term bank loans used to buy all those resources, the interest paid to bondholders (who lend organizations their money), and the dividends (cash payments) and growth in stock value that accrue to shareholders. EVA is positive when company profits (revenues minus expenses minus taxes) exceed the cost of capital in a given year. In other words, if a business is to truly grow, its revenues must be large enough to cover both short-term costs (annual expenses and taxes) and long-term costs (the cost of borrowing capital from bondholders and shareholders). If you're a bit confused, the late Roberto Goizueta, the former CEO of Coca-Cola, explained it this way: "You borrow money at a certain rate and invest it at a higher rate and pocket the difference. It is simple. It is the essence of banking."[48]

Exhibit 16.3 shows how to calculate EVA. First, starting with a company's income statement, you calculate the net operating profit after taxes (NOPAT) by subtracting taxes owed from income from operations. (Remember, a quick review of an income statement is on the Financial Review Card found at the back of your book.) The

Economic value added (EVA) the amount by which company profits (revenues minus expenses minus taxes) exceed the cost of capital in a given year

NOPAT shown in Exhibit 16.3 is $3,500,000. Second, identify how much capital the company has invested (that is, spent). Total liabilities (what the company owes) less accounts payable and less accrued expenses, neither of which you pay interest on, provides a rough approximation of this amount. In Exhibit 16.3, total capital invested is $16,800,000. Third, calculate the cost (that is, rate) paid for capital by determining the interest paid to bondholders (who lend organizations their money), which is usually somewhere between 5 and 8 percent, and the return that stockholders want in terms of dividends and stock price appreciation, which is historically about 13 percent. Take a weighted average of the two to determine the overall cost of capital. In Exhibit 16.3, the cost of capital is 10 percent. Fourth, multiply the total capital ($16,800,000) from Step 2 by the cost of capital (10%) from Step 3. In Exhibit 16.3, this amount is $1,680,000. Fifth, subtract the total dollar cost of capital in Step 4 from the NOPAT in Step 1. In Exhibit 16.3, this value is $1,820,000, which means that our example company has created economic value or wealth this year. If our EVA number had been negative, meaning that the company didn't make enough profit to cover the cost of capital from bondholders and shareholders, then the company would have destroyed economic value or wealth by taking in more money than it returned.[49]

Why is EVA so important? First and most importantly, because it includes the cost of capital, it shows whether a business, division, department, profit center, or product is really paying for itself. The key is to make sure that managers and employees can see how their choices and behaviors affect the company's EVA. For example, because of EVA training and information systems, factory workers at Herman Miller, a leading office furniture manufacturer, understand that using more efficient materials, such as less expensive wood-dust board instead of real wood sheeting, contributes an extra dollar of EVA from each desk the company makes. On its website, Herman Miller explains, "Under the terms of the EVA plan, we shifted our focus from budget performance to long-term continuous improvements and the creation of economic value. When we make plans for improvements around here, we include an EVA analysis. When we make decisions to add or cut programs, we look at the impact on EVA. Every month, we study our performance in terms of EVA, and this measurement system is one of the first things new recruits to the company learn."[50] "The result is a highly motivated and

Apple had an EVA of $50.5 billion in 2015—by far the largest in the world.

Rose Carson/Shutterstock.com

business-literate workforce that challenges convention and strives to create increasingly greater value for both customers and owners. Every month the company and all employees review performance in terms of EVA, which has proven to be a strong corollary to shareholder value."[51]

Second, because EVA can easily be determined for subsets of a company such as divisions, regional offices, manufacturing plants, and sometimes even departments, it makes managers and workers at all levels pay much closer attention to their segment of the business. In other words, EVA motivates managers and workers to think like small-business owners who must scramble to contain costs and generate enough business to meet their bills each month. And, unlike many kinds of financial controls, EVA doesn't specify what should or should not be done to improve performance. Thus, it encourages managers and workers to be creative in looking for ways to improve EVA performance.

Remember that EVA is the amount by which profits exceed the cost of capital in a given year. So the more that EVA exceeds the total dollar cost of capital, the better a company has used investors' money that year. For example, Apple had an EVA of $50.5 billion in 2015, by far the largest EVA in the world. The next-closest company was Alphabet (parent company of Google) at $6.9 billion. Apple's EVA financial performance in 2015 was truly extraordinary and the largest ever achieved by any company.[52]

16-3c The Customer Perspective: Controlling Customer Defections

The second aspect of organizational performance that the balanced scorecard helps managers monitor is customers. It does so by forcing managers to address the question, "How do customers see us?" Unfortunately, most companies try to answer this question through customer satisfaction surveys, but these are often misleadingly positive. Most customers are reluctant to talk about their problems because they don't know who to complain to or think that complaining will not do any good. In fact, a study by the Australian Federal Office of Consumer Affairs found that 96 percent of unhappy customers never complain to anyone in the company.[53]

One reason that customer satisfaction surveys can be misleading is that sometimes even very satisfied customers will leave to do business with competitors. Rather than poring over customer satisfaction surveys from current customers, studies indicate that companies may do a better job of answering the question, "How do customers see us?" by closely monitoring **customer defections**, that is, by identifying which customers are leaving the company and measuring the rate at which they are leaving. Unlike the results of customer satisfaction surveys, customer defections and retention have a great effect on profits.

Because most accounting systems measure the financial impact of a customer's current activity (sales), rather than the lifetime value of each customer, few managers realize the financial impact that even a low rate of customer defection can have on a business. Businesses frequently lose 15–20 percent of their customers each year, so even a small improvement in retention can have a significant impact on profits. In fact, retaining just 5 percent more customers per year can increase annual profits 25–100 percent. Managers, therefore, should pay closer attention to customer defections. John Tschohl, an author and business consultant, worked with a network of seventeen blood plasma donation centers to determine the financial impact of defections. With 40,600 donors each year, analysis of the network showed that the "lifetime" of a typical donor—the time when the donor was active—was 3.4 years. During that time, each lifetime donor contributed roughly $6,000 in profits to the company. Each year, however, a cohort of 2,340 donors defected, making the network's annual customer defection rate 6 percent. While the defection rate was modest, the financial impact was considerable, resulting in more than $100 million in lost revenue and $60 million less in profits each year, or $200 million in profits over the lifetime (3.4 years) of a single cohort (2,430 people) of defectors.[54]

Beyond the clear benefits to the bottom line, the second reason to study customer defections is that customers who have left are much more likely than current customers to tell you what you are doing wrong. Perhaps the best way to tap into this source of good feedback is to have top-level managers from various departments talk directly to customers who have left. It's also worthwhile to have top managers talk to dissatisfied customers who are still with the company. Finally, companies that understand why customers leave not only can take steps to fix ongoing problems but also can identify which customers are likely to leave and can make changes to prevent them from leaving.

Customer defections a performance assessment in which companies identify which customers are leaving and measure the rate at which they are leaving

Value customer perception that the product quality is excellent for the price offered

16-3d The Internal Perspective: Controlling Quality

The third part of the balanced scorecard, the internal perspective, consists of the processes, decisions, and actions that managers and workers make within the organization. In contrast to the financial perspective of EVA and the outward-looking customer perspective, the internal perspective focuses on internal processes and systems that add value to the organization. For McDonald's, it could be processes and systems that enable the company to provide consistent, quick, low-cost food. For Toyota, it could be reliability—when you turn on your car, it starts, regardless of whether it has 20,000 or 200,000 miles on it. Yet, no matter what area a company chooses, the key is to excel in that area. Consequently, the internal perspective of the balanced scorecard usually leads managers to a focus on quality.

Quality is typically defined and measured in three ways: excellence, value, and conformance to expectations.[55] When the company defines its quality goal as *excellence*, managers must try to produce a product or service of unsurpassed performance and features. *Condé Nast Traveler* magazine has been ranking global airlines for twenty-seven years. For twenty-six of those years, Singapore Airlines was named the best airline in the world.[56] Whereas many airlines try to cram passengers into every available inch on a plane, Singapore Airlines delivers creature comforts to encourage repeat business and lure customers willing to pay premium prices. On its newer planes, the first-class cabin is divided into eight private mini-rooms, each with an unusually wide leather seat that folds down flat for sleeping, a twenty-three-inch LCD TV that doubles as a computer monitor, and an adjustable table.

These amenities and services are common for private jets but truly unique in the commercial airline industry. Singapore Airlines was the first airline, in the 1970s, to introduce a choice of meals, complimentary drinks, and earphones in coach class. It was the first to introduce worldwide video, news, telephone, and fax services; was the first to feature personal video monitors for movies, news, and documentaries; and has had AC power outlets and on-board high-speed Internet for some time—well ahead of other airlines.

Value is the customer perception that the product quality is excellent for the price offered. At a higher price, for example, customers may perceive the product to be less of a value. When a company emphasizes value as its quality goal, managers must simultaneously control excellence, price, durability, and any other features of a product or service that customers strongly associate with value. Fresh fruits and vegetables are categorized according to size, uniformity, and appearance. The most attractive produce (about 85%) goes to supermarkets, while the non-conforming produce ends up in processed foods, animal feed, and landfills. British supermarket chain **Asda** recently loosened its produce appearance specifications and began packaging misshapen, cracked, blemished, and unusually sized vegetables into five kilogram boxes. Asda's so-called Wonky Veg Box sells for £3.50 (about $5.00), a 30 percent discount, which 95 percent of Asda's customers think is a tremendous value. Sales quadrupled in the first two months after the box launched.[57] Ian Harrison, Asda's produce technical director, said that the Wonky Veg Box "was always

Luis Santos/Shutterstock.com

British supermarket chain Asda recently began packaging misshapen, cracked, blemished, and unusually sized vegetables into reduced-price Wonky Veg Boxes.

meant as a trial to see how customers reacted to slightly scruffier produce, but this has also enabled us to flex our specifications across a wide variety of our standard produce lines. For example, we're taking 340 more tonnes of standard and organic carrots which would previously have been out of spec."[58] Harrison adds, "We've got a real hit on our hands with Wonky!"[59]

When a company defines its quality goal as conformance to specifications, employees must base decisions and actions on whether services and products measure up to the standard. In contrast to excellence and value-based definitions of quality that can be somewhat ambiguous, measuring whether products and services are "in spec" is relatively easy. Furthermore, while conformance to specifications (for example, precise tolerances for a part's weight or thickness) is usually associated with manufacturing, it can be used equally well to control quality in nonmanufacturing industries like supermarkets. Exhibit 16.4 shows a checklist that a cook or restaurant owner would use to ensure quality when buying fresh fish.

The way in which a company defines quality affects the methods and measures that workers use to control quality. Accordingly, Exhibit 16.5 shows the advantages and disadvantages associated with the excellence, value, and conformance to specification definitions of quality.

16-3e The Innovation and Learning Perspective: Sustainability

The last part of the balanced scorecard, the innovation and learning perspective, addresses the question, "Can we continue to improve and create value?" Thus,

Exhibit 16.4
Conformance to Specifications Checklist for Buying Fresh Fish

Fresh Whole Fish	Acceptable	Not Acceptable
Gills	✔ bright red, free of slime, clear mucus	✗ brown to grayish, thick, yellow mucus
Eyes	✔ clear, bright, bulging, black pupils	✗ dull, sunken, cloudy, gray pupils
Smell	✔ inoffensive, slight ocean smell	✗ ammonia, putrid smell
Skin	✔ opalescent sheen, scales adhere tightly to skin	✗ dull or faded color, scales missing or easily removed
Flesh	✔ firm and elastic to touch, tight to the bone	✗ soft and flabby, separating from the bone
Belly cavity	✔ no viscera or blood visible, lining intact, no bone protruding	✗ incomplete evisceration, cuts or protruding bones, off-odor

iStockphoto.com/Valeriy Evlakhov

Sources: "A Closer Look: Buy It Fresh, Keep It Fresh," *Consumer Reports Online*, accessed June 20, 2005, http://www.seagrant.sunysb.edu/SeafoodTechnology /SeafoodMedia/CR02-2001/CR-SeafoodII020101.htm; "How to Purchase: Buying Fish," *AboutSeafood*, accessed June 20, 2005, http://www.aboutseafood.com/faqs /purchase1.html.

Exhibit 16.5
Advantages and Disadvantages of Different Measures of Quality

Quality Measure	Advantages	Disadvantages
Excellence	Promotes clear organizational vision.	Provides little practical guidance for managers.
	Being/providing the "best" motivates and inspires managers and employees.	Excellence is ambiguous. What is it? Who defines it?
Value	Appeals to customers who know excellence "when they see it."	Difficult to measure and control.
	Customers recognize differences in value.	Can be difficult to determine what factors influence whether a product/service is seen as having value.
	Easier to measure and compare whether products/services differ in value.	Controlling the balance between excellence and cost (that is, affordable excellence) can be difficult.
Conformance to Specifications	If specifications can be written, conformance to specifications is usually measurable.	Many products/services cannot be easily evaluated in terms of conformance to specifications.
	Should lead to increased efficiency.	Promotes standardization, so may hurt performance when adapting to changes is more important.
	Promotes consistency in quality.	May be less appropriate for services, which are dependent on a high degree of human contact.

Source: Briar Cliff Manor, NY, 10510-8020; C. A. Reeves and D. A. Bednar, "Defining Quality: Alternatives and Implications," *Academy of Management Review* 19 (1994): 419–445.

the innovation and learning perspective involves continuous improvement in ongoing products and services (discussed in Chapter 18), as well as relearning and redesigning the processes by which products and services are created (discussed in Chapter 7). Because these are discussed in more detail elsewhere in the text, this section reviews an increasingly important topic, sustainability. Exhibit 16.6 shows the four levels of sustainability, ranging from waste disposal, which produces the smallest minimization of waste, to waste prevention and reduction, which produces the greatest minimization.[60]

The goals of the top level, *waste prevention and reduction*, are to prevent waste and pollution before they occur or to reduce them when they do occur. In its new $1.2 billion stadium in Santa Clara, California, the National Football League's San Francisco 49ers installed Bander Bermuda Grass on the field because it uses half the water of regular sports turf. The stadium has an 18,000 square-foot garden on top of the luxury box suites to provide insulation and reduce energy use, 1,000 solar panels to generate energy, and a rainwater collection system for cooling and irrigation. In all, the stadium is energy neutral, meaning it generates all of its own energy for home games. 49ers President Paraag

Marathe says, "Where we are in Silicon Valley it's sort of our mandate. If it wasn't environmentally responsible, we wouldn't be as successful."[61]

There are three strategies for waste prevention and reduction:

1. *Good housekeeping*—performing regularly scheduled preventive maintenance for offices, plants, and equipment. Examples of good housekeeping include fixing leaky valves quickly to prevent wasted water and making sure machines are running properly so that they don't use more fuel than necessary. Likewise, companies are also beginning to apply good housekeeping practices to their cloud computing services. Companies tend to overestimate their capacity needs, but because cloud computing charges work similarly to a taxicab (the meter is always running), companies can end up spending a lot of money on unused computing power. To remedy this problem, engineers at **Netflix** wrote software that automatically shuts down service during off-peak hours and resumes it when activity picks back up. **ThermoFisher**, a biotechnology company, did likewise and also

downgraded to less powerful cloud computing servers that better matched its needs—and cost a lot less to use.[61]

2. *Material/product substitution*—replacing toxic or hazardous materials with less harmful materials.

3. *Process modification*—changing steps or procedures to eliminate or reduce waste.

At the second level of sustainability, *recycle and reuse*, wastes are reduced by reusing materials as long as possible or by collecting materials for on- or off-site recycling. Primark, a worldwide clothing retailer based in the United Kingdom, has an annual revenue of £5.35 billion and is growing roughly 25 percent per year. The company's flagship store has 44 fitting rooms, 104 cash registers, and can—and often does—hold 3,200 customers. When delivery trucks arrive at the back of the store, merchandise is unpacked and sent straight onto the floor. The cardboard boxes used to ship the merchandise go right back onto the truck to be recycled and later return to the store as Primark's iconic brown paper shopping bags.[62]

A growing trend in recycling is *design for disassembly*, where products are designed from the start for easy disassembly, recycling, and reuse after they are no longer usable. Japan-based Kyocera used design for disassembly

In the new Levi's Stadium, there are 1,000 solar panels that are used to generate energy, and a rainwater collection system for cooling and irrigation.

principles to create laser printers that are cartridge-free (because of their complexity, printer cartridges are difficult to recycle). To make its printers easy to take apart at the end of their life cycle, Kyocera designed them with just five parts, down from seventy, used plastic clips instead of metal fasteners, and marked each part with codes explaining how they should be recycled. Kyocera's careful designs have reduced carbon footprints by 55 percent, waste by 85 percent, and costs by 54 percent.[63]

At the third level of sustainability, waste treatment, companies use biological, chemical, or other processes to turn potentially harmful waste into harmless compounds or useful by-products. Usually, supermarkets throw away the food they don't sell, but in the United Kingdom, several supermarket chains are using warm water and bacteria to convert food waste to a methane-rich biogas that powers electricity plants. Because the supermarkets are taxed $98 for every ton of trash that goes into landfills, Marks & Spencer now sends 89 percent of its food waste for biogas conversion, saving the company $163 million a year.[64]

The fourth and lowest level of sustainability is *waste disposal*. Wastes that cannot be prevented, reduced, recycled, reused, or treated should be safely disposed of in processing plants or in environmentally secure

Exhibit 16.6 **Four Levels of Sustainability**

- Waste Prevention & Reduction
- Recycle & Reuse
- Waste Treatment
- Waste Disposal

Source: D. R. May and B. L. Flannery, "Cutting Waste with Employee Involvement Teams," *Business Horizons*, September–October 1995, pp. 28–38.

MAKING LEGO BRICKS OUT OF AGRICULTURAL WASTE

Since 1963, LEGO has made its iconic plastic bricks from the same petroleum-based formulation—acrylonitrile butadiene styrene (ABS). In 2015, however, LEGO announced that it was launching a research and development effort to reformulate its plastic using biodegradable plant-based materials. Ideally, says senior director for environmental sustainability Tim Guy Brooks, the new plastic will be derived from agricultural waste that doesn't have any other apparent potential use, such as corn stalk. Even though oil prices have plummeted in recent years, LEGO remains committed to replacing its petroleum-based plastics with bio-plastic. The company estimates that it will take fifteen years to develop a bio-based alternative to replace the 77,000 metric tons of petroleum granules it currently uses to make bricks every year—a main contributor to the company's overall carbon footprint. "This is the right thing

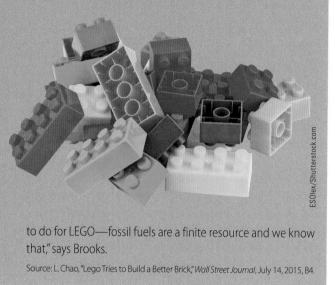

ESOlex/Shutterstock.com

to do for LEGO—fossil fuels are a finite resource and we know that," says Brooks.

Source: L. Chao, "Lego Tries to Build a Better Brick," *Wall Street Journal*, July 14, 2015, B4.

---

landfills that prevent leakage and contamination of soil and underground water supplies. Contrary to common belief, all businesses, not just manufacturing firms, have waste disposal problems. For example, with the average computer lasting just three years, approximately 60 million computers come out of service each year, creating disposal problems for offices all over the world. But organizations can't just throw old computers away because they have lead-containing cathode ray tubes in the monitors, toxic metals in the circuit boards, paint-coated plastic, and metal coatings that can contaminate groundwater.[65] Many companies give old computers and computer equipment to local computer recycling centers that distribute usable computers to nonprofit organizations or safely dispose of lead and other toxic materials. A number of retailers and electronics manufacturers operate recycling programs to keep electronics out of landfills. For example, customers can drop off computers, TVs, DVD players, batteries, and other items at Best Buy stores. There is a $10 recycling fee for anything with a screen, but Best Buy offsets that with a $10 gift card. Best Buy will recycle 80 million pounds of electronics this year. But for those items that still function, Costco and Newegg.com work with Gazelle.com, which buys, refurbishes, and resells 250,000 items overseas and on eBay. College student Bobby Lozano sold his used iPod Nano and LG EnV Touch phone to Gazelle, because he says,

"I got an iPhone, so I no longer needed the other two." Gazelle wiped the devices of personal information and put $70 into his PayPal account.[66]

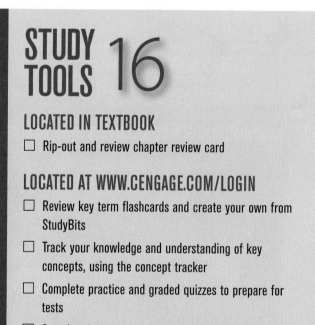

STUDY TOOLS 16

LOCATED IN TEXTBOOK
☐ Rip-out and review chapter review card

LOCATED AT WWW.CENGAGE.COM/LOGIN
☐ Review key term flashcards and create your own from StudyBits

☐ Track your knowledge and understanding of key concepts, using the concept tracker

☐ Complete practice and graded quizzes to prepare for tests

☐ Complete interactive content within the exposition

☐ View chapter highlight box content at the beginning of each chapter

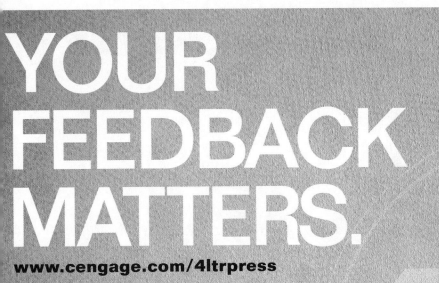

17 Managing Information

 asharkyu/Shutterstock.com

LEARNING OUTCOMES

17-1 Explain the strategic importance of information.

17-2 Describe the characteristics of useful information (that is, its value and costs).

17-3 Explain the basics of capturing, processing, and protecting information.

17-4 Describe how companies can access and share information and knowledge.

After you finish this chapter, go to **PAGE 383** for **STUDY TOOLS**

17-1 STRATEGIC IMPORTANCE OF INFORMATION

A generation ago, computer hardware and software had little to do with managing business information. Rather than storing information on hard drives, managers stored it in filing cabinets. Instead of uploading daily sales and inventory levels by satellite to corporate headquarters, they mailed hard-copy summaries to headquarters at the end of each month. Instead of word processors, reports were typed on electric typewriters. Instead of spreadsheets, calculations were made on adding machines. Managers communicated by sticky notes, not email. Phone messages were written down by assistants and coworkers, not forwarded in your email as a sound file with the message converted to text. Workers did not use desktop, laptop, or tablet computers or smartphones as daily tools to get work done. Instead, they scheduled limited access time to run batch jobs on the mainframe computer (and prayed that the batch job computer code they wrote would work).

Today, a generation later, computer hardware and software are an integral part of managing business information. This is due mainly to something called **Moore's law**. Gordon Moore is one of the founders of Intel Corporation, which makes 75 percent of the integrated processors used in PCs. In 1965, Moore predicted that computer-processing power would double and that its cost would drop by 50 percent every two years.[1] As Exhibit 17.1 shows, Moore was right. Computer power, as measured by the number of transistors per computer chip, *has* more than doubled every few years, as have hard drive sizes and pixel density (that is, screen resolution). Consequently, the computer sitting in your lap or on your desk (or in your hand!) is not only smaller but also much cheaper and more powerful than the large mainframe computers used by *Fortune* 500 companies thirty years ago. For instance, your iPhone replaces thirteen of the fifteen items, such as a desktop computer, mobile phone, CD player, camcorder, and so on, commonly sold by Radio Shack in 1991, items that would have cost you $3,071.21 then, or, after adjusting for inflation, $5,374.46 today. So your $600 iPhone not only replaces a trunkful of 1991 electronics gear, it does so for only 11 percent of the cost.[2] That's Moore's law in action. Likewise, in 2001, the cost of sequencing one human genome was $100 million. Thanks to Moore's law, that cost dropped to just over $1,000 in 2015.[3] Will Moore's law eventually

Frits van Paasschen, CEO of Starwood Hotels & Resorts, values information much more than data. If employees send him a bulky spreadsheet, he sends it back, asking them to summarize the key points instead.

fail and technological progress eventually slow? Perhaps, as the physics and costs of developing faster, more powerful chips (today's chips are already based on circuitry 1 billionth of a meter thin) may eventually slow the rate of development. Indeed, the Semiconductor Industry Associations of the United States, Europe, Japan, South Korea, and Taiwan are moving away from Moore's law for predicting future power outputs and costs of computer chips. On the other hand, Intel CEO Brian Krzanich says, "I have witnessed the advertised death of Moore's law no less than four times."[4]

Raw data are facts and figures. For example, 11, $762, 128, and 26,100 are some data that I used the day I wrote this section of the chapter. However, facts and figures aren't particularly useful unless they have meaning. For example, you probably can't guess what these four pieces of raw data represent, can you? If you can't, these data are useless. That's why researchers make the distinction between raw data and information. Whereas raw data consist of facts and figures, **information** is useful data that can influence someone's choices and behavior. One way to think about the difference between data and information is that information has context. Frits van Paasschen, CEO of **Starwood Hotels & Resorts**, values information much more than data. If employees send him a bulky

> **Moore's law** the prediction that about every two years, computer processing power would double and its cost would drop by 50 percent
>
> **Raw data** facts and figures
>
> **Information** useful data that can influence people's choices and behavior

Exhibit 17.1
Moore's Law

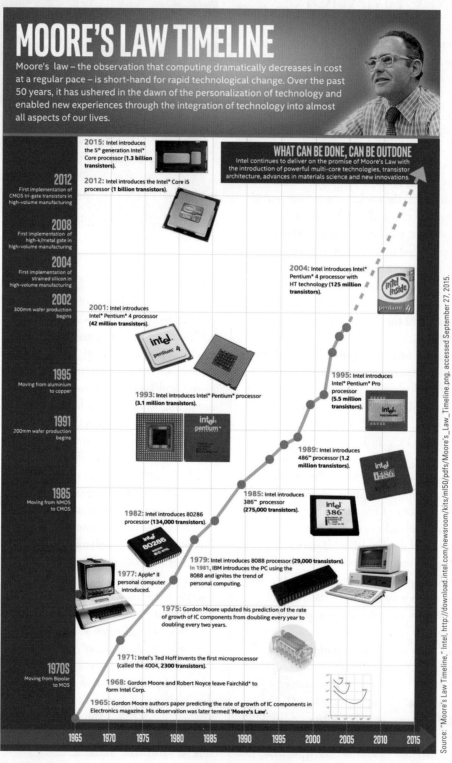

MOORE'S LAW TIMELINE

Moore's law – the observation that computing dramatically decreases in cost at a regular pace – is short-hand for rapid technological change. Over the past 50 years, it has ushered in the dawn of the personalization of technology and enabled new experiences through the integration of technology into almost all aspects of our lives.

2015: Intel introduces the 5th generation Intel® Core processor (**1.3 billion transistors**).

2012: Intel introduces the Intel® Core i5 processor (**1 billion transistors**).

WHAT CAN BE DONE, CAN BE OUTDONE
Intel continues to deliver on the promise of Moore's Law with the introduction of powerful multi-core technologies, transistor architecture, advances in materials science and new innovations.

2012 First implementation of CMOS tri-gate transistors in high-volume manufacturing

2008 First implementation of high-k/metal gate in high-volume manufacturing

2004 First implementation of strained silicon in high-volume manufacturing

2004: Intel introduces Intel® Pentium® 4 processor with HT technology (**125 million transistors**).

2002 300mm wafer production begins

2001: Intel introduces Intel® Pentium® 4 processor (**42 million transistors**).

1995 Moving from aluminium to copper

1995: Intel introduces Intel® Pentium® Pro processor (**5.5 million transistors**).

1993: Intel introduces Intel® Pentium® processor (**3.1 million transistors**).

1991 200mm wafer production begins

1989: Intel introduces 486™ processor (**1.2 million transistors**).

1985 Moving from NMOS to CMOS

1985: Intel introduces 386™ processor (**275,000 transistors**).

1982: Intel introduces 80286 processor (**134,000 transistors**).

1979: Intel introduces 8088 processor (**29,000 transistors**). In 1981, IBM introduces the PC using the 8088 and ignites the trend of personal computing.

1977: Apple® II personal computer introduced.

1975: Gordon Moore updated his prediction of the rate of growth of IC components from doubling every year to doubling every two years.

1970S Moving from Bipolar to MOS

1971: Intel's Ted Hoff invents the first microprocessor (called the 4004, **2300 transistors**).

1968: Gordon Moore and Robert Noyce leave Fairchild® to form Intel Corp.

1965: Gordon Moore authors paper predicting the rate of growth of IC components in Electronics magazine. His observation was later termed '**Moore's Law**'.

1965 1970 1975 1980 1985 1990 1995 2000 2005 2010 2015

Source: "Moore's Law Timeline," Intel, http://download.intel.com/newsroom/kits/ml50/pdfs/Moore's_Law_Timeline.png, accessed September 27, 2015.

"Moore's Law Timeline," Intel, accessed September 27, 2015, http://download.intel.com.

spreadsheet, he won't even open it. "When I get the massive file, the first thing I'll do is send it back and say tell me the key points that I actually need to understand."[5]

So what did those four pieces of data mean to me? Well, 11 stands for Channel 11, the local CBS affiliate on which I watched part of the men's PGA golf tournament; $762 is how much it would cost me to rent a minivan for a week if I go skiing over spring break; 128 is for the 128-gigabyte storage card that I want to add to my digital camera (prices are low, so I'll probably buy it); and 26,100 means that it's time to get the oil changed in my car.

In today's hyper competitive business environments, information is as important as capital (that is, money) for business success, whether it's about product inventory, pricing, or costs. It takes money to get businesses started, but businesses can't survive and grow without the right information.

*Information has strategic importance for organizations because it can be used to **17-1a obtain first-mover advantage** and **17-1b sustain competitive advantage** after it has been created.*

17-1a First-Mover Advantage

First-mover advantage is the strategic advantage that companies earn by being the first in an industry to use new information technology to substantially lower costs or to differentiate a product or service from that of competitors. Pandora, for example, pioneered music streaming and leads this highly competitive market. Free to listeners because it makes money via advertising, Pandora has 79.4 million active listeners, slightly up from 79.2 million in 2015.[6]

While first-mover advantage typically leads to above average profits and market share, it doesn't immunize a company from competition. Pandora faces four primary competitors: Spotify (30 million subscribers), Deezer (6.3 million subscribers), Apple Music (13 million subscribers), and Amazon's Prime Music, which is free for Amazon's estimated 40 million Prime members (who pay $99 a year for Prime membership which includes two-day shipping and a number of other benefits).[7]

> The key to sustaining a competitive advantage is using information technology to continuously improve and support the core functions of a business.

Many first-movers have failed to capitalize on their strategic advantages. Netscape lost first-mover advantage in web browsers, as did MySpace in social media, and Yahoo! in search engines.[8] A study of thirty first-movers found two key factors mattered in terms of sustaining first-mover advantage: the pace at which product technology is changing and how fast the market is growing.[9] As these examples show, if better technology is quickly being introduced by new market entrants, and the market is quickly growing (which attracts new competitors who want a share of that growing market), it can be difficult to sustain first-mover advantage.

17-1b Sustaining Competitive Advantage

As described, companies that use information technology to establish first-mover advantage usually have higher market shares and profits. According to the resource-based view of information technology shown in Exhibit 17.2, companies need to address three critical questions to sustain a competitive advantage through information technology. First, does the information technology create value for the firm by lowering costs or providing a better product or service? If an information technology doesn't add value, then investing in it would put the firm at a competitive disadvantage relative to companies that choose information technologies that do add value.

Second, is the information technology the same or different across competing firms? If all the firms have access to the same information technology and use it in the same way, then no firm has an advantage over another (that is, there is competitive parity).

Third, is it difficult for another company to create or buy the information technology used by the firm? If so, then the firm has established

First-mover advantage
the strategic advantage that companies earn by being the first to use new information technology to substantially lower costs or to make a product or service different from that of competitors

Using Information Technology to Sustain a Competitive Advantage

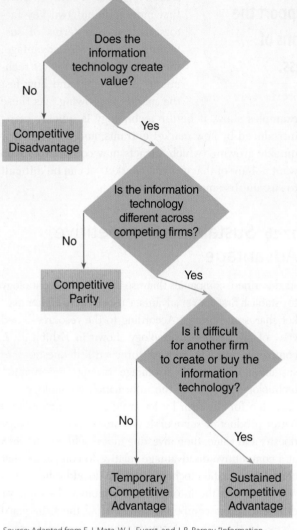

Source: Adapted from F. J. Mata, W. L. Fuerst, and J. B. Barney, "Information Technology and Sustained Competitive Advantage: A Resource-Based Analysis," *MIS Quarterly* 19, no. 4 (December 1995): 487–505.

a sustainable competitive advantage over competitors through information technology. If not, then the competitive advantage is just temporary, and competitors should eventually be able to duplicate the advantages the leading firm has gained from information technology.

In short, the key to sustaining a competitive advantage is not faster computers, more memory, or larger hard drives. The key is using information technology to continuously improve and support the core functions of a business.

17-2 CHARACTERISTICS AND COSTS OF USEFUL INFORMATION

Information and data are more abundant today than ever before. For example, modern Major League Baseball (MLB) teams use iPad Pros loaded with baseball-related software to analyze data and make decisions. MLB Commissioner Rob Manfred says, "I started in this game 25 years ago and the single biggest change has been the emergence and predominance of analytics. It affects the way we judge players, make decisions on the field and the way fans consume the game."[10] Phil Schiller, Apple's senior vice president of marketing, says about the MLB's adoption of iPads, "We're not just replacing binders with tablets, we're actually helping them do things that weren't possible before."[11] Teams can pull up statistics, explore pitching match-ups against specific batters, study game videos, and examine real time spray charts indicating where batters usually hit the ball. While all teams have access to the MLB Dugout App, each team's data are proprietary and are not shared league-wide. New York Mets third base coach Tim Teufel says, "Managers have plans and positions laid out before the game even starts. This won't change that much. But when a relief pitcher comes in, when a pinch hitter comes up, when the game changes in unexpected ways, that's when it'll be really useful [to use the iPads]."[12] Likewise, radio frequency identification tags (discussed in Section 17-3a) in shoulder pads indicate how fast players run, whether they consistently work hard in practice, or how many calories they burn. Pittsburgh Steelers general manager Kevin Colbert is excited about the possibilities, saying, "To be able to tell a quarterback where he should be, to be able to show a defense what an offense looks like at ground level would be great. That would be more realistic."

*As the MLB's use of iPads, data, and analytics demonstrates, information is useful when it is **17-2a accurate, 17-2b complete, 17-2c relevant,** and **17-2d timely.** However, there can be significant **17-2e acquisition, 17-2f processing, 17-2g storage, 17-2h retrieval,** and **17-2i communication costs** associated with useful information.*

17-2a Accurate Information

Information is useful when it is accurate. Before relying on information to make decisions, you must know that the information is correct. But what if it isn't?

In the next twenty-five years, the world's population will grow from 7 billion to 9 billion people. Many of those 9 billion will be moving into the middle class, drastically increasing demand for meat, dairy, and other foods dense with protein and calories. In order to produce the 70 percent more calories needed to feed everyone in 2050, farmers will need to plant, irrigate, and feed their crops much more efficiently. Ohioan Mark Bryant is one of a growing number of farmers using data-driven technologies to do just that. Bryant uses Google's Granular app, which collects data on moisture and soil quality from aircrafts, drones, self-driving tractors, and other sensors. Agricultural machinery manufacturer John Deere produces wireless sensors that map fields and provide farmers with information on which acres need more (or less) water and nutrients. According to Mississippi farmer Jeremy Jack, "If we're really going to be professional farmers and feed everybody in the world, we really have to utilize this technology to do the job."[13]

17-2b Complete Information

Information is useful when it is complete. Incomplete or missing information makes it difficult to recognize problems and identify potential solutions. Following an airplane crash, investigators recover critical information from the plane's black box recordings. If the black box is lost or damaged, then investigators may never understand what happened. "Everyone talks about the black box on an airplane," says Vic Charlebois, vice president of flight operations at Canadian airline First Air, "but it is permanently installed on an airplane, and if the airplane goes missing so does the black box."[14] Indeed, when Malaysia Airlines Flight 370 disappeared en route from Kuala Lumpur to Beijing in March 2014, investigators were left guessing as to the cause because the plane and its black box were still missing after a four-month search.[15]

Regulators have long suggested putting live data systems on planes to transmit real time in-flight data, but airlines have hesitated because of costs estimated at $100,000 per plane.[16] Canadian-based First Air is installing a live data streaming service that can provide much more complete and useful information. Made by Canadian-based Flyht, First Air's FLYHTStream system can be preprogrammed to automatically transmit live data

under certain conditions, or it can be manually activated by the pilot or ground-based flight controllers. First Air's Vic Charlebois says, "Let's take the case of the Malaysian aircraft. If it was being monitored through satellites and a dispatcher did see it wander off course somewhere, the procedure would be to activate the FLYHTStream and then contact the crew to see what was going on."[17]

17-2c Relevant Information

You can have complete, accurate information, but it's not very useful if it doesn't pertain to the problems you're facing. For instance, if you're unlucky enough to contract bullous pemphigoid, a rare skin condition resulting in large, watery blisters on your inner thighs and upper arms, chances are the dermatologist you visit won't have any relevant experience with this condition to be able to recognize and treat it. And that's exactly what happened to Dr. Kavita Mariwalla, who was stumped when a patient came in with these problems. So she turned to Modernizing Medicine, an iPad-based

---

CONTROLLING THE RISKS OF BYOD (BRING YOUR OWN DEVICE) PROGRAMS

At work, millions of employees use their own devices to conduct business. Bring-your-own-device programs are convenient and economical for both employees and employers. Employees no longer have to juggle devices and are often reimbursed for a portion of their wireless bills. Employers don't have to buy everyone at the office the latest smartphone. But BYOD programs are not without drawbacks, particularly in the event of a security breach. Using software developed by Fiberlink, employers can remotely wipe every device in their network completely clean—without differentiating between professional and personal information. That means personal photos, music, and apps are erased along with company emails, contacts, and documents. Fiberlink wipes clean nearly 100,000 devices a year, and although the erasures can be inconvenient for employees, the BYOD trend shows no sign of slowing. According to Gartner Research, by 2017, half of all U.S. employers will stop providing hardware to employees for work purposes and will expect them to use their own.

Source: L. Weber, "Workers' Devices Get a Remote Cleaning," *Wall Street Journal*, September 10, 2014, B7

Volunteers Darby Stanchfield (left) and Ashley Greene hand out fresh fruit at Feeding America's "Put the Heat on Hunger" event in Los Angeles on June 23, 2016.

medical records system to obtain the relevant information needed to determine what was wrong. Modernizing Medicine is a web-based database, containing information from more than 14 million patient visits compiled by 3,700 doctors, that uses the same kind of data mining and artificial intelligence used by websites such as Amazon.com. Dr. Eric Horvitz, Microsoft's managing director of research, says, "Electronic health records [are] like large quarries where there's lots of gold, and we're just beginning to mine them."[18] Dr. Mariwalla was able to quickly access similar cases on Modernizing Medicine's database and find other drugs that had been effective in those cases. Mariwalla said that Modernizing Medicine, "Gives you access to data, and data is king. It's been very helpful, especially in clinically challenging situations."[19]

17-2d Timely Information

Finally, information is useful when it is timely. To be timely, the information must be available when needed to define a problem or to begin to identify possible solutions. If you've ever thought, "I wish I had known that earlier," then you understand the importance of timely information and the opportunity cost of not having it.

Feeding America, a nonprofit organization with more than 200 food banks, collects 4 billion pounds of food every year and distributes it to 46 million people. Until recently, the organization struggled to manage its food inventory because it could not anticipate what types or quantities of food donations it would receive. This uncertainty made it extremely difficult to distribute perishable food items before they spoiled. The problem always got much worse during November and December, when the volume of food donations was twice that donated during the other ten months combined. To reduce the large amount of wasted food, Feeding America uses inventory software made by Exact Macola to track when and where goods are received. Workers are then sent automated alerts indicating which foods are approaching their use-by dates, their locations in the warehouse, and a recommended action (distribute or destroy). Since Feeding America has begun using the software, food waste has declined by more than 50 percent. Kathy Fulton, executive director of the American Logistics Aid Network, which donates logistics services to nonprofits like Feeding America, says, "The last thing you want is this fabulous donation that you can't use quickly enough."[20]

17-2e Acquisition Costs

Acquisition cost is the cost of obtaining data that you don't have. Firms with gigantic databases, like Amazon, Facebook, and Google, have a tremendous advantage over other retailers because they have so much direct data about consumer interests, product searches, and purchase behaviors. Smaller retailers and publishers can overcome this advantage, in part, by banding together to lower the acquisition cost of information. Bombora is a New York data co-op of more than 2,500 publishers that pool their subscriber and website visitor data, demographics, and purchase histories. Any company can purchase information about the consumers in the Bombora database, but co-op members receive a 50 percent discount. Similarly, Skimlinks is a UK-based data co-op of 55,000 digital publishers and 20,000 retailers that have combined their proprietary customer information into a database of 1.3 billion unique users. Advertisers for everything from computers to shoes to toothpaste pay on a cost-per-thousand basis to access information about consumers' intent to purchase. Participating companies get a royalty any time their data is purchased by another firm, which ends up offsetting their own acquisition costs.[21]

17-2f Processing Costs

Companies often have massive amounts of data but not in the form or combination they need. **Processing cost** is the cost of turning raw data into usable information. While Google offers a wide range of online

Acquisition cost the cost of obtaining data that you don't have

Processing cost the cost of turning raw data into usable information

Talk to Your Bar Code Scanner Like a Smart Phone

Logistic and warehouse workers scan up to 3,000 bar codes every day as they move, pack, and track items, so anything that speeds up the process or reduces the number of steps involved has value. With this in mind, Exel Logistics, a unit of delivery company **Deutsche Post DHL**, recently began testing a new bar code scanner that looks and operates sort of like a smartphone. Holding the scanner in front of your face like a magnifying glass, you can see the bar code on a small screen, allowing more precise aiming and reducing uncomfortable wrist angles. Between this scanner's point-and-shoot operation and its ability to use voice confirmations instead of physical buttons, Exel found that the new scanner increased worker productivity by 10–20 percent. James Bonner, Exel Logistics' general manager, said, "In the big scheme of the world, it sounds like nothing. But when you take away three [button] touches, that's like three halves of a second. And you're shipping thousands of shipments a day."

Source: L. Chao, "Bar-Code Readers Get Makeover to Spur Bustling Warehouses," *Wall Street Journal*, January 8, 2016, http://www.wsj.com/articles/bar-code-readers-get-makeover-to-spur-bustling-warehouses-1452162601.

services, most of its revenues come from search-related ads. But those ads are effective only when Google serves up accurate searches that help people find what they're looking for. While Google already operates ten extraordinarily expensive data centers around the world, it's processing needs keep growing, so it has committed to building a new $1 billion data center in Council Bluffs, Iowa (after already building a $1.5 billion data center there in 2007).[22] Likewise in Europe, it will spend $772 million to build a data center in Eemshaven, Holland, where there is low-cost renewable energy, a landing station for underwater international data cables, and a mild climate.[23] The payback from these multibillion dollar investments? They allow Google to process 40,000 searches per second (3.5 billion per day, 1.2 trillion per year), handle email for 500 million+ Gmail accounts, and serve up YouTube videos to 1 billion users, all with the aim of more accurately targeting ads to the people who use its services.[24]

17-2g Storage Costs

Storage cost is the cost of physically or electronically archiving information for later retrieval and use. While your Facebook account is free, Facebook spends billions so that its more than 1 billion users worldwide can connect with their friends, play online games, and share photos. In addition to existing data centers in Oregon,

North Carolina, and Sweden, Facebook is building a 476,000 sq. ft. $300 million data center in Altoona, Iowa. Jay Parikh, Facebook's vice president of Infrastructure Engineering, says, "When complete, Altoona will be among the most advanced and energy-efficient facilities of its kind." Tom Furlong, Facebook's vice president of Site Operations, says, "This location had fiber, power, and a shovel-ready site." Facebook has plans to triple its initial investment in Iowa to more than a billion.[25]

17-2h Retrieval Costs

Retrieval cost is the cost of accessing already-stored and processed information. One of the most common misunderstandings about information is that it is easy and cheap to retrieve after the company has it. Not so. First, you have to find the information. Then, you've got to convince whoever has it to share it with you. Then the information has to be processed into a form that is useful for you. By the time you get the information you need, it may not be timely anymore.

For example, as companies move toward paperless office systems, how will employees quickly and easily retrieve archived emails, file records, website information, word

Storage cost the cost of physically or electronically archiving information for later retrieval and use

Retrieval cost the cost of accessing already-stored and processed information

processing documents, or images? Likewise, how will managers and employees quickly and easily retrieve information about costs, inventory, and sales?

One solution is broadly known as *business intelligence software* (BIS), which transforms stored, unstructured data in real time into meaningful information for business analysis and decision making. For example, retailers now commonly use sensors, video, and bluetooth cell phone tracking to count and monitor the flow of shoppers throughout their stores. These sensors track which entrances and exits are most commonly used, where customers spend most of their time in the store, how long they stay in a particular location, and so on. During the holiday season when stores were crowded, Sunhee Moon, a San Francisco retailer, was surprised to learn that customers spent more time at tables near the back of the store, and not the entrance. So holiday scarves were moved to the back where more customers would see them.[26] Likewise, through bluetooth tracking of your phone, retailers could, for instance, see that you've been to the store four times without buying. The tracking system could then be programmed to send your phone a mobile coupon on entering the store. Because mobile coupons are used ten times more than paper coupons, and smartphone users are 14 percent more likely than those without smartphones to use those mobile coupons while in the store, BIS monitoring gives retailers powerful new tools to track store performance and increase sales.[27]

17-2i Communication Costs

Communication cost is the cost of transmitting information from one place to another. For example, a small business with twenty people needing phone lines, a hosted website, and high-speed Internet access pays Comcast about $1,300 a month for that access. Google, Microsoft, and Facebook do the same for their employees. But because of the size of the data flowing from their websites to customers, they pay millions more in access fees to Comcast and Time Warner Cable, which provide the backbone through which Internet data run. While such payments are rare, it makes sense that generators of heavy Internet traffic pay more, especially because Comcast's Internet traffic is growing at 55 percent per year. Netflix, which accounts for 35 percent of evening traffic on the Internet due to video streaming, has also begun paying Comcast and other Internet providers so that its streaming services are prioritized in network traffic to customers' homes.[28]

> **Communication cost** the cost of transmitting information from one place to another

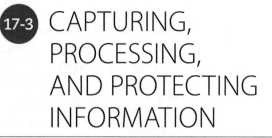

CAPTURING, PROCESSING, AND PROTECTING INFORMATION

In 1907, Metropolitan Life Insurance built a huge office building in New York City for its brand-new, state-of-the-art information technology system. What was this great breakthrough in information management? Card files. That's right, the same card file system that every library in America used before computers. Metropolitan Life's information technology consisted of 20,000 separate file drawers that sat in hundreds of file cabinets more than fifteen feet tall. This filing system held 20 million insurance applications, 700,000 accounting books, and 500,000 death certificates. Metropolitan Life employed sixty-one workers who did nothing but sort, file, and climb ladders to pull files as needed.[29]

How we get and share information has clearly changed. The cost, inefficiency, and ineffectiveness of using this formerly state-of-the-art system would put an insurance company out of business within months. Today, if storms, fire, or accidents damage a policyholder's property, he or she can use the insurance company's smartphone app to photograph and describe the damage. A company representative will then show up and write a check on the spot to cover the losses. As the claims process unfolds, the policyholder can ask questions, fill out forms, and access documents on the company's personalized web portal. From card files to Internet files in just under a century, the rate of change in information technology is spectacular.

*In this section, you will learn about the information technologies that companies use to **17-3a capture, 17-3b process,** and **17-3c protect information.***

17-3a Capturing Information

There are two basic methods of capturing information: manual and electronic. Manual capture of information is a slow, costly, labor-intensive, and often inaccurate process, which entails recording and entering data by hand into a data storage device. For example, when you applied for a driver's license, you probably recorded personal information about yourself by filling out a form. Then, after you passed your driver's test, someone typed your handwritten information into the department of motor vehicles' computer database so that local and state police could access it from their patrol cars in the event they pulled you over for speeding. (Isn't information great?) To avoid the problems inherent in such a system, companies are relying more on electronic capture. They use electronic storage devices such as bar codes, radio frequency identification (RFID) tags, and document scanners to capture and record data electronically.

Bar codes represent numerical data by varying the thickness and pattern of vertical bars. The primary advantage of bar codes is that the data they represent can be read and recorded in an instant with a handheld or pen-type scanner. One pass of the scanner (okay, sometimes several) and "beep!" the information has been captured. Bar codes cut checkout times in half, reduce data entry errors by 75 percent, and save stores money because stockers don't have to go through the labor-intensive process of putting a price tag on each item in the store.[30] And, with mobile phone apps, bar codes are becoming ubiquitous in travel (mobile boarding passes), for customer loyalty and payment programs (Starbucks), and in entertainment, such as movies (Fandango) and live events (LiveNation or TicketMaster). QR (quick response) codes are bar codes with black and white patterns scanned with your smartphone. Chinese consumers can quickly pay for taxi rides by scanning the taxi driver's QR code using Alipay Wallet (China-based Alibaba's PayPal equivalent).[31] Replicon's CloudClock system works by having employees scan a QR code that prompts a camera to take and time-stamp their picture, indicating when they started and stopped work.[32] Finally, BMO Harris Bank is launching cardless ATM machines where customers use their bank app to indicate how much money they want to withdraw. The app generates a QR code that the ATM machine scans and authorizes before dispensing cash in just fifteen seconds, or just one-third of the time of a card-based transaction. Also, QR codes eliminate the risk of card skimming in which hackers tap into the card-reading device in the ATM machine.[33]

Radio frequency identification (RFID) tags contain minuscule microchips and antennas that transmit information via radio waves.[34] Unlike bar codes, which require direct line-of-sight scanning, RFID tags are read by turning on an RFID reader that, like a radio, tunes into a specific frequency to determine the number *and* location of products, parts, or anything else to which the RFID tags are attached. Turn on an RFID reader, and every RFID tag within the reader's range (from several hundred to several thousand feet) is accounted for.

Because they are now so inexpensive, RFID tags and readers are being put to thousands of uses in all kinds

With mobile phone apps, bar codes are becoming ubiquitous in travel (mobile boarding passes), for customer loyalty, payment programs and in entertainment, such as movies (Fandango), and live events (TicketMaster).

of businesses. When Johnson Controls, a $37 billion manufacturer, realized that it was missing thousands of shipping containers and racks used to transport parts and finished products, it bought 830,000 RFID tags and attached them to its remaining equipment. Thanks to the RFID tag readers installed in all of its factories and warehouses, Johnson Controls can now track the location of its 830,000 containers and racks—down to which door they exited the factory from and which customers they got shipped to. Brian Kelly, Johnson Controls' director of supply-chain management, said, "We could get to a point that we not only know where all of our containers are but what is in each one without ever opening them up."[35]

Electronic scanners, which convert printed text and pictures into digital images, have become an increasingly popular method of capturing data electronically because they are inexpensive and easy to use. The first requirement for a good scanner is a document feeder that automatically feeds document pages into the scanner or turns the pages (often with a puff of air) when scanning books or bound documents. Text that has been digitized cannot

Bar code a visual pattern that represents numerical data by varying the thickness and pattern of vertical bars

Radio frequency identification (RFID) tags tags containing minuscule microchips that transmit information via radio waves and can be used to track the number and location of the objects into which the tags have been inserted

Electronic scanner an electronic device that converts printed text and pictures into digital images

be searched or edited like the regular text in your word processing software, however; so the second requirement for a good scanner is **optical character recognition** software to scan and convert original or digitized documents into ASCII (American Standard Code for Information Interchange) text or Adobe PDF documents. ASCII text can be searched, read, and edited with standard word processing, email, desktop publishing, database management, and spreadsheet software, and PDF documents can be searched and edited with Adobe's Acrobat software.

17-3b Processing Information

Processing information means transforming raw data into meaningful information that can be applied to business decision making. Evaluating sales data to determine the best- and worst-selling products, examining repair records to determine product reliability, and monitoring the cost of long-distance phone calls are all examples of processing raw data into meaningful information. And with automated, electronic capture of data, increased processing power, and cheaper and more plentiful ways to store data, managers no longer worry about getting data. Instead, they scratch their heads about how to use the overwhelming amount of data that pours into their businesses every day. Furthermore, most managers know little about statistics and have neither the time nor the inclination to learn how to use them to analyze data.

One promising tool to help managers dig out from under the avalanche of data is data mining. **Data mining** is the process of discovering patterns and relationships in large amounts of data.[36] Data mining is carried out using complex algorithms such as neural networks, rule induction, and decision trees. If you don't know what those are, that's okay. With data mining, you don't have to. Most managers only need to know that data mining looks for patterns that are already in the data but are too complex for them to spot on their own. Many Airbnb hosts who rent their rooms or homes to travelers have trouble deciding how much to charge per night. Data mining showed Airbnb that adjusting prices for *similarity, recency,* and *location* could maximize profits and occupancy rates. Similarity measured factors such as a home versus a private room, the number of bedrooms, the uniqueness of the property (are you renting a room in a castle or in an apartment?) and the number of reviews. Why reviews? They give potential renters confidence regarding the property and its host. Travel is seasonal, and demand for rentals is affected by major events like holidays, trade shows, and sporting events. Taking these and other recency factors into consideration, Airbnb can decide whether last week's, last month's, or last year's pricing should guide how much to charge today. Finally, data mining revealed that a rental's location was critical to renters. Is it safe? Is it near transportation, restaurants, and tourist sites? To measure the value of rentals' locations, Airbnb hired cartographers to "map the boundaries of every neighborhood in our top cities all over the world."[37]

Data mining typically splits a data set in half, finds patterns in one half, and then tests the validity of those patterns by trying to find them again in the second half of the data set. The data typically come from a **data warehouse**, which stores huge amounts of data that have been prepared for data mining analysis by being cleaned of errors and redundancy. The data in a data warehouse can then be analyzed using two kinds of data mining. **Supervised data mining** usually begins with the user telling the data mining software to look and test for specific patterns and relationships in a data set. Typically, this is done through a series of "what-if?" questions or statements. For instance, a grocery store manager might instruct the data mining software to determine if coupons placed in the Sunday paper increase or decrease sales. By contrast, with **unsupervised data mining**, the user simply tells the data mining software to uncover whatever patterns and relationships it can find in a data set. For example, because New York City (NYC) experiences about 3,000 major fires a year, analysts at the NYC Fire Department use data mining to predict which of the 330,000 buildings in New York are at most risk of catching fire. The data mining program checks for sixty different risk factors commonly correlated with fires, such as the building's age, elevators (which allow smoke and super heated air to move from floor to floor), and whether the building is vacant, abandoned, or has had electrical problems, and then generates a risk score for each building,

Optical character recognition the ability of software to convert digitized documents into ASCII (American Standard Code for Information Interchange) text that can be searched, read, and edited by word processing and other kinds of software

Processing information transforming raw data into meaningful information

Data mining the process of discovering unknown patterns and relationships in large amounts of data

Data warehouse a database that stores huge amounts of data that have been prepared for data mining analysis by being cleaned of errors and redundancy

Supervised data mining the process when the user tells the data mining software to look and test for specific patterns and relationships in a data set

Unsupervised data mining the process when the user simply tells the data mining software to uncover whatever patterns and relationships it can find in a data set

allowing fire inspectors to prioritize high-risk buildings for on-site inspections.[38] Unsupervised data mining is particularly good at identifying association or affinity patterns, sequence patterns, and predictive patterns. It can also identify what data mining technicians call data clusters.[39]

Association or affinity patterns occur when two or more database elements tend to occur together in a significant way. Most retailers send flyers and coupons about baby products after a woman has given birth (after the birth announcement is made public), but Target wanted to act earlier, sometime around the first twenty weeks of pregnancy, when mothers-to-be start buying items to get ready for their new baby. So it turned to association and affinity patterns to see if there was a way to identify through purchasing patterns when a woman was pregnant. Target's Guest Marketing Analytics department analyzed consumer data from Target's baby registry and found that around the beginning of their second trimester, pregnant women often bought lotion, mineral and vitamin supplements, unscented soap, hand sanitizer, and washcloths. Target found a pattern of twenty-five products that identified pregnant customers with such accuracy that the company could even estimate a due date. For example, if you're female, are 23 years old, and have bought cocoa-butter lotion, a large purse that doubles as a diaper bag, zinc and magnesium supplements (taken by pregnant women), and a blue or pink throw rug, there's an 87 percent chance that you are pregnant. Why? Because those purchases are almost always associated with being pregnant.[40]

Sequence patterns appear when two or more database elements occur together in a significant pattern in which one of the elements precedes the other. Hospitals employ the Modified Early Warning Score (MEWS), which uses commonly measured vital signs, such as blood pressure, temperature, and heart rate, to predict the likelihood of a patient going Code Blue, that is, respiratory or cardiac arrest. Patients with higher MEWS scores are monitored more closely. Doctors at Chicago's NorthShore University HealthSystem used data mining to see how well seventy-two medical variables predicted the likelihood of a patient going Code Blue. On a data set of 133,000 patients, data mining correctly predicted Code Blues 72 percent of the time—four hours before they happened. By contrast, MEWS scores accurately predicted Code Blues just 30 percent of the time.[41]

Predictive patterns are just the opposite of association or affinity patterns. Whereas association or affinity patterns look for database elements that seem to go together, **predictive patterns** help identify database elements that are different. Banks and credit card companies use data mining to find predictive patterns that distinguish customers who are good credit risks from those who are poor credit risks and less likely to pay their loans and monthly bills. Lending money to people with poor credit or without bank accounts (one out of four adults worldwide) is risky. To better assess that risk, some startup companies are going beyond standard credit scores and are using social media to separate good borrowers from bad ones. For example, you're a better candidate if you access the Internet via an expensive smartphone (versus an Internet cafe where you pay by the hour); don't let your phone battery run down; and you get more phone calls than you make. You are also more likely to get a loan if your phone stays in the same place every day (indicating that you're at work) and you regularly interact with a group of close friends who are good credit risks (meaning that you probably are as well).[42]

Data clusters are the last kind of pattern found by data mining. **Data clusters** occur when three or more database elements occur together (that is, cluster) in a significant way. For example, after analyzing several years' worth of repair and warranty claims, Ford Motor Company might find that, compared with cars built in its Chicago plant, the cars it builds in Kansas City (first element) are more likely to have problems with overtightened fan belts (second element) that break (third element) and result in overheated engines (fourth element), ruined radiators (fifth element), and payments for tow trucks (sixth element), which are paid for by Ford's five-year, 60,000-mile power train warranty.

Traditionally, data mining has been very expensive and very complex. Today, however, data mining services and analyses are much more affordable and within reach of most companies' budgets. And, if it follows the path of most technologies, data mining will become even easier and cheaper to use in the future.

17-3c Protecting Information

Protecting information is the process of ensuring that data are reliably and consistently retrievable in a usable

Association or affinity patterns when two or more database elements tend to occur together in a significant way

Sequence patterns when two or more database elements occur together in a significant pattern in which one of the elements precedes the other

Predictive patterns patterns that help identify database elements that are different

Data clusters when three or more database elements occur together (that is, cluster) in a significant way

Protecting information the process of ensuring that data are reliably and consistently retrievable in a usable format for authorized users but no one else

format for authorized users but no one else. Unfortunately, that didn't happen when North Korean hackers broke into Sony Pictures corporate computers, releasing malware that completely destroyed key databases, and then revealing embarrassing emails in retribution for a movie comedy, *The Interview*, in which two journalists are recruited by the CIA to assassinate North Korean leader Kim Jong Un.[43] The hackers also released copies of five Sony movies on the Internet, as well as sensitive personal information, including Social Security numbers of 47,000 people. The amount of data destroyed made it difficult at first for investigators to identify the hackers. Sony Entertainment CEO Michael Lynton said, "It took me twenty-four or thirty-six hours to fully understand this was not something we were going to be able to recover from in the next week or two."[44]

People inside and outside companies can steal or destroy company data in various ways, including denial-of-service web server attacks that can bring down some of the busiest and best-run sites on the Internet; viruses and malware, spyware, or adware that spread quickly and can result in data loss and business disruption; keystroke monitoring, in which every mouse click and keystroke you make is monitored, stored, and sent to unauthorized users; password-cracking software that steals supposedly secure passwords; and phishing, where fake but real-looking emails and websites trick users into sharing personal information (user names, passwords, account numbers) leading to unauthorized account access. On average, 32 percent of computers are infected with malware. Of those, 57 percent are infected with viruses, and 21 percent are infected with Trojans, which is malware disguised to look like a normal file or program.[45] Studies show that the threats listed in Exhibit 17.3 are so widespread that automatic attacks will begin on an unprotected computer just fifteen seconds after it connects to the Internet.[46]

As shown in the right-hand column of Exhibit 17.3, numerous steps can be taken to secure data and data networks. Some of the most important are authentication and authorization, firewalls, antivirus software for PCs and email servers, data encryption, and virtual private networks.[47] We will review those steps and then finish this section with a brief review of the dangers of wireless networks.

Two critical steps are required to make sure that data can be accessed by authorized users and no one else. One is **authentication**, that is, making sure users are who they claim to be.[48] The other is **authorization**,

Authentication making sure potential users are who they claim to be

Authorization granting authenticated users approved access to data, software, and systems

Exhibit 17.3
Security Threats to Data and Data Networks

Security Problem	Source	Affects	Severity	The Threat	The Solution
Denial of service; web server attacks and corporate network attacks	Internet hackers	All servers	High	Loss of data, disruption of service, and theft of service.	Implement firewall, password control, server-side review, threat monitoring, and bug fixes; turn PCs off when not in use.
Password cracking software and unauthorized access to PCs	Local area network, Internet	All users, especially digital subscriber line and cable Internet users	High	Hackers take over PCs. Privacy can be invaded. Corporate users' systems are exposed to other machines on the network.	Close ports and firewalls, disable file and print sharing, and use strong passwords.
Viruses, worms, Trojan horses, and rootkits	Email, downloaded and distributed software	All users	Moderate to high	Monitor activities and cause data loss and file deletion; compromise security by sometimes concealing their presence.	Use antivirus software and firewalls; control Internet access.
Malware, spyware, adware, malicious scripts, and applets	Rogue web pages	All users	Moderate to high	Invade privacy, intercept passwords, and damage files or file system.	Disable browser script support; use security, blocking, and spyware/adware software.
Email snooping	Hackers on your network and the Internet	All users	Moderate to high	People read your email from intermediate servers or packets, or they physically access your machine.	Encrypt messages, ensure strong password protection, and limit physical access to machines.
Keystroke monitoring	Trojan horses, people with direct access to PCs	All users	High	Records everything typed at the keyboard and intercepts keystrokes before password masking or encryption occurs.	Use antivirus software to catch Trojan horses, control Internet access to transmission, and implement system monitoring and physical access control.
Phishing	Hackers on your network and the Internet	All users, including customers	High	Fake but real-looking emails and websites that trick users into sharing personal information on what they wrongly think is a company's website. This leads to unauthorized account access.	Educate and warn users and customers about the dangers. Encourage both not to click on potentially fake URLs, which might take them to phishing websites. Instead, have them type your company's URL into the web browser.
Spam	Email	All users and corporations	Mild to high	Clogs and overloads email servers and inboxes with junk mail. HTML-based spam may be used for profiling and identifying users.	Filter known spam sources and senders on email servers; have users create further lists of approved and unapproved senders on their PCs.
Cookies	Websites you visit	Individual users	Mild to moderate	Trace web usage and permit the creation of personalized web pages that track behavior and interest profiles.	Use cookie managers to control and edit cookies, and use ad blockers.

Sources: "The 11 Most Common Computer Security Threats . . . And What You Can Do to Protect Yourself from Them," *Symantec-Norton*, accessed May 12, 2015, http://www .symantec-norton.com/11-most-common-computer-security-threats_k13.aspx; K. Bannan, "Look Out: Watching You, Watching Me," *PC Magazine*, July 2002, 99; A. Dragoon, "Fighting Phish, Fakes, and Frauds," *CIO*, September 1, 2004, 33; B. Glass, "Are You Being Watched?" *PC Magazine*, April 23, 2002, 54; K. Karagiannis, "DDoS: Are You Next?" *PC Magazine*, January 2003, 79; B. Machrone, "Protect & Defend," *PC Magazine*, June 27, 2000, 168–181; "Top 10 Security Threats," *PC Magazine*, April 10, 2007, 66; M. Sarrel, "Master End-User Security," *PC Magazine*, May 2008, 101.

CAN YOUR TYPING PATTERN REPLACE YOUR PASSWORDS?

While passwords have long been a staple of digital security, their shortcomings are apparent: simple passwords can be hacked, and complicated passwords can be difficult to remember. A new keyboard that identifies users by their unique typing styles could spur progress toward a "post-password" era, and improve corporate security. The keyboard picks up electrical charges from human skin and uses software to find patterns in users' typing. The scientists behind the keyboard say human typing patterns, comprising rhythm and time between keystrokes, are comparable in uniqueness to fingerprints. The technology does little to advance corporate network security, but it could still be a significant deterrent to hackers targeting individual machines.

Source: C. Boulton, "Keyboard Identifies Computer Users by Their Typing Patterns," *Wall Street Journal*, February 13, 2015, accessed May 13, 2015, http://blogs.wsj.com/cio/2015/02/13/keyboard-identifies-computer-users-by-their-typing-patterns/.

that is, granting authenticated users approved access to data, software, and systems.[49] When an ATM prompts you to enter your personal identification number (PIN), the bank is authenticating that you are you. After you've been authenticated, you are authorized to access your funds and no one else's. Of course, as anyone who has lost a PIN or password or had one stolen knows, user authentication systems are not foolproof. In particular, users create security risks by not changing their default account passwords (such as birth dates) or by using weak passwords such as names ("Larry") or complete words ("football") that are quickly guessed by password-cracking software.[50]

This is why many companies are now turning to **two-factor authentication**, which is based on what users know, such as a password, and what they have, in their possession, such as a secure ID card, their phones, or unique information that only they would know.[51] When logging in, users are first asked for their passwords. But then they must provide a second authentication factor, such as an answer to a security question (that is, unique information) or a validation code that has been sent to their mobile phone. Google, for example, requires two-factor authentication for its Google Apps (Gmail, Calendar, Drive, Docs, and so on). After entering their passwords, users can either use the code sent via text to their phone, or a code generated by Google's Authenticator app. Google Authenticator, which requires a mobile phone or Internet connection, gives you the ability to generate authentication codes for multiple accounts (including non-Google accounts), and generates codes that are only good for sixty seconds.[52]

Unfortunately, stolen or cracked passwords are not the only way for hackers and electronic thieves to gain access to an organization's computer resources. Unless special safeguards are put in place, every time corporate users are online, there's literally nothing between their PCs and the Internet (home users with high-speed Internet access face the same risks). Hackers can access files, run programs, and control key parts of computers if precautions aren't taken. To reduce these risks, companies use **firewalls**, hardware or software devices that sit between the computers in an internal organizational network and outside networks such as the Internet. Firewalls filter and check incoming and outgoing data. They prevent company insiders from accessing unauthorized sites or from sending confidential company information to people outside the company. Firewalls also prevent outsiders from identifying and gaining access to company computers and data. If a firewall is working properly, the computers behind the company firewall literally cannot be seen or accessed by outsiders.

A **virus** is a program or piece of code that, without your knowledge, attaches itself to other programs on your computer and can trigger anything from a harmless flashing message to the reformatting of your hard drive to a system-wide network shutdown. You used to have to do something or run something to get a virus, such as double-clicking an infected email attachment. Today's viruses are much more threatening. In fact, with

Two-factor authentication authentication based on what users know, such as a password and what they have in their possession, such as a secure ID card or key

Firewall a protective hardware or software device that sits between the computers in an internal organizational network and outside networks, such as the Internet

Virus a program or piece of code that, without your knowledge, attaches itself to other programs on your computer and can trigger anything from a harmless flashing message to the reformatting of your hard drive to a system-wide network shutdown

In 2016, Home Depot announced that it would pay as much as $19.5 million to settle a class-action lawsuit brought by customers affected by a massive online security breach at the company.

some viruses, just being connected to a network can infect your computer. *Antivirus software for PCs* scans email, downloaded files, and computer hard drives, disk drives, and memory to detect and stop computer viruses from doing damage. However, this software is effective only to the extent that users of individual computers have and use up-to-date versions. With new viruses appearing all the time, users should update their antivirus software weekly or, even better, configure their virus software to automatically check for, download, and install updates. By contrast, *corporate antivirus software* automatically scans email attachments such as Microsoft Word documents, graphics, or text files as they come across the company email server. It also monitors and scans all file downloads across company databases and network servers. So, while antivirus software for PCs prevents individual computers from being infected, corporate antivirus software for email servers, databases, and network servers adds another layer of protection by preventing infected files from multiplying and being sent to others.

Another way of protecting information is to encrypt sensitive data. **Data encryption** transforms data into complex, scrambled digital codes that can be decrypted only by authorized users who possess unique decryption keys. One method of data encryption is to use products by Symantec (http://buy.symantec.com/estore/clp/home) to encrypt the files stored on PCs or network servers and databases. This is especially important with laptop computers, which are easily stolen, and with sensitive data like customer credit card numbers. Indeed, after being hit by a major security breach in which 56 million customers' unencrypted credit card numbers were stolen by hackers, Home Depot now spends $7 million a year to encrypt data at its 2,200 stores.[53]

With people increasingly gaining unauthorized access to email messages—email snooping—it's also important to encrypt sensitive email messages and file attachments. You can use a system called "public key encryption" to do so. First, give copies of your "public key" to anyone who sends you files or email. Have the sender use the public key, which is actually a piece of software, to encrypt files, before sending them to you. The only way to decrypt the files is with a companion "private key" that you keep to yourself.

Although firewalls can protect PCs and network servers connected to the corporate network, people away from their offices (for example, salespeople, business travelers, telecommuters) who interact with their company networks via the Internet face a security risk. Because Internet data are not encrypted, "packet sniffer" software easily allows hackers to read everything sent or received except files that have been encrypted before sending. Previously, the only practical solution was to have employees dial in to secure company phone lines for direct access to the company network. Of course, with international and long-distance phone calls, the costs quickly added up. Now, **virtual private networks (VPNs)** have solved this problem by using software to encrypt all Internet data at both ends of the transmission process. Instead of making long-distance calls, employees connect to the Internet. But, unlike typical Internet connections in which data packets are decrypted, the VPN encrypts the data sent by employees outside the company computer network, decrypts the data when they arrive within the company network, and does the same when data are sent back to the computer outside the network. VPN connections provide secure access to everything on a company's network. If your employer or university doesn't provide a VPN, you can purchase VPN services for personal use and protection from well-known providers, such as AnchorFree Hotspot Shield (www.anchorfree.com) or Cloak VPN (www.getcloak.com), for about $3 a month. VPN services should be used when connected to

Data encryption the transformation of data into complex, scrambled digital codes that can be decrypted only by authorized users who possess unique decryption keys

Virtual private network (VPN) software that securely encrypts data sent by employees outside the company network, decrypts the data when they arrive within the company computer network, and does the same when data are sent back to employees outside the network

Uber Hires White Hat Hackers

Kamira/Shutterstock.com

If you own a car, chances are you've got a wireless key fob that lets you lock and unlock the vehicle at the touch of a button. While convenient, keyless entry systems are highly susceptible to hacking attacks. German researchers found that at least twenty-four different models from nineteen auto manufacturers could be unlocked, started, and driven away as long as the car owner's key fob was within several hundred meters. In other words, your car keys could be in your house and hackers could drive away with your supposedly locked car. Two hackers, Charlier Miller and Chris Valasek, recently demonstrated that they could remotely control a Jeep Cherokee from ten miles away. They were able to adjust the air conditioning, change the radio, flip on the windshield wipers, and scariest of all, shift the transmission into neutral in the middle of a busy highway. They were also able to kill the engine and slam on the brakes—or disable them altogether. Uber, a ride sharing company that may ultimately become a provider of driverless services, is a common target of hackers. To combat this, the company hired Miller and Valesek to "continue building out a world-class safety and security program at Uber."

Sources: A. Greenberg, "Radio Attack Lets Hackers Steal 24 Different Car Models," *Wired*, March 21, 2016, accessed May 12, 2016, https://www.wired.com/2016/03/study-finds-24-car-models-open-unlocking-ignition-hack/; A. Greenberg, "Hackers Remotely Kill a Jeep on the Highway—With Me in It," *Wired*, July 21, 2015, accessed May 12, 2016, https://www.wired.com/2015/07/hackers-remotely-kill-jeep-highway/; M. Isaac and N. Perlroth, "Uber Hires Two Engineers Who Showed Cars Could Be Hacked," *New York Times*, August 28, 2015, accessed May 12, 2016, http://www.nytimes.com/2015/08/29/technology/uber-hires-two-engineers-who-showed-cars-could-be-hacked.html.

public Wi-Fi systems, such as in hotels, airports, or coffee shops, where anyone on the public network can monitor or spy on what you're doing.

Alternatively, many companies are now adopting web-based **secure sockets layer (SSL) encryption** to provide secure off-site access to data and programs. If you've ever entered your credit card in a web browser to make an online purchase, you've used SSL technology to encrypt and protect that information.

You can tell if SSL encryption is being used on a website if you see a padlock icon or if the URL begins with "https." SSL encryption works the same way in the workplace. Managers and employees who aren't at the office simply connect to the Internet, open a web browser, and then enter a user name and password to gain access to SSL-encrypted data and programs.

Finally, while wireless networks come equipped with security and encryption capabilities that, in theory, permit only authorized users to access the wireless network, those capabilities are easily bypassed with the right tools. Compounding the problem, many wireless network routers are shipped with outdated firmware susceptible to hacking

and with encryption capabilities turned off for ease of installation.[54] To stay safe, organizations should regularly update their wireless network routers' firmware. Also, caution is important even when encryption is turned on, because the WEP (Wired Equivalent Privacy) security protocol is easily compromised. If you work at home or are working on the go, extra care is critical because Wi-Fi networks in homes and public places such as hotel lobbies are among the most targeted by hackers.[55] See the Wi-Fi Alliance site at www.wi-fi.org for the latest information on wireless security and encryption protocols that provide much stronger protection for your company's wireless network.

Finally, companies are combating security threats by hiring *white hat hackers*, so-called good guys, who test security weak points in information systems so that they can be fixed. While this is typically done using traditional hacking tools, as discussed in Exhibit 17.3, white hat hackers also test security via *social engineering*, in which they trick people into giving up passwords and authentication protocols or unknowingly providing unauthorized access to company computers. One test involves emailing a picture of a cat with a purple mohawk and this subject line, "Check out these kitties!" to employees with a link to more cute kitty photos. When you click an embedded link to "more cute kitty photos," you're taken to a

Secure sockets layer (SSL) encryption Internet browser–based encryption that provides secure off-site web access to some data and programs

company website warning about the dangers of phishing scams. Think that you wouldn't fall for this? Forty-eight percent of employees receiving this email click the link.[56] Another test involves "lost or left-behind" USB thumb drives, ostensibly belonging to competitors. When the person who picked up the thumb drive inserts it into a computer, it installs software that uses the webcam to snap a picture of the employee, who then receives a visit from the IT security team.[57]

17-4 ACCESSING AND SHARING INFORMATION AND KNOWLEDGE

Today, information technologies are letting companies communicate data, share data, and provide data access to workers, managers, suppliers, and customers in ways that were unthinkable just a few years ago.

After reading this section, you should be able to explain how companies use information technology to improve 17-4a internal access and sharing of information, 17-4b external access and sharing of information, and 17-4c the sharing of knowledge and expertise.

17-4a Internal Access and Sharing

Executives, managers, and workers inside the company use three kinds of information technology to access and share information: executive information systems, intranets, and portals. An **executive information system (EIS)** uses internal and external sources of data to provide managers and executives the information they need to monitor and analyze organizational performance.[58] The goal of an EIS is to provide accurate, complete, relevant, and timely information to managers. With just a few mouse clicks and basic commands such as *find*, *compare*, and *show*, the EIS displays costs, sales revenues, and other kinds of data in color-coded charts and graphs. Managers can drill down to view and compare data by global region, country, state, time period, and product. Managers at Colgate-Palmolive, which makes dental (Colgate toothpastes), personal (Irish Spring soap and Speed Stick antiperspirants), and home care (Palmolive dish soaps) products, as well as pet nutrition (Hill's Science Diet), use their EIS, which they call their "dashboard," to see how well the company is running. Ruben Panizza, Colgate's global IT director of business intelligence, says, "These real-time dashboards are a change for people who are used to seeing a lot of numbers with their data. But they quickly realize they can use the information as it's presented in the dashboards to make faster decisions. In the past, executives relied on other people to get custom reports and data. Now, they can look at the information themselves. They see the real data as it is in the system much more easily and quickly. For the first time, many of the company's business leaders are running BI [business intelligence] tools—in this case, dashboards—to monitor the business to see what's going on at a high level."[59]

Intranets are private company networks that allow employees to easily access, share, and publish information using Internet software. Intranet websites are just like external websites, but the firewall separating the internal company network from the Internet permits only authorized internal access.[60] Companies typically use intranets to share information (e.g., about benefits) and to replace paper forms with online forms. Many company intranets are built on the web model as it existed a decade ago. Intranets are evolving to include:

- collaboration tools, such as wikis, where team members can post all relevant information for a project they're working on together

- customizable email accounts

- presence awareness (information on whether someone you are looking for on the network is in the office, in a meeting, working from home, and so on)

- instant messaging

- simultaneous access to files for virtual team members

Dorma+kaba, a global provider of security and business access solutions (keys, locks, automatic doors, door and controls), recently launched a company intranet that was recognized in 2015 as one of the world's ten best. With 16,000 employees in 50 countries speaking multiple languages, Dorma+kaba needed an intranet that promoted collaboration and sharing of information. The new intranet's communication platform was designed so that employees could easily create corporate blogs, disseminate company news and videos, and promote events and announcements. What's

> **Executive information system (EIS)** a data processing system that uses internal and external data sources to provide the information needed to monitor and analyze organizational performance
>
> **Intranets** private company networks that allow employees to easily access, share, and publish information using Internet software

more, it made all of this content readily accessible in each user's native language. Dorma+kaba's intranet has other advanced features as well. SmartFeed, which sits on the intranet home page, automatically finds the most important and relevant news for each user. Collaboration is facilitated by building Yammer, a corporate social networking function, directly into the intranet. Within months of launch, more than 500 conversations on new products had taken place on Yammer, allowing global sales and operational teams to answer questions and share best practices. To reach employees no matter where they're located or what devices they're using, dorma+kaba's intranet is synchronized across PCs and Macs and there are native applications for iOS, Android, and Windows phones and tablets.[61]

Finally, **corporate portals** are a hybrid of executive information systems and intranets. While an EIS provides managers and executives with the information they need to monitor and analyze organizational performance, and intranets help companies distribute and publish information and forms within the company, corporate portals allow company managers and employees to access customized information *and* complete specialized transactions using a web browser.

17-4b External Access and Sharing

Historically, companies have been unable or reluctant to let outside groups have access to corporate information. Now, however, a number of information technologies—electronic data interchange, extranets, web services, and the Internet—are making it easier to share company data with external groups such as suppliers and customers. They're also reducing costs, increasing productivity by eliminating manual information processing (70% of the data output from one company, such as a purchase order, ends up as data input at another company, such as a sales invoice or shipping order), reducing data entry errors, improving customer service, and

speeding communications. As a result, managers are scrambling to adopt these technologies.

With **electronic data interchange, or EDI,** two companies convert purchase and ordering information to a standardized format to enable direct electronic transmission of that information from one company's computer system to the other company's system. For example, when a Walmart checkout clerk drags an Apple iPad across the checkout scanner, Walmart's computerized inventory system automatically reorders another iPad through the direct EDI connection that its computer has with Apple's manufacturing and shipping computer. No one at Walmart or Apple fills out paperwork. No one makes phone calls. There are no delays to wait to find out whether Apple has the iPad in stock. The transaction takes place instantly and automatically because the data from both companies were translated into a standardized, shareable, compatible format.

Web services are another way for companies to directly and automatically transmit purchase and ordering data from one company's computer system to another company's computer system. **Web services** use standardized protocols to describe and transfer data from one company in such a way that those data can automatically be read, understood, transcribed, and processed by different computer systems in another company.[62] Route One, which helps automobile dealers process loans for car buyers, was started by the financing companies of DaimlerChrysler, Ford, General Motors, and Toyota. Not surprisingly, each auto company had a different computer system with different operating systems, different programs, and different data structures. RouteOne relies on web services to connect these different computer systems to the wide variety of different databases and software used by various auto dealers, credit bureaus, banks, and other auto financing companies. Without web services, there's no way these different companies and systems could share information.[63]

Now, what's the difference between web services and EDI? For EDI to work, the data in different companies' computer, database, and network systems must adhere to a particular set of standards for data structure and processing. For example, company X, which has a seven-digit parts numbering system, and company Y, which has an eight-digit parts numbering system, would agree to convert their internal parts numbering systems to identical ten-digit parts numbers when their computer systems talk to each other. By contrast, the tools underlying web services such as extensible markup language (or XML) automatically do the describing and transcribing so that data with different structures can be shared across very different computer systems in different companies.

Corporate portal a hybrid of executive information systems and intranets that allows managers and employees to use a web browser to gain access to customized company information and to complete specialized transactions

Electronic data interchange (EDI) when two companies convert their purchase and ordering information to a standardized format to enable the direct electronic transmission of that information from one company's computer system to the other company's computer system

Web services software that uses standardized protocols to describe data from one company in such a way that those data can automatically be read, understood, transcribed, and processed by different computer systems in another company

Self-service kiosks have speed up check-in times for the more than 34 million passengers who pass through Gatwick Airport every year.

example, most airlines have automated the ticketing process by eliminating paper tickets altogether. Simply buy an e-ticket via the Internet, and then check yourself in online via an app on your smart phone, or by printing your boarding pass from your PC or an airport kiosk. Internet purchases, ticketless travel, and automated check-ins have together fully automated the purchase of airline tickets. Use of self-service kiosks is expanding, too.

At London's Gatwick airport, self-service kiosks now offer "self bag drop," which travelers use to check in, weigh, and tag their luggage—all without the help of an agent. The self-service kiosks can process excess, oversized, and overweight baggage, even taking credit card payments for modified or extra charges. After check-in and bag tagging, customers place their luggage on baggage conveyor belts immediately adjacent to the kiosks. While the kiosks are speeding up check-in, some customers still prefer checking bags with gate agents.[66] New Yorker Mark Rosenthal says, "I don't work for the airline. Why should I do their job? If something goes wrong or I have a question, the self-tagging machine isn't going to have an answer."[67]

In the long run, the goal is to link customer Internet sites with company intranets (or EDI) and extranets so that everyone—all the employees and managers within a company as well as the suppliers and distributors outside the company—involved in providing a service or making a product for a customer is automatically notified when a purchase is made. Companies that use EDI, web services, extranets, and the Internet to share data with customers and suppliers achieve increases in productivity 2.7 times larger than those that don't.[68]

(Don't worry if you don't understand how this works, just appreciate what it does.) As a result, by automatically handling those differences, web services allow organizations to communicate data without special knowledge of each other's computer information systems.

In EDI and web services, the different purchasing and ordering applications in each company interact automatically without any human input. No one has to lift a finger to click a mouse, enter data, or hit the Enter key. An **extranet**, by contrast, allows companies to exchange information and conduct transactions by purposely providing outsiders with direct, password-protected, web browser–based access to authorized parts of a company's intranet or information system.[64]

In an attempt to improve the marketing efforts of the contractors that it works with, Mitsubishi Electric Cooling & Heating developed its Creative Center extranet. The site provides a host of tools that contractors can use to grow their business. These include a range of company-approved marketing tools such as newspaper ads, posters, and banners that each contractor can customize to his or her preference and use to promote both the contractor's business and the Mitsubishi Electric Cooling & Heating brand.[65]

Finally, companies are reducing paperwork and manual information processing by using the Internet to electronically automate transactions with customers; this is similar to the way in which extranets are used to handle transactions with suppliers and distributors. For

17-4c Sharing Knowledge and Expertise

At the beginning of the chapter, we distinguished between raw data, which

Extranets networks that allow companies to exchange information and conduct transactions with outsiders by providing them direct, web-based access to authorized parts of a company's intranet or information system

consist of facts and figures, and information, which consists of useful data that influence someone's choices and behavior. One more important distinction needs to be made, namely, that data and information are not the same as knowledge. **Knowledge** is the understanding that one gains from information. Importantly, knowledge does not reside in information. Knowledge resides in people. That's why companies hire consultants and why family doctors refer patients to specialists. Unfortunately, it can be quite expensive to employ consultants, specialists, and experts. So companies have begun using two information technologies to capture and share the knowledge of consultants, specialists, and experts with other managers and workers: decision support systems and expert systems.

Whereas an executive information system speeds up and simplifies the acquisition of information, a **decision support system (DSS)** helps managers understand problems and potential solutions by acquiring and analyzing information with sophisticated models and tools.[69] Furthermore, whereas EIS programs are broad in scope and permit managers to retrieve all kinds of information about a company, DSS programs are usually narrow in scope and targeted toward helping managers solve specific kinds of problems. DSS programs have been developed to help managers pick the shortest and most efficient routes for delivery trucks, select the best combination of stocks for investors, and schedule the flow of inventory through complex manufacturing facilities.

It's important to understand that DSS programs don't replace managerial decision making; they *improve* it by furthering managers' and workers' understanding of the problems they face and the solutions that might work. Though used by just 2 percent of physicians, medical DSS programs hold the promise of helping doctors make more accurate patient diagnoses. A British study of eighty-eight cases misdiagnosed or initially misdiagnosed (to be correctly diagnosed much later) found that a medical DSS made the right diagnosis 69 percent of the time.[70] With a medical DSS, doctors enter patient data such as age, gender, weight, and medical symptoms. The medical DSS then produces a list of diseases and conditions, ranked by probability, low or high, or by medical specialty, such as cardiology or oncology. For instance, when emergency room physician Dr. Harold Cross treated a ten-year-old boy who had been ill with nausea and dizziness for two weeks, he wasn't sure what was wrong because the boy had a healthy appetite, no abdominal pain, and just one brief headache. However, when the medical DSS that Dr. Cross used suggested a

Knowledge the understanding that one gains from information

Decision support system (DSS) an information system that helps managers understand specific kinds of problems and potential solutions

possible problem in the back of the boy's brain, Cross ordered an MRI scan that revealed a tumor, which was successfully removed two days later. Says Dr. Cross, "My personal knowledge of the literature and physical findings would not have prompted me to suspect a brain tumor."[71]

Expert systems are created by capturing the specialized knowledge and decision rules used by experts and experienced decision makers. They permit nonexpert employees to draw on this expert knowledge base to make decisions. Most expert systems work by using a collection of "if–then" rules to sort through information and recommend a course of action. For example, let's say that you're using your American Express card to help your spouse celebrate a promotion. After dinner and a movie, the two of you stroll by a travel office with a Las Vegas poster in its window. Thirty minutes later, caught up in the moment, you find yourselves at the airport ticket counter trying to purchase last-minute tickets to Vegas. But there's just one problem. American Express didn't approve your purchase. In fact, the ticket counter agent is now on the phone with an American Express customer service agent. So what put a temporary halt to your weekend escape to Vegas? An expert system that American Express calls Authorizer's Assistant.[72]

The first "if–then" rule that prevented your purchase was the rule "*if* a purchase is much larger than the cardholder's regular spending habits, *then* deny approval of the purchase." This if–then rule, just one of 3,000, is built into American Express's transaction-processing system that handles thousands of purchase requests per second. Now that the American Express customer service agent is on the line, he or she is prompted by the Authorizer's Assistant to ask the ticket counter agent to examine your identification. You hand over your driver's license and another credit card to prove you're you. Then the ticket agent asks for your address, phone number, and your mother's maiden name and relays the information to American Express. Finally, your ticket purchase is approved. Why? Because you met the last series of "if–then" rules. *If* the purchaser can provide proof of identity and *if* the purchaser can provide personal information that isn't common knowledge, *then* approve the purchase.

> **Expert system** an information system that contains the specialized knowledge and decision rules used by experts and experienced decision makers so that nonexperts can draw on this knowledge base to make decisions

STUDY TOOLS 17

LOCATED IN TEXTBOOK

☐ Rip-out and review chapter review card

LOCATED AT WWW.CENGAGE.COM

☐ Review key term flashcards and create your own from StudyBits

☐ Track your knowledge and understanding of key concepts, using the concept tracker

☐ Complete practice and graded quizzes to prepare for tests

☐ Complete interactive content within the exposition

☐ View chapter highlight box content at the beginning of each chapter

18 Managing Service and Manufacturing Operations

Iskra Antova/Shutterstock.com

LEARNING OUTCOMES

18-1 Discuss the kinds of productivity and their importance in managing operations.

18-2 Explain the role that quality plays in managing operations.

18-3 Explain the essentials of managing a service business.

18-4 Describe the different kinds of manufacturing operations.

18-5 Explain why and how companies should manage inventory levels.

After you finish
this chapter, go
to **PAGE 404** for
STUDY TOOLS

PRODUCTIVITY

Furniture manufacturers, hospitals, restaurants, automakers, airlines, and many other kinds of businesses struggle to find ways to produce quality products and services efficiently and then deliver them in a timely manner. Managing the daily production of goods and services, or **operations management**, is a key part of a manager's job. But an organization depends on the quality of its products and services as well as its productivity.

On turnaround day, Royal Caribbean's Oasis of the Seas cruise ship sails into port at 6:00 a.m., dropping off 6,000 passengers, restocking supplies, taking on 6,000 new passengers, and departing by 4:30 p.m. Provision master Rodolfo Corrales says, "Embarkation day is frantic. It's not just busy, it's crazy busy."[1] Corrales and other crewmembers will load 12,000 bags, 24,000 beer bottles, 1,400 champagne bottles, 15,000 pounds of potatoes, 9,000 pounds of tomatoes, and 9,000 cans of soft drinks onto the ship. In 2,700 rooms, attendants will strip the beds and towels, which go into green and red bags (for easier handling of 93,000 pounds of laundry). One hundred eighty-nine housekeepers clean 2,700 cabins and bathrooms. Precisely choreographed jobs and tasks, as well as a service corridor (which passengers never see), nicknamed I-95 because it runs the length of the ship making it easy to quickly get anything anywhere, make all of this happen. None of it is accidental. In fact, Royal Caribbean brought in productivity experts from Porsche, the German carmaker, and DHL, the delivery logistics firm to learn how to best manage the flow of goods, people, and luggage. The ship's hotel director, Martin Rissley, says, "The minute efficiencies you can create in the process make a big difference in the end."[2]

At their core, organizations are production systems. Companies combine inputs such as labor, raw materials, capital, and knowledge to produce outputs in the form of finished products or services. **Productivity** is a measure of performance that indicates how many inputs it takes to produce or create an output.

$$\text{Productivity} = \frac{\text{Outputs}}{\text{Inputs}}$$

The fewer inputs it takes to create an output (or the greater the output from one input), the higher the productivity.

On calm weather days, London's Heathrow airport lands forty to forty-five planes every hour. Strong headwinds drop that rate to just thirty-two to thirty-eight planes per hour, however. How could Heathrow be more productive on windy days? Arriving planes are typically spaced three to seven miles apart depending on jet size. Heathrow, however, now uses time-based plane separation to improve arrival efficiency. The *Wall Street Journal's* Scott McCartney explains: "If a plane normally needs to be 5 miles behind the one it's following, but the headwind at 3,000 feet above sea level is 50 knots, or 58 miles an hour, now the plane might move a mile closer. Time between touchdowns remains the same, even with the headwinds slowing down the flight." How well does this work? On a blustery March day with nearly 60-miles-per-hour headwinds, sixty more planes than normal landed at Heathrow. Indeed, delays and circling patterns have dropped significantly, and the airport reports a 50 percent increase in landing productivity on windy days.[3]

*Let's examine **18-1a why productivity matters** and **18-1b the different kinds of productivity**.*

18-1a Why Productivity Matters

Why does productivity matter? For companies, higher productivity—that is, doing more with less—results in lower costs for the company, lower prices, faster service, higher market share, and higher profits. In 1989, 85 percent of the items on a UPS delivery truck were shipped to businesses. Today, 60 percent of those items are delivered to consumers, with one-third shipping from Amazon.com. Although UPS earns $11 billion a year from e-commerce deliveries, revenues per package are dropping, while per-package delivery costs are rising, all thanks to rising home deliveries. Consequently, UPS is intensifying its already strong focus on productivity by spending $500 million in preparation for the holiday season where, at its peak, it will deliver 34 million packages in one day (double an average day). It is getting large productivity increases, however, from its "Next Generation Sort Aisle," where sorters scan a package barcode (just like in stores), hear a beep (indicating a successful scan), and then read the name of a color-coded chute to which the packages needs to go. Before the scanning system, employees trained for two weeks on computers to memorize 120 ZIP codes. Now, new employees can be trained in two or three days. Rosemary Etheredge, who has worked at UPS for ten years, says, "For new employees, it is much better."[4] In fact, with the Next Generation

Operations management managing the daily production of goods and services

Productivity a measure of performance that indicates how many inputs it takes to produce or create an output

PACKAGING AND PRODUCTIVITY: "WE HATE AIR AT IKEA"

Ikea, famous for its low prices and assemble-ready furniture, is striving to grow by 10 percent a year. The Swedish retailer expects much of that growth to come from lower prices driving higher sales volumes. And, lower prices will likely come from increasing productivity. When Ikea hollowed out the solid wood legs of its Bjursta dining table, it reduced the table's weight and shipping costs, allowing it to cut the price from $360 to $260. When it cut the number of parts in its Textur lamp from 33 to 9, the lamp was 28 percent lighter and could be packed in smaller boxes. Now, 128 Textur boxes can fit on one pallet instead of 80.

That enabled Ikea to drop the Textur's price by 28 percent. The Ektrop sofa used to be one piece, but redesigning it to have a hinged back and removable arms allowed Ikea to cut the sofa's package size in half, resulting in 7,500 fewer truck loads per year and a 14 percent lower price. CEO Peter Agnefjall says, "We are engineering costs out of our value chain that don't contribute anything . . . We hate [shipping] air at Ikea."

Source: S. Chaudhuri, "IKEA Can't Stop Obsessing About Its Packaging, *Wall Street Journal*, June 17, 2015, accessed May 6, 2016, http://www.wsj.com/articles/ikea-cant-stop-obsessing-about-its-packaging-1434533401.

scanning system, sorters can process 15 percent more packages per day, which means that UPS can hire the same number of temporary holiday season workers as it did two years ago, even though product volumes are rising more than 10 percent per year.[5]

Productivity matters because it results in a higher standard of living in terms of higher wages, charitable giving, and making products more affordable. When companies can do more with less, they can raise employee wages without increasing prices or sacrificing normal profits. For instance, recent government economic data indicated that U.S. companies were paying workers 2.0 percent more than in the previous year. But because workers were only producing 0.6 percent more than they had the year before, real labor costs actually increased.[6]

The average American family earned approximately $66,632 in 2014. If productivity grows 1 percent per year, that family's income will increase to $85,451 in 2039. But if productivity grows 2 percent per year, their income in 2039 will be $109,317, an increase of $23,866, and that's without working longer hours.[7]

Thanks to long-term increases in business productivity, the average American family today earns 15.8 percent more than the average family in 1980 and 35.5 percent more than the average family in 1967—and that's after accounting for inflation.[8] Productivity increased an average of 2.4 percent from 1999 to 2006, 1.3 percent from 2007 to 2012, and 0.6 percent from 2013 to 2015.[9] And, from 2004 to 2014, the U.S. economy created nearly 8.5 million new jobs.[10]

And when more people have jobs that pay more, they give more to charity. For example, in 2014 Americans donated more than $358 billion to charities, compared to 230 billion in 2000 and $261 billion in 2009.[11] Did Americans become more thoughtful, caring, conscientious, and giving? Probably not. Yet, because of increases in productivity during this time, the average American's income increased by 54.5 percent, from $36,433 in 2000 to 56,300 in 2015.[12] Because people earned more money, they were able to share their good fortune with others by giving more to charity.[13]

Another benefit of productivity is that it makes products more affordable or better. One way to demonstrate this is by comparing how many work hours it would take to earn enough money to buy a product now versus in the past. For instance, in 1958 when the average U.S. wage was $1.98 an hour, a 1958 24-inch black-and-white TV (prime time TV shows weren't broadcast in color until 1965) cost $270 and 136.3 work hours compared to a 2016 26-inch LCD HDTV which cost $130 and 4.8 work hours! Finally, a 1958 stereo phonograph that played vinyl records (look in the attic, your grandparents might still have some) cost $84.95 and 43 work hours, while a 2016 iPod Touch, which runs for 40 hours on a charge and holds tens of thousands of songs, costs $249 and just 9.2 work hours.[14] People like to reminisce about the "good 'ol days," when things were "cheaper." But, mostly, they really weren't. Thanks to steady increases in productivity, most goods become better and more affordable over time.

18-1b Kinds of Productivity

Two common measures of productivity are partial productivity and multifactor productivity. **Partial productivity**

> **Partial productivity** a measure of performance that indicates how much of a particular kind of input it takes to produce an output

Exhibit 18.1
Multifactor Productivity Growth Across Industries

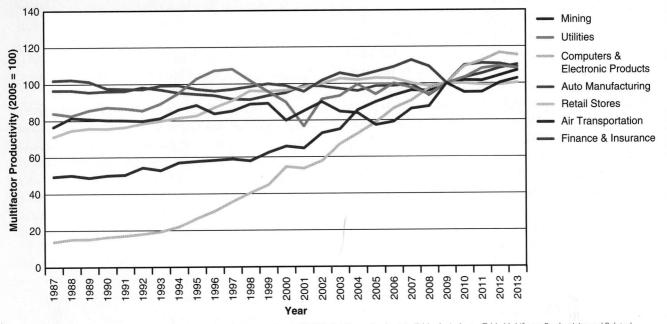

Source: "Nonmanufacturing Sectors and NIPA-level Nonmanufacturing Industries KLEMS Multifactor Productivity Tables by Industry: Table Multifactor Productivity and Related KLEMS Measures from the NIPA Industry Database, 1987 to 2013," Bureau of Labor Statistics, Division of Industry Productivity Studies, July 28, 2015, accessed May 5, 2016. http://www.bls.gov/mfp/special_requests/klemsmfpxg.zip; "Manufacturing Sector and NIPA-level Manufacturing Industries KLEMS Multifactor Productivity Tables by Industry: Table Multifactor Productivity and Related KLEMS Measures from the NIPA Industry Database, 1987 to 2013," Bureau of Labor Statistics, Division of Industry Productivity Studies, February 16, 2016, accessed May 5, 2016. http://www.bls.gov/mfp/special_requests/prod3.klemsmfp.zip.

indicates how much of a particular kind of input it takes to produce an output.

$$\text{Partial Productivity} = \frac{\text{Outputs}}{\text{Single Kind of Input}}$$

Labor is one kind of input that is frequently used when determining partial productivity. *Labor productivity* typically indicates the cost or number of hours of labor it takes to produce an output. In other words, the lower the cost of the labor to produce a unit of output, or the less time it takes to produce a unit of output, the higher the labor productivity. Labor cost as a percentage of revenue is a basic measure of labor productivity used in the airline industry. The lower the percentage of revenue attributable to labor costs, the more productively an airline uses labor to generate a unit of revenue (that is, dollars, euros, and so on). In Europe, for example, Wizz Air (6.5%), Ryanair (9.5%), and easyJet (12.4%) have some of the lowest labor costs per unit of revenue, especially when compared to major carriers such as British Airways (21.7%), Lufthansa

(23.4%), Air France (29.9%), and Scandinavian Airlines (32.1%).[15]

Partial productivity assesses how efficiently companies use only one input, such as labor, when creating outputs. Multifactor productivity is an overall measure of productivity that assesses how efficiently companies use all the inputs it takes to make outputs. More specifically, **multifactor productivity** indicates how much labor, capital, materials, and energy it takes to produce an output.[16]

$$\frac{\text{Multifactor}}{\text{Productivity}} = \frac{\text{Outputs}}{(\text{Labor} + \text{Capital} + \text{Materials} + \text{Energy})}$$

Exhibit 18.1 shows the trends in multifactor productivity across a number of U.S. industries since 1987.

With a 15.3 percent increase between 2009 (scaled at 100) and 2013 and a 8.4 fold increase since 1987, the growth in multifactor productivity

Multifactor productivity
an overall measure of performance that indicates how much labor, capital, materials, and energy it takes to produce an output

in the computer and electronic products industry far exceeded the productivity growth in mining, utilities, auto manufacturing, retail stores, air transportation, and financial and insurance services, as well as most other industries tracked by the U.S. government.

Should managers use multiple or partial productivity measures? In general, they should use both. Multifactor productivity indicates a company's overall level of productivity relative to its competitors. In the end, that's what counts most. However, multifactor productivity measures don't indicate the specific contributions that labor, capital, materials, or energy make to overall productivity. To analyze the contributions of these individual components, managers need to use partial productivity measures. Doing so can help them determine what factors need to be adjusted or in what areas adjustment can make the most difference in overall productivity.

18-2 QUALITY

With the average car costing $33,865, car buyers want to make sure that they're getting good quality for their money.[17] Fortunately, as indicated by the number of problems per 100 cars (PP100), today's cars are of much higher quality than earlier models. In 1981, Japanese cars averaged 240 PP100. GM's cars averaged 670, Ford's averaged 740, and Chrysler's averaged 870 PP100! In other words, as measured by PP100, the quality of American cars was two to three times worse than that of Japanese cars. By 1992, however, U.S. carmakers had made great strides, significantly reducing the number of problems to an average of 155 PP100. Japanese vehicles had improved, too, averaging just 125 PP100. According to the 2015 J. D. Power and Associates survey of initial car quality, as shown in Exhibit 18.2, however, overall

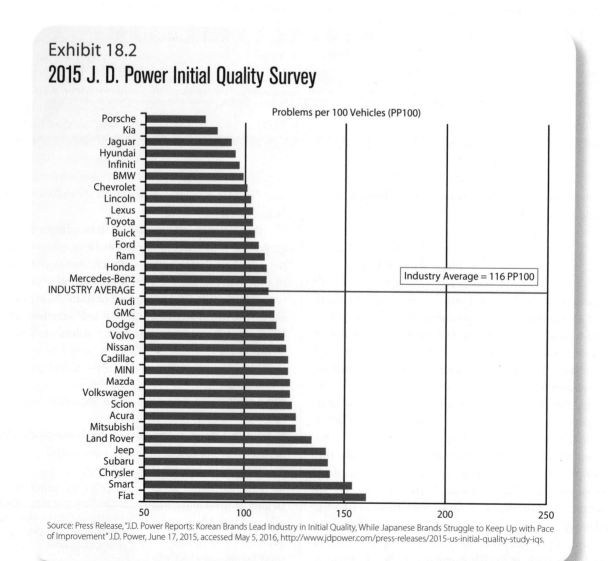

Exhibit 18.2
2015 J. D. Power Initial Quality Survey

Source: Press Release, "J.D. Power Reports: Korean Brands Lead Industry in Initial Quality, While Japanese Brands Struggle to Keep Up with Pace of Improvement," J.D. Power, June 17, 2015, accessed May 5, 2016, http://www.jdpower.com/press-releases/2015-us-initial-quality-study-iqs.

quality improved to 112 problems per 100 vehicles, and even the worst rated cars easily beat the scores of the Japanese cars of decades ago. Category leaders such as Porsche, Kia, Jaguar, Hyundai, Infiniti, and BMW came in with scores under 100. That means less than one problem per car![18]

The American Society for Quality gives two meanings for **quality**. It can mean a product or service free of deficiencies, such as the number of problems per 100 cars, or it can mean the characteristics of a product or service that satisfy customer needs.[19] Today's cars are of higher quality than those produced twenty years ago in both senses. Not only do they have fewer problems per 100 cars, they also have a number of additional standard features (power brakes and steering, Bluetooth connectivity, power windows and locks, keyless entry, cruise control).

*In this part of the chapter, you will learn about **18-2a quality-related characteristics for products and services, 18-2b ISO 9000 and 14000, 18-2c the Baldrige National Quality Award,** and **18-2d total quality management.***

18-2a Quality-Related Characteristics for Products and Services

Quality products usually possess three characteristics: reliability, serviceability, and durability.[20] A breakdown occurs when a product quits working or doesn't do what it was designed to do. The longer it takes for a product to break down, or the longer the time between breakdowns, the more reliable the product. Consequently, many companies define *product reliability* in terms of the average time between breakdowns. *Serviceability* refers to how easy or difficult it is to fix a product. The easier it is to maintain a working product or fix a broken product, the more serviceable that product is.

A product breakdown assumes that a product can be repaired. However, some products don't break down; they fail. *Product failure* means products can't be repaired. They can only be replaced. *Durability* is defined as the mean time to failure. A typical incandescent lightbulb, for example, has a mean time of failure of 1,000 hours. By contrast, LED bulbs, which use the same technology that lights up HDTVs

Video game manufacturer Nintendo has long been known for high-quality games and hardware. Knowing that its products are used largely by children and teens, Nintendo designs its hand held devices, controllers, and consoles to be incredibly durable.

Tinxi/Shutterstock.com

and cell phone screens, have a mean time to failure of between twenty and twenty-five years. Furthermore, the energy savings from one $10 LED bulb means it will pay for itself within two years and then provide twenty more years of lighting while saving $149 in energy costs over the longer lifetime of the bulb.[21]

While high-quality products are characterized by reliability, serviceability, and durability, services are different. There's no point in assessing the durability of a service because services don't last but are consumed the minute they're performed. For example, after a lawn service has mowed your lawn, the job is done until the mowers come back next week to do it again. Services also don't have serviceability. You can't maintain or fix a service. If a service wasn't performed correctly, all you can do is perform it again. Rather than serviceability and durability, the quality of service interactions often depends on how the service provider interacts with the customer. Was the service provider friendly, rude, or helpful? Five characteristics typically distinguish a quality service: reliability, tangibles, responsiveness, assurance, and empathy.[22]

Service reliability is the ability to consistently perform a service well. Studies clearly show that reliability matters more to customers than anything else when buying services. When you take your clothes to the dry cleaner, you don't want them returned with cracked buttons or wrinkles down the front. If your dry cleaner gives you perfectly clean and pressed clothes every time, it's providing a reliable service.

Also, although services themselves are not tangible (you can't see or touch them), services are provided in tangible places. Thus, *tangibles* refer to the appearance of the offices, equipment, and personnel involved with the delivery of a service. One of the best examples of the effect of tangibles on the perception of quality is the restroom. When you eat at a fancy restaurant, you expect clean, upscale restrooms. How different is your perception of a business, say a gas station, if it has clean restrooms rather than filthy ones?

Responsiveness is the promptness and willingness with which service providers give good service. *Assurance* is the

> **Quality** a product or service free of deficiencies, or the characteristics of a product or service that satisfy customer needs

confidence that service providers are knowledgeable, courteous, and trustworthy. *Empathy* is the extent to which service providers give individual attention and care to customers' concerns and problems.

When Apple first launched its retail stores, they were widely predicted to fail given all of the locations where consumers could already buy computer and electronics equipment. Those predictions were wrong, however, as more than 400 million people visit Apple stores every year. Apple's average annual revenue tops $50 million per store, and malls with Apple Stores average 10 percent more overall customer traffic than those without.[23] Why have Apple Stores achieved these extraordinary results? In addition to great products, the stores are great at delivering responsiveness, assurance, and empathy.

At Apple stores, responsiveness manifests itself in a sales philosophy of not selling. Instead, Apple store employees are trained to help customers solve problems. An Apple training manual says, "Your job is to understand all of your customers' needs—some of which they may not even realize they have." David Ambrose, a former Apple store employee, says, "You were never trying to close a sale. It was about finding solutions for a customer and finding their pain points."

Apple store employees demonstrate assurance through the high level of training that they receive. Apple "geniuses," who staff the Genius Bar in each Apple store, are trained at Apple headquarters and, according to Apple's website, "can take care of everything from troubleshooting your problems to actual repairs." Geniuses are regularly tested on their knowledge and problem-solving skills to maintain their certification. Other Apple store employees are highly trained, too, and are not allowed to help customers until they've spent two to four weeks shadowing experienced store employees.

The acronym APPLE instructs employees on how to empathetically engage with customers: "Approach customers with a personalized warm welcome," "Probe politely to understand all the customer's needs," "Present a solution for the customer to take home today," "Listen for and resolve any issues or concerns," and "End with a fond farewell and an invitation to return." And when customers are frustrated and become emotional, the advice is to "listen and limit your responses to simple reassurances that you are doing so. 'Uh-huh,' 'I understand,' etc."

ISO 9000 a series of five international standards, from ISO 9000 to ISO 9004, for achieving consistency in quality management and quality assurance in companies throughout the world

ISO 14000 a series of international standards for managing, monitoring, and minimizing an organization's harmful effects on the environment

In order to improve customer service at its retail stores, Apple recently redesigned the Genius Bar customer service desk to be more welcoming and rebranded it as the Genius Grove. Here, Genius Grove employees help customers solve problems at the company's new flagship store in San Francisco on May 21, 2016.

The results from Apple's retail approach speak for themselves, as Apple retail sales average $5,009 per square foot, higher than Tiffany & Co. jewelry stores ($3,043), Coach luxury retail ($1,532), or Deckers Outdoor ($1,246), a function-oriented footwear company.[24]

18-2b ISO 9000 and 14000

ISO, pronounced *eye-so*, comes from the Greek word *isos*, meaning "equal, similar, alike, or identical" and is also an acronym for the International Organization for Standardization, which helps set standards for 163 countries. The purpose of this agency is to develop and publish standards that facilitate the international exchange of goods and services.[25] **ISO 9000** is a series of five international standards, from ISO 9000 to ISO 9004, for achieving consistency in quality management and quality assurance in companies throughout the world. **ISO 14000** is a series of international standards for managing, monitoring, and minimizing an organization's harmful effects on the environment.[26] (For more on environmental quality and issues, see subsection 16-3e of Chapter 16 on sustainability.)

The ISO 9000 and 14000 standards publications, which are available from the American National Standards Institute (see the end of this section), are general and can be used for manufacturing any kind of product or delivering any kind of service. Importantly, the ISO 9000 standards don't describe how to make a better-quality car, computer, or widget. Instead, they describe how companies can extensively document (and thus standardize) the steps

Robotic Bellhop

The next time you order a spare toothbrush or towel from a hotel's front desk, you may find that the delivering bellhop is a little shorter—and more mechanical—than expected. The aloft Hotel in Cupertino, California, employed a three-foot-tall robot named Botlr to complement its human customer service staff. The automated bellhop might be an obvious addition to aloft's service staff, considering the hotel sits across the street from Apple's corporate campus. Both aloft Hotels and the robot's designer, Savioke, insist Botlr isn't going to replace human talent. Instead, the robot is intended to help deliver small items, such as razors, smartphone chargers, and snacks. Traveling up to four miles per hour, Botlr can reach any of the aloft's 150 rooms in less than three minutes. Botlr works for reviews—which can be input on a frontal display—rather than tips. Best of all, the friendly robot will perform a small dance for guests upon receiving a positive review.

Source: J. Markoff, "'Beep' Says the Bellhop," *New York Times*, August 12, 2014, B1.

they take to create and improve the quality of their products. Why should companies go to the trouble to achieve ISO 9000 certification? Because their customers increasingly want them to. In fact, studies show that customers clearly prefer to buy from companies that are ISO 9000 certified. Companies, in turn, believe that being ISO 9000 certified helps them keep customers who might otherwise switch to an ISO 9000–certified competitor.[27]

To become ISO certified, a process that can take months, a company must show that it is following its own procedures for improving production, updating design plans and specifications, keeping machinery in top condition, educating and training workers, and satisfactorily dealing with customer complaints.[28] An accredited third party oversees the ISO certification process, just as a certified public accountant verifies that a company's financial accounts are up to date and accurate. After a company has been certified as ISO 9000 compliant, the accredited third party will issue an ISO 9000 certificate that the company can use in its advertising and publications. This is the quality equivalent of the *Good Housekeeping* Seal of Approval. But continued ISO 9000 certification is not guaranteed. Accredited third parties typically conduct periodic audits to make sure the company is still following quality procedures. If it is not, its certification is suspended or canceled.

To get additional information on ISO 9000 guidelines and procedures, see the American National Standards Institute (www.webstore.ansi.org; the ISO 9000 and ISO 14000 standards publications are available here for about $550 and $599, respectively), the American Society for Quality (www.asq.org), and the IOS (www.iso.org).

18-2c Baldrige Performance Excellence Program

The Baldrige Performance Excellence Awards, which are administered by the U.S. government's National Institute for Standards and Technology, is given "to recognize U.S. companies for their achievements in quality and business performance and to raise awareness about the importance of quality and performance excellence as a competitive edge."[29] Each year, up to three awards may be given in the categories of manufacturing, education, health care, service, small business, and nonprofit.

The cost of applying for the Baldrige Award includes a $360 eligibility fee, an application fee of $18,000 for manufacturing firms and $9,600 for small businesses, and a site visitation fee of $50,000 to $60,000 for manufacturing firms and $30,000 to $35,000 for small businesses.[30] Why does it cost so much? Because you get a great deal of useful information about your business even if you don't win. At a minimum, each company that applies receives an extensive report based on 300 hours of assessment from at least eight business and quality experts. At $10 an hour for small businesses and about $20 an hour for manufacturing and service businesses, the *Journal for Quality and Participation* called the Baldrige feedback report "the best bargain in consulting in America."[31] Arnold Weimerskirch, former chair of the Baldrige Award panel of judges and former vice president of quality at Honeywell, says, "The application and review process for the Baldrige Award is the best, most cost-effective and comprehensive business health audit you can get."[32]

Businesses that apply for the Baldrige Award are judged on the seven criteria shown in Exhibit 18.3: leadership; strategic planning; customers; measurement, analysis, and knowledge management; workforce; operations; and results.[33] Results are typically the most important category. In other words, in addition to the six other criteria, companies must show that they have achieved superior quality when it comes to products and process, its customers, workforce, leadership, governance (social responsibility), and financial and market results. This emphasis on results is what differentiates the Baldrige Award from the ISO 9000 standards. The Baldrige Award indicates the extent to which companies have actually achieved world-class quality. The ISO 9000 standards simply indicate whether a company is following the management system it put into place to improve quality. In fact, ISO 9000 certification covers less than 10 percent of the requirements for the Baldrige Award.[34]

Why should companies go to the trouble of applying for the Baldrige Award? Baldrige program examiner Betsy Beam explains that it's not just about winning the award; it's about the opportunity to improve. "Ritz-Carlton has won the Baldrige Award twice," Beam says. "Even in … the years they won, there were 35 opportunities for improvement identified. This is a very difficult journey for any organization, but it's well worth it as changes [that are needed] become obvious."[35]

18-2d Total Quality Management

Total quality management (TQM) is an integrated, organization-wide strategy for improving product and service quality.[36] TQM is not a specific tool or technique. Rather, TQM is a philosophy or overall approach to management that is characterized by three principles: customer focus and satisfaction, continuous improvement, and teamwork.[37]

Although most economists, accountants, and financiers argue that companies exist to earn profits for shareholders, TQM suggests that customer focus and customer satisfaction should be a company's primary goals. **Customer focus** means that the entire organization, from top to bottom, should be focused on meeting customers' needs. The result of that customer focus should be **customer satisfaction**, which occurs when the company's products or services meet or exceed customers' expectations.

At companies where customer satisfaction is taken seriously, such as **Alaska Airlines**, paychecks depend on keeping customers satisfied. Everyone at Alaska Airlines, from the CEO to pilots to people who handle baggage, gets a monthly bonus, 70 percent of which is based on earnings, with the remaining 30 percent split among costs, safety, and customer satisfaction. J.D. Power and Associates rates Alaska Airlines as the highest in customer satisfaction among traditional U.S. airlines from 2008 to 2015. Likewise, according to FlightStats, Alaska

Total quality management (TQM) an integrated, principle-based, organization-wide strategy for improving product and service quality

Customer focus an organizational goal to concentrate on meeting customers' needs at all levels of the organization

Customer satisfaction an organizational goal to provide products or services that meet or exceed customers' expectations

Continuous improvement an organization's ongoing commitment to constantly assess and improve the processes and procedures used to create products and services

Exhibit 18.3
Criteria for the Baldrige National Quality Award

2015–2016 Categories/Items

1 Leadership
1.1 Senior Leadership
1.2 Governance and Social Responsibilities

2 Strategic Planning
2.1 Strategy Development
2.2 Strategy Implementation

3 Customers
3.1 Voice of the Customer
3.2 Customer Engagement

4 Measurement, Analysis, and Knowledge Management
4.1 Measurement, Analysis, and Improvement of Organizational Performance
4.2 Knowledge Management, Information, and Information Technology

5 Workforce
5.1 Workforce Environment
5.2 Workforce Engagement

6 Operations
6.1 Work Processes
6.2 Operational Effectiveness

7 Results
7.1 Product and Process Results
7.2 Customer-Focused Results
7.3 Workforce-Focused Results
7.4 Leadership and Governance Results
7.5 Financial and Market Results

Source: "2015–2016 Baldrige Performance Excellence Framework," *Baldrige Performance Excellence Program*, accessed May 11, 2015. http://www.nist.gov/baldrige/publications /upload/2015_2016_Category_and_Item_Commentary_BNP.pdf.

Airlines was the best North American airline in terms of on-time arrivals, a key issue in terms of customer satisfaction, from 2010 to 2015.[38]

Continuous improvement is an ongoing commitment to increase product and service quality by constantly assessing and improving the processes and procedures used to create those products and services. How do companies know whether they're achieving continuous improvement? Invented in 1885, Dr. Pepper is the oldest soft drink in the United States. While soft drink sales have dropped eleven years in a row, Dr. Pepper is increasing profits and lowering

Everyone at Alaska Airlines, from the CEO to the pilots to the people who handle baggage, gets a monthly bonus based, in part, on customer satisfaction.

costs through rapid continuous improvement (RCI). Chief Financial Officer Marty Ellen says, "RCI is about taking the existing baseline and improving it by finding the waste. We walk by waste every day. A team watched the process of fountain-syrup bags being assembled and packed into the cardboard boxes used to ship the bags. Somebody asked, 'Why does that box have the maroon Dr Pepper logo on it when the box isn't a consumer package?' You immediately call on the box supplier and ask, if we took that off, how much could we save a year? They said $60,000, and we said great. Put it in the bank."[39]

Besides higher customer satisfaction, continuous improvement is usually associated with a reduction in variation. **Variation** is a deviation in the form, condition, or appearance of a product from the quality standard for that product. The less a product varies from the quality standard, or the more consistently a company's products meet a quality standard, the higher the quality. Beyond safety, the quality standard for an airline is on-time departure and arrival. Variation from that standard means delays, and even worse, cancellations. On average, 1.7 percent of flights are cancelled each year, sometimes because of weather, but often because of poor management decisions. Delta Airlines, however, cancels only 0.3 percent of its flights because it stocks extra parts (engine starters) that often cause delays, maintains twenty extra planes that are brought into service when a jet encounters mechanical problems, and gets around flight hour limitations for flight crews (typically eight hours within twenty-four hours) by having planes make interim stops (meaning less than eight hours) with new crews taking over. With 15,000 daily flights, Delta cancels just forty-five flights per day. But if Delta had an average cancellation rate, it would cancel 255 flights per day, or more than five times as many.[40]

The third principle of TQM is teamwork. **Teamwork** means collaboration between managers and nonmanagers, across business functions, and between the company and its customers and suppliers. In short, quality improves when everyone in the company is given the incentive to work together and the responsibility and authority to make improvements and solve problems. ArcellorMittal's Gent, Belgium, plant needs only needs 1.3 man-hours to make a ton of steel, or one-third less than average. One of ArcellorMittal's practices is to "twin" its best plants, such as Gent, with its poor performing plants, such as its Burns Harbor, Indiana, plant. Then, it uses teamwork— and competition—to improve both. So it flew 100 Burns Harbor engineers and managers to Gent and told them, "Do as the Belgians do," whereas the Belgians were told to maintain their advantage. Founder Lakshmi Mittal says, "The process doesn't change: melt iron, cast, roll [steel]. But there are always incremental improvements you can make. We wanted Burns Harbor to be more like Gent."[41] Teamwork comes into play as teams from both plants meet regularly to discuss plant performance and share the steps they're taking to improve it. Following practices at Gent, Burns Harbor began using a different high pressure water nozzle to remove flakes (that is, imperfections) from super-heated steel. Not only did steel quality improve, the nozzle used less water and power, saving $1.4 million in annual energy costs. Likewise, Burns Harbor workers began trimming less steel off the sides of steel coils, saving 725 coils of steel per year, the equivalent of 17,000 cars. Today, thanks to twinning and teamwork, Burns Harbor now produces 900 tons of steel per employee each year, close to Gent's 950.

Customer focus and satisfaction, continuous improvement, and teamwork mutually reinforce each other to improve quality throughout a company. Customer-focused, continuous improvement is necessary to increase customer satisfaction. At the same time, continuous improvement depends on teamwork from different functional and hierarchical parts of the company.

18-3 SERVICE OPERATIONS

At the start of this chapter, you learned that operations management means managing the daily production of goods and services. Then you learned that to manage production, you must oversee the factors that affect

Variation a deviation in the form, condition, or appearance of a product from the quality standard for that product

Teamwork collaboration between managers and nonmanagers, across business functions, and between companies, customers, and suppliers

productivity and quality. In this half of the chapter, you will learn about managing operations in service and manufacturing businesses. The chapter ends with a discussion of inventory management, a key factor in a company's profitability.

Imagine that your trusty TiVo digital video recorder (DVR) breaks down as you try to record your favorite TV show. You've got two choices. You can run to Walmart and spend $250 to purchase a new DVR, or you can spend less (you hope) to have it fixed at a repair shop. Either way, you end up with the same thing, a working DVR. However, the first choice, getting a new DVR, involves buying a physical product (a good), while the second, dealing with a repair shop, involves buying a service.

Services differ from goods in several ways. First, goods are produced or made, but services are performed. In other words, services are almost always labor-intensive in that someone typically has to perform the service for you. A repair shop could give you the parts needed to repair your old DVR, but you're still going to have a broken DVR without the technician to perform the repairs. Second, goods are tangible, but services are intangible. You can touch and see that new DVR, but you can't touch or see the service provided by the technician who fixed your old DVR. All you can "see" is that the DVR works. Third, services are perishable and unstorable. If you don't use them when they're available, they're wasted. For example, if your DVR repair shop is backlogged on repair jobs, then you'll just have to wait until next week to get your DVR repaired. You can't store an unused service and use it when you like. By contrast, you can purchase a good, such as motor oil, and store it until you're ready to use it.

Because services are different from goods, managing a service operation is different from managing a manufacturing or production operation.

Exhibit 18.4
Service-Profit Chain

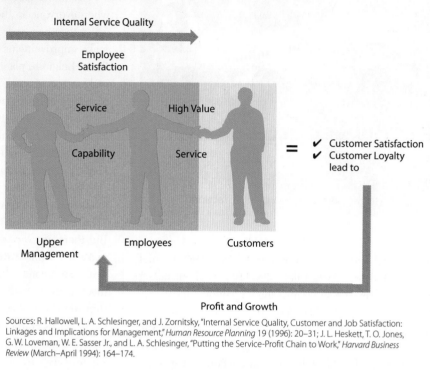

Internal Service Quality

Employee Satisfaction

Service

Capability

High Value

Service

= ✔ Customer Satisfaction
✔ Customer Loyalty
lead to

Upper Management   Employees   Customers

Profit and Growth

Sources: R. Hallowell, L. A. Schlesinger, and J. Zornitsky, "Internal Service Quality, Customer and Job Satisfaction: Linkages and Implications for Management," *Human Resource Planning* 19 (1996): 20–31; J. L. Heskett, T. O. Jones, G. W. Loveman, W. E. Sasser Jr., and L. A. Schlesinger, "Putting the Service-Profit Chain to Work," *Harvard Business Review* (March–April 1994): 164–174.

*Let's look at **18-3a the service-profit chain** and **18-3b service recovery and empowerment.***

18-3a The Service-Profit Chain

One of the key assumptions in the service business is that success depends on how well employees—that is, service providers—deliver their services to customers. But success actually begins with how well management treats service employees, as the service-profit chain, depicted in Exhibit 18.4, demonstrates.[42]

The key concept behind the service-profit chain is **internal service quality**, meaning the quality of treatment that employees receive from a company's internal service providers, such as management, payroll and benefits, human resources, and so forth. An employee at Adobe, a global software company, says, "The company has great perks for their employees that include company parties, outdoor activities, indoor pool and ping-pong tables, and a computer gaming room." Netflix gives new parents a year of *paid* maternity leave. Facebook gives parents $4,000 of "baby cash." Spotify pays for infertility treatments, such as egg freezing. Airbnb gives employees $2,000 a year to stay at any of its listings, anywhere in the world. Burton, which makes snowboarding equipment

Internal service quality the quality of treatment employees receive from management and other divisions of a company

and outdoor gear, pays for season-long ski passes, plus "snow days" to use them. Finally, if a Google employee dies, the surviving spouse or partner gets half of his or her annual salary for ten years.[43] These extraordinary benefits are clearly signs of companies with internal service quality orientations.

As depicted in Exhibit 18.4, good internal service leads to employee satisfaction and service capability. *Employee satisfaction* occurs when companies treat employees in a way that meets or exceeds their expectations. In other words, the better employees are treated, the more satisfied they are, and the more likely they are to give high-value service that satisfies customers. How employers treat employees is important because it affects service capability. *Service capability* is an employee's perception of his or her ability to serve customers well. When an organization serves its employees in ways that help them to do their jobs well, employees, in turn, are more likely to believe that they can and ought to provide high-value service to customers.

Finally, according to the service-profit chain shown in Exhibit 18.4, *high-value service* leads to *customer satisfaction* and *customer loyalty*, which, in turn, lead to *long-term profits and growth*.[44] What's the link between customer satisfaction and loyalty and profits? To start, the average business keeps only 70 to 90 percent of its existing customers each year. No big deal, you say? Just replace leaving customers with new customers. Well, there's one significant problem with that solution. It costs ten times as much to find a new customer as it does to keep an existing customer. Also, new customers typically buy only 20 percent as much as established customers. In fact, keeping existing customers is so cost-effective that most businesses could double their profits by simply keeping 5 percent more customers per year![45] How does this work? Imagine that keeping more of your customers turns some of those customers into customers for life. How much of a difference would that make to company profits? Consider that just one lifetime customer spends $8,000 on pizza and over $330,000 on luxury cars![46]

18-3b Service Recovery and Empowerment

When mistakes are made, when problems occur, and when customers become dissatisfied with the service they've received, service businesses must switch from the process of service delivery to the process of **service recovery**, or restoring customer satisfaction to strongly dissatisfied customers.[47] Or as business consultant Barry Moltz explains, "When a customer says they are dissatisfied, the company gets a chance to fix it and turn them into a more loyal customer."[48] Service recovery

sometimes requires service employees to not only fix whatever mistake was made but also perform heroic service acts that delight highly dissatisfied customers by far surpassing their expectations of fair treatment. Jason Friend, co-founder of 37signals.com, which provides web-based collaboration software such as Basecamp and Campfire, bought a custom bike via the Web from Mission Bicycle Company in San Francisco. When the bike arrived, he found a large gash on the side of the bike's frame. He described what happened when he contacted Mission: "They said sending the whole bike back would be overkill since the only thing that was damaged was the frame. Further, the bike was rideable—it was just a paint problem—so sending the bike back would mean I didn't have a bike for a week or so. They didn't feel good about that. So here's what they did: They called up a local shop (On The Route) and arranged to ship a new frame to them. Then one of their bike techs would drive down to my office and swap the frames and reassemble the bike for me while I waited. All of this at Mission's expense." He concluded by saying, "That's incredible customer service. I'm a happy customer for life. If you're in the market for a great custom bike, check out the good people and products at Mission Bicycle Company."[49]

Unfortunately, when mistakes occur, service employees often don't have the discretion to resolve customer complaints. Customers who want service employees to correct or make up for poor service are frequently told, "I'm not allowed to do that," "I'm just following company rules," or "I'm sorry, only managers are allowed to make changes of any kind." In other words, company rules prevent them from engaging in acts of service recovery meant to turn dissatisfied customers back into satisfied customers. The result is frustration for customers and service employees and lost customers for the company.

Now, however, many companies are empowering their service employees.[50] In Chapter 9, you learned that *empowering workers* means permanently passing decision-making authority and responsibility from managers to workers. With respect to service recovery, empowering workers means giving service employees the authority and responsibility to make decisions that immediately solve customer problems.[51] For example, when customers call into Nicor National, an energy utility, to ask for credits to their accounts, they are not transferred to a billing department. They are not put on hold while the operator looks for a supervisor or manager. Instead, the operator, who is empowered to make this decision, simply awards the credit without having to check with anyone.

Service recovery restoring customer satisfaction to strongly dissatisfied customers

According to Barbara Porter, the company's vice president of business development and customer service, empowering the call centers in this way is a quick, easy resolution. "They're professionals and we trust them to make the right decisions," says Porter.[52]

When things go wrong for customers, how well does service recovery work? Sixty-nine percent of customers see quick resolution of their problems as central to good customer service. Furthermore, about half of customers will stop buying from a company when bad customer service is not resolved. Either way, roughly nine out of ten customers will tell others about their poor customer service or how you fixed their problem.[53]

18-4 MANUFACTURING OPERATIONS

Ford makes cars, and Dell does computers. BP produces gasoline, whereas Sherwin-Williams makes paint. Boeing makes jet planes, but Budweiser makes beer. Maxtor makes hard drives, and Maytag makes appliances. The *manufacturing operations* of these companies all produce physical goods. But not all manufacturing operations, especially these, are the same.

*Let's learn how various manufacturing operations differ in terms of **18-4a the amount of processing that is done to produce and assemble a product** and **18-4b the flexibility to change the number, kind, and characteristics of products that are produced.***

18-4a Amount of Processing in Manufacturing Operations

Manufacturing operations can be classified according to the amount of processing or assembly that occurs after a customer order is received. The highest degree of processing occurs in **make-to-order operations**. A make-to-order operation does not start processing or assembling products until it receives a customer order. In fact, some make-to-order operations may not even order parts until a customer order is received. Not surprisingly, make-to-order operations produce or assemble highly specialized or customized products for customers. The John Deere 8R tractor, for example, comes with thousands of options that can be customized to the needs of a corn farmer in Kansas or a rice farmer in India. Buyers choose from six types of axles, five transmissions, thirteen types of rear hitches, and fifty-four different wheel and tire configurations. There are 354 option bundles for the basic tractor and 114 option bundles for attachments. Thanks to so many option combinations, Deere produced 7,800 unique 8R tractors in the past year. On average, each tractor configuration was built just 1.5 times, and over half of the configurations were built just once—truly a make-to-order operation.[54]

A moderate degree of processing occurs in **assemble-to-order operations**. A company using an assemble-to-order operation divides its manufacturing or assembly process into separate parts or modules. The company orders parts and assembles modules ahead of customer orders. Then, based on actual customer orders or on research forecasting what customers will want, those modules are combined to create semicustomized products. For example, when a customer orders a new car, GM may have already ordered the basic parts or modules it needs from suppliers. In other words, based on sales forecasts, GM may already have ordered enough tires, air-conditioning compressors, brake systems, and seats from suppliers to accommodate nearly all customer orders on a particular day. Special orders from customers and car dealers are then used to determine the final assembly checklist for particular cars as they move down the assembly line.

The lowest degree of processing occurs in **make-to-stock operations** (also called build-to-stock). Because the products are standardized, meaning each product is exactly the same as the next, a company using a make-to-stock operation starts ordering parts and assembling finished products before receiving customer orders. Customers then purchase these standardized products— such as Rubbermaid storage containers, microwave ovens, and vacuum cleaners—at retail stores or directly from the manufacturer. Because parts are ordered and products are assembled before customers order the products, make-to-stock operations are highly dependent on the accuracy of sales forecasts. If sales

Julius Kielaitis/Shutterstock.com

LEGO'S QUEST FOR MANUFACTURING FLEXIBILITY

Manufacturing flexibility allows companies to quickly respond to shifts in the marketplace. By changing the number and kind of products they produce, flexible companies can beat competitors to the punch and better meet customer demand. LEGO, which sells its plastic brick toys to 85 million children in 144 countries, is enhancing manufacturing flexibility to meet surging and difficult to predict global demand. In August 2015, LEGO informed retailers that it was overwhelmed with orders and would not accept new ones until January 2016. Hanne Gundorff, who owns the Den Flyvende Kuffert toy store in Copenhagen, Denmark, said, "It's a positive problem for LEGO, but it's a big problem for small retailers." COO Bali Padda admitted, "It's been a challenge for us to ensure we have the right mix of products in the right volumes at the end of the year." LEGO is improving manufacturing flexibility by spending $480 million to expand factories in Mexico, Europe, and Asia. Likewise, rather than painting the faces and uniforms on its LEGO minifigures in factories, it waits until the last possible moment, painting them at packaging plants. That way, if sales in one part of the world suddenly increase or decrease, or if one toy suddenly becomes more popular than another, LEGO can change what and where it ships to meet customer demand.

Source: S Chaudhiri, "Lego Struggles to Build Up Supplies in Time for Holidays, Wall Street Journal, November 11, 2015, accessed May 6, 2016, http://www.wsj.com /articles/lego-struggles-to-build-up-supplies-in-time-for-holidays-1447237802.

forecasts are incorrect, make-to-stock operations may end up building too many or too few products, or they may make products with the wrong features or without the features that customers want.

18-4b Flexibility of Manufacturing Operations

A second way to categorize manufacturing operations is by **manufacturing flexibility**, meaning the degree to which manufacturing operations can easily and quickly change the number, kind, and characteristics of products they produce. Flexibility allows companies to respond quickly to changes in the marketplace (that is, respond to competitors and customers) and to reduce the lead time between ordering and final delivery of products. There is often a trade-off between flexibility and cost, however, with the most flexible manufacturing operations frequently having higher costs per unit, and the least flexible operations having lower costs per unit. Some common manufacturing operations, arranged in order from the least flexible to the most flexible, are continuous-flow production, line-flow production, batch production, and job shops.

Most production processes generate finished products at a discrete rate. A product is completed, and then—perhaps a few seconds, minutes, or hours later—another is completed, and so on. For instance, if you stood at the end of an automobile assembly line, nothing much would seem to be happening for fifty-five seconds of every minute. In that last five seconds, however, a new car would be started and driven off the assembly line, ready for its new owner. By contrast, in **continuous-flow production**, products are produced continuously rather than at a discrete rate. Like a water hose that is never turned off and just keeps on flowing, production of the final product never stops. Until recently, drug companies used discrete production operations to make drugs, mixing ingredients in huge vats at separate factories. But to cut costs and increase quality, many are switching to continuous-flow production where the raw materials used to make drugs are "fed into a single, continuously running process."[55] Johnson & Johnson, GlaxoSmithKline, and Novartis are building continuous-flow factories, which should reduce operating costs by 30 percent and increase quality because corrections can be made immediately and not after large batches have been produced. Furthermore, continuous-flow pharmaceutical factories are much smaller at 4,000 square feet compared to the typical 100,000 square foot drug making facility, and thus, much less costly to build. Finally, production speeds and output can be dramatically higher. For instance, while it takes four to six weeks to make 100,000 tablets of Vertex's new cystic-fibrosis drug, its new continuous-flow factory will be able to make that many tablets in an hour![56] Despite their many advantages, continuous-flow production processes are the most standardized and least flexible manufacturing operations. In other words, a continuous-flow factory dedicated to making cystic-fibrosis drugs could not be used to make another kind of drug.

Manufacturing flexibility
the degree to which manufacturing operations can easily and quickly change the number, kind, and characteristics of products they produce

Continuous-flow production
a manufacturing operation that produces goods at a continuous, rather than a discrete, rate

Line-flow production processes are preestablished, occur in a serial or linear manner, and are dedicated to making one type of product. In this way, the ten different steps required to make product X can be completed in a separate manufacturing process (with separate machines, parts, treatments, locations, and workers) from the twelve different steps required to make product Y. Line-flow production processes are inflexible because they are typically dedicated to manufacturing one kind of product. For example, the production process for Tesla Motors' Model S car starts with large rolls of aluminum, which are flattened, cut, and then stamped into the shapes of the car's body panels (that is, roof, trunk, left front, and so on). Stamped panels are then moved to the body shop, where the car's underbody, sides, and front are joined via robotic welding machines. After the shell of the car is formed, it is primed, painted, and moved to the assembly line. There, 3,000 workers and 160 robots install the battery, motor, wiring, interior, seats, and the rest of the car's 30,000-plus parts. The assembly process for a car takes three to five days. In total, Tesla's Model S factory produces about 400 cars per week.[57]

The next most flexible manufacturing operation is **batch production**, which involves the manufacture of large batches of different products in standard lot sizes. A worker in a batch production operation will perform the same manufacturing process on 100 copies of product X, followed by 200 copies of product Y, and then 50 copies of product Z. Furthermore, these batches move through each manufacturing department or process in identical order. So, if the paint department follows chemical treatment, and chemical treatment is now processing a batch of 50 copies of product Z, then the paint department's next task will be to paint 50 copies of product Z. Batch production is finding increasing use among restaurant chains. To ensure consistency in the taste and quality of their products, many restaurant chains have central kitchens, or commissaries, that produce batches of food such as mashed potatoes, stuffing, macaroni and cheese, rice, quiche filling, and chili, in volumes ranging from 10 to 200 gallons. These batches are then delivered to the individual restaurant locations, which in turn serve the food to customers.

Next in terms of flexibility is the job shop. **Job shops** are typically small manufacturing operations that handle special manufacturing processes or jobs. In contrast to batch production, which handles large batches of different products, job shops typically handle very small batches, some as small as one product or process per batch. Basically, each job in a job shop is different, and after a job is done, the job shop moves on to a completely different job or manufacturing process for, most likely, a different customer. For example, **Grauch Enterprises** in Philipsburg, Pennsylvania, is a job shop that mills, turns, drills, paints, and finishes everything from plastics, such as nylon, polycarbonates, and laminates, to metals, such as brass, aluminum, stainless and alloy steels, titanium, and cast iron. It made 650 different parts for one customer alone and received one order to make 5,000 units out of 20,000 individual parts. When it comes to making different parts for different customers, owner Fred Grauch says, "There's very little we won't try."[58]

18-5 INVENTORY

Inventory is the amount and number of raw materials, parts, and finished products that a company has in its possession. Inventory issues have plagued fast-growing furniture retailer Restoration Hardware (RH) for years. Customers who purchased a $4,800 desk often waited up to seven months for delivery. The wait for a $1,260 lamp was often more than two months. RH argued that many of its expensive items are custom made, and thus take longer to manufacture and ship. However, analysts at BB&T Capital found that twenty-nine of fifty noncustomized RH items were out of stock, with an average delivery of sixty-three days. In an age of free two-day shipping, many customers were turned off by the company's frequent delays. With more than 90 percent of its items in stock, RH is making progress. But, it's inability to manage inventory contributed to a 22 percent decline in profits.[59]

ducu59us/Shutterstock.com

Pix11/Shutterstock.com

*In this section, you will learn about **18-5a the different types of inventory, 18-5b how to measure inventory levels, 18-5c the costs of maintaining an inventory,** and **18-5d the different systems for managing inventory.***

18-5a Types of Inventory

Exhibit 18.5 shows the four kinds of inventory a manufacturer stores: raw materials, component parts, work-in-process, and finished goods. The flow of inventory through a manufacturing plant begins when the purchasing department buys raw materials from vendors. **Raw material inventories** are the basic inputs in the manufacturing process. For example, to begin making a car, automobile manufacturers purchase raw materials such as steel, iron, aluminum, copper, rubber, and unprocessed plastic.

Next, raw materials are fabricated or processed into **component parts inventories**, meaning the basic parts used in manufacturing a product. For example, in an automobile plant, steel is fabricated or processed into a car's body panels, and steel and iron are melted and shaped into engine parts such as pistons or engine blocks. Some component parts are purchased from vendors rather than fabricated in-house.

The component parts are then assembled to make unfinished **work-in-process inventories**, which are also known as partially finished goods. This process is also called *initial assembly*. For example, steel body panels are welded to each other and to the frame of the car to make a "unibody," which comprises the unpainted interior frame and exterior structure of the car. Likewise, pistons, camshafts, and other engine parts are inserted into the engine block to create a working engine.

Next, all the work-in-process inventories are assembled to create **finished goods inventories**, which are the final outputs of the manufacturing process. This process is also called *final assembly*. For a car, the engine, wheels, brake system, suspension, interior, and electrical system are assembled into a car's painted unibody to make the working automobile, which is the factory's finished product. In the last step in the process, the finished goods are sent to field warehouses, distribution centers, or wholesalers, and then to retailers for final sale to customers.

18-5b Measuring Inventory

As you'll learn next, uncontrolled inventory can lead to huge costs for a manufacturing operation. Consequently, managers need good measures of inventory to prevent inventory costs from becoming too large. Three basic measures of inventory are average aggregate inventory, weeks of supply, and inventory turnover.

If you've ever worked in a retail store and had to take inventory, you probably weren't too excited about the process of counting every item in the store and storeroom. It's an extensive task that's a bit

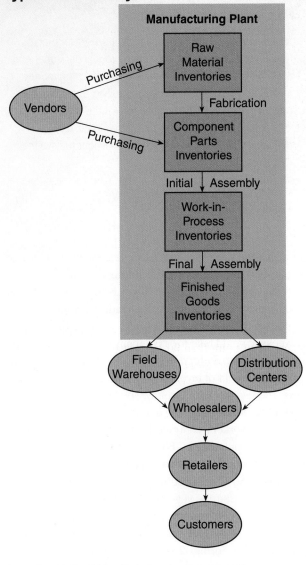

Exhibit 18.5
Types of Inventory

Source: From Markland/Vickery/Davis. *Operations Management*, 2E. Cengage Learning, Inc.

Raw material inventories
the basic inputs in a manufacturing process

Component parts inventories
the basic parts used in manufacturing that are fabricated from raw materials

Work-in-process inventories
partially finished goods consisting of assembled component parts

Finished goods inventories
the final outputs of manufacturing operations

Americans' Addiction to Free Shipping Gives Rise to Reverse Logistics

It is hard to beat e-commerce for convenience. Not sure what size shoe will fit best? Buy two (or three) different sizes from Zappos.com; when they arrive the next day, try them all on, and simply return the ones that are too tight or too loose. Or return them all if you don't like the color. Regardless, all you need to do is pack them up, affix the return shipping label, and let UPS do the rest.

Over the past twenty years, retailers have developed sophisticated logistics operations designed to deliver products ordered over the Internet to the doorsteps of U.S. consumers in a matter of days or, in some places, even hours. In today's retail environment, however, it is no longer the low price and fast delivery of the product that give a company a competitive edge; low-cost shipping and easy customer returns are also part of escalating competition among retailers. According to Gailen Vick of the Reverse Logistics Association, returns come at a hefty price, particularly for companies that don't have a solid program in place. "If they're doing nothing today, they're losing about 5 percent to 7 percent of their bottom line." That figure is much higher at electronics retailer Best Buy, which in 2014 lost 10 percent of its revenue, or $400 million, because of returned

Ethan Miller/Getty Images

products. Companies without an efficient system for processing customer returns and getting returned product back on the shelves risk customer dissatisfaction as well as losing money from stockouts or product obsolescence. Gary Shapiro of the Consumer Electronics Association says that the challenges of reverse logistics are here to stay for one simple reason, "Americans think they have a constitutional right to have their products returned."

Source: E. Phillips, "Do Customers Have a Constitutional Right to Return Stuff Ordered Online?" *Wall Street Journal*, May 1, 2015. http://www.wsj.com/articles/do-customers-have-a-constitutional-right-to-return-stuff-ordered-online-1430490642.

---

easier today because of bar codes that mark items and computers that can count and track them. Nonetheless, inventories still differ from day to day. An inventory count taken at the beginning of the month will likely be different from a count taken at the end of the month. Similarly, an inventory count taken on a Friday will differ from a count taken on a Monday. Because of such differences, companies often measure **average aggregate inventory**, which is the average overall inventory during a particular time period. Average aggregate inventory for a month can be determined by simply averaging the inventory counts at the end of each business day for that month. One way companies know whether they're carrying too much or too little inventory is to compare their average aggregate inventory with the industry average for aggregate inventory. For example, seventy-two days of inventory is the average for the automobile industry.

The automobile industry records inventory in terms of days of supply, but most other industries measure inventory in terms of *weeks of supply*, meaning the number of weeks it would take for a company to run out of its current supply of inventory. In general, there is an acceptable number of weeks of inventory for a particular kind of business. Too few weeks of inventory on hand, and a company risks a **stockout**—running out of inventory. When a West Coast dockworkers' contract dispute slowed shipments of U.S. frozen potatoes by 86 percent, 100 McDonald's in Venezuela found themselves unable to sell french fries to customers. So they substituted fried arepa flatbreads or fried yuca (a starchy vegetable used in South American cooking). Maria Guerreiro left a Caracas McDonald's unhappy because she had wanted to buy a Happy Meal (with fries) as a treat for her 2-year-old. Said Guerreiro, whose daughter won't eat yuca, "It's a total debacle."[60]

Another common inventory measure, **inventory turnover**, is the number of times per year that a company

Average aggregate inventory average overall inventory during a particular time period

Stockout the point when a company runs out of finished product

Inventory turnover the number of times per year that a company sells, or "turns over," its average inventory

> "IN THEORY, MAKE-TO-ORDER COMPANIES HAVE NO INVENTORY. IN FACT, THEY'VE GOT INVENTORY, BUT YOU HAVE TO MEASURE IT IN HOURS."

B Calkins/Shutterstock.com

sells, or "turns over," its average inventory. For example, if a company keeps an average of 100 finished widgets in inventory each month, and it sold 1,000 widgets this year, then it turned its inventory ten times this year.

In general, the higher the number of inventory turns, the better. In practice, a high turnover means that a company can continue its daily operations with just a small amount of inventory on hand. For example, let's take two companies, A and B, which have identical inventory levels (520,000 widget parts and raw materials) over the course of a year. If company A turns its inventories twenty-six times a year, it will completely replenish its inventory every two weeks and have an average inventory of 20,000 widget parts and raw materials. By contrast, if company B turns its inventories only two times a year, it will completely replenish its inventory every twenty-six weeks and have an average inventory of 260,000 widget parts and raw materials. So, by turning its inventory more often, company A has 92 percent less inventory on hand at any one time than company B.

The average number of inventory turns across all kinds of manufacturing plants is approximately eight per year, although the average can be higher or lower for different industries.[61] For example, whereas the average automobile or truck manufacturer turns its entire inventory 7.8 times per year, truck manufacturer Paccar turns its inventory 17.64 times a year—roughly once every three weeks.[62] Turning inventory more frequently than the industry average can cut an auto company's costs by several hundred million dollars per year. Finally, it should be pointed out that even make-to-order companies such as Dell turn their inventory. In theory, make-to-order companies have no inventory. In fact, they've got inventory, but you have to measure it in hours. For example, Dell turns its inventories 500 times a year, which means that on average it has 17 hours of inventory on hand in its factories.[63]

18-5c Costs of Maintaining an Inventory

Maintaining an inventory incurs four kinds of costs: ordering, setup, holding, and stockout. **Ordering cost** is not the cost of the inventory itself but the costs associated with ordering the inventory. It includes the costs of completing paperwork, manually entering data into a computer, making phone calls, getting competing bids, correcting mistakes, and simply determining when and how much new inventory should be reordered. For example, ordering costs are relatively high in the restaurant business because 80 percent of foodservice orders (in which restaurants reorder food supplies) are processed manually. A report, *Enabling Profitable Growth in the Food-Prepared-Away-From-Home Industries*, estimated that the food industry could save $14.3 billion if all restaurants converted to electronic data interchange (see Chapter 17), in which purchase and ordering information from one company's computer system is automatically relayed to another company's computer system. Toward that end, an industry-wide effort, Efficient Foodservice Response (EFR), is underway to improve efficiencies in the foodservice supply chain.[64]

Setup cost is the cost of changing or adjusting a machine so that it can produce a different kind of inventory.[65] For example, 3M uses the same production machinery to make several kinds of industrial tape, but it must adjust the machines whenever it switches from one kind of tape to another. There are two kinds of setup costs: downtime and lost efficiency. *Downtime* occurs whenever a machine is not being used to process inventory. If it takes five hours to switch a machine from processing one kind of inventory to another, then five hours of downtime have occurred. Downtime is costly because companies earn an economic return only when machines are actively turning raw materials into parts or parts into finished products. The second setup cost is *lost efficiency*. Recalibrating a machine to its optimal settings after a switchover typically takes some time. It may take several days of fine-tuning before a machine finally produces the number of high-quality parts that it is supposed to. So, each time a machine has to be

> **Ordering cost** the costs associated with ordering inventory, including the cost of data entry, phone calls, obtaining bids, correcting mistakes, and determining when and how much inventory to order

> **Setup cost** the costs of downtime and lost efficiency that occur when a machine is changed or adjusted to produce a different kind of inventory

changed to handle a different kind of inventory, setup costs (downtime and lost efficiency) rise.

Holding cost, also known as *carrying* or *storage cost*, is the cost of keeping inventory until it is used or sold. Holding cost includes the cost of storage facilities, insurance to protect inventory from damage or theft, inventory taxes, the cost of obsolescence (holding inventory that is no longer useful to the company), and the opportunity cost of spending money on inventory that could have been spent elsewhere in the company. For example, it's estimated that U.S. airlines have a total of $48 billion worth of airplane parts in stock at any one time for maintenance, repair, and overhauling of their planes. The holding cost for managing, storing, and purchasing these parts is nearly $12 billion—or roughly one-fourth of the cost of the parts themselves.[66]

Stockout cost is the cost incurred when a company runs out of a product. There are two basic kinds of stockout costs. First, the company incurs the transaction costs of overtime work, shipping, and the like in trying to quickly replace out-of-stock inventories with new inventories. The second and perhaps more damaging cost is the loss of customers' goodwill when a company cannot deliver the products it promised. Stockouts occur more often than you might think. In the United States, the supermarket industry's average out-of-stock rate (the percentage of items that are unavailable at a given time) is 7.9 percent, according to research firm Market6. Highly promoted items have, as would be expected, a higher average out-of-stock rate of 13.1 percent. How costly is it for stores to run out of stock? Market6 estimates that running out of stock on the twenty-five best-selling product categories reduces a grocery store's revenue by an average of $200,000 per year, per store.[67] In general, retailers can increase sales 4 percent if they never run out of stock.

18-5d Managing Inventory

Inventory management has two basic goals. The first is to avoid running out of stock and thus angering and dissatisfying customers. This goal seeks to increase inventory to a safe level that won't risk stockouts. The second is to efficiently reduce inventory levels and costs as much as possible without impairing daily operations. This goal seeks a minimum level of inventory. The following inventory management techniques—economic order quantity (EOQ), just-in-time inventory (JIT), and materials requirement planning (MRP)—are different ways of balancing these competing goals.

Economic order quantity (EOQ) is a system of formulas that helps determine how much and how often inventory should be ordered. EOQ takes into account the overall demand (D) for a product while trying to minimize ordering costs (O) and holding costs (H). The formula for EOQ is

$$EOQ = \sqrt{\frac{2DO}{H}}$$

For example, if a factory uses 40,000 gallons of paint a year (D), ordering costs (O) are $75 per order, and holding costs (H) are $4 per gallon, then the optimal quantity to order is 1,225 gallons:

$$EOQ = \sqrt{\frac{2(40,000)(75)}{4}} = 1,225$$

With 40,000 gallons of paint being used per year, the factory uses approximately 110 gallons per day:

$$\frac{4,000 \text{ gallons}}{365 \text{ days}} = 110$$

Consequently, the factory would order 1,225 new gallons of paint approximately every eleven days:

$$\frac{1,225 \text{ gallons}}{110 \text{ gallons per day}} = 11.1 \text{ days}$$

In general, EOQ formulas do a good job of letting managers know what size or amount of inventory they should reorder to minimize ordering and holding costs. Mark Lore, former founder of Diapers.com, explains how it used EOQ formulas to decide precisely how much inventory to keep on hand. He says, "We built software with computational algorithms to determine what the optimal number of boxes to have in the warehouse is and what the sizes of those boxes should be. Should we stock five different kinds of boxes to ship product in? Twenty kinds? Fifty kinds? And what size should those boxes be? Right now, it's twenty-three box sizes, given what we sell, in order to minimize the cost of dunnage (those little plastic air-filled bags or peanuts), the cost of corrugated boxes, and the cost of shipping. We rerun the simulation every quarter."[68] As this example makes clear, EOQ formulas and models can become much more complex

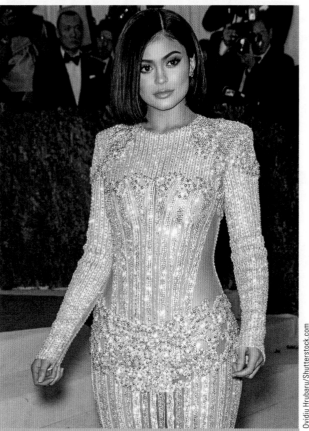

When reality television star Kylie Jenner launched a cosmetics company in November 2015, the company's three debut products sold out in less than five minutes. When Jenner announced that the initial line had been restocked and three new products had been added, the entire inventory sold out in less than 10 minutes, crashing the company's online storefront. Whether an intentional move to create demand or simply poor inventory management, Jenner's frequent stockouts likely frustrate potential customers.

just 6.1 days of inventory of iPhones, iPad Pro tablets, and Mac computers waiting to be shipped. That six days of inventory is equivalent to an inventory turn of 60.05 times a year (remember, more turns is better). Samsung Electronics was next with 17.7 turns a year, followed by Cisco Systems with 12.6 turns a year and Amazon with 8.7.[70]

To have just the right amount of inventory arrive at just the right time requires a tremendous amount of coordination between manufacturing operations and suppliers. One way to promote tight coordination under JIT is close proximity. Most parts suppliers for Toyota's JIT system at its Georgetown, Kentucky, plant are located within 200 miles of the plant. Furthermore, parts are picked up from suppliers and delivered to Toyota as often as sixteen times a day.[71] A second way to promote close coordination under JIT is to have a shared information system that allows a manufacturer and its suppliers to know the quantity and kinds of parts inventory the other has in stock. Generally, factories and suppliers facilitate information sharing by using the same part numbers and names. Ford's seat supplier accomplishes this by sticking a bar code on each seat, and Ford then uses the sticker to route the seat through its factory.

Manufacturing operations and their parts suppliers can also facilitate close coordination by using the system of kanban. **Kanban**, which is Japanese for "sign," is a simple ticket-based system that indicates when it is time to reorder inventory. Suppliers attach kanban cards to batches of parts. Then, when an assembly-line worker uses the first part out of a batch, the kanban card is removed. The cards are then collected, sorted, and quickly returned to the supplier, who begins resupplying the factory with parts that match the order information on the kanban cards. Glenn Uminger, former manager of production control and logistics at Toyota's Georgetown, Kentucky, plant, said they would place, "orders for new parts as the first part is used out of a box." Because prices and batch sizes are typically agreed to ahead of time, kanban tickets greatly reduce paperwork and ordering costs.[72]

A third method for managing inventory is **materials requirement planning (MRP)**. MRP is a production and inventory system that, from beginning to end, precisely determines the production schedule, production batch sizes, and inventories needed to complete final products. The three key parts of MRP systems are the

as adjustments are made for price changes, quantity discounts, setup costs, and many other factors.[69]

While EOQ formulas try to minimize holding and ordering costs, the just-in-time (JIT) approach to inventory management attempts to eliminate holding costs by reducing inventory levels to near zero. With a **just-in-time (JIT) inventory system**, component parts arrive from suppliers just as they are needed at each stage of production. By having parts arrive just in time, the manufacturer has little inventory on hand and thus avoids the costs associated with holding inventory. Thanks to its strict JIT inventory system, Apple carries the smallest amount of inventory among technology companies, averaging

Just-in-time (JIT) inventory system an inventory system in which component parts arrive from suppliers just as they are needed at each stage of production

Kanban a ticket-based JIT system that indicates when to reorder inventory

Materials requirement planning (MRP) a production and inventory system that determines the production schedule, production batch sizes, and inventory needed to complete final products

GM TAKES THE LONG VIEW ON EOQ

General Motors is taking the long view with its inventory management program and asking its vendors to sign long-term contracts, maybe even lasting decades, for automotive parts. Establishing an economic order quantity minimizes costs, but GM is hoping that locking in longer parts contracts—for higher quantities and higher overall dollar values—will produce a host of other benefits. Longer contracts signal greater commitment to vendors, which GM hopes will improve its vendor relationships. (Parts suppliers rank the quality of GM's relationships with its vendors as poor, behind Toyota, Nissan, and Honda.) In turn, GM hopes better relationships will produce greater collaboration with suppliers and give GM access to more advanced technologies earlier in their development cycle. GM Purchasing Chief Steve Keifer justified the change to longer contracts by saying, "We want [our suppliers] to double down on us." By 2017, GM expects

to sign billions of dollars in these contracts with its 30 biggest suppliers.

Source: J. Bennett, "GM Wants Long-Term Parts Contracts," *Wall Street Journal*, April 15, 2015, B3.

master production schedule, the bill of materials, and the inventory records. The *master production schedule* is a detailed schedule that indicates the quantity of each item to be produced, the planned delivery dates for those items, and the time by which each step of the production process must be completed to meet those delivery dates. Based on the quantity and kind of products set forth in the master production schedule, the *bill of materials* identifies all the necessary parts and inventory, the quantity or volume of inventory to be ordered, and the order in which the parts and inventory should be assembled. *Inventory records* indicate the kind, quantity, and location of inventory that is on hand or that has been ordered. When inventory records are combined with the bill of materials, the resulting report indicates what to buy, when to buy it, and what it will cost to order. Today, nearly all MRP systems are available in the form of powerful, flexible computer software.[73]

Which inventory management system should you use? Economic order quantity (EOQ) formulas are intended for use with **independent demand systems**, in which the level of one kind of inventory does not depend on another. For example, because inventory levels for automobile tires are unrelated to the inventory levels of women's dresses, Sears could use EOQ formulas to calculate separate optimal order quantities for

Independent demand system an inventory system in which the level of one kind of inventory does not depend on another

Dependent demand system an inventory system in which the level of inventory depends on the number of finished units to be produced

dresses and tires. By contrast, JIT and MRP are used with **dependent demand systems**, in which the level of inventory depends on the number of finished units to be produced. For example, if Yamaha makes 1,000 motorcycles a day, then it will need 1,000 seats, 1,000 gas tanks, and 2,000 wheels and tires each day. So, when optimal inventory levels depend on the number of products to be produced, use a JIT or MRP management system.

STUDY TOOLS 18

LOCATED IN TEXTBOOK
☐ Rip-out and review chapter review card

LOCATED AT WWW.CENGAGEBRAIN.COM
☐ Review key term flashcards and create your own from StudyBits

☐ Track your knowledge and understanding of key concepts, using the concept tracker

☐ Complete practice and graded quizzes to prepare for tests

☐ Complete interactive content within the exposition

☐ View chapter highlight box content at the beginning of each chapter

Endnotes

1

1. A. Steele, "Sears Revenue Drops 20%," *Wall Street Journal*, December 4, 2015, B3; A. Steele, "Sears Holdings Revenue Slides," *Wall Street Journal*, December 3, 2015, accessed April 15, 2016, http://www.wsj.com/articles/sears-narrows -loss-1449144707; S. Kapner and L. Beilfuss, "Sears Looks to Sell More Assets After Weak Holiday Quarter," *Wall Street Journal*, February 9, 2016, accessed April 15, 2016, http://www.wsj.com/articles /sears-holdings-warns-on-fourth-quarter-sales -moves-to-cut-more-costs-1455019066; S. Kapner, "Sears Bets Big on Technology, but at the Expense of Its Stores," *Wall Street Journal*, December 16, 2014, accessed April 24, 2015, http://www.wsj.com /articles/sears-bets-big-on-technology-but-at-the -expense-of-its-stores-1418787001; K. Gustafson, "Sears to Accelerate Closings, Shutter 235 Stores," *CNBC*, December 4, 2014, accessed April 24, 2015, http://www.cnbc.com/id/102237069.

2. "Industry Snapshot: Management, Scientific, and Technical Consulting Services (NAICS 5416)," *US Census Bureau*, accessed April 24, 2015, http://thedataweb.rm.census.gov/TheDataWeb _HotReport2/econsnapshot/2012/snapshot .hrml?NAICS=5416.

3. "What Do Managers Do?" Adapted from "The Wall Street Journal Guide to Management" by Alan Murray. *Wall Street Journal*, accessed June 3, 2014, http://guides.wsj.com/management/developing-a -leadership-style/what-do-managers-do/.

4. D. Michaels and R. Wall, "Airbus-Boeing Speed Race Increasingly Takes Place on the Ground," *Wall Street Journal*, June 12, 2015, A1.

5. N. Safo, "'Greedy,' 'Heartless,'…but Also 'On-time,'" *Marketplace*, February 10, 2016, accessed April 15, 2016, http://www.marketplace .org/2016/02/09/world/greedy-heartless-also-time.

6. N. Safo, "'Greedy,' 'Heartless,'…but Also 'On-time,'" *Marketplace*, February 10, 2016, accessed April 15, 2016, http://www.marketplace .org/2016/02/09/world/greedy-heartless-also-time; B. Hill, "Time Warner Cable Combats Dreadful Customer Service with One-Hour Service Windows and Self-Deprecating Humor," *HotHardware*, October 5, 2015, accessed April 15, 2016, http://hothardware. com/news/time-warner-cable-combats -dreadful-customer-service-with-one-hour-service -windows-and-self-deprecating-humor; "Time Warner Cable Responds to Its Customers During Customer Service Week: We Hear You Loud and Clear. We're Changing," *BusinessWire*, October 5, 2015, accessed April 15, 2016, http://www.businesswire .com/news/home/20151005005324/en/Time-Warner -Cable-Responds-Customers-Customer-Service; A. Russell, "Read TWC's Open Letter to Customers (Hint: We Get Your Frustration)," *Untangled*, October 5, 2015, accessed April 15, 2016, http://www .twcableuntangled.com/2015/10/read-twcs-open -letter-to-customers-hint-we-get-your-frustration/.

7. "Time Warner Cable Responds to Its Customers During Customer Service Week: We Hear You Loud and Clear. We're Changing," *BusinessWire*, October 5, 2015, http://www.businesswire.com/news /home/20151005005324/en/Time-Warner-Cable -Responds-Customers-Customer-Service, accessed April 15, 2016.

8. D. A. Wren, A. G. Bedeian, and J. D. Breeze, "The Foundations of Henri Fayol's Administrative Theory," *Management Decision* 40 (2002): 906–918.

9. A. Bryant, "Google's Quest to Build a Better Boss," *New York Times*, March 12, 2011, accessed February 23, 2012, http://www.nytimes.com /2011/03/13/business/13hire.html?_r=0; B. Hall, "Google's Project Oxygen Pumps Fresh Air into Management," *The Street*, February 11, 2014, accessed June 11, 2014, http://www.thestreet.com /story/12328981/1/googles-project-oxygen-pumps -fresh-air-into-management.html.

10. H. Fayol, *General and Industrial Management* (London: Pittman & Sons, 1949).

11. R. Stagner, "Corporate Decision Making," *Journal of Applied Psychology* 53 (1969): 1–13.

12. D. W. Bray, R. J. Campbell, and D. L. Grant, *Formative Years in Business: A Long-Term AT&T Study of Managerial Lives* (New York: Wiley, 1993).

13. H. Tabuchi, "Backpack Makers Rethink Student Staple," *New York Times*, September 2, 2015, B1.

14. Ibid.

15. "Our Story," *Walmart*, accessed March 14, 2016, http://corporate.walmart.com/; J. Fox, "Retailers Discover That Labor Isn't Just a Cost," *Bloomberg View*, November 16, 2015, accessed April 16, 2016, http:// www.bloombergview.com/articles/2015-11-16 /retailers-discover-that-labor-isn-t-just-a-cost; L. DePillis, "Walmart Is Rolling Out Big Changes to Worker Schedules This Year," *Washington Post*, February 17, 2016, accessed April 16, 2016, https:// www.washingtonpost.com/news/wonk/wp/2016/02/17 /walmart-is-rolling-out-big-changes-to-worker -schedules-this-year/.

16. E. Martinson, "Corner Office: Eileen Martinson of Sparta Systems on Clarity of Leadership," interview by A. Bryant, *New York Times*, January 9, 2014, accessed June 3, 2014, http://www.nytimes.com /2014/01/10/business/eileen-martinson-of-sparta -systems-on-clarity-of-leadership.html.

17. Ibid.

18. A. Narayan, "An App Gives India's Hotels a Closer Look," *Bloomberg Businessweek*, October 19–25, 2015, 39–40; "How We Do Hotel Audits," Official OYO Blog, April 12, 2016, accessed April 16, 2016, https://www.oyorooms.com/officialoyoblog /2016/04/12/how-we-do-hotel-audits.

19. Ibid.

20. H. S. Jonas III, R. E. Fry, and S. Srivastva, "The Office of the CEO: Understanding the Executive Experience," *Academy of Management Executive* 4 (1990): 36–47.

21. J. Chesto, "Moving to Boston Is Così's Recipe for Success," *Boston Globe*, March 18, 2015, accessed April 24, 2015, http://www.bostonglobe.com /business/2015/03/17/cosi-recipe-for-success-the -boston-way/3dFx7EaJKv10uGKW4FTIWJ/story .html; J. Lublin, "Rookie CEOs Face a Steep Learning Curve," *Wall Street Journal*, June 24, 2014, accessed April 24, 2015, http://www.wsj.com/articles /rookie-ceos-face-a-steep-learning-curve-1403656894.

22. Jonas et al., "The Office of the CEO."

23. Dina Bass, "Beyond Windows," *Bloomberg Businessweek*, February 2–8, 2015, pp. 30–31.

24. Jonas et al., "The Office of the CEO."

25. M. Porter, J. Lorsch, and N. Nohria, "Seven Surprises for New CEOs," *Harvard Business Review* (October 2004): 62.

26. P. Martens, "Corner Office: Phil Martens of Novelis, on Consistent Leadership," interview by A. Bryant, *New York Times*, October 26, 2013, accessed June 3, 2014, http://www.nytimes .com/2013/10/27/business/phil-martens-of-novelis -on-consistent-leadership.html.

27. Novelis, "Sustainability Through Disruptive Innovation: Sustainability Report 2013," 2013, p. 44, accessed June 3, 2014, http://www.novelis.com /Documents/Sustainability/2013_Novelis_Sustainability _Report_En.pdf.

28. Q. Huy, "In Praise of Middle Managers," *Harvard Business Review*. September 2001, 72–79.

29. "Using Their Own Words, Middle Managers Describe the Nature of Their Jobs," *Wall Street Journal*, August 6, 2013, accessed June 12, 2014, www.wsj .com/articles/SB10001424127887323420604578652 110485397972.

30. R. Feintzeig, "Radical New Idea: Middle Managers," *Wall Street Journal*, August 19, 2015, B5.

31. "Using Their Own Words, Middle Managers Describe the Nature of Their Jobs."

32. R. Silverman, "Some Tech Firms Ask: Who Needs Managers?" *Wall Street Journal*, August 6, 2013, accessed June 12, 2014, http://www.wsj.com /articles/SB10001424127887323420604578652051466314748.

33. R. Feintzeig, "Radical New Idea: Middle Managers," *Wall Street Journal*, August 19, 2015, B5.

34. S. Tully, "What Team Leaders Need to Know," *Fortune*, February 20, 1995, 93.

35. B. Francella, "In a Day's Work," *Convenience Store News*, September 25, 2001, 7.

36. L. Liu and A. McMurray, "Frontline Leaders: The Entry Point for Leadership Development in the Manufacturing Industry," *Journal of European Industrial Training* 28, no. 2–4 (2004): 339–352.

37. A. Nowogrodski, "Corner Office: Avinoam Nowogrodski of Clarizen, on the Rewards of Listening," interview by A. Bryant, *New York Times*, March 13, 2014, accessed June 3, 2014, http://www.nytimes .com/2014/03/14/business/avinoam-nowogrodski-of -clarizen-on-the-rewards-of-listening.html.

38. K. Hultman, "The 10 Commandments of Team Leadership," *Training & Development*, February 1, 1998, 12–13.

39. A. Nowogrodski, "Corner Office: Avinoam Nowogrodski of Clarizen, on the Rewards of Listening ".

40. Ibid.

41. R. Silverman, "Who's the Boss? There Isn't One," *Wall Street Journal*, June 20, 2012, B1.

42. N. Steckler and N. Fondas, "Building Team Leader Effectiveness: A Diagnostic Tool," *Organizational Dynamics*, Winter 1995, 20–34.

43. H. Mintzberg, *The Nature of Managerial Work* (New York: Harper & Row, 1973).

44. K. Bowers, "Corner Office: Kim Bowers of CST Brands, on Managing Up vs. Managing Down," interview by A. Bryant, *New York Times*, April 5, 2014, accessed June 3, 2014, http://www.nytimes .com/2014/04/06/business/kim-bowers-of-cst-brands -on-managing-up-vs-managing-down.html.

45. C. P. Hales, "What Do Managers Do? A Critical Review of the Evidence," *Journal of Management Studies* 23, no. 1 (1986): 88–115.

46. B. Kilkha, "FENDI Celebrates the Opening of the New York Flagship Store," *Forbes*, February 14, 2015, accessed April 24, 2015, http:// www.forbes.com/sites/bettinazilkha/2015/02/14 /fendi-celebrates-the-opening-of-the-new-york -flagship-store/.

47. A. Preuschat, "Huawei Enterprise Business Grew More in Europe Than Home Last Year," *Wall Street Journal*, March 10, 2014, accessed June 3, 2014, http://www.wsj.com/articles/SB1000142405270 23047045045794313022826506692.

48. M. Murphy and E. Chasan, "A Boardroom with a View—Outside Directorships Can Offer CFOs Fresh Perspective, Add to Financial Toolbox," *Wall Street Journal*, May 7, 2013, B7.

49. J. Light, "Study Points to Benefits of Outside Board Seats," *Wall Street Journal*, May 23, 2011, B6.

50. "News by Industry," *Business Wire*, accessed April 16, 2016, http://www.businesswire.com/portal /site/home/news/industries/.

51. "Media Monitoring," *CyberAlert*, accessed April 16, 2016, http://www.cyberalert.com.

52. "What Is FNS News Clips Online?" *FNS NewsClips*, accessed April 16, 2016, http://www .fednews.com/.

53. A. Bryant, "Transparency Is Much More Than a Buzzword," *New York Times*, March 2, 2013, accessed May 14, 2013, http://www.nytimes .com/2013/03/03/business/ryan-smith-of-qualtrics -on-building-a-transparent-culture.html.

54. A. Gasparro, "Kraft Heinz Yet to See Lift from Cost Cuts," *Wall Street Journal*, November 6, 2015, B3.

55. B. Stone, "Half Off Whole Foods: Following a Very Bad Year, The Elite Grocer Says It's Ready to Compete Like a Big-Box Chain," *Bloomberg Businessweek*, February 2–8, 2015, pp. 45–49.

56. M. Townsend, "Why Target Is Raking Up Its Maple Leaves," *Bloomberg Businessweek*, January 26–February 1, 2015, pp. 24–25; I. Austen and H. Tabuchi, "Target's Red Ink Runs Out in Canada," *The New York Times*, January 15, 2015, accessed April 24, 2015, http://www.nytimes.com/2015/01/16/business /target-to-close-stores-in-canada.html.

57. M. Ramsey, "Fuel Goal Tests Ford's Mettle," *Wall Street Journal*, January 13, 2014, B1.

58. G. Farley, "Colorful Airline CEO Negotiates Multi-Billion Dollar Deal," *KING 5 News*, September 9, 2014, accessed April 24, 2015, http://www .king5.com/story/tech/science/aerospace/2014/09/09 /michael-oleary-cuts-deal-with-boeing/15364151/; A. Scott, "Ryanair Buys 100 Boeing 737 MAX Jets, Sees Fare Price War," *Reuters*, September 8, 2014, accessed April 24, 2015, http://uk.reuters.com /article/2014/09/08/uk-boeing-ryanairhldgs -idUKKBN0H31E220140908.

59. L. A. Hill, *Becoming a Manager: Mastery of a New Identity* (Boston: Harvard Business School Press, 1992).

60. R. L. Katz, "Skills of an Effective Administrator," *Harvard Business Review*, September–October 1974, 90–102.

61. C. A. Bartlett and S. Ghoshal, "Changing the Role of Top Management: Beyond Systems to People," *Harvard Business Review*, May–June 1995, 132–142.

62. F. L. Schmidt and J. E. Hunter, "Development of a Causal Model of Process Determining Job Performance," *Current Directions in Psychological Science* 1 (1992): 89–92.

63. J. B. Miner, "Sentence Completion Measures in Personnel Research: The Development and Validation of the Miner Sentence Completion Scales," in *Personality Assessment in Organizations*, ed. H. J. Bernardin and D. A. Bownas (New York: Praeger, 1986), 145–176.

64. M. W. McCall, Jr., and M. M. Lombardo, "What Makes a Top Executive?" *Psychology Today*, February 1983, 26–31; E. van Velsor and J. Brittain, "Why Executives Derail: Perspectives Across Time and Cultures," *Academy of Management Executive*, November 1995, 62–72.

65. Ibid.

66. J. Lublin, "How to Delegate the Right Way," *Wall Street Journal*, March 13, 2014, accessed June 3, 2014, http://www.wsj.com/articles/SB10001424052 70230418510457943564080334 5898.

67. A. K. Naj, "Corporate Therapy: The Latest Addition to Executive Suite Is Psychologist's Couch," *Wall Street Journal*, August 29, 1994, A1.

68. Ibid.

69. P. Wallington, "Leadership: How to Spot a Toxic Boss," *CIO*, April 26, 2006, accessed June 13, 2014,

http://www.cio.com/article/20139/Leadership_How _to_Spot_a_Toxic_Boss; P. Wallington, "Management2 Toxic!" *Financial Mail*, July 28, 2006, 48.

70. R. Ashkenas, "First-Time Managers, Don't Do Your Team's Work for Them," *Harvard Business Review*, September 21, 2015, accessed April 16, 2016, https://hbr.org/2015/09/first-time-managers-dont-do -your-teams-work-for-them.

71. J. Sandberg, "Overcontrolling Bosses Aren't Just Annoying; They're Also Inefficient," *Wall Street Journal*, March 30, 2005, B1.

72. P. Drexler, "Managing Up: When Your Boss Is an Obsessive Micromanager," *Forbes*, June 13, 2013, accessed June 3, 2014, http://www.forbes.com/sites /peggydrexler/2013/06/13/managing-up-when-your -boss-is-an-obsessive-micromanager/.

73. Hill, *Becoming a Manager*, p. 17.

74. Ibid., p. 55.

75. Ibid., p. 57.

76. Ibid., p. 64.

77. Ibid., p. 67.

78. Ibid., p. 161.

79. J. Pfeffer, *The Human Equation: Building Profits by Putting People First* (Boston: Harvard Business School Press, 1996); *Competitive Advantage Through People: Unleashing the Power of the Work Force* (Boston: Harvard Business School Press, 1994).

80. M. A. Huselid, "The Impact of Human Resource Management Practices on Turnover, Productivity, and Corporate Financial Performance," *Academy of Management Journal* 38 (1995): 635–672.

81. D. McDonald and A. Smith, "A Proven Connection: Performance Management and Business Results," *Compensation & Benefits Review* 27, no. 6 (January 1, 1995): 59.

82. J. Combs, Y. Liu, A. Hall, and D. Ketchen, "How Much Do High-Performance Work Practices Matter? A Meta-Analyis of Their Effects on Organizational Performance," *Personnel Psychology* 59 (2006): 501–528.

83. I. Fulmer, B. Gerhart, and K. Scott, "Are the 100 Best Better? An Empirical Investigation of the Relationship between Being a 'Great Place to Work' and Firm Performance," *Personnel Psychology*, Winter 2003, 965–993.

84. B. Schneider and D. E. Bowen, "Employee and Customer Perceptions of Service in Banks: Replication and Extension," *Journal of Applied Psychology* 70 (1985): 423–433; B. Schneider, J. J. Parkington, and V. M. Buxton, "Employee and Customer Perceptions of Service in Banks," *Administrative Science Quarterly* 25 (1980): 252–267.

85. "How Investing in Intangibles—Like Employee Satisfaction—Translates into Financial Returns," *Knowledge@Wharton*, January 9, 2008, accessed January 24, 2010, http://knowledge.wharton.upenn .edu/article.cfm ?articleid=1873.

2

1. C. S. George, Jr., *The History of Management Thought* (Englewood Cliffs, NJ: Prentice-Hall, 1972).

2. D. Schmandt-Besserat, *How Writing Came About* (Austin: University of Texas Press, 1997).

3. A. Erman, *Life in Ancient Egypt* (London: Macmillan & Co., 1984).

4. J. Burke, *The Day the Universe Changed* (Boston: Little, Brown, 1985).

5. S. A. Epstein, *Wage Labor and Guilds in Medieval Europe* (Chapel Hill: University of North Carolina Press, 1991).

6. R. Braun, *Industrialization and Everyday Life*, trans. S. Hanbury-Tenison (Cambridge: Cambridge University Press, 1990).

7. J. B. White, "The Line Starts Here: Mass-Production Techniques Changed the Way People Work and Live Throughout the World," *Wall Street Journal*, January 11, 1999, R25.

8. R. B. Reich, *The Next American Frontier* (New York: Time Books, 1983).

9. J. Mickelwait and A. Wooldridge, *The Company: A Short History of a Revolutionary Idea* (New York: Modern Library, 2003).

10. H. Kendall, "Unsystematized, Systematized, and Scientific Management," in *Scientific Management: A Collection of the More Significant Articles Describing the Taylor System of Management*, ed. C. Thompson (Easton, PA: Hive Publishing, 1972), 103–131.

11. United States Congress, House, Special Committee, *Hearings to Investigate the Taylor and Other Systems of Shop Management*, vol. 3 (Washington, DC: Government Printing Office, 1912).

12. Ibid.

13. Ibid.

14. A. Derickson, "Physiological Science and Scientific Management in the Progressive Era: Frederic S. Lee and the Committee on Industrial Fatigue," *Business History Review* 68 (1994): 483–514.

15. U.S. Congress, House, Special Committee, 1912.

16. F. W. Taylor, *The Principles of Scientific Management* (New York: Harper, 1911).

17. C. D. Wrege and R. M. Hodgetts, "Frederick W. Taylor's 1899 Pig Iron Observations: Examining Fact, Fiction, and Lessons for the New Millennium," *Academy of Management Journal* 43 (December 2000): 1283; J. R. Hough and M. A. White, "Using Stories to Create Change: The Object Lesson of Frederick Taylor's 'Pig-tale,'" *Journal of Management* 27, no. 5 (October 2001): 585–601; E. A. Locke, "The Ideas of Frederick W. Taylor: An Evaluation," *Academy of Management Review* 7, no. 1 (1982) 14–24.

18. Locke, "The Ideas of Frederick W. Taylor."

19. George, *The History of Management Thought.*

20. F. Gilbreth and L. Gilbreth, "Applied Motion Study," in *The Writings of the Gilbreths*, ed. W. R. Spriegel and C. E. Myers (1917; reprint, Homewood, IL: Irwin, 1953), 207–274.

21. Ibid.

22. D. Ferguson, "Don't Call It 'Time and Motion Study,'" *IIE Solutions* 29, no. 5 (1997): 22–23.

23. H. Gantt, "A Graphical Daily Balance in Manufacture," *Transactions of the American Society of Mechanical Engineers* 24 (1903): 1325.

24. P. Peterson, "Training and Development: The View of Henry L. Gantt (1861–1919)," *SAM Advanced Management Journal*, Winter 1987, 20–23.

25. H. Gantt, "Industrial Efficiency," *National Civic Federation Report of the 11th Annual Meeting*, New York, January 12, 1991, 103.

26. Ibid.

27. M. Weber, *The Theory of Social and Economic Organization*, trans. A. Henderson and T. Parsons (New York: Free Press, 1947).

28. M. Weber, *The Protestant Ethic and the Spirit of Capitalism* (New York: Scribner's, 1958).

29. George, *The History of Management Thought.*

30. D. A. Wren, "Henri Fayol as Strategist: A Nineteenth Century Corporate Turnaround," *Management Decision* 39, no. 6 (2001): 475–487; D. Reid, "Fayol: From Experience to Theory," *Journal of Management History* (Archive) 1, no. 3 (1995): 21–36.

31. Ibid.

32. Ibid.

33. Ibid.

34. F. Blancpain, "Les cahiers inédits d'Henri Fayol," trans. D. Wren, *Extrait du bulletin de l'institut international d'administration publique* 28–29 (1974): 1–48.

35. D. A. Wren, A. G. Bedeian, and J. D. Breeze, "The Foundations of Henri Fayol's Administrative Theory," *Management Decision* 40 (2002): 906–918.

36. H. Fayol, *General and Industrial Management* (London: Pittman & Sons, 1949); Wren, Bedeian, and Breeze, "Foundations."

37. P. Graham, ed., *Mary Parker Follett—Prophet of Management: A Celebration of Writings from the 1920s* (Boston: Harvard Business School Press, 1995).

38. D. Linden, "The Mother of Them All," *Forbes,* January 16, 1995, 75.

39. J. H. Smith, "The Enduring Legacy of Elton Mayo," *Human Relations* 51, no. 3 (1998): 221–249.

40. E. Mayo, *The Human Problems of an Industrial Civilization* (New York: Macmillan, 1933).

41. Ibid.

42. "Hawthorne Revisited: The Legend and the Legacy," *Organizational Dynamics,* Winter 1975, 66–80.

43. E. Mayo, *The Social Problems of an Industrial Civilization* (Boston: Harvard Graduate School of Business Administration, 1945).

44. "Hawthorne Revisited: The Legend and the Legacy."

45. Mayo, *The Social Problems of an Industrial Civilization,* 45.

46. George, *The History of Management Thought.*

47. C. I. Barnard, *The Functions of the Executive* (Cambridge, MA: Harvard University Press, 1938), 4.

48. C. I. Barnard, *The Functions of the Executive: 30th Anniversary Edition* (Cambridge, MA: Harvard University Press, 1968), 5.

49. J. Fuller and A. Mansour, "Operations Management and Operations Research: A Historical and Relational Perspective," *Management Decision* 41 (2003): 422–426.

50. D. Wren and R. Greenwood, "Business Leaders: A Historical Sketch of Eli Whitney," *Journal of Leadership & Organizational Studies* 6 (1999): 131.

51. "Monge, Gaspard, comte de Péluse," *Britannica Online,* accessed January 9, 2005, http://www .britannica.com/biography/Gaspard-Monge-comte -de-Peluse.

52. M. Schwartz and A. Fish, "Just-in-Time Inventories in Old Detroit," *Business History* 40, no. 3 (July 1998): 48.

53. D. Ashmos and G. Huber, "The Systems Paradigm in Organization Theory: Correcting the Record and Suggesting the Future," *Academy of Management Review* 12 (1987): 607–621; F. Kast and J. Rosenzweig, "General Systems Theory: Applications for Organizations and Management," *Academy of Management Journal* 15 (1972): 447–465; D. Katz and R. Kahn, *The Social Psychology of Organizations* (New York: Wiley, 1966).

54. R. Mockler, "The Systems Approach to Business Organization and Decision Making," *California Management Review* 11, no. 2 (1968): 53–58.

55. F. Luthans and T. Stewart, "A General Contingency Theory of Management," *Academy of Management Review* 2, no. 2 (1977): 181–195.

3

1. L. Fleisher, "Thousands of Taxi Drivers Protest Uber Across Europe," *Wall Street Journal,* June 12, 2014, B2; C. Matlack, "Europe's Cabbies, Fed Up with Uber, Plan a Day of Traffic Chaos," *Bloomberg Businessweek,* June 10, 2014, accessed June 15, 2014, http://www.businessweek.com/articles/2014-06-10 /europes-cabbies-fed-up-with-uber-plan-a-day-of -traffic-chaos.

2. D. Herbert, "Rest in Peace for Less with Caskets Made in China," *Bloomberg Businessweek,* February 20, 2015, accessed April 24, 2015, http://www .bloomberg.com/news/features/2015-02-20/casket -industry-fends-off-chinese-imports-favored-by -vegas-entrepreneur; P. Cain, "The Living Dead: New Embalming Method Aids Surgical Training," *BBC News,* June 15, 2013, accessed April 24, 2015, http://www.bbc.com/news/health-22908661.

3. "iPhone 7 - Apple," *Apple.com,* accessed October 6, 2016, http://www.apple.com/iphone-7/.

4. E. Romanelli and M. L. Tushman, "Organizational Transformation as Punctuated Equilibrium: An Empirical Test," *Academy of Management Journal* 37 (1994): 1141–1166.

5. H. Banks, "A Sixties Industry in a Nineties Economy," *Forbes,* May 9, 1994, 107–112.

6. L. Cowan, "Cheap Fuel Should Carry Many Airlines to More Record Profits for 1st Quarter," *Wall Street Journal,* April 4, 1998, B17A.

7. "Annual Revenues and Earnings: US Airlines—All Services," *Air Transport Association,* accessed January 15, 2005, http://www.airlines.org; S. Carey, "Carrier Makes Deeper Cuts as It Seeks Federal Backing Needed to Exit Chapter 11," *Wall Street Journal,* November 27, 2002, A3; S. Carey, "UAL Will Lay Off 1,500 Workers as Part of Cost-Cutting Strategy," *Wall Street Journal,* January 6, 2003, A3; D. Carty, "Oral Testimony of Mr. Donald J. Carty, Chairman and CEO, American Airlines: United States Senate, Committee on Commerce, Science, and Transportation," accessed January 9, 2003, http://www.amrcorp.com; S. McCartney, M. Trottman, and S. Carey, "Northwest, Continental, America West Post Losses as Delta Cuts Jobs," *Wall Street Journal,* November 18, 2002, B4.

8. "Airlines Still in Upheaval, 5 Years after 9/11," *CNNMoney.com,* September 8, 2006, accessed July 25, 2008, http://money.cnn.com/2006/09/08/news /companies/airlines_sept11/?postversion=200609081 3&eref=yahoo.

9. J. Mouawad, "Airlines Reap Record Profits, and Passengers Get Peanuts," *New York Times,* February 6, 2016, A1.

10. J. Mouawad, "Airlines Reap Record Profits, and Passengers Get Peanuts," *New York Times,* February 6, 2016, accessed August 4, 2016, http:// www.nytimes.com/2016/02/07/business/energy -environment/airlines-reap-record-profits-and -passengers-get-peanuts.html.

11. A. Madrigal, "The Perfect Milk Machine: How Big Data Transformed the Dairy Industry," *The Atlantic,* May 1, 2012, accessed April 25, 2015, http:// www.theatlantic.com/technology/archive/2012/05 /the-perfect-milk-machine-how-big-data-transformed -the-dairy-industry/256423/; "U.S. Dairy: Milk Produced Per Cow in the United States from 1999 to 2015 (in Pounds)," *Statistica,* accessed April 17, 2016, http://www.statista.com.ezproxy.butler.edu /statistics/194935/quantity-of-milk-produced-per -cow-in-the-us-since-1999/.

12. "US Dairy: Total Milk Production 2015," *Statista,* accessed April 17, 2016, http://www.statista .com/statistics/194937/total-us-milk-production -since-1999/.

13. Press Release, "Worldwide PC Shipments Will Continue to Decline into 2016 as the Short-Term Outlook Softens, According To IDC," *International Data Corporation,* December 5, 2015, accessed April 17, 2016, http://www.idc.com/getdoc .jsp?containerId=prUS40704015. K. Bora, "Worldwide PC Shipments Showed Signs of Improvement Despite 1.7% Annual Decline in Q1 2014," *International Business Times,* April 15, 2014, accessed April 25, 2015, http://www.ibtimes.com/worldwide -pc-shipments-showed-signs-improvement-despite -17-annual-decline-q1-2014-1571663; M. Muchmore, "Microsoft Windows 10 Review & Rating," *PCMag .com,* April 15, 2016, accessed April 17, 2016, http:// www.pcmag.com/article2/0,2817,2488631,00.asp.

14. D. Charles, "Thanks to Nutella, The World Needs More Hazelnuts," *All Things Considered,* NPR, September 16, 2014, accessed April 25, 2015, www.npr.org/blogs/thesalt/2014/09/16/347749070 /thanks-to-nutella-the-world-needs-more-hazelnuts; V. Wong, "Nutella Hogs Hazelnuts to Meet the World's Insatiable Craving for Chocolaty Goodness," *Bloomberg Businessweek,* August 14, 2014, accessed April 25, 2015, www.businessweek.com/articles /2014-08-14/nutella-buys-hazelnut-supplier-to -protect-against-worldwide-shortage.

15. G. Wearden, "Chinese Economic Boom Has Been 30 Years in the Making," *The Guardian,* August 16, 2016, accessed April 17, 2016, http://www .theguardian.com/business/2010/aug/16/chinese -economic-boom; "The Economist Explains: Why China's Economy Is Slowing," *The Economist,* March 11, 2015, accessed April 17, 2016, http://www .economist.com/blogs/economist-explains/2015/03 /economist-explains-8.

16. C. Paris, "Dry-Bulk Shipping Firms Face Unprecedented Crisis; Companies Selling Vessels to Survive," *Wall Street Journal,* January 20, 2016, accessed April 17, 2016, http://www.wsj.com/articles /dry-bulk-shipping-firms-face-unprecedented -crisis-1453293892.

17. B. Einhorn and C. Matlack, "The Shipping Industry Is Suffering From China's Trade Slowdown," *Bloomberg BusinessWeek,* February 11, 2016, accessed April 17, 2016, http://www.bloomberg.com /news/articles/2016-02-11/shipping-industry-suffering -from-china-s-trade-slowdown; "Baltic Dry Index," accessed April 17, 2016, http://www.bloomberg.com /quote/BDIY:IND.

18. C. Paris, "Dry-Bulk Shipping Firms Face Unprecedented Crisis; Companies Selling Vessels to Survive," *Wall Street Journal,* January 20, 2016, accessed April 17, 2016, http://www.wsj.com/articles /dry-bulk-shipping-firms-face-unprecedented -crisis-1453293892.

19. A. Lakshmi, "Maersk Line to Face Miserable 2016," *Maritime Professional,* February 11, 2016, accessed April 17, 2016, http:// www.maritimeprofessional.com/news/maersk-line -face-miserable-2016-284942.

20. C. Paris, "Dry-Bulk Shipping Firms Face Unprecedented Crisis; Companies Selling Vessels to Survive," *Wall Street Journal,* January 20, 2016, accessed April 17, 2016, http://www.wsj.com/articles /dry-bulk-shipping-firms-face-unprecedented -crisis-1453293892.

21. OECD (2014), "OECD Forecasts During and After the Financial Crisis: A Post Mortem," OECD Economics Department Policy Notes, No. 23, February 2014.

22. "CEO Confidence Improves Slightly," The Conference Board, April 6, 2016, accessed April 17, 2016, https://www.conference-board.org/data /ceoconfidence.cfm.

23. "Unflinching Small Business Optimism," *WSJ/ Vistage Small Business CEO Survey,* February–March 28, 2015, accessed April 25, 2015, http://www .vistage.com/wp-content/uploads/2015/03/WSJ-CEO -Survey-0215.pdf; http://www.vistage.com/press -center/wallsjvistage-ceo-survey/.

24. C. Paris, "Carnival Sails Toward China Growth," *Wall Street Journal,* January 22, 2015, B7.

25. S. Daneshkhu and L. Whipp, "Hipster Dollar Carries Heavy Weight as Millennials Come to Market," *Financial Times,* January 20, 2016, accessed April 17, 2016, http://www.ft.com/cms/s/0/bfce2878 -c691-11e5-b3b1-7b2481276e45.html.

26. Ibid.

27. "The Civil Rights Act of 1991," US Equal Employment Opportunity Commission, accessed April 17, 2016, http://www.eeoc.gov/policy/cra91.html.

28. "Compliance Assistance—Family and Medical Leave Act (FMLA)," *US Department of Labor: Employment Standards Administration, Wage and Hour Division,* accessed April 17, 2016, http://www .dol.gov/.

29. A Loten, "Small Business Owners Scramble to Prepare for New Tax Form," *Wall Street Journal,* March 4, 2015, B5.

30. R. J. Bies and T. R. Tyler, "The Litigation Mentality in Organizations: A Test of Alternative Psychological Explanations," *Organization Science* 4 (1993): 352–366.

31. M. Orey, "Fear of Firing," *BusinessWeek,* April 23, 2007, 52–62.

32. S. Gardner, G. Gomes, and J. Morgan, "Wrongful Termination and the Expanding Public Policy Exception: Implications and Advice," *SAM Advanced Management Journal* 65 (2000): 38.

33. "Bases by Issue: FY 2010 - FY 2015," *U.S. Equal Employment Opportunity Commission,* accessed April 17, 2016, https://www1.eeoc.gov/eeoc/statistics /enforcement/bases_by_issue.cfm?renderforprint=1.

34. J. Mundy, "Wrongful Termination Lawsuits on the Rise," *LawyersandSettlements.com,* January 5, 2011, accessed June 4, 2014, http://www .lawyersandsettlements.com/articles/wrongful -termination/wrongful-termination-law-11-15747 .html#.U48_GvldWSp.

35. Orey, "Fear of Firing."

36. Ibid.

37. "Little Gym Case Study," Listen360, April 2014, accessed April 4, 2015, http://listen360.com/assets /case_studies/LittleGym_4-2014.pdf.

38. R. Johnston and S. Mehra, "Best-Practice Complaint Management," *Academy of Management Experience* 16 (November 2002): 145–154.

39. D. Smart and C. Martin, "Manufacturer Responsiveness to Consumer Correspondence: An Empirical Investigation of Consumer Perceptions," *Journal of Consumer Affairs* 26 (1992): 104.

40. "Spotify Launches Tool to Let Artists Track their Biggest Fans," Fact, November 18, 2015, accessed April 17, 2016, http://www.factmag.com/2015/11/18 /spotify-fan-insights-tool-artists-track-biggest-fans/. K. Rosman, "Weather Channel Now Also Forecasts What You'll Buy," *Wall Street Journal*, August 14, 2013, accessed June 16, 2014, http://online.wsj.com /news/articles/SB1000142412788732363970457901 2674092402660.

41. Ibid.

42. S. A. Zahra and S. S. Chaples, "Blind Spots in Competitive Analysis," *Academy of Management Executive* 7 (1993): 7–28.

43. K. Hagey and S. Ramachandran, "Pay TV's New Worry: 'Shaving' the Cord," *Wall Street Journal*, October 9, 2014, accessed April 25, 2015, http:// www.wsj.com/articles/pay-tvs-new-worry-shaving -the-cord-1412899121; D. Beres, "150,000 Cable Subscribers Cut the Cord Last Quarter," *Huffington Post*, November 14, 2014, accessed April 25, 2015, http://www.huffingtonpost.com/2014/11/14 /cord-cutting_n_6159502.html; E. Deggans, "Evaluating Whether It's Time to Cut the Cord," *Morning Edition on NPR*, March 27, 2015, accessed April 25, 2015, http://www.npr.org/2015/03/27/395698509 /how-to-evaluate-whether-its-time-for-you-to-cut -the-cord; E. Lee, "TV Subscriptions Fall for First Time as Viewers Cut the Cord," *BloombergBusiness. com*, March 19, 2014, accessed April 25, 2015, http:// www.bloomberg.com/news/articles/2014-03-19/u-s -pay-tv-subscriptions-fall-for-first-time-as-streaming -gains.

44. K. G. Provan, "Embeddedness, Interdependence, and Opportunism in Organizational Supplier-Buyer Networks," *Journal of Management* 19 (1993): 841–856.

45. J. Lessin, L. Luk, and J. Osawa, "Apple Finds It Difficult to Divorce Samsung," *Wall Street Journal*, June 29, 2013, A1.

46. D. Clark, "Samsung's Chip Choice Is a Mixed Verdict for Qualcomm," *Wall Street Journal*, April 3, 2015, accessed April 25, 2015, http://blogs.wsj.com /digits/2015/04/03/samsungs-chip-choice-is-a-mixed -verdict-for-qualcomm/.

47. J. Lee and I. King, "Samsung Said to Win Apple A9 Chip Orders for Next iPhone," *BloombergBusiness*, April 2, 2015, accessed April 25, 2015, http:// www.bloomberg.com/news/articles/2015-04-03 /samsung-said-to-win-apple-a9-chip-orders-for-next -iphone.

48. Ibid.

49. Ibid.

50. Ibid.

51. S. Parker and C. Axtell, "Seeing Another Viewpoint: Antecedents and Outcomes of Employee Perspective Taking," *Academy of Management Journal* 44 (2001): 1085–1100; B. K. Pilling, L. A. Crosby, and D. W. Jackson, "Relational Bonds in Industrial Exchange: An Experimental Test of the Transaction Cost Economic Framework," *Journal of Business Research* 30 (1994): 237–251.

52. M. Hickins, "CIO Journal: H-P Reinvents Itself," *Wall Street Journal*, April 25, 2013, B5.

53. K. O'Brien, "DreamWorks Animation Data Center On-Site," Storage Review, October 24, 2012, accessed June 16, 2014, http://www.storagereview .com/dreamworks_animation_data_center_onsite.

54. "FDA Finalizes Menu and Vending Machine Calorie Labeling Rules," *US Food and Drug Administration*, November 25, 2014, accessed April 25, 2015, http://www.fda.gov/NewsEvents/Newsroom /PressAnnouncements/ucm423952.htm.

55. A. Martin, "Inside the Powerful Lobby Fighting for Your Right to Eat Pizza," *Chicago Tribune*, March 9, 2015, accessed April 25, 2015, http://www .chicagotribune.com/news/sns-wp-blm-news-bc -pizza-lobby09-20150309-story.html#page=2.

56. "CPSC Approves Strong Federal Safety Standard for High-Powered Magnet Sets to Protect Children and Teenagers," *United States Consumer Product Safety Commission*, September 25, 2014, Release number 14-283, accessed April 25, 2015, http://www.cpsc.gov/en/Newsroom/News-Releases /2014/CPSC-Approves-Strong-Federal-Safety -Standard-for-High-Powered-Magnet-Sets-to -Protect-Children-and-Teenagers/; M. Lipka, "After Death and Recalls, Feds Ban High-Powered Magnets," *CBS Moneywatch*, September 25, 2014, accessed April 25, 2015, http://www.cbsnews.com /news/after-deaths-and-recalls-feds-ban-high -powered-magnets/; R. Abrams, "High-Power Magnets Get Temporary Reprieve from Safety Rules," *Boston Globe*, April 4, 2015, accessed April 25, 2015, https://www.bostonglobe.com/business/2015/04/03 /high-power-magnets-get-temporary-reprieve-from -safety-rules/TK26SoOCz82d3XSu2655LK/story.html.

57. J. Hansegard, "Lego Builds Stronger Bridges to Girls: Danish Toy Maker Finally Is Succeeding after Several Failed Attempts to Span the Gender Gap," *Wall Street Journal*, December 30, 2015, B1.

58. SPARKsummit, "Our Letter to LEGO," January 20, 2012, accessed February 17, 2016, http://www .sparksummit.com/2012/01/20/our-letter-to-lego/.

59. J. Hansegard, "Lego Builds Stronger Bridges to Girls: Danish Toy Maker Finally Is Succeeding After Several Failed Attempts to Span the Gender Gap," *Wall Street Journal*, December 30, 2015, B1.

60. Ibid.

61. C. Mims, "Amid Stratospheric Valuations, Google Unearths a Deal with Skybox," *Wall Street Journal*, June 15, 2014, http://online.wsj.com/articles /amid-stratospheric-valuations-google-unearths-a -deal-with-skybox-1402864823?KEYWORDS=google +acquisition+satellite.

62. D. F. Jennings and J. R. Lumpkin, "Insights Between Environmental Scanning Activities and Porter's Generic Strategies: An Empirical Analysis," *Journal of Management* 4 (1992): 791–803.

63. "China's Unsafe Water Is Nestlé's Opportunity," *Bloomberg Businessweek*, January 28–February 3, 2013, 19–20.

64. E. Jackson and J. E. Dutton, "Discerning Threats and Opportunities," *Administrative Science Quarterly* 33 (1988): 370–387.

65. B. Thomas, S. M. Clark, and D. A. Gioia, "Strategic Sensemaking and Organizational Performance: Linkages Among Scanning, Interpretation, Action, and Outcomes," *Academy of Management Journal* 36 (1993): 239–270.

66. R. Daft, J. Sormunen, and D. Parks, "Chief Executive Scanning, Environmental Characteristics, and Company Performance: An Empirical Study," *Strategic Management Journal* 9 (1988): 123–139; V. Garg, B. Walters, and R. Priem, "Chief Executive Scanning Emphases, Environmental Dynamism, and Manufacturing Firm Performance," *Strategic Management Journal* 24 (2003): 725–744; D. Miller and P. H. Friesen, "Strategy-Making and Environment: The Third Link," *Strategic Management Journal* 4 (1983): 221–235.

67. A. Gasparro and A. Prior, "Kellogg's Profit Falls 16% as Cereal Sales Drop," *Wall Street Journal*, July 31, 2014, accessed April 25, 2015, http://www.wsj .com/articles/kelloggs-profit-pressured-by-cereal -sales-1406809902.

68. D. Leonard, "Bad News in Cereal City—Will Kellogg Ever Catch a Break?" *Bloomberg Businessweek*, March 2–8, 2015, pp. 42–47.

69. J. Bunge, "Tastes Like Chicken: The Race Is On to Breed Better Birds as Chicken Emerges as the Protein of the Masses," *Wall Street Journal*, December 4, 2015, 2016, accessed April 17, 2016, http://www.wsj.com/articles/how-to-satisfy-the-worlds -surging-appetite-for-meat-1449238059.

70. K. Paris, "How Cargill Plans to Help Feed the World," *Foodonline.com*, September 25, 2014, accessed April 17, 2016, http://www.foodonline.com /doc/how-cargill-plans-to-help-feed-the-world-0001; S. Lewis, "Cargill's New Poultry Processing Facility Is Up and Running, September 16, 2014, 2016, accessed April 17, 2016, http://www.foodonline.com /doc/cargill-s-new-poultry-processing-facility-is-up -and-running-0001.

71. J. Bunge, "Tastes Like Chicken: The Race Is On to Breed Better Birds as Chicken Emerges as the Protein of the Masses," *Wall Street Journal*, December 4, 2015, accessed April 17, 2016, http://www .wsj.com/articles/how-to-satisfy-the-worlds-surging -appetite-for-meat-1449238059.

72. R. Feitelberg, "Building a Winning Culture," *WWD*, December 1, 2011, SR12; Under Armour, Inc., "2013 Under Armour Annual Report," February 21, 2014, 4.

73. S. Berfield, "Container Store: Conscious Capitalism and the Perils of Going Public," Bloomberg Business, February 19, 2015, accessed April 25, 2015, http://www.bloomberg.com/news/articles/2015-02-19 /container-store-conscious-capitalism-and-the-perils -of-going-public.

74. Ibid.; K. Gustafson, "Retail's Turnover a Plus for Economy But Challenge for Stores," *CNBC*, September 23, 2014, accessed April 25, 2015, http:// www.cnbc.com/id/102021496.

75. D. M. Boje, "The Storytelling Organization: A Study of Story Performance in an Office-Supply Firm," *Administrative Science Quarterly* 36 (1991): 106–126.

76. B. Horowitz, "6 Questions for: Nobody Said Startups Would Be Easy," *Inc.*, April 2014, 39–40.

77. F. D'Souza, "Corner Office: Francisco D'Souza of Cognizant, on Finding Company Heroes," interview by A. Bryant, *New York Times*, August 31, 2013, accessed June 4, 2014, http://www.nytimes .com/2013/09/01/business/francisco-dsouza-of -cognizant-on-finding-company-heroes.html.

78. Ibid.

79. D. R. Denison and A. K. Mishra, "Toward a Theory of Organizational Culture and Effectiveness," *Organization Science* 6 (1995): 204–223.

80. P. Ziobro, "Floundering Mattel Tries to Make Things Fun Again," *Wall Street Journal*, December 22, 2014, accessed April 26, 2015, http://www.wsj .com/articles/floundering-mattel-tries-to-make-things -fun-again-1419305830.

81. "Our Philosophy," *BPV Capital Management*, June 18, 2014, accessed June 18, 2014, http://www .backporchvista.com/about-bpv/our-philosophy/.

82. D. Roberts, "Why U.S. Olympic Swimming Is So Dominant," *Fortune*, April 17, 2015, accessed February 17, 2016, http://fortune.com/2015/04/17 /usa-olympic-swimming-gold/.

83. Ibid.

84. Ibid.

85. A. Zuckerman, "Strong Corporate Cultures and Firm Performance: Are There Tradeoffs?" *Academy of Management Executive*, November 2002, 158–160.

86. E. Schein, *Organizational Culture and Leadership*, 2nd ed. (San Francisco: Jossey-Bass, 1992).

87. S. Albert & D.A. Whetten, "Organizational Identity," *Research in Organizational Behavior* 7 (1985): 263–295. C.M. Fiol, "Managing Culture as a Competitive Resource: An Identity-Based View of Sustainable Competitive Advantage," *Journal of Management* 17 (1991): 191–211.

88. J. Lublin, "This CEO Used to Have an Office— At Dynegy, Boss's Drive for a 'Winning' Culture Means More Cubicles and Fewer Emails," *Wall Street Journal*, March 13, 2013, B1.

89. "Michael O'Leary's Most Memorable Quotes," *The Telegraph*, September 5, 2012, accessed April 17, 2016, http://www.telegraph.co.uk/travel/lists/Michael -OLearys-most-memorable-quotes/.

90. "Ryanair: How the Airline Is Trying to Change Its Image," *The Telegraph*, February 4, 2016, accessed April 17, 2016, http://www.telegraph.co.uk/travel/galleries/Ryanair-how-the-airline-is-trying-to-change-its-image/ryanair4/; C. Osborne, "Ryanair CEO Admits His Loudmouth Ways Are Affecting Carrier's Growth," *ZDNet*, November 22, 2013, accessed April 17, 2016, http://www.zdnet.com/article/ryanair-ceo-admits-personal-behavior-is-affecting-carriers-growth/#!; A. Tovey, "Being Nice Pays Off for Ryanair as Passenger Numbers Soar," *The Telegraph*, September 2, 2015, accessed April 17, 2016, http://www.telegraph.co.uk/finance/newsbysector/transport/11839609/Being-nice-pays-off-for-Ryanair-as-passenger-numbers-soar.html.

91. Tovey, "Being Nice Pays Off for Ryanair as Passenger Numbers Soar."

92. G. Bensinger, "Amazon Recruits Face 'Bar Raisers,'" *Wall Street Journal*, January 8, 2014, B1.

4

1. "2016 Edelman Trust Barometer Annual Global Study," *Edelman Berland*, accessed April 18, 2016, http://www.edelman.com/insights/intellectual-property/2014-edelman-trust-barometer/.

2. D. Meinhert, "Creating an Ethical Workplace," HR Magazine 59 (April 2014): 4, accessed June 4, 2014, https://www.shrm.org/Publications/hrmagazine/EditorialContent/2014/0414/Pages/0414-ethical-workplace-culture.aspx.

3. "2013 National Business Ethics Survey of the U.S. Workforce," *Ethics Resource Center*, 2014, accessed June 4, 2014, http://www.ethics.org/downloads/2013NBESFinalWeb.pdf.

4. C. Smith, "The Ethical Workplace," *Association Management* 52 (2000): 70–73.

5. "Trust in the Workplace: 2010 Ethics & Workplace Survey," *Deloitte LLP*, 2010, accessed June 4, 2014, http://www.deloitte.com/assets/Dcom-United-States/Local%20Assets/Documents/us_2010_Ethics_and_Workplace_Survey_report_071910.pdf.

6. "Communication, Honesty among Traits Most Desired and Lacking in Corporate Leaders, ASQ Survey Says," *Reuters.com*, February 11, 2014, accessed April 11, 2015, http://www.reuters.com/article/2014/02/11/idUSnGNX91ymYv+1c2+GNW20140211.

7. A. Bryant, "In a Word, He Wants Simplicity," *New York Times*, May 23, 2009, accessed August 15, 2010, http://www.nytimes.com/2009/05/24/business/24corner.html?_r=2&pagewanted=1.

8. Association of Certified Fraud Examiners, "Report to the Nation on Occupational Fraud and Abuse: 2014 Global Fraud Study," accessed April 11, 2015, http://www.acfe.com/rttn-summary.aspx. K. Gibson, "Excuses, Excuses: Moral Slippage in the Workplace," *Business Horizons* 43, no. 6 (2000): 65; S. L. Robinson and R. J. Bennett, "A Typology of Deviant Workplace Behaviors: A Multidimensional Scaling Study," *Academy of Management Journal* 38 (1995): 555–572.

9. Harvard Management Update, "Learn by 'Failing Forward,'" *Globe & Mail*, October 31, 2000, B17.

10. "Challenger March Madness Report," Challenger, Gray & Christmas, Inc., March 11, 2015, accessed April 11, 2015, http://www.challengergray.com/download/file/fid/215.

11. B. Falcon, "Oil Thieves Plague Shell in Nigeria," *Wall Street Journal*, April 12, 2013, B1.

12. M. Korolov, "Overall Jump Linked to Increase in Employee Theft and Higher Security Spending," *CSO Online*, November 7, 2014, accessed April 11, 2015, http://www.csoonline.com/article/2845058/loss-prevention/cost-of-retail-crime-skyrockets-nearly-30-percent.html; Global Retail Theft Barometer 2014, accessed April 11, 2015, http://globalretailtheftbarometer.com/.

13. J.L. Hayes, "26th Annual Retail Theft Survey," *Hayes International* press release, June 2015, accessed April 18, 2016 http://hayesinternational.com/wp-content/uploads/2012/01/27th-Annual-Retail-Theft-Survey-Jack-L.-Hayes-Intl-1.pdf

14. A. Wren, "Sweethearting: A Bottom Line Drain for Retailers," *Chain Store Age*, June 21, 2012, accessed April 11, 2015, http://www.chainstoreage.com/article/sweethearting-bottom-line-drain-retailers; M. K. Brady, C. M. Voorhees, and M. J. Brusco, "Service Sweethearting: Its Antecedents and Customer Consequences," *Journal of Marketing* 76 (2012): 81–98.

15. J. Norman, "Cultivating a Culture of Honesty," *The Orange County [California] Register*, October 23, 2006.

16. News Release, "Nonfatal Occupational Injuries and Illnesses Requiring Days Away from Work, 2014," *U.S. Bureau of Labor Statistics*, November 19, 2015, accessed April 18, 2016, http://www.bls.gov/news.release/pdf/osh2.pdf, 28; Economic News Release, "Table 1. Fatal Occupational Injuries by Event or Exposure, 2013–2014," *U.S. Bureau of Labor Statistics*, September 17, 2015, accessed April 18, 2016, http://www.bls.gov/news.release/cfoi.t01.htm.

17. D. Palmer and A. Zakhem, "Bridging the Gap Between Theory and Practice: Using the 1991 Federal Sentencing Guidelines as a Paradigm for Ethics Training," *Journal of Business Ethics* 29, no. 1/2 (2001): 77–84.

18. K. Tyler, "Do the Right Thing: Ethics Training Programs Help Employees Deal with Ethical Dilemmas," *HR Magazine*, February 2005, accessed March 13, 2009, http://www.shrm.org/publications/hrmagazine/editorialcontent/pages/0205tyler.aspx.

19. D. R. Dalton, M. B. Metzger, and J. W. Hill, "The 'New' US Sentencing Commission Guidelines: A Wake-up Call for Corporate America," *Academy of Management Executive* 8 (1994): 7–16.

20. G. Marcias, "Q&A: Gayle Macias, World Vision," interview by B. DiPietro, *Wall Street Journal*, June 12, 2013, accessed June 4, 2014, http://blogs.wsj.com/riskandcompliance/2013/06/12/qa-gayle-macias-world-vision/.

21. B. Ettore, "Crime and Punishment: A Hard Look at White-Collar Crime," *Management Review* 83 (1994): 10–16.

22. F. Robinson and C. C. Pauze, "What Is a Board's Liability for Not Adopting a Compliance Program?" *Healthcare Financial Management* 51, no. 9 (1997): 64.

23. D. Murphy, "The Federal Sentencing Guidelines for Organizations: A Decade of Promoting Compliance and Ethics," *Iowa Law Review* 87 (2002): 697–719.

24. Robinson and Pauze, "What Is a Board's Liability?"

25. B. Schwartz, "The Nuts and Bolts of an Effective Compliance Program," *HR Focus* 74, no. 8 (1997): 13–15.

26. C. Chen, "The CEO Who Saved a Life and Lost His Job," *Bloomberg Businessweek*, January 22, 2015, accessed April 18, 2016, http://www.bloomberg.com/news/articles/2015-01-22/biotech-drug-approvals-social-media-storm-hits-chimerix.

27. S. Morris and R. McDonald, "The Role of Moral Intensity in Moral Judgments: An Empirical Investigation," *Journal of Business Ethics* 14 (1995): 715–726; B. Flannery and D. May, "Environmental Ethical Decision Making in the US Metal-Finishing Industry," *Academy of Management Journal* 43 (2000): 642–662.

28. L. Kohlberg, "Stage and Sequence: The Cognitive-Developmental Approach to Socialization," in *Handbook of Socialization Theory and Research*, ed. D. A. Goslin (Chicago: Rand McNally, 1969); L. Trevino, "Moral Reasoning and Business Ethics: Implications for Research, Education, and Management," *Journal of Business Ethics* 11 (1992): 445–459.

29. L. Trevino and M. Brown, "Managing to be Ethical: Debunking Five Business Ethics Myths," *Academy of Management Executive* 18 (May 2004): 69–81.

30. L. T. Hosmer, "Trust: The Connecting Link Between Organizational Theory and Philosophical Ethics," *Academy of Management Review* 20 (1995): 379–403.

31. A. Edney, "Cost to Develop a Drug More Than Doubles to $2.56 Billion," *Bloomberg BusinessWeek*, November 18, 2014, accessed April 18, 2016, http://www.bloomberg.com/news/articles/2014-11-18/cost-to-develop-a-drug-more-than-doubles-to-2-56-billion.

32. C. Chen, "The CEO Who Saved a Life and Lost His Job," *Bloomberg BusinessWeek*, January 22, 2015, accessed April 18, 2016, http://www.bloomberg.com/news/articles/2015-01-22/biotech-drug-approvals-social-media-storm-hits-chimerix.

33. Ibid.

34. Ibid.

35. Ibid.

36. "2013 National Business Ethics Survey of the U.S. Workforce."

37. H. J. Bernardin, "Validity of an Honesty Test in Predicting Theft Among Convenience Store Employees," *Academy of Management Journal* 36 (1993): 1097–1108.

38. J. M. Collins and F. L. Schmidt, "Personality, Integrity, and White Collar Crime: A Construct Validity Study," *Personnel Psychology* (1993): 295–311.

39. W. C. Borman, M. A. Hanson, and J. W. Hedge, "Personnel Selection," *Annual Review of Psychology* 48 (1997): 299–337.

40. "303A.10 Code of Business Conduct and Ethics," *NYSE Listed Company Manual*, November 25, 2009, accessed April 18, 2016, http://nysemanual.nyse.com/lcm/Help/mapContent.asp?sec=lcm-sections&title=sx-ruling-nyse-policymanual_303A.09&id=chp_1_4_3_11.

41. P. E. Murphy, "Corporate Ethics Statements: Current Status and Future Prospects," *Journal of Business Ethics* 14 (1995): 727–740.

42. "Code of Ethical Business Conduct," *The Hershey Company*, no date, accessed February 26, 2012, http://www.thehersheycompany.com/investors/corporate-governance/code-of-conduct.aspx.

43. "More Corporate Boards Involved in Ethics Programs; Ethics Training Becoming Standard Practice," *PR Newswire*, October 16, 2006.

44. S. J. Harrington, "What Corporate America Is Teaching About Ethics," *Academy of Management Executive* 5 (1991): 21–30.

45. L. A. Berger, "Train All Employees to Solve Ethical Dilemmas," *Best's Review–Life-Health Insurance Edition* 95 (1995): 70–80.

46. Meinhert, "Creating an Ethical Workplace."

47. Ibid.

48. L. Trevino, G. Weaver, D. Gibson, and B. Toffler, "Managing Ethics and Legal Compliance: What Works and What Hurts," *California Management Review* 41, no. 2 (1999): 131–151.

49. M. Swanton, "Compliance Comedy," *Inside Counsel* 22 (2011): 56.

50. "Leader's Guide: A Culture of Trust 2008," *Lockheed Martin*, accessed July 17, 2008, http://www.lockheedmartin.com/data/assets/corporate/documents/ethics/2008_EAT_Leaders_Guide.pdf.

51. Meinhert, "Creating an Ethical Workplace."

52. E. White, "Theory & Practice: What Would You Do? Ethics Courses Get Context; Beyond Checking Boxes, Some Firms Start Talking About Handling Gray Areas," *Wall Street Journal*, June 12, 2006, B3.

53. "The State of Ethics in Large Companies: A Research Report from the National Business Ethics Survey (NBES)," *Ethics Research Center*, 2015, accessed April 11, 2015, http://www.ethics.org/nbes/wp-content/uploads/2015/03/LargeCompaniesExecSummary.pdf.

54. Ibid.

55. G. Weaver and L. Trevino, "Integrated and De-coupled Corporate Social Performance: Management Commitments, External Pressures, and Corporate Ethics Practices," *Academy of Management Journal* 42 (1999): 539–552; Trevino, et al., "Managing Ethics and Legal Compliance."

56. "2013 National Business Ethics Survey of the U.S. Workforce."

57. J. Salopek, "Do the Right Thing," *Training & Development* 55 (July 2001): 38–44.

58. M. Gundlach, S. Douglas, and M. Martinko, "The Decision to Blow the Whistle: A Social Information Processing Framework," *Academy of Management Executive* 17 (2003): 107–123.

59. "Retaliation: When Whistleblowers Become Victims: A Supplemental Report of the 2011 National Business Ethics Survey," *Ethics Resource Center*, 2012, accessed May 21, 2013, http://www.ethics.org /files/u5/RetaliationFinal.pdf.

60. "2013 National Business Ethics Survey of the U.S. Workforce"; "The State of Ethics in Large Companies: A Research Report from the National Business Ethics Survey (NBES)."

61. "OSHA Found Airline Violated Whistleblower Protection Provision of AIR21," *OSHA News Release: 11-1814-ATL*, January 17, 2012, accessed May 22, 2013, http://www.osha.gov/pls/oshaweb/owadisp .show_document?p_id=21651&p_table=NEWS _RELEASES," *Wall Street Journal*, January 18, 2012, B2.

62. J. Deschenaux, "High Court Extends Employee Whistle-blower Protections," *Society for Human Resource Management*, March 5, 2014, accessed June 4, 2014, http://www.shrm.org/LegalIssues /FederalResources/Pages/High-Court-Extends -Employee-Whistle-blower-Protections.aspx.

63. M. Mucci, "Compliance Without Compliance Officer: Q&A with Martin Mucci of Paychex," interview by G. Millman, *Wall Street Journal*, February 6, 2014, accessed June 4, 2014, http://blogs.wsj.com /riskandcompliance/2014/02/06/compliance-without -a-chief-compliance-officer-qa-with-martin-mucci-of -paychex/?KEYWORDS=ethics+training.

64. M. P. Miceli and J. P. Near, "Whistleblowing: Reaping the Benefits," *Academy of Management Executive* 8 (1994): 65–72.

65. M. Mucci, "Compliance Without Compliance Officer."

66. Ibid.

67. M. Master and E. Heresniak, "The Disconnect in Ethics Training," *Across the Board* 39 (September 2002): 51–52.

68. H. R. Bower, *Social Responsibilities of the Businessman* (New York: Harper & Row, 1953).

69. "Beyond the Green Corporation," *Business-Week*, January 29, 2007.

70. S. L. Wartick and P. L. Cochran, "The Evolution of the Corporate Social Performance Model," *Academy of Management Review* 10 (1985): 758–769.

71. J. Nocera, "The Paradox of Businesses as Do-Gooders," *New York Times*, November 11, 2006, C1.

72. S. Waddock, C. Bodwell, and S. Graves, "Responsibility: The New Business Imperative," *Academy of Management Executive* 16 (2002): 132–148.

73. T. Donaldson and L. E. Preston, "The Stakeholder Theory of the Corporation: Concepts, Evidence, and Implications," *Academy of Management Review* 20 (1995): 65–91.

74. D. Gilbert, "Exxon Agrees to Disclose Fracking Risks," *Wall Street Journal*, April 3, 2014, accessed, http://online.wsj.com/news/articles/SB100014240527 023038478045794796403182633438?mod=WSJ_hps _sections_management&mg=reno64-wsj.

75. M. B. E. Clarkson, "A Stakeholder Framework for Analyzing and Evaluating Corporate Social Performance," *Academy of Management Review* 20 (1995): 92–117.

76. B. Agle, R. Mitchell, and J. Sonnenfeld, "Who Matters to CEOs? An Investigation of Stakeholder Attributes and Salience, Corporate Performance, and CEO Values," *Academy of Management Journal* 42 (1999): 507–525.

77. K. Pullen, "Just Below the Surface - The Hidden Side of Triclosan," June 27, 2014, accessed April 18, 2016, https://www.nrdc.org/experts/kristi-pullen/just -below-surface-hidden-side-triclosan.

78. L. Landro, "Antibacterial Soaps Go under the Microscope," *Wall Street Journal*, February 16, 2016, R1.

79. E. W. Orts, "Beyond Shareholders: Interpreting Corporate Constituency Statutes," *George Washington Law Review* 61 (1992): 14–135.

80. A. B. Carroll, "A Three-Dimensional Conceptual Model of Corporate Performance," *Academy of Management Review* 4 (1979): 497–505.

81. Ibid.

82. S. Carey, "Spirit Air Abruptly Replaces CEO," *Wall Street Journal*, January 6, 2016, B1.

83. J. Lublin and M. Murrary, "CEOs Leave Faster Than Ever Before as Boards, Investors Lose Patience," *Wall Street Journal Interactive*, October 27, 2000.

84. "CEO Dismissals in the US at the Lowest Level in a Decade, The Conference Board Finds," The Conference Board, April 14, 2015, accessed April 18, 2016, http://www.prnewswire.com/news-releases /ceo-dismissals-in-the-us-at-the-lowest-level-in-a -decade-the-conference-board-finds-300065351.html.

85. R. Bender, "Secret Dairy Cartel Ends in $204 Million of Fines," *Wall Street Journal*, March 13, 2015, B1.

86. P. Ziobro, "Same Package, Same Price, Less Product," *Wall Street Journal*, June 12, 2015, B1; S. Ng, "P&G Settles Suit on Puffed-Up Packaging," *Wall Street Journal*, July 7, 2015, accessed February 23, 2016, http://www.wsj.com/articles/p-g-settles -suit-on-puffed-up-packaging-1436305037; P. Ziobro, "Same Package, Same Price, Less Product," *Wall Street Journal*, June 12, 2015, B1.

87. Ibid.

88. "JPMorgan Chase Offers Relief Following Hurricane Sandy," *Business Wire*, November 1, 2012, accessed May 22, 2013, http://www.businesswire.com /news/home/20121101006246/en/JPMorgan-Chase -Offers-Relief-Hurricane-Sandy; G. Szalai, "Time Warner to Donate $1 Million for Hurricane Sandy Relief Efforts," *The Hollywood Reporter*, November 2, 2012, accessed May 22, 2013, http://www .hollywoodreporter.com/news/hurricane-sandy -time-warner-donates-million-401982; A. Stonich, "How Outdoor Gear Companies Helped Hurricane Sandy Relief Efforts," *Beyond the Edge-National Geographic Adventure Blog*, December 13, 2012, accessed May 22, 2013, http://adventureblog .nationalgeographic.com/2012/12/13/how-outdoor -gear-companies-helped-hurricane-sandy-relief-efforts/.

89. A. Pasztor, "Helicopter Industry Moves to Improve Safety," *Wall Street Journal*, December 31, 2015, B5.

90. C. Duhigg, "In China, Human Costs Are Built into an iPad," *New York Times*, January 25, 2012, accessed February 28, 2012, http://www.nytimes .com/2012/01/26/business/ieconomy-apples -ipad-and-the-human-costs-for-workers-in-china .html?pagewanted=all; H. Perlberg and T. Culpan, "Apple Says Fair Labor Association Began Foxconn Inspection," *Bloomberg Businessweek*, February 14, 2012, accessed February 28, 2012, http://www .bloomberg.com/news/2012-02-13/apple-says-fair -labor-association-will-inspect-suppliers-including -foxconn.html; J. Stern, "Foxconn, Apple, and the Fair Labor Association Respond to ABC News' Exclusive Report," *ABCNews*, February 22, 2012, accessed February 28, 2012, http://abcnews.go.com /blogs/technology/2012/02/foxconn-apple-and-the -fair-labor-association-respond-to-abc-news -exclusive-report/.

91. J. Stewart, "Chipotle's New Mantra: Safe Food, Not Just Fresh," *The New York Times*, January 15, 2016, B1.

92. J. Jargon and J. Newman, "Chipotle Revamps Following E. coli Crisis," *Wall Street Journal*, February 3, 2016, B1.

93. D. Kesmodel, J. Bunge, and A. Gasparro, "McDonald's to Curb Antibiotics Use," *Wall Street Journal*, March 5, 2015, B1, B2.

94. A. McWilliams and D. Siegel, "Corporate Social Responsibility: A Theory of the Firm Perspective," *Academy of Management Review* 26, no.1 (2001): 117–127; H. Haines, "Noah Joins Ranks of Socially Responsible Funds," *Dow Jones News Service*, October 13, 1995. A meta-analysis of 41 different studies also found no relationship between corporate social responsibility and profitability. Though not reported in the meta-analysis, when confidence intervals are placed around its average sample-weighted correlation of .06, the lower confidence interval includes zero, leading to the conclusion that there is no relationship between corporate social responsibility and profitability. See M. Orlitzky, "Does Firm Size Confound the Relationship Between Corporate Social Responsibility and Firm Performance?" *Journal of Business Ethics* 33 (2001): 167–180; S. Ambec and P. Lanoie, "Does It Pay to Be Green? A Systematic Overview," *Academy of Management Perspectives*, 22 (2008): 45–62.

95. M. Orlitzky, "Payoffs to Social and Environmental Performance," *Journal of Investing* 14 (2005): 48–51.

96. M. Orlitzky, F. Schmidt, and S. Rynes, "Corporate Social and Financial Performance: A Meta-analysis," *Organization Studies* 24 (2003): 403–441.

97. Orlitzky, "Payoffs to Social and Environmental Performance."

98. J. Millman, "After Cutting Cigarettes, CVS Is Encouraging Other Pharmacies to do the Same," *Washington Post*, October 20, 2014, accessed April 13, 2015, http://www.washingtonpost.com /blogs/wonkblog/wp/2014/10/20/after-cutting-tobacco -sales-cvs-is-pressuring-other-pharmacies-to -do-the-same/; T. Martin and M. Esterl, "CVS to Stop Selling Cigarettes," *Wall Street Journal*, February 4, 2014, accessed April 13, 2015, http://www.wsj.com /articles/SB10001424052702304851104579363520905 849600; H. Stuart, "CVS's Cigarette Ban Appears to Have Boosted Sales," *Huffington Post*, November 4, 2014, accessed April 13, 2015, http:// www.huffingtonpost.com/2014/11/04/cvs-cigarettes -sales_n_6101086.html.

99. Orlitzky, et al., "Corporate Social and Financial Performance."

100. "GM Offers Big Discounts to Boost Volt Sales," *Fox News*, September 24, 2012, accessed May 24, 2013, http://www.foxnews.com/leisure/2012/09/24 /gm-offers-big-discounts-to-boost-volt-sales; P. Lienert and B. Woodall, "GM Planning Lower-Priced Version of 2016 Chevy Volt," *Reuters*, April 8, 2014, accessed June 22, 2014, http://www .reuters.com/article/2014/04/08/us-autos-gm-volt -idUSBREA371XW20140408; M. Maynard, "Stunner: GM May be Losing $50,000 on Each Chevrolet Volt," *Forbes*, September 10, 2012, accessed May 24, 2013, http://www.forbes.com/sites /michelinemaynard/2012/09/10/stunner-gm-may-be -losing-50000-on-each-chevrolet-volt/; B. Woodall, P. Lienert, and B. Klayman, "Insight: GM's Volt: The Ugly Math of Low Sales, High Costs," *Reuters*, September 10, 2012, accessed May 24, 2013, http://www.reuters.com/article/2012/09/10/us -generalmotors-autos-volt-idUSBRE88904 J20120910. "GM to Suspend Volt Production for 4 Weeks This Summer," *Petoskey News*, April 13, 2015, accessed April 13, 2015, http://www .petoskeynews.com/news/business/gm-to -suspend-volt-production-for-weeks-this-summer /article_6429471f-8537-5722-9d89-09fc17881ca8 .html; D. Shepardson, "Chevy Volt Sales Fall 30% in November," *Detroit News*, December 2, 2014, accessed April 13, 2015, http://www.detroitnews.com /story/business/autos/general-motors/2014/12/02/gm -chevrolet-volt-sales/19776623/.

5

1. L. A. Hill, *Becoming a Manager: Master a New Identity* (Boston: Harvard Business School Press, 1992).

2. L. Lazo, "VRE Kicks Off Major Expansion Plan with New Spotsylvania Station," *Washington Post*, April 18, 2015, accessed April 26, 2015, http://www .washingtonpost.com/local/trafficandcommuting

/vre-kicks-off-major-expansion-plan-with-a-new
-spotsylvania-county-stop/2015/04/18/63576394
-e1f8-11e4-b510-962fcfabc310_story.html.

3. E. A. Locke and G. P. Latham, *A Theory of Goal Setting & Task Performance* (Englewood Cliffs, NJ: Prentice Hall, 1990).

4. M. E. Tubbs, "Goal-Setting: A Meta-Analytic Examination of the Empirical Evidence," *Journal of Applied Psychology* 71 (1986): 474–483.

5. J. Bavelas and E. S. Lee, "Effect of Goal Level on Performance: A Trade-Off of Quantity and Quality," *Canadian Journal of Psychology* 32 (1978): 219–240.

6. D. Turner, "Ability, Aspirations Fine, But Persistence Is What Gets Results," *Seattle Times*, February 13, 2005, http://community.seattletimes.nwsource .com/archive/?date=20030215&slug=dale15m.

7. I. Wladawsky-Berger, "Managing Innovation Requires Unique Leaders and Goals," *Wall Street Journal*, August 25, 2013, accessed June 5, 2014, http://blogs.wsj.com/cio/2013/08/25/managing -innovation-requires-unique-leaders-and-goals /?KEYWORDS=achieving+goals.

8. C. C. Miller, "Strategic Planning and Firm Performance: A Synthesis of More Than Two Decades of Research," *Academy of Management Performance* 37 (1994): 1649–1665.

9. H. Mintzberg, "Rethinking Strategic Planning: Part I: Pitfalls and Fallacies," *Long Range Planning* 27 (1994): 12–21, and "Part II: New Roles for Planners," 22–30; H. Mintzberg, "The Pitfalls of Strategic Planning," *California Management Review* 36 (1993): 32–47.

10. S. Berfield and L. Rupp, "The Aging of Abercrombie & Fitch: Behind the Decline of Abercrombie & Fitch and the Fall of Its Mastermind, Michael Jeffries," *BloombergBusiness*, January 22, 2015, accessed April 26, 2015, http://www.bloomberg.com /news/features/2015-01-22/the-aging-of-abercrombie -fitch-i58ltcqx; L. Rupp, "Abercrombie's Next CEO Needs to Revamp Outdated Brand, Again," *Bloomberg Business*, December 9, 2014, accessed April 26, 2015, http://www.bloomberg.com/news /articles/2014-12-10/abercrombies-next-ceo-will -have-to-revamp-outdated-brand-again.

11. G. Ip, "China, Oil Show Peril of Faulty Assumptions," *Wall Street Journal*, January 13, 2016, accessed May 7, 2016, http://www.wsj.com/articles /china-oil-show-peril-of-faulty-assumptions -1452705708.

12. Mintzberg, "The Pitfalls of Strategic Planning."

13. P. Sonne and P. Evans, "The $1.6 Billion Grocery Flop: Tesco Poised to Quit US," *Wall Street Journal*, December 6, 2012, accessed May 24, 2013, http://www.wsj.com/articles/SB100014241278873246 40104578160514192695162.

14. Locke and Latham, *A Theory of Goal Setting & Task Performance*.

15. A. King, B. Oliver, B. Sloop, and K. Vaverek, *Planning & Goal Setting for Improved Performance: Participant's Guide* (Cincinnati, OH: Thomson Executive Press, 1995).

16. M. Prior, "Lafly: P&G Getting into Shape," *WWD*, February 20, 2015, 9, *P&G 2014 Annual Report*, accessed April 26, 2015, http://www.pginvestor. com/interactive/lookandfeel/4004124/PG _Annual_Report_2014.pdf; J. Hawkins, "Procter & Gamble Looking to Trim Its Brand Portfolio by Exiting Over 100 Brands," *Mainenewsonline*, February 23, 2015, accessed April 26, 2015, http:// mainenewsonline.com/content/15022993-procter -gamble-looking-trim-its-brand-portfolio-exiting-over.

17. Ibid.

18. Ibid; A. Steele, "Coty Profits Hit by Costs of Merger with PG Brands," *Market Watch*, February 4, 2016, accessed May 7, 2016, http://www.marketwatch .com/story/coty-profit-hit-by-costs-of-merger -with-pg-brands-2016-02-04; "P&G Accepts Coty's Offer of $12.5 Billion to Merge 43 P&G Beauty Brands with Coty," *Business Wire*, July 9, 2015, accessed May 7, 2016, http://www.businesswire .com/news/home/20150709005357/en/PG-Accepts -Coty%e2%80%99s-Offer-12.5-Billion-Merge.

19. C. Loomis, J. Schlosser, J. Sung, M. Boyle, and P. Neering, "The 15% Delusion: Brash Predictions about Earnings Growth Often Lead to Missed Targets, Battered Stock, and Creative Accounting—and That's When Times Are Good," *Fortune*, February 5, 2001, 102; H. Paster, "Manager's Journal: Be Prepared," *Wall Street Journal*, September 24, 2001, A24; P. Sellers, "The New Breed: The Latest Crop of CEOs Is Disciplined, Deferential, Even a Bit Dull," *Fortune*, November 18, 2002, 66; H. Klein and M. Wesson, "Goal and Commitment and the Goal-Setting Process: Conceptual Clarification and Empirical Synthesis," *Journal of Applied Psychology* 84 (1999): 885–896.

20. Locke and Latham, *A Theory of Goal Setting & Task Performance*.

21. J. Jargon, "Wendy's Three-Year Quest to Find Blackberries," *Wall Street Journal*, August 19, 2015, B1; C. Beach. "Wendy's Needs 2 Million Pounds of Blackberries," *The Packer*, August 20, 2015, accessed May 7, 2016, http://www.thepacker.com /news/wendy%E2%80%99s-needs-2-million-pounds -blackberries.

22. A. Bandura and D. H. Schunk, "Cultivating Competence, Self-Efficacy, and Intrinsic Interest Through Proximal Self-Motivation," *Journal of Personality & Social Psychology* 41 (1981): 586–598.

23. Naughton, K., "Driverless in Detroit: Even General Motors Thinks the Age of Autonomous Cars Is Inevitable," *Bloomberg Businessweek*, November 2–8, 2015, 53.

24. Locke and Latham, *A Theory of Goal Setting & Task Performance*.

25. M. J. Neubert, "The Value of Feedback and Goal Setting over Goal Setting Alone and Potential Moderators of This Effect: A Meta-Analysis," *Human Performance* 11 (1998): 321–335.

26. E. H. Bowman and D. Hurry, "Strategy Through the Option Lens: An Integrated View of Resource Investments and the Incremental-Choice Process," *Academy of Management Review* 18 (1993): 760–782.

27. "How Design Thinking Transformed Airbnb from a Failing Startup to a Billion Dollar Business," *Design Magazine*, 2014, http://firstround.com/review /How-design-thinking-transformed-Airbnb-from -failing-startup-to-billion-dollar-business/.

28. M. Lawson, "In Praise of Slack: Time Is of the Essence," *Academy of Management Executive* 15 (2000): 125–135.

29. R. Smith, "Utilities Seek to Stockpile Essential Parts for Disasters," *Wall Street Journal*, April 7, 2016, accessed May 7, 2016, http://www.wsj.com /articles/utilities-seek-to-stockpile-essential-parts-for -disasters-1460076194.

30. M. Prior, "Lafley: P&G Getting Into Shape," *WWD*, February 20, 2015, p. 9; C. Hymowitz and L. Coleman-Lochner, "Lafley Pivots from Builder to Demolition Man as He Shrinks P&G," *Bloomberg News*, April 14, 2015, accessed April 27, 2015, http:// www.bloomberg.com/news/articles/2015-04-14 /lafley-pivots-from-builder-to-demolition-man-as-he -shrinks-p-g.

31. J. C. Collins and J. I. Porras, "Organizational Vision and Visionary Organizations," *California Management Review*, Fall 1991: 30–52.

32. "About Avon," *Avon*, accessed May 7, 2016, http://www.avoncompany.com/aboutavon/index.html.

33. Collins and Porras, "Organizational Vision and Visionary Organization."

34. J. Dulski, "Jennifer Dulski of Change.org, on Problem-Solving," interview by A. Bryant, *New York Times*, November 30, 2013, accessed June 5, 2014, http://www.nytimes.com/2013/12/01/business /jennifer-dulski-of-changeorg-on-problem-solving .html?ref=business.

35. Collins and Porras, "Organizational Vision and Visionary Organizations"; J. A. Pearce II, "The Company Mission as a Strategic Tool," *Sloan Management Review*, Spring 1982: 15–24.

36. J. Jargon, "Sbarro Seeks New Life Outside the Mall," *Wall Street Journal*, October 2, 2015, accessed May 7, 2016, http://www.wsj.com/articles/sbarro -seeks-new-life-outside-the-mall-1443778202.

37. Ibid.

38. E. Musk, "The Secret Tesla Motors Master Plan (just between you and me)," *Tesla Motors* (blog), August 2, 2006, accessed June 5, 2014, http://www .teslamotors.com/blog/secret-tesla-motors-master -plan-just-between-you-and-me.

39. J. Boudreau, "Tesla Motors Begins Delivering Model S Electric Cars in a Silicon Valley Milestone," *San Jose Mercury News*, June 22, 2012, accessed June 5, 2014, http://www.mercurynews.com/business /ci_20919722/silicon-valley-milestone-tesla-motors -begins-delivering-model?refresh=no.

40. T. Randall, "Here's How Elon Musk Takes Tesla to 500,000 Cars in Five Years," *Bloomberg Business-Week*, August 10, 2015, accessed May 7, 2016, http:// www.bloomberg.com/news/articles/2015-08-10 /here-s-how-elon-musk-takes-tesla-to-500-000 -cars-in-five-years; D. Choy, "Tesla Model X Release Date Early 2015: Price Estimated Just Under $70,000," *LA Times*, June 17, 2014, accessed June 23, 2014, http://www.latintimes.com/tesla-model-x -release-date-early-2015-price-estimated-just-under -70000-report-182247; N. Bilton, "Disruptions: The Echo Chamber of Silicon Valley," *New York Times*, June 2, 2013, accessed June 5, 2014, http://bits.blogs. nytimes.com/2013/06/02/disruptions-the-echo -chamber-of-silicon-valley/.

41. J. Jargon, "New Plan at Hostess: Cupcakes Everywhere," *Wall Street Journal*, September 18, 2015, B1.

42. Ibid.

43. R. Smith and G. Tabbing, "Why Radical Transparency Is Good Business," *HBR Blog Network*, October 11, 2012, accessed May 25, 2013, https:// hbr.org/2012/10/why-radical-transparency-is-good -business.

44. A. Bryant, "Transparency Is Much More Than a Buzzword," *New York Times*, March 2, 2013, accessed May 14, 2013, http://www.nytimes.com /2013/03/03/business/ryan-smith-of-qualtrics-on -building-a-transparent-culture.html?_r=0.

45. T. Mann, and V. McGrane, "GE to Cash Out of Banking Business," *Wall Street Journal*, April 11, 2015, A1.

46. S. McCartney, "Inside an Airline's Winter War Room," *Wall Street Journal*, February 5, 2015, D1.

47. J. Paterson, "Presenteeism on the Rise Among UK Workforce," *Employee Benefits*, May 2013, 3.

48. S. Shellenbarger, "The Art of Calling in Sick— Or Not," *Wall Street Journal*, October 12, 2012, D1.

49. S. McCartney, "The Trouble with Keeping Commercial Flights Clean," *Wall Street Journal*, September 18, 2014, D1.

50. N. Humphrey, "References a Tricky Issue for Both Sides," *Nashville Business Journal* 11 (May 8, 1995): 1A.

51. K. R. MacCrimmon, R. N. Taylor, and E. A. Locke, "Decision Making and Problem Solving," in *Handbook of Industrial & Organizational Psychology*, ed. M. D. Dunnette (Chicago: Rand McNally, 1976), 1397–1453.

52. L. Weber, "Businesses Use New Apps for Workplace Scheduling," *Wall Street Journal*, September 15, 2013, accessed June 23, 2014, http://online.wsj .com/news/articles/SB100014241278873241394045790 17193724502688?mg=reno64-wsj.

53. MacCrimmon, et al., "Decision Making and Problem Solving."

54. G. Kress, "The Role of Interpretation in the Decision Process," *Industrial Management* 37 (1995): 10–14.

55. M. Esterl, "Coke Chief's Solution for Lost Fizz: More Soda," *Wall Street Journal*, March 19, 2015, A1, A12.

56. L. Weber, "Businesses Use New Apps for Workplace Scheduling," *Wall Street Journal*, September 15, 2013, accessed June 23, 2014, http://online.wsj .com/news/articles/SB100014241278873241394045790 17193724502688?mg=reno64-wsj.

57. "New-Vehicle Ratings Comparison by Car Category," *ConsumerReports.org*, February 19, 2005, http://www.consumerreports.org/cro/cars/index.htm.

58. P. Djang, "Selecting Personal Computers," *Journal of Research on Computing in Education* 25 (1993): 327.

59. "European Cities Monitor," *Cushman & Wakefield*, 2010, http://www.europeancitiesmonitor.eu /wp-content/uploads/2010/10/ECM-2010-Full -Version.pdf.

60. J. Stiff, "6 Tips to Build Your Social Media Strategy," *CIO*, May 8, 2013, accessed May 26, 2013, http://www.cio.com/article/732975/6_Tips_to_Build _Your_Social_Media_Strategy.

61. "The Critical Role of Teams," *The Ken Blanchard Companies*, March 23, 2006, accessed June 5, 2014, http://www.kenblanchard.com/img /pub/pdf_critical_role_teams.pdf.

62. I. L. Janis, *Groupthink* (Boston: Houghton Mifflin, 1983).

63. C. P. Neck and C. C. Manz, "From Groupthink to Teamthink: Toward the Creation of Constructive Thought Patterns in Self-Managing Work Teams," *Human Relations* 47 (1994): 929–952; J. Schwartz and M. L. Wald, "'Groupthink' Is 30 Years Old, and Still Going Strong," *New York Times*, March 9, 2003, 5.

64. J. McIntosh, "Assumptions of Quality Could Hinder Group Decision-Making Ability," *Medical News Today*, March 10, 2015, accessed April 27, 2015, http://www.medicalnewstoday.com /articles/290618.php.

65. A. Mason, W.A. Hochwarter, and K.R. Thompson, "Conflict: An Important Dimension in Successful Management Teams," *Organizational Dynamics* 24 (1995): 20.

66. D. Merrill, "Corner Office: Douglas Merrill of ZestFinance: Steer Clear of What You Can't Measure," interview by A. Bryant, March 20, 2014, accessed June 5, 2014, http://www.nytimes .com/2014/03/21/business/douglas-merrill-of -zestfinance-steer-clear-of-what-you-cant-measure.html.

67. J. Freeman, "The Soul of a Hedge Fund 'Machine,'" *Wall Street Journal*, June 6, 2014, accessed June 24, 2014, http://online.wsj.com /articles/james-freeman-the-soul-of-a-hedge -fund-machine-1402094722.

68. A. Mason, et al., "Conflict: An Important Dimension in Successful Management Teams."

69. R. Cosier and C. R. Schwenk, "Agreement and Thinking Alike: Ingredients for Poor Decisions," *Academy of Management Executive* 4 (1990): 69–74.

70. K. Jenn and E. Mannix, "The Dynamic Nature of Conflict: A Longitudinal Study of Intragroup Conflict and Group Performance," *Academy of Management Journal* 44, no. 2 (2001): 238–251; R. L. Priem, D. A. Harrison, and N. K. Muir, "Structured Conflict and Consensus Outcomes in Group Decision Making," *Journal of Management* 21 (1995): 691–710.

71. A. Van De Ven and A. L. Delbecq, "Nominal versus Interacting Group Processes for Committee Decision Making Effectiveness," *Academy of Management Journal* 14 (1971): 203–212.

72. P. Gilbert, "Hearing Every Voice in the Room: How IBM Brings Ideas Forward from Its Teams," *New York Times*, December 6, 2014, BU8.

73. A. R. Dennis and J. S. Valicich, "Group, Sub-Group, and Nominal Group Idea Generation: New Rules for a New Media?" *Journal of Management* 20 (1994): 723–736.

74. R. B. Gallupe, W. H. Cooper, M. L. Grise, and L. M. Bastianutti, "Blocking Electronic Brainstorms," *Journal of Applied Psychology* 79 (1994): 77–86.

75. E. Bernstein, "Speaking Up Is Hard to Do: Researchers Explain Why," *Wall Street Journal*, February 7, 2012, accessed May 27, 2013, http:// online.wsj.com/article/SB1000142405297020413640 4577207020525853492.html.

76. R. B. Gallupe and W. H. Cooper, "Brainstorming Electronically," *Sloan Management Review*, Fall 1993, 27–36.

77. Ibid.

78. G. Kay, "Effective Meetings through Electronic Brainstorming," *Management Quarterly* 35 (1995): 15.

6

1. "Microsoft Surface Usage Share Takes Slight Dip in Early 2014," *Chitika*, May 20, 2014, accessed June 24, 2014, http://chitika.com/insights/2014 /surface-over-time D. Resinger, "What Caused the Tablet Sales Slowdown of Q4 2014," *eWeek*, February 3, 2015, 11.

2. "iPad Usage Share Rises Since July, Drops Slightly Year-over-Year," *Chitika*, November 6, 2014, accessed April 27, 2015, https://chitika.com/insights/2014/q4 -tablet-update.

3. J. Barney, "Firm Resources and Sustained Competitive Advantage," *Journal of Management* 17 (1991): 99–120; J. Barney, "Looking Inside for Competitive Advantage," *Academy of Management Executive* 9 (1995): 49–61.

4. D. Bailey, "Is It Time to Say Goodbye to Netbooks?," *The Motley Fool*, April 30, 2011, accessed March 1, 2012, http://www.fool.com/investing /general/2011/04/30/is-it-time-to-say-goodbye-to -netbooks.aspx; S. Lohr, "Netbooks Lose Status as Tablets Like the iPad Rise," *New York Times*, February 13, 2011, accessed March 1, 2012, http:// www.nytimes.com/2011/02/14/technology/14netbook .html?pagewanted=all.

5. C. Arther, "Netbooks Plummet While Tablets and Smartphones Soar, Says Canalys," *The Guardian* (technology blog), February 3, 2012 (5:38), accessed June 5, 2014, http://www.theguardian.com/technology /blog/2012/feb/03/netbooks-pc-canalys-tablet.

6. N. Ralph, "Microsoft Windows 10 Review: Microsoft Gets It Right," *CNet.com*, July 28, 2015, accessed April 20, 2016, http://www.cnet.com/products /microsoft-windows-10/; E. Price, Here's How Nokia Creates Its Maps," *Mashable.com*, November 12, 2012, accessed March 10, 2016, http://mashable .com/2012/11/20/nokia-here-map-car.

7. B. Snyder, "Tech's Bottom Line," *InfoWorld*, April 17, 2015, http://www.infoworld.com/article/2910323 /mobile-security/for-android-adware-is-the-threat -not-malware.html; "One in Six Android Apps Is a Malware, Says Study," *The Times of India*, April 23, 2015, http://timesofindia.indiatimes.com/tech /tech-news/One-in-six-Android-apps-is-a-malware -says-study/articleshow/47021326.cms.

8. "2015 Data Breach Investigations Report, Verizon Enterprise Solutions," accessed April 27, 2015, 18, http://www.verizonenterprises.com/DBIR/2015/.

9. "U.S. Market Reach of the Most Popular iPhone Apps in March 2012," *Statista*, accessed April 20, 2016, http://www.statista.com/statistics/243757/us -market-reach-of-the-most-popular-iphone-app/.

10. N. Carlson, "Apple Has ~7,000 Fewer People Working On Maps Than Google," *Business Insider*, September 21, 2012, accessed April 20, 2016, http:// www.businessinsider.com/apple-has-7000-fewer -people-working-on-maps-than-google-2012-9?op=1.

11. D. Goldman, "Apple CEO: 'We are extremely sorry' for Maps Frustration," *CNN Money*, September 28, 2012, accessed April 20, 2016, http://money .cnn.com/2012/09/28/technology/apple-maps-apology /index.html.

12. P. Elmer-DeWitt, "How Apple Maps Overtook Google Maps," *Fortune*, June 16, 2015, accessed April 20, 2016, http://fortune.com/2015/06/16 /apple-google-maps-ios/.

13. S. Hart and C. Banbury, "How Strategy-Making Processes Can Make a Difference," *Strategic Management Journal* 15 (1994): 251–269.

14. R. A. Burgelman, "Fading Memories: A Process Theory of Strategic Business Exit in Dynamic Environments," *Administrative Science Quarterly* 39 (1994): 24–56; R. A. Burgelman and A. S. Grove, "Strategic Dissonance," *California Management Review* 38 (Winter 1996): 8–28.

15. E. Byron and J. Lublin, "Lackluster Avon Explores Makeover," *Wall Street Journal*, April 27, 2015, accessed April 28, 2015, http://www.wsj .com/articles/lackluster-avon-explores-makeover -1430188201?KEYWORDS=avon.

16. Ibid.

17. J. Lublin and E. Byron, "Avon Explores Strategic Alternatives: Options Include Possible Sale of Struggling North America Business," *Wall Street Journal*, April 14, 2015, accessed April 27, 2015, http://www .wsj.com/articles/avon-explores-strategic-alternatives -1429030371; S. Mitchell, "Sephora to Open Stores in Australia," *Financial Review*, April 8, 2014, accessed April 27, 2015, http://www.afr.com/business /sephora-to-open-stores-in-australia-20140408-ix7ac; R. Duprey, "Why Procter & Gamble Company Is Shedding Its Cosmetics Business," *The Motley Fool. com*, April 23, 2015, accessed April 27, 2015, http:// www.fool.com/investing/general/2015/04/23/putting -lipstick-on-a-pig-ma-heats-up-in-beauty-ca.aspx.

18. Byron and Lublin, "Lackluster Avon Explores Makeover."

19. R. A. Burgelman and A. S. Grove, "Strategic Dissonance," *California Management Review* 38 (Winter 1996): 8–28.

20. Y. Koh, "Airline Learns to Be Nimble—Starting Up Budget Carriers Helped All Nippon Restructure Its Own Operations," *Wall Street Journal*, May 23, 2013, B8.

21. J. Mahler, "For SkyMall, It All Seemed So Cool at Six Miles High," *The New York Times*, January 23, 2015, accessed April 28, 2015, http://www.nytimes .com/2015/01/24/business/it-all-seemed-so-cool-at-six -miles-high.html?_r=0.

22. A. Fiegenbaum, S. Hart, and D. Schendel, "Strategic Reference Point Theory," *Strategic Management Journal* 17 (1996): 219–235.

23. S. Salomon, "'Consumer Reports' Names the 10 Best (and Worst) Cars of 2016," *Boston.com*, March 17, 2016, accessed April 25, 2016, http://www .boston.com/cars/news-and-reviews/2016/03/17 /consumer-reports-names-the-best-and-worst-cars /arJvxL2UNGXRyRH2Qxt2AI/story.html.

24. K. Yakal, "The Best Online Tax Preparation Software for 2016," *PC Magazine*, March 4, 2016, accessed April 25, 2016, http://www.pcmag.com /article2/0,2817,2498447,00.asp.

25. S. Clifford, "Where Wal-Mart Failed, Aldi Succeeds," *New York Times*, March 29, 2011, accessed March 1, 2012, http://www.nytimes.com/2011/03/30 /business/30aldi.html?pagewanted=all.

26. A. Fiegenbaum and H. Thomas, "Strategic Groups as Reference Groups: Theory, Modeling and Empirical Examination of Industry and Competitive Strategy," *Strategic Management Journal* 16 (1995): 461–476.

27. "Expecting 4.7% Home Improvement Sales Growth in 2016," *Home Improvement Research Institute*, March 2, 2016, accessed April 25, 2016, http://www.hiri.org.

28. R. K. Reger and A. S. Huff, "Strategic Groups: A Cognitive Perspective," *Strategic Management Journal* 14 (1993): 103–124.

29. "U.S. Store County by State," *HomeDepot.com*, January 31, 2016, accessed April 25, 2016, http:// ir.homedepot.com/phoenix.zhtml?c=63646&p=irol -factsfaq; Lowe's Companies, Inc., March 3, 2016, accessed April 25, 2016, http://phx.corporate-ir.net /phoenix.zhtml?c=95223&p=irol-IRHome.

30. "About Ace Hardware," *Ace Corporate*, March 3, 2016, accessed April 25, 2016, http://www.acehardware .com/category/index.jsp?categoryId=34453606.

31. "About Aubuchon Hardware," *Aubuchon Hardware*, accessed April 25, 2016, https://www .hardwarestore.com/about-us.

32. "Frequently Asked Questions," *Ace Hardware*, accessed July 29, 2008, http://www.acehardware .com/corp/index.jsp?page=faq; "Company History: 2010s," *Ace Hardware*, accessed June 5, 2014, http:// www.acehardware.com/category/index .jsp?categoryId=34641526.

33. "History of 84 Lumber," accessed April 23, 2015, http://www.84lumber.com/About/History.aspx.

34. J. Mangalindan, "eBay's Back!" *Fortune*, February 5, 2013, 58–65.

35. Ibid.

36. Ibid.

37. G. Bensinger, "eBay's New Goal: Double Its Users," *Wall Street Journal*, March 29, 2013, B5.

38. R. Blumenstein, "How IBM Plans to Thrive as a Digital Company," *Wall Street Journal*, October 27, 2015, R3.

39. "Vision," *Dr. Pepper Snapple Group*, accessed April 25, 2016, http://www.drpeppersnapplegroup.com/company/vision/.

40. M. Lubatkin, "Value-Creating Mergers: Fact or Folklore?" *Academy of Management Executive* 2 (1988): 295–302; M. Lubatkin and S. Chatterjee, "Extending Modern Portfolio Theory Into the Domain of Corporate Diversification: Does It Apply?" *Academy of Management Journal* 37 (1994): 109–136; M. H. Lubatkin and P. J. Lane, "Psst ... The Merger Mavens Still Have It Wrong!" *Academy of Management Executive* 10 (1996): 21–39.

41. "Science Applied to Life, Annual Report 2014," *3M*, accessed April 28, 2015, http://investors.3m.com/files/doc_financials/2014/ar/2014_3M_Annual_Report.pdf.

42. P. Morris, "Why Warren Buffett Just Bought Duracell," *Money*, November 14, 2014, accessed April 28, 2015, http://time.com/money/3585592/warren-buffett-duracell/; P. Ziobro and E. Byron, "P7G to Unload Duracell as CEO Lafley Focuses on Best Sellers," *Wall Street Journal*, October 14, 2014, accessed April 28, 2015, http://online.wsj.com/articles/p-g-to-exit-duracell-battery-ops-1414149781; "Mars to Buy Most of P&G's Pet Food Business for $2.9 Billion," *Reuters.com*, April 9, 2014, accessed April 28, 2015, http://uk.reuters.com/article/2014/04/09/uk-mars-pgpetcare-acquisition-idUKBREA3813B20140409.

43. "Our Brands," *Newell Brands*, accessed April 25, 2016, http://www.newellbrands.com/OurBrands/Pages/our-Brands.aspx.

44. M. Reeves, S. Moose, and T. Venema, "BCG Classics Revisited: The Growth Share Matrix," *BCG Perspectives*, June 4, 2014, accessed April 25, 2016, https://www.bcgperspectives.com/content/articles/corporate_strategy_portfolio_management_strategic_planning_growth_share_matrix_bcg_classics_revisited/.

45. D. Hambrick, I. MacMillan, and D. Day, "Strategic Attributes and Performance in the BCG Matrix—A PIMS-based Analysis of Industrial Product Businesses," *Academy of Management Journal* 25 (1982): 510–531.

46. J. Armstrong and R. Brodie, "Effects of Portfolio Planning Methods on Decision Making: Experimental Results," *International Journal of Research in Marketing* 11 (1994): 73–84.

47. M. Rogowsky, "Microsoft Office: Could the Cash Cow's Long-Awaited Death Finally Be Imminent," *Forbes*, May 5, 2014, accessed April 28, 2015, http://www.forbes.com/sites/markrogowsky/2014/05/05/microsoft-office-could-the-cash-cows-long-awaited-death-finally-be-imminent/.

48. "Up-to-Date Program for Pages, Numbers, and Keynote," *Apple*, accessed April 28, 2015, https://www.apple.com/creativity-apps/mac/up-to-date/; T. Green, "What did Microsoft's Earnings Reveal about Its Biggest Cash Cow?" *The Motley Fool*, April 30, 2014, accessed April 28, 2015, http://www.fool.com/investing/general/2014/04/30/microsofts-stellar-quarter-was-driven-by-office.aspx.

49. S. Ovide, "Microsoft Outperforms Its Low Growth Expectations," *Wall Street Journal*, April 24, 2015, B4.

50. J. A. Pearce II, "Selecting Among Alternative Grand Strategies," *California Management Review* (Spring 1982): 23–31.

51. "AT&T to Buy DirecTV for $48.5 Billion," *CBS News*, May 18, 2014, accessed June 24, 2014, http://

www.cbsnews.com/news/at-t-to-buy-directv-for-49-billion/.

52. M. Reardon, "AT&T Defends Benefits of Proposed DirecTV Merger," *cNet*, June 24, 2014, accessed June 24, 2014, http://www.cnet.com/news/at-t-defends-benefits-of-proposed-directv-merger/.

53. G. Bensinger, "Amazon Plans Hundreds of Brick-and-Mortar Bookstores, Mall CEO Says," *Wall Street Journal*, February 2, 2016, B1; H. Tabuchi, "Amazon Challenges Etsy with Strictly Handmade Marketplace," *New York Times*, October 8, 2015, B3.

54. "ABM Launches New Brand," *ABM Industries*, accessed May 31, 2013, http://www.abm.com/about-abm/pages/our-new-brand.aspx.

55. J. A. Pearce II, "Retrenchment Remains the Foundation of Business Turnaround," *Strategic Management Journal* 15 (1994): 407–417.

56. "Goldsmith Bankers," *Encyclopedia of Money*, accessed June 25, 2014, http://encyclopedia-of-money.blogspot.com/2010/03/goldsmith-bankers.html; "Timeline | 1690: The Start of Barclays," *Barclays Plc*, accessed June 25, 2014, http://www.barclays.com/about-barclays/history.html.

57. M. Colchester and D. Enrich, "Barclays Dashes Its Global Dreams—U.K. Lender to Cut Investment Bank Nearly in Half as Expansion Efforts Falter; 'Bold Simplification,'" *Wall Street Journal*, May 9, 2014, C1.

58. M. Berry, "Barclays to Axe 14,000 Jobs and Create 'Bad Bank,'" *FundWeb*, May 8, 2014, accessed June 25, 2014, http://www.fundweb.co.uk/news-and-analysis/uk/barclays-to-axe-14000-jobs-and-create-bad-bank/2009986.article.

59. J. Jargon, "McDonald's Gets Some Sizzle Back," *Wall Street Journal*, October 23, 2015, B1.

60. J. Jargon, "McDonald's Profit Climbs, Showing Turnaround Is Sustainable," *Wall Street Journal*, April 22, 2016, accessed April 25, 2016, http://www.wsj.com/articles/mcdonalds-profit-climbs-above-expectations-1461327646.

61. M. Ramsey, "Tesla Is Hiring Fast as Rivals Loom," *Wall Street Journal*, December 29, 2015, B1; M. Ramsey, "Tesla Rival Plans $1 Billion Plant," *Wall Street Journal*, November 6, 2015, B6; D. Wakabayashi and M. Ramsey, "Apple Secretly Gears Up to Create Car," *Wall Street Journal*, February 14–16, 2015, A1; "Best Cars: 2015 Tesla Model S," *U.S. News and World Report*, April 25, 2016, http://usnews.rankingsandreviews.com/cars-trucks/Tesla_Model-S/.

62. L. Ellis and L. Stevens, "UPS Tries On 3-D Printing in Bet to Stem New Threat," *Wall Street Journal*, September 19–20, 2015, B1.

63. Ibid.

64. K. Souza, "The Supply Side: Analysts Assess Walmart Supplier Contract Changes," *The City Wire*, October 12, 2015, accessed April 26, 2016, http://talkbusiness.net/2015/10/the-supply-side-analysts-assess-wal-mart-supplier-contract-changes/; S. Pettypiece, M. Townsend, and L. Coleman-Lochner, "Now, Suppliers are Walmart's Main Squeeze," *Bloomberg Businessweek*, September 21–27, 2015, 24–25.

65. D. Sax, "A $99.99 Surfboard Upends the Industry," *Bloomberg Businessweek*, October 29, 2015, April 26, 2016, http://www.bloomberg.com/news/articles/2015-10-29/wavestorm-s-99-99-surfboard-upends-the-industry.

66. Ibid.

67. "Norweb Microfiber," *Norwex*, accessed June 26, 2014, http://www.norwex.biz/pws/home2999999/tabs/microfiber.aspx.

68. E. Byron, "It Cleans, Polishes and Scrubs: It's a $27 Cloth and Water," *Wall Street Journal*, June 25, 2014, D1.

69. "'Our Purpose' Can One Person Change the World? At Norwex—We Think We Can," *Norwex*, accessed June 26, 2014, http://www.norwex.biz/pws/home2999999/tabs/our-purpose.aspx.

70. Pirate Joe's, accessed April 28, 2015, http://www.piratejoes.ca/.

71. C. Dawson, "This Pirate Sells Treasures from Trader Joe's to Canadians: Retailer Drives to US to Stock Up on Grocer's Goodies, Nuts, Coffee, Maple Syrup," *Wall Street Journal*, March 7, 2015, accessed April 28, 2015, http://www.wsj.com/articles/pirate-joes-sells-treasures-from-trader-joes-to-canadians-1425660654.

72. R. E. Miles and C. C. Snow, *Organizational Strategy, Structure, & Process* (New York: McGraw-Hill, 1978); S. Zahra and J. A. Pearce, "Research Evidence on the Miles-Snow Typology," *Journal of Management* 16 (1990): 751–768; W. L. James and K. J. Hatten, "Further Evidence on the Validity of the Self Typing Paragraph Approach: Miles and Snow Strategic Archetypes in Banking," *Strategic Management Journal* 16 (1995): 161–168.

73. W. Boston, "Porsche Tries to Remain Exclusive as Luxury Demand Surges," *Wall Street Journal*, March 17, 2015, http://www.wsj.com/articles/porsche-tries-to-keep-itself-exclusive-as-luxury-demand-surges-1426591087.

74. C. Karmin, "Airbnb Crimps Hotels' Power on Pricing," *Wall Street Journal*, September 29, 2015, accessed April 26, 2016, http://www.wsj.com/articles/airbnb-crimps-hotels-power-on-pricing-1443519181.

75. "About Us," *Airbnb*, accessed April 26, 2016, https://www.airbnb.com/about/about-us.

76. S. Rosenbloom, "Giving Airbnb a Run for Its Money," *New York Times*, February 10, 2015, T2.

77. W. Boston, "In Luxury Race, Profits Get Dented," *Wall Street Journal*, March 13, 2015, B1.

78. M. Chen, "Competitor Analysis and Interfirm Rivalry: Toward a Theoretical Integration," *Academy of Management Review* 21 (1996): 100–134; J. C. Baum and H. J. Korn, "Competitive Dynamics of Interfirm Rivalry," *Academy of Management Journal* 39 (1996): 255–291.

79. M. Chen, "Competitor Analysis and Interfirm Rivalry: Toward a Theoretical Integration," *Academy of Management Review* 21 (1996): 100–124.

80. C. Giammona and L. Patton, "Playing Chicken in the Burger Wars," *BloombergBusiness*, January 19–25, 2015, 28–29.

81. J. White, "Wendy's Wendy Gets a Makeover," *Wall Street Journal*, October 11, 2012, accessed June 5, 2014. http://blogs.wsj.com/corporate-intelligence/2012/10/11/wendy/?KEYWORDS=wendy%27s+strategy.

82. "Wendy's Plans to Double Pace of Image Activation Reimages in 2014," *Yahoo! Finance*, February 27, 2014, accessed June 5, 2014, http://finance.yahoo.com/news/wendys-plans-double-pace-image-123613973.html.

83. A. Gasparro, "McDonald's New Chief Plots Counter Attack," *Wall Street Journal*, March 2, 2015, B1.

84. L. Lavelle, "The Chickens Come Home to Roost, and Boston Market Is Prepared to Expand," *The Record*, October 6, 1996.

85. "2016 Franchise 500—Subway," *Entrepreneur*, accessed April 26, 2016, http://www.entrepreneur.com/franchises/subway/282839; "Discover McDonalds Around the Globe," accessed April 26, 2016, http://www.aboutmcdonalds.com/mcd/country/map.html84. I. Brat, "Jamba Plans to Sell 100 Stores," *Wall Street Journal*, April 2, 2015, B2; "Company Profile—McDonald's Is Global—And in Your Hometown," accessed April 23, 2015, http://www.aboutmcdonalds.com/mcd/investors/company_profile.html.

86. "Our People, Our Communities: Heart Health & Childhood Obesity," *Subway*, accessed April 26, 2016, http://www.subway.com/subwayroot/about_us/Social_Responsibility/OurPeopleOurCommunities.aspx#joy.

87. S. Bertoni, "Razor Wars: Harry's Raises $75 Million to Fight Gillette and Dollar Shave Club," *Forbes*, July 7, 2015, accessed March 9, 2016 http://www.forbes.com/sites/stevenbertoni/2015/07/07/razor-wars-harrys-raises-75-million-to-fight-gillette-and-dollar-shave-club/2/#5ff774d832c9; S. Ng and P. Ziobro, "Razor Sales Move Online, Away from Gillette," *Wall Street Journal*, June 23, 2015, B1.

88. D. Ketchen, Jr., C. Snow, and V. Street, "Improving Firm Performance by Matching Strategic Decision—Making Process to Competitive Dynamics," *Academy of Management Executive* 18 (2004) 29–43.

89. D. Harwell, "Razor Lawsuit: Gillette Takes on Online Service," *New Zealand Herald*, December 21, 2015, accessed April 26, 2016, http://www.nzherald.co.nz/business/news/article.cfm?c_id=3&objectid=11564163.

90. M. Gottfried, "T-Mobile's Shine Dims Sprint's Deal Hopes," *Wall Street Journal*, March 1, 2014, B14.

91. R. Karpinski, "Un-Carrier at Three Years: Assessing T-Mobile's Disruptive Impact," *451 Research*, March 28, 2016, accessed April 26, 2016, https://newsroom.t-mobile.com/content/1020/files/NEWImpactReport.pdf.

92. "Now, More Than 100 Services Stream Free with T-Mobile's Binge On and Music Freedom," *T-Mobile*, April 5, 2016, accessed April 26, 2016, https://newsroom.t-mobile.com/news-and-blogs/binge-on-music-freedom-new-services.htm; "T-Mobile Introduces 'Mobile without Borders': Extends Coverage & Calling Across North America at No Extra Charge," *T-Mobile*, July 9, 2015, accessed April 26, 2016, https://newsroom.t-mobile.com/media-kits/mobile-without-borders.htm; M. Gottfried, "T-Mobile Takes Toll on Verizon," *Wall Street Journal*, April 25, 2014, C8; E. Mason, "T-Mobile's Loss Widens as Costs Press Higher," *Wall Street Journal*, February 26, 2014, B4; T Gryta and B. Rubin, "T-Mobile Posts Big Gain in Subscribers," *Wall Street Journal*, May 1, 2014, accessed June 26, 2014, http://www.wsj.com/articles/SB10001424052702304677904579535291254065308; Z. Epstein, "The Most Important Wireless Carrier in America," *BGR*, October 10, 2013, accessed June 26, 2014, http://bgr.com/2013/10/10/t-mobile-free-international-roaming-analysis/; T. Gryta, "T-Mobile will Waive Data Fees for Music Services," *Wall Street Journal*, June 18, 2014, accessed June 26, 2014, http://online.wsj.com/articles/t-mobile-will-waive-data-fees-for-music-service-1403142678.

93. R. Wall and J. Chow, "Europe's Top Airlines to Spend Billions in Battle to Win Back Passengers," *Wall Street Journal*, June 4, 2015, accessed April 26, 2016, http://www.wsj.com/articles/europes-top-airlines-to-spend-billions-in-battle-to-win-back-passengers-1433425762.

94. Ibid.

95. C. Boulton, "Amazon's Fire Phone Aims for 'Showrooming on Steroids' - The CIO Report," *Wall Street Journal*, June 19, 2014, accessed April 28, 2015, http://blogs.wsj.com/cio/2014/06/19/amazons-fire-phone-aims-for-showrooming-on-steroids/.

96. Associate Press, "Best Buy's Store Closing List: Is Yours on It?" *CBS News*, April 16, 2012, accessed June 1, 2013, http://www.cbsnews.com/8301-505144_162-57414517/best-buys-store-closing-list-is-yours-on-it/; G. Bensinger, "When Apps Attack: Industries Under Pressure," *Wall Street Journal*, March 27, 2013, accessed June 1, 2013, http://online.wsj.com/article/SB1000142412788732439280457835879340982629.html; M. Bustle, "*Best Buy* Pays Price to Rival Amazon," *Wall Street Journal*, December 14, 2011, accessed June 1, 2013, http://online.wsj.com/article/SB1000142405297020351840457709610260252527328.html; A. Zimmerman, "Can Electronics Stores Survive?" *Wall Street Journal*, August 20, 2012, accessed June 1, 2013, http://www.wsj.com/articles/SB10000872396390444772804577621581739401906.

97. "Annual Reports and Proxy Data," Best Buy, accessed May 10, 2016, http://investors.bestbuy.com/investor-relations/financial-info/annual-reports-and-proxy-statements/default.aspx; N. Halter, "Best Buy Closed 30 Stores Last Year; More Are Likely in 2016," *Minneapolis/St. Paul Business Journal*, February 25, 2016, accessed May 10, 2016, http://www.bizjournals.com/twincities/news/2016/02/25/best-buy-store-closures-2015-2016.html; B. Sozzi, "Best Buy Is Very Quietly Shrinking," *TheStreet.com*, February 25, 2016, accessed May 10, 2016, http://www.thestreet.com/story/13472535/1/best-buy-is-very-quietly-shrinking.html.

7

1. T. Randall, "Inside the Connected Future of Architecture," *Bloomberg Businessweek*, September 23, 2015, 72–77.

2. P. Anderson and M. L. Tushman, "Managing Through Cycles of Technological Change," *Research/Technology Management* 34(3) (May–June 1991): 26–31.

3. R. N. Foster, *Innovation: The Attacker's Advantage* (New York: Summit, 1986).

4. "The Silicon Engine: A Timeline of Semiconductors in Computers," *Computer History Museum*, accessed April 22, 2001, http://www.computerhistory.org/semiconductor/; "The Evolution of a Revolution," *Intel*, accessed June 2, 2013, http://download.intel.com/pressroom/kits/IntelProcessorHistory.pdf; T. Smith, "Inside Intel's Haswell: What do 1.4 BEELION Transistors Get You?" *The Register*, June 3, 2013, accessed June 13, 2014, http://www.theregister.co.uk/2013/06/03/feature_inside_haswell_intel_4g_core/; P. Alcorn, "Intel Xeon E5-2600 v4 Broadwell-EP Review," *Tom's Hardware*, March 31, 2016, accessed May 12, 2016, http://www.tomshardware.com/reviews/intel-xeon-e5-2600-v4-broadwell-ep,4514-2.html.

5. J. Burke, *The Day the Universe Changed* (Boston: Little, Brown, 1985).

6. D. Wakabayashi, "The Point-and-Shoot Camera Faces Its Existential Moment," *Wall Street Journal*, July 30, 2013, accessed June 30, 2014, http://online.wsj.com/news/articles/SB10001424127887324251504578580263719432252.

7. J. Osawa, "Phones Imperil Fancy Cameras," *Wall Street Journal*, November 7, 2013, accessed June 13, 2014, http://online.wsj.com/news/articles/SB10001424052702304574591836436962366989?KEYWORDS=high-end+camera&mg=reno64-wsj.

8. "HTC Talks Camera Tech: DSLR-Destroying Optical Zooming '18 Months' Away," *Official Vodafone UK blog* (blog), April 18, 2014, accessed June 13, 2014, http://blog.vodafone.co.uk/2014/04/18/htc-talks-camera-tech-optical-zooming/; J. Osawa, "Are Camera Apps Enough for Photo Enthusiasts?" *Wall Street Journal*, November 8, 2013, accessed June 13, 2014, http://blogs.wsj.com/digits/2013/11/08/are-camera-apps-enough-for-photo-enthusiasts/?KEYWORDS=dslr+camera.

9. M. L. Tushman, P. C. Anderson, and C. O'Reilly, "Technology Cycles, Innovation Streams, and Ambidextrous Organizations: Organization Renewal Through Innovation Streams and Strategic Change," in *Managing Strategic Innovation and Change*, ed. M. L. Tushman and P. Anderson (New York: Oxford Press, 1997), 3–23.

10. L. Grush, "Magnetically Levitating Elevators Could Reshape Skylines—They Go Up, Down, and All Around," *Popular Science*, April 14, 2015, accessed April 26, 2015, http://www.popsci.com/elevator-will-reshape-skylines"; "ThyssenKrupp Develops the World's First Rope-Free Elevator System to Enable the Building Industry to Face the Challenges of Global Urbanization," *ThyssenKrupp*, November 27, 2014, accessed May 4, 2015, http://www.thyssenkrupp-elevator.com/Show-article.104.0.html?&L=1&cHash=08b38cb686f00ec874ad82c44c737427&tx_ttnews%5Btt_news%5D=546.

11. S. J. Blumberg and J. V. Luke, "Wireless Substitution: Early Release of Estimates from the National Health Interview Survey, January–June 2014," *US Department of Health and Human Services, Centers for Disease Control and Prevention*, December 2014, accessed April 25, 2015, http://www.cdc.gov/nchs/data/nhis/earlyrelease/wireless201412.pdf.

12. Staff, "Landline Phone Penetration Dwindles as Cell-Only Households Grow," *Marketing Charts*, June 6, 2012, accessed June 2, 2013, http://www.marketingcharts.com/direct/landline-phone-penetration-dwindles-as-cell-only-households-grow-22577/.

13. Blumberg and Luke, "Wireless Substitution."

14. "AT&T, Verizon Are Leaving Landlines Behind," *Wall Street Journal News Hub*, online video, 17:27, April 8, 2014, accessed June 13, 2014, http://live.wsj.com/video/att-verizon-are-leaving-landlines-behind/7874152A-A635-4092-9B7B-69EB86AE3787.html?KEYWORDS=milestones#!7874152B-A635-4092-9B7B-69EB86AE3787; R. Knutson, "Verizon Union Says Company Is Not Fixing Landline Phones," *Wall Street Journal*, June 10, 2015, B3.

15. R. Knutson, "Who Needs a Wireless Carrier? Go Wi-Fi Only," *Wall Street Journal*, March 2, 2015, B1.

16. Ibid.

17. E. Schlossberg, *Interactive Excellence: Defining and Developing New Standards for the Twenty-First Century* (New York: Ballantine, 1998).

18. W. Abernathy and J. Utterback, "Patterns of Industrial Innovation," *Technology Review* 2 (1978): 40–47.

19. D. Howley, "Wireless Charging Standard Gets One Step Closer," *Laptop Magazine*, February 1, 2014, accessed July 1, 2014, as reported at http://www.techhive.com/article/2096802/wireless-charging-alliances-teaming-up-to-work-toward-a-cable-free-world.html.

20. "Wireless Charging Surge Seen," *Investor's Business Daily*, March 24, 2014, A02.

21. R. Jones, "Wireless Races to Define 5G," *Wall Street Journal*, March 10, 2015, B7.

22. M. Schilling, "Technological Lockout: An Integrative Model of the Economic and Strategic Factors Driving Technology Success and Failure," *Academy of Management Review* 23 (1998): 267–284; M. Schilling, "Technology Success and Failure in Winner-Take-All Markets: The Impact of Learning Orientation, Timing, and Network Externalities," *Academy of Management Journal* 45 (2002): 387–398.

23. R. McMillan, "Tech World Prepares Obituary for Adobe Flash," *Wall Street Journal*, July 20, 2015, B1.

24. T. M. Amabile, R. Conti, H. Coon, J. Lazenby, and M. Herron, "Assessing the Work Environment for Creativity," *Academy of Management Journal* 39 (1996): 1154–1184.

25. Ibid.

26. M. Csikszentmihalyi, *Flow: The Psychology of Optimal Experience* (New York: Harper & Row, 1990).

27. R. Feintzeig, "Can Furniture Help Workers Stay Focused?" *Wall Street Journal*, April 22, 2015, B7.

28. L. Emarian, "Creating Culture of IT Innovation Includes Rewarding Failure," *Computer World*, April 6, 2012, accessed June 2, 2013, http://www.computerworld.com/s/article/9225870/Creating_culture_of_IT_innovation_includes_rewarding_failure.

29. A. Ahrendts, "The Experts: How Should Leaders Spur Innovation?" interview by C. Wiens, March 12, 2013, accessed June 13, 2014, http://online.wsj.com/news/articles/SB10001424127887323826704578352921473825316?mg=reno64-wsj&url=http%3A%2F%2Fonline.wsj.com%2Farticle%2FSB10001424127887323826704578352921473825316.html.

30. R. Tetzeli, "9 Ways GE Executed Its Radical Green Reinvention," *FastCoexist.com*, December 11, 2015, accessed April 27, 2016, http://www.fastcoexist.com/3054441/9-ways-ge-executed-its-radical-green-reinvention.

31. Ibid.

32. T. Higgins, "Distressed Denim: At 162 Years Old, Levi Strauss Confronts the Yoga Pant," *Bloomberg Businessweek*, July 27–August 2, 2015, 48–55.

33. K. M. Eisenhardt, "Accelerating Adaptive Processes: Product Innovation in the Global Computer Industry," *Administrative Science Quarterly* 40 (1995): 84–110.

34. Ibid.

35. R. Fleming, "Oculus Rift has Sold Over 85,000 Prototypes," Digital Trends, April 16, 2014, accessed June 13, 2014, http://www.digitaltrends.com/gaming/oculus-rift-sold-85000-prototypes/#!YqqBJ; B. Chen, "Oculus Rift Review: A Clunky Portal to a Promising

Virtual Reality," *New York Times*, March 28, 2016, accessed April 27, 2016, http://www.nytimes.com /2016/03/31/technology/personaltech/oculus-rift -virtual-reality-review.html; "Oculus Rift Crescent Bay vs Dk2 - How Much Cooler is It?" *RiftInfo.com*, February 23, 2015, accessed April 27, 2016, http:// riftinfo.com/oculus-rift-crescent-bay-vs-dk2-how -much-cooler-is-it.

36. K. Naughton and J. Green, "Crash Test City," *Bloomberg Businessweek*, April 6–12, 2015, pp. 19–20.

37. A. Barr, "Google Lab Puts a Time Limit on In-novation," *Wall Street Journal*, April 1, 2015, B6.

38. D. Wakabayashi and M. Ramsey, "Apple Gears Up to Challenge Tesla in Electric Cars," *Wall Street Journal*, February 13, 2015, B1; T. Bradshaw, "Bat-teries Suit Offers Clues to Apple's Car Ambitions," *Financial Times*, February 19, 2015, accessed April 26, 2015, http://www.ft.com/intl /cms/s/0/b061736c-b874-11e4-a2fb-00144feab7de .html#axzz3YRCCbjHx.

39. D. Gates, "McNerney: No More 'Moonshots' as Boeing Develops New Jets," *The Seattle Times*, May 22, 2014, accessed May 4, 2015, http://www .seattletimes.com/business/mcnerney-no-more -lsquomoonshotsrsquo-as-boeing-develops-new-jets/.

40. Ibid.; J. Ostrower, "At Boeing, Innovation Means Small Steps, Not Giant Leap," *Wall Street Journal*, April 3, 2015, B1.

41. L. Kraar, "25 Who Help the US Win: Innovators Everywhere are Generating Ideas to Make America a Stronger Competitor. They Range from a Boss Who Demands the Impossible to a Mathematician with a Mop," *Fortune*, March 22, 1991.

42. M. W. Lawless and P. C. Anderson, "Genera-tional Technological Change: Effects of Innovation and Local Rivalry on Performance," *Academy of Management Journal* 39 (1996): 1185–1217.

43. "USB.org—Hi-Speed FAQ," *USB Implementers Forum*, accessed April 27, 2016, http://www.usb.org /developers/usb20/faq20/; "USB.org—SuperSpeed USB," USB Implementers Forum, accessed April 27, 2016, http://www.usb.org/developers/ssusb/.

44. A. Satariano, "Apple Gets More Bank for Its R&D Buck," *Bloomberg BusinessWeek*, November 30–December 6, 2015, 38–39.

45. E. Bellman and J. Jai Krishna, "Churning Out Smartphones Like Fast Fashion," *Wall Street Jour-nal*, June 5, 2015, B1.

46. J. Brustein, "Inside RadioShack's Collapse— How Did the Electronics Retailer Go Broke? Gradu-ally, Then All at Once," *Bloomberg Businessweek*, February 9–15, 2015, 56. "Table 13–AT&T Interstate Residential Tariff Rates for 10-Minute Calls," *The Industry Analysis Division's Reference Book* of *Rates, Price Indices, and Household Expenditures for Telephone Service*, March 1997, Federal Trade Com-mission, 69, accessed April 25, 2015, http://transition .fcc.gov/Bureaus/Common_Carrier/Reports/FCC -State_Link/IAD/ref97.pdf.

47. Brustein, "Inside RadioShack's Collapse."

48. P. Strebel, "Choosing the Right Change Path," *California Management Review* 36(2) (Winter 1994): 29–51.

49. E. Steel, "Netflix Refines Its DVD Business, Even as Streaming Unit Booms," *New York Times*, July 27, 2015, B1.

50. D. Fitzgeral and M. Jarzemsky, "Besieged RadioShack Spirals Into Bankruptcy," *Wall Street Journal*, February 6, 2015, accessed May 4, 2015, http://www.wsj.com/articles/SB218109728774777646 94704580441814139751730.

51. P. Brickley and D. FitzGerald, "RadioShack Is Dead, Long Live RadioShack," *Wall Street Journal*, April 2, 2015, B1.

52. K. Lewin, *Field Theory in Social Science*: *Selected Theoretical Papers* (New York: Harper & Brothers, 1951).

53. J. Owen, "Film is Finished–This Could Be Its Last Oscars," *The Independent*, February 24, 2013, accessed June 13, 2014, http://www.independent .co.uk/arts-entertainment/films/news/film-is -finished—this-could-be-its-last-oscars-8508257 .html?printService=print.

54. Lewin, *Field Theory in Social Science*.

55. A. B. Fisher, "Making Change Stick," *Fortune*, April 17, 1995, 121.

56. J. P. Kotter and L. A. Schlesinger, "Choosing Strategies for Change," *Harvard Business Review* (March–April 1979): 106–114.

57. S. Giessner, G. Viki, T. Otten, S. Terry, and D. Tauber, "The Challenge of Merging: Merger Patterns, Premerger Status, and Merger Support," *Personality and Social Psychology Bulletin* 32, no. 3 (2006): 339–352.

58. E. Cassano, "How Vince Donnelly Led PMA Companies Through an Acquisition by Involving Everyone," *Smart Business*, February 1, 2012, accessed March 7, 2012, http://www.sbnonline .com/article/how-vince-donnelly-led-pma -companies-through-an-acquisition-by-involving -everyone/.

59. D. Bennett, "Marriage at 30,000 Feet," *Bloom-berg Businessweek*, February 6–12, 2012, 58–63.

60. D. Meinert, "An Open Book," *HR Magazine*, April 2013, 42–46.

61. J. P. Kotter, "Leading Change: Why Transforma-tion Efforts Fail," *Harvard Business Review* 73, no. 2 (March–April 1995): 59.

62. "Nordstrom Company History," Nordstrom, ac-cessed March 23, 2016, http://shop.nordstrom.com/c /company-history.

63. S. Kapner, "Macy's Seeks Answers as Sales Slide," *Wall Street Journal*, November 12, 2015, A1, A14.

64. R. Tetzeli, "9 Ways GE Executed Its Radical Green Reinvention," *FastCoexist.com*, December 11, 2015, accessed March 22, 2016, http://www .fastcoexist.com/3054441/9-ways-ge-executed-its -radical-green-reinvention.

65. Ibid.

66. P. Burrows, "Stephen Elop's Nokia Adventure," *Bloomberg Businessweek*, June 2, 2011, accessed June 3, 2013, http://www .businessweek.com/magazine/content/11_24 /b4232056703101.htm.

67. J. Rossi, "Nokia Releases New Lumia Phone," *Wall Street Journal*, May 14, 2013, accessed June 5, 2013, http://online.wsj.com/article/SB100014241278 87323716304578482822129616580.html; T. Warren, "Windows Phone is Dead," *The Verge*, January 28, 2016, accessed April 27, 2016, http://www.theverge .com/2016/1/28/10864034/windows-phone-is-dead; M. Singh, "Microsoft CEO Admits Windows Phone Market Share Is Unsustainable: Report," *NDTV Gadgets360.com*, January 4, 2016, accessed April 27, 2016, http://gadgets.ndtv.com/mobiles/news /microsoft-ceo-admits-windows-phones-market -share-is-unsustainable-report-785310.

68. S. Cramm, "A Change of Hearts," *CIO*, April 1, 2003, May 20, 2003, http://www.cio.com /archive/040103/hsleadership.html.

69. J. Scheck, "New Shell CEO Van Beurden Lays Out Turnaround Plan," *Wall Street Journal*, April 27, 2014, accessed July 1, 2014, http://online.wsj.com/news/articles /SB10001424052702304163604579527901868370442 ?KEYWORDS=Ben+van+Beurden+CEO+Royal +Dutch+Shell&mg=reno64-wsj.

70. R. N. Ashkenas and T. D. Jick, "From Dialogue to Action in GE WorkOut: Developmental Learning in a Change Process," in *Research in Organizational Change and Development*, vol. 6, ed. W. A. Pasmore and R. W. Woodman (Greenwich, CT: JAI Press, 1992), 267–287.

71. T. Stewart, "GE Keeps Those Ideas Coming," *Fortune*, August 12, 1991, 40.

72. W. J. Rothwell, R. Sullivan, and G. M. McLean, *Practicing Organizational Development: A Guide for Consultants* (San Diego, CA: Pfeiffer & Co., 1995).

73. Ibid.

8

1. "Web Table 34. Number of Parent Corporations and Foreign Affiliates, by Region and Economy," *World Investment Report 2011*, United Nations Con-ference on Trade and Development, accessed April 28, 2016, http://unctad.org/Sections/dite_dir /docs/WIR11_web%20tab%2034.pdf.

2. M. Scott, "Cap Gemini Agrees to Buy IGATE, Merging Rivals Focused on Tech and Outsourcing," New York Times, April 27, 2015, accessed May 5, 2015, http://www.nytimes.com/2015/04/28/business /dealbook/capgemini-agrees-to-buy-igate-for-4 -billion.html.

3. L. Stevens, M. van Tartwijk, and T. Fairless, "FedEx's Priority: Bulk Up in Europe," *Wall Street Journal*, April 8, 2015, B1.

4. K. Ellis, "Mexican Import Rules Hit US Fashion Firms," *WWD*, March 3, 2015, pp. 1, 8.

5. "Govt May Hike Sugar Import Duty to 40% to Check Price Fall," *Times of India*, April 21, 2015, accessed May 5, 2015, http://timesofindia .indiatimes.com/business/india-business/Govt-may -hike-sugar-import-duty-to-40-to-check-price-fall /articleshow/47002065.cms.

6. G. Kantchev and E. Ballard, "Ground Shifts under Wheat Export Market," *Wall Street Journal*, February 7, 2016, accessed May 19, 2016, http:// www.wsj.com/articles/ground-shifts-under-wheat -export-market-1454754785; "Argentina Cuts Tariffs, Affects Grain Markets," *WHOTV.com*, December 16, 2015, accessed April 8, 2016, http://whotv .com/2015/12/16/argentina-cuts-tariffs-affects-grain -markets/; "Macri Eliminates Argentine Farm Export Taxes on Wheat, Corn," *AgWeb.com*, December 14, 2015, accessed April 8, 2016, http://www.agweb.com /article/macri-eliminates-argentine-farm-export -taxes-on-wheat-corn-blmg/.

7. P. Prengaman, "Argentine President's Decision to Lift Agricultural Export Taxes Puts Country on New Course," *Canada.com*, December 14, 2015, accessed April 8, 2016, http://www.canada.com/business/argent ine+president+eliminates+export+taxes+corn+wheat +meat+products/11588534/story.html.

8. B. Fritz and L. Burkitt, "Chinese Film Company Takes Role in Hollywood," *Wall Street Journal*, April 20, 2015, B1.

9. Reuters, "Mexico Bows to Brazilian Pressure on Auto Exports," *Reuters*, March 15, 2012, accessed June 8, 2013, http://www.reuters.com /article/2012/03/16/mexico-brazil-autos -idUSL2E8EF3G420120316.

10. "Understanding the WTO," *World Trade Organi-zation*, accessed April 28, 2016, http://www.wto.org /english/thewto_e/whatis_e/tif_e/agrm9_e.htm.

11. "Pangasius June 2014," *Globefish*, June 2014, http://www.globefish.org/pangasius-june -2014.html; T. Tracy, "U.S. Catfish Farmers Go After Asian Rival," *Wall Street Journal*, March 24, 2015, B6.

12. Tracy, "U.S. Catfish Farmers Go After Asian Rival."

13. Ibid.

14. J. Wehrman, "Farm Bill's Subsidy for Sugar Under Pressure," *The Columbus Dispatch*, June 20, 2013, accessed July 2, 2014, http://www.dispatch .com/content/stories/local/2013/06/20/farm-bills -subsidy-for-sugar-under-pressure.html.

15. A. Wexler, "Big Sugar Is Set for a Sweet Bail-out," *Wall Street Journal*, March 13, 2013, accessed July 2, 2014, http://online.wsj.com/news/articles/SB10 001424127887324096404578356740206766164.

16. J. Wehrman, "Farm Bill's Subsidy for Sugar Under Pressure," The Columbus Dispatch, June 20, 2013, https://duckduckgo.com/?q=Farm%20 Bill's%20Subsidy%20for%20Sugar%20Under%20 Pressure, accessed August 25, 2015.

17. T. Shields, "'Costumes or Clothes?' H.R. 3128 Department of Homeland Security Appropriations, 2016," *Bloomberg Businessweek*, October 19–25, 2015, 35.

18. "GATT/WTO," *Duke Law: Library & Technology*, accessed June 12, 2009, https://law.duke.edu/lib/researchguides/gatt/.

19. "IFPI Digital Music Report 2015," *International Federation of the Phonographic Industry*, January 2015, accessed April 28, 2016, http://www.ifpi.org/downloads/Digital-Music-Report-2015.pdf.

20. "The Compliance Gap: 2014 BSA Global Software Piracy Study," *BSA*, June 2014, accessed April 9, 2016, http://globalstudy.bsa.org/2013/downloads/studies/2013GlobalSurvey_inbrief_en.pdf.

21. C. Bialik, "Putting a Price Tag on Film Piracy," *Wall Street Journal*, April 5, 2013, accessed June 8, 2013, http://blogs.wsj.com/numbersguy/putting-a-price-tag-on-film-piracy-1228/.

22. "Countries: On the Road to EU Membership," *European Union*, accessed April 28, 2016, http://europa.eu/about-eu/countries/index_en.htm.

23. M. Villarreal and I. Ferguson, "North American Free Trade Agreement," *Congressional Research Service*, April 16, 2015, accessed April 28, 2016, http://www.fas.org/sgp/crs/row/R42965.pdf.

24. "Dominican Republic-Central America-United States Free Trade Agreement," US Department of Commerce, April 29, 2014, "Trade in Goods with CAFTA-DR," U.S. Census Bureau, accessed April 28, 2016, https://www.census.gov/foreign-trade/balance/c0017.html.

25. "UNASUR: Union of South American Nations," *Comunidad Andina*, accessed April 8, 2016, http://unasursg.org/; "La Región en Cifras: UNASUR: Espacio de Cooperación e Integración para al Desarrollo," accessed April 28, 2016, http://unasursg.org/.

26. "ASEAN Includes Ten Southeast Asian Countries with a $2.4 Trillion Economy and Population of 626 Million That Will Form the ASEAN Economic Community (AEC) in 2015—One of the Largest Markets in the World," *US-ASEAN*, accessed April 28, 2016, https://www.usasean.org/why-asean/what-is-asean; "Almost $100 Billion of US Goods and Services Exports Go to ASEAN," *US-ASEAN*, accessed April 28, 2016, https://www.usasean.org/why-asean/trade.

27. "Almost $100 Billion of US Goods and Services Exports Go to ASEAN," *US-ASEAN*, accessed April 28, 2016, https://www.usasean.org/why-asean/trade; "ASEAN 2025—Forging Ahead Together," *US-ASEAN*, November 2015, accessed April 28, 2016, http://www.asean.org/storage/images/2015/November/KL-Declaration/ASEAN%202025%20Forging%20Ahead%20Together%20final.pdf.

28. "Trade Raises Living Standards in APEC Region: Report," *Asia-Pacific Economic Cooperation*, accessed April 28, 2016, http://www.apec.org/Press/News-Releases/2016/0331_development.aspx; "StatsAPEC—Data for the Asia-Pacific Region—Economic and Social Statistics & Bilateral Trade and Investment Flows," *StatsAPEC*, accessed April 28, 2016, http://statistics.apec.org/index.php/apec_psu/index.

29. "Member Economies," *Asia Pacific Economic Cooperation*, accessed August 6, 2008, http://www.apec.org/About-Us/About-APEC/Member-Economies.aspx; "Frequently Asked Questions (FAQs)," *Asia-Pacific Economic Cooperation*, accessed August 6, 2008, http://www.apec.org/FAQ.aspx.

30. B. R. Williams, "Trans-Pacific Partnership (TPP) Countries: Comparative Trade and Economic Analysis," *Congressional Research Service*, June 10, 2013, accessed April 8, 2016, https://www.fas.org/sgp/crs/row/R42344.pdf.

31. R. Howard and M. Perry, "Trans-Pacific Partnership Trade Deal Signed, But Years of Negotiations Still to Come," *Reuters*, February 4, 2016, accessed April 28, 2016, http://www.reuters.com/article/us-trade-tpp-idUSKCN0VD08S.

32. "Gross National Income (GNI) per Capita 2014, Atlas Method and PPP," *The World Bank*, February 17, 2016, http://databank.worldbank.org/data/download/GNIPC.pdf.

33. Ibid.

34. "The Global Competitiveness Report: 2015–2016," *World Economic Forum*, accessed April 28, 2016, http://www3.weforum.org/docs/gcr/2015-2016/Global_Competitiveness_Report_2015-2016.pdf.

35. M. Yamaguchi, "Japan-US Talks on Pacific Trade Accord Get Push from 'Fast-Track' Proposal in US Congress," *US News & World Report*, April 17, 2015, accessed April 28, 2015, http://www.usnews.com/news/business/articles/2015/04/17/trade-talks-in-tokyo-get-push-from-fast-track-deal-in-us; "Commodity Policies," *US Department of Agriculture, Economic Research Service*, August 7, 2014, accessed April 28, 2015, http://www.ers.usda.gov/topics/international-markets-trade/countries-regions/japan/policy.aspx.

36. L. Lockwood, "Ralph's Brazilian Vibe," *WWD*, April 13, 2015, p. 2.

37. S. Schechner, "Netflix Launches in France in First Phase of Expansion," *Wall Street Journal*, September 16, 2014, B1.

38. M. Gao, "Culture Determines Business Models: Analyzing Home Depot's Failure Case in China for International Retailers from a Communication Perspective," *Thunderbird International Business Review*, March/April 2013, 173–191.

39. L. Burkitt, "Home Depot Learns Chinese Prefer 'Do-It-for-Me,'" *Wall Street Journal*, September 14, 2012, accessed June 8, 2013, http://online.wsj.com/article/SB10000872396390444433504577651072911154602.html.

40. Katie Englehart, "Starbucks Go Home," *Macleans*, January 25, 2013, accessed July 2, 2014, http://online.wsj.com/news/articles/SB10001424052702304607104579209971318755960.

41. A. Sundaram and J. S. Black, "The Environment and Internal Organization of Multinational Enterprises," *Academy of Management Review* 17 (1992): 729–757.

42. H. S. James, Jr. and M. Weidenbaum, *When Businesses Cross International Borders: Strategic Alliances & Their Alternatives* (Westport, CT: Praeger Publishers, 1993).

43. I. Brat and K. Gee, "U.S. Dairies Get Crash Course in Exporting," *Wall Street Journal*, January 9, 2015, accessed May 5, 2015, http://www.wsj.com/articles/dairy-factory-gears-up-for-production-1420765811

44. Ibid.

45. A. Whitley, "Giving a New Meaning to Cattle Class," *Bloomberg Businessweek*, November 23–29, 2015, 24–25.

46. A. Sharma, "TV Studios Court Licensing Deals in Bustling Foreign Markets: For Warner Bros. and Other U.S. Studios, the International TV-Licensing Bazaar Has Never Been More Lucrative," *Wall Street Journal*, November 19, 2014, accessed April 28, 2016 http://www.wsj.com/articles/tv-studios-court-licensing-deals-in-bustling-foreign-markets-1416454383.

47. M. Willens, "NBCUniversal to Produce American TV Shows for European Broadcasters," *International Business Times*, April 14, 2015, accessed April 28, 2016, http://www.ibtimes.com/nbcuniversal-produce-american-tv-shows-european-broadcasters-1881835.

48. K. Chu and M. Fujikawa, "Burberry Gets Grip on Brand in Japan," *Wall Street Journal*, August 15–16, 2015, B4.

49. "2016 Franchise 500—McDonald's at a Glance," Entrepreneur.com, accessed April 28, 2016, http://www.entrepreneur.com/franchises/mcdonalds/282570-0.html; "New Restaurants," *McDonald's.com*, accessed April 28, 2016, http://www.aboutmcdonalds.com/mcd/franchising/us_franchising/acquiring_a_franchise.html.

50. B. Gruley and L. Patton, "McRevolt: The Frustrating Life of the McDonald's Franchisee—Not Lovin' it," *Bloomberg BusinessWeek*, September 16, 2015, accessed April 28, 2016, http://www.bloomberg.com/features/2015-mcdonalds-franchises/.

51. K. Le Mesurier, "Overseas and Overwhelmed," *BRW*, January 25, 2007, 51.

52. P. Rana, "Dipping into India, Dunkin' Donuts Changes Menu," *Wall Street Journal*, November 28, 2014, http://online.wsj.com/articles/dipping-into-india-dunkin-donuts-changes-menu-1417211158.

53. E. Dou, "Hewlett-Packard, Foxconn Launch Joint Server Venture," *Wall Street Journal*, April 30, 2014, accessed April 28, 2016, http://www.wsj.com/articles/SB10001424052702303948104579533080961860334.

54. S. Chaudhuri, "Tesco Caps Tumultuous Year with Huge Loss," *Wall Street Journal*, April 22, 2015, http://www.wsj.com/articles/tesco-reports-full-year-loss-1429683249; "Supermarket Operator Kroger Ends Joint Venture with Dunnhumby, Starts Customer Data Subsidiary," *Associated Press*, April 27, 2015, accessed April 28, 2016, http://www.foxbusiness.com/markets/2015/04/27/supermarket-operator-kroger-ends-joint-venture-with-dunnhumby-starts-customer/; S. Watkins, "Kroger Executive: Dunnhumby Sale Won't Keep Us from Data," *Cincinnati Business Courier*, March 27, 2015, accessed April 28, 2016, http://www.bizjournals.com/cincinnati/news/2015/03/27/kroger-executive-nothing-would-preclude-us-from.html?page=all.

55. J. Hagerty, "In Alabama, Chinese Firm Struggles to Fit In," *Wall Street Journal*, February 29, 2016, B1.

56. K. Chu, "Garment Maker Retreats as China Shifts Policy," *Wall Street Journal*, December 2, 2015, accessed April 28, 2016, http://www.wsj.com/articles/garment-maker-succumbs-to-shift-in-chinas-policy-1449082802.

57. W. Hordes, J. A. Clancy, and J. Baddaley, "A Primer for Global Start-Ups," *Academy of Management Executive*, May 1995, 7–11.

58. P. Dimitratos, J. Johnson, J. Slow, and S. Young, "Micromultinationals: New Types of Firms for the Global Competitive Landscape," *European Management Journal* 21, no. 2 (April 2003): 164; B. M. Oviatt and P. P. McDougall, "Toward a Theory of International New Ventures," *Journal of International Business Studies*, Spring 1994, 45–64; S. Zahra, "A Theory of International New Ventures: A Decade of Research," *Journal of International Business Studies*, January 2005, 20–28.

59. B. Keplesky, "MakerBot's Bre Pettis on the Next Industrial Revolution," *Entrepreneur*, March 9, 2013, accessed June 10, 2013, http://www.entrepreneur.com/article/226044; M. Wolf, "How 3D Printing Is Now Helping NASA Get to Space," *Forbes*, January 12, 2013, accessed June 10, 2013, http://www.forbes.com/sites/michaelwolf/2013/01/12/how-3d-printing-is-now-helping-nasa-get-to-space/; "Official International MakerBot Distributors," *MakerBot*, accessed June 10, 2013, http://www.makerbot.com/distributors/.

60. "Shaping Our Future: 2014 Annual Review," *Coca-Cola*, accessed May 5, 2015, http://assets.coca-colacompany.com/6c/70/b23ba5fe42bb8684672 6cf4779c4/2014-year-in-review-pdf.pdf.

61. "Coca-Cola Bottle (500ml) Prices," *Humuch.com*, accessed April 28, 2016, http://www.humuch.com/prices/CocaCola-Bottle-20oz500ml//40#.VT_FdiFVhBc.

62. "2010 Annual Report," *The Coca-Cola Company*.

63. L. Craymer, "China's Changing Tastes Offer Upside for Coffee," *Wall Street Journal*, September 6, 2015, accessed April 28, 2016, http://www.wsj.com/articles/chinas-changing-tastes-offer-upside-for-coffee-1442431980; D. Harashima, "China's Coffee Market: Cafe Competition Perks Up Amid Slowdown," *Nikkei Asian Review*, October 31, 2015, accessed April 28, 2016, http://asia.nikkei.com/Business/Trends/Cafe-competition-perks-up-amid-slowdown.

64. J. Stoll, "Volvo to Open Plant in the US," *Wall Street Journal*, March 30, 2015, accessed May 5, 2015, http://www.wsj.com/articles/volvo-to-open-plant-in-the-u-s-1427688301.

65. D. Shepardson, "Volvo Plans $500M Factory in US to Revive Sales," *The Detroit News*, March 30, 2015, accessed May 5, 2015, http://www.detroitnews

.com/story/business/autos/foreign/2015/03/30/volvo
-us-plant/70657920/.

66. "Tax Environment," *NFIA*, accessed April 28, 2016, http://www.nfia.com/tax.html; D. Dzombak, "The Highest Corporate Tax Rates in the World," *The Motley Fool*, March 1, 2014, accessed April 28, 2016, http://www.fool.com/investing/general/2014/03/01 /the-highest-corporate-tax-rates-in-the-world.aspx.

67. "Special Eurobarometer 386: Europeans and Their Languages," *European Commission*, June 2012, accessed April 28, 2016, http://ec.europa.eu /public_opinion/archives/ebs/ebs_386_en.pdf.

68. "IMD World Talent Report 2014," *IMD World Competitiveness Center*, November 2014, accessed April 28, 2016, http://www.imd.org/uupload/imd .website/wcc/NewTalentReport/IMD_World _Talent_Report_2014bis.pdf.

69. C. Passariello and S. Kapner, "Search for Cheaper Labor Leads to Africa," *Wall Street Journal*, July 13, 2015, B1.

70. S. Adams, "2015's Most and Least Reliable Countries to Do Business In," *Forbes*, March 31, 2015, accessed April 28, 2016, http://www.forbes .com/sites/susanadams/2015/03/31/2015s-most-and -least-reliable-countries-to-do-business-in/; "Resilience Index," FM Global, http://www.fmglobal.com /assets/pdf/Resilience_Methodology.pdf.

71. J. Oetzel, R. Bettis, and M. Zenner, "How Risky Are They?" *Journal of World Business* 36, no. 2 (Summer 2001): 128–145.

72. K. D. Miller, "A Framework for Integrated Risk Management in International Business," *Journal of International Business Studies*, 2nd Quarter 1992, 311.

73. M. Bahree, "Foreign Retailers Regroup in India," *Wall Street Journal*, December 12, 2011, B3.

74. J. Bennett and J. Stoll, "GM's Hopes for Russia Go in Reverse," *Wall Street Journal*, March 19, 2015, B1, B2; D. Levin, "GM Exits Russia," *Fortune*, March 27, 2015, accessed April 28, 2016, http:// fortune.com/2015/03/27/gm-exits-russia/.

75. Levin, "GM Exits Russia."

76. "Chapter 1: Political Outlook," *UAE Business Forecast Report*, 1st Quarter 2007, 5–10.

77. A. Irrera, "Uber Hires Uber-Lobbyist for European Expansion," *Wall Street Journal*, September 5, 2014, accessed April 28, 2016, http://blogs.wsj .com/digits/2014/09/05/uber-hires-uber-lobbyist-for -european-expansion/.

78. D. Kerr, "Uber Fights Back in Europe, Files Complaints Against Governments," *Cnet*, April 10, 2015, accessed April 28, 2016, http://www.cnet.com /news/uber-fights-back-in-europe-files-complaints -against-governments/; S. Schechner, "Uber's Europe Policy Chief Exits," *Wall Street Journal*, November 16, 2015, B4.

79. C. Alessi, "India Invests in Germany's Family Firms," *Wall Street Journal*, April 11–12, 2015, B4.

80. G. Hofstede, "The Cultural Relativity of the Quality of Life Concept," *Academy of Management Review* 9 (1984): 389–398; G. Hofstede, "The Cultural Relativity of Organizational Practices and Theories," *Journal of International Business Studies*, Fall 1983, 75–89; G. Hofstede, "The Interaction Between National and Organizational Value Systems," *Journal of Management Studies*, July 1985, 347–357; M. Hoppe, "An Interview with Geert Hofstede," *Academy of Management Executive*, February 2004, 75–79.

81. Alessi, "India Invests in Germany's Family Firms."

82. Ibid.

83. Ibid.

84. R. Hodgetts, "A Conversation with Geert Hofstede," *Organizational Dynamics*, Spring 1993, 53–61.

85. T. Lenartowicz and K. Roth, "Does Subculture within a Country Matter? A Cross-Cultural Study of Motivational Domains and Business Performance in Brazil," *Journal of International Business Studies* 32 (2001): 305–325.

86. M. Koren, "Why Russians Aren't Smiling at You in Sochi," *National Journal*, February 7, 2014, accessed June 13, 2014, http://www.nationaljournal .com/politics/why-russians-aren-t-smiling-at-you-in -sochi-20140207.

87. J. S. Black, M. Mendenhall, and G. Oddou, "Toward a Comprehensive Model of International Adjustment: An Integration of Multiple Theoretical Perspectives," *Academy of Management Review* 16 (1991): 291–317; R. L. Tung, "American Expatriates Abroad: From Neophytes to Cosmopolitans," *Columbia Journal of World Business*, June 22, 1998, 125; A. Harzing, "The Persistent Myth of High Expatriate Failure Rates," *International Journal of Human Resource Management* 6 (1995): 457–475; A. Harzing, "Are Our Referencing Errors Undermining Our Scholarship and Credibility? The Case of Expatriate Failure Rates," *Journal of Organizational Behavior* 23 (2002): 127–148; N. Forster, "The Persistent Myth of High Expatriate Failure Rates: A Reappraisal," *International Journal of Human Resource Management* 8 (1997): 414–433.

88. J. Black, "The Right Way to Manage Expats," *Harvard Business Review* 77 (March–April 1999): 52; C. Joinson, "No Returns," *HR Magazine*, November 1, 2002, 70.

89. "International Assignment Perspectives: Critical Issues Facing the Globally Mobile Workforce," *PricewaterhouseCoopers*, Vol. 5, November 2011, accessed June 13, 2014, http://www.pwc.com/en_US /us/hr-international-assignment-services/publications /assets/ny-12-0258_ias_journal_volume_5_new _images.pdf.

90. R. Feintzeig, "After Stints Abroad, Re-Entry Can be Hard," *Wall Street Journal*, September 17, 2013, accessed June 14, 2014, http://online.wsj.com /news/articles/SB10001424127887323342404579081 382781895274?KEYWORDS=after+stints+abroad& mg=reno64-wsj.

91. "Ten Examples of Cross-Cultural Blunders," *UKProEdits*, June 7, 2012, accessed June 10, 2013, http://ukproedits.com/uncategorized/ten-examples -of-cross-cultural-mistakes.

92. J. S. Black and M. Mendenhall, "Cross-Cultural Training Effectiveness: A Review and Theoretical Framework for Future Research," *Academy of Management Review* 15 (1990): 113–136.

93. K. Essick, "Executive Education: Transferees Prep for Life, Work in Far-Flung Lands," *Wall Street Journal*, November 12, 2004, A6.

94. Ibid.

95. P. W. Tam, "Culture Course—'Awareness Training' Helps US Workers Better Know Their Counterparts in India," *Wall Street Journal*, May 25, 2004, B1.

96. S. Hamm, "Aperian: Helping Companies Bridge Cultures," *BusinessWeek*, September 8, 2008, 16.

97. W. Arthur, Jr. and W. Bennett, Jr., "The International Assignee: The Relative Importance of Factors Perceived to Contribute to Success," *Personnel Psychology* 48 (1995): 99–114; B. Cheng, "Home Truths About Foreign Postings; To Make an Overseas Assignment Work, Employers Need More Than an Eager Exec with a Suitcase. They Must Also Motivate the Staffer's Spouse," *BusinessWeek Online*, accessed March 20, 2009, http://www.businessweek .com/careers/content/jul2002/ca20020715_9110.htm.

98. B. Groysberg and R. Abrahams, "A Successful International Assignment Depends on These Factors," *Harvard Business Review* (blog), February 13, 2014, 10:00, accessed June 15, 2014, http://blogs.hbr .org/2014/02/a-successful-international-assignment -depends-on-these-factors/.

99. "OAI: Overseas Assignment Inventory," *Prudential Real Estate and Relocation Services Intercultural Group*, May 11, 2011, http://www.performance programs.com/self-assessments/work-across-cultures /overseas-assignment-inventory/.

100. S. P. Deshpande and C. Visweswaran, "Is Cross-Cultural Training of Expatriate Managers Effective? A Meta-Analysis," *International Journal of Intercultural Relations* 16, no. 3 (1992): 295–310.

101. D. M. Eschbach, G. Parker, and P. Stoeberl, "American Repatriate Employees' Retrospective Assessments of the Effects of Cross-Cultural Training on Their Adaptation to International Assignments," *International Journal of Human Resource Management* 12 (2001): 270–287; "Culture Training: How to Prepare Your Expatriate Employees for Cross-Cultural Work Environments," *Managing Training & Development*, February 1, 2005.

102. I. Driscoll, "You Love Going Abroad for Work. Your Spouse Hates It." *BBC*, November 11, 2014, accessed May 5, 2015, http://www.bbc.com/capital /story/20141110-the-reluctant-expat-spouse.

103. Ibid.

9

1. M. Lia, "Thomson Reuters Restructures," *Wall Street Journal*, September 28, 2011, accessed June 12, 2013, http://www.wsj.com/articles/SB100014240 52970204138204576598671601828928; "About Us 2015," *Thomson Reuters*, accessed April 28, 2016, http://thomsonreuters.com/en/about-us.html.

2. M. Hammer and J. Champy, *Reengineering the Corporation: A Manifesto for Business Revolution* (New York: Harper & Row, 1993).

3. J. Mick, "Windows 8 Public 'Consumer Preview' Beta Is Live," *Daily Tech*, February 29, 2012, accessed March 11, 2012, http://www .dailytech.com/Windows+8+Public+Consumer +Preview+Beta+is+Live/article24123.htm; J. Mick, "Microsoft's Windows 10 Now Has Over 2 Million Public Testers," *Daily Tech*, January 28, 2015, accessed May 1, 2015, http://www.dailytech.com /Microsofts+Windows+10+Now+Has+Over+2 +Million+Public+Testers/article37113.htm.

4. J. G. March and H. A. Simon, *Organizations* (New York: John Wiley & Sons, 1958).

5. M. Isaac, "EBay to Cut 2,400 Jobs, and Weighs 2nd Spinoff," *New York Times*, January 22, 2015, B4.

6. "Global Human Capital Trends 2016-The New Organization: Different by Design," *Deloitte University Press*, accessed April 29, 2016, http:// www2.deloitte.com/content/dam/Deloitte/global /Documents/HumanCapital/gx-dup-global-human -capital-trends-2016.pdf.

7. "At a Glance," *UTC*, accessed April 29, 2016, http://www.utc.com/Our-Businesses/Pages/At-A -Glance.aspx.

8. "United Technologies 2015 Annual Report," *United Technologies*, accessed April 29, 2016, http://2015ar.utc.com/assets/pdf/UTC_AR15 _Annual_Report.pdf.

9. "Structure—Group Structure & Corporate Management," *Swisscom AG*, accessed June 16, 2014, http://www.swisscom.ch/en/about/company /structure.html.

10. "Anheuser-Busch InBev Annual Report 2015," *Anheuser-Busch InBev*, accessed April 14, 2016, http://annualreport.ab-inbev.com/.

11. Ibid.

12. Ibid.

13. "P&G 2015 Annual Report," *Procter & Gamble*, accessed April 13, 2016, http://www.pginvestor.com /Cache/1001201800.PDF?O=PDF&T=&Y=&D=&F ID=1001201800&iid=4004124.

14. "Corporate Structure," *Procter & Gamble*, accessed April 14, 2016, http://us.pg.com/who_we_are /structure_governance/corporate_structure.

15. L. R. Burns, "Adoption and Abandonment of Matrix Management Programs: Effects of Organizational Characteristics and Interorganizational Networks," *Academy of Management Journal* 36 (1993): 106–138.

16. H. Fayol, *General and Industrial Management*, trans. C. Storrs (London: Pitman Publishing, 1949).

17. M. Weber, *The Theory of Social and Economic Organization*, trans. and ed. A. M. Henderson and T. Parsons (New York: Free Press, 1947).

18. Fayol, *General and Industrial Management.*

19. J. Vanian, "Amazon Now Has Three CEOs," *Fortune*, April 7, 2016, accessed April 29, 2016, http://fortune.com/2016/04/07/amazon-three-ceos-wilke-jassy-bezos/.

20. C. Zillman, "With Co-CEOs, Companies Flirt with Disaster," *Fortune*, September 20, 2014, accessed April 29, 2016, http://fortune.com/2014/09/20/oracle-two-ceos-disaster/.

21. A. Lashinsky, "Inside Apple, from Steve Jobs Down to the Janitor: How America's Most Successful—and Most Secretive—Big Company Really Works," *Fortune*, May 23, 2011, 125–134.

22. B. Borzykowski, "Why You Can't Delegate and How to Fix It," *BBC Capital*, April 2, 2015, accessed April 18, 2016, http://www.bbc.com/capital/story/20150401-why-you-find-it-hard-to-delegate.

23. Ibid.

24. I. Brat, "Whole Foods Reworks Approach," *Wall Street Journal*, February 16, 2016, B2.

25. J. Jargon, "McDonald's Plans to Change U.S. Structure," *Wall Street Journal*, October 20, 2014, accessed May 5, 2015, http://www.wsj.com/articles/mcdonalds-to-change-u-s-structure-1414695278.

26. E. E. Lawler, S. A. Mohrman, and G. E. Ledford, *Creating High Performance Organizations: Practices and Results of Employee Involvement and Quality Management in Fortune 1000 Companies* (San Francisco: Jossey-Bass, 1995).

27. Y. Kubota, "Toyota Unveils Revamped *Manufacturing* Process," *Wall Street Journal*, March 26, 2015, accessed May 1, 2015, http://www.wsj.com/articles/toyota-unveils-revamped-manufacturing-process-1427371432.

28. "Employee Turnover Rate Tops 70% in 2015," *National Restaurant Association*, March 22, 2016, accessed April 29, 2016, http://www.restaurant.org/News-Research/News/Employee-turnover-rate-tops-70-in-2015.

29. R. W. Griffin, *Task Design* (Glenview, IL: Scott, Foresman, 1982).

30. F. Herzberg, *Work and the Nature of Man* (Cleveland, OH: World Press, 1966).

31. R. Hackman and G. R. Oldham, *Work Redesign* (Reading, MA: Addison-Wesley, 1980).

32. T. Burns and G. M. Stalker, *The Management of Innovation* (London: Tavistock, 1961).

33. Hammer and Champy, *Reengineering the Corporation.*

34. Ibid.

35. J. D. Thompson, *Organizations in Action* (New York: McGraw-Hill, 1967).

36. G. James, "World's Worst Management Fads," *Inc.*, May 10, 2013, accessed May 1, 2015 http://www.inc.com/geoffrey-james/worlds-worst-management-fads.html.

37. J. B. White, " 'Next Big Thing': Re-Engineering Gurus Take Steps to Remodel Their Stalling Vehicles," *Wall Street Journal Interactive*, November 26, 1996.

38. C. Tuna, "Remembrances: Champion of 'Re-Engineering' Saved Companies, Challenged Thinking," *Wall Street Journal*, September 6, 2008, A12.

39. G. M. Spreitzer, "Individual Empowerment in the Workplace: Dimensions, Measurement, and Validation," *Academy of Management Journal* 38 (1995): 1442–1465.

40. D. Vidalon and P. Denis, "Carrefour Bets on Store Bosses in French Revamp," *cNBC*, March 12, 2013, accessed July 8, 2014, http://article.wn.com/view/2013/03/12/Carrefour_bets_on_store_bosses_in_French_revamp/.

41. K. W. Thomas and B. A. Velthouse, "Cognitive Elements of Empowerment," *Academy of Management Review* 15 (1990): 666–681.

42. C. Gallo, "How Wegmans, Apple Store and Ritz-Carlton Empower Employees to Offer Best-in-Class Service," *Retail Customer Experience*, December 27, 2012, accessed June 12, 2013, http://www.retailcustomerexperience.com/article/205849/How

-Wegmans-Apple-Store-and-Ritz-Carlton-empower-employees-to-offer-best-in-class-service.

43. J. Lee, "Finding Gooey Goodness in Nutella's Huge Supply Chain," *Triple Pundit*, January 10, 2014, accessed April 29, 2016, http://www.triplepundit.com/2014/01/nutella-supply-chain/; D. Mitzman, "Nutella, How the World Went Nuts for a Hazelnut Spread," *BBC News*, May 18, 2014, accessed May 19, 2016, http://www.bbc.com/news/magazine-27438001.

44. W. Bulkeley, "New IBM Jobs Can Mean Fewer Jobs Elsewhere," *Wall Street Journal*, March 8, 2004, B1.

45. A. Satariano and S. Soper, "Yuletemps," *Bloomberg Businessweek*, December 14–20, 2015, 30–31; "Amazon.com Announces Fourth Quarter Sales up 22% to $35.7 Billion," *Business Wire*, January 28, 2016, accessed April 29, 2016, http://www.businesswire.com/news/home/20160128006357/en/Amazon.com-Announces-Fourth-Quarter-Sales-22-35.7.

46. C. C. Snow, R. E. Miles, and H. J. Coleman, Jr., "Managing 21st Century Network Organizations," *Organizational Dynamics* 20 (Winter 1992): 5–20.

47. J. H. Sheridan, "The Agile Web: A Model for the Future?" *Industry Week*, March 4, 1996, 31.

10

1. B. Dumaine, "The Trouble with Teams," *Fortune*, September 5, 1994, 86–92.

2. K. C. Stag, E. Salas, and S. M. Fiore, "Best Practices in Cross Training Teams," in *Workforce Cross Training Handbook*, ed. D. A. Nembhard (Boca Raton, FL: CRC Press), 156–175.

3. M. Marks, "The Science of Team Effectiveness," *Psychological Science in the Public Interest* 7 (December 2006): pi–i.

4. J. R. Katzenbach and D. K. Smith, *The Wisdom of Teams* (Boston: Harvard Business School Press, 1993).

5. S. G. Cohen and D. E. Bailey, "What Makes Teams Work: Group Effectiveness Research from the Shop Floor to the Executive Suite," *Journal of Management* 23, no. 3 (1997): 239–290.

6. S. E. Gross, *Compensation for Teams* (New York: American Management Association, 1995); B. L. Kirkman and B. Rosen, "Beyond Self-Management: Antecedents and Consequences of Team Empowerment," *Academy of Management Journal* 42 (1999): 58–74; G. Stalk and T. M. Hout, *Competing Against Time: How Time-Based Competition Is Reshaping Global Markets* (New York: Free Press, 1990); S. C. Wheelwright and K. B. Clark, *Revolutionizing New Product Development* (New York: Free Press, 1992).

7. D. A. Harrison, S. Mohamed, J. E. McGrath, A. T. Florey, and S. W. Vanderstoep, "Time Matters in Team Performance: Effects of Member Familiarity, Entrainment, and Task Discontinuity on Speed and Quality," *Personnel Psychology* 56, no. 3 (August 2003): 633–669.

8. R. Cross, R. Rebele, and A. Grant, "Collaborative Overload," *Harvard Business Review*, January–February 2016, accessed April 30, 2016, https://hbr.org/2016/01/collaborative-overload.

9. L. Chao, "Auto Makers, Others Explore New Roles for 3-D Printing," *Wall Street Journal*, April 25, 2016, accessed April 30, 2016, http://www.wsj.com/articles/auto-makers-others-explore-new-roles-for-3-d-printing-1461626635; "Hunton & Williams Launches 3D Printing Team to Guide Clients Through Emerging Technology's Legal Complexities," *Business Wire*, April 30, 2016, accessed May 19, 2016, http://www.businesswire.com/news/home/20160420006044/en/Hunton-Williams-Launches-3D-Printing-Team-Guide.

10. R. D. Banker, J. M. Field, R. G. Schroeder, and K. K. Sinha, "Impact of Work Teams on Manufacturing Performance: A Longitudinal Field Study," *Academy of Management Journal* 39 (1996): 867–890.

11. L. Chao, "Trucker Teams Drive to the Rescue of Online Shipping," *Wall Street Journal*, December 24, 2015, accessed April 30, 2016, http://www.wsj.com/articles/trucker-teams-drive-to-the-rescue-of-online-shipping-1450953001.

12. Ibid.

13. J. L. Cordery, W. S. Mueller, and L. M. Smith, "Attitudinal and Behavioral Effects of Autonomous Group Working: A Longitudinal Field Study," *Academy of Management Journal* 34 (1991): 464–476; T. D. Wall, N. J. Kemp, P. R. Jackson, and C. W. Clegg, "Outcomes of Autonomous Workgroups: A Long-Term Field Experiment," *Academy of Management Journal* 29 (1986): 280–304.

14. "Great Little Box Company: A Team Approach to Success," *Industry Canada*, May 7, 2012, accessed June 13, 2013, http://www.ic.gc.ca/eic/site/061.nsf/eng/rd02456.html.

15. R. Silverman, "At Zappos, Some Employees Find Offer to Leave Too Good to Refuse," *Wall Street Journal*, May 7, 2015, accessed May 8, 2015, http://www.wsj.com/articles/at-zappos-some-employees-find-offer-to-leave-too-good-to-refuse-1431047917?KEYWORDS=zappos; D. Gelles, "The Zappos Exodus Continues after a Radical Management Experiment," *New York Times*, January 13, 2016, accessed April 30, 2016, http://bits.blogs.nytimes.com/2016/01/13/after-a-radical-management-experiment-the-zappos-exodus-continues/.

16. R. Liden, S. Wayne, R. Jaworski, and N. Bennett, "Social Loafing: A Field Investigation," *Journal of Management* 30 (2004): 285–304.

17. J. George, "Extrinsic and Intrinsic Origins of Perceived Social Loafing in Organizations," *Academy of Management Journal* 35 (1992): 191–202.

18. T. T. Baldwin, M. D. Bedell, and J. L. Johnson, "The Social Fabric of a Team-Based M.B.A. Program: Network Effects on Student Satisfaction and Performance," *Academy of Management Journal* 40 (1997): 1369–1397.

19. S. Perry, N. Lorinkova, E. Hunter, A Hubbard, and J. McMahon, "When Does Virtuality Really Work? Examining the Role of Work-Family and Virtuality in Social Loafing," *Journal of Management* 42 (2016), 449–479.

20. K. H. Price, D. A. Harrison, and J. H. Gavin, "Withholding Inputs in Team Contexts: Member Composition, Interaction Processes, Evaluation Structure and Social Loafing," *Journal of Applied Psychology* 91(6) (2006): 1375–1384.

21. L. P. Tost, F. Gino, and R. P. Larrick, "When Power Makes Others Speechless: The Negative Impact of Leader Power on Team Performance," *Academy of Management Journal* 35, no. 5 (October 1, 2013): 1465–1486.

22. C. Joinson, "Teams at Work," *HR Magazine*, May 1, 1999, 30.

23. R. Wageman, "Critical Success Factors for Creating Superb Self-Managing Teams," *Organizational Dynamics* 26, no. 1 (1997): 49–61.

24. R. Etherington, "Audi Announces New Design Strategy," *Dezeen*, December 19, 2012, accessed June 13, 2013, http://www.dezeen.com/2012/12/19/audi-announces-new-car-design-strategy/.

25. Kirkman and Rosen, "Beyond Self-Management: B. L. Kirkman and B. Rosen, "Beyond Self-Management: Antecedents and Consequences of Team Empowerment," *Academy of Management Journal* (1999): 58–74;

26. K. Kelly, "Managing Workers Is Tough Enough in Theory. When Human Nature Enters the Picture, It's Worse," *BusinessWeek*, October 21, 1996, 32.

27. S. Easton and G. Porter, "Selecting the Right Team Structure to Work in Your Organization," in *Handbook of Best Practices for Teams*, vol. 1, ed. G. M. Parker (Amherst, MA: Irwin, 1996).

28. S. Wilhelm, "Quadrupling 787 Production Won't Be Easy for Boeing, Just Necessary," *Puget Sound Business Journal*, February 10, 2012, accessed March 12, 2012, http://www.bizjournals.com/seattle/print-edition/2012/02/10/quadrupling-787-production-wont-be.html?page=all.

29. R. M. Yandrick, "A Team Effort: The Promise of Teams Isn't Achieved Without Attention to Skills

and Training," *HR Magazine* 46, no. 6 (June 2001): 136–144.

30. "Self-Directed Teams Improve On-Time Delivery and Quality," *Manufacturing.net*, June 29, 2012, accessed June 13, 2013, http://www.manufacturing.net/articles/2012/06/self-directed-teams-improve-on-time-delivery-and-quality.

31. R. Williams, "Self-Directed Work Teams: A Competitive Advantage," *Quality Digest*, accessed November 18, 2009, http://www.qualitydigest.com.

32. Yandrick, "A Team Effort."

33. "Valve: Handbook for New Employees," *Valve*, accessed May 8, 2015, http://media.steampowered.com/apps/valve/Valve_Handbook_LowRes.pdf.

34. Ibid.

35. R. Silverman, "Who's the Boss? There Isn't One," *Wall Street Journal*, June 19, 2012, accessed May 8, 2015, http://www.wsj.com/articles/SB10001424052702303379204577474953586363604.

36. R. J. Recardo, D. Wade, C. A. Mention, and J. Jolly, *Teams* (Houston: Gulf Publishing Co., 1996).

37. D. R. Denison, S. L. Hart, and J. A. Kahn, "From Chimneys to Cross-Functional Teams: Developing and Validating a Diagnostic Model," *Academy of Management Journal* 39, no. 4 (1996): 1005–1023.

38. A. M. Townsend, S. M. DeMarie, and A. R. Hendrickson, "Virtual Teams: Technology and the Workplace of the Future," *Academy of Management Executive* 13, no. 3 (1998): 17–29.

39. F. Rendón, "Understanding the Proliferation of Virtual Teams in the Global Economy," *Huffington Post*, April 28, 2014, accessed June 16, 2014, http://www.huffingtonpost.com/frankie-rendon/understanding-the-prolife_b_5212366.html.

40. M.E. Slater, "How to Effectively Delegate to Your Remote Team," *Startup Collective*, accessed May 8, 2015, http://startupcollective.com/effectively-delegate-remote-team/.

41. N. Radley, "Survey: How Team Members Prefer to Communicate on Virtual Projects," *Software Advice*, July 17, 2014, accessed May 8, 2015, http://blog.softwareadvice.com/articles/project-management/survey-communication-virtual-projects-0714/.

42. Slater, "How to Effective Delegate to Your Remote Team."

43. Ibid.

44. D. Mankin, S. G. Cohen, and T. K. Bikson, *Teams and Technology: Fulfilling the Promise of the New Organization* (Boston: Harvard Business School Press, 1996).

45. A. P. Ammeter and J. M. Dukerich, "Leadership, Team Building, and Team Member Characteristics in High Performance Project Teams," *Engineering Management* 14, no. 4 (December 2002): 3–11.

46. K. Lovelace, D. Shapiro, and L. Weingart, "Maximizing Cross-Functional New Product Teams' Innovativeness and Constraint Adherence: A Conflict Communications Perspective," *Academy of Management Journal* 44 (2001): 779–793.

47. L. Holpp and H. P. Phillips, "When Is a Team Its Own Worst Enemy?" *Training*, September 1, 1995, 71.

48. S. Asche, "Opinions and Social Pressure," *Scientific American* 193 (1995): 31–35.

49. J. Stephens, "Corner Office: Rah-Rah Isn't for Everyone," interview by A. Bryant, *New York Times*, April 9, 2010, accessed June 11, 2010, http://www.nytimes.com/2010/04/11/business/11corner.html?pagewanted=.

50. S. G. Cohen, G. E. Ledford, and G. M. Spreitzer, "A Predictive Model of Self-Managing Work Team Effectiveness," *Human Relations* 49, no. 5 (1996): 643–676.

51. C. Duhigg, "Group Study: What Google Learned from Its Quest to Build the Perfect Team," *New York Times*, February 28, 2016, MM20.

52. A. Edmondson, "Psychological Safety and Learning Behavior in Work Teams," *Administrative Science Quarterly* 44 (1999): 350–383.

53. A. Wooley, C. Chabris, A. Pentland, N. Hashmi, and T. Malone, "Evidence for a Collective Intelligence Factor in the Performance of Human Groups," *Science* 330 (2010): 686–688.

54. K. Bettenhausen and J. K. Murnighan, "The Emergence of Norms in Competitive Decision-Making Groups," *Administrative Science Quarterly* 30 (1985): 350–372.

55. M. E. Shaw, *Group Dynamics* (New York: McGraw Hill, 1981).

56. F. Rees, *Teamwork from Start to Finish* (San Francisco: Josey-Bass, 1997).

57. R. E. Silverman, "Tracking Sensors Invade the Workplace," *Wall Street Journal*, March 7, 2013, accessed June 16, 2014, http://online.wsj.com/news/articles/SB10001424127887324034804578344303429080678.

58. S. M. Gully, D. S. Devine, and D. J. Whitney, "A Meta-Analysis of Cohesion and Performance: Effects of Level of Analysis and Task Interdependence," *Small Group Research* 26, no. 4 (1995): 497–520.

59. B. Cohen, "Golden State: The Team That Eats Together," *Wall Street Journal*, February 11, 2015, accessed May 8, 2015, http://www.wsj.com/articles/golden-state-the-team-that-eats-together-1423682960.

60. J. Bersin, J. Geller, N. Wakefield & B. Walsh, *Global Human Capital Trends 2016—The New Organization: Different by Design*, eds. B. Pelster and J. Schwartz (Deloitte University Press), 20.

61. Gully, et al., "A Meta-Analysis of Cohesion and Performance." F. Tschan and M. V. Cranach, "Group Task Structure, Processes and Outcomes," in *Handbook of Work Group Psychology*, ed. M. A. West (Chichester, UK: Wiley, 1966).

62. D. E. Yeatts and C. Hyten, *High-Performing Self-Managed Work Teams* (Thousand Oaks, CA: Sage Publications, 1998).

63. J. Lublin, "Smaller Boards Get Bigger Returns," *Wall Street Journal*, August 26, 2014, accessed April 30, 2016, 8, 2015, http://www.wsj.com/articles/smaller-boards-get-bigger-returns-1409078628.

64. Ibid.

65. Ibid.

66. Yeatts and Hyten, *High-Performing Self-Managed Work Teams*; J. Colquitt, R. Noe, and C. Jackson, "Justice in Teams: Antecedents and Consequences of Procedural Justice Climate," *Personnel Psychology*, April 1, 2002, 83.

67. D. S. Kezsbom, "Re-Opening Pandora's Box: Sources of Project Team Conflict in the '90s," *Industrial Engineering* 24, no. 5 (1992): 54–59.

68. A. C. Amason, W. A. Hochwarter, and K. R. Thompson, "Conflict: An Important Dimension in Successful Management Teams," *Organizational Dynamics* 24 (1995): 20.

69. A. C. Amason, "Distinguishing the Effects of Functional and Dysfunctional Conflict on Strategic Decision Making: Resolving a Paradox for Top Management Teams," *Academy of Management Journal* 39, no. 1 (1996): 123–148.

70. K. M. Eisenhardt, J. L. Kahwajy, and L. J. Bourgeois III, "How Management Teams Disagree," *California Management Review* 39, no. 2 (Winter 1997): 42–62.

71. K. M. Eisenhardt, J. L. Kahwajy, and L. J. Bourgeois III, "How Management Teams Can Have a Good Fight," *Harvard Business Review* 75, no. 4 (July–August 1997): 77–85.

72. S. Shellenbarger, "Meet the Meeting Killers," *Wall Street Journal*, May 15, 2012, accessed May 8, 2015, http://www.wsj.com/articles/SB10001424052702304192704577404434001058726.

73. C. Nemeth and P. Owens, "Making Work Groups More Effective: The Value of Minority Dissent," in *Handbook of Work Group Psychology*, ed. M. A. West (Chichester, UK: Wiley, 1996).

74. J. M. Levin and R. L. Moreland, "Progress in Small Group Research," *Annual Review of Psychology* 9 (1990): 72–78; S. E. Jackson, "Team Composition in Organizational Settings: Issues in Managing a Diverse Work Force," in *Group Processes and Productivity*, ed. S. Worchel, W. Wood, and J. Simpson (Beverly Hills, CA: Sage, 1992).

75. Eisenhardt, et al., "How Management Teams Can Have a Good Fight."

76. Ibid.

77. J. Lublin, "Arguing with the Boss: A Winning Career Strategy," *Wall Street Journal*, August 9, 2012, accessed May 8, 2015, http://www.wsj.com/articles/SB10000872396390443991704577579201122821724.

78. Eisenhardt, et al., "How Management Teams Can Have a Good Fight."

79. B. W. Tuckman, "Development Sequence in Small Groups," *Psychological Bulletin* 63, no. 6 (1965): 384–399.

80. Gross, *Compensation for Teams*.

81. J. F. McGrew, J. G. Bilotta, and J. M. Deeney, "Software Team Formation and Decay: Extending the Standard Model for Small Groups," *Small Group Research* 30, no. 2 (1999): 209–234.

82. Ibid.

83. J. Case, "What the Experts Forgot to Mention: Management Teams Create New Difficulties, But Succeed for XEL Communication," *Inc.*, September 1, 1993, 66.

84. J. R. Hackman, "The Psychology of Self-Management in Organizations," in *Psychology and Work: Productivity, Change, and Employment*, ed. M. S. Pallak and R. Perloff (Washington, DC: American Psychological Association, 1986), 85–136.

85. A. O'Leary-Kelly, J. J. Martocchio, and D. D. Frink, "A Review of the Influence of Group Goals on Group Performance," *Academy of Management Journal* 37, no. 5 (1994): 1285–1301.

86. A. Zander, "The Origins and Consequences of Group Goals," in *Retrospections on Social Psychology*, ed. L. Festinger (New York: Oxford University Press, 1980), 205–235.

87. M. Erez and A. Somech, "Is Group Productivity Loss the Rule or the Exception? Effects of Culture and Group-Based Motivation," *Academy of Management Journal* 39, no. 6 (1996): 1513–1537.

88. S. Sherman, "Stretch Goals: The Dark Side of Asking for Miracles," *Fortune*, November 13, 1995.

89. J. Muller, "GM's New Goal Is a Stretch: Auto Industry's MVP," *Forbes*, January 31, 2013, accessed June 13, 2013, http://www.forbes.com/sites/joannmuller/2013/01/31/gms-new-goal-seems-a-bit-of-a-stretch-auto-industrys-mvp/.

90. K. R. Thompson, W. A. Hochwarter, and N. J. Mathys, "Stretch Targets: What Makes Them Effective?" *Academy of Management Executive* 11, no. 3 (1997): 48–60.

91. B. Stone, "Inside Google's Secret Lab—Businessweek," May 22, 2013, accessed July 9, 2014, http://www.businessweek.com/articles/2013-05-22/inside-googles-secret-lab.

92. B. Dumaine, "The Trouble with Teams," *Fortune*, 5 September 1994, 86–92.

93. G. A. Neuman, S. H. Wagner, and N. D. Christiansen, "The Relationship Between Work-Team Personality Composition and the Job Performance of Teams," *Group & Organization Management* 24, no. 1 (1999): 28–45.

94. M. A. Campion, G. J. Medsker, and A. C. Higgs, "Relations Between Work Group Characteristics and Effectiveness: Implications for Designing Effective Work Groups," *Personnel Psychology* 46, no. 4 (1993): 823–850.

95. B. L. Kirkman and D. L. Shapiro, "The Impact of Cultural Values on Employee Resistance to Teams: Toward a Model of Globalized Self-Managing Work Team Effectiveness," *Academy of Management Review* 22, no. 3 (1997): 730–757.

96. J. Pavlus, "SAP Looks to XRX for R&D Inspiration," *Bloomberg Businessweek*, February 2–8, 2015, p. 32.

97. A. Galinsky, "Is Your Team Too Talented," *Columbia Ideas at Work*, October 30, 2014, accessed May 8, 2015, http://www8.gsb.columbia.edu/ideas-at-work/publication/1700.

98. J. Bunderson and K. Sutcliffe, "Comparing Alternative Conceptualizations of Functional Diversity in Management Teams: Process and Performance Effects," *Academy of Management Journal* 45 (2002): 875–893.

99. A. Zynga, "The Cognitive Bias Keeping Us from Innovating," *Harvard Business Review*, June 13, 2013, accessed June 16, 2014, http://blogs.hbr .org/2013/06/the-cognitive-bias-keeping-us-from /#disqus_thread.

100. "Rebel Alliance: To Develop Star Wars and Jurassic World, in VR, Industrial Light & Magic Has Formed a Supergroup," *Bloomberg Businessweek*, April 11–24, 2016, 48.

101. J. Hackman, "New Rules for Team Building—The Times Are Changing—And So Are the Guidelines for Maximizing Team Performance," *Optimize*, July 1, 2002, 50.

102. Joinson, "Teams at Work."

103. Strozniak, "Teams at Work."

104. Ibid.

105. P. Nicholas, "It's All About Flight or Fight," *Weekend Australian*, March 14, 2009, 1.

106. Wellins, et al., *Inside Teams*.

107. E. Salas, D. DiazGranados, C. Klein, C. Burke, K. Stagl, G. Goodwin, and S. Halpin, "Does Team Training Improve Team Performance? A Meta-Analysis," *Human Factors* 50, no. 6 (2008): 903–933.

108. S. Caudron, "Tie Individual Pay to Team Success," *Personnel Journal* 73, no. 10 (October 1994): 40.

109. Ibid.

110. Gross, *Compensation for Teams*.

111. G. Ledford, "Three Case Studies on Skill-Based Pay: An Overview," *Compensation & Benefits Review* 23, no. 2 (1991): 11–24.

112. T. Law, "Where Loyalty Is Rewarded," *The Press*, September 29, 2008, *Business Day* 4.

113. J. R. Schuster and P. K. Zingheim, *The New Pay: Linking Employee and Organizational Performance* (New York: Lexington Books, 1992).

114. Cohen and Bailey, "What Makes Teams Work."

115. R. Allen and R. Kilmann, "Aligning Reward Practices in Support of Total Quality Management," *Business Horizons* 44 (May 2001): 77–85.

11

1. J. Emshwiller and G. Fields, "Decadeslong Arrest Wave Vexes Employers," *Wall Street Journal*, December 12, 2014, accessed May 7, 2015, http://www .wsj.com/articles/decadeslong-arrest-wave-vexes -employers-1418438092.

2. S. Thurm, "Background Checks Fuel Jobs Debate," *Wall Street Journal*, June 11, 2013, accessed May 6, 2016, http://www.wsj.com/articles/SB1000142 4127887323495604578539283518855020.

3. Ibid.

4. Emshwiller and Fields, "Decadeslong Arrest Wave Vexes Employers."

5. "Genetic Information Discrimination," *U.S. Equal Employment Opportunity Commission*, accessed May 6, 2016, http://www.eeoc.gov/laws/types /genetic.cfm.

6. K. McGowan, "Barring Male Guards for Female Inmates Might Violate Title VII, Ninth Circuit Rules," *Bloomberg BNA*, July 8, 2014, accessed May 6, 2016, http://www.bna.com/barring-male-guards -n17179891923/.

7. P. S. Greenlaw and J. P. Kohl, "Employer 'Business' and 'Job' Defenses in Civil Rights Actions," *Public Personnel Management* 23, no. 4 (1994): 573.

8. M. Miller, "SeaWorld Fined for Improperly Protecting Employees from Killer Whales," *Washington Post*, May 1, 2015, accessed May 1, 2016, http://www .washingtonpost.com/news/morning-mix/wp/2015 /05/01/seaworld-fined-for-improperly-protecting -employees-from-killer-whales/.

9. Greenlaw and Kohl, "Employer 'Business' and 'Job' Defenses in Civil Rights Actions."

10. City News Service, "66-Year-Old Man Awarded $26 Million in Age Discrimination Lawsuit," *Los Angeles Daily News*, February 27, 2014, accessed May 6, 2016, http://www.dailynews.com/general -news/20140227/66-year-old-man-awarded-26 -million-in-age-discrimination-lawsuit-against-staples.

11. P. Lee and C. Hymowitz, "No Place for Old Waiters at Texas Roadhouse?" *Bloomberg Businessweek*, September 28–October 4, 2015, 23–24.

12. E. Coe, "Steakhouse Chain Says EEOC Age Bias Suit Too Vague," *Law 360*, accessed April 30, 2016, http://www.law360.com/articles/305259 /steakhouse-chain-says-eeoc-age-bias-suit-too-vague.

13. W. Peirce, C. A. Smolinski, and B. Rosen, "Why Sexual Harassment Complaints Fall on Deaf Ears," *Academy of Management Executive* 12, no. 3 (1998): 41–54.

14. R. Gray, "First Student to Pay $150K to Settle Sexual Harassment, Retaliation Suit," *School Transportation News*, February 4, 2011, accessed May 6, 2016, http://stnonline.com/index.php/news/blogs /item/3104-first-student-to-pay-$150k-to-settle -sexual-harassment-retaliation-suit.

15. E. Francis, "$168 Million Awarded to Woman Harassed in 'Raunchy' Cardiac Surgery Unit," *ABC News*, March 2, 2012, accessed May 6, 2016, http:// abcnews.go.com/US/LegalCenter/168-million -awarded-woman-harassed-raunchy-cardiac-surgery /story?id=15835342&singlePage=true.

16. Peirce, et al., "Why Sexual Harassment Complaints Fall on Deaf Ears."

17. Ibid.

18. E. Larson, "The Economic Costs of Sexual Harassment," *The Freeman* 46, August 1996, accessed May 6, 2016, http://fee.org/freeman/the-economic -costs-of-sexual-harassment.

19. L. Weber, "Firms Flock to Cities with Top Talent," *Wall Street Journal*, April 13, 2016, B11.

20. R. D. Gatewood and H. S. Field, *Human Resource Selection* (Fort Worth, TX: Dryden Press, 1998).

21. Ibid.

22. E. Gaydos, "Three Awesome Examples of Great Job Descriptions," *TLNT*, August 2, 2012, accessed May 6, 2016, http://www.tlnt.com/2012/08/02/three -awesome-examples-of-great-job-descriptions/.

23. *Griggs v. Duke Power Co.*, 401 US 424, 436 (1971); *Albemarle Paper Co. v. Moody*, 422 US 405 (1975).

24. R. E. Silverman and N. Waller, "The Algorithm That Tells the Boss Who Might Quit," *Wall Street Journal*, March 13, 2015, accessed May 6, 2016, http://www.wsj.com/articles/the-algorithm-that-tells -the-boss-who-might-quit-1426287935.

25. J. A. Breaugh, *Recruitment: Science and Practice* (Boston: PWSKent, 1992).

26. R. Albergotti, "LinkedIn Wants to Help You Stay at Your Company," *Wall Street Journal* (blog), April 10, 2014, accessed May 6, 2016, http://blogs.wsj.com /atwork/2014/04/10/linkedin-wants-to-help-you-stay -at-your-company/.

27. Ibid.

28. R. Silverman and L. Weber, "An Inside Job: More Firms Opt to Recruit from Within," *Wall Street Journal*, May 29, 2012, accessed May 6, 2016, http:// online.wsj.com/article/SB10001424052702303395604 577434563715828218.html.

29. L. Klaff, "New Internal Hiring Systems Reduce Cost and Boost Morale," *Workforce Management* 83 (March 2004): 76–79.

30. R. Silverman and L. Weber, "An Inside Job: More Firms Opt to Recruit from Within," *Wall Street Journal*, May 29, 2012, accessed May 6, 2016, http:// online.wsj.com/article/SB10001424052702303395604 577434563715828218.html.

31. R. E. Silverman, "Climbing the Career Ladder with Help," *Wall Street Journal*, January 14, 2015, B6.

32. Ibid.

33. C. Hymowitz, "Diebold's New Executive Suite," *Bloomberg Businessweek*, August 10–23, 2015, 21–22.

34. J. Breaugh and M. Starke, "Research on Employee Recruitment: So Many Studies, So Many Remaining Questions," *Journal of Management* 26 (2000): 405–434.

35. J. J. Colao, "The Facebook Job Board Is Here: Recruiting Will Never Look the Same," *Forbes*, November 14, 2012, accessed May 6, 2016, http://www .forbes.com/sites/jjcolao/2012/11/14/the-facebook -job-board-is-here-recruiting-will-never-look-the -same/; J. Zappe, "Now Almost Gone: The Decline of Print-Based Help-Wanted Ads," *Source Con*, March 20, 2012, accessed May 5, 2015, http://www .sourcecon.com/news/2012/03/20/now-almost-gone -the-decline-of-print-based-help-wanted-ads/.

36. "2016 Jobvite Job Seeker Nation Study," *Jobvite*, accessed May 1, 2016, http://www.jobvite.com /wp-content/uploads/2016/03/Jobvite_Jobseeker _Nation_2016.pdf.

37. S. Akiode, "The Social Recruiting Pocket Guide," *Herd Wisdom*, June 9, 2013, accessed May 5, 2015, http://socialmeep.com/infographic-the-social -recruiting-pocket-guide/.

38. R. E. Silverman, "New Year, New Job? Read This First," *Wall Street Journal*, January 2, 2015, B1, B4.

39. Ibid.

40. N. Buhayar, "Be a Grand Pooh-Bah of Probability," *Bloomberg Businessweek*, March 16–22, 2015, 34–35.

41. S. Shellenbarger, "How to Deal with a Long Hiring Process," *Wall Street Journal*, January 19, 2016, B1; R. Feintzeig, "Hiring on the Fast Track," *Wall Street Journal*, September 17, 2015, B1.

42. Feintzeig, "Hiring on the Fast Track."

43. C. Camden and B. Wallace, "Job Application Forms: A Hazardous Employment Practice," *Personnel Administrator* 28 (1983): 31–32.

44. J. Valentino-Devries, "Bosses May Use Social Media to Discriminate Against Job Seekers," *Wall Street Journal*, November 20, 2013, accessed May 6, 2016, http://online.wsj.com/news/articles/SB1000142 4052702303755504579208304255139392.

45. "Fifty-Eight Percent of Employers Have Caught a Lie on a Résumé, According to a New Career-Builder Survey," *CareerBuilder.com*, August 7, 2014, accessed May 6, 2016, http://www.careerbuilder.com /share/aboutus/pressreleasesdetail.aspx?sd=8%2F7% 2F2014&id=pr837&ed=12%2F31%2F2014.

46. D. Kerr, "Uber's Background Checks Don't Catch Criminals," *Cnet.com*, April 17, 2015, accessed May 6, 2016, http://www.cnet.com/news/ubers -background-checks-dont-catch-criminals-says-houston/.

47. S. Adler, "Verifying a Job Candidate's Background: The State of Practice in a Vital Human Resources Activity," *Review of Business* 15, no. 2 (1993/1994): 3–8.

48. W. Woska, "Legal Issues for HR Professionals: Reference Checking/Background Investigations," *Public Personnel Management* 36 (Spring 2007): 79–89.

49. "More Than 70 Percent of HR Professionals Say Reference Checking Is Effective in Identifying Poor Performers," *Society for Human Resource Management*, accessed May 6, 2016, http://www.shrm.org /press_published/CMS_011240.asp.

50. P. Babcock, "Spotting Lies: The High Cost of Careless Hiring," *HR Magazine* 48, no. 10 (October 2003).

51. E. Leizerman, "Oregon Jury Renders $5.2M Verdict Against Trucking Broker and Driver in Negligent Hiring Case," *PRWeb*, March 6, 2012, accessed May 6, 2016, http://www.prweb.com/releases/2012/3 /prweb9258166.htm.

52. M. Le, T. Nguyen, and B. Kleiner, "Legal Counsel: Don't Be Sued for Negligent Hiring," *Nonprofit World*, May 1, 2003, 14–15.

53. "SHRM FInds Fewer Employers Using Background Checks in Hiring," accessed May 6, 2016, accessed May 5, 2015, http://www.shrm.org/about/pressroom/pressreleases/pages/backgroundchecks.aspx.

54. D. Belkin, "More Job Seekers Scramble to Erase Their Criminal Past," *Wall Street Journal*, November 11, 2009, A1.

55. Emshwiller and Fields, "Decadeslong Arrest Wave Vexes Employers."; S. Thurm, "Background Checks Fuel Jobs Debate," *Wall Street Journal*, June 11, 2013, accessed May 6, 2016, http://www.wsj.com/articles/SB10001424127887323495604578539283518855020.

56. A. Athavaley, "Job References You Can't Control," *Wall Street Journal*, September 27, 2007, D1.

57. C. Cohen, "Reference Checks," *CA Magazine*, November 2004, 41.

58. Keith J. Winstein, "Inflated Credentials Surface in Executive Suite," *Wall Street Journal*, November 13, 2008, accessed May 6, 2016, http://online.wsj.com/article/SB122652836844922165.html.

59. B. Ellis, "For Hire: Professional Liars for Job Seekers," *CNN Money*, July 17, 2013, accessed May 6, 2016, http://money.cnn.com/2013/07/17/pf/professional-liars/.

60. L. Weber, "To Get a Job, New Hires Are Put to the Test," *Wall Street Journal*, April 15, 2015, A1, A10.

61. J. Pierson and N. Schaefer Riley, "Here's Why Tests Matter," *Wall Street Journal*, March 31, 2016, accessed May 6, 2016, http://www.wsj.com/articles/heres-why-tests-matter-1459379670.

62. J. Hunter, "Cognitive Ability, Cognitive Aptitudes, Job Knowledge, and Job Performance," *Journal of Vocational Behavior* 29 (1986): 340–362.

63. F. L. Schmidt, "The Role of General Cognitive Ability and Job Performance: Why There Cannot Be a Debate," *Human Performance* 15 (2002): 187–210.

64. "D. Hambrick and C. Chabris, "Yes, IQ Really Matters," *Slate*, April 14, 2014, accessed July 10, 2014, http://www.slate.com/articles/health_and_science/science/2014/04/what_do_sat_and_iq_tests_measure_general_intelligence_predicts_school_and.html.

65. E. E. Cureton, "Comment," in *Research Conference on the Use of Autobiographical Data as Psychological Predictors*, ed. E. R. Henry (Greensboro, NC: The Richardson Foundation, 1965), 13.

66. J. R. Glennon, L. E. Albright, and W. A. Owens, *A Catalog of Life History Items* (Greensboro, NC: The Richardson Foundation, 1966).

67. Gatewood and Field, *Human Resource Selection*.

68. J. M. Digman, "Personality Structure: Emergence of the Five-Factor Model," *Annual Review of Psychology* 41 (1990): 417–440; M. R. Barrick and M. K. Mount, "The Big Five Personality Dimensions and Job Performance: A Meta-Analysis," *Personnel Psychology* 44 (1991): 1–26.

69. N. Schmitt, "Beyond the Big Five: Increases in Understanding and Practical Utility," *Human Performance* 17 (2004): 347–357.

70. R. E. Silverman, "New Year, New Job? Read This First," *Wall Street Journal*, January 2, 2015, B1, B4.

71. L. Weber, "Today's Personality Tests Raise the Bar for Job Seekers," *Wall Street Journal*, April 14, 2015, accessed May 6, 2016, http://www.wsj.com/articles/a-personality-test-could-stand-in-the-way-of-your-next-job-1429065001.

72. M. S. Taylor and J. A. Sniezek, "The College Recruitment Interview: Topical Content and Applicant Reactions," *Journal of Occupational Psychology* 57 (1984): 157–168.

73. M. Harris, "Reconsidering the Employment Interview: A Review of Recent Literature and Suggestions for Future Research," *Personnel Psychology* 42 (Winter 1989): 691–726.

74. Taylor and Sniezek, "The College Recruitment Interview."

75. C. Mims, "At Google, The Science of Working Better," *Wall Street Journal*, March 29, 2015, B1.

76. R. Burnett, C. Fan, S. J. Motowidlo, and T. DeGroot, "Interview Notes and Validity," *Personnel Psychology* 51, (1998): 375–396; M. A. Campion, D. K. Palmer, and J. E. Campion, "A Review of Structure in the Selection Interview," *Personnel Psychology* 50, no. 3 (1997): 655–702.

77. T. Judge, "The Employment Interview: A Review of Recent Research and Recommendations for Future Research," *Human Resource Management Review* 10, no. 4 (2000): 383–406.

78. J. Cortina, N. Goldstein, S. Payne, K. Davison, and S. Gilliland, "The Incremental Validity of Interview Scores Over and Above Cognitive Ability and Conscientiousness Scores," *Personnel Psychology* 53, no. 2 (2000): 325–351; F. L. Schmidt and J. E. Hunter, "The Validity and Utility of Selection Methods in Personnel Psychology: Practical and Theoretical Implications of 85 Years of Research Findings," *Psychological Bulletin* 124, no. 2 (1998): 262–274.

79. K. Tyler, "Training Revs Up," *HR Magazine* (April 2005), *Society for Human Resource Management*, accessed March 23, 2009, http://www.shrm.org.

80. "2013 State of the Industry," *ASTD Research*, 2013, accessed May 6, 2016, https://www.td.org/Publications/Research-Reports/2013/2013-State-of-the-Industry.

81. S. Lupkin, "Texas Health Workers Use Tabasco to Help Train for Ebola," *Good Morning America*, October 23, 2014, accessed May 7, 2015, http://abcnews.go.com/Health/texas-health-workers-tabasco-train-ebola/story?id=26385702.

82. Ibid.

83. T. Jacoby, "Wal-Mart Tries to Skill Up," *Wall Street Journal*, September 5–6, 2015, C3.

84. L. Kolodny, "The Latest Approach to Employee Training," *Wall Street Journal*, March 13, 2016, accessed May 6, 2016, http://www.wsj.com/articles/the-latest-approach-to-employee-training-1457921560.

85. D. L. Kirkpatrick, "Four Steps to Measuring Training Effectiveness," *Personnel Administrator* 28 (1983): 19–25.

86. L. Bassi, J. Ludwig, D. McMurrer, and M. Van Buren, "Profiting from Learning: Do Firms' Investments in Education and Training Pay Off?" *American Society for Training and Development*, accessed August 14, 2008, https://www.td.org/Publications/Research-Reports/2000/Profiting-from-Learning

87. Daley, "It's Shaping Up to Be a Good Year," *Entrepreneur*, January 2014, 92.

88. S. Culbert, "Get Rid of the Performance Review!," *Wall Street Journal*, June 21, 2012, accessed May 6, 2016, http://www.wsj.com/articles/SB122426318874844933.

89. D. Meinert, "Is It Time to Put the Performance Appraisal on a PIP?," *Society of Human Resource Management*, April 1, 2015, accessed May 6, 2016, https://www.shrm.org/publications/hrmagazine/editorialcontent/2015/0415/pages/0415-qualitative-performance-reviews.aspx.

90. M. Nisen, "Why GE Had to Kill Its Annual Performance Reviews after More than Three Decades," *Quartz*, August 13, 2015, accessed May 6, 2016, http://qz.com/428813/ge-performance-review-strategy-shift/

91. Ibid.

92. K. R. Murphy and J. N. Cleveland, *Understanding Performance Appraisal: Social, Organizational and Goal-Based Perspectives* (Thousand Oaks, CA: Sage, 1995).

93. R. Feintzeig, "The Trouble with Grading Employees," *Wall Street Journal*, April 22, 2015, B1, B7.

94. U. J. Wiersma and G. P. Latham, "The Practicality of Behavioral Observation Scales, Behavioral Expectation Scales, and Trait Scales," *Personnel Psychology* 39 (1986): 619–628; U. J. Wiersma, P. T. Van Den Berg, and G. P. Latham, "Dutch Reactions to Behavioral Observation, Behavioral Expectation, and Trait Scales," *Group & Organization Management* 20 (1995): 297–309.

95. D. J. Schleicher, D. V. Day, B. T. Mayes, and R. E. Riggio, "A New Frame for Frame-of-Reference Training: Enhancing the Construct Validity of Assessment Centers," *Journal of Applied Psychology* (August 2002): 735–746.

96. R. Feintzeig, "Everything Is Awesome! Why You Can't Tell Employees They're Doing a Bad Job," *Wall Street Journal*, February 10, 2015, accessed May 6, 2016, http://www.wsj.com/articles/everything-is-awesome-why-you-cant-tell-employees-theyre-doing-a-bad-job-1423613936.

97. R. Feintzeig, "The Trouble with Grading Employees," *Wall Street Journal*, April 22, 2015, B1, B7.

98. H. H. Meyer, "A Solution to the Performance Appraisal Feedback Enigma," *Academy of Management Executive* 5, no. 1 (1991): 68–76; G. C. Thornton, "Psychometric Properties of Self-Appraisals of Job Performance," *Personnel Psychology* 33 (1980): 263–271.

99. Thornton, "Psychometric Properties of Self-Appraisals of Job Performance."

100. K. Mullaney, "It's Not OK to 'Rate' Employees," *CNBC*, April 18, 2016, accessed May 6, 2016, http://www.cnbc.com/2016/04/18/its-not-ok-to-rate-employees-commentary.html.

101. J. Smither, M. London, R. Flautt, Y. Vargas, and I. Kucine, "Can Working with an Executive Coach Improve Multisource Feedback Ratings Over Time? A Quasi-Experimental Field Study," *Personnel Psychology* (Spring 2003): 21–43.

102. A. Walker and J. Smither, "A Five-Year Study of Upward Feedback: What Managers Do with Their Results Matters," *Personnel Psychology* 52 (Summer 1999): 393–422.

103. K. Chu, "China: A Billion Strong But Short on Workers," *Wall Street Journal*, May 1, 2013, accessed May 6, 2016, http://www.wsj.com/articles/SB10001424127887323797810457845515399965831

104. K. Chu, "China Factories Try Karaoke, Speed Dating to Keep Workers," *Wall Street Journal*, May 2, 2013, accessed May 6, 2016, http://www.wsj.com/articles/SB1000142412788732379810457845263407551923

105. G. T. Milkovich and J. M. Newman, *Compensation*, 4th ed. (Homewood, IL: Irwin, 1993).

106. M. L. Williams and G. F. Dreher, "Compensation System Attributes and Applicant Pool Characteristics," *Academy of Management Journal* 35, no. 3 (1992): 571–595.

107. S. Quinton, "The Trader Joe's Lesson: How to Pay a Living Wage and Still Make Money in Retail," *The Atlantic*, March 25, 2013, accessed May 6, 2016, http://www.theatlantic.com/business/archive/2013/03/the-trader-joes-lesson-how-to-pay-a-living-wage-and-still-make-money-in-retail/274322/.

108. D. K. Williams and M. M. Scott, "Why We Pay All Our Employees a Commission," *Harvard Business Review*, March 26, 2013, accessed May 6, 2016, https://hbr.org/2013/03/why-we-pay-all-our-employees-a/.

109. R. Solomon, "Delta Pays Out Biggest Profit Sharing in U.S. History," *Delta*, February 12, 2016, accessed May 6, 2016, http://news.delta.com/delta-pays-out-biggest-profit-sharing-us-history.

110. M. Josephs, "The Millionaire Truck Driver and Other ESOP Miracles," *Forbes*, April 30, 2014, accessed May 6, 2016, http://www.forbes.com/sites/maryjosephs/2014/04/30/the-millionaire-truck-driver-and-other-esop-miracles/.

111. S. Strom, "At Chobani, Now It's Not Just the Yogurt That's Rich," *New York Times*, April 26, 2016, accessed July 26, 2016, http://www.nytimes.com/2016/04/27/business/a-windfall-for-chobani-employees-stakes-in-the-company.html?_r=0.

112. Y. Naguchi, "Why Chobani Gave Employees a Financial Stake in Company's Future," *All Things Considered*, NPR, April 28, 2016, accessed May 6, 2016, http://www.npr.org/templates/transcript/transcript.php?storyId=476021520.

113. A. Loten, "Founders Cash Out, But Do Workers Gain?—US Employee-Owned Firms Top 10,000,

with More Expected as Owners Retire; Critics Point to Potential Drawbacks," *Wall Street Journal*, April 18, 2013, B4.

114. M. Bloom, "The Performance Effects of Pay Dispersion on Individuals and Organizations," *Academy of Management Journal* 42, no. 1 (1999): 25–40.

115. P. Hodgson, "Top CEOs Make More Than 300 Times the Average Worker," *Fortune*, June 22, 2015, accessed May 6, 2016, http://fortune.com/2015/06/22 /ceo-vs-worker-pay/.

116. W. Grossman and R. E. Hoskisson, "CEO Pay at the Crossroads of Wall Street and Main: Toward the Strategic Design of Executive Compensation," *Academy of Management Executive* 12, no. 1 (1998): 43–57.

117. Bloom, "The Performance Effects of Pay Dispersion."

118. M. Bloom and J. Michel, "The Relationships Among Organizational Context, Pay Dispersion, and Managerial Turnover," *Academy of Management Journal* 45 (2002): 33–42.

119. S. Needleman, "Bad Firings Can Hurt Firm's Reputation," *Wall Street Journal*, July 8, 2008, D4.

120. J. Strickland, "Zynga Layoffs: The Aftermath," *Inc*, June 3, 2013, accessed May 6, 2016, http://www .inc.com/julie-strickland/zynga-lay-off-eighteen -percent-staff-close-three-offices.html.

121. A. Rupe, "Horrors from the Bad-Firing File," *Workforce Management*, November 2003, 16.

122. D. Mattel, J. Lublin, and R. Silverman, "Bad Call: How Not to Fire a Worker," *Wall Street Journal*, September 9, 2011, B2.

123. P. Michal-Johnson, *Saying Good-Bye: A Manager's Guide to Employee Dismissal* (Glenview, IL: Scott, Foresman & Co., 1985).

124. M. Bordwin, "Employment Law: Beware of Time Bombs and Shark-Infested Waters," *HR Focus*, April 1, 1995, 19; D. Jones, "Fired Workers Fight Back ... and Win; Laws, Juries Shift Protection to Terminated Employees," *USA Today*, April 2, 1998, 01B.

125. Economic News Release, "Extended Mass Layoffs (Quarterly) News Release," *Bureau of Labor Statistics, Mass Layoff Statistics, 2009–2012*, May 13, 2013, accessed May 6, 2016, http://www.bls.gov/news .release/archives/mslo_05132013.htm.

126. J. Bort, "Microsoft's Layoffs Are Not *Yet* Done," *Business Insider*, January 27, 2015, accessed May 6, 2016, http://www.businessinsider.com/microsofts -layoffs-are-not-yet-done-2015-1.

127. B. Brown, "Microsoft, Blackberry, and NetApp among Those Trimming Workforces," *Network World*, July 22, 2015, accessed May 6, 2016, http:// www.networkworld.com/article/2951484/microsoft -subnet/biggest-tech-industry-layoffs-of-2015.

128. W. F. Cascio, "Employment Downsizing and Its Alternatives: Strategies for Long-Term Success," *SHRM Foundation's Effective Practice Guideline Series, Society for Human Resource Management Foundation*, accessed May 6, 2016, http://www.shrm .org/about/foundation/products/Documents /Downsizing%20EPG-%20Final.pdf.

129. K. E. Mishra, G. M. Spreitzer, and A. K. Mishra, "Preserving Employee Morale During Downsizing," *Sloan Management Review* 39, no. 2 (1998): 83–95.

130. K. Frieswick, "Until We Meet Again?" *CFO*, October 1, 2001, 41; Cascio, "Employment Downsizing and Its Alternatives: Strategies for Long-Term Success"; L. Weber and R. Feintzeig, "Assistance for Laid-Off Workers Gets Downsized," *Wall Street Journal*, February 18, 2013, accessed May 6, 2016, http://www.wsj.com/news/articles/SB1000142405270 2304899704579391254047535652

131. Cascio, "Employment Downsizing and Its Alternatives: Strategies for Long-Term Success."

132. C. Jones and L. Scott, "Layoffs Are Awful, but Don't Forget the Survivors," *Oilweek*, January 14, 2016, accessed May 6, 2016, http://www.oilweek.com /index.php/columnists/699-layoffs-are-awful-but-don -t-forget-the-survivors.

133. J. Ackerman, "Helping Layoff Survivors Cope: Companies Strive to Keep Morale High," *Boston Globe*, December 30, 2001, H1.

134. D. Ferrari, "Designing and Evaluating Early Retirement Programs: The State of Wyoming Experience," *Government Finance Review* 15, no. 1 (1999): 29–31.

135. J. Hilsenrath, "Adventures in Cost Cutting," *Wall Street Journal*, May 10, 2004, R1.

136. J. Lublin and S. Thurm, "How Companies Calculate Odds in Buyout Offers," *Wall Street Journal*, March 27, 2009, B1.

137. M. Willett, "Early Retirement and Phased Retirement Programs for the Public Sector," *Benefits & Compensation Digest*, April 2005, 31.

138. "2016 Jobvite Job Seeker Nation Study," *Jobvite*, accessed May 6, 2016, http://www.jobvite.com /wp-content/uploads/2016/03/Jobvite_Jobseeker _Nation_2016.pdf.

139. D. R. Dalton, W. D. Todor, and D. M. Krackhardt, "Turnover Overstated: The Functional Taxonomy," *Academy of Management Review* 7 (1982): 117–123.

140. J. R. Hollenbeck and C. R. Williams, "Turnover Functionality versus Turnover Frequency: A Note on Work Attitudes and Organizational Effectiveness," *Journal of Applied Psychology* 71 (1986): 606–611.

141. Silverman and Waller, "The Algorithm That Tells the Boss Who Might Quit."

142. C. R. Williams, "Reward Contingency, Unemployment, and Functional Turnover," *Human Resource Management Review* 9 (1999): 549–576.

12

1. "Table 11. Percent of the Projected Population by Hispanic Origin and Race for the United States: 2015 to 2060 (NP2014-T11)," *Census Bureau*, accessed May 8, 2016, https://www.census.gov /population/projections/data/national/2014 /summarytables.html.

2. "Table 3.4. Continued—Civilian Labor Force, by Age, Gender, Race, and Ethnicity, 1994, 2004, 2014, and Projected 2024," *Bureau of Labor Statistics*, December 2015, accessed May 8, 2016, http://www.bls.gov/emp/ep_table_304.htm; "Labor Force Projections to 2020: A More Slowly Growing Workforce," *Monthly Labor Review*, January 2012, 43–64.

3. "Table 3.4. Continued- Civilian Labor Force, by Age, Gender, Race, and Ethnicity, 1994, 2004, 2014, and Projected 2024," *Bureau of Labor Statistics*, December 2015, accessed May 8, 2016, http://www .bls.gov/emp/ep_table_304.htm.

4. "Discover McDonald's Around the Globe," McDonald's, accessed May 8, 2016, http://www .aboutmcdonalds.com/mcd/country/map.html.

5. O. Putnal, "11 Global McDonald's Menu Items," *Women's Day*, March 2010, accessed May 8, 2016, http://www.womansday.com/food-recipes/11-global -mcdonalds-menu-items-104999.

6. E. York, "In Speech, McDonald's Thompson Puts Focus on Diversity," *Chicago Tribune*, May 2, 2012, accessed May 8, 2016, http://articles.chicagotribune .com/2012-05-02/business/chi-in-speech-mcdonalds -thompson-puts-focus-on-diversity-20120502_1 _diversity-women-and-minority-owned-businesses -mcbites.

7. Equal Employment Opportunity Commission, "Affirmative Action Appropriate Under Title VII of the Civil Rights Act of 1964, as Amended. Chapter XIV—Equal Employment Opportunity Commission, Part 1608," *Government Publishing Office*, accessed May 8, 2016, http://www.access.gpo.gov/nara/cfr /waisidx_04/29cfr1608_04.html.

8. Equal Employment Opportunity Commission, "Federal Laws Prohibiting Job Discrimination: Questions and Answers," *Equal Employment Opportunity Commission*, accessed May 8, 2016, http://www.eeoc .gov/facts/qanda.html.

9. A. P. Carnevale and S. C. Stone, *The American Mosaic: An In-Depth Report on the Future of Diversity at Work* (New York: McGraw-Hill, 1995).

10. T. Roosevelt, "From Affirmative Action to Affirming Diversity," *Harvard Business Review* 68, no. 2 (1990): 107–117.

11. A. M. Konrad and F. Linnehan, "Formalized HRM Structures: Coordinating Equal Employment Opportunity or Concealing Organizational Practices?" *Academy of Management Journal* 38, no. 3 (1995): 787–820; see, for example, *Hopwood v. Texas*, 78 F.3d 932 (5th Cir., March 18, 1996). The U.S. Supreme Court has upheld the principle of affirmative action but has struck down some specific programs.

12. J. Bravin, "Court Backs Affirmative Action Ban—Justices Uphold State Initiative to End Race-Based Admissions, But Are Divided on Broader Issue," *Wall Street Journal*, April 23, 2014, A1.

13. P. Schmidt, "5 More States May Curtail Affirmative Action," *The Chronicle of Higher Education*, October 19, 2007, A1.

14. M. E. Heilman, C. J. Block, and P. Stathatos, "The Affirmative Action Stigma of Incompetence: Effects of Performance Information Ambiguity," *Academy of Management Journal* 40, no. 3 (1997): 603–625; D. Evans, "A Comparison of the Other-Directed Stigmatization Produced by Legal and Illegal Forms of Affirmative Action," *Journal of Applied Psychology* 88, no. 1 (2003): 121–130.

15. L. Leslie, D. Mayer, and D. Kravitz, "The Stigma of Affirmative Action: A Stereotyping-Based Theory and Meta-Analytic Test of the Consequences for Performance." *Academy of Management Journal* 57, no. 4 (2014): 964–989.

16. E. Orenstein, "The Business Case for Diversity," *Financial Executive*, May 2005, 22–25; G. Robinson and K. Dechant, "Building a Business Case for Diversity," *Academy of Management Executive* 11, no. 3 (1997): 21–31.

17. E. Esen, "2005 Workplace Diversity Practices: Survey Report," *Society for Human Resource Management*, accessed March 24, 2009, http://www .shrm.org/research.

18. Orenstein, "Business Case for Diversity."

19. Esen, "2005 Workplace Diversity Practices: Survey Report."

20. Orenstein, "Business Case for Diversity."

21. P. Wright and S. P. Ferris, "Competitiveness Through Management of Diversity: Effects on Stock Price Valuation," *Academy of Management Journal* 38 (1995): 272–285.

22. I. Bohnet, "Real Fixes for Workplace Bias," *Wall Street Journal*, March 12–13, 2016, C3; K. Lachance Shandrow, "10 U.S. Companies with Radically Awesome Parental Leave Policies," *Entrepreneur*, August 11, 2015, accessed May 8, 2016, https://www .entrepreneur.com/slideshow/249467.

23. P. Wright and S. P. Ferris, "Competitiveness Through Management of Diversity: Effects on Stock Price Valuation."

24. "State & Country QuickFacts," *Census Bureau*, July 1, 2014, accessed May 8, 2016, http://quickfacts .census.gov/qfd/states/00000.html; J. Humphreys, "The Multicultural Economy 2012," Selig Center for Economic Growth, Terry College of Business, University of Georgia, 2012.

25. J. Boudreau and N. Kieu Giang, "More Women May Sit in the Front of the Plane," *Bloomberg Businessweek*, April 11–25, 2016, 20–21.

26. Anonymous, "Bumpkin Bosses; Schumpeter," *The Economist*, May 10, 2014, 70.

27. W. W. Watson, K. Kumar, and L. K. Michaelsen, "Cultural Diversity's Impact on Interaction Process and Performance: Comparing Homogeneous and Diverse Task Groups," *Academy of Management Journal* 36 (1993): 590–602; K. A. Jehn, G. B. Northcraft, and M. A. Neale, "Why Differences Make a Difference: A Field Study of Diversity, Conflict, and Performance in Workgroups," *Administrative Science Quarterly* 44 (1999): 741–763; E. Kearney, D. Gebert, and S. Voelpel, "When and How Diversity

Benefits Teams: The Importance of Team Members' Need for Cognition," *Academy of Management Journal* 52 (2009): 581–598.

28. C. Palmieri, "Carnival Rocks the Boat," *Bloomberg Businessweek*, November 16–22, 2015, 22–23.

29. M. R. Carrell and E. E. Mann, "Defining Workplace Diversity Programs and Practices in Organizations," *Labor Law Journal* 44 (1993): 743–764.

30. D. A. Harrison, K. H. Price, and M. P. Bell, "Beyond Relational Demography: Time and the Effects of Surface- and Deep-Level Diversity on Work Group Cohesion," *Academy of Management Journal* 41 (1998): 96–107.

31. D. Harrison, K. Price, J. Gavin, and A. Florey, "Time, Teams, and Task Performance: Changing Effects of Surface- and Deep-Level Diversity on Group Functioning," *Academy of Management Journal* 45 (2002): 1029–1045.

32. Harrison, et al., "Beyond Relational Demography."

33. Ibid.

34. J. Haidt and L. Jussim, "Hard Truths About Race on Campus," *Wall Street Journal*, May 6, 2016, accessed May 8, 2016, http://www.wsj.com/articles /hard-truths-about-race-on-campus-1462544543; T. Pettigrew and L. Tropp, "A Meta-Analytic Test of Intergroup Contact Theory," *Journal of Personality and Social Psychology* 90 (2006): 751–783.

35. R. Alsop, "Why Your Grandfather Might Land a Job Before You Do," *BBC*, October 25, 2013, accessed May 8, 2016, http://www.bbc.com/capital /story/20131024-older-workers-fogey-or-find; E. White, "The New Recruits: Older Workers," *Wall Street Journal*, January 14, 2008, B3.

36. M. Kane, "Say What? 'Young People are Just Smarter,'" *CNET*, March 28, 2007, accessed May 9, 2015, http://www.cnet.com/news/say-what-young -people-are-just-smarter/.

37. V. Giang, "This Is the Latest Way Employers Mask Age Bias, Lawyers Say," *Fortune*, May 4, 2015, http://fortune.com/2015/05/04/digital-native -employers-bias/, accessed May 9, 2015;

38. Ibid.

39. "Age Discrimination in Employment Act (includes Concurrent Charges with Title VII, ADA and EPA) FY 1997–FY 2014," *US Equal Employment Opportunity Commission*, accessed May 9, 2015, http://www.eeoc.gov/eeoc/statistics/enforcement /adea.cfm.

40. S. R. Rhodes, "Age-Related Differences in Work Attitudes and Behavior," *Psychological Bulletin* 92 (1983): 328–367.

41. T. Ng and D. Feldman, "The Relationship of Age to Ten Dimensions of Job Performance," *Journal of Applied Psychology* 93, no. 2 (2008): 392–423.

42. G. M. McEvoy and W. F. Cascio, "Cumulative Evidence of the Relationship Between Employee Age and Job Performance," *Journal of Applied Psychology* 74 (1989): 11–17; T. Ng and D. Feldman, "The Relationship of Age to Ten Dimensions of Job Performance," *Journal of Applied Psychology* 93, no. 2 (2008): 392–423; A. Tergesen, "Why Everything You Think about Aging May Be Wrong," *Wall Street Journal*, November 30, 2014, accessed May 9, 2015, http://www.wsj.com/articles/why-everything-you -think-about-aging-may-be-wrong-1417408057.

43. S. E. Sullivan and E. A. Duplaga, "Recruiting and Retaining Older Workers for the Millennium," *Business Horizons* 40 (November 12, 1997): 65; E. Townsend, "To Keep Older Workers, Consider New Responsibilities and Guard Against Discrimination," *SHRM Foundation*, accessed May 3, 2016, http://www.shrm.org/about/foundation/pages /researchthatmatters.aspx.

44. N. Timiraos, "How Older Women Are Reshaping U.S. Job Market," *Wall Street Journal*, February 22, 2016, accessed May 8, 2016, http://www.wsj .com/articles/older-women-reshape-u-s-job-market -1456192536?mod=djem10point.

45. T. Maurer and N. Rafuse, "Learning, Not Litigating: Managing Employee Development and Avoiding Claims of Age Discrimination," *Academy of Management Executive* 15, no. 4 (2001): 110–121.

46. D. Brady, "The Bottom-Line Reasons for Mixing the Young and Old at Work," *Bloomberg Businessweek*, April 10, 2014, accessed July 11, 2014, http:// www.businessweek.com/articles/2014-02-10 /workplaces-boost-profits-when-young-and-old-workers -mentor-each-other; B. L. Hassell and P. L. Perrewe, "An Examination of Beliefs About Older Workers: Do Stereotypes Still Exist?" *Journal of Organizational Behavior* 16 (1995): 457–468.

47. "Charge Statistics: FY 1997 Through FY 2015," *Equal Employment Opportunity Commission*, accessed May 8, 2016, http://eeoc.gov/eeoc/statistics /enforcement/charges.cfm.

48. "Women in the Labor Force: A Databook," *Bureau of Labor Statistics*, December 2015, accessed May 8, 2016, http://www.bls.gov/opub/reports/cps /women-in-the-labor-force-a-databook-2015.pdf.

49. "The 2015 State of Women-Owned Businesses Report: A Summary of Important Trends 1997–2015," *Commissioned by American Express OPEN*, with the assistance of the Economic Census Branch of the Company Statistics Division of the US Census Bureau, May 2015, accessed May 8, 2016, http://www.womenable.com/content/userfiles /Amex_OPEN_State_of_WOBs_2015_Executive _Report_finalsm.pdf.

50. "Table 16. Median Usual Weekly Earnings of Full-Time Wage and Salary Workers, in Current Dollars, by Race, Hispanic or Latino Ethnicity, and Gender, 1979–2014 Annual Averages," *Bureau of Labor Statistics*, accessed May 8, 2016, http://www.bls .gov/opub/reports/womens-databook/archive/women -in-the-labor-force-a-databook-2015.pdf.

51. "US Women in Business," *Catalyst*, June 10, 2014, accessed July 11, 2014, http://www.catalyst.org /knowledge/us-women-business-0.

52. R. Molla, "Meet the Women CEOs of the Fortune 500," *Wall Street Journal*, March 7, 2014, accessed May 8, 2016, http://blogs.wsj.com /atwork/2014/03/07/meet-the-women-ceos-of-the -fortune-500/; "Statistical Overview of Women in the Workplace," *Catalyst*, March 3, 2014, accessed May 8, 2016, http://www.catalyst.org/knowledge/statistical -overview-women-workplace.

53. K. Bellstrom, "Why 2015 Was a Terrible Year to Be a *Fortune* 500 CEO," *Fortune*, December 23, 2015, accessed May 8, 2016, http://fortune.com /2015/12/23/2015-women-fortune-500-ceos/.

54. "Women in S&P 500 Companies." *Catalyst*, February 3, 2016, accessed May 8, 2016, http://www .catalyst.org/knowledge/women-sp-500-companies.

55. A. Joshi, J. Son, and H. Roh, "When Can Women Close the Gap? A Meta-Analytic Test of Sex Differences in Performance and Rewards," *Academy of Management Journal* 58 (2015): 1516–1545.

56. M. Bertrand and K. Hallock, "The Gender Gap in Top Corporate Jobs," *Industrial & Labor Relations Review* 55 (2001): 3–21.

57. J. R. Hollenbeck, D. R. Ilgen, C. Ostroff, and J. B. Vancouver, "Sex Differences in Occupational Choice, Pay, and Worth: A Supply-Side Approach to Understanding the Male-Female Wage Gap," *Personnel Psychology* 40 (1987): 715–744.

58. S. Shellenbarger, "Does Having Kids Dull Career Opportunities?" *WSJ Blogs: The Juggle*, Wall Street Journal, April 6, 2011, accessed May 28, 2011, http://blogs.wsj.com/juggle/2011/04/06/does-having -kids-dull-job-ambition/.

59. C. Friedersdorf, "Why PepsiCo CEO Indra K. Nooyi Can't Have It All," *The Atlantic*, July 1, 2014, accessed July 12, 2014, http://www.theatlantic.com /business/archive/2014/07/why-pepsico-ceo-indra-k -nooyi-cant-have-it-all/373750/.

60. Department of Industry, Labor and Human Relations, Report of the Governor's Task Force on the Glass Ceiling Commission (Madison, WI: State of Wisconsin, 1993); S. Devillard, S. Sancier, C. Werner, I. Maller, and C. Kossoff, "Women Matter 2013, Gender Diversity in Top Management: Moving Corporate Culture, Moving Boundaries," *McKinsey &*

Company, November 2013, 10–11; E. O. Wright and J. Baxter, "The Glass Ceiling Hypothesis: A Reply to Critics," *Gender & Society* 14 (2000): 814–821.

61. M. Fix, G. C. Galster, and R. J. Struyk, "An Overview of Auditing for Discrimination," in *Clear and Convincing Evidence: Measurement of Discrimination in America*, ed. M. Fix and R. Struyk (Washington, DC: Urban Institute Press, 1993), 1–68.

62. S. Devillard, S. Sancier, C. Werner, I. Maller, and C. Kossoff, "Women Matter 2013, Gender Diversity in Top Management: Moving Corporate Culture, Moving Boundaries," *McKinsey & Company*, November 2013, 13–14.

63. S. Shellenbarger, "One Way to Get Unstuck and Move Up? All You Have to Do Is Ask" *Wall Street Journal*, April 15, 2015, D3.

64. J. Lublin, "Men Enlist in Fight for Gender Equality," *Wall Street Journal*, March 11, 2015, B7.

65. "How to Report Sexual Harassment at Work," *Schwin Law*, accessed August 17, 2016, http://www .schwinlaw.com/uncategorized/how-to-report-sexual -harassment-at-work.

66. "Charge Statistics: FY 1997 Through FY 2014," *Equal Employment Opportunity Commission*, accessed May 8, 2016, http://eeoc.gov/eeoc/statistics /enforcement/charges.cfm

67. G. Wallace, "Only 5 Black CEOs at 500 Biggest Companies," *CNN*, January 29, 2015, accessed May 8, 2016, http://money.cnn.com/2015/01/29/news /economy/mcdonalds-ceo-diversity/?iid=EL; A. Garcia, "Only 9 Hispanic CEOs at Top 500 Companies," *CNN*, September 9, 2015, accessed May 8, 2016, http://money.cnn.com/2015/09/09/news/hispanic -ceo-fortune-500-companies/index.html.

68. "Household Data Annual Averages: Table 11. Employed Persons by Detailed Occupation, Sex, Race, and Hispanic or Latino Ethnicity," *Bureau of Labor Statistics, Department of Labor*, accessed May 2, 2016, http://www.bls.gov/cps/cpsaat11.htm.

69. D. A. Neal and W. R. Johnson, "The Role of Premarket Factors in Black-White Wage Differences," *Journal of Political Economy* 104, no. 5 (1996): 869–895.

70. Fix, et al., "An Overview of Auditing for Discrimination."

71. M. Bendick, Jr., C. W. Jackson, and V. A. Reinoso, "Measuring Employment Discrimination through Controlled Experiments," in *African-Americans and Post-Industrial Labor Markets*, ed. James B. Stewart (New Brunswick, NJ: Transaction Publishers, 1997), 77–100.

72. S. Mullainathan, "Racial Bias Even When We Have Good Intentions," *New York Times*, January 3, 2015, BU6.

73. P. B. Riach and J. Rich, "Measuring Discrimination by Direct Experimental Methods: Seeking Gunsmoke," *Journal of Post Keynesian Economics* 14, no. 2 (Winter 1991–1992): 143–150.

74. A. P. Brief, R. T. Buttram, R. M. Reizenstein, and S. D. Pugh, "Beyond Good Intentions: The Next Steps Toward Racial Equality in the American Workplace," *Academy of Management Executive* 11 (1997): 59–72.

75. L. E. Wynter, "Business & Race: Federal Agencies, Spurred on by Nonprofit Groups, Are Increasingly Embracing the Use of Undercover Investigators to Identify Discrimination in the Marketplace," *Wall Street Journal*, July 1, 1998, B1; E. Dwoskin, "Social Bias Creeps Into New Web Technology," *Wall Street Journal*, August 21, 2015, B1, B4.

76. E. Dwoskin, "Social Bias Creeps into New Web Technology," *Wall Street Journal*, August 21, 2015, B1, B4.

77. "Americans with Disabilities Act Questions and Answers," *US Department of Justice*, accessed July 12, 2014, http://www.ada.gov/qandaeng.htm.

78. D. Devlin, "Rutgers Study: Employers Discriminate Against Qualified Workers with Disabilities," *Rutgers University*, accessed August 17, 2016, http:// news.rutgers.edu/research-news/rutgers-study -employers-discriminate-against-qualified-workers -disabilities/20151104#.VjuCCflVikq.

79. N. Scheiber, "Fake Cover Letters Expose Discrimination Against Disabled," *New York Times*, November 2, 2015, accessed May 8, 2016, http://www.nytimes.com/2015/11/02/upshot/fake-cover-letters-expose-discrimination-against-disabled.html.

80. M. Brault, "Americans with Disabilities: 2010, Household Economic Studies," in "Current Population Reports," *Census Bureau*, issued July 2012, 70–131.

81. R. Greenwood and V. A. Johnson, "Employer Perspectives on Workers with Disabilities," *Journal of Rehabilitation* 53 (1987): 37–45.

82. M. Zelley and R. Keys, "Give Michigan's Disabled a Chance to Work," *Detroit News*, November 14, 2014, accessed May 3, 2016, http://www.detroitnews.com/story/opinion/2014/11/06/give-disabled-workers-chance/18553557/. http://www.washingtonpost.com/blogs/on-leadership/wp/2015/04/06/microsoft-launches-a-pilot-program-for-hiring-autistic-workers/.

83. B. Loy, "Accommodation and Compliance Series Workplace Accommodations: Low Cost, High Impact," *Job Accommodation Network*, September 1, 2015, accessed May 2, 2016, https://askjan.org/media/lowcosthighimpact.html.

84. T. E. Narashimhan and G. Babu, "The Chosen Ones," *Business Standard*, March 11, 2012, accessed May 8, 2016, http://www.business-standard.com/india/news/the-chosen-ones/467290/.

85. "Study on the Financing of Assistive Technology Devices and Services for Individuals with Disabilities: A Report to the President and the Congress of the United States," *National Council on Disability*, accessed May 8, 2016, http://www.ncd.gov/newsroom/publications/assistive.html.

86. R. B. Cattell, "Personality Pinned Down," *Psychology Today* 7 (1973): 40–46; C. S. Carver and M. F. Scheier, *Perspectives on Personality* (Boston: Allyn & Bacon, 1992).

87. S. Berfield, "Will Investors Put the Lid on the Container Store's Generous Wages," *Bloomberg BusinessWeek*, February 19, 2015, accessed May 8, 2016, http://www.bloomberg.com/news/articles/2015-02-19/container-store-conscious-capitalism-and-the-perils-of-going-public.

88. J. M. Digman, "Personality Structure: Emergence of the Five-Factor Model," *Annual Review of Psychology* 41 (1990): 417–440; M. R. Barrick and M. K. Mount, "The Big Five Personality Dimensions and Job Performance: A Meta-Analysis," *Personnel Psychology* 44 (1991): 1–26.

89. C. Anderson and G. Kilduff, "Why Do Dominant Personalities Attain Influence in Face-to-Face Groups? The Competence Signaling Effects of Trait Dominance," *Journal of Personal and Social Psychology* 96, no. 2 (2001): 1160–1175.

90. K. D. Lassila, "A Brief History of Groupthink: Why Two, Three, or Many Heads Aren't Always Better Than One," *Yale Alumni Magazine*, January/February 2008, accessed May 8, 2016, http://yalealumnimagazine.com/articles/1947.

91. R. Wall, "Germanwings Co-Pilot Andreas Lubitz Appeared to Rehearse Crash, Investigators Say," *Wall Street Journal*, May 6, 2015, accessed May 9, 2015, http://www.wsj.com/articles/germanwings-co-pilot-andreas-lubitz-altered-settings-of-earlier-flight-investigators-say-1430908536.

92. A. George, "How Airlines Screen Their Pilots and Watch Out for Warning Signs," *Popular Mechanics*, April 10, 2015, accessed May 8, 2016, http://www.popularmechanics.com/flight/a14776/how-airlines-screen-pilots-germanwings-9525/.

93. O. Behling, "Employee Selection: Will Intelligence and Conscientiousness Do the Job?" *Academy of Management Executive* 12 (1998): 77–86.

94. R. S. Dalal, "A Meta-Analysis of the Relationship Between Organizational Citizenship Behavior and Counterproductive Work Behavior," *Journal of Applied Psychology* 90 (2005): 1241–1255.

95. Barrick and Mount, "The Big Five Personality Dimensions and Job Performance"; M. K. Mount and M. R. Barrick, "The Big Five Personality Dimensions: Implications for Research and Practice in Human Resource Management," *Research in Personnel & Human Resources Management* 13 (1995): 153–200; M. K. Mount and M. R. Barrick, "Five Reasons Why the 'Big Five' Article Has Been Frequently Cited," *Personnel Psychology* 51 (1998): 849–857; D. S. Ones, M. K. Mount, M. R. Barrick, and J. E. Hunter, "Personality and Job Performance: A Critique of the Tett, Jackson, and Rothstein (1991) Meta-Analysis," *Personnel Psychology* 47 (1994): 147–156.

96. Mount and Barrick, "Five Reasons Why the 'Big Five' Article Has Been Frequently Cited."

97. J. A. Lopez, "Talking Desks: Personality Types Revealed in State Workstations," *Arizona Republic*, January 7, 1996, D1.

98. D. A. Thomas and R. J. Ely, "Making Differences Matter: A New Paradigm for Managing Diversity," *Harvard Business Review* 74 (September–October 1996): 79–90.

99. Esen, "2005 Workplace Diversity Practices."

100. D. A. Thomas and S. Wetlaufer, "A Question of Color: A Debate on Race in the US Workplace," *Harvard Business Review* 75 (September–October 1997): 118–132.

101. E. Esen, "2007 State of Workplace Diversity Management. A Survey Report by the Society for Human Resource Management," 2008.

102. "Oshkosh Corporation—Diversity & Inclusion," *Oshkosh*, accessed July 12, 2014, http://www.oshkoshcorporation.com/about/diversity.html.

103. J. Espinoza, "Working to Prove Benefits of More Women at the Top," *Wall Street Journal*, February 27, 2011, accessed March 15, 2011, http://www.wsj.com/articles/SB10001424052748704150604576166483012821352.

104. J. R. Norton and R. E. Fox, *The Change Equation: Capitalizing on Diversity for Effective Organizational Change* (Washington, DC: American Psychological Association, 1997).

105. Ibid.

106. Thomas and Ely, "Making Differences Matter."

107. R. Thomas, Jr., *Beyond Race and Gender: Unleashing the Power of Your Total Workforce by Managing Diversity* (New York: AMACOM, 1991).

108. Ibid.

109. T. Cox, Jr., "The Multicultural Organization," *Academy of Management Executive* 5 (1991): 34–47.

110. S. Lubove, "Damned If You Do, Damned If You Don't: Preference Programs Are on the Defensive in the Public Sector, but Plaintiffs' Attorneys and Bureaucrats Keep Diversity Inc. Thriving in Corporate America," *Forbes*, December 15, 1997, 122.

111. L. S. Gottfredson, "Dilemmas in Developing Diversity Programs," in *Diversity in the Workplace*, ed. S. E. Jackson and Associates (New York: Guilford Press, 1992).

112. J. Graham and S. Kerr, "Mentoring," in *Diversity in Engineering: Managing the Workforce of the Future* (Washington, DC: National Academies Press, 2002), accessed June 16, 2013, http://www.nap.edu/openbook.php?record_id=10377&page=99.

113. J. Longman, "Pioneer of a Crossover Move: How Becky Hammon Became NBA's First Full-Time Female Assistant Coach," *New York Times*, August 12, 2014, B8.

114. Carnevale and Stone, *The American Mosaic*.

115. J. Lublin, "Men Enlist in Fight for Gender Equality," *Wall Street Journal*, March 11, 2015, B7.

116. A. Greenwald, B. Nosek, and M. Banaji, "Understanding and Using the Implicit Association Test: I. An Improved Scoring Algorithm," *Journal of Personality & Social Psychology* (August 2003): 197–206; J. S. Lublin, "Bringing Hidden Biases Into the Light," *Wall Street Journal*, January 9, 2014, accessed May 9, 2016, http://online.wsj.com/news/articles/SB10001424052702303754404579308562690896896; "The IAT | The Blind Spot," *The Blind Spot*, accessed July 13, 2014, http://spottheblindspot.com/the-iat/.

117. H. Blanton, J. Jaccard, E. Strauts, G. Mitchell and P. Tetlock, "Toward a Meaningful Metric of Implicit Prejudice," *Journal of Applied Psychology* 100 (2015): 1468–1481; F. Oswald, G. Mitchell, H. Blanton, J. Jaccard, and P. Tetlock, "Predicting Ethnic and Racial Discrimination: A Meta-Analysis of IAT Criterion Studies," *Journal of Personality and Social Psychology* 105 (2013): 171–192; H. Blanton, J. Jaccard, J. Klick, B. Mellers, G. Mitchell, and P. Tetlock, "Strong Claims and Weak Evidence: Reassessing the Predictive Validity of the IAT," *Journal of Applied Psychology* 94 (2009): 567–582.

118. Bohnet, "Real Fixes for Workplace Bias."

119. Ibid.

120. R. Joplin and C. S. Daus, "Challenges of Leading a Diverse Workforce," *Academy of Management Executive* 11 (1997): 32–47.

121. A. Fisher, "Should People Choose Their Own Mentors?" *Fortune*, November 29, 2004, 72.

122. N. Byrnes and R. O. Crocket, "An Historic Succession at Xerox," *Business Week*, June 8, 2009, 18–22.

123. P. Dvorak, "How Executives Are Pushed to Foster Diversity," *Wall Street Journal*, December 18, 2006, accessed May 8, 2016, http://online.wsj.com/article/SB116640764543853102.html?mod=rss_build.

124. A. Kalev, F. Dobbin, and E. Kelly. "Best Practices or Best Guesses? Diversity Management and the Remediation of Inequality." *American Sociological Review* 71 (2006): 589–617; A. Eagly, "When Passionate Advocates Meet Research on Diversity, Does the Honest Broker Stand a Chance," *Journal of Social Issues* 72 (2016): 199–122; C. Moss-Racusin, J. van der Toorn, J. Dovidio, V. Brescoll, M. Graham, and J. Handelsman, "Scientific Diversity Interventions," *Science* 343 (2014): 615–616.

125. F. Dobbin, A. Kalev, and E. Kelley, "Diversity Management in Corporate America," *Contexts* 6 (2007): 21–27.

126. E. Paluck and D. Green, "Prejudice Reduction: What Works? A Review and Assessment of Research and Practice," *Annual Review of Psychology* 60 (2009): 339–367.

127. Haidt and Jussim, "Hard Truths About Race on Campus."

13

1. "State of the Global Workplace: Employee Engagement Insights for Business Leaders Worldwide," *Gallup*, October 8, 2013, accessed May 4, 2016, http://www.gallup.com/services/178517/state-global-workplace.aspx

2. P. Campbell and R. D. Pritchard, "Motivation Theory in Industrial and Organizational Psychology," in *Handbook of Industrial and Organizational Psychology*, ed. M. D. Dunnette (Chicago: Rand McNally, 1976).

3. K. Clark, "The Cardinals Way: Yell, Hug, Repeat," *Wall Street Journal*, October 20, 2015, accessed May 4, 2016, http://www.wsj.com/articles/the-cardinals-way-yell-hug-repeat-1445371413.

4. K. Belson, "No Foul Mouths on This Field: Football With a New Age Twist," *New York Times*, September 6, 2015, accessed May 4, 2016, http://www.nytimes.com/2015/09/07/sports/football/no-foul-mouths-on-pete-carrolls-field-football-with-a-new-age-twist.html?_r=0.

5. A. Locke, "The Nature and Causes of Job Satisfaction," in *Handbook of Industrial and Organizational Psychology*, ed. M. D. Dunnette (Chicago: Rand McNally, 1976).

6. Mr. Everyday Dollar, "I Just Became a Millionaire at Age 35, and It's a Huge Letdown," *Business Insider*, March 27, 2015, accessed May 10, 2015, http://www.businessinsider.com/i-just-became-a-millionaire-at-age-35-and-its-a-huge-letdown-2015-3.

7. H. Maslow, "A Theory of Human Motivation," *Psychological Review* 50 (1943): 370–396.

8. P. Alderfer, *Existence, Relatedness, and Growth: Human Needs in Organizational Settings* (New York: Free Press, 1972).

9. C. McClelland, "Toward a Theory of Motive Acquisition," *American Psychologist* 20 (1965): 321–333; D. C. McClelland and D. H. Burnham, "Power Is the Great Motivator," *Harvard Business Review* 54, no. 2 (1976): 100–110.

10. J. H. Turner, "Entrepreneurial Environments and the Emergence of Achievement Motivation in Adolescent Males," *Sociometry* 33 (1970): 147–165.

11. L. W. Porter, E. E. Lawler III, and J. R. Hackman, *Behavior in Organizations* (New York: McGraw-Hill, 1975).

12. C. Ajila, "Maslow's Hierarchy of Needs Theory: Applicability to the Nigerian Industrial Setting," *IFE Psychology* 5 (1997): 162–174.

13. M. A. Wahba and L. B. Birdwell, "Maslow Reconsidered: A Review of Research on the Need Hierarchy Theory," *Organizational Behavior & Human Performance* 15 (1976): 212–240; J. Rauschenberger, N. Schmitt, and J. E. Hunter, "A Test of the Need Hierarchy Concept by a Markov Model of Change in Need Strength," *Administrative Science Quarterly* 25 (1980): 654–670.

14. E. E. Lawler III and L. W. Porter, "The Effect of Performance on Job Satisfaction," *Industrial Relations* 7 (1967): 20–28.

15. Porter, et al., *Behavior in Organizations*.

16. P. Cohen, "One-Time Bonuses and Perks Muscle Out Pay Raises for Workers," *New York Times*, May 25, 2016, accessed May 4, 2016, http://www.nytimes.com/2015/05/26/business/one-time-bonuses-and-perks-muscle-out-pay-raises-for-workers.html?_r=0.

17. F. Koller, "Lincoln Electric, 67 Straight Years Without Layoffs, 82 Straight Years of Profit-Sharing Bonuses," *FrankKoller.com*, December 11, 2015, accessed May 4, 2016, http://www.frankkoller.com/2015/12/lincoln-electric-67-straight-years-without-layoffs-82-straight-years-of-profit-sharing-bonuses/.

18. Porter, et al., *Behavior in Organizations*.

19. J. Bohannon, "One Type of Motivation May Be Key to Success," *Science*, July 1, 2014, accessed May 8, 2015, http://news.sciencemag.org/brain-behavior/2014/07/one-type-motivation-may-be-key-success; A. Wrzesniewski, B. Schwartz, X. Cong, M. Kane, A. Omar, and T. Kolditz, "Multiple Types of Motives Don't Multiply the Motivation of West Point Cadets," *Proceedings of the National Academy of Sciences of the United States of America* 111 no. 30 (2014): 10990–10995.

20. C. Caggiano, "What Do Workers Want?" *Inc.*, November 1992, 101–104; "National Study of the Changing Workforce," *Families & Work Institute*, accessed May 31, 2005, http://www.familiesandwork.org/summary/nscw.pdf.

21. C. Lee, A. Alonso, E. Esen, J. Coombs, T. Mulvey, K. Wessels, and H. Ng, "Employee Job Satisfaction and Engagement: Revitalizing a Changing Workforce," *Society for Human Resource Management*, April 18, 2016, accessed May 4, 2016, https://www.shrm.org/Research/SurveyFindings/Articles/Documents/2016-Employee-Job-Satisfaction-and-Engagement-Report.pdf.

22. N. Jackson, "5 Ways to Reward Employees When Raises Aren't an Option," *Entrepreneur*, August 24, 2012, accessed June 16, 2013, http://www.entrepreneur.com/article/224249.

23. Lee, et. al., "Employee Job Satisfaction and Engagement."

24. S. Berfield, "Will Investors Put the Lid on the Container Store's Generous Wages," *Bloomberg Businessweek*, February 19, 2015, accessed May 9, 2015, http://www.bloomberg.com/news/articles/2015-02-19/container-store-conscious-capitalism-and-the-perils-of-going-public.

25. J. Laabs, "Satisfy Them with More Than Money," *Personnel Journal* 77, no. 11 (1998): 40.

26. R. Kanfer and P. Ackerman, "Aging, Adult Development, and Work Motivation," *Academy of Management Review* (2004): 440–458.

27. L. Mishel and A. Davis, "Top CEOs Make 300 Times More than Typical Workers: Pay Growth Surpasses Stock Gains and Wage Growth of Top 0.1 Percent," *Economic Policy Institute*, June 21, 2015, accessed May 4, 2016, http://www.epi.org/publication/top-ceos-make-300-times-more-than-workers-pay-growth-surpasses-market-gains-and-the-rest-of-the-0-1-percent/.

28. K. Hagey, "Discovery Communications CEO Gets 2014 Compensation of $156.1 Million," *Wall Street Journal*, April 4, 2015, accessed May 10, 2015, http://www.wsj.com/articles/discovery-communications-ceo-gets-2014-compensation-of-156-1-million-1428164100.

29. "Data Tables for the Overview of May 2015 Occupational Employment and Wages," *Bureau of Labor Statistics*, March 30, 2016, accessed May 4, 2016, http://www.bls.gov/oes/2015/may/featured_data.htm#education2; "Occupational Employment and Wages, May 2015: 11-1011 Chief Executives," *Bureau of Labor Statistics*, March 30, 2016, accessed May 4, 2016, http://www.bls.gov/oes/current/oes111011.htm.

30. C. T. Kulik and M. L. Ambrose, "Personal and Situational Determinants of Referent Choice," *Academy of Management Review* 17 (1992): 212–237.

31. L. Weber & R. Silverman, "Worker Share Their Secret Salaries," *Wall Street Journal*, April 6, 2013, accessed May 4, 2016, http://www.wsj.com/articles/SB10001424127887324345804578426744168583824.

32. Ibid.

33. Ibid.

34. J. S. Adams, "Toward an Understanding of Inequity," *Journal of Abnormal Social Psychology* 67 (1963): 422–436.

35. L. Weber and R. Silverman, "Worker Share Their Secret Salaries," *Wall Street Journal*, April 6, 2013, accessed May 4, 2016, http://www.wsj.com/articles/SB1000142412788732434580457842674168583824.

36. S. Shellenbarger, "Open Salaries: The Good, the Bad and the Awkward," *Wall Street Journal*, January 12, 2016, accessed May 4, 2016, http://www.wsj.com/articles/open-salaries-the-good-the-bad-and-the-awkward-1452624480.

37. D. Primack, "CEO Gives Back Bonus, Says He Doesn't Deserve It," *Fortune*, December 18, 2014, accessed May 8, 2015, http://fortune.com/2014/12/18/ceo-gives-back-bonus-says-he-doesnt-deserve-it/.

38. C. Elliott, "When Labor Woes Cause Turbulence for Fliers," *Washington Post*, September 30, 2012, F2; G. Karp, "American Airlines Cancels Flights on Alleged Pilots' 'Sickout,'" *Chicago Tribune*, September 18, 2012, accessed June 16, 2013, http://articles.chicagotribune.com/2012-09-18/business/chi-american-airlines-cancels-flights-on-pilots-sickout-20120918_1_dennis-tajer-sickout-american-airlines.

39. "General Information on the Fair Labor Standards Act (FLSA)," *Department of Labor*, July 2009, accessed May 4, 2016, https://www.dol.gov/whd/regs/compliance/mwposter.htm; "Overtime Pay—Wage and Hour Division (WHD)," *Department of Labor*, accessed May 4, 2016, https://www.dol.gov/whd/overtime_pay.htm.

40. News Release, "Halliburton Pays Nearly $18.3 Million in Overtime Owed to More Than 1,000 Employees Nationwide After US Labor Department Investigation, *Department of Labor*, September 22, 2015, accessed May 4, 2016, https://www.dol.gov/opa/media/press/whd/whd20151647.htm.

41. Wage and Hour Division, "2008 Statistical Fact Sheet," *United States Department of Labor*, December 2008, accessed May 4, 2016, http://www.dol.gov/whd/statistics/2008FiscalYear.htm.

42. L. Badoux, "Trends in Wage and Hour Litigation Over Unpaid Work Time and the Precautions Employers Should Take," *ADP*, accessed May 4, 2016, https://www.adp.com/workforce-management/docs/whitepaper/trendsinwageandhourlitigation_05292012.pdf.

43. C. Chen, J. Choi, and S. Chi, "Making Justice Sense of Local-Expatriate Compensation Disparity: Mitigation by Local Referents, Ideological Explanations, and Interpersonal Sensitivity in China-Foreign Joint Ventures," *Academy of Management Journal* 45 (2002): 807–817.

44. K. Bradsher, "Even as Wages Rise, China Exports Grow," *The New York Times*, January 9, 2014, accessed July 15, 2014, http://www.nytimes.com/2014/01/10/business/international/chinese-exports-withstand-rising-labor-costs.html?_r=0; M. Gimein, "If US Wages Rose as Fast as China's, Factories Would Now Pay $50 an Hour," *Bloomberg*, March 27, 2013, accessed July 15, 2014, http://go.bloomberg.com/market-now/2013/03/27/if-u-s-wages-rose-as-fast-as-chinas-factories-would-now-pay-50-an-hour/.

45. J. Quigley, "Lenovo CEO to Share $3 Million Bonus with 10,000 Employees," *The Diplomat*, September 3, 2013, accessed July 15, 2014, http://thediplomat.com/2013/09/lenovo-ceo-to-share-3-million-bonus-with-10000-employees/.

46. Bloomberg News, "Lenovo Chief Yang Shares Bonus with Workers a Second Year," *BloombergBusinessweek*, September 2, 2013, accessed July 15, 2014, http://www.bloomberg.com/news/articles/2013-09-01/lenovo-chief-yang-shares-bonus-with-workers-for-second-year.

47. R. Feintzeig, "Radical Idea at the Office: A 40-Hour Workweek," *Wall Street Journal*, October 13, 2015, accessed May 4, 2016, http://www.wsj.com/articles/radical-idea-at-the-office-a-40-hour-workweek-1444754956.

48. Ibid.

49. Ibid.

50. R. Folger and M. A. Konovsky, "Effects of Procedural and Distributive Justice on Reactions to Pay Raise Decisions," *Academy of Management Journal* 32 (1989): 115–130; M. A. Konovsky, "Understanding Procedural Justice and Its Impact on Business Organizations," *Journal of Management* 26 (2000): 489–512.

51. "Four Air France Employees Sacked Over Violent Protest," *BBC News*, November 12, 2015, accessed May 4, 2016, http://www.bbc.com/news/world-europe-34804611.

52. E. Barret-Howard and T. R. Tyler, "Procedural Justice as a Criterion in Allocation Decisions," *Journal of Personality & Social Psychology* 50 (1986): 296–305; Folger and Konovsky, "Effects of Procedural and Distributive Justice on Reactions to Pay Raise Decisions."

53. R. Folger and J. Greenberg, "Procedural Justice: An Interpretive Analysis of Personnel Systems," in *Research in Personnel and Human Resources Management*, vol. 3, ed. K. Rowland and G. Ferris (Greenwich, CT: JAI, 1985); R. Folger, D. Rosenfield, J. Grove, and L. Corkran, "Effects of 'Voice' and Peer Opinions on Responses to Inequity," *Journal of Personality & Social Psychology* 37 (1979): 2253–2261; E. A. Lind and T. R. Tyler, *The Social Psychology of Procedural Justice* (New York: Plenum, 1988); Konovsky, "Understanding Procedural Justice and Its Impact on Business Organizations."

54. V. H. Vroom, *Work and Motivation* (New York: John Wiley & Sons, 1964); L. W. Porter and E. E. Lawler III, *Managerial Attitudes and Performance* (Homewood, IL: Dorsey & Richard D. Irwin, 1968).

55. C. Schultz, "When You Reward, Make It About the Employee—Not the Employer," *TLNT*, May 16, 2012, accessed June 16, 2013, http://www.tlnt.com/2012/05/16/when-you-reward-make-it-about-the-employee-not-the-employer/.

56. S. Miller, "Countering the Employee Recognition Gap," SHRM Library, *Society for Human Resource Management*, February 2006, accessed March 25, 2009, http://www.shrm.org.

57. G. Douglas, "Survey Finds Many Employers Not Satisfied with Their Pay-for-Performance Programs," *Bloomberg BNA*, December 30, 2013, accessed July 15, 2014, http://www.bna.com/survey-finds-employers-n17179881003/.

58. E. Bernstein and H. Blunden, "The Sales Director Who Turned Work Into a Fantasy Sports Competition," *Harvard Business Review*, March 27, 2015, accessed May 10, 2015, https://hbr.org/2015/03/the-sales-director-who-turned-work-into-a-fantasy-sports-competition.

59. Ibid.

60. K. W. Thomas and B. A. Velthouse, "Cognitive Elements of Empowerment," *Academy of Management Review* 15 (1990): 666–681.

61. E. L. Thorndike, *Animal Intelligence* (New York: Macmillan, 1911).

62. "Fox Urine and Christmas Tree Theft," Today I Found Out, December 7, 2015, accessed May 4, 2016, http://www.todayifoundout.com/index.php/2015/12/fox-urine-stops-christmas-tree-theft/.

63. B. F. Skinner, *Science and Human Behavior* (New York: Macmillan, 1954); B. F. Skinner, *Beyond Freedom and Dignity* (New York: Bantam, 1971); B. F. Skinner, *A Matter of Consequences* (New York: New York University Press, 1984).

64. A. M. Dickinson and A. D. Poling, "Schedules of Monetary Reinforcement in Organizational Behavior Management: Latham and Huber Revisited," *Journal of Organizational Behavior Management* 16, no. 1 (1992): 71–91.

65. L. Weber, "Wellness Programs Get a Health Check," *Wall Street Journal*, October 10, 2014, accessed May 10, 2015, http://www.wsj.com/articles/wellness-programs-get-a-health-check-1412725776.

66. M. Jamrisko, "Bosses Bribe Workers to Take Vacation in Healing U.S. Job Market," *Bloomberg Business*, October 1, 2015, accessed May 4, 2016, http://www.bloomberg.com/news/articles/2015-10-01/bosses-bribe-workers-to-take-vacation-in-healing-u-s-job-market.

67. D. Fitzgerald, "Staples Defends Executive Bonuses," *Wall Street Journal*, May 26, 2014, accessed July 15, 2014, http://online.wsj.com/news/articles/SB10001424052702304811904579586173092378940.

68. J. B. Miner, *Theories of Organizational Behavior* (Hinsdale, IL: Dryden, 1980).

69. Dickinson and Poling, "Schedules of Monetary Reinforcement in Organizational Behavior Management."

70. F. Luthans and A. D. Stajkovic, "Reinforce for Performance: The Need to Go Beyond Pay and Even Rewards," *Academy of Management Executive* 13, no. 2 (1999): 49–57.

71. K. Hovland, "Electric-Car Perks Put Norway in a Pinch," *Wall Street Journal*, September 18, 2015, accessed May 5, 2016, http://www.wsj.com/articles/electric-car-perks-put-norway-in-a-pinch-1442601936.

72. K. D. Butterfield, L. K. Trevino, and G. A. Ball, "Punishment from the Manager's Perspective: A Grounded Investigation and Inductive Model," *Academy of Management Journal* 39 (1996): 1479–1512.

73. R. D. Arvey and J. M. Ivancevich, "Punishment in Organizations: A Review, Propositions, and Research Suggestions," *Academy of Management Review* 5 (1980): 123–132.

74. R. D. Arvey, G. A. Davis, and S. M. Nelson, "Use of Discipline in an Organization: A Field Study," *Journal of Applied Psychology* 69 (1984): 448–460; M. E. Schnake, "Vicarious Punishment in a Work Setting," *Journal of Applied Psychology* 71 (1986): 343–345.

75. G. A. Yukl and G. P. Latham, "Consequences of Reinforcement Schedules and Incentive Magnitudes for Employee Performance: Problems Encountered in a Field Setting," *Journal of Applied Psychology* 60 (1975): 294–298.

76. E. A. Locke and G. P. Latham, *Goal Setting: A Motivational Technique That Works* (Englewood Cliffs, NJ: Prentice-Hall, 1984); E. A. Locke and G. P. Latham, *A Theory of Goal Setting and Task Performance* (Englewood Cliffs, NJ: Prentice-Hall, 1990).

77. L. Baldassarre and Brian Finken, "GE's Real-Time Performance Development," *Harvard Business Review*, August 12, 2015, accessed May 5, 2016, https://hbr.org/2015/08/ges-real-time-performance-development.

78. S. Berfield, "Will Investors Put the Lid on the Container Store's Generous Wages," *Bloomberg Businessweek*, February 19, 2015, accessed May 10, 2015, http://www.bloomberg.com/news/articles/2015-02-19/container-store-conscious-capitalism-and-the-perils-of-going-public.

79. G. P. Latham and E. A. Locke, "Goal Setting—A Motivational Technique That Works," *Organizational Dynamics* 8, no. 2 (1979): 68.

80. Ibid.

14

1. A. Bryant, "Before the Meeting Adjourns, Tell Me What You'll Do Next," *New York Times*, August 11, 2012, accessed May 9, 2016, http://www.nytimes.com/2012/08/12/business/bill-flemming-of-skanska-usa-building-on-leadership.html?_r=0.

2. W. Bennis, "Why Leaders Can't Lead," *Training & Development Journal* 43, no. 4 (1989): 35–39.

3. J. Haden, "What No One Ever Tells You About Being the Boss," *LinkedIn Pulse*, August 18, 2015, accessed May 9, 2016, https://www.linkedin.com/pulse/inside-story-what-being-boss-really-means-jeff-haden.

4. M. Langley, "IBM Chief Searches for Big Blue's Next Act," *Wall Street Journal*, April 21, 2015, A1, A16.

5. A. Zaleznik, "Managers and Leaders: Are They Different?" *Harvard Business Review* 55 (1977): 76–78; A. Zaleznik, "The Leadership Gap," *Washington Quarterly* 6 (1983): 32–39.

6. Bennis, "Why Leaders Can't Lead."

7. D. Clark, "New CEO Is Insider, Sales Pro," *Wall Street Journal*, May 5, 2015, B1, B5.

8. B. Fritz, "Sony Names New Movie Chief," *Wall Street Journal*, February 24, 2015, accessed May 9, 2016, http://www.wsj.com/articles/sony-pictures-names-tom-rothman-new-movie-chief-1424802775.

9. D. Jones, "Not All Successful CEOs Are Extroverts," *USA Today*, June 7, 2006, B.1.

10. S. Cole, "7 Famous Leaders Who Prove Introverts Can Be Wildly Successful," *Fast Company*, June 18, 2014, accessed May 9, 2016, http://www.fastcompany.com/3032028/the-future-of-work/7-famous-leaders-who-prove-introverts-can-be-wildly-successful.

11. G. Murray, "Caveman Politics," *Psychology Today*, December 15, 2011, accessed May 9, 2016, http://www.psychologytoday.com/blog/caveman-politics/201112/are-you-sure-we-prefer-taller-leaders; G. Murray and J. Schmitz, "Caveman Politics: Evolutionary Leadership Preferences and Physical Stature," *Social Science Quarterly* 92 (2011): 1215–1235.

12. M. Gladwell, "Why Do We Love Tall Men?" Gladwell.com, accessed July 16, 2014, http://gladwell.com/blink/why-do-we-love-tall-men/.

13. Schumpeter, "The Look of a Leader," *The Economist*, September 27, 2014, accessed May 6, 2016, http://www.economist.com/news/business/21620197-getting-top-much-do-how-you-look-what-you-achieve-look-leader.

14. E. Wong, M. Ormiston, and M. Haselhuhn, "A Face Only an Investor Could Love: CEO's Facial Structure Predicts Their Firms' Financial Performance," *Psychological Science* 22 (2011): 1478–1483; S. Knapton, "Successful Male Leaders Have Wider Faces than Average Man," *Telegraph*, August 16, 2015, accessed May 9, 2016, http://www.telegraph.co.uk/news/science/science-news/11806360/Successful-male-leaders-have-wider-faces-than-average-man.html.

15. S. Zaccaro, "Trait-Based Perspectives of Leadership," *American Psychologist* 62 (2007): 6-16; R. J. House and R. M Aditya, "The Social Scientific Study of Leadership: Quo Vadis?" *Journal of Management* 23 (1997): 409–473; T. Judge, R. Illies, J. Bono, and M. Gerhardt, "Personality and Leadership: A Qualitative and Quantitative Review," *Journal of Applied Psychology* 89 (August 2002): 765–782; S. A. Kirkpatrick and E. A. Locke, "Leadership: Do Traits Matter?" *Academy of Management Executive* 5, no. 2 (1991): 48–60.

16. House and Aditya, "The Social Scientific Study of Leadership"; Kirkpatrick and Locke, "Leadership: Do Traits Matter?"

17. C. Rose, "Charlie Rose Talks to . . . Jack Ma," *BloombergBusinessweek*, January 29, 2015, 36.

18. J. Jurgensen, "How to Run a Creative Hothouse," *Wall Street Journal*, March 13, 2015, D1, D2.

19. J. Lublin, "The Case for Humble Executives," *Wall Street Journal*, October 20, 2015, accessed May 9, 2016, http://www.wsj.com/articles/the-case-for-humble-executives-1445385076.

20. J. Cheng, "Samsung Picks New Mobile Leader," *Wall Street Journal*, December 2, 2015, B4.

21. B. Fritz and E. Schwartzel, "Iger 'Clone' Rises in Disney's Ranks," *Wall Street Journal*, February 14–15, 2015, B1, B3.

22. Kirkpatrick and Locke, "Leadership: Do Traits Matter?"

23. E. A. Fleishman, "The Description of Supervisory Behavior," *Journal of Applied Psychology* 37 (1953): 1–6; L. R. Katz, *New Patterns of Management* (New York: McGraw-Hill, 1961).

24. L. Alpert and J. Marshall, "Bezos is Hands-On Boss at the Washington Post," *Wall Street Journal*, December 21, 2015, B1.

25. J. Jargon, "At Popeye's, Recipe for a Turnaround," *Wall Street Journal*, March 9, 2014, accessed May 9, 2016, http://www.wsj.com/articles/SB10001424052702304181204579368983741915774.

26. J. Goudreau, "The CEO of Popeyes Says Becoming a 'Servant Leader' Helped Her Turn Around the Struggling Restaurant Chain," *Business Insider*, March 24, 2015, accessed May 9, 2016, http://www.businessinsider.com/popeyes-ceo-servant-leadership-traits-2015-3.

27. P. Weissenberg and M. H. Kavanagh, "The Independence of Initiating Structure and Consideration: A Review of the Evidence," *Personnel Psychology* 25 (1972): 119–130.

28. R. J. House and T. R. Mitchell, "Path-Goal Theory of Leadership," *Journal of Contemporary Business* 3 (1974): 81–97; F. E. Fiedler, "A Contingency Model of Leadership Effectiveness," in *Advances in Experimental Social Psychology*, ed. L. Berkowitz (New York: Academic Press, 1964); V. H. Vroom and P. W. Yetton, *Leadership and Decision Making* (Pittsburgh: University of Pittsburgh Press, 1973); P. Hersey and K. H. Blanchard, The *Management of Organizational Behavior*, 4th ed. (Englewood Cliffs, NJ: Prentice Hall, 1984); S. Kerr and J. M. Jermier, "Substitutes for Leadership: Their Meaning and Measurement," *Organizational Behavior & Human Performance* 22 (1978): 375–403.

29. A. Grant, F. Gino, and D. Hofmann, "The Hidden Advantage of Quiet Bosses," *Harvard Business Review* 88, no. 12 (2010): 28.

30. F. E. Fiedler and M. M. Chemers, *Leadership and Effective Management* (Glenview, IL: Scott, Foresman, 1974); F. E. Fiedler and M. M. Chemers, *Improving Leadership Effectiveness: The Leader Match Concept*, 2nd ed. (New York: Wiley, 1984).

31. E. Chasan, "A Startup in Transition: The CFO of Evernote on Where It Is," *Wall Street Journal*, October 29, 2015, R9.

32. Fiedler and Chemers, *Improving Leadership Effectiveness*.

33. F. E. Fiedler, "The Effects of Leadership Training and Experience: A Contingency Model Interpretation," *Administrative Science Quarterly* 17, no. 4 (1972): 455; F. E. Fiedler, *A Theory of Leadership Effectiveness* (New York: McGraw-Hill, 1967).

34. L. S. Csoka and F. E. Fiedler, "The Effect of Military Leadership Training: A Test of the Contingency Model," *Organizational Behavior & Human Performance* 8 (1972): 395–407.

35. House and Mitchell, "Path-Goal Theory of Leadership."

36. "Up and Coming Leaders," *Entrepreneur*, March 26, 2014, accessed July 17, 2014, http://www.entrepreneur.com/article/231531.

37. M. Tenney, "More Than Money," *Collector*, October 2013, 26–28.

38. House and Mitchell, "Path-Goal Theory of Leadership."

39. X. Huang, E. Xu, W. Chiu, C. Lam & J. Farh, "When Authoritarian Leaders Outperform Transformational Leaders: Firm Performance in a Harsh Economic Environment," *Academy of Management Discoveries* 1, no. 2 (2015): 180–200.

40. B. M. Fisher and J. E. Edwards, "Consideration and Initiating Structure and Their Relationships with Leader Effectiveness: A Meta-Analysis," *Proceedings of the Academy of Management*, August 1988, 201–205.

41. Kotter International, "Leadership Lessons from Domino's Pizza: NFL Draft Edition," *Forbes*, May 12, 2014, accessed May 9, 2016, http://www.forbes.com/sites/johnkotter/2014/05/12/leadership-lessons-from-dominos-pizza-nfl-draft-edition/.

42. L. Faw, "For Domino's, 'Failure Is an Option,'" *Mediapost Agency Daily*, April 14, 2014, accessed May 9, 2016, http://www.mediapost.com/publications/article/223604/for-dominos-failure-is-an-option.html.

43. Domino's TV Commercial, "Failure Is an Option," *YouTube.com*, 2014, April 15, 2014, accessed May 9, 2016, https://www.youtube.com/watch?v=wRaM3x78FEw

44. Kotter International, "Innovation Secrets from Domino's Pizza," *Forbes*, March 27, 2012, accessed May 9, 2016, http://www.forbes.com/sites/johnkotter/2012/03/27/innovation-secrets-from-dominos-pizza/.

45. S. Boardman, "The Pygmalion Effect: Do Expectations Shape Reality?" *Huffington Post*, May 21, 2015, accessed May 9, 2016, http://www.huffingtonpost.com/samantha-boardman-md/the-pygmalion-effect-do-expectations-shape-reality_b_7322780.html.

46. Ibid.

47. J. C. Wofford and L. Z. Liska, "Path-Goal Theories of Leadership: A Meta-Analysis," *Journal of Management* 19 (1993): 857–876.

48. House and Aditya, "The Social Scientific Study of Leadership."

49. V. H. Vroom and A. G. Jago, *The New Leadership: Managing Participation in Organizations* (Englewood Cliffs, NJ: Prentice Hall, 1988).

50. C. Fishman, "How Teamwork Took Flight: This Team Built a Commercial Engine—and Self-Managing GE Plant—from Scratch," *Fast Company*, October 1, 1999, 188.

51. Ibid.

52. Ibid.

53. N. Fallon, "Is Your Management Style Hurting Your Team?" *Business News Daily*, May 14, 2014, accessed May 9, 2016, http://www.businessnewsdaily.com/6409-management-styles-strategies.html.

54. G. A. Yukl, *Leadership in Organizations,* 3rd ed. (Englewood Cliffs, NJ: Prentice Hall, 1995).

55. B. M. Bass, *Bass & Stogdill's Handbook of Leadership: Theory, Research, and Managerial Applications* (New York: Free Press, 1990).

56. R. D. Ireland and M. A. Hitt, "Achieving and Maintaining Strategic Competitiveness in the 21st Century: The Role of Strategic Leadership," *Academy of Management Executive* 13, no. 1 (1999): 43–57.

57. J. Lublin, "Rookie CEOs Face a Steep Learning Curve," June 24, 2014, accessed May 10, 2015, http://www.wsj.com/articles/rookie-ceos-face-a-steep-learning-curve-1403656894.

58. P. Thoms and D. B. Greenberger, "Training Business Leaders to Create Positive Organizational Visions of the Future: Is It Successful?" *Academy of Management Journal*, Best Papers & Proceedings 1995, 212–216.

59. M. Weber, *The Theory of Social and Economic Organizations*, trans. R. A. Henderson and T. Parsons (New York: Free Press, 1947).

60. D. A. Waldman and F. J. Yammarino, "CEO Charismatic Leadership: Levels-of-Management and Levels-of-Analysis Effects," *Academy of Management Review* 24, no. 2 (1999): 266–285.

61. K. B. Lowe, K. G. Kroeck, and N. Sivasubramaniam, "Effectiveness Correlates of Transformational and Transactional Leadership: A Meta-Analytic Review of the MLQ Literature," *Leadership Quarterly* 7 (1996): 385–425.

62. J. M. Howell and B. J. Avolio, "The Ethics of Charismatic Leadership: Submission or Liberation?" *Academy of Management Executive* 6, no. 2 (1992): 43–54.

63. G. Colvin, "The Greatest Business Decisions of All Time: Tata Steel," *Fortune*, October 1, 2012, accessed May 9, 2016, http://money.cnn.com/gallery/news/companies/2012/10/01/greatest-business-decisions.fortune/4.html.

64. H. Perlberg and K. Burton, "The Softer Side of Stevie Cohen" *Bloomberg BusinessWeek*, November 6–December 15, 2015, 41–43; A. Viswanatha & J. Chung, "Deal Ends SEC's Pursuit of Steven Cohen," *Wall Street Journal*, January 8, 2016, accessed October 20, 2016, http://www.wsj.com/articles/sec-bars-steven-cohen-from-supervising-hedge-funds-for-two-years-1452278527.

65. D. J. Chandler, "The Perfect Storm of Leaders' Unethical Behavior: A Conceptual Framework," *International Journal of Leadership Studies* 5, no.1 (2009): 69–93.

66. Howell and Avolio, "The Ethics of Charismatic Leadership."

67. B. M. Bass, "From Transactional to Transformational Leadership: Learning to Share the Vision," *Organizational Dynamics* 18 (1990): 19–36.

68. B. M. Bass, *A New Paradigm of Leadership: An Inquiry into Transformational Leadership* (Alexandra, VA: US Army Research Institute for the Behavioral and Social Sciences, 1996).

69. CNN Wire Staff, "Network: Leno Took 50% Pay Cut to Reduce 'Tonight Show' Layoffs," CNN, September 8, 2012, accessed May 9, 2016, http://www.cnn.com/2012/09/07/showbiz/jay-leno-tonight-show/; A. Farnham, "Bosses Who Volunteer for Pay Cuts," ABC News, September 11, 2012, accessed May 9, 2016, http://abcnews.go.com/Business/bosses-pay-cuts/story?id=17209062.

70. J. Gapper and T. Powley, "Inside the Dyson Dynasty," *Financial Times*, April 10, 2015, accessed May 9, 2016, http://www.ft.com/intl/cms/s/2/528c518c-de2e-11e4-8d14-00144feab7de.html.

71. Bass, "From Transactional to Transformational Leadership."

15

1. E. E. Lawler III, L. W. Porter, and A. Tannenbaum, "Manager's Attitudes Toward Interaction Episodes," *Journal of Applied Psychology* 52 (1968): 423–439; H. Mintzberg, *The Nature of Managerial Work* (New York: Harper & Row, 1973).

2. J. D. Maes, T. G. Weldy, and M. L. Icenogle, "A Managerial Perspective: Oral Communication Competency Is Most Important for Business Students in the Workplace," *Journal of Business Communication* 34 (1997): 67–80.

3. E. E. Jones and K. E. Davis, "From Acts to Dispositions: The Attribution Process in Person Perception," in *Advances in Experimental and Social Psychology*, vol. 2, ed. L. Berkowitz (New York: Academic Press, 1965), 219–266; R. G. Lord and J. E. Smith, "Theoretical, Information-Processing, and Situational Factors Affecting Attribution Theory Models of Organizational Behavior," *Academy of Management Review* 8 (1983): 50–60.

4. D. Simons and C. Chabris, "Gorillas in Our Midst: Sustained Inattentional Blindness for Dynamic Events," *Perception* 28 (1999): 1059–1074.

5. J. Zadney and H. B. Gerard, "Attributed Intentions and Informational Selectivity," *Journal of Experimental Social Psychology* 10 (1974): 34–52.

6. M. Beck, "What Cocktail Parties Teach Us," *Wall Street Journal*, April 23, 2012, D1.

7. H. H. Kelly, *Attribution in Social Interaction* (Morristown, NJ: General Learning Press, 1971).

8. J. M. Burger, "Motivational Biases in the Attribution of Responsibility for an Accident: A Meta-Analysis of the Defensive-Attribution Hypothesis," *Psychological Bulletin* 90 (1981): 496–512.

9. D. A. Hofmann and A. Stetzer, "The Role of Safety Climate and Communication in Accident Interpretation: Implications for Learning from Negative Events," *Academy of Management Journal* 41, no. 6 (1998): 644–657.

10. C. Perrow, *Normal Accidents: Living with High-Risk Technologies* (New York: Basic Books, 1984).

11. A. G. Miller and T. Lawson, "The Effect of an Informational Opinion on the Fundamental Attribution Error," *Journal of Personality & Social Psychology* 47 (1989): 873–896; J. M. Burger, "Changes in Attribution Errors Over Time: The Ephemeral Fundamental Attribution Error," *Social Cognition* 9 (1991): 182–193.

12. F. Heider, *The Psychology of Interpersonal Relations* (New York: Wiley, 1958); D. T. Miller and M. Ross, "Self-Serving Biases in Attribution of Causality: Fact or Fiction?" *Psychological Bulletin* 82 (1975): 213–225.

13. J. R. Larson, Jr., "The Dynamic Interplay Between Employees' Feedback-Seeking Strategies and Supervisors' Delivery of Performance Feedback," *Academy of Management Review* 14, no. 3 (1989): 408–422.

14. R. C. Rabin, "15-Minute Visits Take a Toll on the Doctor-Patient Relationship," *Kaiser Health News*, April 21, 2014, accessed May 10, 2016, http://www.kaiserhealthnews.org/Stories/2014/April/21/15-minute-doctor-visits.aspx; S. Wilkins, "The Truth About Those High Patient Satisfaction Scores for Doctor-Patient Communication," *Center For Advancing Health* (Prepared Patient Blog), April 11, 2013, accessed May 10, 2016, http://www.cfah.org/blog/2013/the-truth-about-those-high-patient-satisfaction-scores-for-doctor-patient-communication.

15. Ibid.

16. S. Brownlee, "The Doctor Will See You—If You're Quick," *The Daily Beast*, April 16, 2012, accessed May 10, 2016, http://www.thedailybeast.com/newsweek/2012/04/15/why-your-doctor-has-no-time-to-see-you.html.

17. S. Wilkins, "The Truth About Those High Patient Satisfaction Scores for Doctor-Patient Communication."

18. "The Experts: How to Improve Doctor-Patient Communication," *Wall Street Journal*, April 12, 2013, accessed May 10, 2016, http://www.wsj.com/articles/SB10001424127887324050304578411251805908228.

19. Ibid.

20. S. Wilkins, "The Truth About Those High Patient Satisfaction Scores for Doctor-Patient Communication," Center for Advancing Health (Prepared Patient Blog), April 11, 2013, accessed May 10, 2016, http://www.cfah.org/blog/2013/the-truth-about-those-high-patient-satisfaction-scores-for-doctor-patient-communication.

21. "The Experts: How to Improve Doctor-Patient Communication."

22. L. Davey, "Managing Emotional Outbursts on Your Team," *Harvard Business Review*, April 30, 2015, accessed May 13, 2015, https://hbr.org/2015/04/handling-emotional-outbursts-on-your-team.

23. L. Lagnado, "What Patients Need to Remember after Leaving the Hospital," *Wall Street Journal*, November 30, 2015, accessed May 10, 2016, http://www.wsj.com/articles/what-patients-need-to-remember-after-leaving-the-hospital-1448908354.

24. Ibid.

25. Ibid.

26. G. L. Kreps, *Organizational Communication: Theory and Practice* (New York: Longman, 1990).

27. Ibid.

28. J. Jusko, "A Little More Communication," *Industry Week*, March 1, 2010, 19.

29. "S. Shellenbarger, "To Fight or Not to Fight? How to Pick Your Battles in the Workplace," *Wall Street Journal*, December 14, 2014, B1.

30. Ibid.

31. Ibid.

32. E. Swallow, "How Rumors Could Actually Strengthen Your Company Culture," *Forbes*, March 1, 2013, accessed May 10, 2016, http://www.forbes.com/sites/ericaswallow/2013/03/01/rumor-jar/.

33. J. Sandberg, "Ruthless Rumors and the Managers Who Enable Them," *Wall Street Journal*, October 29, 2003, B1.

34. E. Holm and J. S. Lublin, "Loose Lips Trip Up a Good Hands Executive," *Wall Street Journal*, August 1, 2011, C1.

35. K. Voight, "Office Intelligence," *Asian Wall Street Journal*, January 21, 2005, P1.

36. A. Aschale, "Review of the Grapevine Communication," June 2013, accessed May 10, 2016, http://www.academia.edu/4362950/Review_of_the_Grapevine_Communication.

37. W. C. Redding, *Communication within the Organization: An Interpretive View of Theory and Research* (New York: Industrial Communication Council, 1972).

38. D. T. Hall, K. L. Otazo, and G. P. Hollenbeck, "Behind Closed Doors: What Really Happens in Executive Coaching," *Organizational Dynamics* 27, no. 3 (1999): 39–53.

39. J. Kelly, "Blowing the Whistle on the Boss," *PR Newswire*, November 15, 2004, accessed May 10, 2016, http://www.prnewswire.com/news-releases/blowing-the-whistle-on-the-boss-75393797.html.$$G1Ref.

40. R. McGarvey, "Lords of Discipline," *Entrepreneur Magazine*, January 1, 2000, page number not available.

41. Jack Welch, "'Rank-and-Yank'? That's Not How It's Done," *Wall Street Journal*, November 15, 2013, A.15.

42. N. Goodman, "Jack Welch on How to Manage Employees," *Entrepreneur*, October 5, 2012, accessed May 10, 2016, http://www.entrepreneur.com/blog/224604.

43. C. Hirschman, "Firm Ground: EAP Training for HR and Managers Improves Supervisor-Employee Communication and Helps Organizations Avoid Legal Quagmires," *Employee Benefit News*, June 13, 2005, accessed May 10, 2016, http://www.highbeam.com/doc/1G1-121455684.html.

44. L. Zamosky, "A Little-Known Worker Benefit: Employee Assistance Programs," *Los Angeles Times*, June 15, 2014, accessed May 10, 2016, http://www.latimes.com/business/la-fi-healthcare-watch-20140615-story.html.

45. Ibid.

46. A. Mehrabian, "Communication without Words," *Psychology Today* 3 (1968): 53; A. Mehrabian, *Silent Messages* (Belmont, CA: Wadsworth, 1971); R. Harrison, *Beyond Words: An Introduction to Nonverbal Communication* (Upper Saddle River, NJ: Prentice Hall, 1974); A. Mehrabian, *Non-Verbal Communication* (Chicago: Aldine, 1972).

47. M. L. Knapp, *Nonverbal Communication in Human Interaction*, 2nd ed. (New York: Holt, Rinehart & Winston, 1978).

48. H. M. Rosenfeld, "Instrumental Affiliative Functions of Facial and Gestural Expressions," *Journal of Personality & Social Psychology* 24 (1966): 65–72; P. Ekman, "Differential Communication of Affect by Head and Body Cues," *Journal of Personality & Social Psychology* 23 (1965): 726–735; A. Mehrabian, "Significance of Posture and Position in the Communication of Attitude and Status Relationships," *Psychological Bulletin* 71 (1969): 359–372.

49. J. Gottman and R. Levenson, "The Timing of Divorce: Predicting When a Couple Will Divorce over a 14-Year Period," *Journal of Marriage & the Family* 62 (August 2000): 737–745; J. Gottman, R. Levenson, and E. Woodin, "Facial Expressions During Marital Conflict," *Journal of Family Communication* 1, no. 1 (2001): 37–57.

50. T. Bradberry and K. Kruse, "Why Successful People Never Bring Smartphones Into Meetings," *LinkedIn*, September 22, 2014, accessed May 10, 2016, https://www.linkedin.com/pulse/20140922000612-50578967-why-successful-people-never-bring-smartphones-into-meetings.

51. Ibid.

52. Ibid.

53. S. Shellenbarger, "Is This How You Really Talk?" *Wall Street Journal*, accessed May 10, 2016, accessed June 20, 2014, http://www.wsj.com/news/articles/SB10001424127887323735604578440851083674898.

54. C. A. Bartlett and S. Ghoshal, "Changing the Role of Top Management: Beyond Systems to People," *Harvard Business Review*, May–June 1995, 132–142.

55. J. Lublin, "Managers Need to Make Time for Face Time," *Wall Street Journal*, March 18, 2015, B6.

56. A. Bryant, "Amit Singh of Google for Work: A Respectful Clash of Ideas," *New York Times*, January 22, 2016, BU2.

57. J. Fry, "When Talk Isn't Cheap: Is Emailing Colleagues Who Sit Feet Away a Sign of Office Dysfunction, or a Wise Move?" *Wall Street Journal*, November 28, 2005, accessed May 10, 2016, http://www.wsj.com/articles/SB113293718044406629.

58. L. Clarke-Billings, "Psychologists Warn Constant Email Notifications Are 'Toxic Source of Stress,'" *Daily Telegraph*, January 2, 2016, http://www.telegraph.co.uk/news/2016/03/22/psycholo-gists-warn-constant-email-notifications-are-toxic-source/.

59. E. Bernstein, "Thou Shalt Not Send in Anger: Recovering from a Snippy Email to Friends, Even the Boss, Is Possible If You Grovel," *Wall Street Journal*, October 14, 2014, D1, D4.

60. C. Matlack, "One Company Tries Life Without (Much) E-mail," *Bloomberg BusinessWeek*, October 12–18, 2015, 36–37.

61. S. Shellenbarger, "The Challenge of Managing a Long-Distance Relationship with Your Boss," *Wall Street Journal*, March 15, 2016, http://www.wsj.com/articles/the-challenge-of-managing-a-long-distance-relationship-with-your-boss-1458065121.

62. D. F. Larcker, S. Miles, B. Tayan, and M. E. Gutman, "2013 CEO Performance Evaluation Survey," *Stanford Graduate School of Business*, accessed May 10, 2016, http://www.gsb.stanford.edu/cldr/research/surveys/performance.html.

63. E. Atwater, *I Hear You*, revised ed. (New York: Walker, 1992).

64. R. G. Nichols, "Do We Know How to Listen? Practical Helps in a Modern Age," in *Communication Concepts and Processes*, ed. J. DeVitor (Englewood Cliffs, NJ: Prentice Hall, 1971); P. V. Lewis, *Organizational Communication: The Essence of Effective Management* (Columbus, OH: Grid Publishing Company, 1975); S. Khan, "Why Long Lectures Are Ineffective," *Time*, October 2, 2012, accessed May 10, 2016, http://ideas.time.com/2012/10/02/why-lectures-are-ineffective/.

65. A. Stevenson, "T-Mobile CEO to Cramer: 'Shut Up and Listen,'"*CNBC*, April 28, 2015, accessed May 10, 2016, http://www.cnbc.com/id/102628529.

66. D. A. Kaplan, "Undercover Employee: A Day on the Job at Three Best Companies," *CNNMoney*, January 20, 2011, accessed May 10, 2016, 2012, http://features.blogs.fortune.cnn.com/2011/01/20/undercover-employee-a-day-on-the-job-at-three-best-companies/.

67. L. Gurkow, "The Art of Active Listening," *Jerusalem Post*, May 11, 2014, accessed June 20, 2014, http://www.jpost.com/Jewish-World/Judaism/Active-listening-351878.

68. E. Bernstein, "How 'Active Listening ' Makes Both Participants in a Conversation Feel Better," *Wall Street Journal*, January 12, 2015, accessed May 10, 2016, http://www.wsj.com/articles/how-active-listening-makes-both-sides-of-a-conversation-feel-better-1421082684.

69. S. Turkle, "Stop Googling. Let's Talk," *New York Times*, September 26, 2015, accessed May 10, 2016, http://www.nytimes.com/2015/09/27/opinion/sunday/stop-googling-lets-talk.html?_r=0.

70. S. Konrath, E. O'Brien, and C. Hsing, "Changes in Dispositional Empathy in American College Students Over Time: A Meta-Analysis," *Personality and Social Psychology Review* 15 (2011): 180–198.

71. S. Wolpert, "In Our Digital World, Are Young People Losing the Ability to Read Emotions?," *UCLA Newsroom*, August 21, 2014, accessed May 10, 2016, http://newsroom.ucla.edu/releases/in-our-digital-world-are-young-people-losing-the-ability-to-read-emotions; Y. Uhls, M Michikyan, J. Morris, D. Garcia, G. Small, E. Zgourou, and P. Greenfield, "Five Days at Outdoor Education Camp Without Screens Improves Preteen Skills with Nonverbal Emotion Cues," *Computers in Human Behavior* 39 (2014): 387–392.

72. Turkle, "Stop Googling. Let's Talk."

73. Atwater, *I Hear You*.

74. C. Edwards, "Death of a Pushy Salesman," *BusinessWeek*, July 3, 2006, 108.

75. J. Sandberg, "Not Communicating with Your Boss? Count Your Blessings," *Wall Street Journal*, May 22, 2007, B1.

76. A. Tugend, "You've Been Doing a Fantastic Job. Just One Thing …," *The New York Times*, April 6, 2013, B5.

77. L. Weber and R.E. Silverman, "Workers Get New Tools for Airing Their Gripes," *Wall Street Journal*, August 26, 2015, B1, B4.

78. M. Flatt, "How to Give Feedback That Works," *Inc.*, December 21, 2011, accessed March 27, 2012, http://www.inc.com/michael-flatt/how-to-give-feedback-that-works.html.

79. "Satya Nadella's Email to Employees: Bold Ambition and Our Core," *Microsoft*, July 18, 2014, accessed July 20, 2014, http://www.microsoft.comMay 7, 2016/en-us/news/ceo/index.html, http://news.microsoft.com/ceo/index.html.

80. Ibid.

81. W. Mossberg, "Slack Beats EMail, But Still Needs to Get Better," *The Verge*, April 13, 2016, accessed May 10, 2016, http://www.theverge.com/2016/4/13/11417726/slack-app-walt-mossberg-stewart-butterfield-interview.

82. F. Manjoo, "Slack, the Office Messaging App That May Finally Sink Email," *New York Times*, March 22, 2015, B1.

83. A. Bryant, "The Memo List: Where Everyone Has an Opinion," *New York Times*, March 10, 2012, accessed May 10, 2016, http://www.nytimes.com/2012/03/11/business/jim-whitehurst-of-red-hat-on-merits-of-an-open-culture.html.

84. S. Ovide, "Companies Get the Message on Chatting," *Wall Street Journal*, October 14, 2015, R7.

85. E. W. Morrison, "Organizational Silence: A Barrier to Change and Development in a Pluralistic World," *Academy of Management Review* 25 (2000): 706–725.

86. M. Heffernan, "Encourage Employees to Speak Up," *Inc*, April 9, 2014, accessed July 21, 2014, http://www.inc.com/margaret-heffernan/encourage-employees-to-speak-up.html.

87. R. Willingham, "Jetstar Pilots 'Afraid to Report Risks,'" *The Age*, March 19, 2011, accessed June 17, 2011, http://www.theage.com.au/travel/travel-news/jetstar-pilots-afraid-to-report-risks-20110318-1c0mi.html.

88. Ibid.

89. E. O'Mara, "Three Key Findings from Our 2016 Hotline Benchmark Report," *JD Supra Business Advisor*, April 25, 2016, http://www.jdsupra.com/legalnews/three-key-findings-from-our-2016-67770/.

Full NAVEXGlobal 2016 Hotline Benchmark Report available http://trust.navexglobal.com/rs/852-MYR-807/images/NAVEX-Global_2016_Hotline_BenchmarkReport.pdf.

90. Lublin, "Managers Need to Make Time for Face Time."

91. C. Hymowitz, "Sometimes, Moving Up Makes It Harder to See What Goes on Below," *Wall Street Journal*, October 15, 2007, B1.

92. A. Bryant, "Every Team Should Have a Devil's Advocate," *New York Times*, December 24, 2011, accessed May 7, 2016, http://www.nytimes.com/2011/12/25/business/ori-hadomi-of-mazor-robotics-on-choosing-devils-advocates.html?pagewanted=all.

93. J. Olson, "We Messed Up," *The Hours Blog*, March 25, 2016, accessed May 10, 2016, https://medium.com/the-hours-blog/we-messed-up-256e13d2caf5#.l8ha0guyg.

94. G. Kane, "How McDonalds Cooked Up More Transparency," *MIT Sloan Management Review* 57 (Winter 2016), accessed May 11, 2016, http://sloan-review.mit.edu/article/how-mcdonalds-cooked-up-more-transparency/.

95. Ibid.

96. R. Jones, "Labor Strife at Emirates Air," *Wall Street Journal*, March 23, 2015, B3.

16

1. R. Leifer and P. K. Mills, "An Information Processing Approach for Deciding Upon Control Strategies and Reducing Control Loss in Emerging Organizations," *Journal of Management* 22 (1996): 113–137.

2. D. Winning, "More Companies Are Outfitting Warehouses With 'Smart' Lights," *Wall Street Journal*, September 13, 2015, accessed May 11, 2016, http://www.wsj.com/articles/more-companies-are-outfitting-1442197722.

3. Ibid.

4. J. Dunn, "Criminals Steal Money from ATMs by Gluing Down Keys," *TechWorld* March 18, 2011, accessed May 11, 2016, http://www.techworld.com/news/security/criminals-steal-money-from-atms-by-gluing-down-keys-3265904/.

5. B. Barrett, "Your Phone Will Replace Your Wallet at the ATM, Too," *Wired*, January 28, 2016, accessed May 11, 2016, http://www.wired.com/2016/01/cardless-atms/.

6. "Our Green Filter," *Green Depot*, accessed May 11, 2016, http://www.greendepot.com/greendepot/dept.asp?dept_id=12; N. Leiber, "With Eco-Friendly Building Supplies, Green Depot Thrives in the Construction Rebound," *Bloomberg Businessweek*, accessed May 11, 2016, accessed June 21, 2013, http://www.businessweek.com/articles/2013-04-11/with-eco-friendly-building-supplies-green-depot-thrives-in-the-construction-rebound.

7. R. Upson and K. Notarianni, "Quantitative Evaluaton of Fire and EMS Mobilization Times," The Fire Protection Research Foundation, May 2010, p. 1.

8. D. Robb, "Is Big Data Right for Small Business?" *Tech Page One*, June 26, 2014, accessed May 11, 2016, http://techpageone.dell.com/technology/is-big-data-right-for-small-business/.

9. L. Landro, "Why Hospitals Want Patients to Ask Doctors, 'Have You Washed Your Hands?'" *Wall Street Journal*, September 30, 2013, accessed May 11, 2016, http://wsj.com/news/articles/SB10001424052702303918804579107202360565642.

10. University Health Network, "HealthCare Worker Hand Hygiene Rates Increase Three-Fold When Auditors Visible," *Science Daily*, July 8, 2014, accessed May 11, 2016, http://www.sciencedaily.com/releases/2014/07/140708165727.htm.

11. T. Rosenberg, "An Electronic Eye on Hospital Hand-Washing," *New York Times*, November 24, 2011, accessed May 11, 2016, http://opinionator.blogs.nytimes.com/2011/11/24/an-electronic-eye-on-hospital-hand-washing.

12. N. Wiener, *Cybernetics; Or Control and Communication in the Animal and the Machine* (New York: Wiley, 1948).

13. A. Levin, "Pilots Can't Stop Cockpit Video Forever," *Bloomberg Businessweek*, October 12–18, 2015, 27–28.

14. Ibid.

15. S. Ovide, "Microsoft Hopes Sneak Peaks Will Pay Off," *Wall Street Journal*, July 29, 2015, B6.

16. M. Griggs, "In Nasty Weather, High-Tech Sensors Get the Lights Back on Faster," *Popular Science*, December 23, 2014, accessed May 11, 2016, http://www.popsci.com/high-tech-power-line-sensors-get-lights-turned-faster.

17. D. Cardwell, "Grid Sensors Could Ease Disruptions of Power," *New York Times*, February 3, 2015, B4.

18. Leifer and Mills, "An Information Processing Approach."

19. A Gasparro and J. Newman, "Blue Bell Recall Shows Difficulty of Controlling Listeria," *Wall Street Journal*, April 21, 2015, accessed May 11, 2016, http://www.wsj.com/articles/blue-bell-recall-shows-difficulty-of-controlling-listeria-1429653383.

20. S. Ng, "Big Cracks Spread in Glass Recycling," *Wall Street Journal*, April 23, 2015, B8.

21. Ibid.

22. "Test Security and Fairness: Know Your Rights and Responsibilities, https://collegereadiness.collegeboard.org/sat/taking-the-test/test-security-fairness.

23. R. Dudley, S. Stecklow, A. Harney & I. Liu, "College Board Gave Sat Tests That It Knew Had Been Compromised in Asia," Reuters, March 28, 2016, accessed May 11, 2016, http://www.reuters.com/investigates/special-report/college-sat-one/.

24. J. Koffler, "China Uses a Drone to Curb Cheating on College Placement Exams," *Time*, June 9, 2015, accessed May 11, 2016, http://time.com/3914087/china-drones-cheating-exams/.

25. M. Weber, *The Protestant Ethic and the Spirit of Capitalism* (New York: Scribner's, 1958).

26. B. Morris, "Truckers Tire of Government Sleep Rules," *Wall Street Journal*, accessed May 11, 2016, http://wsj.com/news/articles/SB10001424052702304672404579182522881942740.

27. C. Zakrzewski, "The Key to Getting Workers to Stop Wasting Time Online," *Wall Street Journal*, March 13, 2016, accessed May 11, 2016, http://www.wsj.com/articles/the-key-to-getting-workers-to-stop-wasting-time-online-1457921545.

28. L. Scism, "State Farm Is There: As You Drive," *Wall Street Journal*, August 4, 2013, accessed May 11, 2016, http://wsj.com/news/articles/SB10001424127887323420604578647950497541958.

29. H. Son, "'Bob in Accounting Is Going to Fix Currency Rates.'—'I'll tell Jamie Dimon,'" *BloombergBusinessweek*, April 13–19, 2015, pp. 34–35.

30. Rajul, "Four Seasons Park Lane Shares Hiring Secrets," London Hotel Insight, January 24, 2011, accessed May 11, 2016, http://londonhotelsinsight.com/2011/01/24/four-seasons-park-lane-shares-hiring-secrets/.

31. "About Four Seasons: Nick Mutton," Four Seasons, accessed May 11, 2016, 2014, http://www.fourseasons.com/about_four_seasons/nick-mutton/.

32. A. Kadet, "City News—Metro Money/Jerks Need Not Apply," *Wall Street Journal*, January 18, 2014, accessed May 11, 2016, http://www.wsj.com/articles/SB10001424052702304149404579326730931946454.

33. J. R. Barker, "Tightening the Iron Cage: Concertive Control in Self-Managing Teams," *Administrative Science Quarterly* 38 (1993): 408–437.

34. N. Byrnes, "The Art of Motivation," *BusinessWeek*, May 1, 2006, 56–62.

35. Barker, "Tightening the Iron Cage."

36. C. Manz and H. Sims, "Leading Workers to Lead Themselves: The External Leadership of Self-Managed Work Teams," *Administrative Science Quarterly* 32 (1987): 106–128.

37. J. Slocum and H. A. Sims, "Typology for Integrating Technology, Organization and Job Design," *Human Relations* 33 (1980): 193–212.

38. C. C. Manz and H. P. Sims, Jr., "Self-Management as a Substitute for Leadership: A Social Learning Perspective," *Academy of Management Review* 5 (1980): 361–367.

39. C. Manz and C. Neck, *Mastering Self-Leadership*, 3rd ed. (Upper Saddle River, NJ: Pearson, Prentice Hall, 2004).

40. S. Nassauer, "Welcome Back, Wal-Mart Greeters," *Wall Street Journal*, June 19, 2015, B1.S. Nassauer, "Welcome Back, Wal-Mart Greeters," *Wall Street Journal*, June 19, 2015, accessed May 11, 2016, http://www.wsj.com/articles/wal-mart-ushers-greeters-back-to-the-front-1434651944.

41. Ibid.

42. R. S. Kaplan and D. P. Norton, "Using the Balanced Scorecard as a Strategic Management System," *Harvard Business Review* (January–February 1996): 75–85; R. S. Kaplan and D. P. Norton, "The Balanced Scorecard: Measures That Drive Performance," *Harvard Business Review* (January–February 1992): 71–79.

43. J. Meliones, "Saving Money, Saving Lives," *Harvard Business Review* (November–December 2000): 57–65.

44. A. Wilde Mathews and A. Steele, "Aetna Lifts Forecast; Net Tops Expectations as Key Measure Falls," *Wall Street Journal*, October 30, 2015, B4.

45. D. Kesmodel and A. Gasparro, "Lean Recipe Fuels Food Deals," *Wall Street Journal*, March 26, 2015, A1, A6.

46. S. L. Fawcett, "Fear of Accounts: Improving Managers' Competence and Confidence Through Simulation Exercises," *Journal of European Industrial Training* (February 1996): 17.

47. M. H. Stocks and A. Harrell, "The Impact of an Increase in Accounting Information Level on the Judgment Quality of Individuals and Groups," *Accounting, Organizations & Society* (October–November 1995): 685–700.

48. B. Morris, "Roberto Goizueta and Jack Welch: The Wealth Builders," *Fortune*, December 11, 1995, 80–94.

49. G. Colvin, "America's Best & Worst Wealth Creators: The Real Champions Aren't Always Who You Think. Here's an Eye-Opening Look at Which Companies Produce and Destroy the Most Money for Investors—Plus a New Tool for Spotting Future Winners," *Fortune*, December 18, 2000, 207.

50. "About Herman Miller: Operational Excellence," *Herman Miller*, accessed June 20, 2011, http://www.hermanmiller.com/About-Us/About-Herman-Miller/Operational-Excellence.

51. M. Schurman, "A Herman Miller Primer," *Herman Miller*, accessed June 20, 2011, http://www.hermanmiller.com/MarketFacingTech/hmc/about_us/News_Events_Media/Corporate_Backgrounder.pdf.

52. B. Stewart, *Best-Practice EVA: The Definitive Guide to Measuring and Maximizing Shareholder Value* (New York: Wiley Finance, 2013); "Apple, Inc.: Economic Value Added," *Stock Analysis on Net*, accessed May 11, 2016, https://www.stock-analysis-on.net/NASDAQ/Company/Apple-Inc/Performance-Measure/Economic-Value-Added; "Alphabet, Inc.: Economic Value Added," *Stock Analysis on Net*, accessed May 11, 2016, https://www.stock-analysis-on.net/NASDAQ/Company/Alphabet-Inc/Performance-Measure/Economic-Value-Added.

53. "Welcome Complaints," *Office of Consumer and Business Affairs*, Government of South Australia, accessed June 20, 2005, http://www.ocba.sa.gov.au/businessadvice/complaints/03_welcome.html.

54. J. Tschohl, "Cultivate Loyal Customers: The Value of Defection Management," Desk.com, May

23, 2013, accessed May 11, 2016, http://www.desk
.com/blog/loyal-customers/.

55. C. A. Reeves and D. A. Bednar, "Defining
Quality: Alternatives and Implications," *Academy of
Management Review* 19 (1994): 419–445.

56. "The Best Airlines in the World: Readers'
Choice Awards 2015," *Condé Nast Traveler*, October
19, 2015, accessed May 10, 2016, http://www
.cntraveler.com/galleries/2015-10-07/top-international
-airlines-readers-choice-awards; "About Us: *Singapore
Airlines*—Our Awards," Singapore Airlines, accessed
May 10, 2016, http:// www.singaporeair.com/en_UK
/about-us/sia-history/sia-awards/.

57. R. Smithers, "Asda Puts UK's First Supermarket
Wonky Veg Box on Sale," *The Guardian*, February 5,
2016, accessed May 11, 2016, http://www.theguardian
.com/environment/2016/feb/05/asda-puts-uks-first
-supermarket-wonky-veg-box-on-sale.

58. L. Neel, "Wonky Veg Introduced in Ongoing
Supermarket Price War," *Fresh Business* Thinking,
February 9, 2016, accessed May 11, 2016 http://www
.freshbusinessthinking.com/wonky-veg-introduced
-in-ongoing-supermarket-price-war/.

59. Ibid.

60. D. R. May and B. L. Flannery, "Cutting Waste
with Employee Involvement Teams," *Business Horizons*, September–October 1995, 28–38.

61. J. Carlton, "Some NFL Teams Are Going
Green," *Wall Street Journal*, May 18, 2014, accessed
May 10, 2016, http://wsj.com/news/articles/SB100
0142405270230467790457953788269155049; C.
Boulton, "Exposing the Hidden Waste and Expense
of Cloud Computing," *Wall Street Journal*, February
17, 2015, B4.

62. M. Perella, "How HP and Kyocera Are Applying
Circular Economy to Printing," *The Guardian*, May
28, 2014, accessed May 10, 2016, http://www
.theguardian.com/sustainable-business/hp-kyocera
-circular-economy-printing.

63. Ibid.

64. L. Downing, "British Retailers Turn Waste into
Power," *Bloomberg Businessweek*, June 14, 2012, accessed June 21, 2013, http://www.businessweek
.com/articles/2012-06-14/british-retailers-turn-waste
-into-power.

65. "The End of the Road: Schools and Computer
Recycling," *Intel*, accessed September 5, 2008, http://
www.intel.com/education/recycling_computers
/recycling.htm.

66. M. Meece, "Giving Those Old Gadgets a Proper
Green Burial," *New York Times*, January 6, 2011,
accessed March 5, 2011, http://www.nytimes
.com/2011/01/06/technology/personaltech/06basics
.html?ref=recyclingofwastematerials.

17

1. R. Lenzner, "The Reluctant Entrepreneur,"
Forbes, September 11, 1995, 162–166.

2. "Inflation Calculator | Find US Dollar's Value from
1913-2014," US Inflation Calculator, accessed July 24,
2014, http://www.usinflationcalculator.com/; T. Lee,
"Today's iPhone Is More Useful Than $3,000 Worth
of Gadgets from a 1991 Radio Shack," *The Washington Post*, January 31, 2014, accessed July 24, 2014,
http://www.washingtonpost.com/blogs/the-switch
/wp/2014/01/31/todays-iphone-is-more-useful-than
-3000-worth-of-gadgets-from-a-1991-radio-shack/.

3. K. Wetterstrand, "DNA Sequencing Costs: Data
from the NHGRI Genome Sequencing Program,"
National Human Genome Research Institute, January 15, 2016, accessed May 12, 2016, www.genome
.gov/sequencingcosts/.

4. J. Markoff, "Moore's Law Running Out of Room,
Tech Looks for a Successor," *New York Times*, May 4,
2016, accessed May 12, 2016, http://www.nytimes
.com/2016/05/05/technology/moores-law-running
-out-of-room-tech-looks-for-a-successor.html.

5. S. Norton, "A Post-PC CEO: No Desk, No Desktop," *Wall Street Journal*, November 20, 2014, B5.

6. "Pandora Reports Q1 2016 Financial Results,"
Business Wire, April 28, 2016, accessed May 12,
2016, http://www.businesswire.com/news
/home/20160428006873/en/.

7. M. Singleton, "Spotify Hits 30 Million Subscribers," *The Verge*, March 21, 2016, accessed May 12,
2016, http://www.theverge.com/2016/3/21/11220398
/spotify-hits-30-million-subscribers; M. Singleton,
"Apple Music Now Has 13 Million Subscribers," *The
Verge*, April 26, 2016, accessed May 12, 2016, http://
www.theverge.com/2016/4/26/11513410/apple-music
-13-million-subscribers; R. Dillet, "Deezer Is Losing
Subscribers But Growing Revenue," *TechCrunch*,
October 15, 2015, accessed May 12, 2016, http://
techcrunch.com/2015/10/15/deezer-is-losing
-subscribers-but-growing-revenue/; E. Weise,·
"Amazon Prime Is Big, But How Big?" *USA Today*,
February 3, 2015, accessed May 12, 2015, http://
www.usatoday.com/story/tech/2015/02/03/amazon
-prime-10-years-old-anniversary/22755509/.

8. D. A. Fields, "The Myth of First-Mover Advantage," *Industry Week*, June 12, 2013, accessed May
12, 2016, http://www.industryweek.com/innovation
/myth-first-mover-advantage.

9. F. Suarez and G. Lanzolla, "The Half-Truth of
First Mover Advantage," *Harvard Business Review*,
April 2005, accessed May 12, 2016, http://hbr
.org/2005/04/the-half-truth-of-first-mover-advantage
/ar/1.

10. N. Olivarez-Giles, "Baseball's Latest Recruit Is
an iPad," *Wall Street Journal*, March 29, 2016, accessed May 12, 2016, http://www.wsj.com/articles
/baseballs-latest-recruit-is-an-ipad-1459310403.

11. Ibid.

12. Ibid.

13. C. Mims, "To Feed Billions, Farms Are about
Data as Much as Dirt," *Wall Street Journal*, April 9,
2015, accessed May 12, 2016, http://www.wsj.com
/articles/to-feed-billions-farms-are-about-data-as
-much-as-dirt-1439160264.

14. N. Bogart, "Canadian Airline First Air to Live
Stream Black Box Data," *Global News*, May 6, 2014,
accessed May 12, 2016, http://globalnews.ca
/news/1314398/canadian-airline-first-air-to-live
-stream-black-box-data/.

15. D. Stacey and G. Raghuvanshi, "Malaysia
Airlines Flight 370: Contractor Will Get 300 Days to
Complete Search," *Wall Street Journal*, June 4, 2014,
accessed May 12, 2016, http://online.wsj.com/articles
/contractor-will-get-300-days-to-complete-malaysia
-airlines-flight-370-search-1401849756.

16. A. Pasztor and J. Ostrower, "Missing Malaysia Jet
Adds Fuel to 'Live Black Box' Debate," *Wall Street
Journal*, March 9, 2014, accessed May 12, 2016,
http://online.wsj.com/news/articles/SB100014240527
0230402010457942923351669201 4?KEYWORDS
=missing+malaysia+jet+adds+fuel&mg=reno64-wsj.

17. Bogart, "Canadian Airline First Air to Live
Stream Black Box Data."

18. D. Hernandez, "Artificial Intelligence Is Now
Telling Doctors How to Treat You," *Wired*, June 2,
2014, accessed May 12, 2016, http://www.wired
.com/2014/06/ai-healthcare/.

19. Ibid.

20. E. Phillips, "Technology Helps Food Banks
Handle Holiday Surge," *Wall Street Journal*, December 3, 2015, accessed May 12, 2016, http://www.wsj
.com/articles/technology-helps-food-banks-handle
-holiday-surge-1449101555.

21. B. Levine, "Facing Facebook, Google, and
Amazon, Brands Pool Their Data: Sharing Data in
Cooperatives Is Becoming a Way for the Non-Giants
to Survive," *Marketing Land*, May 2, 2016, accessed
May 12, 2016, http://marketingland.com/facing
-facebook-google-amazon-brands-pool-data-175424.

22. D. Chernicoff, "Another Billion Dollar Data
Center Investment for Google," *ZDNet*, April, 21,
2015, accessed May 12, 2016, http://www.zdnet.com
/article/another-billion-dollar-data-center-investment
-for-google/.

23. D. Meyer, "Google to Build Gigantic "120-mega-
watt" Data Center in the Netherlands," Gigaom,

September 23, 2014, accessed May 12, 2016, https://
gigaom.com/2014/09/23/google-to-build-gigantic
-120-megawatt-data-center-in-the-netherlands/.

24. "Google Search Statistics - Internet Live Stats,"
Google, accessed May 12, 2015, http://www
.internetlivestats.com/google-search-statistics/#trend;
"Statistics - YouTube," YouTube, accessed May 12,
2015, http://www.youtube.com/yt/press/statistics.html.

25. R. Miller, "Facebook Decloaks, Confirms Plans
for Iowa Server Farm," *Data Center Knowledge*,
April 23, 2013, accessed May 12, 2016, http://www
.datacenterknowledge.com/archives/2013/04/23
/facebook-decloaks-confirms-plans-for-iowa-server
-farm/.

26. E. Dwoskin and G. Bensinger, "Hot New Thing
at the Mall: Heat Maps Track Shoppers," *Wall Street
Journal*, December 9, 2013, B1.

27. K. Kamenec, "How Apples iBeacon Could
Upend Retail Shopping," *PC Magazine*, October 24,
2013, accessed May 12, 2016, http://www.pcmag
.com/article2/0,2817,2425052,00.asp.

28. S. Ramachandran, "Netflix Will Pay Comcast
for Speed," *Wall Street Journal*, February 24, 2014,
A1; S. Ramachandran and D. Fitzgerald, "For Web
Firms, Faster Access Comes at a Price," *Wall Street
Journal*, June 19, 2013, B1; "Netflix Still Dominates
Internet Traffic," Advanced Television, November
20, 2014, accessed May 12, 2015, http://advanced
-television.com/2014/11/20/netflix-still-dominates
-internet-traffic/.

29. S. Lubar, *Infoculture: The Smithsonian Book
of Information Age Inventions* (Boston: Houghton
Mifflin, 1993).

30. Ibid.

31. P. Mozur and J. Osawa, "Can Alibab's Taxi App
Be New Growth Driver," *Wall Street Journal*, March
17, 2014, B4.

32. Anonymous, "Home & Digital: #ASKWSJD,"
Wall Street Journal, March 5, 2014, D3.

33. R. Trichur, "Global Finance: No Cards Necessary with New ATM Grid," *Wall Street Journal*,
March 16, 2015, C3.

34. B. Worthen, "Bar Codes on Steroids," *CIO*,
December 15, 2002, 53.

35. J. Bennett, "Johnson Controls Unravels Riddle
of Missing Crates," Wall Street Journal, April 29,
2016, accessed May 12, 2016, http://www.wsj.com
/articles/johnson-controls-unravels-riddle-of-missing
-crates-1461943710.

36. N. Rubenking, "Hidden Messages," *PC Magazine*, May 22, 2001, 86.

37. D. Hill, "The Secret of Airbnb's Pricing Algorithm," *IEEE Spectrum*, August 20, 2015, accessed
May 12, 2016, http://spectrum.ieee.org/computing
/software/the-secret-of-airbnbs-pricing-algorithm.

38. E. Dwoskin, "How New York's Fire Department
Uses Data Mining," *Wall Street Journal* (Digits blog),
January 24, 2014, 2:12 p.m., accessed May 12, 2016,
http://blogs.wsj.com/digits/2014/01/24/how-new
-yorks-fire-department-uses-data-mining/.

39. Rubenking, "Hidden Messages."

40. C. Duhigg, "How Companies Learn Your Secrets," *New York Times*, February 16, 2012, accessed
May 12, 2016, http://www.nytimes.com/2012/02/19
/magazine/shopping-habits.html?pagewanted=all.

41. A. Rutkin, "Machine Predicts Heart Attacks 4
Hours before Doctors," *NewScientist*, August 11,
2014, accessed May 12, 2016, http://www
.newscientist.com/article/mg22329814.400-machine
-predicts-heart-attacks-4-hours-before-doctors.html#
.VVKi5mBtEkE.

42. S. Yoon, "Lot of Contacts in Your Mobile
Phone May Get You Loans," *BloombergBusiness
Week*, November 15, 2015, accessed May 12, 2016,
http://www.bloomberg.com/news/articles/2015-11-15
/lot-of-contacts-in-your-mobile-phone-you-may
-qualify-for-a-loan; S. Armour, "Lenders Use Social
Media to Screen Borrowers," *Wall Street Journal*,
January 8, 2014, accessed May 12, 2016, http://www
.wsj.com/articles/SB1000142405270230477310457926
6423512930050.

43. K. Johnson, O. Dorell, and E. Weise, "Official: North Korea behind Sony Hack," *USA Today*, December 18, 2014, accessed May 12, 2016, http://www.usatoday.com/story/news/world/2014/12/17/north-korea-sony-hack/20558135/.

44. B. Fritz, D. Yadron, and E. Schwartzel, "Behind the Scenes at Sony as Hacking Crisis Unfolded," *Wall Street Journal*, December 30, 2014, accessed May 12, 2016, http://www.wsj.com/articles/behind-the-scenes-at-sony-as-hacking-crisis-unfolded-1419985719.

45. "Cloud Infographic: Computer Virus Facts and Stats, CloudTweaks, April 11, accessed May 12, 2016, http://cloudtweaks.com/2014/04/cloud-infographic-computer-virus-facts-stats/.

46. B. Gottesman and K. Karagiannis, "A False Sense of Security," *PC Magazine*, February 22, 2005, 72.

47. F. J. Derfler, Jr., "Secure Your Network," *PC Magazine*, June 27, 2000, 183–200.

48. "Authentication," *PC Magazine*, accessed May 12, 2016, http://www.pcmag.com/encyclopedia/term/38192/authentication.

49. "Authorization," *PC Magazine*, accessed May 12, 2016, http://www.pcmag.com/encyclopedia/term/38202/authorization.

50. L. Seltzer, "Password Crackers," *PC Magazine*, February 12, 2002, 68.

51. "Two-Factor Authentication," *Information Security Glossary*, accessed May 12, 2016, http://www.rsa.kz/node/glossary/default4b75.html?id=1056.

52. W. Gordon, "Here's Everywhere You Should Enable Two-Factor Authentication Right Now," *LifeHacker*, December 10, 2013, accessed July 26, 2014, http://lifehacker.com/5938565/heres-everywhere-you-should-enable-two-factor-authentication-right-now; L. Tung, "Google to Slap Two-Factor Across Apps via Suspicious Logins Trigger," *ZD Net*, May 15, 2014, accessed June 24, 2014, http://www.zdnet.com/google-to-slap-two-factor-across-apps-via-suspicious-logins-trigger-7000029476/.

53. D. Yadron, "Five Simple Steps to Protect Corporate Data," *Wall Street Journal*, April 19, 2015, accessed May 12, 2016, http://www.wsj.com/articles/five-simple-steps-to-protect-corporate-data-1429499477.

54. J. Valentino-Devries, "Rarely Patched Software Bugs in Home Routers Cripple Security," *Wall Street Journal*, accessed May 12, 2016, http://www.wsj.com/articles/rarely-patched-software-bugs-in-home-routers-cripple-security-1453136285.

55. J. DeAvila, "Wi-Fi Users, Beware: Hot Spots Are Weak Spots," *Wall Street Journal*, January 16, 2008, D1; J. Vijayan, "Hotel Router Vulnerability a Reminder of Untrusted WiFi Risks," March 27, 2015, Information Week Dark Reading, accessed May 12, 2016, http://www.darkreading.com/perimeter/hotel-router-vulnerability-a-reminder-of-untrusted-wifi-risks/d/d-id/1319668.

56. G. A. Fowler, "You Won't Believe How Adorable This Kitty Is! Click For More!" *Wall Street Journal*, March 26, 2013, accessed May 12, 2016, http://online.wsj.com/news/articles/SB10001424127887324373204578373011392662962?mg=reno64-wsj.

57. Ibid.

58. J. van den Hoven, "Executive Support Systems & Decision Making," *Journal of Systems Management* 47, no. 8 (March–April 1996): 48.

59. D. Hannon, "Colgate-Palmolive Empowers Senior Leaders with Executive Dashboards," *InsiderProfiles*, April 1, 2011, accessed May 13, 2016, http://insiderprofiles.wispubs.com/article.aspx?iArticleId=5720.

60. "Intranet," *PC Magazine*, accessed May 13, 2016, http://www.pcmag.com/encyclopedia/term/45310/intranet.

61. "2016 Intranet Design Annual Winners," Nielsen Norman Group, January 9, 2016, accessed May 12, 2016, https://www.nngroup.com/news/item/2016-intranet-design-awards/; "DORMA Delivers Access To Innovation For 7000 Global Users With a Unily intranet," Unily, accessed May 12,

2016, https://www.unily.com/insights/dorma-delivers-access-to-innovation-for-7000-global-users-with-unily; "Dorma-Supporting Employees with Access to Innovation," Unily, accessed May 12, 2016, https://www.unily.com/media/23157/unily-dorma-case-study-2.pdf; M. Gibson, "dorma+kaba Pan-European Intranet Wins Nielsen Norman Best Intranet 2016," Unily, January 11, 2016, accessed May 12, 2016, https://www.unily.com/insights/dormakaba-wins-nielsen-norman-award-for-best-intranet-of-2016.

62. "Web Services," *PC Magazine*, accessed May 13, 2016, http://www.pcmag.com/encyclopedia/term/54345/web-services.

63. S. Overby, "This Could Be the Start of Something Small," *CIO*, February 15, 2003, 54.

64. "Extranet," *PC Magazine*, accessed May 13, 2016, http://www.pcmag.com/encyclopedia/term/42945/extranet.

65. "Mitsubishi Opens Sales/Training Center; Establishes Online Creative Centers," *ContractingBusiness.com*, March 27, 2012, accessed May 13, 2016, http://contractingbusiness.com/news/Mitsubishi-training-creative-centers-0328/.

66. "Travellers Embracing Efficiencies of Self-Service Bag Drop," *Airport Business*, April 14, 2016, accessed May 12, 2016, http://www.airport-business.com/2016/04/travellers-embracing-efficiencies-self-service-bag-drop/.

67. J. Nicas & T. Shukla, "The Next Frontier in Airline Baggage: Digital Bag Tags," *Wall Street Journal*, July 1, 2015, accessed May 12, 2016, http://www.wsj.com/articles/bag-tags-1435340070.

68. S. Hamm, D. Welch, W. Zellner, F. Keenan, and F. Engardio, "Down But Hardly Out: Downturn Be Damned, Companies Are Still Anxious to Expand Online," *BusinessWeek*, March 26, 2001, 126.

69. K. C. Laudon and J. P. Laudon, *Management Information Systems: Organization and Technology* (Upper Saddle River, NJ: Prentice Hall, 1996).

70. J. Borzo, "Software for Symptoms," *Wall Street Journal*, May 23, 2005, R10.

71. Ibid.

72. R. Hernandez, "American Express Authorizer's Assistant," *Business Rules Journal*, August 2001, accessed May 13, 2016, http://bizrules.info/page/art_amexaa.htm.

18

1. J. Mouawad, "A Luxury Liner Docks, and the Countdown's On," *The New York Times*, March 22, 2015, BU1.

2. Ibid.

3. S. McCartney, "How Heathrow Airport Cut Down on Flight Delays," *Wall Street Journal*, September 16, 2015, accessed May 5, 2016, http://www.wsj.com/articles/how-heathrow-airport-cut-down-on-flight-delays-1442423115.

4. L. Stevens, "For UPS, E-Commerce Brings Big Business and Big Problems," *Wall Street Journal*, September 11, 2014, accessed May 11, 2015, http://www.wsj.com/articles/for-ups-e-commerce-brings-big-business-and-big-problems-1410489642.

5. Ibid.

6. "Employment Cost Index News Release Text," Bureau of Labor Statistics, April 29, 2016, accessed May 5, 2016, http://www.bls.gov/news.release/eci.nr0.htm; "Productivity and Costs: First Quarter 2016, Preliminary," Bureau of Labor Statistics, May 4, 2016, accessed May 5, 2016, http://www.bls.gov/news.release/prod2.nr0.htm.

7. "Historical Income Tables—Families: Table F-23—Families by Total Money Income, Race, and Hispanic Origin of Householder: 1967 to 2014," U.S. Census Bureau, Current Population Survey, Annual Social and Economic Supplements, accessed May 5, 2016, http://www.census.gov/hhes/www/income/data/historical/families/2014/f23.xls.

8. Ibid.

9. The Conference Board Total Economy Data Base, Summary Tables, May 2015, "Table 3: Growth of Labor Productivity, Total Hours Worked, and Real GDB for Major Mature Economies, 1999–2015," *The Conference Board*, accessed accessed May 5, 2016, https://www.conference-board.org/retrievefile.cfm?filename=The-Conference-Board-2015-Productivity-Brief-Summary-Tables-1999–2015.pdf&type=subsite.

10. "Employment Projections, Table 3.1: Civilian Labor Force by Sex, Age, Race, and Ethnicity, 1994, 2004, 2014, and projected 2014," Bureau of Labor Statistics, December 8, 2015, accessed May 5, 2016, http://www.bls.gov/emp/ep_table_301.htm.

11. "Charitable Giving Statistics," *National Philanthropic Trust*, accessed accessed May 5, 2016, http://www.nptrust.org/philanthropic-resources/charitable-giving-statistics/; C. Lourosa-Ricardo, "How America Gives to Charity," Wall Street Journal, December 14, 2014, http://www.wsj.com/articles/how-america-gives-to-charity-1418619046, accessed May 11, 2015.

12. "North America: United States," The World Factbook, April 26, 2016, accessed May 5, 2016, https://www.cia.gov/library/publications/the-world-factbook/geos/us.html.

13. "Philanthropy in the American Economy," *Council of Economic Advisers*, February 19, 2002, accessed April 13, 2009, http://clinton4.nara.gov/media/pdf/philanthropy.pdf.

14. M. Perry, "Christmas Shopping 1958 vs. 2012 Illustrates the 'Miracle of the Marketplace' Which Delivers Better and Cheaper Goods," *American Enterprise Institute*, December 28, 2013, accessed May 5, 2016, http://www.aei-ideas.org/2013/12/christmas-shopping-1958-vs-2012-illustrates-the-miracle-of-the-marketplace-which-delivers-better-and-cheaper-goods/.

15. "European Airline Labor Productivity: CAPA Rankings," *CAPA Centre for Aviation*, April 9, 2013, accessed May 11, 2015, http://centreforaviation.com/analysis/european-airline-labour-productivity-capa-rankings-104204.

16. "Multifactor Productivity: Frequently Asked Questions," Bureau of Labor Statistics, accessed May 5, 2016, http://www.bls.gov/mfp/mprfaq.htm#1.

17. Press Release, "New-Car Transaction Prices Increase Nearly 2 Percent In April 2016, According To Kelley Blue Book," *Kelley Blue Book*, May 3, 2016, accessed May 5, 2016, http://mediaroom.kbb.com/new-car-transaction-prices-increase-nearly-2-percent-april-2016.

18. Press Release, "J.D. Power Reports: Korean Brands Lead Industry in Initial Quality, While Japanese Brands Struggle to Keep Up with Pace of Improvement," J.D. Power, June 17, 2015, accessed May 5, 2016, http://www.jdpower.com/press-releases/2015-us-initial-quality-study-iqs.

19. "Basic Quality Concepts," *American Society for Quality*, accessed August 2, 2009, http://www.asq.org/learn-about-quality/basic-concepts.html.

20. R. E. Markland, S. K. Vickery, and R. A. Davis, "Managing Quality" (Chapter 7), in *Operations Management: Concepts in Manufacturing and Services* (Cincinnati, OH: South-Western College Publishing, 1998).

21. J. Ewoldt, "A Brighter Day for LED Bulbs," *StarTribune*, April 3, 2013, accessed June 23, 2013, http://www.startribune.com/business/201357281.html?refer=y; M. White, "Light Switch: Why You'll Start Using LED Bulbs This Year," *Time*, April 25, 2013, accessed June 23, 2013, http://business.time.com/2013/04/25/light-switch-why-youll-start-using-led-bulbs-this-year/.

22. L. L. Berry and A. Parasuraman, *Marketing Services* (New York: Free Press, 1991).

23. S. Kapner, "Apple Gets Sweet Deals From Mall Operators," *Wall Street Journal*, March 10, 2015, accessed May 5, 2016, http://www.wsj.com/articles/apple-gets-sweet-deals-from-mall-operators-1426007804; S. Kovach, "10 Mind-Blowing Facts about the Apple Store," *Business Insider*, March 13,

2015, accessed May 5, 2016, http://www
.businessinsider.com/apple-store-facts-2015-3?op=1.

24. "Apple Still Sells the Most per Square Foot,"
May 22, 2015, accessed May 5, 2016, eMarketer,
http://www.emarketer.com/Article/Apple-Still-Sells
-Most-per-Square-Foot/1012523; "Apple, Murphy
USA, Tiffany & Co. Top New eMarketer Store Productivity Rankings," *eMarketer Retail*, May 26, 2014,
accessed May 5, 2016, http://retail.emarketer.com
/apple-murphy-usa-tiffany-co-top-new-emarketer
-store-productivity-rankings/.

25. "About ISO," *International Organization for
Standardization*, accessed May 5, 2016, 2014, http://
www.iso.org/iso/home/about.htm.

26. "ISO 9000 Essentials," and "ISO 14000 Essentials," *International Organization for Standardization*, accessed May 5, 2016, http://www.iso.org
/iso/iso_catalogue/management_standards/iso_9000
_iso_14000.htm.

27. J. Briscoe, S. Fawcett, and R. Todd, "The
Implementation and Impact of ISO 9000 Among
Small Manufacturing Enterprises," *Journal of Small
Business Management* 43 (July 1, 2005): 309.

28. R. Henkoff, "The Hot New Seal of Quality (ISO
9000 Standard of Quality Management)," *Fortune*,
June 28, 1993, 116.

29. "Baldrige Frequently Asked Questions: Baldrige Performance Excellence Program," *National
Institute of Standards and Technology*, accessed May
5, 2016, http://www.nist.gov/baldrige/about
/baldrige_faqs.cfm.

30. "Baldrige Award Process Fees," *National Institute of Standards and Technology*, accessed May 11,
2015, http://www.nist.gov/baldrige/enter/award_fees
.cfm.

31. "Frequently Asked Questions About the Malcolm Baldrige National Quality Award."

32. Ibid.

33. "Criteria for Performance Excellence,"
Baldrige National Quality Program 2008, accessed
September 15, 2008, http://www.quality.nist.gov
/PDF_files/2008_Business_Criteria.pdf.

34. Ibid.

35. D. C. Moody, "Beam Integral Part of Prestigious
Baldridge Program," *theeasleyprogress.com*,
June 4, 2014, accessed June 25, 2014, http://www
.theeasleyprogress.com/news/home_top-news/4915403
/Beam-integral-part-of-prestigious-Baldridge-Program.

36. J. W. Dean, Jr., and J. Evans, *Total Quality:
Management, Organization, and Strategy* (St. Paul,
MN: West, 1994).

37. J. W. Dean, Jr., and D. E. Bowen, "Management
Theory and Total Quality: Improving Research and
Practice Through Theory Development," *Academy of
Management Review* 19 (1994): 392–418.

38. "7th Annual On-time Performance Service
Awards," FlightStats, accessed May 5, 2016, http://
www.flightstats.com/company/media/on-time
-performance-awards/; Press Release, "2015 North
America Airline Satisfaction Study," J.D. Power, May
13, 2015, accessed May 5, 2016, http://www
.jdpower.com/press-releases/2015-north-america
-airline-satisfaction-study. "Alaska Airlines Awards
and Recognition," Alaska Airlines, accessed May 11,
2015, http://www.alaskaair.com/content/about-us
/newsroom/alaska-awards.aspx; M. Kaminsky, "The
Weekend Interview with Bill Ayer: An Airline That
Makes Money—Really," *Wall Street Journal*, February 4, 2012, A13; T. Maxon, "JetBlue Leads American
Customer Satisfaction Index for Second Year," *Dallas
Morning News*, June 18, 2012, accessed June 23,
2013, http://aviationblog.dallasnews.com/2013/06
/jetblue-leads-american-consumer-satisfaction-index
-for-second-year.html/.

39. M. Esterl, "How Dr Pepper Cuts Costs. And
Keeps Cutting," *Wall Street Journal*, February 21,
2016, accessed May 6, 2016, http://www.wsj.com
/articles/how-dr-pepper-cuts-costs-and-keeps
-cutting-1456110339.

40. S. McCartney, "A World Where Flights Aren't
Canceled," *Wall Street Journal*, April 2, 2014,
accessed July 28, 2014, http://www.wsj.com/articles
/SB10001424052702303987004579477412359027
986.

41. J. Miller, "Remade in the USA: Indiana Steel
Mill Revived with Lessons from Abroad," *Wall Street
Journal*, May 21, 2012, A1.

42. R. Hallowell, L. A. Schlesinger, and J. Zornitsky,
"Internal Service Quality, Customer and Job Satisfac-
tion: Linkages and Implications for Management,"
Human Resource Planning 19 (1996): 20–31; J. L.
Heskett, T. O. Jones, G. W. Loveman, W. E. Sasser,
Jr., and L. A. Schlesinger, "Putting the Service-Profit
Chain to Work," *Harvard Business Review* (March–
April 1994): 164–174.

43. L. Dishman, "These are the Best Employee
Benefits and Perks," *Fast Company*, February 3,
2016, accessed May 5, 2016, http://www.fastcompany
.com/3056205/the-future-of-work/these-are-the-best
-employee-benefits-and-perks.

44. J. Paravantis, N. Bouranta, and L. Chitiris, "The
Relationship Between Internal and External Service
Quality," *International Journal of Contemporary
Hospital Management* 21 (2009): 275–293.

45. G. Brewer, "The Ultimate Guide to Winning
Customers: The Customer Stops Here," *Sales &
Marketing Management* 150 (March 1998): 30; F. F.
Reichheld, *The Loyalty Effect: The Hidden Force Be-
hind Growth, Profits, and Lasting Value* (Cambridge,
MA: Harvard Business School Press, 2001).

46. J. Heskett, T. Jones, G. Loveman, E. Sasser, and
L. Schlesinger, "Putting the Service-Profit Chain to
Work," *Harvard Business Review* 86 (July–August
2008): 118–129.

47. L. L. Berry and A. Parasuraman, "Listening to
the Customer—The Concept of a Service-Quality
Information System," *Sloan Management Review* 38,
no. 3 (Spring 1997): 65; C. W. L. Hart, J. L. Heskett,
and W. E. Sasser, Jr., "The Profitable Art of Service
Recovery," *Harvard Business Review* (July–August
1990): 148–156.

48. A. L. Rodgers, "A 5-Point Plan for Making the
Most of Customer Complaints," *Inc.*, January 14,
2014, accessed June 25, 2014, http://www.inc.com
/the-build-network/a-5-point-plan-for-making-the
-most-of-customer-complaints.html.

49. "Great Customer Service from the Mission
Bicycle Company," *37signals.com*, August 16, 2011,
accessed April 9, 2012, http://37signals.com/svn
/posts/2989-great-customer-service-from-the
-mission-bicycle-company.

50. D. E. Bowen and E. E. Lawler III, "The
Empowerment of Service Workers: What, Why, How,
and When," *Sloan Management Review* 33 (Spring
1992): 31–39; D. E. Bowen and E. E. Lawler III,
"Empowering Service Employees," *Sloan Management Review* 36 (Summer 1995): 73–84.

51. Bowen and Lawler, "The Empowerment of
Service Workers: What, Why, How, and When."

52. J. Shelly, "Empowering Employees," *Human
Resource Executive*, October 2, 2011, accessed April
9, 2012, http://www.hreonline.com/HRE/view/story
.jhtml?id=533341639.

53. "Customer Service and Business Results: A Survey of Customer Service from Mid-Size Companies,"
ZenDesk, April 2013, accessed July 28, 2014, http://
cdn.zendesk.com/resources/whitepapers/Zendesk
_WP_Customer_Service_and_Business_Results.pdf.

54. B. Gruel and S. Singh, "Deere's Big Green Profit
Machine," *Bloomberg Businessweek*, July 5, 2012, accessed June 23, 2013, http://www.businessweek.com
/articles/2012-07-05/deeres-big-green-profit-machine.

55. J. Rockoff, "Drug Making Breaks Away from Its
Old Ways," *Wall Street Journal*, February 8, 2015,
accessed May 11, 2015, http://www.wsj.com/articles
/drug-making-breaks-away-from-its-old-ways
-1423444049.

56. Ibid.

57. D. Lavrinc, "Peek Inside Tesla's Robotic Factory," *Wired*, July 16, 2013, accessed June 25, 2014,
http://www.wired.com/2013/07/tesla-plant-video/.

58. "Job Shop Hits Bull's Eye with Multitasking,"
Manufacturing Engineering (November 2008):
43–105.

59. Unfortunately, inventory issues are hurting fast
growing retailer, Restoration Hardware (RH), which
sells high-end furniture. Customers purchasing a
$4,800 desk are waiting 7 months for delivery. The
wait for a $1,260 lamp is 2.5 months. RH argues
that many of its expensive items are custom made,
and thus take longer to manufacture and ship.
However, analysts at BB&T Capital found that 29
of 50 non-customized RH items were out of stock,
with with an average delivery of 63 days. In an age
of free 2-day shipping from most major retailers, RH
customers are unhappy about the delays. With more
than 90% of its items now in stock, RH is making
progress. But, it's inability to manage inventory has
contributed to a 22% decline in profits.

60. H. Dreier, "McDonald's Runs Out of French
Fries in Venezuela," Yahoo News (Associated Press),
January 6, 2015, accessed May 11, 2015, http://
news.yahoo.com/mcdonalds-runs-french-fries
-venezuela-172701168.html.

61. D. Drickhamer, "Reality Check," *Industry Week*,
November 2001, 29.

62. "Paccar Inc., Efficiency Comparisons," CSIMarket, accessed May 6, 2016, http://csimarket.com
/stocks/PCAR-Efficiency-Comparisons.html; "GM's
Management Effectiveness versus its Competition,"
CSIMarket, accessed May 6, 2016, http://csimarket
.com/stocks/competitionNO6.php?code=GM.

63. J. Zeiler, "The Need for Speed," *Operations &
Fulfillment*, April 1, 2004, 38.

64. "Efficient Foodservice Response (EFR)," accessed August 3, 2009, http://www.ifdaonline.org
/webarticles.

65. J. R. Henry, "Minimized Setup Will Make Your
Packaging Line S.M.I.L.E.," *Packaging Technology &
Engineering*, February 1, 1998, 24.

66. M. McFadden, "Global Outsourcing of Aircraft
Maintenance," *Journal of Aviation Technology and
Engineering*, 1 no 2 (2012): 63–73.

67. K. Clark, "An Eagle Eye for Inventory," *Chain
Store Age*, May 2005, Supplement, 8A.

68. "The Way I Work: Marc Lore of Diapers.com,"
Inc., September 1, 2009, accessed March 15, 2010,
http://www.inc.com/magazine/20090901/the-way-i
-work-marc-lore-of-diaperscom.html.

69. E. Powell, Jr., and F. Sahin, "Economic Production Lot Sizing with Periodic Costs and Overtime,"
Decision Sciences 32 (2001): 423–452.

70. Apple Inc's Management Effectiveness Versus
Its Competition, CSIMarket, accessed May 6,
2016, http://csimarket.com/stocks/competitionNO6.
php?code=AAPL; 63. Press Release, "Gartner Announces Rankings of Its 2015 Supply Chain Top 25,"
May 14, 2015, accessed May 6, 2016, http://www
.gartner.com/newsroom/id/3053118.

71. N. Shirouzu, "Why Toyota Wins Such High
Marks on Quality Surveys," *Wall Street Journal*,
March 15, 2001, A1.

72. Ibid.

73. G. Gruman, "Supply on Demand; Manufacturers Need to Know What's Selling Before They Can
Produce and Deliver Their Wares in the Right Quantities," *InfoWorld*, April 18, 2005, accessed April 15,
2009, http://www.infoworld.com/article/2669692
/database/supply-on-demand.html.

Index

A

AB InBev, 40, 185–186
ABC Fine Wine & Spirits, 233
Abercrombie & Fitch (A&F), 94
Ability, 276
AbleData, 265
ABM Industries, 125
Abrasiveness, in managers, 16
Absenteeism, 102
Absolute comparison, 104
Academic journals, 25
Academy of Management, 25
Academy of Management Perspectives, 25
Accenture, 54
Access and legitimacy paradigm, 268–269
Accommodative strategy, 88
Accurate information, 367
Ace Hardware, 118, 119
Acer Group, 47
Achievement-oriented leadership, 308
Acorda Therapeutics, 249
Acquisitions, 122
Acroyoga studio, 219
Action plans, 96
Active listening, 334
Adaptability, 62
Adaptability screening, 178
Adaptive strategies, 130–131
Additive manufacturing, 203
Adequate capital, 34
Adequate manpower, 34
Adidas, 61
Adidas AG, 124
"The Administration of Big Business," 34
Administrative ability, 4
Administrative management, 32–33
Administrative Science Quarterly, 25
Adobe, 242
Adobe's Flash software, 142
Advanced Technology and Projects (ATAP), 146
Adverse impact, 226
Advertising agency, departmentalization, 182
Advertising budget, 34
Advocacy groups, 56–57
Adworkshop, 248
A&E Network, 333
Affective conflict, 108, 213
Affiliation, 277
Affirmative action, 256–257
African Americans
    as CEOs, 263
    population, 255
    turnover rates for, 257
African Free Trade Zone Agreement (AFTZ), 161
Agarwal, Ritesh, 6
Age, changing demographics in, 255
Age discrimination, 259–261
Age Discrimination in Employment Act (1967), 259
Aggressive behavior, 71
Agnefjall, Peter, 386
Agreeableness, 266
Agricultural work, 23
Air ambulances, 87
Air France-KLM, 134, 135
Air Methods, 87
AirAsia Japan, 116
Airbnb, 98, 131, 372

Airbus, 3
Airline industry, 46–47, 116
AirTran Airways, 47, 82
Alaska Airlines, 392, 393
Aldi, 117
Al-Farabi, 24
Alibaba, 299
All Nippon Airways (ANA), 116
Allaire, Jeremy, 142
Allaire, Paul A., 272
Allen, Doug, 93
Allen, Michael, 88
Alliance for Wireless Power (A4WP), 140
Allstate, 231
Aloha, 219
Aloof personality, 16–17
Altos Research, 127
"Always Getting Better" campaign, 65
Amazon, 66, 113, 125, 134, 135, 189, 199, 212
Amazon Firefly app, 135
Amazon Home Services, 125
Amazon Instant Video, 54
Amazon Kindle Fire, 113
Amazon Video, 134
Amazon Web Services (AWS), 127, 189
Ambitious, managers being overly, 17
American Airlines, 46, 47
American Civil Rights, 257
American College of Cardiologists, 133
American Electric Power, 98
American Heart Association, 133
American Society of Mechanical Engineers, 28
Amirshahi, Bobby, 3–4
Ammann, Daniel, 174
AMP, 179
Analyzers, 131
Anand, P., 75
Ancient Egypt, 23
Ancient Sumer, 23
Anderson, Heather, 53
Andreessen, Mark, 62
Andreessen Horowitz (AH), 61–62
Andres, Mike, 191
Android devices, 113, 114
Angie's List, 125
Anthes, G., 353
Antibiotic-free livestock, 89
Antivirus software, 377
Aon Hewitt, 102
APEC (Asia-Pacific Economic Cooperation), 161, 162, 163
Apparel industry, 172
AppDynamics, 231
Apple, 45, 46, 54, 55, 56, 61, 65, 87, 88, 113, 115, 131, 142, 145, 148, 190, 214
Apple App Store, 114
Apple iTunes, 54
Apple Mac personal computers, 114
Apple Maps, 115
Apple Music, 134
Apple Pencil, 113
Apple TV, 54
Apple Watch, 131
Applicant selection, changing company culture and, 65–66
Application forms and résumés, 231–232
Aptitude tests, 234
Arnold, Chris, 89
Arrivers, 16
Arrogance, in managers, 16–17
Artman, Tuomas, 152

ASCII (American Standard Code for Information Interchange), 372
Asda, 357
ASEAN (Association of Southeast Asian Nations), 161, 162, 163
Ashkenas, R., 37
Ashton-Martin, 130
Asian airlines, 258
Asian Americans
    as CEOs, 263
    population, 255
Asia-Pacific Economic Cooperation (APEC), 161, 163
Assemble-to-order operation, 396
Assessment centers, 236
Assistive technology, 265
Association of Southeast Asian Nations (ASEAN), 161, 163
Association or affinity patterns, 373
Asus, 47
Atos, 333
AT&T, 16–17, 125, 134, 140, 208
Attack, 134
Attention, 321
Attribution theory, 323
Atwater, E., 335
A-type conflict, 108–109, 213
Aubrey, A., 88
Audi, 131
Audi Group, 206
Authentication, 374
Authority. *See also* Organizational authority
    acceptance of, 38
    defined, 188
    in Fayol's fourteen principles of management, 33
    necessities of management, 34
Authority-compliance leadership, 301
Authorization, 374
Auto advertisements, 127
Autocratic decisions, 310
Autodesk, 334
Automobile industry, 127
Autonomy, 194, 206, 207
Average aggregate inventory, 400
Avis, 247
Avoidance, 288
Avoidance strategy, 173
Avon, 99, 116
AvtoVaz, 6
Awareness training, 271
Axe, 86
Axis Performance Advisors, 208

B

Baby Jogger strollers, 122
Bachelder, Cheryl, 301
"Back porch vista," 63
Background checks, 233
Backpacks, 5
Badstübner, Achim, 206
Bain & Company, 40
Balance sheets, 352
Balanced scorecard, 352
Baldrige Performance Excellence Program, 391–392
Bales, Suzanne, 331
Ball canning jars, 122
Bandwidth Consulting, 54
Bank Wiring Room, 38
Bar codes, 371
Bar Raisers, 66
Barbarigo, 24

Barclays Plc, 126
Bargaining power of buyers, 128
Bargaining power of suppliers, 128
Barnard, Chester, 34, 38
Barnes, Dave, 128
Barnes & Noble's Nook, 113
Barney, J. B., 366
Barwick, K. D., 97
Base fines, 72
Batch production, 398
Bayod, Marion, 166
BCG matrix, 122
Beauchamp, Katia, 6
Beccari, Pietro, 11
Beck, Vicki Dobbs, 218
Becoming a Manager: Mastery of a New Identity (Hill), 17
Beer market, 52
Behavior
    change after training, 241
    establishing new patterns of, 64–65
Behavior control, 348
Behavior observation scale (BOS), 242
Behavioral addition, 64–65
Behavioral substitution, 64–65
"Being Nicer" campaign, 65
Bell, Alexander Graham, 143
Belongingness, 277
Benchmarking, 118, 344
Berg, Natalie, 94
Berger, Ron, 56
Bergh, Chip, 145
Berkenstock, Dan, 58
Berkshire Hathaway, 121
Bernard, Suzanne, 177
Berning, Mel, 333
Bernstein, Elizabeth, 111
BestBuy, 135, 148
Beta testing process, 181
Betraying a trust, 17
Beurden, Ben van, 153
Bezos, Jeff, 66, 189, 212, 300, 301
Biases, hiring, 262
Big Bazaar, 173
Big Mac Index, 172
Bill of materials, 404
Bilotta, J. G., 214
Bing, 177
Biodata, 235
Biographical data. *See* **Biodata**
Birchbox, 6
Bishop, Toby, 267
Biying, 177
BlackBerry, 45
Blacklist, 167
Blake/Mouton leadership grid, 302
Blaze, 131
Blind hiring, 262
Blinded stage, 149
Blog, 340
Bloomberg Business Week, 78
Bloomberg Financial, 127
"Blue box" device, 148
Blu-ray, 140
BMW, 131
Bock, Laszlo, 4
Boeing, 13, 147, 208, 258
Bogut, Andrew, 212
Bohnet, Iris, 272
Bolsinger, Lorraine, 144, 152
Bona fide occupational qualification (BFOQ), 224
Bonner, James, 369
Booking.com, 131
Bortunk, Shmuli, 200

A GUIDE FOR NEW MANAGERS: SIX STEPS TO BECOME A SUCCESSFUL MANAGER
—ED MUZIO

If you've recently been hired as a manager, you know the dirty secret: Management positions come with surprisingly little guidance. Whether you were promoted internally or brought in from outside, you were probably expected to hit the ground running, toward only the vaguest of goals.

Many of the problems new managers experience stem from that secret. They are faced with an ill-defined job and equally intense pressure from above and below. Plus, as the pivot points in the information revolution, they are barraged with queries about the work of their groups.

It's easy to see why capable, well-meaning managers resort to micromanagement, detachment, grandstanding, or sheer blockheadedness in an effort to find some sort of stability for themselves and their employees.

How can you avoid these pitfalls? The following six steps will help you define your purpose as manager:

1. DEFINE YOUR OWN JOB CLEARLY.

If you're a new manager, this is your first and most important step. You need a memorable, meaningful definition, something that you can figuratively (or literally) write across your bathroom mirror so that you see it every morning.

I suggest "engender useful output." Your primary responsibility as a manager is to maximize the likelihood that your employees will be productive; your task is to create an environment in which employee output is clearly defined and realistically achievable. If you're not doing that, then it doesn't matter what data you're gathering, which employees you're monitoring, or whose ear you're bending. You may be busy, you may be stressed, and you may look managerial, but you're not doing your job.

2. DEFINE YOUR GROUP'S OUTPUT.

To engender output you must first define it. This task is easier said than done. Today's workplace changes quickly, and managers at all levels are expected to turn the work of their groups on a dime. Your own manager may not be terribly clear on long range company plans, so neither of you may fully understand how the work of your group will change in the next quarter, month, or even week.

Uncertainty about the future is not an excuse for lack of productivity in the present. If your plan is to wait around until everything is known before doing anything, you might as well lock the doors and go home for good! Things will change again and again, and only by delivering on current plans will you and your company learn what works, and what changes to make next. Besides, the definition of your group's required output is the definition of YOUR required output as manager. Defining it is one part good management practice and one part career survival.

3. SEEK MOMENTARY CLARITY RATHER THAN PERMANENT ANSWERS.

Speak with your leaders about what your group can reasonably produce right now and then agree to task your group with producing it right now. Make it clear that unless you hear otherwise, until the next scheduled check-in you will follow the current plan. Then, verbally summarize the output you are committing to engender in about 90 seconds. During follow-up discussions with your management, use that mini-commercial as a way to gently remind them what you are working on so that they can edit your understanding if needed.

When changes, do come, don't fight them. Welcome the new information, openly revise your understanding of what you need to produce, and clearly explain the time and resources you need to accomplish the change. If you can't turn the boat in an hour, say so. It's far better to be up front when something isn't possible than to agree to it under duress but fail to deliver.

4. BECOME AN EXPERT IN DEFINING AND COMMUNICATING EXPECTATIONS.

Of course, your definition is only half the story. To engender output from your group, you need to convert from the commitment you made as manager into what each of your employees must do individually.

Contrary to popular opinion, this doesn't mean telling your employees what to do. It means teaching them to discuss what they are doing themselves—to create their own 90-second mini-commercials—and then working with them on a shared understanding of what's needed. You haven't successfully taught an employee his or her expected output until you hear that person say it to you spontaneously, in a way that matches your own understanding. Then you know it's happening.

This also means your employees must be in the habit of speaking openly about what they are doing. To get honesty, avoid using discussions about current objectives as pop quizzes! When you need to adjust an employee's understanding of his or her work, frame your conversation as being about expectations for the future and defining how to succeed. Don't let it degrade into how the employee should already know these things. Remember: When your employees don't know what they're supposed to be doing, it's at least as likely to be your fault as theirs.

5. KEEP TALKING ABOUT OUTPUT.

A VSO, or *verbalized summary objective statement*, is a kind of mini-commercial in which you state the output you're trying to deliver at the moment. It should take about 90 seconds and should list about 5–7 output goals that together cover about 80% of what you are working on. It's yours to change, adjust, and modify whenever you see fit. It's also yours to use as your introduction whenever you're talking to people in or about your workplace. Use VSOs with your management and teach your employees to use them with you.

Why? Your VSO trains people as to what to expect—and not expect—from you. It provides an avenue for a manager to edit an employee's understanding of the job, and a basis for you to accept or decline requests for additional work. As time goes by, and you deliver on your VSO, you also increase your credibility within the organization as people see that you are following through on your commitments.

6. KEEP AT IT.

Management is like exercise: it's often difficult, you're never done, and it requires self-discipline.

Get in the habit of having conversations with superiors about the output needed from your group and discussions with your employees about their individual contributions to that output. Then remind yourself that your job is to maximize the chances that your employees will produce. This won't make management easy, but it's the first step in making you better at it.

AUTHOR BIO

Edward G. Muzio, CEO of Group Harmonics, is the author of the award winning books *Make Work Great: Supercharge Your Team, Reinvent the Culture, and Gain Influence One Person at a Time* and *Four Secrets to Liking Your Work: You May Not Need to Quit to Get the Job You Want*. An expert in workplace improvement and its relationship to individual enjoyment, Muzio has been featured on Fox Business Network, CBS, and other national media. For more information visit *Make Work Great* and follow the author on Facebook.

N

CHAPTER 1 LEARNING OUTCOMES / KEY TERMS

1-1 **Describe what management is.** Good management is working through others to accomplish tasks that help fulfill organizational objectives as efficiently as possible.

Management getting work done through others (p. 3)

Efficiency getting work done with a minimum of effort, expense, or waste (p. 3)

Effectiveness accomplishing tasks that help fulfill organizational objectives (p. 3)

1-2 **Explain the four functions of management.** Henri Fayol's classic management functions are known today as planning, organizing, leading, and controlling. Planning is determining organizational goals and a means for achieving them. Organizing is deciding where decisions will be made, who will do what jobs and tasks, and who will work for whom. Leading is inspiring and motivating workers to work hard to achieve organizational goals. Controlling is monitoring progress toward goal achievement and taking corrective action when needed. Studies show that performing the management functions well leads to better managerial performance.

Planning determining organizational goals and a means for achieving them (p. 5)

Organizing deciding where decisions will be made, who will do what jobs and tasks, and who will work for whom (p. 5)

Leading inspiring and motivating workers to work hard to achieve organizational goals (p. 5)

Controlling monitoring progress toward goal achievement and taking corrective action when needed (p. 6)

1-3 **Describe different kinds of managers.** There are four different kinds of managers. Top managers are responsible for creating a context for change, developing attitudes of commitment and ownership, creating a positive organizational culture through words and actions, and monitoring their companies' business environments. Middle managers are responsible for planning and allocating resources, coordinating and linking groups and departments, monitoring and managing the performance of subunits and managers, and implementing the changes or strategies generated by top managers. First-line managers are responsible for managing the performance of nonmanagerial employees, teaching entry-level employees how to do their jobs, and making detailed schedules and operating plans based on middle management's intermediate-range plans. Team leaders are responsible for facilitating team performance, fostering good relationships among team members, and managing external relationships.

Top managers executives responsible for the overall direction of the organization (p. 7)

Middle managers responsible for setting objectives consistent with top management's goals and for planning and implementing subunit strategies for achieving these objectives (p. 8)

First-line managers responsible for training and supervising the performance of nonmanagerial employees who are directly responsible for producing the company's products or services (p. 9)

Team leaders managers responsible for facilitating team activities toward goal accomplishment (p. 9)

1-4 **Explain the major roles and subroles that managers perform in their jobs.** Managers perform interpersonal, informational, and decisional roles in their jobs. In fulfilling interpersonal roles, managers act as figureheads by performing ceremonial duties, as leaders by motivating and encouraging workers, and as liaisons by dealing with people outside their units. In performing informational roles, managers act as monitors by scanning their environment for information, as disseminators by sharing information with others in their companies, and as spokespeople by sharing information with people outside their departments or companies. In fulfilling decisional roles, managers act as entrepreneurs by adapting their units to change, as disturbance handlers by responding to larger problems that demand immediate action, as resource allocators by deciding resource recipients and amounts, and as negotiators by bargaining with others about schedules, projects, goals, outcomes, and resources.

Figurehead role the interpersonal role managers play when they perform ceremonial duties (p. 11)

Leader role the interpersonal role managers play when they motivate and encourage workers to accomplish organizational objectives (p. 11)

Liaison role the interpersonal role managers play when they deal with people outside their units (p. 11)

Monitor role the informational role managers play when they scan their environment for information (p. 12)

Disseminator role the informational role managers play when they share information with others in their departments or companies (p. 12)

Spokesperson role the informational role managers play when they share information with people outside their departments or companies (p. 12)

Entrepreneur role the decisional role managers play when they adapt themselves, their subordinates, and their units to change (p. 13)

Disturbance handler role the decisional role managers play when they respond to severe pressures and problems that demand immediate action (p. 13)

Resource allocator role the decisional role managers play when they decide who gets what resources and in what amounts (p. 13)

Negotiator role the decisional role managers play when they negotiate schedules, projects, goals, outcomes, resources, and employee raises (p. 13)

1-5 **Explain what companies look for in managers.** Companies do not want one-dimensional managers. They want managers with a balance of skills. Managers need to have the knowledge and abilities to get the job done (technical skills), must be able to work effectively in groups and be good listeners and communicators (human skills), must be able to assess the relationships between the different parts of their companies and the external environment and position their companies for success (conceptual skills), and should want to assume positions of leadership and power (motivation to manage). Technical skills are most important for team leaders and lower-level managers, human skills are equally important at all levels of management, and conceptual skills as well as motivation to manage both increase in importance as managers rise through the managerial ranks.

Technical skills the specialized procedures, techniques, and knowledge required to get the job done (p. 14)

Human skills the ability to work well with others (p. 15)

Conceptual skills the ability to see the organization as a whole, understand how the different parts affect each other, and recognize how the company fits into or is affected by its environment (p. 15)

Motivation to manage an assessment of how enthusiastic employees are about managing the work of others (p. 15)

1-6 **Discuss the top mistakes that managers make in their jobs.** Another way to understand what it takes to be a manager is to look at the top mistakes managers make. Five of the most important mistakes made by managers are being abrasive and intimidating; being cold, aloof, or arrogant; betraying trust; being overly ambitious; and being unable to delegate, build a team, and staff effectively.

1-7 **Describe the transition that employees go through when they are promoted to management.** Managers often begin their jobs by using more formal authority and less people management skills. However, most managers find that being a manager has little to do with "bossing" their subordinates. According to a study of managers in their first year, after six months on the job, the managers were surprised by the fast pace and heavy workload and by the fact that "helping" their subordinates was viewed as interference. After a year on the job, most of the managers had come to think of themselves not as doers but as managers who get things done through others. And, because they finally realized that people management was the most important part of their job, most of them had abandoned their authoritarian approach for one based on communication, listening, and positive reinforcement.

Exhibit 1.6
Stages in the Transition to Management

MANAGERS' INITIAL EXPECTATIONS			AFTER SIX MONTHS AS A MANAGER			AFTER A YEAR AS A MANAGER					
JAN	FEB	MAR	APR	MAY	JUN	JUL	AUG	SEP	OCT	NOV	DEC

- ⊙ Be the boss
- ⊙ Formal authority
- ⊙ Manage tasks
- ⊙ Job is not managing people

- ⊙ Initial expectations were wrong
- ⊙ Fast pace
- ⊙ Heavy workload
- ⊙ Job is to be problem solver and troubleshooter for subordinates

- ⊙ No longer a doer
- ⊙ Communication, listening, and positive reinforcement
- ⊙ Learning to adapt to and control stress
- ⊙ Job is people development

Source: L.A. Hill, *Becoming a Manager: Mastery of a New Identity* (Boston: Harvard Business School Press, 1992).

1-8 **Explain how and why companies can create competitive advantage through people.** Why does management matter? Well-managed companies are competitive because their workforces are smarter, better trained, more motivated, and more committed. Furthermore, companies that practice good management consistently have greater sales revenues, profits, and stock market performance than companies that don't. Finally, good management matters because it leads to satisfied employees who, in turn, provide better service to customers. Because employees tend to treat customers the same way that their managers treat them, good management can improve customer satisfaction.

CHAPTER 2 LEARNING OUTCOMES / KEY TERMS

2-1 Explain the origins of management. Management as a field of study is just 125 years old, but management ideas and practices have actually been used since 5000 BCE. From ancient Sumer to sixteenth-century Europe, there are historical antecedents for each of the functions of management discussed in this textbook: planning, organizing, leading, and controlling. However, there was no compelling need for managers until systematic changes in the nature of work and organizations occurred during the past two centuries. As work shifted from families to factories; from skilled laborers to specialized, unskilled laborers; from small, self-organized groups to large factories employing thousands under one roof; and from unique, small batches of production to standardized mass production; managers were needed to impose order and structure, to motivate and direct large groups of workers, and to plan and make decisions that optimized overall performance by effectively coordinating the different parts of an organizational system.

2-2 Explain the history of scientific management. Scientific management involves studying and testing different work methods to identify the best, most efficient way to complete a job. According to Frederick W. Taylor, the father of scientific management, managers should follow four scientific management principles. First, study each element of work to determine the one best way to do it. Second, scientifically select, train, teach, and develop workers to reach their full potential. Third, cooperate with employees to ensure that the scientific principles are implemented. Fourth, divide the work and the responsibility equally between management and workers. Above all, Taylor believed these principles could be used to align managers and employees by determining a fair day's work (what an average worker could produce at a reasonable pace) and a fair day's pay (what management should pay workers for that effort). Taylor believed that incentives were one of the best ways to align management and employees.

Frank and Lillian Gilbreth are best known for their use of motion studies to simplify work. Whereas Taylor used time study to determine a fair day's work based on how long it took a "first-class man" to complete each part of his job, Frank Gilbreth used motion-picture films and microchronometers to conduct motion studies to improve efficiency by eliminating unnecessary or repetitive motions. Henry Gantt is best known for the Gantt chart, which graphically indicates when a series of tasks must be completed in order to complete a job or project, but he also developed ideas regarding worker training, specifically, that all workers should be trained and their managers should be rewarded for training them.

Scientific management thoroughly studying and testing different work methods to identify the best, most efficient way to complete a job (p. 25)

Soldiering when workers deliberately slow their pace or restrict their work output (p. 25)

Rate buster a group member whose work pace is significantly faster than the normal pace in his or her group (p. 26)

Motion study breaking each task or job into its separate motions and then eliminating those that are unnecessary or repetitive (p. 28)

Time study timing how long it takes good workers to complete each part of their jobs (p. 28)

Gantt chart a graphical chart that shows which tasks must be completed at which times in order to complete a project or task (p. 29)

2-3 Discuss the history of bureaucratic and administrative management. Today, we associate bureaucracy with inefficiency and red tape. Yet German sociologist Max Weber thought that bureaucracy—that is, running organizations on the basis of knowledge, fairness, and logical rules and procedures—would accomplish organizational goals much more efficiently than monarchies and patriarchies, where decisions were based on personal or family connections, personal gain, and arbitrary decision making. Bureaucracies are characterized by seven elements: qualification-based hiring; merit-based promotion; chain of command; division of labor; impartial application of rules and procedures; recording rules, procedures, and decisions in writing; and separating managers from owners. Nonetheless, bureaucracies are often inefficient and can be highly resistant to change.

The Frenchman Henri Fayol, whose ideas were shaped by his more than twenty years of experience as a CEO, is best known for developing five management functions (planning, organizing, coordinating, commanding, and controlling) and fourteen principles of management (division of work, authority and responsibility, discipline, unity of command, unity of direction, subordination of individual interests to the general interest, remuneration, centralization, scalar chain, order, equity, stability of tenure of personnel, initiative, and *esprit de corps*).

Bureaucracy the exercise of control on the basis of knowledge, expertise, or experience (p. 30)

2-4 Explain the history of human relations management. Unlike most people who view conflict as bad, Mary Parker Follett believed that it should be embraced rather than avoided. Of the three ways of dealing with conflict—domination, compromise, and integration—she argued that the latter was the best because it focuses on developing creative methods for meeting conflicting parties' needs.

Elton Mayo is best known for his role in the Hawthorne Studies at the Western Electric Company. In the first stage of the Hawthorne Studies, production went up because both the increased attention paid to the workers in the study and their development into a cohesive work group led to significantly higher levels of job satisfaction and productivity. In the second stage, productivity dropped because the workers had already developed strong negative norms. The Hawthorne Studies demonstrated that workers' feelings and attitudes affect their work, that financial incentives aren't necessarily the most important motivator for workers, and that group norms and behavior play a critical role in behavior at work.

Chester Barnard, president of New Jersey Bell Telephone, emphasized the critical importance of willing cooperation in organizations. In general, Barnard argued that people will be indifferent to managerial directives or orders if they (1) are understood, (2) are consistent with the purpose of the organization, (3) are compatible with the people's personal interests, and (4) can actually be carried out by those people. Acceptance of managerial authority (that is, cooperation) is not automatic, however.

Domination an approach to dealing with conflict in which one party satisfies its desires and objectives at the expense of the other party's desires and objectives (p. 35)

Compromise an approach to dealing with conflict in which both parties give up some of what they want in order to reach agreement on a plan to reduce or settle the conflict (p. 35)

Integrative conflict resolution an approach to dealing with conflict in which both parties indicate their preferences and then work together to find an alternative that meets the needs of both (p. 35)

Organization a system of consciously coordinated activities or forces created by two or more people (p. 38)

2-5 **Discuss the history of operations, information, systems, and contingency management.** Operations management uses a quantitative or mathematical approach to find ways to increase productivity, improve quality, and manage or reduce costly inventories. The manufacture of standardized, interchangeable parts; the graphical and computerized design of parts; and the accidental discovery of just-in-time inventory systems were some of the most important historical events in operations management.

Throughout history, organizations have pushed for and quickly adopted new information technologies that reduce the cost or increase the speed with which they can acquire, store, retrieve, or communicate information. Historically, some of the most important technologies that have revolutionized information management were the invention of machines to produce pulp for paper and the printing press in the fourteenth and fifteenth centuries,

the manual typewriter in 1850, the telephone in the 1880s, the personal computer in the 1980s, and the Internet in the 1990s.

A system is a set of interrelated elements or parts (subsystems) that function as a whole. Organizational systems obtain inputs from both general and specific environments. Managers and workers then use their management knowledge and manufacturing techniques to transform those inputs into outputs that, in turn, provide feedback to the organization. Organizational systems must also address the issues of synergy and open versus closed systems.

Finally, the contingency approach to management clearly states that there are no universal management theories. The most effective management theory or idea depends on the kinds of problems or situations that managers or organizations are facing at a particular time. This means that management is much harder than it looks.

System a set of interrelated elements or parts that function as a whole (p. 41)

Subsystems smaller systems that operate within the context of a larger system (p. 41)

Synergy when two or more subsystems working together can produce more than they can working apart (p. 41)

Closed systems systems that can sustain themselves without interacting with their environments (p. 41)

Open systems systems that can sustain themselves only by interacting with their environments, on which they depend for their survival (p. 41)

Contingency approach holds that there are no universal management theories and that the most effective management theory or idea depends on the kinds of problems or situations that managers are facing at a particular time and place (p. 43)

Exhibit 2.7
Systems View of Organizations

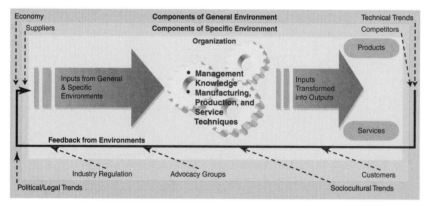

CHAPTER 3 LEARNING OUTCOMES / KEY TERMS

3-1 **Discuss how changing environments affect organizations.** Environmental change, environmental complexity, and resource scarcity are the basic components of external environments. Environmental change is the rate of variation in a company's general and specific environments. Environmental complexity is the number and intensity of factors in the external environment. Resource scarcity is the abundance or shortage of critical resources in the external environment. As the rate of environmental change increases, as the environment becomes more complex, and as resources become more scarce, managers become less confident that they can understand, predict, and effectively react to the trends affecting their businesses. According to punctuated equilibrium theory, companies experience long periods of stability followed by short periods of dynamic, fundamental change, followed by a return to stability.

External environments all events outside a company that have the potential to influence or affect it (p. 45)

Environmental change the rate at which a company's general and specific environments change (p. 45)

Stable environment an environment in which the rate of change is slow (p. 45)

Dynamic environment an environment in which the rate of change is fast (p. 45)

Punctuated equilibrium theory the theory that companies go through long periods of stability (equilibrium), followed by short periods of dynamic, fundamental change (revolutionary periods), and then a new equilibrium (p. 46)

Environmental complexity the number and the intensity of external factors in the environment that affect organizations (p. 47)

Simple environment an environment with few environmental factors (p. 47)

Complex environment an environment with many environmental factors (p. 47)

Resource scarcity the abundance or shortage of critical organizational resources in an organization's external environment (p. 47)

Uncertainty extent to which managers can understand or predict which environmental changes and trends will affect their businesses (p. 48)

3-2 **Describe the four components of the general environment.** The general environment consists of trends that affect all organizations. Because the economy influences basic business decisions, managers often use economic statistics and business confidence indices to predict future economic activity. Changes in technology, which transforms inputs into outputs, can be a benefit or a threat to a business. Sociocultural trends, such as changing demographic characteristics, affect how companies staff their businesses. Similarly, sociocultural changes in behavior, attitudes, and beliefs affect the demand for businesses' products and services. Court decisions and new federal and state laws have imposed much greater political/legal responsibility on companies. The best way to manage legal responsibilities is to educate managers and employees about laws and regulations as well as potential lawsuits that could affect a business.

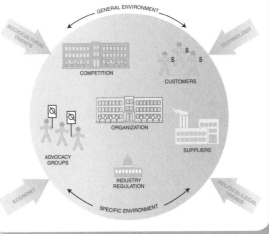

Exhibit 3.2
General and Specific Environments

General environment the economic, technological, sociocultural, and political/legal trends that indirectly affect all organizations (p. 49)

Specific environment the customers, competitors, suppliers, industry regulations, and advocacy groups that are unique to an industry and directly affect how a company does business (p. 49)

Business confidence indices indices that show managers' level of confidence about future business growth (p. 51)

Technology the knowledge, tools, and techniques used to transform inputs into outputs (p. 51)

3-3 **Explain the five components of the specific environment.** The specific environment is made up of five components: customers, competitors, suppliers, industry regulations, and advocacy groups. Companies can monitor customers' needs by identifying customer problems after they occur or by anticipating problems before they occur. Because they tend to focus on well-known competitors, managers often underestimate their competition or do a poor job of identifying future competitors. Suppliers and buyers are very dependent on each other, and that dependence sometimes leads to opportunistic behavior in which one party benefits at the expense of the other. Regulatory agencies affect businesses by creating rules and then enforcing them. Advocacy groups cannot regulate organizations' practices. Nevertheless, through public communications, media advocacy, and product boycotts, they try to convince companies to change their practices.

Competitors companies in the same industry that sell similar products or services to customers (p. 53)

Competitive analysis a process for monitoring the competition that involves identifying competition, anticipating their moves, and determining their strengths and weaknesses (p. 53)

Suppliers companies that provide material, human, financial, and informational resources to other companies (p. 54)

Supplier dependence the degree to which a company relies on a supplier because of the importance of the supplier's product to the company and the difficulty of finding other sources of that product (p. 54)

Buyer dependence the degree to which a supplier relies on a buyer because of the importance of that buyer to the supplier and the difficulty of finding other buyers for its products (p. 55)

Opportunistic behavior a transaction in which one party in the relationship benefits at the expense of the other (p. 55)

Relationship behavior the establishment of mutually beneficial, long-term exchanges between buyers and suppliers (p. 56)

Industry regulation regulations and rules that govern the business practices and procedures of specific industries, businesses, and professions (p. 56)

Advocacy groups concerned citizens who band together to try to influence the business practices of specific industries, businesses, and professions (p. 56)

Public communications an advocacy group tactic that relies on voluntary participation by the news media and the advertising industry to get the advocacy group's message out (p. 56)

Media advocacy an advocacy group tactic that involves framing issues as public issues; exposing questionable, exploitative, or unethical practices; and forcing media coverage by buying media time or creating controversy that is likely to receive extensive news coverage (p. 57)

Product boycott an advocacy group tactic that involves protesting a company's actions by persuading consumers not to purchase its product or service (p. 57)

3-4 **Describe the process that companies use to make sense of their changing environments.** Managers use a three-step process to make sense of external environments: environmental scanning, interpreting information, and acting on threats and opportunities. Managers scan their environments in order to keep up to date on factors influencing their industries, to reduce uncertainty, and to detect potential problems. When managers identify environmental events as threats, they take steps to protect their companies from harm. When managers identify environmental events as opportunities, they formulate alternatives for taking advantage of them to improve company performance. Using cognitive maps can help managers visually summarize the relationships between environmental factors and the actions they might take to deal with them.

Environmental scanning searching the environment for important events or issues that might affect an organization (p. 58)

Cognitive maps graphic depictions of how managers believe environmental factors relate to possible organizational actions (p. 60)

3-5 **Explain how organizational cultures are created and how they can help companies be successful.** Organizational culture is the set of key values, beliefs, and attitudes shared by members of an organization. Organizational cultures are often created by company founders and then sustained through repetition of organizational stories and recognition of organizational heroes. Companies with adaptable cultures that promote employee involvement, make clear the organization's strategic purpose and direction, and actively define and teach organizational values and beliefs can achieve higher sales growth, return on assets, profits, quality, and employee satisfaction. Organizational cultures exist on three levels: the surface level, where visible artifacts and behaviors can be observed; just below the surface, where values and beliefs are expressed; and deep below the surface, where unconsciously held assumptions and beliefs exist. Managers can begin to change company cultures by focusing on the top two levels. Techniques for changing organizational cultures include using behavioral substitution and behavioral addition, changing visible artifacts, and selecting job applicants who have values and beliefs consistent with the desired company culture.

Internal environment the events and trends inside an organization that affect management, employees, and organizational culture (p. 61)

Organizational culture the values, beliefs, and attitudes shared by organizational members (p. 61)

Organizational stories stories told by organizational members to make sense of organizational events and changes and to emphasize culturally consistent assumptions, decisions, and actions (p. 61)

Organizational heroes people celebrated for their qualities and achievements within an organization (p. 62)

Company mission a company's purpose or reason for existing (p. 62)

Consistent organizational culture a company culture in which the company actively defines and teaches organizational values, beliefs, and attitudes (p. 63)

Behavioral addition the process of having managers and employees perform new behaviors that are central to and symbolic of the new organizational culture that a company wants to create (p. 64)

Behavioral substitution the process of having managers and employees perform new behaviors central to the new organizational culture in place of behaviors that were central to the old organizational culture (p. 64)

Visible artifacts visible signs of an organization's culture, such as the office design and layout, company dress code, and company benefits and perks, such as stock options, personal parking spaces, or the private company dining room (p. 65)

4

CHAPTER 4 LEARNING OUTCOMES / KEY TERMS

4-1

Identify common kinds of workplace deviance. Ethics is the set of moral principles or values that define right and wrong. Workplace deviance is behavior that violates organizational norms about right and wrong and harms the organization or its workers.

There are four different types of workplace deviance. Production deviance and property deviance harm the company, whereas political deviance and personal aggression harm individuals within the company.

Ethics the set of moral principles or values that defines right and wrong for a person or group (p. 69)

Ethical behavior behavior that conforms to a society's accepted principles of right and wrong (p. 69)

Workplace deviance unethical behavior that violates organizational norms about right and wrong (p. 70)

Production deviance unethical behavior that hurts the quality and quantity of work produced (p. 70)

Property deviance unethical behavior aimed at the organization's property or products (p. 70)

Employee shrinkage employee theft of company merchandise (p. 71)

Political deviance using one's influence to harm others in the company (p. 71)

Personal aggression hostile or aggressive behavior toward others (p. 71)

4-2

Describe the U.S. Sentencing Commission Guidelines for Organizations, and explain how they both encourage ethical behavior and punish unethical behavior by businesses. Under the U.S. Sentencing Commission guidelines, companies can be prosecuted and fined up to $600 million for employees' illegal actions. Fines are computed by multiplying the base fine by a culpability score. Companies that establish compliance programs to encourage ethical behavior can reduce their culpability scores and their fines.

4-3

Describe what influences ethical decision making. Three factors influence ethical decisions: the ethical intensity of the decision, the moral development of the manager, and the ethical principles used to solve the problem. Ethical intensity is high when decisions have large, certain, immediate consequences and when the decision maker is physically or psychologically close to those affected by the decision. There are three levels of moral development. At the preconventional level, decisions are made for selfish reasons. At the conventional level, decisions conform to societal expectations. At the postconventional level, internalized principles are used to make ethical decisions. Each of these levels has two stages. Managers can use a number of different principles when making ethical decisions: long-term self-interest, religious injunctions, government requirements, individual rights, personal virtue, distributive justice, and utilitarian benefits.

Ethical intensity the degree of concern people have about an ethical issue (p. 74)

Magnitude of consequences the total harm or benefit derived from an ethical decision (p. 75)

Social consensus agreement on whether behavior is bad or good (p. 75)

Probability of effect the chance that something will happen that results in harm to others (p. 75)

Temporal immediacy the time between an act and the consequences the act produces (p. 75)

Proximity of effect the social, psychological, cultural, or physical distance between a decision maker and those affected by his or her decisions (p. 75)

Concentration of effect the total harm or benefit that an act produces on the average person (p. 75)

Preconventional level of moral development the first level of moral development, in which people make decisions based on selfish reasons (p. 76)

Conventional level of moral development the second level of moral development, in which people make decisions that conform to societal expectation (p. 76)

Postconventional level of moral development the third level of moral development, in which people make decisions based on internalized principles (p. 76)

Principle of long-term self-interest an ethical principle that holds that you should never take any action that is not in your or your organization's long-term self-interest (p. 77)

Principle of religious injunctions an ethical principle that holds that you should never take any action that is not kind and that does not build a sense of community (p. 77)

Principle of government requirements an ethical principle that holds that you should never take any action that violates the law, for the law represents the minimal moral standard (p. 77)

Principle of individual rights an ethical principle that holds that you should never take any action that infringes on others' agreed-upon rights (p. 77)

Principle of personal virtue an ethical principle that holds that you should never do anything that is not honest, open, and truthful and that you would not be glad to see reported in the newspapers or on TV (p. 77)

Principle of distributive justice an ethical principle that holds that you should never take any action that harms the least fortunate among us: the poor, the uneducated, the unemployed (p. 78)

Principle of utilitarian benefits an ethical principle that holds that you should never take any action that does not result in greater good for society (p. 78)

4-4 **Explain what practical steps managers can take to improve ethical decision making.** Employers can increase their chances of hiring ethical employees by testing all job applicants. Most large companies now have corporate codes of ethics. In addition to offering general rules, ethics codes must also provide specific, practical advice. Ethics training seeks to increase employees' awareness of ethical issues; make ethics a serious, credible factor in organizational decisions; and teach employees a practical model of ethical decision making. The most important factors in creating an ethical business climate are the personal examples set by company managers, the involvement of management in the company ethics program, a reporting system that encourages whistle-blowers to report potential ethics violations, and fair but consistent punishment of violators.

Overt integrity test a written test that estimates job applicants' honesty by directly asking them what they think or feel about theft or about punishment of unethical behaviors (p. 79)

Personality-based integrity test a written test that indirectly estimates job applicants' honesty by measuring psychological traits, such as dependability and conscientiousness (p. 79)

Whistle-blowing reporting others' ethics violations to management or legal authorities (p. 82)

4-5 **Explain to whom organizations are socially responsible.** Social responsibility is a business's obligation to benefit society. According to the shareholder model, a company's only social responsibility is to maximize shareholder wealth by maximizing company profits. According to the stakeholder model, companies must satisfy the needs and interests of multiple corporate stakeholders, not just shareholders. The needs of primary stakeholders, on which the organization relies for its existence, take precedence over those of secondary stakeholders.

Social responsibility a business's obligation to pursue policies, make decisions, and take actions that benefit society (p. 83)

Shareholder model a view of social responsibility that holds that an organization's overriding goal should be profit maximization for the benefit of shareholders (p. 83)

Stakeholder model a theory of corporate responsibility that holds that management's most important responsibility, long-term survival, is achieved by satisfying the interests of multiple corporate stakeholders (p. 83)

Stakeholders persons or groups with a stake, or legitimate interest, in a company's actions (p. 83)

Primary stakeholder any group on which an organization relies for its long-term survival (p. 84)

Secondary stakeholder any group that can influence or be influenced by a company and can affect public perceptions about the company's socially responsible behavior (p. 84)

4-6 **Explain for what organizations are socially responsible.** Companies can best benefit their stakeholders by fulfilling their economic, legal, ethical, and discretionary responsibilities. Being profitable, or meeting its economic responsibility, is a business's most basic social responsibility. Legal responsibility consists of following a society's laws and regulations. Ethical responsibility means not violating accepted principles of right and wrong when doing business. Discretionary responsibilities are social responsibilities beyond basic economic, legal, and ethical responsibilities.

Economic responsibility a company's social responsibility to make a profit by producing a valued product or service (p. 85)

Legal responsibility a company's social responsibility to obey society's laws and regulations (p. 85)

Ethical responsibility a company's social responsibility not to violate accepted principles of right and wrong when conducting its business (p. 85)

Discretionary responsibilities the social roles that a company fulfills beyond its economic, legal, and ethical responsibilities (p. 86)

4-7 **Explain how organizations can respond to societal demands for social responsibility.** Social responsiveness is a company's response to stakeholders' expectations concerning socially responsible behavior. There are four social responsiveness strategies. When a company uses a reactive strategy, it denies responsibility for a problem. When it uses a defensive strategy, a company takes responsibility for a problem but does the minimum required to solve it. When a company uses an accommodative strategy, it accepts responsibility for problems and does all that society expects to solve them. Finally, when a company uses a proactive strategy, it does much more than expected to solve social responsibility problems.

Social responsiveness a company's strategy to respond to stakeholders' economic, legal, ethical, or discretionary expectations concerning social responsibility (p. 87)

Reactive strategy a social responsiveness strategy in which a company does less than society expects (p. 87)

Defensive strategy a social responsiveness strategy in which a company admits responsibility for a problem but does the least required to meet societal expectations (p. 87)

Accommodative strategy a social responsiveness strategy in which a company accepts responsibility for a problem and does all that society expects to solve that problem (p. 88)

Proactive strategy a social responsiveness strategy in which a company anticipates a problem before it occurs and does more than society expects to take responsibility for and address the problem (p. 89)

4-8 **Explain whether social responsibility hurts or helps an organization's economic performance.** Does it pay to be socially responsible? Studies show that there is generally no trade-off between social responsibility and economic performance. In most circumstances, there is generally a small positive relationship between social responsibility and economic performance that becomes stronger when a company or its products have a positive reputation. Social responsibility, however, does not guarantee profitability, as socially responsible companies experience the same ups and downs as other companies.

CHAPTER 5 LEARNING OUTCOMES / KEY TERMS

CHAPTER REVIEW

5-1 **Discuss the benefits and pitfalls of planning.** Planning is choosing a goal and developing a method or strategy for achieving it. Planning is one of the best ways to improve organizational and individual performance. It encourages people to work harder (intensified effort), to work hard for extended periods (persistence), to engage in behaviors directly related to goal accomplishment (directed behavior), and to think of better ways to do their jobs (task strategies). However, planning also has three potential pitfalls. Companies that are overly committed to their plans may be slow to adapt to environmental changes. Planning can create a false sense of security: planning is based on assumptions about the future, and when those assumptions are wrong, plans can fail. Finally, planning can fail when planners are detached from the implementation of their plans.

Planning choosing a goal and developing a strategy to achieve that goal (p. 93)

5-2 **Describe how to make a plan that works.** There are five steps to making a plan that works: (1) Set S.M.A.R.T. goals—goals that are **S**pecific, **M**easurable, **A**ttainable, **R**ealistic, and **T**imely. (2) Develop commitment to the goals. Managers can increase workers' goal commitment by encouraging their participation in goal setting, making goals public, and getting top management to show support for goals. (3) Develop action plans for goal accomplishment. (4) Track progress toward goal achievement by setting both proximal and distal goals and by providing workers with regular performance feedback. (5) Maintain flexibility by keeping options open.

Exhibit 5.1

How to Make a Plan That Works

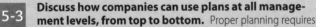

1 Set goals.	2 Develop commitment.	3 Develop effective action plans: ☑ Who ☑ What ☑ When ☑ How	4 Track progress toward goal achievement.	5 Maintain flexibility.

Revise existing plan or Begin planning process anew.

S.M.A.R.T. goals goals that are specific, measurable, attainable, realistic, and timely (p. 95)

Goal commitment the determination to achieve a goal (p. 96)

Action plan a plan that lists the specific steps, people, resources, and time period needed to attain a goal (p. 96)

Proximal goals short-term goals or subgoals (p. 96)

Distal goals long-term or primary goals (p. 96)

Options-based planning maintaining planning flexibility by making small, simultaneous investments in many alternative plans (p. 97)

Slack resources a cushion of extra resources that can be used with options-based planning to adapt to unanticipated changes, problems, or opportunities (p. 97)

5-3 **Discuss how companies can use plans at all management levels, from top to bottom.** Proper planning requires that the goals at the bottom and middle of the organization support the objectives at the top of the organization. The goals at the top will be longer range than those at the bottom. Top management develops strategic plans, which start with the creation of an organizational purpose statement and strategic objectives. Middle managers use techniques such as management by objectives to develop tactical plans that direct behavior, efforts, and priorities. Finally, lower-level managers develop operational plans that guide daily activities in producing or delivering an organization's products and services. There are three kinds of operational plans: single-use plans, standing plans (policies, procedures, and rules and regulations), and budgets.

Strategic plans overall company plans that clarify how the company will serve customers and position itself against competitors over the next two to five years (p. 99)

Purpose statement a statement of a company's purpose or reason for existing (p. 99)

Strategic objective a more specific goal that unifies company-wide efforts, stretches and challenges the organization, and possesses a finish line and a time frame (p. 100)

Tactical plans plans created and implemented by middle managers that direct behavior, efforts, and attention over the next six months to two years (p. 100)

Management by objectives a four-step process in which managers and employees discuss and select goals, develop tactical plans, and meet regularly to review progress toward goal accomplishment (p. 101)

Operational plans day-to-day plans, developed and implemented by lower-level managers, for producing or delivering the organization's products and services over a thirty-day to six-month period (p. 101)

Single-use plans plans that cover unique, one-time-only events (p. 101)

Standing plans plans used repeatedly to handle frequently recurring events (p. 101)

Policies standing plans that indicate the general course of action that should be taken in response to a particular event or situation (p. 102)

Procedures standing plans that indicate the specific steps that should be taken in response to a particular event (p. 102)

Rules and regulations standing plans that describe how a particular action should be performed or what must happen or not happen in response to a particular event (p. 102)

Budgeting quantitative planning through which managers decide how to allocate available money to best accomplish company goals (p. 103)

5-4 **Explain the steps and limits to rational decision making.** Rational decision making is a six-step process in which managers define problems, evaluate alternatives, and compute optimal solutions. Step 1 is identifying and defining the problem. Problems are gaps between desired and existing states. Managers won't begin the decision-making process unless they are aware of a gap, are motivated to reduce it, and possess the necessary resources to fix it. Step 2 is defining the decision criteria used to judge alternatives. In Step 3, an absolute or relative comparison process is used to rate the importance of the decision criteria. Step 4 involves generating many alternative courses of action (that is,

solutions). Potential solutions are assessed in Step 5 by systematically gathering information and evaluating each alternative against each criterion. In Step 6, criterion ratings and weights are used to compute the weighted average for each alternative course of action. Rational managers then choose the alternative with the highest value.

The rational decision-making model describes how decisions should be made in an ideal world without constraints. However, managers' limited resources, incomplete and imperfect information, and limited decision-making capabilities restrict their decision-making processes in the real world.

Decision making the process of choosing a solution from available alternatives (p. 103)

Rational decision making a systematic process of defining problems, evaluating alternatives, and choosing optimal solutions (p. 103)

Problem a gap between a desired state and an existing state (p. 103)

Decision criteria the standards used to guide judgments and decisions (p. 104)

Absolute comparisons a process in which each decision criterion is compared to a standard or ranked on its own merits (p. 104)

Relative comparisons a process in which each decision criterion is

compared directly with every other criterion (p. 105)

Maximize choosing the best alternative (p. 107)

Satisficing choosing a "good-enough" alternative (p. 107)

5-5 **Explain how group decisions and group decision-making techniques can improve decision making.** When groups view problems from multiple perspectives, use more information, have a diversity of knowledge and experience, and become committed to solutions they help choose, they can produce better solutions than do individual decision makers. However, group decisions can suffer from several disadvantages: groupthink, slowness, discussions dominated by just a few individuals, and unfelt responsibility for decisions. Group decision making works

best when group members encourage c-type (cognitive) conflict. Group decision making doesn't work as well when groups become mired in a-type (affective) conflict. The devil's advocacy approach improves group decisions because it brings structured c-type conflict into the decision-making process. By contrast, the nominal group technique improves decision making by reducing a-type conflict. Because it overcomes the problems of production blocking and evaluation apprehension, electronic brainstorming is more effective than face-to-face brainstorming.

Groupthink a barrier to good decision making caused by pressure within the group for members to agree with each other (p. 107)

C-type conflict (cognitive conflict) disagreement that focuses on problem- and issue-related differences of opinion (p. 108)

A-type conflict (affective conflict) disagreement that focuses on individuals or personal issues (p. 108)

Devil's advocacy a decision-making method in which an individual or a subgroup is assigned the role of critic (p. 109)

Dialectical inquiry a decision-making method in which decision makers state the

assumptions of a proposed solution (a thesis) and generate a solution that is the opposite (antithesis) of that solution (p. 109)

Nominal group technique a decision-making method that begins and ends by having group members quietly write down and evaluate ideas to be shared with the group (p. 109)

Delphi technique a decision-making method in which members of a panel of experts respond to questions and to each other until reaching agreement on an issue (p. 109)

Brainstorming a decision-making method in which group members build on each others' ideas to generate as many alternative solutions as possible (p. 110)

Electronic brainstorming a decision-making method in which group members use computers to build on each others' ideas and generate as many alternative solutions as possible (p. 110)

Production blocking a disadvantage of face-to-face brainstorming in which a group member must wait to share an idea because another member is presenting an idea (p. 110)

Evaluation apprehension fear of what others will think of your ideas (p. 110)

6-1 **Specify the components of sustainable competitive advantage, and explain why it is important.** Firms can use their resources to create and sustain a competitive advantage, that is, to provide greater value for customers than competitors can. A competitive advantage becomes sustainable when other companies cannot duplicate the benefits it provides and have, for now, stopped trying. Four conditions must be met if a firm's resources are to be used to achieve a sustainable competitive advantage. The resources must be valuable, rare, imperfectly imitable, and nonsubstitutable.

Resources the assets, capabilities, processes, employee time, information, and knowledge that an organization uses to improve its effectiveness and efficiency and create and sustain competitive advantage (p. 113)

Competitive advantage providing greater value for customers than competitors can (p. 113)

Sustainable competitive advantage a competitive advantage that other companies have tried unsuccessfully to duplicate and have, for the moment, stopped trying to duplicate (p. 113)

Valuable resource a resource that allows companies to improve efficiency and effectiveness (p. 113)

Rare resource a resource that is not controlled or possessed by many competing firms (p. 114)

Imperfectly imitable resource a resource that is impossible or extremely costly or difficult for other firms to duplicate (p. 114)

Nonsubstitutable resource a resource that produces value or competitive advantage and has no equivalent substitutes or replacements (p. 115)

6-2 **Describe the steps involved in the strategy-making process.** The first step in strategy making is determining whether a strategy needs to be changed to sustain a competitive advantage. The second step is to conduct a situational (SWOT) analysis that examines internal strengths and weaknesses as well as external opportunities and threats. The third step involves choosing a strategy. Strategic reference point theory suggests that when companies are performing better than their strategic reference points, top management will typically choose a risk-averse strategy. When performance is below strategic reference points, risk-seeking strategies are more likely to be chosen.

Competitive inertia a reluctance to change strategies or competitive practices that have been successful in the past (p. 116)

Strategic dissonance a discrepancy between a company's intended strategy and the strategic actions managers take when implementing that strategy (p. 116)

Situational (SWOT) analysis an assessment of the strengths and weaknesses in an organization's internal environment and the opportunities and threats in its external environment (p. 117)

Distinctive competence what a company can make, do, or perform better than its competitors (p. 117)

Core capabilities the internal decision-making routines, problem-solving processes, and organizational cultures that determine how efficiently inputs can be turned into outputs (p. 117)

Shadow-strategy task force a committee within a company that analyzes the company's own weaknesses to determine how competitors could exploit them for competitive advantage (p. 118)

Strategic group a group of companies within an industry against which top managers compare, evaluate, and benchmark strategic threats and opportunities (p. 118)

Core firms the central companies in a strategic group (p. 118)

Secondary firms the firms in a strategic group that follow strategies related to but somewhat different from those of the core firms (p. 118)

Strategic reference points the strategic targets managers use to measure whether a firm has developed the core competencies it needs to achieve a sustainable competitive advantage (p. 119)

6-3 **Explain the different kinds of corporate-level strategies.** Corporate-level strategies, consisting of portfolio strategies and grand strategies, help managers determine what businesses they should be in. Portfolio strategy focuses on lowering business risk by being in multiple, unrelated businesses and by investing the cash flows from slow-growing businesses into faster-growing businesses. One portfolio strategy is based on the BCG matrix. The most successful way to use the portfolio approach to corporate strategy is to reduce risk through related diversification.

The three kinds of grand strategies are growth, stability, and retrenchment/recovery. Companies can grow externally by merging with or acquiring other companies, or they can grow internally through direct expansion or creating new businesses. Companies choose a stability strategy when their external environment changes very little or after they have dealt with periods of explosive growth. Retrenchment strategy, shrinking the size or scope of a business, is used to turn around poor performance. If retrenchment works, it is often followed by a recovery strategy that focuses on growing the business again.

Corporate-level strategy the overall organizational strategy that addresses the question, "What business or businesses are we in or should we be in?" (p. 121)

Diversification a strategy for reducing risk by buying a variety of items (stocks or, in the case of a corporation, types of businesses) so that the failure of one stock or one business does not doom the entire portfolio (p. 121)

Portfolio strategy a corporate-level strategy that minimizes risk by diversifying investment among various businesses or product lines (p. 121)

Acquisition the purchase of a company by another company (p. 122)

Unrelated diversification creating or acquiring companies in completely unrelated businesses (p. 122)

BCG matrix a portfolio strategy developed by the Boston Consulting Group that categorizes a corporation's businesses by growth rate and relative market share and helps managers decide how to invest corporate funds (p. 122)

Star a company with a large share of a fast-growing market (p. 122)

Question mark a company with a small share of a fast-growing market (p. 122)

Cash cow a company with a large share of a slow-growing market (p. 123)

Dog a company with a small share of a slow-growing market (p. 123)

Related diversification creating or acquiring companies that share similar products, manufacturing, marketing, technology, or cultures (p. 125)

Grand strategy a broad corporate-level strategic plan used to achieve strategic goals and guide the strategic alternatives that managers of individual businesses or subunits may use (p. 125)

Growth strategy a strategy that focuses on increasing profits, revenues, market

share, or the number of places in which the company does business (p. 125)

Stability strategy a strategy that focuses on improving the way in which the company sells the same products or services to the same customers (p. 125)

Retrenchment strategy a strategy that focuses on turning around very poor company performance by shrinking the size or scope of the business (p. 126)

Recovery the strategic actions taken after retrenchment to return to a growth strategy (p. 126)

6-4 **Describe the different kinds of industry-level strategies.** The five industry forces determine an industry's overall attractiveness to corporate investors and its potential for long-term profitability. Together, a high level of these elements combine to increase competition and decrease profits. Industry-level strategies focus on how companies choose to compete in their industries. The three positioning strategies can help companies protect themselves from the negative effects of industry-wide competition. The four adaptive strategies help companies adapt to changes in the external environment. Defenders want to defend their current strategic positions. Prospectors look for new market opportunities to bring innovative new products to market. Analyzers minimize risk by following the proven successes of prospectors. Reactors do not follow a consistent adaptive strategy but instead react to changes in the external environment after they occur.

Industry-level strategy a corporate strategy that addresses the question, "How should we compete in this industry?" (p. 126)

Character of the rivalry a measure of the intensity of competitive behavior between companies in an industry (p. 127)

Threat of new entrants a measure of the degree to which barriers to entry make it easy or difficult for new companies to get started in an industry (p. 127)

Threat of substitute products or services a measure of the ease with which customers can find substitutes for an industry's products or services (p. 128)

Bargaining power of suppliers a measure of the influence that suppliers of parts, materials, and services to firms in an industry have on the prices of these inputs (p. 128)

Bargaining power of buyers a measure of the influence that customers have on a firm's prices (p. 128)

Cost leadership the positioning strategy of producing a product or service of acceptable quality at consistently lower production costs than competitors can, so that the firm can offer the product or service at the lowest price in the industry (p. 129)

Differentiation the positioning strategy of providing a product or service that is sufficiently different from competitors' offerings that customers are willing to pay a premium price for it (p. 129)

Focus strategy the positioning strategy of using cost leadership or differentiation to produce a specialized product or service for a limited, specially targeted group of customers in a particular geographic region or market segment (p. 129)

Defenders companies using an adaptive strategy aimed at defending strategic positions by seeking moderate, steady growth and by offering a limited range of high-quality products and services to a well-defined set of customers (p. 130)

Prospectors companies using an adaptive strategy that seeks fast growth by searching for new market opportunities, encouraging risk taking, and being the first to bring innovative new products to market (p. 130)

Analyzers companies using an adaptive strategy that seeks to minimize risk and maximize profits by following or imitating the proven successes of prospectors (p. 131)

Reactors companies that do not follow a consistent adaptive strategy but instead react to changes in the external environment after they occur (p. 131)

6-5 **Explain the components and kinds of firm-level strategies.** Firm-level strategies are concerned with direct competition between firms. Market commonality and resource similarity determine whether firms are in direct competition and thus likely to attack each other and respond to each other's attacks. In general, the more markets in which there is product, service, or customer overlap and the greater the resource similarity between two firms, the more intense the direct competition between them will be.

Firm-level strategy a corporate strategy that addresses the question, "How should we compete against a particular firm?" (p. 131)

Direct competition the rivalry between two companies that offer similar products and services, acknowledge each other as rivals, and act and react to each other's strategic actions (p. 132)

Market commonality the degree to which two companies have overlapping products, services, or customers in multiple markets (p. 132)

Resource similarity the extent to which a competitor has similar amounts and kinds of resources (p. 132)

Attack a competitive move designed to reduce a rival's market share or profits (p. 134)

Response a competitive countermove, prompted by a rival's attack, to defend or improve a company's market share or profit (p. 134)

7-1 Explain why innovation matters to companies.

Technology cycles typically follow an S-curve pattern of innovation. Early in the cycle, technological progress is slow, and improvements in technological performance are small. As a technology matures, however, performance improves quickly. Finally, as the limits of a technology are reached, only small improvements occur. At this point, significant improvements in performance must come from new technologies. The best way to protect a competitive advantage is to create a stream of innovative ideas and products. Innovation streams begin with technological discontinuities that create significant breakthroughs in performance or function. Technological discontinuities are followed by discontinuous change, in which customers purchase new technologies, and companies compete to establish the new dominant design. Dominant designs emerge because of critical mass, because they solve a practical problem, or because of the negotiations of independent standards bodies. Because technological innovation both enhances and destroys competence, companies that bet on the wrong design often struggle, while companies that bet on the eventual dominant design usually prosper. When a dominant design emerges, companies focus on incremental change, lowering costs, and making small but steady improvements in the dominant design. This focus continues until the next technological discontinuity occurs.

Organizational innovation the successful implementation of creative ideas in organizations (p. 137)

Technology cycle a cycle that begins with the birth of a new technology and ends when that technology reaches its limits and is replaced by a newer, substantially better technology (p. 137)

S-curve pattern of innovation a pattern of technological innovation characterized by slow initial progress, then rapid progress, and then slow progress again as a technology matures and reaches its limits (p. 137)

Innovation streams patterns of innovation over time that can create sustainable competitive advantage (p. 139)

Technological discontinuity the phase of an innovation stream in which a scientific advance or unique combination of existing technologies creates a significant breakthrough in performance or function (p. 139)

Discontinuous change the phase of a technology cycle characterized by technological substitution and design competition (p. 139)

Technological substitution the purchase of new technologies to replace older ones (p. 140)

Design competition competition between old and new technologies to establish a new technological standard or dominant design (p. 140)

Dominant design a new technological design or process that becomes the accepted market standard (p. 140)

Technological lockout the inability of a company to competitively sell its products because it relies on old technology or a nondominant design (p. 142)

Incremental change the phase of a technology cycle in which companies innovate by lowering costs and improving the functioning and performance of the dominant technological design (p. 142)

7-2 Discuss the different methods that managers can use to effectively manage innovation in their organizations.

To successfully manage innovation streams, companies must manage the sources of innovation and learn to manage innovation during both discontinuous and incremental change. Because innovation begins with creativity, companies can manage the sources of innovation by supporting a work environment in which creative thoughts and ideas are welcomed, valued, and encouraged. Creative work environments provide challenging work; offer organizational, supervisory, and work group encouragement; allow significant freedom; and remove organizational impediments to creativity. Discontinuous and incremental change require different strategies. Companies that succeed in periods of discontinuous change typically follow an experiential approach to innovation. The experiential approach assumes that intuition, flexible options, and hands-on experience can reduce uncertainty and accelerate learning and understanding. A compression approach to innovation works best during periods of incremental change. This approach assumes that innovation can be planned using a series of steps and that compressing the time it takes to complete those steps can speed up innovation.

Creative work environments workplace cultures in which workers perceive that new ideas are welcomed, valued, and encouraged (p. 143)

Flow a psychological state of effortlessness, in which you become completely absorbed in what you're doing, and time seems to pass quickly (p. 143)

Experiential approach to innovation an approach to innovation that assumes a highly uncertain environment and uses intuition, flexible options, and hands-on experience to reduce uncertainty and accelerate learning and understanding (p. 145)

Design iteration a cycle of repetition in which a company tests a prototype of a new product or service, improves on that design, and then builds and tests the improved prototype (p. 145)

Product prototype a full-scale, working model that is being tested for design, function, and reliability (p. 145)

Testing the systematic comparison of different product designs or design iterations (p. 146)

Milestones formal project review points used to assess progress and performance (p. 146)

Multifunctional teams work teams composed of people from different departments (p. 146)

Compression approach to innovation an approach to innovation that assumes that incremental innovation can be planned using a series of steps and that compressing those steps can speed innovation (p. 147)

Generational change change based on incremental improvements to a dominant technological design such that the improved technology is fully backward compatible with the older technology (p. 147)

CHAPTER REVIEW

CHAPTER 7 LEARNING OUTCOMES / KEY TERMS

7-3 **Discuss why not changing can lead to organizational decline.** The five-stage process of organizational decline begins when organizations don't recognize the need for change. In the blinded stage, managers fail to recognize the changes that threaten their organization's survival. In the inaction stage, management recognizes the need to change but doesn't act, hoping that the problems will correct themselves. In the faulty action stage, management focuses on cost cutting and efficiency rather than facing up to the fundamental changes needed to ensure survival. In the crisis stage, failure is likely unless fundamental reorganization occurs. Finally, in the dissolution stage, the company is dissolved through bankruptcy proceedings; by selling assets to pay creditors; or through the closing of stores, offices, and facilities. If companies recognize the need to change early enough, however, dissolution may be avoided.

Organizational decline a large decrease in organizational performance that occurs when companies don't anticipate, recognize, neutralize, or adapt to the internal or external pressures that threaten their survival (p. 148)

7-4 **Discuss the different methods that managers can use to better manage change as it occurs.** The basic change process involves unfreezing, change intervention, and refreezing. Resistance to change stems from self-interest, misunderstanding, and distrust as well as a general intolerance for change. Resistance can be managed through education and communication, participation, negotiation, top management support, and coercion. Knowing what *not* to do is as important as knowing what to do to achieve successful change. Managers should avoid these errors when leading change: not establishing a sense of urgency, not creating a guiding coalition, lacking a vision, undercommunicating the vision, not removing obstacles to the vision, not creating short-term wins, declaring victory too soon, and not anchoring changes in the corporation's culture. Finally, managers can use a number of change techniques. Results-driven change and the General Electric workout reduce resistance to change by getting change efforts off to a fast start. Organizational development is a collection of planned change interventions (large-system, small-group, person-focused), guided by a change agent, that are designed to improve an organization's long-term health and performance.

Change forces forces that produce differences in the form, quality, or condition of an organization over time (p. 149)

Resistance forces forces that support the existing conditions in organizations (p. 149)

Resistance to change opposition to change resulting from self-interest, misunderstanding and distrust, and a general intolerance for change (p. 150)

Unfreezing getting the people affected by change to believe that change is needed (p. 150)

Change intervention the process used to get workers and managers to change their behaviors and work practices (p. 150)

Refreezing supporting and reinforcing new changes so that they stick (p. 150)

Coercion the use of formal power and authority to force others to change (p. 151)

Results-driven change change created quickly by focusing on the measurement and improvement of results (p. 153)

General Electric workout a three-day meeting in which managers and employees from different levels and parts of an organization quickly generate and act on solutions to specific business problems (p. 154)

Organizational development a philosophy and collection of planned change interventions designed to improve an organization's long-term health and performance (p. 154)

Change agent the person formally in charge of guiding a change effort (p. 154)

Exhibit 7.6
Different Kinds of Organizational Development Interventions

Large-System Interventions	
Sociotechnical systems	An intervention designed to improve how well employees use and adjust to the work technology used in an organization.
Survey feedback	An intervention that uses surveys to collect information from the members of the system, reports the results of that survey to the members, and then uses those results to develop action plans for improvement.
Small-Group Interventions	
Team building	An intervention designed to increase the cohesion and cooperation of work group members.
Unit goal setting	An intervention designed to help a work group establish short- and long-term goals.
Person-Focused Interventions	
Counseling/ coaching	An intervention designed so that a formal helper or coach listens to managers or employees and advises them on how to deal with work or interpersonal problems.
Training	An intervention designed to provide individuals with the knowledge, skills, or attitudes they need to become more effective at their jobs.

Source: W. J. Rothwell, R. Sullivan, and G. M. McLean, *Practicing Organizational Development: A Guide for Consultants* (San Diego: Pfeiffer & Co., 1995).

8-1 **Discuss the impact of global business and the trade rules and agreements that govern it.** Today, there are 103,000 multinational corporations worldwide; just 9.4 percent are based in the United States. Global business affects the United States in two ways: through direct foreign investment in the United States by foreign companies and through U.S. companies' investment in businesses in other countries. U.S. direct foreign investment throughout the world amounts to more than $4.9 trillion per year, whereas direct foreign investment by foreign companies in the United States amounts to more than $2.9 trillion per year. Historically, tariffs and nontariff trade barriers such as quotas, voluntary export restraints, government import standards, government subsidies, and customs classifications have made buying foreign goods much harder or more expensive than buying domestically produced products. In recent years, however, worldwide trade agreements such as GATT and the WTO, along with regional trading agreements such as the Maastricht Treaty of Europe, NAFTA, CAFTA-DR, UNASUR, ASEAN, and APEC, TPP, and TFTA have substantially reduced tariffs and nontariff barriers to international trade. Companies have responded by investing in growing markets in Asia, Eastern Europe, and Latin America. Consumers have responded by purchasing products based on value rather than geography.

Global business the buying and selling of goods and services by people from different countries (p. 157)

Multinational corporation a corporation that owns businesses in two or more countries (p. 157)

Direct foreign investment a method of investment in which a company builds a new business or buys an existing business in a foreign country (p. 157)

Trade barriers government-imposed regulations that increase the cost and restrict the number of imported goods (p. 158)

Protectionism a government's use of trade barriers to shield domestic companies and their workers from foreign competition (p. 158)

Tariff a direct tax on imported Goods (p. 158)

Nontariff barriers nontax methods of increasing the cost or reducing the volume of imported goods (p. 159)

Quota a limit on the number or volume of imported products (p. 159)

Voluntary export restraints voluntarily imposed limits on the number or volume of products exported to a particular country (p. 159)

Government import standard a standard ostensibly established to protect the health and safety of citizens but, in reality, is often used to restrict imports (p. 159)

Subsidies government loans, grants, and tax deferments given to domestic companies to protect them from foreign competition (p. 159)

Customs classification a classification assigned to imported products by government officials that affects the size of the tariff and the imposition of import quotas (p. 159)

General Agreement on Tariffs and Trade (GATT) a worldwide trade agreement that reduced and eliminated tariffs, limited government subsidies, and established protections for intellectual property (p. 160)

World Trade Organization (WTO) the successor to GATT; the only international organization dealing with the global rules of trade between nations; its main function is to ensure that trade flows as smoothly, predictably, and freely as possible (p. 160)

Regional trading zones areas in which tariff and nontariff barriers on trade between countries are reduced or eliminated (p. 161)

Maastricht Treaty of Europe a regional trade agreement among most European countries (p. 161)

North American Free Trade Agreement (NAFTA) a regional trade agreement among the United States, Canada, and Mexico (p. 162)

Dominican Republic–Central America Free Trade Agreement (CAFTA-DR) a regional trade agreement among Costa Rica, the Dominican Republic, El Salvador, Guatemala, Honduras, Nicaragua, and the United States (p. 162)

Union of South American Nations (UNASUR) a regional trade agreement among Argentina, Brazil, Paraguay, Uruguay, Venezuela, Bolivia, Colombia, Ecuador, Peru, Guyana, Suriname, and Chile (p. 163)

Association of Southeast Asian Nations (ASEAN) a regional trade agreement among Brunei Darussalam, Cambodia, Indonesia, Laos, Malaysia, Myanmar, the Philippines, Singapore, Thailand, and Vietnam (p. 163)

Asia-Pacific Economic Cooperation (APEC) a regional trade agreement among Australia, Canada, Chile, the People's Republic of China, Hong Kong, Japan, Mexico, New Zealand, Papua New Guinea, Peru, Russia, South Korea, Taiwan, the United States, and all the members of ASEAN except Cambodia, Lao PDR, and Myanmar (p. 163)

Trans-Pacific Partnership (TPP) a proposed regional trade agreement among Australia, Brunei, Canada, Chile, Japan, Malaysia, Mexico, New Zealand, Peru, Singapore, United States, and Vietnam (p. 163)

Tripartite Free Trade Agreement (TFTA) a regional trade agreement among twenty-seven African countries (p. 163)

8-2 **Explain why companies choose to standardize or adapt their business procedures.** Global business requires a balance between global consistency and local adaptation. Global consistency means using the same rules, guidelines, policies, and procedures in each location. Managers at company headquarters like global consistency because it simplifies decisions. Local adaptation means adapting standard procedures to differences in markets. Local managers prefer a policy of local adaptation because it gives them more control. Not all businesses need the same combination of global consistency and local adaptation. Some thrive by emphasizing global consistency and ignoring local adaptation. Others succeed by ignoring global consistency and emphasizing local adaptation.

Global consistency when a multinational company has offices, manufacturing plants, and distribution facilities in different countries and runs them all using the same rules, guidelines, policies, and procedures (p. 164)

Local adaptation modifying rules, guidelines, policies, and procedures to adapt to differences in foreign customers, governments, and regulatory agencies (p. 165)

8-3 Explain the different ways that companies can organize to do business globally. The phase model of globalization says that, as companies move from a domestic to a global orientation, they use these organizational forms in sequence: exporting, cooperative contracts (licensing and franchising), strategic alliances, and wholly owned affiliates. Yet, not all companies follow the phase model. For example, global new ventures are global from their inception.

Exporting selling domestically produced products to customers in foreign countries (p. 166)

Cooperative contract an agreement in which a foreign business owner pays a company a fee for the right to conduct that business in his or her country (p. 167)

Licensing an agreement in which a domestic company, the licensor, receives royalty payments for allowing another company, the licensee, to produce the licensor's product, sell its service, or use its brand name in a specified foreign market (p. 167)

Franchise a collection of networked firms in which the manufacturer or marketer of a product or service, the franchisor, licenses the entire business to another person or organization, the franchisee (p. 167)

Strategic alliance an agreement in which companies combine key resources, costs, risks, technology, and people (p. 168)

Joint venture a strategic alliance in which two existing companies collaborate to form a third, independent company (p. 168)

Wholly owned affiliates foreign offices, facilities, and manufacturing plants that are 100 percent owned by the parent company (p. 169)

Global new ventures new companies that are founded with an active global strategy and have sales, employees, and financing in different countries (p. 169)

8-4 Explain how to find a favorable business climate. The first step in deciding where to take your company global is finding an attractive business climate. Be sure to look for a growing market where consumers have strong purchasing power, and foreign competitors are weak. When locating an office or manufacturing facility, consider both qualitative and quantitative factors. In assessing political risk, be sure to examine both political uncertainty and policy uncertainty. If the location you choose has considerable political risk, you can avoid it, try to control the risk, or use a cooperation strategy.

Purchasing power the relative cost of a standard set of goods and services in different countries (p. 170)

Political uncertainty the risk of major changes in political regimes that can result from war, revolution, death of political leaders, social unrest, or other influential events (p. 172)

Policy uncertainty the risk associated with changes in laws and government policies that directly affect the way foreign companies conduct business (p. 172)

8-5 Discuss the importance of identifying and adapting to cultural differences. National culture is the set of shared values and beliefs that affects the perceptions, decisions, and behavior of the people from a particular country. The first step in dealing with culture is to recognize meaningful differences such as power distance, individualism, masculinity, uncertainty avoidance, and short-term/long-term orientation. Cultural differences should be interpreted carefully because they are based on generalizations rather than specific individuals. Adapting managerial practices to cultural differences is difficult because policies and practices can be perceived differently in different cultures.

National culture the set of shared values and beliefs that affects the perceptions, decisions, and behavior of the people from a particular country (p. 175)

8-6 Explain how to successfully prepare workers for international assignments. Many expatriates return prematurely from international assignments because of poor performance. This is much less likely to happen if employees receive language and cross-cultural training, such as documentary training, cultural simulations, or field experiences, before going on assignment. Adjustment of expatriates' spouses and families, which is the most important determinant of success in international assignments, can be improved through adaptability screening and language and cross-cultural training.

Expatriate someone who lives and works outside his or her native country (p. 177)

9-1 **Describe the departmentalization approach to organizational structure.** There are five traditional departmental structures: functional, product, customer, geographic, and matrix. Functional departmentalization is based on the different business functions or types of expertise used to run a business. Product departmentalization is organized according to the different products or services a company sells. Customer departmentalization focuses its divisions on the different kinds of customers a company has. Geographic departmentalization is based on the different geographic areas or markets in which the company does business. Matrix departmentalization is a hybrid form that combines two or more forms of departmentalization, the most common being the product and functional forms. There is no single best departmental structure. Each structure has advantages and disadvantages.

Organizational structure the vertical and horizontal configuration of departments, authority, and jobs within a company (p. 181)

Organizational process the collection of activities that transforms inputs into outputs that customers value (p. 181)

Departmentalization subdividing work and workers into separate organizational units responsible for completing particular tasks (p. 182)

Functional departmentalization organizing work and workers into separate units responsible for particular business functions or areas of expertise (p. 182)

Product departmentalization organizing work and workers into separate units responsible for producing particular products or services (p. 183)

Customer departmentalization organizing work and workers into separate units responsible for particular kinds of customers (p. 184)

Geographic departmentalization organizing work and workers into separate units responsible for doing business in particular geographic areas (p. 185)

Matrix departmentalization a hybrid organizational structure in which two or more forms of departmentalization, most often product and functional, are used together (p. 186)

Simple matrix a form of matrix departmentalization in which managers in different parts of the matrix negotiate conflicts and resources (p. 188)

Complex matrix a form of matrix departmentalization in which managers in different parts of the matrix report to matrix managers, who help them sort out conflicts and problems (p. 188)

9-2 **Explain organizational authority.** Organizational authority is determined by the chain of command, line versus staff authority, delegation, and the degree of centralization in a company. The chain of command vertically connects every job in the company to higher levels of management and makes clear who reports to whom. Managers have line authority to command employees below them in the chain of command but have only staff, or advisory, authority over employees not below them in the chain of command. Managers delegate authority by transferring to subordinates the authority and responsibility needed to do a task; in exchange, subordinates become accountable for task completion. In centralized companies, most authority to make decisions lies with managers in the upper levels of the company. In decentralized companies, much of the authority is delegated to the workers closest to the problems, who can then make the decisions necessary for solving the problems themselves.

Authority the right to give commands, take action, and make decisions to achieve organizational objectives (p. 188)

Chain of command the vertical line of authority that clarifies who reports to whom throughout the organization (p. 189)

Unity of command a management principle that workers should report to just one boss (p. 189)

Line authority the right to command immediate subordinates in the chain of command (p. 189)

Staff authority the right to advise, but not command, others who are not subordinates in the chain of command (p. 189)

Line function an activity that contributes directly to creating or selling the company's products (p. 190)

Staff function an activity that does not contribute directly to creating or selling the company's products but instead supports line activities (p. 190)

Delegation of authority the assignment of direct authority and responsibility to a subordinate to complete tasks for which the manager is normally responsible (p. 190)

Centralization of authority the location of most authority at the upper levels of the organization (p. 191)

Decentralization the location of a significant amount of authority in the lower levels of the organization (p. 191)

Standardization solving problems by consistently applying the same rules, procedures, and processes (p. 191)

9-3 **Discuss the different methods for job design.** Companies use specialized jobs because they are economical, easy to learn, and don't require highly paid workers. However, specialized jobs aren't motivating or particularly satisfying for employees. Companies have used job rotation, job enlargement, job enrichment, and the job characteristics model to make specialized jobs more interesting and motivating. The goal of the job characteristics model is to make jobs intrinsically motivating. For this to happen, jobs must be strong on five core job characteristics (skill variety, task identity, task significance, autonomy, and feedback), and workers must experience three critical psychological states (knowledge of results, responsibility for work outcomes, and meaningful work). If jobs aren't internally motivating, they can be redesigned by combining tasks, forming natural work units, establishing client relationships, using vertical loading, and opening feedback channels.

Job design the number, kind, and variety of tasks that individual workers perform in doing their jobs (p. 192)

Job specialization a job composed of a small part of a larger task or process (p. 192)

Job rotation periodically moving workers from one specialized job to another to give them more variety and the opportunity to use different skills (p. 192)

Job enlargement increasing the number of different tasks that a worker performs within one particular job (p. 192)

Job enrichment increasing the number of tasks in a particular job and giving workers the authority and control to make meaningful decisions about their work (p. 193)

Job characteristics model (JCM) an approach to job redesign that seeks to formulate jobs in ways that motivate workers and lead to positive work outcomes (p. 193)

Internal motivation motivation that comes from the job itself rather than from outside rewards (p. 193)

Skill variety the number of different activities performed in a job (p. 194)

Task identity the degree to which a job, from beginning to end, requires the completion of a whole and identifiable piece of work (p. 194)

Task significance the degree to which a job is perceived to have a substantial impact on others inside or outside the organization (p. 194)

Autonomy the degree to which a job gives workers the discretion, freedom, and independence to decide how and when to accomplish the job (p. 194)

Feedback the amount of information the job provides to workers about their work performance (p. 194)

9-4 **Explain the methods that companies are using to redesign internal organizational processes (that is, intraorganizational processes).** Today, companies are using reengineering and empowerment to change their intraorganizational processes. Reengineering changes an organization's orientation from vertical to horizontal and changes its work processes by decreasing sequential and pooled interdependence and by increasing reciprocal interdependence. Reengineering promises dramatic increases in productivity and customer satisfaction, but it has been criticized as simply an excuse to cut costs and lay off workers. Empowering workers means taking decision-making authority and responsibility from managers and giving it to workers. Empowered workers develop feelings of competence and self-determination and believe that their work has meaning and impact.

Mechanistic organization an organization characterized by specialized jobs and responsibilities; precisely defined, unchanging roles; and a rigid chain of command based on centralized authority and vertical communication (p. 195)

Organic organization an organization characterized by broadly defined jobs and responsibilities; loosely defined, frequently changing roles; and decentralized authority and horizontal communication based on task knowledge (p. 195)

Intraorganizational process the collection of activities that take place within an organization to transform inputs into outputs that customers value (p. 195)

Reengineering fundamental rethinking and radical redesign of business processes to achieve dramatic improvements in critical measures of performance, such as cost, quality, service, and speed (p. 195)

Task interdependence the extent to which collective action is required to complete an entire piece of work (p. 196)

Pooled interdependence work completed by having each job or department independently contribute to the whole (p. 196)

Sequential interdependence work completed in succession, with one group's or job's outputs becoming the inputs for the next group or job (p. 197)

Reciprocal interdependence work completed by different jobs or groups working together in a back-and-forth manner (p. 197)

Empowering workers permanently passing decision-making authority and responsibility from managers to workers by giving them the information and resources they need to make and carry out good decisions (p. 197)

Empowerment feeling of intrinsic motivation in which workers perceive their work to have impact and meaning and perceive themselves to be competent and capable of self-determination (p. 198)

9-5 **Describe the methods that companies are using to redesign external organizational processes (that is, interorganizational processes).** Organizations are using modular and virtual organizations to change interorganizational processes. Because modular organizations outsource all noncore activities to other businesses, they are less expensive to run than traditional companies. However, modular organizations require extremely close relationships with suppliers, may result in a loss of control, and could create new competitors if the wrong business activities are outsourced. Virtual organizations participate in a network in which they share skills, costs, capabilities, markets, and customers. Virtual organizations can reduce costs, respond quickly, and, if they can successfully coordinate their efforts, produce outstanding products and services.

Interorganizational process a collection of activities that take place among companies to transform inputs into outputs that customers value (p. 198)

Modular organization an organization that outsources noncore business activities to outside companies, suppliers, specialists, or consultants (p. 198)

Virtual organization an organization that is part of a network in which many companies share skills, costs, capabilities, markets, and customers to collectively solve customer problems or provide specific products or services (p. 199)

CHAPTER REVIEW

10-1 **Explain the good and bad of using teams.** In many industries, teams are growing in importance because they help organizations respond to specific problems and challenges. Teams have been shown to increase customer satisfaction (specific customer teams), product and service quality (direct responsibility), and employee job satisfaction (cross-training, unique opportunities, and leadership responsibilities). Although teams can produce significant improvements in these areas, using teams does not guarantee these positive outcomes. Teams and teamwork have the disadvantages of initially high turnover and social loafing (especially in large groups). Teams also share many of the advantages (multiple perspectives, generation of more alternatives, and more commitment) and disadvantages (groupthink, time, poorly run meetings, domination by a few team members, and weak accountability) of group decision making. Teams should be used for a clear purpose, when the work requires that people work together, when rewards can be provided for both teamwork and team performance, and when ample resources can be provided.

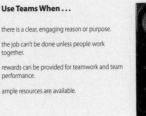

Exhibit 10.1
When to Use and When Not to Use Teams

Use Teams When . . .
- ✓ there is a clear, engaging reason or purpose.
- ✓ the job can't be done unless people work together.
- ✓ rewards can be provided for teamwork and team performance.
- ✓ ample resources are available.

Don't Use Teams When . . .
- ✗ there isn't a clear, engaging reason or purpose.
- ✗ the job can be done by people working independently.
- ✗ rewards are provided for individual effort and performance.
- ✗ the necessary resources are not available.

Source: R. Wageman, "Critical Success Factors for Creating Superb Self-Managing Teams," *Organizational Dynamics* 26, no. 1 (1997): 49–61.

Work team a small number of people with complementary skills who hold themselves mutually accountable for pursuing a common purpose, achieving performance goals, and improving interdependent work processes (p. 203)

Cross-training training team members to do all or most of the jobs performed by the other team members (p. 203)

Social loafing behavior in which team members withhold their efforts and fail to perform their share of the work (p. 205)

10-2 **Recognize and understand the different kinds of teams.** Companies use different kinds of teams to make themselves more competitive. Autonomy is the key dimension that makes teams different. Traditional work groups (which execute tasks) and employee involvement groups (which make suggestions) have the lowest levels of autonomy. Semi-autonomous work groups (which control major direct tasks) have more autonomy, while self-managing teams (which control all direct tasks) and self-designing teams (which control membership and how tasks are done) have the highest levels of autonomy. Cross-functional, virtual, and project teams are common but are not easily categorized in terms of autonomy. Cross-functional teams combine employees from different functional areas to help teams attack problems from multiple perspectives and generate more ideas and solutions. Virtual teams use telecommunications and information technologies to bring coworkers together, regardless of physical location or time zone. Virtual teams reduce travel and work time, but communication may suffer because team members don't work face-to-face. Finally, project teams are used for specific, one-time projects or tasks that must be completed within a limited time. Project teams reduce communication barriers and promote flexibility; teams and team members are reassigned to their departments or to new projects as their current projects are completed.

Traditional work group a group composed of two or more people who work together to achieve a shared goal (p. 207)

Employee involvement team team that provides advice or makes suggestions to management concerning specific issues (p. 208)

Semi-autonomous work group a group that has the authority to make decisions and solve problems related to the major tasks of producing a product or service (p. 208)

Self-managing team a team that manages and controls all of the major tasks of producing a product or service (p. 208)

Self-designing team a team that has the characteristics of self-managing teams but also controls team design, work tasks, and team membership (p. 208)

Cross-functional team a team composed of employees from different functional areas of the organization (p. 209)

Virtual team a team composed of geographically and/or organizationally dispersed coworkers who use telecommunication and information technologies to accomplish an organizational task (p. 209)

Project team a team created to complete specific, one-time projects or tasks within a limited time (p. 210)

10-3 Understand the general characteristics of work teams.

The most important characteristics of work teams are team norms, cohesiveness, size, conflict, and development. Norms let team members know what is expected of them and can influence team behavior in positive and negative ways. Positive team norms are associated with organizational commitment, trust, and job satisfaction. Team cohesiveness helps teams retain members, promotes cooperative behavior, increases motivation, and facilitates team performance. Attending team meetings and activities, creating opportunities to work together, and engaging in nonwork activities can increase cohesiveness. Team size has a curvilinear relationship with team performance: teams that are very small or very large do not perform as well as moderate-sized teams of six to nine members. Teams of this size are cohesive and small enough for team members to get to know each other and contribute in a meaningful way but are large enough to take advantage of team members' diverse skills, knowledge, and perspectives. Conflict and disagreement are inevitable in most teams. The key to dealing with team conflict is to maximize cognitive conflict, which focuses on issue-related differences, and minimize affective conflict, the emotional reactions that occur when disagreements become personal rather than professional. As teams develop and grow, they pass through four stages of development: forming, storming, norming, and performing. If a team is not managed well, its performance may decline after a period of time as the team regresses through the stages of de-norming, de-storming, and de-forming.

Norms informally agreed-on standards that regulate team behavior (p. 210)

Cohesiveness the extent to which team members are attracted to a team and motivated to remain in it (p. 211)

Forming the first stage of team development, in which team members meet each other, form initial impressions, and begin to establish team norms (p. 214)

Storming the second stage of development, characterized by conflict and disagreement, in which team members disagree over what the team should do and how it should do it (p. 215)

Norming the third stage of team development, in which team members begin to settle into their roles, group cohesion grows, and positive team norms develop (p. 215)

Performing the fourth and final stage of team development, in which performance improves because the team has matured into an effective, fully functioning team (p. 215)

De-norming a reversal of the norming stage, in which team performance begins to decline as the size, scope, goal, or members of the team change (p. 215)

De-storming a reversal of the storming phase, in which the team's comfort level decreases, team cohesion weakens, and angry emotions and conflict may flare (p. 215)

De-forming a reversal of the forming stage, in which team members position themselves to control pieces of the team, avoid each other, and isolate themselves from team leaders (p. 215)

10-4 Explain how to enhance work team effectiveness.

Companies can make teams more effective by setting team goals and managing how team members are selected, trained, and compensated. Team goals provide a clear focus and purpose, reduce the incidence of social loafing, and lead to higher team performance 93 percent of the time. Extremely difficult stretch goals can be used to motivate teams as long as teams have autonomy, control over resources, structural accommodation, and bureaucratic immunity. Not everyone is suited for teamwork. When selecting team members, companies should select people who have a preference for teamwork (that is, are more collectivists than individualists) and should consider team level (average ability of a team) and team diversity (different abilities of a team). Organizations that use teams successfully provide thousands of hours of training to make sure that teams work. The most common types of team training are for interpersonal skills, decision-making and problem-solving skills, conflict resolution, technical training to help team members learn multiple jobs (that is, cross-training), and training for team leaders. Employees can be compensated for team participation and accomplishments in three ways: skill-based pay, gainsharing, and nonfinancial rewards.

Structural accommodation the ability to change organizational structures, policies, and practices in order to meet stretch goals (p. 216)

Bureaucratic immunity the ability to make changes without first getting approval from managers or other parts of an organization (p. 216)

Individualism-collectivism the degree to which a person believes that people should be self-sufficient and that loyalty to one's self is more important than loyalty to team or company (p. 217)

Team level the average level of ability, experience, personality, or any other factor on a team (p. 217)

Team diversity the variances or differences in ability, experience, personality, or any other factor on a team (p. 217)

Interpersonal skills skills, such as listening, communicating, questioning, and providing feedback, that enable people to have effective working relationships with others (p. 219)

Skill-based pay compensation system that pays employees for learning additional skills or knowledge (p. 220)

Gainsharing a compensation system in which companies share the financial value of performance gains, such as increased productivity, cost savings, or quality, with their workers (p. 220)

CHAPTER 11 LEARNING OUTCOMES / KEY TERMS

11-1 **Explain how different employment laws affect human resource practice.** Human resource management is subject to numerous major federal employment laws and subject to review by several federal agencies. In general, these laws indicate that sex, age, religion, color, national origin, race, disability, and genetic history may not be considered in employment decisions unless these factors reasonably qualify as BFOQs. Two important criteria, disparate treatment (intentional discrimination) and adverse impact (unintentional discrimination), are used to decide whether companies have wrongly discriminated against someone. The two kinds of sexual harassment are quid pro quo sexual harassment and hostile work environment.

Human resource management (HRM) the process of finding, developing, and keeping the right people to form a qualified workforce (p. 223)

Bona fide occupational qualification (BFOQ) an exception in employment law that permits sex, age, religion, and the like to be used when making employment decisions, but only if they are "reasonably necessary to the normal operation of that particular business." BFOQs are strictly monitored by the Equal Employment Opportunity Commission (p. 224)

Disparate treatment intentional discrimination that occurs when people are purposely not given the same hiring, promotion, or membership opportunities because of their race, color, sex, age, ethnic group, national origin, or religious beliefs (p. 225)

Adverse impact unintentional discrimination that occurs when members of a particular race, sex, or ethnic group are unintentionally harmed or disadvantaged because they are hired, promoted, or trained (or any other employment decision) at substantially lower rates than others (p. 226)

Four-fifths (or 80%) rule a rule of thumb used by the courts and the EEOC to determine whether there is evidence of adverse impact; a violation of this rule occurs when the impact ratio (calculated by dividing the decision ratio for a protected group by the decision ratio for a nonprotected group) is less than 80 percent, or four-fifths (p. 226)

Sexual harassment a form of discrimination in which unwelcome sexual advances, requests for sexual favors, or other verbal or physical conduct of a sexual nature occurs while performing one's job (p. 226)

Quid pro quo sexual harassment a form of sexual harassment in which employment outcomes, such as hiring, promotion, or simply keeping one's job, depend on whether an individual submits to sexual harassment (p. 226)

Hostile work environment a form of sexual harassment in which unwelcome and demeaning sexually related behavior creates an intimidating and offensive work environment (p. 226)

11-2 **Explain how companies use recruiting to find qualified job applicants.** Recruiting is the process of finding qualified job applicants. The first step in recruiting is to conduct a job analysis, which is used to write a job description of basic tasks, duties, and responsibilities and to write job specifications indicating the knowledge, skills, and abilities needed to perform the job. Whereas internal recruiting involves finding qualified job applicants from inside the company, external recruiting involves finding qualified job applicants from outside the company.

Recruiting the process of developing a pool of qualified job applicants (p. 227)

Job analysis a purposeful, systematic process for collecting information on the important work-related aspects of a job (p. 227)

Job description a written description of the basic tasks, duties, and responsibilities required of an employee holding a particular job (p. 227)

Job specifications a written summary of the qualifications needed to successfully perform a particular job (p. 228)

Internal recruiting the process of developing a pool of qualified job applicants from people who already work in the company (p. 229)

External recruiting the process of developing a pool of qualified job applicants from outside the company (p. 229)

11-3 **Describe the selection techniques and procedures that companies use when deciding which applicants should receive job offers.** Selection is the process of gathering information about job applicants to decide who should be offered a job. Accurate selection procedures are valid, are legally defendable, and improve organizational performance. Application forms and résumés are the most common selection devices. Managers should check references and conduct background checks even though previous employers are often reluctant to provide such information for fear of being sued for defamation. Unfortunately, without this information, other employers are at risk of negligent hiring lawsuits. Selection tests generally do the best job of predicting applicants' future job performance. The three kinds of job interviews are unstructured, structured, and semistructured.

Selection the process of gathering information about job applicants to decide who should be offered a job (p. 231)

Validation the process of determining how well a selection test or procedure predicts future job performance; the better or more accurate the prediction of future job performance, the more valid a test is said to be (p. 231)

Human resource information system (HRIS) a computerized system for gathering, analyzing, storing, and disseminating information related to the HRM process (p. 231)

Employment references sources such as previous employers or coworkers who can provide job-related information about job candidates (p. 233)

Background checks procedures used to verify the truthfulness and accuracy of information that applicants provide about themselves and to uncover negative, job-related background information not provided by applicants (p. 233)

Specific ability tests (aptitude tests) tests that measure the extent to which an applicant possesses the particular kind of ability needed to do a job well (p. 234)

Cognitive ability tests tests that measure the extent to which applicants have abilities in perceptual speed, verbal comprehension, numerical aptitude, general reasoning, and spatial aptitude (p. 235)

Biographical data (biodata) extensive surveys that ask applicants questions about their personal backgrounds and life experiences (p. 235)

Personality test an assessment that measures the extent to which an applicant possesses different kinds of job-related personality dimensions (p. 235)

Work sample tests tests that require applicants to perform tasks that are actually done on the job (p. 236)

Assessment centers a series of managerial simulations, graded by trained observers, that are used to determine applicants' capability for managerial work (p. 236)

Interview a selection tool in which company representatives ask job applicants job-related questions to determine whether they are qualified for the job (p. 237)

Unstructured interviews interviews in which interviewers are free to ask the applicants anything they want (p. 237)

Structured interviews interviews in which all applicants are asked the same set of standardized questions, usually including situational, behavioral, background, and job-knowledge questions (p. 237)

11-4 Describe how to determine training needs, and select the appropriate training methods.
Training is used to give employees the job-specific skills, experience, and knowledge they need to do their jobs or improve their job performance. To make sure training dollars are well spent, companies need to determine specific training needs, select appropriate training methods, and then evaluate the training.

Training developing the skills, experience, and knowledge employees need to perform their jobs or improve their performance (p. 238)

Needs assessment the process of identifying and prioritizing the learning needs of employees (p. 238)

11-5 Discuss how to use performance appraisal to give meaningful performance feedback.
The keys to successful performance appraisals are accurately measuring job performance and effectively sharing performance feedback with employees. Organizations should develop good performance appraisal scales; train raters how to accurately evaluate performance; and impress upon managers the value of providing feedback in a clear, consistent, and fair manner, as well as setting goals and monitoring progress toward those goals.

Performance appraisal the process of assessing how well employees are doing their jobs (p. 241)

Objective performance measures measures of job performance that are easily and directly counted or quantified (p. 242)

Subjective performance measures measures of job performance that require

someone to judge or assess a worker's performance (p. 242)

Behavior observation scales (BOSs) rating scales that indicate the frequency with which workers perform specific behaviors that are representative of the job dimensions critical to successful job performance (p. 242)

Rater training training performance appraisal raters in how to avoid rating errors and increase rating accuracy (p. 243)

360-degree feedback a performance appraisal process in which feedback is obtained from the boss, subordinates, peers and coworkers, and the employees themselves (p. 244)

11-6 Describe basic compensation strategies, and discuss the four kinds of employee separations.
Compensation includes both the financial and the nonfinancial rewards that organizations give employees in exchange for their work. There are three basic kinds of compensation decisions: pay level, pay variability, and pay structure. Employee separation is the loss of an employee, which can occur voluntarily or involuntarily. Companies use downsizing and early retirement incentive programs (ERIPs) to reduce the number of employees in the organization and lower costs. However, companies generally try to keep the rate of employee turnover low to reduce costs associated with finding and developing new employees. Functional turnover, on the other hand, can be good for organizations.

Compensation the financial and nonfinancial rewards that organizations give employees in exchange for their work (p. 246)

Employee separation the voluntary or involuntary loss of an employee (p. 246)

Job evaluation a process that determines the worth of each job in a company by evaluating the market value of the knowledge, skills, and requirements needed to perform it (p. 246)

Piecework a compensation system in which employees are paid a set rate for each item they produce (p. 247)

Commission a compensation system in which employees earn a percentage of each sale they make (p. 247)

Profit sharing a compensation system in which a company pays a percentage of its profits to employees in addition to their regular compensation (p. 247)

Employee stock ownership plan (ESOP) a compensation system that awards employees shares of company stock in addition to their regular compensation (p. 247)

Stock options a compensation system that gives employees the right to purchase shares of stock at a set price, even if the value of the stock increases above that price (p. 248)

Wrongful discharge a legal doctrine that requires employers to have a job-related reason to terminate employees (p. 249)

Downsizing the planned elimination of jobs in a company (p. 250)

Outplacement services employment-counseling services offered to employees who are losing their jobs because of downsizing (p. 251)

Early retirement incentive programs (ERIPs) programs that offer financial benefits to employees to encourage them to retire early (p. 251)

Phased retirement employees transition to retirement by working reduced hours over a period of time before completely retiring (p. 251)

Employee turnover loss of employees who voluntarily choose to leave the company (p. 251)

Functional turnover loss of poor-performing employees who voluntarily choose to leave a company (p. 252)

Dysfunctional turnover loss of high-performing employees who voluntarily choose to leave a company (p. 252)

12-1 **Describe diversity and explain why it matters.** Diversity exists in organizations when there are demographic, cultural, and personal differences among the employees and the customers. A common misconception is that workplace diversity and affirmative action are the same. However, affirmative action is more narrowly focused on demographics; is required by law; and is used to punish companies that discriminate on the basis of race/ethnicity, religion, sex, or national origin. By contrast, diversity is broader in focus (going beyond demographics); voluntary; more positive in that it encourages companies to value all kinds of differences; and, at this time, substantially less controversial than affirmative action. Affirmative action and diversity thus differ in purpose, practice, and the reactions they produce. Diversity also makes good business sense in terms of reducing costs (decreasing turnover and absenteeism and avoiding lawsuits), attracting and retaining talent, and driving business growth (improving marketplace understanding and promoting higher-quality problem solving).

Diversity a variety of demographic, cultural, and personal differences among an organization's employees and customers (p. 255)

Affirmative action purposeful steps taken by an organization to create employment opportunities for minorities and women (p. 256)

12-2 **Understand the special challenges that the dimensions of surface-level diversity pose for managers.** Age, sex, race/ethnicity, and physical and mental disabilities are dimensions of surface-level diversity. Because those dimensions are (usually) easily observed, managers and workers tend to rely on them to form initial impressions and stereotypes. Sometimes this can lead to age, sex, racial/ethnic, or disability discrimination (that is, treating people differently) in the workplace. In general, older workers, women, people of color or different national origins, and people with disabilities may be less likely to be hired or promoted than are white males. This disparity is often due to incorrect beliefs or stereotypes such as "job performance declines with age," or "women aren't willing to travel on business," or "workers with disabilities aren't as competent as able workers." To reduce discrimination, companies can determine the hiring and promotion rates for different groups, train managers to make hiring and promotion decisions on the basis of specific criteria, and make sure that everyone has equal access to training, mentors, reasonable work accommodations, and assistive technology. Finally, companies need to designate a go-to person to whom employees can talk if they believe they have suffered discrimination.

Surface-level diversity differences such as age, sex, race/ethnicity, and physical disabilities that are observable, typically unchangeable, and easy to measure (p. 259)

Deep-level diversity differences such as personality and attitudes that are communicated through verbal and nonverbal behaviors and are learned only through extended interaction with others (p. 259)

Social integration the degree to which group members are psychologically attracted to working with each other to accomplish a common objective (p. 259)

Age discrimination treating people differently (for example in hiring and firing, promotion, and compensation decisions) because of their age (p. 259)

Sex discrimination treating people differently because of their sex (p. 261)

Glass ceiling the invisible barrier that prevents women and minorities from advancing to the top jobs in organizations (p. 261)

Racial and ethnic discrimination treating people differently because of their race or ethnicity (p. 263)

Disability a mental or physical impairment that substantially limits one or more major life activities (p. 264)

Disability discrimination treating people differently because of their disabilities (p. 264)

12-3 **Explain how the dimensions of deep-level diversity affect individual behavior and interactions in the workplace.** Deep-level diversity matters because it can reduce prejudice, discrimination, and conflict while increasing social integration. It consists of dispositional and personality differences that can be recognized only through extended interaction with others. Research conducted in different cultures, settings, and languages indicates that there are five basic dimensions of personality: extraversion, emotional stability, agreeableness, conscientiousness, and openness to experience. Of these, conscientiousness is perhaps the most important because conscientious workers tend to be better performers on virtually any job. Extraversion is also related to performance in jobs that require significant interaction with others.

Disposition the tendency to respond to situations and events in a predetermined manner (p. 265)

Personality the relatively stable set of behaviors, attitudes, and emotions displayed over time that makes people different from each other (p. 265)

Extraversion the degree to which someone is active, assertive, gregarious, sociable, talkative, and energized by others (p. 266)

Emotional stability the degree to which someone is not angry, depressed, anxious, emotional, insecure, and excitable (p. 266)

Agreeableness the degree to which someone is cooperative, polite, flexible, forgiving, good-natured, tolerant, and trusting (p. 266)

Conscientiousness the degree to which someone is organized, hardworking, responsible, persevering, thorough, and achievement oriented (p. 266)

Openness to experience the degree to which someone is curious, broad-minded, and open to new ideas, things, and experiences; is spontaneous; and has a high tolerance for ambiguity (p. 267)

12-4 **Explain the basic principles and practices that can be used to manage diversity.** The three paradigms for managing diversity are the discrimination and fairness paradigm (equal opportunity, fair treatment, strict compliance with the law), the access and legitimacy paradigm (matching internal diversity to external diversity), and the learning and effectiveness paradigm (achieving organizational plurality by integrating deep-level diversity into the work of the organization). Unlike the other paradigms that focus on surface-level differences, the learning and effectiveness paradigm values common ground, distinguishes between individual and group differences, minimizes conflict and divisiveness, and focuses on bringing different talents and perspectives together. What principles can companies use when managing diversity? Follow and enforce federal and state laws regarding equal employment opportunity. Treat group differences as important but not special. Find the common ground. Tailor opportunities to individuals, not groups. Solicit negative as well as positive feedback. Set high but realistic goals. The two types of diversity training are awareness training and skills-based diversity training. Companies also manage diversity through diversity audits and diversity pairing and by having top executives experience what it is like to be in the minority.

Organizational plurality a work environment where (1) all members are empowered to contribute in a way that maximizes the benefits to the organization, customers, and themselves, and (2) the individuality of each member is respected by not segmenting or polarizing people on the basis of their membership in a particular group (p. 269)

Skills-based diversity training training that teaches employees the practical skills they need for managing a diverse workforce, such as flexibility and adaptability, negotiation, problem solving, and conflict resolution (p. 271)

Awareness training training that is designed to raise employees' awareness of diversity issues and to challenge the underlying assumptions or stereotypes they may have about others (p. 271)

Diversity audits formal assessments that measure employee and management attitudes, investigate the extent to which people are advantaged or disadvantaged with respect to hiring and promotions, and review companies' diversity-related policies and procedures (p. 272)

Diversity pairing a mentoring program in which people of different cultural backgrounds, sexes, or races/ethnicities are paired together to get to know each other and change stereotypical beliefs and attitudes (p. 272)

Paradigms for Managing Diversity

Diversity Paradigm	Focus	Success Measured By	Benefits	Limitations
Discrimination & Fairness	Equal opportunity; Fair treatment; Recruitment of minorities; Strict compliance with laws	Recruitment, promotion, and retention goals for underrepresented groups	Fairer treatment; Increased demographic diversity	Focus on surface-level diversity
Access & Legitimacy	Acceptance and celebration of differences	Diversity in company matches diversity of primary stakeholders	Establishes a clear business reason for diversity	Focus on surface-level diversity
Learning & Effectiveness	Integrating deep-level differences into organization	Valuing people on the basis of individual knowledge, skills, and abilities	Values common ground; Distinction between individual and group differences; Less conflict, backlash, and divisiveness; Bringing different talents and perspectives together	Focus on deep-level diversity, which is more difficult to measure and quantify

13-1 **Explain the basics of motivation.** Motivation is the set of forces that initiates, directs, and makes people persist in their efforts over time to accomplish a goal. Managers often confuse motivation and performance, but job performance is a multiplicative function of motivation times ability times situational constraints. Needs are the physical or psychological requirements that must be met to ensure survival and well-being. Different motivational theories (Maslow's Hierarchy of Needs, Alderfer's ERG Theory, and McClelland's Learned Needs Theory) specify a number of different needs. However, studies show that there are only two general kinds of needs: lower-order needs and higher-order needs. Both extrinsic and intrinsic rewards motivate people.

Motivation the set of forces that initiates, directs, and makes people persist in their efforts to accomplish a goal (p.275)

Needs the physical or psychological requirements that must be met to ensure survival and well-being (p. 276)

Extrinsic reward a reward that is tangible, visible to others, and given to employees contingent on the performance of specific tasks or behaviors (p. 278)

Intrinsic reward a natural reward associated with performing a task or activity for its own sake (p. 278)

13-2 **Use equity theory to explain how employees' perceptions of fairness affect motivation.** The basic components of equity theory are inputs, outcomes, and referents. After an internal comparison in which employees compare their outcomes to their inputs, they then make an external comparison in which they compare their O/I ratio with the O/I ratio of a referent, a person who works in a similar job or is otherwise similar. When their O/I ratio is equal to the referent's O/I ratio, employees perceive that they are being treated fairly. But, when their O/I ratio is lower than or higher than their referent's O/I ratio, they perceive that they have been treated inequitably or unfairly. There are two kinds of inequity: underreward and overreward. Underreward, which occurs when a referent's O/I ratio is higher than the employee's O/I ratio, leads to anger or frustration. Overreward, which occurs when a referent's O/I ratio is lower than the employee's O/I ratio, can lead to guilt but only when the level of overreward is extreme.

Equity theory a theory that states that people will be motivated when they perceive that they are being treated fairly (p. 280)

Inputs in equity theory, the contributions employees make to the organization (p. 280)

Outcomes in equity theory, the rewards employees receive for their contributions to the organization (p. 280)

Referents in equity theory, others with whom people compare themselves to determine if they have been treated fairly (p. 280)

Outcome/input (O/I) ratio in equity theory, an employee's perception of how the rewards received from an organization compare with the employee's contributions to that organization (p. 281)

Underreward a form of inequity in which you are getting fewer outcomes relative to inputs than your referent is getting (p. 281)

Overreward a form of inequity in which you are getting more outcomes relative to inputs than your referent (p. 281)

Distributive justice the perceived degree to which outcomes and rewards are fairly distributed or allocated (p. 283)

Procedural justice the perceived fairness of the process used to make reward allocation decisions (p. 284)

13-3 **Use expectancy theory to describe how workers' expectations about rewards, effort, and the link between rewards and performance influence motivation.** Expectancy theory holds that three factors affect the conscious choices people make about their motivation: valence, expectancy, and instrumentality. Expectancy theory holds that all three factors must be high for people to be highly motivated. If any one of these factors declines, overall motivation will decline, too.

Expectancy theory the theory that people will be motivated to the extent to which they believe that their efforts will lead to good performance, that good performance will be rewarded, and that they will be offered attractive rewards (p. 284)

Valence the attractiveness or desirability of a reward or outcome (p. 284)

Expectancy the perceived relationship between effort and performance (p. 285)

Instrumentality the perceived relationship between performance and rewards (p. 285)

13-4 **Explain how reinforcement theory works and how it can be used to motivate.** Reinforcement theory says that behavior is a function of its consequences. Reinforcement has two parts: reinforcement contingencies and schedules of reinforcement. The four kinds of reinforcement contingencies are positive reinforcement and negative reinforcement, which strengthen behavior, and punishment and extinction, which weaken behavior. There are two kinds of reinforcement schedules, continuous and intermittent; intermittent schedules, in turn, can be divided into fixed and variable interval schedules and fixed and variable ratio schedules.

Reinforcement theory the theory that behavior is a function of its consequences, that behaviors followed by positive consequences will occur more frequently, and that behaviors followed by negative consequences, or not followed by positive consequences, will occur less frequently (p. 287)

Reinforcement the process of changing behavior by changing the consequences that follow behavior (p. 287)

Reinforcement contingencies cause-and-effect relationships between the performance of specific behaviors and specific consequences (p. 288)

Schedule of reinforcement rules that specify which behaviors will be reinforced, which consequences will follow those behaviors, and the schedule by which those consequences will be delivered (p. 288)

Positive reinforcement reinforcement that strengthens behavior by following behaviors with desirable consequences (p. 288)

Negative reinforcement reinforcement that strengthens behavior by withholding an unpleasant consequence when employees perform a specific behavior (p. 288)

Punishment reinforcement that weakens behavior by following behaviors with undesirable consequences (p. 289)

Extinction reinforcement in which a positive consequence is no longer allowed

to follow a previously reinforced behavior, thus weakening the behavior (p. 289)

Continuous reinforcement schedule a schedule that requires a consequence to be administered following every instance of a behavior (p. 290)

Intermittent reinforcement schedule a schedule in which consequences are delivered after a specified or average time has elapsed or after a specified or average number of behaviors has occurred (p. 290)

Fixed interval reinforcement schedule an intermittent schedule in which consequences follow a behavior only after a fixed time has elapsed (p. 290)

Variable interval reinforcement schedule an intermittent schedule in which the time between a behavior and the following consequences varies around a specified average (p. 290)

Fixed ratio reinforcement schedule an intermittent schedule in which consequences are delivered following a specific number of behaviors (p. 290)

Variable ratio reinforcement schedule an intermittent schedule in which consequences are delivered following a different number of behaviors, sometimes more and sometimes less, that vary around a specified average number of behaviors (p. 290)

13-5 **Describe the components of goal-setting theory and how managers can use them to motivate workers.** A goal is a target, objective, or result that someone tries to accomplish. Goal-setting theory says that people will be motivated to the extent to which they accept specific, challenging goals and receive feedback that indicates their progress toward goal achievement. The basic components of goal-setting theory are goal specificity, goal difficulty, goal acceptance, and performance feedback.

Goal specificity is the extent to which goals are detailed, exact, and unambiguous. Goal difficulty is the extent to which a goal is hard or challenging to accomplish. Goal acceptance is the extent to which people consciously understand and agree to goals. Performance feedback is information about the quality or quantity of past performance and indicates whether progress is being made toward the accomplishment of a goal.

Goal a target, objective, or result that someone tries to accomplish (p. 293)

Goal-setting theory the theory that people will be motivated to the extent to which they accept specific, challenging goals and receive feedback that indicates their progress toward goal achievement (p. 293)

Goal specificity the extent to which goals are detailed, exact, and unambiguous (p. 293)

Goal difficulty the extent to which a goal is hard or challenging to accomplish (p. 293)

Goal acceptance the extent to which people consciously understand and agree to goals (p. 293)

Performance feedback information about the quality or quantity of past performance that indicates whether progress is being made toward the accomplishment of a goal (p. 293)

13-6 **Discuss how the entire motivation model can be used to motivate workers.**

Motivating with the Integrated Model

Motivating with	Managers should . . .
The Basics	• Ask people what their needs are. • Satisfy lower-order needs first. • Expect people's needs to change. • As needs change and lower-order needs are satisfied, satisfy higher-order needs by looking for ways to allow employees to experience intrinsic rewards.
Equity Theory	• Look for and correct major inequities. • Reduce employees' inputs. • Make sure decision-making processes are fair.
Expectancy Theory	• Systematically gather information to find out what employees want from their jobs. • Take specific steps to link rewards to individual performance in a way that is clear and understandable to employees. • Empower employees to make decisions if management really wants them to believe that their hard work and efforts will lead to good performance.
Reinforcement Theory	• Identify, measure, analyze, intervene, and evaluate critical performance-related behaviors. • Don't reinforce the wrong behaviors. • Correctly administer punishment at the appropriate time. • Choose the simplest and most effective schedules of reinforcement.
Goal-Setting Theory	• Assign specific, challenging goals. • Make sure workers truly accept organizational goals. • Provide frequent, specific, performance-related feedback.

CHAPTER 14 LEARNING OUTCOMES / KEY TERMS

14-1 **Explain what leadership is.** Management is getting work done through others; leadership is the process of influencing others to achieve group or organizational goals. Leaders are different from managers. The primary difference is that leaders are concerned with doing the right thing, while managers are concerned with doing things right. Organizations need both managers and leaders. But, in general, companies are overmanaged and underled.

Leadership the process of influencing others to achieve group or organizational goals (p. 297)

14-2 **Describe who leaders are and what effective leaders do.** Trait theory says that effective leaders possess traits or characteristics that differentiate them from nonleaders. Those traits are drive, the desire to lead, honesty/integrity, self-confidence, emotional stability, cognitive ability, and knowledge of the business. These traits alone aren't enough for successful leadership; leaders who have many or all of them must also behave in ways that encourage people to achieve group or organizational goals. Two key leader behaviors are initiating structure, which improves subordinate performance, and consideration, which improves subordinate satisfaction. There is no ideal combination of these behaviors. The best leadership style depends on the situation.

Trait theory a leadership theory that holds that effective leaders possess a similar set of traits or characteristics (p. 298)

Traits relatively stable characteristics, such as abilities, psychological motives, or consistent patterns of behavior (p. 298)

Initiating structure the degree to which a leader structures the roles of followers by setting goals, giving directions, setting deadlines, and assigning tasks (p. 300)

Consideration the extent to which a leader is friendly, approachable, and supportive and shows concern for employees (p. 301)

14-3 **Explain Fiedler's contingency theory.** Fiedler's contingency theory assumes that leaders are effective when their work groups perform well, that leaders are unable to change their leadership styles, that leadership styles must be matched to the proper situations, and that favorable situations permit leaders to influence group members. According to the Least Preferred Coworker (LPC) scale, there are two basic leadership styles. People who describe their LPC in a positive way have a relationship-oriented leadership style. By contrast, people who describe their LPC in a negative way have a task-oriented leadership style. Situational favorableness, which occurs when leaders can influence followers, is determined by leader-member relations, task structure, and position power. In general, relationship-oriented leaders with high LPC scores are better leaders under moderately favorable situations, whereas task-oriented leaders with low LPC scores are better leaders in highly favorable and highly unfavorable situations. Because Fiedler assumes that leaders are incapable of changing their leadership styles, the key is to accurately measure and match leaders to situations or to teach leaders how to change situational factors. Though matching or placing leaders in appropriate situations works well, reengineering situations to fit leadership styles doesn't because the complexity of the model makes it difficult for people to understand.

Leadership style the way a leader generally behaves toward followers (p. 302)

Contingency theory a leadership theory states that to maximize work group performance, leaders must be matched to the situation that best fits their leadership style (p. 303)

Situational favorableness the degree to which a particular situation either permits or denies a leader the chance to influence the behavior of group members (p. 304)

Leader-member relations the degree to which followers respect, trust, and like their leaders (p. 304)

Task structure the degree to which the requirements of a subordinate's tasks are clearly specified (p. 304)

Position power the degree to which leaders are able to hire, fire, reward, and punish workers (p. 304)

14-4 **Describe how path-goal theory works.** Path-goal theory states that leaders can increase subordinate satisfaction and performance by clarifying and clearing the paths to goals and by increasing the number and kinds of rewards available for goal attainment. For this to work, however, leader behavior must be a source of immediate or future satisfaction for followers and must complement and not duplicate the characteristics of followers' work environments. In contrast to Fiedler's contingency theory, path-goal theory assumes that leaders can and do change their leadership styles (directive, supportive, participative, and achievement-oriented), depending on their subordinates (experience, perceived ability, and internal or external locus of control) and the environment in which those subordinates work (task structure, formal authority system, and primary work group).

Path-goal theory a leadership theory states that leaders can increase subordinate satisfaction and performance by clarifying and clearing the paths to goals and by increasing the number and kinds of rewards available for goal attainment (p. 306)

Directive leadership a leadership style in which the leader lets employees know precisely what is expected of them, gives them specific guidelines for performing tasks, schedules work, sets standards of performance, and makes sure that people follow standard rules and regulations (p. 307)

Supportive leadership a leadership style in which the leader is friendly and approachable to employees, shows concern for employees and their welfare, treats them as equals, and creates a friendly climate (p. 307)

Participative leadership a leadership style in which the leader consults employees for their suggestions and input before making decisions (p. 307)

Achievement-oriented leadership a leadership style in which the leader sets challenging goals, has high expectations of employees, and displays confidence that employees will assume responsibility and put forth extraordinary effort (p. 308)

14-5   **Explain the normative decision theory.** The normative decision theory helps leaders decide how much employee participation should be used when making decisions. Using the right degree of employee participation improves the quality of decisions and the extent to which employees accept and are committed to decisions. The theory specifies five different decision styles or ways of making decisions: autocratic decisions (AI or AII), consultative decisions (CI or CII), and group decisions (GII). The theory improves decision quality via decision rules concerning quality, leader information, subordinate information, goal congruence, and problem structure. The theory improves employee commitment and acceptance via decision rules related to commitment probability, subordinate conflict, and commitment requirement. These decision rules help leaders improve decision quality and follower acceptance and commitment by eliminating decision styles that don't fit the decision or situation the group or organization is facing. Normative decision theory operationalizes these decision rules in the form of yes/no questions, as shown in the decision tree displayed in Exhibit 14.8.

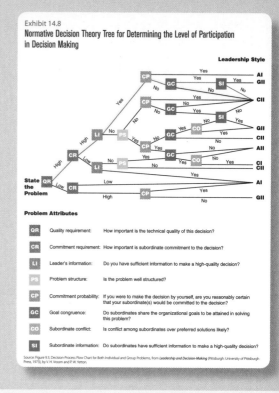

Exhibit 14.8
Normative Decision Theory Tree for Determining the Level of Participation in Decision Making

Problem Attributes

QR	Quality requirement:	How important is the technical quality of this decision?
CR	Commitment requirement:	How important is subordinate commitment to the decision?
LI	Leader's information:	Do you have sufficient information to make a high-quality decision?
PS	Problem structure:	Is the problem well structured?
CP	Commitment probability:	If you were to make the decision by yourself, are you reasonably certain that your subordinate(s) would be committed to the decision?
GC	Goal congruence:	Do subordinates share the organizational goals to be attained in solving this problem?
CO	Subordinate conflict:	Is conflict among subordinates over preferred solutions likely?
SI	Subordinate information:	Do subordinates have sufficient information to make a high-quality decision?

Source: Figure 9.3, Decision-Process Flow Chart for Both Individual and Group Problems, from *Leadership and Decision-Making* (Pittsburgh: University of Pittsburgh Press, 1973), by V. H. Vroom and P. W. Yetton.

Normative decision theory a theory that suggests how leaders can determine an appropriate amount of employee participation when making decisions (p. 309)

14-6   **Explain how visionary leadership (that is, charismatic or transformational) helps leaders achieve strategic leadership.** Strategic leadership requires visionary leadership, which can be charismatic or transformational. Visionary leadership creates a positive image of the future that motivates organizational members and provides direction for future planning and goal setting. Charismatic leaders have strong, confident, dynamic personalities that attract followers, enable the leader to create strong bonds, and inspire followers to accomplish the leader's vision. Followers of ethical charismatic leaders work harder, are more committed and satisfied, are better performers, and are more likely to trust their leaders. Followers can be just as supportive and committed to unethical charismatics, but these leaders can pose a tremendous risk for companies. Unethical charismatics control and manipulate followers and do what is best for themselves instead of their organizations. Transformational leadership goes beyond charismatic leadership by generating awareness and acceptance of a group's purpose and mission and by getting employees to see beyond their own needs and self-interests for the good of the group. The four components of transformational leadership are charismatic leadership or idealized influence, inspirational motivation, intellectual stimulation, and individualized consideration.

Strategic leadership the ability to anticipate, envision, maintain flexibility, think strategically, and work with others to initiate changes that will create a positive future for an organization (p. 314)

Visionary leadership leadership that creates a positive image of the future that motivates organizational members and provides direction for future planning and goal setting (p. 314)

Charismatic leadership the behavioral tendencies and personal characteristics of leaders that create an exceptionally strong relationship between them and their followers (p. 314)

Ethical charismatics charismatic leaders who provide developmental opportunities for followers, are open to positive and negative feedback, recognize others' contributions, share information, and have moral standards that emphasize the larger interests of the group, organization, or society (p. 314)

Unethical charismatics charismatic leaders who control and manipulate followers, do what is best for themselves instead of their organizations, want to hear only positive feedback, share only information that is beneficial to themselves, and have moral standards that put their interests before everyone else's (p. 315)

Transformational leadership leadership that generates awareness and acceptance of a group's purpose and mission and gets employees to see beyond their own needs and self-interests for the good of the group (p. 316)

Transactional leadership leadership based on an exchange process in which followers are rewarded for good performance and punished for poor performance (p. 318)

CHAPTER 15 LEARNING OUTCOMES / KEY TERMS

15-1 **Explain the role that perception plays in communication and communication problems.** Perception is the process by which people attend to, organize, interpret, and retain information from their environments. Perception is not a straightforward process. Because of perceptual filters such as selective perception and closure, people exposed to the same information or stimuli often end up with very different perceptions and understandings. Perception-based differences can also lead to differences in the attributions (internal or external) that managers and workers make when explaining workplace behavior. In general, workers are more likely to explain behavior from a defensive bias, in which they attribute problems to external causes (that is, the situation). Managers, on the other hand, tend to commit the fundamental attribution error, attributing problems to internal causes (that is, the worker made a mistake or error). Consequently, when things go wrong, it's common for managers to blame workers and for workers to blame the situation or context in which they do their jobs. Finally, this problem is compounded by a self-serving bias that leads people to attribute successes to internal causes and failures to external causes. So, when workers receive negative feedback from managers, they may become defensive and emotional and not hear what their managers have to say. In short, perceptions and attributions represent a significant challenge to effective communication and understanding in organizations.

Communication the process of transmitting information from one person or place to another (p. 321)

Perception the process by which individuals attend to, organize, interpret, and retain information from their environments (p. 321)

Perceptual filters the personality-, psychology-, or experience-based differences that influence people to ignore or pay attention to particular stimuli (p. 321)

Selective perception the tendency to notice and accept objects and information consistent with our values, beliefs, and expectations, while ignoring or screening inconsistent information (p. 322)

Closure the tendency to fill in gaps of missing information by assuming that what we don't know is consistent with what we already know (p. 323)

Attribution theory the theory that we all have a basic need to understand and explain the causes of other people's behavior (p. 323)

Defensive bias the tendency for people to perceive themselves as personally and situationally similar to someone who is having difficulty or trouble (p. 323)

Fundamental attribution error the tendency to ignore external causes of behavior and to attribute other people's actions to internal causes (p. 323)

Self-serving bias the tendency to overestimate our value by attributing successes to ourselves (internal causes) and attributing failures to others or the environment (external causes) (p. 324)

15-2 **Describe the communication process and the various kinds of communication in organizations.** Organizational communication depends on the communication process, formal and informal communication channels, one-on-one communication, and nonverbal communication. The major components of the communication process are the sender, the receiver, noise, and feedback. Senders often mistakenly assume that they can pipe their intended messages directly into receivers' heads with perfect clarity. Formal communication channels such as downward, upward, and horizontal communication carry organizationally approved messages and information. By contrast, the informal communication channel, called the *grapevine*, arises out of curiosity and is carried out through gossip or cluster chains. There are two kinds of one-on-one communication. Coaching is used to improve on-the-job performance, while counseling is used to communicate about nonjob-related issues affecting job performance. Nonverbal communication, such as kinesics and paralanguage, accounts for as much as 93 percent of the transmission of a message's content.

Encoding putting a message into a written, verbal, or symbolic form that can be recognized and understood by the receiver (p. 325)

Decoding the process by which the receiver translates the written, verbal, or symbolic form of a message into an understood message (p. 326)

Feedback to sender in the communication process, a return message to the sender that indicates the receiver's understanding of the message (p. 326)

Noise anything that interferes with the transmission of the intended message (p. 326)

Jargon vocabulary particular to a profession or group that interferes with communication in the workplace (p. 327)

Formal communication channel the system of official channels that carry organizationally approved messages and information (p. 327)

Downward communication communication that flows from higher to lower levels in an organization (p. 328)

Upward communication communication that flows from lower to higher levels in an organization (p. 328)

Horizontal communication communication that flows among managers and workers who are at the same organizational level (p. 328)

Informal communication channel (grapevine) the transmission of messages from employee to employee outside of formal communication channels (p. 328)

Coaching communicating with someone for the direct purpose of improving the person's on-the-job performance or behavior (p. 330)

Counseling communicating with someone about non-job-related issues that may be affecting or interfering with the person's performance (p. 330)

Nonverbal communication any communication that doesn't involve words (p. 331)

Kinesics movements of the body and face (p. 331)

Paralanguage the pitch, rate, tone, volume, and speaking pattern (that is, use of silences, pauses, or hesitations) of one's voice (p. 332)

15-3 **Explain how managers can manage effective one-on-one communication.** One-on-one communication can be managed by choosing the right communication medium, being a good listener, and giving effective feedback. Managers generally prefer oral communication because it provides the opportunity to ask questions and assess nonverbal communication. Oral communication is best suited to complex, ambiguous, or emotionally laden topics. Written communication is best suited for delivering straightforward messages and information. Listening is important for managerial success, but most people are terrible listeners. To improve your listening skills, choose to be an active listener (clarify responses, paraphrase, and summarize) and an empathetic listener (show your desire to understand, reflect feelings). Feedback can be constructive or destructive. To be constructive, feedback must be immediate, focused on specific behaviors, and problem-oriented.

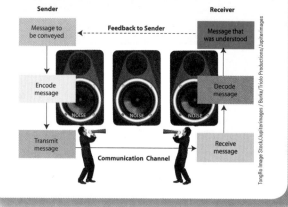

Exhibit 15.3
The Interpersonal Communication Process

Communication medium the method used to deliver an oral or written message (p. 332)

Hearing the act or process of perceiving sounds (p. 334)

Listening making a conscious effort to hear (p. 334)

Active listening assuming half the responsibility for successful communication by actively giving the speaker

nonjudgmental feedback that shows you've accurately heard what he or she said (p. 334)

Empathetic listening understanding the speaker's perspective and personal frame of reference and giving feedback that conveys that understanding to the speaker (p. 335)

Destructive feedback feedback that disapproves without any intention of being

helpful and almost always causes a negative or defensive reaction in the recipient (p. 336)

Constructive feedback feedback intended to be helpful, corrective, and/or encouraging (p. 336)

15-4 **Describe how managers can manage effective organization-wide communication.** Managers need methods for managing organization-wide communication and for making themselves accessible so that they can hear what employees throughout their organizations are feeling and thinking. Email, collaborative discussion sites, televised/videotaped speeches and conferences, and broadcast voice mail make it much easier for managers to improve message

transmission and get the message out. By contrast, anonymous company hotlines, survey feedback, frequent informal meetings, town halls and surprise visits help managers avoid organizational silence and improve reception by giving them the opportunity to hear what others in the organization think and feel. Monitoring internal and external blogs is another way to find out what people are saying and thinking about your organization.

Online discussion forums the in-house equivalent of Internet newsgroups. By using web- or software-based discussion tools that are available across the company, employees can easily ask questions and share knowledge with each other (p. 337)

Televised/videotaped speeches and meetings speeches and meetings originally made to a smaller audience that are either simultaneously broadcast

to other locations in the company or videotaped for subsequent distribution and viewing (p. 338)

Organizational silence when employees withhold information about organizational problems or issues (p. 339)

Company hotlines phone numbers that anyone in the company can call anonymously to leave information for upper management (p. 339)

Survey feedback information that is collected by surveys from organizational members and then compiled, disseminated, and used to develop action plans for improvement (p. 339)

Blog a personal website that provides personal opinions or recommendations, news summaries, and reader comments (p. 340)

16-1 Describe the basic control process. The control process begins by setting standards and then measuring performance and comparing performance to the standards. The better a company's information and measurement systems, the easier it is to make these comparisons. The control process continues by identifying and analyzing performance deviations and then developing and implementing programs for corrective action. Control is a continuous, dynamic, cybernetic process, not a one-time achievement or result. Control requires frequent managerial attention. The three basic control methods are feedback control (after-the-fact performance information), concurrent control (simultaneous performance information), and feedforward control (preventive performance information). Control has regulation costs and unanticipated consequences and therefore isn't always worthwhile or possible.

Exhibit 16.1
Cybernetic Control Process

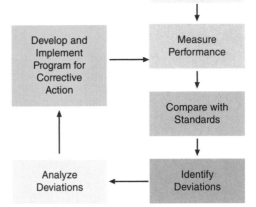

Source: From *Business Horizons*, June 1972, H. Koontz and R. W. Bradspies, "Managing through Feedforward Control: A Future Directed View," pp. 25–36.

Control a regulatory process of establishing standards to achieve organizational goals, comparing actual performance against the standards, and taking corrective action when necessary (p. 343)

Standards a basis of comparison for measuring the extent to which various kinds of organizational performance are satisfactory or unsatisfactory (p. 343)

Benchmarking the process of identifying outstanding practices, processes, and standards in other companies and adapting them to your company (p. 344)

Cybernetic the process of steering or keeping on course (p. 345)

Feedback control a mechanism for gathering information about performance deficiencies after they occur (p. 345)

Concurrent control a mechanism for gathering information about performance deficiencies as they occur, thereby eliminating or shortening the delay between performance and feedback (p. 346)

Feedforward control a mechanism for monitoring performance inputs rather than outputs to prevent or minimize performance deficiencies before they occur (p. 346)

Control loss the situation in which behavior and work procedures do not conform to standards (p. 347)

Regulation costs the costs associated with implementing or maintaining control (p. 347)

Cybernetic feasibility the extent to which it is possible to implement each step in the control process (p. 347)

16-2 Discuss the various methods that managers can use to maintain control. There are five methods of control: bureaucratic, objective, normative, concertive, and self-control (self-management). Bureaucratic and objective controls are top down, management based, and measurement based. Normative and concertive controls represent shared forms of control because they evolve from company-wide or team-based beliefs and values. Self-control, or self-management, is a control system in which managers and workers control their own behavior.

Bureaucratic control is based on organizational policies, rules, and procedures. Objective control is based on reliable measures of behavior or outputs. Normative control is based on strong corporate beliefs and careful hiring practices. Concertive control is based on the development of values, beliefs, and rules in autonomous work groups. Self-control is based on individuals setting their own goals, monitoring themselves, and rewarding or punishing themselves with respect to goal achievement.

Each of these control methods may be more or less appropriate depending on the circumstances.

Bureaucratic control the use of hierarchical authority to influence employee behavior by rewarding or punishing employees for compliance or noncompliance with organizational policies, rules, and procedures (p. 348)

Objective control the use of observable measures of worker behavior or outputs to assess performance and influence behavior (p. 348)

Behavior control the regulation of the behaviors and actions that workers perform on the job (p. 348)

Output control the regulation of workers' results or outputs through rewards and incentives (p. 348)

Normative control the regulation of workers' behavior and decisions through widely shared organizational values and beliefs (p. 349)

Concertive control the regulation of workers' behavior and decisions through work group values and beliefs (p. 350)

Self-control (self-management) a control system in which managers and workers control their own behavior by setting their own goals, monitoring their own progress, and rewarding themselves for goal achievement (p. 351)

16-3 **Describe the behaviors, processes, and outcomes that today's managers are choosing to control in their organizations.** Deciding what to control is just as important as deciding whether to control or how to control. In most companies, performance is measured using financial measures alone. However, the balanced scorecard encourages managers to measure and control company performance from four perspectives: financial, customer, internal, and innovation and learning. Traditionally, financial control has been achieved through cash flow analysis, balance sheets, income statements, financial ratios, and budgets. (For a refresher on these traditional financial control tools, see the Financial Review Card.) Another way to measure and control financial performance is to evaluate economic value added (EVA). Unlike traditional financial measures, EVA helps managers assess whether they are performing well enough to pay the cost of the capital needed to run the business. Instead of using customer satisfaction surveys to measure performance, companies should pay attention to customer defections, as customers who leave are more likely to speak up about what the company is doing wrong. From the internal perspective, performance is often measured in terms of quality, which is defined in three ways: excellence, value, and conformance to specifications. Sustainability has become an important part of innovation and learning in companies. The four levels of sustainability are waste prevention and reduction, recycling and reuse, waste treatment, and waste disposal.

Exhibit 16.5
Advantages and Disadvantages of Different Measures of Quality

Quality Measure	Advantages	Disadvantages
Excellence	Promotes clear organizational vision.	Provides little practical guidance for managers.
	Being/providing the "best" motivates and inspires managers and employees.	Excellence is ambiguous. What is it? Who defines it?
Value	Appeals to customers who know excellence "when they see it."	Difficult to measure and control.
	Customers recognize differences in value.	Can be difficult to determine what factors influence whether a product/service is seen as having value.
	Easier to measure and compare whether products/services differ in value.	Controlling the balance between excellence and cost (that is, affordable excellence) can be difficult.
Conformance to Specifications	If specifications can be written, conformance to specifications is usually measurable.	Many products/services cannot be easily evaluated in terms of conformance to specifications.
	Should lead to increased efficiency.	Promotes standardization, so may hurt performance when adapting to changes is more important.
	Promotes consistency in quality.	May be less appropriate for services, which are dependent on a high degree of human contact.

Source: Briar Cliff Manor, NY, 10510-8020; C. A. Reeves and D. A. Bednar, "Defining Quality: Alternatives and Implications," *Academy of Management Review* 19 (1994): 419–445.

Balanced scorecard measurement of organizational performance in four equally important areas: finances, customers, internal operations, and innovation and learning (p. 352)

Suboptimization performance improvement in one part of an organization but only at the expense of decreased performance in another part (p. 352)

Cash flow analysis a type of analysis that predicts how changes in a business will affect its ability to take in more cash than it pays out (p. 352)

Balance sheets accounting statements that provide a snapshot of a company's financial position at a particular time (p. 352)

Income statements accounting statements, also called "profit and loss statements," that show what has happened to an organization's income, expenses, and net profit over a period of time (p. 352)

Financial ratios calculations typically used to track a business's liquidity (cash), efficiency, and profitability over time compared to other businesses in its industry (p. 353)

Budgets quantitative plans through which managers decide how to allocate available money to best accomplish company goals (p. 353)

Zero-based budgeting a budgeting technique that requires managers to justify every expenditure every year (p. 353)

Economic value added (EVA) the amount by which company profits (revenues minus expenses minus taxes) exceed the cost of capital in a given year (p. 354)

Customer defections a performance assessment in which companies identify which customers are leaving and measure the rate at which they are leaving (p. 356)

Value customer perception that the product quality is excellent for the price offered (p. 356)

Basic Accounting Tools for Controlling Financial Performance

Steps for a Basic Cash Flow Analysis

1. Forecast sales (steady, up, or down).
2. Project changes in anticipated cash inflows (as a result of changes).
3. Project anticipated cash outflows (as a result of changes).
4. Project net cash flows by combining anticipated cash inflows and outflows.

Parts of a Basic Balance Sheet (Assets = Liabilities + Owner's Equity)

1. Assets
   a. Current assets (cash, short-term investment, marketable securities, accounts receivable, and so on)
   b. Fixed assets (land, buildings, machinery, equipment, and so on)
2. Liabilities
   a. Current liabilities (accounts payable, notes payable, taxes payable, and so on)
   b. Long-term liabilities (long-term debt, deferred income taxes, and so on)
3. Owner's Equity
   a. Preferred stock and common stock
   b. Additional paid-in capital
   c. Retained earnings

Basic Income Statement

SALES REVENUE
− sales returns and allowances
+ other income
= NET REVENUE
− cost of goods sold (beginning inventory, costs of goods purchased, ending inventory)
= GROSS PROFIT
− total operating expenses (selling, general, and administrative expenses)
= INCOME FROM OPERATIONS
− interest expense
= PRETAX INCOME
− income taxes
= NET INCOME

Common Kinds of Budgets

Revenue Budgets—used to project or forecast future sales.	• Accuracy of projection depends on economy, competitors, sales force estimates, and so on • Determined by estimating future sales volume and sales prices for all products and services.
Expense Budgets—used within departments and divisions to determine how much will be spent on various supplies, projects, or activities.	• One of the first places that companies look for cuts when trying to lower expenses.
Profit Budgets—used by profit centers, which have "profit and loss" responsibility.	• Profit budgets combine revenue and expense budgets into one budget. • Typically used in large businesses with multiple plants and divisions.
Cash Budgets—used to forecast how much cash a company will have on hand to meet expenses.	• Similar to cash-flow analyses. • Used to identify cash shortfalls, which must be covered to pay bills, or cash excesses, which should be invested for a higher return.
Capital Expenditure Budgets—used to forecast large, long-lasting investments in equipment, buildings, and property.	• Help managers identify funding that will be needed to pay for future expansion or strategic moves designed to increase competitive advantage.
Variable Budgets—used to project costs across varying levels of sales and revenues.	• Important because it is difficult to accurately predict sales revenue and volume. • Lead to more accurate budgeting with respect to labor, materials, and administrative expenses, which vary with sales volume and revenues. • Build flexibility into the budgeting process.

Common Financial Ratios

Ratios	Formula	What It Means	When to Use
Liquidity Ratios			
Current Ratio	$\dfrac{\text{Current Assets}}{\text{Current Liabilities}}$	• Whether you have enough assets on hand to pay for short-term bills and obligations. • Higher is better. • Recommended level is two times as many current assets as current liabilities.	• Track monthly and quarterly. • Basic measure of your company's health.
Quick (Acid Test) Ratio	$\dfrac{(\text{Current Assets} - \text{Inventories})}{\text{Current Liabilities}}$	• Stricter than current ratio. • Whether you have enough (that is, cash) to pay short-term bills and obligations. • Higher is better. • Recommended level is one or higher.	• Track monthly. • Also calculate quick ratio with potential customers to evaluate whether they're likely to pay you in a timely manner.
Leverage Ratios			
Debt to Equity	$\dfrac{\text{Total Liabilities}}{\text{Total Equity}}$	• Indicates how much the company is leveraged (in debt) by comparing what is owed (liabilities) to what is owned (equity). • Lower is better. A high debt-to-equity ratio could indicate that the company has too much debt. • Recommended level depends on industry.	• Track monthly. • Lenders often use this to determine the creditworthiness of a business (that is, whether to approve additional loans).
Debt Coverage	$\dfrac{(\text{Net Profit} + \text{Noncash Expense})}{\text{Debt}}$	• Indicates how well cash flow covers debt payments. • Higher is better.	• Track monthly. • Lenders look at this ratio to determine if there is adequate cash to make loan payments.
Efficiency Ratios			
Inventory Turnover	$\dfrac{\text{Cost of Goods Sold}}{\text{Average Value of Inventory}}$	• Whether you're making efficient use of inventory. • Higher is better, indicating that inventory (dollars) isn't purchased (spent) until needed. • Recommended level depends on industry.	• Track monthly by using a twelve-month rolling average.
Average Collections Period	$\dfrac{\text{Accounts Receivable}}{(\text{Annual Net Credit Sales} \div 365)}$	• Shows on average how quickly your customers are paying their bills. • Recommended level is no more than fifteen days longer than credit terms. If credit is net thirty days, then average should not be longer than forty-five days.	• Track monthly. • Use to determine how long company's money is being tied up in customer credit.
Profitability Ratios			
Gross Profit Margin	$\dfrac{\text{Gross Profit}}{\text{Total Sales}}$	• Shows how efficiently a business is using its materials and labor in the production process. • Higher is better, indicating that a profit can be made if fixed costs are controlled.	• Track monthly. • Analyze when unsure about product or service pricing. • Low margin compared to competitors means you're underpricing.
Return on Equity	$\dfrac{\text{Net Income}}{\text{Owner's Equity}}$	• Shows what was earned on your investment in the business during a particular period. Often called "return on investment." • Higher is better.	• Track quarterly and annually. • Use to compare to what you might have earned on the stock market, bonds, or government Treasury bills during the same period.

CHAPTER 17 LEARNING OUTCOMES / KEY TERMS

17-1 **Explain the strategic importance of information.** The first company to use new information technology to substantially lower costs or differentiate products or services often gains a first-mover advantage, higher profits, and a larger market share. Creating a first-mover advantage can be difficult, expensive, and risky, however. According to the resource-based view of information technology, sustainable competitive advantage occurs when information technology adds value, is different across firms, and is difficult to create or acquire.

Moore's law the prediction that about every two years, computer processing power would double and its cost would drop by 50 percent (p. 363)

Raw data facts and figures (p. 363)

Information useful data that can influence people's choices and behavior (p. 363)

First-mover advantage the strategic advantage that companies earn by being the first to use new information technology to substantially lower costs or to make a product or service different from that of competitors (p. 365)

17-2 **Describe the characteristics of useful information (that is, its value and costs).** Raw data are facts and figures. Raw data do not become information until they are in a form that can affect decisions and behavior. For information to be useful, it has to be reliable and valid (accurate), of sufficient quantity (complete), pertinent to the problems you're facing (relevant), and available when you need it (timely). Useful information is not cheap. The five costs of obtaining good information are the costs of acquiring, processing, storing, retrieving, and communicating information.

Acquisition cost the cost of obtaining data that you don't have (p. 368)

Processing cost the cost of turning raw data into usable information (p. 368)

Storage cost the cost of physically or electronically archiving information for later retrieval and use (p. 369)

Retrieval cost the cost of accessing already-stored and processed information (p. 369)

Communication cost the cost of transmitting information from one place to another (p. 370)

17-3 **Explain the basics of capturing, processing, and protecting information.** Electronic data capture (using bar codes, radio frequency identification [RFID] tags, scanners, or optical character recognition), is much faster, easier, and cheaper than manual data capture. Processing information means transforming raw data into meaningful information that can be applied to business decision making. Data mining helps managers with this transformation by discovering unknown patterns and relationships in data. Supervised data mining looks for patterns specified by managers, while unsupervised data mining looks for four general kinds of data patterns: association or affinity patterns, sequence patterns, predictive patterns, and data clusters. Protecting information ensures that data are reliably and consistently retrievable in a usable format by authorized users but no one else. Authentication and authorization, firewalls, antivirus software for PCs and corporate email and network servers, data encryption, virtual private networks (VPNs), and web-based secure sockets layer (SSL) encryption are some of the best ways to protect information. Be careful when using wireless networks, which are easily compromised even when security and encryption protocols are in place.

Exhibit 17.3

Security Threats to Data and Data Networks

Security Problem	Source	Affects	Severity	The Threat	The Solution
Denial of service; web server attacks and corporate network attacks	Internet hackers	All servers	High	Loss of data, disruption of service, and theft of service.	Implement firewall, password control, server-side review, threat monitoring, and bug fixes; turn PCs off when not in use.
Password cracking software and unauthorized access to PCs	Local area network, Internet	All users, especially digital subscriber line and cable Internet users	High	Hackers take over PCs. Privacy can be invaded. Corporate users' systems are exposed to other machines on the network.	Close ports and firewalls, disable file and print sharing, and use strong passwords.
Viruses, worms, Trojan horses, and rootkits	Email, downloaded and distributed software	All users	Moderate to high	Monitor activities and cause data loss and file deletion; compromise security by sometimes concealing their presence.	Use antivirus software and firewalls; control Internet access.
Malware, spyware, adware, malicious scripts, and applets	Rogue web pages	All users	Moderate to high	Invade privacy, intercept passwords, and damage files or file system.	Disable browser script support; use security, blocking, and spyware/adware software.
Email snooping	Hackers on your network and the Internet	All users	Moderate to high	People read your email from intermediate servers or packets, or they physically access your machine.	Encrypt messages, ensure strong password protection, and limit physical access to machines.
Keystroke monitoring	Trojan horses, people with direct access to PCs	All users	High	Records everything typed at the keyboard and intercepts keystrokes before password masking or encryption occurs.	Use antivirus software to catch Trojan horses, control Internet access to transmission, and implement system monitoring and physical access control.
Phishing	Hackers on your network and the Internet	All users, including customers	High	Fake but real-looking emails and websites that trick users into sharing personal information on what they wrongly think is a company's website. This leads to unauthorized account access.	Educate and warn users and customers about the dangers. Encourage both not to click on potentially fake URLs, which might take them to phishing websites. Instead, have them type your company's URL into the web browser.
Spam	Email	All users and corporations	Mild to high	Clogs and overloads email servers and inboxes with junk mail. HTML-based spam may be used for profiling and identifying users.	Filter known spam sources and senders on email servers; have users create further lists of approved and unapproved senders on their PCs.
Cookies	Websites you visit	Individual users	Mild to moderate	Trace web usage and permit the creation of personalized web pages that track behavior and interest profiles.	Use cookie managers to control and edit cookies, and use ad blockers.

Sources: "The 11 Most Common Computer Security Threats . . . And What You Can Do to Protect Yourself from Them," Symantec-Norton, accessed May 12, 2015. http://www.symantec-norton.com/11-most-common-computer-security-threats_k13.aspx; K. Bannan, "Look Out: Watching You, Watching Me," PC Magazine, July 2002, 99; A. Dragoon, "Fighting Phish, Fakes, and Frauds," CIO, September 1, 2004, 33; B. Glass, "Are You Being Watched?" PC Magazine, April 23, 2002, 54; K. Karagiannis, "DDoS: Are You Next?" PC Magazine, January 2003, 79; B. Machrone, "Protect & Defend," PC Magazine, June 27, 2000, 168–181; "Top 10 Security Threats," PC Magazine, April 10, 2007, 66; M. Sarrel, "Master End-User Security," PC Magazine, May 2008, 101.

Bar code a visual pattern that represents numerical data by varying the thickness and pattern of vertical bars (p. 371)

Radio frequency identification (RFID) tags tags containing minuscule microchips that transmit information via radio waves and can be used to track the number and location of the objects into which the tags have been inserted (p. 371)

Electronic scanner an electronic device that converts printed text and pictures into digital images (p. 371)

Optical character recognition the ability of software to convert digitized documents into ASCII (American Standard Code for Information Interchange) text that can be searched, read, and edited by word processing and other kinds of software (p. 372)

Processing information transforming raw data into meaningful information (p. 372)

Data mining the process of discovering unknown patterns and relationships in large amounts of data (p. 372)

Data warehouse a database that stores huge amounts of data that have been prepared for data mining analysis by being cleaned of errors and redundancy (p. 372)

Supervised data mining the process when the user tells the data mining software to look and test for specific patterns and relationships in a data set (p. 372)

Unsupervised data mining the process when the user simply tells the data mining software to uncover whatever patterns and relationships it can find in a data set (p. 372)

Association or affinity patterns when two or more database elements tend to occur together in a significant way (p. 373)

Sequence patterns when two or more database elements occur together in a significant pattern in which one of the elements precedes the other (p. 373)

Predictive patterns patterns that help identify database elements that are different (p. 373)

Data clusters when three or more database elements occur together (that is, cluster) in a significant way (p. 373)

Protecting information the process of ensuring that data are reliably and consistently retrievable in a usable format for authorized users but no one else (p. 373)

Authentication making sure potential users are who they claim to be (p. 374)

Authorization granting authenticated users approved access to data, software, and systems (p. 374)

Two-factor authentication authentication based on what users know, such as a password and what they have in their possession, such as a secure ID card or key (p. 376)

Firewall a protective hardware or software device that sits between the computers in an internal organizational network and outside networks, such as the Internet (p. 376)

Virus a program or piece of code that, without your knowledge, attaches itself to other programs on your computer and can trigger anything from a harmless flashing message to the reformatting of your hard drive to a system-wide network shutdown (p. 376)

Data encryption the transformation of data into complex, scrambled digital codes that can be decrypted only by authorized users who possess unique decryption keys (p. 377)

Virtual private network (VPN) software that securely encrypts data sent by employees outside the company network, decrypts the data when they arrive within the company computer network, and does the same when data are sent back to employees outside the network (p. 377)

Secure sockets layer (SSL) encryption Internet browser–based encryption that provides secure off-site web access to some data and programs (p. 378)

17-4 **Describe how companies can access and share information and knowledge.** Executive information systems, intranets, and corporate portals facilitate internal sharing and access to company information and transactions. Electronic data interchange and the Internet allow external groups such as suppliers and customers to easily access company information. Both decrease costs by reducing or eliminating data entry, data errors, and paperwork and by speeding up communication. Organizations use decision support systems and expert systems to capture and share specialized knowledge with nonexpert employees.

Executive information system (EIS) a data processing system that uses internal and external data sources to provide the information needed to monitor and analyze organizational performance (p. 379)

Intranets private company networks that allow employees to easily access, share, and publish information using Internet software (p. 379)

Corporate portal a hybrid of executive information systems and intranets that allows managers and employees to use a web browser to gain access to customized company information and to complete specialized transactions (p. 380)

Electronic data interchange (EDI) when two companies convert their purchase and ordering information to a standardized format to enable the direct electronic transmission of that information from one company's computer system to the other company's computer system (p. 380)

Web services software that uses standardized protocols to describe data from one company in such a way that those data can automatically be read, understood, transcribed, and processed by different computer systems in another company (p. 380)

Extranets networks that allow companies to exchange information and conduct transactions with outsiders by providing them direct, web-based access to authorized parts of a company's intranet or information system (p. 381)

Knowledge the understanding that one gains from information (p. 381)

Decision support system (DSS) an information system that helps managers understand specific kinds of problems and potential solutions (p. 382)

Expert system an information system that contains the specialized knowledge and decision rules used by experts and experienced decision makers so that nonexperts can draw on this knowledge base to make decisions (p. 383)

18-1 Discuss the kinds of productivity and their importance in managing operations. Productivity is a measure of how many inputs it takes to produce or create an output. The greater the output from one input, or the fewer inputs it takes to create an output, the higher the productivity. Partial productivity measures how much of a single kind of input, such as labor, is needed to produce an output. Multifactor productivity is an overall measure of productivity that indicates how much labor, capital, materials, and energy are needed to produce an output.

$$\text{Partial Productivity} = \frac{\text{Outputs}}{\text{Single Kind of Input}}$$

Operations management managing the daily production of goods and services (p. 385)

Productivity a measure of performance that indicates how many inputs it takes to produce or create an output (p. 385)

Partial productivity a measure of performance that indicates how much of a particular kind of input it takes to produce an output (p. 386)

Multifactor productivity an overall measure of performance that indicates how much labor, capital, materials, and energy it takes to produce an output (p. 387)

18-2 Explain the role that quality plays in managing operations. Quality can mean that a product or service is practically free of deficiencies or has characteristics that satisfy customer needs. Quality products usually possess three characteristics: reliability, serviceability, and durability. Quality service includes reliability, tangibles, responsiveness, assurance, and empathy. ISO 9000 is a series of five international standards for achieving consistency in quality management and quality assurance, while ISO 14000 is a set of standards for minimizing an organization's harmful effects on the environment. The Baldrige Performance Excellence Program recognizes U.S. companies for their achievements in quality and business performance. Each year, up to three Baldrige Awards may be given in the categories of manufacturing, service, small business, education, nonprofit, and health care. Total quality management (TQM) is an integrated organization-wide strategy for improving product and service quality. TQM is based on three mutually reinforcing principles: customer focus and satisfaction, continuous improvement, and teamwork.

Quality a product or service free of deficiencies, or the characteristics of a product or service that satisfy customer needs (p. 389)

ISO 9000 a series of five international standards, from ISO 9000 to ISO 9004, for achieving consistency in quality management and quality assurance in companies throughout the world (p. 390)

ISO 14000 a series of international standards for managing, monitoring, and minimizing an organization's harmful effects on the environment (p. 390)

Total quality management (TQM) an integrated, principle-based, organization-wide strategy for improving product and service quality (p. 392)

Customer focus an organizational goal to concentrate on meeting customers' needs at all levels of the organization (p. 392)

Customer satisfaction an organizational goal to provide products or services that meet or exceed customers' expectations (p. 392)

Continuous improvement an organization's ongoing commitment to constantly assess and improve the processes and procedures used to create products and services (p. 392)

Variation a deviation in the form, condition, or appearance of a product from the quality standard for that product (p. 393)

Teamwork collaboration between managers and nonmanagers, across business functions, and between companies, customers, and suppliers (p. 393)

18-3 Explain the essentials of managing a service business. Services are different from goods. Goods are produced, tangible, and storable. Services are performed, intangible, and perishable. Likewise, managing service operations is different from managing production operations. The service-profit chain indicates that success begins with internal service quality, meaning how well management treats employees. Internal service quality leads to employee satisfaction and service capability, which, in turn, lead to high-value service to customers, customer satisfaction, customer loyalty, and long-term profits and growth. Keeping existing customers is far more cost-effective than finding new ones. Consequently, to prevent disgruntled customers from leaving, some companies are empowering service employees to perform service recovery—restoring customer satisfaction to strongly dissatisfied customers—by giving employees the authority and responsibility to immediately solve customer problems. The hope is that empowered service recovery will prevent customer defections.

Internal service quality the quality of treatment employees receive from management and other divisions of a company (p. 394)

Service recovery restoring customer satisfaction to strongly dissatisfied customers (p. 395)

18-4 Describe the different kinds of manufacturing operations. Manufacturing operations produce physical goods. Manufacturing operations can be classified according to the amount of processing or assembly that occurs after receiving an order from a customer. Manufacturing operations can also be classified in terms of flexibility, the degree to which the number, kind, and characteristics of products can easily and quickly be changed. Flexibility allows companies to respond quickly to competitors and customers and to reduce order lead times, but it can also lead to higher unit costs.

Make-to-order operation a manufacturing operation that does not start processing or assembling products until a customer order is received (p. 396)

Assemble-to-order operation a manufacturing operation that divides manufacturing processes into separate parts or modules that are combined to create semicustomized products (p. 396)

Make-to-stock operation a manufacturing operation that orders parts and assembles standardized products before receiving customer orders (p. 396)

Manufacturing flexibility the degree to which manufacturing operations can easily and quickly change the number, kind, and characteristics of products they produce (p. 397)

Continuous-flow production a manufacturing operation that produces goods at a continuous, rather than a discrete, rate (p. 397)

Line-flow production manufacturing processes that are preestablished, occur in a serial or linear manner, and are dedicated to making one type of product (p. 398)

Batch production a manufacturing operation that produces goods in large batches in standard lot sizes (p. 398)

Job shops manufacturing operations that handle custom orders or small batch jobs (p. 398)

18-5 **Explain why and how companies should manage inventory levels.** There are four kinds of inventory: raw materials, component parts, work-in-process, and finished goods. Because companies incur ordering, setup, holding, and stockout costs when handling inventory, inventory costs can be enormous. To control those costs, companies measure and track inventory in three ways: average aggregate inventory, weeks of supply, and turnover. Companies meet the basic goals of inventory management (avoiding stockouts and reducing inventory without hurting daily operations) through economic order quantity (EOQ) formulas, just-in-time (JIT) inventory systems, and materials requirement planning (MRP). The formula for EOQ is

$$EOQ = \sqrt{\frac{2DO}{H}}$$

Use EOQ formulas when inventory levels are independent, and use JIT and MRP when inventory levels are dependent on the number of products to be produced.

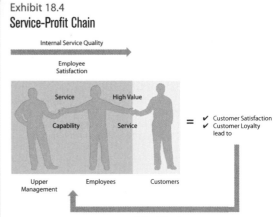

Exhibit 18.4
Service-Profit Chain

Internal Service Quality

Employee Satisfaction

Service — High Value

Capability — Service

= ✔ Customer Satisfaction
✔ Customer Loyalty lead to

Upper Management — Employees — Customers

Profit and Growth

Sources: R. Hallowell, L. A. Schlesinger, and J. Zornitsky, "Internal Service Quality, Customer and Job Satisfaction: Linkages and Implications for Management," *Human Resource Planning* 19 (1996): 20–31; J. L. Heskett, T. O. Jones, G. W. Loveman, W. E. Sasser Jr., and L. A. Schlesinger, "Putting the Service-Profit Chain to Work," *Harvard Business Review* (March–April 1994): 164–174.

Inventory the amount and number of raw materials, parts, and finished products that a company has in its possession (p. 398)

Raw material inventories the basic inputs in a manufacturing process (p. 399)

Component parts inventories the basic parts used in manufacturing that are fabricated from raw materials (p. 399)

Work-in-process inventories partially finished goods consisting of assembled component parts (p. 399)

Finished goods inventories the final outputs of manufacturing operations (p. 399)

Average aggregate inventory average overall inventory during a particular time period (p. 400)

Stockout the point when a company runs out of finished product (p. 400)

Inventory turnover the number of times per year that a company sells, or "turns over," its average inventory (p. 400)

Ordering cost the costs associated with ordering inventory, including the cost of data entry, phone calls, obtaining bids, correcting mistakes, and determining when and how much inventory to order (p. 401)

Setup cost the costs of downtime and lost efficiency that occur when a machine is changed or adjusted to produce a different kind of inventory (p. 401)

Holding cost the cost of keeping inventory until it is used or sold, including storage, insurance, taxes, obsolescence, and opportunity costs (p. 402)

Stockout cost the cost incurred when a company runs out of a product, including transaction costs to replace inventory and the loss of customers' goodwill (p. 402)

Economic order quantity (EOQ) a system of formulas that minimizes ordering and holding costs and helps determine how much and how often inventory should be ordered (p. 402)

Just-in-time (JIT) inventory system an inventory system in which component parts arrive from suppliers just as they are needed at each stage of production (p. 403)

Kanban a ticket-based JIT system that indicates when to reorder inventory (p. 403)

Materials requirement planning (MRP) a production and inventory system that determines the production schedule, production batch sizes, and inventory needed to complete final products (p. 403)

Independent demand system an inventory system in which the level of one kind of inventory does not depend on another (p. 404)

Dependent demand system an inventory system in which the level of inventory depends on the number of finished units to be produced (p. 404)